COLLINS

POSTCODE ATLAS

BRITAIN

& NORTHERN IRELAND

CONTENTS

◌ Collins

Published by Collins
An imprint of HarperCollins Publishers
Westerhill Road, Bishopbriggs, Glasgow, G64 2QT

www.harpercollins.co.uk

Copyright © HarperCollins Publishers Ltd 2012
Reprint with changes 2013

Collins® is a registered trademark of HarperCollins Publishers Limited

Mapping generated from Collins Bartholomew digital databases

Postcode boundaries and codes copyright © Royal Mail Group plc

The postcode boundary information published in this atlas is compiled from the Postcode Address File (PAF) and reproduced with the permission of Royal Mail Group plc. The copyright and database rights in PAF are owned by Royal Mail Group plc. Details included in this atlas are subject to change without notice.

The grid on this map is the National Grid taken from the Ordnance Survey map with the permission of the Controller of Her Majesty's Stationery Office.

British population figures are derived from the 2001 census.
Source: National Statistics website: www.statistics.gov.uk
Crown copyright material is reproduced with the permission of the Controller of HMSO.
Northern Ireland populations derived from the 2001 Census.
Source: Northern Ireland Statistics and Research Agency www.nisra.gov.uk
Reproduced by permission.

The contents of this publication are believed correct at the time of printing. Nevertheless, the publisher can accept no responsibility for errors or omissions, changes in the detail given, or for any expense or loss thereby caused.

The representation of a road, track or footpath is no evidence of a right of way.

Printed in China

ISBN 978 0 00 744307 9   Imp 002

e-mail: roadcheck@harpercollins.co.uk   Twitter @Collinsmaps

Key to map symbols

Postcode information

PL   Area code

Area boundary

35   District code

District boundary

Britain map symbols (pages 2-107)

M4   Motorway

M6 Toll   Toll Motorway

8   9   Motorway junction with full / limited access

Maidstone   Motorway service areas (off road, full, limited access)

Birch   Sarn

A48   Primary route dual / single carriageway

A5   'A' road dual / single carriageway

B1403   'B' road dual / single carriageway

Minor road

Restricted access due to road condition or private ownership

Roads with passing places

Roads proposed or under construction

32b   Multi-level junction (occasionally with junction number)

Roundabout

Road tunnel

Steep hill (arrows point downhill)

Level crossing

Toll   Toll

Railway line and station

Preserved railway line and station

Railway tunnel

✈   Airport with / without scheduled services

Ⓗ   Heliport

Built up area

□ □ ▫   Towns, villages and other settlements

National boundary

County / Unitary Authority boundary

468   941   Spot / Summit height in metres

Lake, dam and river

Canal / Dry canal / Canal tunnel

Beach

1:260,000 (approx)

0   2   4   6   8   10 miles

0   2   4   6   8   10   12   14   16 km

4.1 miles to 1 inch   2.6 km to 1 cm

Northern Ireland map symbols (pages 108-109)

M1   Motorway

5   9   Motorway junction with full / limited access

A28   N4   Primary / National primary route

A29   N52   'A' road / National secondary route

B113   R408   'B' road / Regional road

Minor road

Road under construction

Multi-level junction / roundabout

»   Steep hill (arrows point downhill)

⊕   ✈   International / domestic airport

Canal

International boundary

District / County boundary

754   Summit height (in metres)

Built up areas

Beach

Conurbation map symbols (pages 110-122)

M73   Motorway

M6 Toll   Toll motorway

3   4   Motorway junctions with full / limited access

FRANKLEY SERVICES   Motorway service area

A725   Primary route dual / single carriageway

A4054   'A' road dual / single carriageway

B7078   'B' road dual / single carriageway

Minor road dual / single carriageway

○ ○ ○ ○   Roundabout

Railway line and station

Ⓤ Ⓢ Ⓜ ▣   London Underground / Subway / Metro / Light rail station

Railway tunnel

Airport with scheduled services

Built up areas

Public building

County / Unitary Authority boundary

Woodland / Park

▲ 266   Spot height in metres

Congestion charging zone

Postcodes operate at five levels.

Level 1. Areas are denoted by the first one or two letters of the code, eg GL. These areas are then divided into districts.

Level 2. Districts are denoted by the number or numbers in the first part of the postcode, eg GL52. Districts are further subdivided into sectors.

Level 3. Subdistricts are a further special division of districts and only occur in London, eg EC1A.

Level 4. Sectors are denoted by the number in the second part of the postcode, eg GL52 5.

Level 5. The final two letters of the code denote a group of houses or an individual building, eg GL52 5HH.

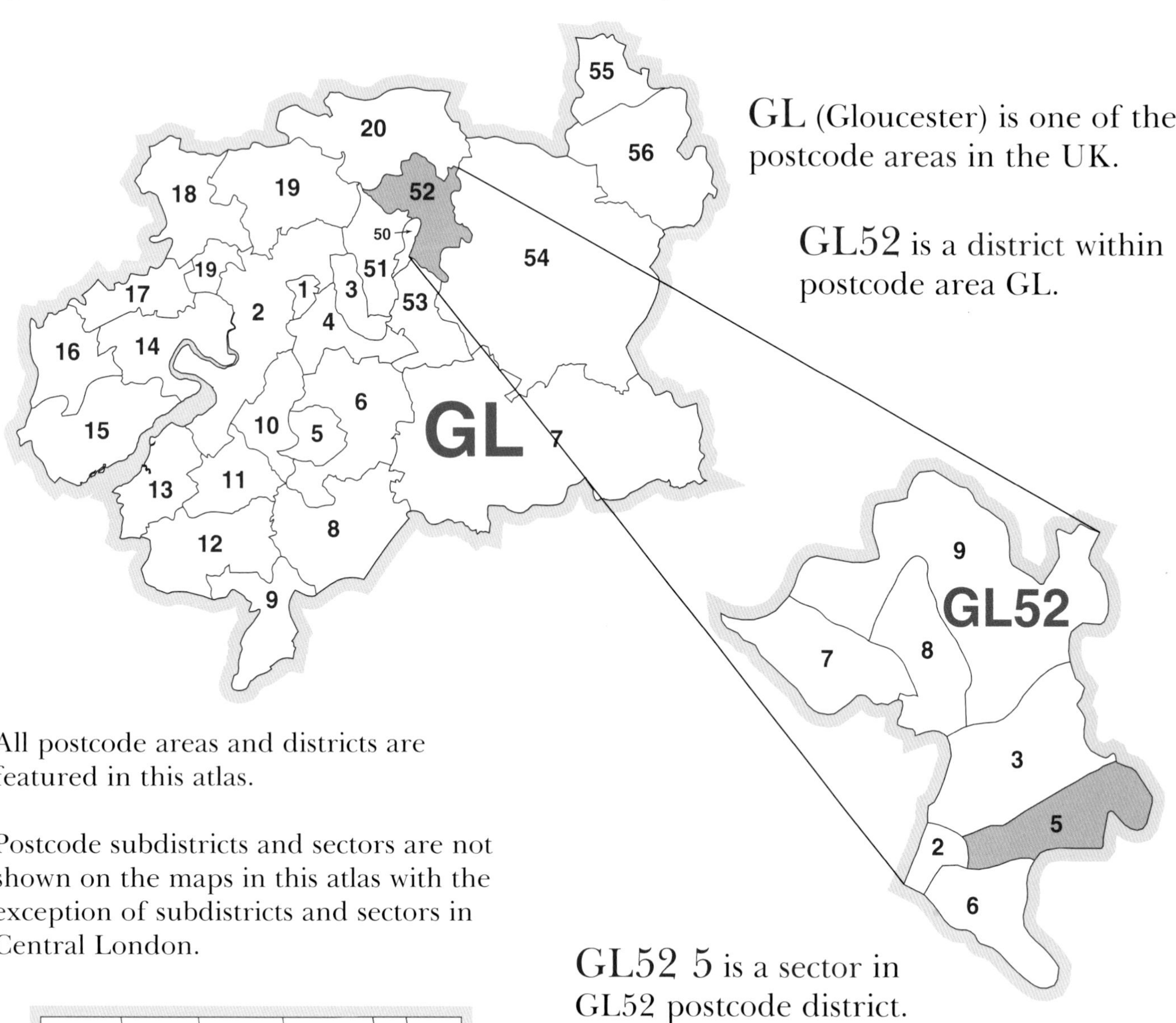

GL (Gloucester) is one of the postcode areas in the UK.

GL52 is a district within postcode area GL.

All postcode areas and districts are featured in this atlas.

Postcode subdistricts and sectors are not shown on the maps in this atlas with the exception of subdistricts and sectors in Central London.

GL52 5 is a sector in GL52 postcode district.

GL52 5HH is the postcode. It pinpoints a group of houses and in some cases individual business premises.

Postcode areas

Postcode & Area	
AB	Aberdeen
AL	St Albans
B	Birmingham
BA	Bath
BB	Blackburn
BD	Bradford
BH	Bournemouth
BL	Bolton
BN	Brighton
BR	Bromley
BS	Bristol
BT	Northern Ireland
CA	Carlisle
CB	Cambridge
CF	Cardiff
CH	Chester
CM	Chelmsford
CO	Colchester
CR	Croydon
CT	Canterbury
CV	Coventry
CW	Crewe
DA	Dartford
DD	Dundee
DE	Derby
DG	Dumfries
DH	Durham
DL	Darlington
DN	Doncaster
DT	Dorchester
DY	Dudley
E	London E
EC	London EC
EH	Edinburgh
EN	Enfield
EX	Exeter
FK	Falkirk
FY	Blackpool
G	Glasgow
GL	Gloucester
GU	Guildford
GY	Guernsey
HA	Harrow
HD	Huddersfield
HG	Harrogate
HP	Hemel Hempstead

Postcode & Area	
HR	Hereford
HS	Hebrides
HU	Kingston upon Hull
HX	Halifax
IG	Ilford
IM	Isle of Man
IP	Ipswich
IV	Inverness
JE	Jersey
KA	Kilmarnock
KT	Kingston-upon-Thames
KW	Kirkwall
KY	Kirkcaldy
L	Liverpool
LA	Lancaster
LD	Llandrindod Wells
LE	Leicester
LL	Llandudno
LN	Lincoln
LS	Leeds
LU	Luton
M	Manchester
ME	Medway
MK	Milton Keynes
ML	Motherwell
N	London N
NE	Newcastle upon Tyne
NG	Nottingham
NN	Northampton
NP	Newport
NR	Norwich
NW	London NW
OL	Oldham
OX	Oxford
PA	Paisley
PE	Peterborough
PH	Perth
PL	Plymouth
PO	Portsmouth
PR	Preston
RG	Reading
RH	Redhill
RM	Romford
S	Sheffield

Postcode & Area	
SA	Swansea
SE	London SE
SG	Stevenage
SK	Stockport
SL	Slough
SM	Sutton
SN	Swindon
SO	Southampton
SP	Salisbury
SR	Sunderland
SS	Southend-on-Sea
ST	Stoke-on-Trent
SW	London SW
SY	Shrewsbury
TA	Taunton
TD	Galashiels
TF	Telford
TN	Royal Tunbridge Wells
TQ	Torquay
TR	Truro
TS	Teesside
TW	Twickenham
UB	Southall
W	London W
WA	Warrington
WC	London WC
WD	Watford
WF	Wakefield
WN	Wigan
WR	Worcester
WS	Walsall
WV	Wolverhampton
YO	York
ZE	Shetland

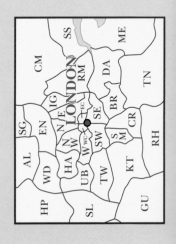

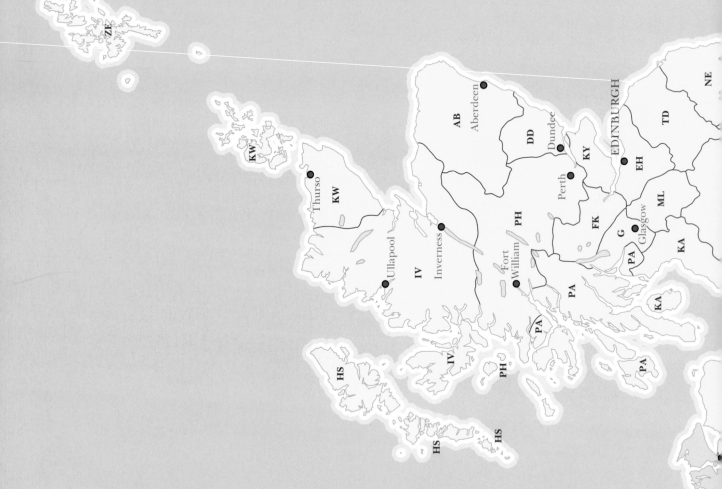

FRANCE

English Channel

Channel
Islands ◁GY

JE

Irish
Sea

Isle of
Man
IM

BELFAST

BT

IRELAND

Isles of
Scilly
TR

Carlisle
CA

Middlesbrough
TS

SR

DH

DL

LA

FY

PR

BB

BD

HG

YO

HU

DN

Leeds
LS
WF
HX
HD
OL
BL
WN
M
Manchester
WA
L
Liverpool
CH
CW

SK
S

Lincoln
LN

NG
Nottingham

DE

ST

TF

SY

LL

LL

Aberystwyth

SA

LD

CF
CARDIFF

Swansea

NP

BS
Bristol

HR

WR

GL

TA

EX
Exeter

PL
Plymouth

TQ

TR

DT

BA

SP

BH

SN

SO
Southampton

RG

Oxford
OX

GU

PO

PO

PO

SL

HP

LU

AL

MK

NN

LE

WS
Birmingham
B
CV
DY
WV

PE

Norwich
NR

IP
Cambridge
CB
Ipswich

CM

CO

SG

SS

EN
WD
HA
UB
TW
KT

LONDON
N
IG
E
RM
EC
WC
W
SW
CR
BR
DA

ME

CT
Folkestone

TN

RH

BN
Brighton

A
B
C
D
E
1
2
3
4
5
6
7
St Helen's
White Island
Tean
St Martin's
Old Grimsby
Lower Town
Middle Town
Higher Town
25
Eastern Isles
24
Bryher
New Grimsby
Tresco
23
Samson
Crow Sound
North West Channel
The Road
TR
A3110
St Mary's
Maypole
Hugh Town
Old Town
ST. MARY'S
21
Crim Rocks
22
Broad Sound
Annet
Gugh
Bishop Rock
Western Rocks
Smith Sound
St Agnes
ISLES OF SCILLY
same scale as main map
Towan Head
Newquay
Kelsey Head
West Pentire
Crantock
Holywell Bay
Penhale Point
Holywell
Ligger Pt
Cubert
Penhale Sands
Ligger Bay (Perran Bay)
6
Perranporth
Goonhavern
Bawden Rocks (Man and his Man)
St Agnes Head
Trevellas
Bolingey
5
St Agnes
Goonvrea
Mithian
Towan Cross
Mount Hawke
Three Burrows
Porthtowan
Blackwater
Nancekuke
Portreath
Chacewater
Crane Islands
Bridge
Illogan
Threemilestone
Godrevy Island
Navax Point
St Day
Twelveheads
Gwithian
Coombe
Pool
Redruth
Carharrack
St Ives Bay
15
Carn Naun Pt
The Island
St Ives
Camborne
Brea
Lanner
Gwennap
The Carracks
26
Trevarnon
14
16
Gurnard's Head
Trendrine Hill
Zennor
Halsetown
Towednack
Connor Downs
Barripper
Four Lanes
Perranarworthal
Treen
Porthmeor
Phillack
Angarrack
Troon
Ponsanooth
Longstone
Lelant
Gwinear
Carnhell Green
Stithians
Pendeen Watch
Trencrom Hill
Hayle
27
Praze-an-Beeble
Morvah
Nancledra
Lower Boscaswell
20
Canon's Town
St Erth Praze
Crowan
Pendeen
New Mill
Castle Gate
St Erth
Fraddam
Burras
Trewellard
Chysauster
Whitecross
Kerthen Wood
Paul's Green
Leedstown
Crowan Beacon
Carnyorth
Boswarthan
Crowlas
Townshend
Porkellis
Rame
Botallack
Kenidjack
Ludgvan
Relubbus
Releath
Lezerea
Mabe Burnthouse
Cape Cornwall
Madron
Heamoor
Gulval
17
Edgcumbe
10
Budock Water
The Brisons
St Just
Newbridge
Penzance
Goldsithney
St Hilary
Godolphin Cross
Nancegollan
Crelly
Bosavern
Tremethick Cross
Marazion
Trescowe
Tregonning Hill
Crowntown
Wendron
Trenear
Seworgan
Kelynack
18
Trevarrack
Perran Downs
Pollardras
13
11
Grumbla
Sancreed
Penzance
Rosudgeon
Newtown
Germoe
Carleen
Lower Town
Trevenen
Constantine
LAND'S END
Drift Reservoir
Lower Drift
Kenneggy Downs
Tresowes Green
Sithney
Trewennack
Whitesand Bay
Brane
Catchall
Tredavoe
Newlyn
Perranuthnoe
Prussia Cove
Cudden Point
Praa Sands
Ashton
Breage
Helston
Port Navas
Sennen Cove
Crows-an-wra
Kerris
Paul
Mousehole
Rinsey
Gweek
Durgan
LAND'S END
Sennen
St Buryan
MOUNT'S BAY
Trewavas Head
Porthleven
Helford
Longships
Trevescan
St Clement's Isle
Mawgan
Manaccan
19
Boleigh
Lamorna
Garras
St Martin
Trethewey
Lamorna Cove
The Loe
Tregidden
Porthcurno
Treen
Berepper
Newtown-in-St-Martin
Tregarne
Cribba Head
Gunwalloe
Tregowris
Gwennap Head
St Levan
Logan Rock
A3083
Cury
Cross Lanes
Traboe
Lanarth
12
Poldhu Cove
Poldhu Point
Goonhilly Downs
Mullion
Erisey Barton
Trelan
Mullion Cove
Penhale
Gwenter
Ponsongath
Mullion Island
Gwendreath
Predannack Wollas
Ruan Major
Kuggar
Vellan Head
St Ruan
Ruan Minor
Cadgwith
Grade
Toll
Kynance Cove
Landewednack
Lizard
Hot Point
LIZARD POINT
Wolf Rock
PENINSULA
LIZARD
0 2 4 6 miles
0 2 4 6 8 10 km
B
C
D
E

F
G
H
J
K
3
4
1
2
3
4
5
6
7
BODMIN
MOOR
PL
CORNWALL
GY
JE
ALDERNEY
GUERNSEY
JERSEY
same scale as main map
same scale as main map
same scale as main map
CHANNEL ISLANDS location map
Alderney
Guernsey
Herm
Sark
Jersey
Newland
Rumps Point
Pentire Point
Port Isaac
Port Quin
Port Gaverne
Westdowns
Trewalder
Helstone
Lanteglos
Pencarrow
Trewint
Altarnun
Fivelanes
Polyphant
Lewannick
Tresinney
Watergate
Bowithick
Buttern Hill
Bray Down
Brown Willy
Garrow Tor
Gulland Rock
New Polzeath
Pentireglaze
Trelights
St Teath
Treveighan
Pendoggett
Michaelstow
Codda
Trevadlock
Congdon's Shop
Newtown
Trebullett
Gunver Head
Polzeath
Trebetherick
St Endellion
St Minver
Trelill
St Kew
Trequite
St Kew Highway
St Breward
Row
Lank
St Tudy
Bolventor
Trebartha
North Hill
Coad's Green
Trevose Head
Quies
Harlyn
Crugmeer
Trevone
Pityme
Rock
Stoptide
Chapel Amble
Trewornan
Kelly
Wenfordbridge
Bradford
Smallacombe Downs
Berriowbridge
Kilmar Tor
Constantine Bay
Treyarnon
St Merryn
Shop
Padstow
Bodieve
Trevanson
St Mabyn
Blisland
Temple
Henwood
Rilla Mill
Upton Cross
Porthcothan Beach
Porthcothan
St Issey
Edmonton
Wadebridge
Egloshayle
Tregolds
Little Petherick
Whitecross
St Breock
Sladesbridge
Hellandbridge
Helland
Cardinham Moor
Millpool
Maidenwell
Brown Gelly
Siblyback Reservoir
Minions
Caradon Hill
Caradon Town
Pensilva
Common Moor
Park Head
Penrose
St Ervan
Rumford
Trenance
Treburrick
Tredinnick
St Eval
Burlawn
Washaway
Lane-end
Cardinham
Treslea
Warleggan
Draynes
Darite
Crow's Nest
Middlehill
Charaton
Trenance
Mawgan Porth
Berryl's Point
Trevarrian
St Mawgan
Lanvean
Vale of Mawgan
St Breock Downs
Rutherbridge
Boscarne
Nanstallon
Dunmere
Bodmin
Mount
St Neot
St Cleer
Tremar
Gang
St Ive
Tregurrian
Carloggas
NEWQUAY CORNWALL INTERNATIONAL
Winnard's Perch
Rosenannon
St. Wenn
Withiel
Withielgoose
Tremore
St Lawrence
Fletchersbridge
Ley
Liskeard
Merrymeet
Pengover Green
St Columb Major
Talskiddy
Reterth
Tregonetha
Lanivet
Tregullon
Respryn
Middle Draft
West Taphouse
Middle Taphouse
Doublebois
Dobwalls
Trevelmond
East Taphouse
St Pinnock
Menheniot
Tregaswith
Trebudannon
Colan
Quintrell Downs
Mountjoy
Black Cross
Ruthvoes
Belowda
Victoria
Higher Town
Criggan
Lockengate
Bokiddick
Trebyan
Sweetshouse
Redmoor
Restormel
Braddock
Boconnoc
Bodrane
Herodsfoot
St Keyne
Trewidland
Horningtops
Doddycross
White Cross
St Columb Road
Trevarren
Indian Queens
Fraddon
Enniscaven
Tregoss
Roche
Trezaise
Bilberry
Bodwen
Lanlivery
Lostwithiel
Bridgend
Couch's Mill
Duloe
Budge's Shop
Roseclisten
Kestle Mill
Retyn
St Dennis
Gothers
Coldvreath
Hensbarrow Downs
Bugle
Rosevean
Rescorla
Luxulyan
Milltown
Saint Winnow
Lerryn
Boraddon
Lanreath
Tredinnick
Tregarland
Widegates
Hessenford
Newlyn East
St Enoder
Blue Anchor
Retew
Whitemoor
Stenalees
Nanpean
Carthew
Penwithick
Trethurgy
Tywardreath Highway
Penpillick
Muchlarnick
Sandplace
Morval
No Man's Land
Tidewalla
Summercourt
Treviscoe
Meledor
Ruddlemoor
Tregrehan Mills
St Blazey
St Blazey Gate
Treesmill
Tywardreath
Torfrey
Golant
St Veep
Pelynt
St Martin
Downderry
Carland Cross
Mitchell
Chapel Town
Brighton
Foxhole
Sarcewater
High Street
Lanteglos Highway
Penpoll
Trenewan
Looe
East Looe
West Looe
Newlyn Downs
New Mills
St Stephen
Coombe
Trewoon
Mount Charles
Par
Polkerris
Fowey
Bodinnick
Lansallos
Portlooe
Looe Bay
Talland
St George's Island (Looe Island)
Treliassick
Carlyon Bay
Charlestown
St Austell Bay
St Mewan
St Austell
Porthpean
Menabilly
Polruan
Pencarrow Head
Lantivet Bay
Polperro
Porthallow
St Allen
Truthan
Trispen
Tregear
Ladock
Grampound Road
Polgooth
Sticker
Hewas Water
London Apprentice
Gribbin Head
St Erme
Shortlanesend
Idless
Probus
Grampound
Creed
Trenarren
Black Head
Pentewan
Tregiskey
Tresillian
Polmassick
St Ewe
Kestle
Penare Point
Mevagissey Bay
Mevagissey
Portmellon
Chapel Point
TRURO
Merther
St Clement
Malpas
Tregony
Trewarthenick
Ruan Lanihorne
Trevarrick
St Michael Caerhays
Gorran Churchtown
Gorran Haven
Maenease Point
Playing Place
Old Kea
Penelewey
St Michael Penkevil
Lamorran
Coombe
Portholland
Boswinger
Treworga
Trelissick
Philleigh
Veryan Green
Veryan
Portloe
Veryan Bay
Penare
Dodman Point
Treworthal
Treworlas
Feock
Mylor Bridge
St Just in Roseland
Trewithian
Gerrans Bay
Nare Head
Portscatho
Gerrans
Flushing
St Mawes
Greeb Point
Castle Pt
Bohortha
St Anthony
Pendennis Point
Zone Point
FALMOUTH BAY
Mullion Head
Meneage
Porthoustock
Manacle Point
The Manacles
ALDERNEY
St Anne
Grande Havre
L'Islet
Bordeaux
Grandes Rocques
St Sampson
Herm
Albecq
Vazon Bay
Kings Mills
St Peter Port
Lihou
Jethou
Rocquaine Bay
St Saviour
Sark
Pleinmont Pt
GUERNSEY
St Martin
Brecqhou
Little Sark
Jerbourg Pt
Plémont Pt
Greve de Lecq Bay
St John
Bouley Bay
St Mary
Trinity
Rozel
St Ouen
Carrefour Selous
St Martin
St Catherine's Bay
St Ouen's Bay
St Peter
JERSEY
Five Oaks
Maufant
Beaumont
St Aubin's Bay
St Saviour
Gorey
St Brelade
St Aubin
ST HELIER
Grouville
St Clement
Noirmont Pt
La Rocque Pt
A30
A39
A389
A38
A390
A391
A392
A3058
A3059
A3075
A3076
A3078
A3082
A387
A3
A4
A8
A10
A12
A13

4
A
B
C
D
E
6
3
1
2
3
4
5
6
7
Widemouth Bay
Box's Shop
Week St Mary
Bridgerule
Pyworthy
Chasty
Whimble
Hollacombe
Halwill Forest
21
Chilla
Odham
Dizzard Point
Poundstock
Treskinnick Cross
Tinney
Coppathorne
23
22
St Gennys
Tregole
Trewint
Penlean
Whitstone
North Tamerton
Clawton
Corfcott Green
Halwill
Halwill Junction
Beaworthy
Whiddon
Crackington Haven
Cambeak
Week St Mary
Crackington
Rosecare
Jacobstow
Wainhouse Corner
Trebarrow
Tetcott
Lana
Quoditch
Higher Prestacott
Upcott
Broadbury
Ashwater
Henford
Germansweek
Eworthy
Higher Whiteleigh
West Curry
Fire Beacon Point
Tresparrett Posts
Trengune
South Wheatley
Maxworthy
Clubworthy
Northcott
Chapmans Well
Virginstow
Bratton Clovelly
Beeny
Marshgate
Collamoor Head
Langdon
Canworthy Water
Boyton
Bennacott
Hele
West Panson
East Panson
St Giles on the Heath
Boscastle
Trevalga
35
Lesnewth
Tresparrett
Otterham
Trelash
Warbstow
Troswell
Brazacott
Langdon
Bridgetown
Broadwoodwidger
Tintagel Head
Bossiney
Tintagel
34
Trewarmett
Penpethy
Treknow
Start Point
Trebarwith
Hendraburnick
Hallworthy
Davidstow
Trewassa
Tremail
Treneglos
Three Hammers
Tresmeer
Tremaine
15
Penrose
North Petherwin
Trebeath
Egloskerry
Tregeare
Langore
Ladycross
Leat
Polapit Tamar
Werrington
Yeolmbridge
Cross Green
Kellacott
Thrushelton
Stowford
Portgate
Lewdown
Lobhillcross
Lewtrenchard
Cold Northcott
Badgall
Truscott
St Stephens
Newport
Dutson
Launceston
Lifton
Tinhay
Sprytown
Allerford
Rockhead
Delabole
Treligga
33
Camelford
32
Tregoodwell
St Clether
Trevivian
Downhead
Laneast
Red Down
Pipers Pool
Tregadillett
Lower Moor
New Park
Tregunnon
Trewen
Polyphant
Kennards House
Daw's House
16
Coryton
Liddaton Green
Westdowns
Trewalder
Valley Truckle
Lanteglos
Pencarrow
Trevinney
Bowithick
Buttern Hill
346
Bray Down
Port Isaac Bay
Port Isaac
Port Gaverne
29
St Teath
Helstone
Watergate
Rough Tor
400
Brown Willy
420
Altarnun
Trewint
Tredaule
Fivelanes
Lewannick
South Petherwin
Trecrogo
Lawhitton
Bradstone
Kelly
Meadwell
Marystow
Chillaton
North Brentor
Brentor Tor
335
Pendoggett
Trevighan
Michaelstow
Garrow Tor
331
369
Plusha
Lezant
Trekenner
Treburley
Felldownhead
Dunterton
Milton Abbot
Longcross
Mary
St Endellion
Trelill
St Breward
Row
Trevadlock
Congdon's Shop
Newtown
Trebullett
Lower Trebullett
Rezare
Bealsmill
Sydenham Damerel
Tutwell
Lamerton
Rushford
19
Minver
Trewethern
St Kew
Trequite
St Kew Highway
St Tudy
Lank
Wenfordbridge
30
Bradford
B O D M I N
M O O R
Bolventor
Codda
Trebartha
North Hill
Coad's Green
Berriowbridge
Smallacombe Downs
390
Kilmar Tor
Laney
Bray Shop
Kingston
Venterdon
Cholwell
Horsebridge
Tavistock
Chapel
Kellys
C O R N W A L L
St Mabyn
Blisland
Temple
Colliford Reservoir
Dozmary Pool
Siblyback Reservoir
Henwood
Rilla Mill
Rillaton
Linkinhorne
Stoke Climsland
17
Downgate
Kit Hill
333
Luckett
Latchley
Whitchurch
Wadebridge
Egloshayle
Hellandbridge
Helland
Cardinham Moor
Millpool
342
Brown Gelly
PL
Upton
Upton Cross
Plushabridge
Mornick
South Hill
Maders
Kelly Bray
Caradon Hill
369
Caradon Town
Minions
Common Moor
Pensilva
Golberdon
Callington
Monkscross
Coxpark
Chilsworthy
18
Gunnislake
Higher Walreddon
Sladesbridge
Burlawn
Washaway
Lane-end
Maidenwell
Trezlea
Cardinham
Warleggan
Draynes
Darite
Crow's Nest
Middlehill
Charaton
Trevigro
Harrowbarrow
St Ann's Chapel
Norris Green
Albaston
Metherell
Calstock
Bunmere
Dunmere
31
Bodmin
Mount
St Neot
St Cleer
Tremar
Gang
Frogwell
Newbridge
Ashton
Rumleigh
Buckland Monachorum
Rutherbridge
Boscarne
Nanstallon
St Lawrence
Fletchersbridge
Ley
14
Liskeard
Merrymeet
St Ive
A390
Parkfield
St Dominick
St Mellion
Burraton
Bohetherick
Bere Alston
Withielgoose
Tremore
Tregullon
Respryn
Middle Drift
Doublebois
Dobwalls
Pengover Green
Quethiock
Weir Quay
Cotts
Maristow House
Lanivet
Bodmin Parkway Sta
West Taphouse
Middle Taphouse
East Taphouse
Trevelmond
St Pinnock
Lamellion
Menheniot
Doddycross
Blunts
Pillaton
12
Ellbridge
Cargreen
Bere Ferrers
Victoria
Trebyan
Bokiddick
Sweetshouse
Braddock
Bodrane
Horningtops
Hatt
Landulph
5
Tamerton Foliot
Higher Town
Criggan
Lockengate
Bodwen
Restormel
Redmoor
Boconnoc
Herodsfoot
St Keyne
Trewidland
Tideford Cross
Botusfleming
Roche
Trezaise
Bilberry
Lanlivery
Bridgend
Lostwithiel
22
Couch's Mill
Duloe
Bylane End
Budge's Shop
Tideford
Landrake
Carkeel
Saltash
Toll charged eastbound only
Coldvreath
Hensbarrow Downs
Bugle
Roseveare
Rescorla
Luxulyan
Milltown
Saint Winnow
Boconnon
Lanreath
Tredinnick
Tregarland
Widegates
Hessenford
Saint Erney
Trerulefoot
Markwell
Trematon
St Germans
Trehan
Burraton
St Stephens
PLYMOUTH
26
Stenalees
Penwithick
Penpillick
Tywardreath Highway
24
Lerryn
Sandplace
Morval
No Man's Land
Polbathic
Narkurs
Maryfield
Torpoint
2
3
4
1
Devonport
Stonehouse
Carthew
Trethurgy
Tregrehan Mills
St Blazey
St Blazey Gate
Treesmill
Tywardreath
Tolfrey
Golant
Lanteglos Highway
St Veep
Peppill
Muchlarnick
Pelynt
St Martin
Seaton
Downderry
11
Portwrinkle
Sheviock
Crafthole
Antony
St John
Cremyll
Drake's Tumchi Island
25
Par
Polkerris
23
Trenewan
13
Looe
West Looe
East Looe
Looe Bay
Trewoon
St Mewan
Mount Charles
Charlestown
Carlyon Bay
Menabilly
Fowey
Bodinnick
Lansallos
Porthallow
Talland
Portlooe
St George's Island (Looe Island)
Whitsand Bay
Freathy
Millbrook
10
Kingsand
Cawsand
Rame
Polgooth
St Austell
St Austell Bay
Sticker
Porthpean
London Apprentice
Polruan
Lantivet Bay
Pencarrow Head
Polperro
Gribbin Head
Plymouth Breakwater
Penlee Point
Rame Head
Trenarren
Black Head
Pentewan
Tregiskey
Penare Point
Mevagissey Bay
Mevagissey
Portmellon
Chapel Point
Gorran Churchtown
Gorran Haven
Maenease Point
Kestle
Penare
Dodman Point
Eddystone
0
2
4
6 miles
0
2
4
6
8
10 km
B
C
D
E

F
G
H
J
K
5
7
DEVON
DARTMOOR
TORBAY
EXETER
TORQUAY
NEWTON ABBOT
PLYMOUTH
Jacobstowe
Exbourne
Sampford Courtenay
North Tawton
Bow
Copplestone
Crediton
Shobrooke
Thorverton
Killerton
Okehampton
Inwardleigh
Folly Gate
Belstone
Sticklepath
South Tawton
South Zeal
Spreyton
Whiddon Down
Yeoford
Cheriton Bishop
Tedburn St Mary
Crockernwell
Drewsteignton
Throwleigh
Chagford
Moretonhampstead
North Bovey
Manaton
Lustleigh
Bovey Tracey
Dunsford
Bridford
Christow
Doddiscombsleigh
Exminster
Kenn
Kenton
Topsham
Clyst St Mary
Woodbury
Exton
Lympstone
Starcross
Exmouth
Dawlish
Teignmouth
Shaldon
Chudleigh
Ideford
Kingsteignton
Bishopsteignton
Ashburton
Buckfastleigh
Buckfast
Widecombe in the Moor
Postbridge
Princetown
Yes Tor
High Willhays
Cawsand Hill
Sittaford Tor
Cut Hill
Rippon Tor
Haytor Vale
Yelverton
Meavy
Walkhampton
Sheepstor
Ivybridge
Cornwood
Harford
Ugborough Moor
Dean Moor
South Brent
Totnes
Dartington
Staverton
Ipplepen
Kingskerswell
Marldon
Paignton
Brixham
Berry Head
Tor Bay
Hope's Nose
Babbacombe Bay
Dartmouth
Kingswear
Stoke Fleming
Strete
Slapton
Start Bay
Start Point
Kingsbridge
Salcombe
Bolt Head
Bolt Tail
Prawle Point
Modbury
Yealmpton
Newton Ferrers
Noss Mayo
Wembury
Bigbury-on-Sea
Bigbury Bay
Burgh Island
Thurlestone
Hope
Loddiswell
Moreleigh
Halwell
Harbertonford
Diptford
Avonwick
Ugborough
Ermington
Aveton Gifford
Churchstow
Chillington
Torcross
Hallsands
Beesands
East Portlemouth
Mew Stone
Sharkham Point
Scabbacombe Head

A
B
C
D
E
1
2
3
4
5
6
7
North West Point
EX
LUNDY
34
Rat Island
Shutter Rock
Heddon's Mouth
Widmouth Head
Ilfracombe
Hele
Berrynarbor
Combe Martin Bay
Trentishoe
Martinhoe
Bull Point
Rockham Bay
Morte Point
Mortehoe
Lee
Slade
Sterridge
Combe Martin
Hunter's Inn
Heale
Kemacott
Killington
Parracombe
Mullacott Cross
Seymour Villas
Woolacombe
Trimstone
Dean Cross
Cheglinch
West Down
Berry Down Cross
Kentisbury
Churchtown
Morte Bay
Bradwell
Blackmoor Gate
Challacombe
Patchole
Kentisbury Ford
Arlington
Arlington Beccott
East Down
Clifton
Baggy Point
Putsborough
Pickwell
North Buckland
Georgeham
Bittadon
Churchill
Croyde Bay
Croyde
33
Knowle
Halsinger
Winsham
Middle Marwood
Milltown
31
Muddiford
Upcott
Knightacott
Loxhore
Lobb
Boode
Marwood
Higher Muddiford
Shirwell
Shirwell Cross
Lower Loxhore
Bratton Fleming
Benton
Leworthy
Saunton
Saunton Sands
Braunton
Pippacott
Heanton Punchardon
Kingsheanton
Prixford
West Ashford
Ashford
Stoke Rivers
Braunton Burrows
Toll
Wrafton
Chivenor
Bradiford
Pilton
Northleigh
BARNSTAPLE
Bickington
Newport
Lilly
Goodleigh
Willesleigh
Gunn
32
Stoodleigh
West Buckland
East Buckland
BARNSTAPLE BAY (BIDEFORD BAY)
The Neck
Appledore
Yelland
Fremington
Lake
Landkey
Swimbridge Newland
Yarnacott
Instow
Bickleton
Tawstock
Bishop's Tawton
Riverton
Westward Ho!
Tapeley
Northam
Westleigh
St John's Chapel
Swimbridge
Hartland Point
Titchberry
Windbury Point
Gallantry Bower
Eastleigh
Horwood
Lower Lovacott
Harracott
Cobbaton
Stowford
Filleigh
East-the-Water
Bideford
Woodtown
Newton Tracey
Hiscott
Ensis
Herner
Chapelton
Chittlehampton
Abbotsham
Clovelly
Clovelly Bay
Gammaton
Alverdiscott
Hartland Quay
Stoke
Hartland
Sierra
Dyke
Clovelly Cross
Fairy Cross
Buck's Mills
Buck's Cross
Horns Cross
Ford
Yeo Vale
Gammaton Moor
Landcross
Huntshaw Water
Yarnscombe
Fishleigh Barton
Atherington
Umberleigh
Hudscott
Milford
Alwington
Littleham
Eastacott
Clapworthy
Elmscott
Edistone
Philham
Goldworthy
Buckland Brewer
Saltrens
Weare Giffard
Huntshaw
Huntshaw Cross
Langridgeford
Langridge
Warkleigh
Satterleigh
Tosberry
Woolfardisworthy
Cranford
Parkham
Parkham Ash
Monkleigh
High Bickington
Chittlehamholt
37
South Hole
Almiston Cross
39
Sherwood Green
High Bullen
Portsmouth Arms Sta
Knaps Longpeak
Welcombe
Melbury
Frithelstock Stone
Frithelstock
Great Torrington
Dodscott
St Giles in the Wood
Kingscott
Head Bridge
Mead
Ashmansworthy
Fowler's Piece
Taddiport
38
Northcote Manor
Darracott
Meddon
Kimbaldon Bridge
Little Torrington
Roborough
Gooseham
Woolley
East Putford
Burrington
Eastcott
East Youlstone
Langtree
Langtree Week
Villavin
Elstone
Dinworthy
West Putford
Beaford
West Youlstone
Stibb Cross
Berry Cross
Great Potheridge
Little Potheridge
Cottwood
Riddlecombe
Ashreigney
Shop
Woodford
Bradworthy
Haytown
Bulkworthy
Peters Marland
Winswell
Lower Sharpnose Point
Brendon
Abbots Bickington
Woollaton
Merton
Heanton Satchville
Dolton
Coombe
Taylors Cross
Kilkhampton
Alfardisworthy
Sutcombe
Newton St Petrock
Huish
Little Marland
Hollacombe Town
Thurdon
Upper Tamar Lake
Lower Tamar Lake
Soldon
Sutcombemill
Venngreen
Eggesford Barton
Hollocombe
Ashley
Stibb
Soldon Cross
Milton Damerel
Dowland
23
Youldonmoor Cross
Youldon
North Town
Petrockstowe
19
Shebbear
Buckland Filleigh
Wembworthy
Maer
Poughill
Flexbury
Hersham
Bush
Holsworthy Beacon
Thornbury
Ash Barton
Meeth
Iddesleigh
Winkleigh
Bude Haven
Bude
Grimscott
Woodacott
Bradford
Lashbrook
Inglegh Green
D
Stratton
Launcells Cross
Chilsworthy
Brendon
Sheepwash
Hele Bridge
Brushford
Lana
Pancrasweek
22
Cookbury
Middlecott
Black Torrington
Broadwood Kelly
Launcells
Red Post
Cookbury Wick
Monkokehampton
Bondleigh
A3072
Derril
Rydon
Brandis Corner
Highampton
Hatherleigh
Lowton
Helebridge
Marhamchurch
Bridgerule
Holsworthy
Anvil Corner
Dunsland Cross
Derriton
Chasty
Whimble
Hollacombe
Graddon Moor
Lydacott
Basset's Cross
Honeychurch
North Tawton
Widemouth Bay
Pyworthy
Odham
Chilla
Ekbourne
Sampford Courtenay
Titson
Box's Shop
Yeomadon
Halwill Forest
21
Jacobstowe
Week Orchard
Shilstone
Coppathorne
Whiddon
Trecott
Tamar
Poundstock
Treskinnick Cross
Tinney
Clawton
Halwill
Halwill Junction
Beaworthy
Northlew
Inwardleigh
Belstone Corner
Sampford Courtenay Sta
Tregole
Penlean
Whitstone
Corfcott Green
East Kimber
Ashbury
Oak Cross
Folly Gate
Trewint
Week St Mary
North Tamerton
Upcott
Patchacott
Rowden
Taw Green
Quoditch
Higher Prestacott
Broadbury
20
Chichacott
CORNWALL
Tetcott
Jacobstow
Trebarrow
Lana
Ashwater
Okehampton
Southcott
South Tawton
Higher Whiteleigh
Luffincott
Henford
Eworthy
Thorndon Cross
Yelland
Sticklepath
Trengune
Maxworthy
West Curry
Clubworthy
Germansweek
Boasley Cross
Belstone
South Zeal
Small Wheatley
Northcott
Chapmans Well
Roadford Reservoir
Hewton
Okehampton Camp
Canworthy Water
Bennacott
Boyton
Virginstow
Bratton Clovelly
Meldon
Meldon Sta
Cawsand Hill
Troswell
Brazacott
Hele
West Panson
Thrushel
Throwleigh
Warbstow
Langdon
St Giles on the Heath
Ebsworthy Town
Forda
Sourton
Yes Tor
619
Penrose
North Petherwin
Bridgetown
Broadwoodwidger
621
High Willhays
Wonson
Tremaine
15
Bridestowe
Bidlake
Hallworthy
Treneglos
Ladycross
Polapit Tamar
Werrington
Cross Green
Kellacott
Thrushelton
Southerly
Bridestowe and Sourton Common
Okement Hill
Gidleigh
413
Murchington
Three Hammers
Tresmeer
Trebeath
Tregeare
Egloskerry
Yeolmbridge
Leat
Hangingstone Hill
604
Chagford
Cold Northcott
Badgall
Truscott
St Stephens
Newport
Dutson
Lifton Down
Stowford
Lewdown
Lobhillcross
Shortacombe
Cranmere Pool
Whitehorse Hill
601
Frenchbeer
A395
Red Down
Pipers Pool
PL
Launceston
Tinhay
Lifton
Sprytown
Portgate
Allerford
Lewtrenchard
Lydford
Amicombe Hill
Great Kneeset
568
Downhead
Tregadillett
Downton
Fernworthy Reservoir
Corndon
Laneast
Trewen
16
Corytown
Black Ridge
Sittaford Tor
Tregunnon
Polyphant
Kennards House
Daw's House
Lawhitton
Marystow
Liddaton Green
Beardon
Cut Hill
604
White Ridge
Bray Down
346
Altarnun
Tredaule
South Petherwin
Kelly
Meadwell
Chillaton
North Brentor
Black Down
Willsworthy
504
Warren House
Trewint
Fivelanes
Lewannick
Tregrogo
Bradstone
Brent Tor
335
South Brentor
Lynch Tor
517
Rough Tor
546
Higher White Tor
525
Plusha
Fellownhead
Horndon
DARTMOOR
Lezant
Mary Tavy
Blackdown
Cocks Hill
Cowsic Head
Postbridge
20
369
0 2 4 6 miles
0 2 4 6 8 10 km
Dunterton
Lamerton
19
Cudlipptown
Peter Tavy
Great Mis Tor
Bellever
Trebartha
Coad's Green
Trebullett
Bealsmill
Sydenham
Cox Tor
Bolventor
4
4

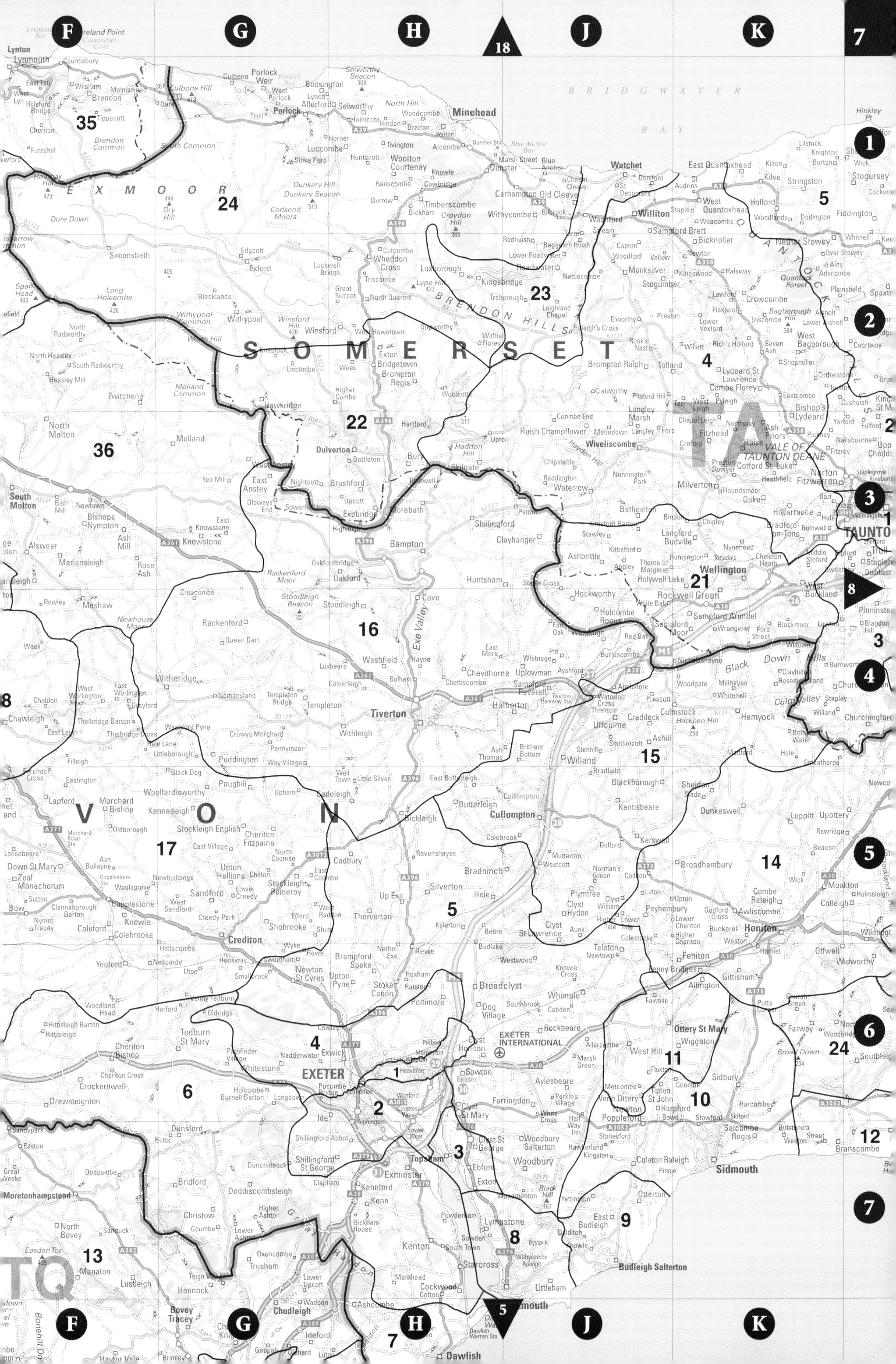
F
G
H
18
J
K
Foreland Point
Countisbury Cove
Lynton
Lynmouth
Countisbury
East Lyn
West Lyn
Hillsford Bridge
Wilsham
Brendon
Malmsmead
Oare
Culbone Hill
Culbone
Porlock Weir
Porlock Bay
Porlock
West Porlock
Bossington
Selworthy Beacon
Lynch
Allerford
Selworthy
North Hill
Woodcombe
Minehead
Bratton
Hindon
Holnicote
Tippacott
Brendon Common
Cheriton
Furzehill
35
South Common
B R I D G W A T E R
B A Y
Hinkley Pt
Horner
Tivington
Luccombe
Huntscott
Alcombe
Dunster Sta
Blue Anchor Bay
Marsh Street
Blue Anchor
Dunster
Stoke Pero
Wootton Courtenay
Knowle
Cowbridge
Ranscombe
Watchet
Doniford
East Quantoxhead
Kilton
Lilstock
Knighton
Burton
Wick
Stogursey
Kilve
Stringston
5
Holford
Dodington
Fiddington
Woodlands
1
Hoaroak Hill
473
E X M O O R
Dry Hill
444
24
Dunkery Hill
Dunkery Beacon
519
Codsend Moors
Burrow
Timberscombe
Bickham
Croydon Hill
365
Carhampton
Old Cleeve
Chapel Cleeve
Withycombe
Bilbrook
Washford
Williton
St Decumans
St Audries
West Quantoxhead
Staple
Weacombe
Sampford Brett
Bicknoller
Nether Stowey
Over Stowey
Whitnell
Dure Down
Simonsbath
Edgcott
Exford
Luckwell Bridge
Cutcombe
Wheddon Cross
Luxborough
Rodhuish
Beggearn Huish
Roadwater
Lower Roadwater
Nettlecombe
Capton
Woodford
Monksilver
Yellow
Newton
Halsway
Kingswood
Stogumber
Aley
Adscombe
Quantock Forest
Span Head
493
Long Holcombe
436
409
Blacklands
Great Nurcot
Triscombe
North Quarme
Lype Hill
423
Kingsbridge
Treborough
23
Leighland Chapel
B R E N D O N   H I L L S
Raleigh's Cross
Elworthy
Preston
Lawford
Crowcombe
Flaxpool
Bagborough Hill
384
Triscombe
Plainsfield
Aisholt
Lower Aisholt
2
Lower Vexford
North Radworthy
Withypool Common
Withypool
Winsford Hill
426
Winsford
West Howetown
Gupworthy
Withiel Florey
Rook's Nest
Willett
Rich's Holford
Seven Ash
West Bagborough
Courtway
Worth Hill
S O M E R S E T
North Heasley
South Radworthy
Heasley Mill
Shaplock
Liscombe
Exton
Week
Bridgetown
Brompton Regis
Brompton Ralph
Tolland
4
Lydeard St Lawrence
Combe Florey
Shopnoller
Cothelstone
Twitchen
Molland Common
Hawkridge
Higher Combe
Woolcotts
Clatworthy
Pitsford Hill
Terr
West Leigh
Pyleigh
Eastcombe
Bishop's Lydeard
Cushuish
North Molton
22
Hartford
317
Coombe End
Langley Marsh
Langley
Ford
Chapel Leigh
Northway
Ash Priors
Yarford
Fulford
Huish Champflower
Maundown
Fitzhead
Pickney
Nailsbourne
36
Molland
Dulverton
Battleton
Haddon Hill
Upton
Wiveliscombe
Heydon Hill
Croford
Halse
VALE OF TAUNTON DEANE
Fitzroy
West Anstey
Yeo Mill
East Anstey
Bury
Skilgate
Chipstable
Raddington
Preston Bowyer
Cotford St Luke
Heathfield
Norton Fitzwarren
Nightcott
Brushford
Hele
Waterrow
Nunnington Park
Milverton
Houndsmoor
Oake
3
South Molton
Bish Mill
Newtown
Oldways End
Sowerhill
Upcott
Exebridge
Morebath
Petton
Bathealton
Bindon
Chipley
Hillfarrance
Bradford-on-Tone
Rumwell
TAUNTON
Bishops Nympton
Knowstone
East Knowstone
Highleigh
Bampton
Shillingford
Clayhanger
Kittisford Barton
Stawley
Langford Budville
Nynehead
Alswear
Ash Mill
Marianslleigh
Rose Ash
Rackenford Moor
Oakfordbridge
Oakford
Huntsham
Ashbrittle
Kittisford
Thorne St Margaret
Appley
Runnington
Tonedale
Chelston Heath
Middle Stoford
Wellington
West Buckland
Holywell Lake
21
8
Creacombe
Stoodleigh Beacon
301
Stoodleigh
Cove
Exe Valley
Stapple Cross
Hockworthy
Rockwell Green
White Ball
Rowley
Meshaw
Newhouse Moor
Rackenford
Queen Dart
16
Holcombe Rogus
Fairy Oak
Waddeigh
Sampford Moor
Sampford Arundel
Wrangway
Ford Street
Blackmoor
Pitminster
Blagdon Hill
Red Ball
Burlescombe
East Mere
Pitt
Whitnage
Washfield
Hayne
Loxbeare
Chevithorne
Uplowman
Ayshford
Nicholashayne
Black Down Hills
Witheridge
West Worlington
East Worlington
Calverleigh
Bolham
Chettiscombe
Sampford Peverell
Tiverton Parkway Sta
Appledore
Woodgate
Millhayes
Whitehall
Clayhidon
Rosemary Lane
Churchinford
Week
Cheldon
Chawleigh
Drayford
Nomansland
Templeton Bridge
Templeton
Halberton
Waterloo Cross
Prescott
Culmstock
Hackpen Hill
258
Hemyock
Culm Valley
Stapley
Willand
Thelbridge Barton
East Leigh
Thelbridge Cross
Washford Pyne
Cruwys Morchard
Tiverton
Withleigh
Craddock
Uffculme
Ashill
Bolham Water
Hele Lane
Littleborough
Pennymoor
Way Village
Ash Thomas
Brithem Bottom
Stenhill
Smithincott
Willand
15
Madford
Hole
Smeatharpe
Filleigh
Forches Cross
Eastington
Puddington
Black Dog
Well Town
Little Silver
East Butterleigh
Bradfield
Blackborough
Sheldon
Luppitt
Upottery
Lapford
Morchard Bishop
Woolfardisworthy
Poughill
Upham
Cadeleigh
Butterleigh
Cullompton
Kentisbeare
Dunkeswell
Rawridge
V
O
N
Kennerleigh
Bickleigh
Morchard Road Sta
Oldborough
Stockleigh English
17
East Village
Cheriton Fitzpaine
North Coombe
Cadbury
Ravenshayes
Colebrook
Mutterton
Westcott
Dulford
Kerswell
Broadhembury
14
Beacon
5
Loosebeare
Down St Mary
Zeal Monachorum
Ash
Bullayne
Copplestone Sta
Upton Hellions
Chilton
Stockleigh Pomeroy
East Coombe
Silverton
Bradninch
Norman's Green
Colliton
Wick
Monkton
Holmsleigh
Sutton
Bow
Clannaborough Barton
Woolsgrove
Copplestone
Newbuildings
Sandford
Lower Creedy
Up Exe
Hele
Plymtree
Clyst William
Luton
Upton
Payhembury
Combe Raleigh
Awliscombe
Cotleigh
Nymet Tracey
Coleford
Knowle
Colebrooke
West Sandford
Creedy Park
Shobrooke
West Raddon
Shute
Thorverton
Killerton
Clyst Hydon
Higher Tale
Lower Tale
Godford Cross
Lower Cheriton
Buckerell
Honiton
Wilmington
Crediton
Hollacombe
Wyke
Rewe
Beare
Clyst St Lawrence
Aunk
Colestocks
Higher Cheriton
Weston
Yeoford
Neopardy
Hookway
Sweetham
Brampford Speke
Nether Exe
Rewe
Budlake
Talaton
Newtown
Feniton
Hamlet
Offwell
Widworthy
Uton
Smallbrook
Newton St Cyres
Upton Pyne
Huxham
Westwood
Knowle Cross
Fenny Bridges
Gittisham
Stoke Canon
Ratsloe
Broadclyst
Whimple
Alfington
Woodland Head
Venny Tedburn
Harford
Poltimore
Dog Village
Cobden
Fairmile
Putts Corner
Church Green
Hittisleigh Barton
Hittisleigh
Oldridge
Tedburn St Mary
Cowley
Pinhoe
Southbrook
Rockbeare
Ottery St Mary
Wiggaton
North Farway
Farway
Woodbridge
6
Cheriton Bishop
Pathfinder Village
Nadderwater
Exwick
4
Monkerton
Clyst Honiton
EXETER INTERNATIONAL
Allercombe
West Hill
11
Broad Down
234
24
Southleigh
Cheriton Cross
Whitestone
EXETER
Heavitree
1
Sowton
Marsh Green
Crockernwell
Holcombe Burnell Barton
Longdown
Pocombe Bridge
St Thomas
Wonford
Aylesbeare
Fluxton
Sidbury
Drewsteignton
6
Ide
Alphington
2
Countess Wear
Clyst St Mary
Farringdon
Perkin's Village
Metcombe
Venn Ottery
Tipton St John
Coombe
10
Harcombe
Lower Wear
Newton Poppleford
Harpford
Bowd
Stowford
Sidford
Salcombe Regis
Bulstone
Street
Weston
12
Branscombe
Sandypark
Dunsford
Butts
Shillingford Abbot
White Cross
Half Way Inn
Easton
Clyst St George
Woodbury Salterton
Stoneyford
Great Weeke
Doccombe
Dunchideock
Shillingford St George
Topsham
3
Ebford
Hawkerland
Kingston
Colaton Raleigh
Exminster
Woodbury
Sidmouth
Moretonhampstead
Bridford
Clapham
Kennford
Exton
Pinn
Doddiscombsleigh
Kenn
Woodmanton
Black Hill
167
Otterton
Yettington
Higher Ashton
Powderham
Lympstone
North Bovey
Christow
Bickham House
Sowden
8
East Budleigh
9
Sanduck
Coombe
Lower Ashton
Kenton
South Town
Bystock
Withycombe Raleigh
Dalditch
Knowle
13
Easdon Tor
439
Manaton
Oxencombe
Trusham
Starcross
Budleigh Salterton
TQ
Lustleigh
Lower Upcott
Mamhead
Cockwood
Cofton
Littleham
Hennock
Teign Village
Bovey Tracey
Chudleigh
Ashcombe
Exmouth
5
Waddon
Ideford
Dawlish Warren Sta
Dawlish
7
Haytor Vale
Brimley
Gappah
Luton
Bonehill Down

8
A
B
C
D
E
19
7
1
2
3
4
5
6
7
SOMERSET
DEVON
D
BRIDGWATER
TAUNTON
Wellington
Glastonbury
Street
Somerton
Langport
Martock
South Petherton
Ilminster
Chard
Crewkerne
YEOVIL
Beaminster
Bridport
Lyme Regis
Axminster
Honiton
Seaton
Sidmouth
Ottery St Mary
Budleigh Salterton
LYME BAY
Seaton Bay
Beer Head
POLDEN HILLS
QUANTOCK HILLS
VALE OF TAUNTON DEANE
Black Down Hills
Culm Valley
King's Sedge Moor
West Sedge Moor
Marshwood Vale
Golden Cap
Pilsdon Pen
Hackpen Hill
Bagborough Hill
Glastonbury Tor
Kingsdon Hill
Bradley Hill
Eggardon Hill
North Hill
Staple Hill
Dunkeswell
Hemyock
Upottery
Yarcombe
Colyton
Kilmington
Hawkchurch
Charmouth
Chideock
West Bay
Burton Bradstock
Abbotsbury
Ilchester
Montacute
Stoke-sub-Hamdon
Castle Cary
North Petherton
Cannington
Nether Stowey
Bishop's Lydeard
Milverton
Wiveliscombe
Chilton Polden
Westonzoyland
Middlezoy
Othery
Burrow Bridge
Curry Rivel
Isle Abbotts
Hatch Beauchamp
Broadway
Whitestaunton
Winsham
Thorncombe
Broadwindsor
Netherbury
Mosterton
Misterton
Haselbury Plucknett
East Coker
Halstock
0
2
4
6 miles
0
2
4
6
8
10 km

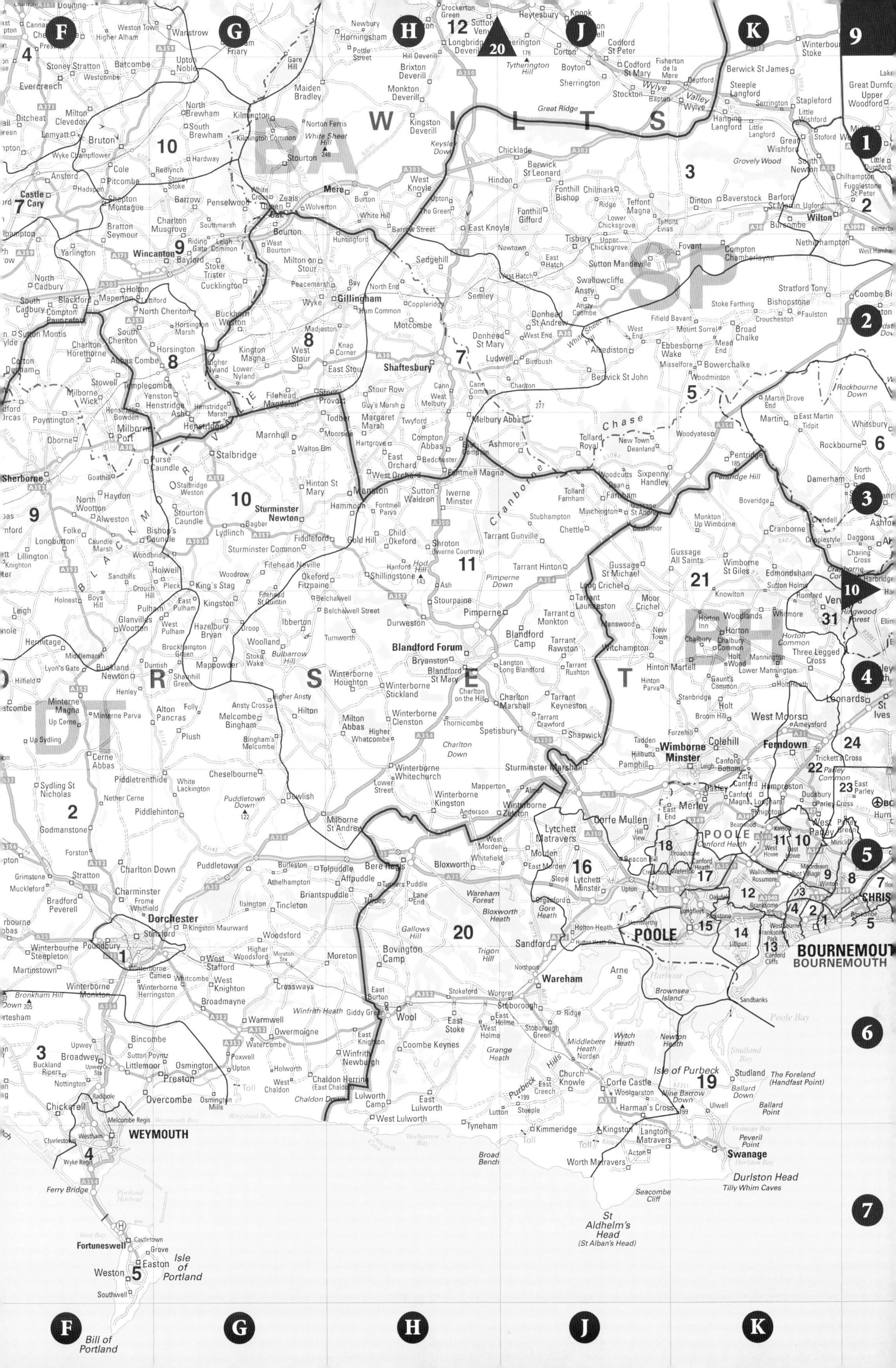

9
F
G
H
J
K
12
20
W I L T S
BA
SP
BH
DT
D O R S E T
B L A C K M O R E V A L E
Cranborne Chase
Wylye Valley
Great Ridge
Grovely Wood
Cranborne Chase
Shepton Montague
Castle Cary
Bruton
Wincanton
Mere
Gillingham
Shaftesbury
Sherborne
Milborne Port
Stalbridge
Sturminster Newton
Blandford Forum
Wimborne Minster
Ferndown
Colehill
Verwood
Wilton
Dorchester
Puddletown
Bere Regis
Wareham
Wool
Sandford
POOLE
BOURNEMOUTH
Swanage
Corfe Castle
WEYMOUTH
Fortuneswell
Isle of Portland
Bill of Portland
Poole Harbour
Brownsea Island
Poole Bay
Isle of Purbeck
Studland
The Foreland (Handfast Point)
Ballard Point
Durlston Head
Tilly Whim Caves
Seacombe Cliff
St Aldhelm's Head (St Alban's Head)
Worth Matravers
Kimmeridge
Tyneham
Lulworth Camp
West Lulworth
Broad Bench
Ferry Bridge
Weston
Easton
Southwell
Chickerell
Preston
Osmington
Winfrith Newburgh
Bovington Camp
Crossways
Tolpuddle
Charminster
Cerne Abbas
Maiden Newton
Milton Abbas
Sturminster Marshall
Corfe Mullen
Lytchett Matravers
Lytchett Minster
Merley
Canford Heath
Broadstone
West Moors
St Leonards
Three Legged Cross
Cranborne
Sixpenny Handley
Tollard Royal
Ashmore
Fontmell Magna
Iwerne Minster
Shillingstone
Okeford Fitzpaine
Child Okeford
Marnhull
Henstridge
Templecombe
Bishopstone
Broad Chalke
Tisbury
Hindon
Chicklade
Stourton
Zeals
Kilmington
Warminster
Heytesbury
Codford St Peter
Wilton

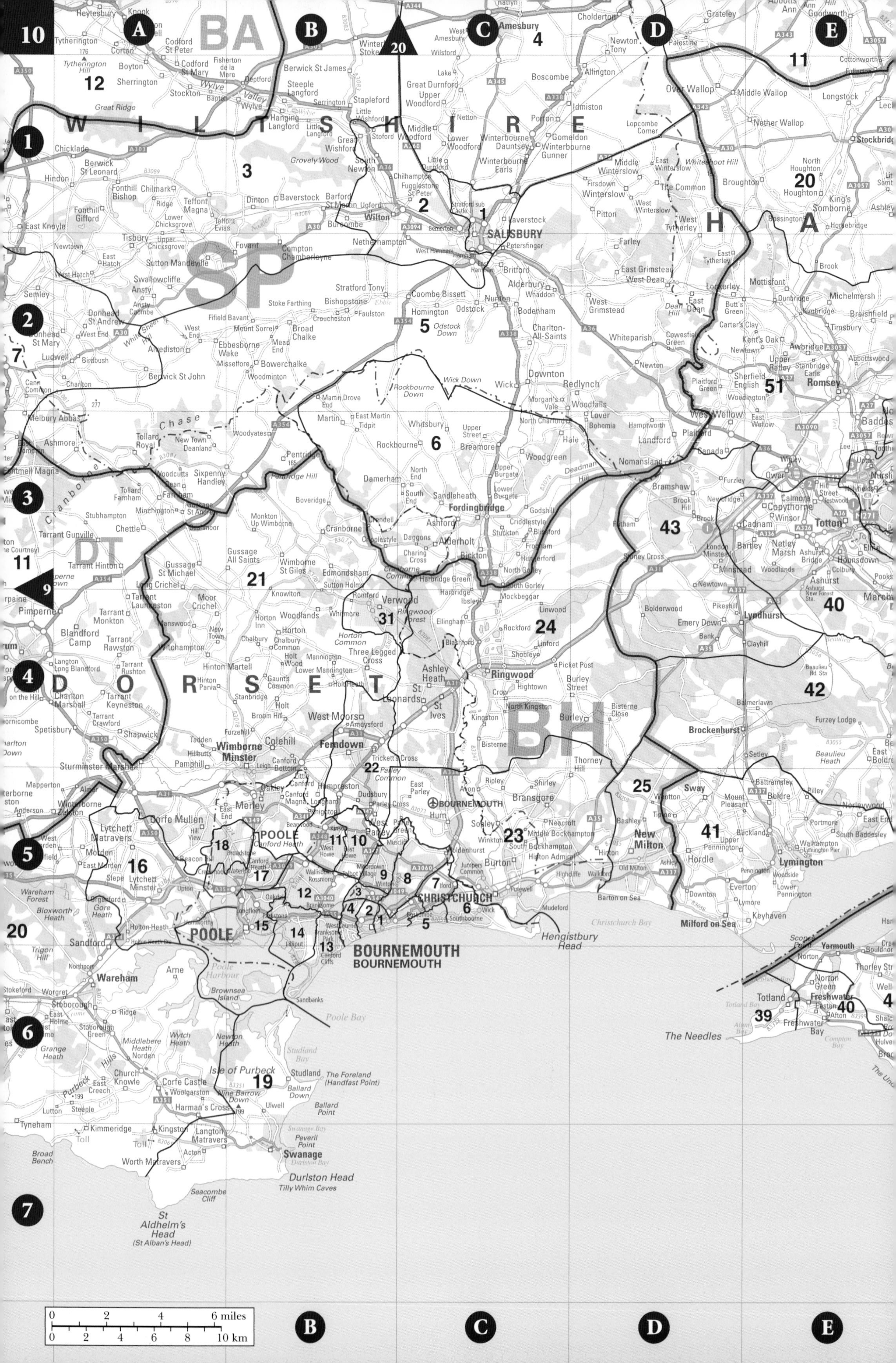
A
B
C
D
E
1
2
3
4
5
6
7
BA
SP
DT
BH
WILTSHIRE
DORSET
HA
20
9
Heytesbury
Tytherington
Codford St Peter
Codford St Mary
Boyton
Sherrington
Stockton
Wylye
Great Ridge
Berwick St James
Steeple Langford
Stapleford
Amesbury
West Amesbury
Wilsford
Lake
Great Durnford
Upper Woodford
Boscombe
Allington
Newton Tony
Cholderton
Grateley
Palestine
Over Wallop
Middle Wallop
Nether Wallop
Longstock
Idmiston
Porton
Gomeldon
Winterbourne Gunner
Winterbourne Dauntsey
Winterbourne Earls
Lopcombe Corner
Stockbridge
Houghton
Chicklade
Berwick St Leonard
Hindon
Fonthill Bishop
Fonthill Gifford
Chilmark
Teffont Magna
Grovely Wood
Dinton
Baverstock
Barford St Martin
Wilton
Burcombe
Netherhampton
SALISBURY
Laverstock
Petersfinger
Middle Winterslow
Winterslow
The Common
Firsdown
Pitton
West Winterslow
West Tytherley
East Tytherley
Broughton
King's Somborne
Bossington
Horsebridge
Brook
East Knoyle
Tisbury
Newtown
East Hatch
Sutton Mandeville
Fovant
Compton Chamberlayne
Swallowcliffe
Ansty
Semley
Donhead St Andrew
Donhead St Mary
West End
Ludwell
Birdbush
Charlton
Alvediston
Ebbesburne Wake
Berwick St John
Broad Chalke
Bowerchalke
Stratford Tony
Bishopstone
Coombe Bissett
Homington
Odstock
Nunton
Britford
Alderbury
Whaddon
Bodenham
Charlton-All-Saints
Farley
East Grimstead
West Dean
West Grimstead
Whiteparish
Lockerley
Mottisfont
Michelmersh
Timsbury
Romsey
Sherfield English
Plaitford
West Wellow
Landford
Nomansland
Hamptworth
Downton
Redlynch
Woodfalls
Wick
Hale
Woodgreen
Breamore
Whitsbury
Rockbourne
Martin
Damerham
Fordingbridge
Sandleheath
Ashford
Alderholt
Cranborne
Godshill
Frogham
Hyde
North Gorley
South Gorley
Mockbeggar
Linwood
Rockford
Ringwood
Picket Post
Burley
Burley Street
Bisterne
Kingston
Crow
Cadnam
Totton
Netley Marsh
Ashurst
Lyndhurst
Minstead
Brockenhurst
Beaulieu
Sway
Boldre
Lymington
New Milton
Milford on Sea
Hordle
Everton
Keyhaven
Barton on Sea
Highcliffe
Bransgore
Sopley
Burton
CHRISTCHURCH
Hengistbury Head
Christchurch Bay
BOURNEMOUTH
POOLE
Poole Harbour
Brownsea Island
Sandbanks
Poole Bay
Wimborne Minster
Colehill
Ferndown
West Moors
St Leonards
St Ives
Verwood
Ashley Heath
Three Legged Cross
Corfe Mullen
Merley
Lytchett Matravers
Lytchett Minster
Upton
Blandford Camp
Pimperne
Spetisbury
Sturminster Marshall
Shapwick
Wareham
Sandford
Arne
Isle of Purbeck
Studland
Studland Bay
The Foreland (Handfast Point)
Ballard Down
Ballard Point
Corfe Castle
Church Knowle
Kimmeridge
Tyneham
Kingston
Langton Matravers
Swanage
Peveril Point
Durlston Head
Tilly Whim Caves
Worth Matravers
St Aldhelm's Head
(St Alban's Head)
Seacombe Cliff
Broad Bench
Yarmouth
Totland
Freshwater
Freshwater Bay
The Needles
0 2 4 6 miles
0 2 4 6 8 10 km

F
G
H
21
J
K
1
2
3
4
5
6
7
12
SO
GU
PO
P S H I R E
W E S T
S U S S E X
SOUTH DOWNS
Proposed National Park
ISLE OF WIGHT
THE SOLENT
WINCHESTER
EASTLEIGH
SOUTHAMPTON
Hedge End
Botley
Bishop's Waltham
Swanmore
New Alresford
Alton
Bordon
Haslemere
Hindhead
Grayshott
Liphook
Petersfield
Liss
Midhurst
Horndean
WATERLOOVILLE
HAVANT
Emsworth
FAREHAM
GOSPORT
PORTSMOUTH
Lee-on-the-Solent
Stubbington
Locks Heath
Whiteley
Wickham
Denmead
Fawley
Hamble-le-Rice
Netley Abbey
Bursledon
Cowes
East Cowes
Ryde
Seaview
NEWPORT
Sandown
Shanklin
Ventnor
CHICHESTER
Selsey
Selsey Bill
East Wittering
South Hayling
Hayling Island
Thorney Island
Pagham
Bosham
Southbourne
Westbourne
Rowland's Castle
Clanfield
East Meon
West Meon
Droxford
Meonstoke
Hambledon
Twyford
Colden Common
Otterbourne
Kings Worthy
Headbourne Worthy
Alresford
Bishop's Sutton
Ropley
Four Marks
Medstead
Selborne
Greatham
Longmoor Camp
Rake
Rogate
Sheet
Steep
Stroud
Froxfield Green
Langrish
Wootton Bridge
Bembridge
Brading
Godshill
Wroxall
Niton
St Catherine's Point
Culver Cliff
Dunnose
Gilkicker Point
Stone Point
Calshot
Blackfield
Langley

A
B
C
D
E
1
2
3
4
5
6
7
CAMBERLEY
FARNBOROUGH
ALDERSHOT
WOKING
GUILDFORD
GODALMING
Haslemere
Petersfield
Midhurst
Petworth
HORSHAM
CHICHESTER
BOGNOR REGIS
LITTLEHAMPTON
WORTHING
HAVANT
Farnham
Alton
Dorking
Cranleigh
Arundel
Selsey
Selsey Bill
NORTH DOWNS
HANTS
SURREY
WEST SUSSEX
SOUTH DOWNS
0 2 4 6 miles
0 2 4 6 8 10 km

13
F
G
H
J
K
1
2
3
4
5
6
7
23
14
Banstead
Warlingham
Biggin Hill
Caterham
Westerham
Oxted
Sevenoaks
Redhill
Reigate
Horley
London Gatwick
Crawley
East Grinstead
Edenbridge
Tonbridge
Southborough
Royal Tunbridge Wells
Crowborough
Wadhurst
Haywards Heath
Burgess Hill
Hurstpierpoint
Heathfield
Hailsham
Lewes
Newhaven
Peacehaven
Seaford
Eastbourne
Brighton & Hove
Hove
Brighton
Shoreham-by-Sea
Portslade-by-Sea
Southwick
Polegate
Uckfield
Maresfield
Rottingdean
Pevensey Bay
Pevensey Levels
Beachy Head
West Malling
Aylesford
Paddock Wood
Kent
East Sussex
The Weald
Ashdown Forest

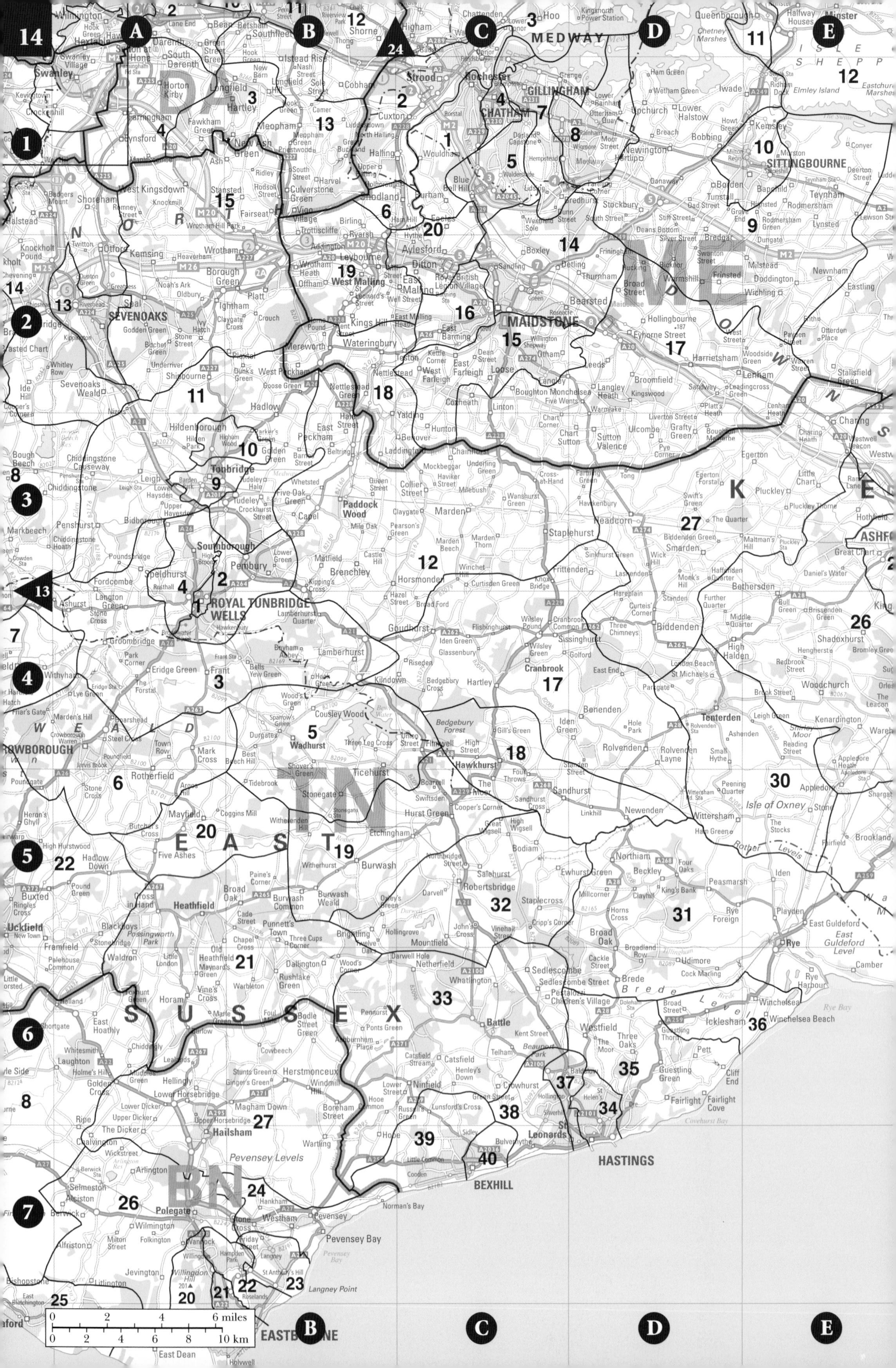
14
A
B
C
D
E
1
2
3
4
5
6
7
24
13
MEDWAY
ISLE
SHEPP
Swanley
Dartford
Longfield
Hartley
Strood
Rochester
GILLINGHAM
CHATHAM
Queenborough
Minster
Sittingbourne
SITTINGBOURNE
Teynham
Faversham
West Kingsdown
Shoreham
Otford
Kemsing
Wrotham
Borough Green
SEVENOAKS
Ightham
Snodland
Aylesford
West Malling
Kings Hill
Wateringbury
MAIDSTONE
Bearsted
Hollingbourne
Harrietsham
Lenham
Charing
Tonbridge
Hildenborough
Paddock Wood
Marden
Staplehurst
Headcorn
Southborough
Pembury
ROYAL TUNBRIDGE WELLS
Horsmonden
Goudhurst
Lamberhurst
Cranbrook
Biddenden
Tenterden
Hawkhurst
Wadhurst
Ticehurst
Mayfield
Heathfield
Uckfield
Burwash
Robertsbridge
Battle
Rye
Winchelsea
Hailsham
Polegate
Pevensey
Pevensey Bay
BEXHILL
HASTINGS
St Leonards
EASTBOURNE
Langney Point
Isle of Oxney
Pevensey Levels
ME
TN
BN
EAST
SUSSEX
K
E
0 2 4 6 miles
0 2 4 6 8 10 km

15
F
G
H
J
K
25
1
2
3
4
5
6
7
Warden Point
Long Nose Spit
Foreness Point
White Ness
North Foreland
Broadstairs
Ramsgate
Herne Bay
Reculver
Birchington
Whitstable
Shell Ness
Seasalter
ISLE OF THANET
KENT INTERNATIONAL
Minster
Manston
Monkton
Acol
St Nicholas at Wade
Sarre
Chislet
Hoath
Upstreet
West Stourmouth
East Stourmouth
Pegwell Bay
Sandwich Flats
Sandwich Bay
Sandwich
Cliffs End
Graveney
Faversham
Goodnestone
Boughton Street
Dunkirk
Blean
Tyler Hill
Sturry
Broadoak
Hersden
Westbere
Fordwich
CANTERBURY
Wickhambreaux
Ickham
Littlebourne
Wingham
Staple
Ash
Woodnesborough
Eastry
Worth
Deal
Great Mongeham
Ripple
Kingsdown
Ringwould
Sholden
Northbourne
Betteshanger
Tilmanstone
Eythorne
Shepherdswell
Coldred
Lydden
Whitfield
Temple Ewell
River
Guston
East Langdon
West Langdon
St Margaret's at Cliffe
South Foreland
DOVER
Chartham
Shalmsford Street
Chilham
Molash
Challock
Godmersham
Selling
Bridge
Patrixbourne
Bekesbourne
Adisham
Aylesham
Nonington
Goodnestone
Chillenden
Lower Hardres
Bishopsbourne
Kingston
Barham
Womenswold
Petham
Waltham
Bossingham
Stelling Minnis
Elham
Lyminge Forest
Wye
Brook
Hastingleigh
West Brabourne
Smeeth
Sellindge
Stanford
Mersham
Aldington
Bonnington
Bilsington
Lympne
Hythe
Saltwood
Sandgate
FOLKESTONE
Capel le Ferne
Hawkinge
Paddlesworth
Etchinghill
Densole
Swingfield Minnis
Alkham
West Hougham
Ewell Minnis
Romney Marsh
Burmarsh
Newchurch
Dymchurch
Ivychurch
St Mary in the Marsh
St Mary's Bay
Old Romney
New Romney
Littlestone-on-Sea
Romney Sands
Greatstone-on-Sea
LYDD (LONDON ASHFORD)
Lydd
Lydd-on-Sea
Denge Marsh
Denge Beach
Dungeness
Channel Tunnel Folkestone to Calais 35mins
STRAIT OF DOVER
8
9
10
11
12
13
14
15
16
17
18
19
20
21
24
25
28
29

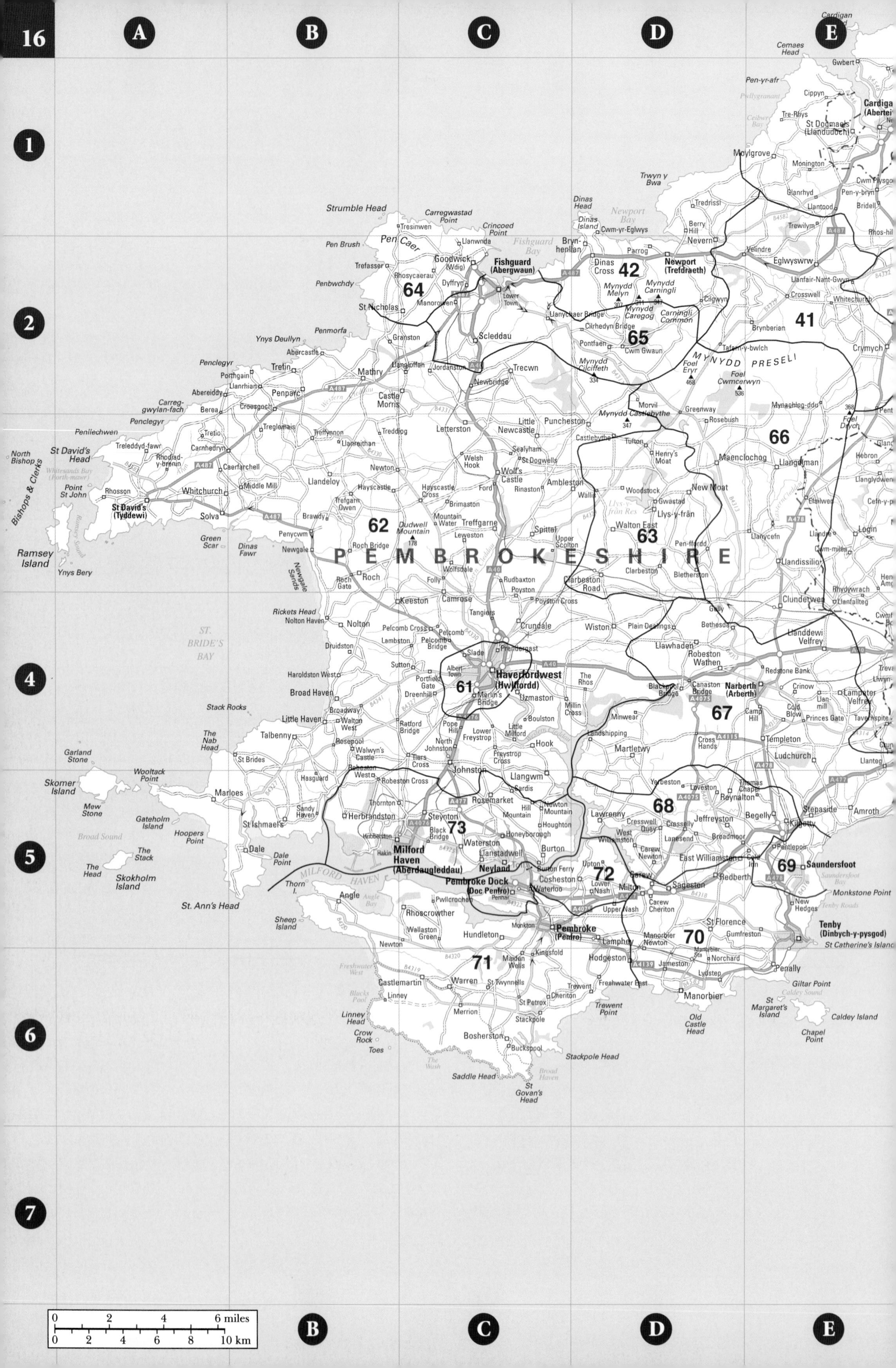
16
A
B
C
D
E
1
2
3
4
5
6
7
Cardigan
Cemaes Head
Gwbert
Pen-yr-afr
Cippyn
Tre-Rhys
St Dogmaels (Llandudoch)
Cardiga (Abertei
Moylgrove
Monington
Trwyn y Bwa
Glanrhyd
Cwm Plysgo
Pen-y-bryn
Bridell
Dinas Head
Newport Bay
Tredrissi
Llantood
Berry Hill
Trewilym
Rhos-hil
Strumble Head
Carregwastad Point
Crincoed Point
Tresinwen
Dinas Island
Cwm-yr-Eglwys
Pen Caer
Pen Brush
Llanwnda
Fishguard Bay
Bryn-henllan
Nevern
Parrog
Velindre
Goodwick (Wdig)
Fishguard (Abergwaun)
Dinas Cross
42
Newport (Trefdraeth)
Eglwyswrw
Trefasser
Rhosycaerau
Penbwchdy
64
Dyffryn
Mynydd Melyn
Mynydd Carningli
Llanfair-Nant-Gwyn
Crosswell
Whitechurch
Manorowen
Lower Town
St Nicholas
Llanychaer Bridge
Mynydd Caregog
Carningli Common
Cilgwyn
41
Cilrhedyn Bridge
Brynberian
Penmorfa
Granston
Scleddau
Pontfaen
65
Cwm Gwaun
Ynys Deullyn
Abercastle
Tafarn-y-bwlch
Crymych
Penclegyr
Porthgain
Trefin
Llangloffan
Mathry
Jordanston
Trecwn
Mynydd Cilciffeth
Foel Eryr
MYNYDD PRESELI
Llanrhian
Newbridge
Foel Cwmcerwyn
Carreg-gwylan-fach
Abereiddy
Penparc
Castle Morris
Morvil
Mynachlog-ddu
Berea
Croesgoch
Penclegyr
Tretio
Treglemais
Treffynnon
Treddiog
Letterston
Little Newcastle
Puncheston
Mynydd Castlebythe
Greenway
Foel Dyrch
Penllechwen
Llanreithan
Castlebythe
Rosebush
66
North Bishop
St David's Head
Treleddyd-fawr
Carnhedryn
Tufton
Seafyham
St Dogwells
Henry's Moat
Maenclochog
Hebron
Llangolman
Rhodiad-y-brenin
Caerfarchell
Welsh Hook
Whitesands Bay (Porth-mawr)
Newton
Wolf's Castle
Llandeloy
Ambleston
Point St John
Middle Mill
Hayscastle
Hayscastle Cross
Ford
Rinaston
New Moat
Bishops & Clerks
Rhosson
Whitchurch
Wallis
Woodstock
St David's (Tyddewi)
Trefgarn Owen
Brimaston
Gwastad
Llys-y-frân
Llys-y-frân Res
Ramsey Sound
Solva
Brawdy
Mountain Water
Treffgarne
62
Dudwell Mountain
Spittal
Walton East
63
Llanycefn
Login
Green Scar
Dinas Fawr
Penycwm
Leweston
Upper Scolton
Ramsey Island
Newgale
Roch Bridge
PEMBROKESHIRE
Pen-ffordd
Llandissilio
Ynys Bery
Newgale Sands
Roch Gate
Roch
Wolfsdale
Rudbaxton
Clarbeston
Blethersten
Folly
Clarbeston Road
Poyston
Rickets Head
Keeston
Camrose
Poyston Cross
Clunderwen
Nolton Haven
Tangiers
Nolton
Crundale
Wiston
Plain Dealings
Bethesda
Gelly
ST. BRIDE'S BAY
Pelcomb Cross
Pelcomb
Lambston
Pelcomb Bridge
Llanddewi Velfrey
Druidston
Llawhaden
Robeston Wathen
Slade
Prendergast
Sutton
Albert Town
Haverfordwest (Hwlffordd)
Redstone Bank
Haroldston West
Portfield Gate
The Rhos
Crinow
Broad Haven
61
Merlin's Bridge
Blackpool Bridge
Canaston Bridge
Narberth (Arberth)
Lampeter Velfrey
Dreenhill
Uzmaston
Stack Rocks
Millin Cross
67
Little Haven
Broadway
Walton West
Boulston
Minwear
Camp Hill
Cold Blow
Llan-mill
Princes Gate
Tavernspite
Ratford Bridge
Pope Hill
Lower Freystrop
Little Milford
Landshipping
Cross Hands
The Nab Head
Talbenny
Rosepool
North Johnston
Hook
Martletwy
Templeton
Walwyn's Castle
Freystrop Cross
Ludchurch
Garland Stone
St Brides
Tiers Cross
Llanteg
Wooltack Point
Robeston West
Hasguard
Johnston
Llangwm
Skomer Island
Robeston Cross
Sardis
Yerbeston
Loveston
Thomas Chapel
Reynalton
Marloes
Thornton
Rosemarket
Newton Mountain
68
Mew Stone
Sandy Haven
Hill Mountain
Lawrenny
Jeffreyston
Begelly
Kilgetty
Stepaside
Amroth
Gateholm Island
St Ishmael's
Herbrandston
Steynton
73
Cresswell Quay
Crosselly
Hubberston
Black Bridge
Honeyborough
Houghton
West Williamston
Lanesend
Broadmoor
Hooper's Point
Broad Sound
Waterston
Burton
Pentlepoir
The Stack
Dale
Milford Haven (Aberdaugleddau)
Hakin
Llanstadwell
Neyland
Carew Newton
East Williamston
Cold Inn
69
Saundersfoot
The Head
Dale Point
Burton Ferry
Upton
72
Skokholm Island
Thorn I.
MILFORD HAVEN
Pembroke Dock (Doc Penfro)
Cosheston
Carew
Redberth
Saundersfoot Bay
Angle
Angle Bay
Pwllcrochan
Waterloo
Pennar
Lower Nash
Milton
Sageston
Monkstone Point
St. Ann's Head
Rhoscrowther
Upper Nash
Carew Cheriton
New Hedges
Tenby Roads
Sheep Island
Monkton
Pembroke (Penfro)
St Florence
Tenby (Dinbych-y-pysgod)
Wallaston Green
Hundleton
Lamphey
Manorbier Newton
70
Gumfreston
Newton
St Catherine's Island
Freshwater West
71
Maiden Wells
Kingsfold
Hodgeston
Jameston
Norchard
Penally
Castlemartin
Warren
St Twynnells
Trewent
Freshwater East
Lydstep
Gilter Point
Blacks Pool
Linney
Cheriton
Caldey Sound
Manorbier
St Margaret's Island
St Petrox
Trewent Point
Caldey Island
Linney Head
Merrion
Stackpole
Old Castle Head
Chapel Point
Crow Rock
Bosherston
Toes
Buckspool
Stackpole Head
The Wash
Saddle Head
Broad Haven
St Govan's Head
0 2 4 6 miles
0 2 4 6 8 10 km
B
C
D
E

F
G
H
J
K
17
26
48
44
40
38
37
39
35
32
33
31
17
15
16
14
18
19
4
5
6
3
2
1
CARMARTHENSHIRE
SWANSEA
Abertawe
PORT TAL
CARMARTHEN BAY
SA
Lampeter
(Llanbedr Pont Steffan)
Newcastle Emlyn
(Castell Newydd Emlyn)
Carmarthen
(Caerfyrddin)
St Clears
(Sanclêr)
Llandeilo
Ammanford
(Rhydaman)
Kidwelly
(Cydweli)
Llanelli
Gorseinon
Loughor
Gowerton
Pontarddulais
Pontardawe
Clydach
Burry Port
Pembrey
(Pen-bre)
Ferryside
(Glanyferi)
Laugharne
(Lacharn)
Pendine
(Pentywyn)
Pendine Sands
Laugharne Sands
Llansteffan
Cross Hands
Tumble
(Y Tymbl)
Llanybydder
Llandysul
Abergwili
Brechfa
Talley
(Talyllychau)
Llangadog
Brynamman
Glanaman
Cenarth
Abercych
Aberporth
Blaenporth
Tresaith
Talgarreg
Ffostrasol
Rhydowen
Llanwenog
Cwrt-newydd
Alltyblaca
Llanllwni
Pencader
New Inn
Llanpumsaint
Cynwyl Elfed
Trelech
Llanfyrnach
Whitland Abbey
Meidrim
Bancyfelin
Llangain
Llangynog
Llandyfaelog
Pontyates
Pontyberem
Llannon
Hendy
Llangennech
Penllergaer
Gorslas
Llandybie
Llanarthney
Nantgaredig
Crugybar
Pumsaint
Caio
Llansawel
Abergorlech
Cefn Sidan Sands
Pembrey Forest
Whiteford Point
Llanrhidian Sands
Burry Holms
Rhossili
Rhossili Downs
Llangennith
Cheriton
Llanmadoc
Reynoldston
Knelston
Scurlage
Port Eynon
Port Eynon Point
Oxwich
Horton
Penmaen
Parkmill
Bishopston
Pennard
Southgate
Murton
Newton
The Mumbles
Mumbles Head
Black Pill
West Cross
Mayals
Killay
Dunvant
Three Crosses
Llanrhidian
Cefn Bryn
Worms Head
Pwlldu Head
Oxwich Bay
Kilvey Hill
Jersey Marine
Morriston
Landore
Sketty
Uplands
Cockett
Llangyfelach
Pontlliw
Grovesend
Mynydd Llanllwni
Mynydd Cerrig
Mynydd Sylen
Mynydd Pen-bre
Mynydd Garn-fach
Mynydd y Betws
Banc Cwmhelen
Tair Carn Isaf
Trichrug
Mynydd Cynros
Craig Twrch
Pen Tas-eithin
DYFFRYN TYWI
LOUGHOR
Ginst Point
Wharley Point
St Ishmael
East Marsh
Laugharne Burrows

18
A
B
C
D
E
27
48
22
23
1
2
3
4
5
6
7
17
7
NEATH
PORT TALBOT
RHONDDA
CYNON
TAFF
MERTHYR
TYDFIL
CAERPHILLY
BRIDGEND
VALE OF GLAMORGAN
CARDIFF
DEVON
EXMOOR
BRISTOL CHANNEL
BRIDGWATER BAY
SWANSEA BAY
Gwaun-Cae-Gurwen
Ystradgynlais
Ystalyfera
Pontardawe
Seven Sisters
Glynneath
Resolven
Neath (Castell-nedd)
Briton Ferry (Llansawel)
Baglan
Cwmafan
PORT TALBOT
Tonna
Skewen
Cimla
Glyncorrwg
Hirwaun
Aberdare
Mountain Ash (Abercynon)
Treherbert
Treorchy
Ferndale
Tonypandy
Porth
Pontypridd
Merthyr Tydfil
Rhymney
Tredegar
Ebbw Vale (Glynebwy)
New Tredegar
Bargoed
Ystrad Mynach
Nelson
Caerphilly
Maesteg
Pontycymer
Ogmore Vale
Tonyrefail
Llantrisant
Llanharan
Pontyclun
Pencoed
Pyle
Porthcawl
BRIDGEND (Pen-y-bont ar Ogwr)
Cowbridge
Llantwit Major
St Athan
Rhoose
BARRY
Barry Island
Penarth
Dinas Powys
Sully Island
Ogmore-by-Sea
Southerndown
Nash Point
Breaksea Pt
Sker Point
Kenfig
Taffs Well
Radyr
St Fagans
Foreland Point
Lynton
Lynmouth
Porlock
Minehead
Dunster
Watchet
Williton
Blue Anchor
Dunkery Beacon
Dunkery Hill
Brendon Common
Challacombe
Tusker Rock
CARDIFF INT
0 2 4 6 miles
0 2 4 6 8 10 km

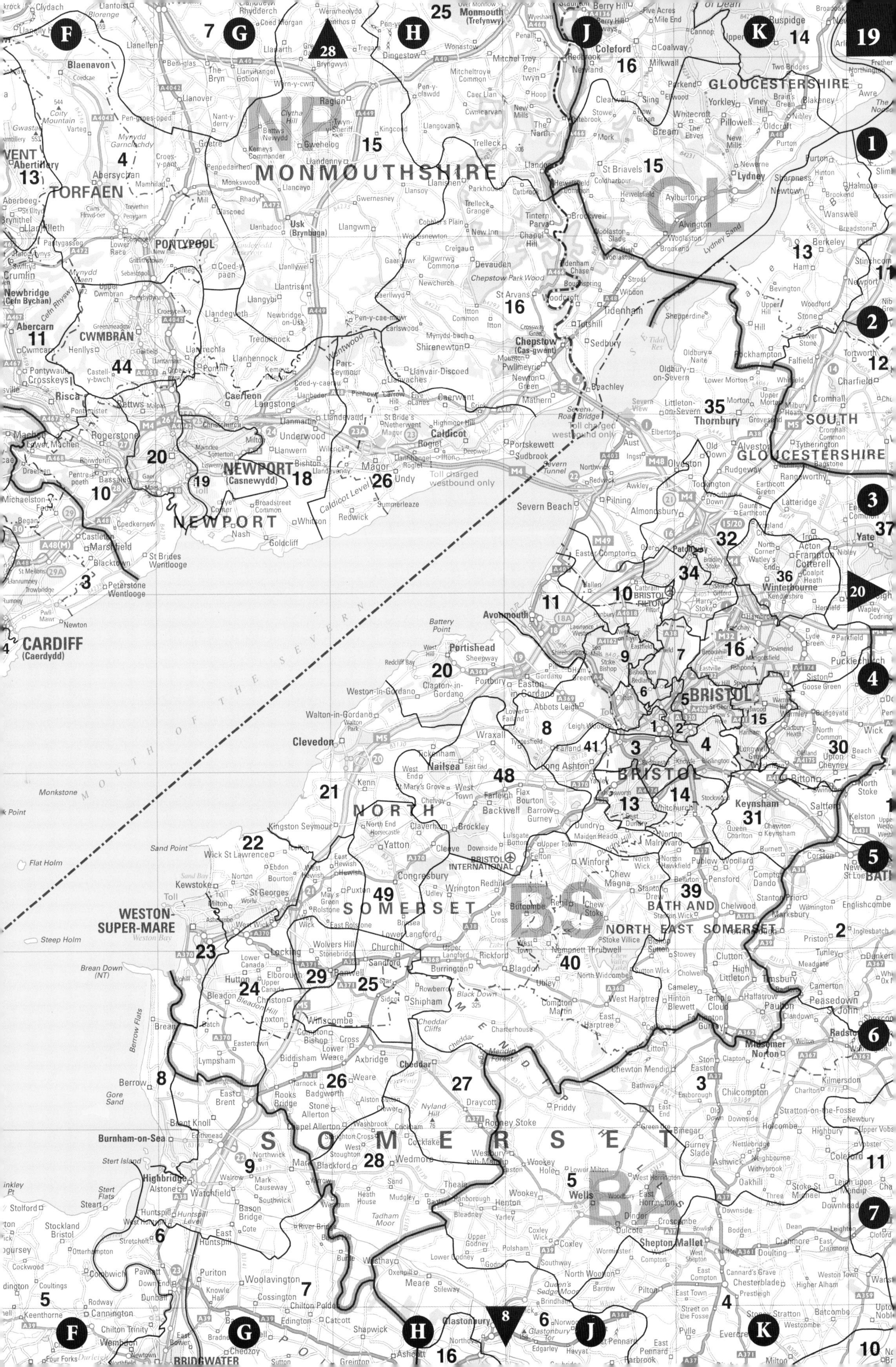

19
F
G
H
J
K
28
20
8
1
2
3
4
5
6
7
MONMOUTHSHIRE
TORFAEN
NP
GL
GLOUCESTERSHIRE
SOUTH GLOUCESTERSHIRE
BS
BA
NEWPORT
NORTH SOMERSET
BATH AND NORTH EAST SOMERSET
SOMERSET
MOUTH OF THE SEVERN
Blaenavon
Abertillery
Pontypool
Cwmbrân
Risca
Newport (Casnewydd)
Caerleon
Usk (Brynbuga)
Raglan
Monmouth (Trefynwy)
Chepstow (Cas-gwent)
Caldicot
Magor
Coleford
Lydney
Berkeley
Thornbury
Yate
Winterbourne
Avonmouth
Portishead
Clevedon
Nailsea
Bristol
Keynsham
Weston-super-Mare
Cheddar
Wells
Shepton Mallet
Midsomer Norton
Glastonbury
Burnham-on-Sea
Highbridge
Bridgwater
Cardiff (Caerdydd)
Severn Road Bridge
Toll charged westbound only
Second Severn Crossing
Severn Beach
Flat Holm
Steep Holm
Bristol International

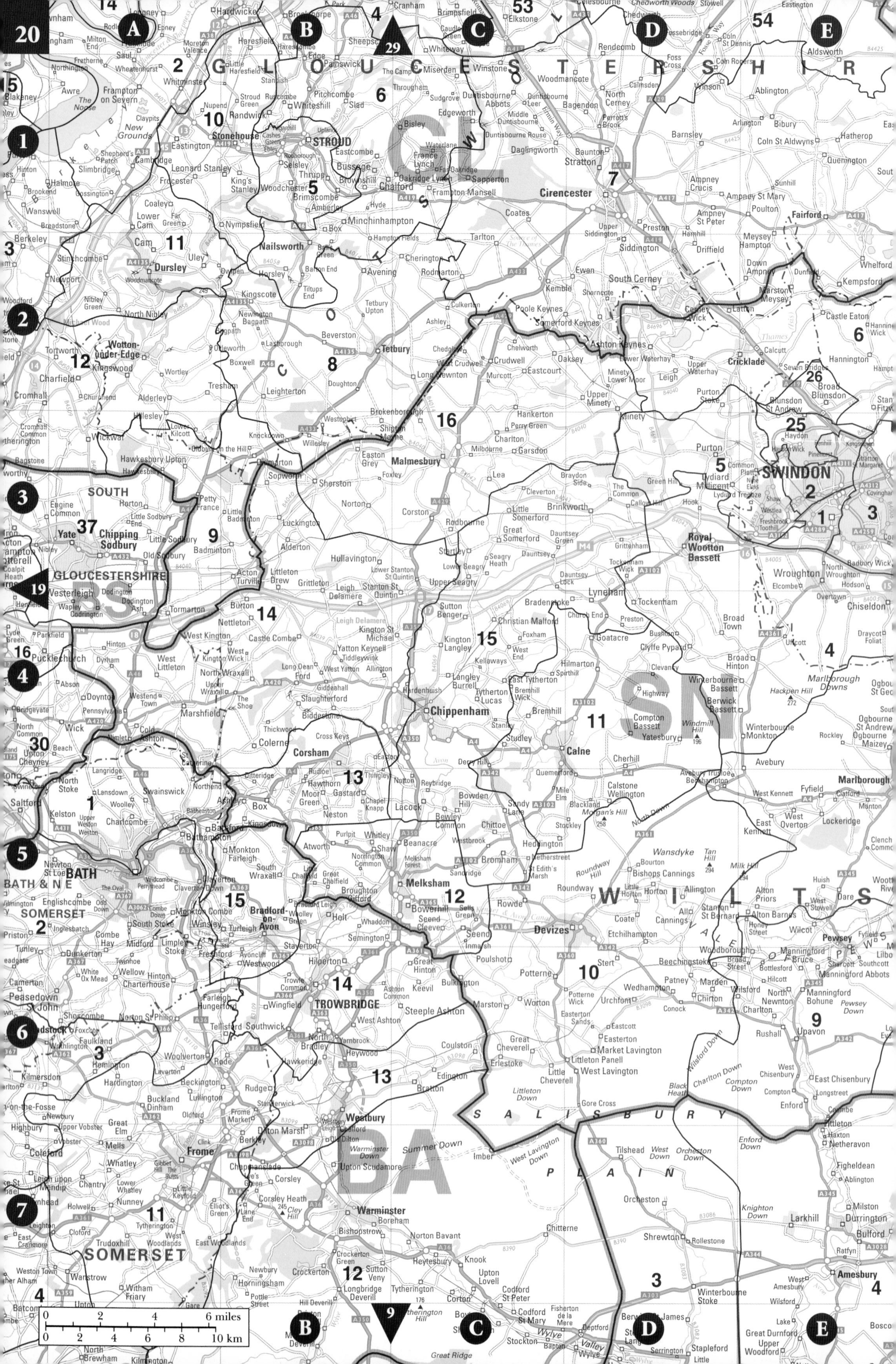
A
B
C
D
E
1
2
3
4
5
6
7
29
19
9
G L O U C E S T E R S H I R E
GL
SN
BA
W I L T S
S A L I S B U R Y
P L A I N
SOUTH
GLOUCESTERSHIRE
BS
BATH & N E
SOMERSET
SOMERSET
STROUD
Stonehouse
Nailsworth
Dursley
Wotton-under-Edge
Tetbury
Cirencester
Malmesbury
Cricklade
SWINDON
Royal Wootton Bassett
Chipping Sodbury
Yate
Chippenham
Corsham
Calne
Marlborough
BATH
Bradford-on-Avon
Melksham
Devizes
TROWBRIDGE
Westbury
Frome
Warminster
Pewsey
Amesbury
Fairford
Lechlade
Kemble
Lyneham
Hardwicke
Painswick
Bisley
Chalford
Minchinhampton
Avening
Badminton
Marshfield
Box
Lacock
Bowerhill
Upavon
Tidworth
Bulford
Durrington
Larkhill
Shrewton
Heytesbury
Codford St Mary
Mere
Wylye
Wansdyke
Marlborough Downs
Cley Hill
Summer Down
West Lavington Down
Warminster Down
Great Ridge
Kennet and Avon Canal
0 2 4 6 miles
0 2 4 6 8 10 km

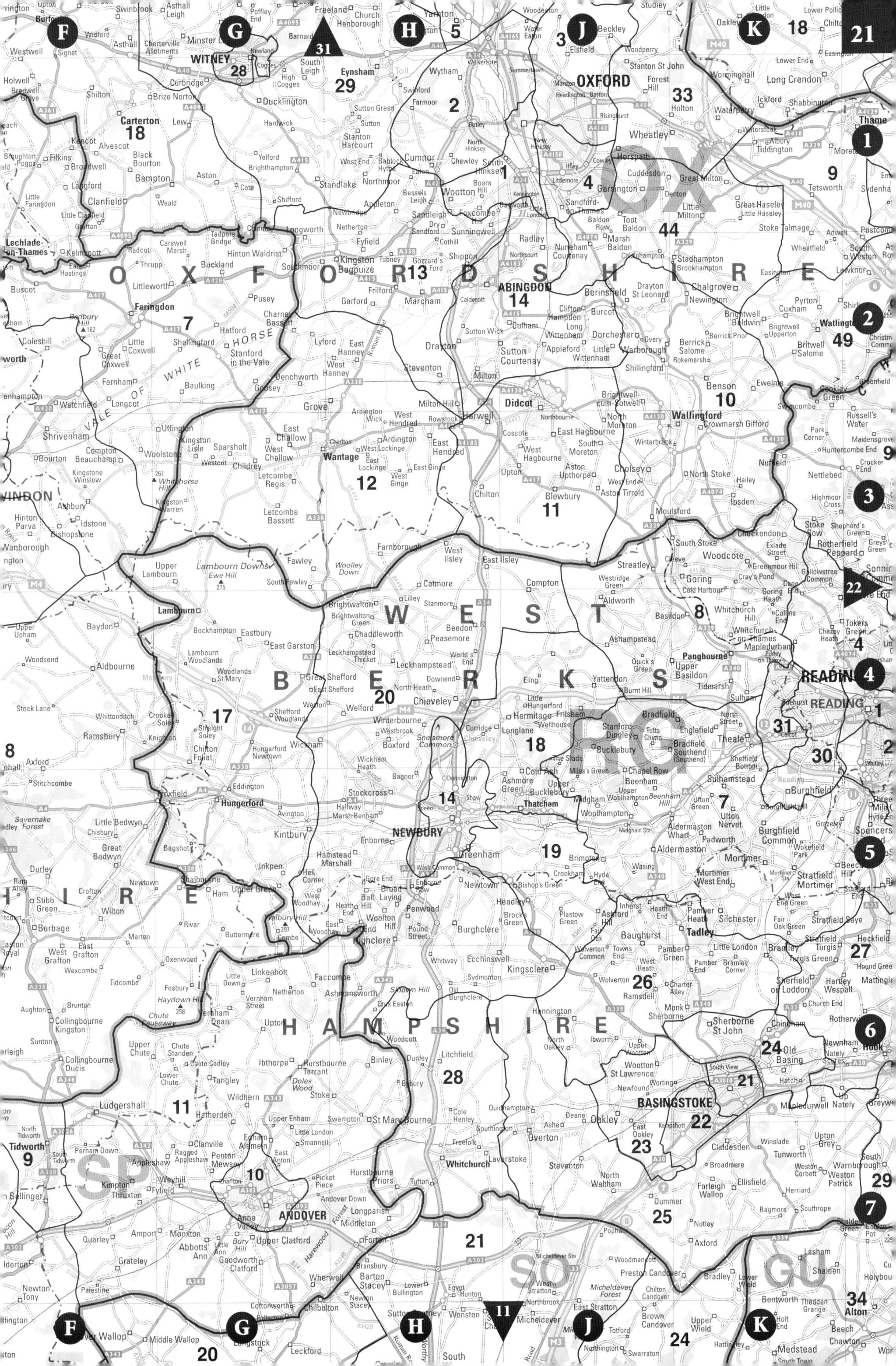
OXFORD
OXFORDSHIRE
WEST BERKSHIRE
HAMPSHIRE
VALE OF WHITE HORSE
OX
RG
SP
SO
GU
WITNEY
Carterton
Eynsham
Faringdon
Wantage
ABINGDON
Didcot
Wallingford
Watlington
Thame
Lambourn
Hungerford
NEWBURY
Thatcham
READING
BASINGSTOKE
ANDOVER
Whitchurch
Tadley
Alton
Tidworth
Ludgershall
Kingsclere
Pangbourne
Theale
Goring
Wheatley
Long Crendon
Chalgrove
Benson
Harwell
Grove
Kintbury
Overton
Oakley
Hook
Old Basing
Burghfield
Mortimer
Lambourn Downs
Savernake Forest
Harewood Forest
Micheldever Forest
Snelsmore Common
Whitehorse Hill
Walbury Hill
Haydown Hill
Sidown Hill
Woolley Down
Lechlade-on-Thames
Swindon
M4
M40
M3
A34
A4
A338
A339
A303
A417
A40
F
G
H
J
K
1
2
3
4
5
6
7
22
31
11

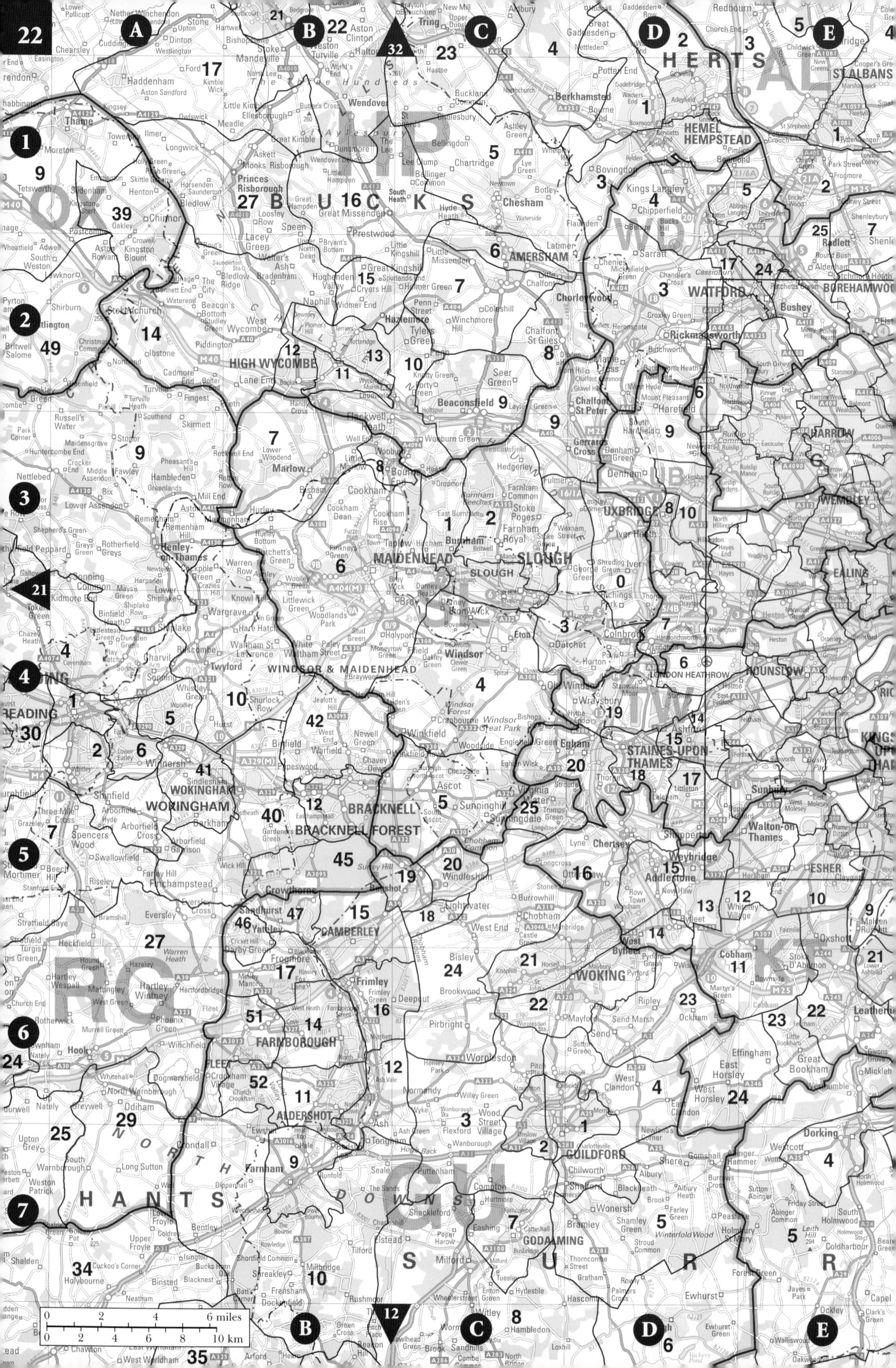

A
B
C
D
E
1
2
3
4
5
6
7
32
21
12
HERTS
BUCKS
HANTS
SURREY
OX
HP
AL
WD
UB
SL
RG
GU
TW
KT
HA
ST ALBANS
HEMEL HEMPSTEAD
WATFORD
BOREHAMWOOD
Berkhamsted
Chesham
AMERSHAM
Rickmansworth
Bushey
Radlett
HARROW
WEMBLEY
EALING
HOUNSLOW
UXBRIDGE
LONDON HEATHROW
STAINES-UPON-THAMES
Thame
Princes Risborough
Wendover
Tring
HIGH WYCOMBE
Beaconsfield
Marlow
MAIDENHEAD
SLOUGH
Windsor
WINDSOR & MAIDENHEAD
Henley-on-Thames
READING
WOKINGHAM
BRACKNELL
BRACKNELL FOREST
Ascot
Egham
Chertsey
Weybridge
Addlestone
Walton-on-Thames
ESHER
Sunbury
Camberley
Sandhurst
Yateley
Crowthorne
Frimley
FARNBOROUGH
FLEET
ALDERSHOT
Farnham
WOKING
GUILDFORD
GODALMING
Cobham
Dorking
Hook
Odiham
Fleet
Bagshot
Windlesham
Chobham
NORTH DOWNS
0
2
4
6 miles
10 km

See pages 110 - 113 for postcode detail
WELWYN GARDEN CITY
Hatfield
Potters Bar
Hoddesdon
CHESHUNT
Waltham Abbey
HARLOW
Epping
North Weald Bassett
Chipping Ongar
ENFIELD
BARNET
Loughton
Chigwell
WOOD GREEN
WALTHAMSTOW
ILFORD
Barking
ROMFORD
BRENTWOOD
Billericay
Ingatestone
THURROCK
Stanford-le-Hope
GRAYS
Tilbury
LONDON CITY
WESTMINSTER
LONDON
WOOLWICH
LEWISHAM
DARTFORD
GRAVESEND
Northfleet
Swanscombe
WANDSWORTH
Wimbledon
BROMLEY
Orpington
Swanley
CROYDON
SUTTON
EPSOM
Banstead
Caterham
Warlingham
Biggin Hill
Westerham
Oxted
SEVENOAKS
West Malling
Redhill
REIGATE
Horley
LONDON GATWICK
CRAWLEY
East Grinstead
Edenbridge
Tonbridge
Southborough
ROYAL TUNBRIDGE WELLS
Paddock Wood
ESSEX
KENT
SG
EN
CM
RM
DA
BR
CR
RH
TN
ME
SS
F
G
H
J
K
33
24
14
13

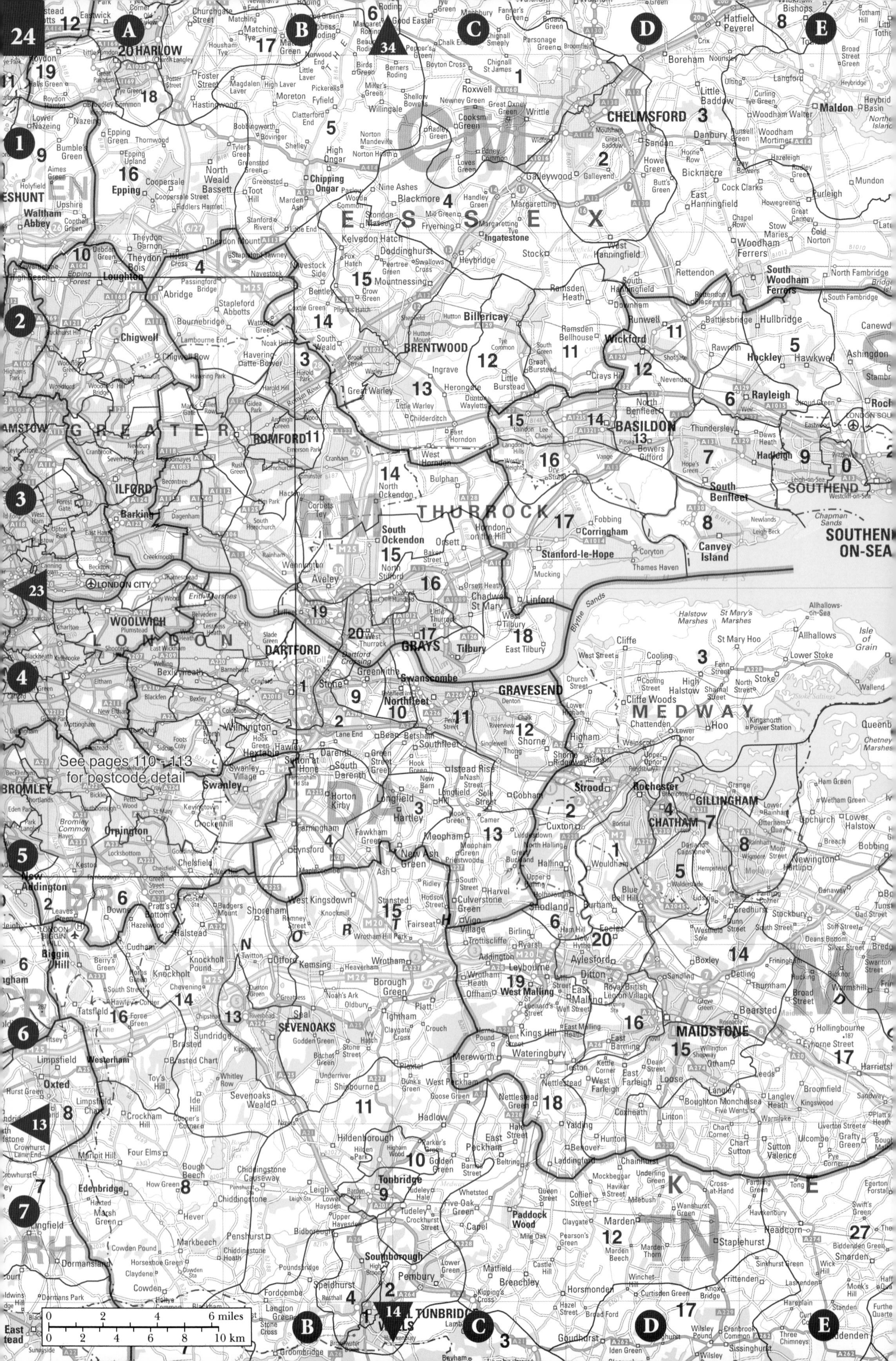
A
B
C
D
E
1
2
3
4
5
6
7
34
23
13
14
27
HARLOW
Epping
CHESHUNT
Waltham Abbey
Loughton
Chigwell
Chipping Ongar
North Weald Bassett
Theydon Bois
Abridge
Stapleford Abbotts
Havering-atte-Bower
ROMFORD
ILFORD
Barking
Dagenham
LONDON CITY
WOOLWICH
LONDON
GREATER
Bexleyheath
DARTFORD
BROMLEY
Orpington
Swanley
See pages 110 - 113 for postcode detail
New Addington
Biggin Hill
Westerham
Oxted
Limpsfield
Edenbridge
Dormansland
CHELMSFORD
ESSEX
Maldon
Hatfield Peverel
Boreham
Danbury
Galleywood
Ingatestone
Writtle
Roxwell
Blackmore
Fryerning
Kelvedon Hatch
Doddinghurst
Mountnessing
BRENTWOOD
Billericay
Wickford
South Woodham Ferrers
Rayleigh
Hockley
Hadleigh
SOUTHEND
SOUTHEND-ON-SEA
BASILDON
Canvey Island
THURROCK
Stanford-le-Hope
Corringham
South Ockendon
North Ockendon
Aveley
Purfleet
GRAYS
Tilbury
Swanscombe
Northfleet
GRAVESEND
MEDWAY
Strood
Rochester
CHATHAM
GILLINGHAM
Hoo
Higham
Cliffe
Isle of Grain
Allhallows
Longfield
Hartley
Meopham
Snodland
West Malling
Aylesford
Ditton
MAIDSTONE
Bearsted
Harrietsham
Kemsing
Otford
Borough Green
SEVENOAKS
Sevenoaks Weald
Hildenborough
Tonbridge
Paddock Wood
Marden
Staplehurst
Headcorn
Southborough
Pembury
TUNBRIDGE WELLS
Horsmonden
Goudhurst
Brenchley
Matfield
Yalding
Wateringbury
Kings Hill
Edenbridge
Hever
Penshurst
Chiddingstone
Langton Green
Groombridge
THAMES
0
2
4
6 miles
0
2
4
6
8
10 km

F
G
H
J
K
35
1
2
3
4
5
6
7
Tollesbury
West Mersea
Cobmarsh Island
Great Cob Island
Colne Point
Bradwell Waterside
Sales Point
St Peter's Flat
East End
Osea Island
Ramsey Island
Bradwell-on-Sea
St Lawrence
Tillingham
Dengie Flat
Steeple
Dengie
Mayland
Asheldham
Dengie Marshes
Southminster
Ray Sand
Stoneyhills
Eves Corner
Old Montsale
Deal Hall
Burnham-on-Crouch
Foulness Sands
Holliwell Point
Foulness Point
Courtsend
Paglesham Churchend
Wallasea Island
Churchend
Paglesham Eastend
Potton Island
Foulness Island
Barling
Havengore Island
Little Wakering
Maplin Sands
Great Wakering
North Shoebury
Shoeburyness
Shoebury Ness
Sheerness
Marine Town
East End
Warden Point
Halfway Houses
Minster
Eastchurch
Warden
Leysdown-on-Sea
ISLE OF SHEPPEY
Elmley Island
Eastchurch Marshes
Isle of Harty
Shell Ness
Whitstable
Seasalter
Tankerton
Swalecliffe
Hampton
Herne Bay
Beltinge
Reculver
Hillborough
Broomfield
Herne
Herne Common
Hunters Forstal
Maypole
Highstead
Boyden Gate
Chislet
St Nicholas at Wade
Sarre
Birchington
Acol
ISLE OF THANET
KENT INTERNATIONAL
Minster
Monkton
Manston
MARGATE
Westgate on Sea
Westbrook
Cliftonville
Kingsgate
Long Nose Spit
Foreness Point
White Ness
North Foreland
Broadstairs
Ramsgate
Pegwell
Cliffs End
Pegwell Bay
Sandwich Flats
Stonar Cut
Great Stonar
Sandwich
Sandwich Bay
Conyer
SITTINGBOURNE
Teynham
Rodmersham
Deerton Street
Uplees
Oare
Luddenham Court
Graveney
Faversham
Preston
Goodnestone
Lewson Street
Lynsted
Ospringe
Yorkletts
Highstreet
Dargate
Hernhill
Staplestreet
Boughton Street
Dunkirk
Clapham Hill
Pean Hill
Honey Hill
Blean
Tyler Hill
Broadoak
Calcott
Sturry
Westbere
Hersden
Fordwich
Stodmarsh
Upstreet
West Stourmouth
Plucks Gutter
Grove
East Stourmouth
Westmarsh
Ware
Preston
Elmstone
Hoaden
Cop Street
CANTERBURY
Harbledown
Wickhambreaux
Ickham
Littlebourne
Bramling
Wingham
Wingham Well
Staple
Shatterling
Ash
Marshborough
Barnsole
Woodnesborough
Worth
Hackling
Finglesham
Deal
Sholden
Walmer
Newnham
Eastling
North Street
Sheldwich
Sheldwich Lees
Gushmere
Overland
Selling
Chartham Hatch
Throwley
Badlesmere
Old Wives Lees
Chartham
Shalmsford Street
Nackington
Bridge
Bekesbourne
Patrixbourne
Adisham
Goodnestone
Chillenden
Knowlton
Eastry
Ham
Betteshanger
Northbourne
Great Mongeham
Otterden Place
Leaveland
Shottenden
Chilham
Lower Hardres
Bishopsbourne
Kingston
Aylesham
Ratling
Nonington
Easole Street
Tilmanstone
Womenswold
Garlinge Green
Petham
Molash
Godmersham
Challock
Stalisfield Green
Warren Street
Upper Hardres Court
Barham
Derringstone
Woolage Village
Woolage Green
Elvington
Barfrestone
Eythorne
Lower Eythorne
East Studdal
Sutton
Ripple
Charing
Charing Heath
Westwell Leacon
Westwell
Paddock
Eastwell Park
Boughton Aluph
Bilting
Crundale
Sole Street
Waltham
Bossingham
Breach
Denton
Shepherdswell (Sibertswold)
Ashley
West Langdon
Kingsdown
Ringwould
Little Chart
Rank Lane
Boughton Lees
Kempe's Corner
Wye
Hassell Street
Bodsham Green
Stone Street
Stelling Minnis
Lyminge Forest
Bladbean
Wingmore
Wootton
Coldred
Lydden
Martin Mill Sta
East Langdon
Pluckley Thorne
Hothfield
Kennington
Brook
Hastingleigh
Whatsole Street
Maxted Street
Sixmile
Elham
Selsted
Temple Ewell
Whitfield
Guston
West Cliffe
St Margaret's at Cliffe
St Margaret's Bay
ASHFORD
Willesborough Lees
West Brabourne
Lymbridge Green
Rhodes Minnis
Mount
Acrise Place
Swingfield Minnis
Ewell Minnis
Alkham
River
Buckland
South Foreland
Great Chart
Hinxhill
Stowting
Densole
South Alkham
DOVER
Daniel's Water
Beaver Green
Willesborough
Sevington
Brabourne
Brabourne Lees
Woodland
Ottinge
Lyminge
Paddlesworth
Hawkinge
West Hougham
Maxton
Bull Green
Kingsnorth
Cheeseman's Green
Mersham
Smeeth
Broad Street
Newbarn
Etchinghill
Capel le Ferne
Forstal
Sellindge
Stanford
Postling
Shadoxhurst
Stone Cross
Stonestreet Green
Aldington
Newington
East Wear Bay
Folkestone to Calais
South Channel
Gunfleet
Roman Road
M2
M20
A2
A20
A28
A249
A250
A251
A252
A253
A254
A255
A256
A257
A258
A260
A290
A291
A299
B1021
B1018
B1017
B2205
B2231
B2068
CO
CT
N
S
T
W

A
B
C
D
E
1
2
3
4
5
6
7
CEREDIGION
PEMBROKESHIRE
CARMARTHENSHIRE
SA
Cardigan Island
Cemaes Head
Pen-yr-afr
Gwbert
Cardigan (Aberteifi)
St Dogmaels (Llandudoch)
Moylgrove
Penparc
Aberporth
Tresaith
Pencribach
Llangrannog
Ynys-Lochtyn
New Quay Head
New Quay (Ceinewydd)
New Quay Bay
Cwmtudu
Aberaeron
Aberarth
Ffos-y-ffin
Llanrhystud
Llansanffraid
Llan-non
Carreg Ti-pw
Lampeter (Llanbedr Pont Steffan)
Newcastle Emlyn (Castell Newydd Emlyn)
Llandysul
Cenarth
Cilgerran
Crymych
Boncath
Eglwyswrw
Mynydd Preseli
Foel Cwmcerwyn
Mynachlog-ddu
Maenclochog
Llangolman
Whitland (Hendy-Gwyn)
St Clears (Sanclêr)
Carmarthen (Caerfyrddin)
Abergwili
Johnstown
Llanarthney
Nantgaredig
Cwmffrwd
Llangain
Llansteffan
Laugharne (Lacharn)
Laugharne Burrows
Pendine Sands
Kidwelly (Cydweli)
Ferryside
Llangendeirne
Llandyfaelog
Pontyberem
Tumble (Y Tymbl)
Cross Hands
Gorslas
Brechfa
Pencader
New Inn
Llanybydder
Alltwalis
Cynwyl Elfed
Meidrim
Llanboidy
Narberth (Arberth)
Templeton
Ludchurch
Red Roses
Llanddowror
Whitland Abbey
Llanfyrnach
Tegryn
Hermon
Rhos
Saron
Drefach
Felindre
Pontweli
Llanfihangel-ar-arth
Rhydcymerau
Mynydd Llanllwni
Talgarreg
Synod Inn (Post-mawr)
Cross Inn
Llanarth
Mydroilyn
Ffostrasol
Rhydowen
Horeb
Capel Iwan
Blaenffos
Pentre Galar
Llanddewi Velfrey
Lampeter Velfrey
Bancyfelin
Llangynog
Llanybri
Brook
Pendine
Llanmiloe
Plashett
East Marsh
Ginst Point
Wharley Point
Llanfynydd
Llangathen
Court Henry
Llanddarog
Porthyrhyd
Crwbin
Mynydd Cerrig
Pont-Henri
Cynheidre
Mynydd-y-Garreg
Carmel
Cefneithin
Drefach
Llanllwni
Aber-Giâr
Pen Tas-eithin
Gwernogle
Abergorlech
Llanllawddog
Pontarsais
Llanpumsaint
Rhydargaeau
Peniel
Bronwydd Arms
Newchurch
Talog
Cwmfelin Mynach
Login
Llanglydwen
Llandissilio
Clunderwen
Efailwen
Rhydywrach
Henllan Amgoed
Castell Gorfod
Llangynin
Trelech
Dinas
Pen-y-bont
Blaen-y-coed
Bwlchnewydd
Merthyr
Cwmduad
Gorllwyn
Talgarreg
Capel Cynon
Wstrws
Glynarthen
Blaenporth
Tremain
Sarnau
Penbryn
Brynhoffnant
Beulah
Betws Ifan
Brongest
Rhydlewis
Penrhiw-llan
Llandyfriog
Aber-banc
Henllan
Pentre-cwrt
Llangeler
Cwmpengraig
Penboyr
Moelfre
Bwlch-clawdd
Dolgran
Gwyddgrug
Pentrecagal
Cwm-cou
Abercych
Penrhiw
Clynfyw
Newchapel
Cilwendeg
Capel Tygwydd
Llandygwydd
Llechryd
Manordeifi
Pen-y-bryn
Bridell
Rhos-hill
Crosswall
Whitechurch
Brynberian
Tafarn-y-bwlch
Nevern
Velindre
Tredrissi
Glanrhyd
Llantood
Trewilym
Monington
Cippyn
Tre-Rhys
Ceibwr Bay
Pwllgranant
Llangoedmor
Ferwig
Blaenannerch
Tan-y-groes
Parcllyn
Morfa
Pontgarreg
Wervil Grange
Plwmp
Pentregat
Blaencelyn
Caerwedros
Llwyndafydd
Nanternis
Maen-y-groes
Gilfachreda
Llwyn-onn
Llaingarreglwyd
Llwyncelyn
Neuadd
Oakford
Pen-cae
Dihewyd
Ystrad Aeron
Felinfach
Temple Bar
Cilcennin
Ciliau Aeron
Llanaeron
Monachty
Pennant
Cross Inn
Nebo
Rhyd-Rosser
Llanddeiniol
Blaenplwyf
Chancery
Rhydyfelin
Allt Wen
The Bar
Brynog
Trefilan
Llundain-fach
Tal-sarn
Abermeurig
Felindre
Caledrhydiau
Cribyn
Gorsgoch
Capel St Silin
Silian
Aber
Cwm-newydd
Llanwnnen
Castell Howell
Pont-siân
Cwmsychbant
Alltyblaca
Pentre-bach
Cwmann
Llanwenog
Drefach
Highmead
Pencarreg
Glan-Duar
Capel Dewi
Maesycrugiau
Tre-groes
Croes-lan
Pren-gwyn
Maesllyn
Penrhiw-pâl
Coed-y-bryn
Llangynllo
Troedyraur
Falin-Wnda
Pontgarreg
Llanfair-Orllwyn
Bancyffordd
Llidiad-Nenog
Felingwmisaf
Felingwmuchaf
Llanfihangel-uwch-Gwili
Capel Gwyn
White Mill
Pontargothi
Broad Oak
Llanegwad
Dryslwyn
Capel Dewi
Tanerdy
Tre-vaughan
Golden Grove
Nantycaws
Croesyceiliog
Bancycapel
Pontantwn
Cwmisfael
Foelgastell
Bancffosfelen
Meinciau
Pontyates
Broadlay
Llansaint
Mynyddygarreg
Cwmgwili
Maesybont
Cwm-mawr
Llanllwch
Bron-y-gaer
Sarnau
Aberrant
Brandy Hill
Pwll-trap
Backe
Llandeilo Abercywyn
Llandawke
Llansadurnen
Cwmllyfri
Ffynnon
Llwyn-y-brain
Trevaughan
Cwmfelin Boeth
Llanfallteg
Llandre
Cwm-miles
Llanycefn
Maesgwynne
Cwmbach
Gellywen
Llanwinio
Cefn-y-pant
Blaenwaun
Hebron
Glandwr
Foel Drych
Glogue
Freni-fawr
Star
Clydey
Bwlch-y-groes
Glanpant
Cilrhedyn
Cwm Morgan
Tavernspite
Princes Gate
Cold Blow
Llan-mill
Crinow
Redstone Bank
Camp Hill
Robeston Wathen
Bethesda
Gelly
Lanteg
Crunwere
Cross Hands
Jeffreyston
Begelly
Kilgetty
Clifton
A487
A484
A486
A475
A485
A482
A478
A40
A477
A4066
A484
A476
A48
6 miles
10 km
0
2
4
8
16
17
14
15
31
32
33
34
35
36
37
38
39
40
41
42
43
44
45
46
47
48
66
67

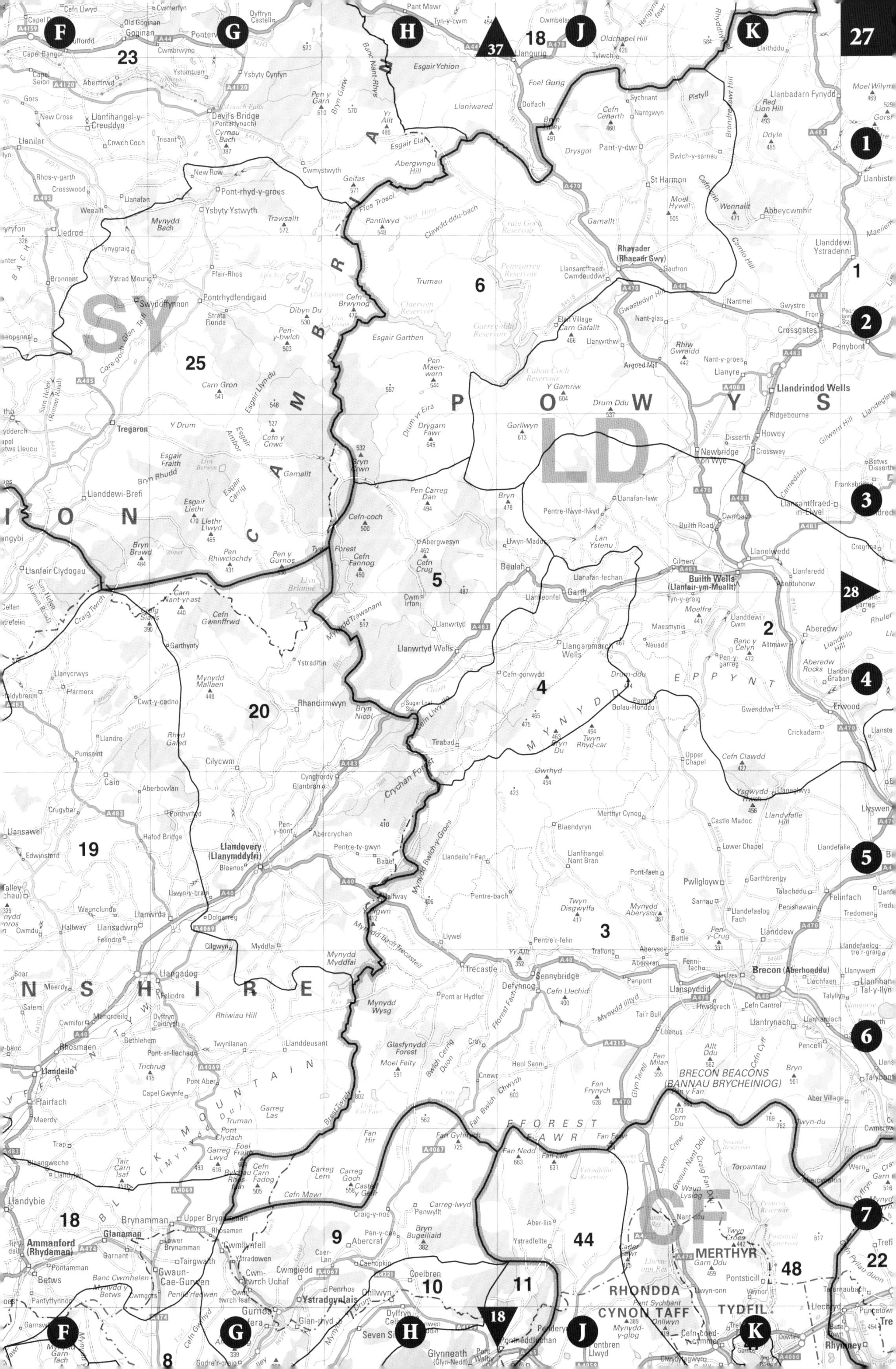

F
G
H
37
18
J
K
23
Capel Bangor
Goginan
Aberffrwd
Devil's Bridge (Pontarfynach)
Ysbyty Cynfyn
Llangurig
Esgair Ychion
Llaniwared
Foel Gurig
Oldchapel Hill
Tylwch
Llaithddu
Llanbadarn Fynydd
Moel Wilym
Red Lion Hill
Pistyll
Sychnant
Nantgwyn
Cefn Cenarth
Pant-y-dwr
Drysgol
Bwlch-y-sarnau
St Harmon
Moel Hywel
Wennallt
Abbeycwmhir
Gamallt
Rhayader (Rhaeadr Gwy)
Gaufron
Llansantffraed-Cwmdeuddwr
Craig Goch Reservoir
Penygarreg Reservoir
Claerwen Reservoir
Garreg-ddu Reservoir
Caban Coch Reservoir
Elan Village
Carn Gafallt
Llanwrthwl
Nantmel
Gwystre
Crossgates
Penybont
Llanbister
Llanddewi Ystradenni
Nant-glas
Rhiw Gwraidd
Nant-y-groes
Llanyre
Llandrindod Wells
Argoed Mill
Trumau
6
Esgair Elan
Abergwngu Hill
Ffos Trosol
Pantllwyd
Clawdd-ddu-bach
Cefn Brwynog
Esgair Garthen
Pen Maen-wern
Drum yr Eira
Drygarn Fawr
Y Gamriw
Gorllwyn
Drum Ddu
POWYS
LD
Ridgebourne
Howey
Disserth
Crossway
Newbridge on Wye
Franksbridge
Llansantffraed-in-Elwel
Llanafan-fawr
Pentre-llwyn-llwyd
Lan Ystenu
Builth Road
Cwmbach
Llanelwedd
Cilmery
Builth Wells (Llanfair-ym-Muallt)
Llanfaredd
Aberduhonw
Beulah
Llwyn-Madoc
Llanafan-fechan
Garth
Llanlleonfel
Tyn-y-graig
Moelfre
Llanddewi'r Cwm
Maesmynis
Aberedw
Aberedw Rocks
Alltmawr
Banc y Celyn
Pen-y-garreg
EPPYNT
MYNYDD
Erwood
Gwenddwr
Crickadarn
Cefn Clawdd
Upper Chapel
Ysgwydd Hwch
Llaneglwys
Llyswen
Llandyfalle Hill
Castle Madoc
Lower Chapel
Llandefalle
Merthyr Cynog
Blaendryn
Llanfihangel Nant Bran
Pont-faen
Pwllgloyw
Garthbrengy
Felinfach
Talachddu
Penishawain
Sarnau
Llandefaelog Fach
Battle
Pen-y-Crug
Llanddew
Twyn Disgwylfa
Mynydd Aberysgir
3
Pentre'r-felin
Trallong
Aberyscir
Aberbran
Fenni-fach
Brecon (Aberhonddu)
Llanfaes
Llanspyddid
Penpont
Sennybridge
Defynnog
Cefn Llechid
Mynydd Illtyd
Trecastle
Yr Allt
Llwel
Pentre-bach
Llandeilo'r-Fan
Tai'r Bull
Libanus
Ffrwdgrech
Cefn Cantref
Llanfrynach
Llechfaen
Pencelli
Allt Ddu
Pen Milan
Cefn Cyff
Bryn
BRECON BEACONS (BANNAU BRYCHEINIOG)
Pen y Fan
Corn Du
Aber Village
Twyn-du
Talybont
Heol Senni
Cnewr
Fan Frynych
Glyn Tarell
Fan Bwlch Chwyth
FFOREST FAWR
Fan Gyhirych
Fan Fawr
Fan Nedd
Fan Llia
Ystradfellte Reservoir
Torpantau
Neuadd Reservoirs
Gwaun Nant Ddu
Craig Fan Ddu
Waun Lysiog
Nant-ddu
Pentwyn Reservoir
Pontsticill Reservoir
Twyn Croes
MERTHYR
Garn Ddu
Pontsticill
48
TYDFIL
Llwyn-onn
RHONDDA
CYNON TAFF
Pant Sychbant
Mynydd-y-glog
Cefn-coed-y-cymmer
Aber-llia
Ystradfellte
44
Coelbren
10
11
Penderyn
Pontbren Llwyd
Cwm
Glynneath (Glyn-Nedd)
Pont Walby
Onllwyn
Dyffryn Cellwen
Seven Sisters
Ystradgynlais
Penrhos
Caehopkin
Cwmgiedd
Abercraf
Pen-y-cae
Craig-y-nos
Penwyllt
Carreg-lwyd
Bryn Bugeiliaid
9
Cefn Mawr
Carreg Lem
Carreg Goch
Castell y Geifr
Cefn Carn Fadog
Fan Hir
Cray
Glasfynydd Forest
Moel Feity
Bwlch Cerrig Duon
Mynydd Wysg
Usk Res
Mynydd Myddfai
Mynydd-bach Trecastell
Halfway
Babel
Pentre-ty-gwyn
Llandovery (Llanymddyfri)
Blaenos
Llwyn-y-brain
Abercrychan
Pen-y-bont
Crychan Forest
Cynghordy
Glanbran
Tirabad
Cefn Llwyd
Sugar Loaf
Bryn Nicol
Rhandirmwyn
20
Cilycwm
Ystradffin
Mynydd Trawsnant
Cwm Irfon
Llanwrtyd
Llanwrtyd Wells
Llangammarch Wells
Cefn-gorwydd
Drum-ddu
4
Gwrhyd
Twyn Rhyd-car
Bryn Du
Abergwesyn
Cefn Crug
5
Cefn Fannog
Cefn-coch
Pen Carreg Dan
Llyn Brianne
Bryn Crwn
CAMBRIAN
Gamallt
Cefn y Cnwc
Esgair Ambor
Esgair Carrig
Esgair Llethr
Llethr Llwyd
Pen Rhiwclochdy
Pen y Gurnos
Bryn Brawd
Carn Nant-yr-ast
Cefn Gwenffrwd
Craig Swais
Garthynty
Mynydd Mallaen
Rhyd Galed
Tregaron
Y Drum
Carn Gron
25
SY
Swyddffynnon
Pontrhydfendigaid
Strata Florida
Ystrad Meurig
Ffair-Rhos
Pen-y-bwlch
Dibyn Du
Mynydd Bach
Ysbyty Ystwyth
Trawsallt
Pont-rhyd-y-groes
New Row
Llanafan
Lledrod
Tynygraig
Bronnant
Wenallt
Crosswood
Rhos-y-garth
Llanilar
Trisant
Cwmystwyth
Geifas
Yr Allt
Pen y Garn
Bryn Garw
Cnwch Coch
Llanfihangel-y-Creuddyn
New Cross
Gors
Capel Seion
Cwmbrwyno
Cefn Llwyd
Pant Mawr
Tyn-y-cwm
Cwmbelan
Esgair Fraith
Bryn Rhudd
Llanddewi-Brefi
CEREDIGION
Llanfair Clydogau
Craig Twrch
Llanycrwys
Ffarmers
Cwrt-y-cadno
Llandre
Pumsaint
Caio
Crugybar
Porthyrhyd
Hafod Bridge
19
Edwinsford
Llansawel
Waunclunda
Llanwrda
Halfway
Llansadwrn
Dolgarreg
Felindre
Cilgwyn
Myddfai
Llangadog
Maerdy
Salem
Manordeilo
Cwmifor
Dyffryn Ceidrych
Bethlehem
Rhosmaen
Llandeilo
Rhiwiau Hill
Twynllanan
Llanddeusant
Pont-ar-llechau
Trichrug
Pont Aber
Capel Gwynfe
Garreg Las
Ffairfach
Maerdy
Trap
BLACK MOUNTAIN
Pont Clydach
Foel Fraith
Garreg Lwyd
Tair Carn Isaf
Llandyfan
Bwlch y Rhos-fain
Llandybie
18
Ammanford (Rhydaman)
Glanaman
Garnant
Brynamman
Upper Brynamman
Rhosaman
Lower Brynamman
Cwmllynfell
Tairgwaith
Gwaun-Cae-Gurwen
Cwm-twrch Uchaf
Cwm-twrch Isaf
Gurnos
Glan-rhyd
Ystalyfera
Pontamman
Betws
Banc Cwmhelen
Mynydd y Betws
Cwmgors
Pantyffynnon
Godre'r-graig
Cefn Gwrhyd
8
1
2
3
28
4
5
6
7
22
Llangorse Lake
Cwmcrawnon
Dyffryn Crawnon
Rhymney
Tredegar

A
B
C
D
E
38
1
2
3
4
5
6
7
SHROPSHIRE
POWYS
HEREFORDSHIRE
MONMOUTHSHIRE
BLACK MOUNTAINS
(MYNYDDOEDD DUON)
BLAENAU GWENT
TORFAEN
LD
SY
HR
NP
CF
Newcastle
Clunton
Aston on Clun
Craven Arms
Culmington
Beguildy
(Bugeildy)
Black Mountains
Dutlas
Llanfair Waterdine
Lloyney
Knucklas
(Cnwclas)
Skyborry Green
Heyop
Hobarris
Pentre
Obley
Hopton Castle
Hopton Titterhill
Clunbury
Clungunford
Onibury
Stokesay
Broome
Bromfield
Ludlow
Middleton
Bitterley
Stanton Lacy
Caynham
Caynham Camp
Knowbury
Bedstone
Bucknell
Stowe
Weston
Knighton
(Tref-y-clawdd)
Milebrook
Kinton
Leintwardine
Marlow
Buckton
Walford
Downton on the Rock
Burrington
Aston
Elton
Overton
Bringewood Chase
Brampton Bryan
Adforton
Richards Castle
Ashford Carbonel
Ashford Bowdler
Little Hereford
Brimfield
Woofferton
Orleton
Orleton Common
Comberton
Wigmore
Leinthall Starkes
Leinthall Earls
Birtley
Letton
Newton
Lingen
Ongar Street
Upper Lye
Lower Lye
Aymestrey
Yatton
Croft
Yarpole
Lucton
Bircher
Bircher Common
Mortimer's Cross
Moel Wilym
Gorslydan
Moelfre Hill
Beacon Hill
Pool Hill
Brynmelyn
Llanbadarn Fynydd
Llanbister
Llanbister Rd Sta
Crug
Llangunllo
Bailey Hill
Maelienydd
Llanddewi Ystradenni
Little Hill
Dolau
Llanfihangel Rhydithon
Bleddfa
Glog Hill
Fforest-fach
Black Mixen
Radnor Forest
Great Rhos
Bache Hill
Esgairnantau
Penybont
Llandegley
Llandrindod Wells
Llandegley Rhos
Fron Hill
New Radnor
(Maesyfed)
Kinnerton
Evenjobb
Cascob
Pilleth
Whitton
Norton
Rhos-y-Meirch
Llan-wen Hill
Hawthorn Hill
Stapleton
Presteigne
(Llanandras)
Kinsham
Discoed
Beggar's Bush
Maes-Treylow
Barland
Burfa
Nash
Rodd
Combe
Knill
Combes Moor
Wapley Hill
Byton
Upnampton
Easthampton
Shobdon
Ledicot
Kingsland
Bicton
Luston
Eyton
The Broad
Eye
Moreton
Ashton
Leysters
Kimbolton
Stockton
Grantsfield
Hamnish Clifford
Bach Camp
Pudleston
Leominster
Stretford
Steen's Bridge
Docklow
Stoke Prior
Humber
Buckland
Risbury
Womaston
Walton
Lower Harpton
Old Radnor
(Pencraig)
Wolfpits
Yardro
Burlingjobb
Bradnor Hill
Bradnor Green
Dolyhir
Hergest Ridge
Kington
Titley
Eywood
Staunton on Arrow
Stansbatch
Shirl Heath
Lawton
Cobnash
Cholstrey
Pembridge
Eardisland
The Forge
Marston
Barewood
Lower Barewood
Monkland
Ivington
Ivington Green
Barons' Cross
Newtown
Wharton
Llanfihangel-nant-Melan
Bryn-y-maen
Gwaunceste Hill
Betws Disserth
Franksbridge
Hundred House
Colva Hill
Colva
Glascwm
Gladestry
Lower Hergest
Upper Hergest
Huntington
Kingswood
Lyonshall
Holme Marsh
Weston
Moorcot
Luntley
Broxwood
Lower Burton
Sollers Dilwyn
Dilwyn Common
Dilwyn
Aulden
Upper Hill
Brierley
Hope under Dinmore
Bowley Town
Hengoed
Cregrina
Glascwm Hill
Vaaullt
Newchurch
Brilley Mountain
Upper Welson
Lower Welson
Almeley Wootton
Almeley
Woonton
Upcott
Meer Common
Sarnesfield
Weobley
Weobley Marsh
Bush Bank
Westhope
Bodenham
Bodenham Moor
King's Pyon
Ledgemoor
Canon Pyon
Llanfaredd
Rhulen
Red Hill
Rhulen Hill
Llanbedr Hill
Llanbadarn-y-garreg
Michaelchurch-on-Arrow
Bryngwyn
Dol-y-cannau
Rhosgoch
Clyro Hill
Brilley
Woods Eaves
Millhalf
Eardisley
Kinnersley
Ailey
Norton Wood
Eccles Green
Wormsley
Yarsop
Foxley
Wellington
Auberrow
Marden
Sutton Walls
Burley Gate
Preston Wynne
Rhydspence
Whitney-on-Wye
Toll
Winforton
Willersley
Letton
Norton Canon
Moorhampton
Mansell Lacy
Mansell Gamage
Tillington
Tillington Common
Burghill
Portway
Moreton on Lugg
Sutton St Nicholas
Withington Marsh
Aberedw
Llandeilo Hill
Llanbedr
Painscastle
Bronydd
Clifford
Priory Wood
Merbach
Bredwardine
Brobury
Staunton on Wye
Yazor
Bishopstone
Credenhill
Brinsop
Pipe and Lyde
Shelwick
Llandeilo Graban
Erwood
The Begwns
Clyro
Pen-y-Park
Hardwicke
The Bage
Dorstone
Moccas
Monnington on Wye
Byford
Bridge Sollers
Kenchester
Sugwas Pool
Swainshill
Stretton Sugwas
King's Acre
Huntington
Holmer
HEREFORD
Lugwardine
Hagley
Bartestree
Crickadarn
Llanstephan
Llowes
Hay-on-Wye
(Y Gelli Gandryll)
Cusop
Blakemere
Preston on Wye
Lulham
Canon Bridge
Upper Breinton
Breinton Common
Breinton
Warham
White Cross
Tupsley
Hampton Bishop
Boughrood
Glasbury
Llanigon
Ffordd-fawr
Cwmbach
Snodhill
Vagar Hill
Cefn Hill
Hinton
Golden Valley
Peterchurch
Shenmore
Tyberton
Madley
Cublington
Eaton Bishop
Clehonger
Lower Bullingham
Dinedor
Holme Lacy
Mordiford
Llyswen
Pipton
Tregoyd
Three Cocks
(Aberllynfi)
Velindre
Urishay Common
Monnington Court
Turnastone
Vowchurch
Goose Pool
Grafton
Allensmore
Kingstone
Webton
Cobhall Common
Twyford Common
Fownhope
Bronllys
Talgarth
Llanelieu
Twmpa
Rhos Dirion
Craswall
Michaelchurch Escley
Upper Maes-coed
Middle Maes-coed
St Margarets
Newton
Thruxton
Kerry's Gate
Whitfield
Tram Inn
Callow
Dewsall Court
Aconbury
Felinfach
Llanfilo
Tredustan
Trefecca
Penishawain
Tredomen
Llandefaelog-tre'r-graig
Pen y Manllwyn
Capel-y-ffin
Olchon Valley
Llanveynoe
Bacton
Lower Maes-coed
Abbey Dore
Didley
Crizeley
Kivernoll
Much Dewchurch
Wormbridge
Kingsthorne
Little Birch
Little Dewchurch
Much Birch
Bolstone
Ballingham
Pengenffordd
Waun Fach
Longtown
Kilpeck
Wormelow Tump
Orcop Hill
Hoarwithy
Llandinabo
Kings Caple
Carey
Brecon
(Aberhonddu)
Llechfaen
Llanywern
Llanfihangel Tal-y-llyn
Talyllyn
Llangorse
Llangorse Lake
Mynydd Troed
Mynydd Llysiau
Pen Twyn Mawr
Llanthony
Clodock
Mynydd Merddin
Ewyas Harold
Howton
Kenderchurch
Pontrilas
Llanwarne
Harewood End
Sellack
Llanhamlach
Pennorth
Llangasty-Talyllyn
Scethrog
Cathedine
Pen Allt-mawr
Pen Gwyllt Meirch
Hatterall Hill
Walterstone
Oldcastle
Rowlestone
Kentchurch
Bagwyllydiart
Garway Hill
Orcop
Pencoyd
Michaelchurch
Sandyway
St Owen's Cross
Tretire
Peterstow
Bridstow
Upper Grove Common
Llansantffraed
Talybont-on-Usk
Cwmdu
Felindre
Pen Cerrig-calch
Crug Mawr
Cwmyoy
Tre-wyn
Pandy
Grosmont
Hoaldalbert
Graig Syfyrddin
Little Garway
St Weonards
White Rocks
Garway
Llangarron
Glewstone
Pencraig
Aber Village
Pen-y-gaer
Gaer
Bwlch
Tretower
Myarth
Coed-yr-ynys
Cwmcrawnon
Llanbedr
Forest Coal Pit
Partrishow
Llanvihangel Crucorney
(Llanfihangel Crucornau)
Llangattock Lingoed
Bont
Upper Green
Cross Ash
Norton
Skenfrith
Crossway
Broad Oak
Llangrove
Goodrich
Marstow
Welsh Newton
Whitchurch
Trewen
Llangynidr
Ffawyddog
Crickhowell
Llangenny
Sugar Loaf
(Mynydd Pen-y-fâl)
Blaenawey
Bryn arw
Deri
Pantygelli
Ysgyryd Fawr
Caggle Street
Llanvetherine
Llanfaenor
Llanrothal
Newcastle
St Maughans Green
Buckholt
Ganarew
Great Doward
Symonds Yat
Wern
Crawnon
Garn Caws
Llangattock
Cwrt-y-gollen
Rholben
Mynydd Llanwenarth
Llantilio Pertholey
Mardy
Llanddewi Skirrid
Brynygwenin
Croes Hywel
Llantilio Crossenny
Llangattock-Vibon-Avel
Tal-y-coed
Maypole
Rockfield
Dixton
Abercynafon
Dyffryn Crawnon
Mynydd Llangynidr
Cefn Onneu
Mynydd Llangatwg
Glangrwyney
Gilwern
Llanelly
Govilon
Abergavenny
(Y Fenni)
Llanvapley
Llanvihangel-Ystern-Llewern
Monmouth
(Trefynwy)
Christchurch
Berry Hill
Trefil
BLAENAU GWENT
Rassau
Beaufort
Clydach Terrace
Blackrock
Clydach
Llanfoist
Blorenge
Llanddewi Rhydderch
Coed Morgan
Wernrheolydd
Penrhos
Pen-yr-heol
Osbaston
Wyesham
Staunton
Lower Berry Hill
Crossways
Penallt
Brynmawr
Ebbw Vale
(Glynebwy)
Nantyglo
Dukestown
Sirhowy
Tafarnaubach
Cefn Pyllau-duon
Llangattock
Llanelly Hill
Llanellen
Llanarth
Great Oak
Tregare
Dingestow
Mitchel Troy
Mitchel Troy Common
Wonastow
Redbrook
Coleford
Newland
Pen-twyn
Blaenavon
The Bryn
Bryngwyn
Raglan
Wern-y-cwrt
Pen-clawdd
Caer Llan
Cwmcarvan
Hoop
Clearwell
Trow Green
Whitebrook
Coity
Llanover
Clytha
Waun-Lwyd
Princetown
TORFAEN
22
23
4
15
25
16
19
27
48
0 2 4 6 miles
0 2 4 6 8 10 km

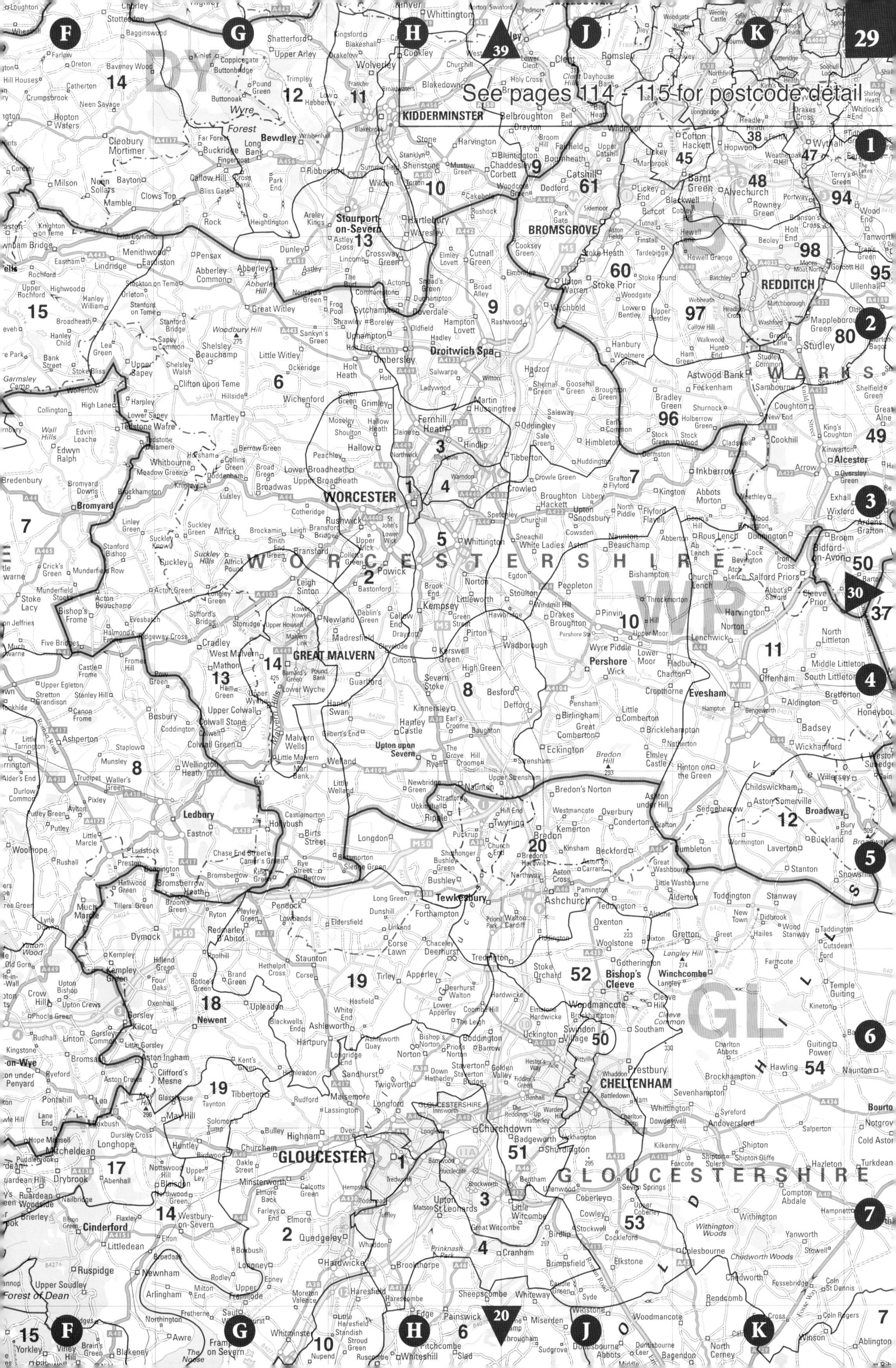

29
F
G
H
J
K
39
See pages 114 - 115 for postcode detail
DY
KIDDERMINSTER
Bewdley
Wyre Forest
Stourport-on-Severn
BROMSGROVE
REDDITCH
Droitwich Spa
WORCESTER
WORCESTERSHIRE
WARKS
WR
GREAT MALVERN
Bromyard
Ledbury
Evesham
Pershore
Upton upon Severn
Tewkesbury
Alcester
Broadway
Bishop's Cleeve
Winchcombe
CHELTENHAM
GL
GLOUCESTER
GLOUCESTERSHIRE
Newent
Cinderford
Forest of Dean
30
37
20
1
2
3
4
5
6
7

30
A
B
C
D
E
40
See pages 114 - 115 for postcode detail
SOLIHULL
COVENTRY
Bickenhill
Hampton in Arden
Berkswell
Balsall Common
Kenilworth
Stoneleigh
ROYAL LEAMINGTON SPA
WARWICK
Bromsgrove
Catshill
Alvechurch
Hockley Heath
Knowle
REDDITCH
Studley
Henley-in-Arden
Astwood Bank
Feckenham
Alcester
Bidford-on-Avon
STRATFORD-UPON-AVON
Wellesbourne
Kineton
WARWICKSHIRE
CV
WORCESTERSHIRE
WR
Inkberrow
Pershore
Evesham
Mickleton
Chipping Campden
Broadway
Ilmington
Shipston on Stour
Moreton-in-Marsh
Stow-on-the-Wold
Bourton-on-the-Water
Winchcombe
Bishop's Cleeve
CHELTENHAM
Prestbury
Charlton Kings
Tewkesbury
Ashchurch
Bredon
GL
GLOUCESTERSHIRE
COTSWOLD HILLS
Chipping Norton
Charlbury
OX
Burford
WITNEY
Northleach
Andoversford
Guiting Power
1
2
3
4
5
6
7
29
20
0 2 4 6 miles
0 2 4 6 8 10 km

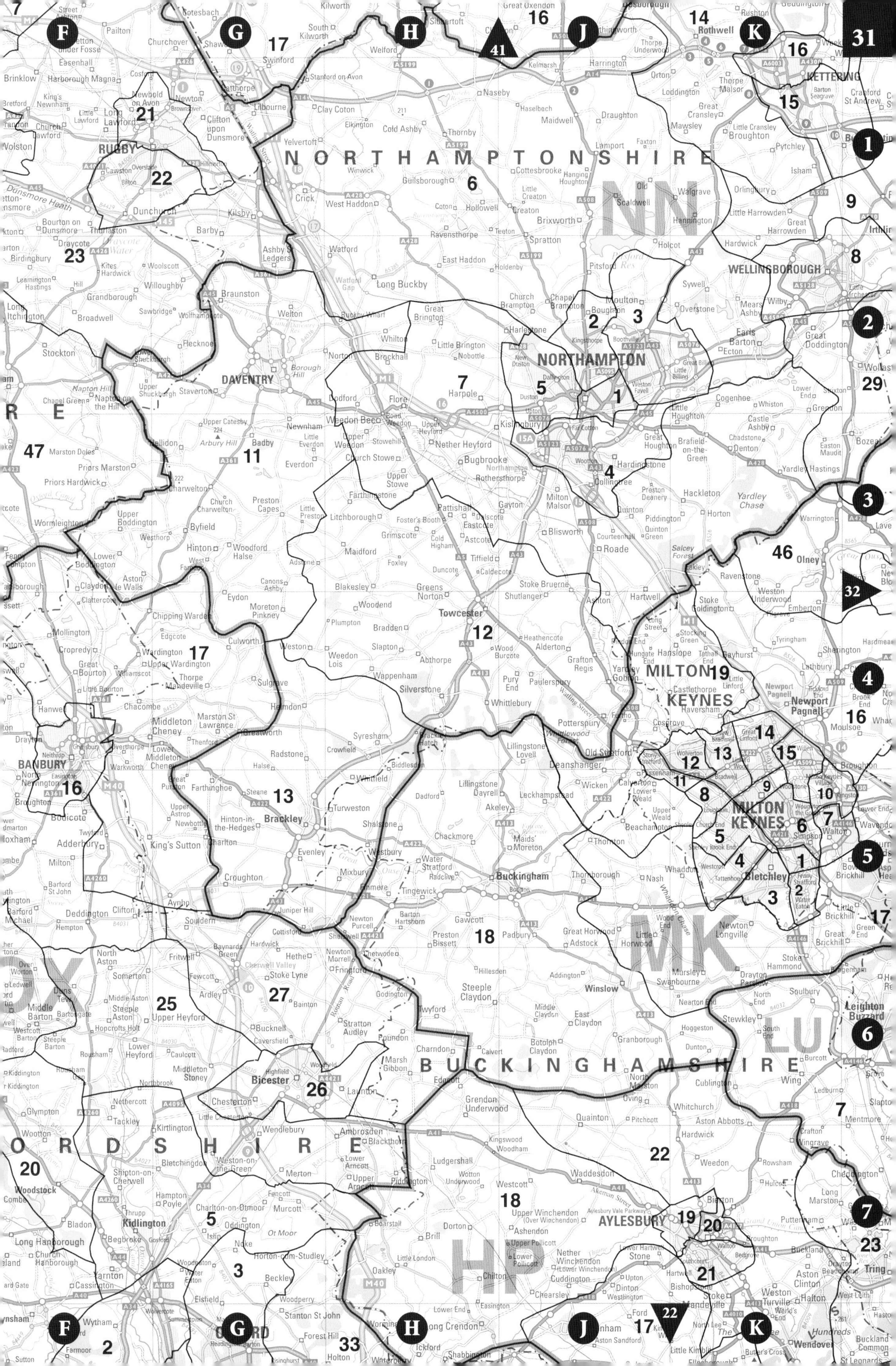

NORTHAMPTONSHIRE
BUCKINGHAMSHIRE
NN
MK
HP
LU
NORTHAMPTON
MILTON KEYNES
KETTERING
WELLINGBOROUGH
RUGBY
DAVENTRY
BANBURY
Bicester
AYLESBURY
Towcester
Brackley
Buckingham
Newport Pagnell
Bletchley
Kidlington
Olney
Winslow
Leighton Buzzard
Rothwell
Long Buckby
Woodstock
Wendover
Tring
Stony Stratford
Wolverton
Old Stratford
Deanshanger
Potterspury
Silverstone
Roade
Blisworth
Brixworth
Naseby
Crick
Kilsby
Braunston
Byfield
Badby
Weedon Bec
Bugbrooke
Hackleton
Yardley Hastings
Denton
Earls Barton
Moulton
Lilbourne
Swinford
Welford
Harrington
Desborough
Great Oxendon
Kilworth
Stanford on Avon
Clay Coton
Cold Ashby
Guilsborough
West Haddon
Ravensthorpe
Watford
Ashby St Ledgers
Barby
Dunchurch
Hillmorton
Bilton
Draycote
Thurlaston
Bourton on Dunsmore
Dunsmore Heath
Long Itchington
Stockton
Napton on the Hill
Priors Marston
Priors Hardwick
Marston Doles
Wormleighton
Chipping Warden
Culworth
Sulgrave
Helmdon
Greatworth
Middleton Cheney
Marston St Lawrence
Thenford
Farthinghoe
Hinton-in-the-Hedges
King's Sutton
Adderbury
Bodicote
Deddington
Aynho
Croughton
Evenley
Turweston
Westbury
Biddlesden
Syresham
Whittlebury
Paulerspury
Alderton
Grafton Regis
Hanslope
Castlethorpe
Haversham
Lathbury
Sherington
Emberton
Stoke Goldington
Ravenstone
Weston Underwood
Salcey Forest
Hartwell
Ashton
Stoke Bruerne
Shutlanger
Courteenhall
Quinton
Piddington
Horton
Yardley Chase
Castle Ashby
Whiston
Cogenhoe
Grendon
Bozeat
Wollaston
Great Doddington
Wilby
Mears Ashby
Sywell
Overstone
Holcot
Walgrave
Hannington
Old
Scaldwell
Lamport
Maidwell
Draughton
Kelmarsh
Great Cransley
Little Cransley
Broughton
Pytchley
Isham
Orlingbury
Harrowden
Finedon
Irthlingborough
Hardwick
Great Harrowden
Little Harrowden
Barton Seagrave
Cranford St Andrew
Loddington
Mawsley
Orton
Thorpe Malsor
Thorpe Underwood
Rushton
Geddington
Weekley
Cottesbrooke
Hollowell
Creaton
Spratton
Teeton
East Haddon
Holdenby
Church Brampton
Chapel Brampton
Pitsford
Boughton
Harlestone
Duston
Dallington
Kingsthorpe
Weston Favell
Great Billing
Little Billing
Far Cotton
Hardingstone
Great Houghton
Little Houghton
Brafield-on-the-Green
Collingtree
Milton Malsor
Rothersthorpe
Gayton
Kislingbury
Upper Heyford
Nether Heyford
Harpole
Flore
Dodford
Brockhall
Norton
Whilton
Great Brington
Little Brington
Nobottle
Newnham
Everdon
Farthingstone
Litchborough
Pattishall
Eastcote
Astcote
Tiffield
Caldecote
Maidford
Grimscote
Foxley
Adstone
Blakesley
Woodend
Greens Norton
Plumpton
Bradden
Slapton
Abthorpe
Wappenham
Weedon Lois
Weston
Moreton Pinkney
Canons Ashby
Eydon
Woodford Halse
Hinton
Preston Capes
Charwelton
Hellidon
Staverton
Welton
Norton
Lower Boddington
Upper Boddington
Aston le Walls
Claydon
Mollington
Cropredy
Wardington
Edgcote
Thorpe Mandeville
Chacombe
Warkworth
Hanwell
Drayton
Broughton
Milton
Clifton
Souldern
Fritwell
Somerton
North Aston
Upper Heyford
Lower Heyford
Ardley
Fewcott
Stoke Lyne
Hethe
Cottisford
Hardwick
Bucknell
Caversfield
Middleton Stoney
Launton
Marsh Gibbon
Poundon
Stratton Audley
Godington
Fringford
Twyford
Charndon
Steeple Claydon
Middle Claydon
East Claydon
Botolph Claydon
Calvert
Granborough
North Marston
Oving
Whitchurch
Cublington
Aston Abbotts
Wing
Stewkley
Soulbury
Mursley
Swanbourne
Little Horwood
Great Horwood
Adstock
Addington
Padbury
Gawcott
Preston Bissett
Barton Hartshorn
Tingewick
Water Stratford
Radclive
Maids' Moreton
Chackmore
Akeley
Leckhampstead
Lillingstone Dayrell
Lillingstone Lovell
Wicken
Thornton
Beachampton
Calverton
Thornborough
Nash
Whaddon
Newton Longville
Drayton Parslow
Stoke Hammond
Great Brickhill
Little Brickhill
Bow Brickhill
Wavendon
Walton
Simpson
Fenny Stratford
Water Eaton
Broughton
Moulsoe
Chicheley
Tyringham
Chesterton
Ambrosden
Blackthorn
Piddington
Merton
Arncott
Ludgershall
Wotton Underwood
Grendon Underwood
Edgcott
Kingswood
Woodham
Quainton
Pitchcott
Waddesdon
Westcott
Upper Winchendon
Ashendon
Dorton
Brill
Oakley
Long Crendon
Chilton
Chearsley
Cuddington
Nether Winchendon
Stone
Dinton
Hartwell
Bishopstone
Stoke Mandeville
Weston Turville
Halton
Aston Clinton
Buckland
Bierton
Hardwick
Weedon
Rowsham
Hulcott
Puttenham
Long Marston
Cheddington
Mentmore
Slapton
Ledburn
Wingrave
Oxford
Weston-on-the-Green
Bletchingdon
Kirtlington
Tackley
Shipton-on-Cherwell
Hampton Poyle
Charlton-on-Otmoor
Oddington
Islip
Noke
Murcott
Fencott
Horton-cum-Studley
Beckley
Elsfield
Woodeaton
Stanton St John
Forest Hill
Wheatley
Woodperry
Wytham
Cassington
Yarnton
Begbroke
Bladon
Long Hanborough
Combe
Wootton
Glympton
Rousham
Steeple Aston
Middle Aston
Middle Barton
Westcott Barton
Hopcrofts Holt
Ot Moor
Ickford
Shabbington
Worminghall
Haddenham
Ford
Aston Sandford
Little Kimble
Butler's Cross
Lower Hartwell
Upper Pollicott
Lower Pollicott
Bourton
Great Oxendon
Sibbertoft
Clipston
Cotesbach
South Kilworth
Shawell
Churchover
Pailton
Monks Kirby
Easenhall
Harborough Magna
Brinklow
Newbold on Avon
Brownsover
Clifton upon Dunsmore
Newton
Long Lawford
Little Lawford
Church Lawford
Wolston
Birdingbury
Leamington Hastings
Grandborough
Broadwell
Willoughby
Kites Hardwick
Woolscott
Sawbridge
Wolfhampcote
Flecknoe
Lower Shuckburgh
Upper Shuckburgh
Upper Catesby
Arbury Hill
Borough Hill
F
G
H
J
K
1
2
3
4
5
6
7
41
22
32

NORTHAMPTONSHIRE
NN
NORTHAMPTON
KETTERING
WELLINGBOROUGH
Rothwell
Burton Latimer
Finedon
Irthlingborough
Higham Ferrers
Rushden
Raunds
Thrapston
BEDFORD
BEDFORD
MK
MILTON KEYNES
MILTON KEYNES
Newport Pagnell
Bletchley
Olney
CENTRAL
BEDFORDSHIRE
Kempston
Flitwick
Buckingham
Winslow
Leighton Buzzard
LU
DUNSTABLE
LUTON
LUTON
Harpenden
BUCKINGHAMSHIRE
AYLESBURY
Tring
Wendover
Berkhamsted
HEMEL HEMPSTEAD
Hitchin
Shefford
Sandy
Chicksands
Toddington
HP
CAM
PE
AL
Salcey Forest
Yardley Chase
Whaddon Chase
Grafham Water
Pitsford Res
31
42
22
0 2 4 6 miles
0 2 4 6 8 10 km

F
G
H
J
K
43
34
23
CAMBRIDGESHIRE
HERTFORDSHIRE
ESSEX
Huntingdon
Godmanchester
St Ives
Somersham
Warboys
Chatteris
Sutton
Haddenham
Ely
Witchford
Soham
Mildenhall
Fordham
Newmarket
Waterbeach
Cottenham
Histon
Girton
Impington
Milton
Cambourne
CAMBRIDGE
Fulbourn
Great Shelford
Sawston
Linton
Haverhill
Royston
Melbourn
Saffron Walden
Thaxted
Great Dunmow
Baldock
STEVENAGE
Buntingford
Puckeridge
BISHOP'S STORTFORD
Stansted Mountfitchet
LONDON STANSTED
Sawbridgeworth
Ware
HERTFORD
WELWYN GARDEN CITY
HARLOW
Hoddesdon
Knebworth
Great Waltham
Stebbing
Finchingfield
Steeple Bumpstead
Newport
Great Chesterford
Duxford
Whittlesford
Bassingbourn
Gamlingay
Papworth Everard
Willingham
Swavesey
Burwell
Bottisham
Balsham

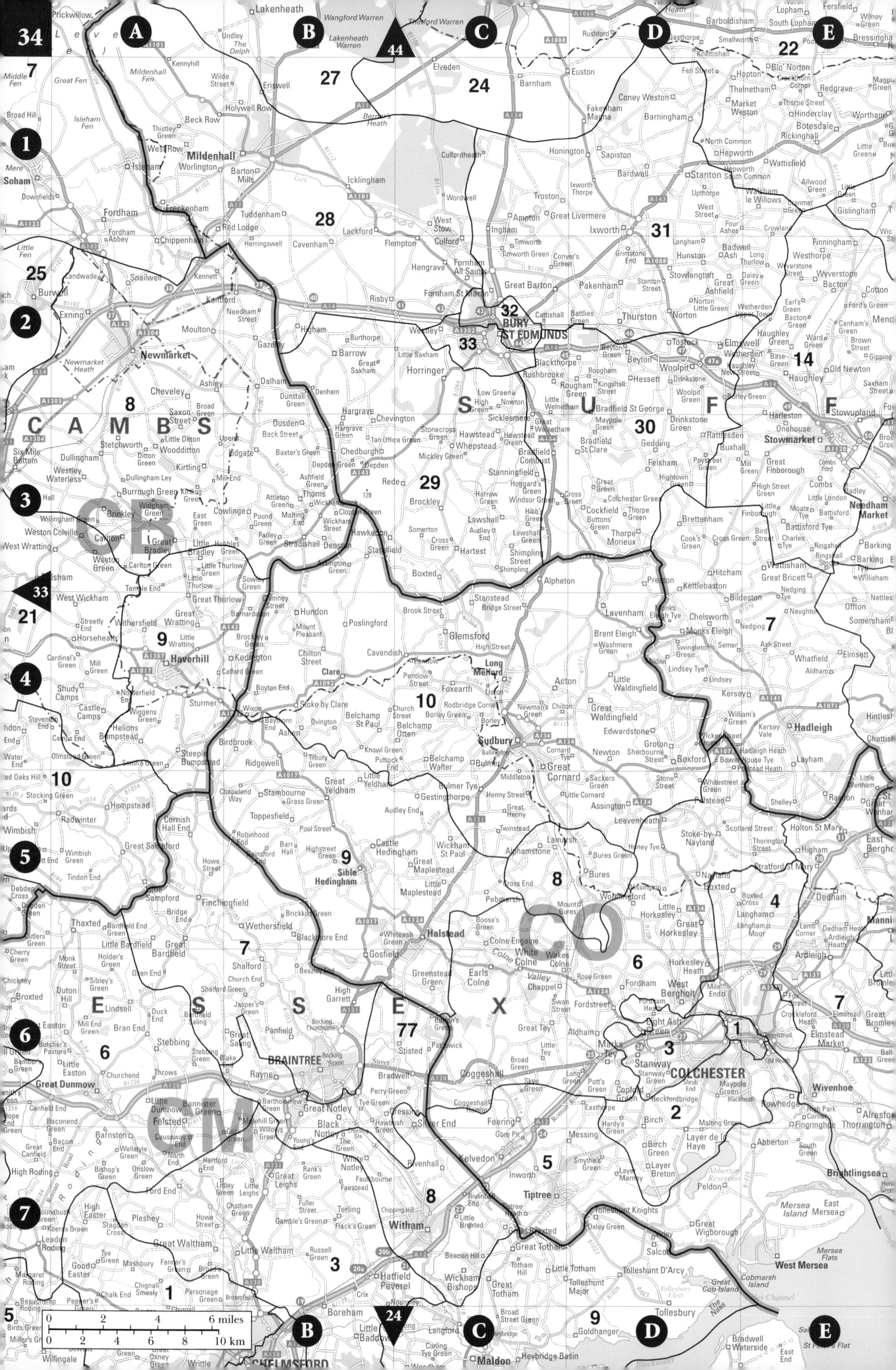

34
A
B
C
D
E
1
2
3
4
5
6
7
44
33
24
Lakenheath
Mildenhall
Soham
Fordham
Burwell
Exning
Newmarket
Kentford
Moulton
Gazeley
Higham
Barrow
Risby
Elveden
Barnham
Euston
Icklingham
Tuddenham
Red Lodge
Chippenham
Cavenham
Flempton
Hengrave
Culford
Ingham
Ampton
Ixworth
Pakenham
Great Barton
BURY ST EDMUNDS
Horringer
Thurston
Norton
Woolpit
Elmswell
Haughley
Stowmarket
Needham Market
Stowupland
Rattlesden
Felsham
Gedding
Bradfield St George
Rougham
Beyton
Tostock
Hessett
Drinkstone
Cockfield
Lavenham
Chelsworth
Bildeston
Hadleigh
Kersey
Boxford
Nayland
Stoke-by-Nayland
Sudbury
Long Melford
Glemsford
Cavendish
Clare
Stoke by Clare
Haverhill
Kedington
Withersfield
Great Thurlow
Little Thurlow
Great Bradley
Kirtling
Cheveley
Dullingham
Stetchworth
Wickhambrook
Denston
Stradishall
Hundon
Poslingford
Chevington
Hawkedon
Brockley
Hartest
Lawshall
Shimpling
Stanstead
Alpheton
Acton
Great Waldingfield
Little Waldingfield
Great Cornard
Bures
Assington
Leavenheath
Wormingford
Halstead
Sible Hedingham
Castle Hedingham
Great Yeldham
Gosfield
Coggeshall
Kelvedon
Witham
BRAINTREE
Great Notley
Black Notley
Rayne
Felsted
Great Dunmow
Thaxted
Finchingfield
Wethersfield
Shalford
Great Bardfield
Stebbing
Great Leighs
Terling
Hatfield Peverel
Boreham
CHELMSFORD
Maldon
Heybridge Basin
Tiptree
Tolleshunt D'Arcy
Tollesbury
Great Totham
Wickham Bishops
Great Braxted
Feering
Marks Tey
Stanway
COLCHESTER
Wivenhoe
Alresford
Brightlingsea
West Mersea
Mersea Island
Abberton
Peldon
Layer de la Haye
Dedham
Langham
Ardleigh
Great Horkesley
West Bergholt
Fordham
Earls Colne
White Colne
Chappel
Great Tey
Messing
Birch
Elmstead Market
CAMBS
CB
SUFF
CO
ESSEX
CM
Colne Valley
0 2 4 6 miles
0 2 4 6 8 10 km

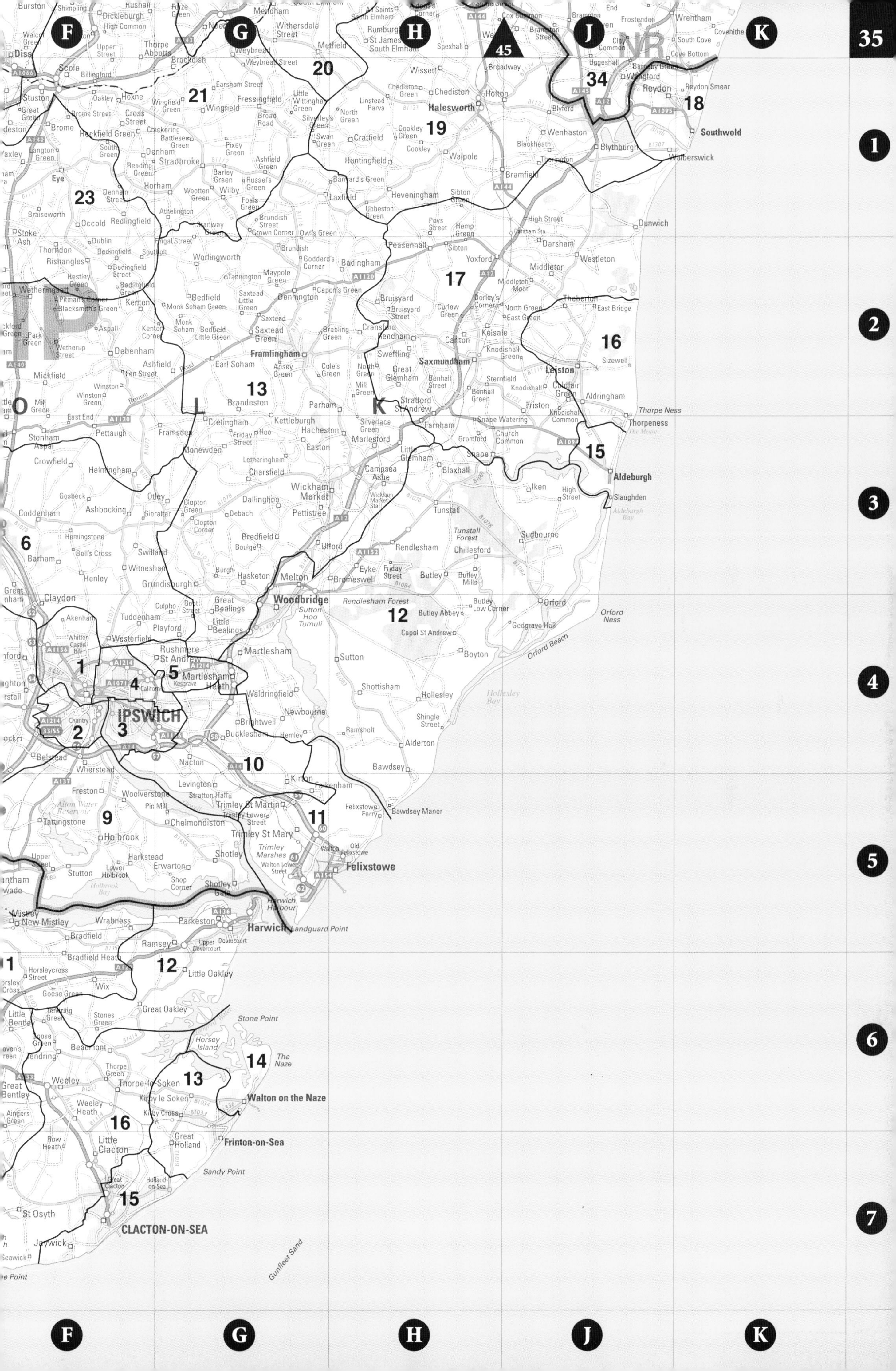
F
G
H
J
K
1
2
3
4
5
6
7
45
Diss
Scole
Dickleburgh
Thorpe Abbotts
Brockdish
Weybread
Withersdale Street
Metfield
Mendham
Rumburgh
St James South Elmham
Wissett
Chediston
Halesworth
Holton
Spexhall
Wenhaston
Blythburgh
Walberswick
Southwold
Reydon
Wangford
Uggeshall
South Cove
Covehithe
Wrentham
Frostenden
Blyford
Blackheath
Thorington
Walpole
Cookley
Huntingfield
Cratfield
Linstead Parva
Fressingfield
Wingfield
Stradbroke
Eye
Occold
Redlingfield
Horham
Wilby
Laxfield
Heveningham
Ubbeston Green
Sibton Green
Peasenhall
Badingham
Yoxford
Darsham
Middleton
Westleton
Dunwich
Theberton
East Bridge
Leiston
Sizewell
Aldringham
Thorpe Ness
Thorpeness
Aldeburgh
Slaughden
Saxmundham
Kelsale
Carlton
Knodishall
Friston
Sternfield
Benhall Street
Farnham
Snape
Blaxhall
Iken
Tunstall
Tunstall Forest
Chillesford
Sudbourne
Orford
Orford Ness
Orford Beach
Gedgrave Hall
Butley
Butley Abbey
Capel St Andrew
Boyton
Hollesley
Hollesley Bay
Shingle Street
Alderton
Bawdsey
Bawdsey Manor
Felixstowe Ferry
Felixstowe
Trimley St Martin
Trimley St Mary
Trimley Marshes
Kirton
Falkenham
Levington
Nacton
Bucklesham
Brightwell
Newbourne
Waldringfield
Martlesham
Martlesham Heath
Kesgrave
Rushmere St Andrew
IPSWICH
Westerfield
Whitton
Claydon
Akenham
Belstead
Wherstead
Freston
Woolverstone
Pin Mill
Chelmondiston
Holbrook
Tattingstone
Alton Water Reservoir
Stutton
Harkstead
Erwarton
Shotley
Shotley Gate
Harwich Harbour
Harwich
Landguard Point
Parkeston
Dovercourt
Ramsey
Little Oakley
Great Oakley
Wrabness
Mistley
New Mistley
Bradfield
Bradfield Heath
Wix
Stone Point
Horsey Island
The Naze
Walton on the Naze
Kirby le Soken
Kirby Cross
Thorpe-le-Soken
Weeley
Weeley Heath
Beaumont
Great Holland
Frinton-on-Sea
Sandy Point
Little Clacton
Great Clacton
Holland-on-Sea
CLACTON-ON-SEA
St Osyth
Jaywick
Gunfleet Sand
Woodbridge
Melton
Sutton Hoo Tumuli
Sutton
Shottisham
Ramsholt
Rendlesham Forest
Rendlesham
Eyke
Bromeswell
Ufford
Wickham Market
Pettistree
Campsea Ashe
Little Glemham
Marlesford
Hacheston
Easton
Parham
Framlingham
Saxtead Green
Dennington
Brandeston
Kettleburgh
Cretingham
Monewden
Charsfield
Dallinghoo
Debach
Bredfield
Hasketon
Burgh
Grundisburgh
Witnesham
Swilland
Otley
Clopton Green
Great Bealings
Little Bealings
Playford
Tuddenham
Culpho
Henley
Barham
Coddenham
Ashbocking
Helmingham
Crowfield
Pettaugh
Framsden
Earl Soham
Ashfield
Debenham
Aspall
Kenton
Mickfield
Stonham Aspal
Winston
Bedfield
Worlingworth
Tannington
Brundish
Thorndon
Rishangles
Wetheringsett
Mendlesham
Bruisyard
Rendham
Sweffling
Great Glemham
Stratford St Andrew
Cransford
Snape Watering
Church Common
12
13
14
15
16
17
18
19
20
21
23
34
IP
NR
O
L
K
A12
A14
A140
A144
A1120
A1152
A1094
A1156
A1214
A137
A120
A133

A **B** **C** **D** **E**

1 **2** **3** **4** **5** **6** **7**

Pontllyfni
Talysarn
Llyn Nantlle Uchaf
Y Garn
Trum
Fridd
Trwyn Maen Dylan
Aberdesach
Llanllyfni
A487
Craig Cwm Silyn 734
Edgelert Forest
46
Clynnog-fawr
Tai'n Lôn
221
Nebo
54
Garneddgoch
700
Moel Hebog 782
Gyrn Goch
Capeluchaf
Nasareth
Mynydd Craig Goch 610
Pass Aberglas
Aberglas
Bwlch Mawr 509
Pant Glas
Trefor
Gyrn Ddu 522
Bwlch-derwin
51
Trwyn y Gorlech
Mynydd Cennin
Cennin
Moel-de 552
Yr Eifl 561
Llanaelhaearn
Pen-sarn
Glan-Dwyfach
Brynci
Llanfihangel-y-pennant
Tremadog
Carreg Ddu
Pistyll
Cefn-caer-Ferch
Pencaenewydd
Garndolbenmaen
A487
Porth Dinllaen
Llithfaen
Llwyndyrys
Llangybi
Dolbenmaen
Tremadog
Morfa Nefyn
Nefyn
LLEYN PENINSULA
Fron
Llanarmon
Golan
Pentrefelin
Penmorfa Wern
Groesffordd
Edern
Garn Boduan
Rhos-fawr
Y Ffôr
B4354
Chwilog
Gell
52
Llanystumdwy
Moel-y-Gest 262
Porthmadog
Rhos-y-llan
Ceidio Fawr
Tân-y-graig
Hendre
B4354
Afon Wen
Criccieth
Morfa Bychan
Borth-y
Porth Ysgaden
Tudweiliog
Bodfuan
B4417
Llannor
Abererch
Penychain Sta
Black Rock Sands
Penmein
Dinas
B4417
Efailnewydd
Denio
Pen-ychain
Harlech Point
Traeth Bach
Penllech
Porth Colmon
Carn Fadryn
Rhyd-y-clafdy
Pwllheli
Morfa Harlech
Porth Colmon
Pen-y-Graig
Bryn-mawr
Garnfadryn 371
53
Penrhos
Carreg yr Imbill
Penrhyn Mawr
Llangwnnadl
Llaniestyn
T R E M A D O G
Rhedyn
Y Gamlas
Ty-hen
Sarn Meyllteyrn
B4413
Llanbedrog
B A Y
Llandanwg
Bryncroes
Botwnnog
Nanhoron
Llandegwning
Mynytho
A499
Llangian
Trwyn Llanbedrog
Llanfihangel
Methlem
Porth Oer
Rhydlios
Rhydlios
Mynydd Rhiw 305
Abersoch
Pen-
Braich Anelog
Rhoshirwaun
Rhiw
Llawr-y-dref
St Tudwal's Road
Mynydd Anelog
Anelog 191
Rhydolion
Llanengan
Llandanwg
Braich y Pwll
Pwlldefaid
Llanfaelrhys
Sarn Bach
Bwlchtocyn
Coed Ystumgwern
3 Uwchmynydd
Aberdaron
Aberdaron Bay
St Tudwal's Islands
Dyffryn Ardudwy Sta
Pen y Cil
Ynys Gwylan-fawr
Porth Neigwl (Hell's Mouth)
Porth Ceiriad
Dyffryn Ardudwy
Bardsey Sound (Swnt Enlli)
Cilan Uchaf
Trwyn yr Wylfa
Llanddwywe
Tal-y-bont
Bardsey Island (Ynys Enlli)
Trwyn Cilan

4
Barmouth B (Bae Berme)

5
Llangelyn
Rhosle
A49
Tonfanau
Llanfendigaid
Tywyn

C A R D I G A N

6
B A Y
Aberdyfi B
(B A E C E R E D I G I O N)

7
Sarn Cynfelyn
Llang
Aberystwyth
The Bar
Penparcau
Sou
Afon Wen
Chancery
Rhydyfelir

0 2 4 6 miles
0 2 4 6 8 10 km

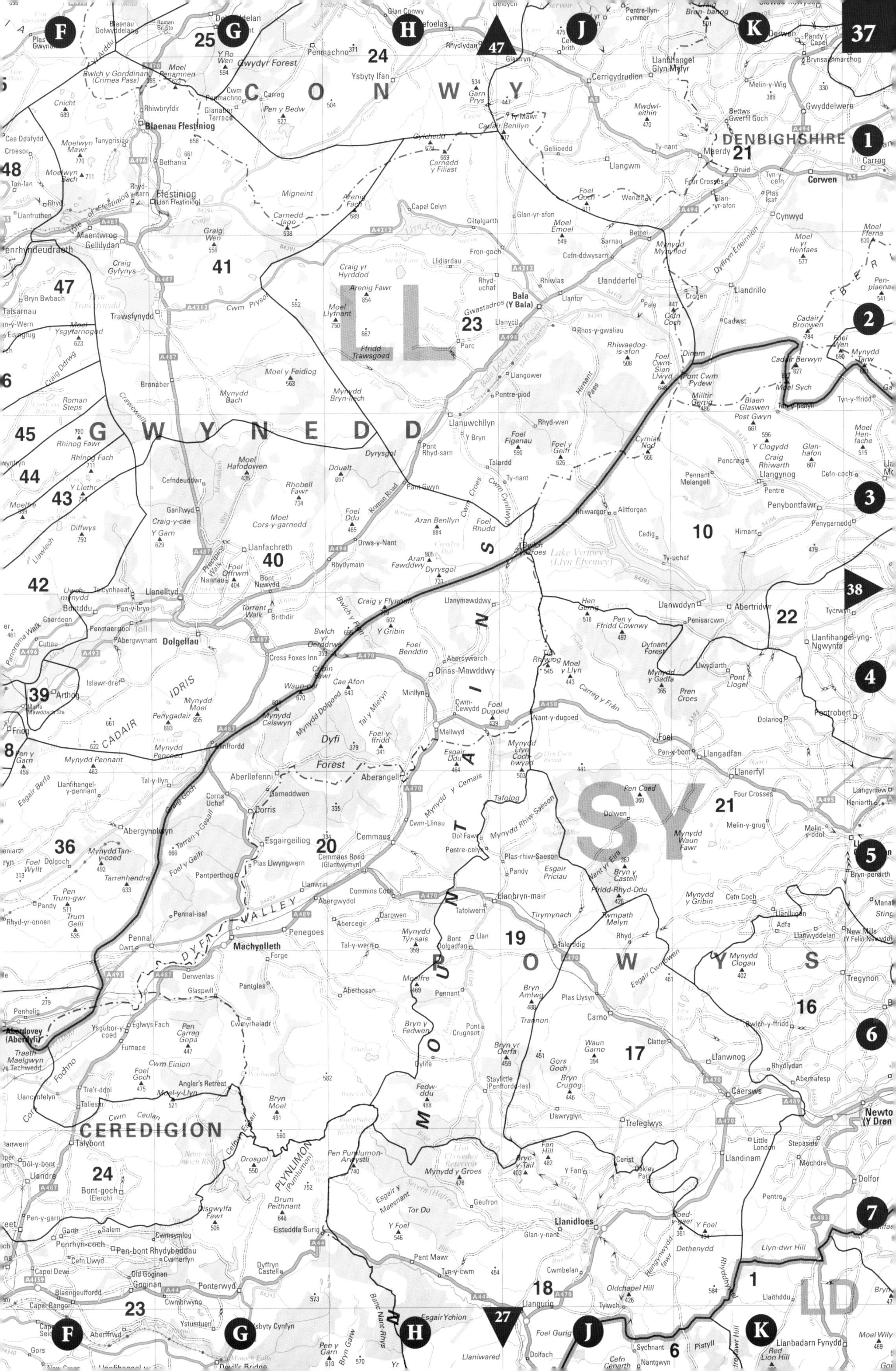
F
G
H
47
J
K
CONWY
DENBIGHSHIRE
GWYNEDD
POWYS
CEREDIGION
LL
SY
LD
38
27
1
2
3
4
5
6
7
Blaenau Ffestiniog
Ffestiniog
Maentwrog
Gellilydan
Trawsfynydd
Penmachno
Ysbyty Ifan
Cerrigydrudion
Gwyddelwern
Corwen
Carrog
Llandrillo
Llandderfel
Bala (Y Bala)
Llanuwchllyn
Dolgellau
Llanelltyd
Barmouth
Dinas-Mawddwy
Mallwyd
Aberangell
Corris
Machynlleth
Cemmaes
Llanbryn-mair
Talerddig
Carno
Llanidloes
Llangurig
Caersws
Llandinam
Llanwnog
Trefeglwys
Newtown (Y Drenewydd)
Tregynon
Llanfair Caereinion
Llangadfan
Llanerfyl
Llanwddyn
Lake Vyrnwy (Llyn Efyrnwy)
Llangynog
Penybontfawr
Bala Lake (Llyn Tegid)
Arenig Fawr
Aran Fawddwy
Cadair Idris
Cadair Berwyn
Moel Sych
Plynlimon (Pumlumon)
Aberdovey (Aberdyfi)
Talybont
Goginan
Ponterwyd
Devil's Bridge
Dyfi Forest
Gwydyr Forest
Dyfi Valley
Mynydd Moel
Precipice Walk
Torrent Walk
Panorama Walk
Cross Foxes Inn
Clywedog Reservoir
Migneint
Rhinog Fawr
Rhinog Fach
Moelwyn Mawr
Cnicht
Hirnant Pass
Bwlch y Groes

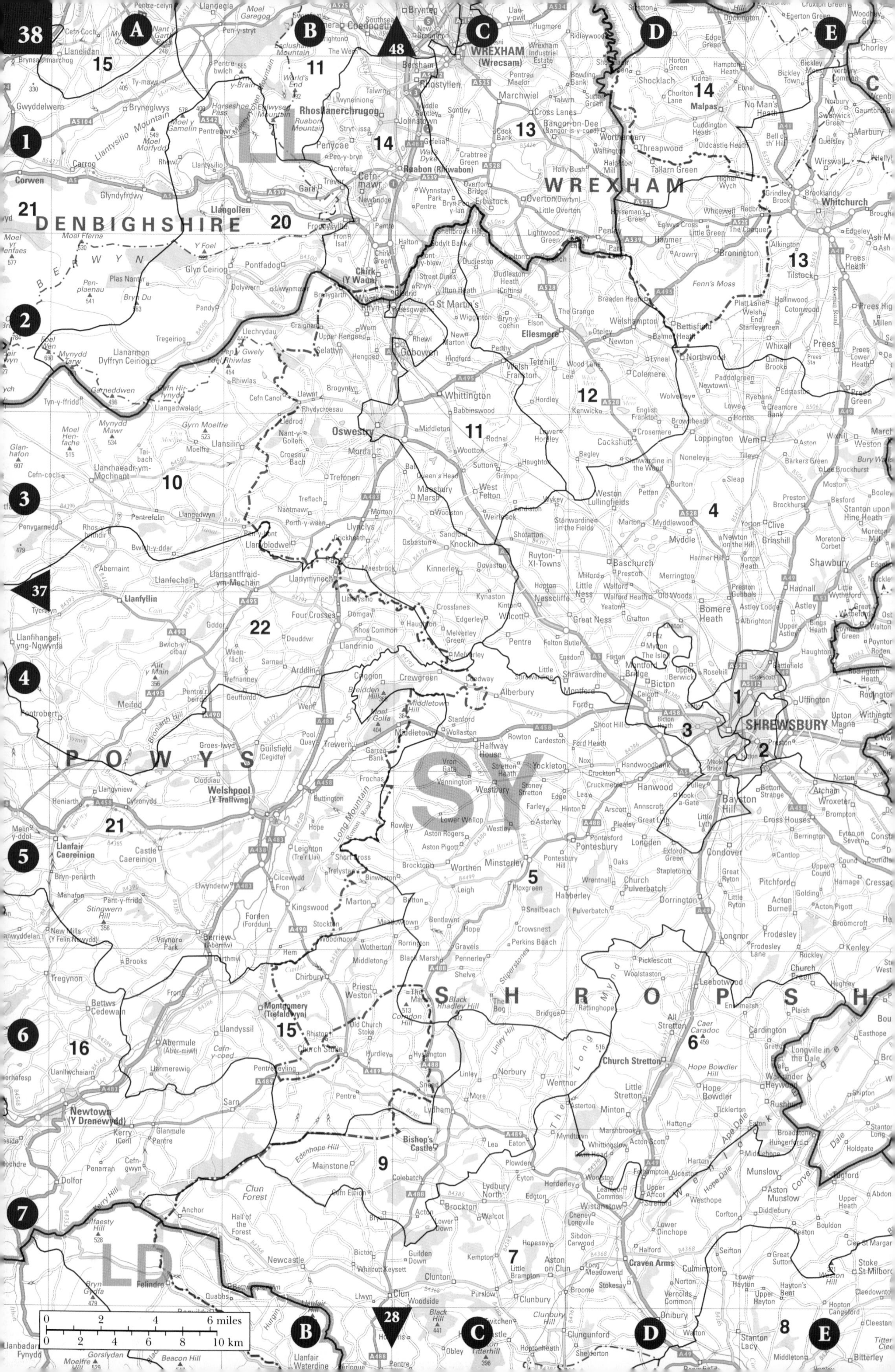
A
B
C
D
E
48
37
28
1
2
3
4
5
6
7
LL
SY
LD
DENBIGHSHIRE
WREXHAM
POWYS
SHROPSH
WREXHAM (Wrecsam)
Rhosllanerchrugog
Ruabon (Rhiwabon)
Corwen
Llangollen
Chirk (Y Waun)
Oswestry
Ellesmere
Malpas
Whitchurch
Bangor-on-Dee
Overton
Whittington
Llanfyllin
Welshpool (Y Trallwng)
Llanfair Caereinion
SHREWSBURY
Montgomery (Trefaldwyn)
Newtown (Y Drenewydd)
Bishop's Castle
Church Stretton
Craven Arms
Clun
Pontesbury
Baschurch
Wem
Prees
Shawbury
Minsterley
Westbury
Berriew
Chirbury
Lydham
Lydbury North
Aston on Clun
Felindre
Clun Forest
Long Mountain
Long Mynd
Stiperstones
Berwyn
Llantysilio Mountain
Horseshoe Pass
Ruabon Mountain
Breidden Hill
Corndon Hill
Caer Caradoc
Wenlock Edge
Fenn's Moss
0 2 4 6 miles
0 2 4 6 8 10 km

STAFFORDSHIRE
TELFORD & WREKIN
WEST MIDLANDS
NEWCASTLE-UNDER-LYME
STOKE-ON-TRENT
STAFFORD
CANNOCK
LICHFIELD
WOLVERHAMPTON
WALSALL
WEST BROMWICH
DUDLEY
OLDBURY
SMETHWICK
STOURBRIDGE
HALESOWEN
KIDDERMINSTER
TELFORD
Market Drayton
Eccleshall
Stone
Uttoxeter
Cheadle
Rugeley
Hednesford
Burntwood
Penkridge
Newport
Shifnal
Bridgnorth
Much Wenlock
Codsall
Wombourne
Brownhills
Aldridge
See pages 114 - 115 for postcode detail
ST
TF
WS
WV
DY
CW
49
40
29
F
G
H
J
K
1
2
3
4
5
6
7

A
B
C
D
E
1
2
3
4
5
6
7
50
39
30
65
NEWCASTLE-UNDER-LYME
STOKE-ON-TRENT
STOKE-ON-TRENT
Cheadle
Ashbourne
Uttoxeter
Stone
STAFFORDSHIRE
Eccleshall
STAFFORD
Rugeley
Cannock Chase
BURTON UPON TRENT
Penkridge
Hednesford
CANNOCK
LICHFIELD
Burntwood
Brownhills
TAMWORTH
Codsall
WOLVERHAMPTON
WALSALL
Aldridge
SUTTON COLDFIELD
WEST MIDLANDS
See pages 114 - 115 for postcode detail
DUDLEY
WEST BROMWICH
OLDBURY
SMETHWICK
BIRMINGHAM
BIRMINGHAM INT
Wombourne
STOURBRIDGE
HALESOWEN
Coleshill
SOLIHULL
KIDDERMINSTER
WARWIC
DERB
DE
ST
WS
WV
B
0 2 4 6 miles
0 2 4 6 8 10 km

NOTTINGHAM
NOTTINGHAMSHIRE
NG
DERBY
SHIRE
LEICESTER
LEICESTERSHIRE
LE
NORTHANTS
NN
CV
LOUGHBOROUGH
MELTON MOWBRAY
COALVILLE
HINCKLEY
NUNEATON
ILKESTON
BEESTON
WEST BRIDGFORD
EAST MIDLANDS
WIGSTON
Market Harborough
Lutterworth
Bingham
Hucknall
Arnold
Carlton
Eastwood
Heanor
Ripley
Belper
Kimberley
Stapleford
Long Eaton
Castle Donington
Melbourne
Ashby de la Zouch
Shepshed
Syston
Oadby
Market Bosworth
Earl Shilton
Bedworth
Atherstone
Keyworth
Radcliffe on Trent
Charnwood Forest
F
G
H
J
K
1
2
3
4
5
6
7
51
42
31

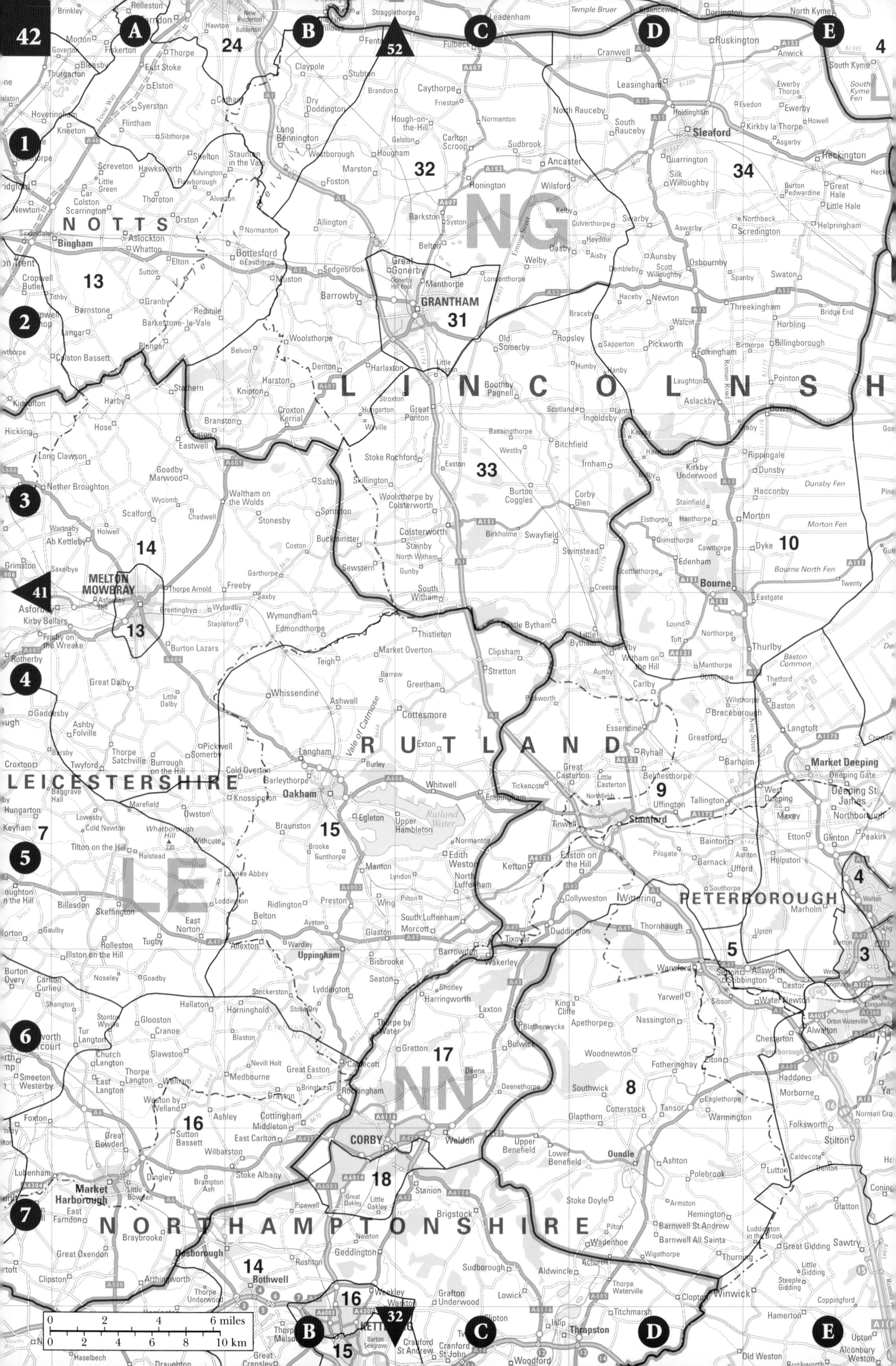

42
A
B
C
D
E
52
41
32
1
2
3
4
5
6
7
NOTTS
LINCOLNSH
RUTLAND
LEICESTERSHIRE
NORTHAMPTONSHIRE
PETERBOROUGH
NG
LE
NN
Bingham
Sleaford
GRANTHAM
MELTON MOWBRAY
Oakham
Uppingham
Stamford
Bourne
Market Deeping
CORBY
Oundle
Market Harborough
Desborough
Rothwell
Kettering
Thrapston
Brinkley
Rolleston
Farndon
Morton
Fiskerton
Thurgarton
Bleasby
Hoveringham
Kneeton
Syerston
Elston
East Stoke
Thorpe
Hawton
Flintham
Sibthorpe
Shelton
Staunton in the Vale
Kilvington
Flawborough
Alverton
Screveton
Hawksworth
Car Colston
Little Green
Scarrington
Thoroton
Orston
Aslockton
Whatton
Normanton
Bottesford
Easthorpe
Elton
Sutton
Granby
Cropwell Butler
Tithby
Barnstone
Langar
Redmile
Barkestone-le-Vale
Plungar
Colston Bassett
Belvoir
Muston
Sedgebrook
Barrowby
Woolsthorpe
Denton
Harlaxton
Harston
Knipton
Stathern
Branston
Croxton Kerrial
Eaton
Eastwell
Harby
Hose
Hickling
Long Clawson
Goadby Marwood
Nether Broughton
Wycomb
Chadwell
Scalford
Waltham on the Wolds
Wartnaby
Ab Kettleby
Holwell
Grimston
Saxelbye
Asfordby
Kirby Bellars
Frisby on the Wreake
Rotherby
Thorpe Arnold
Freeby
Brentingby
Wyfordby
Stapleford
Burton Lazars
Saxby
Garthorpe
Wymondham
Edmondthorpe
Teigh
Market Overton
Thistleton
Barrow
Greetham
Whissendine
Ashwell
Cottesmore
Exton
Langham
Burley
Barleythorpe
Cold Overton
Knossington
Owston
Somerby
Pickwell
Burrough on the Hill
Thorpe Satchville
Twyford
Great Dalby
Little Dalby
Ashby Folville
Gaddesby
Croxton
Baggrave Hall
Hungarton
Keyham
Lowesby
Cold Newton
Marefield
Whatborough Hill
Tilton on the Hill
Halstead
Withcote
Launde Abbey
Loddington
Billesdon
Skeffington
East Norton
Rolleston
Tugby
Illston on the Hill
Noseley
Goadby
Gaulby
Carlton Curlieu
Burton Overy
Shangton
Stonton Wyville
Tur Langton
Church Langton
Glooston
Cranoe
Hallaton
Horninghold
Blaston
Slawston
Thorpe Langton
Welham
East Langton
Smeeton Westerby
Foxton
Great Bowden
Weston by Welland
Sutton Bassett
Ashley
Medbourne
Nevill Holt
Drayton
Great Easton
Bringhurst
Cottingham
Middleton
East Carlton
Wilbarston
Stoke Albany
Brampton Ash
Dingley
Little Bowden
Lubenham
East Farndon
Braybrooke
Great Oxendon
Clipston
Arthingworth
Thorpe Underwood
Haselbech
Pipewell
Rushton
Geddington
Newton
Great Oakley
Little Oakley
Stanion
Brigstock
Weldon
Rockingham
Caldecott
Gretton
Thorpe by Water
Harringworth
Shotley
Laxton
Lyddington
Stoke Dry
Seaton
Bisbrooke
Glaston
Wardley
Allexton
Belton
Ridlington
Preston
Ayston
Wing
Morcott
South Luffenham
North Luffenham
Pilton
Lyndon
Manton
Edith Weston
Normanton
Brooke
Gunthorpe
Braunston
Egleton
Upper Hambleton
Rutland Water
Whitwell
Empingham
Tickencote
Great Casterton
Little Casterton
Ryhall
Belmesthorpe
Uffington
Tallington
Essendine
Carlby
Aunby
Pickworth
Clipsham
Stretton
Tinwell
Easton on the Hill
Ketton
Collyweston
Duddington
Tixover
Wakerley
Barrowden
Wittering
Thornhaugh
Wansford
Sutton
Sibbington
Yarwell
Nassington
King's Cliffe
Apethorpe
Blatherwycke
Bulwick
Deene
Deenethorpe
Woodnewton
Fotheringhay
Southwick
Cotterstock
Glapthorn
Tansor
Eaglethorpe
Warmington
Upper Benefield
Lower Benefield
Ashton
Polebrook
Stoke Doyle
Armston
Hemington
Barnwell St Andrew
Barnwell All Saints
Pilton
Wadenhoe
Wigsthorpe
Thurning
Luddington in the Brook
Great Gidding
Little Gidding
Steeple Gidding
Sawtry
Coppingford
Hamerton
Winwick
Clopton
Achurch
Aldwincle
Thorpe Waterville
Titchmarsh
Sudborough
Lowick
Islip
Grafton Underwood
Cranford St Andrew
Cranford St John
Barton Seagrave
Weekley
Warkton
Woodford
Old Weston
Alconbury Weston
Upton
Glatton
Conington
Caldecote
Denton
Lutton
Stilton
Folksworth
Norman Cross
Haddon
Morborne
Chesterton
Elton
Alwalton
Orton Waterville
Orton Longueville
Castor
Water Newton
Ailsworth
Sibson
Upton
Marholm
Walton
Westwood
Southorpe
Ufford
Barnack
Ashton
Bainton
Pilsgate
Helpston
Etton
Glinton
Peakirk
Northborough
Maxey
West Deeping
Deeping St James
Deeping Gate
Barholm
Greatford
Braceborough
Wilsthorpe
Langtoft
Baston
Thetford
Baston Common
Obthorpe
Manthorpe
Thurlby
Witham on the Hill
Little Bytham
Castle Bytham
Creeton
Swinstead
Toft
Lound
Northorpe
Eastgate
Twenty
Bourne North Fen
Dyke
Cawthorpe
Edenham
Grimsthorpe
Elsthorpe
Scottlethorpe
Hanthorpe
Morton
Morton Fen
Stainfield
Hacconby
Dunsby
Dunsby Fen
Rippingale
Kirkby Underwood
Haconby
Hawthorpe
Bulby
Kelby
Dowsby
Graby
Aslackby
Pointon
Laughton
Billingborough
Birthorpe
Horbling
Bridge End
Threekingham
Walcot
Pickworth
Folkingham
Sapperton
Braceby
Haceby
Newton
Spanby
Swaton
Osbournby
Scott Willoughby
Aunsby
Dembleby
Aisby
Heydour
Culverthorpe
Oasby
Welby
Kelby
Swarby
Aswarby
Northbeck
Scredington
Helpringham
Burton Pedwardine
Great Hale
Little Hale
Heckington
Asgarby
Kirkby la Thorpe
Howell
Evedon
Ewerby
Ewerby Thorpe
South Kyme
South Kyme Fen
North Kyme
Anwick
Ruskington
Dorrington
Leasingham
Holdingham
Quarrington
Silk Willoughby
South Rauceby
North Rauceby
Cranwell
Brauncewell
Temple Bruer
Leadenham
Fulbeck
Caythorpe
Frieston
Normanton
Hough-on-the-Hill
Carlton Scroop
Gelston
Sudbrook
Ancaster
Wilsford
Honington
Barkston
Syston
Belton
Marston
Foston
Hougham
Westborough
Long Bennington
Dry Doddington
Claypole
Stubton
Brandon
Fenton
Stragglethorpe
Allington
Great Gonerby
Gonerby Hill Foot
Manthorpe
Londonthorpe
Little Ponton
Old Somerby
Ropsley
Humby
Hanby
Boothby Pagnell
Scotland
Ingoldsby
Lenton
Bassingthorpe
Westby
Bitchfield
Irnham
Great Ponton
Stroxton
Hungerton
Wyville
Stoke Rochford
Easton
Saltby
Skillington
Woolsthorpe by Colsterworth
Burton Coggles
Corby Glen
Sproxton
Buckminster
Colsterworth
Stainby
North Witham
Gunby
Sewstern
Coston
Stonesby
Birkholme
Swayfield
South Witham
Vale of Catmose
Frosse Way
Ermine Street
Roman Road
King Street
0 2 4 6 miles
0 2 4 6 8 10 km

F
G
H
J
K
22
53
44
33
Wildmore Fen
Leake Commonside
Lowgate
Friskney Flats
Frithville
Gipsey Bridge
Hollandgen
Wrangle
Fishtoft Drove
High Ferry
Langrick
Leake Hurn's End
Leverton Outgate
Holland Fen
Amber Hill
Frith Bank
Hill Dyke
Leverton
Leverton Lucasgate
Langrick Bridge
Anton's Gowt
Benington
Benington Sea End
Brothertoft
BOSTON
Butterwick
Haltoft End
Long Sand
Hubbert's Bridge
21
Freiston
Butterwick Low
Swineshead Bridge
Skirbeck Quarter
Skirbeck
Frampton West End
Fishtoft
Freiston Shore
Tamworth Green
Roger Sand
Kirton Holme
Wyberton
Scrane End
Fenhouses
Kirton End
Toft Sand
Frampton
Gat Sand
Drayton
20
Black Buoy Sand
Mare Tail
THE WASH
Asperton
Kirton
Sandholme
The Scalp
Hoffleet Stow
Skeldyke
Wigtoft
Sutterton
Seadyke
Old South
Algarkirk
Church End
Quadring Eaudike
Quadring
Fosdyke
Seal Sand
Holbeach St Matthew
Holbeach St Marks
Gosberton
RE
Westhorpe
Belnie
Whaplode Marsh
Dawsmere
Peter Black Sand
Gedney Marsh
Gedney Drove End
Holbeach Marsh
Surfleet
Surfleet Seas End
Crossgate
Moulton Seas End
Holbeach Clough
Holbeach Hurn
Holbeach Bank
Saracen's Head
Gedney Dyke
Lutton Marsh
Spalding Marsh
Halesgate
Pinchbeck
Weston
Loosegate
Lutton
Guy's Head
Bulldog Sand
Breast Sand
Holbeach
Moulton
Whaplode
Fleet Hargate
Fleet
Chapelgate
Gedney
Little London
Long Sutton
SPALDING
12
Gedney Broadgate
Delph Bank
Sutton Bridge
Pode Hole
Little London
Weston Hills
Sutton Crosses
Whaplode Fen
Whaplode St Catherine
Moulton Chapel
Cowbit
Holbeach St Johns
PE
Moulton Fen
Deeping St Nicholas
Tydd St Mary
Tydd Gote
Sutton St James
Four Gotes
Tydd St Giles
Newton
Tydd St Giles Fen
Aswick Grange
Whaplode Drove
Great Postland
Sutton St Edmund
Shepeau Stow
Holbeach Drove
Gedney Hill
Crowland
Fitton End
Gorefield
Leverington
Church End
Throckenholt
North Fen
Parson Drove
13
Wisbech St Mary
Murrow
Morris Fen
Wryde Croft
6
Tholomas Drove
Bedford Level
Eye Green
Thorney
Eye
(North Level)
Adventurers' Land
Guyhirn
Waldersey
Priors Fen
Rings End
Hobbs Lots Bridge
North Side
TERBOROUGH
Whittlesey
Coates
Eldernell
Eastrea
Oldeamere
King's Delph
West Fen
Flag Fen
White Moor
Westry
West End
March
Town End
15
CAMBRIDGESHIRE
Glass Moor
Flood's Ferry
Hook
Wimblington
Ranson Moor
Eastwood End
Pondersbridge
White Fen
Whittlesey Mere
Bedford Level
The Herne
Benwick
New World
Doddington
(Middle Level)
Middle Moor
Ramsey Mereside
Mere Side
Ramsey St Mary's
Ramsey Forty Foot
Forty Foot Drain
West Moor
Chatteris
16
Horseway
Ramsey Heights
26
Ramsey
Ramsey Hollow
Tick Fen
Langwood Fen
Upwood
Bury
Ferry Hill
Woodwalton
Great Raveley
Wistow
Somersham High North Fen
Warboys
Pidley Fen
Little Raveley
Fenton
Chatteris Fen
Broughton
Pidley
Somersham
Old Hurst
Holme next the Sea
Ringstead
Hunstanton
36
Heacham
Sedgeford
Eaton
Snettisham
Southgate
Ingoldisthorpe
Shernborne
31
Dersingham
Wolferton
35
Sandringham
West Newton
Flitcham
Castle Rising
North Wootton
30
Congham
Roydon
South Wootton
32
Ongar Hill
Terrington Marsh
Wingland Marsh
KING'S LYNN
Gaywood
Bawsey
Pott Row
Terrington St Clement
Little London
Walpole Cross Keys
Clenchwarton
Walpole Marsh
Hay Green
Tilney All Saints
Walpole St Andrew
Walpole St Peter
Tilney High End
Saddle Bow
West Winch
Ashwicken
Tower End
Middleton
East Winch
North Runcton
Blackborough End
Blackborough
Pentney
Setchey
Ingleborough
West Walton
Terrington St John
Tilney St Lawrence
Wiggenhall St Germans
Walpole Highway
St John's Highway
Wiggenhall St Mary the Virgin
Wiggenhall St Peter
Walton Highway
Marshland
34
Tottenhill Row
Wormegay
Tottenhill
Wisbech
Walsoken
New Walsoken
St John's Fen End
Tilney Fen End
Wiggenhall St Mary Magdalen
Watlington
33
Marshland St James
Emneth Hungate
Runcton Holme
Shouldham
Marham
Elm
Emneth
Holly End
Marshland Fen
Thorpland
NORFOLK
Stowbridge
South Runcton
Shouldham Thorpe
Barton Bendish
Beggdale
Friday Bridge
West Head
Stow Bardolph
Wimbotsham
Fincham
Stradsett
14
Outwell
Stow Bardolph Fen
Downham Market
Crimplesham
Bexwell
Upwell
Barroway Drove
Coldham
Laddus Fens
North District
Nordelph
Denver
Boughton
Three Holes
Wereham
West Dereham
Wretton
Euximoor Fen
Upwell Fen
Fordham
Stoke Ferry
South District
Hilgay
Binnimoor Fen
Christchurch
Ten Mile Bank
38
Lakes End
Upwell Fen
Hilgay Fen
Southery
Tipps End
Methwold Fens
Methwold Hythe
Stonea
Welney
Southery Fens
26
Queen's Ground
Gold Hill
Brandon Creek
The Apes Hall
Feltwell
Wimblington Fen
Manea
Little Ouse
Brandon Bank
Feltwell Fens
Mare Fen
Purls Bridge
Welches Dam
Fodder Fen
Burnt Fen
IP
Hockwold Fens
Littleport
Pymore (Pymoor)
CB
Shippea Hill
Little Street
Little Downham
Shippea Hill Sta.
27
Chettisham
Padnal Fen
SUFFOLK
Lakenheath
Coveney
Queen Adelaide
Prickwillow
Wardy Hill
West Fen
Bedford Level
Undley
The Delph
(South Level)
Mepal
Witcham
Ely
Middle Fen
7
Great Fen
Kennyhill
28
Wentworth
Witchford
Stuntney
Wilde Street
Holywell Row
North Fen

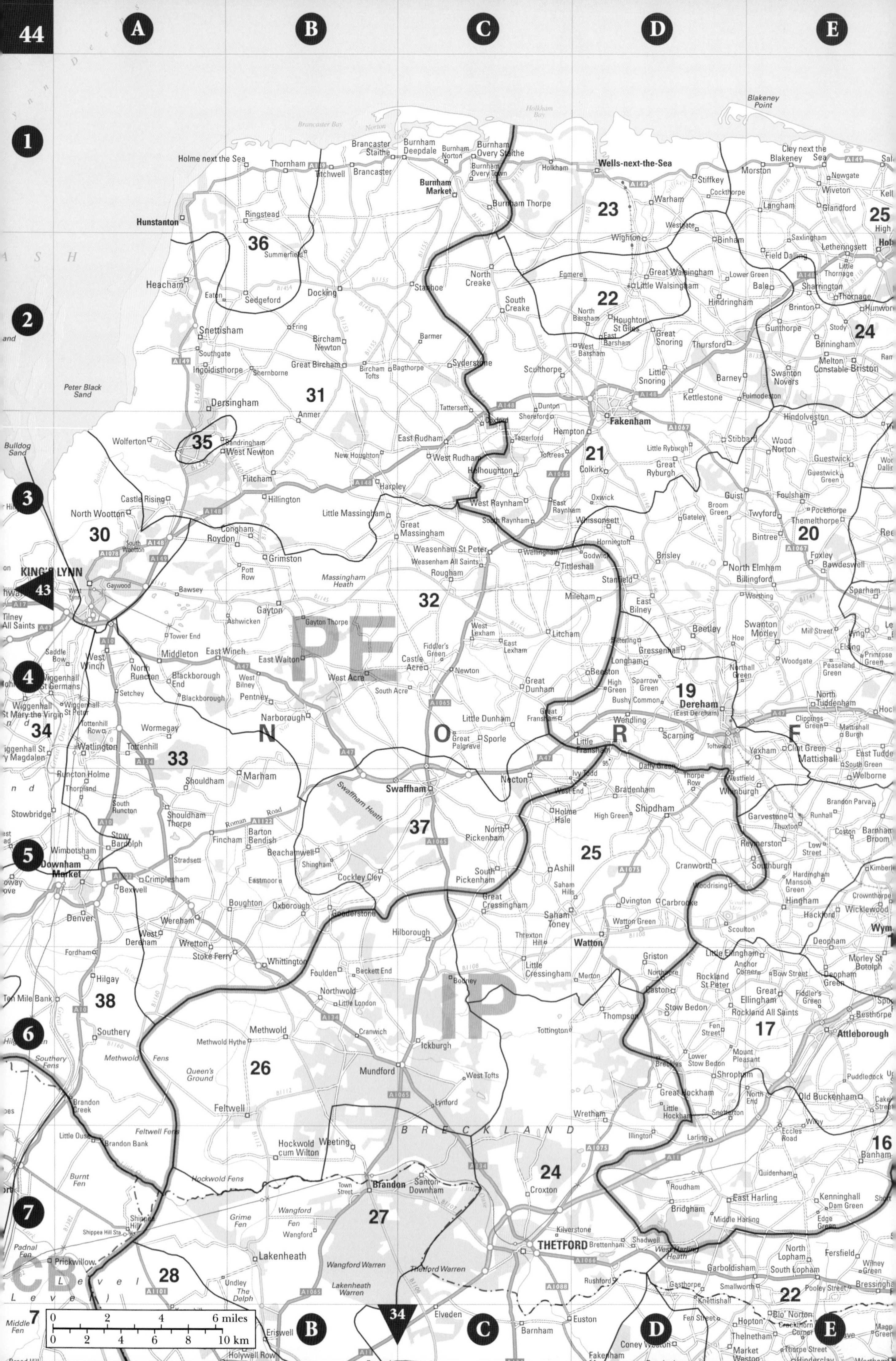
A
B
C
D
E
1
2
3
4
5
6
7
Hunstanton
Holme next the Sea
Thornham
Titchwell
Brancaster
Brancaster Staithe
Burnham Deepdale
Burnham Market
Burnham Thorpe
Holkham
Wells-next-the-Sea
Blakeney Point
Cley next the Sea
Blakeney
Stiffkey
Morston
Warham
Wighton
Binham
Langham
Wiveton
Glandford
Heacham
Ringstead
Sedgeford
Docking
Stanhoe
North Creake
South Creake
Great Walsingham
Little Walsingham
Houghton St Giles
Great Snoring
Little Snoring
Thursford
Snettisham
Ingoldisthorpe
Dersingham
Great Bircham
Bircham Newton
Syderstone
Sculthorpe
Fakenham
Barney
Kettlestone
Hindolveston
Wolferton
Sandringham
West Newton
Flitcham
Anmer
East Rudham
West Rudham
Helhoughton
Hempton
Colkirk
Great Ryburgh
Guist
Foulsham
Castle Rising
North Wootton
Hillington
Little Massingham
Great Massingham
West Raynham
East Raynham
South Raynham
Whissonsett
KING'S LYNN
Gaywood
Bawsey
Roydon
Grimston
Congham
Weasenham St Peter
Weasenham All Saints
Rougham
Massingham Heath
Tittleshall
Mileham
Litcham
Brisley
North Elmham
Billingford
Bawdeswell
Foxley
Gayton
Gayton Thorpe
Ashwicken
Middleton
East Winch
East Walton
Castle Acre
West Acre
South Acre
Newton
West Lexham
East Lexham
Great Dunham
Little Dunham
Beeston
Longham
Gressenhall
Dereham (East Dereham)
Scarning
Wendling
Swanton Morley
Beetley
Yaxham
Mattishall
West Winch
North Runcton
Setchey
Blackborough End
Pentney
Narborough
Wormegay
Tottenhill
Watlington
Marham
Shouldham
Shouldham Thorpe
Runcton Holme
Stow Bardolph
Fincham
Barton Bendish
Swaffham
Sporle
Great Palgrave
Necton
Little Fransham
Great Fransham
Shipdham
Holme Hale
North Pickenham
South Pickenham
Beachamwell
Cockley Cley
Ashill
Saham Toney
Watton
Carbrooke
Ovington
Scoulton
Hingham
Wicklewood
Deopham
Downham Market
Wimbotsham
Crimplesham
Bexwell
Denver
Stradsett
Boughton
Oxborough
Gooderstone
West Dereham
Wereham
Wretton
Stoke Ferry
Whittington
Hilborough
Little Cressingham
Great Cressingham
Threxton Hill
Griston
Caston
Rockland St Peter
Great Ellingham
Attleborough
Hilgay
Southery
Ten Mile Bank
Methwold
Methwold Hythe
Methwold Fens
Northwold
Foulden
Mundford
Ickburgh
Cranwich
Bodney
Tottington
Thompson
Stow Bedon
Queen's Ground
Feltwell
Brandon Creek
Little Ouse
Brandon Bank
Feltwell Fens
Hockwold cum Wilton
Weeting
Lynford
West Tofts
BRECKLAND
Wretham
Illington
Larling
Snetterton
Banham
Old Buckenham
Brandon
Santon Downham
Croxton
Hockwold Fens
Burnt Fen
Grime Fen
Wangford Fen
Wangford
Lakenheath
Lakenheath Warren
Wangford Warren
Thetford Warren
THETFORD
Kilverstone
Brettenham
Shadwell
Roudham
Bridgham
East Harling
Quidenham
Kenninghall
Garboldisham
South Lopham
North Lopham
Rushford
Euston
Barnham
Elveden
Eriswell
Undley
Prickwillow
Shippea Hill
Knettishall
Hopton
Thelnetham
Blo' Norton
Market Weston
Coney Weston
Bressingham
Fersfield
Middle Fen
PE
IP
CB
N
O
R
F
43
34
0 2 4 6 miles
0 2 4 6 8 10 km

F
G
H
J
K
1
2
3
4
5
6
7
Sheringham
West Runton
East Runton
Cromer
Beeston Regis
East Beckham
West Beckham
Aylmerton
Felbrigg
Overstrand
Sidestrand
Trimingham
Northrepps
Gresham
Roughton
Baconsthorpe
Bessingham
Southrepps
Gimingham
Mundesley
Matlaske
Plumstead
Little Barningham
Aldborough
Thorpe Market
Lower Street
Trunch
Knapton
Paston
Bacton
Keswick
Walcott
Wickmere
Antingham
Suffield
Swafield
Edingthorpe
Ridlington
Happisburgh
Whimpwell Green
Eccles-on-Sea
Erpingham
Calthorpe
Colby
North Walsham
Saxthorpe
Itteringham
Ingworth
Banningham
Felmingham
Crostwight
Happisburgh Common
Lessingham
Hempstead
Ingham Corner
Sea Palling
Waxham
Heydon
Blickling
Aylsham
Oulton Street
Tuttington
Skeyton
Westwick
Honing
East Ruston
Worstead
Ingham
Stalham
Burgh next Aylsham
Swanton Abbot
Dilham
Brampton
Oxnead
Scottow
Smallburgh
Stalham Green
Hickling
Hickling Green
Horsey Corner
Horsey
Cawston
Marsham
Buxton
Buxton Heath
Lamas
Little Hautbois
Sco Ruston
Market Street
Beeston St Lawrence
Barton Turf
Catfield
Hill Common
Hevingham
Stratton Strawless
Tunstead
Neatishead
Coltishall
Horstead
Potter Heigham
West Somerton
East Somerton
Winterton-on-Sea
Swannington
Hainford
Frettenham
Belaugh
Hoveton
Wroxham
NORFOLK
Ludham
Mustard Hyrn
Martham
Bastwick
Attlebridge
Felthorpe
St Helena
Newton St Faith
Horning
BROADS
Thurne
Repps
Rollesby
Hemsby
Ormesby St Margaret
Scratby
California
Newport
Horsford
Horsham St Faith
Crostwick
Spixworth
Woodbastwick
Ranworth
Clippesby
Ormesby St Michael
Weston Longville
Ringland
Taverham
NORWICH INTERNATIONAL
Rackheath
Salhouse
New Rackheath
Little Plumstead
Panxworth
South Walsham
Upton
Fleggburgh
Filby
Caister-on-Sea
Costessey
Hellesdon
Sprowston
Thorpe End
Blofield Heath
Pedham
North Burlingham
Acle
Stokesby
Runham
West Caister
Easton
NORWICH
Great Plumstead
Blofield
Lingwood
Damgate
Marlingford
Bawburgh
Colney
Brundall
Strumpshaw
Beighton
Halvergate
Halvergate Marshes
GREAT YARMOUTH
Little Melton
Hethersett
Cringleford
Keswick
Trowse Newton
Postwick
Surlingham
Buckenham
Hassingham
Moulton St Mary
Freethorpe
Wickhampton
Freethorpe Common
Burgh Castle
Gorleston-on-Sea
Lynch Green
Arminghall
Caistor St Edmund
Kirby Bedon
Bramerton
Rockland St Mary
Claxton
Cantley
Limpenhoe
Belton
Ketteringham
Swardeston
Poringland
Framingham Pigot
Hellington
Yelverton
Ashby St Mary
Carleton St Peter
Hardley Street
Reedham
Bradwell
Browston Green
Hobland Hall
East Carleton
Mulbarton
Stoke Holy Cross
Framingham Earl
Bergh Apton
Thurton
Langley Street
Norton Marshes
Nogdam End
Swainsthorpe
Bracon Ash
Shotesham
Howe
Brooke
Chedgrave
Norton Subcourse
Lower Thurlton
Fritton
Ashby Dell
Lound
Hopton
Wreningham
Newton Flotman
Sisland
Loddon
Heckingham
Thurlton
Thorpe
Blundeston
Corton
Ashwellthorpe
Fundenhall
Flordon
Saxlingham Nethergate
Saxlingham Thorpe
Saxlingham Green
Mundham
Seething
Kirstead Green
Stubbs Green
Hales
Herringfleet
Haddiscoe
Somerleyton
Hapton
Tasburgh
Raveningham
Tacolneston
Forncett St Mary
Forncett End
Forncett St Peter
Hempnall
Brundish
Maypole Green
Toft Monks
Waterheath
Wheatacre
Camps Heath
Oulton
Normanston
Lowestoft Ness
LOWESTOFT
Long Stratton
Stratton St Michael
Thwaite St Mary
Kirby Green
Kirby Cane
Woodton
Hedenham
Stockton
Bull's Green
Burgh St Peter
Aldeby
Bunwell Street
Bunwell
Pottergate Street
Fritton
Silver Green
Hempnall Green
Topcroft
Bedingham Green
Ellingham
Kirby Row
Gillingham
Aslacton
Great Moulton
Wacton
Morningthorpe
Shelton
Topcroft Street
Upgate Street
Ditchingham
Broome
Geldeston
Beccles
Oulton Broad
Kirkley
Pakefield
Carlton Colville
Tibenham
Hardwick
Harris Green
Darrow Green
Bungay
Wainford
Earsham
Shipmeadow
Barsham
North Cove
Barnby
Mettingham
Worlingham
Gisleham
Mutford
Pristow Green
Cole's Common
North Green
Denton
Great Green
The City
Ringsfield
Ellough
Ellough Moor
Rushmere
Black Street
Kessingland
Kessingland Beach
Tivetshall St Margaret
Tivetshall St Mary
Colegate End
Bush Green
Alburgh
Flixton
Ilketshall St Andrew
Ilketshall St Margaret
Ringsfield Corner
Halver Street
Henstead
Gissing
Pulham Market
Pulham St Mary
Piccadilly Corner
Homersfield
Starston
Wortwell
SUFFOLK
Beck's Green
Shadingfield
Sotterley
Benacre
Dickleburgh Moor
Rushall
Harleston
Redenhall
St Margaret South Elmham
St Michael South Elmham
St Cross South Elmham
Ilketshall St Lawrence
Redisham
Brampton Sta
Cuckold's Green
West End
Burston
Shimpling
Dickleburgh
High Common
Needham
Mendham
Withersdale Street
All Saints South Elmham
Alder's Corner
High Street
Stone Street
Cox Common
Brampton
Stoven
Frostenden
Wrentham
Covehithe
Thelveton
Upper Street
Thorpe Abbotts
Weybread
Metfield
Rumburgh
St James South Elmham
Westhall
Brampton Street
Spexhall
Clay Common
South Cove
Cove Bottom
Diss
Brockdish
Weybread Street
Uggeshall
Barnaby Green
Wangford
Reydon Smear
Reydon
Billingford
Stuston
Oakley
Hoxne
Wingfield Green
Wingfield
Fressingfield
Little Wittingham Green
Linstead Parva
Chediston
Halesworth
Holton
Blyford
Brome Street
Cross
North
Yarmouth Roads
Hemsby Hole
Hundred Stream
Horsey Mere
Hickling Broad
Barton Broad
Sutton Broad
Filby Broad
A149
A148
A1082
A140
A1151
A1062
A1064
A47
A1074
A1042
A11
A146
A1242
A143
A12
A145
A144
A1095
A1117
B1145
B1149
B1140
B1136
B1062
B1127
B1123
26
27
11
28
12
10
29
9
8
6
7
5
3
1
2
4
13
30
14
31
15
32
35
33
34
20
19
21
18
NR
O
L
K
35

A
B
C
D
E
1
2
3
4
5
6
7
The Skerries
Middle Mouse
West Mouse
Carmel Head
Cemlyn Bay
Cemaes Bay
Porth Wen Bay
Bull Bay (Porth Llechog)
Point Lynas
Cemaes
Llanbadrig
Neuadd
Burwen
Amlwch
Amlwch Port
Llaneilian
Tregele
67
68
Llanfechell
Llanfairynghornwy
Pengorffwysfa
Pen-y-sarn
Bodewryd
66
Mynydd-mechell
Parys Mountain
69
Nebo
Ynys Dulas
HOLYHEAD BAY
Church Bay
Llanrhyddlad
Rhyd-wyn
Llanfflewyn
Carreglefn
Rhos-goch
Rhosybol
Dulas
Dulas Bay
Lligwy Bay
Llaneuddog
City Dulas
70
ISLE OF
Llanfaethlu
Llanbabo
Capel Parc
Llyn Alaw
Brynrefail
Rhosllugwy
Moelfre
72
73
A5025
Gwredog
Ceidio
Llandyfrydog
North Stack
Llanddeusant
Elim
Llannerch-y-medd
71
Holyhead Mountain
220
Holyhead (Caergybi)
Llanfwrog
Stryd y Facsen
Bachau
Maenaddwyn
Marian-glas
Llanallgo
Tyn-y-gongl
Benllech
Salt Island
Llanfachraeth
Llantrisant
Llanfigael
ANGLESEY
Bryn-teg
Capel Coch
74
Puffin Island (Priestholm)
South Stack
Llaingoch
Penrhos
Pen-llyn
Llyn Llywenan
ANGLESEY
Red Wharf Bay
Kingsland
A5
Llanynghenedl
Llechcynfarwy
78
Red Wharf Bay (Traeth Coch)
Mariandyrys
Glan-yr-afon
Cairn
Penmon
Bodedern
Llanbedrgoch
76
58
Penrhyn Mawr
Trearddur
Valley (Y Fali)
65
Trefor
(YNYS MON)
Tregaian
75
Mynydd Llwydiarth
Llanddona
Llangoed
Llyn Frogwy
Llanddyfnan
Pentraeth
Llan-faes
Dutchman Bank
Four Mile Bridge
Caergeiliog
Bryngwran
Llynfaes
Bodffordd
Rhosmeirch
77
Talwrn
Beaumaris (Biwmares)
HOLY ISLAND
Llanfihangel-yn-Nhywyn
Gwalchmai
Bodior
Llanfair-yn-neubwll
Capel Gwyn
Heneglwys
Llangefni
Llansadwrn
59
Rhoscolyn
Tywyn Trewan
Rhostrehwfa
Pen-mynydd
Llandegfan
Lavan Sands
Llanfairfechan
Cymyran Bay
A4080
Cefni
Rhosneigr
64
Pencarnisiog
Llanfaelog
Ty Croes
Ty Croes Sta
Corrigceinwen
Llangristiolus
Llanfairpwllgwyngyll
Bangor
Port Penrhyn
Gorddinog
Abergwyngregyn
63
Capel Mawr
Pentre Berw
Gaerwen
Menai Bridge (Porthaethwy)
A4087
Minffordd
Llandygai
Crymlyn
62
Bethel
Trefdraeth
Malltraeth Marsh
Llanddaniel Fab
Penrhos-garnedd
Tal-y-bont
Moel Wnion
580
Llangadwaladr
60
Capel-y-graig
Aberffraw
Hermon
Malltraeth
Llangaffo
Waun-wen
Glasinfryn
Llanllechid
Rachub
Drosgl
758
Aberffraw Bay
Y Felinheli
56
Rhyd-y-groes
Tal-y-Cae
Tregarth
Bethesda
Gerlan
Carned G
Bodorgan
Malltraeth Sands
A4080
Brynsiencyn
Seion
Pentir
Coed-y-parc
Braichmelyn
Newborough (Niwbwrch)
Dwyran
Saron
Llanddeiniolen
Rhiwlas
Foel Grach
Mynydd Llandygai
57
Carnedd Ll
Pen-lôn
61
Bethel
Penisa'r Waun
Malltraeth Bay
Newborough Warren
Waterloo Port
Carnedd Dafydd
1044
Llanddwyn Island
Caernarfon
A4086
Pont-rug
Llanrug
Deiniolen
Clwt-y-bont
Galltyfoel
Mynydd Perfedd
812
Nant Ffrancon
Caeathro
Brynrefail
Fachwen
Cwm-y-glo
Elidyr Fawr
923
Llyn Padarn
Dinorwig
Abermenai Point
The Bar
Ceunant
Groeslon
Llanberis
Foel Goch
831
Llanfaglan
Bontnewydd
Pont Pen-y-benglog
Foryd Bay
Saron
Dinas
Croesywaun
Waunfawr
Y Garn
946
Glyder Fach
994
Betws Garmon
Moel Eilio
726
Llyn Peris
Nant Peris
Gwastadnant
Glyder Fawr
999
Llanwnda
Rhostryfan
Rhosgadfan
A4085
A4086
CAERNARFON BAY
55
Dinas Dinlle
Penyffridd
Moel Tryfan
Salem
Pass of Llanberis
Pen-y-Pass
356
Llandwrog
Groeslon
GWYNEDD
SNOWDONIA (ERYRI)
Pen-y-Gwryd Hotel
Carmel
Bwlchyllyn
Mynydd Mawr
698
Llyn Cwellyn
1085
Glaslyn
Snowdon (Yr Wyddfa)
898
Llyn Llydaw
Y Fron (Upper Llandwrog)
A499
Carnedd y Cribau
591
Penygroes
Talysarn
Nantlle
B4418
Y Garn
634
Pontllyfni
Llyn Nantlle Uchaf
Rhyd-Ddu
A498
Trwyn Maen Dylan
Llyn Gwynant
Aberdesach
Llanllyfni
54
Craig Cwm Silyn
Trum y Ddysgl
709
Ffridd Uchaf
747
Yr Aran
Plas Gwynant
Dolwyddelan
A487
Nebo
734
Beddgelert Forest
605
Tai'n Lôn
221
Nasareth
700
A4085
36
Capeluchaf
Bwlch Mawr
509
Gyrn Goch
610
Mynydd Craig Goch
Garneddgoch
Beddgelert
Llyn Dinas
Cnicht
689
Bwlch y Gorddinan (Crimea Pass)
41
Trefor
Gyrn Ddu
Bwlch-derwin
Pant Glas
Moel Hebog
Pass of Aberglaslyn
Rhiwbryfdir
0 2 4 6 miles
0 2 4 6 8 10 km

F
G
H
J
K
1
2
3
4
5
6
7
LIVERPOOL BAY
West Hoyle Bank
Hilbre Island
West Kirby
Welsh Channel
Point of Ayr
Talacre
Mostyn Bank
Mostyn Quay
Great Ormes Head
Llandudno
Little Ormes Head
Penrhyn Bay (Bae Penrhyn)
Colwyn Bay (Bae Colwyn)
Conwy Sands
Conwy
Abergele
Rhyl
Prestatyn
Kinmel Bay (Bae Cinmel)
Rhuddlan
St Asaph (Llanelwy)
Holywell
FLINTSHIRE
CONWY
DENBIGHSHIRE
VALE OF CLWYD
CLWYDIAN RANGE
Denbigh (Dinbych)
Ruthin (Rhuthun)
Mold (Yr Wyddgrug)
Llanrwst
Betws-y-coed
Capel Curig
Vale of Conwy
Mynydd Hiraethog
Clocaenog Forest
Gwydyr Forest
Moel Famau
Halkyn Mountain
Greenfield (Maes-Glas)
Llandegla
Horseshoe Pass
Cerrigydrudion
Pentrefoelas
Penmachno
Ysbyty Ifan
Llansannan
Llanfair Talhaiarn
Trefriw
Dolgarrog
Rhyl
37
48

48
A
B
C
D
E
55
1
2
3
4
5
6
7
47
38
Horse Bank
Angry Brow
SOUTHPORT
Banks
Tarleton
Bretherton
LEYLAND
Croston
Euxton
CHORLEY
Eccleston
L A N C A S H
Holmeswood
Rufford
Mawdesley
Birkdale
Ainsdale-on-Sea
Scarisbrick
Bescar
Burscough Bridge
Burscough
Parbold
Halsall
Newburgh
Appley Bridge
Shevington
Standish
WIGAN
Orrell
Formby Point
Mad Wharf
Formby
Haskayne
ORMSKIRK
Skelmersdale
Hightown
Ince Blundell
Maghull
Aughton
Bickerstaffe
Little Crosby
Lydiate
Rainford
CROSBY
Melling
Kirkby
Litherland
Haydock
Newton-le-Willows
BOOTLE
Knowsley
ST HELENS
Prescot
LIVERPOOL BAY
WALLASEY
LIVERPOOL
HUYTON
See page 120 for postcode detail
Hoylake
BIRKENHEAD
Hilbre Island
West Kirby
M E R S E Y S I D E
Greasby
Point of Ayr
Talacre
Mostyn Bank
BEBINGTON
Garston
Speke
WIDNES
RUNCORN
Heswall
Dawpool Bank
Mostyn Quay
Mostyn
HALTON
LIVERPOOL JOHN LENNON
Eastham Sands
Dungeon Banks
Stanlow Banks
Ince Banks
Frodsham
Holywell Bank
Greenfield (Maes-Glas)
Neston
Willaston
ELLESMERE PORT
Whitford
Holywell (Treffynnon)
Bagillt Bank
Helsby
Kingsley
FLINTSHIRE
Flint (Y Fflint)
CH
CHESHIRE
Halkyn
White Sands
Connah's Quay
Shotton
Queensferry
CHESTER
WEST
Northop
Mold (Yr Wyddgrug)
Buckley (Bwcle)
Hawarden (Penarlâg)
&
CHESTER
Tarporley
DENBIGHSHIRE
Ruthin (Rhuthun)
WREXHAM
WREXHAM (Wrecsam)
Malpas
0 2 4 6 miles
0 2 4 6 8 10 km

BLACKBURN WITH DARWEN
Darwen
Hoddlesden
Rawtenstall
Edenfield
Ramsbottom
Whitworth
Wardle
Littleborough
Calderbrook
Walsden
Todmorden
Ripponden
Holywell Green
Stainland
Rishworth Moor
Huddersfield
Slaithwaite
Marsden
Meltham
WEST YORKS
Egerton
Tottington
Horwich
Rivington
BOLTON
BURY
ROCHDALE
Heywood
Milnrow
Shaw
Royton
Radcliffe
Little Lever
Whitefield
Middleton
Chadderton
OLDHAM
Delph
Diggle
Dobcross
Uppermill
Greenfield
Saddleworth Moor
Westhoughton
Hindley
Atherton
Tyldesley
Walkden
Farnworth
Swinton
Pendlebury
Prestwich
SALFORD
Failsworth
ASHTON-UNDER-LYNE
Mossley
Stalybridge
Dukinfield
Droylsden
GREATER MANCHESTER
MANCHESTER
Leigh
Glazebury
Culcheth
Irlam
Urmston
Stretford
Denton
Hyde
Hollingworth
Tintwistle
Hadfield
Glossop
Longdendale
Charlesworth
Sale
Partington
Carrington
Romiley
STOCKPORT
Marple
WARRINGTON
Lymm
Altrincham
Hale
Gatley
Cheadle
Hazel Grove
Bramhall
Disley
New Mills
High Lane
Hayfield
Little Hayfield
High Peak
MANCHESTER
Styal
Handforth
Poynton
Whaley Bridge
Chapel-en-le-Frith
Wilmslow
Knutsford
Mobberley
Alderley Edge
Bollington
Prestbury
Northwich
Winsford
Middlewich
MACCLESFIELD
CHESHIRE EAST
DERBYSHIRE
Buxton
Holmes Chapel
Goostrey
Congleton
Sandbach
CREWE
Alsager
Kidsgrove
Biddulph
Leek
STAFFS
Nantwich
NEWCASTLE-UNDER-LYME
See pages 116 - 117 for postcode detail

A
B
C
D
E
1
2
3
4
5
6
7
56
57
49
40
See pages 116 - 117
for postcode detail
HX
OL
HD
SK
ST
DE
WA
CW
P E N N I N E S
D E R B Y S H I R E
CHESHIRE
EAST
S T A F F S
GREATER
MANCHESTER
Rochdale
Bury
Heywood
Middleton
Oldham
Chadderton
Royton
Shaw
Milnrow
Littleborough
Whitworth
Edenfield
Prestwich
Salford
Pendlebury
Eccles
Manchester
Droylsden
Failsworth
Ashton-under-Lyne
Dukinfield
Stalybridge
Mossley
Hyde
Denton
Stockport
Romiley
Marple
Sale
Altrincham
Hale
Cheadle
Gatley
Hazel Grove
Bramhall
Poynton
Wilmslow
Alderley Edge
Knutsford
Macclesfield
Bollington
Prestbury
Congleton
Kidsgrove
Biddulph
Leek
Buxton
Chapel-en-le-Frith
Whaley Bridge
New Mills
Hayfield
Glossop
Hadfield
Marsden
Slaithwaite
Huddersfield
Holmfirth
Honley
Meltham
Kirkburton
Skelmanthorpe
Denby Dale
Penistone
Stocksbridge
Dewsbury
Mirfield
Ossett
Ripponden
Elland
Castleton
Hope
Bradwell
Hathersage
Tideswell
Bakewell
Youlgreave
Hartington
Wirksworth
Uppermill
Delph
Diggle
Greenfield
Edale
Kinder Scout
High Peak
Longdendale
Saddleworth Moor
Hope Woodlands
Derwent Dale
Ladybower Reservoir
Howden Reservoir
Featherbed Moss
Bleaklow Hill
Snake Pass
Castleshaw Moor
Black Hill
Tittesworth Reservoir
Manchester Airport
Under-Lyme
0 2 4 6 miles
0 2 4 6 8 10 km

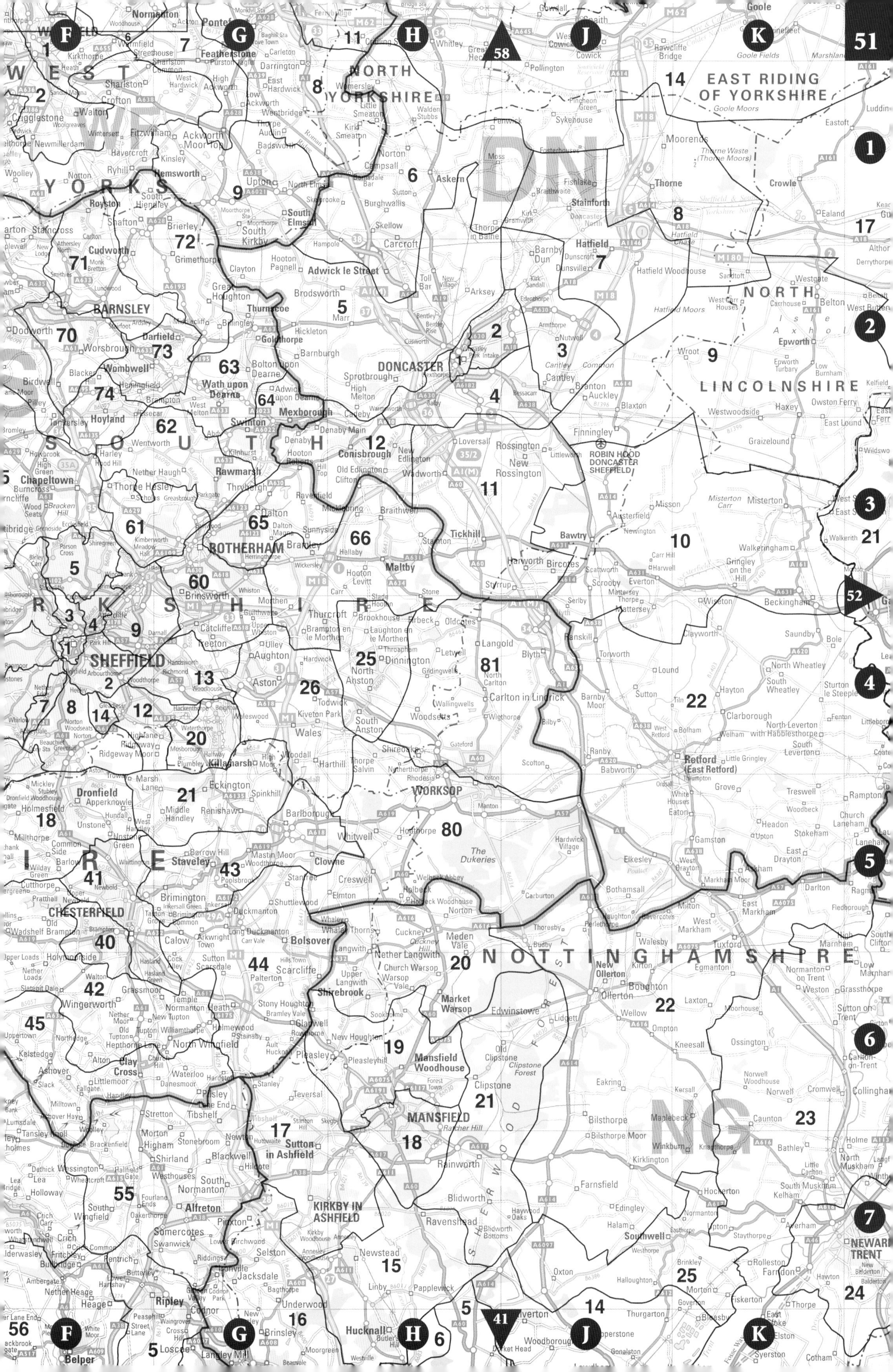
F
G
H
J
K
58
1
2
3
4
5
6
7
52
41
WEST YORKS
SOUTH YORKSHIRE
NORTH YORKSHIRE
EAST RIDING OF YORKSHIRE
NORTH LINCOLNSHIRE
NOTTINGHAMSHIRE
DN
NG
WF
Normanton
Pontefract
Featherstone
Goole
Goole Fields
Marshland
Goole Moors
Cowick
Pollington
Whitley
Kirkthorpe
Sharlston
Crofton
Walton
Crigglestone
Newmillerdam
Wintersett
Ackworth Moor Top
Fitzwilliam
Havercroft
Ryhill
Kinsley
Hemsworth
Notton
Woolley
Royston
South Hiendley
Shafton
Brierley
Grimethorpe
Cudworth
Staincross
Barnsley
Dodworth
Worsbrough
Darfield
Wombwell
Hoyland
Birdwell
Pilley
Tankersley
Chapeltown
Wentworth
Thorpe Hesley
Kimberworth
Rotherham
Dalton
Sunnyside
Bramley
Wickersley
Brinsworth
Catcliffe
Treeton
Sheffield
Aughton
Aston
Swallownest
Dronfield
Apperknowle
Holmesfield
Unstone
Eckington
Renishaw
Marsh Lane
Killamarsh
Mosborough
Ridgeway
Staveley
Barlborough
Clowne
Whitwell
Creswell
Elmton
Bolsover
Chesterfield
Brimington
Calow
Duckmanton
Wingerworth
Clay Cross
North Wingfield
Ashover
Tibshelf
Stonebroom
Shirland
Higham
South Normanton
Alfreton
Somercotes
Swanwick
Ripley
Codnor
Heage
Belper
Langley Mill
Eastwood
Brinsley
Selston
Jacksdale
Underwood
Pinxton
Kirkby in Ashfield
Sutton in Ashfield
Mansfield
Mansfield Woodhouse
Rainworth
Blidworth
Ravenshead
Newstead
Hucknall
Linby
Papplewick
Calverton
Woodborough
Lowdham
Epperstone
Oxton
Southwell
Farnsfield
Bilsthorpe
Eakring
Kneesall
Ollerton
New Ollerton
Boughton
Edwinstowe
Clipstone
Clipstone Forest
Forest Town
Sherwood Forest
Market Warsop
Church Warsop
Shirebrook
Pleasley
Langwith
Cuckney
Worksop
Manton
Rhodesia
Shireoaks
Carlton in Lindrick
Langold
North Carlton
Blyth
Tickhill
Maltby
Dinnington
North Anston
South Anston
Kiveton Park
Todwick
Wales
Harthill
Thorpe Salvin
Thurcroft
Laughton en le Morthen
Stainton
Wadworth
Rossington
New Rossington
Doncaster
Bessacarr
Cantley
Armthorpe
Branton
Auckley
Finningley
Robin Hood Doncaster Sheffield
Hatfield
Dunscroft
Dunsville
Stainforth
Thorne
Moorends
Thorne Waste (Thorne Moors)
Crowle
Eastoft
Luddington
Fishlake
Sykehouse
Askern
Moss
Campsall
Norton
Burghwallis
Skellow
Carcroft
Adwick le Street
Brodsworth
Marr
Hickleton
Barnburgh
Goldthorpe
Thurnscoe
Bolton upon Dearne
Wath upon Dearne
Mexborough
Swinton
Conisbrough
Denaby Main
Edlington
Sprotbrough
Warmsworth
Balby
Bentley
Arksey
Kirk Sandall
Barnby Dun
Epworth
Westwoodside
Haxey
Owston Ferry
Belton
Westgate
Misterton
Walkeringham
Gringley on the Hill
Beckingham
Everton
Bawtry
Austerfield
Harworth
Bircotes
Scrooby
Mattersey
Ranskill
Torworth
Barnby Moor
Sutton
Lound
Clayworth
Hayton
Clarborough
North Wheatley
South Wheatley
Sturton le Steeple
Retford (East Retford)
Ordsall
Babworth
Ranby
Grove
Gamston
Eaton
Elkesley
Headon
Rampton
Treswell
Church Laneham
East Drayton
Darlton
Tuxford
Egmanton
Laxton
Walesby
Kirton
Wellow
Ompton
Ossington
Norwell
Cromwell
Collingham
Caunton
Bathley
North Muskham
South Muskham
Kelham
Averham
Newark-on-Trent
Farndon
Rolleston
Hawton
Thorpe
East Stoke
Elston
Syerston
Fiskerton
Bleasby
Morton
Thurgarton
Halam
Edingley
Kirklington
Winkburn
Maplebeck
Kersall
Hockerton
Upton
Sutton on Trent
Carlton-on-Trent
Weston
Normanton on Trent
Marnham
Skegby
Teversal
The Dukeries
Hardwick Village
Carburton
Bothamsall
Welbeck Abbey
Holbeck
Nether Langwith
Meden Vale
Budby
Thoresby
Perlethorpe

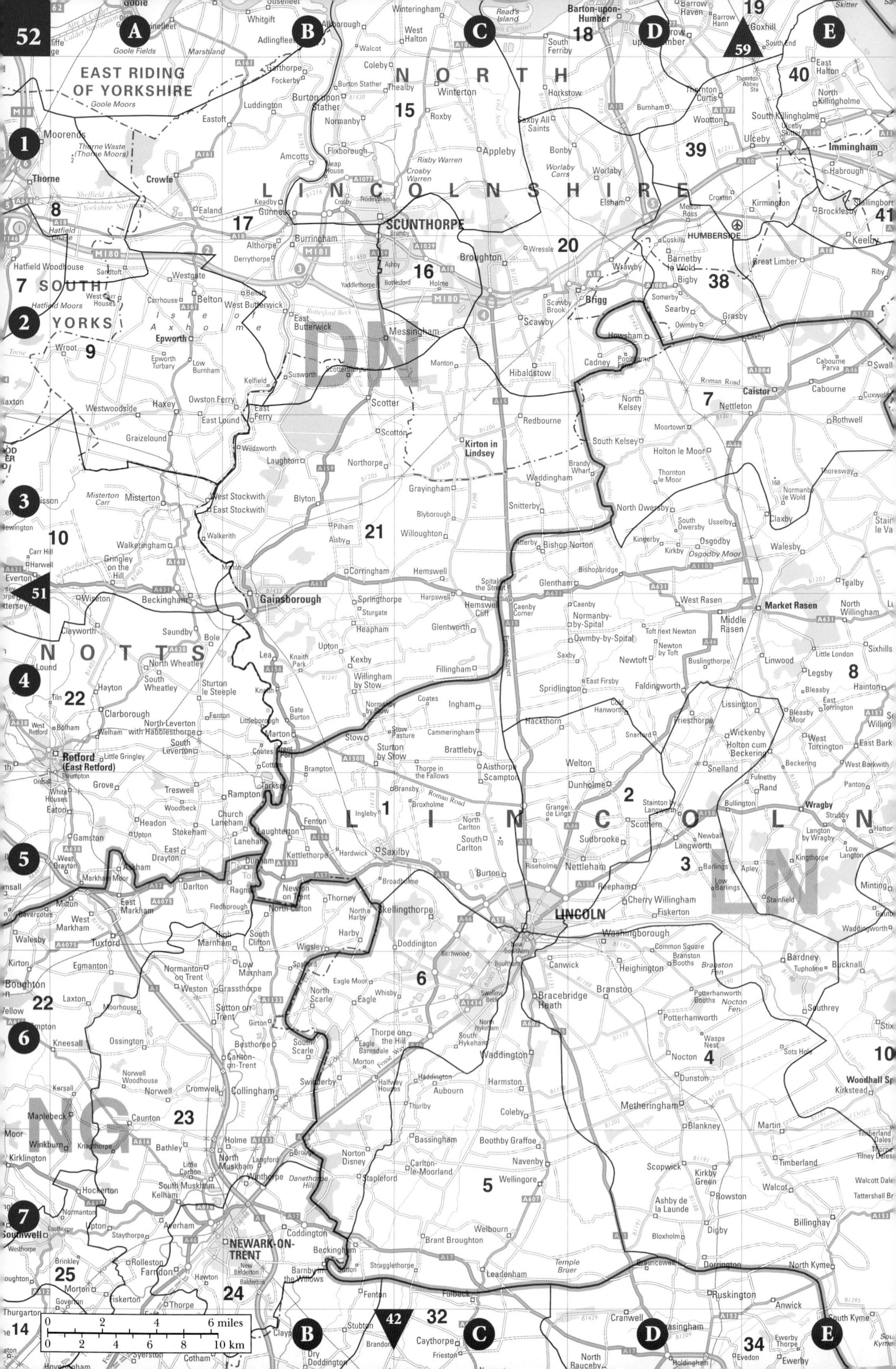
A
B
C
D
E
1
2
3
4
5
6
7
59
51
42
EAST RIDING OF YORKSHIRE
NORTH
LINCOLNSHIRE
SOUTH YORKS
NOTTS
LINCOLN
DN
LN
NG
Goole
Swinefleet
Goole Fields
Marshland
Whitgift
Adlingfleet
Alkborough
Ousefleet
Winteringham
West Halton
Walcot
Coleby
Read's Island
Barton-upon-Humber
South Ferriby
Barrow Haven
Barrow Hann
Barrow upon Humber
Goxhill
South End
East Halton
North Killingholme
South Killingholme
Ulceby Skitter
Ulceby
Immingham
Habrough
Thornton Curtis
Thornton Abbey Sta
Wootton
Horkstow
Saxby All Saints
Bonby
Worlaby Carrs
Worlaby
Elsham
Burnham
Croxton
Kirmington
Melton Ross
HUMBERSIDE
Brocklesby
Stallingborough
Keelby
Riby
Great Limber
Coskills
Barnetby le Wold
Bigby
Somerby
Searby
Owmby
Grasby
Clixby
Wrawby
Brigg
Scawby Brook
Scawby
Wressle
Broughton
Appleby
Winterton
Roxby
Thealby
Burton Stather
Burton upon Stather
Normanby
Flixborough
Risby Warren
Crosby Warren
Neap House
Garthorpe
Fockerby
Luddington
Eastoft
Amcotts
Goole Moors
Moorends
Thorne Waste (Thorne Moors)
Thorne
Crowle
Eaolam
Keadby
Gunness
Crosby
Frodingham
SCUNTHORPE
Brumby
Burringham
Althorpe
Derrythorpe
Ashby
Bottesford
Yaddlethorpe
Holme
Hatfield Chase
Hatfield Woodhouse
Sandtoft
Westgate
Belton
West Carr Houses
Carrhouse
West Butterwick
East Butterwick
Bottesford Beck
Messingham
Isle of Axholme
Epworth
Epworth Turbary
Hatfield Moors
Wroot
Low Burnham
Kelfield
Susworth
Scotter
Scotterthorpe
Manton
Hibaldstow
Cadney
Howsham
North Kelsey
Caistor
Nettleton
Cabourne
Cabourne Parva
Roman Road
Rothwell
Cuxwold
Swallow
Moortown
South Kelsey
Holton le Moor
Thornton le Moor
Redbourne
Kirton in Lindsey
Brandy Wharf
Waddingham
Thoresway
North Owersby
South Owersby
Usselby
North Owersby
Claxby
Normanby le Wold
Kingerby
Kirkby
Osgodby
Osgodby Moor
Walesby
Tealby
Owston Ferry
East Ferry
Haxey
Westwoodside
East Lound
Graizelound
Wildsworth
Laughton
Scotton
Northorpe
Grayingham
Snitterby
Atterby
Bishop Norton
Bishopbridge
Blyton
Blyborough
Willoughton
Pilham
Aisby
Misterton
Misterton Carr
West Stockwith
East Stockwith
Walkerith
Walkeringham
Gringley on the Hill
Carr Hill
Harwell
Everton
Corringham
Hemswell
Glentham
West Rasen
Middle Rasen
Market Rasen
North Willingham
Wiseton
Beckingham
Gainsborough
Morton
Springthorpe
Sturgate
Harpswell
Spital in the Street
Caenby Corner
Caenby
Hemswell Cliff
Normanby-by-Spital
Owmby-by-Spital
Toft next Newton
Newton by Toft
Clayworth
Saundby
Bole
Heapham
Glentworth
Lea
Knaith Park
Upton
Kexby
Willingham by Stow
Fillingham
Saxby
Newtoft
Buslingthorpe
Linwood
Little London
Sixhills
Lound
North Wheatley
South Wheatley
Hayton
Sturton le Steeple
Knaith
Gate Burton
Spridlington
East Firsby
Faldingworth
Legsby
Bleasby
Hainton
Tiln
Clarborough
Fenton
Littleborough
North Leverton with Habblesthorpe
South Leverton
Welham
Bolham
West Retford
Retford (East Retford)
Little Gringley
Marton
Normanby by Stow
Coates
Ingham
Cammeringham
Stow
Stow Pasture
Sturton by Stow
Brattleby
Hackthorn
Cold Hanworth
Snarford
Friesthorpe
Lissington
East Torrington
Wickenby
Holton cum Beckering
West Torrington
Bleasby Moor
East Bark
Ordsall
Thrumpton
Grove
Treswell
Rampton
Coates
Cottam
Brampton
Thorpe in the Fallows
Aisthorpe
Scampton
Welton
Dunholme
Snelland
Beckering
West Barkwith
Fulnetby
Rand
Panton
Wragby
Bullington
Strubby
White Houses
Eaton
Headon
Woodbeck
Church Laneham
Torksey
Bransby
Broxholme
Roman Road
Ingleby
Grange de Lings
Stainton by Langworth
Scothern
Newball
Langworth
Langton by Wragby
Low Langton
Gamston
Upton
Stokeham
Laneham
Laughterton
Fenton
North Carlton
South Carlton
Sudbrooke
Nettleham
Barlings
Apley
Kingthorpe
West Drayton
East Drayton
Askham
Dunham
Kettlethorpe
Hardwick
Saxilby
Broadholme
Burton
Riseholme
Reepham
Low Barlings
Stainfield
Minting
Markham Moor
Milton
Bevercotes
West Markham
East Markham
Darlton
Ragnall
Newton on Trent
Thorney
North Clifton
Fledborough
North Harby
Skellingthorpe
LINCOLN
Cherry Willingham
Fiskerton
Washingborough
Waddingworth
Walesby
Tuxford
High Marnham
South Clifton
Harby
Wigsley
Doddington
Birchwood
New Boultham
Boultham
Canwick
Heighington
Common Square
Branston Booths
Branston Fen
Bardney
Tupholme
Bucknall
Kirton
Egmanton
Normanton on Trent
Low Marnham
Spalford
Eagle Moor
Whisby
Swallow Beck
Bracebridge Heath
Branston
Potterhanworth Booths
Nocton Fen
Southrey
Boughton
Laxton
Moorhouse
Weston
Grassthorpe
North Scarle
Eagle
North Hykeham
Potterhanworth
Wellow
Ompton
Sutton on Trent
Girton
Thorpe on the Hill
South Hykeham
Wasps Nest
Sots Hole
Kneesall
Ossington
Besthorpe
South Scarle
Eagle Barnsdale
Morton
Fosse Way
Waddington
Nocton
Woodhall Spa
Carlton-on-Trent
Swinderby
Haddington
Halfway Houses
Harmston
Dunston
Kirkstead
Norwell Woodhouse
Norwell
Cromwell
Collingham
Aubourn
Thurlby
Coleby
Metheringham
Timberland Delph
Kersall
Caunton
Bassingham
Boothby Graffoe
Blankney
Martin
Timberland Dales
Thorpe Tilney Dales
Maplebeck
Winkburn
Knapthorpe
Bathley
Holme
Norton Disney
Navenby
Scopwick
Kirkby Green
Timberland
Walcott Dale
Tattershall Bri
Moor
Kirklington
Little Carlton
North Muskham
Langford
Carlton-le-Moorland
Stapleford
Wellingore
Walcott
Brough
Winthorpe
Danethorpe Hill
Rowston
Ashby de la Launde
Hockerton
South Muskham
Kelham
Billinghay
Normanton
Upton
Averham
Coddington
Bloxholm
Digby
Southwell
Westhorpe
Staythorpe
NEWARK-ON-TRENT
Brant Broughton
Welbourn
Brinkley
Rolleston
Farndon
New Balderton
Balderton
Beckingham
Stragglethorpe
Leadenham
Temple Bruer
Brauncewell
Dorrington
North Kyme
Morton
Hawton
Barnby in the Willows
Fenton
Fulbeck
Ruskington
Anwick
Goverton
Fiskerton
Thorpe
South Kyme
Thurgarton
Claypole
Stubton
Caythorpe
Cranwell
Leasingham
Dry Doddington
Brandon
Frieston
North Rauceby
Holdingham
Evedon
Ewerby Thorpe
Ewerby
Syerston
Cotham
Hoveringham
Temple
Sleaford
Ermine Street
Trent
0 2 4 6 miles
0 2 4 6 8 10 km

53
F
G
H
J
K
1
2
3
4
5
6
7
12
19
31
32
33
34
35
36
7
11
12
13
9
23
24
25
22
20
43
EAST RIDING OF YORKSHIRE
NORTH
EAST
LINCOLNSHIRE
THE WOLDS
SHIRE
PE
THE
WASH
Patrington
Patrington Haven
Welwick
Out Newton
Weeton
Skeffling
Easington
Sunk Island
Old Hall
Skeffling Clays
Sunk Island Sands
Kilnsea
Kilnsea Clays
Mouth of The Humber
Spurn Head
Healing
GRIMSBY
Cleethorpes
Humberston
Scartho
Bradley
Laceby
Waltham
New Waltham
Barnoldby le Beck
Holton le Clay
Tetney Lock
Brigsley
Ashby cum Fenby
Tetney
North Cotes
Ravendale
North Thoresby
Marshchapel
Donna Nook
Grainthorpe
Meals
North Somercotes
Fulstow
Ludborough
Covenham St Bartholomew
Covenham St Mary
Conisholme
Church End
Skidbrooke North End
South Somercotes
Saltfleet
Utterby
North Ormsby
Yarburgh
Skidbrooke
Saltfleetby St Clements
Saltfleetby All Saints
Saltfleetby St Peter
Alvingham
North Cockerington
South Cockerington
Fotherby
Little Grimsby
North Elkington
Keddington Corner
Keddington
Theddlethorpe St Helen
Theddlethorpe All Saints
South Elkington
Welton le Wold
Louth
Stewton
Grimoldby
Manby
Burgh on Bain
Gayton le Wold
Hallington
Little Carlton
Great Carlton
Legbourne
Mablethorpe
Trusthorpe
Biscathorpe
Raithby
Withcall
Maltby
Gayton le Marsh
North Reston
South Reston
Little Cawthorpe
Donington on Bain
Tathwell
Strubby
Withern
Thorpe
Sutton on Sea
Sandilands
Sutton le Marsh
Maltby le Marsh
Stenigot
Haugham
Muckton
Authorpe
Tothill
Woodthorpe
Beesby
Hagnaby
Market Stainton
Cawkwell
Asterby
Maidenwell
Goulceby
Ranby
Scamblesby
Farforth
Ruckland
Burwell
Claythorpe
Aby
Belleau
Greenfield
Saleby
Markby
Hannah
Walmsgate
Oxcombe
Worlaby
Flint Hill
White Pit
Swaby
South Thoresby
Ailby
Thoresthorpe
Asserby
The Grange
Bilsby
Thurlby
Huttoft
Anderby Creek
Anderby
Mumby
Alford
Bilsby Field
Farlesthorpe
Rigsby
Haugh
Hemingby
Belchford
Tetford
Little London
South Ormsby
Calceby
Driby
Ketsby
Well
Authorpe Row
Fulletby
Salmonby
Brinkhill
Ulceby Cross
Mawthorpe
Cumberworth
Hogsthorpe
Chapel St Leonards
Farthorpe
Midthorpe
West Ashby
Ashby Puerorum
Somersby
Harrington
Ulceby
Skendleby Psalter
Bonthorpe
Helsey
Willoughby
Edlington
Low Toynton
Horncastle
Bag Enderby
Aswardby
Langton
Claxby St Andrew
Sloothby
Thimbleby
Greetham
Salmsby
Hagworthingham
Sausthorpe
Dalby
Skendleby
Welton le Marsh
Hasthorpe
Ingoldmells
Ingoldmells Point
Addlethorpe
High Toynton
Scrafield
Winceby
Lusby
Partney
Candlesby
Orby
Thornton
Woodhall
Martin
Mareham on the Hill
Hameringham
Asgarby
Raithby
Scremby
Ashby by Partney
Gunby
Orby Marsh
Spilsby
Halton Holegate
Dalderby
Claxby Pluckacre
Mavis Enderby
Hareby
Hundleby
Burgh le Marsh
Winthorpe
Seathorne
Great Steeping
Bratoft
Roughton
Wood Enderby
Moorby
Miningsby
Bolingbroke
Old Bolingbroke
East Keal
Toynton All Saints
Burgh Marsh
Skegness
West Keal
Irby in the Marsh
Haltham
Wilksby
East Kirkby
Toynton Fen Side
Toynton St Peter
Little Steeping
Firsby
Kirkby on Bain
Hagnaby
Mareham le Fen
Revesby
Revesby Bridge
Keal Cotes
Thorpe Culvert
Thorpe St Peter
Croft
Seacroft
Croft Marsh
Fendike Corner
Stickford
Tumby
Coningsby
Wainfleet All Saints
Havenhouse Sta
Wainfleet Bank
New Bolingbroke
Moor Side
Gibraltar
Key's Toft
Wainfleet St. Mary
Gibraltar Pt
Tumby Woodside
New Leake
Midville
Hawthorn Hill
New York
Sandy Bank
Stickney
Carrington
East Fen
Friskney Eaudyke
Friskney
Wainfleet Sand
Scrub Hill
Bunker's Hill
Lade Bank
West Fen
Northlands
Wildmore Fen
Leake Commonside
Wrangle Lowgate
Frithville
Gipsey Bridge
Sibsey
Old Leake
Wrangle
Friskney Flats
Boston Deeps
Lynn Deeps
Holland Fen
Langrick
Fishtoft Drove
Langrick Bridge
Amber Hill
Antons Gowt
Frith Bank
Dyke
Leverton
Leverton Outgate
Leverton Lucasgate
Leake Hurn's End
Long Sand
A180
A1098
A16
A46
A1243
A18
A1031
A631
A157
A153
A1104
A52
A1028
A158
A155
A1111
B1200
B1449
B1195
B1183
B1184

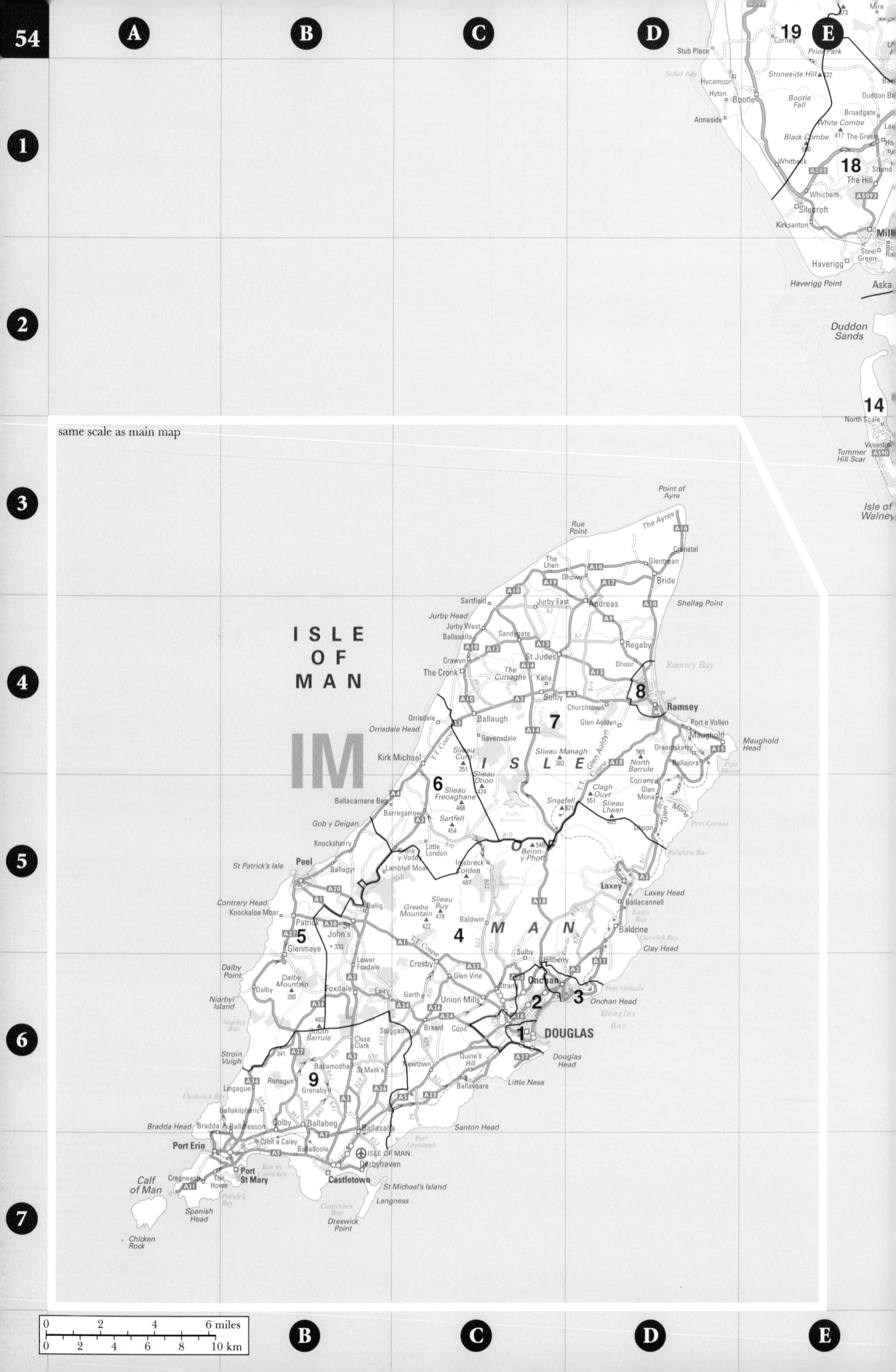

same scale as main map
ISLE OF MAN
IM
Point of Ayre
Rue Point
The Ayres
Cranstal
Glentruan
Bride
The Lhen
Dhowin
Sartfield
Jurby East
Andreas
Shellag Point
Jurby Head
Jurby West
Ballasalla
Sandygate
Regaby
St Judes
Dhoor
Ramsey Bay
Crawyn
The Cronk
The Curraghs
Kella
Sulby
Churchtown
Ramsey
Orrisdale
Orrisdale Head
Ballaugh
Ravensdale
Glen Auldyn
Port e Vullen
Maughold
Maughold Head
Dreemskerry
Kirk Michael
Slieau Curn
Slieau Dhoo
Slieau Managh
North Barrule
Ballajora
Slieau Freoaghane
Clagh Ouyr
Corrany
Glen Mona
Ballacarnane Beg
Barregarrow
Sartfell
Snaefell
Slieau Lhean
Port Cornaa
Gob y Deigan
Dhoon
Knocksharry
Little London
Beinn-y-Phott
Ballaglass
St Patrick's Isle
Peel
Ballagyr
Cronk-y-Voddy
Lambfell Moar
Injebreck
Colden
Laxey
Laxey Head
Ballacannell
Contrary Head
Knockaloe Moar
Ballig
Greeba Mountain
Slieau Ruy
Baldwin
Patrick
St John's
Baldrine
Garwick Bay
Clay Head
Glenmaye
Crosby
Sulby
Hillberry
Dalby Point
Lower Foxdale
Glen Vine
Onchan
Port Groudle
Dalby Mountain
Niarbyl Island
Dalby
Foxdale
Eairy
Garth
Union Mills
Strang
Onchan Head
Douglas Bay
South Barrule
Stuggadhoo
Braaid
Cooil
DOUGLAS
Stroin Vuigh
Close Clark
Quine's Hill
Douglas Head
Ballamodha
St Mark's
Newtown
Ronague
Grenaby
Little Ness
Lingague
Ballaveare
Fleshwick Bay
Ballakilpheric
Bradda Head
Bradda
Ballafesson
Colby
Ballabeg
Ballasalla
Santon Head
Port Erin
Croit e Caley
Balladoole
ISLE OF MAN
Derbyhaven
Port Grenaugh
Calf of Man
Cregneash
The Howe
Port St Mary
Bay ny Carrickey
Castletown
St Michael's Island
Langness
Perwick Bay
Spanish Head
Castletown Bay
Dreswick Point
Chicken Rock
Stub Place
Corney
Prior Park
Selker Bay
Hycemoor
Hyton
Bootle
Stoneside Hill
Bootle Fell
Annaside
Broadgate
White Combe
Black Combe
The Green
Whitbeck
The Hill
Whicham
Silecroft
Kirksanton
Haverigg
Steel Green
Haverigg Point
Aska
Duddon Sands
North Scale
Vickerstown
Tummer Hill Scar
Isle of Walney
A5
A7
A3
A1
A2
A18
A10
T.T. Course
0 2 4 6 miles
0 2 4 6 8 10 km

CUMBRIA
LA
LANCASHIRE
PR
BB
BLACKPOOL
BLACKBURN WITH DARWEN
MORECAMBE BAY
Forest of Bowland
Kendal
Sedbergh
Killington Lake
Oxenholme
Dent
Kirkby Lonsdale
Milnthorpe
Arnside
Grange-over-Sands
Ulverston
Newby Bridge
Haverthwaite
Cartmel
Flookburgh
Broughton in Furness
Barrow-in-Furness
Dalton-in-Furness
Carnforth
Silverdale
Warton
Bolton-le-Sands
Morecambe
Heysham
LANCASTER
Galgate
Glasson Dock
Cockerham
Garstang
Fleetwood
Cleveleys
Thornton
Poulton-le-Fylde
Knott End-on-Sea
Preesall
Pilling
Kirkham
Wesham
BLACKPOOL INTERNATIONAL
LYTHAM ST ANNE'S
PRESTON
Longridge
Chipping
Slaidburn
BLACKBURN
Darwen
Bamber Bridge
LEYLAND
CHORLEY
SOUTHPORT
Tarleton
Ingleton
High Bentham
Halton
Caton
Hornby
Clougha Pike
Ward's Stone
Parlick
Walney Island
Piel Island
Hilpsford Point
Sunderland Point
Humphrey Head Point
Banks Sands
Horse Bank
60
56
48
F
G
H
J
K
1
2
3
4
5
6
7

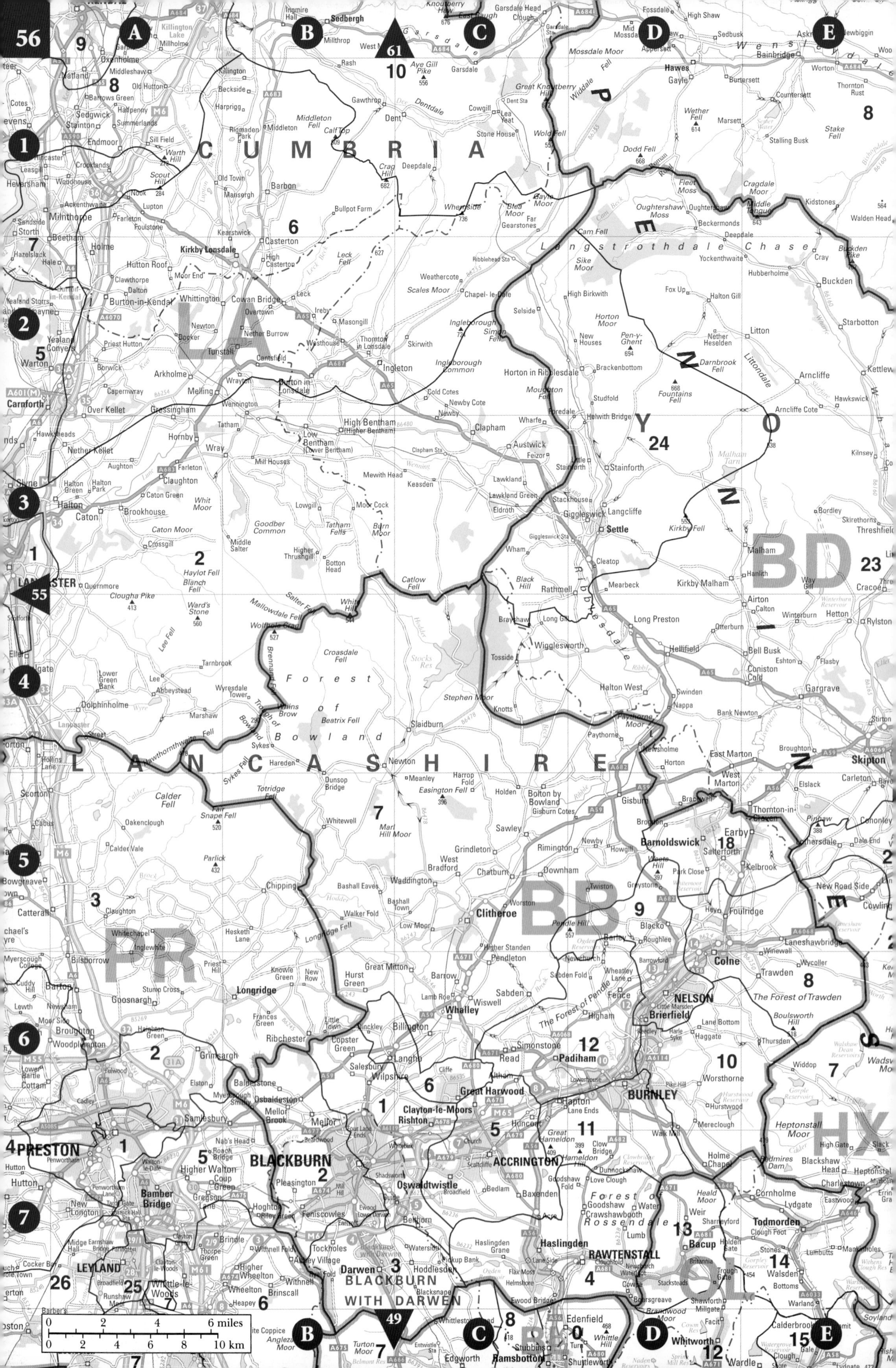

A
B
C
D
E
61
49
55
1
2
3
4
5
6
7
CUMBRIA
LA
LANCASHIRE
YORKSHIRE DALES
PENNINE
BD
BB
PR
HX
OL
Sedbergh
Killington Lake
Oxenholme
Natland
Sedgwick
Stainton
Endmoor
Milnthorpe
Heversham
Beetham
Storth
Holme
Burton-in-Kendal
Yealand Conyers
Warton
Carnforth
Over Kellet
Nether Kellet
Halton
Caton
Slyne
Lancaster
Quernmore
Clougha Pike
Ward's Stone
Dolphinholme
Kirkby Lonsdale
Casterton
Barbon
Cowan Bridge
Whittington
Tunstall
Arkholme
Melling
Wray
Hornby
Claughton
Wennington
Burton in Lonsdale
Ingleton
High Bentham
Low Bentham
Clapham
Austwick
Dent
Dentdale
Garsdale
Hawes
Gayle
Bainbridge
Wensleydale
Whernside
Ingleborough
Pen-y-Ghent
Horton in Ribblesdale
Langstrothdale Chase
Buckden
Litton
Arncliffe
Settle
Giggleswick
Langcliffe
Stainforth
Malham
Kirkby Malham
Airton
Hellifield
Long Preston
Gargrave
Skipton
Forest of Bowland
Slaidburn
Newton
Dunsop Bridge
Whitewell
Gisburn
Bolton by Bowland
Sawley
Barnoldswick
Earby
Clitheroe
Waddington
Chatburn
Pendle Hill
Colne
Nelson
Brierfield
Burnley
Padiham
Whalley
Longridge
Chipping
Goosnargh
Broughton
Preston
Bamber Bridge
Leyland
Blackburn
Darwen
Blackburn with Darwen
Oswaldtwistle
Accrington
Clayton-le-Moors
Rishton
Great Harwood
Haslingden
Rawtenstall
Bacup
Todmorden
Whitworth
Ramsbottom
Edenfield
The Forest of Pendle
The Forest of Trawden
Forest of Rossendale
0 2 4 6 miles
0 2 4 6 8 10 km

F
G
H
J
K
62
50
58
1
2
3
4
5
6
7
NORTH YORKSHIRE
WEST YORKS
HG
LS
YO
See pages 118 - 119 for postcode detail
Castle Bolton
Leyburn
Constable Burton
Patrick Brompton
Scruton
Ainderby Steeple
Morton-on-Swale
Leeming Bar
Leeming
Bedale
Aiskew
Great Crakehall
Newton-le-Willows
Middleham
Thornton Steward
Thornton Watlass
East Witton
West Witton
West Burton
Carlton
West Scrafton
Coverdale
Masham
Swinton
Fearby
Healey
Snape
Burneston
Carthorpe
Pickhill
Kirby Wiske
Sinderby
Kirklington
Thirsk
Sowerby
South Kilvington
Sandhutton
Carlton Miniott
Baldersby
Skipton-on-Swale
Topcliffe
Dalton
Asenby
Rainton
Dishforth
Sessay
Hutton Sessay
Thormanby
Cundall
Raskelf
Brafferton
Helperby
Norton-le-Clay
Kirby Hill
Boroughbridge
Langthorpe
Aldborough
Roecliffe
Myton-on-Swale
Tholthorpe
Minskip
Grafton
Marton
Staveley
Arkendale
Ferrensby
Farnham
Knaresborough
Goldsborough
Flaxby
Whixley
Green Hammerton
Kirk Hammerton
Marston Moor
Tockwith
Cattal
Hunsingore
Cowthorpe
Bickerton
Walton
Wetherby
Thorp Arch
Boston Spa
Clifford
Bramham
Tadcaster
Newton Kyme
Wighill
Bilton-in-Ainsty
Long Marston
Linton-on-Ouse
Tollerton
Aldwark
Great Ouseburn
Little Ouseburn
Thorpe Underwood
Ripon
Sharow
Bishop Monkton
Markington
South Stainley
Burton Leonard
Ripley
Killinghall
Scotton
Nidd
Harrogate
Pannal
Beckwithshaw
Spofforth
Follifoot
Little Ribston
North Deighton
Kirk Deighton
Sicklinghall
Kirkby Overblow
Linton
Collingham
Harewood
East Keswick
East Rigton
Bardsey
Scarcroft
Thorner
Shadwell
Barwick in Elmet
Aberford
Scholes
Garforth
Kippax
Great Preston
Swillington
Allerton Bywater
Castleford
Pontefract
Featherstone
Knottingley
Ferrybridge
Sherburn in Elmet
South Milford
Monk Fryston
Micklefield
Ledsham
Grewelthorpe
Kirkby Malzeard
Laverton
Galphay
Winksley
Grantley
Sawley
Aldfield
Eavestone
Pateley Bridge
Glasshouses
Summer Bridge
Dacre Banks
Darley
Birstwith
Hampsthwaite
Burnt Yates
Clint
Bishop Thornton
Shaw Mills
Kettlesing
Fewston
Blubberhouses
Timble
Lofthouse
Ramsgill
Middlesmoor
Nidderdale
Kirkby Malzeard Moor
Hambleton Hill
Dallowgill Moor
Pateley Moor
Heathfield Moor
Greenhow Hill
Bewerley
Hebden
Burnsall
Appletreewick
Simon's Seat
Grassington Moor
Bolton Abbey
Halton East
Draughton
Langbar
Addingham
Ilkley
Middleton
Denton
Askwith
Burley in Wharfedale
Otley
Pool
Leathley
Farnley
Lindley
Stainburn
Huby
Weeton
Dunkeswick
Arthington
Bramhope
Weardley
Eccup
Menston
Guiseley
Yeadon
Leeds Bradford International
Horsforth
Silsden
Steeton
Riddlesden
Keighley
Bingley
Baildon
Shipley
Haworth
Cullingworth
Denholme
Oxenhope
Harden
Bradford
Queensbury
Thornton
Pudsey
Calverley
Leeds
Morley
Rothwell
Oulton
Woodlesford
Methley
Batley
Birstall
Cleckheaton
Heckmondwike
Liversedge
Gomersal
Dewsbury
Mirfield
Ossett
Horbury
Wakefield
Normanton
Altofts
Stanley
Lofthouse
East Ardsley
Tingley
Halifax
Sowerby Bridge
Brighouse
Elland
Hipperholme
Northowram
Shelf
Luddenden
Ripponden
Holywell Green
Stainland
Greetland
Sharlston
Crofton
Walton
Middlestown
Calder Grove
Whitley Lower
Thornhill
Kirkheaton

A
B
C
D
E
63
1
2
3
4
5
6
7
57
51
NORTH YORKSHIRE
EAST OF YORKS
WEST YORKS
YORK
LS
DN
YO
Landmoth
Nether Silton
Arden Great Moor
Helmsley Moor
Hutton-le-Hole
Lastingham
Keldy Castle
Lockton Low Moor
Thornton-le-Beans
Thornton-le-Moor
South Otterington
Borrowby
Kepwick
Cowesby
Boltby Moor
Hawnby
Hambleton Hills
Gillamoor
Fadmoor
Spaunton
Appleton-le-Moors
Cropton
Cawthorn
Newton-on-Rawcliffe
Levisham
Lockton
Newton Dale
Stain Dale
Dalby Forest
Knayton
Kirby Knowle
Upsall
Thornton-le-Street
North Kilvington
Old Byland
Rievaulx
Carlton
Pockley
Kirkbymoorside
Keldholme
Sinnington
Wrelton
Aislaby
Middleton
Newbridge
High Kingthorpe
Low Kingthorpe
Thirsk
South Kilvington
Felixkirk
Thirlby
Sutton-under-Whitestonecliffe
Cold Kirby
Scawton
Helmsley
Beadlam
Nawton
Welburn
Wombleton
Great Edstone
Marton
Pickering
Wilton
Thornton-le-Dale
Allerston
Sandhutton
Old Thirsk
Sowerby
Caravans prohibited Sutton Bank
Scawton Moor
Rye Dale
Harome
Sproxton
Normanby
Vale of Pickering
Wilton Carr
Carlton Miniott
Thorpefield
Skipton-on-Swale
Bagby
Kilburn
High Kilburn
Oldstead
Wass
Ampleforth College
Ampleforth
Byland Abbey
Oswaldkirk
Nunnington
West Ness
East Ness
Salton
Great Barugh
Little Barugh
Kirby Misperton
Brawby
Butterwick
High Marishes
Thirkleby
Stonegrave
South Holme
Little Habton
Great Habton
Low Marishes
Topcliffe
Dalton
Little Hutton
Hutton Sessay
Carlton Husthwaite
Coxwold
Thorpe Hall
Gilling East
Cawton
Hovingham
Ryton
Wykeham
West Knapton
Scampston
Sessay
Birdforth
Thormanby
Husthwaite
Oulston
Yearsley
Coulton
Slingsby
Barton-le-Street
Amotherby
Old Malton Moor
Rillington
Dishforth
Crakehill
Fawdington
Cundall
Scackleton
Howardian Hills
Appleton-le-Street
Broughton
Swinton
Old Malton
Thorpe Bassett
Scagglethorpe
Norton-le-Clay
Thornton Bridge
Brandsby
Stearsby
Wiganthorpe
Dalby
Skewsby
Terrington
Coneysthorpe
Hildenley
Malton
Norton
Settrington
Raskelf
Crayke
Ganthorpe
Great Lake
Bafferton
Helperby
Humberton
Kirby Hill
Boroughbridge
Aldborough
Easingwold
Marton Abbey
Marton-in-the-Forest
Whenby
High Hutton
Menethorpe
Low Hutton
Langton Wold
Langton
North Grimston
Welburn
Bulmer
Stillington
Farlington
Sheriff Hutton
Whitwell-on-the-Hill
Crambeck Village
Firby
Kennythorpe
Birdsall
Wharram le Street
Wharram Percy
Myton-on-Swale
Tholthorpe
Flawith
Alne
Huby
Kirkham
Westow
Burythorpe
Lower Dunsforth
Cross Lanes
Sutton-on-the-Forest
West Lilling
Lilling Green
Foston
Thornton-le-Clay
Crambe
Barton Hill
Barton-le-Willows
Howsham
Leavening
Grafton
Upper Dunsforth
Aldwark
Tollerton
Youlton
Flaxton
Harton
Acklam
Burdale
Thixendale
Great Ouseburn
Little Ouseburn
Linton-on-Ouse
Newton-on-Ouse
Strensall
Leppington
Claxton
Bossall
Strensall Common
Thorpe Underwood
Whixley
Green Hammerton
Allerton Mauleverer
Hopperton
Nun Monkton
Beningbrough
Shipton
Wigginton
Towthorpe
Haxby
Earswick
Sand Hutton
Scrayingham
Buttercrambe
Upper Helmsley
Skirpenbeck
Bugthorpe
Kirby Underdale
Fridaythorpe
Moor Monkton
Kirk Hammerton
Roman Road
Skelton
Overton
Nether Poppleton
Upper Poppleton
Huntington
New Earswick
Stockton on the Forest
Warthill
Gate Helmsley
Stamford Bridge
Full Sutton
Youlthorpe
Bishop Wilton
Great Givendale
Gowthorpe
Fangfoss
Cattal
Marston Moor
Rawcliffe
Clifton
Heworth
Holtby
Low Catton
High Catton
Walshford
Hunsingore
Hessay
Tockwith
Knapton
Acomb
Tang Hall
Osbaldwick
Murton
Dunnington
Bolton
Meltonby
Yapham
Millington
Warter Wold
North Deighton
Cowthorpe
Rufforth
Holgate
Four Lane Ends
Wilberfoss
Kilnwick Percy
Warter
Kirk Deighton
Wetherby
Bickerton
Long Marston
Hutton Wandesley
Woodthorpe
Dringhouses
Heslington
Fulford
Kexby
Newton upon Derwent
Barmby Moor
Pocklington
Nunburnholme
Bilton-in-Ainsty
Angram
Askham Bryan
Askham Richard
Walton
Wighill
Healaugh
Bilbrough
Bishopthorpe
Copmanthorpe
Crockey Hill
Elvington
Sutton upon Derwent
Allerthorpe
Hayton
Burnby
Londesborough
Linton
Boston Spa
Thorp Arch
Catterton
Acaster Malbis
Naburn
Wheldrake
Thornton
Shiptonthorpe
Market Weighton
Newton Kyme
Street Houses
Colton
Deighton
Escrick
Storwood
Ross Moor
Melbourne
Thorpe le Street
East Rigton
Compton
Clifford
Bramham
Tadcaster
Appleton Roebuck
Acaster Selby
Bolton Percy
Stillingfleet
Thorganby
East Cottingwith
Bielby
Everingham
Wothersome
Kirkby Wharfe
Ulleskelf
Stutton
Ellerton
Seaton Ross
Harswell
Weighton Common
Moor End
Ryther
Towton
Laytham
Holme-on-Spalding-Moor
Potterton
Barwick in Elmet
Aberford
Parlington
Scarthingwell
Saxton
Cawood
Kelfield
Skipwith
Aughton
Water End
North Duffield
Harlthorpe
Foggathorpe
Church Fenton
Barkston Ash
Little Fenton
Biggin
Riccall
Wistow
Highfield
Bubwith
Gribthorpe
Holme Common
South Cliffe
Willitoft
Micklefield
Sherburn in Elmet
Barlby
Osgodby
Lund
South Duffield
Breighton
Spaldington
Bursea
Garforth
Newthorpe
Thorpe Willoughby
Selby
Cliffe
Wressle
Portington
Sandholme
Newport
South Milford
Hambleton
Brayton
Howden Sta
Eastrington
Scalby
Swillington
Kippax
Ledsham
Lumby
Monk Fryston
Hemingbrough
Newsholme
Gilberdyke
Staddlethorpe
Great Preston
Hillam
Barlow
Barmby on the Marsh
Asselby
Howden
Allerton Bywater
Ledston
Fairburn
Gateforth
Burn
Long Drax
Knedlington
Balkholme
Mickleton
Methley
Methley Junction
Newton
Brotherton
Burton Salmon
Birkin
Camblesforth
Drax
Kilpin Pike
Kilpin
Saltmarshe Sta
Castleford
West Haddlesey
Chapel Haddlesey
Temple Hirst
Hook
Skelton
Laxton
Airmyn
Newland
Blacktoft
Faxfleet
Whitwood
Glasshoughton
Ferrybridge
Knottingley
Beal
Kellington
Hirst Courtney
Carlton
Rawcliffe
Goole
Saltmarshe
Reedness
Yokefleet
Ousefleet
Normanton
Pontefract
Eggborough
Hensall
Whitley Bridge Sta
Gowdall
Snaith
Old Goole
Swinefleet
Whitgift
Adlingfleet
Alkborough
Altofts
Woodhouse
Ackton
Wheldale
Baghill Sta
Grove Town
Carleton
Cridling Stubbs
Whitley
West Cowick
East Cowick
Rawcliffe Bridge
Goole Fields
Marshland
Warmfield
Streethouse
Sharlston
Featherstone
Purston Jaglin
Great Heck
Pollington
Garthorpe
Fockerby
Burton Stather
Burton upon Stather
Crofton
Sharlston
Wentbridge
Little Smeaton
Walden Stubbs
Pinkerton Green
Goole Moors
Luddington
Aire & Calder Navigation
0 2 4 6 miles
0 2 4 6 8 10 km

F
G
H
J
K
1
2
3
4
5
6
7
SCARBOROUGH
Cromer Point
Scalby
Hackness
Suffield
Silpho
Langdale End
Wrench Green
Everley
Newby
Barrowcliff
Irton Moor
Falsgrave
South Bay
Black Rocks
Wykeham Forest
West Ayton
East Ayton
Hutton Buscel
Sawdon
Osgodby
Cayton Bay
Eastfield
Crossgates
Irton
Seamer
Cayton
Ruston
Wykeham
Brompton
Snainton
Lebberston
Gristhorpe
The Wyke
Filey Brigg
Filey
Filey Bay
Flixton
Folkton
Staxton
Willerby
The Carrs
Muston
West Flotmanby
Potter Brompton
Ganton
Sherburn
East Heslerton
West Heslerton
Hunmanby
Sherburn Wold
Fordon
Reighton
Reighton Sands
Speeton
Crab Rocks
Buckton
Bempton
Flamborough
Flamborough Head
Marton
Sewerby
Foxholes
Wold Newton
Burton Fleming
Grindale
Butterwick
Weaverthorpe
Helperthorpe
Octon
Thwing
East Lutton
West Lutton
Grindalythe
Swaythorpe
Boynton
Bridlington
Langtoft
Rudston
Gypsey Race
Cowlam Manor
Roman Road
Carnaby
Bessingby
West Hill
Hilderthorpe
Haisthorpe
Wilsthorpe
West End
Kilham
Thornholme
Carnaby Moor
Ruston Parva
Burton Agnes
BRIDLINGTON BAY
Harpham
Fraisthorpe
Garton-on-the-Wolds
Lowthorpe
Nafferton
Gransmoor
Barmston
Wetwang
Elmswell
Driffield
Lissett
Great Kelk
Little Driffield
Kelleythorpe
Wansford
Gembling
Ulrome
Tibthorpe Wold
Foston on the Wolds
Tibthorpe
Kirkburn
Eastburn
Southburn
Skerne
Skipsea
Upton
Old
Beeford
Skipsea Brough
Sunderlandwick
Brigham
Church End
North Frodingham
Dunnington
Bainton
Hutton Cranswick
Rotsea
North End
Atwick
Cawkeld
Hempholme
Bewholme
Middleton-on-the-Wolds
Watton
Kilnwick
Watton Carrs
Hornsea
Lund
Beswick
Burshill
Little Burton
Lockington
Brandesburton
Seaton
Thorpe
Aike
Holme on the Wolds
South Dalton
Scorborough
Leven
Catwick
Sigglesthorne
Goxhill
Little Catwick
Rolston
Mappleton
Etton
New Arram
Arram
Little Hatfield
Leconfield
Great Hatfield
Great Cowden
Gardham
Cherry Burton
Routh
Long Riston
Arras
Tickton
Rise
North End
Withernwick
Molescroft
Arnold
Bishop Burton
New Ellerby
BEVERLEY
Weel
Skirlaugh
Bishop Burton Wold
Marton
Old Ellerby
West Newton
Aldbrough
East Newton
Woodmansey
Walkington
Wawne
Etherdwick Grange
North Newbald
South Newbald
Thearne
Swine
Rimton
Bentley
Dunswell
High Bransholme
Coniston
Barton
Grimston
Risby
High Hunsley
Bransholme
Ganstead
Thirtleby
Sproatley
Humbleton
Hilston
Skidby
Little Weighton
Fitling
Sutton-on-Hull
Wyton
Lelley
Danthorpe
Owstwick
Tunstall
Cottingham
Riplingham
Eppleworth
Newland
Sutton Ings
Bilton
Elstronwick
Haltemprice Farm
Burton Pidsea
North End
South Cave
Willerby
KINGSTON UPON HULL
Preston
East End
Roos
Dairy House
Waxholme
Brantingham
Kirk Ella
Marfleet
Wadworth Hill
West Ella
Anlaby
Hedon
Ellerton
Brough
Welton
Swanland
Rimswell
Burstwick
Withernsea
Halsham
East End
Melton
Thorngumbald
North Ferriby
Camerton
Ryehill
Keyingham
Hessle
Paull
Hollym
Whitton Ness
Humber Bridge
Paull Holme
Winestead
Redcliff Channel
Paull Holme Sands
East Halton Skitter
New Holland
Holmpton
Read's Island
Barton-upon-Humber
Barrow Haven
Barrow Hann
Goxhill
Patrington
Cherry Cobb Sands
Out Newton
South Ferriby
Barrow upon Humber
South End
Salthaugh Grange
Patrington Haven
Welwick
Weeton
NORTH LINCOLNSHIRE
Foulholme Sands
East Halton
Sunk Island
Skeffling
Easington
Winteringham
Horkstow
Thornton Curtis
Killingholme
Old Hall
Skeffling Clays
Roxby
Burnham
South Killingholme
Immingham Dock
Sunk Island
WOLDS
RIDING
YORKSHIRE
HU
A165
A171
A170
A64
A1039
B1261
B1229
B1255
B1259
B1253
B1249
A614
A166
A1079
A1035
A174
A164
A1174
A1033
A15
A1077
B1242
B1362
B1244
52
40
13
12
11
14
15
16
25
17
18
20
10
5
2
3
4
1
6
7
8
9
19

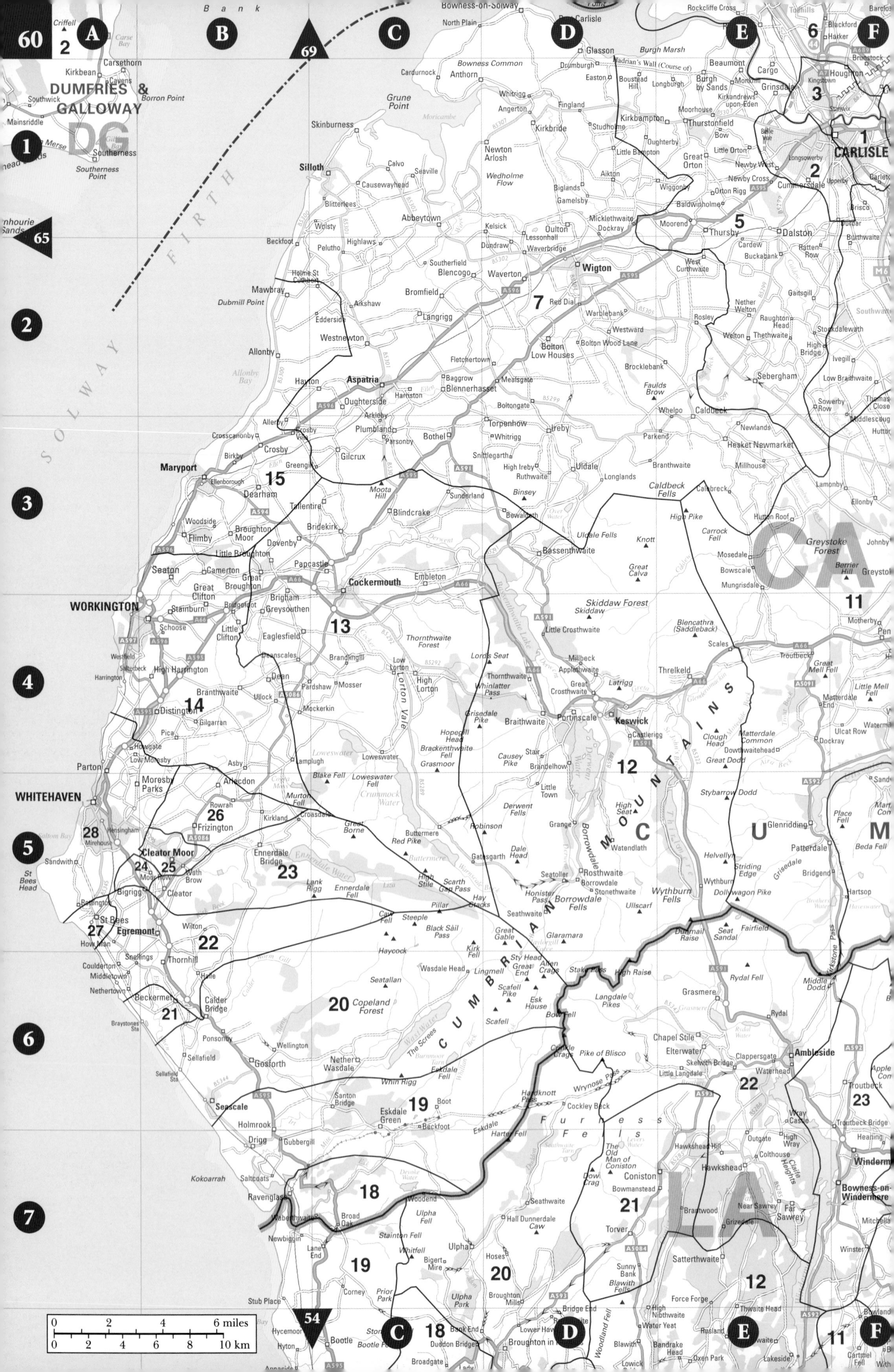
2
A
B
C
D
E
F
69
65
54
6
1
2
3
4
5
6
7
Criffell
Bank
Carse Bay
Carsethorn
Kirkbean
Cavens
DUMFRIES & GALLOWAY
DG
Borron Point
Southwick
Mainsriddle
Southerness
Southerness Point
Bowness-on-Solway
North Plain
Port Carlisle
Glasson
Burgh Marsh
Rockcliffe Cross
Todhills
Blackford
Harker
Barclose
Cardurnock
Anthorn
Bowness Common
Drumburgh
Hadrian's Wall (Course of)
Easton
Boustead Hill
Longburgh
Burgh by Sands
Beaumont
Monkhill
Cargo
Grinsdale
Kingstown
Houghton
Brunstock
Stanwix
Kirkandrews-upon-Eden
Moorhouse
Thurstonfield
Kirkbampton
Oughterby
Little Bampton
Bow
Little Orton
Belle Vue
CARLISLE
Longsowerby
Newby West
Great Orton
Newby Cross
Cummersdale
Upperby
Carleton
Grune Point
Whitrigg
Angerton
Fingland
Kirkbride
Studholme
Moricambe
Skinburness
Newton Arlosh
Wedholme Flow
Aikton
Wiggonby
Biglands
Gamelsby
Orton Rigg
Baldwinholme
Silloth
Calvo
Seaville
Causewayhead
Blitterlees
Abbeytown
Wolsty
Highlaws
Beckfoot
Pelutho
Kelsick
Dundraw
Lessonhall
Oulton
Micklethwaite
Dockray
Moorend
Thursby
Dalston
Brisco
Durdar
Cardew
Buckabank
Raiten Row
Blackwell
Waverbridge
Southerfield
Blencogo
Waverton
Wigton
West Curthwaite
Holme St Cuthbert
Mawbray
Dubmill Point
Aikshaw
Edderside
Bromfield
Langrigg
Red Dial
Warblebank
Westward
Rosley
Nether Welton
Raughton Head
Gaitsgill
Southwaite
Welton
Thethwaite
Stockdalewath
High Bridge
Ivegill
Westnewton
Allonby
Allonby Bay
Bolton Low Houses
Bolton Wood Lane
Brocklebank
Fletchertown
Baggrow
Blennerhasset
Mealsgate
Hayton
Aspatria
Oughterside
Harriston
Sebergham
Low Braithwaite
Faulds Brow
Arkleby
Boltongate
Whelpo
Caldbeck
Sowerby Row
Thomas Close
Middlesceugh
Allerby
Crosby Villa
Crosscanonby
Birkby
Crosby
Plumbland
Parsonby
Bothel
Torpenhow
Whitrigg
Ireby
Parkend
Newlands
Hesket Newmarket
Hutton
Maryport
Ellenborough
Greengill
Gilcrux
Snittlegarth
High Ireby
Ruthwaite
Uldale
Longlands
Branthwaite
Millhouse
Moota Hill
Sunderland
Binsey
Caldbeck Fells
Calebreck
Lamonby
Ellonby
Dearham
Tallentire
Blindcrake
Bewaldeth
Over Water
High Pike
Woodside
Flimby
Broughton Moor
Bridekirk
Dovenby
Uldale Fells
Knott
Carrock Fell
Hutton Roof
Greystoke Forest
Johnby
Little Broughton
Derwent
Bassenthwaite
Mosedale
Bowscale
Mungrisdale
Great Calva
Berrier Hill
Greystoke
CA
Seaton
Camerton
Papcastle
Great Clifton
Great Broughton
Cockermouth
Embleton
Skiddaw Forest
Skiddaw
WORKINGTON
Stainburn
Bridgefoot
Brigham
Greysouthen
Schoose
Little Clifton
Eaglesfield
Thornthwaite Forest
Little Crosthwaite
Bassenthwaite Lake
Blencathra (Saddleback)
Scales
Motherby
Penruddock
Westfield
Salterbeck
Harrington
High Harrington
Deanscales
Brandlingill
Low Lorton
Lords Seat
Millbeck
Applethwaite
Troutbeck
Great Mell Fell
Dean
Pardshaw
Mosser
High Lorton
Lorton Vale
Thornthwaite
Whinlatter Pass
Great Crosthwaite
Latrigg
Threlkeld
Little Mell Fell
Matterdale End
Branthwaite
Distington
Ullock
Mockerkin
Grisedale Pike
Braithwaite
Portinscale
Keswick
Gilgarran
Pica
Howgate
Low Moresby
Parton
Asby
Lamplugh
Loweswater
Hopegill Head
Brackenthwaite Fell
Grasmoor
Causey Pike
Stair
Brandelhow
Castlerigg
Derwent Water
Clough Head
Matterdale Common
Dowthwaitehead
Great Dodd
Ulcat Row
Dockray
Watermillock
WHITEHAVEN
Moresby Parks
Arlecdon
Rowrah
Frizington
Blake Fell
Loweswater Fell
Crummock Water
Murton Fell
Little Town
Stybarrow Dodd
Kirkland
Croasdale
Great Borne
Buttermere
Red Pike
Robinson
Derwent Fells
High Seat
Grange
Borrowdale
Watendlath
Glenridding
Place Fell
Patterdale
Beda Fell
Saltom Bay
Hensingham
Mirehouse
Cleator Moor
Wath Brow
Ennerdale Bridge
Ennerdale Water
Gatesgarth
Dale Head
Seatoller
Rosthwaite
Stonethwaite
Helvellyn
Striding Edge
Grisedale
Bridgend
St Bees Head
Sandwith
Moor Row
Cleator
Bigrigg
Lank Rigg
Ennerdale Fell
High Stile
Scarth Gap Pass
Hay Stacks
Honister Pass
Borrowdale Fells
Ullscarf
Wythburn Fells
Wythburn
Dollywagon Pike
Hartsop
Rottington
St Bees
Egremont
Pillar
Caw Fell
Steeple
Black Sail Pass
Seathwaite
Great Gable
Glaramara
Dunmail Raise
Seat Sandal
Fairfield
Wilton
How Man
Haycock
Kirk Fell
Sty Head
Great End
Allen Crags
Stake Pass
High Raise
Rydal Fell
Middle Dodd
Kirkstone Pass
Coulderton
Snellings
Middletown
Thornhill
Nethertown
Haile
Wasdale Head
Lingmell
Seatallan
Copeland Forest
Scafell Pike
Esk Hause
Langdale Pikes
Grasmere
Rydal
Beckermet
Calder Bridge
Braystones Sta
Bow Fell
Scafell
Ponsonby
Wellington
CUMBRIAN MOUNTAINS
Chapel Stile
Elterwater
Ambleside
Sellafield
Sellafield Sta
Gosforth
Nether Wasdale
The Screes
Wast Water
Burnmoor Tarn
Crinkle Crags
Pike of Blisco
Skelwith Bridge
Clappersgate
Little Langdale
Waterhead
Apple Tree
Eskdale Fell
Whin Rigg
Wrynose Pass
Troutbeck
Seascale
Santon Bridge
Hardknott Pass
Cockley Beck
Boot
Holmrook
Eskdale Green
Beckfoot
Eskdale
Harter Fell
Furness Fells
Wray Castle
Troutbeck Bridge
Drigg
Gubbergill
The Old Man of Coniston
Hawkshead Hill
Outgate
High Wray
Colthouse
Claife Heights
Windermere
Kokoarrah
Saltcoats
Devoke Water
Dow Crag
Coniston
Hawkshead
Ravenglass
Bowmanstead
Bowness-on-Windermere
Woodend
Seathwaite
Brantwood
Near Sawrey
Far Sawrey
Waberthwaite
Broad Oak
Ulpha Fell
Hall Dunnerdale
Caw
Torver
Grizedale
LA
Mitchelland
Newbiggin
Stainton Fell
Whitfell
Lane End
Bigert Mire
Ulpha
Hoses
Sunny Bank
Blawith Fells
Satterthwaite
Winster
Corney
Prior Park
Ulpha Park
Broughton Mills
Stub Place
Force Forge
Thwaite Head
Bridge End
High Nibthwaite
Water Yeat
Woodland Fell
Hycemoor
Bootle
Bootle Fell
Bank End
Lower Haw
Broughton in Furness
Duddon Bridge
Rusland
Blawith
Bandrake Head
Oxen Park
Lakeside
Cartmel Fell
Bowland
Hyton
Broadgate
Lowick
0 2 4 6 miles
0 2 4 6 8 10 km
A595
A596
A594
A597
A66
A5086
A591
A5091
A592
A593
A5084
A689
A7
A6
M6
B5307
B5302
B5305
B5299
B5300
B5301
B5292
B5289
B5344
B5343
B5285
B5286
B5322
SOLWAY FIRTH
1
2
3
5
7
15
13
14
12
11
26
28
24
25
23
22
27
21
20
19
18
U
M
C

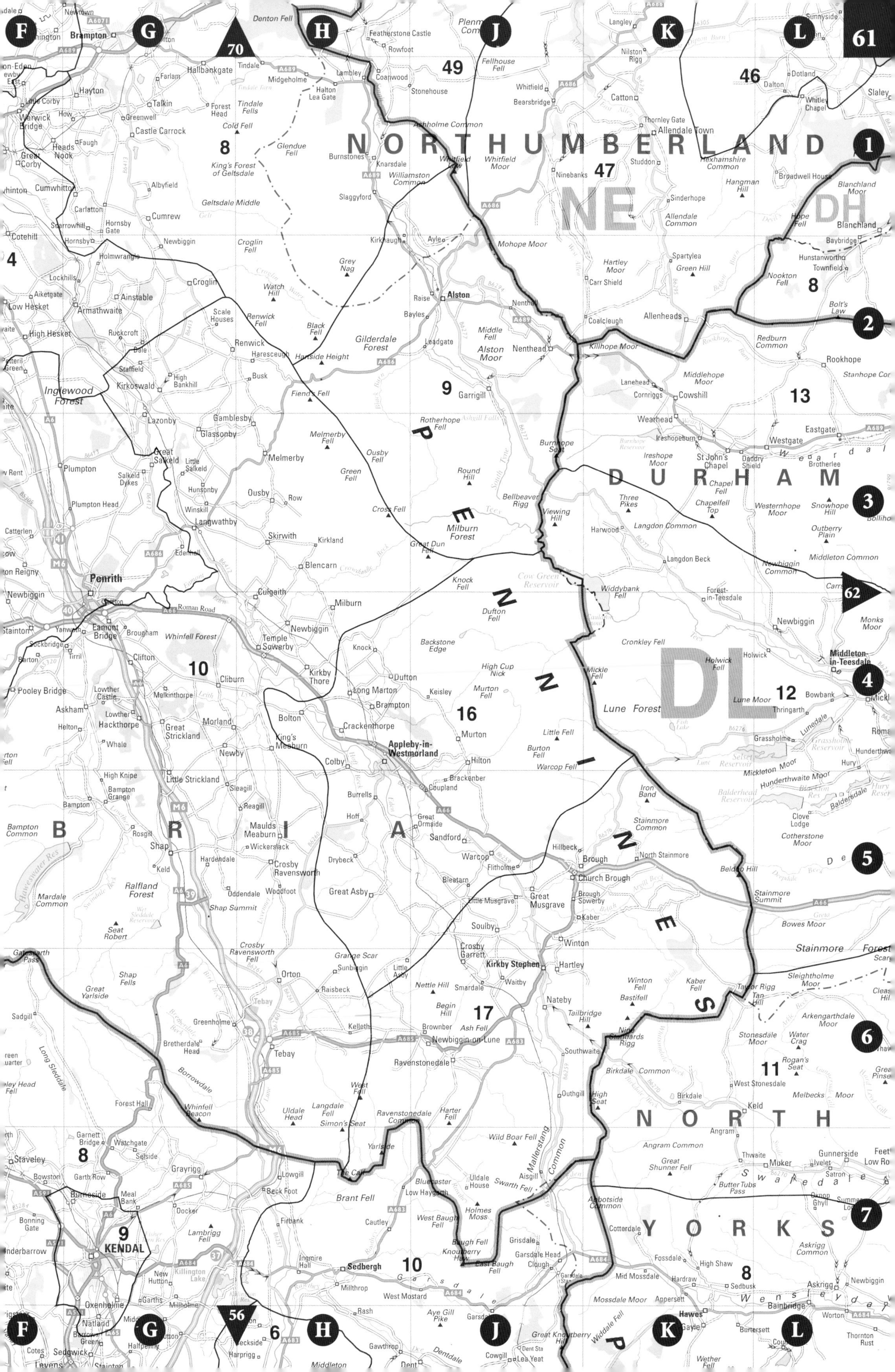
F
G
H
J
K
L
70
62
56
NORTHUMBERLAND
DURHAM
NORTH YORKS
BRIA
PENNINES
NE
DH
DL
Brampton
Denton Fell
Featherstone Castle
Rowfoot
Plenmeller Common
Langley
Nilston Rigg
Sunnyside
Dotland
Dalton
Whitley Chapel
Slaley
Newtown
Hallbankgate
Tindale
Farlam
Midgeholme
Lambley
Coanwood
Halton Lea Gate
Stonehouse
Fellhouse Fell
Whitfield
Bearsbridge
Catton
Thornley Gate
Allendale Town
Hayton
Talkin
Forest Head
Tindale Fells
Cold Fell
Warwick Bridge
Little Corby
How
Greenwell
Castle Carrock
Heads Nook
Faugh
Great Corby
Glendue Fell
Ashholme Common
Burnstones
Knarsdale
Whitfield Law
Whitfield Moor
Williamston Common
Ninebanks
Studdon
Hexhamshire Common
Broadwell House
Blanchland Moor
Blanchland
Hangman Hill
King's Forest of Geltsdale
Cumwhitton
Albyfield
Slaggyford
Sinderhope
Allendale Common
Geltsdale Middle
Carlatton
Cumrew
Hornsby Gate
Scarrowhill
Hornsby
Cotehill
Newbiggin
Croglin Fell
Kirkhaugh
Ayle
Mohope Moor
Hope Fell
Baybridge
Hunstanworth
Townfield
Holmwrangle
Grey Nag
Hartley Moor
Carr Shield
Spartylea
Green Hill
Nookton Fell
Lockhills
Croglin
Watch Hill
Alston
Raise
Nenthall
Aiketgate
Ainstable
Low Hesket
Armathwaite
Scale Houses
Renwick Fell
Black Fell
Bayles
Coalcleugh
Allenheads
Bolt's Law
High Hesket
Ruckcroft
Renwick
Gilderdale Forest
Leadgate
Middle Fell
Alston Moor
Nenthead
Killhope Moor
Redburn Common
Rookhope
Hartside Height
Harescough
Dale
Staffield
High Bankhill
Busk
Inglewood Forest
Kirkoswald
Fiend's Fell
Garrigill
Lanehead
Cornriggs
Cowshill
Middlehope Moor
Stanhope Common
Lazonby
Gamblesby
Glassonby
Melmerby Fell
Rotherhope Fell
Ashgill Falls
Wearhead
Ireshopeburn
Burnhope Seat
Burnhope Reservoir
Westgate
Eastgate
Great Salkeld
Little Salkeld
Melmerby
Ousby Fell
Green Fell
Round Hill
Ireshope Moor
St John's Chapel
Daddry Shield
Brotherlee
Plumpton
Salkeld Dykes
Hunsonby
Ousby
Row
Bellbeaver Rigg
Viewing Hill
Three Pikes
Chapel Fell
Chapelfell Top
Westernhope Moor
Snowhope Hill
Plumpton Head
Winskill
Cross Fell
Milburn Forest
Harwood
Langdon Common
Outberry Plain
Catterlen
Langwathby
Skirwith
Kirkland
Great Dun Fell
Langdon Beck
Newbiggin Common
Middleton Common
Edenhall
Blencarn
Knock Fell
Cow Green Reservoir
Widdybank Fell
Forest-in-Teesdale
Carrs
Penrith
Culgaith
Milburn
Dufton Fell
Newbiggin
Monks Moor
Roman Road
Whinfell Forest
Yanwath
Eamont Bridge
Brougham
Temple Sowerby
Cronkley Fell
Stainton
Sockbridge
Tirril
Barton
Clifton
Knock
Backstone Edge
Holwick
Holwick Fell
Middleton-in-Teesdale
Cliburn
High Cup Nick
Mickle Fell
Kirkby Thore
Dufton
Pooley Bridge
Lowther Castle
Melkinthorpe
Long Marton
Keisley
Murton Fell
Lune Forest
Lune Moor
Bowbank
Thringarth
Askham
Lowther
Hackthorpe
Great Strickland
Morland
Bolton
Brampton
Crackenthorpe
Murton
Little Fell
Helton
Whale
King's Meaburn
Appleby-in-Westmorland
Burton Fell
Grassholme
Grassholme Reservoir
Lunedale
Hunderthwaite
Newby
Colby
Hilton
Selset Reservoir
Mickleton Moor
Hury
Warcop Fell
High Knipe
Little Strickland
Brackenber
Coupland
Hunderthwaite Moor
Blackton Reservoir
Baldersdale
Balderhead Reservoir
Bampton Grange
Sleagill
Reagill
Burrells
Iron Band
Bampton
Hoff
Great Ormside
Clove Lodge
Bampton Common
Rosgill
Maulds Meaburn
Sandford
Stainmore Common
Cotherstone Moor
Shap
Wickerslack
Hillbeck
Warcop
Flitholme
Brough
North Stainmore
Haweswater Reservoir
Keld
Hardendale
Crosby Ravensworth
Drybeck
Church Brough
Beldoo Hill
Ralfland Forest
Mardale Common
Oddendale
Woodfoot
Great Asby
Bleatarn
Little Musgrave
Great Musgrave
Brough Sowerby
Stainmore Summit
Shap Summit
Wet Sleddale Reservoir
Kaber
Bowes Moor
Seat Robert
Soulby
Winton
Stainmore Forest
Crosby Ravensworth Fell
Grange Scar
Sunbiggin
Crosby Garrett
Kirkby Stephen
Hartley
Gatesgarth Pass
Shap Fells
Orton
Little Asby
Raisbeck
Nettle Hill
Smardale
Waitby
Winton Fell
Kaber Fell
Sleightholme Moor
Great Yarlside
Tebay
Begin Hill
Nateby
Bastifell
Taylor Rigg
Tan Hill
Sadgill
Greenholme
Tailbridge Hill
Nine Standards Rigg
Arkengarthdale Moor
Long Sleddale
Bretherdale Head
Kelleth
Brownber
Ash Fell
Newbiggin-on-Lune
Stonesdale Moor
Water Crag
Ravenstonedale
Southwaite
Rogan's Seat
Borrowdale
Birkdale Common
West Stonesdale
Melbecks Moor
West Fell
Outhgill
High Seat
Birkdale
Forest Hall
Whinfell Beacon
Uldale Head
Langdale Fell
Simon's Seat
Ravenstonedale Common
Harter Fell
Keld
Angram
Angram Common
Garnett Bridge
Watchgate
Selside
Wild Boar Fell
Mallerstang Common
Staveley
Grayrigg
Yarlside
The Calf
Lowgill
Great Shunner Fell
Thwaite
Muker
Gunnerside
Ivelet
Satron
Swaledale
Bowston
Garth Row
Bluecaster
Low Haygarth
Uldale House
Swarth Fell
Aisgill
Butter Tubs Pass
Oxnop Ghyll
Burneside
Meal Bank
Beck Foot
Brant Fell
Abbotside Common
Docker
Firbank
Holmes Moss
West Baugh Fell
Cotterdale
Askrigg Common
Bonning Gate
Lambrigg Fell
Cautley
Baugh Fell
Grisdale
KENDAL
Knoutberry Haw
Garsdale Head
Fossdale
High Shaw
Ingmire Hall
Sedbergh
Clough
East Baugh Fell
Mid Mossdale
Hardraw
Sedbusk
Askrigg
Newbiggin
New Hutton
Killington Lake
Garths
Millholme
Millthrop
Garsdale
Mossdale Moor
Appersett
Bainbridge
Wensleydale
Oxenholme
West Mostard
Rash
Aye Gill Pike
Widdale Fell
Hawes
Gayle
Burtersett
Worton
Natland
Great Knoutberry Hill
Thornton Rust
Sedgwick
Halfpenny
Beckside
Harprigg
Gawthrop
Dentdale
Cowgill
Dent Sta
Lea Yeat
Dent
Middleton
Wether Fell
Levens
Cotes
M6
A6
A66
A686
A689
A685
A683
A684
A69
A591
A65
A6071
A689
B6413
B6412
B6295
B6276
B6259
B6270
B6277
B6294
B6260
B6261
B5320
B5284
49
46
47
8
9
13
10
12
16
17
11
6
4
1
2
3
5
7

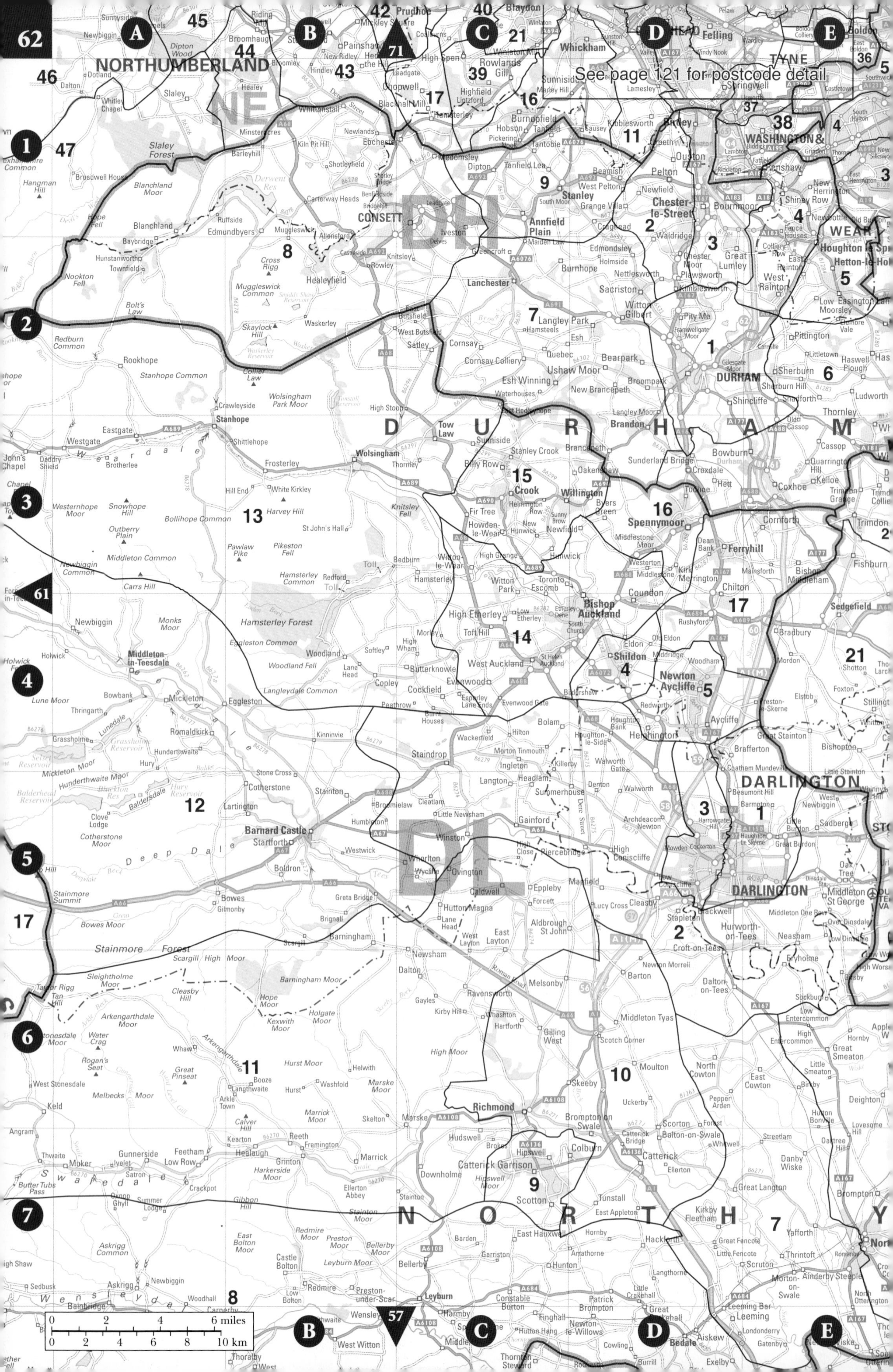
A
B
C
D
E
1
2
3
4
5
6
7
71
61
57
NORTHUMBERLAND
NE
DH
DL
DURHAM
DARLINGTON
TYNE
WEAR
NORTH
See page 121 for postcode detail
Prudhoe
Blaydon
Felling
Whickham
Riding Mill
Broomhaugh
Dipton Wood
Newbiggin
Dotland
Dalton
Whitley Chapel
Slaley
Healey
Whittonstall
Painshawfield
New Ridley
Hindley
Mickley Square
High Spen
Rowlands Gill
Chopwell
Highfield
Lintzford
Blackhall Mill
Hamsterley
Burnopfield
Hobson
Tanfield
Pickering Nook
Tantobie
Sunniside
Marley Hill
Lamesley
Springwell
Kibblesworth
Birtley
Washington
Ouston
Pelton
Beamish
West Pelton
Newfield
Chester-le-Street
Bournmoor
Shiney Row
New Herrington
Penshaw
Houghton le Spring
Hetton-le-Hole
Minsteracres
Slaley Forest
Barleyhill
Kiln Pit Hill
Newlands
Ebchester
Medomsley
Shotleyfield
Dipton
Tanfield Lea
Stanley
South Moor
Grange Villa
Craghead
Annfield Plain
Consett
Leadgate
Iveston
Delves
Knitsley
Greencroft
Maiden Law
Broadwell House
Blanchland Moor
Derwent Res
Carterway Heads
Blanchland
Ruffside
Edmundbyers
Muggleswick
Allensford
Castleside
Rowley
Baybridge
Hunstanworth
Townfield
Cross Rigg
Healeyfield
Muggleswick Common
Nookton Fell
Bolt's Law
Skaylock Hill
Waskerley
East Butsfield
West Butsfield
Satley
Cornsay
Cornsay Colliery
Lanchester
Langley Park
Hamsteels
Esh
Quebec
Ushaw Moor
Esh Winning
Bearpark
Waterhouses
Broompark
New Brancepeth
Edmondsley
Holmside
Burnhope
Nettlesworth
Sacriston
Witton Gilbert
Chester Moor
Plawsworth
Kimblesworth
Great Lumley
West Rainton
East Rainton
Pity Me
Framwellgate Moor
Durham
Gilesgate Moor
Carrville
Sherburn
Sherburn Hill
Shincliffe
Shadforth
Pittington
Littletown
Haswell Plough
Low Moorsley
Easington Lane
Ludworth
Thornley
Old Cassop
Cassop
Quarrington Hill
Kelloe
Coxhoe
Trimdon Grange
Trimdon
Bowburn
Croxdale
Hett
Tudhoe
Sunderland Bridge
Brandon
Langley Moor
Brancepeth
Redburn Common
Rookhope
Stanhope Common
Collier Law
Crawleyside
Stanhope
Wolsingham Park Moor
High Stoop
East Hedleyhope
Tow Law
Sunniside
Stanley Crook
Billy Row
Crook
Willington
Oakenshaw
Spennymoor
Middlestone Moor
Byers Green
Newfield
Westgate
Eastgate
Weardale
Daddry Shield
Brotherlee
Shittlehope
Frosterley
Wolsingham
Thornley
St John's Chapel
Westernhope Moor
Snowhope Hill
Hill End
White Kirkley
Harvey Hill
Bollihope Common
Knitsley Fell
Fir Tree
Helmington Row
Howden-le-Wear
New Hunwick
Sunny Brow
Hunwick
High Grange
St John's Hall
Outberry Plain
Middleton Common
Pawlaw Pike
Pikeston Fell
Newbiggin Common
Carrs Hill
Bedburn
Hamsterley
Witton-le-Wear
Hamsterley Common
Redford
Witton Park
Toronto
Escomb
Bishop Auckland
Westerton
Middlestone
Kirk Merrington
Dean Bank
Ferryhill
Mainsforth
Bishop Middleham
Fishburn
Cornforth
Chilton
Coundon
Hamsterley Forest
Monks Moor
High Etherley
Low Etherley
Etherley Dene
South Church
Rushyford
Sedgefield
Bradbury
Newbiggin
Holwick
Middleton-in-Teesdale
Eggleston Common
Woodland
Woodland Fell
Morley
Toft Hill
High Wham
Softley
Lane Head
Butterknowle
West Auckland
St Helen Auckland
Eldon
Old Eldon
Shildon
Middridge
Newton Aycliffe
Woodham
Mordon
Shotton
Lune Moor
Bowbank
Thringarth
Mickleton
Eggleston
Langleydale Common
Copley
Cockfield
Evenwood
Evenwood Gate
Esperley Lane Ends
Peathrow
Burnt Houses
Bolam
Redworth
Heighington
Houghton Bank
Houghton-le-Side
Aycliffe
Preston-le-Skerne
Elstob
Foxton
Stillington
Lunedale
Grassholme
Grassholme Reservoir
Selset Reservoir
Romaldkirk
Hunderthwaite
Kinninvie
Staindrop
Wackerfield
Hilton
Morton Tinmouth
Ingleton
Killerby
Walworth Gate
Great Stainton
Brafferton
Bishopton
Mickleton Moor
Hunderthwaite Moor
Balderhead Reservoir
Blackton Res
Baldersdale
Hury Reservoir
Hury
Stone Cross
Cotherstone
Lartington
Stainton
Brommielaw
Cleatlam
Langton
Headlam
Summerhouse
Denton
Walworth
Coatham Mundeville
Little Stainton
Beaumont Hill
Barmpton
Whinny Hill
West Newbiggin
Sadberge
Clove Lodge
Cotherstone Moor
Barnard Castle
Startforth
Humbleton
Little Newsham
Winston
Gainford
Archdeacon Newton
Harrowgate Hill
Haughton le Skerne
Great Burdon
Little Burdon
Deep Dale
Westwick
Whorlton
Wycliffe
Ovington
High Close
Piercebridge
High Coniscliffe
Cockerton
Mowden
Darlington
Middleton St George
Oak Tree
Boldron
Bowes
Gilmonby
Stainmore Summit
Bowes Moor
Greta Bridge
Brignall
Caldwell
Eppleby
Forcett
Manfield
Lucy Cross
Cleasby
Low Coniscliffe
Stapleton
Blackwell
Hurworth-on-Tees
Neasham
Middleton One Row
Over Dinsdale
Low Dinsdale
Hutton Magna
Lane Head
West Layton
East Layton
Aldbrough St John
Croft-on-Tees
Stainmore Forest
Scargill
Barningham
Newsham
Dalton
Newton Morrell
Barton
Dalton-on-Tees
Eryholme
Girsby
Sockburn
Tan Hill
Sleightholme Moor
Scargill High Moor
Cleasby Hill
Barningham Moor
Hope Moor
Holgate Moor
Kexwith Moor
Melsonby
Ravensworth
Gayles
Kirby Hill
Whashton
Hartforth
Gilling West
Scotch Corner
Middleton Tyas
Low Entercommon
High Entercommon
Great Smeaton
Hornby
Arkengarthdale Moor
Water Crag
Whaw
Arkengarthdale
Stonesdale Moor
Rogan's Seat
Great Pinseat
Booze
Langthwaite
Hurst Moor
Helwith
High Moor
Moulton
North Cowton
East Cowton
Little Smeaton
Birkby
Deighton
West Stonesdale
Melbecks Moor
Hurst
Washfold
Marske Moor
Skeeby
Uckerby
Pepper Arden
Keld
Arkle Town
Marrick Moor
Skelton
Marske
Richmond
Brompton on Swale
Scorton
Bolton-on-Swale
Whitwell
Hutton Bonville
Lovesome Hill
Angram
Calver Hill
Reeth
Fremington
Kearton
Healaugh
Hudswell
Brokes
Hipswell
Colburn
Catterick Bridge
Catterick
Ellerton
Streetlam
Danby Wiske
Oaktree Hill
Thwaite
Muker
Ivelet
Gunnerside
Feetham
Low Row
Grinton
Harkerside Moor
Marrick
Swaledale
Satron
Crackpot
Downholme
Catterick Garrison
Hipswell Moor
Great Langton
Brompton
Butter Tubs Pass
Oxnop Ghyll
Summer Lodge
Gibbon Hill
Ellerton Abbey
Stainton
Stainton Moor
Scotton
Tunstall
East Appleton
Kirkby Fleetham
Yafforth
Northallerton
Askrigg Common
Redmire Moor
Preston Moor
Bellerby Moor
Barden
East Hauxwell
Hornby
Great Fencote
Little Fencote
Thrintoft
East Bolton Moor
Castle Bolton
Leyburn Moor
Garriston
Arrathorne
Hackforth
Scruton
Romanby
High Shaw
Newbiggin
Sedbusk
Askrigg
Low Bolton
Redmire
Preston-under-Scar
Bellerby
Hunton
Langthorne
Ainderby Steeple
Morton-on-Swale
North Otterington
Wensleydale
Bainbridge
Woodhall
Carperby
Wensley
Leyburn
Constable Burton
Patrick Brompton
Little Crakehall
Great Crakehall
Leeming Bar
Leeming
Harmby
Finghall
Hutton Hang
Newton-le-Willows
Aiskew
Bedale
Londonderry
Gatenby
West Witton
Middleham
Thornton Steward
Cowling
Burrill
Exelby
Thoralby
0 2 4 6 miles
0 2 4 6 8 10 km

F
G
H
J
K
same scale as main map
1
2
3
4
5
6
7
Mulgrave
Hinderwell
Runswick Bay
Kettle Ness
Kettleness
Goldsborough
Sandsend Ness
Lythe
East Barnby
West Barnby
Sandsend
Whitby
Saltwick Bay
East Row
21
Dunsley
Newholm
Hutton Mulgrave
Ruswarp
Briggswath
Aislaby
A171
Egton Low Moor
Sleights
Stainsacre
High Hawsker
Sneaton
Low Hawsker
Ugglebarnby
Ness Point (North Cheek)
Sneatonthorpe
Raw
Robin Hood's Bay
Fylingthorpe
Grosmont
Egton Bridge
Littlebeck
Sleights
Moor
22
Falling Foss
Low Moor
Beck Hole
Thomason Foss
Old Peak (South Cheek)
Ravenscar
Goathland
A169
Flask Inn
Fylingdales Moor
Hunt House
YO
Burn Howe Rigg
Staintondale
NORTH
YORKS
Lockton High Moor
Allerston High Moor
Cloughton Newlands
Cloughton Wyke
Harwood Dale
Saltergate
Broxa Forest
Cloughton
Burniston
Cromer Point
13
Silpho
Lockton Low Moor
18
Levisham
Suffield
Scalby Ness Rocks
Broxa
Langdale End
Hackness
Scalby
Toll
A165
UNDERLAND
SR
Seaham
Nose's Point
Hawthorn
Easington Colliery
Easington
8
Horden
Peterlee
Dene Mouth
Blackhall Colliery
Blackhall Rocks
Hesleden
High Hesleden
Eden Vale
Monk Hesleden
Crimdon Park
Hutton Henry
Sheraton
Hart
A179
A1049
24
The Headland
27
High Throston
26
Hartlepool Bay
Elwick
Dalton Piercy
Rift House
HARTLEPOOL
Tees
Bay
Seaton Carew
25
Embleton
Brierton
22
Claxton Grange
Greatham
Newton Bewley
Wolviston
Billingham
Cowpen Bewley
Haverton Hill
Seal Sands
TS
Coatham
Redcar
Warrenby
10
Dormanstown
A1042
Marske-by-the-Sea
Kirkleatham
20
23
2
Salt Holme
Port Clarence
MIDDLESBROUGH
19
18
South Bank
Grangetown
Lazenby
Yearby
Wilton
11
New Marske
Upleatham
Saltburn-by-the-Sea
Warsett Hill
Brotton
Skinningrove
6
1
3
Normanby
Eston
Dunsdale
Skelton
(Skelton-in-Cleveland)
REDCAR
AND
CLEVELAND
Carlin How
Loftus
Boulby
Staithes
North Skelton
Kilton
Kilton Thorpe
Easington
13
Dalehouse
Port Mulgrave
Hinderwell
Roxby
Runswick Bay
Kettle Ness
MIDDLESBROUGH
Acklam
Ormesby
Thornaby-on-Tees
17
5
4
A171
Nunthorpe
7
Pinchinthorpe
14
Guisborough
Margrove Park
12
Boosbeck
Lingdale
Charltons
Stanghow
Lockwood Beck Res.
Liverton
Handale
Borrowby
Newton Mulgrave
Ellerby
Lythe
Sandsend Ness
Kettleness
Goldsborough
Sandsend
East Barnby
West Barnby
Mickleby
Whitby
Hemlington
Stainton
Thornton
Coulby Newham
Maltby
8
Newby
Hilton
Newton under Roseberry
Roseberry Topping
Gisborough Moor
Freebrough Hill
Moorsholm
Moorsholm Moor
Roxby Low Moor
Scaling
Scaling Reservoir
Roxby High Moor
Lealholm Moor
Danby Beacon
Danby Low Moor
Commondale Moor
Commondale
Ugthorpe
East Row
Dunsley
Newholm
Hutton Mulgrave
Ruswarp
Briggswath
Aislaby
Egton Low Moor
Stainsacre
Sneaton
Low Hawsker
Ugglebarnby
Sleights
Langbaurgh
Great Ayton
Little Ayton
Easby Moor
Seamer
Middleton-on-Leven
15
Crathorne
Hutton Rudby
Rudby
Enterpen
Stokesley
A173
Easby
Kildale
Kildale Moor
Battersby
Baysdale
Danby
Castleton
Ainthorpe
Houlsyke
Stonegate
Lealholm
21
Esk Dale
Egton
Grosmont
Egton Bridge
Glaisdale
Westerdale
Brawith
Great Broughton
Kirkby
Ingleby Greenhow
Great Busby
Carlton-in-Cleveland
9
Potto
East Rounton
West Lees
Faceby
Whorlton
Swainby
Ingleby Arncliffe
Ingleby Cross
Cleveland Tontine Inn
Urra
Round Hill
Baysdale Moor
Westerdale Moor
Castleton Ridge
Danby High Moor
Street
Glaisdale Rigg
Glaisdale Moor
Egton High Moor
Pike Hill Moss
Littlebeck
22
Moor
Beck Hole
Goathland
Falling Foss
Flask Inn
Seave Green
Chop Gate
Cockayne Ridge
Cockayne
Farndale Moor
Rosedale Moor
Wheeldale Moor
Hunt House
Fylingdales Moor
Burn Howe Rigg
YO
Whorlton Moor
Osmotherley
Snilesworth Moor
Arnsgill Ridge
Bilsdale West Moor
Bilsdale East Moor
Church Houses
Hill Cottages
Thorgill
Rosedale Abbey
Lockton High Moor
Allerston High Moor
Ellerbeck
Thimbleby
Jeater Houses
Black Hambleton
Over Silton
Nether Silton
O
R
K
S
H
I
R
E
Fangdale Beck
Rudland Rigg
Low Mill
Blakey Ridge
Spaunton Moor
Hartoft End
Cropton Forest
Toll
Saltergate
Lockton Low Moor
13
Arden Great Moor
Helmsley Moor
62
Bransdale
Keldy Castle
18
Levisham
7
Kepwick
Cowesby
Boltby Moor
Kirby Knowle
Gillamoor
Lastingham
Spaunton
Fadmoor
Appleton-le-Moors
Newton-on-Rawcliffe
Newton Dale
Lockton
Stain Dale
Dalby Forest
Cawthorn
High Kingthorpe
Kirkbymoorside
58
CLEVELAND HILLS
Hambleton Hills
Cow Ridge

A
B
C
D
E
1
2
3
4
5
6
7
67
66
19
6
26
8
9
Ailsa Craig
SOUTH
CARRICK
AYRSHIRE
KA
DUMFRIES AN
THE RHINNS OF GALLOWAY
THE MACHARS
LUCE BAY
LOCH RYAN
Girvan
Dipple
Low Craighead
Chapeldonan
Grangeston
Dailly
Old Dailly
Penkill
Houdston
Saugh Hill
Glendoune
Glendrissaig
Pinminnoch
Black Neuk
Kennedy's Pass
Ardwell
Grey Hill
Hadyard Hill
Glengennet
North Balloch
South Balloch
Barr
Changue Forest
Nick of the Balloch Pass
Garleffin Fell
Craig
Tairlaw
Maratz Hill
Craigengillan
Craiglee
Waterhead
Shiel Hill
Shalloch
Shalloch on Minnoch
Polmaddie Hill
Pinmore
Lendalfoot
Carleton Fishery
Aldons
Daljarrock
Pinwherry
Poundland
Colmonell
Dalreoch
Craigneil
Bennane Head
Knockdolian
Mains of Tig
Ballantrae Bay
Ballantrae
Glenapp Castle
Downan Point
Auchairne
Balkissock
Glenduisk
Ballochmorrie
Black Clauchrie
Shiel Hill
Barrhill
Eldrick
Lochton
Corwar House
Kirriereoch Hill
Merrick
Garwall Hill
Palgowan
Craignaw
Buchan Hill
Glen Trool Lodge
Smyrton
Craigie Fell
Benerairds
Milljoan Hill
Altimeg Hill
Carlock Hill
Glen App
Finnarts Point
Milleur Point
Chirmorrie
Drumlamford House
Glentrool
Bargrennan
Mulldonoch
Lamachan Hill
Larg Hill
Millfore
Markdhu
Miltonise
Glenwhilly
Clachaneasy
Larg
Polbae
Cordorcan
Knockville
Knowe
Garlick Hill
Urrall Fell
Barnhills
North Cairn
Dalnigap
Cairnryan
Cairn Point
Kirkcolm
Corsewall
Ervie
Airies
Penninghame
Boreland
Garlies Castle
Dallash
Glenrazie
Carseriggan
Cumloden
Artfield Fell
Challoch
Minnigaff
Newton Stewart
Creebridge
Bargaly
Blackcraig
St Mary's Croft
Soleburn
Leswalt
Brad Fell
Balminnoch
Tarf Bridge
Culvennan Fell
Benfield
Nether Barr
Palnure
Innermessan
New Luce
Shennanton
Auchmantle
Galdenoch
Lochinch Castle
Craig Fell
Stranraer
Castle Kennedy
Dunragit Moor
Carscreugh
Barlae
Craighlaw
Kirkcowan
Barraer
Baltersan
Spittal
Portslogan
Causeway End
Carsegowan
Barholm Mains
Creetown
Whiteleys
Lochans
Dunragit
Whitecairn
Glenluce
Spittal
Wigtown Sands
Cairn Pat
Genoch
Whitecrook
Knock Moss
Knock Fell
Culquhirk
Black Head
Dinvin
Portpatrick
Kildrochet House
Colfin
Genoch Square
Sands of Luce
Milton
Bladnoch
Wigtown
Crow's Nest
Awhirk
Stoneykirk
Auchenmalg
Culmalzie
Braehead
Kirkinner
Culshabbin
Barnbarroch
Port of Spittal Bay
Balgreggan
Sandhead
Alticry
Barrachan
Whauphill
Stewarton
Loch Head
Elrig
Cairngarroch Bay
Money Head
Kirkland of Longcastle
Airyhassen
Sorbie
Clachanmore
Ardwell
Chapel Rossan
Mochrum
Barr Point
Barwinnock
Port William
Cults
Logan
Balgowan
Castlewigg
Mull of Logan
Barsalloch Point
Monreith
Monreith Bay
Craigdhu
Whithorn
Port Logan
Terally
Cairndoon
Glasserton
Portyerrock
Fell of Carleton
Kilstay
Drummore
Kidsdale
Isle of Whithorn
Laggantalluch Head
Kirkmaiden
Cailiness Point
St. Ninian's Cave
Cutcloy
Damnaglaur
Maryport
Burrow Head
Crammag Head
Dunman
Nick of Kindram
East Tarbet
West Tarbet
Mull of Galloway
A77
A714
A75
A747
A716
A746
A751
A712
B734
B7027
0 2 4 6 miles
0 2 4 6 8 10 km

F
G
H
J
K
65
68
69
60
11
14
1
2
3
4
5
6
7
GALLOWAY
DUMFRIES
Windy Standard 698
Countam 475
Cairnkinna Hill 552
Breconside
Gateslack
Benbrack 448
Drumjohn
Cairnsmore of Carsphairn 797
Dodd Hill 498
Colt Hill 598
Countam 500
Auchenbrack
Holm of Drumlanrig
Carronbridge
Rashy Height 380
Queensberry 697
Wee Queensberry 512
Minnygap Height 399
Black Shoulder 688
Benbuie
Bail Hill 516
Torbraehead 400
Auchenhessnane
Dabton
Thornhill
Gatelawbridge
Brochloch
Craig of Knockgray 383
Bennan
Burnhead
Penpont
Keir Mill
Forest of Ae
Garryhorn
Carsphairn
Knockgray
Marscalloch Hill 381
Wether Hill
Cornharrow Hill
Clonrae
Tynron
Great Hill 353
Bardennoch
Carroch
Closeburn
Croalchapel
Moniaive
Kirkland
Craigdarroch
Crawfordton
Keir Hills
Ae Village
Dalshangan
Glencrosh
Crossford
Barndennoch
Dalswinton Common
Blackwood
Parkgate
Forrest Lodge
Wether Hill 385
Castlefairn
Glenhead
Auldgirth
Burnhead
Holmhead
Bogrie Hill 432
Crawston Hill 217
Knocknalling
Lochurr
Sundaywell
Dunscore
Allanton
Friars Carse
Dalswinton
Glenae
Meikle Millyea 746
Waterhead
Milton
Stroquhan
Duncow
Amisfield Town
Corriedoo
Blackcraig Hill 406
Craigenputtock
Speddoch
Kirkton
Tinwald
St John's Town of Dalry
Garroch
Bogue
Blackcraig
Drumwhirn
Newtonairds
Holywood
Locharbriggs
Glenlee
Bennan 381
Garcrogo Forest
Knocklearn
Slongaber
Skeoch Hill
Gribton
New Bridge
New Galloway
Balmaclellan
Gibbshill
Margreig
Scaur
Terregles
Lincluden
Lochar Moss
Clatteringshaws
Cairnsmore of Dee 493
Larglear Hill 282
Corsock
398
Glen
Shawhead
Maxwelltown
Noblehill
Henderland
Cargenbridge
Forest Drive (summer only)
Merkland
Crofts
Brae
Lochfoot
Goldielea
Kingholm Quay
Round Fell 402
Fell of Fleet 471
Shaw Hill 385
Bennan Cottage
Toll
Drumrash
Glenlair
Square Point
Brooklands
Crocketford or Ninemile Bar
Dalskairth
Cargen
Netherwood
Mossdale
Parton
Walton Park
Kirkpatrick Durham
Milton
Mabie
Gillfoot
Kelton
Auchencloy Hill 209
Airie Hill 291
Slogarie
Springholm
Whinny Hill
Beeswing
Gleneaple
Craig
Auchendolly
Hermitage
Stonehouse
Lotus Hill 321
Kirkconnell
Shambellie
Crossmichael
Old Bridge of Urr
Clarebrand
Mollance
Kirkgunzeon
Kinharvie
New Abbey
Townhead of Greenlaw
Haugh of Urr
Glenlochar
White Top of Culreoch 344
Laurieston
Darngarroch
Hillowton
Cuil Hill
Criffell 569
Castle Douglas
Buchan
Craignair
Dalbeattie
Castramont
Bridge of Dee
Glenquicken Moor
Glengap
Low Barlay
Rusko
Rhonehouse (Kelton Hill)
Dildawn
Breoch
Kirkbean
Carsethorn
Argrennan House
Gelston
Palnackie
Dalbeattie Forest
Cavens
Borron Point
Glen
Lauchentyre
Ringford
Caulkerbush
Southwick
Gatehouse of Fleet
Barcaple
Airieland
Barnbarroch
Fairgirth
Mainsriddle
Cairnharrow 456
Valleyfield
Screel Hill 343
Kippford (Scaur)
Anwoth
Netherthird
Bengairn 391
Sandyhills
Preston Merse
Ardwall
Barwhinnock
Kirkdale House
Cardoness
Girthon
Twynholm
Tongland
Colvend
Mersehead Sands
Southerness
Southerness Point
Cumstoun
Rockcliffe
Port o' Warren
Sandgreen
Barharrow
Langlands
Castlehill Point
Fleet Bay
High Borgue
Auchencairn
Almorness Point
Lennox Plunton
Kirkcudbright
Hestan Island
Barnhourie Sands
Auchencairn Bay
Murray's Isles
Islands of Fleet
Knockbrex
Bombie
Bankhead
Hazlefield
Balcary Point
Ardwall Island
Borgue
St Mary's Isle
Auchnabony
Rascarrel
Barlocco Island
Dundrennan
Rascarrel Bay
Kirkandrews
Orroland
Townhead
Barlocco Bay
Senwick
Ringdoo Point
Borness
Ross
Balmae
Port Mary
Abbey Head
Little Ross
Kirkcudbright Bay
WIGTOWN BAY
SOLWAY
NITHSDALE
Seaton
Great Clifton
WORKINGTON
Westfield
A713
A702
A76
A712
A762
A75
A711
A755
A745
A710
A701
A780
A756
A596
B729
B7000
B7075
B794
B795
B796
B727
B736
B793
B725

A
B
C
D
E
1
2
3
4
5
6
7
ARGYLL
AND
BUTE
PA
28
NORTH
AYRSHIRE
KA
27
73
9
Bellochantuy
Killocraw
Corrylach
Lussa Loch
Saddell
Bunlarie
Saddell Bay
Sgreadan Hill
397
Ugadale Point
Tangy
Ballochgair
Westport
Skeroblingarry
Drumgarve
Glen Lussa
Low Ballevain
Calliburn
Machrihanish Bay
Kilchenzie
Peninver
Ardnacross Bay
East Darlochan
A83
Kilmichael
CAMPBELTOWN
Drumore
Campbeltown
(Ceann Loch
Chille Chiarain)
Machrihanish
Dalivaddy
Witchburn
Davaar Island
Drumlemble
B843
Kilkerran
Davaar
Chiscan
Glenramskill
Knocknaha
Kilchrist
New Orleans
Beinn Ghuilean
352
The Slate
385
Oatfield
Cnoc Moy
446
Killellan
312
Arinarach Hill
Largybaan
273
Cnoc Reamhar
Cnoc Odhar
277
Conie Glen
Glen Kerran
Feochaig
Ru Stafnish
Sheanachie
Glen Breackerie
Brocklate
Keprigan
Kildavie
Strone Glen
Machariochi
Polliwilline Bay
Beinn na Lice
428
Carrine
Southend
Garveld
Keil
Feorlan
Carskey Bay
Mull of Kintyre
Borgadelmore Point
Sanda Sound
Sheep Island
Sanda Island
Tormore
Ballymichael
512
Beinn
Clauchlands P
Torbeg
Shiskine
Cnoc a' Chapuill
417
Benlister Glen
Glenkiln
Lamlash
Lamlash Bay
Holy Isla
A841
Blackwaterfoot
Drumadoon Bay
Kilpatrick
Brown Head
458
Tighvein
Kingscross Po
Kingscross
Knockenkelly
Whiting Bay
Kiscadale
Glen Scorrodale
Whiting Bay
Ashdale
Largymore
Corriecravie
Largybeg
Largybeg Point
Sliddery
Dippen
Kilmory
Levencorroch
Dippin Head
Lagg
Shannochie
Kildonan
Bennan Head
Sound of Pladda
Pladda
Ailsa Craig
Bennane Head
Ballantrae Bay
Ballantrae
Glenapp Castle
Downan Point
Carlock Hill
Finnarts Point
Glen App
Milleur Point
Corsewall Point
A77
LOCH RYAN
Barnhills
North Cairn
South Cairn
Kirkcolm
Corsewall
Cairnryan
Dounan Bay
Airies
Ervie
Loch Connell
Cairn Point
Portobello
A718
St Mary's Croft
Knocknain
Soleburn
Leswalt
Innermessan
B7043
B738
THE RHINNS
Stranraer
Broadsea Bay
Portslogan
Whiteleys
Lochans
Black
0 2 4 6 miles
0 2 4 6 8 10 km

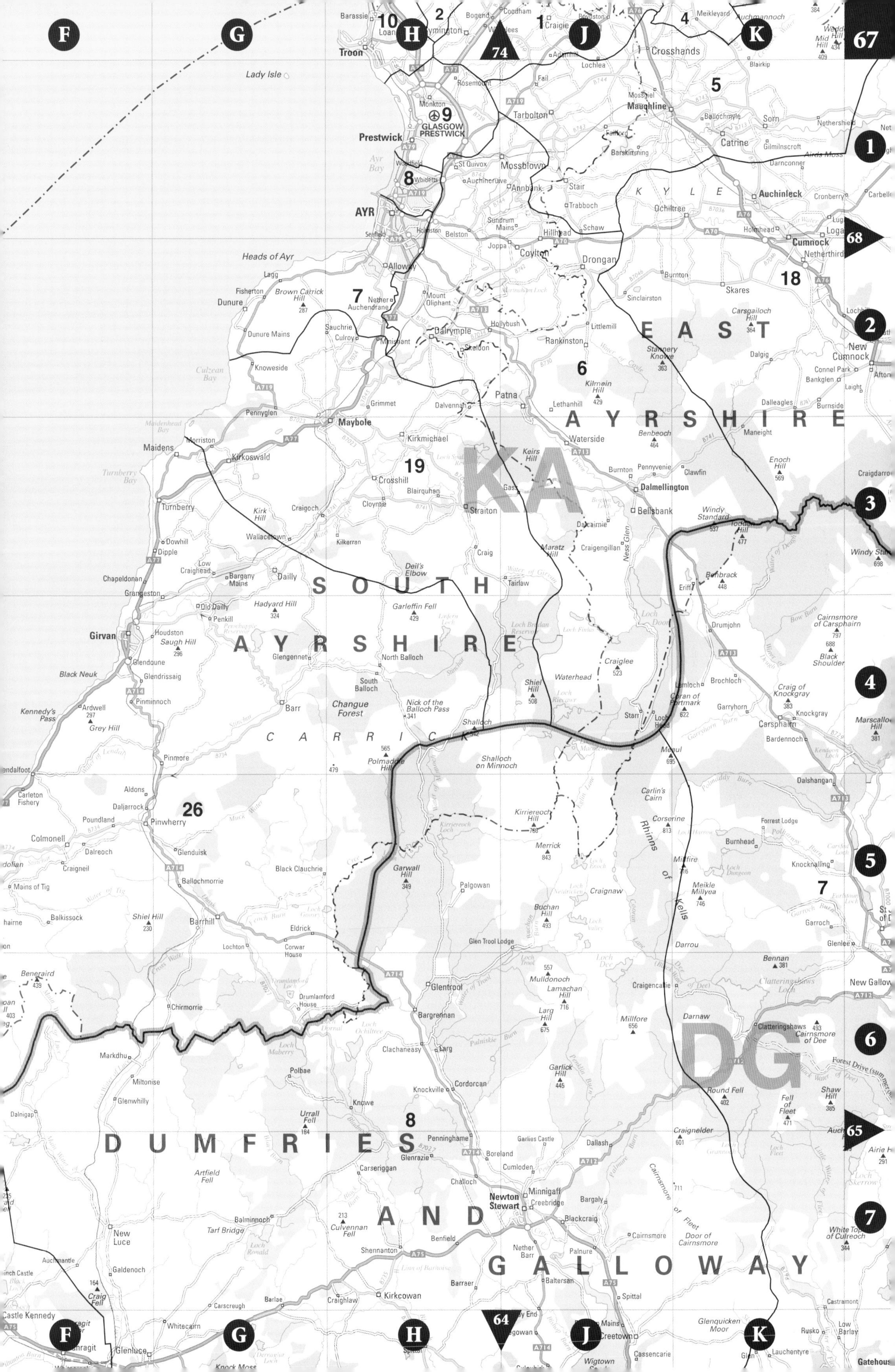

F
G
H
J
K
74
67
68
65
64
1
2
3
4
5
6
7
Troon
Barassie
Prestwick
GLASGOW PRESTWICK
AYR
Lady Isle
Ayr Bay
Heads of Ayr
Monkton
Tarbolton
Mauchline
Catrine
Sorn
Crosshands
Craigie
Auchinleck
Cumnock
New Cumnock
Ochiltree
Mossblown
Annbank
Stair
Drongan
Coylton
Alloway
Dunure
Maybole
Kirkoswald
Turnberry
Maidens
Girvan
Dailly
Kirkmichael
Crosshill
Straiton
Patna
Waterside
Dalmellington
Bellsbank
Dalrymple
Hollybush
Barr
Pinwherry
Colmonell
Barrhill
Pinmore
Lendalfoot
Ballantrae
Carsphairn
Dalry
Glentrool
Bargrennan
Newton Stewart
Minnigaff
Creebridge
Kirkcowan
Glenluce
New Luce
Castle Kennedy
Creetown
Clatteringshaws
Clatteringshaws Loch
Loch Doon
Rhinns of Kells
Merrick
843
Kirriereoch Hill
Shalloch on Minnoch
Changue Forest
Nick of the Balloch Pass
Cairnsmore of Fleet
Cairnsmore of Carsphairn
797
Windy Standard
Blackcraig
Palnure
Kyle
Carrick
KA
DG
EAST AYRSHIRE
SOUTH AYRSHIRE
DUMFRIES AND GALLOWAY
A77
A70
A76
A713
A714
A712
A75
A719
Craiglee
Waterhead
Dalshangan
Forrest Lodge
Knocknalling
Garroch
Glenlee
New Galloway
Forest Drive (summer only)
Round Fell
Craignelder
Auchenleck
Penninghame
Glenrazie
Challoch
Cumloden
Bargaly
Balminnoch
Tarf Bridge
Barlae
Craighlaw
Carscreugh
Whitecairn
Knock Moss
Wigtown
Cassencarie
Spittal
Baltersan
Glenquicken Moor
Castramont
Low Barlay
Rusko
Lauchentyre
Gatehouse
Markdhu
Miltonise
Glenwhilly
Chirmorrie
Drumlamford House
Eldrick
Corwar House
Lochton
Shiel Hill
Balkissock
Craigneil
Mains of Tig
Dalreoch
Ballochmorrie
Glenduisk
Black Clauchrie
Daljarrock
Aldons
Poundland
Carleton Fishery
Kennedy's Pass
Ardwell
Grey Hill
Black Neuk
Glendrissaig
Glendoune
Pinminnoch
Houston
Saugh Hill
Old Dailly
Penkill
Hadyard Hill
Glengennet
North Balloch
South Balloch
Garleffin Fell
Tairlaw
Deil's Elbow
Craig
Kilkerran
Wallacetown
Kirk Hill
Craigoch
Cloyntie
Blairquhan
Dowhill
Dipple
Chapeldonan
Grangeston
Low Craighead
Bargany Mains
Morriston
Pennyglen
Knoweside
Culzean Bay
Dunure Mains
Culroy
Sauchrie
Minishant
Auchendrane
Mount Oliphant
Skeldon
Fisherton
Lagg
Brown Carrick Hill
Grimmet
Dalvennan
Rankinston
Littlemill
Kilmein Hill
Lethanhill
Benbeoch
Burnton
Pennyvenie
Clawfin
Keirs Hill
Gass
Dalcairnie
Craigengillan
Ness Glen
Maratz Hill
Loch Bradan Reservoir
Loch Finlas
Shiel Hill
Loch Riecawr
Shalloch
Polmaddie Hill
Palgowan
Garwall Hill
Glen Trool Lodge
Buchan Hill
Craignaw
Mullwharchar
Lamachan Hill
Larg Hill
Mulldonoch
Millfore
Garlick Hill
Darrou
Craigencallie
Darnaw
Meaul
Carlin's Cairn
Corserine
Millfire
Meikle Millyea
Burnhead
Corran of Portmark
Lamloch
Starr
Loch Head
Brochloch
Garryhorn
Craig of Knockgray
Knockgray
Bardennoch
Marscalloch Hill
Black Shoulder
Drumjohn
Eriff
Benbrack
Todd Hill
Windy Standard
Enoch Hill
Maneight
Dalleagles
Dalgig
Carsgailoch Hill
Stannery Knowe
Skares
Burnton
Sinclairston
Netherthird
Holmhead
Cronberry
Darnconner
Gilmilnscroft
Airds Moss
Nethershield
Ballochmyle
Barskimming
Failford
Mossgiel
Lochlea
Adamhill
Fail
Rosemount
St Quivox
Auchincruive
Whitletts
Woodfield
Holmston
Belston
Sundrum Mains
Joppa
Hillhead
Trabboch
Schaw
Seafield
Symington
Loans
Bogend
Coodham
Meikleyard
Auchmannoch
Blairkip
Knockville
Cordorcan
Polbae
Knowe
Urrall Fell
Clachaneasy
Larg
Garlies Castle
Boreland
Dallash
Artfield Fell
Culvennan Fell
Benfield
Shennanton
Nether Barr
Barraer
Cairnsmore
Door of Cairnsmore
Shaw Hill
Fell of Fleet
Cairnsmore of Dee
White Top of Culreoch
Airie Hill
Bennan
Craig Fell
Auchmantle
Galdenoch
Beneraird
Lochinch Castle
Dunragit

A
B
C
D
E
75
1
2
3
4
5
6
7
67
64
65
SOUTH
LANARKSHIRE
ML
KA
EAST
AYRSHIRE
DUMFRIES
AND
DG
NITHSDALE
LOWTHER HILLS
Auchmannoch Muir
Meikleyard
Wedder Hill
Mid Hill
Blairkip
Dun Rig
Middlefield Law
Priesthill Height
Douglas
Robert Law
Scaur Hill
Wiston
Newton
Mossgiel
Mauchline
Ballochmyle
Sorn
Catrine
Gilmilnscroft
Nethershield
Airds Moss
Netherwood
Muirkirk
Smallburn
Kames
Nether Wellwood
Black Hill
Parish Holm
Hazelside
Glespin
Redshaw
Carmacoup
Glentaggart
Wildshaw Hill
Roberton
Wandel
Abington
Cold Chapel
Arbory Hill
Rome Hill
Darnconner
Auchinleck
Boghead
Cronberry
Carbellow
Lugar
Wardlaw Hill
Cairn Table
Dryrigs Hill
Crawfordjohn
Drake Law
Crawford
Ochiltree
Holmhead
Logan
Cumnock
Netherthird
Stony Hill
Duneaton Water
Lettershaws
Burnton
Skares
Dalblair
Mount Stuart
Fingland
Wellgrain Dod
Elvanfoot
Watchman Hill
Sinclairston
Craigdullyeart Hill
Halfmerk Hill
Corsebank
Lochhill
Cocker Hill
Leadhills
Carsgailoch Hill
Pathhead
New Cumnock
Lagrae
Kirkland
Carco
Wanlock Dod
Glenochar
Beat Sum
Stannery Knowe
Dalgig
Connel Park
Bankglen
Afton Bridgend
Laight
Kirkconnel
Wanlockhead
Willowgrain Hill
Green Lowther
Watermeetings
Tomont Hill
Roman Road
Dalleagles
Burnside
Kelloholm
Drumbuie
Crawick
Sanquhar
Mennock Pass
Lowther Hill
Winter
Benbeoch
Maneight
Hare Hill
Ulzieside
Mennock
Eliock
Wintercleuch
Pennyvenie
Clawfin
Dalmellington
Enoch Hill
Craigdarroch
Blackcraig Hill
Cloud Hill
Glengenny Muir
Ardoch
Dalveen Pass
Comb Law
Ballencleuch Law
Daer Reservoir
Windy Standard
Todden Hill
Blacklorg Hill
Cruffell
Polgown
Dalgonar
Wether Hill
Enterkinfoot
Durisdeer
Gateslack
Wedder Law
Craigengillan
Afton Res
Windy Standard
Countam
Glenmanna
Cairnkinna Hill
Breconside
Gana Hill
Earncraig Hill
Alhang
Eriff
Benbrack
Dodd Hill
Colt Hill
Rashy Height
Queensberry
Drumjohn
Cairnsmore of Carsphairn
Holm of Drumlanrig
Carronbridge
Auchenbrack
Torbraehead
Auchenhessnane
Dabton
Thornhill
Gatelawbridge
Black Shoulder
Benbuie
Bail Hill
Burnhead
Penpont
Bennan
Lamloch
Brochloch
Craig of Knockgray
Coran of Portmark
Garryhorn
Loch Head
Carsphairn
Knockgray
Marscalloch Hill
Cornharrow Hill
Tynron
Clonrae
Keir Mill
Closeburn
Great Hill
Forest of Ae
Bardennoch
Carroch
Craigdarroch
Moniaive
Crawfordton
Kirkland
Keir Hills
Croalchapel
Meaul
Carlin's Cairn
Dalshangan
Glencrosh
Crossford
Barndennoch
Dalswinton Common
Blackwood
Ae Village
Corserine
Forrest Lodge
Wether Hill
Castlefairn
Holmhead
Bogrie Hill
Glenhead
Auldgirth
Crawston Hill
Rhinns of Kells
Burnhead
Knocknalling
Millfire
Lochurr
Sundaywell
Dunscore
Allanton
Friars Carse
Dalswinton
Meikle Millyea
Corriedoo
Waterhead
Blackcraig Hill
Stroquhan
Milton
Duncow
Craigenputtock
Speddoch
Garroch
St John's Town of Dalry
Bogue
Kirkton
Darrou
Glenlee
Blackcraig
Drumwhirn
Newtonairds
Holywood
Locharbriggs
Bennan
Garcrogo Forest
Knocklearn
Slongaber
Skeoch Hill
Gribton
New Bridge
Craigencallie
New Galloway
Balmaclellan
Gibbshill
Margreig
Scaur
Terregles
Lincluden
Clatteringshaws Loch
Larglear Hill
Corsock
Glen
Shawhead
Darnaw
Clatteringshaws
Cairnsmore of Dee
Maxwelltown
Cargenbridge
Forest Drive (summer only)
Merkland
Crofts
Henderland
Lochfoot
Goldielea
Glenlair
Brooklands
Crocketford or Ninemile Bar
Dalskairth
Round Fell
Shaw Hill
Bennan Cottage
Drumrash
Square Point
Milton Loch
Cargen
Fell of Fleet
Toll
Mossdale
Walton Park
Milton
Mabie
Gillfoot
Craignelder
Auchencloy Hill
Parton
Kirkpatrick Durham
Springholm
Beeswing
Whinny Hill
Airie Hill
Slogarie
Loch Grannoch
Auchendolly
Hermitage
Stonehouse
Kirkconnell
Craig
Old Bridge of Urr
Lotus Hill
Shambell
Cairnsmore of Fleet
Crossmichael
Mollance
Haugh of Urr
Kirkgunzeon
Kinharvie
Loch Skerrow
Townhead of Greenlaw
Clarebrand
New Abbey
Door of Cairnsmore
White Top of Culreoch
Laurieston
Glenlochar
Hillowton
Cairnsmore
Darngarroch
Cuil Hill
Castle Douglas
Criffell
Loch Whinyeon
Buchan
Craignair
Dalbeattie
Castramont
Bridge of Dee
Glengap
Rhonehouse or Kelton
Breoch
Kirkbean
Creetown
Ringford
Dildawn
Gelston
Palnackie
Caulkerbush
Southwick
Cassencarie
Gatehouse
Barcaple
Tongland
Airieland
Barnbarroch
Fairgirth
0 2 4 6 miles
0 2 4 6 8 10 km

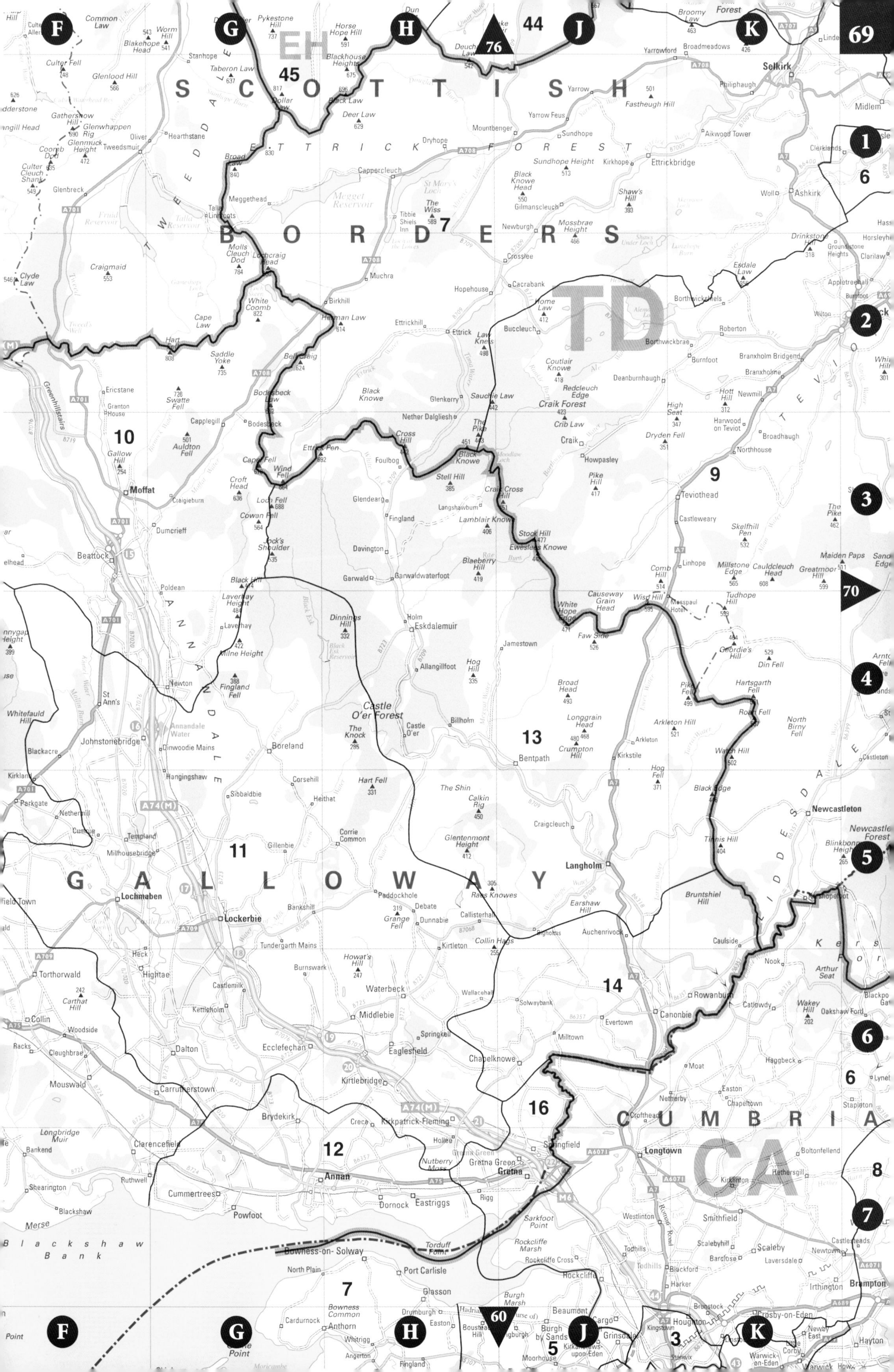
69
F
G
H
J
K
76
44
70
60
EH
45
SCOTTISH BORDERS
ETTRICK FOREST
TD
TWEEDDALE
ANNANDALE
TEVIOTDALE
LIDDESDALE
DUMFRIES AND GALLOWAY
CUMBRIA
CA
Selkirk
Philiphaugh
Midlem
Yarrowford
Broadmeadows
Yarrow
Fastheugh Hill
Yarrow Feus
Mountbenger
Sundhope
Aikwood Tower
Dryhope
Sundhope Height
Kirkhope
Ettrickbridge
Black Knowe Head
Shaw's Hill
Gilmanscleuch
Newburgh
Mossbrae Height
Crosslee
Cacrabank
Hopehouse
Ashkirk
Woll
Clerklands
Drinkstone Hill
Groundistone Heights
Horsleyhill
Clarilaw
Hassendean
Esdale Law
Appletreehall
Borthwickshiels
Borthwickbrae
Roberton
Wilton
Burnfoot
Branxholm Bridgend
Branxholme
Newmill
Hott Hill
Harwood on Teviot
Broadhaugh
Northhouse
Teviothead
Castleweary
Skelfhill Pen
The Pike
Linhope
Millstone Edge
Cauldcleuch Head
Greatmoor Hill
Maiden Paps
Tudhope Hill
Mosspaul Hotel
Geordie's Hill
Din Fell
Hartsgarth Fell
Roan Fell
North Birny Fell
Arkleton Hill
Arkleton
Kirkstile
Watch Hill
Hog Fell
Black Edge
Newcastleton
Newcastleton Forest
Blinkbonny Height
Tinnis Hill
Kershopefoot
Bruntshiel Hill
Caulside
Nook
Arthur Seat
Rowanburn
Catlowdy
Wakey Hill
Oakshaw Ford
Canonbie
Evertown
Milltown
Moat
Haggbeck
Lynebank
Easton
Netherby
Chapeltown
Stapleton
Crofthead
Longtown
Boltonfellend
Hethersgill
Kirklinton
Smithfield
Westlinton
Scalebyhill
Scaleby
Barclose
Laversdale
Newtown
Castlesteads
Irthington
Brampton
Crosby-on-Eden
Newby East
Warwick Bridge
Warwick-on-Eden
Corby
Hayton
Houghton
Kingstown
Stanwix
Harker
Blackford
Todhills
Rockcliffe
Rockcliffe Cross
Rockcliffe Marsh
Sarkfoot Point
Beaumont
Burgh Marsh
Burgh by Sands
Grinsdale
Kirkandrews-upon-Eden
Moorhouse
Cargo
Springfield
Gretna
Gretna Green
Rigg
Nutberry Moss
Hollee
Kirkpatrick-Fleming
Creca
Brydekirk
Annan
Dornock
Eastriggs
Cummertrees
Powfoot
Clarencefield
Ruthwell
Shearington
Blackshaw
Bankend
Longbridge Muir
Mouswald
Carrutherstown
Dalton
Cleughbrae
Racks
Collin
Woodside
Carthat Hill
Torthorwald
Heck
Hightae
Castlemilk
Kettleholm
Lockerbie
Lochmaben
Tundergarth Mains
Bankshill
Burnswark
Howat's Hill
Ecclefechan
Middlebie
Eaglesfield
Springkell
Kirtlebridge
Waterbeck
Kirtleton
Paddockhole
Debate
Grange Fell
Dunnabie
Callisterhall
Collin Hags
Wallacehall
Solwaybank
Chapelknowe
Bigholms
Auchenrivock
Earshaw Hill
Raes Knowes
Langholm
Craigcleuch
Glentenmont Height
Calkin Rig
The Shin
Bentpath
Crumpton Hill
Longgrain Head
Broad Head
Jamestown
Faw Side
Causeway Grain Head
White Hope Edge
Wisp Hill
Comb Hill
Ewes Knowe
Stock Hill
Blaeberry Hill
Lamblair Knowe
Craik Cross Hill
Langshawburn
Stell Hill
Black Knowe
The Pike
Sauchie Law
Glenkerry
Nether Dalgliesh
Craik Forest
Crib Law
Craik
Howpasley
Pike Hill
Dryden Fell
High Seat
Redcleuch Edge
Coutlair Knowe
Deanburnhaugh
Buccleuch
Home Law
Law Kneis
Ettrick
Ettrickhill
Cross Hill
Ettrick Pen
Foulbog
Glendearg
Fingland
Davington
Garwald
Garwaldwaterfoot
Holm
Eskdalemuir
Allangillfoot
Hog Hill
Dinnings Hill
Black Esk Reservoir
Castle O'er Forest
Castle O'er
The Knock
Billholm
Boreland
Corsehill
Hart Fell
Heithat
Corrie Common
Gillenbie
Sibbaldbie
Hangingshaw
Dinwoodie Mains
Annandale Water
Johnstonebridge
Newton
Fingland Fell
Milne Height
Laverhay
Laverhay Height
Black Hill
Poldean
Jock's Shoulder
Cowan Fell
Loch Fell
Croft Head
Wind Fell
Capel Fell
Bodesbeck
Bodesbeck Law
Bell Craig
Capplegill
Auldton Fell
Swatte Fell
Ericstane
Granton House
Gallow Hill
Moffat
Craigieburn
Dumcrieff
Beattock
Greenhillstairs
Saddle Yoke
Hart Fell
Cape Law
White Coomb
Herman Law
Birkhill
Muchra
Lochcraig Head
Molls Cleuch Dod
Craigmaid
Clyde Law
Tibbie Shiels Inn
The Wiss
St Mary's Loch
Megget Reservoir
Cappercleuch
Meggethead
Talla Linnfoots
Talla Reservoir
Fruid Reservoir
Broad Law
Glenbreck
Culter Cleuch Shank
Coomb Dod
Glenmuck Height
Glenwhappen Rig
Gathersnow Hill
Tweedsmuir
Oliver
Hearthstane
Dollar Law
Black Law
Deer Law
Blackhouse Heights
Horse Hope Hill
Pykestone Hill
Stanhope
Taberon Law
Glenlood Hill
Culter Fell
Common Law
Blakehope Head
Worm Hill
Deuchar Law
Broomy Law
Forest
Lindean
St Ann's
Whitefauld Hill
Blackacre
Kirkland
Parkgate
Nethermill
Cumrue
Templand
Millhousebridge
Mouswald
Merse
Blackshaw Bank
Bowness-on-Solway
Torduff Point
North Plain
Port Carlisle
Glasson
Bowness Common
Cardurnock
Anthorn
Drumburgh
Easton
Whitrigg
Angerton
Fingland
Boustead Hill
Longburgh
A708
A701
A74(M)
A709
A75
A7
A6071
A689
M6

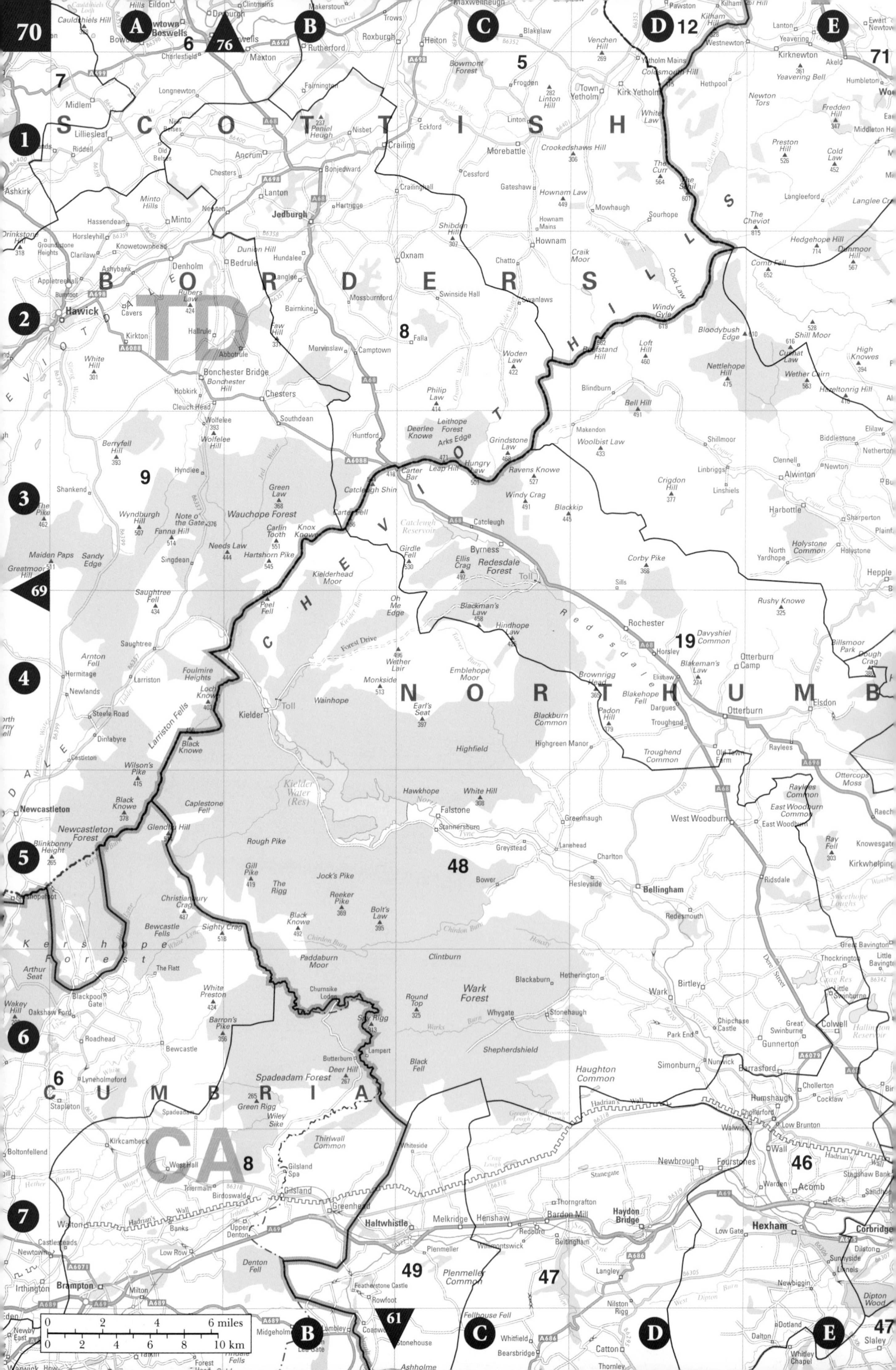
70
A
B
C
D
E
12
71
76
69
61
47
1
2
3
4
5
6
7
SCOTTISH
BORDERS
TD
CHEVIOT HILLS
NORTHUMB
CUMBRIA
CA
Cauldshiels Hill
Eildon
Newtown St Boswells
Dryburgh
Clintmains
Makerstoun
Maxwellheugh
Pawston
Kilham
Lanton
Ewart
Newtown
Bowden
Charlesfield
St Boswells
Maxton
Rutherford
Trows
Roxburgh
Heiton
Blakelaw
Venchen Hill
Yetholm Mains
Westnewton
Kirknewton
Yeavering
Yeavering Bell
Akeld
Bowmont Forest
Colesmouth Hill
Humbleton
Midlem
Longnewton
Fairnington
Frogden
Linton Hill
Town Yetholm
Kirk Yetholm
Hethpool
Newton Tors
Fredden Hill
Lilliesleaf
New Belses
Peniel Heugh
Nisbet
Eckford
Linton
White Law
Middleton Hall
Riddell
Old Belses
Ancrum
Crailing
Morebattle
Crookedshaws Hill
Preston Hill
Cold Law
Chesters
Bonjedward
Cessford
The Curr
Ashkirk
Lanton
Crailinghall
Gateshaw
The Schil
Langleeford
Langlee Crags
Minto Hills
Minto
Hartrigge
Hownam Law
Mowhaugh
Hassendean
Newton
Jedburgh
Sourhope
The Cheviot
Drinkstone Hill
Horsleyhill
Hownam Mains
Hedgehope Hill
Dunmoor Hill
Groundistone Heights
Knowetownhead
Shibden Hill
Hownam
Clarilaw
Dunion Hill
Oxnam
Craik Moor
Bedrule
Hundalee
Chatto
Ashybank
Denholm
Comb Fell
Appletreehall
Langlee
Cock Law
Burnfoot
Rubers Law
Mossburnford
Swinside Hall
Swanlaws
Hawick
Cavers
Bairnkine
Windy Gyle
Bloodybush Edge
Shill Moor
Faw Hill
Hallrule
Falla
Kirkton
Abbotrule
Mervinslaw
Camptown
Beefstand Hill
Loft Hill
Cushat Law
High Knowes
White Hill
Bonchester Bridge
Bonchester Hill
Woden Law
Nettlehope Hill
Wether Cairn
Hobkirk
Chesters
Philip Law
Blindburn
Hazeltonrig Hill
Cleuch Head
Wolfelee
Southdean
Leithope Forest
Bell Hill
Wolfelee Hill
Deerlee Knowe
Makendon
Eilaw
Berryfell Hill
Huntford
Arks Edge
Grindstone Law
Woolbist Law
Shillmoor
Biddlestone
Netherton
Hyndlee
Leap Hill
Hungry Law
Ravens Knowe
Linbriggs
Clennell
Alwinton
Newton
Carter Bar
Crigdon Hill
Linshiels
Shankend
Green Law
Catcleugh Shin
Windy Crag
Harbottle
The Pike
Wyndburgh Hill
Note o' the Gate
Wauchope Forest
Blackkip
Carter Fell
Catcleugh
Sharperton
Fanna Hill
Carlin Tooth
Knox Knowe
Catcleugh Reservoir
Byrness
Holystone Common
Holystone
Maiden Paps
Sandy Edge
Needs Law
Hartshorn Pike
Girdle Fell
Ellis Crag
Redesdale Forest
North Yardhope
Greatmoor Hill
Singdean
Kielderhead Moor
Corby Pike
Hepple
Saughtree Fell
Peel Fell
Oh Me Edge
Sills
Toll
Blackman's Law
Rushy Knowe
Redesdale
Hindhope Law
Rochester
Davyshiel Common
Saughtree
Forest Drive
Horsley
Billsmoor Park
Arnton Fell
Wether Lair
Blakeman's Law
Otterburn Camp
Dough Crag
Hermitage
Foulmire Heights
Emblehope Moor
Elishaw
Brownrigg Head
Larriston
Monkside
Newlands
Loch Knowe
Wainhope
Blakehope Fell
Dargues
Otterburn
Elsdon
Kielder
Earl's Seat
Blackburn Common
Padon Hill
Troughend
Steele Road
Dinlabyre
Larriston Fells
Black Knowe
Highfield
Highgreen Manor
Raylees
Castleton
Troughend Common
Old Town Farm
Wilson's Pike
Kielder Water (Res)
Ottercops Moss
Raylees Common
Newcastleton
Black Knowe
Caplestone Fell
Hawkhope
White Hill
East Woodburn Common
Falstone
Greenhaugh
West Woodburn
East Woodburn
Reachl
Newcastleton Forest
Glendhu Hill
Stannersburn
Blinkbonny Height
Rough Pike
Greystead
Lanehead
Ray Fell
Knowesgate
Charlton
Kirkwhelpington
Gill Pike
Jock's Pike
Bower
Hesleyside
Ridsdale
Kershopefoot
The Rigg
Bellingham
Christianbury Crag
Reeker Pike
Sweethope Loughs
Black Knowe
Bolt's Law
Redesmouth
Bewcastle Fells
Sighty Crag
Chirdon Burn
Kershope Forest
Great Bavington
Arthur Seat
Paddaburn Moor
Clintburn
Thockrington
Little Bavington
The Flatt
Blackaburn
Hetherington
Birtley
Colt Crag Res
Churnsike Lodge
Wark Forest
Wark
Little Swinburne
Wakey Hill
Oakshaw Ford
Blackpool Gate
White Preston
Round Top
Whygate
Stonehaugh
Chipchase Castle
Great Swinburne
Colwell
Hallington Reservoir
Roadhead
Barron's Pike
Sky Rigg
Park End
Gunnerton
Bewcastle
Lampert
Shepherdshield
Butterburn
Black Fell
Simonburn
Nunwick
Barrasford
Lyneholmeford
Deer Hill
Haughton Common
Chollerton
Spadeadam Forest
Humshaugh
Stapleton
Spadeadam
Green Rigg
Hadrian's Wall
Cocklaw
Wiley Sike
Chollerford
Walwick
Low Brunton
Kirkcambeck
Whiteside
Thirlwall Common
Boltonfellend
Wall
West Hall
Gilsland Spa
Newbrough
Fourstones
Stagshaw Bank
Stanegate
Warden
Acomb
Sandhoe
Triermain
Birdoswald
Gilsland
Greenhead
Thorngrafton
Anick
Walton
Banks
Haltwhistle
Melkridge
Henshaw
Bardon Mill
Haydon Bridge
Hexham
Corbridge
Castlesteads
Upper Denton
Redburn
Beltingham
Low Gate
Newtown
Low Row
Plenmeller
Willimontswick
Dilston
Sunnyside
Denton Fell
Plenmeller Common
Langley
Linnels
Irthington
Brampton
Milton
Featherstone Castle
Newbiggin
Rowfoot
Nilston Rigg
Dipton Wood
Fellhouse Fell
Midgeholme
Lambley
Coanwood
Stonehouse
Whitfield
Catton
Dotland
Dalton
Slaley
Whitley Chapel
Lea Gate
Bearsbridge
Talkin
Forest Head
Fells
Ashholme
Thornley
Newby East
Warwick
How
0 2 4 6 miles
0 2 4 6 8 10 km

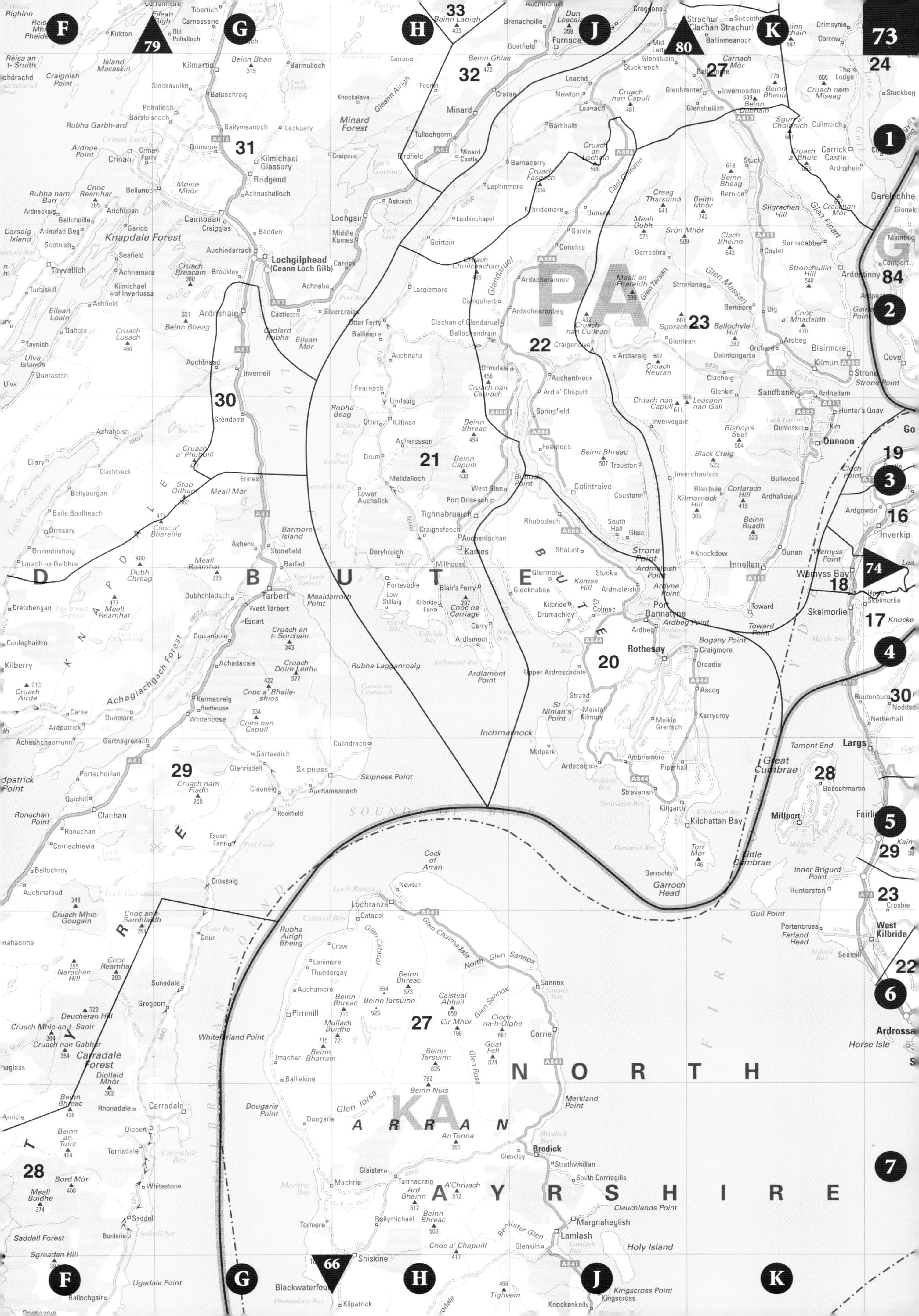

73
F
G
H
J
K
79
80
74
66
33
32
31
30
29
28
27
23
22
21
20
24
84
19
16
18
17
1
2
3
4
5
6
7
D
B
U
T
E
PA
KA
N O R T H
A Y R S H I R E
A R R A N
Lochgilphead
(Ceann Loch Gilb)
Ardrishaig
Tarbert
West Tarbert
Kennacraig
Whitehouse
Clachan
Skipness
Skipness Point
Tighnabruaich
Kames
Portavadie
Rothesay
Port Bannatyne
Dunoon
Sandbank
Kilmun
Strone Point
Hunter's Quay
Innellan
Toward
Toward Point
Colintraive
Wemyss Bay
Skelmorlie
Largs
Millport
Great Cumbrae
Little Cumbrae
Kilchattan Bay
Garroch Head
Inchmarnock
Lochranza
Catacol
Pirnmill
Sannox
Corrie
Brodick
Lamlash
Holy Island
Blackwaterfoot
Shiskine
Kilpatrick
Kingscross
Kingscross Point
Carradale
Saddell
Saddell Forest
Torrisdale
Dippen
Grogport
Crossaig
Ronachan
Ronachan Point
Ballochroy
Knapdale Forest
Achaglachgach Forest
Carradale Forest
Minard Forest
Minard
Furnace
Strachur
(Clachan Strachur)
Kilmartin
Crinan
Cairnbaan
Bridgend
Kilmichael Glassary
Lochgair
Otter Ferry
Kilfinan
Glendaruel
Clachan of Glendaruel
Sound of Bute
Firth of Clyde
Cock of Arran
Goat Fell
874
Cir Mhòr
798
Caisteal Abhail
859
Beinn Tarsuinn
825
Beinn Bharrain
Beinn Nuis
792
Glen Iorsa
Glen Sannox
North Glen Sannox
Glen Chalmadale
Glen Catacol
Machrie
Dougarie
Dougarie Point
Imachar
Tormore
Ballymichael
Glencloy
Strathwhillan
South Corriegills
Clauchlands Point
Margnaheglish
Merkland Point
Whitefarland Point
Rubha Airigh Bheirg
Loch Fyne
Loch Striven
Holy Loch
Loch Eck
Glen Finart
Glen Massan
Ardentinny
Coulport
Blairmore
Cove
Kilcreggan
Garelochhead
Inverkip
Fairlie
West Kilbride
Seamill
Portencross
Farland Head
Hunterston
Ardrossan
Horse Isle
Ugadale Point
Ballochgair
Sgreadan Hill
Tighvein
Knockenkelly
Kilmory
Ettrick Bay
Ascog
Kerrycroy
Ardbeg
Ardbeg Point
Bogany Point
Craigmore
Straad
St Ninian's Point
Ardscalpsie
Stravanan
Kingarth
Ambrismore
Piperhall
Barmore Island
Stonefield
Barfad
Erines
Inverneil
Auchbraad
Srondoire
Castleton
Achnaba
Silvercraigs
Ardlamont Point
Rubha Lagganroaig
Blair's Ferry
Millhouse
Auchenlochan
Port Driseach
Melldalloch
Acharosson
Otter
Lindsaig
Fearnoch
Ballimore
Auchnaha
Ormidale
Auchenbreck
Springfield
Glenmore
Stuck
Ardmaleish
Ardmaleish Point
Ardyne Point
Strone Point
Glaic
South Hall
Coustonn
Troustan
Inverchaolain
Blairbuie
Knockdow
Dunan

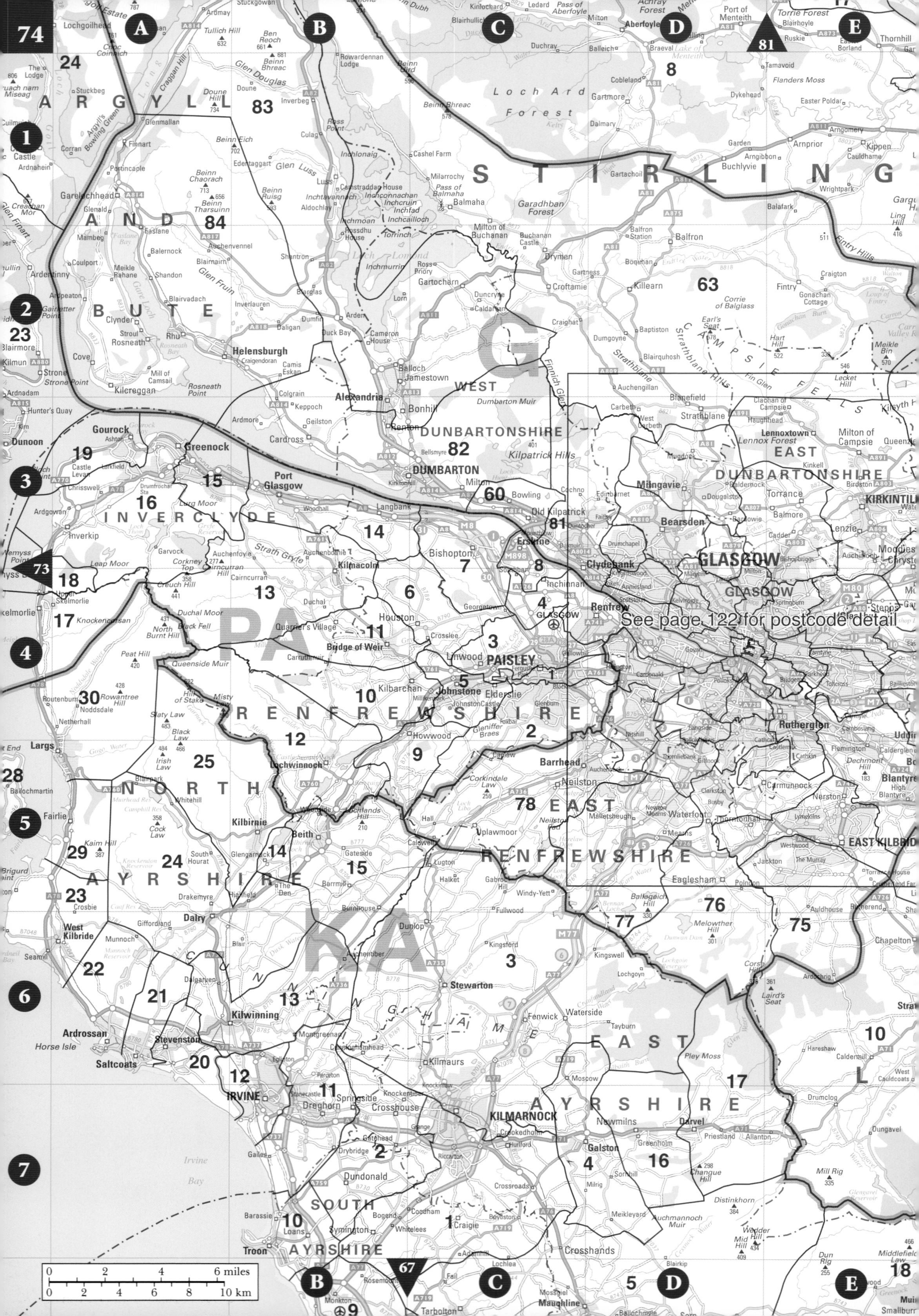
A
B
C
D
E
1
2
3
4
5
6
7
81
73
67
ARGYLL AND BUTE
STIRLING
WEST DUNBARTONSHIRE
EAST DUNBARTONSHIRE
INVERCLYDE
RENFREWSHIRE
EAST RENFREWSHIRE
NORTH AYRSHIRE
EAST AYRSHIRE
SOUTH AYRSHIRE
GLASGOW
G
PA
KA
L
See page 122 for postcode detail
Lochgoilhead
Loch Ard Forest
Aberfoyle
Port of Menteith
Garadhban Forest
Drymen
Balfron
Killearn
Fintry
Campsie Fells
Strathblane
Blanefield
Lennoxtown
Milton of Campsie
Kilsyth
Kirkintilloch
Lenzie
Milngavie
Bearsden
Clydebank
Helensburgh
Garelochhead
Kilcreggan
Rosneath
Balloch
Alexandria
Dumbarton
Kilpatrick Hills
Old Kilpatrick
Bowling
Erskine
Renfrew
Paisley
Johnstone
Elderslie
Kilbarchan
Bridge of Weir
Houston
Bishopton
Kilmacolm
Port Glasgow
Greenock
Gourock
Dunoon
Inverkip
Wemyss Bay
Skelmorlie
Largs
Fairlie
West Kilbride
Seamill
Ardrossan
Saltcoats
Stevenston
Kilwinning
Irvine
Dreghorn
Dundonald
Troon
Loans
Symington
Kilmarnock
Kilmaurs
Stewarton
Fenwick
Galston
Newmilns
Darvel
Beith
Dalry
Kilbirnie
Lochwinnoch
Howwood
Barrhead
Neilston
Newton Mearns
Eaglesham
Clarkston
Giffnock
Rutherglen
Cambuslang
Blantyre
East Kilbride
Strathaven
Mauchline
Tarbolton
Irvine Bay
Horse Isle
0 2 4 6 miles
0 2 4 6 8 10 km

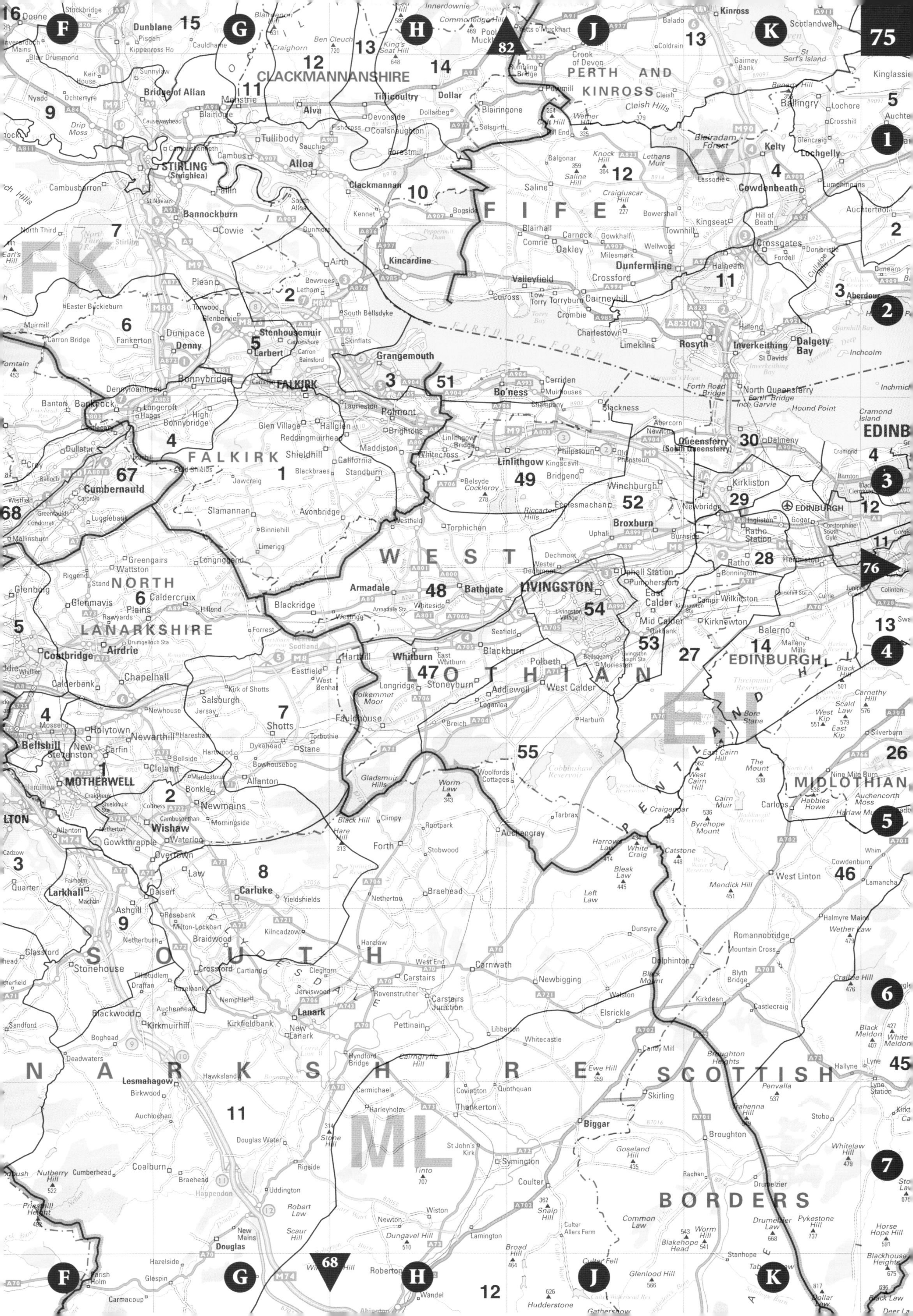
CLACKMANNANSHIRE
PERTH AND KINROSS
FIFE
KY
FK
FALKIRK
WEST LOTHIAN
EDINBURGH
EH
MIDLOTHIAN
NORTH LANARKSHIRE
SOUTH LANARKSHIRE
ML
SCOTTISH BORDERS
FIRTH OF FORTH
PENTLAND HILLS
CLYDESDALE
Dunblane
Bridge of Allan
STIRLING (Sruighlea)
Bannockburn
Alloa
Alva
Tillicoultry
Dollar
Menstrie
Tullibody
Clackmannan
Kincardine
Kinross
Cowdenbeath
Lochgelly
Kelty
Dunfermline
Rosyth
Inverkeithing
Dalgety Bay
North Queensferry
Queensferry (South Queensferry)
Larbert
Stenhousemuir
Denny
Grangemouth
FALKIRK
Bo'ness
Polmont
Linlithgow
Cumbernauld
Broxburn
Bathgate
Armadale
LIVINGSTON
Whitburn
West Calder
Airdrie
Coatbridge
Bellshill
MOTHERWELL
Wishaw
Shotts
Carluke
Larkhall
Lanark
Lesmahagow
Biggar
Douglas
West Linton
EDINBURGH
76
82
68
F
G
H
J
K
1
2
3
4
5
6
7

A
B
C
D
E
1
2
3
4
5
6
7
FIFE
KY
FIRTH OF FORTH
EDINBURGH
EAST LOTHIAN
MIDLOTHIAN
LAMMERMUIR HILLS
MOORFOOT HILLS
SCOTTISH BORDERS
LAUDERDALE
EH
75
83
69
Glenrothes
Markinch
Kingsdale
Lundin Links
Largo
Kilconquhar
Pittenweem
St Monans
Auchmuirbridge
Windygates
Leven
Innerleven
Methil
Buckhaven
Milton of Balgonie
Coaltown of Balgonie
Kinglassie
Thornton
Lochore
Crosshill
Auchterderran
Cardenden
East Wemyss
Coaltown of Wemyss
West Wemyss
Dysart
Kirkcaldy
Lumphinnans
Auchtertool
Kinghorn
Burntisland
Pettycur
Aberdour
Hawkcraig Point
Inchcolm
Inchkeith
Inchmickery
Earlsferry
Rudd Point
Kincraig Point
Chapel Ness
Saucher Point
Isle of May
South Ness
Fidra
Lamb
North Berwick
Craigleith
Bass Rock
St Baldred's Boat
Dirleton
Gullane Point
Gullane
Fenton Barns
Kingston
Auldhame
Scoughall
Whitekirk
St Baldred's Cradle
Tyne Mouth
Aberlady
Aberlady Bay
Luffness
Drem
Craigielaw
Craigielaw Point
Gosford Bay
Mungoswells
Ballencrieff
East Fortune
Athelstaneford
Preston
East Linton
Tyninghame
West Barns
Spittal
Longniddry
Garleton Hills
Cockenzie and Port Seton
Prestonpans
Meadowmill
Tranent
Macmerry
Elvingston
Gladsmuir
Haddington
Traprain
Luggate Burn
Stenton
Pitcox
Spott
Halls
Cramond Island
Cramond
Granton
Black Rocks
Leith
Portobello
Musselburgh
Newcraighall
Corstorphine
Gorgie
Morningside
Blackford Hill
Braid Hills
Colinton
Currie
Swanston
Hillend
Loanhead
Lasswade
Bonnyrigg
Dalkeith
Eskbank
Newbattle
Easthouses
Mayfield
Newtongrange
Roslin
Bilston
Penicuik
Auchendinny
Rosewell
Gorebridge
Carrington
Wallyford
Elphinstone
Penston
New Winton
New Town
Samuelston
Bolton
Whitelaw Hill
Garvald
Papple
Deuchrie Dod
Dunbar Common
Inveresk
Whitecraig
Crossgatehall
Ormiston
Cousland
Pencaitland
West Saltoun
East Saltoun
Peastonbank
Peaston
Gilchriston
Gifford
Carfrae
Danskine
Longyester
Clints Dod
Rangely Kip
Spartleton Edge
Newlands Hill
Lammer Law
Penshiel Hill
Cranshaws Hill
Meikle Says Law
Edgehead
Ford
Pathhead
Crichton
Fala
Fala Dam
Humbie
West Hill
Soutra Hill
Fala Moor
Tynehead
North Middleton
Borthwick
Temple
Middleton
Gilston
Dun Law
Turf Law
Hunt Law
Blythe Edge
Longformacus
Wrunk Law
Falahill
Heriot
Oxton
Carfraemill
Hogs Law
Collie Law
Inchkeith Hill
Scoured Rig
Edgarhope Wood
Westruther
Lauder
Lauder Common
Thirlestane
Whiteburn
Houndslow
Fountainhall
Torquhan
Galabank
Killochyett
Stow
Torsonce
Nether Blainslie
Legerwood
Huntlywood
Birkhill
East Morriston
West Morriston
Gordon
Fans
Silverburn
Nine Mile Burn
Howgate
Cauldhall Moor
Auchencorth Moss
Leadburn
Whim
Cowdenburn
Lamancha
Westloch
Halmyre Mains
Wether Law
Eddleston
Blackhope Scar
Dewar
Dun Law
Ladyside Height
Eastside Heights
Totto Hill
Whitehope Law
Cringletie
Redscarhead
Black Meldon
White Meldon
Dunslair Heights
Black Law
Glentress Forest
Black Knowe
Colquhar
Windlestraw Law
Yardstone Knowe
Great Law
Hallyne
Lyne
Peebles
Lyne Station
Kings Muir
Glentress
Cardrona
Cardrona Forest
Lee Pen
Priesthope Hill
Seathope Law
Innerleithen
Walkerburn
Elibank and Traquair Forest
Traquair
Kirkton Manor
Cadmuir Hill
Wallace's Hill
Preston Law
Stob Law
Hundleshope Heights
Horse Hope Hill
Dun Rig
Blake Muir
Deuchar Law
Blackhouse
Minch Moor
William Law
Langshaw
Buckholm
Knowes Hill
Blackhaugh
Glendearg
Earlston
Galashiels
Thornylee
Clovenfords
Meigle Hill
Caddonfoot
Ashiestiel Hill
Ashiestiel
Gala Hill
Yair Hill Forest
Broomy Law
Boleside
Melrose
Darnick
Gattonside
Drygrange
Redpath
Leaderfoot
Newstead
Bemersyde
Clintmains
Smailholm
Makerstoun
Eildon Hills
Eildon
Dryburgh
Newtown St Boswells
St Boswells
Lindean
Cauldshiels Hill
Bowden
Peat Law
Broadmeadows
Yarrowford
Selkirk
Charlesfield
Maxton
Rutherford
Longnewton
Midlem
Fastheugh Hill
Philiphaugh
Kirkhill
0 2 4 6 miles
0 2 4 6 8 10 km

F   G   H   J   K

1

2

3

Barns Ness
Skateraw Harbour
Skateraw
Thorntonloch
ck
Reed Point
cklaw Hill
Bigdean
Cove
S
Pease Bay
Cockburnspath
dhamstocks
Siccar Point
Wheat Stack
Telegraph Hill
174
13
Ecclaw
245
Meikle Black Law
A1
Lumsdaine
St Abb's Head
Heart Law
391
277
Ecclaw Hill
A1107
Coldingham Moor
Coldingham Loch
Northfield
St Abbs
Blackburn Rig
Grantshouse
Coldingham
Coldingham Bay
Laughing Law
307
Houndwood
14
A1107
Eyemouth

Longstone
Farne Islands
loss
Budle Point
Budle Bay
Supie Sound
Bamburgh
Budle
B1341
Mill
Gloror um
Monks House Rocks
Inner Sound
Bradford
Sandlestone
Burton
New Shoreston
69
68
Seahouses
rstone
Lucker
Elford
North Sunderland
same scale as main map
East

4

ERMUIR
I   S   H
Abbey St Bathans
emford
Horseley Hill
262
Drakemire
Cockburn Law
325
A6112
Marygold
B6438
Auchencrow
B6438
Reston
A1
Ayton
Cairncross
Burnmouth
Millerton Hill
132
199
Ayton Hill
Hilton Bay
Lamberton Beach
11
Preston
Lintlaw
Blanerne
B6355
Chirnside
Chirnsidebridge
Whiteadder Water
A6105
Allanton
Foulden
A6105
Lamberton
Mordington Holdings
Clappers
Halidon Hill
163
Needles Eye
Marshall Meadows
Sharper's Head
Highfields

5

law
Law
TD
105
Edrom
S
H
Duns
Gavinton
Blackadder
B6460
Hutton
Paxton
B6461
Berwick-upon-Tweed
Tweedmouth
Spittal
Choicelee
A6112
Whitelaw
B6460
B6437
Sunwick
Fishwick
East Ord
A1167
Realshin Cove
Greenlaw
Polwarth
Sinclair's Hill
Whitsome
B6461
Horncliffe
Horndean
Longridge Towers
Murton
Scremerston
Cheswick Black Rocks

6

Fogo
Fogorig
Swinton
Swinton Quarter
Ladykirk
B6470
Thornton Park
Thornton
West Allerdean
Cheswick
Goswick
Holy Island (Lindisfarne)
Emmanuel Head
R   S   **12**
Purves Hall
Leitholm
Simprim
Upsettlington
Norham
A698
Grindon
Shoreswood
Shoresdean
Ancroft
Cheswick Buildings
A1
Berrington
Haggerston
Beal
West Mains
Holy Island
Holy Island Sands
Castle Point
Barrows Hole
Easter owlaws
Lambden
Eccles
Orange Lane
Felkington
Duddo
15
Bowsden
Lowick
West Kyloe
Cotham
Guile Point
Fenham Flats
Humhall
egars
Birgham
Lennel
Castle Heaton
Barmoor Lane End
B6353
Holburn
B6525
East Kyloe
Buckton
Kyloe Hills

7

Stichill
Ednam
Hendersyde Park
Carham
Wark
West Learmouth
New Heaton
Crookham Eastfield
Pallinsburn House
al
Crookham
Cornhill on Tweed
A697
Ford
Lowick
Middleton
70
Elwick
Low Middleton
Ross
Budle Point
Kelso
Maxwellheugh
Hadden
B6350
East Learmouth
Pressen
Branxton
Mardon
Flodden
Kimmerston
Fenton
Nesbit
Hoburn
ckenheugh
Middleton
North Hazelrigg
Belford
Easington
Budle
Bamburgh
Glororum
Sandlestone
Bradford
69
New Shoreston
Farne Island
House Ro
Heiton
B6352
Sprouston
Downham
Milfield
NORTHUMBERLAND
B6354
Howtel
Mindrummill
Mindrum
Pawston
Kilham
267 Hill
Houden on Hill
Lanton
A697
Doddington
South Hazelrigg
66
NE
Warenton
Bellshill
Adderstone
68
North Sunderland
Elford
East Fleetham
West Fleetham
Blakelaw
Kilham Hill
Yeavering Bell
Coupland
Ewart Newtown
West Horton
East Horton
Lucker
Newham Hall
Swinhoe

F   **5**   Frogden   G   **71**   H   **71**   J   K   **67**
Bowmon Forest
Town Yetholm
282 Linton Hill
Venchen Hill
269
Yetholm Mains
Kirk Yetholm
Hill
Hethpool
Newton Tors
Fredden Hill
Kirknewton
Yeavering Bell
Westnewton
Humbleton
Wooler
Greendykes
Chatton
Twizell House
Rosebrough
Chathill
Wandon
Newham

A
B
C
D
E
85
1
2
3
4
5
6
7
SEA OF THE HEBRIDES
INNER HEBRIDES
PA
Eag na Maoile
Eilean Mòr
Rubha Mòr
Rubha Sgor-Innis
Bousd
Sorisdale
Rubh' a' Bhinnein
Torastan
Grishipoll
Arnabost
Grishipoll Bay
Clabhach
Ballyhaugh
Ben Hogh
104
Hogh Bay
73
Arinagour
Totronald
Totamore
78
COLL
Loch Eatharna
Arileod
Feall Bay
Acha
Uig
B8070
Eilean Ornsay
Port Mine
Calgary Point
Crossapol
Gorton
Crossapol Bay
Friesland Bay
Rubha Fasachd
Soa
Gunna
Urvaig
Port a' Mhurain
Miodar
Sgeir Bharrach
Salum Bay
Salum
Caolas
Rubha Dubh
The Green
Clachan Mòr
Balephetrish Bay
Balephetrish Hill
Vaul
Ruaig
Brock
Port Bàn
Hough Bay
Kenovay
Gott Bay
Rubha Liath
Soa
TIREE
Kilkenneth
77
Scarinish
Moss
Crossapoll
Heanish
Sandaig
Heylipoll
Baugh
Barrapoll
Hynish Bay
B8067
Balemartine
Balephuil
Mannal
Rinn Thorbhais
Hynish
Caliach Point
Sunipol
Langamull
Mornish
Cruach Sleibhe
166
Calgary
Rubha nan Oirean
Calgary Bay
Treshnish Point
Treshnish
Ensay
191
Beinn Duill
74
Burg
Rubh' a' Chaoil
Rubh' an t-Suibhein
Cairn na Burgh More
Cairn na Burgh Beg
Loch Tuath
Treshnish Isles
Sgeir a' Chaisteil
Fladda
Lunga
Eilean Dioghlum
Gometra
Gometra House
Rubha Maol na Mine
Maisgeir
Bac Mòr (Dutchman's Cap)
Bac Beag
Little Colonsay
Staffa
Eilean Dubh
Fingal's Cave
A R
Réidh Eilean
Eilean Chalbha
Rubha nan Cearc
Port an Duine Mhairbh
Dun I
100
76
Kintra
Beinn Chladan
81
Fionnphort
Ruanaich
Baile Mòr
IONA
Stac an Aoineidh
Aridhglas
A849
Fidden
66
Rubha na Carraig-gèire
Sound of Iona
Ross of M
Knockvologan
87
Torr Fada
Ardalanish
Soa Island
Erraid
Eilean Dubh
Aird Mòr
89
67
Eilean a' Chalmain
Eilean Mòr
Rubh' Ardalanish
Dearg Sgeir
Ruadh Sgeir
Torran Rocks
Na Torrain
West Reef
McPhail's Anvil
Torran Sgoilte
Sgeir Ghobhlach
Otter Rock
Dubh Artach
0 2 4 6 miles
0 2 4 6 8 10 km
Kilora

F
G
H
J
K
86
Ockle
Sanna Point
Fascadale
Achateny
Kilmory
Swordle
Sanna
Branault
Carn Mòr
Ardtoe
Shielfoot
Kinlochmoidart
Glen Moidart
Glen Forsa
Gaskan
Gorstanvorran
Beinn Bhreac
Dalnabreck
Kentra
Cliff
Achnaha
Meall nan Con
Beinn an Leathaid
Beinn Bhreac
36
Portuairk
Achosnich
Grigadale
Gorteneorn
Anvegaig
Acharacle
Ardshealach
Claish Moss
Dalelia
Polloch
Achnanellan
Sgurr na Greine
37
Glen Hurich
Glenhurich
Kinlochan
Carn na Nathrach
Druim Garbh
Sgurr Dhomhnuill
Meall an Tarmachain
A R D N A M U R C H A N
Beinn nan Losgann
Caim
Leac Shoilleir
Salen
Resipole
S U N A R T
Beinn Resipol
PH
Scotstown
Sgurr nan Cnamh
1
Beinn na Seilg
Kilchoan
Ormsaigmore
Ben Hiant
Beinn Bhuidhe
Glenbeg
Tarbert
Ardery
Anaheilt
Drumnatorran
Strontian
(Sròn an t-Sìthein)
Garbh Bheinn
33
Sròn Bheag
Maclean's Nose
Ardslignish
Eilean Mòr
Glenborrodale
Laga
Ben Laga
Gearr Chreag
Meall a' Bhroin
Ranachan
Woodend
Ardnastang
Achnalea
Glen Tarbert
Eilean Mòr
Oronsay
Risga
Carna
Glencripesdale
Liddesdale
Achleek
Meall a' Choirein Luachraich
Ardmore Point
Sorne Point
Auliston Point
H I G H L A N D
Creach Bheinn
Meall an Inbhire
Beinn Ghormaig
Taobh Dubh
Glas Bheinn
Fuar Bheinn
Meall nan Each
Mishnish
Tobermory
Calve Island
Rahoy
Meall a' Chaise
Achagavel
Lochuisge
Quinish
75
'S Airdhe Beinn
Barr
Kinloch
Beinn Iadain
Beinn Na Cille
2
Achleanan
Drimnin
M O R V E R N
Ardantiobairt
Beinn Bhuidhe
Beinn na h-Uamha
Gleann Dubh
Beinn Chlaonleud
Meall a' Chaorainn
Loch Uisge
Beach
Sgurr Shalachain
Glengalmadale
Rubha na h-Airde Uinnsinn
Camasnacroise
Achnadrish
Dervaig
Sidhean na Raplaich
Durinemast
80
Clounlaid
Rhemore
Gleann Geal
Beinn Mheadhoin
Sgurr a' Bhuic
Cuanna Mòr
AROS
Speinne Mòr
Claggan
Alltachonaich
38
Shuna Island
Cruachan na' Ghairbh
Lettermore
Ardnacross
Killundine
Beinn an t-Sruthain
Creag Bhan Ard
Beinn Bhan
Larachbeg
Bràigh na Glaice Mòire
Meall Damh
Beinn a' Chaisil
Glensanda
Aoinacraig
Salen Forest
Meall na Caorach
Fiunary Forest
Fiunary
Ardtornish
Loch Tearnait
Eilean Loch Oscair
Eilean Ramsay
Port Ramsay
73
Beinn nan Clach-corra
Cnoc an da Chinn
Druim an Fhraoich Mhin
Ledmore
Tenga
Glen Aros
Eileanan Glasa
Achnaha
Tighachnoic
Glais Bheinn
Mam a' Chullaich
Meall a' Chaorainn
An Sleaghach
Eignaig
3
Fanmore
Ballygown
Beinn Bhuidhe
Meall an Fhiar Mhaim
72
Lochaline
(Loch Alainn)
Appin Rocks
Eriska
North Shian
Kilbrennan
Beinn na Drise
Salen
Pennygown
Fishnish Point
Fishnish
Inninbeg
Ardtornish Point
Clachan
Eilean Dubh
South Shian
(Sithean a Deas)
Rubha nan Gall
Lagganulva
Killiechronan
Kellan
Cruach Torran Lochain
Killbeg
Beinn Bhuidhe
Glen Forsa
Beinn Chreagach Mhòr
Balmeanach
Garmony
Achnacroish
Lynn of Morven
Rubha an Ridire
Seabank
VA
Acharonich
Killiemor
Gruline
Loch Ba
Lismore
Baligrundle
80
Culcharry
A'Chrannag
Loch Na Keal
71
Na Binneinean
Beinn Mheadhon
Salen Forest
Scallastle
Bernera
34
Kilcheran
Balure
37
Benderloch
Ledaig
Eorsa
Knock
Beinn a' Ghraig
Gaodhail
Beinn na Duatharach
Dun da Ghaoithe
PA
Craignure
Eilean Dubh
Pladda Island
Rubha Garbh-àird
South Ledaig
Samalan Island
Maol nan Uan
Duart Point
North Connel
Inch Kenneth
Clachandhu
Balnahard
68
Dhiseig
M U L L
Beinn Fhada
Beinn Talaidh
65
Sgurr Dearg
Eilean Musdile
Eilean Mòr
Ledaig Point
4
Y L L
A N D
B U T E
Gortenbuie
Lochdon
Lady's Rock
Dunbeg
(An Dùn Beag)
Coirc Bheinn
Ben More
Cruachan Dearg
Beinn Chaisgidle
Balmeanach
Guibean Uluvailt
Corra-bheinn
Cruach Choireadail
Glen More
Oakbank
Gorten
Ganavan Bay
Dunbeg
Cruach Ardura
Maiden Island
Rubh' a' Bhearnaig
Pennyfuir
Beinn na Sreine
Maol na Coille Moire
Balevulin
Derrerach
Craig
Ishriff
Ardachoil
Ardnadrochit
64
Grass Point
Eilean nan Gamhna
Gib Bheinn
Uluvalt
Creag na h-Iolaire
Beinn Fhada
Glas Bheinn
Ardura
Cruach Ardura
Auchnacraig
Carn Bàn
Ruba na Lice
Ardantrive
Balliemore
Oban
(An t-Oban)
Glencruitten
69
Aird of Kinloch
70
Cruach nan Con
Ben Buie
Creach Beinn
Fellonmore
Kerrera
Soroba
Upper Gylen
Glenamachrie
L O C H S C R I D A I N
Pennyghael
Beinn na Croise
Kinlochspelve
Loch Spelve
Croggan
Dalnahaa
Rubha na Faoilinn
Ardmore
Bach Island
Gallanach
Kilbride
Cleigh
Kilmore
5
Killunaig
Maol nan Uan
Lochbuie
Creag nam Fitheach
Maol Ban
63
Portfield
Loch Uisg
Loch Buie
62
Druim Fada
Dubh Sgeir
Rubha Seanach
Lerags
Dunach
Glenfeochan
Brolass
Glenbyre
Beinn a' Bhainne
Minard Point
Ardentallan
Knipoch
34
A'Chruach
Cruachan Min
Beinn Chreagach
Carsaig
Rubha Dubh
Barnacarry
Eilean Dùin
Kilninver
Scammadale
Bragleenbeg
Nuns' Pass
Rubha Garbh Airde
Duachy
Glen Euchar
Shellachan
Creachan Mòr
Frank Lockwood's Island
Ardencaple House
Ardfad
Insh Island
F I R T H O F L O R N
Clachan-Seil
Ardshellach
Corrielorne
Rubha nam Bràithrean
Malcolm's Point
Ellenabeich
Dùn-Mòr
Seil
Easdale
Balvicar
Caddleton
Henderson's Rock
Cruach nam Fearna
6
Pass of Melfort
Melfort
Ardanstur
Garvellachs
Cullipool
Torsay Island
Kilchoan
Kilmelford
Maolachy
35
Isles of the Sea
A'Chùli
Garbh Eileach
Belnahua
Glas Eilean
Degnish
Ardinamar
Eilean Gamhna
Degnish Point
Tullich
Lagalochan
Carn Duchan
Eilean Dubh Mòr
Luing
Kames
Arduaine
Tom Soilleir
Eileach an Naoimh
Lunga
Toberonochy
Shuna
Barravullin
Gleann Domhain
Cruach an Eachlaich
Guirasdeal
Eilean Arsa
Craobh Haven
Lunga
Arichamish
Inverliever
Shuna Point
Gemmil
Kintraw
7
Cruach Scarba
Ardfern
Torran
Scarba
Barrackan
Eilean Mhic Chrion
Ford
Corranmore
Tibertich
Rubha Righinn
Reisa Mhic Phaidean
Eilean Righ
Carnassarie
Old Poltalloch
Eurach
Eilean Dubh
Kirkton
31
Beinn nan Capull
60
Rèisa an t- Sruith
Island Macaskin
73
Kilmartin
Beinn Bhan
Barmolloch
Inahard
Rubh' a' Geodha
Cruach na Seilcheig
Kinuachdrachd
Kinuachdrachd Harbour
Ockavullin
Baluachraig
Knockalava
Port Ceann a' Gharraidh
Gleann Speireig
Glengarrisdale
Poltalloch
F
G
H
J
K

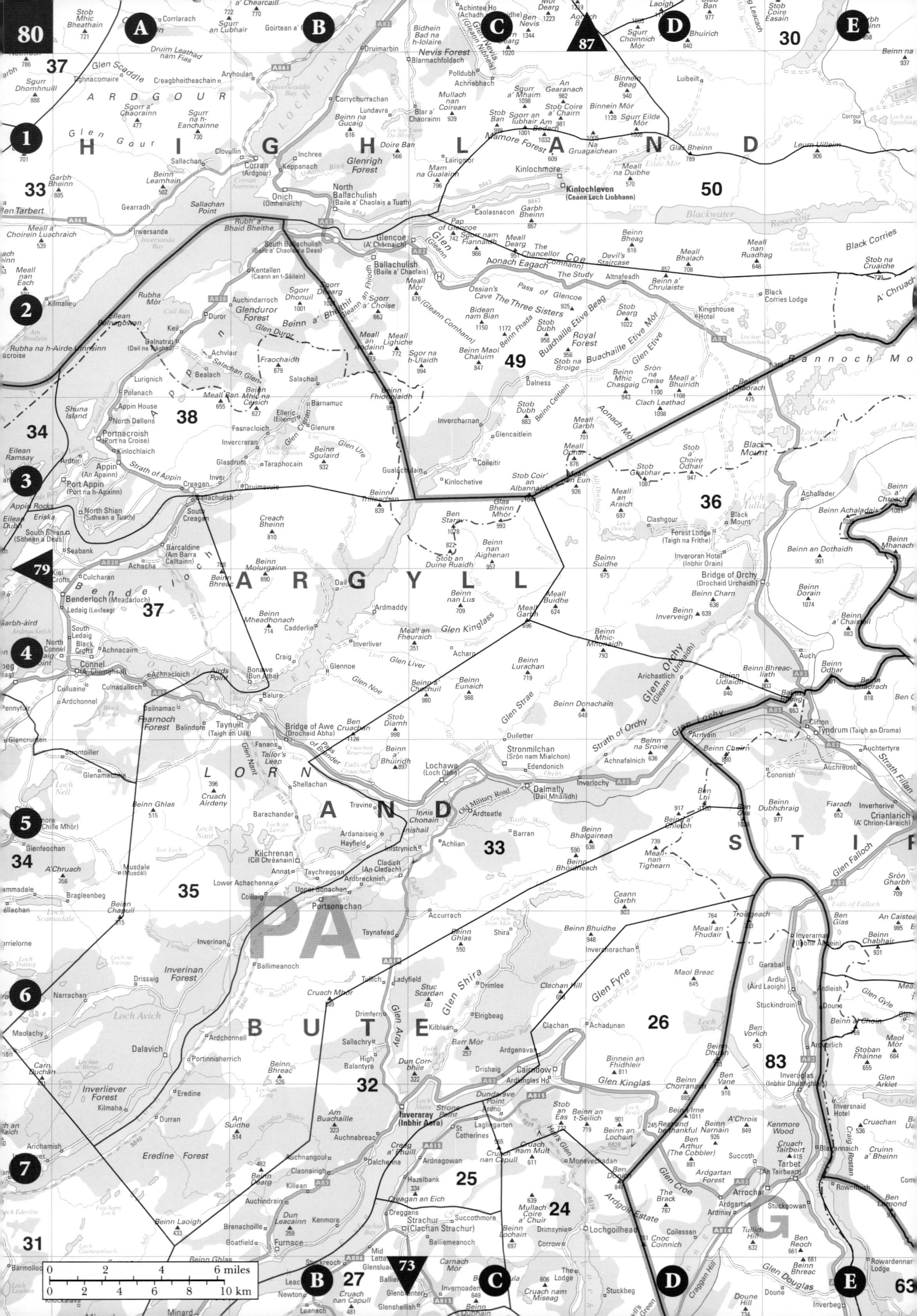
A
B
C
D
E
87
1
2
3
4
5
6
7
79
73
HIGHLAND
ARGYLL
AND
BUTE
PA
STIR
ARDGOUR
Glen Scaddle
Glen Gour
Druim Leathad nam Fias
Corrarlach
Sgurr an Lubhair
Goirtean a' Eòin
Stob Mhic Bheathain
Sgurr Dhomhnuill
Tighnacomaire
Creagbheitheachain
Aryhoulan
Sgorr a' Chaorainn
Sgurr na h-Eanchainne
Clovullin
Sallachan
Corran (Ardgour)
Corran Narrows
Inchree
Keppanach
Glenrigh Forest
Beinn Leamhain
Garbh Bheinn
Gearradh
Sallachan Point
Glen Tarbert
Inversanda
Meall a' Choirein Luachraich
Onich (Omhanaich)
North Ballachulish (Baile a' Chaolais a Tuath)
Rubh' a' Bhaid Bheithe
South Ballachulish (Baile a' Chaolais a Deas)
Glencoe (A' Chàrnaich)
Ballachulish (Baile a' Chaolais)
Kentallen (Ceann an t-Sàilein)
Rubha Mòr
Kilmalieu
Meall nan Each
Auchindarroch
Glenduror Forest
Duror
Glen Duror
Keil
Eilean Balnagowan
Rubha na h-Airde Uinnsinn
Cuil Bay
Sgorr Dhonuil
Sgorr Dhearg
Beinn a' Bheithir
Gleann an Fhiodh
Sgorr a' Choise
Meall Mòr
Meall an Aodainn
Meall Lighiche
Sgor na h-Ulaidh
Druimarbin
Blarmachfoldach
Nevis Forest
Polldubh
Achriabhach
Glen Nevis
Ben Nevis
Mullach nan Coirean
Corrychurrachan
Lundavra
Blar a' Chaorainn
Beinn na Gucaig
Doire Ban
Lairigmor
Mam na Gualainn
Mamore Forest
Kinlochmore
Kinlochleven (Ceann Loch Liobhann)
Sgurr a' Mhaim
Stob Ban
Sgorr an Iubhair
Am Bodach
An Gearanach
Stob Coire a' Chairn
Binnein Mòr
Binnein Beag
Na Gruagaichean
Sgurr Eilde Mòr
Glas Bheinn
Loch Eilde Mòr
Meall na Duibhe
Caolasnacon
Garbh Bheinn
Pap of Glencoe
Sgorr nam Fiannaidh
Meall Dearg
The Chancellor
Aonach Eagach
Devil's Staircase
The Study
Altnafeadh
Glen Coe
Pass of Glencoe
The Three Sisters
Ossian's Cave
Bidean nam Bian
Beinn Fhada
Stob Dubh
Buachaille Etive Beag
Buachaille Etive Mòr
Stob Dearg
Royal Forest
Stob na Broige
Beinn Maol Chaluim
Glen Etive
Blackwater Reservoir
Leven
Beinn Bheag
Meall Bhalach
Meall nan Ruadhag
Black Corries
Stob na Cruaiche
Black Corries Lodge
Kingshouse Hotel
Beinn a' Chrulaiste
Rannoch Moor
Sròn na Creise
Meall a' Bhuiridh
Clach Leathad
Meall a' Bhuiridh
Beinn Mhic Chasgaig
Dalness
Beinn Ceitlein
Aonach Mòr
Stob Dubh
Inverchamnan
Glenceitlein
Coileitir
Kinlochetive
Gualachulain
Meall Garbh
Meall Odhar
Meall an Eun
Stob Coir' an Albannaich
Stob Ghabhar
Stob a' Choire Odhair
Black Mount
Loch Tulla
Achallader
Meall an Araich
Clashgour
Forest Lodge (Taigh na Frithe)
Inveroran Hotel (Inbhir Orain)
Bridge of Orchy (Drochaid Urchaidh)
Beinn Achaladair
Beinn an Dothaidh
Beinn Dorain
Loch Ba
Beinn Chaorach
Leum Uilleim
Corrour Sta
Luibeilt
Sgurr Choinnich Mòr
Stob Coire Easain
Stob Ban
Beinn na Lap
Loch Treig
Appin
Strath of Appin
Port Appin (Port na h-Apainn)
Appin House
North Dallens
Portnacroish (Port na Croise)
Kinlochlaich
Shuna Island
Eilean Ramsay
Lurignich
Polanach
Achvlair
Bealach
Salachan Glen
Fraochaidh
Meall Ban
Beinn Mhic na Ceisich
Salachail
Creran
Barnamuc
Elleric (Eileirig)
Glen Creran
Glenure
Glen Ure
Beinn Sgulaird
Fasnacloich
Invercreran
Glasdrum
Taraphocain
Beinn Fhionnlaidh
Creagan
Inver
Druimavuic
Ballachulish
South Creagan
North Shian (Sithean a Tuath)
South Shian (Sithean a Deas)
Appin Rocks
Eriska
Eilean Dubh
Seabank
Barcaldine (Am Barra Calltainn)
Creach Bheinn
Beinn Trilleachan
Ben Starav
Glas Bheinn Mhòr
Stob an Duine Ruaidh
Beinn nan Aighenan
Beinn Suidhe
Achacha
Kiel Crofts
Culcharan
Benderloch (Meadarloch)
Ledaig (Leideag)
Beinn Molurgainn
Beinn Bhreac
Dail
Ardmaddy
Beinn Mheadhonach
Cadderlie
Beinn nan Lus
Meall Buidhe
Meall Garbh
Glen Kinglass
Meall an Fheuraich
Acharn
Inverliver
Glen Liver
Glen Noe
Craig
Glennoe
South Ledaig
North Connel
Black Crofts
Achnacairn
Connel (A' Choingheal)
Culnadalloch
Achnacloich
Airds Point
Bonawe (Bun Atha)
Balure
Ardchonnel
Cuilvaine
Dailnamac
Fearnoch Forest
Balindore
Taynuilt (Taigh an Uillt)
Bridge of Awe (Drochaid Abha)
Pass of Brander
Ben Cruachan
Stob Diamh
Beinn a' Bhùiridh
Beinn a' Chochuil
Beinn Eunaich
Beinn Lurachan
Glen Strae
Beinn Donachain
Beinn Mhic-Mhonaidh
Glen Orchy (Gleann Urchaidh)
Arichastlich
Beinn Udlaidh
Beinn Bhreac-liath
Beinn Odhar
Beinn Chaorach
Auch
Beinn Inverveigh
Beinn Chaisteil
Beinn a' Chreachain
Beinn Mhanach
Ben Lui
Beinn a' Chleibh
Ben Oss
Beinn Dubhchraig
Tyndrum (Taigh an Droma)
Clifton
Auchtertyre
Strath Fillan
Auchreoch
Cononish
Crianlarich (A' Chrìon-Làraich)
Inverherive
Fiarach
Glen Lochy
Arrivain
Beinn Chuirn
Strath of Orchy
Beinn na Sroine
Achnafalnich
Duiletter
Stronmilchan (Sròn nam Mialchon)
Edendonich
Inverlochy
Dalmally (Dail Mhàilidh)
Lochawe (Loch Obha)
Falls of Cruachan
Glencruitten
Strontoiller
Glenamachrie
Loch Nell
Fanans
Tailor's Leap
Glen Nant
Cruach Airdeny
Shellachan
Beinn Ghlas
Barachander
Trevine
Innis Chonain
Inishail
Old Military Road
Ardteatle
Barran
Beinn Bhalgairean
Achlian
Meall nan Tighearn
Ardanaiseig
Hayfield
Kilchrenan (Cill Chrèanain)
Annat
Cladich (An Cladach)
Taychreggan
Ardbrecknish
Upper Sonachan
Portsonachan
Lower Achachenna
Coillaig
Musdale
A'Chruach
Glenfeochan
Kilmore (Cille Mhòr)
Bragleenbeg
Beinn Chapull
Accurrach
Taynafead
Inverinan
Inverinan Forest
Drissaig
Ballimeanoch
Narrachan
Loch Avich
Maolachy
Dalavich
Ardchonnell
Portinnisherrich
Carn Dubhan
Inverliever Forest
Kilmaha
Eredine
Durran
Eredine Forest
Arichamish
Cruach Mhòr
Tullich
Ladyfield
Stuc Scardan
Glen Shira
Beinn Ghlas
Shira
Drimlee
Elrigbeag
Kilblaan
Drimfern
Glen Aray
Sallachry
Barr Mòr
High Balantyre
Dun Corr-bhile
Beinn Bhreac
An Suidhe
Am Buachaille
Auchnabreac
Inveraray (Inbhir Aora)
St Catherines
Ardgenavan
Drishaig
Cairndow
Ardkinglas Ho
Dundarave Point
Strone Point
Lagingarten
Creag a' Phuill
Dalchenna
Ardnagowan
Hazelbank
Creagan an Eich
Creggans
Strachur (Clachan Strachur)
Succothmore
Balliemeanoch
Auchnangoul
Claonairigh
Killean
Auchindrain
Beinn Dearg
Dun Leacainn
Kenmore
Brenachoille
Goatfield
Furnace
Beinn Laoigh
Mid Letter
Glensluain
Stuckreoch
Newton
Leacann
Cruach nan Capull
Glenbranter
Glenshellish
Carnach Mòr
Beinn Dubhain
Invernoaden
Beinn Ghlas
Cruach nan Capull
Cruach nam Mult
Mullach Coire a' Chuir
Drimsynie
Lochgoilhead
Corrow
Beinn Lochain
The Lodge
Cruach nam Miseag
Stuckbeg
Hell's Glen
Monevechadan
Stob an Eas
Beinn an t-Seilich
Beinn an Lochain
Glen Kinglass
Ben Donich
Ardgoil Estate
The Brack
Cnoc Coinnich
Coilessan
Glen Croe
Beinn Ime
Beinn Narnain
Rest and be thankful
Ben Arthur (The Cobbler)
A'Chrois
Succoth
Ardgartan Forest
Arrochar
Ardgartan
Ardmay
Stuckgowan
Tullich Hill
Ben Reoch
Beinn Bhreac
Glen Douglas
Doune Hill
Douné
Inverbeg
Craggan Hill
Beinn Chorranach
Ben Vane
Binnein an Fhidhleir
Clachan Hill
Glen Fyne
Achadunan
Clachan
Loch Sloy
Ben Vorlich
Beinn Dubh
Inveruglas (Inbhir Dhubhghlais)
Kenmore Wood
Cruach Tairbeirt
Tarbet (An Tairbeart)
Blarennaich
Rowchoish
Ben Lomond
Craig Rostan
Cruinn a' Bheinn
Cruachan
Inversnaid Hotel
Glen Arklet
Stoban Fhàinne
Maol Mor
Beinn a' Choin
Ardvorlich
Doune
Ardleish
Glen Gyle
Ardlui (Àird Laoigh)
Stuckindroin
Garabal
Maol Breac
Beinn Bhuidhe
Invercorrachan
Meall an Fhudair
Troisgeach
Inverarnan (Inbhir Àirnein)
Beinn Chabhair
Ben Glas
An Caisteal
Sròn Gharbh
Glen Falloch
Falls of Falloch
Ceann Garbh
Beinn Bhuidhe
Rowardennan Lodge
Miseag
Barmollo
Carnach Mòr
0 2 4 6 miles
0 2 4 6 8 10 km
37
33
34
38
37
34
35
31
27
25
24
32
26
83
33
36
49
50
30
63
A82
A861
A828
A85
A819
A83
A815
A886
A814
B863
B8074
B840
B845

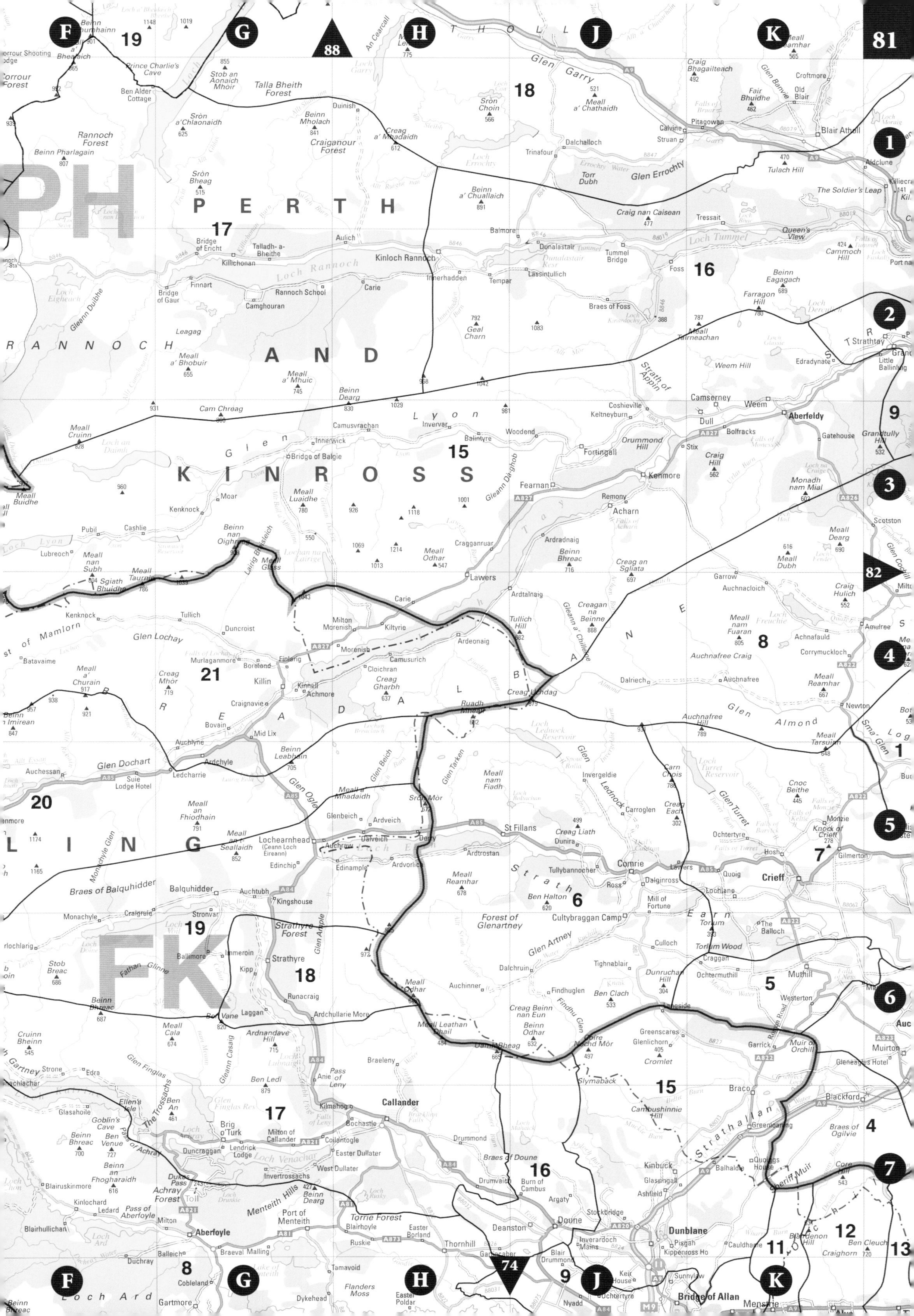
F
G
H
J
K
88
82
74
PH
FK
P E R T H
A N D
K I N R O S S
R A N N O C H
A T H O L L
B R E A D A L B A N E
S T R A T H
L I N G
Beinn Bhrotain
19
Corrour Shooting Lodge
Corrour Forest
Prince Charlie's Cave
Stob an Aonaich Mhoir
Talla Bheith Forest
Ben Alder Cottage
Sròn a'Chlaonaidh
Rannoch Forest
Beinn Pharlagain
Duinish
Beinn Mholach
Craiganour Forest
Creag a' Mhadaidh
Sròn Choin
18
Glen Garry
Meall a' Chathaidh
Craig Bhagailteach
Fair Bhuidhe
Old Blair
Croftmore
Glen Banvie
Calvine
Struan
Pitagowan
Blair Atholl
Dalchalloch
Trinafour
Loch Errochty
Torr Dubh
Glen Errochty
Tulach Hill
Aldclune
Killiecrankie
The Soldier's Leap
Sròn Bheag
Beinn a' Chuallaich
Craig nan Caisean
Tressait
Balmore
Queen's View
Cammoch Hill
Port na Craig
17
Bridge of Ericht
Talladh-a-Bheithe
Aulich
Killichonan
Loch Rannoch
Kinloch Rannoch
Dunalastair
Dunalastair Resr
Tummel Bridge
Loch Tummel
Foss
16
Finnart
Innerhadden
Tempar
Lassintullich
Beinn Eagagach
Bridge of Gaur
Rannoch School
Carie
Camghouran
Loch Eigheach
Gleann Duibhe
Geal Charn
Braes of Foss
Farragon Hill
Meall Tairneachan
Leagag
Meall a' Bhobuir
Meall a' Mhuic
Strath of Appin
Weem Hill
Strathtay
Edradynate
Little Ballinluig
Grandtully
Beinn Dearg
Carn Chreag
Meall Cruinn
Loch an Daimh
Camusvrachan
Innerwick
Inververar
Lyon
Balintyre
Woodend
Coshieville
Keltneyburn
Camserney
Weem
Aberfeldy
Dull
Bolfracks
Gatehouse
Grandtully Hill
Glen
Bridge of Balgie
15
Fortingall
Drummond Hill
Stix
Craig Hill
Kenmore
Monadh nam Mial
Meall Buidhe
Moar
Meall Luaidhe
Gleann Da-ghob
Fearnan
Remony
Acharn
Kenknock
Pubil
Cashlie
Loch Lyon
Lubreoch
Meall nan Subh
Beinn nan Oighreag
Lairig Breisleich
Meall Glas
Meall Odhar
Cragganruar
Ardradnaig
Beinn Bhreac
Creag an Sgliata
Meall Dubh
Meall Dearg
Scotston
Glen Cochill
Sgiath Bhuidhe
Meall Taurnie
Lawers
Garrow
Auchnacloich
Craig Hulich
Milton
Carie
Ardtalnaig
Creagan na Beinne
Kenknock
Tullich
Milton Morenish
Kiltyrie
Tullich Hill
Gleann a' Chilleine
Meall nam Fuaran
Amulree
Forest of Mamlorn
Glen Lochay
Duncroist
Morenish
Ardeonaig
8
Achnafauld
Corrymuckloch
Batavaime
Murlaganmore
Boreland
Finlarig
Camusurich
Auchnafree Craig
Meall a' Churain
Creag Mhòr
21
Killin
Kinnell
Achmore
Cloichran
Creag Gharbh
Dalriech
Auchnafree
Meall Reamhar
Craignavie
Creag Uchdag
Ruadh Mheall
Newton
Beinn Imirean
Bovain
Mid Lix
Loch Lednock Reservoir
Auchnafree Hill
Glen Almond
Meall Tarsuinn
Sma' Glen
Auchlyne
Beinn Leabhain
Ardchyle
Glen Dochart
Auchessan
Suie Lodge Hotel
Ledcharrie
Glen Ogle
Glen Beich
Meall a' Mhadaidh
Glen Tarken
Meall nam Fiadh
Invergeldie
Glen Lednock
Carn Chois
Loch Turret Reservoir
Glen Turret
Cnoc Beithe
20
Meall an Fhiodhain
Glenbeich
Ardveich
Sròn Mòr
Carroglen
Creag Each
Monzie
Knock of Crieff
Glenmore
Monachyle Glen
Meall an t-Seallaidh
Lochearnhead (Ceann Loch Eireann)
Dalveich
Derry
St Fillans
Creag Liath
Dunira
Ochtertyre
Auchraw
Loch Earn
Ardtrostan
Edinchip
Ednample
Ardvorlich
Comrie
Lawers
Hosh
Gilmerton
Braes of Balquhidder
Balquhidder
Auchtubh
Kingshouse
Meall Reamhar
Tullybannocher
Dalginross
Quoig
Crieff
Ross
Lochlane
Ben Halton
6
Mill of Fortune
Monachyle
Craigruie
Stronvar
19
Strathyre Forest
Glen Ample
Forest of Glenartney
Cultybraggan Camp
Dalreoch
Torlum
The Balloch
Glen Artney
Culloch
Torlum Wood
Craggan
Ochtermuthill
Muthill
Stob Breac
Fathan Glinne
Ballimore
Immeroin
Kipp
Strathyre
18
Dalchruin
Tighnablair
Dunruchan Hill
5
Auchinner
Findhuglen
Ben Clach
Westerton
Beinn Bhreac
Runacraig
Meall Odhar
Creag Beinn nan Eun
Findhu Glen
Langside
Ben Vane
Laggan
Ardchullarie More
Meall Cala
Ardnandave Hill
Meall Leathan Dhail
Beinn Odhar
Greenscares
Glenlichorn
Cromlet
Garrick
Muir of Orchill
Muirton
Cruinn Bheinn
Damh Bheag
Coire Odhar Mòr
Gleneagles Hotel
Glen Finglas
Glen Casaig
Braeleny
Slymaback
15
Glen Gartney
Strone
Edra
Anie
Pass of Leny
Braco
Blackford
Ben Ledi
Cambushinnie Hill
Ellen's Isle
Glasahoile
The Trossachs
Ben An
Glen Finglas Res
17
Kilmahog
Callander
Greenloaning
Braes of Ogilvie
4
Goblin's Cave
Beinn Bhreac
Ben Venue
Pass of Achray
Brig o'Turk
Milton of Callander
Bochastle
Coilantogle
Easter Dullater
West Dullater
Falls of Leny
Drummond
Strathallan
Duncraggan
Lendrick Lodge
Loch Vennachar
Beinn an Fhogharaidh
Invertrossachs
Braes of Doune
16
Kinbuck
Balhaldie
Quoiggs House
Core Hill
7
Blairuskinmore
Dukes Pass
Achray Forest
Beinn Dearg
Drumvaich
Burn of Cambus
Glassingall
Ashfield
Sheriff Muir
Kinlochard
Ledard
Pass of Aberfoyle
Loch Drunkie
Menteith Hills
Torrie Forest
Port of Menteith
Argaty
Stockbridge
Blairhullichan
Milton
Aberfoyle
Blairhoyle
Ruskie
Easter Borland
Deanston
Thornhill
Doune
Inverardoch Mains
Dunblane
Pisgah
Kippenross Ho
Cauldhame
Blairdenon Hill
Ochil Hills
12
Ben Cleuch
Craighorn
11
13
Loch Ard
Balleich
Braeval
Malling
Duchray
8
Cobleland
Tamavoid
Gargunnock
Blair Drummond
9
Keir House
Sunnylaw
Bridge of Allan
Flanders Moss
Dykehead
Easter Poldar
Gartmore
Nyadd
Ochtertyre
Menstrie
Beinn Bhreac
A9
A827
A826
A822
A85
A84
A821
A81
A873
A820
M9
B8019
B846
B847
B8079
B8062
B8031
B8033
B8032
B8075
B822

A
B
C
D
E
89
Ben Vuirich
Meall Choire Bhuidhe
Dalmunzie House Hotel
Ben Gulabin
Spittal of Glenshee
Ben Earb
Carn an Daimh
Monamenach
Auchavan
Mid Hill
Cairn Baddoch
Mount Bouie
Cairn of Barns
Wheen
Rottal
18
Meall Breac
Gleann Fearnach
Meall Uaine
Mealna Letter (Duchray Hill)
Badandun Hill
Cairn Daunie
The Drums
Runtaleave
Balnaboth
Glenprosen Village
Hill of Couternach
Eskielawn
Cairnwhorn
Glen Prosen
Glen Uig
Glen Finlet
Glen Damff
Glen Girnaig
Creag an-t Sithein
Finegand
Dalnaglar Castle
Forter
1
16
Aldclune
Killiecrankie
Pass of Killiecrankie
The Soldier's Leap
Ben Vrackie
Tarvie
Straloch
Dalnacarn
Glen Brerachan
Kindrogan Field Centre
Enochdhu
Balvarran
Lamh Dhearg
Glen Shee
Lair
Cray
Mount Blair
Folda
11
Glenisla Forest
Hare Cairn
Tomnun
Glenarm
Glenhead Farm
Easter Lednathie
Tulloch Hill
Craigower
Creag Dhubh
Badyo
10
Kirkmichael
Bridge of Brewlands
Kirkton of Glenisla
Alrick
Meall Mòr
Blacklunans
Cairn Gibbs
Backwater Reservoir
Cat Law
Dykehead
Moulin
Pitlochry
Port na Craig
Cammoch Hill
Strathardle
Ballinluig
Dalrulzian
Knockton
Druim Dearg
Bellaty
Cragh Hill
A
N
Balintore
Pearsie
Meall Reamhar
Knock of Balmyle
Balmyle
Ballintuim
Forest of Alyth
Dykends
Mile Hill
Ascreavie
Balloch
8
2
Milton of Dalcapon
Persie House
Drumderg
Loch of Lintrathen
Bridgend of Lintrathen
Kingoldrum
Kirkton of Kingoldrum
Kinnordy
Strath Tay
Pitnacree
Ballechin
Strathtay
Grandtully
Little Ballinluig
Creag nam Mial
Ashmore
Netherton
Bridge of Craigisla
Balduff Hill
Baldovie
Kirriemuir
Logierait
Tulliemet
Blackcraig Hill
Tullymurdoch
Auchrannie
Westmuir
Balnaguard
Bishopric
9
15
Forest of Clunie
Blackcraig Forest
Bridge of Cally
Rochallie
Bamff
Kirkton of Airlie
Lindertis
Balmacneil
Kindallachan
Guay
Benachally
Hill of Alyth
Shanzie
Craigton
Gatehouse
Grandtully Hill
Kincraigie
Deuchary Hill
Riechip
Cochrage Muir
PH
Tullyfergus
Alyth
Ruthven
Meall Reamhar
Elrick More
Dowally
PERTH
Arlick
Middleton
New Alyth
Jordanstone
Balendoch
3
Craigvinean Forest
Dalguise
Butterstone
Loch of Butterstone
Achalader
Parkhill
Balhary
Castleton
Glamis
Charleston
Dalmarnock
Creag an Eunaich
Craig a' Barns
Forneth
Kinloch
Rattray
Blairgowrie
Leitfie
Meigle
Eassie
Balkeerie
Scotston
8
Druim Mòr
Dunkeld
Concraigie
Craigie
Loch of Lowes
Clunie
Loch of Drumellie
Muirton of Ardblair
Carsie
Rosemount
Kinloch
Arthurstone
Ardler
12
Kirkinch
Newbigging
Newtyle
Kinpurney Hill
Ark Hill
Milton
Meall Dearg
Little Dunkeld
Birnam
Newtyle Hill
Inver
Dunkeld & Birnam Sta
Kirkton of Lethendy
Auchtertyre
Nether Handwick
Glen Cochill
Ballinlick
Drumour
Birnam Hill
Stenton
Thornton
Spittalfield
Keillor
Auchterhouse Hill
81
Craig Hulich
Aldville
Trochry
Caputh
Delvine
Meikleour
Coupar Angus
Kettins
Milton
Obney Hills
AND
Gellyburn
Murthly
Ardoch
Muir of Thorn
Kinclaven
Keithick
Bonnyton
Kirkton of Auchterhouse
Strathbraan
Amulree
Creag Liath
Upper Obney
Waterloo
Laguna
Woodside
Barrelton
Campmuir
Pitcur
Thriepley
Lundie
Auchterhouse
Leoch
3
Meall nan Caoraich
Findowie Hill
Creag na Criche
Bankfoot
Cargill
13
4
Crochan Hill
Little Glenshee
Airntully
West Tofts
Cargieholm
Whitefield
Springfield
Hallyburton Forest
Blacklaw Hill
Littleton
Muirhead
Liff
Birkhill
Fowlis
Craig Lea
Tullybelton
Stanley
Wolfhill
Dunsinnan
Kinrossie
Saucher
Collace
King's Seat
Abernyte
Newton
Botich
KINROSS
Strathord Forest
Guildtown
Kirkton of Collace
Knapp
Denhead of Gray
Benvie
2
DUNDEE
Logiealmond
Harrietfield
Chapelhill
1
Moneydie
Luncarty
Newmiln
Colenden
Stormontfield
St Martins
Pitmiddle Wood
Rossie Priory
14
Ballindean
Kinnaird
Craigdallie
Longforgan
Kingoodie
Sma' Glen
Tulchan
Pickston
Scones Lethendy
Balbeggie
Inchture
Buchanty
Glen Almond
Busby
Pitcairngreen
Almondbank
Old Scone
Scone
Braes of the Carse
Rait
Kilspindie
Pitroddie
Pole Hill
Murray's Hill
Grundcruie
Methven
Keillour
5
Fowlis Wester
Braegrum
Huntingtower
Bridgend
Grange
Kirkton
Balmerino
Gilmerton
Keillour Forest
Forebrae
Tibbermore
PERTH (Real)
Kinnoull Hill
Balthayock
Kinfauns
Kinfauns Forest
Glendoick
Errol
Carse of Gowrie
Dog Bank
Madderty
Newmiln
Dubheads
Crossgates
Findo Gask
Milltown of Aberdalgie
Friarton
Tarsappie
Elcho
Glencarse
Chapelhill
St Madoes
Port Allen
Carthagena Bank
Hazelton Walls
Creich
Rathillet
Kilmany
St David's
Clathy
Craigend
Moncreiffe Hill
Rhynd
Inchyra
Mugdrum Island
Glenduckie Hill
Glenduckie
Norman's Law
Luthrie
Prospect Hill
Kirkton
Gask
Aberdalgie
2
Chapelbank
Bridge of Earn
Newburgh
Dunbog
Moonzie
Broom of Dalreach
Forteviot
Forgandenny
Kintillo
Ormiston Hill
Lindores
Grange of Lindores
Lindifferon
Mount Hill
Cairney
5
Millearne
Kinkell Bridge
Aberuthven
Glenearn
Abernethy
Aberargie
Pitcairlie Hill
Cunnoquhie
Letham
Fernie
Invermay
Duncrub
Garvock
Culteuchar Hill
Dron
Glenfoot
Ayton
Pitmedden Forest
Monimail
Collessie
Cupar
Cupar Muir
6
Machany
Damside
Dunning
Rossie Ochill
Balmanno Hill
Auchterarder
Pitcairns
Kippen
14
Pleasance
Over Rankeilour
Bow of Fife
Muirton
Craig Rossie
Path of Condie
Beins Law
Auchtermuchty
Kinloch
Giffordtown
Springfield
KY
Gleneagles Hotel
3
Balquhandy Hill
Glenfarg Reservoir
Glenfarg
Newton of Balcanquhal
Arngask
Strathmiglo
Dunshalt
Howe of Fife
Ladybank
Craigrothie
Blackford
Gleneagles House
Eastbow Hill
Steele's Knowe
Common of Dunning
Middle Rigg
Duncrievie
Gateside
Nether Urquhart
Lathrisk
Kingskettle
Pitlessie
Struthers
Braes of Ogilvie
4
Glen Eagles
Innerdouny Hill
Dochrie Hill
Slungie Hill
Craigow
Middleton
Burnside
Balmalcolm
Kettlebridge
Newton of Falkland
Falkland
FIFE
Sim's Hill
Glendevon Forest
Upper Tillyrie
West Lomond
Lomond Hills
East Lomond
Freuchie
Clatto Hill
Montrave
7
Glendevon
Dalqueich
Arlary
Glasslie
Muirhead
Langdyke
Kilmux
Glen Devon
Burnfoot
Innerdownie
Warroch
Milnathort
Bishop Hill
Easter Balgedie
Wester Balgedie
Kinnesswood
New Inn
Bonnybank
FK
Scad Hill
Lendrick Hill
Commonedge Hill
Carnbo
Kinross
Loch Leven
Pitkevy
Bandon
Star
7
Kennoway
Broom
12
Ben Cleuch
Craighorn
13
King's Seat Hill
14
Pool of Muckhart
Yetts o' Muckhart
Balado
13
Coldrain
Scotlandwell
St Serf's Island
6
Leslie
GLENROTHES
Cadham
Markinch
Kingsdale
Windygates
Balcurvie
Milton of Balgonie
Drum
Crook of Devon
Gairney Bank
Auchmuirbridge
Woodside
Coaltown of Balgonie
Buckhaven
Methil
0 2 4 6 miles
0 2 4 6 8 10 km
B
75
C
D
E
Pow Mill
Cleish
Cleish Hills
4
Ballingry
Lochore
Kinglassie
5
Thornton
1
Blairingone
Tillicoultry

F
G
H
J
K
90
30
76
1
2
3
4
5
6
7
ABERDEENSHIRE
AB
DD
G U S
Inverbervie
Gourdon
Knox Hill
Laurencekirk
Edzell
Luthermuir
Fettercairn
Marykirk
North Water Bridge
Logie Pert
Johnshaven
St Cyrus
Milton Ness
Morphie
Hillside
Kinnaber
Brechin
Little Brechin
Trinity
Stracathro
Keithock
Templewood
Bridge of Dun
Dun
Montrose
Montrose Basin
Ferryden
Scurdie Ness
Fishtown of Usan
Long Craig
Boddin Point
Braehead of Lunan
Lunan
Lunan Bay
Redcastle
Inverkeilor
Red Head
Ethie Mains
Auchmithie
Meg's Craig
The Deil's Heid
Arbroath
St Vigeans
Colliston
Friockheim
Guthrie
Letham
Carmyllie
Arbirlot
Elliot
East Haven
Carnoustie
Barry Links
Buddon Ness
Monifieth
Monikie
Muirdrum
Panbride
Forfar
Lunanhead
Kingsmuir
Aberlemno
Finavon
Tannadice
Oathlaw
Careston
Memus
Fern
Noranside
Menmuir
Montreathmont Forest
Montreathmont Moor
Farnell
Rossie Moor
Wuddy Law
Tay Road Bridge
Newport-on-Tay
Tayport
Tentsmuir Point
Tentsmuir Forest
Leuchars
Guardbridge
Eden Mouth
Out Head
St Andrews Bay
St Andrews
Kinkell Ness
Buddo Ness
Boarhills
Babbet Ness
Kingsbarns
Cambo Ness
North Carr
Tullybothy Craigs
Craighead
Fife Ness
Crail
West Ness
Kilrenny
Anstruther
Pittenweem
St Monans
Elie
Earlsferry
Colinsburgh
Largoward
Peat Inn
Largo Bay
Lower Largo
Ruddons Point
Chapel Ness
Sauchar Point
Bell Rock (Inchcape)
North Ness
Isle of May
South Ness
A90
A92
A94
A932
A933
A934
A935
A937
A91
A914
A915
A917
A919
A930

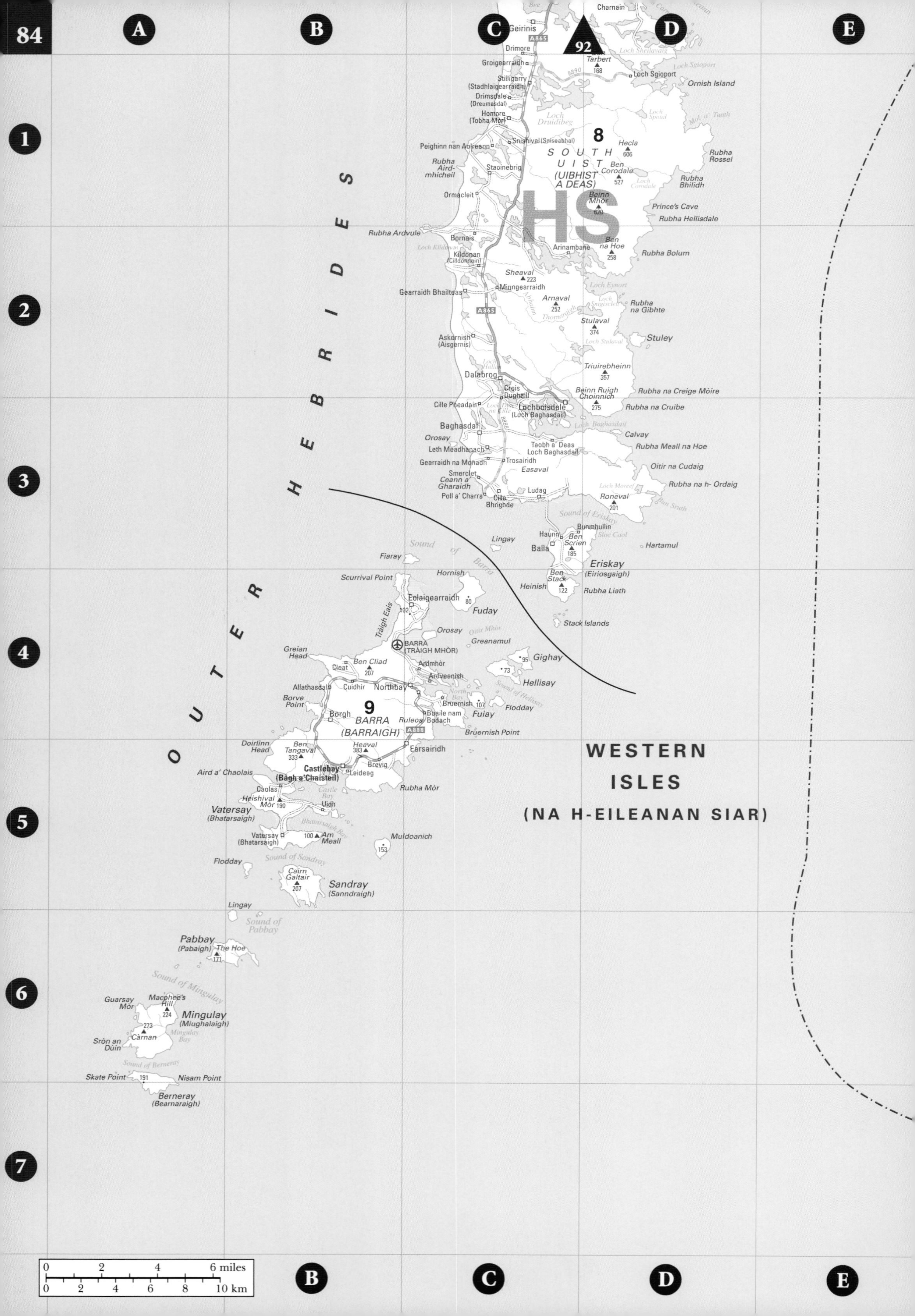
A
B
C
D
E
1
2
3
4
5
6
7
92
OUTER HEBRIDES
WESTERN ISLES
(NA H-EILEANAN SIAR)
HS
8
SOUTH UIST
(UIBHIST A DEAS)
9
BARRA
(BARRAIGH)
Geirinis
Drimore
Charnain
Tarbert
Loch Sgioport
Ornish Island
Groigearraidh
Stilligarry
(Stadhlaigearraidh)
Drimsdale
(Dreumasdal)
Homore
(Tobha Mòr)
Snishival (Sniseabhal)
Peighinn nan Aoireann
Rubha Aird-mhicheil
Stoinebrig
Hecla
Ben Corodale
Rubha Rossel
Rubha Bhilidh
Ormacleit
Beinn Mhòr
Prince's Cave
Rubha Hellisdale
Rubha Ardvule
Bornais
Kildonan
(Cilldonnain)
Arinambane
Ben na Hoe
Rubha Bolum
Sheaval
Minngearraidh
Gearraidh Bhailteas
Arnaval
Rubha na Gibhte
Stulaval
Stuley
Askernish
(Aisgernis)
Triuirebheinn
Dalabrog
Crois Dughaill
Beinn Ruigh Choinnich
Rubha na Creige Mòire
Rubha na Cruibe
Cille Pheadair
Lochboisdale
(Loch Baghasdail)
Baghasdal
Orosay
Calvay
Rubha Meall na Hoe
Leth Meadhanach
Taobh a' Deas Loch Baghasdail
Gearraidh na Monadh
Trosairidh
Oitir na Cudaig
Easaval
Smerclet
Ceann a' Gharaidh
Rubha na h- Ordaig
Poll a' Charra
Cille Bhrighde
Ludag
Roneval
Lingay
Haunn
Ben Scrien
Eriskay
(Eiriosgaigh)
Balla
Hartamul
Fiaray
Hornish
Scurrival Point
Ben Stack
Heinish
Rubha Liath
Eolaigearraidh
Fuday
Stack Islands
Tràigh Eais
Orosay
Greanamul
Greian Head
BARRA
(TRÀIGH MHÒR)
Gighay
Ben Cliad
Ardmhòr
Cleat
Hellisay
Allathasdal
Cuidhir
Northbay
Ardveenish
Borve Point
Bruernish
Flodday
Borgh
Buaile nam Bodach
Fuiay
Ruleos
Bruernish Point
Doirlinn Head
Ben Tangaval
Heaval
Eàrsairidh
Castlebay
(Bàgh a'Chaisteil)
Brevig
Leideag
Aird a' Chaolais
Caolas
Rubha Mòr
Heishival Mòr
Vatersay
(Bhatarsaigh)
Uidh
Am Meall
Muldoanich
Flodday
Cairn Galtair
Sandray
(Sanndraigh)
Lingay
Pabbay
(Pabaigh)
The Hoe
Guarsay Mòr
Macphee's Hill
Mingulay
(Miughalaigh)
Sròn an Dùin
Càrnan
Skate Point
Nisam Point
Berneray
(Bearnaraigh)
0 2 4 6 miles
0 2 4 6 8 10 km

F
G
H
J
K
1
2
3
4
5
6
7
93
86
78
The Hoe
233
Lorgill
Table South)
488
Ben Connan
244
55
Beinn na Boineid
371
Ben Idrigill
340
Harlosh Point
Harlosh Island
Balmore
Ose
Ebost
Tarner Island
Ullinish
Beinn na Cloiche
232
Am Maol
212
Bracadale
56
Coillore
Struan
Ben Duagrich
304
Mugeary
400
Stroc-bheinn
S K Y E
(ANT-EILEAN SGITHEANACH)
Beinn Totaig
51
Roneval
439
291
Meall an Fhuarain
Camastianavaig
Lower Ollach
Ben Lee
445
Peinchorran
Glen Varragill
Broc-bheinn
An Dubh Sgeir
MacLeod's Maidens
Idrigill Point
Loch Bracadale
Wiay
Oronsay
Ardtreck Point
Portnalong
Fernilea
Rubha nan Clach
A863
A87
INNER HEBRIDES
Arnaval
369
Carbost
Drynoch
Glen Drynoch
48
Glenn Oraid
Talisker
Merkadale
HIGHLAND
Sligachan
Glamaig
775
Stockval
416
Glen Eynort
Biod Mòr
383
Eynort
IV
47
Beinn Bhreac
445
Beinn Dearg
Glen Sligachan
Cuillin Hills
Grula
Beinn a' Bhràghad
461
Minginish
Bruach na Frìthe
958
Am Basteir
935
Sgurr nan Gillean
965
Sgurr Thuilm
879
Sgurr a' Mhadaidh
918
Harta Corrie
Sgurr a' Ghreadaidh
973
Beinn Staic
411
Loch Eynort
An Cruachan
435
965
Sgurr na Banachdich
Sgurr Dearg (Inaccessible Pinnacle)
986
Sgurr Mhic Choinnich
948
Glenbrittle
Bualintur
Beinn an Eòin
312
Cuinamean
Sgurr Alasdair
993
Sgurr Dubh Mòr
944
49
Druim Hain
Loch Coruisk
Sgurr na Stri
497
Strath
Camas
Rubha Thearna Sgurr
Sgurr nan Eag
924
Gars-bheinn
895
Loch Brittle
Ceann na Beinne
225
Rubh' an Dùnain
Beinn Bhreac
141
Loch Scavaig
Leac nam Faoileann
41
Soay
Molchlach
Camas nan Gall
Elgol
Prince Charles's Cave
CUILLIN SOUND
SEA OF THE HEBRIDES
CANNA
Carn a' Ghaill
210
Compass Hill
140
44
A'Chill
Camas Tharbernish
Garrisdale Point
Sròn Ruail
Canna Harbour
Sanday
Tarbert Bay
Rubha Shamhnan Insir
Kilmory
Sound of Canna
278
Sgaorishal
Mullach Mòr
304
PH
Rubha na Roinne
Humla
Bloodstone Hill
388
A'Bhrideanach
Kinloch
Orval
571
RUM (RHUM)
43
Sgor Reidh
263
An Dornabac
591
Barkeval
Hallival
723
Askival
812
Bagh na h-Uamha
Garbh Sgeir
Oigh-sgeir
Harris
Ainshval
781
Ival
528
764
Sgurr nan Gillean
Rubha Sgor an t-Snidhe
Rubha nam Meirleach
SOUND OF RUM
Cleadale
Bay of Laig
An Cruachan
299
Rubha an Fhasaidh
Beinn Tighe
315
Laig
EIGG
42
Kildonnan
393
An Sgurr
Galmisdale
Sound of Eigg
Eilean nan Each
Gòdag
Rubh' Leam na Làraich
Beinn Airein
137
41
Port Mòr
Muck
Sanna Point
Fascadale
Achateny
Sanna
36
Sanna Bay
Achnaha
Meall nan Con
437
401
Beinn an Leathaid
Point of Ardnamurchan
Portuairk
Achosnich
Grigadale

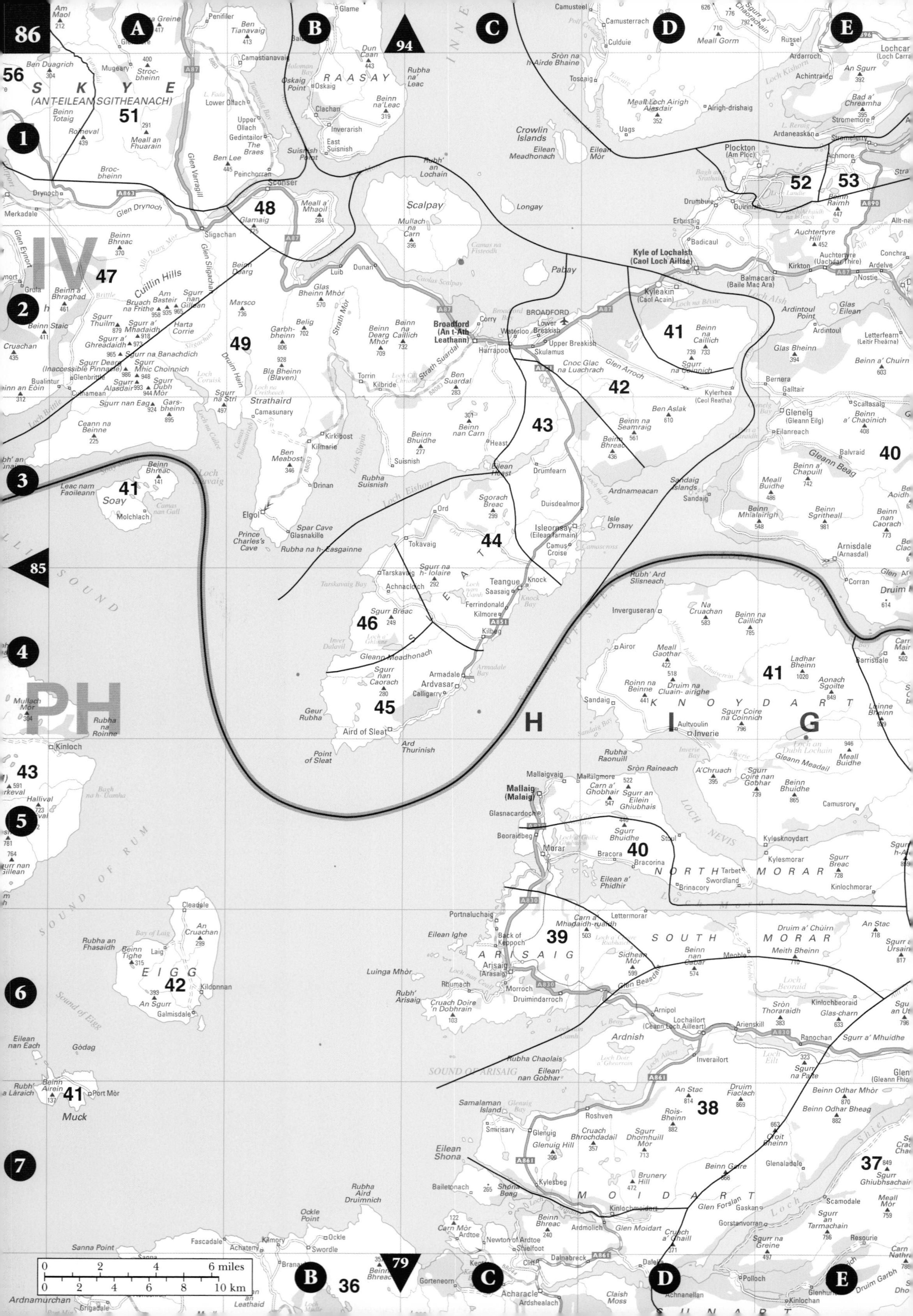

A
B
C
D
E
94
85
79
1
2
3
4
5
6
7
56
47
51
48
49
47
41
43
42
44
45
46
40
39
38
37
36
52
53
IV
PH
H
I
G
S K Y E
(ANT-EILEAN SGITHEANACH)
R A A S A Y
Scalpay
Pabay
Soay
Crowlin Islands
K N O Y D A R T
N O R T H M O R A R
S O U T H M O R A R
A R I S A I G
M O I D A R T
E I G G
Muck
Am Maol
Ben Duagrich
Beinn Totaig
Roineval
Broc-bheinn
Drynoch
Merkadale
Glen Drynoch
Glen Eynort
Sligachan
Glen Sligachan
Glen Varragill
Sconser
Glamaig
Beinn Dearg
Marsco
Cuillin Hills
Am Basteir
Sgurr nan Gillean
Bruach na Frithe
Sgurr Thuilm
Sgurr a' Mhadaidh
Sgurr a' Ghreadaidh
Sgurr na Banachdich
Sgurr Dearg (Inaccessible Pinnacle)
Sgurr Mhic Choinnich
Sgurr Alasdair
Sgurr Dubh Mòr
Sgurr nan Eag
Gars-bheinn
Harta Corrie
Glenbrittle
Bualintur
Cuilnamean
Beinn Staic
Cruachan
Ceann na Beinne
Loch Brittle
Loch Coruisk
Druim Hain
Sgurr na Stri
Camasunary
Strathaird
Leac nam Faoileann
Molchlach
Soay Sound
Loch Scavaig
Elgol
Prince Charles's Cave
Glasnakille
Spar Cave
Rubha na h-Easgainne
Drinan
Ben Meabost
Kirkibost
Kilmarie
Bla Bheinn (Blaven)
Garbh-bheinn
Belig
Glas Bheinn Mhòr
Strath Mòr
Torrin
Kilbride
Strath Suardal
Beinn Dearg Mhòr
Beinn na Caillich
Ben Suardal
Beinn Bhuidhe
Beinn nan Carn
Suisnish
Rubha Suisnish
Loch Slapin
Loch Eishort
Heast
Luib
Dunan
Broadford (An t-Ath Leathann)
BROADFORD
Corry
Waterloo
Lower Breakish
Upper Breakish
Harrapool
Skulamus
Cnoc Glac na Luachrach
Glen Arroch
Kylerhea (Ceol Reatha)
Ben Aslak
Beinn na Seamraig
Beinn Bhreac
Kyleakin (Caol Acain)
Kyle of Lochalsh (Caol Loch Aillse)
Beinn na Caillich
Sgurr na Coinnich
Loch Alsh
Eilean Heast
Drumfearn
Duisdealmor
Sgorach Breac
Ord
Isleornsay (Eilean Iarmain)
Isle Ornsay
Camus Croise
Tokavaig
Tarskavaig
Tarskavaig Bay
Sgurr na h-Iolaire
Achnacloich
Teangue
Saasaig
Knock
Knock Bay
Ferrindonald
Kilmore
Kilbeg
Sgurr Breac
Gleann Meadhonach
Sgurr nan Caorach
Armadale
Armadale Bay
Ardvasar
Calligarry
Geur Rubha
Aird of Sleat
Point of Sleat
Ard Thurinish
S L E A T
Inver Dalavil
Glame
Balachuirn
Dun Caan
Oskaig Point
Oskaig
Holoman Bay
Rubha na' Leac
Beinn na' Leac
Clachan
Inverarish
East Suisnish
Suisnish Point
Rubh' an Lochain
Meall a' Mhaoil
Mullach na Carn
Camas na Fìsteodh
Caolas Scalpay
Eilean Meadhonach
Eilean Mòr
Longay
Penifiler
Ben Tianavaig
Camastianavaig
Mugeary
Stroc-bheinn
Meall an Fhuarain
Lower Ollach
Upper Ollach
Gedintailor
The Braes
Ben Lee
Peinchorran
Camusteel
Camusterrach
Culduie
Sròn na h-Airde Bhaine
Toscaig
Meall Loch Airigh Alasdair
Airigh-drishaig
Uags
Meall Gorm
Sgurr a' Chaorachain
Russel
Ardarroch
Achintraid
Loch Kishorn
An Sgurr
Bad a' Chreamha
Stromemore
Ardaneaskan
Strome Ferry
Achmore
Plockton (Am Ploc)
Drumbuie
Duirinish
Erbusaig
Badicaul
Balmacara (Baile Mac Ara)
Beinn Raimh
Auchtertyre Hill
Auchtertyre (Uachdar Thìre)
Kirkton
Conchra
Ardelve
Nostie
Lochcarron (Loch Carron)
Ardintoul Point
Ardintoul
Glas Eilean
Letterfearn (Leitir Fhearna)
Glas Bheinn
Beinn a' Chuirn
Bernera
Galltair
Glenelg (Gleann Eilg)
Eilanreach
Scallasaig
Beinn a' Chaoinich
Balvraid
Gleann Beag
Beinn a' Chapuill
Meall Buidhe
Beinn Mhialairigh
Beinn Sgritheall
Beinn nan Caorach
Arnisdale (Arnasdal)
Corran
Sandaig Islands
Sandaig
Ardnameacan
Rubh' Ard Slisneach
Loch Hourn
Inverguseran
Na Cruachan
Beinn na Caillich
Airor
Meall Gaothar
Druim na Cluain-airighe
Ladhar Bheinn
Aonach Sgoilte
Barrisdale
Roinn na Beinne
Sandaig
Sgurr Coire na Coinnich
Aultvoulin
Inverie
Inverie Bay
Rubha Raonuill
Sròn Raineach
Loch an Dubh Lochain
Gleann Meadail
Meall Buidhe
A' Chruach
Sgurr Coire nan Gobhar
Beinn Bhuidhe
Camusrory
Mallaigvaig
Mallaigmore
Mallaig (Malaig)
Carn a' Ghobhair
Sgurr an Eilein Ghiubhais
Glasnacardoch
Beoraidbeg
Morar
Sgurr Bhuidhe
Bracora
Bracorina
Stoul
Loch Nevis
Kylesknoydart
Kylesmorar
Tarbet
Swordland
Brinacory
Eilean a' Phidhir
Sgurr Breac
Kinlochmorar
Loch Morar
Portnaluchaig
Lettermorar
Carn a' Mhadaidh-ruadh
Eilean Ighe
Back of Keppoch
Arisaig (Arasaig)
Sidhean Mòr
Beinn nan Cabar
Meoble
Meith Bheinn
Druim a' Chùirn
An Stac
Luinga Mhòr
Rhumach
Loch nan Ceall
Morroch
Druimindarroch
Glen Beasdale
Rubh' Arisaig
Cruach Doire 'n Dobhrain
Loch Beoraid
Sròn Thoraraidh
Kinlochbeoraid
Glas-charn
Arnipol
Lochailort (Ceann Loch Ailleart)
Arienskill
Ranochan
Sgurr a' Mhuidhe
Ardnish
Loch Eilt
Sgurr na Paiteachan
Rubha Chaolais
Sound of Arisaig
Eilean nan Gobhar
Inverailort
Loch Ailort
An Stac
Druim Fiaclach
Rois-Bheinn
Beinn Odhar Mhòr
Beinn Odhar Bheag
Samalaman Island
Roshven
Smirisary
Glenuig
Glenuig Hill
Cruach Bhrochdadail
Sgurr Dhomhuill Mòr
Croit Bheinn
Glenaladale
Eilean Shona
Brunery Hill
Beinn Gaire
Loch Shiel
Scamodale
Sgurr Ghiubhsachain
Meall Mòr
Kylesbeg
Shona Beag
Bailetonach
Kinlochmoidart
Glen Forslan
Gaskan
Glen Moidart
Ardmolich
Beinn Bhreac
Carn Mòr
Ardtoe
Newton of Ardtoe
Shielfoot
Cruach a' Ghaill
Gorstanvorran
Sgurr an Tarmachain
Sgurr na Greine
Resourie
Dalnabreck
Dalelia
Polloch
Glenhurich
Kinlochan
Achnanellan
Acharacle
Ardshealach
Claish Moss
Gorteneorn
Ockle
Ockle Point
Swordle
Kilmory
Fascadale
Achateny
Sanna Point
Branault
Ardnamurchan
Grigadale
Rubha Aird Druimnich
Kinloch
Mullach Mòr
Rubha na Roinne
Hallival
Askival
Sgurr nan Gillean
Bagh na h-Uamha
Sound of Rum
Cleadale
Bay of Laig
An Cruachan
Rubha an Fhasaidh
Beinn Tighe
Laig
An Sgurr
Kildonnan
Galmisdale
Sound of Eigg
Eilean nan Each
Gòdag
Beinn Airein
Port Mòr
Rubh' a Làraich
Sound of Sleat
0 2 4 6 miles
0 2 4 6 8 10 km

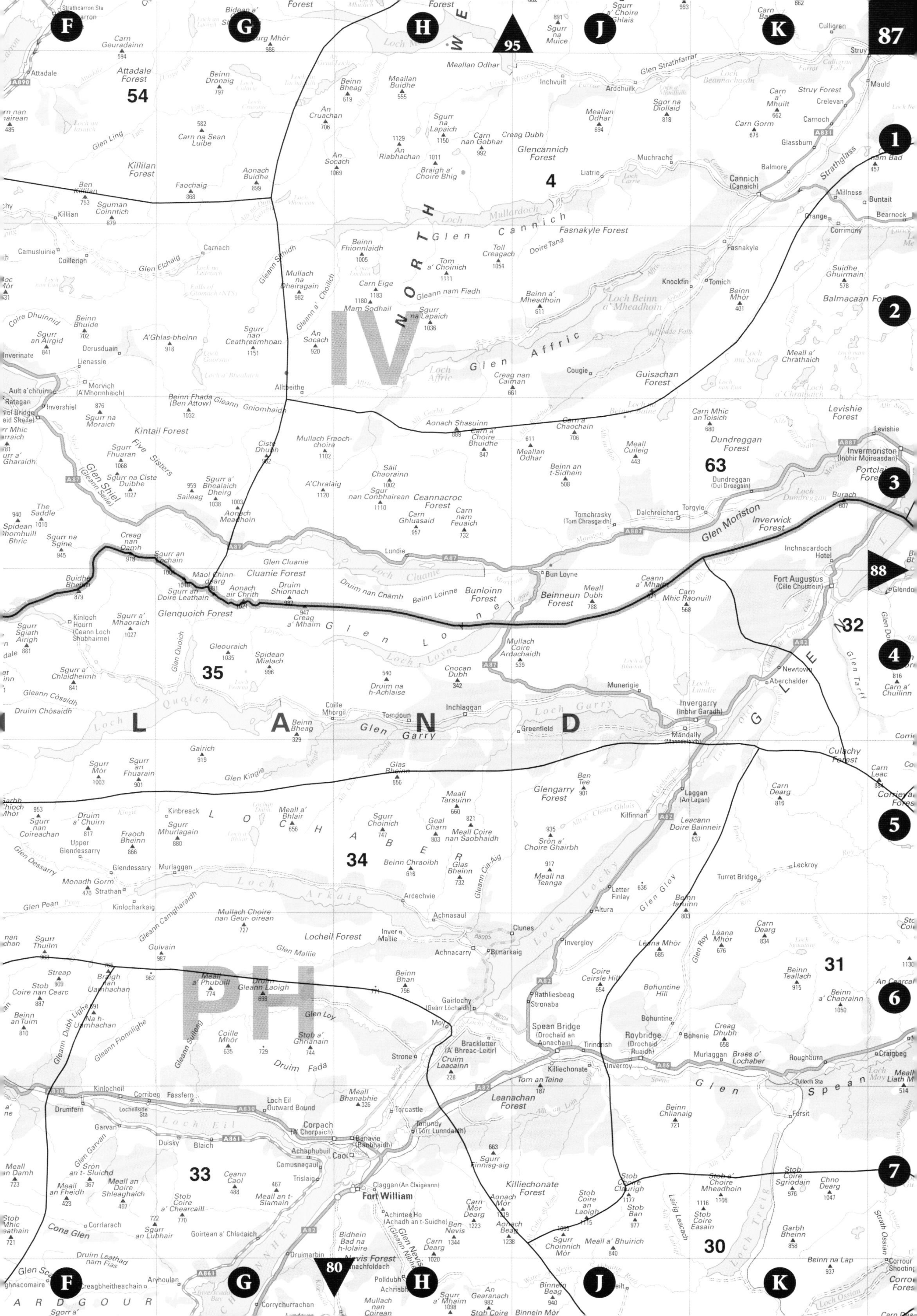
F
G
H
95
J
K
Strathcarron Sta
Carn Geuradainn
594
Bidean a' Ghlas
Sgurr a' Choire Ghlais
Sgurr na Muice
891
993
Culligran
Struy
Attadale
A890
Attadale Forest
54
Beinn Dronaig
797
Beinn Bheag
619
Meallan Buidhe
555
Meallan Odhar
Inchvuilt
Glen Strathfarrar
Ardchuilk
Loch Beannacharan
Carn a' Mhuilt
662
Struy Forest
Crelevan
Mauld
An Cruachan
706
Sgurr na Lapaich
1150
Carn nan Gobhar
992
Creag Dubh
Meallan Odhar
694
Sgor na Diollaid
818
Carn Gorm
676
Carnoch
A831
582
Carn na Sean Luibe
Glen Ling
1129
An Riabhachan
1011
Braigh a' Choire Bhig
Glencannich Forest
Muchrachd
Glassburn
1
Killilan Forest
Aonach Buidhe
899
An Socach
1069
4
Liatrie
Cannich (Canaich)
Balmore
Strathglass
Carn nam Bad
457
Ben Killilan
753
Faochaig
868
Sguman Coinntich
879
Loch Mullardoch
Millness
Buntait
Killilan
Glen Cannich
Fasnakyle Forest
Grange
Bearnock
Corrimony
Camusluinie
Carnach
Beinn Fhionnlaidh
1005
Toll Creagach
1054
Doire Tana
Fasnakyle
Coillerigh
Glen Elchaig
Gleann Sithidh
Tom a' Choinich
1111
NORTH
Falls of Glomach (NTS)
Mullach na Dheiragain
982
Carn Eige
1183
Gleann nam Fiadh
Beinn a' Mheadhoin
611
Knockfin
Tomich
Loch Beinn a' Mheadhoin
Beinn Mhòr
401
Suidhe Ghuirmain
578
Balmacaan Forest
1180
Mam Sodhail
Sgurr na Lapaich
1036
2
Coire Dhuinnid
Beinn Bhuide
702
Sgurr an Airgid
841
A'Ghlas-bheinn
918
Sgurr nan Ceathreamhnan
1151
An Socach
920
IV
Glen Affric
Plodda Falls
Loch ma Stac
Meall a' Chrathaich
Dorusduain
Invernate
Lienassie
Loch Affric
Creag nan Caiman
661
Cougie
Guisachan Forest
Morvich (A'Mhormhaich)
Alltbeithe
Ault a'chruinn
Ratagan
Inversheil
876
Sgurr na Moraich
Beinn Fhada (Ben Attow)
1032
Gleann Gniomhaidh
Aonach Shasuinn
889
Carn a' Choire Bhuidhe
847
611
Meallan Odhar
Carn a' Chaochain
706
Carn Mhic an Toisich
680
Levishie Forest
Levishie
Kintail Forest
Five Sisters
Ciste Dhubh
982
Mullach Fraoch-choire
1102
Beinn an t-Sidhein
508
Meall Cuileig
443
Dundreggan Forest
63
Invermoriston (Inbhir Moireasdan)
A887
Portclair Forest
Sgurr Fhuaran
1068
Sgurr na Ciste Duibhe
1027
Sàil Chaorainn
1002
Dundreggan (Dul Dreagain)
Glen Shiel (Gleann Seile)
A87
959
Saileag
Sgurr a' Bhealaich Dheirg
1038
A'Chralaig
1120
Sgurr nan Conbhairean
1110
Ceannacroc Forest
Loch Dundreggan
Burach
607
3
940
The Saddle
1010
Spidean Dhomhuill Bhric
1003
Aonach Meadhoin
Carn Ghluasaid
957
Carn nam Feuaich
732
Tomchrasky (Tom Chrasgaidh)
Dalchreichart
Torgyle
Glen Moriston
Inverwick Forest
Sgurr na Sgine
945
Creag nan Damh
918
Sgurr an Lochain
1004
A887
Lundie
Glen Cluanie
Inchnacardoch Hotel
Buidhe Bheinn
879
Maol Chinn-dearg
981
1010
Sgurr an Doire Leathain
Cluanie Forest
Loch Cluanie
Bun Loyne
Ceann a' Mhaim
Fort Augustus (Cille Chuimein)
88
Aonach air Chrith
1021
Druim Shionnach
987
Druim nan Cnamh
Beinn Loinne
Bunloinn Forest
Beinneun Forest
Meall Dubh
788
Carn Mhic Raonuill
568
32
Sgurr Sgiath Airigh
881
Kinloch Hourn (Ceann Loch Shubhairne)
Sgurr a' Mhaoraich
1027
Glenquoich Forest
947
Creag a' Mhaim
Glen Loyne
4
Glen Quoich
Gleouraich
1035
Spidean Mialach
996
Loch Loyne
Mullach Coire Ardachaidh
539
Newtown
Aberchalder
Glen Tarff
Sgurr a' Chlaidheimh
841
35
540
Druim na h-Achlaise
Cnocan Dubh
342
Munerigie
Carn a' Chuilinn
816
Gleann Còsaidh
Druim Chòsaidh
Coille Mhorgil
Inchlaggan
Tomdoun
Loch Garry
Invergarry (Inbhir Garadh)
LAND
Loch Quoich
Beinn Bheag
329
Glen Garry
Greenfield
Mandally (Manndalaidh)
Gairich
919
Glas Bheinn
656
Culachy Forest
Sgurr Mòr
1003
Sgurr an Fhuarain
901
Glen Kingie
Ben Tee
901
Glengarry Forest
Laggan (An Lagan)
Carn Leac
Carn Dearg
816
Corrieyairack Forest
953
Kinbreack
LOCHABER
Meall a' Bhlair
656
Meall Tarsuinn
660
821
Kilfinnan
Sgurr nan Coireachan
Druim a' Chuirn
817
Sgurr Mhurlagain
880
Sgurr Choinich
747
Geal Charn
803
Meall Coire nan Saobhaidh
935
Sròn a' Choire Ghairbh
Leacann Doire Bainneir
637
A82
5
Upper Glendessarry
Fraoch Bheinn
866
Glen Dessarry
Glendessary
Murlaggan
34
Beinn Chraoibh
616
Glas Bheinn
732
Gleann Cia-Aig
917
Meall na Teanga
Leckroy
Turret Bridge
Monadh Gorm
470
Strathan
Loch Arkaig
Ardechvie
636
Letter Finlay
Glen Gloy
Beinn Iaruinn
803
Glen Pean
Kinlocharkaig
Gleann Camgharaidh
Mullach Choire nan Geur-oirean
727
Achnasaul
Altura
Loch Lochy
Carn Dearg
834
Sgurr Thuilm
963
Gulvain
987
Locheil Forest
Inver Mallie
Clunes
Invergloy
Lèana Mhòr
685
Glen Roy
Lèana Mhor
676
31
Glen Mallie
Achnacarry
Bunarkaig
Streap
909
Braigh nan Uamhachan
962
Meall a' Phubuill
774
Druim Gleann Laoigh
698
771
Beinn Bhan
796
Coire Ceirsle Hill
654
Bohuntine Hill
Beinn Teallach
915
Beinn a' Chaorainn
1050
An Cearcal
6
Stob Coire nan Cearc
887
PH
Gairlochy (Geàrr Lòchaidh)
Rathliesbeag
Stronaba
891
Na h-Uamhachan
Glen Loy
Moy
Bohuntine
Beinn an Tuim
810
Gleann Dubh Lighe
Gleann Fionnlighe
Gleann Suileag
Coille Mhòr
635
729
Stob a' Ghrianain
744
Brackletter (A' Bhreac-Leitir)
Spean Bridge (Drochaid an Aonachain)
Tirindrish
Roybridge (Drochaid Ruaidh)
Bohenie
Creag Dhubh
658
Murlaggan
Braes o' Lochaber
Roughburn
Craigbeg
Druim Fada
Strone
Cruim Leacainn
228
Killiechonate
Inverroy
A86
Tulloch Sta
Loch Moy
Meall Liath M
514
Kinlocheil
Corribeg
Fassfern
A830
Tom an Teine
187
Glen Spean
Drumfern
Lochielside Sta
Loch Eil
Loch Eil Outward Bound
Meall Bhanabhie
326
Torcastle
Leanachan Forest
Beinn Chlianaig
721
Fersit
Garvan
A861
Duisky
Blaich
Corpach (A' Chorpaich)
Banavie (Banbhaidh)
Tomacharich
Torlundy (Torr Lunndaidh)
Glen Garvan
Achaphubuil
Caol
663
Sgurr Finnisg-aig
Meall nan Damh
723
Sròn an t-Sluichd
367
Meall an Fheidh
423
Meall an Doire Shleaghaich
407
33
Ceann Caol
488
467
Meall an t-Slamain
Camusnagaul
Trislaig
Claggan (An Claigeann)
Fort William
Killiechonate Forest
Stob Choire Claurigh
1177
Stob a' Choire Mheadhoin
1106
Stob Coire Sgriodain
976
Chno Dearg
1047
7
Stob Coire a' Chearcaill
770
1116
Stob Coire Easain
Stob Coire an Laoigh
1115
Stob Ban
977
Lairig Leacach
Stob Mhic Bheathain
721
Corrlarach
Cona Glen
722
Sgurr an Lubhair
Goirtean a' Chladaich
A82
Achintee Ho (Achadh an t-Suidhe)
Carn Mor Dearg
1223
Aonach Mor
1219
Aonach Beag
1236
Ben Nevis
1344
1055
Sgurr Choinnich Mòr
Meall a' Bhuiridh
840
Loch Treig
30
Garbh Bheinn
858
Strath Ossian
Druim Leathad nam Fias
Drumarbin
Bidhein Bad na h-Iolaire
Nevis Forest
Achnachfoldach
Glen Nevis (Gleann Nibheis)
Carn Dearg
1020
Beinn na Lap
937
Corrour Shooting Lodge
Corrour Forest
Glen Scaddle
F
Creagbheitheachain
Aryhoulan
A861
G
80
Polldubh
Achriabhach
H
Binnein Beag
940
J
K
Loch Ossian
ARDGOUR
Sgorr a'
Corrychurrachan
Mullach nan Coirean
Sgurr a' Mhaim
1098
An Gearanach
982
Stob Coire
Binnein Mòr
Carn Dearg

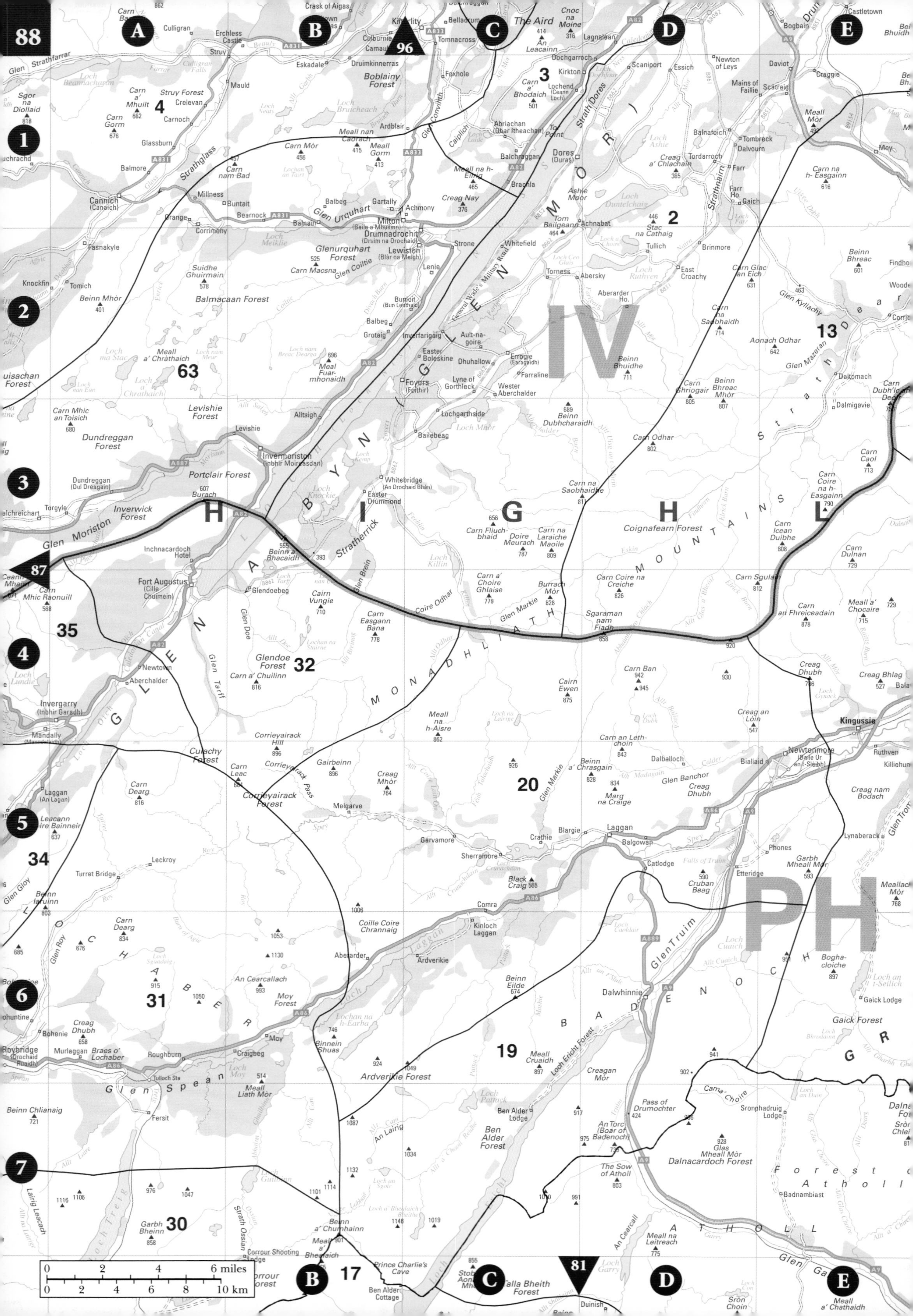
A
B
C
D
E
96
81
87
1
2
3
4
5
6
7
IV
PH
H I G H L
The Aird
Crask of Aigas
Kiltarlity
Beauly
Culligran
Erchless Castle
Struy
Glen Strathfarrar
Loch Beannacharan
Sgor na Diollaid
818
Carn a' Mhuilt
662
Struy Forest
Crelevan
Mauld
Carnoch
Carn Gorm
676
Glassburn
Eskadale
Druimkinnerras
Boblainy Forest
Culburnie
Camault
Belladrum
Tomnacross
Foxhole
Loch Bruicheach
Ardblair
Meall nan Caorach
415
Meall Gorm
413
Carn Mòr
456
Strathglass
Carn nam Bad
457
Balmore
Cannich (Canaich)
Millness
Buntait
Orange
Corrimony
Bearnock
Balbeg
Gartally
Achmony
Balnain
Glen Urquhart
Milton (Baile a' Mhuilinn)
Drumnadrochit (Druim na Drochaid)
Lewiston (Blàr na Maigh)
Loch Meiklie
Glenurquhart Forest
Carn Macsna
525
Glen Coiltie
Fasnakyle
Suidhe Ghuirmain
578
Balmacaan Forest
Knockfin
Tomich
Beinn Mhòr
401
Loch ma Stac
Meall a' Chràthaich
63
Carn Mhic an Toisich
680
Dundreggan Forest
Levishie Forest
Levishie
Invermoriston (Inbhir Moireasdan)
Portclair Forest
Dundreggan (Dul Dreagain)
Torgyle
Inverwick Forest
Glen Moriston
Burach
607
Inchnacardoch Hotel
Fort Augustus (Cille Chuimein)
Glendoebeg
Carn Mhic Raonuill
568
35
Glen Doe
Glen Tarff
Newtown
Aberchalder
Invergarry (Inbhir Garadh)
Mandally
Loch Lundie
Glendoe Forest
32
Carn a' Chuilinn
816
Culachy Forest
Corrieyairack Hill
896
Corrieyairack Pass
Corrieyairack Forest
Carn Leac
884
Carn Dearg
816
Laggan (An Lagan)
Leacann Doire Bainneir
637
34
Leckroy
Turret Bridge
Beinn Iaruinn
803
Glen Gloy
Glen Roy
Carn Dearg
834
31
1053
1130
1050
An Cearcallach
993
Moy Forest
Creag Dhubh
658
Bohenie
Roybridge (Drochaid Ruaidh)
Murlaggan
Braes o' Lochaber
Roughburn
Craigbeg
Tulloch Sta
Glen Spean
Loch Moy
Meall Liath Mòr
514
Beinn Chlianaig
721
Fersit
Lairig Leacach
1116
1106
976
1047
Garbh Bheinn
858
30
Strath Ossian
Corrour Shooting Lodge
Corrour Forest
17
Beinn a' Chumhainn
901
Meall a' Bhealaich
865
Prince Charlie's Cave
Ben Alder Cottage
Loch Ericht
Talla Bheith Forest
855
Duinish
Kirkton
Lochend (Ceann Loch)
Carn a' Bhodaich
501
3
Dochgarroch
Lagnalean
Cnoc na Moine
316
An Leacainn
414
Scaniport
Essich
Newton of Leys
Abriachan (Obar Itheachan)
Caiplich
Dores (Duras)
Balchraggan
Meall na h-Eilrig
465
Creag Nay
376
Brachla
Strath Dores
Loch Ashie
Creag a' Chlachain
365
Ashie Moor
Loch Duntelchaig
Tom Bailgeann
464
Achnabat
Stac na Cathaig
446
2
Tullich
Whitefield
Strone
Lenie
Bunloit (Bun Loidh)
Balbeg
Grotaig
Inverfarigaig
Aultnagoire
Torness
Abersky
Loch Ruthven
Aberarder Ho.
Easter Boleskine
Dhuhallow
Errogie (Eargaidh)
Farraline
Foyers (Foithir)
Lyne of Gorthleck
Wester Aberchalder
Meal Fuar-mhonaidh
696
Alltsigh
Lochgarthside
Loch Mhòr
Bailebeag
Beinn Dubhcharaidh
689
Whitebridge (An Drochaid Bhàn)
Loch Knockie
Easter Drummond
Stratherrick
Beinn a' Bhacaidh
555
393
Glen Brein
Cairn Vungie
710
Carn Easgann Bana
778
Coire Odhar
Carn Fliuch-bhaid
656
Doire Meurach
787
Carn na Laraiche Maoile
809
Carn a' Choire Ghlaise
779
Burrach Mòr
828
Glen Markie
Carn na Saobhaidhe
811
Carn Coire na Creiche
826
Sgaraman nam Fiadh
858
Coignafearn Forest
M O N A D H L I A T H
M O U N T A I N S
Meall na h-Aisre
862
Cairn Ewen
875
Carn Ban
942
945
930
Gairbeinn
896
Creag Mhòr
764
926
20
Carn an Leth-choin
843
Beinn a' Chrasgain
828
834
Marg na Craige
Dalballoch
Glen Banchor
Creag Dhubh
Melgarve
Garvamore
Sherramore
Crathie
Blargie
Laggan
Balgowan
Catlodge
Black Craig
565
Comra
1006
Coille Coire Chrannaig
Kinloch Laggan
Aberarder
Ardverikie
Loch Laggan
Binnein Shuas
746
924
1049
Ardverikie Forest
Beinn Eilde
674
19
Meall Cruaidh
897
Loch Ericht Forest
Creagan Mòr
Loch Pattack
Ben Alder Lodge
Ben Alder Forest
An Lairig
1087
1034
1132
1114
1101
1148
1019
Pass of Drumochter
424
917
An Torc (Boar of Badenoch)
739
975
The Sow of Atholl
803
1010
991
An Cearcall
Meall na Leitreach
775
Glen Truim
Dalwhinnie
B A D E N O C H
Falls of Truim
Cruban Beag
590
Etteridge
Garbh Mheall Mòr
593
Phones
Kingussie
Newtonmore (Baile Ùr an t-Slèibh)
Bialaid
Ruthven
Creag nam Bodach
Lynaberack
Loch Cuaich
Bogha-cloiche
897
Gaick Lodge
Gaick Forest
941
902
Sronphadruig Lodge
Glas Mheall Mòr
928
Dalnacardoch Forest
Forest of Atholl
Badnambiast
A T H O L L
Glen Garry
Meall a' Chathaidh
Sròn Choin
Bogbain
Castletown
Daviot
Craggie
Mains of Faillie
Scatraig
Meall Mòr
492
Balnafoich
Tombreck
Dalvourn
Farr
Moy
Carn na h-Easgainn
616
Farr Ho.
Gaich
Strathnairn
Brinmore
East Croachy
Carn Glac an Eich
631
Beinn Bhreac
601
Glen Kyllachy
Carn na Saobhaidh
714
Aonach Odhar
642
13
Glen Mazeran
Strath Dearn
Dalmigavie
Carn Ghriogair
805
Beinn Bhreac Mhòr
807
Beinn Bhuidhe
711
Carn Odhar
802
Carn Caol
713
Carn Coire na h-Easgainn
790
Carn Icean Duibhe
808
Carn Dulnan
729
Carn Sgulain
812
Carn an Fhreiceadain
878
Meall a' Chocaire
715
729
920
Creag Dhubh
756
Creag Bhlag
527
Creag an Loin
547
Meallach Mòr
768
Loch Killin
General Wade's Military Road
Caledonian Canal
Loch Ness
Loch Oich
Glen Urquhart
Glen Convinth
Glen Gloy
L O C H A B E R
G L E N M O R E
0 2 4 6 miles
0 2 4 6 8 10 km

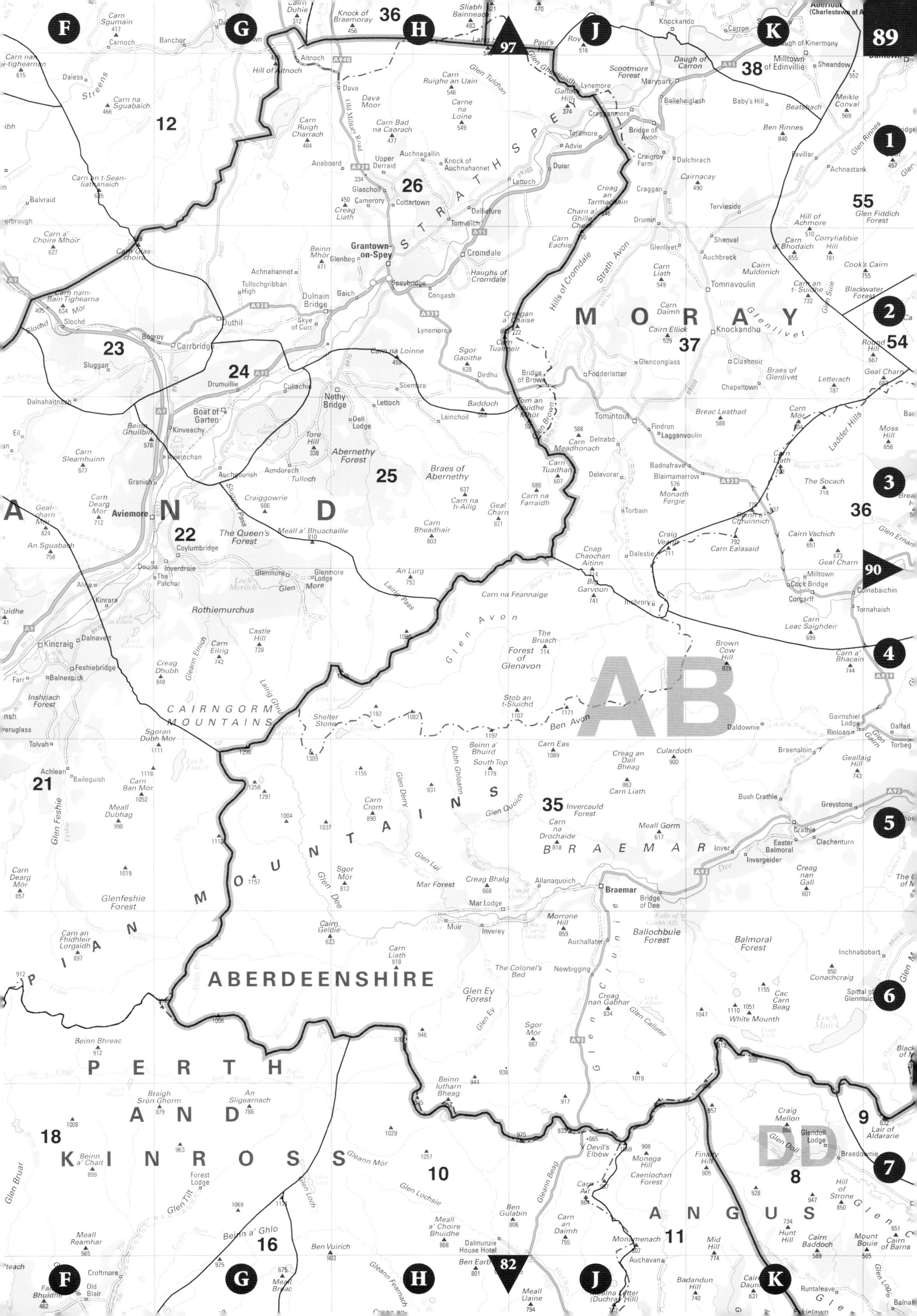
F
G
H
J
K
36
97
38
12
26
55
1
2
54
23
24
25
37
3
36
90
22
4
AB
21
35
5
6
9
18
10
16
11
82
8
7
DD
MORAY
STRATHSPEY
AND
CAIRNGORM MOUNTAINS
GRAMPIAN MOUNTAINS
ABERDEENSHIRE
PERTH AND KINROSS
ANGUS
BRAEMAR
Grantown-on-Spey
Aviemore
Carrbridge
Nethy Bridge
Boat of Garten
Kincraig
Tomintoul
Braemar
Cromdale
Dava
Duthil
Knockandhu
Glenlivet
Tomnavoulin
Dulnain Bridge
Rothiemurchus
Abernethy Forest
Glenmore
Coylumbridge
Inverdruie
Feshiebridge
Glenfeshie Forest
Mar Lodge
Inverey
Crathie
Balmoral Forest
Ballochbuie Forest
Glen Ey Forest
Glen Clunie
Devil's Elbow
Glen Doll
Glendoll Lodge
Forest Lodge
Glen Tilt
Dalmunzie House Hotel
Spittal of Glenmuick
Loch Muick
White Mounth
Lochnagar
Cock Bridge
Corgarff
Milltown of Edinvillie
Marypark
Bridge of Avon
Ladder Hills
Glen Avon
Ben Avon
Invercauld Forest
Glen Derry
Glen Lui
Glen Quoich
Glen Dee
Lairig Ghru
Lairig Pass
The Queen's Forest
Braes of Abernethy
Hills of Cromdale
Strath Avon
Glen Fiddich Forest
Ben Rinnes
Bridge of Brown
Tom an Uidhe Mhòr
Glen Brown
Old Military Road
Streens
Slochd
Kinveachy
Achnahannet
Skye of Curr
Speybridge
Lynemore
Dirdhu
Baddoch
Dell Lodge
Tulloch
Lettoch
Granish
Auchgourish
Aundorach
Craiggowrie
Carn Eilrig
Castle Hill
Creag Dhubh
Sgoran Dubh Mòr
Meall Dubhag
Carn Ban Mòr
Achlean
Baileguish
Tolvah
Insriach Forest
Balnespick
Dalnavert
Kinrara
Alvie
Doune
The Polchar
Meall a' Bhuachaille
An Lurg
Carn na Feannaige
The Bruach
Forest of Glenavon
Stob an t-Sluichd
Beinn a' Bhuird
South Top
Carn Eas
Creag an Dail Bheag
Culardoch
Carn Liath
Carn na Drochaide
Meall Gorm
Creag Bhalg
Allanaquoich
Morrone Hill
Auchallater
Newbigging
Creag nan Gabhar
Glen Callater
Sgor Mòr
Carn Crom
Sgor Mòr
Cairn Geldie
Carn Liath
The Colonel's Bed
Beinn Iutharn Bheag
Beinn Bhreac
Braigh Sròn Ghorm
An Sligearnach
Beinn a' Chait
Gleann Mòr
Glen Lochsie
Beinn a' Ghlo
Ben Vuirich
Meall Reamhar
Croftmore
Old Blair
Fenderbridge
Meall Breac
Glen Loch
Gleann Fearnach
Ben Gulabin
Carn an Daimh
Meall a' Choire Bhuidhe
Ben Earb
Meall Uaine
Gleann Beag
Monamenach
Auchavan
Mid Hill
Badandun Hill
Cairn Daunie
Runtaleave
Mount Bouie
Cairn of Barns
Hunt Hill
Cairn Baddoch
Hill of Strone
Craig Mellon
Braedownie
Loch of Aldararie
Monega Hill
Caenlochan Forest
Finalty Hill
Carn an Fhidhleir Lorgaidh
Carn Dearg Mòr
Glen Feshie
Glen Bruar
Conachcraig
Inchnabobart
Bush Crathie
Greystone
Clachanturn
Easter Balmoral
Invergelder
Creag nan Gall
Inver
Gairnshiel Lodge
Rinloan
Braenaloin
Geallaig Hill
Daldownie
Brown Cow Hill
Carn a' Bhacain
Leac Saighdeir
Tornahaish
Colnabaichin
Milltown
Cairn Vachich
Geal Charn
The Socach
Carn Ealasaid
Craig Veann
Dalestie
Inchrory
Cnap Chaochan Aitinn
Big Garvoun
Delnabo
Carn Meadhonach
Carn Tuadhan
Carn na Farraidh
Geal Charn
Carn na h-Ailig
Carn Bheadhair
Delavorar
Torbain
Badnafrave
Blairnamarrow
Monadh Fergie
Findron
Lagganvoulin
Breac Leathad
Chapeltown
Braes of Glenlivet
Clashnoir
Glenconglass
Fodderletter
Cairn Ellick
Carn Daimh
Letterach
Round Hill
Geal Charn
Carn Mòr
Moss Hill
Carn Liath
Blackwater Forest
Cook's Cairn
Carn an t-Suidhe
Cairn Muldonich
Carn a' Bhodaich
Corryhabbie Hill
Hill of Achmore
Auchbreck
Shenval
Tervieside
Cairnacay
Craggan
Drumin
Dalchirach
Craigroy Farm
Advie
Tormore
Cragganmore
Ballieheiglash
Lynemore
Gallow Hill
Glen Tulchan
Daugh of Carron
Scootmore Forest
Knockando
Carron
Baby's Hill
Beatshach
Meikle Conval
Sheandow
Pavillar
Achnastank
Glen Rinnes
Creag an Tarmachain
Charn a' Ghille Chearr
Carn Eachie
Haughs of Cromdale
Congash
Gaich
Glenbeg
Beinn Mhòr
Tullochgribban High
Dellefure
Tomvaich
Cottartown
Camerory
Creag Liath
Glaschoil
Upper Derraid
Auchnagallin
Knock of Auchnahannet
Anaboard
Carn Ruigh Charrach
Carn Bad na Caorach
Carne na Loine
Carn Ruighe an Uain
Dava Moor
Aitnoch
Hill of Aitnoch
Knock of Braemoray
Carn Duhie
Sliabh Bainneach
Lang Hill
Paul's Hill
Roy
Carn Sgumain
Carnoch
Banchor
Daless
Carn na Sguabaich
Carn an t-Sean-liathanaich
Balvraid
Carn a' Choire Mhòir
Carn Glas-choire
Carn nam-Bain Tighearna
Sluggan
Drumuillie
Cullachie
Dalnahaitnach
Beinn Ghuilbin
Avielochan
Carn Sleamhuinn
Carn Dearg Mor
Geal-charn Mòr
An Sguabach
Carn na Loinne
Sgor Gaoithe
Creagan a' Chaise
Carn Tuairneir
Lainchoil
Sliemore
Tore Hill
Glen More
Loch Morlich
Shelter Stone
Gleann Einich
Mar Forest
Muir
Bridge of Dee

A
B
C
D
E
1
2
3
4
5
6
7
98
89
83
Aberlour
(Charlestown of Aberlour)
Carron
Daugh of Carron
38
Milltown of Edinvillie
Kinermony
Sheandow
Marypark
Belleheiglash
Baby's Hill
Beatshach
Meikle Conval
569
Ben Rinnes
840
Glen Rinnes
Tullich
Dufftown
Keithmore
Milltown of Auchindoun
Aultnapaddock
Bakebare
Braehead
Daugh of Cairnborrow
Milton of Cairnborrow
Drumdelgie
313 The Bin Forest
Corse of Kinnoir
Huntly
Cruchie
Lessendrum
Frendraught
Denmoss
Drumblade
Corse
Auchaber
Haugh of Glass
Torry
Cairnargat
Clashmach Hill
375
Mosshead
Brideswell
Ythanwells
Sliach
Beggshill
Dumeath
Muckle Long Hill
391
Balieswärd
54
Strathbogie
Strath Bogie
Denend
Millburn
Thomastown
Laggan
The Scalp
487
Bridgehaugh
Backside
Succoth
Tillathrowie
Bridgend
Kirkstile
Winds Eye
314
Bainshole
Hill of Tillymorgan
381
Craigroy Farm
Dalchirach
Cairnacay
490
Pavillar
Achnastank
Laird's Seat
457
Glen Fiddich
Carn Chrom
502
Glacks of Balloch Pass
365
Ballochford
Coynachie
Culdrain
Kirkney
Gartly
Backburn
Wishach Hill
419
Glens of Foudland
Hill of Foudland
Skares
Kirkton of Culsalmond
Cairnhill
Colpy
Craggan
MORAY
55
Glen Fiddich Forest
A941
Tomnaven
525
Clashindarroch Forest
Quarry Hill
440
Cransmill Hill
Clashindarroch
Black Hill
505
Cults
Knockandy Hill
434
Largie
Wrangham
Tervieside
Bridgend
Inverharroch Farm
Newnoth
Slack
Wardhouse
Bonnyton
Hill of Achmore
510
Ardwell
Tap o' Noth
563
Upper Boddam
Greenhall
Glenlivet
Shenval
Auchbreck
Carn a' Bhodaich
855
Corryhabbie Hill
781
Meikle Firbriggs
539
Auchmair
Mount of Haddoch
521
Milton of Noth
Kennethmont
Glanderston
Aulton
52
Insch
Cairn Muldonich
Carn Liath
549
Cook's Cairn
755
Round Hill
571
Aldunie
Bruntland
Belhinnie
Rhynie
Cottown
Towie
Ardlair
Rothney
Ardoyne
Tomnavoulin
Carn an t-Suidhe
732
Blackwater Forest
Glen Suie
Aldivalloch
Cabrach
Elrick
Wheedlemont
Longlands
Craik
Clatt
Duncanston
Hill of Christ's Kirk
Christskirk
Westhall
Oyne
Cairnbrallan
618
New Leslie
Old Leslie
Kirkton
Ryehill
Glenlivet
Cairn Ellick
529
37
Knockandhu
Bracklach
Leslie
Auchleven
Garioch
Clashnoir
Round Hill
667
Hill of Three Stones
629
The Buck
721
Clova
Mire of Midgates
487
Whitehaugh Forest
Suie Hill
415
Knock Saul
412
Black Hill
430
Bennachie
Mither Tap
518
Glenconglass
Braes of Glenlivet
Letterach
787
Geal Charn
Sand Hill
548
Mount Meddin
Hill of John's Cairn
532
Lumsden
Correen Hills
Brux Hill
475
AB
Millburn
Muckletown
Teperse Castle
Chapeltown
Lord Arthur's Cairn
518
Redhouse
Glenton
Millstone Hill
408
Breac Leathad
588
Carn Mòr
804
Ladder Hills
Badenyon
Creag an Fhuarain
632
Peat Hill
566
Mossat
Edinbanchory
Tullynessle
Keig
Findron
Lagganvoulin
Moss Hill
658
Dulax
Ladylea Hill
609
Rinmore
Glencuie
Kildrummy
Delphorrie
Milltown of Kildrummy
Montgarrie
Bankhead
Rorandle
Carn Liath
792
Torrancroy
Bridge of Alford
Alford
Cairn William
448
Pitfichie
Pitfichie Forest
Badnafrave
A939
The Socach
718
Kirkton of Glenbuchat
Mains of Glenbuchat
532
Coiliochbhar Hill
Auchintoul
Asloun
Dorsell
Kingsford
Howe of Alford
33
Gateside
Pitmunie
Whitehouse
Todlachie
A944
36
Breagach Hill
556
Bellabeg
Forbestown
Strathdon
Glenkindie
Fichlie
Sinnahard
Towie
Hillockhead
Bridgeton
Muir of Fowlis
Kirkton
Tillyfourie
Black Hill
185
Bonnh a' Chruinnich
Carn Ealasaid
792
Cairn Vachich
651
Glen Ernan
Waterside
Heugh-head
Craig of Bunzeach
531
Tornashean Forest
Bellabeg
Milltown of Towie
Scar Hill
525
Ley
Muirhead
A980
Ardgowse
Tillycairn Castle
Little Ley
Craig Veann
711
Geal Charn
673
Milltown
Cock Bridge
Corgarff
Colnabaichin
Fleuchats
Hillockhead
Bogston
Boultenstone Hotel
Badenyon Hill
Frosty Hill
412
574
Broom Hill
Pressendye
619
Milton of Cushnie
Leochel-Cushnie
Tillyfour
Corrennie Forest
Corrennie Moor
Benaquhallie
494
Ordhead
Shiels
Tornahaish
Tillypronie
East Davoch
Melgum
Bogfields
Kintocher
Bankhead
Corsindae
Carn Leac Saighdeir
699
Cairn Mona Gowan
749
Migvie
Bogfern
Oldmill
Collmuir
Craiglich
476
Douneside
Tullochvenus
Glenshalg
Tornaveen
Drumlasie
Brown Cow Hill
829
Carn a' Bhacain
744
Glen Fenzie
Coynach
Logie Coldstone
Corrachree
Tarland
Craskins
CROMAR
Perkhill
Wartle
Lumphanan
Milton of Auchinhove
Cairnbeathie
East Learney
Auchorrie
Morven
871
ABERDEENSHIRE
Leys
Coull
Mortlich
380
Hill of Fare
471
Torphins
Craigmyle Ho.
Milton of Campfield
Gairnshiel Lodge
Rinloan
Dalfad
Glen Gairn
Lary
Culblean Hill
604
Davan
Ordie
Scar Hill
299
Kincardine O'Neil
Mid Beltie
Daldownie
Peter's Hill
34
Rosehill
Glassel
Kennerty
Culardoch
900
Braenaloin
Geallaig Hill
743
Torbeg
Candacraig
A939
Milton of Tullich
Cambus o' May
Dinnet
Heugh-head
Aboyne
Tillydrine
Brathens
Culsh
Bridge of Gairn
Muir of Dinnet
Oldhall
Bridge o' Ess
Birsemore
Birse
Cordach
Potarch
Backhill of Trustach
Inchmarlo
Bridge of Canny
Bush Crathie
A93
Greystone
Ballater
Glascorrie
Deecastle
Ballaterach
The Fungle Road
Allancreich
Balfour
Ballogie
Marywell
Blackhall Forest
Bridge of Canny
Strathgirnock
Pannanich Hill
601
Black Craig
529
Glen Tanar
Forest of Glentanar
Tom's Cairn
310
Hill of Goauch
337
Scolty
299
Crathie
Easter Balmoral
Clachanturn
35
Birkhall
Bridge of Muick
Carnferg
525
Glencat
Finzean
Bauids
31
MAR
Inver
Invergelder
Creag nan Gall
601
The Coyles of Muick
601
Aucholzie
Cairn Leuchan
669
Clachan Yell
626
Red Craig
640
Forest of Birse
Ballochan
Lamahip
Drumhead
Percie
Whitestone
Bridge of Bogendreip
Bridge of Dee
Falls of Garbh Allt
Ballochbuie Forest
Linn of Muick Cottage
Craigmahandle
574
Craig of Dalfro
317
Greendams
Balmoral Forest
Inchnabobart
Cock Cairn
727
Braid Cairn
White Hill
571
Peter Hill
617
Cock Hill
598
Clachnaben
589
Glendye Lodge
Bridge of Dye
Conachcraig
850
Glen Muick
Fasheilach
721
839
Hill of Cat
742
Mudlee Bracks
688
577
Hill of Edendocher
1155
Cac Carn Beag
1110
1051
1047
White Mounth
Spittal of Glenmuick
Loch Muick
Hill of Saughs
Glen Tennet
Mount Battock
778
Glen Mark
Glen Dye
Meluncart
525
369
Cairn o' Mount
455
Glen Lee
Black Hill of Mark
998
Easter Balloch
834
Monawee
696
Glenlee
Auchronie
Tarfside
Cairncross
Hill of Fingray
485
Hound Hillock
518
Inchgrundle
Loch Lee
Glen Effock
Glen Esk
Fernybank
Sturdy Hill
Clatterin Brig
Craig Mellon
866
Glendoll Lodge
Glen Doll
Lair of Aldararie
832
9
Braedownie
Green Hill
870
Muckle Cairn
826
Ben Tirran
896
Cruys
741
West Knock
691
DD
Bulg
607
Thainston
908
Finalty Hill
905
11
8
928
947
Hill of Strone
850
Clova
Glen Clova
ANGUS
778
White Hill
Hill of Wirren
678
Auchmull
Fettercairn
PH
Hunt Hill
734
Cairn Baddoch
589
Mount Bouie
585
Cairn of Barns
651
Wheen
Rottal
Finbracks
756
Dog Hillock
722
726
Hill of Berran
Hill of Formal
343
Witton
Dalbog
Gannochy
Burn
Thornyhill
Meikle Strath
Inch of Arnhall
Arnhall
Howe of the Mearns
Mid Hill
774
Hill of Glansie
Hill of Wirren
Hill of Garbet
581
Bridgend
Tillyarblet
Dunlappie
Edzell
Inglismaldie Forest
Balnaboth
Auld
Peat Hill
481
0 2 4 6 miles
0 2 4 6 8 10 km

F
G
H
J
K
99
ABERDEEN
(Obar Dheathain)
Ellon
Oldmeldrum
Inverurie
Kintore
Stonehaven
Newburgh
Cruden Bay
Portlethen
Newtonhill
Inverbervie
Westhill
Kingswells
Dyce
Peterculter
Balmedie
Cove Bay
Laurencekirk
1
2
3
4
5
6
7

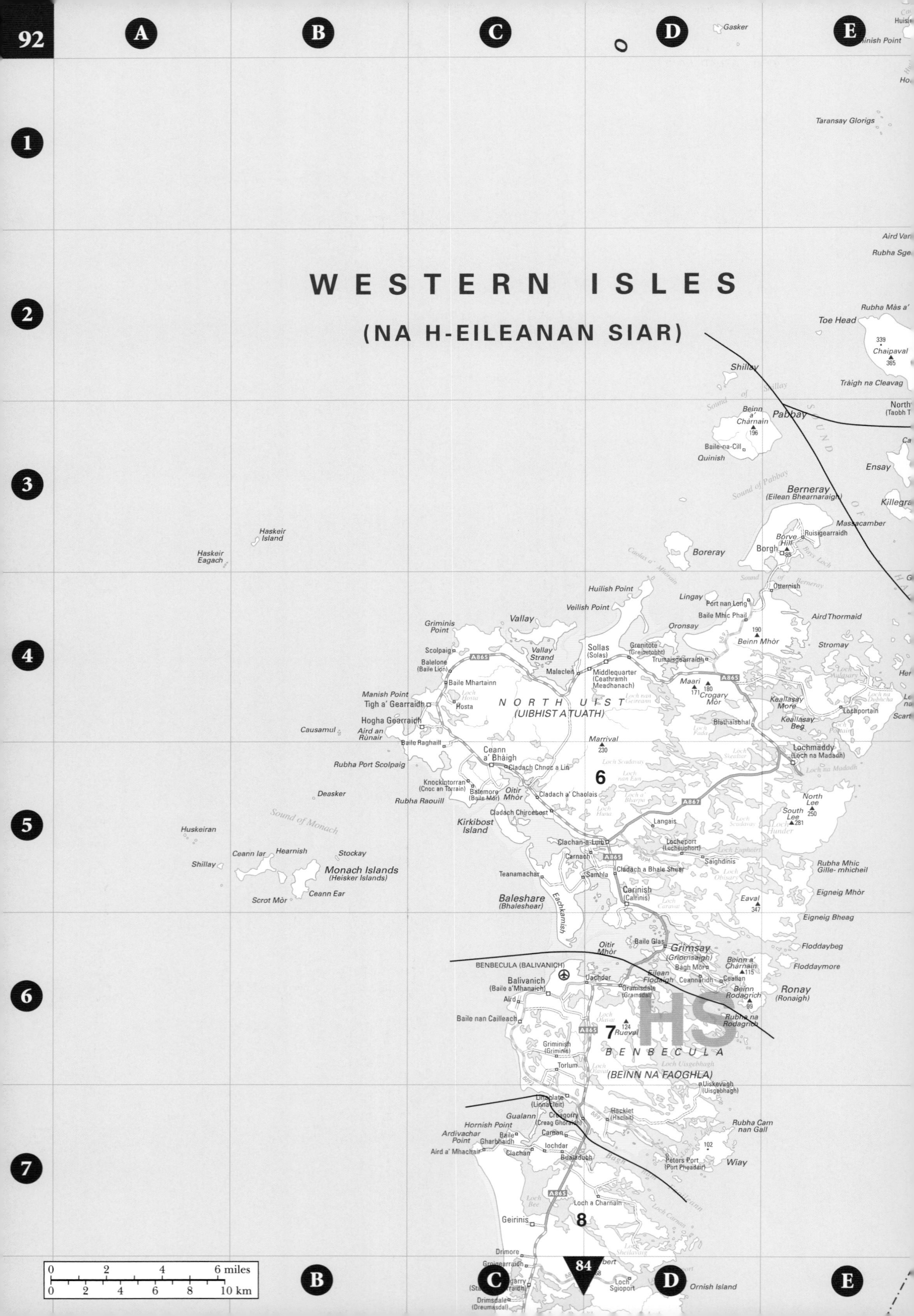

1

WESTERN ISLES
(NA H-EILEANAN SIAR)

2

3

4

5

6

7

Gasker

Uishi

inish Point

Ho

Taransay Glorigs

Aird Vari

Rubha Sge

Rubha Mâs a'

Toe Head

339
• Chaipaval
365

North
(Taobh T

Shillay

Sound of Shillay

Beinn
a'
Chárnain
196

Pabbay

Tràigh na Cleavag

Ca

Ensay

Baile-na-Cill
Quinish

Sound of Pabbay

Berneray
(Eilean Bhearnaraigh)

Killegra

Haskeir
Island

Haskeir
Eagach

Boreray

Caolas a' Mhòrain

Borve
Hill
85

Borgh

Ruisigearraidh

Massacamber

Sound of Berneray

Otternish

Bass Loch

H

Huilish Point

Griminis
Point

Valley

Veilish Point

Lingay

Pòrt nan Long

Aird Thormaid

Oronsay

Baile Mhic Phail

Scolpaig

Valley
Strand

Sollas
(Solas)

Grenitote
(Greinetobht)

190
Beinn Mhòr

Stromay

Balelone
(Baile Lión)

A865

Middlequarter
(Ceathramh
Meadhanach)

Trumaisgearraidh

Maari
171   180
Crogary
Mòr

A865

Keallasay
More

Her

Baile Mhartainn

Malaclet

Keallasay
Beg

Manish Point

Tigh a' Gearraidh

Hosta

N O R T H   U I S T
(UIBHIST A TUATH)

*Loch nan
Geireann*

Blathaisbhal

Lochportain

Le

Hogha Gearraidh

Aird an
Rùnair

*Loch
Hosta*

Marrival
230

A865

Lochmaddy
(Loch na Madadh)

Causamul

Baile Raghaill

Ceann
a' Bhàigh

Cladach Chnoc a Lin

*Loch
nan Ean*

*Loch a
Siadair*

Loch na Madadh

Rubha Port Scolpaig

Deasker

Knockintorran
(Cnoc an Torrain)

Batemore
(Baile Mòr)

Oitir
Mhòr

Cladach a' Chaolais

*Loch
Huna*

A867

North
Lee
250

Rubha Raouill

Cladach Chircebost

*Loch
Bharpa*

South
Lee
281

*Loch
Scadavay*

*Loch
Eford*

Kirkibost
Island

Langais

Locheport
(Locheuphort)

Loch Euphort

Rubha Mhic
Gille- mhicheil

Huskeiran

Sound of Monach

Clachan-a-Luib

A865

Saighdinis

Hearnish

Stockay

Carnach

Cladach a Bhale Shear

Samhla

Eigneig Mhòr

Ceann Iar

Shillay

Monach Islands
(Heisker Islands)

Teanamachar

Carinish
(Cairinis)

*Loch
Obisary*

Eaval
347

Eigneig Bheag

Scrot Mòr

Ceann Ear

Baleshare
(Bhaleshear)

Eachkamish

*Loch
Caravat*

Baile Glas

Floddaybeg

Oitir
Mhòr

Grimsay
(Griomsaigh)

Beinn a'
Chárnain
115

Floddaymore

BENBECULA (BALIVANICH)

Uachdar

Bàgh Mòra

Ceannaidh

Cealtan

Ronay
(Ronaigh)

Balivanich
(Baile a' Mhanaich)

Eilean
Flodaigh

Grimsdale
(Gramsdal)

Beinn
Rodagrich
99

Aird

Rubha na
Rodagrich

Baile nan Cailleach

*Loch
Olavat*

124
Rueval

B E N B E C U L A

HS

Griminish
(Griminis)

A865

(BEINN NA FAOGHLA)

Loch Uiscebhagh

Torlum

Uiskevagh
(Uisgebhagh)

Liniclate
(Linnacleit)

Gualann

Creagorry
(Creag Ghoraidh)

Hacklet
(Haclait)

Rubha Cam
nan Gall

Hornish Point

Baile
Gharbhaidh

Carnan

Ardivachar
Point

Clachan

102

Aird a' Mhachair

Iochdar

Bualadubh

Peter's Port
(Port Pheadair)

Wiay

Loch Bee

A865

Loch a Charnain

Loch Carnan

Geirinis

8

Drimore

*Loch
Skipport*

Ornish Island

Groigearraidh
(Sta   raidh)

Drimsdale
(Dreumasdal)

*Loch
Sgioport*

84

0   2   4   6 miles
0   2   4   6   8   10 km

F
G
H
J
K
1
2
3
4
5
6
7
100
94
85
NORTH HARRIS
(CEANN A TUATH NA HEARADH)
Forest of Harris
Ullaval
659
Oreval
662
Stulaval
579
Tullach a' Ruisg
Ath Linne
Aird a' Mhulaidh
Leosaval
412
Cleiseval
511
Uisgnaval Mòr
729
Mulla-fo-dheas
743
Clisham
799
Clett Ard
328
Abhainnsuidhe
Soay Beg
Soay Mòr
Miabhag
Tolmachan
WEST LOCH TARBERT
Bun Abhainn Eadarra
Sgaoth Aird
559
Straiaval
389
Toddun
528
Maraig (Maaruig)
Kenmore
A859
Beinn na h-Uamha
389
Beinn Mhòr
572
Beannan Mòr
242
2
Park
Corlabhadh
298
Eisgean
Orasaigh
Leumrabhagh
Gob na h-
Srianach
Eilean Iubhard
Loch Shell
Uisenis
371
Mulhagery
470
Crionaig
Caiteshal
449
Tathas Mhòr
Mol Truisg
Gob Rubh' Uisenis
SOUND OF SHIANT
Rubha Bhrollum
Bhalamus
Rhenigidale (Reinigeadal)
Beinn a' Chaolais
Ben Raah
267
Beinn Dhubh
506
3
Beesdale
Aird Asaig
Taobh Siar
Tarbert (Tairbeart)
Urgha
Paible
Losgaintir
Ceann Reamhar
467
South Harris Forest
287
Corran Seilebost
Sound of Taransay
Uieseval
334
Eilean Mòr a' Bhàigh
Sgeir na h-Eigheach
Rubh' a' Bhaird
Garbh Eilean
161
Eilean Mhuire
Eilean an Tighe
Shiant Islands
Carragrich
Kyles Scalpay (Caolas Scalpaigh)
Sgeotasaigh
Loch Ceann Dibig
Miabhag
East Loch Tarbert
Scalpay
4
Ben Scoravick
104
Scalpay (Eilean Scalpaigh)
Kennavay
Meall Challibost
HS
Seilebost
158
Clett Nisabost
175
East Stocklett
Bulabhall
354
Heileasbhal Mòr
384
An Coileach
386
Drinishader
Kennacley
Plocropol
Greosabhagh
Aird Mhige
Lacklee (Leac a' Li)
Liceasto
Scadabhagh
Bleaval
398
SOUTH HARRIS
(CEANN A DEAS NA HEARADH)
Cluer (Cliuthar)
Geocrab
Beacravik
Stockinish (Stocinis)
Rubha Bocaig
Braigh-nam-bagh
Manish (Manais)
Aird Leimhe
Rubha Cluer
Fleoideabhagh
Ard Manish
Aird Mhighe
Màs Garbh
Quidinish (Cuidhtinis)
5
Roneval
459
Finsbay (Fionnsbhagh)
Rubha Quidnish
Boirseam
Strondeval
211
Ceann a' Bhàigh
Lingarabay Island
Rodel (Roghadal)
Rubha Vallarip
Renish Point
Gilsay
Fladda-chuain
Gaeilavore Island
Gearran Island
Eilean Trodday
Rubha Hunish
Rubha na h- Aiseig
Loch Hunish
Duntulm Bay
The Aird
Tulm Island
Kilmaluag
Kilmaluag Bay
Balmaqueen
Duntulm
Score Bay
Galta Mòr
A855
Sgeir Eirin
Eilean Flodigarry
Flodigarry
Ru Bornaskitaig
Bornisketaig
Hunglader
Camas Mòr
Kilmuir
Quiraing
Meall na Suiramach
543
The Needle
Digg
Staffin Island
Kilvaxter
Suidh' a' Mhinn
350
Balgown
Staffin
Rubha Garbhaig
Monkstadt
Stenscholl
Kilbride Point
Linicro
Totscore
Bioda Buidhe
466
Stack of Skudiburgh
Idrigil
Ben Gorm
Maligar
Elishader
Ascrib Islands
South Ascrib
Rubha Idrigil
Uig (Uige)
Uig Bay
Balnaknock
Beinn Edra
611
Marishader
Garros
Culnaknock
Rubha Chorachan
Earlish
Lealt
LOCH SNIZORT
Cuidrach
Trotternish
Peinlich
Glenuachdarach
Creag a' Lain
608
Baca Ruadh
637
A87
Lyndale Point
Vaternish Point
Sròn Ochrulan
251
Ben Geary
284
Geary
Trumpan
Vaternish
Aros Bay
Loch Losait
Ardmore Point
Halistra
Gillen
Stac a' Bhothain
Hallin
Isay
Mingay Island
Dunvegan Head
Rubha Maol
Stein
Lusta
Bàrd nan Laogh
Greshornish Point
Ben Diubaig
214
Lyndale Ho.
Kingsburgh
Beinn a' Sga
452
Hartaval
668
Rigg
Lampay Islands
Claigan
Beinn Bhreac
327
Beinn Chreagach
326
Greshornish
The Storr
719
313
Ben Skriaig
307
Galtrigill
Boreraig
Uig
Husabost
Loch Dunvegan
Flashader
Treaslane
The Aird
Romesdal
Eyre
51
HIGHLAND
Milovaig
Feriniquarrie
Totaig
Ben Horneval
264
Edinbane
Kensaleyre
Ben Dearg
552
Upper Milovaig
Lephin
Colbost
55
A850
Ben Uigshader
246
Bernisdale
Tote
Waterstein Head
296
Beinn na Creiche
264
Skinidin
Uiginish
Dunvegan
Kilmuir
Lonmore
IV
Ben Sca
286
Cruachan Beinn a' Chearcaill
271
Skeabost
Carbost
Borve
Sithean Bhealaich Chumhaing
392
Neist Point
Ben Corkeval
Glen Dale
Healabhal Mhòr (Macleod's Table North)
468
Roskhill
A863
Ben Aketil
265
Drumuie
Beinn a' Ghlinne Bhig
208
Uigshader
Glengrasco
Torvaig
Ramasaig
Hoe Rape
Roag
Vatten
Orbost
Harlosh
Balmore
Glen Ose
Beinn na Cloiche
232
Am Maol
212
Portree (Port Righ)
The Hoe
233
Lorgill
488
Healabhal Bheag (Macleod's Table South)
Ose
56
417
Beinn na Greine
Penifiler
Ben Tianavaig
413
Ben Connan
244
Beinn na Boineid
371
Harlosh Point
Glenmore
Mugeary
400
Camastianavaig
Ben Idrigill
340
Harlosh Island
Tarner Island
Ebost
Ben Duagrich
304
Coillore
SKYE
(ANT-EILEAN SGITHEANACH)
Ullinish
Loch Bracadale
An Dubh Sgeir
Lower Ollach
LITTLE MINCH

94
A
B
C
D
E
1
2
3
4
5
6
7
WESTERN ISLES
(NA H-EILEANAN SIAR)
HS
Sound of Shiant
Srianach
Eilean Iubhard
Garbh Eilean
Eilean Mhuire
Eilean an Tighe
Shiant Islands
93
Eilean Trodday
Rubha Hunish
Rubha na h- Aiseig
The Aird
Kilmaluag
Duntulm
Balmaqueen
Galta Mòr
Flodigarry
Sgeir Eirin
Eilean Flodigarry
Hunglader
Kilmuir
Quiraing
Meall na Suiramach
Digg
Staffin Island
Staffin
Rubha Garbhaig
Suidh' a' Mhinn
The Needle
Stenscholl
Kilvaxter
Balgown
Linicro
Totscore
Bioda Buidhe
Ben Gorm
Maligar
Elishader
Uig
(Uige)
Marishader
Balnaknock
Beinn Edra
Garros
Rubha nam Brathairean
Culnaknock
Earlish
Lealt
Trotternish
Peinlich
Glenuachdarach
Creag a' Lain
Baca Ruadh
Leac Tressirnish
Beinn a' Sga
Hartaval
Rigg
The Storr
Romesdal
Eyre
The Aird
51
Kensaleyre
Ben Dearg
Bernisdale
Tote
Prince Charles's Cave
Borve
Skeabost
Carbost
Drumuie
Sithean Bhealaich Chumhaing
Uigshader
Glengrasco
Torvaig
Portree
(Port Righ)
Am Maol
Penifiler
Beinn na Greine
Ben Tianavaig
Glenmore
Camastianavaig
56
(AN T-EILEAN SGITHEANACH)
Lower Ollach
Sound of Raasay
Loch a' Bhràigh
Dry Harbour
RONA
Eilean Tigh
Eilean Fladday
Beinn na h-Iolaire
Torran
Manish Point
Arnish
Brochel
RAASAY
40
Glame
Balachuirn
Dun Caan
86
Rubha na' Leac
Beinn na' Leac
Clachan
Inner Sound
Sròn na h-Airde Bhaine
Greenstone Point
Opinan
Rubha Mòr
Mellon Udrigle
Achgarve
Eilean Furadh Mòr
Rubha Reidh
Cove
Mellon Charles
Ormiscaig
Aultbea
(An t-Allt Beithe)
Isle of Ewe
An Cuaidh
Loch Ewe
Melvaig
Inverasdale
Aultgrishan
Midtown
Cnoc Breac
Naast
Peterburn
North Erradale
Boor
Londubh
Poolewe
Big Sand
Mial
Meall A' Ghiuthais Mhic Craidh
Longa Island
Carn Dearg
Smithstown
Gairloch
(Geàrrloch)
Auchtercairn
Gair Loch
Eilean Horrisdale
Charlestown
Port Henderson
Badachro
Kerrysdale
Opinan
Meall Aundrary
Shieldaig
South Erradale
Mullach nan Cadhaichean
Red Point
Maol Ruadh
21
Red Point
Meall na h-Uamha
Baosbheinn
Shieldaig Forest
Loch Torridon
Beinn Bhreac
Craig
Rubha na Fearn
An Ruadh-mheallan
Sgurr Mhòr
Lower Diabaig
Upper Diabaig
Fearnmore
Fearnbeg
Beinn Alligin
Cuaig
Arinacrinachd
Kenmore
Alligin Shuas
Inverallligin
Ardheslaig
Rubha na Feola
Shieldaig Island
(NTS)
Callakille
Inverbain
Balgy
An Garbh-mheall
Shieldaig
Lonbain
Croic-bheinn
Ben Shieldaig
Ben-damph Forest
Meall na Fhuaid
An Fur
Glenshieldaig
Forest
Applecross Forest
An Staonach
Meall na Saobhaidhe
Hartfield
Beinn Bhan
Applecross
Milton
Camusteel
Bealach na Ba
Camusterrach
Sgurr a' Chaorachain
Culduie
Meall Gorm
Russel
Lochcarron
Ardarroch
Toscaig
Meall Loch Airigh Alasdair
Airigh-drishaig
Bad a' Chreamha
0 2 4 6 miles
0 2 4 6 8 10 km

F
G
H
J
K
102
Isle Ristol
Polbain
Aird of Coigach
Stac Pollaidh
Cul Mòr 849
Drumrunie Forest
Ledmore
Elphin
Knockan
An Stuc 364
Beinn an Eòin 544
Glas-leac Mòr
Achiltibuie (Achd-'Ille-Bhuidhe)
Ardnagoine
Polglass
Tanera Beg
Garadheancal
An t-Sàil 490
Cul Beag 769
A835
Loch Urigill
Cnoc na Glas Choille 307
A837
Glen Oykel
Summer Isles
Glas-leac Beag
Achvraie
Beinn an Eòin 618
Cromalt Hills
Drumrunie
Horse Island
Ben Mòr Coigach 743
Culnacraig
C O I G A C H
Achduart
Eilean Dubh
330 Fionn Bheinn Mhòr
Meall an Fhuarain 578
Coire a' Chonachair
Lubcroy
Geodha Mòr
Strathcanaird
Bottle Island
Càrn nan Sgeir
Strath Canaird
26
Na Dromannan 408
Strath nan Lòn
Rappach
27
N O R T H
Oykel Bridge
Langwell
A837
Leac Dhonn
Isle Martin
Cailleach Head
Cùl a' Bhogha
Rhidorroch Forest
Glen Einig
Ardmair
Rhue
Achmore
Gruinard Island
Stattic Point
Scoraig
Carnach
Rhireavach
Meall Liath Choire 548
Creag Loisgte 412
Morefield
Rhidorroch
Glen Achall
Knockdamph
Badluarach
Beinn Ghobhlach 635
Ullapool (Ullapul)
Braes of Ullapool (Bruthaicheann Ullapuil)
2
Dumamuck
Cnoc a' Bhaid-rallaich 545
Mungasdale
Badcaul
Badrallach
Allt na h-Airbhe
558 Beinn Eilideach
Strath Mulzie
Carn a' Choin Deirg 701
Second Coast
Blarnalearoch
Loggie (An Lagaidh)
Rhiroy
Lockmelm (Leac Mailm)
642 Meall Dubh
Meall nam Bradhan 677
Carn na Beiste 302
Little Gruinard
Ardessie
Sàil Mhòr 767
Camusnagaul
Ardcharnich
Glen Douchary
Freevater Forest
Bodach Mòr 822
A832
Dundonnell (Ach-Dà-Dhòmhnaill)
Eilean Darach
Ardindrean
Letters
Seana Bhraigh 927
Carn nam Buailtean 384
Gruinard Forest
A835
Carn Bàn 845
24
Sròn Gun Aran
Creag-mheall Beag 347
Strath Beag
649 Carn Mòr
Inverlael Forest
Strathnasheallag
An Teallach
Bidein a' Ghlas Thuill 1062
Inverlael
Eididh nan Clach Geala 928
3
Inverbroom
Gleann Beag
Glenbeg
Beinn Tharsuinn 714
Beinn a' Chaisgein Beag 680
Fisherfield
Auchlunachan
Meall nan Ceapraichean 977
Meall a' Chuaille 628
1059 Sgurr Fiona
Forest
Loch na Sealga
Glackour
Strath More
Cona Mheall 980
Dundonnell Forest
Forest
Auchindrean
Fasagrianach
Braemore
1084 Beinn Dearg
Tollomuick Forest
Beinn Deargh Mhòr 908
Strath na Sealga
889 Beinn Enaiglair
96
Am Faochagach 954
Beinn a' Chaisgein Mòr 857
Fain
22
Beinn a' Chlaidheimh 914
Meall Leacachain 618
23
Strathvaich Forest
Inchbae Forest
Meall an t-Sithe 601
A832
Dirrie More
Ruadh Stac Mòr 918
Beinn Airigh Charr 791
Tom Ban Mòr 742
Loch Vaich
Loch a' Bhraoin
522 Creag Dhubh
Lochdrum
A835
4
A'Mhaighdean 967
Sgurr Ban 989
Creag Rainich 807
Loch Glascarnoch
Strathrannoch
Meall Mheannaidh
Mullach Coire Mhic Fhearchair 1019
Meall a' Chrasgaidh 934
Beinn Liath Bheag 665
Strath Vaich
Strath Rannoch
Beinn Lair 860
954 Beinn Liath Mhòr Fannaich
Sgurr nan Clach Geala 1093
Sgurr Mòr 1110
Beinn Liath Mhòr a' Ghiubhais Li 766
Carn Mòr 640
936 Beinn Tarsuinn
Beinn Bheag 668
Groban 748
A'Chailleach 999
Eilean Subhainn
Letterewe
Lochan Fada
IV
Aultguish Inn
Lubfearn
Furnace
1000 Sgurr Breac
Sgurr nan Each 923
Kinlochluichart Forest
Inchbae Lodge
Garbat Forest
Garbat
Slioch 980
Meallan Chuaich 690
949 Meall Gorm
Beinn Dearg 687
Strath Lungard
Gleann Bianasdail
Gleann Tanagaidh
Fannich Forest
An Coileachan 923
Meall Mhic Iomhair 607
Corriemoillie Forest
Carn na Dubh Choille 479
E S T E R
R O S S
Gleann na Muice
Beinn a' Mhuinidh 692
Beinn nan Ramh 711
Loch Fannich
A835
Kinlochewe Forest
Lockie
Carn na Beiste 518
Beinn a' Bhric 442
5
A832
Heights of Kinlochewe
Strath Chrombuill
Beinn a' Chearcaill
Meall a' Ghiubhais 878
Taagan
Lochrosque Forest
465 Carn Daraich
An Cabar 558
A832
Lochluichart
Strathgarve Forest
Gorstan
I G H L A N D
Ruadh-stac Mòr 1010
933 Fionn Bheinn
Lochluichart Sta
Garve (Clachan Ghairbh)
Kinlochewe
Carn a' Ghlinne 539
Knockban
A832
Carn Chaiseachain 312
Loch Luichart
Sàil Mhòr 981
Beinn Eighe
Glen Docherty
Meall a' Chaorainn 705
Glen Torridon
Spidean a' Choire Leith 1054
A832
Badavanich
Lubmore
Achnasheen
S T R A T H B R A N
Carn na Cre 461
Sgurr Marcasaidh 580
14
Glen
Carn Loisgte 446
An Liathanach
Loch a' Chroisg
Sgurr a' Ghlas Leathaid 844
Creag Loch nan Dearcag 536
Little Scatwell
Liathach
A896
Ledgowan Forest
Sgurr a' Mhuilinn 879
Milton
Porin
Seana Mheallan 436
Sgurr Dubh 782
Carn Beag 550
H I G H L A N D S
6
Meallan nan Uan 840
Coulin Forest
Carn Breac 678
A890
Cnoc an t-Sidhein 372
538 Carn Mhartuin
Carn an Leanaidh 574
Gleann Meinich
Carn na Cloiche Moire
Glenmeanie
6
Beinn Liath Mhòr 925
876
680 Meall na Faochaig
Meall nan Damh 591
Scardroy
671
Sròn nan Saobhaidh 408
Maol Chean-dearg 933
Sgorr Ruadh 960
Glen Carron
Carn Liath
Carnoch
Meall Giubhais 662
Carn na Coinnich 673
Carn Gorm 875 857
Moruisg 928
Inverchoran
Fuar Tholl 907
Achnashellach Sta
A890
Craig
Sgurr nan Ceannaichean 913
Bac an Eich 849
Glen Orrin Reservoir
Glencarron and Glenuig Forest
Gleann Go
Ruadh-stac 892
Achnashellach Forest
Gleann Fhiodhaig
Sgurr Choire nan Eun 789
Strathconon Forest
Corriehallie Forest
Beinn nam Fith 494
Balnacra
Maoile Lunndaidh 1007
Coulags
Sgurr na Feartaig 862
Sgurr a' Chaorachain 1053
686 Sgurr na Cairbe
Meallan Buidhe 766
Sgurr a' Phollain 854
Erchless
7
W E S T
A890
999 Sgurr Choinnich
Beinn a' Bha'ach Ard 862
New Kelso
Creag a' Chaorainn
Beinn Tharsuinn 863
West Monar Forest
East Monar Forest
Carn Eiteige 882
Sgurr Fhuar-thuill 1049
Sgurr a' Choire Ghlais 1083
Carn nan Gobhar 992
Sgurr na Ruaidhe 993
4
Strathcarron Sta
Strathcarron
Achintee
Bidean a' Choire Sheasgaich 945
Sgurr na Muice 891
Carn Ban 736
Culligran
Lurg Mhòr 986
Loch Monar
Carn Geuradainn 594
Erchless Castle
Struy
A831
87
Meallan Odhar
Glen Strathfarrar
Attadale
Attadale Forest
Beinn Dronaig 797
Beinn Bheag 619
Meall Buidhe 555
Inchvuilt
Loch Beannacharan
Mauld
Struy Forest
Crelevan
Mhuilt
Sgor na Diollaid
A890

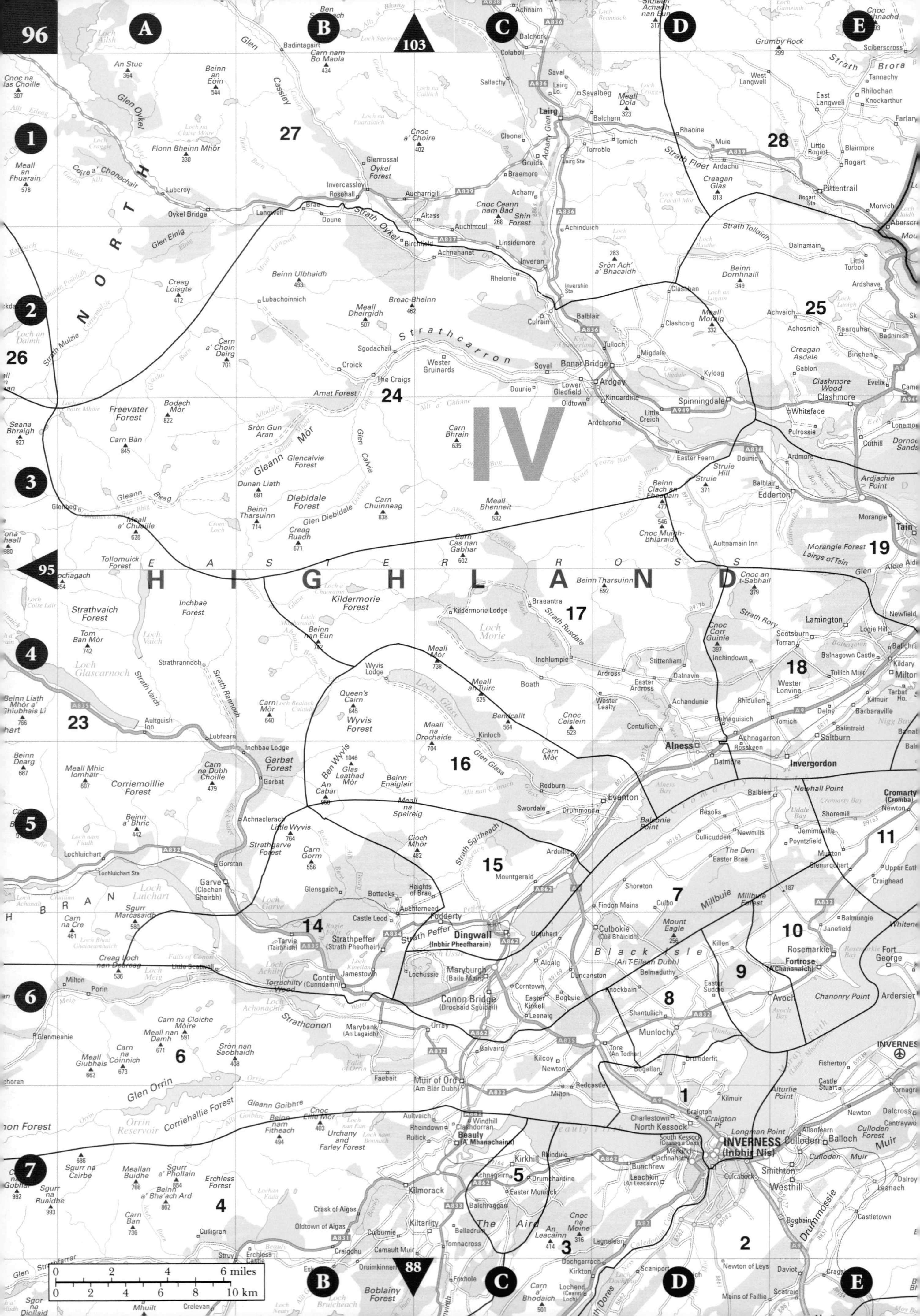
A
B
C
D
E
1
2
3
4
5
6
7
103
95
88
NORTH
EASTER ROSS
HIGHLAND
IV
26
27
28
25
24
23
19
17
18
16
15
14
11
10
9
8
7
6
5
4
3
2
1
An Stuc
Beinn an Eòin
Glen Oykel
Glen Cassley
Badintagairt
Carn nam Bo Maola
Cnoc na Glas Choille
Fionn Bheinn Mhòr
Meall an Fhuarain
Coire a' Chonachair
Lubcroy
Oykel Bridge
Glen Einig
Creag Loisgte
Strath Mulzie
Loch an Daimh
Carn a' Choin Deirg
Freevater Forest
Bodach Mòr
Seana Bhraigh
Carn Bàn
Glenbeg
Meall a' Chuaille
Tollomuick Forest
Langwell
Invercassley
Rosehall
Glenrossal
Oykel Forest
Cnoc a' Choire
Brae
Doune
Strath Oykel
Aucharrigill
Altass
Auchintoul
Birchfield
Achnahanat
Beinn Ulbhaidh
Lubachoinnich
Meall Dheirgidh
Breac-Bheinn
Strathcarron
Sgodachail
Croick
The Craigs
Wester Gruinards
Amat Forest
Sròn Gun Aran
Gleann Mòr
Glencalvie Forest
Glen Calvie
Dunan Liath
Diebidale Forest
Glen Diebidale
Gleann Beag
Beinn Tharsuinn
Creag Ruadh
Carn Chuinneag
Carn Bhrain
Meall Bhenneit
Carn Cas nan Gabhar
Achnairn
Dalchork
Colaboll
Sallachy
Saval
Lairg
Savalbeg
Meall Dola
Balcharn
Tomich
Torroble
Claonel
Gruids
Braemore
Achany
Cnoc Ceann nam Bad
Shin Forest
Linsidemore
Inveran
Rhelonie
Achinduich
Sròn Ach' a' Bhacaidh
Culrain
Invershin
Balblair
Kyle of Sutherland
Tulloch
Bonar Bridge
Ardgay
Soyal
Dounie
Lower Gledfield
Kincardine
Oldtown
Ardchronie
Spinningdale
Little Creich
Migdale
Clashcoig
Kyloag
Meall Moraig
Clashban
Rhaoine
Muie
Strath Fleet
Ardachu
Creagan Glas
Grumby Rock
West Langwell
East Langwell
Strath Brora
Sciberscross
Tannachy
Rhilochan
Knockarthur
Farlary
Little Rogart
Blairmore
Rogart
Pittentrail
Morvich
Strath Tollaich
Dalnamain
Little Torboll
Beinn Domhnaill
Ardshave
Achvaich
Achosnich
Rearquhar
Badninish
Creagan Asdale
Gablon
Clashmore Wood
Clashmore
Evelix
Whiteface
Pulrossie
Cuthill
Easter Fearn
Struie Hill
Struie
Beinn Clach an Fheadain
Cnoc Muigh-bhlàraidh
Edderton
Ardmore
Ardjachie Point
Morangie
Tain
Morangie Forest
Aultnamain Inn
Lairgs of Tain
Cnoc an t-Sabhail
Beinn Tharsuinn
Strathvaich Forest
Inchbae Forest
Kildermorie Forest
Kildermorie Lodge
Braeantra
Strath Rusdale
Loch Morie
Tom Ban Mòr
Loch Vaich
Beinn nan Eun
Loch Glascarnoch
Strathrannoch
Strath Vaich
Strath Rannoch
Wyvis Lodge
Meall Mòr
Meall an Tuirc
Queen's Cairn
Wyvis Forest
Loch Glass
Inchlumpie
Boath
Ardross
Easter Ardross
Stittenham
Dalnavie
Cnoc Corr Guinie
Inchindown
Strath Rory
Scotsburn
Lamington
Logie Hill
Newfield
Balnagown Castle
Kildary
Milton
Tullich Muir
Wester Lonvine
Rhicullen
Kilmuir
Tarbat Ho.
Delny
Barbaraville
Balintraid
Saltburn
Nigg Bay
Invergordon
Beinn Liath Mhòr a' Ghiubhais Li
Aultguish Inn
Lubfearn
Inchbae Lodge
Garbat Forest
Garbat
Carn Mòr
Ben Wyvis
Glas Leathad Mòr
An Cabar
Beinn Enaiglair
Meall na Drochaide
Kinloch
Glen Glass
Bendeallt
Cnoc Ceislein
Carn Mòr
Wester Lealty
Achandunie
Contullich
Alness
Dalmore
Rosskeen
Achnagarron
Redburn
Evanton
Swordale
Drummond
Balconie Point
Meall Mhic Iomhair
Corriemoillie Forest
Carn na Dubh Choille
Beinn Dearg
Meall na Speireig
Little Wyvis
Strathgarve Forest
Beinn a' Bhric
Carn Gorm
Cloch Mhòr
Strath Sgitheach
Moungerald
Ardullie
Lochluichart
Gorstan
Loch Luichart
Garve (Clachan Ghairbh)
Glensgaich
Bottacks
Heights of Brae
Auchterneed
Fodderty
Sgurr Marcasaidh
Carn na Cre
Tarvie
Castle Leod
Strathpeffer (Strath Pheofhair)
Strath Peffer
Dingwall (Inbhir Pheofharain)
Loch Achilty
Creag Loch nan Dearcag
Little Scatwell
Contin (Cunndainn)
Jamestown
Lochussie
Maryburgh (Baile Màiri)
Conon Bridge (Drochaid Sgùideil)
Torrachilty Wood
Milton
Porin
Strathconon
Glenmeanie
Carn na Cloiche Mòire
Meall nan Damh
Carn a' Choinnich
Meall Ghiubhais
Sròn nan Saobhaidh
Marybank (An Lagaidh)
Urray
Glen Orrin
Orrin Reservoir
Corriehallie Forest
Gleann Goibhre
Cnoc Eille Mòr
Beinn nan Fitheach
Urchany and Farley Forest
Faebait
Muir of Ord (Am Blàr Dubh)
Balvaird
Kilcoy
Newton
Redcastle
Milton
Aultvaich
Rheindown
Ruilick
Windhill
Clashdorran
Beauly (A' Mhanachainn)
Kirkhill
Achnagairn
Drumchardine
Easter Moniack
Balchraggan
The Aird
Kilmorack
Crask of Aigas
Oldtown of Aigas
Culburnie
Kiltarlity
Belladrum
Tomnacross
Camault Muir
Craigdhu
Erchless Castle
Struy
Druimkinnerras
Boblainy Forest
Foxhole
Carn a' Bhodaich
Lochend
Dochgarroch
Kirkton
Sgurr na Cairbe
Meallan Buidhe
Sgurr a' Phollain
Erchless Forest
Beinn a' Bha'ach Ard
Carn Ban
Culligran
Sgurr na Ruaidhe
Urquhart
Findon Mains
Culbokie (Cùil Bhàicidh)
Alcaig
Duncanston
Corntown
Easter Kinkell
Bogbuie
Leanaig
Knockbain
Shantullich
Munlochy
Belmaduthy
Easter Suddie
Tore (An Todhar)
Bogallan
Drumderfit
Black Isle (An T-Eilean Dubh)
Mount Eagle
Millbuie
Millbuie Forest
Culbo
Shoreton
Cromarty Firth
Resolis
Cullicudden
Newmills
The Den
Easter Brae
Balblair
Newhall Point
Cromarty Bay
Udale Bay
Shoremill
Jemimaville
Poyntzfield
Cromarty (Cromba)
Newton
Muirton
Glenurquhart
Upper Eathie
Craighead
Balmungie
Janefield
Rosemarkie
Rosemarkie Bay
Fortrose (A' Chananaich)
Fort George
Ardersier
Chanonry Point
Avoch
Avoch Bay
Killen
Kilmuir
Craigton
Craigton Pt
Charlestown
North Kessock
South Kessock
Merkinch
Clachnaharry
Bunchrew
Leachkin (An Leacainn)
Beauly Firth
Moray Firth
Alturlie Point
Longman Point
INVERNESS (Inbhir Nis)
Culloden
Balloch
Culloden Forest
Culloden Muir
Smithton
Westhill
Culcabock
Allanfearn
Dalcross
Cantraywood
Castle Stuart
Fisherton
Tornagrain
Drummossie
Bogbain
Leanach
Castletown
Newton of Leys
Daviot
Mains of Faillie
Scatraig
An Leacainn
Cnoc na Moine
Lagnalean
Scaniport
Dores
Muir
Glen Strathfarrar
Mhuilt
Crelevan
Sgor na Diollaid
Loch Bruicheach
0 2 4 6 miles
0 2 4 6 8 10 km

F
G
H
J
K
1
2
3
4
5
6
7
104
98
89
Brora
Golspie
Embo
Portmahomack
Tarbat Ness
Wilkhaven
Inver
Balintore
Hill of Fearn
Shandwick
North Sutor
MORAY FIRTH
Nairn
Forres
Kinloss
Burghead
Hopeman
Lossiemouth
ELGIN
Lhanbryde
Rothes
Aberlour
Dufftown
Archiestown
Dallas
Rafford
Auldearn
Cawdor
Findhorn
Culbin Forest
Darnaway Forest
Covesea Skerries
Halliman Skerries
Lothbeg Point
KW
IV
AB
PH
MORAY
SPEY
STRATHSPEY
9
20
12
36
30
31
32
38
37
26
55

A
B
C
D
E
1
2
3
4
5
6
7
97
90
Halliman Skerries
Stotfield
Branderburgh
Lossiemouth
Gordonstoun
Oakenhead
Boar's Head Rock
31
Lossie Forest
Innes Links
Salterhill
Spey Mouth
Kingston
Spey Bay
Portgordon
Findochty
Portknockie
Scar Nose
Cullen Bay
Logie Head
Portessie
Ianstown
Bauds of Cullen
Rathven
Buckie
Seatown
Cullen
Sandend
Sandend Bay
Redhythe Point
Portsoy
Boyne Bay
Knock Head
Whitehills
Easter Whyntie
Lochhill
Bishopmill
ELGIN
Urquhart
Garmouth
Nether Dallachy
Upper Dallachy
Bogmoor
Mains of Tannachy
Slackhead
Arradoul
56
Hill of Maud
Bin of Cullen
Lintmill
Clune
Mains of Glassaugh
Fordyce
Durn Hill
Fordyce Hill
Boyndie
Auds
Blairshinnoch
Wester Culbeuchly
Muir of Lochs
Newton
Auchenhalrig
Broadley
Drybridge
Slate Haugh
Weston
Milton
Kirktown of Deskford
Ardiecow
Hill of Culbirnie
45
Palmerscross
New Elgin
Moss of Barmuckity
Lhanbryde
Newlands of Tynet
Bridge of Tynet
Clochan
Black Hill
Shiel Muir
Berryhillock
Hoggie
Mosstodloch
Fochabers
Braes of Enzie
Addie Hill
Craibstone
Canterbury
Oldtown of Ord
Paddockhaugh
Cloddach
Longmorn
Blackhills
Clackmarras
Altonside
Orbliston
Dipple
Whiteash Hill
Millstone Hill
Aultmore
Black Hill
Backies
Lurg Hill
Cornhill
Fattahead
30
Thornhill
Fogwatt
Whitewreath
Ordiequish
32
Inchberry
Deerhill
Gordonstown
Glen Barry
Park
Weachyburn
Teindland Forest
Wood of Ordiequish
Speymouth Forest
Thief's Hill
Broadrashes
Garralburn
Grange Crossroads
Crannoch
Sillyearn
Knock Hill
Mill of Kebholes
Linhead
M
O
R
A
Y
Glenlatterach
Bardon
Coleburn
Findlay's Seat
Forgie
Aultmore
Bracobrae
Wether Hill
Culvie
Finnygaud
Knowes of Elrick
Gallow Hill
Boghead
Brylach Hill
Wood of Dunduras
Boat o' Brig
North Bogbain
Hill of Mulderie
Newmill
Floors
Knock
Drumnagorrach
Limehillock
Knabbygates
Auchintoul
Crannach
Aberchirder
Cairn Uish
Pikey Hill
The Kettles
Glen of Rothes
Auchinroath
Orton
Mulben
Fife Keith
Keith
Davoch of Grange
Farmtown
Old Crombie
Bognie
Rothes
Knock More
Tauchers
Auchlunkart
Rosarie
Meikle Balloch Hill
Moss-side
Marnoch
Clunie
Carnousie
Haughs
Mayen
Carn na Cailliche
Hill of Stob
Cairn Cattoch
Hunt Hill
38
Whiteacen
Ben Aigan
Rosarie Forest
Hill of Towie
Blackhillock
Balloch Wood
Milltown of Rothiemay
Hillbrae
Inverkeithny
Yonder Bognie
Auchininna
Knockan
Towiemore
Edintore
The Balloch
Glen of Coachford
Ruthven
Redhill
Fortrie
Bognie brae
Sochies Forest
Dandaleith
Maggieknockater
Coachford
Newton
Fourman Hill
Hill of Carlincraig
Archiestown
Robertstown
Craigellachie
55
Drummuir Castle
Drummuir
Hillend
Cairnie
Conland
Feithhill
Cardow
Ringorm
Aberlour (Charlestown of Aberlour)
Braehead
The Bin
The Bin Forest
Cobairdy
Drumblair
Knockando
Carron
Speyview
Tullich
Aultnapaddock
Daugh of Invermarkie
Drumdelgie
Daugh of Cairnborrow
Milton of Cairnborrow
Corse of Kinnoir
Cruchie
Lessendrum
Largue
Denmoss
A
B
E
R
D
E
Daugh of Kinermony
Milltown of Edinvillie
Parkmore
Milltown of Auchindoun
Huntly
Frendraught
Auchamie
Corse
Daugh of Carron
Sheandow
Dufftown
Torry
Drumblade
Marypark
Keithmore
Bakebare
Haugh of Glass
Cairnargat
54
Clashmach Hill
Mosshead
Brideswell
Bellehiglash
37
Baby's Hill
Meikle Conval
Beatshach
Laggan
Dumeath
Muckle Long Hill
Baillieswal
Strathbogie
Beggshill
Denend
Ythanwells
Bridgehaugh
The Scalp
Backside
Succoth
Tillathrowie
Bridgend
Thomastown
Millburn
Ben Rinnes
Favillar
Glen Rinnes
Laird's Seat
Glen Fiddich
Glacks of Balloch Pass
Ballochford
Carn Chrom
Tomnaven
Coynachie
Kirkstile
Winds Eye
Bainshole
Hill of Tillymorgan
Dalchirach
Achnastank
Clashindarroch Forest
Quarry Hill
Cransmill Hill
Clashindarroch
Kirkney
Gartly
Culdrain
Backburn
Wishach Hill
Glens of Foudland
Hill of Foudland
Skares
Kirkton of Culsalmond
Cairnhill
Cairnacay
Craggan
Tervieside
Hill of Achmore
Glen Fiddich Forest
Bridgend
Inverharroch Farm
Ardwell
Black Hill
Newnoth
Tap o' North
Cults
Knockandy Hill
Slack
Wardhouse
Largie
Wrangham
Colpy
Upper Boddam
Meikle Firriggs
Mount of Haddoch
Milton of Noth
Kennethmont
Glanderston
Aulton
52
Glenlivet
Carn Liath
Muldonich
Aldunie
Belhinnie
Rhynie
Towie
Cottown
Rothney
Hill of Christ's Kirk
Ardoyne
0
2
4
6 miles
0
2
4
6
8
10 km

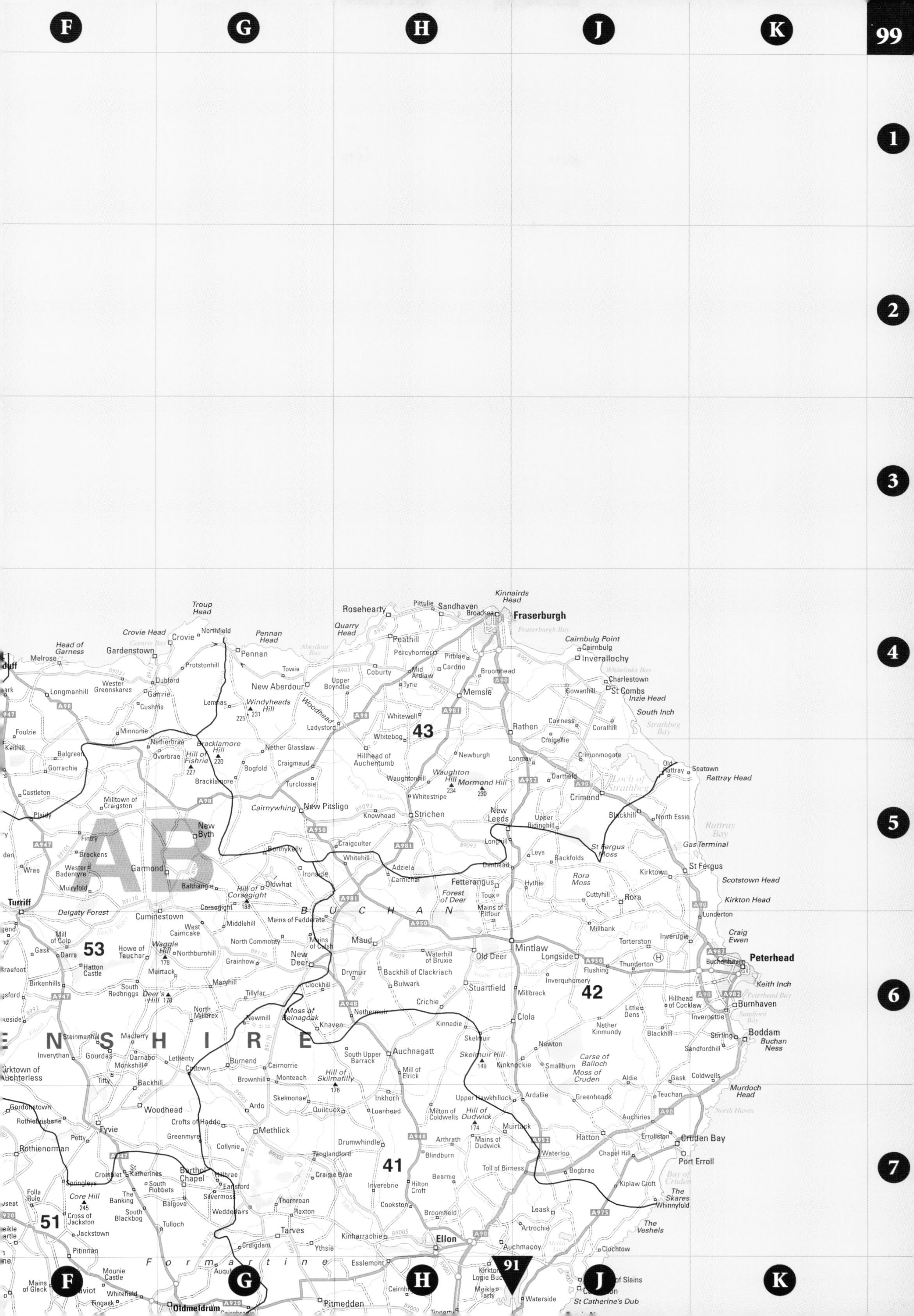
F
G
H
J
K
1
2
3
4
5
6
7
Fraserburgh
Peterhead
Kinnairds Head
Rosehearty
Sandhaven
Pittulie
Troup Head
Crovie Head
Crovie
Northfield
Pennan Head
Pennan
Gardenstown
Head of Garness
Melrose
New Aberdour
Memsie
Rathen
Inverallochy
Cairnbulg
Cairnbulg Point
Charlestown
St Combs
Inzie Head
South Inch
Strathbeg Bay
Loch of Strathbeg
Crimond
Rattray Head
Seatown
Old Rattray
St Fergus
Scotstown Head
Kirkton Head
Craig Ewen
Keith Inch
Burnhaven
Boddam
Buchan Ness
Murdoch Head
Cruden Bay
Port Erroll
The Skares
Whinnyfold
The Veshels
43
42
41
53
51
AB
B U C H A N
E N S H I R E
F o r m a r t i n e
Turriff
Delgaty Forest
Cuminestown
New Byth
Garmond
Fyvie
Rothienorman
Oldmeldrum
Methlick
Tarves
Ellon
Auchmacoy
Maud
New Deer
Mintlaw
Longside
Old Deer
Stuartfield
Fetterangus
Strichen
New Pitsligo
New Leeds
Mormond Hill
Waughton Hill
Forest of Deer
Auchnagatt
Hatton
Clola
Boddam
91

A
B
C
D
E
1
2
3
4
5
6
7
WESTERN ISLES
(NA H-EILEANAN SIAR)
OUTER HEBRIDES
Aird Mhòr Bragair
Labost
Fibhig
Rubh' an Dùnain
Shawbost (Siabost)
Siabost Bho Dheas
Siabost Bho
Pairc
Dail Beag
Aird Mhòr
Gearrannan
Dail Mòr
Mullach Charlabhaigh
Craigeam
Beinn Bragar
261
248
Beinn Rahacleit
Borghastan
Carloway (Carlabhagh)
Cirbhig
Creag Mhòr
Little Bernera
West Loch Roag
Crothair
Bostadh
Gallan Head
Pabaidh Mòr
Tobson
Great
Bernera
East Loch Roag
Tolastadh a' Chaolais
Aird Uig
Bhaltos
Breacleit
Vacsay
Geodha Nasavig
Forsnaval
205
Miavaig (Miabhaig)
Nisa Mhòr
Reef (Riof)
Vuia Mòr
Hacklete (Tacleit)
Barragiom
Kirkibost (Circebost)
Breascleit
Cradhlastadh
Timsgearraidh
Uigen
Iarsiadar
Crùlabhig
Eilean Kearstay
Vuia Beg
Callanish (Calanais)
Aird Mhòr Mangurstadh
Cairisiadar
Floday
Lundale
Geisiadar
A858
Mangurstadh
Eadar dha Fhadhail
Ben Drovinish
185
Linsiadar
Garrynahine (Gearraidh na h-Aibhne)
Suainaval
429
Teahaval
256
Griomarstaidh
Aird Fenish
Ungisiadar
Loch Suainaval
Einacleit
Islibhig
Mealisval
574
Tahaval
515
Scealascro
B8011
Aird Breanais
Breanais
2
Cracaval
514
Loch Grunavat
Giosla
Skeun
265
Calltraiseal Bheag
226
Beinn Mohal
207
HS
Mealasta
Tamanaisval
467
Beinn Mheadhonach
397
Kinlochroag (Ceann Lochroag)
241
Coduinn
228
Calltraiseal Mhòr
Roineval
281
Mealasta Island
Griomaval
Maghannan
Loch na Craobhaig
Scalaval
260
Liongam
Aird Bheag
Loch Benisvat
Sleiteachal Mhòr
248
Kintarvie
Airidh a' Bhruaich
Kearstay
Gob na h-Airde Mòire
Aird Mhòr
Morsgail Forest
Beinn a' Bhoth
308
Sgeir Moil Duinn
Sròn Romul
308
Scarp
Màs a' Chnoic-chuairtich
386
Mullach na Reidheachd
295
Kearnaval
378
Aird an Troim
A859
Loch Langavat
Beinn a' Mhuil
370
Sidhean an Airgid
381
Mòr Mhonadh
401
Sgianait
425
Rapaire
Liuthaid
Beinn na h-Uamha
389
Gasker
Huisinis
Tirga Mòr
679
Stulaval
579
473
Mullach a' Ruisg
Ath Linne
424
Husival Mòr
489
Ullaval
659
NORTH HARRIS
Seaforth Island
Muaithabhal
Hushinish Point
Aird a' Mhulaidh
Arda Beaga
Leosaval
412
Forest of Harris
Oreval
662
(CEANN A TUATH NA HEARADH)
572
Beinn Mhòr
Gobhaig
Cleiseval
511
Uisgnaval Mòr
729
Horsanish
Abhainnsuidhe
Rubha Bhuic
Mulla-fo-dheas
743
Clisham
799
Clett Ard
328
3
Maraig (Maaruig)
Kenmore
Taransay Glorigs
Soay Beg
Soay Mòr
Miabhag
Tolmachan
A859
Bun Abhainn Eadarra
Sgaoth Aird
559
Straiaval
389
Toddun
528
Caiteshal
449
Taransay (Tarasaigh)
WEST LOCH TARBERT
Ben Raah
267
Aird Asaig
Rhenigidale (Reinigeadal)
Beinn Dhubh
506
Tarbert (Tairbeart)
Taobh Siar
Beinn a' Chaolais
Beesdale
Urgha
Ueiseval
334
Aird Vanish
Paible
Losgaintir
93
Reamhar
467
Carragrich
Eilean Mòr a' Bhàigh
Rubha Sgeirigin
South Harris Forest
Kyles Scalpay (Caolas Scalpaigh)
Sgeotasaigh
Scalpay
0 2 4 6 miles
0 2 4 6 8 10 km

101
F
G
H
J
K
1
2
3
4
5
6
7
102
Butt of Lewis
(Rubha Robhanais)
Eoropaidh
Còig Peighinnean
Bad an Fhithich
Lionel
(Lional)
Port of Ness (Port Nis)
Swainbost
(Suainebost)
Harbost
(Tabost)
Eorodal
Aird Dhail
South Dell (Dail Bho Dheas)
North Dell
(Dail Bho Thuath)
Cross (Cros)
Sgiogarstaigh
Ness
(Niss)
Glen Cross
Meall Geal
Toa Galson
A857
Gabhsunn Bho Thuath
Gabhsunn Bho Dheas
Melbost Borve
(Mealabost)
Roinn a' Bhuic
Cuidhaseadair
Laimhrig
Airigh na Glaice
Ben Dell
Airighean Beinn nan Caorach
Borve
(Borgh)
High Borve
Cellar Head
Siadar Iarach
Rubha Leathann
Siadar Uarach
Baile an Truiseil
Airighean Loch Breihavat
Diaval
Glen Shader
Upper Barvas
Brue
(Bru)
Barvas
(Barabhas)
A858
Muirneag
248
Tolastadh Ùr
Tolastadh
Tolsta Head
Gleann Mòr Bharabhais
Gleann Tholastaidh
Gleann Bhruthadail
Roishal Mòr
174
Gress
(Griais)
Creag Fhraoch
E O F L E W I S
EILEAN LEODHAIS)
Bac
Col
Col Uarach
Breibhig
Rubha Bhataisgeir
Beinn Mholach
292
Col Sands
Tiumpan Head
(Rubha an Tiumpain)
Portnaguran
(Port nan Giùran)
Portvoller
Rubha Deas
Tunga
Aird Thunga
Sròn Ruadh
LOCH A' TUATH
Flesherin
Aird
New Valley
Newmarket
Stornoway
(Steornabhagh)
Laxdale
(Lacasdail)
Melbost Sands
Siulaisiadar
East Roisnish
Seisiadar
Marybank
Steinis
STORNOWAY
Melbost Pt
Melbost
Garrabost
Eye Peninsula
(An Rubha)
Rubha na Greine
1
2
A858
A866
Sandwick
(Sanndabhaig)
Aiginis
Cnoc
Rubha na Bearnaich
Upper Bayble (Pabail Uarach)
Holm
(Tolm)
Branahuie Banks
Suardail
Lower Bayble
(Pabail Iarach)
149
Beinn a' Bhuna
Arnish Pt
Arnish Moor
Achadh Mòr
Rubh' a' Bhàigh Uaine
Ceann na Circ
A859
Leurbost
(Liurbost)
Grimshader
(Griomsiadar)
Crosbost
Ranish
(Ranais)
Raerinish Point
Tabhaigh Mhòr
Eilean Chaluim Chille
Keose
(Ceos)
Cromore
Orasaigh
acasaigh
Cearsiadar
Cabharstadh
Torraigh
Tabost
Gearraidh Bhaird
Marbhig
Calbost
Rubha Iosal
Grabhair
Tom an Fhuadain
Kebock Head
Orasaigh
Leumrabhagh
Gob na Milaid
Srianach
Eilean Iubhard
Uisenis
371
Mulhagery
Gob Rubh' Uisenis
Rubha Bhrollum
THE MINCH
SOUND OF SHIANT
Garbh Eilean
161
Eilean an Tighe

A   B   C   D   E

1   Cape Wrath
Duslic
Geodha Ruadh na Fola
Cnoc a'
Ghiubhais
297

2   Am Balg
Sandwood
Bay
Am Buachaille
Sandwood
Loch
Beinn De
423
Rubh' an Fhir Leithe
Strath
An
Grianan
467
Creag
Riabha
485
Mea
M
Shinary

Sheigra
Blairmore
Balchrick
Oldshore Beg
Oldshoremore
Beinn
a' Chraisg
257
An
Socach
358
Eilean an
Ròin Mòr

3   Kinlochbervie
Rubha na Leacaig
Badcall
Achlyness
Achriesgill
Rhiconich
Ardmore
Point
Ceathramh
Garbh
Rubha Ruadh
Fanagmore
Tarbet
Foindle
A838

101   Handa
Island
Laxford Bridge
Badnabay
A894
Loch
St

4   Scourie Morell
Scourie
A838
Rubh' Aird
an t- Sionnaich
Ben
Stack
721
Badcall

Ben
Auskaird
386
Reay
Fores
S

Eilean
a' Bhreitheimh
Rubh'
a' Mhucard
Calbha Beag
H
Loch an
Leathaid
Bhuain
Ben
Strome
426
Meall Mòr
Meall Beag
Calbha
Mòr

5   Point
of Stoer
Sgeir nan Gall
Oldany
Island
Eddrachillis
Bay
Kylestrome
Glendhu
Forest
Cirean Geardail
161
Rubha nan Còsan
Ardvar
Kylesku
Be
Al
da L
Culkein
Eilean
Chrona
Drumbeg
Newton
Cluas Deas
Raffin
Achnacarnin
Nedd
Clashmore
Sàil Gorm
776
Gleann Leireag
Balchladich
Cleshnessie
Quinag
808
Rubh' a'
Mhill Dheirg
Stoer
Spidean Coinich
764
A894
Clachtoll
Glas Bheinn
776
Rubha Leumair
Little Assynt
A837
Bein
Uid
740

6   Achmelvich
Rhicarn
Loch Assynt
Ardroe
Beinn Gharbh
540
Inchnada
Rubha Rodha
Baddidarach
Lochinver
(Loch an Inbhir)
Inchnadamph
Soyea
Island
A'Chleit
Kirkaig Point
Badnabàn
Strathan
Glencanisp Forest
Stronechrubie
Inverkirkaig
Rubha na Brèige
Suilven
731
Canisp
846
A837
Rubha Coigeach
Eilean Mòr
Rhegreanoch
Bre
Me
Bhra

7   Feochag Bay
Enard
Bay
Rubh'
a' Choin
Ledbeg
Ledmore
Camas Eilean
Glilais
Rubha Mòr
Reiff
Polly Bay
Cul
Mòr
Loch
Sionascaig
Loch
Urigill
Altandhu
Brae of Achnahaird
26
Eilean
Mullagrach
Isle
Ristol
Aird of
Coigach
Inverpolly
Forest
Cul
Beg
Drumrunie
Forest
Elphin
Polbain
Stac
Pollaidh
613
Knockan
Glas-leac
95
Cnoc na
Glas Choire
307

B   Ardnagoine   C   D   E
Tanera Beg
Garadheancal
Achiltibuie
(Achd-'Ille
Polglass
An
t-Sàil
490
Beinn
na Eòin
A835
Loch
Largann

0   2   4   6 miles
0   2   4   6   8   10 km

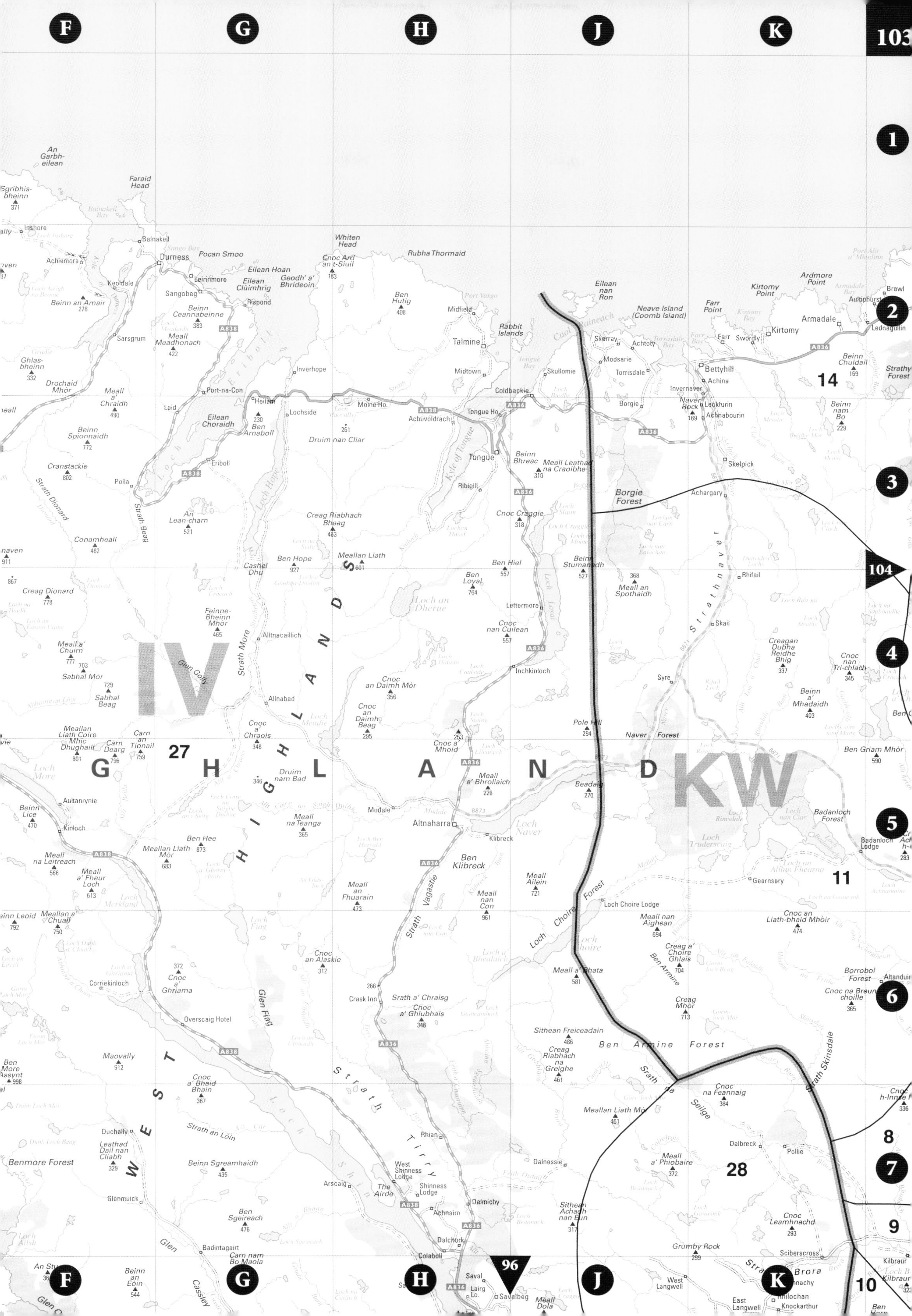
F
G
H
J
K
1
2
3
4
5
6
7
8
9
10
104
96
An Garbh-eilean
Faraid Head
Sgribhis-bheinn 371
Balnakeil Bay
Inshore
Balnakeil
Durness
Pocan Smoo
Whiten Head
Cnoc Ard an t-Siuil 183
Rubha Thormaid
Achiemore
Keoldale
Leirinmore
Eilean Hoan
Eilean Clùimhrig
Geodh' a' Bhrideoin
Sangobeg
Rispond
Beinn an Amair 278
Beinn Ceannabeinne 383
Ben Hutig 408
Midfield
Eilean nan Ron
Caol Raineach
Neave Island (Coomb Island)
Farr Point
Kirtomy Point
Ardmore Point
Brawl
Aultiphurst
Lednagullin
Armadale
Kirtomy
Swordly
Farr
Sarsgrum
Meall Meadhonach 422
Rabbit Islands
Talmine
Skerray
Achtoty
Torrisdale Bay
Ghlas-bheinn 332
Inverhope
Midtown
Skullomie
Modsarie
Torrisdale
Bettyhill
Achina
Beinn Chuldail 169
Strathy Forest
14
Drochaid Mhòr
Meall a' Chraidh 490
Port-na-Con
Coldbackie
Invernaver
Naver Rock 169
Leckfurin
Achnabourin
Laid
Heilam
Lochside
Moine Ho.
Achuvoldrach
Tongue Ho.
Borgie
Beinn nam Bo 229
Eilean Choraidh
230 Ben Arnaboll
261
Druim nan Cliar
Beinn Spionnaidh 772
Tongue
Beinn Bhreac
Meall Leathad na Craoibhe 310
Skelpick
Cranstackie 802
Eriboll
Kyle of Tongue
Polla
Ribigill
Borgie Forest
Achargary
Strath Dionard
Strath Beag
An Lean-charn 521
Creag Riabhach Bheag 463
Cnoc Craggie 318
Conamheall 482
Ben Hope 927
Meallan Liath 801
Cashel Dhu
Ben Hiel 557
Beinn Stumanadh 527
Rhifail
Creag Dionard 778
Ben Loyal 764
368 Meall an Spothaidh
Strathnaver
Loch an Dherue
Lettermore
Feinne-Bheinn Mhòr 465
Loch Loyal
Alltnacaillich
Cnoc nan Cuilean 557
Skail
Meall a' Chuirn 777
703
Strath More
Glen Golly
IV
Inchkinloch
Creagan Dubha Reidhe Bhig 337
Cnoc nan Tri-chlach 345
Sabhal Mòr
729 Sabhal Beag
Cnoc an Daimh Mòr 356
Syre
Beinn a' Mhadaidh 403
Allnabad
Cnoc an Daimh Beag 295
Pole Hill 294
Meallan Liath Coire Mhic Dhughaill 801
Carn Dearg 796
Carn an Tionail 759
27
Cnoc a' Chraois 348
Cnoc a' Mhoid 253
Naver Forest
Ben Griam Mhòr 590
HIGHLANDS
H I G H L A N D
KW
Loch More
Druim nam Bad
346
Meall a' Bhrollaich 226
Beadaig 270
Aultanrynie
Beinn Lice 470
Kinloch
Mudale
Meall na Teanga 365
Altnaharra
Klibreck
Loch Naver
Loch Rimsdale
Loch nan Clar
Badanloch Forest
Badanloch Lodge
Ben Hee 873
Loch Truderscaig
Meall na Leitreach 566
Meallan Liath Mòr 683
Ben Klibreck
Loch an Alltan Fhearna
Meall a' Fheur Loch 613
Meall Ailein 721
Gearnsary
11
Meall an Fhuarain 473
Strath Vagastie
Meall nan Con 961
Loch Choire Forest
Loch Choire Lodge
Loch Merkland
Meallan a' Chuail 750
Meall nan Aighean 694
Cnoc an Liath-bhaid Mhòir 474
Loch Fiag
Loch Choire
Creag a' Choire Ghlais 704
Ben Armine
Cnoc an Alaskie 312
Meall a' Bhata 581
Borrobol Forest
Altanduin
372 Cnoc a' Ghriama
Corriekinloch
266
Crask Inn
Srath a' Chraisg
Cnoc a' Ghiubhais 346
Glen Fiag
Creag Mhor 713
Cnoc na Breun-choille 365
Overscaig Hotel
Sithean Freiceadain 486
Ben Armine Forest
Strath Skinsdale
Maovally 512
Creag Riabhach na Greighe 461
Ben More Assynt 998
Cnoc a' Bhaid Bhain 367
Strath Tirry
Srath na Seilge
Cnoc na Feannaig 384
Meallan Liath Mòr 461
WEST
Duchally
Leathad Dail nan Cliabh 329
Strath an Lòin
Rhian
Dalbreck
Pollie
Benmore Forest
Beinn Sgreamhaidh 435
Loch Shin
West Shinness Lodge
Dalnessie
Meall a' Phiobaire 372
28
Arscaig
The Airde
Shinness Lodge
Glenquick
Dalmichy
Achnairn
Ben Sgeireach 476
Sithean Achadh nan Eun 317
Cnoc Leamhnachd 293
Loch Ailsh
Glen Cassley
Badintagairt
Carn nam Bo Maola
Dalchork
Grumby Rock 299
Sciberscross
Colaboll
Brora
Kilbraur
Beinn an Eoin 544
Saval
Lairg Lo.
Savalbeg
Meall Dola
West Langwell
East Langwell
Knockarthur
A838
A836
B873
B871

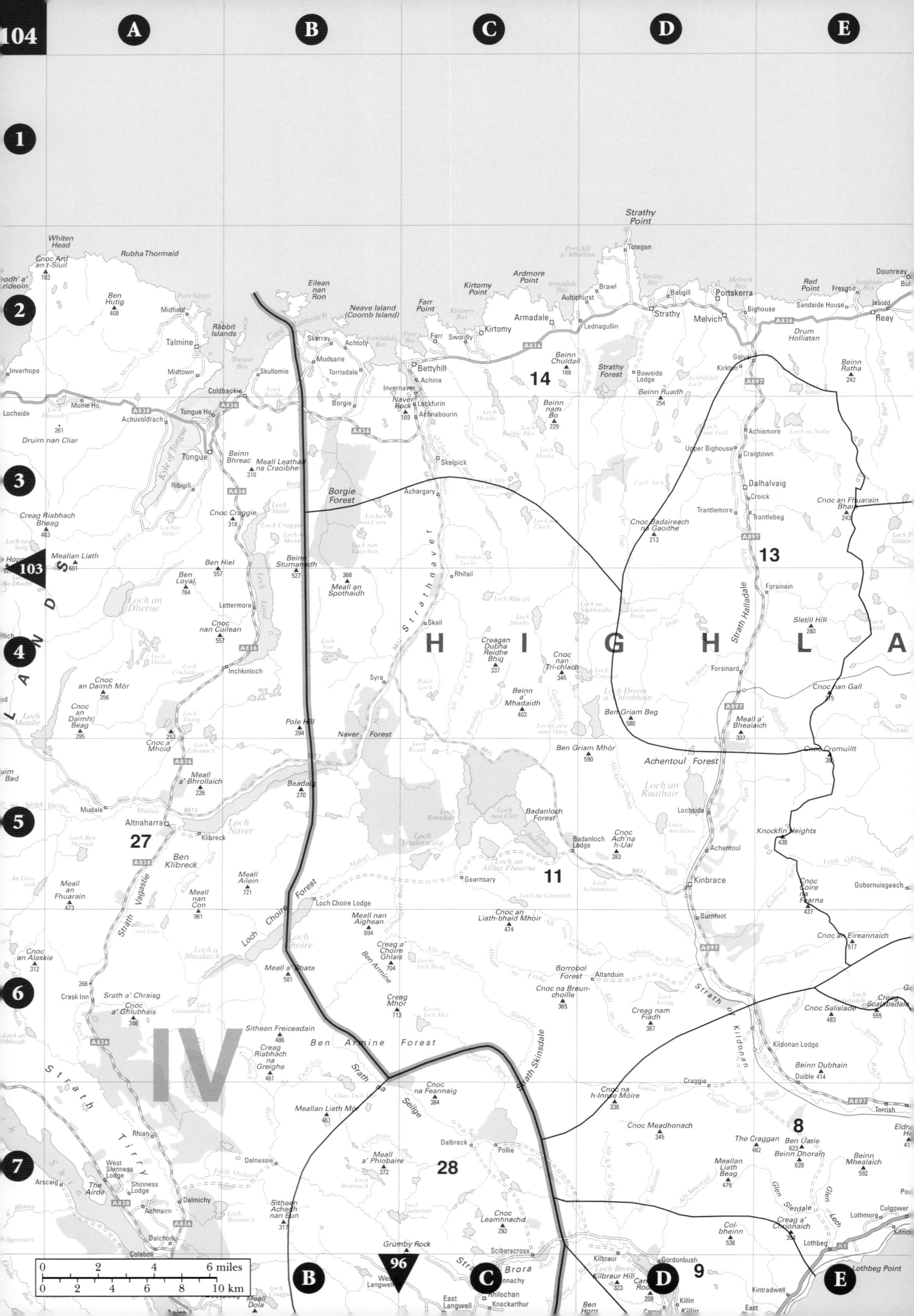
A
B
C
D
E
1
2
3
4
5
6
7
Strathy Point
Whiten Head
Rubha Thormaid
Cnoc Ard an t-Siuil
Ben Hutig
Eilean nan Ron
Neave Island (Coomb Island)
Farr Point
Kirtomy Point
Ardmore Point
Red Point
Dounreay
Talmine
Midfield
Rabbit Islands
Skerray
Achtoty
Modsarie
Torrisdale
Skullomie
Bettyhill
Achina
Farr
Swordly
Kirtomy
Armadale
Strathy
Melvich
Portskerra
Bighouse
Reay
Sandside House
Fresgoe
Isauld
Baligill
Brawl
Aultiphurst
Lednagullin
Totegan
Drum Hollistan
Inverhope
Midtown
Coldbackie
Tongue Ho.
Moine Ho.
Lochside
Achuvoldrach
Druim nan Cliar
Borgie
Invernaver
Naver Rock
Lackfurin
Achnabourin
Beinn Chuldail
Strathy Forest
Bowside Lodge
Beinn Ruadh
Golval
Kirkton
Beinn Ratha
Beinn nam Bo
14
Tongue
Beinn Bhreac
Meall Leathad na Craoibhe
Ribigill
Skelpick
Achiemore
Upper Bighouse
Craigtown
Dalhalvaig
Croick
Trantlemore
Trantlebeg
Borgie Forest
Achargary
Cnoc Craggie
Creag Riabhach Bheag
Cnoc Badaireach na Gaoithe
Cnoc an Fhuarain Bhain
Meallan Liath
103
Ben Hiel
Beinn Stumanadh
Meall an Spothaidh
Rhifail
Strathnaver
13
Forsinain
Ben Loyal
Loch an Dheruė
Lettermore
Loch Loyal
Cnoc nan Cuilean
Skail
Strath Halladale
Sletill Hill
H I G H L A
Creagan Dubha Reidhe Bhig
Cnoc nan Tri-chlach
Inchkinloch
Cnoc an Daimh Mòr
Syre
Beinn a' Mhadaidh
Loch Druim a' Chliabhain
Ben Griam Beg
Forsinard
Cnoc nan Gall
Cnoc an Daimh Beag
Pole Hill
Naver Forest
Meall a' Bhealaich
Cnoc a' Mhoid
Ben Griam Mhòr
Achentoul Forest
Cnoc Cromuillt
Meall a' Bhrollaich
Beadaig
Loch an Ruathair
Mudale
Altnaharra
Loch Naver
Badanloch Forest
Lochside
27
Klibreck
Ben Klibreck
Badanloch Lodge
Cnoc Ach'na h-Uai
Knockfin Heights
Achentoul
Loch an Alltan Fhearna
11
Gearnsary
Kinbrace
Meall an Fhuarain
Meall Ailein
Meall nan Con
Strath Vagastie
Loch Choire Forest
Loch Choire Lodge
Cnoc Coire na Fearna
Gobernuisgeach
Meall nan Aighean
Cnoc an Liath-bhaid Mhoir
Burnfoot
Cnoc an Alaskie
Loch Choire
Creag a' Choire Ghlais
Ben Armine
Cnoc an Eireannaich
Meall a' Bhata
Borrobol Forest
Altanduin
Crask Inn
Strath a' Chraisg
Cnoc a' Ghubhais
Creag Mhor
Cnoc na Breun-choille
Strath of Kildonan
Cnoc Salislade
Creag Scalabsdale
IV
Sithean Freiceadain
Creag Riabhach na Greighe
Ben Armine Forest
Creag nam Fiadh
Kildonan Lodge
Strath na Seilge
Cnoc na Feannaig
Strath Skinsdale
Beinn Dubhain
Duible
Strath Tirry
Meallan Liath Mòr
Cnoc na h-Innse Mòire
Craggie
Torrish
Cnoc Meadhonach
8
Rhian
Dalbreck
Pollie
The Craggan
Ben Uarie
Beinn Dhorain
Beinn Mhealaich
West Shinness Lodge
Dalnessie
Meall a' Phiobaire
28
Meallan Liath Beag
Glen Sletdale
Glen Loth
Arscaig
The Airde
Shinness Lodge
Dalmichy
Lothmore
Culgower
Achnairn
Sithean Achadh nan Eun
Cnoc Leamhnachd
Creag a' Chrionaich
Col-bheinn
Dalchork
Colaboll
Grumby Rock
Sciberscross
Lothbeg
Kilbraur
Gordonbush
96
Loch Brora
Kilbraur Hill
9
Lothbeg Point
West Langwell
Rhilochan
Knockarthur
East Langwell
Carrol
Killin
Ben Horn
Kintradwell
Meall Dola
A836
A838
A897
B871
B873
A9
0 2 4 6 miles
0 2 4 6 8 10 km

F
G
H
J
K
106
PENTLAND FIRTH
Dunnet Head
Easter Head
Island of Stroma
Langaton Point
Nethertown
Red Head
Mell Head
Uppertown
Muckle Skerry
Pentland Skerries
Men of Mey
St John's Point
Skarfskerry Point
Tang Head
Dunnet Hill
Scarfskerry
Harrow
East Mey
Head of Crees
Ness of Duncansby
Duncansby Head
Stacks of Duncansby
The Thirl
Brough
Ham
Rattar
Hunspow
West Dunnet
Whitebridge
Barrock
Mey
Rigga
Gills
Kirkstyle
Canisbay
John o' Groats
Upper Gills
Huna
Brims Ness
Ness of Litter
Clett
Holborn Head
Scrabster
Clardon Head
Dwarwick Head
The Spur
Dunnet
Inkstack
Warth Hill
Wife Geo
Crosskirk
Thurso (Inbhir Theòrsa)
Murkle
Links of Dunnet
Brabster
Everley
Tofts
Skirza
Skirza Head
Lybster
Bridge of Forss
Clardon
Castletown
Greenland
Lochend
Viewfield
Ormlie
Thurdistoft
Slickly
Freswick
Ness Head
Lythmore
Haimer
Olrig House
Hayfield
Tain
Janetstown
Glengolly
Newlands of Geise
Lochside
Alterwall
Auckengill
Shalmstry
Reaster
Hilliclay
Durran
Weydale
Westfield
Hoy
Bowermadden
Ruthers of Howe
Nybster
Shebster
Forsie
Lieurary
Buckies
Carsgoe
Achingills
Lyth
Sortat
Brough Head
14
Loch Calder
Ainster
Sordale
Stemster
Tister
Bowertower
Howe
Keiss
Skinnet
Knockdee
Stemster House
Halcro
Hastigrow
Mireland
Tang Head
Broubster
Calder Mains
Braal Castle
Roadside
Corsback
Stain
Gerston
Halkirk
Clayock
Gillock
Kirk
Georgemas Junc. Sta
North Watten
Westerloch
Shurrery
Brawlbin
Lynegar
Sinclair's Bay
Killimster
Quoys of Reiss
Shurrery Lodge
Scotscalder Sta
Bloody Moss
Harpsdale
Spittal Hill
Dunn
Oldhall
Mains of Watten
1
Ben Dorrery
Olgrinmore
Achies
Houstry of Dunn
Loch Watten
Noss Head
Dorrery
Spital
Newton
Watten
Winless
Reiss
Backlass
Whitefield
Bilbster
Ackergill
WICK
Mybster
Sibster
Staxigoe
Strath
Thuster
KW
Westerdale
Haster
Milton
Broadhaven
Tormsdale
Stirkoke House
Janetstown
Wick (Inbhir Ùige)
North Head
Newton
South Head
Badlipster
Whiterow
Northfield
Puldagon
Tannach
Hempriggs House
Loch Hempriggs
Tacher
Toftcarl
N
D
Lower Camster
Ires Geo
Stemster
Ballharn Hill
Thrumster
Achnoduhu Hotel
Corbiegoe
Hill of Yarrows
Sarclet
Loch More
Whiteleen
Sarclet Head
12
Achavanich
Stemster Hill
Cnoc an Earrannaiche
Upper Camster
Stack of Ulbster
2
Ulbster
Whaligoe
Coire na Beinne
3
Sheppardstown
Roster
East Clyth
Bruan
Ben Alisky
5
Crofts of Benachielt
Ben-a-chielt
Rumster Forest
Upper Lybster
Mid Clyth
Blackness
Cnocan Conachreag
Reisgill
Occumster
Houstry
Nottingham
Swiney
Lybster
Inver shore
Achnaclyth
6
Gillivoan
Forse
Landhallow
Smerral
Latheron
Badnagie
Latheronwheel
Braemore
Achorn
Dunbeath
Toremore
Maiden Pap
Inver
Knockally
Dunbeath Bay
Meall na Caorach
Ramscraigs
Scaraben
Wag
Borgue
Langwell Forest
7
Aultibea
Newport
Ceann Leathad nam Bo
Mid Hill
Langwell House
Berriedale
Braigh na h-Eaglaise
Ousdale
Creag Thoraraidh
Badbea
Navidale
East Helmsdale
Helmsdale
A836
A9
A882
A99
B874
B870
B876
B855

A B C D E F G H

1

2

3

4

5

6

7

8

9

10

11

ORKNEY ISLANDS

Mull Head

17 Papa Westray

Bow Head

WESTRAY 17 PAPA WESTRAY

Noup Head

Holland

Rackwick

North Ronaldsay

Point of Sinsoss

17

NORTH RONALDSAY 17 Hollandstoun

Strom Ness

North Ronaldsay Firth

Pierowall

WESTRAY 17

Midbea Skelwick

THE NORTH SOUND

Tofts Ness

Sandquoy

Linklet Bay

Berst Ness

Stanger Head

Rapness

Burness

Otters Wick

Roadside Newark

Start Point

WESTRAY FIRTH

Calf of Eday

Broughtown

SANDAY

SANDAY

Kettletoft

17

Quoy Ness

Tres Ness

SACQUOY Head

ROUSAY

Wasbister

Faray

Calfsound

Guith Millbounds

EDAY

Braeswick

SANDAY SOUND

Costa Head

Sourin

Egilsay

17 EDAY

Loth

Spur Ness

Brough Head

Birsay

Costa

Westness

17

STRONSAY

Papa Stronsay

Whitehall

A966

KW

Evie

Redland

Brinian

Wyre

Linga Holm

STRONSAY

Marwick Head

Matwick Twatt

Kirbister

Woodwick

Gairsay Sound

Rothiesholm

Aith Everbay

STRONSAY FIRTH

Grobister

17

Burgh Head

Isbister

17 Downby

Gairsay

Quoyno

Skaill

Settiscarth

Bimbister

Edmonstone

SHAPINSAY

Lamb Head

A986

A966

17

Auskerry

Yesnaby

Voy

Finstown

Bay of Firth

Balfour

Sandgarth

A967

16

A965

Wide Firth

Shapinsay Sound

Rerwick Head

Stromness

Ward Hill

15

Kirkwall

A965

Scapa

KIRKWALL

Mull Head

Hoy Sound

Kirbister

Hobbister

Greenigo

17

Toab

Skaill

Clestrain

Gyre

A961

A960

Gritley

Graemsay

Houton

ORKNEY

17

Linksness

Upper Sanday

Point of Ayre

Ward Hill 479

Scapa Flow

St Mary's

Cornquoy

Copinsay

Rora Head

Rackwick

Knap of Trowieglen 399

Cava

Rysa Little

Hunda

Rose Ness

HOY

Fara

Oil Terminal

Flotta

Burray

16

Lyness

Bow

Southtown

St Margaret's Hope

Grim Ness

Sneuk Head

Heldale Water

Herston

Widewall

Melsetter

Langhope

Cantick Head

SOUTH RONALDSAY

17

Lythes

Tor Ness

South Walls

Burwick

Ward Hill

Swona

Cleat

Brough Ness

Old Head

PENTLAND FIRTH

Island of Stroma

1

Muckle Skerry

Dunnet Head

Mell Head

Pentland Skerries

Ness of Duncansby

Duncansby Head

Scrabster

Holborn Head

Clett

Scarfskerry

Brough Hunspow

Ham Rattar

Mey

Gills

Huna

John o' Groats

Thurso (Inbhir Theòrsa)

Dunnet

Barrock

Kirkstyle Canisby

Murkle Castletown

Inkstack

124

Warth Hill

Skirza

Olrig House

Lochend

Tofts

Freswick

KW

Bowermadden

Slickly

1

Freswick Bay

14

Lyth

Altarwall

Auckengill

Ness Head

HIGHLAND

12

Sordale Knockdee

Bowertower

Hastigrow

Howe

Keiss

Braal Castle

Roadside

Gillock

Mireland

Halkirk

North Watten

Westerloch

Kirk

0 2 4 6 miles
0 2 4 6 8 10 km

Noss Head

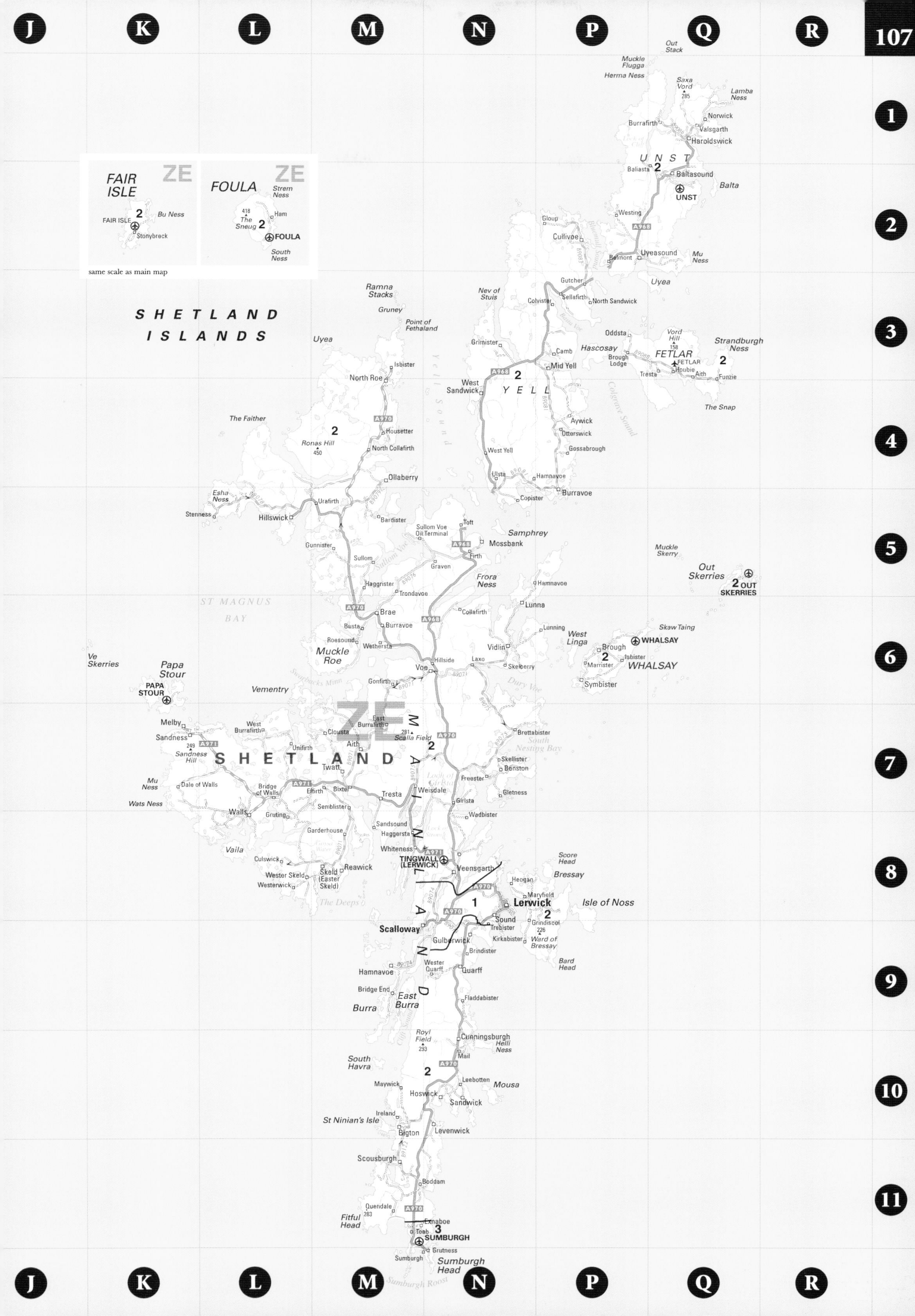
SHETLAND ISLANDS
FAIR ISLE
ZE
Bu Ness
FAIR ISLE
Stonybreck
FOULA
Strem Ness
Ham
418
The Sneug
FOULA
South Ness
same scale as main map
Out Stack
Muckle Flugga
Herma Ness
Saxa Vord
285
Lamba Ness
Norwick
Burrafirth
Valsgarth
Haroldswick
UNST
Baliasta
Baltasound
Balta
UNST
Westing
A968
Gloup
Cullivoe
Belmont
Uyeasound
Mu Ness
Uyea
Gutcher
Sellafirth
North Sandwick
Nev of Stuis
Colvister
Ramna Stacks
Gruney
Point of Fethaland
Uyea
Oddsta
Vord Hill
158
Strandburgh Ness
Grimister
Hascosay
Brough Lodge
FETLAR
FETLAR
Houbie
Aith
Funzie
Tresta
Camb
Mid Yell
Isbister
North Roe
West Sandwick
YELL
The Snap
The Faither
Housetter
Ronas Hill
450
North Collafirth
Aywick
Otterswick
Gossabrough
West Yell
Ulsta
Hamnavoe
Ollaberry
Burravoe
Copister
Esha Ness
Stenness
Urafirth
Hillswick
Bardister
Toft
Sullom Voe Oil Terminal
Samphrey
Mossbank
Firth
Gunnister
Sullom
Graven
Muckle Skerry
Out Skerries
OUT SKERRIES
Frora Ness
Haggrister
Trondavoe
Hamnavoe
ST MAGNUS BAY
Lunna
Brae
Busta
Burravoe
Collafirth
Lunning
Skaw Taing
West Linga
WHALSAY
Roesound
Muckle Roe
Wethersta
Vidlin
Brough
Isbister
Marrister
WHALSAY
Ve Skerries
Papa Stour
PAPA STOUR
Hillside
Laxo
Skelberry
Voe
Gonfirth
Symbister
Vementry
ZE
East Burrafirth
Melby
West Burrafirth
Clousta
281
Scalla Field
Brettabister
Sandness
249
Sandness Hill
Aith
Unifirth
South Nesting Bay
SHETLAND
MAINLAND
Twatt
Skellister
Benston
Mu Ness
Dale of Walls
Bridge of Walls
Effirth
Bixter
Tresta
Weisdale
Freester
Girlsta
Gletness
Wats Ness
Walls
Gruting
Semblister
Wadbister
Garderhouse
Sandsound
Haggersta
Whiteness
Vaila
TINGWALL (LERWICK)
Veensgarth
Score Head
Bressay
Culswick
Reawick
Wester Skeld
Skeld (Easter Skeld)
Westerwick
The Deeps
Heogan
Maryfield
Lerwick
Isle of Noss
Sound
Grindiscol
Scalloway
Trebister
Gulberwick
Kirkabister
226
Ward of Bressay
Brindister
Bard Head
Wester Quarff
Quarff
Hamnavoe
Bridge End
East Burra
Burra
Fladdabister
Royl Field
293
Cunningsburgh
Helli Ness
Mail
South Havra
Leebotten
Mousa
Maywick
Hoswick
Sandwick
Ireland
St Ninian's Isle
Bigton
Levenwick
Scousburgh
Boddam
Quendale
283
Fitful Head
Exnaboe
Toab
SUMBURGH
Grutness
Sumburgh
Sumburgh Head
Sumburgh Roost

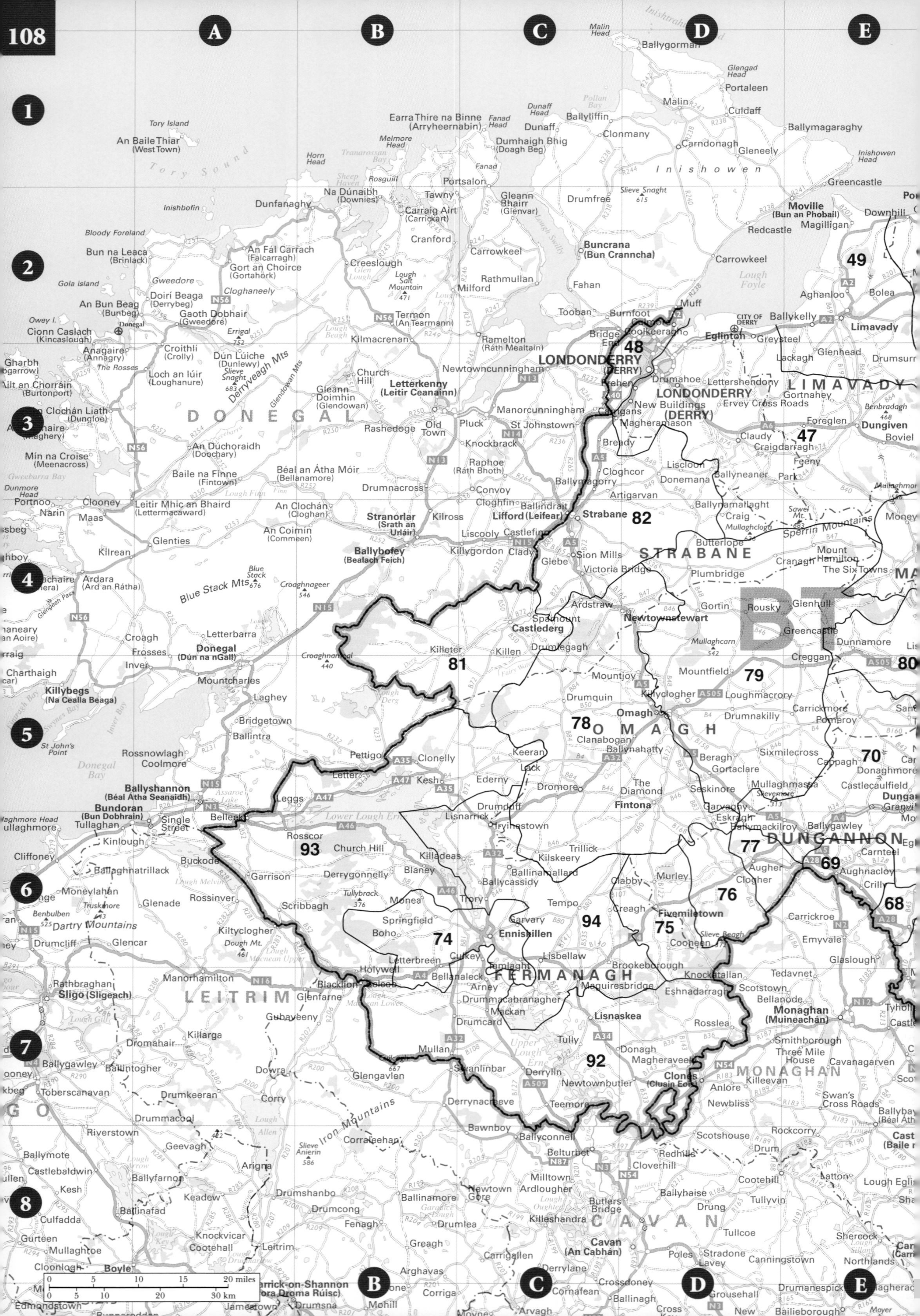
A
B
C
D
E
1
2
3
4
5
6
7
8
Tory Island
An Baile Thiar (West Town)
Tory Sound
Inishbofin
Bloody Foreland
Bun na Leaca (Brinlack)
Gola Island
An Bun Beag (Bunbeg)
Owey I.
Cionn Caslach (Kincaslough)
Donegal
Anagaire (Annagry)
The Rosses
Gharbh
Ailt an Chorráin (Burtonport)
An Clochán Liath (Dungloe)
Mín na Croise (Meenacross)
Gweebarra Bay
Dunmore Head
Portnoo
Narin
Clooney
Maas
Kilrean
Glenties
Ardara (Ard an Rátha)
Glengesh Pass
Croagh
Frosses
Inver
Killybegs (Na Cealla Beaga)
Charthaigh
St John's Point
Donegal Bay
Mountcharles
Donegal (Dún na nGall)
Letterbarra
Blue Stack Mts
Blue Stack 676
Croaghnageer 546
Croaghnameal 440
Laghey
Bridgetown
Ballintra
Rossnowlagh
Coolmore
Ballyshannon (Béal Átha Seanaidh)
Bundoran (Bun Dobhráin)
Tullaghan
Mullaghmore Head
Single Street
Belleek
Kinlough
Cliffoney
Ballaghnatrillack
Buckode
Garrison
Lough Melvin
Moneylahan
Rossinver
Glenade
Benbulben 525
Truskmore 643
Dartry Mountains
Drumcliff
Glencar
Kiltyclogher
Dough Mt. 461
Rathbraghan
Sligo (Sligeach)
Manorhamilton
LEITRIM
Lough Gill
Dromahair
Killarga
Ballygawley
Ballintogher
Toberscanavan
Drumkeeran
Dowra
Drummacool
Riverstown
Geevagh
Ballymote
Castlebaldwin
Arigna
Ballyfarnon
Kesh
Keadew
Ballinafad
Culfadda
Gurteen
Mullaghroe
Knockvicar
Cootehall
Leitrim
Cloonloogh
Boyle
Edmondstown
Carrick-on-Shannon
Horn Head
Dunfanaghy
Na Dúnaibh (Downies)
Sheep Haven
Rosguill
Melmore Head
Earra Thíre na Binne (Arryheernabin)
Fanad Head
An Fál Carrach (Falcarragh)
Gort an Choirce (Gortahork)
Gweedore
Doirí Beaga (Derrybeg)
Cloghaneely
Gaoth Dobhair (Gweedore)
Errigal 752
Croithlí (Crolly)
Dún Lúiche (Dunlewy)
Slieve Snaght 683
Derryveagh Mts
Glendowan Mts
Loch an Iúir (Loughanure)
DONEGAL
An Dúchoraidh (Doochary)
Baile na Finne (Fintown)
Lough Finn
Leitir Mhic an Bhaird (Lettermacaward)
An Clochán (Cloghan)
An Coimín (Commeen)
Creeslough
Lough Salt Mountain 471
Termon (An Tearmann)
Kilmacrenan
Church Hill
Gleann Doimhin (Glendowan)
Letterkenny (Leitir Ceanainn)
Rashedoge
Béal an Átha Móir (Bellanamore)
Drumnacross
Stranorlar (Srath an Urláir)
Ballybofey (Bealach Feich)
Kilross
Tawny
Carraig Airt (Carrickart)
Portsalon
Cranford
Carrowkeel
Milford
Gleann Bhairr (Glenvar)
Rathmullan
Ramelton (Ráth Mealtain)
Newtowncunningham
Old Town
Manorcunningham
Pluck
Knockbrack
Raphoe (Ráth Bhoth)
Convoy
Cloghfin
Ballindrait
Lifford (Leifear)
Liscooly
Castlefinn
Killygordon
Clady
St Johnstown
Lough Swilly
Malin Head
Ballygorman
Inishtrahull
Glengad Head
Portaleen
Malin
Culdaff
Pollan Bay
Dunaff Head
Dunaff
Ballyliffin
Clonmany
Dumhaigh Bhig (Doagh Beg)
Carndonagh
Gleneely
Inishowen
Slieve Snaght 615
Drumfree
Buncrana (Bun Cranncha)
Fahan
Tooban
Burnfoot
Muff
Culmore
Bridge End
Ballymagaraghy
Inishowen Head
Greencastle
Moville (Bun an Phobail)
Redcastle
Carrowkeel
Lough Foyle
Magilligan
Downhill
Aghanloo
Bolea
Limavady
Ballykelly
City of Derry
Eglinton
Greysteel
Lackagh
Glenhead
Drumsurn
LIMAVADY
Gortnahey
Benbradagh 468
Dungiven
Boviel
LONDONDERRY (DERRY)
48
Prehen
Drumahoe
Lettershendony
New Buildings
Ervey Cross Roads
Carrigans
Magheramason
Bready
Foreglen
Claudy
Craigdarragh
47
Feeny
Park
Lisclool
Cloghcor
Donemana
Ballyneaner
Ballymagorry
Artigarvan
Ballymamallaght
Strabane
82
Craig
Mullaghclogha
Sawel Mt. 683
Sperrin Mountains
Butterlope
STRABANE
Mount Hamilton
Cranagh
The Six Towns
Glebe
Sion Mills
Victoria Bridge
Plumbridge
Ardstraw
Gortin
Rousky
Glenhull
Newtownstewart
Spamount
Castlederg
Killeter
Killen
81
Drumlegagh
Mullaghcarn 542
Greencastle
Dunnamore
Creggan
BT
Mountfield
79
Mountjoy
Killyclogher
Loughmacrory
Drumquin
Omagh
Drumnakilly
Carrickmore
Pomeroy
78
Clanabogan
OMAGH
Ballynahatty
Beragh
Sixmilecross
Gortaclare
Cappagh
70
Donaghmore
Castlecaulfield
Keeran
Lack
Ederny
Seskinore
Mullaghmassa
Dromore
The Diamond
Fintona
Garvaghy
Eskragh
Ballymackilroy
Ballygawley
DUNGANNON
Carnteel
77
Augher
Clogher
69
Aughnacloy
Kilskeery
Trillick
Clabby
Murley
76
68
Crilly
Fivemiletown
75
Slieve Beagh
Creagh
Tempo
94
Cooneen
Lough Derg
Pettigo
Clonelly
Letter
Kesh
Leggs
Lower Lough Erne
Rosscor
93
Church Hill
Killadeas
Lisnarrick
Drumduff
Irvinestown
Ballinamallard
Ballycassidy
Derrygonnelly
Blaney
Tullybrack 376
Trory
Monea
Scribbagh
Springfield
Boho
74
Enniskillen
Garvary
Letterbreen
Cuilkey
Holywell
Bellanaleck
Tamlaght
Lisbellaw
Brookeborough
FERMANAGH
Knockatallan
Blacklion
Belcoo
Glenfarne
Arney
Drummacabranagher
Maguiresbridge
Eshnadarragh
Mackan
Lisnaskea
Gubaveeny
Drumcard
Tully
Upper Lough Erne
Rosslea
Mullan
Cuilcagh 667
Swanlinbar
Glengavlen
Derrylin
Donagh
Magheraveely
92
Newtownbutler
Clones (Cluain Eois)
Teemore
Derrynacreeve
Iron Mountains
Slieve Anierin 586
Corry
Corratechan
Bawnboy
Ballyconnell
Belturbet
Redhills
Cloverhill
Milltown
Newtown Gore
Ardlougher
Drumshanbo
Ballinamore
Drumcong
Garadice Lough
Fenagh
Drumlea
Killeshandra
Butlers Bridge
CAVAN
Cavan (An Cabhán)
Greagh
Carrigallen
Arghavas
Derrylane
Crossdoney
Corriga
Cornafean
Ballinagh
Mohill
Arvagh
Jamestown
Drumsna
Ballyhaise
Drung
Tullyvin
Tullcoe
Cootehill
Stradone
Lavey
Poles
Canningstown
Tedavnet
Scotstown
Bellanode
Monaghan (Muineachán)
Emyvale
Glaslough
Carrickroe
Smithborough
Three Mile House
Cavanagarven
MONAGHAN
Anlore
Killeevan
Newbliss
Swan's Cross Roads
Scotshouse
Rockcorry
Drum
Latton
Lough Egish
Shercock
Northlands
Drumanespick
Bailieborough
0 5 10 15 20 miles
0 5 10 20 30 km

F
G
H
J
K
1
2
3
4
5
6
7
8
NORTH CHANNEL
Mull of Kintyre
Feochaig
Macharioch
Southend
Sanda Island
Ailsa Craig
Bull Point
Rathlin Island
54
Giants Causeway
Fair Head
Torr Head
Ballintoy
Portballintrae
Lagavara
Carnduff
Ballycastle
Ballyvoy
56
57
Bushmills
Moyarget
MOYLE
Knocklayd
Ballyloughbeg
Liscolman
Cloyfin
52
Moss-side
Armoy
53
Dervock
Ballybogy
Damhead
Stranocum
The Drones
Ballyhoe Bridge
Castleroe
Killyrammer
Cushendun
Knocknacarry
Cushendall
Red Bay
Garron Point
Ballymoney
Balnamore
Dunaghy
Kilraghts
Loughguile
Glenariff
Trostan
Bendooragh
Corkey
Antrim Hills
Killagan Bridge
Aghadowey
44
Finvoy
Dunloy
Newtown Crommelin
Cargan
Carnlough
Moneydig
BALLYMONEY
Cloughmills
43
Martinstown
Glenarm
ERAINE
Glarryford
Clogh
McGregor's Corner
Bovedy
Kilrea
BALLYMENA
Black Hill
The Maidens or Hulin Rocks
Craigs
The Sheddings
Ballygalley
Lisnagh
Tamlaght O'Crilly
Cullybackey
Carncastle
LARNE
Portglenone
Broughshane
Slemish
40
Inishrush
Gracehill
BALLYMENA
Millbrook
Larne
46
Culnady
Clady
42
Ahoghill
Maghera
Shoptown
Kilwaughter
Glynn
Island Magee
Gulladuff
New Ferry
Straid
Cromkill
Moorfields
Millbay
Bellaghy
Kells
Glenoe
Grange Corner
Caddy
Ballystrudder
Curran
Moneyglass
Chapeltown
Ballyeaston
Ballynure
Ballycarry
Castledawson
Roxhill
Burnside
39
Straid
Black Head
Toome
Randalstown
Ballyclare
CARRICKFERGUS
Whitehead
Newmill
Doagh
38
Belmont
45
Magherafelt
Parkgate
Eden
41
Mill Town
NEWTOWNABBEY
CARRICKFERGUS
Staffordstown
ANTRIM
Templepatrick
36
Mossley
Greenisland
NORTH DOWN
Groomsport
Mew Island
Ballyronan
The Loup
Helen's Bay
Copeland Island
ANTRIM
Mallusk
37
20
BANGOR
BELFAST INTERNATIONAL
NEWTOWNABBEY
Loanends
Belfast Lough
Holywood
18
Derrychrin
80
Aldergrove
14
Coagh
Moortown
29
Nutt's Corner
Ligoniel
BELFAST CITY
19
Donaghadee
Crumlin
Conlig
21
Ardboe
Craigantlet
Millisle
Dundrod
BELFAST
16
The Diamond
17
COOKSTOWN
Glenavy
Hannahstown
See inset for postcode detail
Dundonald
NEWTOWNARDS
ARDS
Stonyford
Stewartstown
Killeen
Mountjoy
Dunmurry
Ballywalter
Coalisland
Lower Ballinderry
Upper Ballinderry
CASTLEREAGH
Comber
CRAIGAVON
Greyabbey
Ards Peninsula
Moneyreagh
22
Clonoe
Aughamullan
66
Aghalee
28
Drumbo
8
Carryduff
Aghagallon
LISBURN
23
Lisbane
Maghery
Bannfoot
Maghaberry
Hillhall
Ballygowan
Ardmillan
Ballyhalbert
Milltown
Derrytrasna
Derrymacash
Soldierstown
27
Kilmood
Kircubbin
67
Mazetown
The Temple
Killinchy
Rubane
Portavogie
64
Lurgan
Moira
Culcavy
Ravernet
Strangford Lough
62
Magheralin
Saintfield
Curragh
Kirkistown
Craigavon
65
Dollingstown
Hillsborough
Darragh Cross
Raffrey
Ringboy
Charlemont
Waringstown
Gamblestown
26
24
Annahilt
Scotch Street
Bleary
LISBURN
Shrigley
Cloghy
Blackwatertown
Portadown
Donaghcloney
Dromore
Ballynahinch
Listooder
Crossgar
Killyleagh
Cox's Hill
Ballykeel
Kearney
Kearney Pt.
Loughgall
63
Kilmore
Portaferry
61
Bellylany
Lawrencetown
Kinallen
The Spa
DOWN
Strangford
Richhill
Laurelvale
Gilford
Seapatrick
Waringsford
25
Dromara
Drumaness
Raholp
Tandragee
Banbridge
Slieve Croob
Saul
Churchtown
Armagh
Hamilton's Bawn
Loughinisland
Downpatrick
30
Ballyquintin Point
Clare
Scarva
32
BANBRIDGE
Drumaroad
Milford
Loughbrickland
Annaclone
Seaforde
Ballyhornan
ARMAGH
Acton
Monteith
Katesbridge
31
Markethill
Poyntz Pass
Moneyslane
Church Ballee
Leitrim
Clough
Ballynoe
Ballyward
Ballykinler
Scollogstown
Ardglass
Clady Milltown
Mount Norris
May's Corner
Ballyroney
Annsborough
Killough
Castlewellan
Dundrum
Minerstown
Milltown
Keady
Glenanne
Rathfriland
Maghera
Carrigatuke
Lurganare
Kilcoo
Bryansford
Whitecross
33
Newcastle
Bessbrook
Slieve Donard
Dundrum Bay
Hamilton
Belleek
Cloughreagh
Hilltown
Mayobridge
Camlough
NEWRY
34
35
NEWRY & MOURNE
Eagle Mountain
Mourne Mountains
Cullyhanna
Meigh
Burren
Rostrevor
Attical
Annalong
Mullaghbane
Jonesborough
Warrenpoint
Omeath
Creggan
Forkhill
Killowen
Ballymartin
Crossmaglen
Cullaville
Slieve Foye
Riverside
Kilkeel
Ravensdale
Carlingford
DUNDALK (DÚN DEALGAN)
Kilcurry
Greenore
Jenkinstown
Inishkeen
Castletown
Kilcurly
Mullabohy
Ballybarrack
South Marsh
Grange
Ballagan Pt.
Knockbridge
Cooley Point
Sandymount
Haggardstown
Blackrock
Dundalk Bay
Louth
Readypenny
Dromiskin
Mansfieldstown
Castlebellingham
Kirkcolm
Cairnryan
Leswalt
Portpatrick
Sandhead
Rinns of Galloway
Holywood
BELFAST CITY
BELFAST
14
15
3
18
4
16
17
13
1
2
5
12
7
6
Castlereagh
11
9
CASTLEREAGH
10
23
8

112
See pages 124-131 for complete postcode detail
LONDON WEST
0 1 2 3 miles
0 1 2 3 4 5 kilometres
HERTFORDSHIRE
BUCKINGHAMSHIRE
WD
HA
NW
N
G R E A T E R
WATFORD
Holywell
Oxhey
South Oxhey
Watford Heath
Carpenders Park
BUSHEY
Bushey Heath
Merry Hill
Elstree
Elstree Aerodrome
BOREHAMWOOD
Aldenham Reservoir
Hatch End
Pinnerwood Park
Pinner Green
Pinner
Eastcote Village
Eastcote
RUISLIP
Ruislip Manor
Ruislip Gardens
South Ruislip
Northolt
Northolt Aerodrome
Rayners Lane
North Harrow
West Harrow
HARROW
Harrow on the Hill
HARROW WEALD
Headstone
Wealdstone
Kenton
Belmont
Stanmore
Stanmore Common
EDGWARE
Canons Park
Queensbury
Burnt Oak
Kingsbury
North Wembley
WEMBLEY
Wembley Park
Tokyngton
Sudbury
South Harrow
Greenford
Perivale
Alperton
Park Royal
North Acton
West Acton
Stonebridge
Harlesden
Willesden
Neasden
Dollis Hill
Cricklewood
HENDON
West Hendon
Holders Hill
MILL HILL
Highwood Hill
Arkley
Barnet Gate
Rowley Green
Chipping Barnet
High Barnet
BARNET
Hadley
New Barnet
Underhill
Ducks Island
Totteridge
Whetstone
North Finchley
FINCHLEY
Church End
East Finchley
Golders Green
Hampstead Garden Suburb
Childs Hill
HAMPSTEAD
Highgate
Muswell Hill
HORNSEY
Crouch End
HARRINGAY
Stroud Green
Finsbury Park
WOOD GREEN
Noel Park
Bowes Park
FRIERN BARNET
New Southgate
Southgate
Oakwood
Winchmore Hill
Grange Park
Palmers Green
Cockfosters
East Barnet
Oakleigh Park
Upper Holloway
Tufnell Park
Holloway
Dartmouth Park
Kentish Town
Camden
King's Cross
ST. PANCRAS
Bloomsbury
HOLBORN
FINSBURY
Barnsbury
Belsize Park
Primrose Hill
St. John's Wood
Regent's Park
MARYLEBONE
PADDINGTON
Maida Vale
Kilburn
Brondesbury
Kensal Rise
Westbourne Green
Wormwood Scrubs
Yeading
Hayes End
North Hillingdon

113
WESTMINSTER
LAMBETH
KENSINGTON
CHELSEA
HAMMERSMITH
FULHAM
BATTERSEA
WANDSWORTH
STREATHAM
MITCHAM
MERTON
WIMBLEDON
MORDEN
CARSHALTON
BEDDINGTON
WALLINGTON
CHISWICK
BARNES
RICHMOND
KINGSTON UPON THAMES
TWICKENHAM
ISLEWORTH
HOUNSLOW
HESTON
FELTHAM
SURBITON
ESHER
SURREY
L O N D O N
SW
SM
KT
TW
CR
Richmond Park
Wimbledon Common
Bushy Park
Royal Botanic Gardens Kew
Putney
Mortlake
Brentford
Teddington
Hampton
Sunbury
East Molesey
West Molesey
Walton-on-Thames
Hersham
Tolworth
Worcester Park
New Malden
Raynes Park
Tooting Graveney
Earlsfield
Southfields
Balham
Clapham Park
Brixton
Stockwell
Vauxhall
Pimlico
Norbury
Streatham Vale
Hackbridge
North Cheam
Old Malden
Hook
Thames Ditton
Hinchley Wood
Long Ditton
Hampton Wick
Ham
Petersham
East Sheen
Roehampton
Kew
Gunnersbury
South Acton
Bedford Park
Hanwell
Osterley
Norwood Green
North Hyde
Hounslow West
Hatton
East Bedfont
Lower Feltham
Upper Halliford
Ashley Park
Oatlands Park
Burwood Park
Rydens

LONDON EAST
0 1 2 3 miles
0 1 2 3 4 5 kilometres
110
E S S E X
G R E A T E R
RM
IG
E
N
EN
ROMFORD
HORNCHURCH
Harold Hill
Noak Hill
Gidea Park
Ardleigh Green
Collier Row
Chase Cross
Havering-atte-Bower
Stapleford Abbotts
Nuper's Hatch
Lambourne End
Havering Park
Mark's Gate
Chadwell Heath
Rush Green
Becontree Heath
Becontree
Dagenham
Rainham
South Hornchurch
Elm Park
Goodmayes
Seven Kings
Creekmouth
Abridge
Chigwell Row
CHIGWELL
HAINAULT
Grange Hill
Aldborough Hatch
Newbury Park
Barkingside
Fullwell Cross
ILFORD
Loxford
BARKING
Debden
Loughton
Buckhurst Hill
Woodford Bridge
Clayhall
Gants Hill
REDBRIDGE
Cranbrook
Little Ilford
EAST HAM
Beckton
Custom House
Woodford Wells
Woodford Green
WOODFORD
South Woodford
Snaresbrook
Wanstead
Aldersbrook
Manor Park
Forest Gate
Upton
Upton Park
WEST HAM
Plaistow
Canning Town
Epping Forest
Sewardstonebury
Chingford Green
Friday Hill
Chingford Hatch
CHINGFORD
Highams Park
Hale End
WALTHAMSTOW
Upper Walthamstow
Higham Hill
South Chingford
Leytonstone
LEYTON
Stratford
Hackney Wick
Homerton
Lower Clapton
Clapton Park
Lea Bridge
Upper Clapton
Old Ford
Bow
Bromley
Mile End
Stepney
Whitechapel
Bethnal Green
Haggerston
Hoxton
SHOREDITCH
Dalston
Hackney
Shacklewell
Stamford Hill
STOKE NEWINGTON
South Tottenham
Tottenham Hale
TOTTENHAM
Upper Edmonton
EDMONTON
Lower Edmonton
Ponders End
Enfield Highway
Brimsdown
Bush Hill Park
Grange Park
Palmers Green
West Green
Finsbury Park
Highbury
Holloway
Barnsbury
FINSBURY
St. Luke's
HOLBORN
Stroud Green
River Thames

DARTFORD
KENT
DA
SE
LONDON
BR
CR
SW
Wilmington
Swanley Village
Hextable
SWANLEY
Crockenhill
Joydens Wood
Coldblow
Crayford
Barnes Cray
Barnehurst
Northumberland Heath
Erith
Belvedere
Lessness Heath
Abbey Wood
Thamesmead
Thamesmead West
North Woolwich
WOOLWICH
Plumstead
East Wickham
Welling
Bexley
Bexleyheath
Old Bexley
North Cray
Foots Cray
SIDCUP
Blackfen
Lamorbey
Falconwood
Avery Hill
New Eltham
Longlands
Eltham
Shooter's Hill
Charlton
New Charlton
Silvertown
GREENWICH
Kidbrooke
Blackheath
Blackheath Park
Lee
Hither Green
Mottingham
Elmstead
Chislehurst West
CHISLEHURST
St. Paul's Cray
St. Mary Cray
Petts Wood
ORPINGTON
Poverest
Derry Downs
Ramsden
Goddington
Chelsfield
Farnborough
Bromley Common
Southborough
Bickley
BROMLEY
Widmore
Sundridge
Plaistow
Grove Park
Downham
Shortlands
Hayes
Coney Hall
Keston
West Wickham
Park Langley
Eden Park
Upper Elmers End
Elmers End
BECKENHAM
New Beckenham
Southend
Catford
Bellingham
Lewisham
Ladywell
Brockley
Deptford
Millwall
Cubitt Town
Rotherhithe
BERMONDSEY
New Cross
New Cross Gate
Peckham
CAMBERWELL
Walworth
SOUTHWARK
Kennington
LAMBETH
Brixton
Herne Hill
Nunhead
East Dulwich
DULWICH
Honor Oak
Forest Hill
Lower Sydenham
SYDENHAM
Upper Sydenham
Penge
Anerley
South Norwood
Upper Norwood
Norwood
West Norwood
West Dulwich
Tulse Hill
Streatham Hill
Norwood New Town
Thornton Heath
Selhurst
Woodside
Addiscombe
CROYDON
Shirley
Monks Orchard
Waddon
See pages 124-131 for complete postcode detail
111

Bilbrook
Codsall
Lane Green
Moseley
Bushbury
Essington
6
Pelsall Wood
Pelsa

Oaken
9
Fordhouses
Bloxwich North
Wallington Heath
Little Bloxwich
Bloxwich
Heath End

7
8
Wrottesley
Palmers Cross
Oxley
10
Old Fallings
Wood Hayes
11
Ashmore Park
Wood End
New Invention
12
Leamore
3
Harden
Coal Pool

Werg
Claregate
Park Village
Wednesfield
Ashmore Lake
Lane Head
Bentley
2
Birchills
WALS

Perton
Tettenhall
WV
Dunstall Hill
Heath Town
Springfield
13
Willenhall
Darlaston Green
Pleck
1

6
Tettenhall Wood
Compton
Wolves RFC
Wolverhampton
St George's
1
Monmore Green
Moseley
Portobello
Darlaston
Kings Hill
Wood Green
Bescot
Caldmore
Palfrey
The Chucke

Nurton
Old Purton
3
Castlecroft
Bradmore
Merry Hill
2
Stow Lawn
Bilston
Darlaston
Woods Bank
Fallings Heath
Wednesbury
10
The Delves

Trescott
Lower Penn
4
Spring Hill
Penn
Colton Hills
Blakenhall
Goldthorn Park
Parkfield
Preestfield
Ettingshall
Spring Vale
14
Bradley
Moxley
Lower Bradley
Church Hill
Mesty Croft
The Woods
Yew

Seisdon
STAFFORDSHIRE
Orton
Cinder Hill
Ettingshall Park
Lanesfield
Coseley
Hurst Hill
Roseville
Wallbrook
Wednesbury Oak
Princes End
Summer Hill
Ocker Hill
Top End
Golds Green
Balls Hill
Hateley Heath
Charlemont
Stone Cross
Friar Park

5
Trysull
Wombourne
Sedgley
Bramford
Bloomfield
4
Tipton Green
Tipton
Horseley Heath
Harvills Hawthorn
Hill Top
Black Lake
71
Churchfield
Lyndon

Swindon
Wall Heath
Upper Gornal
Woodsetton
New Town
Dudley Port
WEST BROMWICH
70
Swan Village
Guns Village

Hinksford
6
Ruiton
Lower Gornal
1
Redhall
Gornalwood
London Fields
Eve Hill
DUDLEY
Kate's Hill
Dixon's Green
Burnt Tree
Tividale
Brades Village
69
Rounds Green
SANDWELL
66

Ashwood
Summer Hill
Mount Pleasant
Kingswinford
Bromley
Brockmoor
Pennett
Waterfront
Russell's Hall
Baptist End
Netherton
2
Oakham
Darby's Hill
Oldbury
Portway
Langley
Rood End
Langley Green
67

7
Prestwood
Wordsley
Buckpool
Hawbush
5
Brierley Hill
Primrose Hill
Bowling Green
Darby End
The Knowle
Rowley Regis
65
Ross
Blackheath
Causeway Green
Bristnall Fields
68
Smethwick
Bearwo

Audnam
Withymoor Village
Dudley Wood
Cradley Heath
64
Old Hill
Cakemore
Coombeswood
Hurst Green
Warley

Amblecote
Amblecote Bank
Quarry Bank
Netherend
Cradley
Haden Cross
Quinton
Ridgacre
Harborn

Wollaston
Holloway End
STOURBRIDGE
Dunn's Bank
Lye
The Hayes
Belle Vale
Hawne
Lapal
32
California

High Park
8
Gigmill
Stambermill
Wollescote
HALESOWEN
63
Hasbury
Spring Hill
Moor Street
Woodgate
Bartley Green
Weoley Castle
Shenley Fields

Kinver
Dunsley
DY
Norton
Swindford
Pedmore
Hunnington
62
Illey
31

Blakeshall
Caunsall
11
Hagley
West Hagley
Lower Clent
Clent
Romsley
Frankley
45

Cookley
Wolverley
Churchill
9
Holy Cross
Romsley Hill
Rubery
Rednal

Broadwaters
10
Blakedown
Broome
WORCESTERSHIRE
Bell End
Bell Heath

Greenhill
KIDDERMINSTER
Stone

WEST MIDLANDS

0   1   2   3   4 miles
0 1 2 3 4 5 6 kilometres

61
60
Fairfield
Cofton Hackett

STAFFORDSHIRE
WARWICKSHIRE
WEST MIDLANDS
BIRMINGHAM
SUTTON COLDFIELD
SOLIHULL
TAMWORTH
WS
B
CV
Shenstone
Stonnall
Lower Stonnall
Thornes
Walsall Wood
Vigo
Leighswood
Druid's Heath
Aldridge
Mill Green
Pool Green
Hardwick
Little Aston
Four Oaks
Streetly
Roughley
Mere Green
Ley Hill
Little Sutton
Four Oaks Park
Daisy Bank
Sutton Park
Doe Bank
Whitehouse Common
Tudor Hill
Falcon Lodge
Pheasey
Banners Gate
Maney
Reddicap Heath
Queslett
Kingstanding
Great Barr
New Oscott
Boldmere
Perry Beeches
Old Oscott
Wylde Green
Hamstead
Tower Hill
Perry
Perry Common
Short Heath
Chester Road
Walmley
Thimble End
Minworth
Upper Witton
Perry Barr
Erdington
Pype Hayes
Brown's Green
Handsworth Wood
Witton
Tyburn
Castle Vale
Birches Green
Gravelly Hill
Birchfield
Nechells
Bromford
Castle Bromwich
Lozells
Aston
Washwood Heath
Hodgehill
Buckland End
Shard End
Gib Heath
Hockley
Newtown
Ward End
Colehall
Winson Green
Vauxhall
Saltley
Kingshurst
Rotton Park
Glebe Farm
Alum Rock
Kitt's Green
Fordbridge
Stechford
Tile Cross
Chelmsley Wood
Lea Hall
Ladywood
Little Bromwich
Bordesley
Digbeth
Lee Bank
Yardley
Garrett's Green
Chad Valley
Highgate
Small Heath
Lyndon Green
Marston Green
Sparkbrook
Hay Mills
South Yardley
Gilbertstone
Balsall Heath
Edgbaston
Birmingham International Airport
National Exhibition Centre
Sheldon
Wells Green
Sparkhill
Tyseley
Acock's Green
Moseley
Bournbrook
Moor Green
Wake Green
Olton
Elmdon
Bickenhill
King's Heath
Kineton Green
Hall Green
Ulverley Green
Elmdon Heath
Stirchley
Billesley
Worlds End
Hampton in Arden
Cotteridge
Brandwood End
Billesley Common
Yardley Wood
Lode Heath
Catherine-de-Barnes
King's Norton
Warstock
Shirley Street
Sharmans Cross
Hasluck's Green
Shirley
Walkers Heath
Highter's Heath
Solihull Lodge
Blossomfield
Eastcote
Copt Heath
Barston
Hawkesley
Major's Green
Shirley Heath
Hollywood
Headley Heath
Trueman's Heath
Drakes Cross
Bateman's Green
Whitlocks End
Knowle
Dickens Heath
Balsall Common
Tilehouse Green
Bentley Heath
Grimes Hill
Wythall
Tidbury Green
Cheswick Green
Temple Balsall
Sedgemere
The Leys
Bolehall
Kettlebrook
Glascote
Fazeley
Bonehill
Mile Oak
Hints
Weeford
Belgrave
Wilnecote
Two Gates
Drayton Bassett
Hockley
Dosthill
Whateley
Middleton
Kingsbury
Bodymoor Heath
Marston
Wishaw
Over Green
Lea Marston
Curdworth
Whitacre Heath
Nether Whitacre
Water Orton
Gibson
Cole End
Coleshill
Shustoke
Duke End
Bacon's End
Little Packington
Middle Bickenhill
Stonebridge
Hoggrill's End
Blythe End
Fillongley
M6 Toll
M6
M42
A38
A452
A45
A41
A34
A435
A4040
A47
A446
A4097
A5127
M6 Toll
8
9
14
74
75
78
79
77
43
44
73
72
76
20
42
23
24
35
21
6
19
36
46
18
7
8
34
1
3
4
33
2
9
16
5
10
25
37
15
12
40
26
11
29
13
27
92
28
30
14
91
90
38
47
94
93

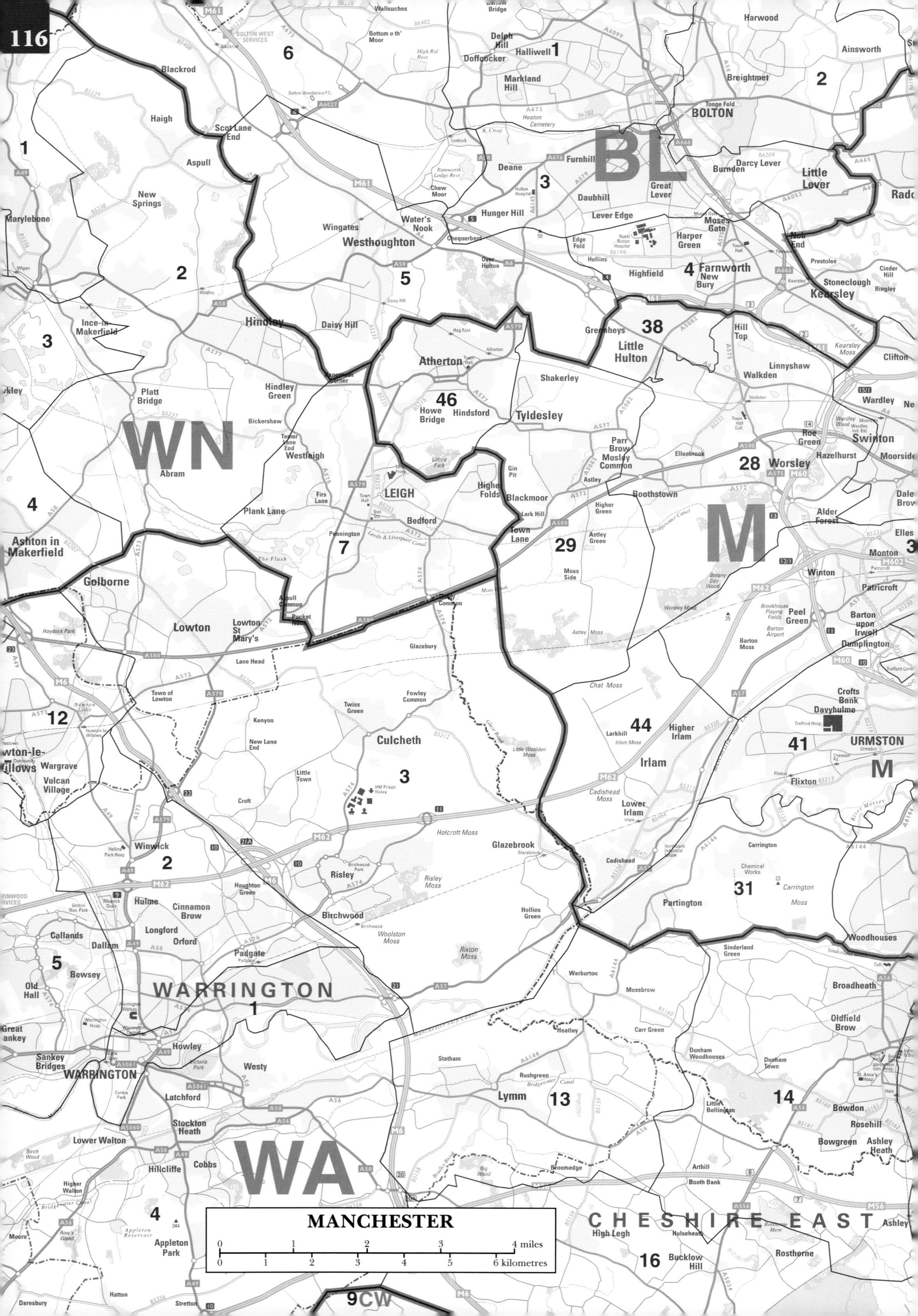

Wallsuches
Bottom o th' Moor
Delph Hill
Halliwell
Doffcocker
Harwood
Ainsworth
Breightmet
Markland Hill
BOLTON
Tonge Fold
Heaton Cemetery
Blackrod
BOLTON WEST SERVICES
Haigh
Scot Lane End
Aspull
New Springs
Marylebone
Wigan
Hindley
Ince-in-Makerfield
Daisy Hill
Westhoughton
Wingates
Water's Nook
Chequerbent
Hunger Hill
Chew Moor
Deane
Furnhill
BL
Great Lever
Daubhill
Lever Edge
Burnden
Darcy Lever
Little Lever
Moses Gate
Harper Green
Farnworth
New Bury
Highfield
Nob End
Prestolee
Stoneclough
Kearsley
Cinder Hill
Ringley
Over Hulton
Greenheys
Little Hulton
Hill Top
Kearsley Moss
Clifton
Linnyshaw
Walkden
Atherton
Shakerley
Tyldesley
Hindsford
Howe Bridge
Platt Bridge
Hindley Green
Bickershaw
WN
Abram
Westleigh
Tamer Lane End
Parr Brow
Mosley Common
Ellenbrook
Roe Green
Worsley
Swinton
Wardley
Hazelhurst
Moorside
Astley
Boothstown
Higher Folds
Gin Pit
Blackmoor
Lark Hill
Town Lane
LEIGH
Firs Lane
Bedford
Pennington
Plank Lane
Ashton in Makerfield
Golborne
Lowton
Lowton St Mary's
Aspull Common
Pocket Nook
Higher Green
Astley Green
Moss Side
M
Alder Forest
Monton
Winton
Patricroft
Botany Bay Wood
Peel Green
Barton upon Irwell
Dumplington
Barton Airport
Barton Moss
Astley Moss
Chat Moss
Crofts Bank
Davyhulme
URMSTON
Flixton
Larkhill
Higher Irlam
Irlam
Irlam Moss
Cadishead Moss
Lower Irlam
Cadishead
Carrington
Chemical Works
Carrington Moss
Partington
Woodhouses
Sinderland Green
Glazebury
Lane Head
Town of Lowton
Twiss Green
Fowley Common
Kenyon
New Lane End
Culcheth
Little Town
HM Prison Risley
Croft
Holcroft Moss
Glazebrook
Little Woolden Moss
Winwick
Houghton Green
Risley
Risley Moss
Birchwood
Woolston Moss
Rixton Moss
Hollins Green
Hulme
Cinnamon Brow
Callands
Longford
Orford
Dallam
Padgate
Bewsey
Old Hall
WARRINGTON
Warburton
Mossbrow
Broadheath
Oldfield Brow
Carr Green
Heatley
Statham
Rushgreen
Lymm
Dunham Woodhouses
Dunham Town
Little Bollington
Bowdon
Rosehill
Bowgreen
Ashley Heath
Great Sankey
Sankey Bridges
Howley
Westy
Latchford
Stockton Heath
Lower Walton
Hillcliffe
Cobbs
WA
Higher Walton
Appleton Park
Appleton Reservoir
Broomedge
Arthill
Booth Bank
High Legh
Hulseheath
Rostherne
Bucklow Hill
CHESHIRE EAST
Ashley
Moore
Hatton
Stretton
Daresbury
Vulcan Village
Wargrave
Newton-le-Willows
Haydock Park
MANCHESTER
0 1 2 3 4 miles
0 1 2 3 4 5 6 kilometres
CW

BURY
Elton
Heap Bridge
Heady Hill
HEYWOOD
Castleton
Beursil
Balderstone
Beursil Head
Gravel Hole
Burnedge
Wood End
High Crompton
Crompton Fold
Crompton
Denshaw
Slackcote
Fishpool
Gigg
Three Lane Ends
Hopwood
Slattocks
Birch Services
Blackford Bridge
Hollins
Sunny Bank
Unsworth
Whittle Hill
Birch
Industrial Estate
Thorp
Royton
Luzley Brook
Heyside
Sholver
Besom Hill
Top of Hebers
Stanycliffe
Langley
Hollins
Higher Boarshaw
Healds Green
Chadderton Fold
Haggate
Holden Fold
Long Sight
Higginshaw
Moorside
Roebuck Low
Thurston Clough
High Moor
Watersheddings
Top o' th' Meadows
Radcliffe
Bowlee
Middleton
Moor Close
Chadderton
Busk
Oldham Edge
Derker
Spring Hill
OL
Scouthead
Saddleworth
Chapel Field
Stand
Whitefield
Oak Bank
Simister
Rhodes
Mumps
Greenacres
Austerlands
Besses o' th' Barn
Kirkhams
Heaton Park Resr.
Alkrington
Middleton Junction
Coppice
Werneth
Moorhey
Lees
Grotton
Grasscroft
Park Lane
Heaton Park
Higher Blackley
Nimble Nook
Alexandra Park
Glodwick
Springhead
Lydgate
Prestwich
Charlestown
White Gate
OLDHAM
Holts
Alt
Quick Edge
Clifton Junction
Sedgley Park
Crumpsall
Chain Bar
Hathershaw
Copster Hill
Brook Bottom
Green
Hilton Park
Boggart Hole Clough
Blackley
Lime Side
Park Bridge
Alt Hill
Hartshead Pike
Hartshead Green
Mossley
Mossley Brow
Micklehurst
Rainsough
New Moston
Hollinwood
Pendlebury
Broughton Park
Moston
Bardsley
Knott Lanes
Kersal
GREATER
Cheetham Hill
Harpurhey
Failsworth
Limehurst
Smallshaw
Hurst
Hazelhurst
Lower Kersal
The Cliff
Higher Broughton
Cheetham
Woodhouses
Daisy Nook
Waterloo
Charlestown
Newton Heath
Littlemoss
Taunton
Crowhill
Heyrod
Brindle Heath
Pendleton
Collyhurst
Cheetwood
Lower Broughton
Miles Platting
Medlock Vale
ASHTON-UNDER-LYNE
Ridge Hill
Millbrook
Seedley
Wallness
Strangeways
Clayton Bridge
Little Bolton
SALFORD
MANCHESTER
Ancoats
Bradford
Clayton
Copley
Droylsden
Guide Bridge
Stalybridge
Weaste
Ordsall
Beswick
Openshaw
Fairfield
Audenshaw
Dukinfield
Yew Tree
Ardwick
Brunswick
West Gorton
St. George's
Trafford Park
Hulme
Longsight
Abbey Hey
Gorton
Debdale
Old Trafford
Newton
Flowery Field
Gorse Hill
Moss Side
Rusholme
Dane Bank
Denton
Kingston
Godley
Godley Hill
Hyde
STRETFORD
Whalley Range
Levenshulme
North Reddish
Backbower
NCHESTER
Chorlton-cum-Hardy
Fallowfield
Ladybarn
Reddish
Haughton Green
Gee Cross
Heaton Chapel
Castle Hill
Idle Hill
Sale Ees
Barlow Moor
Withington
Burnage
South Reddish
Brinnington
Woodley
Werneth Low
West Didsbury
Green End
Heaton Moor
Greave
SALE
Lane End
Portwood
Bredbury
Compstall
Didsbury
Heaton Mersey
Heaton Norris
Norris Bank
Lower Bredbury
Romiley
Cherry Tree
Brooklands
Northern Moor
Bredbury Green
Northenden
East Didsbury
STOCKPORT
Stockport Little Moor
Bunkers Hill
Marple Dale
Ley Hey Park
Marple Bridge
Edgeley
Cheadle Heath
Offerton Fold
Foggbrook
Offerton Green
Chadkirk
Baguley
Shaw Heath
Heaviley
Roundthorn
Sharston
Gatley
Cheadle
Adswood
Cale Green
Great Moor
Marple
Benchill
Davenport
Woods Moor
Stepping Hill
Newall Green
SK
CHAM
Wythenshawe
Cheadle Royal
Cheadle Hulme
Bramhall Moor
Hawk Green
Marpleridge
Torkington
Hazel Grove
Well Green
Peel Hall
Woodhouse Park
Bramhall Park
Heald Green
Windlehurst
Strines
Woodend
Long Lane
Norbury Moor
High Lane
Heyhead
Moss Nook
Smithy Green
Halebarns
Warburton Green
Manchester Airport
Stanley Green
Bramhall
Disley
Thorns Green
Kitt's Moss
Middlewood
Handforth
Poynton
Higher Poynton
Country Park
Woodford
Hope Green
Lacey Green

LEEDS AND BRADFORD
0 1 2 3 4 miles
0 1 2 3 4 5 6 kilometres
N O R T H Y
W E S T
BD
HX
HD
Addingham
Middleton
Denton
Askwith
Farnley
Ilkley
29
Silsden
Rombalds Moor
Ilkley Moor
Burley in Wharfedale
Otley
Steeton
20
Menston
Utley
Riddlesden
East Morton
Hawksworth
20
Guiseley
Keighley
Laycock
21
Thwaites Brow
Micklethwaite
16
Eldwick
Yeadon
Ingrow
17
Baildon
Bogthorn
Oakworth
Harewood Hill
Lane End
Bingley
Myrtle Park
Baildon Green
Thackley End
Thackley
Harden
Simpson Green
22
Haworth
Saltaire
Nab Wood
Moorhead
West Royd
Windhill
Idle
10
Apperley Bridge
Cottingley
Shipley
18
Cullingworth
Wilsden
Idle Moor
Swain House
Bank Top
Eccleshill
Greengates
Sandy Lane
Noon Nick
Heaton Shay
Frizinghall
2
Ravenscliffe
Oxenhope
15
Daisy Hill
9
Heaton
Fagley
Farsley
Leeming
Allerton
Four Lane Ends
8
Thornbury
Denholme
Hill Top
Thornton
School Green
Lower Grange
Crossley Hall
1
BRADFORD
3
Laisterdyke
Denholme Clough
13
Chat Hill
Lidget Green
7
Tyresal
Scholemoor
Bowling
14
Clayton
Great Horton
Little Horton
5
West Bowling
4
Holme Shay
West Scholes
Mountain
Dudley Hill
Ogden
Old Dolphin
Wibsey
Bierley
Tong Street
Queensbury
Buttershaw
6
Odsal
Ambler Thorn
Holdsworth
East Bierley
Shibden Head
Moor End
Illingworth
Shelf
Low Moor
11
Mixenden
2
Holmfield
Moor Side
12
Stone Chair
Wyke
Ovenden
Boothtown
Coley
Hunsworth
Merchant Fields
Gomersal
Midgley
Wyke Common
Northowram
Akroydon
3
Norwood Green
Priestley Green
Hipperholme
Scholes
19
Mt. Pellon
Cleckheaton
1
HALIFAX
Warley Town
Luddenden Foot
Bailiff Bridge
Birkhouse
Hightown Heights
Hightown
Littletown
Hove Edge
6
Southowram
Siddal
Sowerby
Sowerby Bridge
6
Brookfoot
Liversedge
15
Clifton
Brighouse
Norristhorpe
Robertown
5
Norland
4
Rastrick
Woodhouse
14

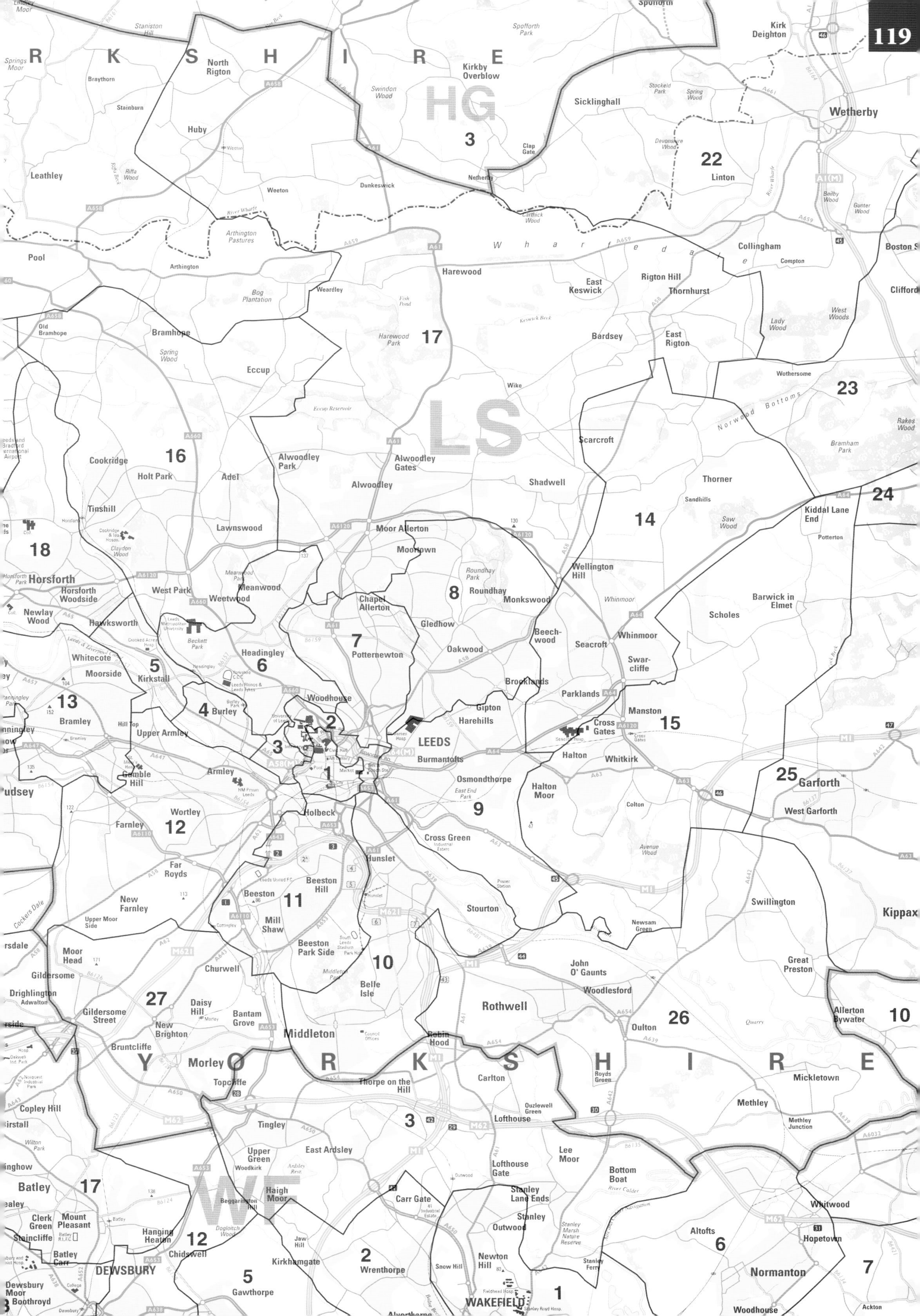
Y O R K S H I R E
HG
3
LS
WF
Spofforth Park
Kirk Deighton
North Rigton
Kirkby Overblow
Braythorn
Stainburn
Swindon Wood
Sicklinghall
Stockeld Park
Spring Wood
Wetherby
Huby
Clap Gate
Devonshire Wood
22
Linton
Leathley
Riffa Wood
Weeton
Dunkeswick
Netherby
Pool
Arthington Pastures
Arthington
Carthick Wood
Wharfedale
Harewood
Collingham
Compton
Boston Spa
East Keswick
Rigton Hill
Thornhurst
Clifford
Weardley
Bog Plantation
Old Bramhope
Bramhope
Spring Wood
Harewood Park
17
Bardsey
East Rigton
Lady Wood
West Woods
Eccup
Eccup Reservoir
Wike
Wothersome
23
Norwood Bottoms
Rakes Wood
Bramham Park
Cookridge
16
Holt Park
Alwoodley Park
Alwoodley Gates
Alwoodley
Adel
Scarcroft
Shadwell
Thorner
Sandhills
Saw Wood
Tinshill
Lawnswood
Moor Allerton
14
Kiddal Lane End
Potterton
24
18
Horsforth
Moortown
Roundhay Park
Roundhay
Wellington Hill
Horsforth Woodside
West Park
Meanwood
Weetwood
8
Monkswood
Whinmoor
Barwick in Elmet
Scholes
Newlay Wood
Hawksworth
Chapel Allerton
Gledhow
Beckett Park
7
Potternewton
Oakwood
Beech-wood
Seacroft
Swar-cliffe
Whitecote
Headingley
6
5
Kirkstall
Moorside
Brooklands
13
Bramley
4 Burley
Woodhouse
Gipton
Harehills
Parklands
Manston
Cross Gates
15
Upper Armley
2
3
LEEDS
Burmantofts
Halton
Whitkirk
Armley
Gamble Hill
1
Osmondthorpe
East End Park
9
Halton Moor
25
Garforth
West Garforth
Colton
Pudsey
Farnley
Wortley
12
Holbeck
Cross Green
Hunslet
Avenue Wood
Far Royds
Beeston Hill
Beeston
11
Mill Shaw
New Farnley
Stourton
Swillington
Kippax
Upper Moor Side
Newsam Green
Beeston Park Side
10
Moor Head
Gildersome
Churwell
John O' Gaunts
Great Preston
Drighlington
Adwalton
Belle Isle
Woodlesford
27
Daisy Hill
Bantam Grove
Rothwell
Gildersome Street
New Brighton
Middleton
Oulton
26
Allerton Bywater
10
Bruntcliffe
Robin Hood
Morley
Carlton
Royds Green
Mickletown
Topcliffe
Thorpe on the Hill
Methley
Copley Hill
3
Oulzewell Green
Lofthouse
Methley Junction
Tingley
East Ardsley
Lee Moor
Upper Green
Woodkirk
Lofthouse Gate
Bottom Boat
Batley
17
Haigh Moor
Carr Gate
Stanley Lane Ends
Beggarington Hill
Whitwood
Clerk Green
Mount Pleasant
Stanley
Outwood
Staincliffe
Batley Carr
Hanging Heaton
12
Chidswell
Jaw Hill
Altofts
6
Hopetown
Kirkhamgate
2
Wrenthorpe
Snow Hill
Newton Hill
Stanley Ferry
DEWSBURY
5
Normanton
7
Dewsbury Moor
Boothroyd
Gawthorpe
WAKEFIELD
1
Woodhouse
Ackton
Alverthorpe

LIVERPOOL
0 1 2 3 4 miles
0 1 2 3 4 5 6 kilometres
LANCS
MERSEYSIDE
CHESHIRE WEST & CHESTER
LIVERPOOL BAY
Crosby Channel
River Mersey
Manchester Ship Canal
Hightown
Ince Blundell
Lydiate
Aughton
Town Green
Bowker's Green
Stanley Gate
SKELMER
Maghull
Little Crosby
Thornton
Blundellsands
Great Crosby
CROSBY
Buckley Hill
Aintree
Waterloo
Waterloo Park
Litherland
Seaforth
Orrell
Northwood
Westvale
Kirkby
Southdene
Fazakerley
Gillmoss
Croxteth
Knowsley
Knowsley Park
BOOTLE
Walton
Dog and Gun
Norris Green
Kirkdale
Anfield
Clubmoor
Tuebrook
New Brighton
WALLASEY
Egremont
Liscard
Stoneycroft
West Derby
Fincham
Woolfall Heath
Prescot
Longview
Poulton
Seacombe
Everton
Fairfield
LIVERPOOL
Old Swan
Knotty Ash
Swanside
Dovecot
Page Moss
Roby
Huyton with Roby
Huyton
Whiston Cross
Huyton Park
Huyton Quarry
Windy Arbor
Bidston Hill
Bidston
Ford
Claughton
BIRKENHEAD
Edge Hill
Wavertree
Childwall
Court Hey
Bowring Park
Princes Park
Toxteth
Netherley
Belle Vale
Upton
Noctorum
Oxton
Tranmere
Dingle
St Michael's
Hamlet
Mossley Hill
Gateacre
Arrowe Hill
Woodchurch
Prenton
Rock Ferry
Calderstones
Allerton
Woolton
Landican
Aigburth
Otterspool
Grassendale
Halewood
Higher Bebington
Woodhey
New Ferry
Hunts Cross
Storeton
BEBINGTON
Bromborough Pool
Thingwall
Lower Bebington
Port Sunlight
Garston
Speke
Barnston
Brimstage
Poulton
Heswall
Bromborough
Liverpool John Lennon Airport
Thornton Hough
Eastham
Gayton
Brookhurst
Raby
Parkgate
Willaston
Hooton
Childer Thornton
Neston
ELLESMERE PORT
Overpool
Little
CH
L
WA
WN
37 38 40 8 39 29 31 23 11 33 30 22 21 32 10 20 9 10 34 11 4 12 28 45 5 6 44 3 14 36 46 13 2 7 41 1 15 16 27 35 8 43 17 42 18 25 49 26 19 61 24 8 62 63 60 64 66 65 2

NEWCASTLE UPON TYNE
1 2 3 4 miles
1 2 3 4 5 6 kilometres
NORTHUMBERLAND
NE
TYNE & WEAR
SR
Morpeth
Stakeford
Sheepwash
Guide Post
Scotland Gate
East Sleekburn
Cambois
Bedlington
Nedderton
Blyth
Bedside
Cowpen
Stannington
East Hartford
New Delaval
Newsham
Shankhouse
Nelson Village
Cramlington
East Cramlington
New Hartley
Seaton Delaval
Seaton Sluice
Hartley
Holywell
Seghill
Seaton Burn
Annitsford
Dudley
Dinnington
Prestwick
Brunswick Village
Wide Open
Camperdown
Killingworth
Backworth
Earsdon
Monkseaton
Whitley Bay
Shiremoor
Cullercoats
Marden
Tynemouth
North Shields
Wallsend
Gosforth
Jesmond
Newcastle upon Tyne
Gateshead
Jarrow
Hebburn
South Shields
Blaydon
Whickham
Washington
Sunderland
Felling
Heworth
Boldon
Birtley
Heaton
Byker
Walker
Benwell
Fenham
Kenton
Longbenton
Benton
Westerhope
Lemington
Dunston
Swalwell
Sunniside
Lamesley
Kibblesworth
Stephenson
Usworth
Sulgrave
Hylton Castle
Castletown
Southwick
Whiteleas
Harton
Hedworth
Primrose
Fellgate
Wardley
Wrekenton
Springwell
Eighton Banks
Low Fell
Team Valley
Lobley Hill
Winlaton Mill
Dunston Hill
Scotswood
Elswick
Blakelaw
Cowgate
West Denton
East Denton
Woolsington
Kenton Bank
Ponteland

GLASGOW
0 1 2 3 4 miles
0 1 2 3 4 5 6 kilometres
STIRLING
63
Strathblane
Blanefield
Carbeth
Clachan of Campsie
Haughhead
Lennoxtown
65
Queenziebum
STIRLIN
Lennox Forest
EAST
Mugdock
Milton of Campsie
Kinkell
66
Twechar
81
62
Milngavie
Baldernock
Birdston
DUNBARTONSHIRE
Harestanes
Dougalston
Torrance
Kirkintilloch
Bardowie
Balmore
Gallowhill
Oxgang
Waterside
Bearsden
64
Cadder
Buckhey
G
61
Lenzie
15
Drumchapel
23
Auchinloch
Bridgend
Moodiesburn
Summerston
Kenmure
Woodhill
NORTH
Chryston
Bishopbriggs
LANARKSHIRE
Knightswood
Milton
Crowhill
Maryhill
Gilshochill
Lambhill
22
Auchinairn
Muirhead
69
Temple
Springburn
Stepps
Gartcosh
Yoker
13
Kelvindale
20
Balornock
Scotstounhill
Anniesland
12
21
Craigendmuir
Kelvinside
Possilpark
Barmulloch
Millerston
Scotstoun
14
Dowanhill
GLASGOW
Provanmill
33
4
PA
Partick
11
4
Royston
Riddrie
Ruchazie
Garthamlock
Lochwood
Dean Park
Whiteinch
Shieldhall
Easterhouse
3
Finnieston
2
Dennistoun
31
Carntyne
34
3
51
1
Springboig
Barlanark
Swinton
Govan
Ibrox
Bridgeton
Baillieston
Hillington
Cardonald
Barrachnie
Garrowhill
Craigton
52
Shettleston
Crosshill
Ralston
1
Crookston
5
GLASGOW
Parkhead
40
32
41
Pollokshields
Muirhead
Mosspark
Dumbreck
Oatlands
Braidfauld
Mount Vernon
Crossmyloof
Broomhouse
Pollok
Govanhill
Polmadie
Hawkhead
Rutherglen
Carmyle
42
Birkenshaw
2
43
Shawlands
Langside
Mount Florida
Eastfield
Hurlet
Pollokshaws
King's Park
73
Kylepark
Battlefield
Cathcart
Newton
53
High Crosshill
Uddingston
Priesthill
Newlands
Nitshill
Mansewood
44
Croftfoot
Hallside
Arden
Merrylee
Muirend
Burnside
Carnwardric
Cambuslang
72
Darnley
Flemington
Thornliebank
Giffnock
Netherlee
Castlemilk
Barrhead
46
45
Dalton
SOUTH
Low Blantyre
78
Stamperland
Williamwood
Carmunnock
Blantyre
EAST
Nerston
Crookfur
Whitecraigs
Clarkston
Sheddens
76
High Blantyre
Rogerton
Broom
74
RENFREWSHIRE
Busby
LANARKSHIRE
Stewartfield
Calderwood
Hillhouse
Malletsheugh
Braehead
Netherplace
Newton Mearns
Mearns
Thorntonhall
East Mains
Auchentibber
Waterfoot
EAST KILBRIDE
Earnock
77
West Mains
3
St. Leonards
Westwood
The Murray
ML
Birniehill
Jackton
Lawmuir
75
Eaglesham
Greenhills
Torrance House
10

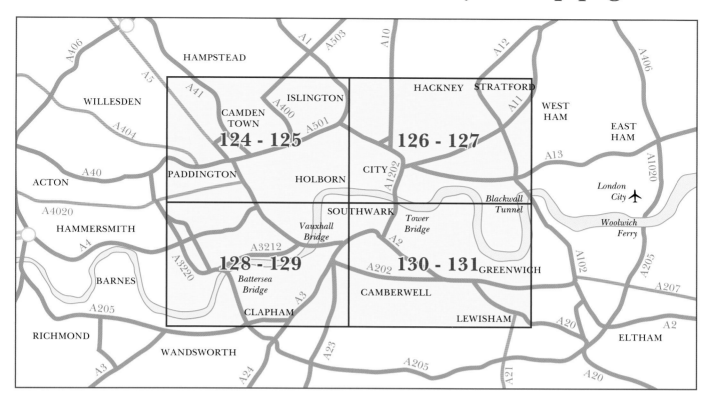

London key to symbols

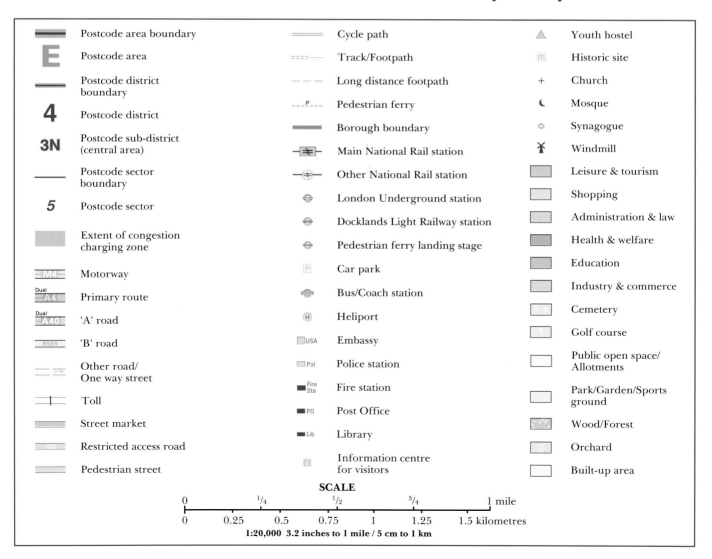

Symbol	Description	Symbol	Description	Symbol	Description
	Postcode area boundary		Cycle path	▲	Youth hostel
E	Postcode area		Track/Footpath	m	Historic site
	Postcode district boundary		Long distance footpath	+	Church
4	Postcode district	P	Pedestrian ferry	☾	Mosque
3N	Postcode sub-district (central area)		Borough boundary	✡	Synagogue
	Postcode sector boundary		Main National Rail station	✗	Windmill
5	Postcode sector		Other National Rail station		Leisure & tourism
	Extent of congestion charging zone		London Underground station		Shopping
M4	Motorway		Docklands Light Railway station		Administration & law
Dual A4	Primary route		Pedestrian ferry landing stage		Health & welfare
Dual A40	'A' road	P	Car park		Education
B504	'B' road		Bus/Coach station		Industry & commerce
	Other road/ One way street	H	Heliport		Cemetery
	Toll	USA	Embassy		Golf course
	Street market	Pol	Police station		Public open space/ Allotments
	Restricted access road	Fire Sta	Fire station		Park/Garden/Sports ground
	Pedestrian street	PO	Post Office		Wood/Forest
		Lib	Library		Orchard
		i	Information centre for visitors		Built-up area

SCALE

| 0 | ¼ | ½ | ¾ | 1 mile |

| 0 | 0.25 | 0.5 | 0.75 | 1 | 1.25 | 1.5 kilometres |

1:20,000 3.2 inches to 1 mile / 5 cm to 1 km

WEST HAMPSTEAD
SOUTH HAMPSTEAD
BELSIZE PARK
PRIMROSE HILL
NW
KILBURN
ST. JOHN'S WOOD
MAIDA VALE
MAIDA HILL
LISSON GROVE
MARYLEBONE
THE REGENT'S PARK
LONDON ZOO
QUEEN MARY'S GARDENS
WESTBOURNE GREEN
PADDINGTON
BAYSWATER
W
KENSINGTON GARDENS
HYDE PARK
THE SERPENTINE
THE LONG WATER
ROUND POND
KENSINGTON PALACE
KENSINGTON
HOLLAND PARK
NOTTING HILL GATE
LORD'S CRICKET GROUND
ST. MARY'S HOSP
WELLINGTON HOSP
HOSPITAL OF ST. JOHN & ST. ELIZ.
PADDINGTON RECREATION GROUND
PADDINGTON OLD CEMETERY
SWISS COTTAGE
CHALK FARM
SPEAKER'S CORNER
MARBLE ARCH
OXFORD STREET where marked is closed to through traffic (except buses & taxis) from 7a.m.-7p.m. Monday - Saturday
128
A
B
C
D
E
F
G
1
2
3
4
5
6
7
8
9
10
11

H
J
K
L
M
N
P
KENTISH TOWN
LOWER HOLLOWAY
HIGHBURY
CANONBURY
CAMDEN TOWN
KING'S CROSS
BARNSBURY
ISLINGTON
PENTONVILLE PRISON
CALEDONIAN PARK
SOMERS TOWN
EUSTON
ST. PANCRAS
FINSBURY
CLERKENWELL
BLOOMSBURY
BRITISH MUSEUM
HOLBORN
SOHO
STRAND
ALDWYCH
EMBANKMENT
VICTORIA EMBANKMENT
BARBICAN
ST. PAUL'S CATH
BLACKFRIARS
SOUTHWARK
THE BOROUGH
WATERLOO
LAMBETH
ST. JAMES'S
ST. JAMES'S PARK
THE GREEN PARK
BUCKINGHAM PALACE
TRAFALGAR
CHARING CROSS
SHAKESPEARE GLOBE THEATRE
TATE MODERN
REGENT'S PARK
EUSTON ROAD
PENTONVILLE RD
OXFORD STREET
FARRINGDON
THEOBALD'S ROAD
FLEET ST
HOLBORN
RIVER
WC
EC
SE
SW
126
129
1
2
3
4
5
6
7
8
9
10

A
B
C
D
E
F
G
1
2
3
4
5
6
7
8
9
10
HIGHBURY
CANONBURY
KINGSLAND
DE BEAUVOIR TOWN
DALSTON
HACKNEY
SOUTH HACKNEY
HAGGERSTON
HOXTON
SHOREDITCH PARK
BETHNAL GREEN
SHOREDITCH
CLERKENWELL
BARBICAN
BROADGATE
WHITECHAPEL
WAPPING
SHADWELL
STEPNEY
SOUTHWARK
THE BOROUGH
TOWER OF LONDON
LONDON BRIDGE HOSP
GUY'S HOSPITAL
SHAKESPEARE GLOBE THEATRE
TATE MODERN
ROYAL LONDON HOSP
MOORFIELDS EYE HOSP
MILDMAY MISS. HOSP
ST. JOSEPH'S HOSPICE
LONDON FIELDS
REGENT'S CANAL
TOWER BRIDGE EXHIBITION
ST. KATHARINE'S PIER
BALLS POND ROAD
KINGSLAND ROAD
NEW NORTH ROAD
CITY ROAD
GOSWELL ROAD
OLD STREET
GREAT EASTERN ST
COMMERCIAL ROAD
WHITECHAPEL ROAD
MILE END ROAD
CAMBRIDGE HEATH ROAD
MARE ST
VICTORIA PARK
EAST SMITHFIELD
THE HIGHWAY
TOOLEY ST
SOUTHWARK ST
UPPER THAMES ST
LONDON WALL
HOUNDSDITCH
MINORIES
TOWER BR APP
DRUID ST
BLACKFRIARS BR
N
SE
16
125
130

HOMERTON
HACKNEY WICK
LONDON 2012 OLYMPIC PARK
OLYMPIC VILLAGE
STRATFORD INTERNATIONAL
STRATFORD
VICTORIA PARK
OLD FORD
Olympic Stadium
Aquatics Centre
Water Polo Arena
Handball Arena
Basketball Arena
PUDDING MILL LANE
BOW
MILE END
BROMLEY
LEE VALLEY REGIONAL PARK
TOWER HAMLETS CEMETERY PARK
LIMEHOUSE
POPLAR
CANARY WHARF
ISLE
WEST INDIA DOCKS
RIVER THAMES
CANNING TOWN
NORTH GREENWICH
ROYAL LON. HOSP (ST. CLEMENTS)
MILE END HOSP
Queen Mary University of London
EAST INDIA DOCK BASIN
E
SE
131

A
B
C
D
E
F
G
KENSINGTON GARDENS
HYDE PARK
124
ROUND POND
THE SERPENTINE
SERPENTINE GALLERY
KENSINGTON PALACE
KENSINGTON
HOLLAND PARK
W
8
7
1
14
2
3
4
5
6
7
8
9
10
15
SOUTH KENSINGTON
NATURAL HISTORY MUSEUM
SCIENCE MUSEUM
VICTORIA & ALBERT MUSEUM
ROYAL ALBERT HALL
KNIGHTSBRIDGE
HARRODS
BROMPTON
BELGRAVIA
1X
1W
PIMLICO
CROMWELL ROAD
EARLS COURT
EARLS COURT EXHIBITION CENTRE
WEST BROMPTON
BROMPTON CEMETERY
THE ROYAL MARSDEN
ROYAL BROMPTON HOSP
CHELSEA
CHELSEA & WEST. HOSP
ROYAL HOSPITAL CHELSEA
KING'S ROAD
FULHAM ROAD
STAMFORD BRIDGE CHELSEA FC
FULHAM BROADWAY
WALHAM GREEN
PARSONS GREEN
EEL BROOK COMMON
SANDS END
CHELSEA REACH
EMBANKMENT
KENSINGTON & CHELSEA
WANDSWORTH
SW
BATTERSEA PARK
CHILDREN'S ZOO
BATTERSEA BRIDGE
ALBERT BRIDGE
HURLINGHAM PARK
HURLINGHAM CLUB
SOUTH PARK
LONDON BATTERSEA HELIPORT
CLAPHAM JUNCTION
CLAPHAM COMMON
LAVENDER HILL
WANDSWORTH BRIDGE
HAMMERSMITH & FULHAM
WANDSWORTH TOWN
WANDSWORTH COMMON
NORTHCOTE ROAD
11
18
0
10
A3220
A308
A3217
A3212
A3205
A3036
A217
A3209
A205
A4

H
J
K
L
M
N
P
125
130
THE GREEN PARK
ST. JAMES'S PARK
BUCKINGHAM PALACE
WESTMINSTER
HOUSES OF PARLIAMENT
ST. THOMAS' HOSP
WATERLOO
SOUTHWARK
THE BOROUGH
NEWINGTON
LAMBETH
SE
11
17
VICTORIA
PIMLICO
VAUXHALL
KENNINGTON
THE OVAL (SURREY C.C.C.)
KENNINGTON PARK
NINE ELMS
RIVER THAMES
Battersea Power Station (Disused)
New Covent Garden Market
SOUTH LAMBETH
STOCKWELL
BRIXTON
CLAPHAM
LAMBETH HOSPITAL
TRINITY HOSPICE
KING'S COLL HOSPITAL
MYATT'S FIELDS PARK
LOUGHBOROUGH JUNCTION
COLDHARBOUR LANE
CAMBERWELL NEW ROAD
CLAPHAM HIGH STREET
CLAPHAM ROAD
BRIXTON ROAD
KENNINGTON ROAD
WANDSWORTH ROAD
VAUXHALL BRIDGE ROAD
GROSVENOR ROAD
1A
1E
1H
1J
1P
1V
1Y
8
9
24
5
2
4

A
B
C
D
E
F
G
1W
WAPPING
SOUTHWARK
THE BOROUGH
NEWINGTON
BERMONDSEY
WALWORTH
CAMBERWELL
PECKHAM
BURGESS PARK
MYATT'S FIELDS PARK
RUSKIN PARK
PECKHAM RYE COMMON
PECKHAM RYE PARK
SOUTHWARK PARK
KING'S COLLEGE HOSPITAL
MAUDSLEY HOSPITAL
GUY'S HOSPITAL
DULWICH COMMUNITY HOSP
TOWER BRIDGE EXHIBITION
LONDON BRIDGE
ELEPHANT & CASTLE
SE
SW
16
17
15
22
24
126
129
1
2
3
4
5
6
7
8
9
10

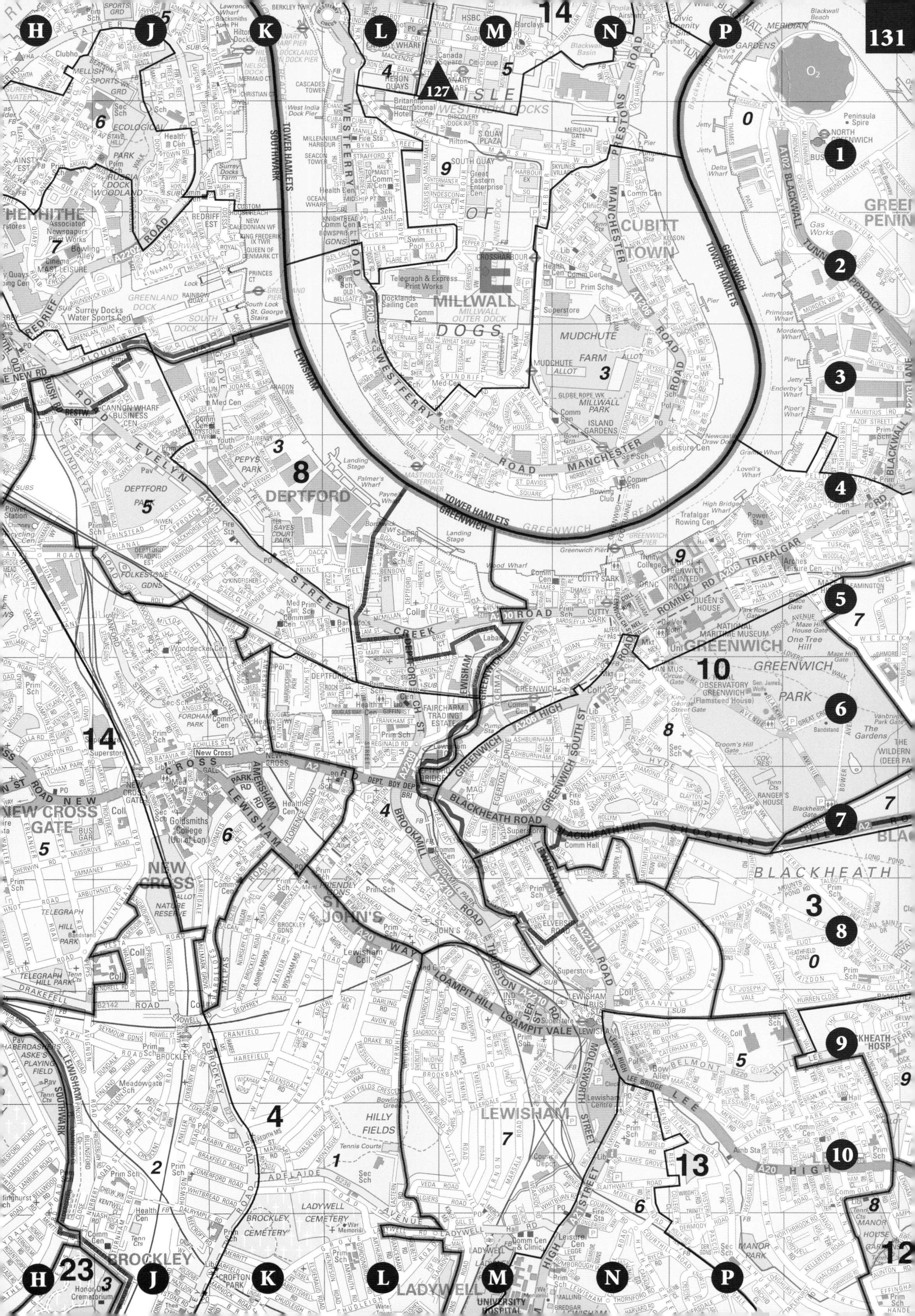

H
J
K
L
M
N
P
14
127
ISLE OF DOGS
WEST INDIA DOCKS
MILLWALL
MILLWALL OUTER DOCK
MUDCHUTE FARM
CUBITT TOWN
ISLAND GARDENS
MILLWALL PARK
TOWER HAMLETS
SOUTHWARK
LEWISHAM
GREENWICH
ROTHERHITHE
DEPTFORD
DEPTFORD PARK
PEPYS PARK
SURREY DOCKS FARM
RUSSIA DOCK WOODLAND
GREENLAND DOCK
SOUTH DOCK
Surrey Docks Water Sports Cen
CANNON WHARF BUSINESS CEN
DEPTFORD TRADING EST
FOLKESTONE GDNS
NEW CROSS
NEW CROSS GATE
Goldsmiths College (Uni of Lon)
NATURE RESERVE
TELEGRAPH HILL PARK
ST JOHN'S
BROCKLEY
BROCKLEY CEMETERY
LADYWELL CEMETERY
HILLY FIELDS
LEWISHAM
LADYWELL
UNIVERSITY HOSPITAL
MANOR PARK
BLACKHEATH
GREENWICH PARK
ROYAL OBSERVATORY GREENWICH (Flamsteed House)
NATIONAL MARITIME MUSEUM
QUEEN'S HOUSE
CUTTY SARK
Uni of Greenwich PAINTED ROOM
Trinity College
Trafalgar Rowing Cen
Greenwich Pier
RANGER'S HOUSE
One Tree Hill
The Wilderness (Deer Park)
O₂
Peninsula Spire
NORTH GREENWICH
GREENWICH PENINSULA
Gas Works
Canada Square
Citigroup
HSBC
Barclays
Britannia International Hotel
Millennium Harbour
Telegraph & Express Print Works
Docklands Sailing Cen
Great Eastern Enterprise Cen
FAIRCHARM TRADING ESTATE
Lewisham Centre
Superstore
Honor Oak Crematorium
Meadowgate Sch
A2
A20
A200
A206
A209
A2210
A2211
A102 BLACKWALL
A1206
BLACKHEATH ROAD
LEWISHAM HIGH STREET
LEE HIGH RD
SHOOTERS HILL
EVELYN STREET
MANCHESTER ROAD
WESTFERRY ROAD
TUNNEL APPROACH
LOAMPIT VALE
LOAMPIT HILL
MOLESWORTH STREET
BROCKLEY ROAD
GREENWICH SOUTH ST
ROMNEY RD
TRAFALGAR
DEPTFORD CREEK
1
2
3
4
5
6
7
8
9
10
12
13
23

Notes: Listed below are the administrative areas for Great Britain, Northern Ireland and Isle of Man used in this Postcode Atlas. Where an area is dual language, the English form is given first, followed by the alternative in parenthesis. Each entry includes its standard abbreviation in *italics* which will appear in the index. Population figures are derived from 2001 Census information. A brief description of the area then follows, which includes: adjoining administrative areas; main centres (based on descending order of population); historical, physical and economic characteristics. For English counties or former Metropolitan counties, each district, city or borough authority is listed under the heading, **Districts.**

Aberdeen *Aberdeen* Population: 212,125.
Unitary authority surrounding Aberdeen, Scotland's third largest city, on the NE coast and neighbouring Aberdeenshire. Aberdeen is the major commercial and administrative centre for N Scotland. It is the second largest fishing port in Scotland, with docks at the mouth of the River Dee, and is the oil and gas capital of Europe.

Aberdeenshire *Aber.* Population: 226,871.
Unitary authority on the NE coast of Scotland neighbouring Aberdeen, Angus, Highland, Moray and Perth & Kinross. Main centres are Peterhead, Fraserburgh, Inverurie, Stonehaven, Ellon, Banchory, Portlethan and Huntly. Aberdeenshire is split geographically into two main areas. The W is dominated by the Grampian Mountains and is largely unpopulated. The undulating lowlands of the E are mainly rural and are populated by farming and fishing communities. The major rivers are the Dee, which flows through Royal Deeside, and the Don.

Angus *Angus* Population: 108,400.
Unitary authority on the E coast of Scotland neighbouring Aberdeenshire, Dundee and Perth & Kinross. The chief centres are Arbroath, Forfar, Montrose, Carnoustie, the ancient cathedral city of Brechin, Kirriemuir and Monifieth. Angus occupies an area of 2200 square km and is an important agricultural area. It combines ancient relics and castles with highland terrain and market towns. Rivers include the North Esk, Isla and Prosen Water.

Antrim *Antrim* Population: 48,366
Covering around 4% of the total area of Northern Ireland, Antrim borders the eastern and northern shores of Lough Neagh, the largest freshwater lake in the United Kingdom. Major towns include Antrim, Crumlin, Templepatrick, Toombridge, internationally famous for its eel industry and Randalstown. Chief industries are heavy engineering, construction, transport and distribution, plus agriculture and tourism.

Ards *Ards* Population: 73,244
Designated as an Area of Outstanding Natural Beauty (AONB). Over half the area is a peninsula created by Strangford Lough. Newtownards is the largest town, with smaller ones being Donaghdee, Portaferry, where the ferry can be caught to the other side of the lough, Kircubbin, Ballygowan, Comber, Millisle and Portavogie. The Copeland Islands lie about a mile offshore and there are several small islands in Strangford Lough itself. Main industries are agriculture and tourism.

Argyll & Bute *Arg. & B.* Population: 91,306.
Unitary authority on the W coast of Scotland combining mainland and island life and neighbouring Highland, Inverclyde, North Ayrshire, Perth & Kinross, Stirling and West Dunbartonshire. The main towns are Helensburgh, Dunoon, Oban, Campbeltown, Rothesay and Lochgilphead. It includes the former districts of Argyll and Bute as well as the islands of Islay, Jura, Colonsay and Mull. The main industries are fishing, agriculture, whisky production and tourism.

Armagh *Armagh* Population: 54,263.
The southern border of Armagh abuts the Republic of Ireland and the city of Armagh is home to the Archbishops of both the Church of Ireland and the Roman Catholic Church. Other towns include Keady, Tandragee, Richill, Loughgall and Markethill. Chief industries are agriculture (particularly orchard fruits), food processing, small scale manufacturing and tourism, with IT as an emerging sector.

Bath & North East Somerset *B. & N.E.Som.* Population: 169,040.
Unitary authority in SW England neighbouring Bristol, North Somerset, Somerset, South Gloucestershire and Wiltshire. It surrounds the city of Bath, and includes the towns of Keynsham, Radstock and Midsomer Norton. The Georgian spa of Bath is considered to be one of the most beautiful cities in Britain, and is an important commercial and ecclesiastical centre popular with tourists. The River Avon flows through the area.

Ballymena *Ballymena* Population: 58,610.
The river Bann, which forms the western border, affords some of the best coarse fishing in Europe. To the east are the Antrim Hills. The main town is Ballymena, where around half the population live. Other towns include Broughshane, Cullybackey and Ahoghill. Main industries are agriculture, textiles, manufacturing and tourism.

Ballymoney *Ballymoney* Population: 26,894.
This predominantly rural district contains much of the Antrim Coast & Glens AONB, in the north-east corner of Northern Ireland. Ballymoney is the principle town, lying on the main A26 road. Many small villages dot the area, with agriculture being the main industry. There are a high proportion of self-employed and small businesses, along with textiles and pharmaceuticals.

Banbridge *Banbr.* Population: 41,392.
Crossed by the river Bann and dotted with glacial drumlins, Banbridge is a peaceful, unspoilt district, with the rugged Slieve Croob mountain in the east. Banbridge is the main town, while the historic cathedral town of Dromore on the river Lagan is the other major settlement. Other villages include Scarva, Loughbrickland and Gilford. Main industries are textiles (linen), construction, light engineering and agriculture.

Bedford *Bed.* Population: 154,700
Unitary authority in England formed in April 2009 from the northern part of Bedfordshire county. Bounded by Milton Keynes, Northamptonshire, Cambridgeshire and Central Bedfordshire. The main centres are Bedford and Kempston. The main river is the Great Ouse.

Belfast *Belfast.* Population: 277,391.
Belfast has the highest population and population density of all the Northern Ireland Districts. The city of Belfast sits on the river Lagan at the mouth of Belfast Lough and is a lively, vibrant city. There are no other settlements of significance within the area. A busy port, shipbuilding is still a major industry, the Titanic was built here, along with aircraft manufacturing, textiles, construction, oil refining, brewing, retail and tourism. Belfast city airport handles tourist and business flights.

Blackburn with Darwen *B'burn.* Population: 137,470.
Unitary authority in NW England surrounding Blackburn and Darwen and neighbouring Greater Manchester and Lancashire. Blackburn is a market and retail centre with a wide spread of industry including textiles, brewing and electronic engineering.

Blackpool *B'pool* Population: 142,283.
Unitary authority on the NW coast of England surrounding Blackpool and neighbouring Lancashire. Blackpool receives around 7.2 million visitors each year, making it the most popular seaside resort in Europe. Attractions including the Tower, Pleasure Beach, Winter Gardens and Illuminations.

Blaenau Gwent *B.Gwent* Population: 70,064.
Unitary authority in S Wales bounded by Caerphilly, Monmouthshire, Powys and Torfaen. The chief towns are Ebbw Vale, Tredegar, Bryn-mawr and Abertillery. The area was previously dependent upon coal, iron and steel industries but has since developed a broader industrial base. Part of the Brecon Beacons are in the N of the area.

Bournemouth *Bourne.* Population: 163,444.
Unitary authority on the S coast of England surrounding Bournemouth and neighbouring Dorset and Poole. Bournemouth is a major resort, conference and commercial centre.

Bracknell Forest *Brack.F.* Population: 109,617.
Unitary authority to the W of Greater London and bounded by Hampshire, Surrey, Windsor & Maidenhead and Wokingham. Bracknell is the chief town, while to the N of the area there are the villages of Winkfield and Binfield. To the S lies forest and heathland, and the towns of Crowthorne and Sandhurst. Bracknell has many hi-tech industries, and is a shopping and leisure centre.

Bridgend (Pen-y-Bont ar Ogwr). *Bridgend* Population: 128,645.
Unitary authority in S Wales bounded by Neath Port Talbot, Rhondda Cynon Taff, Vale of Glamorgan and the sea. Main centres are Bridgend, Maesteg and Porthcawl. The area is mountainous to the N, having ribbon development along river valleys; there is greater urbanisation in the S.

Brighton & Hove *B. & H.* Population: 247,817.
Unitary authority on the S coast of England neighbouring East Sussex and West Sussex. It encompasses the seaside resort of Brighton, which is a major commercial and conference centre, and the surrounding area which includes Hove, Portslade-by-Sea, Portslade, Rottingdean, Saltdean and part of the South Downs.

Bristol *Bristol* Population: 380,615.
Unitary authority in SW England neighbouring Bath & North East Somerset, North Somerset, South Gloucestershire and the Bristol Channel. The area includes the city of Bristol and surrounding urban area, including Avonmouth. Bristol is an important industrial and commercial centre of W England. A former major port, its character varies from docks and a busy city centre, to parks and gardens and Georgian terracing. The city hosts the Balloon Fiesta and Harbour Regatta. River Avon forms part of the W border of the area.

Buckinghamshire *Bucks.* Population: 479,026.
S midland county of England bounded by Central Bedfordshire, Greater London, Hertfordshire, Northamptonshire, Oxfordshire, Surrey, Windsor & Maidenhead and Wokingham. Chief towns are High Wycombe, the county town of Aylesbury, Amersham, Chesham, Marlow and Beaconsfield, around which, and other smaller towns, is a variety of light industry, as well as extensive residential areas. The chalk downs of the Chiltern Hills traverse the S part of the county, which is otherwise mostly flat. The River Thames flows along its S border.
Districts: Aylesbury Vale; Chiltern; South Bucks; Wycombe.

Caerphilly (Caerffili). *Caerp.* Population: 169,519.
Unitary authority in S Wales bordered by Blaenau Gwent, Cardiff, Merthyr Tydfil, Rhondda Cynon Taff and Torfaen. The chief centres are Caerphilly, Gelligaer, Risca, Bargoed, Blackwood and Bedwas. The geography of the area varies from open moorland to busy market towns. The former mining industry has been replaced by electronics and automotive companies, with tourism also being important to the local economy. Rivers include the Rhymney and Sirhowy.

Cambridgeshire *Cambs.* Population: 552,658.
County of E England bounded by Bedford, Central Bedfordshire, Essex, Hertfordshire, Lincolnshire, Norfolk, Northamptonshire, Peterborough and Suffolk. Cambridgeshire is mostly flat, with fenland to N and E, although there are low chalk hills in the S and SE. Chief centres are the city and county town of Cambridge, Wisbech, St. Ives, March, Huntingdon, St. Neots and the cathedral city of Ely. Agriculture is a major industry with sugar beet, potatoes and corn all important crops; soft fruit and vegetable cultivation and canning are also significant rural industries. There has been recent growth of medical, pharmaceutical and hi-tech industries around Cambridge. Rivers include the Cam, Nene, and Great Ouse.
Districts: Cambridge; East Cambridgeshire; Fenland; Huntingdonshire; South Cambridgeshire.

Cardiff (Caerdydd). *Cardiff* Population: 305,353.
Unitary authority in S Wales surrounding the city of Cardiff and bordered by Caerphilly, Newport, Rhondda Cynon Taff, Vale of Glamorgan and the Bristol Channel. Cardiff, the capital of Wales, is a major administrative, commercial, cultural and tourism centre. It contains the Welsh Office, Welsh National Stadium, remains of medieval castle, cathedral at Llandarff and university. Cardiff docks, which were formerly used to export Welsh coal, are part of an ongoing major redevelopment. The city has excellent shopping facilities, notably at the St. David's Centre. The birthplace of Roald Dahl.

Carmarthenshire (Sir Gaerfyrddin). *Carmar.*
Population: 172,842.
Unitary authority in S Wales bounded by Ceredigion, Neath Port Talbot, Pembrokeshire, Powys, Swansea and the sea. The chief towns are Llanelli, Carmarthen and Ammanford. The geography varies from the Brecon Beacons in the E, to the river valleys in the N, and the fishing villages, beaches and coastal towns in the S. The 50m coastline runs along the S of the area. Rivers include the Tywi, Cothi, Gwendaeth Fach and Gwendaeth Fawr.

Carrickfergus *Carrick.* Population: 37,659.
A small district, with Belfast Lough at its eastern boundary. The main town of Carrickfergus is an ancient harbour with the impressive Carrickfergus Norman Castle built on a volcanic dyke. Smaller towns include Greenisland and Whitehead. Main industries are construction, manufacturing, retailing and tourism.

Castlereagh *Castle.* Population: 66,488.
To the south-east of Belfast, the main town of the district is Castlereagh, with other towns being Carryduff and Dundonald, which still has a Norman motte. Agriculture is the main industry but many people work in the shipbuilding and aircraft industries in Belfast.

Central Bedfordshire *Cen Beds.* Population: 249,200
Unitary authority in England formed in April 2009 from the southern part of Bedfordshire county (the former districts of Mid and South Bedfordshire). Bounded by Milton Keynes, Bedford, Cambridgeshire, Hertfordshire, Luton and Buckinghamshire. The main centres are Dunstable, Leighton Buzzard and Biggleswade. It includes the N end of the Chiltern Hills but is otherwise flat.

Ceredigion *Cere.* Population: 74,941.
Unitary authority in W Wales bounded by Carmarthenshire, Gwynedd, Pembrokeshire, Powys and the sea at Cardigan Bay. The main towns are Aberystwyth, Cardigan, Aberaeron, Lampeter, Tregaron and Llandysul. Part of the Cambrian Mountains lie in the E of the area and the 50m coast has many sandy beaches. Tourism and agriculture are the most important industries. The main river is the Teifi.

Cheshire East *Ches.E.* Population: 359,000
Unitary authority of NW England formed in April 2009 from three former districts of the county of Cheshire. Bounded by Warrington, Greater Manchester, Derbyshire, Staffordshire, Shropshire and Cheshire West & Chester. Chief centres are Crewe, Macclesfield, Nantwich, Wilmslow and Congleton. The foothills of the Pennines enter the NW of the area.

Cheshire West & Chester *Ches.W & C.* Population: 327,600
Unitary authority of NW England formed in April 2009 from three former districts of the county of Cheshire. Bounded by Merseyside, Halton, Warrington, Cheshire East, Shropshire and the Welsh authorities of Wrexham and Flintshire. Chief centres are the cathedral city of Chester and the towns of Ellesmere Port, Northwich and Winsford. The country is mainly flat with rural areas of the S and W noted for dairy products. To the N and W are the estuaries of the River Dee and River Mersey.

Clackmannanshire *Clack.* Population: 48,077.
Unitary authority in central Scotland neighbouring Fife, Perth & Kinross and Stirling. The N includes the Ochil Hills, while the lowland surrounding the Forth estuary contains the chief towns which are Alloa, Tullibody, Tillicoultry and Alva. Clackmannanshire has over 50 sites of nature conservation and five historic castles and towers. The main rivers are the Devon and the Forth.

Coleraine *Coleraine* Population: 56,315.
This beautiful district borders the coast on its northern edge, with

the ports of Portrush, Portstewart and Portballintrae. The resorts of Downhill and Castlerock are popular with tourists, the latter at the outlet of the River Bann. Coleraine is the main town, an ancient but busy shopping centre. Smaller towns include Garvagh and Kilrea. Industries centre on agriculture and tourism.

Conwy *Conwy* Population: 109,596.
Unitary authority in N Wales bordered by Denbighshire, Gwynedd and the sea. The chief towns are Colwyn Bay, Llandudno, Abergele, Rhôs-on-Sea and Conwy. Around 40 per cent of Conwy is within Snowdonia National Park and there are 29m of coastline. The coastal resorts attract tourism which is a key industry, but agriculture and light manufacturing are also important to the local economy. The main river is the Conwy.

Cookstown *Cookstown* Population: 32,581.
With Lough Neagh at its eastern border and the foothills of the Sperrin Mountains to the west, Cookstown has been designated an AONB. The main town of Cookstown has the longest main street in Northern Ireland, with one mile of shops. Another town of significance is Moneymore, with other settlements being scattered, smaller villages. Industries are based around small businesses, agriculture and tourism.

Cornwall *Cornw.* Population: 499,114.
Unitary authority of SW England bounded by Devon and the sea. Chief centres are St. Austell, Falmouth, Penzance, the cathedral city and administrative centre of Truro, Redruth, Camborne and Newquay. The coastline is wild and rocky; headlands and cliffs are interspersed with large sandy beaches in the N, and deeply indented with river estuaries in the S. The interior is dominated by areas of moorland, notably the granite mass of Bodmin Moor in the NE. There are also farmlands providing rich cattle-grazing, and deep river valleys. The climate is mild, and flower cultivation is carried on extensively. The many derelict tin mines are witness to the former importance of this industry; there has recently been a partial revival. The chief industry is tourism. China clay is produced in large quantities in the St. Austell area, and there is some fishing. Rivers include the Tamar, forming the boundary with Devon; Fowey, East and West Looe, Fal, Camel, and Lynher.

Craigavon *Craigavon* Population: 80,671.
Craigavon's northern boundary is the southern shore of Lough Neagh. The M1 motorway crosses east-west, providing a link to Lisburn, Belfast and Antrim. Its principle towns are Craigavon itself, Lurgan, home to the Carnegie library and Portadown. Main industries include manufacturing, retail, public service and construction.

Cumbria *Cumb.* Population: 487,607.
County of NW England bounded by Durham, Lancashire, Northumberland and North Yorkshire; the Scottish authorities of Dumfries & Galloway and Scottish Borders; and the Solway Firth and Irish Sea. Chief centres are the city of Carlisle and the towns of Barrow-in-Furness, Whitehaven, Workington, Kendal, Penrith and Ulverston. A narrow strip of flat country along the coast widens to a plain in the N and around Carlisle. Otherwise the county is composed of mountains, moorland and lakes, and includes the scenically famous Lake District. Cumbria is mostly rural and uncultivated, with industry centred on Carlisle and the urban centres. Whitehaven, Workington, and Maryport all once relied on coal, while Barrow-in-Furness developed due to shipbuilding and heavy industry. There are links with nuclear technology: Calder Hall, N of Seascale, was Britain's first atomic power station, Sellafield is the site of a nuclear reprocessing plant and Trident submarines were built at Barrow-in-Furness. Tourism in the Lake District and sheep farming are also important industries. The area is noted for its radial drainage, with Windermere and Ullswater being the largest of the lakes and the River Eden being the chief of many rivers.
Districts: Allerdale; Barrow-in-Furness; Carlisle; Copeland; Eden; South Lakeland.

Darlington *Darl.* Population: 97,838.
Unitary authority in NE England surrounding Darlington and neighbouring Durham, North Yorkshire and Stockton-on-Tees. Darlington has a variety of industries, including iron, steel and textiles. The River Tees forms the S border.

Denbighshire (Sir Ddinbych). *Denb.* Population: 93,065.
Unitary authority in N Wales neighbouring Conwy, Flintshire, Gwynedd, Powys, Wrexham and the sea. The chief towns are Rhyl, Prestatyn, Denbigh, Ruthin, the ancient city of St. Asaph, and Llangollen. Main industries are tourism, centred on the coastal resorts of Rhyl and Prestatyn, and agriculture. Rivers include the Morwynion.

Derby *Derby* Population: 221,708.
Unitary authority in central England surrounding the city of Derby and bordered by Derbyshire. Derby has a history dating back to Roman times and is now important in the rail industry; other key industries are manufacturing and aerospace engineering. The River Derwent passes through the area.

Derbyshire *Derbys.* Population: 734,585.
Midland county of England bounded by Cheshire East, Derby, Greater Manchester, Leicestershire, Nottinghamshire, South Yorkshire, Staffordshire and West Yorkshire. Chief towns are Chesterfield, Long Eaton, Swadlincote, Ilkeston, Staveley, Dronfield, Alfreton, Heanor and Buxton. The high steep hills in the N, which include the dramatic scenery of The Peak, are the S extremity of The Pennines, and provide grazing for sheep and cattle. There is some textile industry in the towns of the N and W, while the S of the county is dominated by heavy industry, mining, and quarrying. Tourism is based on the scenic Peak District National Park, most of which falls in the county. Principal rivers are the Dove, forming much of the boundary with Staffordshire and noted for its scenery and fishing, and the Derwent; the Trent flows through the S corner of the county.
Districts: Amber Valley; Bolsover; Chesterfield; Derbyshire Dales; Erewash; High Peak; North East Derbyshire; South Derbyshire.

Devon *Devon* Population: 704,493.
Large county in SW peninsula of England bounded by Cornwall, Dorset, Plymouth, Somerset, Torbay and the Bristol and English Channels. The chief centres are the city of Exeter, Exmouth, Barnstaple, Newton Abbot, Tiverton, Bideford and Teignmouth. The county includes the W end of Exmoor and the whole of the granite mass of Dartmoor, whose summit, High Willhays, is the highest point in S England. Moorland areas apart, the county is largely given over to agriculture, and on the coast, to fishing and tourism. On Dartmoor there are quarries and a military training area; there are china clay workings in the S. Daffodils are grown commercially in River Tamar valley. Chief rivers are Exe, Teign, Dart, Avon, Erme, Tamar and Tavy in the S; and Taw and Torridge in the N. The granite island of Lundy is included in the county for administrative purposes.
Districts: East Devon; Exeter; Mid Devon; North Devon; South Hams; Teignbridge; Torridge; West Devon.

Dorset *Dorset* Population: 390,980.
County in SW England bounded by Bournemouth, Devon, Hampshire, Poole, Somerset, Wiltshire and the English Channel. The chief towns are Weymouth, Christchurch, Wimborne Minster, the county town of Dorchester, Bridport, Swanage and Blandford Forum. The county is hilly, with chalk downs and impressive geological formations along the coastline. Sand, gravel, stone and oil extraction takes place around the Isle of Portland and the Isle of Purbeck. Dorset is also noted for its agricultural and dairy produce. Tourism is an important industry due to the beautiful scenery, the proliferation of prehistoric and Roman remains, and the connection with Thomas Hardy's Wessex. Among numerous minor rivers are the Stour, Frome, and Piddle or Trent.
Districts: Christchurch; East Dorset; North Dorset; Purbeck; West Dorset; Weymouth & Portland.

Down *Down* Population: 63,828.
The southern tip of Down includes part of the beautiful Mourne Mountains, and the eastern edge consists of a long coastline, with the long sandy beach of Dundrum Bay and the shores of Strangford Lough. The main town is Downpatrick, others being Ballynahinch, Crossgar and Saintfield along with the coastal towns of Killyleagh, Newcastle and Ardglass. Industries include engineering and agriculture.

Dumfries & Galloway *D. & G.* Population: 147,765.
Unitary authority in SW Scotland neighbouring East Ayrshire, Scottish Borders, South Ayrshire, South Lanarkshire, the English county of Cumbria and the sea. It comprises the former

counties of Dumfries, Kirkcudbright and Wigtown. Chief towns are Dumfries, Stranraer, Annan, Dalbeattie, Lockerbie, Castle Douglas, Newton Stewart and Kirkcudbright. The hilly area to the N is largely given over to sheep-grazing and afforestation, while farther S there is some good-quality arable farmland. At the extreme W of the area is the peninsula known as the Rinns of Galloway, and the port of Stranraer, which provides passenger and car ferry services to Larne in Northern Ireland. Main rivers are the Esk, Annan, Nith, Dee and Cree which descend S to the Solway Firth from the Tweedsmuir Hills, Lowther Hills and the Rhinns of Kells in the N.

Dundee *Dundee* Population: 145,663.
Unitary authority on the E coast of Scotland surrounding the city of Dundee and neighbouring Angus and Perth & Kinross. Dundee is Scotland's fourth largest city and is a centre of excellence in a variety of areas from telecommunications to medical research. The Firth of Tay borders Dundee to the S.

Dungannon *Dungannon* Population: 47,735.
Dungannon includes the scenic Clogher valley, and the Republic of Ireland forms its southern boundary. The north-east corner meets Lough Neagh and the main A4 road bisects it east-west. Dungannon town has almost a quarter of the whole population, with the rest of the area being basically rural. Coalisland still has a linen industry and Tyrone Crystal is famous worldwide. Industries include agriculture, construction, retail and manufacturing.

Durham *Dur.* Population: 493,470.
Unitary authority in NE England bounded by Cumbria, Darlington, Hartlepool, Northumberland, North Yorkshire, Stockton-on-Tees, Tyne & Wear and the North Sea. Chief centres are the cathedral city of Durham; and the towns of Chester-le-Street, Peterlee, Newton Aycliffe, Bishop Auckland, Seaham and Consett. The W part includes The Peninnes and consists mostly of open moorlands which provide rough sheep-grazing and water for the urban areas from a number of large reservoirs. Economic activity is concentrated on the lowland in the E which is more heavily populated, and was formerly a centre for coal-mining and heavy industry. Diversification has since provided a broad industrial base. The principal rivers are the Tees and the Wear.

East Ayrshire *E.Ayr.* Population: 120,235.
Unitary authority in SW Scotland bounded by Dumfries & Galloway, East Renfrewshire, North Ayrshire, South Ayrshire and South Lanarkshire. The principal towns are Kilmarnock, Cumnock, Stewarton, Galston and Auchinleck. Traditional industries centred on textiles and lace in the Irvine valley, coal mining and engineering. Dairy farming is also an important industry, particularly beef and sheep production. The area is a popular tourist destination, with several castles, battle sites and associations with Robert Burns and Keir Hardie. Rivers include the Irvine, Annick and Cessnock.

East Dunbartonshire *E.Dun.* Population: 108,243.
Unitary authority in central Scotland bounded by Glasgow, North Lanarkshire, Stirling and West Dunbartonshire. The chief centres are Bearsden, Bishopbriggs, Kirkintilloch and Milngavie. Much of the urban and industrial development occurs on the N periphery of Greater Glasgow. The Campsie Fells lie in the N of the area.

East Lothian *E.Loth.* Population: 90,088.
Unitary authority in central Scotland neighbouring Edinburgh, Midlothian, Scottish Borders and the North Sea. The main towns are Musselburgh, Haddington, Tranent, Prestonpans, Dunbar, North Berwick and Cockenzie and Port Seton. There are 43m of varied coastline and the topography includes the Lammermuir Hills in the S, and the ancient volcanoes at North Berwick and Traprain. Much of the urban and industrial development is in the NW and N of the area. Rivers include Whitehead Water, the Tyne, Peffer Burn and Gifford Water.

East Renfrewshire *E.Renf.* Population: 89,311.
Unitary authority in SW Scotland bounded by East Ayrshire, Glasgow, Inverclyde, North Ayrshire, Renfrewshire and South Lanarkshire. The principal centres are Newton Mearns, Clarkston,

Barrhead and Giffnock, which lie on the S periphery of Greater Glasgow. Over two-thirds of East Renfrewshire is farmland; the rest being mostly residential, with some light industry.

East Riding of Yorkshire *E.Riding* Population: 314,113.
Unitary authority on the E coast of England neighbouring Kingston upon Hull, North Lincolnshire, North Yorkshire, South Yorkshire and York. The chief centres are Bridlington, Beverley, Goole, Great Driffield, Hornsea, Brough, Hedon and Withernsea. The area is mostly low-lying, except for the central ridge which forms part of The Wolds. The coastline is subject to much erosion, with material being moved from Flamborough Head to the large spit of Spurn Head, at the mouth of the River Humber. Key industries in the area include agriculture, aerospace, gas and oil industries.

East Sussex *E.Suss.* Population: 492,324.
County of SE England bounded by Brighton & Hove, Kent, Surrey, West Sussex and the English Channel. Main towns are Eastbourne, Hastings, Bexhill, Seaford, Crowborough, Hailsham, Peacehaven and the county town of Lewes; Rye is a small historic town in the E of the county. In the W, the coast is backed by the chalk ridge of the South Downs, ending with the white cliffs of the Seven Sisters and Beachy Head, just W of Eastbourne. E of this point, there are extensive areas of reclaimed marshland, which provide good sheep-grazing. Inland is the heavily wooded Weald, a former centre of the iron industry, interspersed with hill ridges, the largest being the open heathland of Ashdown Forest. Rivers, none large, include the Cuckmere, Ouse, Rother, and upper reaches of the Medway.
Districts: Eastbourne; Hastings; Lewes; Rother; Wealden.

Edinburgh *Edin.* Population: 448,624.
Unitary authority on the E coast of central Scotland surrounding the city of Edinburgh and neighbouring East Lothian, Midlothian, West Lothian and the sea at the Firth of Forth. Edinburgh as the capital of Scotland, is a major administrative, cultural, commercial and tourist centre. It contains most of Scotland's national and cultural institutions. Its historic core is centred around Edinburgh Castle and the Royal Mile, attracting much tourism. The city is also a centre for education and scientific research; other important industries are electronics and food and drink production. The river Water of Leith runs through the city to the docks at Leith.

Essex *Essex* Population: 1,310,835.
County of SE England bounded by Cambridgeshire, Greater London, Hertfordshire, Southend, Suffolk, Thurrock and the sea at the Thames estuary and North Sea. Chief towns are Basildon, the county town of Chelmsford, Colchester, Harlow, Brentwood, Clacton-on-Sea, Loughton, Canvey Island, Billericay and Braintree. The landscape is mostly flat or gently undulating, and the low-lying coast is deeply indented with river estuaries. Along the county's S and W sides, there is a concentration of urban development, with a mixture of light engineering and service industries. In the N and central parts are farmlands, orchards, market and nursery gardens. The NE coast has the busy passenger and container port of Harwich, and the popular seaside resort of Clacton-on-Sea. Rivers include the Stour, forming part of the boundary with Suffolk, the Lea, forming part of the boundary with Hertfordshire, and the Blackwater.
Districts: Basildon; Braintree; Brentwood; Castle Point; Chelmsford; Colchester; Epping Forest; Harlow; Maldon; Rochford; Tendring; Uttlesford.

Falkirk *Falk.* Population: 145,191.
Unitary authority in central Scotland surrounding Falkirk and neighbouring Clackmannanshire, Fife, North Lanarkshire, Stirling and West Lothian. Main towns are Falkirk, Grangemouth, Polmont, Stenhousemuir and Bo'ness. Petrochemical and chemical industries are important to the local economy, as well as bus manufacturing, toffees and paper-making. The Firth of Forth borders Falkirk to the N. Other rivers include the Carron and Pow Burn.

Fermanagh *Ferm.* Population: 57,527.
One third of this district is water, mainly taken up by Upper and Lower Lough Erne. Consequently, there are around 150 inland islands, and the population density is one of the lowest in Northern Ireland. Large areas have been planted with conifers for timber. The north-west and south-west boundaries border the Republic of Ireland. The main town of Enniskillen lies on

the River Erne at the junction of the two major loughs and other towns include Irvinestown, Rosslea and Lisnaskea. Main industries are agriculture and tourism, engineering and timber milling.

Fife *Fife* Population: 349,429.
Unitary authority in E Scotland neighbouring Clackmannanshire and Perth & Kinross, and lying between the Firth of Tay and Firth of Forth. Main towns are Dunfermline, Kirkcaldy, Glenrothes, Buckhaven, Cowdenbeath and St. Andrews. Fife comprises the former county of the same name, known since ancient times as the Kingdom of Fife, and is noted for its fine coastline with many distinctive small towns and fishing ports. The historic town of St. Andrews, on the coast between the two firths, is a university town, and the home of the world's premier golf club. Inland, the area is outstandingly fertile, with agriculture being an important industry. The SW of the area is a former coal-mining area.

Flintshire (Sir y Fflint). *Flints.* Population: 148,594.
Unitary authority in N Wales neighbouring Conwy, Denbighshire, Wrexham, Cheshire West & Chester and the mouth of the River Dee. Main towns are Buckley, Connah's Quay, Flint, Hawarden, Shotton, Queensferry, Mold and Holywell. Known as the Gateway to N Wales, the landscape varies from the mountains which form the Clwydian Range, to small villages and woodlands.

Glasgow *Glas.* Population: 577,869.
Unitary authority in SW Scotland surrounding Glasgow and bounded by East Dunbartonshire, East Renfrewshire, North Lanarkshire, Renfrewshire, South Lanarkshire and West Dunbartonshire. Glasgow is Scotland's largest city and its principal industrial and shopping centre. The city developed significantly due to heavy industry, notably shipbuilding, being centred on the Clyde. While such industry has declined, Glasgow has emerged as a major cultural centre of Europe, due to its impressive arts and cultural scene. The River Clyde runs through the city.

Gloucestershire *Glos.* Population: 564,559.
County of W England bounded by Herefordshire, Oxfordshire, South Gloucestershire, Swindon, Warwickshire, Wiltshire, Worcestershire and the Welsh authority of Monmouthshire. Main centres are the cathedral city and county town of Gloucester and the towns of Cheltenham, Stroud, Cirencester and Dursley. The limestone mass of the Cotswold Hills dominates the centre of the county, and provides the characteristic pale golden stone of many of its buildings. The River Severn forms a wide valley to the W, ending in a long tidal estuary, beyond which are the hills of the Forest of Dean. Industry is centred on the fertile Severn Vale, with aerospace, light engineering, food production, and service industries in and around the towns; in rural areas market gardening and orchards dominate. The River Thames rises in the county, and forms part of its S boundary in the vicinity of Lechlade. Apart from the Severn and the Thames, there is the River Wye, which forms part of the boundary with Monmouthshire, and many smaller rivers, among them the Chelt, Coln, Evenlode, Leach, Leadon, and Windrush.
Districts: Cheltenham; Cotswold; Forest of Dean; Gloucester; Stroud; Tewkesbury.

Greater London *Gt.Lon.* Population: 7,172,091.
Former metropolitan county of 32 boroughs and the City of London which together form the conurbation of London, the capital of the UK. Greater London is the largest financial, commercial, cultural, distribution and communications centre in the country, including all but primary industrial sectors. London developed from the City of London, a walled Roman settlement on the Thames, and Westminster, which was a Saxon religious settlement and later a Norman seat of government. The Great Fire of 1666 destroyed most of the medieval city, and was followed by a period of rebuilding and rapid, unplanned expansion. Industrialisation and improved public transport over the last two centuries have caused major suburban growth, and the absorption of most of the surrounding settlements and countryside. Tourism is a major industry, with most attractions situated in and around the historic core, and along the Thames bankside. Other notable tourist areas include Greenwich, Hampstead, Kew and Richmond. Industrial activity is widespread, with major concentrations in the E along the Thames. Leisure facilities include national and major sports stadiums, and many big parks and gardens. Airports at

Heathrow and docklands. The main river is the Thames.
Districts: Barking & Dagenham; Barnet; Bexley; Brent; Bromley; Camden; City of London; City of Westminster; Croydon; Ealing; Enfield; Greenwich; Hackney; Hammersmith & Fulham; Haringey; Harrow; Havering; Hillingdon; Hounslow; Islington; Kensington & Chelsea; Kingston upon Thames; Lambeth; Lewisham; Merton; Newham; Redbridge; Richmond upon Thames; Southwark; Sutton; Tower Hamlets; Waltham Forest; Wandsworth.

Greater Manchester *Gt.Man.* Population: 2,482,328.
Former metropolitan county of NW England neighbouring Blackburn with Darwen, Cheshire East, Derbyshire, Lancashire, Merseyside, Warrington and West Yorkshire. It comprises the near-continuous urban complex which includes the adjoining cities of Manchester and Salford; and towns including Bolton, Stockport, Oldham, Rochdale, Wigan, Bury and Sale. The conurbation is framed by the wild moorland of The Pennines to the N and the Peak District and Cheshire Plain to the S. Development occurred during the 18c and 19c, creating a series of cotton producing textile towns, while Manchester established itself as the commercial and trading hub, later becoming an inland port linked to Liverpool via the canal network. As textile production declined, the industrial base of the area broadened to include brewing, food production, electronics, plastics, printing, light engineering, financial, leisure and service sectors. Retail is based on town shopping centres and malls such as the Arndale and Trafford Centres. There are many major sporting venues in the area, and cultural facilities include the G-MEX centre, numerous universities, museums and galleries and a diverse nightlife. The area is served by Manchester Airport. Main rivers are Irwell and Mersey.
Districts: Bolton; Bury; Manchester; Oldham; Rochdale; Salford; Stockport; Tameside; Trafford; Wigan.

Gwynedd *Gwyn.* Population: 116,843.
Unitary authority in NW Wales bounded by Ceredigion, Conwy, Denbighshire, Isle of Anglesey, Powys and the sea. Main centres are the cathedral city of Bangor, Caernarfon, Ffestiniog, Blaenau Ffestiniog, Llanddeiniolen, Pwllheli, Llanllynfi, Bethesda and Porthmadog. The whole mainland area, except the Lleyn Peninsula in the NW, is extremely mountainous and contains the scenically famous Snowdonia National Park. There is slate-quarrying in the Ffestiniog valley, otherwise sheep-farming and tourism are the principal occupations; the coastline has been much developed for the holiday trade. The area contains many lakes and reservoirs, among them are Llyn Trawsfynedd, Llyn Celyn and Llyn Tegid. Of the many rivers, the Wnion and the Dyfi, which flows through part of the area, are most significant.

Halton *Halton* Population: 118,208.
Unitary authority in NW England neighbouring Cheshire West & Chester, Merseyside and Warrington. The principal towns are Runcorn and Widnes, separated by the River Mersey. The area is industrialised, being dominated by petro-chemicals and chemicals industries due to the nearby salt mines and port facilities.

Hampshire *Hants.* Population: 1,240,103.
County of S England bounded by Bracknell Forest, Dorset, Portsmouth, Southampton, Surrey, West Berkshire, West Sussex, Wiltshire, Wokingham and the English Channel. Main towns are Basingstoke, Gosport, Waterlooville, Farnborough, Aldershot, Eastleigh, Havant, the ancient city and county town of Winchester, Andover and Fleet. The centre of the county consists largely of chalk downs interspersed with fertile valleys. In the SW is the New Forest, while in the NE is the military area centred on Aldershot. The much indented coastline borders The Solent and looks across to the Isle of Wight. Main industries are in the service sector, with chemicals and pharmaceuticals also important. The chief rivers are the Itchen and Test, both chalk streams flowing into Southampton Water, and the Meon flowing into The Solent.
Districts: Basingstoke & Deane; East Hampshire; Eastleigh; Fareham; Gosport; Hart; Havant; New Forest; Rushmoor; Test Valley; Winchester.

Hartlepool *Hart.* Population: 88,611.
Unitary authority on the NE coast of England surrounding Hartlepool and bordering Darlington, Durham, Stockton-on-Tees and the North Sea. Fishing is a major industry and a marina has been created from part of the old docks. The mouth of the River Tees forms part of the E border.

Herefordshire *Here.* Population: 174,871.
Unitary authority in W England bounded by Gloucestershire, Shropshire, Worcestershire and the Welsh authorities of Monmouthshire and Powys. Main centres are the cathedral city of Hereford and the towns of Ross-on-Wye, Leominster and Ledbury. Herefordshire lies between the Malvern Hills to the E and the Black Mountains to the W. It is mainly rural, with dairy farming, orchards and market gardening in evidence. The main river is the Wye, which provides excellent fishing.

Hertfordshire *Herts.* Population: 1,033,977.
S midland county of England bounded by Central Bedfordshire, Buckinghamshire, Cambridgeshire, Essex, Greater London and Luton. Chief centres are Watford, the cathedral city of St. Albans, Hemel Hempstead, Stevenage, Cheshunt, Welwyn Garden City, Hoddesdon, Hitchin, Letchworth and Hatfield; the county town is Hertford. The Chilterns rise along the W border, and there are chalk hills in the N around Royston; otherwise the landscape is mostly flat or gently undulating. There is a mixture of rural and urban life, with agricultural and hi-tech industries represented. While the urban centres in the S lie on the N periphery of the Greater London conurbation, there are many villages with the traditional large green or common. The more urban S part of the county includes a dense network of major roads bypassing, and leading N from London. Rivers include the Colne, Ivel, and Lee.
Districts: Broxbourne; Dacorum; East Herts; Hertsmere; North Hertfordshire; St. Albans; Stevenage; Three Rivers; Watford; Welwyn Hatfield.

Highland *High.* Population: 208,914.
Unitary authority covering a large part of N Scotland and neighbouring Aberdeenshire, Argyll & Bute, Moray and Perth & Kinross. It contains a mixture of mainland and island life, comprising the former districts of Badenoch and Strathspey, Caithness, Inverness, Lochaber, Nairn, Ross and Cromarty, Skye and Lochalsh and Sutherland. Main towns are Inverness, Fort William, Thurso, Nairn, Wick, Alness and Dingwall. Overall, Highland is very sparsely inhabited, being wild and remote in character. It is scenically outstanding, containing as it does part of the Cairngorm Mountains, Ben Nevis, and the North West Highlands. Many of the finest sea and inland lochs in Scotland are also here, such as Loch Ness, Loch Linnhe, Loch Torridon and Loch Broom. The discovery of North Sea oil has made an impact on the towns and villages around the Moray Firth. Elsewhere, tourism, crofting, fishing and skiing are important locally.

Inverclyde *Inclyde* Population: 84,203.
Unitary authority on the W coast of central Scotland, on the S bank of the River Clyde. It is bordered by North Ayrshire, Renfrewshire and the Firth of Clyde. The chief towns are Greenock, Port Glasgow, Gourock and Kilmacolm.

Isle of Anglesey (Sir Ynys Môn). *I.o.A.* Population: 66,829.
Unitary authority island of NW Wales divided from Gwynedd and the mainland by the Menai Strait, and with Holy Island lying to the W. Main towns are Holyhead, Llangefni, Amlwch and Menai Bridge. Anglesey has 125m of coastline and 16 beaches. Agriculture is an important industry to the island, with other industries including aluminium smelting and food processing. Holyhead is an important port terminus for the Republic of Ireland. Rivers include the Braint and Cefni.

Isle of Man *I.o.M.* Population: 76,315.
Self-governing island in the Irish Sea, situated in the centre of the British Isles. The chief towns are Douglas, Ramsey, Peel, Castletown, Port St. Mary, Port Erin and Laxey. Apart from the N tip, the topography is generally mountainous, rising to a peak at Snaefell. The main industries are agriculture, fishing and tourism as well as financial services and manufacturing. The island is synonymous with motorsport, being the home of the internationally renowned Tourist Trophy Circuit. Rivers include the Glen Auldyn and Neb.

Isle of Wight *I.o.W.* Population: 132,731.
County and island with an area of 147 square miles or 381 square km, separated from the S coast of England by The Solent. Chief towns are the capital, Newport, Ryde, Cowes, Shanklin, Sandown, Ventnor and Yarmouth. The island is geologically diverse, composed of sedimentary rocks and contains many important fossil remains. Tourism flourishes owing to the mild climate and the natural beauty of the island. There are Royal associations as Queen Victoria lived and died at Osborne House in the N of the island. There is a strong naval tradition, with the island historically acting as a defence for Portsmouth. Cowes is internationally famous for yachting. There are ferry and hovercraft connections at Cowes, Ryde, and Yarmouth (ferry to Lymington). Chief river is the Medina.

Isles of Scilly *I.o.S.* Population: 2153.
Group of some 140 islands 48m/45km SW of Land's End, Cornwall, of which five are inhabited: Bryher, St. Agnes, St. Martin's, St. Mary's and Tresco. Chief industries are fishing, and the growing of early flowers and vegetables due to the exceptionally mild climate.

Kent *Kent* Population: 1,329,718.
South-easternmost county of England bounded by East Sussex, Greater London, Medway, Surrey and the sea at the Thames estuary and the Strait of Dover. Chief centres are the county town of Maidstone, Royal Tunbridge Wells, Dartford, Margate, Ashford, Gravesend, Folkestone, Sittingbourne, Ramsgate, the cathedral city of Canterbury, Tonbridge and Dover. The chalk ridge of the North Downs runs along the N side, then SE to Folkestone and Dover. The River Medway cuts through the chalk in the vicinity of Maidstone, and there are low lying areas to the E of Canterbury and of Tonbridge, on Romney Marsh in the S, and bordering the Thames estuary in the N. Chief industrial areas are around Maidstone, Ashford and Tonbridge; Dover and Folkestone are major ports, with the Channel Tunnel terminus to the N of Folkestone; Sheerness is a port of growing importance. Industrial activity includes mineral extraction, cement manufacture and papermaking. On the highly productive agricultural land, Kent's reputation as the Garden of England is earned, with market gardening, fruit and hop production. Romney Marsh is used for extensive sheep-grazing. Rivers include the Medway, Stour, and Beult.
Districts: Ashford; Canterbury; Dartford; Dover; Gravesham; Maidstone; Sevenoaks; Shepway; Swale; Thanet; Tonbridge & Malling; Tunbridge Wells.

Kingston upon Hull *Hull* Population: 243,589.
Unitary authority on the E coast of England surrounding the city of Kingston upon Hull and bounded by East Riding of Yorkshire and the mouth of the River Humber. Kingston upon Hull is a major sea port and a great industrial city, with key industries including chemicals, food processing, pharmaceuticals and engineering. The River Hull passes through the area, and the River Humber forms the S border.

Lancashire *Lancs.* Population: 1,134,974.
County of NW England bounded by Blackburn with Darwen, Cumbria, Greater Manchester, Merseyside, North Yorkshire, West Yorkshire and the Irish Sea. Chief centres are the administrative city of Preston, Burnley, Morecambe, the historic county town of Lancaster, Skelmersdale, Lytham St. Anne's, Leyland, Accrington and Chorley; Fleetwood and Heysham are ports. The inland side of the county is hilly and includes the wild and impressive Forest of Bowland. The W side contains the coastal plain, where vegetables are extensively cultivated. The S is largely urban; industries include cotton spinning and weaving, chemicals, glass, rubber, electrical goods, and motor vehicles. The principal rivers are the Lune and the Ribble.
Districts: Burnley; Chorley; Fylde; Hyndburn; Lancaster; Pendle; Preston; Ribble Valley; Rossendale; South Ribble; West Lancashire; Wyre.

Larne *Larne* Population: 30,832.
On the east coast of Northern Ireland, Larne port is one of the main points of entry to Northern Ireland and is also an important centre for freight. The northern part of the district contains the southern tip of the Antrim Hills and the coastline has an amazing range of geological features, from the most ancient rocks, to remains from the last glaciation. Other towns include Carnlough, Ballygalley and Portmuck on the coast, and Kilwaughter, Ballynure and Ballycarry inland. Industries are based around freight, agriculture and tourism.

Leicester *Leic.* Population: 279,921.
Unitary authority in central England surrounding Leicester and bounded by Leicestershire. It is one of the leading shopping

regions in the Midlands. Traditional industries such as hosiery and footwear, as well as hi-tech industries, are important to the local economy. Leicester is aiming to be one of the most environmentally-friendly cities in Europe. It is involved in pioneering electronic toll road schemes in order to encourage the use of public transport. The Rivers Sence and Soar run through the area.

Leicestershire *Leics.* Population: 609,578.
Midland county of England bounded by Derbyshire, Leicester, Lincolnshire, Northamptonshire, Nottinghamshire, Rutland, Staffordshire and Warwickshire. Chief towns are Loughborough, Hinckley, Wigston, Coalville, Melton Mowbray, Oadby, Market Harborough, Shepshed and Ashby de la Zouch. The landscape is mostly of low, rolling hills. E and W of Leicester are areas of higher ground, notably Charnwood Forest. The W is largely industrial; industries include light engineering, hosiery, and footwear. The E is rural, with large fields and scattered woods, and is noted for field sports and food production. Part of the legacy left by the Roman occupation of Leicestershire are the Great North Road, Watling Street and Fosse Way which dissect the county. River Soar traverses the county from S to N, while River Welland forms part of the boundary with Northamptonshire to the S.
Districts: Blaby; Charnwood; Harborough; Hinckley & Bosworth; Melton; North West Leicestershire; Oadby & Wigston.

Limavady *Limavady* Population: 32,422.
There are two AONBs in this district, which contains the Sperrin mountains to the south and the wide, fertile valley of the river Roe in the centre. To the north is Lough Foyle and the long, sandy beach of Magilligan Strand. Main towns are Limavady, Dungiven and Ballykelly and a car ferry runs across Lough Foyle from Magilligan Point to the Inishowen Peninsula in the Republic of Ireland. Industries include agriculture, services, small-scale manufacturing, construction and tourism.

Lincolnshire *Lincs.* Population: 646,645.
County of E England bounded by Cambridgeshire, Leicestershire, Norfolk, Northamptonshire, North East Lincolnshire, North Lincolnshire, Nottinghamshire, Peterborough, Rutland and the North Sea. Main towns are the cathedral city and county town of Lincoln and the towns of Boston, Grantham, Gainsborough, Spalding, Stamford, Skegness and Louth. Much of the county is flat and includes a large area of The Fens in the S. This reclaimed marshland is richly fertile, producing large crops of peas (for canning), sugar beet, potatoes, corn, and around Spalding, flower bulbs. Two ranges of hills traverse the county N and S: the narrow limestone ridge, a continuation of the Cotswold Hills, running from Grantham to Scunthorpe, and the chalk Wolds, about 12m/20km wide, running N from Spilsby and Horncastle. Apart from agriculture, industries include manufacture of agricultural machinery and tourism, which is centred on historic Lincoln, and the coastal resorts of Skegness and Mablethorpe. The rivers, of which the chief are the Witham and Welland, are largely incorporated into the extensive land-drainage system, and scarcely distinguishable from man-made channels.
Districts: Boston; East Lindsey; Lincoln; North Kesteven; South Holland; South Kesteven; West Lindsey.

Lisburn *Lisburn* Population: 108,694.
This district borders Belfast in the east and touches Lough Neagh in the west. Lisburn city itself sits in the valley of the River Lagan, with other towns being Dunmurry, Hillsborough, Magheraberry and Derriaghy. The Giants' Ring is a massive 656 feet (200m) diameter earthwork near the village of Drumbo. Industries include textiles (linen) and light engineering.

Londonderry/Derry *London.* Population: 105,066.
The city of Londonderry (Derry) is an important seaport and the second city of Northern Ireland, sitting astride the wide estuary of the river Foyle. The city walls, erected in 1619, are complete and some of the finest in Europe. Other towns include New Buildings and Eglinton, with several small villages scattered in the rural areas. In the south, are the forested glens of the Sperrin Mountains. Agriculture is the main industry, along with textiles (linen), distilling and chemicals.

Luton *Luton* Population: 184,371.
Unitary authority in SE England surrounding Luton and bounded by Central Bedfordshire and Hertfordshire. Luton is one of the major centres of employment and manufacturing in SE England, with automotive, electrical and retail industries among the most important. The production and export of high fashion and straw hats remains a feature of the local economy. London Luton Airport is situated in the SE of the area, and the River Lea rises nearby.

Magherafelt *Magh.* Population: 39,780.
The Sperrin Mountains form the western boundary and the River Bann, the eastern. The main town of Magherafelt is the administrative and marketing centre of the district and is also well known for its arts festival. Other small towns include Maghera and Draperstown. Agriculture is the main industry, along with some manufacturing and construction.

Medway *Med.* Population: 249,488.
Unitary authority on SE coast of England S of the River Thames estuary and neighbouring Kent. The chief centres are Gillingham, the naval base of Chatham, Strood and the cathedral city of Rochester. The S part of the area, surrounding the River Medway, is largely urban and industrialised. The marshland to the N includes Kingsnorth Power Station and the Isle of Grain, but is mostly rural, and contains Northward Hill Nature Reserve which is a haven for birds.

Merseyside *Mersey.* Population: 1,362,026.
Former metropolitan county of NW England. It neighbours Cheshire West & Chester, Greater Manchester, Halton, Lancashire, Warrington and the sea. It comprises the near-continuous urban complex which includes the city of Liverpool and the towns of St. Helens, Birkenhead, Southport, Bootle, Wallasey, Bebington, Huyton and Crosby. The county straddles the long, wide estuary of the River Mersey, which accounts for the development of the area. During the 18c, growing Imperial trade of goods and slaves, led to the explosion of urban development surrounding the docks at Liverpool, Birkenhead and Bootle. Liverpool went on to become Britain's premier transatlantic port and a significant terminus during the migration flows of the 19c, leading to an ethnically diverse city culture. Over the last century the docks have declined, leaving behind an impressive waterfront and cityscape as testament to a mercantile and maritime heritage. Inland, the urban spread has reached the industrial town of St. Helens which is famed for glass production. To the N are the residential areas of Crosby, Formby and the coastal resort of Southport. The area includes race courses at Aintree and Haydock, and an airport at Speke.
Districts: Knowsley; Liverpool; St. Helens; Sefton; Wirral.

Merthyr Tydfil *M.Tyd.* Population: 55,981.
Unitary authority in S Wales bounded by Caerphilly, Powys and Rhondda Cynon Taff. Main centres are the town of Merthyr Tydfil and the villages of Treharris, Abercanaid and Troedyrhiw. The area stretches from the Brecon Beacons, along the Taff Valley, to the centre of the former Welsh coal mining district. The local economy has diversified from primary industry, with Merthyr Tydfil being an important centre for public administration, shopping and employment for the region. The River Taff flows through the area.

Middlesbrough *Middbro.* Population: 134,855.
Unitary authority in NE England surrounding Middlesbrough and bounded by North Yorkshire, Redcar & Cleveland and Stockton-on-Tees. Middlesbrough is an industrial town, with chemical and petro-chemical industries in evidence. It is also an important sub-regional shopping and entertainment centre between Leeds and Newcastle upon Tyne.

Midlothian *Midloth.* Population: 80,941.
Unitary authority in central Scotland neighbouring East Lothian, Edinburgh and Scottish Borders. Main towns are Penicuik, Bonnyrigg, Dalkeith, Gorebridge and Loanhead. The area is mostly rural, including the rolling moorland of the Pentland Hills and Moorfoot Hills in the S. To the N, the urban area is comprised of satellite towns to the SE of Edinburgh. Rivers include Tyne Water and South Esk.

Milton Keynes *M.K.* Population: 207,057.
S midland unitary authority of England bounded by Bedford,

Central Bedfordshire, Buckinghamshire and Northamptonshire. The area includes the city of Milton Keynes, Bletchley, Newport Pagnell, Great Linford, Stony Stratford and Wolverton. Over the past 30 years, the area has undergone the fastest rate of growth in the country, attracting numerous industries. The Great Ouse and Ouzel rivers pass through the area.

Monmouthshire (Sir Fynwy). *Mon.* Population: 84,885.
Unitary authority in SE Wales bounded by Blaenau Gwent, Newport, Powys, Torfaen, the English areas of Gloucestershire, Herefordshire and the Bristol Channel. The main towns are Abergavenny, Caldicot, Chepstow and Monmouth. Part of the Brecon Beacons are found in NW Monmouthshire, whereas the SW area is mainly flat. Agriculture, mineral extraction and the service sector are important to the local economy. Rivers include the Wye, which forms part of E border, and the Usk, Trothy and Monnow.

Moray *Moray* Population: 86,940.
Unitary authority in N Scotland neighboured by Aberdeenshire, Highland and the sea. Main towns are Elgin, Forres, Buckie, Lossiemouth and Keith. The area is mainly mountainous, including part of the Cairngorm Mountains in the S. It is dissected by many deep river valleys, most notably that of the River Spey. Along with the local grain and peat, the abundant waters provide the raw materials for half of Scotland's malt whisky distilleries, leading to the Whisky Trail and much tourism through Speyside.

Moyle *Moyle* Population: 15,933.
This is Northern Ireland's smallest district by population but it is famous for the amazing basalt columns of the Giant's Causeway on the north coast, a UNESCO World Heritage Site. The entire Causeway Coast has been designated as an AONB. Ballycastle is the largest town, others being Cushendun, Cushendall and Bushmills, which has the world's oldest licensed distillery. Off the north coast is Rathlin Island where Northern Ireland's largest seabird colony breeds under the management of the RSPB. The main industry is agriculture, with some light industry and tourism.

Neath Port Talbot (Castell-nedd Port Talbot). *N.P.T.* Population: 134,468.
Unitary authority in S Wales neighbouring Bridgend, Powys, Rhondda Cynon Taff, Swansea and the sea. The chief centres are Neath, Port Talbot, Pontardawe, Baglan, Glyncorrwg and Briton Ferry. The area is mostly mountainous, divided up by the river valleys of the Tawe, Neath, Afan and Dulais, which all flow out to sea at Swansea Bay. The lower valley of the River Neath is heavily industrialised.

Newport (Casnewydd). *Newport* Population: 137,011.
Unitary authority on the S coast of Wales, N of the mouth of the River Severn, and bounded by Caerphilly, Cardiff, Monmouthshire and Torfaen. Main centres are Newport, Liswerry, Malpas and Caerleon. Steel manufacturing and hi-tech industries are important to the local economy. The rivers Ebbw and Usk run through the area.

Newry & Mourne *N. & M.* Population: 87,058.
Bordering the Republic of Ireland on its southern edge, the district contains the beautiful Mourne mountains in the east and has two areas designated as AONBs. Newry is the main town and has been an important centre for cross-border trade development. Warrenpoint is a modern port. Other towns include Killkeel, with its important fishing industry, Rostrevor, Bessbrook and Annalong. Besides fishing, industries are mainly agriculture and tourism.

Newtownabbey *Newtown.* Population: 79,995.
Bordering the north-western shore of Belfast Lough, this small district is a mix of the urban and rural. It has a high population density compared to the rest of Northern Ireland. The main town is Newtownabbey, others being Ballyclare, which hosts one of the oldest horse fairs in Ireland, Mossley and Mallusk which is a busy commercial centre. There are many small businesses in the area as well as agriculture.

Norfolk *Norf.* Population: 796,728.
County of E England bounded by Cambridgeshire, Lincolnshire, Suffolk and the North Sea. Chief centres are the cathedral city and county town of Norwich, Great Yarmouth on the E coast, the expanding port of King's Lynn near the mouth of the Great Ouse and The Wash, Thetford, which is known as the Breckland 'capital', East Dereham and Wymondham. Norfolk is mainly flat or gently undulating, with fenland in the W characterised by large drainage channels emptying into The Wash. In the SW is Breckland, an expanse of heath and conifer forest used for military training; other afforested areas are near King's Lynn and North Walsham. NE of Norwich are The Broads, an area of meres and rivers popular for boating; reeds for thatching are grown here. The N Norfolk coastline is an Area of Outstanding Natural Beauty and Heritage Coast, and includes the popular resorts of Cromer and Sheringham. Otherwise the county is almost entirely agricultural, with farming an important activity; service and manufacturing industries are also significant. Rivers include the Great Ouse, Bure, Nar, Wensum, Wissey, and Yare; the Little Ouse and Waveney both enter the county briefly, but mainly form the boundary with Suffolk.
Districts: Breckland; Broadland; Great Yarmouth; King's Lynn & West Norfolk; North Norfolk; Norwich; South Norfolk.

North Ayrshire *N.Ayr.* Population: 135,817.
Unitary authority in central Scotland including the islands of Arran, Great Cumbrae and Little Cumbrae. It is bounded by East Ayrshire, East Renfrewshire, Inverclyde, Renfrewshire, South Ayrshire and the sea. The principal towns are Irvine, Kilwinning, Saltcoats, Largs, Ardrossan, Stevenston and Kirbirnie. The area includes mountains and part of Clyde Muirshiel Regional Park in the N, and the lower lands of Cunninghame in the S. There is a maritime heritage to the area; ferry routes operate from Largs and Ardrossan. Rivers include the Garnock, Dusk Water and Noddsdale Water.

North Down *N.Down* Population: 76,323.
On the southern shore of Belfast Lough, this is another high population density district. The main town of Bangor is an important maritime resort with a large, modern marina and shopping centre. Other towns are Helen's Bay and Holywood. Main industries include light engineering, food processing, retail and tourism.

North East Lincolnshire *N.E.Lincs.* Population: 157,979.
Unitary authority in NE England, S of the mouth of the River Humber and bounded by Lincolnshire, North Lincolnshire and the North Sea. Chief towns are Grimsby, Cleethorpes and Immingham. Grimsby and Cleethorpes together are the shopping and commercial centres of the area. Fishing, food, tourism, chemical and port industries are all important to the local economy. The main rivers are the Humber and Freshney.

North Lanarkshire *N.Lan.* Population: 321,067.
Unitary authority in central Scotland neighbouring East Dunbartonshire, Falkirk, Glasgow, South Lanarkshire, Stirling and West Lothian. The chief centres are Cumbernauld, Coatbridge, Airdrie, Motherwell, Wishaw and Bellshill. North Lanarkshsire contains a mixture of urban and rural areas, and formerly depended heavily upon the coal, engineering and steel industries. Regeneration and diversification have occurred in recent years.

North Lincolnshire *N.Lincs.* Population: 152,849.
Unitary authority in NE England neighbouring East Riding of Yorkshire, Leicestershire, Norfolk, North East Lincolnshire, Nottinghamshire, Peterborough, Rutland, South Yorkshire and the River Humber. The main centres are Scunthorpe, Bottesford, Barton-upon-Humber and Brigg. The area is mainly rural, but does include oil refineries, steel and manufacturing industries; the River Humber provides pool and wharf facilities. Rivers include the Humber, Trent and the Old Ancholme.

North Somerset *N.Som.* Population: 188,564.
Unitary authority in W England, S of the mouth of the River Severn, and neighbouring Bath & North East Somerset, Bristol, Somerset and the Bristol Channel. Chief towns are Weston-super-Mare, Clevedon, Nailsea and Portishead. The area is largely rural with tourism, centred on the coastal resort of Weston-super-Mare, being a major industry. Bristol International Airport is located in the E of the area.

North Yorkshire *N.Yorks.* Population: 569,660.
Large county of N England bounded by Cumbria, Darlington,

Durham, East Riding of Yorkshire, Lancashire, Middlesbrough, Redcar & Cleveland, South Yorkshire, Stockton-on-Tees, West Yorkshire, York and the North Sea. Main centres are Harrogate, Scarborough, Hetton, Selby, the cathedral city of Ripon, the county town of Northallerton, Whitby, Skipton and Knaresborough. Apart from the wide plain around York, through which flow River Ouse and its tributaries, and the smaller Vale of Pickering, watered by the Derwent and its tributary the Rye, the county is dominated by two ranges of hills; The Pennines in the W and the Cleveland Hills in the NE. The plains are pastoral and agricultural, while the hills provide rough sheep-grazing. The county includes the popular resorts of Scarborough and Whitby, and the majority of the North York Moors and Yorkshire Dales National Parks which promote tourism. Other economic activities include light engineering, service and hi-tech industries. Principal rivers are the Ouse, fed by the Derwent, Swale, Ure, Nidd and Wharfe, and draining into the Humber; the Esk, flowing into the North Sea at Whitby; and in the W, the Ribble, passing out into Lancashire and the Irish Sea.

Districts: Craven; Hambleton; Harrogate; Richmondshire; Ryedale; Scarborough; Selby.

Northamptonshire *Northants.* Population: 629,676.
Midland county of England bounded by Bedford, Buckinghamshire, Cambridgeshire, Leicestershire, Lincolnshire, Milton Keynes, Oxfordshire, Peterborough, Rutland and Warwickshire. Chief towns are Northampton, Corby, Kettering, Wellingborough, Rushden and Daventry. The county consists largely of undulating agricultural country rising locally to low hills, especially along the W border. Large fields and scattered woods provide terrain for field sports. Northamptonshire still retains its rural and agricultural charm, despite undergoing rapid population growth recently. There are many villages of architectural, scenic and historic interest. Industrial development is modest, concentrating on the traditional footwear manufacture. Corby is undergoing regeneration following the decline of its steel industry. Tourism is set to increase due to the county's natural Middle England ambience, and the seasonal opening of the Althorp Estate, the family home and resting place of Diana, Princess of Wales. The principal rivers are the Nene and Welland.

Districts: Corby; Daventry; East Northamptonshire; Kettering; Northampton; South Northamptonshire; Wellingborough.

Northumberland *Northumb.* Population: 307,190.
Northernmost unitary authority of England bounded by Cumbria, Durham and Tyne & Wear, the Scottish authority of Scottish Borders and the North Sea. The principal towns are Blyth, Ashington, Cramlington, Bedlington, Morpeth, Berwick-upon-Tweed, Prudhoe and Hexham. There is some industry in the SE coastal area, otherwise it is almost entirely rural, the greater part being high moorland, culminating in the Cheviot Hills along the Scottish border. The most spectacular stretches of Hadrian's Wall traverse the area to the N of Haltwhistle and Hexham. There is extensive afforestation, including Kielder Forest Park and part of the Northumberland National Park in the NW; parts of these forests are used for military training. The large reservoir, Kielder Water, also occurs in the NW of the area. Rivers include the Aln, Blyth, Breamish, Coquet, East and West Allen, North and South Tyne, Till, and Wansbeck. The Tweed forms part of the Scottish border and flows out to sea at Berwick-upon-Tweed.

Nottingham *Nott.* Population: 266,988.
Unitary authority in central England surrounding the city of Nottingham and bounded by Nottinghamshire. The city of Nottingham has a long history, having been granted many Royal Charters; Nottingham Castle and Wollaton Hall are among its many historical buildings. It is also an industrial and engineering centre, and a university city. Its main industries include the manufacture of chemicals, tobacco, cycles, lace and hosiery. The River Trent flows through the city.

Nottinghamshire *Notts.* Population: 748,510.
Midland county of England bounded by Derbyshire, Leicestershire, Lincolnshire, North Lincolnshire, Nottingham and South Yorkshire. Principal towns are Mansfield, Carlton, Sutton in Ashfield, Arnold, Worksop, Newark-on-Trent, West Bridgford, Beeston, Stapleford, Hucknall and Kirkby in Ashfield. Much of the county is rural, with extensive woodlands in the central area of The Dukeries, part of the larger Sherwood

Forest. Cattle-grazing is the chief farming activity. Around the large towns there is much industry, including iron and steel, engineering, knitwear, pharmaceuticals, and coal-mining. The county has associations with Robin Hood, at Sherwood Forest, and D.H. Lawrence, at Eastwood. The most important river is the Trent.

Districts: Ashfield; Bassetlaw; Broxtowe; Gedling; Mansfield; Newark & Sherwood; Rushcliffe.

Omagh *Omagh.* Population: 47,952.
One of the largest districts by area of Northern Ireland, the borders are mainly hills, with the town of Omagh in a central valley, at the confluence of several rivers where almost one third of the total population live. The area is primarily rural, with small towns and villages scattered throughout the landscape. These include Fintona, Dromore and Carrickmore. Agriculture is the main industry.

Orkney *Ork.* Population: 19,245.
Group of some fifteen main islands and numerous smaller islands, islets and rocks. Designated an Islands Area for administrative purposes, and lying N of the NE end of the Scottish mainland across the Pentland Firth. Kirkwall is the capital, situated on the island Mainland, 24m/38km N of Duncansby Head. Stromness is the only other town. About twenty of the islands are inhabited. In general the islands are low-lying but have steep, high cliffs on W side. The climate is generally mild for the latitude but storms are frequent. Fishing and farming (mainly cattle-rearing) are the chief industries. The oil industry is also represented, with an oil terminal on the island of Flotta, and oil service bases at Car Ness and Stromness, Mainland and at Lyness, Hoy. Lesser industries include whisky distilling, knitwear and tourism. The islands are noted for their unique prehistoric and archaeological remains. The main airport is at Grimsetter, near Kirkwall, with most of the populated islands being served by airstrips. Ferries also operate from the Scottish mainland, and between islands in the group.

Oxfordshire *Oxon.* Population: 605,488.
S midland county of England bounded by Buckinghamshire, Gloucestershire, Northamptonshire, Reading, Swindon, Warwickshire, West Berkshire, Wiltshire and Wokingham. Chief centres are the county town, cathedral and university city of Oxford and towns of Banbury, Abingdon, Bicester, Witney, Didcot, Thame and Henley-on-Thames. Burford and Chipping Norton are small Cotswold towns in the W and NW respectively. The landscape is predominantly flat or gently undulating, forming part of the Thames Valley. High ground occurs where the Chiltern Hills enter the county in the SE and the Cotswold Hills in the NW. The county is largely agricultural, with industries centred on the towns. Scientific, medical and research establishments are attracted by the proximity of Oxford's universities. Printing and publishing industries have their greatest concentration outside London. The motor industry is well represented with car manufacture at Cowley, Oxford, and the county has the world's largest concentration of performance car development and manufacturing. Tourism, attracted to stately homes, notably Blenheim Palace, and Oxford city centre, is also important. Chief rivers are the Thames (or Isis), Cherwell, Ock, Thame, and Windrush.

Districts: Cherwell; Oxford; South Oxfordshire; Vale of White Horse; West Oxfordshire.

Pembrokeshire (Sir Benfro). *Pembs.* Population: 114,131.
Unitary authority in the SW corner of Wales neighbouring Carmarthenshire, Ceredigion and the sea. The chief centres are Haverfordwest, Pembroke Dock, Pembroke, Tenby, Saundersfoot, Neyland, Fishguard and the ancient cathedral city of St. David's. Key industries are tourism, agriculture and oil refining. The deep estuarial waters of Milford Haven provide a berth for oil tankers. A large part of Pembrokeshire's coastline forms Britain's only coastal National Park. Ferries sail from Fishguard and Pembroke Dock to Rosslare in the Republic of Ireland.

Perth & Kinross *P. & K.* Population: 134,949.
Unitary authority in Scotland bounded by Aberdeenshire, Angus, Argyll & Bute, Clackmannanshire, Fife, Highland and Stirling. Chief centres are the city of Perth, Blairgowrie, Crieff, Kinross, Auchterader and Pitlochry. The area is mountainous, containing large areas of remote open moorland, especially in the N and W; the vast upland expanses of Breadalbane, Rannoch and Atholl,

form the S edge of the Grampian Mountains. The lower land of the S and E is more heavily populated and is dominated by the ancient city of Perth. The area is rich in history as it links the Highlands to the N with the central belt and lowlands to the S via important mountain passes, most notably the Pass of Dromochter. The area has many castles, and Scottish Kings were traditionally enthroned at Scone Abbey, to the N of Perth. There are many lochs, including Loch Rannoch and Loch Tay. Main industries are tourism and whisky production. The world famous Gleneagles golf course is in the S of the area. Rivers include the Tay, Almond and Earn.

Peterborough *Peter.* Population: 156,061.
Unitary authority in E England neighbouring Cambridgeshire, Lincolnshire, Northamptonshire and Rutland. The area includes the city of Peterborough, which lies at the heart of an important agricultural area. Developing as a railway hub, it has become a major industrial, distribution and shopping centre. The River Nene passes through Peterborough.

Plymouth *Plym.* Population: 240,720.
Unitary authority on the SW coast of England surrounding the city of Plymouth and neighbouring Cornwall and Devon. Plymouth stands at the mouth of the River Tamar and is the largest city on the S coast of England. It has strong mercantile and naval traditions; it is closely linked with Sir Francis Drake, and has maintained a Royal Naval Dockyard for 300 years. Plymouth is a regional shopping centre and a popular resort.

Poole *Poole* Population: 138,288.
Unitary authority on S coast of England surrounding Poole and bordered by Bournemouth and Dorset. Poole Harbour is the second largest natural harbour in the world, which enabled Poole to prosper through trading, especially with Newfoundland. Poole has now attracted a variety of industries including boat-building, fishing, pottery, engineering and electronics. Ferries run to the Channel Islands and France.

Portsmouth *Ports.* Population: 186,701.
Unitary authority on the S coast of England surrounding the city of Portsmouth and bordered by Hampshire. Portsmouth developed as a strategic port around Portsmouth Harbour, and it is still the home of the Royal Navy. It has become a culturally diverse centre, attracting a wide range of industries which include leisure, tourism, financial services, distribution, manufacturing and hi-tech industries.

Powys *Powys* Population: 126,354.
Large unitary authority in central Wales bordering Blaenau Gwent, Caerphilly, Carmarthenshire, Ceredigion, Denbighshire, Gwynedd, Merthyr Tydfil, Monmouthshire, Neath Port Talbot, Rhondda Cynon Taff, Wrexham and the English areas of Herefordshire and Shropshire. Main centres are Newtown, Gurnos, Brecon, Welshpool, Ystradgynlais, Llanllwchaiarn, Llandrindod Wells, Knighton, Llanidloes, Builth Wells and Machynlleth. Powys is almost entirely rural, with mountainous terrain; most of the Brecon Beacons National Park falls within the S part of the area, while the Cambrian Mountains are in the W. There is considerable afforestation, and a number of large reservoirs, including Lake Vyrnwy. To the N of Brecon, on Mynydd Eppynt, is an extensive military training area. Main economic activities are agriculture, which is predominantly based around hill farming. Tourism is significant, owing to the natural beauty of the area, and innovative attractions such as the Centre for Alternative Technology. Industrial development is gradually increasing. Among the many rivers, the largest are the Severn, Usk, and Wye.

Reading *Read.* Population: 143,096.
Unitary authority in S England to W of Greater London, surrounding Reading and bordered by Oxfordshire, West Berkshire, Windsor & Maidenhead and Wokingham. Reading developed as a crossing point of the River Thames and River Kennet. Traditional industries include brewing and food production, notably biscuits. These are accompanied by an increasing sector of hi-tech and computer-based companies, attracted by Reading's location in the M4 corridor. Reading has also established itself as a major entertainments centre.

Redcar & Cleveland *R. & C.* Population: 139,132.
Unitary authority on the NE coast of England neighbouring

Hartlepool, Middlesbrough and North Yorkshire. The main centres are Redcar, South Bank, Eston, Guisborough, Marske-by-the-Sea, Saltburn-by-the-Sea, Loftus and Skelton. The area is one of great contrasts. It combines rural villages, market towns and coastal resorts, along with heavily populated urban areas and industrialised port facilities. Industries include steel-making, due to the local ironstone, and chemicals, based around the River Tees to the NW of the area. The coastal towns attract some tourism. The River Tees forms part of the border to the W.

Renfrewshire *Renf.* Population: 172,867.
Unitary authority in central Scotland bordering East Renfrewshire, Glasgow, Inverclyde, North Ayrshire, West Dunbartonshire and the Firth of Clyde. Main centres are Paisley, Renfrew, Johnstone, Erskine and Linwood. The area emerges W from the Greater Glasgow periphery into a contrasting countryside of highlands, lochs and glens. Industry is centred on the urban area and includes electronics, engineering, food and drink production and service sectors; in rural areas to the W, agriculture is still important. The W part of the area includes some of Clyde Muirshiels Regional Park; Glasgow Airport is in the E.

Rhondda Cynon Taff (Rhondda Cynon Taf). *R.C.T.* Population: 231,946.
Unitary authority in S Wales bounded by Bridgend, Caerphilly, Cardiff, Merthyr Tydfil, Neath Port Talbot, Powys and Vale of Glamorgan. The principal towns are Treorchy, Aberdare, Pontypridd, Ferndale and Mountain Ash. Rhondda Cynon Taff is a mountainous area, dissected by deep narrow valleys, with urbanisation typified by ribbon development. The area was the former heart of the Welsh coal mining industry, and has experienced a sharp economic decline as pits closed. Diversification into light engineering and service sectors are gradually improving the industrial base. Main rivers are the Rhondda and Cynon.

Rutland *Rut.* Population: 34,563.
Unitary authority in E England neighbouring Leicestershire, Lincolnshire, Northamptonshire and Peterborough. The main town is Oakham. Agriculture is the main industry; other important industries are engineering, cement-making, plastics, clothing and tourism. The area includes the large reservoir, Rutland Water, which is an important feature for leisure, tourism and wildlife.

Scottish Borders *Sc.Bord.* Population: 106,764.
Administrative region of SE Scotland bordering Dumfries & Galloway, East Lothian, Midlothian, South Lanarkshire, West Lothian, the English counties of Cumbria and Northumberland and the North Sea. It comprises the former counties of Berwick, Peebles, Roxburgh and Selkirk. Main towns are Hawick, Galashiels, Peebles, Kelso, Selkirk and Jedburgh. It extends from the Tweedsmuir Hills in the W to the North Sea on either side of St. Abb's Head in the E, and from the Pentland, Moorfoot and Lammermuir Hills in the N to the Cheviot Hills and the English border in the S. The fertile area of rich farmland between the hills to N and S is known as The Merse. The area around Peebles and Galashiels is noted for woollen manufacture. Elsewhere, the electronics industry is of growing importance. The River Tweed rises in the extreme W and flows between Kelso and Coldstream, finally passing into England, 4m/6km W of Berwick-upon-Tweed.

Shetland *Shet.* Population: 21,988.
Group of over 100 islands, lying beyond Orkney to the NE of the Scottish mainland; Sumburgh Head being about 100m/160km from Duncansby Head. Designated an Islands Area for administrative purposes, the chief islands are Mainland, on which the capital and chief port of Lerwick is situated, Unst and Yell. Some twenty of the islands are inhabited. The islands are mainly low-lying, the highest point being Ronas Hill, on Mainland. The oil industry has made an impact on Shetland, with oil service bases at Lerwick and Sandwick, and a large terminal at Sullom Voe. Other industries include cattle and sheep-rearing, knitwear and fishing. The climate is mild, considering the latitude, but severe storms are frequent. The islands are famous for the small Shetland breed of pony, which is renowned for its strength and hardiness. There is an airport at Sumburgh, on S part of Mainland.

Shropshire *Shrop.* Population: 283,173.
W midland unitary authority of England bounded by Cheshire
East, Cheshire West & Chester, Herefordshire, Staffordshire,
Telford & Wrekin, Worcestershire and the Welsh authorities of
Powys and Wrexham. Main towns are Shrewsbury, Oswestry,
Bridgnorth, Market Drayton, Ludlow and Whitchurch. The
S and W borders are hilly, with large areas of open moorland,
including The Long Mynd and Wenlock Edge, which provide
good sheep-grazing. Elsewhere the county undulates towards the
Severn Valley, which provides fertile agricultural land served by
prosperous market towns. Agricultural output includes dairy,
poultry and pig farming, along with corn crops. As the former
heart of the Marches of Wales, Shropshire contains the remains of
numerous border defences. There are also the remains of
several monasteries, for instance, at Much Wenlock and Buildwas.
The most important river is the Severn, which flows across the
county from W to SE; others include the Clun, Corve, Perry, Rea
Brook, and Teme.

Slough *Slo.* Population: 119,067.
Unitary authority in SE England to the W of London,
surrounding Slough and bordering Buckinghamshire, Greater
London, Surrey and Windsor & Maidenhead. Slough has
grown significantly over the past 30 years, and is a major
regional shopping centre. Industry is centred on the large
Slough Trading Estate, which was planned after World War
I. Numerous sectors are represented in Slough, among them is
confectionery.

Somerset *Som.* Population: 498,093.
County in SW England bounded by Bath & North East Somerset,
Devon, Dorset, North Somerset, Wiltshire and the Bristol
Channel. The chief centres are the county town of Taunton,
Yeovil, Bridgwater, Frome, Chard, Street, Burnham-on-Sea,
Highbridge, the small cathedral city of Wells, Wellington and
Minehead. Somerset consists of several hill ranges, including
the Mendip, Polden, Quantock, Brendon Hills, along with most
of Exmoor. These uplands are separated by valleys, or, on
either side of the River Parrett, by the extensive marshy flats of
Sedgemoor. Economic activity is mainly based on agriculture
in the fertile vales, with manufacturing, distribution and service
industries centred on the urban areas. Tourism is important with
attractions including Exmoor National Park, a holiday complex
at Minehead and the county's natural rural charm. Somerset
also holds one of Europe's largest music festivals at Glastonbury.
The chief rivers are Axe, Brue, Parrett, and Tone, draining into
the Bristol Channel; and Barle and Exe, rising on Exmoor and
flowing into Devon and the English Channel.
Districts: Mendip; Sedgemoor; South Somerset; Taunton Deane; West
Somerset.

South Ayrshire *S.Ayr.* Population: 112,097.
Unitary authority in SW Scotland bounded by Dumfries &
Galloway, East Ayrshire, North Ayrshire and the sea. The chief
towns are Ayr, Troon, Prestwick, Girvan and Maybole. The
area consists of a long coastline, with lowlands surrounding Ayr
Bay and higher ground to the S. Agriculture is a major economic
activity on the uplands. To the N, aerospace and hi-tech
industries are located near Prestwick International Airport and
Ayr, the main retail centre. Notable sporting venues include a
race course at Ayr and open championship golf courses at Troon
and Turnberry. Tourism is a major feature of the local economy.
The area was the birthplace of Robert the Bruce and Robert
Burns; it contains Scotland's first country park at Culzean Castle;
and it has a holiday camp on the coast near Ayr. Rivers include
the Ayr, Water of Girvan and Stinchar.

South Gloucestershire *S.Glos.* Population: 245,641.
Unitary authority in SW England neighbouring Bath & North
East Somerset, Bristol, Gloucestershire and Wiltshire. The
chief centres are Kingswood, Chipping Sodbury, Mangotsfield,
Frampton Cotterell, Yate, Thornbury, Patchway and Filton.
The S part of the area lies on the N and E fringes of Bristol.
The Cotswold hills are in the E, and the Severn Vale in the W.
Main industries are in the S, and include aerospace
engineering; the N is mainly agricultural. South Gloucestershire
includes the English side of both Severn road bridges.
Badminton Park in the E of the area, is the location for the
Badminton Horse Trials. The River Severn borders the area to
the NW.

South Lanarkshire *S.Lan.* Population: 302,216.
Unitary authority in central Scotland bordering Dumfries &
Galloway, East Ayrshire, East Renfrewshire, Glasgow, North
Lanarkshire, Scottish Borders and West Lothian. The main towns
are East Kilbride, Hamilton, Blantyre, Larkhall, Carluke, Lanark
and Bothwell. Urban development is mainly in the N, merging
with the SE periphery of Greater Glasgow. The S part is mostly
farmland and not highly populated. Tourism is mainly centred
on the picturesque valley of the upper Clyde; there is a race
course at Hamilton. The area has associations with the industrial
philanthropist, Robert Owen, who built a model village at New
Lanark. Rivers include the Clyde, Avon and Dippool Water.

South Yorkshire *S.Yorks.* Population: 1,266,338.
Former metropolitan county of N England bordered by
Derbyshire, East Riding of Yorkshire, North Lincolnshire, North
Yorkshire, Nottinghamshire and West Yorkshire. It comprises
the industrial and urban area around the city of Sheffield and
the towns of Rotherham, Barnsley and Doncaster. Located
at the heart of a major coalfield, South Yorkshire prospered
through the development of heavy industry. Barnsley and
Rotherham were coal mining towns, with steel and fine cutlery
centred on Sheffield. The decline of these industries has led
to the area redefining itself. Sheffield has become a centre of
learning, tourism and conferences, aided by its environmental
improvements. Barnsley, Rotherham and Doncaster have
increased their industrial base, especially via light industries.
Leisure and recreation are an important feature of the area, with
venues including Barnsley's Metrodome, Doncaster's race course
and Dome, and Sheffield's Arena and Don Valley Stadium.
Retail has increased with city and town centre redevelopment,
and the Meadowhall complex. The surrounding countryside
includes country parks at Rother Valley and Thrybergh, with
part of the Peak District National Park W and NW of Sheffield.
The chief river is the Don.
Districts: Barnsley; Doncaster; Rotherham; Sheffield.

Southampton *S'ham.* Population: 217,445.
Unitary authority on the S coast of England surrounding the city
of Southampton, and bordered by Hampshire. Southampton
owes much to the deep waters of Southampton Water, which
have enabled the development of Europe's busiest cruise port.
Water and the waterfront remain very important to the local
economy, with marine technology, oceanography, boat shows
and yacht races all prominent. The city is also a leading media,
recreational, entertainment and retail centre. The chief river is
the Itchen.

Southend *S'end* Population: 160,257.
Unitary authority in SE England, N of the mouth of the River
Thames, surrounding Southend-on-Sea and bordering Essex.
Southend is a commerical, residential, shopping and holiday
centre, with tourism among its main industries. It includes a 7m
shoreline from Leigh-on-Sea to Shoeburyness, a famous pier and
a sea life centre.

Staffordshire *Staffs.* Population: 806,744.
Midland county of England bounded by Cheshire East,
Derbyshire, Leicestershire, Shropshire, Stoke-on-Trent, Telford
& Wrekin, Warwickshire, West Midlands and Worcestershire.
Chief centres are Newcastle-under-Lyme, Tamworth, the county
town of Stafford, Burton upon Trent, Cannock, Burntwood,
the cathedral city of Lichfield, Kidsgrove, Rugeley and Leek.
The urban development occurs around the West Midlands
conurbation in the S, where main industries include engineering,
iron and steel, rubber goods and leather production, while to
the N, there is an urban concentration around Stoke-on-Trent.
Burton upon Trent is noted for brewing. The ancient hunting
forest and former mining district of Cannock Chase is in the
centre of the county and contains preserved tracts of moorland.
In the NE lies part of the Peak District National Park. The rest
of the county is predominantly agricultural, with milk, wheat
and sugar beet produced. To the E of Leek, moorland broken
up by limestone walls extends across the Manifold valley to the
Derbyshire border. In additon to the Trent, which dominates
much of the county, rivers include the Blithe, Manifold, Sow and
Tame. River Dove forms the boundary with Derbyshire.
Districts: Cannock Chase; East Staffordshire; Lichfield;
Newcastle-under-Lyme; South Staffordshire; Stafford; Staffordshire
Moorlands; Tamworth.

Stirling *Stir.* Population: 86,212.

Unitary authority in central Scotland neighbouring Argyll & Bute, Clackmannanshire, East Dunbartonshire, Falkirk, North Lanarkshire, Perth & Kinross and West Dunbartonshire. The chief centres are Stirling, the ancient cathedral city of Dunblane, Bannockburn, Bridge of Allan and Callander. The fertile agricultural lands of the Forth valley are in the centre of the area, bounded by mountains: The Trossachs and the mountain peaks of Ben Lomond, Ben More and Ben Lui in the N, while in the S are the Campsie Fells. Tourism is an important industry with Stirling including many sites of historical significance to Scotland, particularly during the struggle to retain independence. There are associations with Rob Roy, and the battle site of Bannockburn. Other features include The Trossachs, part of the Loch Lomond Regional Park and the Queen Elizabeth Forest Park. There are several lochs, including Loch Lomond, which forms part of the W border, and Loch Katrine. Scotland's only lake named as such, Lake of Menteith, is also in Stirling. The main river is the Forth.

Stockton-on-Tees *Stock.* Population: 178,408.

Unitary authority in NE England neighbouring Darlington, Durham, Hartlepool, Middlesbrough, North Yorkshire and Redcar & Cleveland. The main centres are Stockton-on-Tees, Billingham, Thornaby-on-Tees, Eaglescliffe, Egglescliffe and Yarm. The area has a diverse mix of picturesque villages, large-scale urbanisation and heavy industry. The area has recently undergone major renewal and regeneration, with industries now including electronics, food technology and chemical production. Stockton is the main shopping centre for the area, and includes the Teesside Retail Park. The main river is the Tees, which is controlled by the Tees Barrage. This has created Britain's largest purpose-built whitewater canoeing course.

Stoke-on-Trent *Stoke* Population: 240,636.

Unitary authority in England surrounding the city of Stoke-on-Trent and neighbouring Staffordshire. The city has six town centres: Burslem, Fenton, Hanley, Longton, Stoke-upon-Trent and Tunstall. Hanley is where most current city centre activities are located. The area forms The Potteries, and is the largest claywear producer in the world, although now it is largely a finishing centre for imported pottery. There are a wide variety of other industries, including steel, engineering, paper, glass and furniture. Stoke-on-Trent is a centre of employment, leisure and shopping for the surrounding areas. It is noted for its environmental approach, particularly with land reclamation which accounts for around 10 per cent of the city area; sites include Festival Park, Central Forest Park and Westport Lake. The River Trent flows through the area.

Strabane *Strabane* Population: 38,248.

To the east lie the Sperrin Mountains (an AONB) with the Republic of Ireland border and the River Mourne to the west. The main town of the district is Strabane, an historic market town. Other towns include Castlederg in the Derg valley, Newtonstewart, with Baronscourt Forest nearby, Sion Mills, with its model linen village, Plumbridge and Mount Hamilton. Main industries are agriculture, manufacturing and tourism.

Suffolk *Suff.* Population: 668,553.

Easternmost county of England bounded by Cambridgeshire, Essex, Norfolk and the North Sea. Main towns are the county town of Ipswich, Lowestoft, Bury St. Edmunds, Felixstowe, Sudbury, Haverhill, Newmarket, Stowmarket and Woodbridge. The county is low-lying and gently undulating. It is almost entirely agricultural, with cereal crops and oil seed rape in abundance. The low coastline, behind which are areas of heath and marsh, afforested in places, is subject to much erosion; it is deeply indented with long river estuaries which provide good sailing. The NW corner of the county forms part of Breckland. The central region includes many notable historic Wool Towns, for instance, Lavenham. Apart from agriculture, industries include electronics, telecommunications, printing and port facilities. Lowestoft is a prominent fishing port and Felixstowe is a container port of growing importance. River Stour forms the S boundary with Essex, and the Little Ouse and Waveney form most of the N boundary with Norfolk. The many other small rivers include the Alde with its estuary the Ore, Deben, and Gipping with its estuary the Orwell, in the E and Lark in the W.

Districts: Babergh; Forest Heath; Ipswich; Mid Suffolk; St. Edmundsbury; Suffolk Coastal; Waveney.

Surrey *Surr.* Population: 1,059,015.

County of SE England bounded by Bracknell Forest, East Sussex, Greater London, Hampshire, Kent, Slough, West Sussex and Windsor & Maidenhead. The principal towns are Woking, the cathedral and university town of Guildford, Staines, Leatherhead, Farnham, Epsom, Ewell, Sunbury, Walton-on-Thames, Weybridge, Egham, Redhill, Reigate, Esher, Camberley, Frimley and Godalming. The chalk ridge of the North Downs, gently sloping on the N side but forming a steep escarpment on the S, traverses the county from E to W. Extensive sandy heaths in the W are much used for military training. The county is heavily wooded, and contains many traces of the former iron industry in the predominantly rural S. Much of the urbanised E and N areas include commuter or dormitory towns which form the residential outskirts of the Greater London conurbation. Industries include the agricultural activites of dairy farming and horticulture. Tourism and recreation are also important, with Surrey including numerous stately homes, Wentworth golf course, four race courses, and a theme park at Thorpe Park. The chief river is the Thames, into which flow the Wey and the Mole.

Districts: Elmbridge; Epsom & Ewell; Guildford; Mole Valley; Reigate & Banstead; Runnymede; Spelthorne; Surrey Heath; Tandridge; Waverley; Woking.

Swansea (Abertawe). *Swan.* Population: 223,301.

Unitary authority in S Wales bordering Carmarthenshire, Neath Port Talbot and the sea. Main centres are the city of Swansea, Gorseinon, The Mumbles, Sketty, Cockett and Clydach. The area includes mountains in the N, the urban centre surrounding Swansea, and the Gower peninsula in the S. Swansea originally developed as a port serving the W coalfield of S Wales. The area gained an international reputation for tin-plating and copper and nickel production. Swansea is now a regional shopping and commercial centre, including a university and marina development. The Gower peninsula attracts many tourists with its fine beaches and cliff scenery; hang-gliding is popular at Rhossili Down, and there are associations with Dylan Thomas. The Mumbles is a popular resort, formerly connected to Swansea via a tramway. The chief river is the Tawe.

Swindon *Swin.* Population: 180,051.

Unitary authority in SW England neighbouring Gloucestershire, Oxfordshire and Wiltshire. Main centres are Swindon, Stratton St. Margaret, Highworth and Wroughton. The area is located between the Cotswold Hills and Wiltshire Downs, on the fringes of the Thames Valley. Originally a railway town, Swindon has experienced rapid recent growth and is now a centre for car manufacture and central commercial operations. The town is a regional shopping centre with a redeveloped town centre and the Designer Outlet Village. The River Thames borders the area to the N and the River Cole to the E.

Telford & Wrekin *Tel. & W.* Population: 158,325.

Unitary authority in W England bordered by Shropshire and Staffordshire. Main centres are Telford, Wellington, Madeley, Donnington, Oakengates, Hadley and Newport. The area was the cradle of the Industrial Revolution, with notable firsts including Darby's discovery of the iron smelting process at Coalbrookdale, the casting and construction of the first cold blast iron bridge at Ironbridge, and the construction of the first iron ship. The new town of Telford, named after the famous engineer, surveyor and road builder, Thomas Telford, is the major commercial centre. The River Severn runs S through the area.

Thurrock *Thur.* Population: 143,128.

Unitary authority in SE England, N of the mouth of the River Thames. It is bounded by Essex and Greater London. The main centres are Grays, South Ockendon, Stanford-le-Hope, Corringham and Tilbury. The area is a mix of old and modern, rural and urban. In the N there are historic villages set in agricultural land, while in the S, there are the modern urban developments, and industrial activities surrounding oil refining and the container port of Tilbury. Grays is the commercial centre of Thurrock, with the major retail centre being Thurrock Lakeside. The area includes the N stretch of the Dartford Tunnel and Queen Elizabeth II Bridge, both of which cross the River Thames.

Torbay *Torbay* Population: 129,706.

Unitary authority located on the SW coast of England

neighbouring Devon. The major towns are Torquay, Paignton and Brixham. The area, situated on Tor Bay, is among Britain's main holiday resorts, and is widely regarded as the English Riviera. Tourism is the main industry, with Torbay receiving over 1.5 million visitors per year. Excellent leisure, recreation and conference facilities are added attractions.

Torfaen (Tor-faen). *Torfaen* Population: 90,949.
Unitary authority in S Wales bounded by Blaenau Gwent, Caerphilly, Monmouthshire and Newport. The principal towns are Cwmbran, Pontypool and Blaenavon. Torfaen contains rugged mountains with a 12-mile-long valley running N to S from Blaenavon to Cwmbran. The area is a manufacturing centre which includes electronics, engineering and automotive companies. The industrial past of the area has led to the growth of tourist attractions, with notable sites including The Valley Inheritance at Pontypool, and Big Pit National Mining Museum of Wales and 19c ironworks at Blaenavon. The river Afon Llwyd runs through the area.

Tyne & Wear *T. & W.* Population: 1,075,938.
Maritime county of NE England bordered by Durham and Northumberland. It comprises the urban complex around the cities of Newcastle upon Tyne and Sunderland, South Shields, Gateshead, Washington and Wallsend. Named after its two important rivers, the area developed largely through the coal mining and ship-building industries. As these industries declined, the area has undergone urban and industrial regeneration. Newcastle upon Tyne is now a commercial, university and cultural centre, with a historic heart including a cathedral, 12c castle and the Tyne Bridge; the historic Quayside has recently been developed. Sunderland gained city status in 1992, and is now a centre for car manufacture, with recreational facilities including the Crowtree Leisure Complex and the National Glass Centre. Elsewhere, Wallsend has hi-tech and off-shore industries; South Tyneside has electronics industries, and tourism, via its Catherine Cookson links. Gateshead has an international athletics stadium, Europe's largest undercover shopping centre, the Metrocentre, and the modern symbol of renewal, the Angel of the North. The area is served by the Port of Tyne and Newcastle International Airport.
Districts: Gateshead; Newcastle upon Tyne; North Tyneside; South Tyneside; Sunderland.

Vale of Glamorgan (Bro Morgannwg). *V. of Glam.*
Population: 119,292.
Unitary authority on the S coast of Wales neighbouring Bridgend, Cardiff and Rhondda Cynon Taff. The chief towns are Barry, Penarth and Llantwit Major. Vale of Glamorgan is a lowland area between Cardiff and Bridgend, with some agricultural activities, and tourism at the resorts of Barry and Penarth. Cardiff International Airport is situated in the SE near Rhoose. Main river is the Ely, which passes through the area.

Warrington *Warr.* Population: 191,080.
Unitary authority in NW England surrounding Warrington and bounded by Cheshire East, Cheshire West & Chester, Greater Manchester, Halton and Merseyside. The area developed as a main crossing point of the River Mersey and latterly the Manchester Ship Canal. During industrialisation it became an important strategic trading centre for the NW region. In 1968, Warrington was granted New Town status, leading to traditional industries such as chemicals, brewing and food processing being joined by hi-tech industries and research and development facilities. Warrington retains its importance as a regional shopping, leisure and commercial centre. The River Mersey flows through the area.

Warwickshire *Warks.* Population: 505,860.
Midland county of England bounded by Gloucestershire, Leicestershire, Northamptonshire, Oxfordshire, Staffordshire, West Midlands and Worcestershire. Chief towns are Nuneaton, Rugby, Royal Leamington Spa, Bedworth, the county town of Warwick, Stratford-upon-Avon and Kenilworth. Warwickshire consists of mostly flat or undulating farmland, although the foothills of the Cotswold Hills spill over the SW border. Main manufacturing activites occur in an industrial belt extending NW from Rugby to the boundary with Staffordshire. They include motor and component industries, service sectors, electrical and

general engineering. Tourism is centred on the historic town of Warwick with its medieval castle, and Stratford-upon-Avon with its Shakespeare associations. The principal river is the Avon.
Districts: North Warwickshire; Nuneaton & Bedworth; Rugby; Stratford-on-Avon; Warwick.

West Berkshire *W.Berks.* Population: 144,483.
Unitary authority in S England bordered by Hampshire, Oxfordshire, Reading, Wiltshire and Wokingham. The chief centres are Newbury, Thatcham and Hungerford. West Berkshire is a mixture of old market towns, historic buildings and waterways, and includes the famous Newbury racecourse. Rivers include the Kennet and the Pang.

West Dunbartonshire *W.Dun.* Population: 93,378.
Unitary authority in central Scotland bordered by Argyll & Bute, East Dunbartonshire, Glasgow, Inverclyde, Renfrewshire and Stirling. The chief towns are Clydebank, Dumbarton, Alexandria and Bonhill. The area is mountainous, containing the Kilpatrick Hills, and is bounded by Loch Lomond in the N and the Firth of Clyde in the S. The urban SE area of West Dunbartonshire forms part of the NW periphery of Greater Glasgow. There is a broad base of light manufacturing and service sector industries. Tourism and leisure are a feature, with the SE tip of Loch Lomond Regional Park and the whole of Balloch Castle Country Park falling within the area. West Dunbartonshire includes the Erskine Bridge which spans the River Clyde, other rivers include the Leven.

West Lothian *W.Loth.* Population: 158,714.
Unitary authority in central Scotland neighbouring Edinburgh, Falkirk, Midlothian, North Lanarkshire, Scottish Borders and South Lanarkshire. The chief towns are Livingston, Bathgate, Linlithgow, Broxburn, Whitburn and Armadale. The area undulates to the S of the Firth of Forth, and rises to moorland at the foot of the Pentland Hills in the S. The main urban areas are situated along commuter corridors between Glasgow, Edinburgh and Falkirk; elsewhere the area is mostly rural. Hi-tech and computing industries are in evidence.

West Midlands *W.Mid.* Population: 2,555,592.
Former metropolitan county of central England bordered by Staffordshire, Warwickshire and Worcestershire. It comprises the urban complex around the cities of Birmingham and Coventry, and the towns of Wolverhampton, Dudley, Walsall, West Bromwich, Sutton Coldfield and Solihull. The West Midlands developed as a manufacturing and engineering centre which specialised in the metalworking and motor trades. The area around Dudley, Walsall and Wolverhampton became known as the Black Country, with heavy industry centred on the local deposits of coal, iron ore and limestone. Other local trades included glassware, saddlery and lock-making. Birmingham became Britain's second city by specialising in 1001 trades from confectionery to cars, and has developed into the major business, industrial, commercial and cultural centre for the area. As the traditional industries have declined, there has been a shift towards service, leisure and recreation sectors of the economy; several significant corporate service centres and venues, such as the National Exhibition Centre and the Indoor Arena, are in the West Midlands. The area is served by Birmingham International Airport. Rivers include the Tame and the Cole.
Districts: Birmingham; Coventry; Dudley; Sandwell; Solihull; Walsall; Wolverhampton.

West Sussex *W.Suss.* Population: 753,614.
County of S England bounded by Brighton & Hove, East Sussex, Hampshire, Surrey and the English Channel. Main towns are Worthing, Crawley, Bognor Regis, Littlehampton, Horsham, Haywards Heath, East Grinstead, the cathedral city and county town of Chichester, Burgess Hill and Shoreham-by-Sea. N of a level coastal strip run the South Downs, a steep-sided chalk ridge which is thickly wooded in parts. The remaining inland area, The Weald, is largely well-wooded farmland, although there is industrial development around Crawley, Gatwick (London) Airport, Horsham, and Haywards Heath, as well as among the predominantly residential towns on the coast. Tourism is a major activity throughout the county. There are many castles and stately homes, such as Arundel Castle and Goodwood House, the popular seaside resorts of Bognor Regis and Worthing, race courses at Goodwood and Fontwell, Chichester Harbour, which is a centre for yachtsmen and wildfowl, historic Chichester itself,

and numerous picturesque villages. The N of the county includes Gatwick (London) Airport. The rivers, none large, include the Adur and Arun, with its tributary the Rother; the Medway rises in the E of the county.

Districts: Adur; Arun; Chichester; Crawley; Horsham; Mid Sussex; Worthing.

West Yorkshire *W.Yorks.* Population: 2,079,211.
Former metropolitan county of N England bordering Derbyshire, Greater Manchester, Lancashire, North Yorkshire and South Yorkshire. It comprises the area around the cities of Leeds, Bradford and Wakefield, and the towns of Huddersfield, Halifax, Dewsbury, Keighley, Batley, Morley, Castleford, Brighouse, Pudsey, Pontefract and Shipley. West Yorkshire developed as a centre for wool and textiles, manufacturing and engineering, creating an industrial urban landscape set against rural moorland. As the traditional industries have declined, the area has undergone regeneration and diversification, moving towards tertiary economic sectors. Leeds is the industrial, administrative, commercial and cultural centre of the area, containing regional government offices and many corporate service centres and head offices. Emerging economic activities across West Yorkshire have included printing, distribution, chemicals, food and drink production, hi-tech industries and financial services. Haworth with its Brontë associations, Holmfirth and the moorlands are the centres of tourism. The area includes Leeds Bradford International Airport. The chief rivers are the Aire and the Calder, while the Wharfe forms its N boundary below Addingham.

Districts: Bradford; Calderdale; Kirklees; Leeds; Wakefield.

Western Isles (Na h-Eileanan Siar. Also known as Outer Hebrides.) *W.Isles* Population: 26,502.
String of islands off the W coast of Scotland and separated from Skye and the mainland by The Minch. They extend for some 130m/209km from Butt of Lewis in the N, to Barra Head in the S. Stornoway, situated on the Isle of Lewis, is the main town; elsewhere, there are mainly scattered coastal villages and settlements. The chief islands are Isle of Lewis, North Uist, Benbecula, South Uist and Barra. North Harris and South Harris form significant areas in the S part of the Isle of Lewis. The topography of the islands consists of undulating moorland, mountains and lochs. The main industries are fishing, grazing and, on the Isle of Lewis, tweed manufacture. There are airfields with scheduled passenger flights on the Isle of Lewis, Benbecula and Barra.

Wiltshire *Wilts.* Population: 432,973.
Unitary authority of S England bounded by Bath & North East Somerset, Dorset, Gloucestershire, Hampshire, Oxfordshire, Somerset, South Gloucestershire, Swindon and West Berkshire. Main centres are the cathedral city of Salisbury, Trowbridge, Chippenham, Warminster, Devizes and Melksham. Wiltshire consists of extensive chalk uplands scattered with prehistoric remains, notably at Avebury and Stonehenge, and interspersed with wide, well-watered valleys. The N of the county is dominated by the Marlborough Downs which are much used for racehorse training, while in the S, the chalk plateau of Salisbury Plain is an important military training area. Between these two upland areas lies the fertile Vale of Pewsey where dairy production and bacon-curing are important agricultural activities. Other industries include electronics, computing, pharmaceuticals, plastics, telecommunications and service sector activities. Wiltshire attracts tourism with its prehistoric remains, stately houses and picturesque market towns and villages. Rivers include the so-called Bristol and Wiltshire Avons, Ebble, Kennet, Nadder, Wylye, and the upper reaches of the Thames.

Windsor & Maidenhead *W. & M.* Population: 133,626.
Unitary authority in SE England to the W of Greater London, and bounded by Bracknell Forest, Buckinghamshire, Slough, Surrey and Wokingham. The towns of Maidenhead and Windsor are the main centres for industry, leisure and recreation. The area is particularly noted for its strong Royal connections as it includes Windsor Castle and the former Royal hunting estate of Windsor Great Park. Other popular tourist attractions include Ascot race course, Windsor Legoland and Eton College. The River Thames forms the N boundary.

Wokingham *W'ham* Population: 150,229.
Unitary authority in SE England, to the W of Greater London.

The area encompasses Wokingham and is bordered by Bracknell Forest, Buckinghamshire, Hampshire, Oxfordshire, Reading, West Berkshire and Windsor & Maidenhead. The area includes riverside villages in the N, with undulating ridges covered by woodlands and commons in the S. Wokingham is a growing centre for hi-tech and computer industries. The River Thames forms the N border, and the River Blackwater forms the border to the S.

Worcestershire *Worcs.* Population: 542,107.
S midland county of England neighbouring Gloucestershire, Herefordshire, Shropshire, Warwickshire and West Midlands. Main centres are the cathedral city and the county town of Worcester, and the towns of Redditch, Kidderminster, Great Malvern, Bromsgrove, Droitwich Spa, Stourport-on-Severn and Evesham. The urban areas in the N of the county form part of the periphery and commuter belt of the West Midlands conurbation, and attract much of the industrial development. The central and S sections of the county are largely rural, containing the fertile Severn Valley and Vale of Evesham, with market gardening and orchard-growing being the main agricultural activities. Tourism is an important industry, much of it being centred on historic Worcester, with its cathedral, the triennial Three Choirs Festival, Worcester Sauce and china factories. Other popular attractions include boating on the River Severn and visiting the Vale of Evesham whilst the flowers are in full bloom. The main river is the Severn.

Districts: Bromsgrove; Malvern Hills; Redditch; Worcester; Wychavon; Wyre Forest.

Wrexham (Wrecsam). *Wrex.* Population: 128,476.
Unitary authority in NE Wales bordering Denbighshire, Flintshire, Powys and the English counties of Cheshire and Shropshire. Main centres are Wrexham, Rhosllanerchrugog, Gwersyllt, Cefn-mawr and Coedpoeth. The area is mountainous in the SW, containing part of the Berwyn range; the Dee valley lies in the NE. The area was formerly dominated by the iron, coal and limestone industries. Food manufacture, brewing, plastics and hi-tech industries are now important to the local economy. Wrexham is the largest commercial and shopping centre in N Wales. The River Dee flows through the area.

York *York* Population: 181,094.
Unitary authority in N England surrounding the historic cathedral city of York and bordered by East Riding of Yorkshire and North Yorkshire. York is a major archaeological, episcopal, industrial, commercial and cultural centre, situated at the confluence of the River Foss and the River Ouse. The city has a unique history dating from the original Roman military camp, which has led to it becoming one of the main museum and tourist centres in the country. The historic core, situated around the centrepiece of the medieval Minster, is well preserved. Other major attractions include the Jorvik Viking Centre, the medieval city walls and the National Railway Museum. Economic sectors include the confectionery industry, company head offices, Government departmental offices, and research and development establishments. The main river is the Ouse.

WALES Counties

BLAENAU GWENT
BRIDGEND
CAERPHILLY
CARDIFF
CARMARTHENSHIRE
CEREDIGION
CONWY
DENBIGHSHIRE
FLINTSHIRE
GWYNEDD
ISLE OF ANGLESEY
MERTHYR TYDFIL
MONMOUTHSHIRE
NEATH PORT TALBOT
NEWPORT
PEMBROKESHIRE
POWYS
RHONDDA CYNON TAFF
SWANSEA
TORFAEN
VALE OF GLAMORGAN
WREXHAM

**ENGLAND
Counties & Districts**

BATH AND NORTH EAST SOMERSET	**CENTRAL BEDFORDSHIRE**	3 Mid Devon
		4 East Devon
BEDFORD	**CHESHIRE EAST**	5 Exeter
BOURNEMOUTH	**CHESHIRE WEST & CHESTER**	6 Teignbridge
BRACKNELL FOREST		7 West Devon
	CORNWALL	8 South Hams
BRIGHTON & HOVE	**DERBY**	
BRISTOL		**DORSET**
BUCKINGHAMSHIRE	**DERBYSHIRE**	1 North Dorset
1 Aylesbury Vale	1 High Peak	2 East Dorset
2 Wycombe	2 Derbyshire Dales	3 Christchurch
3 Chiltern	3 North East Derbyshire	4 Purbeck
4 South Buckinghamshire	4 Chesterfield	5 West Dorset
	5 Bolsover	6 Weymouth & Portland
CAMBRIDGESHIRE	6 Amber Valley	
1 Fenland	7 Erewash	**EAST SUSSEX**
2 Huntingdonshire	8 South Derbyshire	1 Lewes
3 East Cambridgeshire		2 Wealden
4 South Cambridgeshire	**DEVON**	3 Eastbourne
5 Cambridge	1 North Devon	4 Rother
	2 Torridge	5 Hastings

0   10   20   30   40 kilometres

0   10   20   30 miles

1:1,250,000 20 miles to 1 inch/12.5 km to 1 cm

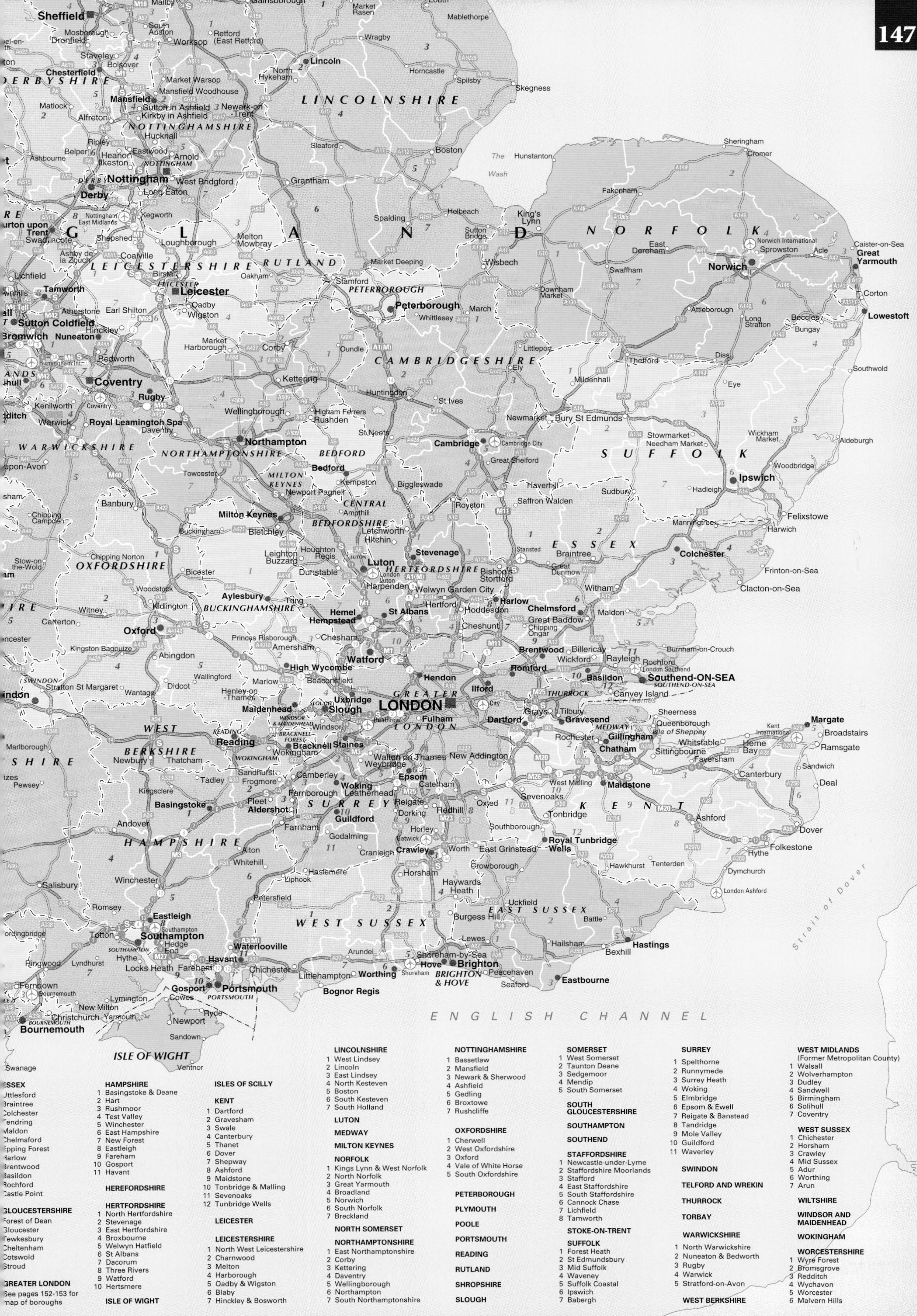

LINCOLNSHIRE
NOTTINGHAMSHIRE
LEICESTERSHIRE
RUTLAND
NORFOLK
SUFFOLK
CAMBRIDGESHIRE
PETERBOROUGH
NORTHAMPTONSHIRE
WARWICKSHIRE
OXFORDSHIRE
BUCKINGHAMSHIRE
MILTON KEYNES
BEDFORD
CENTRAL BEDFORDSHIRE
HERTFORDSHIRE
ESSEX
GREATER LONDON
KENT
SURREY
WEST SUSSEX
EAST SUSSEX
HAMPSHIRE
WEST BERKSHIRE
ISLE OF WIGHT
ENGLISH CHANNEL
Strait of Dover
The Wash
Sheffield
Lincoln
Nottingham
Derby
Leicester
Coventry
Northampton
Peterborough
Cambridge
Norwich
Great Yarmouth
Lowestoft
Ipswich
Colchester
Chelmsford
Luton
Stevenage
Oxford
Reading
Slough
Watford
LONDON
Southend-ON-SEA
Basildon
Gillingham
Chatham
Maidstone
Canterbury
Margate
Dover
Folkestone
Hastings
Eastbourne
Brighton
Worthing
Crawley
Guildford
Portsmouth
Southampton
Bournemouth
Winchester
Salisbury
Basingstoke
Aylesbury
Milton Keynes
Bedford
Kettering
Huntingdon
Bury St Edmunds
Newmarket
King's Lynn
Skegness
Boston
Grantham
Stamford
Wisbech

ESSEX
Uttlesford
Braintree
Colchester
Tendring
Maldon
Chelmsford
Epping Forest
Harlow
Brentwood
Basildon
Rochford
Castle Point
GLOUCESTERSHIRE
Forest of Dean
Gloucester
Tewkesbury
Cheltenham
Cotswold
Stroud
GREATER LONDON
See pages 152-153 for map of boroughs
HAMPSHIRE
1 Basingstoke & Deane
2 Hart
3 Rushmoor
4 Test Valley
5 Winchester
6 East Hampshire
7 New Forest
8 Eastleigh
9 Fareham
10 Gosport
11 Havant
HEREFORDSHIRE
HERTFORDSHIRE
1 North Hertfordshire
2 Stevenage
3 East Hertfordshire
4 Broxbourne
5 Welwyn Hatfield
6 St Albans
7 Dacorum
8 Three Rivers
9 Watford
10 Hertsmere
ISLE OF WIGHT
ISLES OF SCILLY
KENT
1 Dartford
2 Gravesham
3 Swale
4 Canterbury
5 Thanet
6 Dover
7 Shepway
8 Ashford
9 Maidstone
10 Tonbridge & Malling
11 Sevenoaks
12 Tunbridge Wells
LEICESTER
LEICESTERSHIRE
1 North West Leicestershire
2 Charnwood
3 Melton
4 Harborough
5 Oadby & Wigston
6 Blaby
7 Hinckley & Bosworth
LINCOLNSHIRE
1 West Lindsey
2 Lincoln
3 East Lindsey
4 North Kesteven
5 Boston
6 South Kesteven
7 South Holland
LUTON
MEDWAY
MILTON KEYNES
NORFOLK
1 Kings Lynn & West Norfolk
2 North Norfolk
3 Great Yarmouth
4 Broadland
5 Norwich
6 South Norfolk
7 Breckland
NORTH SOMERSET
NORTHAMPTONSHIRE
1 East Northamptonshire
2 Corby
3 Kettering
4 Daventry
5 Wellingborough
6 Northampton
7 South Northamptonshire
NOTTINGHAMSHIRE
1 Bassetlaw
2 Mansfield
3 Newark & Sherwood
4 Ashfield
5 Gedling
6 Broxtowe
7 Rushcliffe
OXFORDSHIRE
1 Cherwell
2 West Oxfordshire
3 Oxford
4 Vale of White Horse
5 South Oxfordshire
PETERBOROUGH
PLYMOUTH
POOLE
PORTSMOUTH
READING
RUTLAND
SHROPSHIRE
SLOUGH
SOMERSET
1 West Somerset
2 Taunton Deane
3 Sedgemoor
4 Mendip
5 South Somerset
SOUTH GLOUCESTERSHIRE
SOUTHAMPTON
SOUTHEND
STAFFORDSHIRE
1 Newcastle-under-Lyme
2 Staffordshire Moorlands
3 Stafford
4 East Staffordshire
5 South Staffordshire
6 Cannock Chase
7 Lichfield
8 Tamworth
STOKE-ON-TRENT
SUFFOLK
1 Forest Heath
2 St Edmundsbury
3 Mid Suffolk
4 Waveney
5 Suffolk Coastal
6 Ipswich
7 Babergh
SURREY
1 Spelthorne
2 Runnymede
3 Surrey Heath
4 Woking
5 Elmbridge
6 Epsom & Ewell
7 Reigate & Banstead
8 Tandridge
9 Mole Valley
10 Guildford
11 Waverley
SWINDON
TELFORD AND WREKIN
THURROCK
TORBAY
WARWICKSHIRE
1 North Warwickshire
2 Nuneaton & Bedworth
3 Rugby
4 Warwick
5 Stratford-on-Avon
WEST BERKSHIRE
WEST MIDLANDS
(Former Metropolitan County)
1 Walsall
2 Wolverhampton
3 Dudley
4 Sandwell
5 Birmingham
6 Solihull
7 Coventry
WEST SUSSEX
1 Chichester
2 Horsham
3 Crawley
4 Mid Sussex
5 Adur
6 Worthing
7 Arun
WILTSHIRE
WINDSOR AND MAIDENHEAD
WOKINGHAM
WORCESTERSHIRE
1 Wyre Forest
2 Bromsgrove
3 Redditch
4 Wychavon
5 Worcester
6 Malvern Hills

KINROSS

SCOTLAND

Tiree
Tiree

Mull
Craignure
Oban
Taynuilt
Dalmally
Bridge of Orchy
Tyndrum
Killin
Crianlarich
Lochearnhead
STIRLING
Auchterarder
Gleneagles
Crieff

Iona
Fionnphort

Colonsay
Scalasaig

Jura
Lochgilphead

ARGYLL
AND
BUTE

Dunkeld

Callander

Aberfoyle
Dunblane
CLACKMANNAN-
SHIRE
Alloa
Tillicoultry
Cowden
Clackmannan
Dunfermline

Garelochhead

Helensburgh
WEST
DUNBARTON-
SHIRE
Denny
Grangemouth
Bo'ness

Islay
Bowmore

Port
Askaig

Portnahaven

Port
Ellen

Islay

Lochranza

NORTH
AYRSHIRE

Brodick

Arran

Carradale

Campbeltown

Tarbert

Largs
Millport

Bute

Dunoon
Wemyss
Bay
INVERCLYDE
Greenock
Port Glasgow

Alexandria
Dumbarton
EAST
DUNBARTON-
SHIRE
Milngavie
Bearsden
Clydebank
Glasgow
GLASGOW
Paisley
RENFREW-
SHIRE
Barrhead
Newton
Mearns
EAST
RENFREW-
SHIRE

Kilsyth
Cumbernauld
NORTH
LANARKSHIRE
Kirkintilloch
Airdrie
Coatbridge
GLASGOW
Hamilton
East
Kilbride
Motherwell
Wishaw
Carluke
WEST
LOTHIAN
Falkirk
FALKIRK
Linlithgow
Bathgate
Whitburn
Livi
Broxbu

Ardrossan
Saltcoats
Irvine
Stevenston
Kilwinning
Dalry
Dunlop
Stewarton
Beith

Troon
Prestwick
Glasgow Prestwick
Ayr

Kilmarnock
Galston
Mauchline
EAST
AYRSHIRE
Cumnock
Muirkirk

SOUTH
LANARKSHIRE
Strathaven
Lanark
Douglas
Abington
Carnwath
Big

SOUTH
AYRSHIRE

Maybole
Dalmellington
New Cumnock
Sanquhar

Girvan

Ailsa Craig

Ballantrae

Moniaive
Thornhill
New Galloway
DUMFRIES & GALL
Dumfries
Lochmaben

Cairnryan
Newton Stewart
Wigtown
Kirkcudbright

Stranraer

Glenluce

Portpatrick

Sandhead

Port William

Whithorn

Drummore

SOLWAY FIRTH
Maryport

Workington

Whitehaven

Egremont

NORTHERN IRELAND Districts

ANTRIM	BALLYMONEY	DOWN	MOYLE
ARDS	BANBRIDGE	DUNGANNON	NEWRY & MOURNE
ARMAGH	BELFAST	FERMANAGH	NEWTOWNABBEY
BALLYMENA	CARRICKFERGUS	LARNE	NORTH DOWN
	CASTLEREAGH	LIMAVADY	OMAGH
	COLERAINE	LISBURN	STRABANE
	COOKSTOWN	LONDONDERRY (DERRY)	
	CRAIGAVON	MAGHERAFELT	

Inishtrahull Sound

0 10 20 30 40 kilometres
0 10 20 30 miles

Rathlin
Island

ISLE
OF
MAN

Andreas
Ramsey
Kirk Michael
Peel
Laxey
Dalby
Foxdale
Onchan
Douglas
Port Erin
Port
St Mary
Castletown
Isle of Man
Castletown

IRISH

SEA

North Channel

Camdonagh
Portrush
Portstewart
Bushmills
Ballycastle
MOYLE
Armoy

Buncrana
Moville

Lough
Swilly

Lough
Foyle

City of Derry
Limavady
Coleraine
Ballymoney
COLERAINE
BALLYMONEY
Camlough
Larne

Londonderry
(Derry)
LONDON-
DERRY
Eglinton
Ballykelly
LIMAVADY
Garvagh
Kilrea
Dungiven
Maghera
BALLYMENA
Ballymena
Broughshane
LARNE
Larne

Letterkenny

Lifford
Strabane
Sion Mills
STRABANE
Ballybofey

NORTHERN IRELAND

Draperstown
MAGHERAFELT
Magherafelt
Randalstown
ANTRIM
Antrim
Ballyclare
NEWTOWN
CARRICKFERGUS
Whitehead
Carrickfergus

enties

Donegal

Castlederg
Newtownstewart

OMAGH
Omagh
Pomeroy
COOKSTOWN
Cookstown
Moneymore

Crumlin
Newtownabbey
Belfast
City
NORTH
DOWN
Bangor
Donaghadee

Ballyshannon

Beragh
Sixmilecross
Donaghmore
Dungannon
DUNGANNON

Dromore

Ballygawley
Augher
Aughnacloy

CRAIGAVON
Lurgan
Craigavon
Portadown

Dunmurry
LISBURN
Lisburn
BELFAST
CASTLEREAGH
Dundonald
Newtownards
Comber
ARDS

Ards
Peninsula

Killinchy
Kirkcubbin
Portavogie

FERMANAGH
Enniskillen
Lisbellaw

Fivemiletown
Lisnaskea
Belcoo

Manorhamilton

Belcoo

Newtownbutler
Clones

Monaghan
(Muineachán)

Armagh
ARMAGH
Tandragee
Markethill
Keady

Banbridge
BANBRIDGE
Dromore
Ballynahinch
Crossgar
Saintfield
Strangford
Portaferry

Downpatrick
Dundrum
DOWN
Ardglass

Carrick-on-Shannon
Mohill

Ballyconnell

Carrickmacross

Rathfriland
Newry
NEWRY & MOURNE
Castleblayney
Warrenpoint
Annalong
Kilkeel
Newcastle

Arvagh

Cavan

Virginia

M1
Dundalk
(Dun Dealgan)
Dundalk Bay
Ardee
Dunleer

ISLE OF ANGLESEY

Amlwch

Holyhead
Holy
Island

Anglesey

Llandudno
Colwyn
Bay
Abergele
Pres

Llangefni
Menai Bridge
Bangor
Caernarfon

CONWY

ENGLAND Counties & Districts

BLACKBURN WITH DARWEN

BLACKPOOL

CHESHIRE
1 Ellesmere Port & Neston
2 Vale Royal
3 Macclesfield
4 Chester
6 Congleton

CUMBRIA
1 Carlisle
2 Allerdale
3 Eden
4 Copeland
5 South Lakeland
6 Barrow-in-Furness

DARLINGTON

DERBYSHIRE
1 High Peak
2 Derbyshire Dales
3 North East Derbyshire
4 Chesterfield
5 Bolsover

DURHAM

EAST RIDING OF YORKSHIRE

GREATER MANCHESTER
(Former Metropolitan County)
1 Wigan
2 Bolton
3 Bury
4 Rochdale
5 Oldham
6 Tameside
7 Stockport
8 Manchester
9 Salford
10 Trafford

HALTON

HARTLEPOOL

ISLE OF MAN

KINGSTON UPON HULL

LANCASHIRE
1 Lancaster
2 Wyre
3 Fylde
4 Preston
5 Ribble Valley
6 Pendle
7 Burnley
8 Rossendale
9 Hyndburn
10 Chorley
11 South Ribble
12 West Lancashire

LINCOLNSHIRE
1 West Lindsey
2 Lincoln
3 East Lindsey
4 North Kesteven

MERSEYSIDE
(Former Metropolitan County)
1 Wirral
2 Sefton
3 Liverpool
4 Knowsley
5 St Helens

MIDDLESBROUGH

NORTH EAST LINCOLNSHIRE

NORTH LINCOLNSHIRE

NORTH YORKSHIRE
1 Scarborough
2 Ryedale
3 Hambleton
4 Richmondshire
5 Craven
6 Harrogate
7 Selby

NORTHUMBERLAND

NOTTINGHAM

NOTTINGHAMSHIRE
1 Bassetlaw
2 Mansfield
3 Newark & Sherwood
4 Ashfield

REDCAR AND CLEVELAND

SOUTH YORKSHIRE
(Former Metropolitan County)
1 Barnsley
2 Doncaster
3 Rotherham
4 Sheffield

STOCKTON-ON-TEES

TYNE AND WEAR
(Former Metropolitan County)
1 Newcastle upon Tyne
2 North Tyneside
3 South Tyneside
4 Gateshead
5 Sunderland

WARRINGTON

WEST YORKSHIRE
(Former Metropolitan County)
1 Calderdale
2 Bradford
3 Leeds
4 Wakefield
5 Kirklees

YORK

1:1,250,000   20 miles to 1 inch/12.5 km to 1 cm

Pen

Scrab

Durness

Bettyhill

Tongue

Kinbrace

Rhiconich

Laxford
Bridge

Sutherland

Ca

Scourie

Port of Ness

Portnaguran

Lochinver

Brora

Golspie

Stornoway

Garrynahine

Lewis

Ledmore

Bonar
Bridge

Portmahoma

Dornoch Firth

Ullapool

*North
Harris*

Summer
Isles

*E a s t e r
R o s s*

Invergordon

Cromarty

Moray Firth

Tarbert

Aultbea

H I G H L A N D

Cromarty Firth

M

Poolewe

Garve

Dingwall

Nairn

*South
Harris*

Gairloch

*W e s t e r
R o s s*

Kinlochewe

Strathpeffer

Fortrose

WESTERN ISLES
(NA H-EILEANAN SIAR)

Rodel

Achnasheen

Muir of Ord

Inverness

Beauly

Inverness

Uig

Shieldaig

Lochmaddy

North Uist

Portree

Raasay

Lochcarron

Drumnadrochit

Grantown
-on-Spey

Dunvegan

Skye

Benbecula

Benbecula

Stromeferry

Carrbridge

Sligachan

Kyle of Lochalsh

Invermoriston

Aviemore

South Uist

Broadford

Kylenkin

Lochboisdale

Elgol

Fort Augustus

Kingussie

Newtonmore

Barra

Barra

Canna

Ardvasar

Invergarry

Castlebay

*Rum
(Rhum)*

Mallaig

Vatersay

Eigg

Arisaig

Dalwhinnie

Glenfinnan

Spean
Bridge

Coll

Salen

Fort William

Blair Atholl

Kinlochleven

Rannoch
Sta

Kinloch
Rannoch

Pitloch

Tiree

Tiree

Tobermory

Ballachulish

P E R T H

Aberfeldy

Lochaline

Bridge of Orchy

K I N R O

Mull

Craignure

S C O T L A N

Tyndrum

Killin

Oban

Taynuilt

Iona

Fionnphort

Dalmally

Crianlarich

Lochearnhead

Crieff

ARGYLL

STIRLING

AND

Lochgoilhead

Callander

BUTE

Auch

Colonsay

Scalasaig

Aberfoyle

Dunblane

Glen

Bridge
of Allan

CLACKMANNAN
SHIRE

Lochgilphead

Garelochhead

Stirling

Alloa

Tillicoul

Jura

Helensburgh

*WEST
DUNBARTON
SHIRE*

Kilsyth

Clackma

Kincardine

Dunk

Port
Askaig

Alexandra

Dumbarton

*EAST
DUNBARTON
SHIRE*

Milngavie

Kirkintilloch

Falkirk

Denn

Gran

Cumbernauld

Linli

Dunoon

Bearsden

*NORTH
LANARKSHIRE*

Bathgate

WE

Islay

Port
Glasgow

Greenock

Wemyss
Bay

INVERCLYDE

Clydebank

Glasgow

GLASGOW

Airdrie

Whitbu

Bowmore

Bute

Jchnstone

Paisley

Coatbridge

*RENFREW-
SHIRE*

Barrhead

Largs

Portnahaven

Port
Ellen

Beith

Newton
Mearns

*EAST
RENFREW-
SHIRE*

Hamilton

Motherwell

**East
Kilbride**

Wishaw

Millport

Dalry

Dunlop

Carluke

NORTH

Lochranza

Stewarton

Kilwinning

Lanark

AYRSHIRE

Ardrossan

Stevenston

Saltcoats

Irvine

Kilmarnock

Galston

Strathaven

SOUTH
LANARKSHIR

Carradale

Brodick

Troon

Glasgow
Prestwick

Mauchline

Muirkirk

EAST

Douglas

Arran

Prestwick

AYRSHIRE

Cumnock

Ayr

New Cumnock

Sanquhar

Ab

Campbeltown

SOUTH

Maybole

Dalmellington

Inishtrahull Sound

AYRSHIRE

DUMFRIES &

Carndonagh

Rathlin
Island

Ailsa Craig

The Minch

Little Minch

Inner Sound

Sound of Sleat

Loch Linnhe

Firth of Lorn

Sound of Jura

Kilbrannan Sound

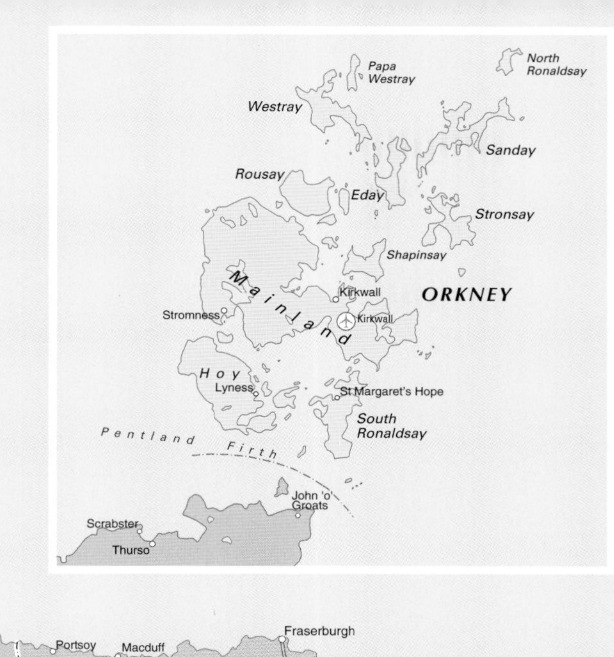

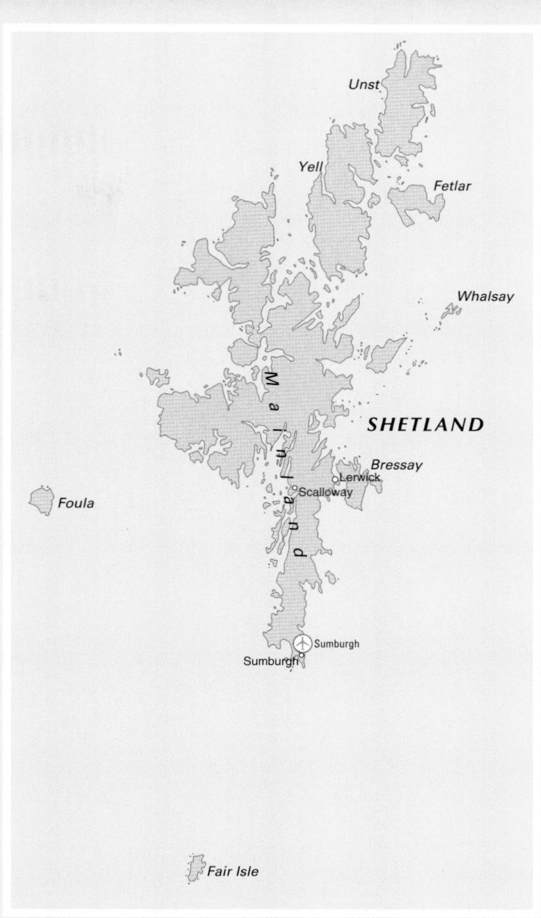

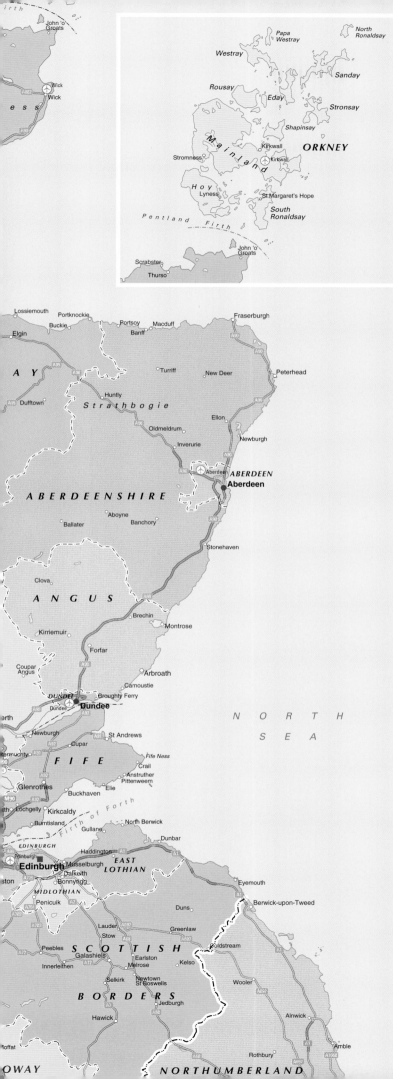

Orkney

Papa Westray

North Ronaldsay

Westray

Sanday

Rousay

Eday

Stronsay

Shapinsay

Mainland

Kirkwall
Kirkwall

ORKNEY

Stromness

Hoy

Lyness

St Margaret's Hope

South Ronaldsay

Pentland Firth

Scrabster

Thurso

John o'
Groats

Shetland

Unst

Yell

Fetlar

Whalsay

Mainland

SHETLAND

Bressay

Lerwick

Scalloway

Foula

Sumburgh

Sumburgh

Fair Isle

'rth

John 'o
Groats

Wick
Wick

ess

OWAY

Lossiemouth
Portknockie
Portsoy Macduff
Buckie   Banff

Fraserburgh

Elgin

AY

Dufftown

Strathbogie

Turriff   New Deer

Peterhead

Huntly

Oldmeldrum

Ellon

Inverurie

Newburgh

Aberdeen ABERDEEN
Aberdeen

ABERDEENSHIRE

Aboyne

Ballater   Banchory

Stonehaven

Clova

ANGUS

Kirriemuir

Brechin

Montrose

Forfar

Coupar
Angus

Arbroath

Carnoustie

DUNDEE
Dundee

Broughty Ferry

Dundee

erth

Newburgh   St Andrews

Cupar

Fife Ness

FIFE

Crail

Anstruther
Pittenweem

Glenrothes   Elie

Buckhaven

rth
Lochgelly Kirkcaldy

Burntisland

Firth of Forth

North Berwick

Gullane

Dunbar

EDINBURGH

Haddington

Musselburgh   EAST
Dalkeith   LOTHIAN

Edinburgh

Bonnyrigg

MIDLOTHIAN

Eyemouth

Penicuik

Duns

Berwick-upon-Tweed

Lauder

Greenlaw

Stow

Peebles

SCOTTISH

Galashiels
Earlston
Melrose

Coldstream

Innerleithen   Selkirk

Kelso

Newtown
St Boswells

Wooler

BORDERS

Jedburgh

Hawick

Alnwick

Moffat

Rothbury   Amble

NORTHUMBERLAND

NORTH
SEA

SCOTLAND Councils

ABERDEEN
ABERDEENSHIRE
ANGUS
ARGYLL AND BUTE
CLACKMANNANSHIRE
DUMFRIES AND GALLOWAY
DUNDEE
EAST AYRSHIRE
EAST DUNBARTONSHIRE
EAST LOTHIAN
EAST RENFREWSHIRE
EDINBURGH
FALKIRK
FIFE
GLASGOW
HIGHLAND
INVERCLYDE
MIDLOTHIAN
MORAY
NORTH AYRSHIRE
NORTH LANARKSHIRE
ORKNEY
PERTH AND KINROSS
RENFREWSHIRE
SCOTTISH BORDERS
SHETLAND
SOUTH AYRSHIRE
SOUTH LANARKSHIRE
STIRLING
WEST DUNBARTONSHIRE
WEST LOTHIAN
WESTERN ISLES (NA H-EILEANAN SIAR)

0	10	20	30	40 kilometres
0	10		20	30 miles

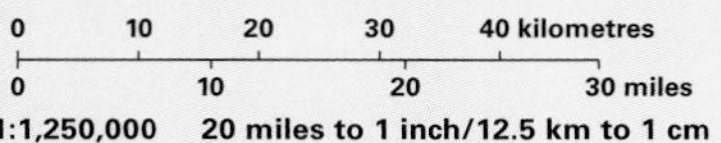

1:1,250,000   20 miles to 1 inch/12.5 km to 1 cm

DACORUM

ST. ALBANS

WELWYN
HATFIELD B

THREE

RIVERS

WATFORD

HERTSMERE

EN

Borehamwood

Barnet

CHILTERN

Watford

Rickmansworth

BARNET

Finchley

HARROW

HARIN

T

SOUTH
BUCKS

HILLINGDON

Harrow

BRENT

Hampstead

ISLINGTO

CAMDEN

Islin

Uxbridge

Wembley

EALING

WESTMINSTER

KENSINGTON &
CHELSEA

HAMMERSMITH &
FULHAM

Ealing

SLOUGH

Heathrow
Airport

HOUNSLOW

River Thames

Richmond
upon
Thames

Wandsworth

LAMBETH

Brix

WINDSOR &
MAIDENHEAD

Hounslow

RICHMOND

WANDSWORTH

UPON THAMES

SPELTHORNE

Wimbledon

Kingston
upon Thames

MERTON

RUNNYMEDE

KINGSTON
UPON THAMES

Esher

SUTTON

ELMBRIDGE

Sutton

EPSOM
& EWELL

Epsom

Woking

Banstead

WOKING

REIGATE &

Leatherhead

GUILDFORD

MOLE VALLEY

BANSTEAD

OURNE

Waltham
Abbey

E P P I N G

B R E N T W O O D

F O R E S T

eld

ELD

monton

Brentwood

WALTHAM
FOREST

Woodford

n

REDBRIDGE

Walthamstow

H A V E R I N G

Romford

CKNEY

Ilford

Upminster

Hackney

West Ham

Barking

Dagenham

TOWER
HAMLETS

NEWHAM

BARKING &
DAGENHAM

Stepney

Beckton

River Thames

T H U R R O C K

London City
Airport

outhwark

GREENWICH

Greenwich

Tilbury

ark

Lewisham

B E X L E Y

LEWISHAM

Bexley

Dartford

D A R T F O R D

G R A V E S H A M

Bromley

GREATER LONDON BOROUGHS

BARKING & DAGENHAM	HOUNSLOW
BARNET	ISLINGTON
BEXLEY	ROYAL BOROUGH OF
BRENT	KENSINGTON & CHELSEA
BROMLEY	ROYAL BOROUGH OF
CAMDEN	KINGSTON UPON
CORPORATION OF	THAMES
LONDON (CITY)	LAMBETH
CROYDON	LEWISHAM
EALING	MERTON
ENFIELD	NEWHAM
GREENWICH	REDBRIDGE
HACKNEY	RICHMOND UPON THAMES
HAMMERSMITH & FULHAM	SOUTHWARK
HARINGEY	SUTTON
HARROW	TOWER HAMLETS
HAVERING	WALTHAM FOREST
HILLINGDON	WANDSWORTH

don

B R O M L E Y

OYDON

S E V E N O A K S

T O N B R I D G E

& M A L L I N G

Sevenoaks

ANDRIDGE

INDEX TO CENTRAL LONDON

General Abbreviations

All	Alley	Conv	Convent	Gar	Garage	Mkts	Markets	Sch	School
Allot	Allotments	Cor	Corner	Gdn	Garden	Ms	Mews	Sec	Secondary
Amb	Ambulance	Coron	Coroners	Gdns	Gardens	Mt	Mount	Shop	Shopping
App	Approach	Cors	Corners	Govt	Government	Mus	Museum	Sq	Square
Apts	Apartments	Cotts	Cottages	Gra	Grange	N	North	St.	Saint
Arc	Arcade	Cov	Covered	Grd	Ground	NT	National Trust	St	Street
Av/Ave	Avenue	Crem	Crematorium	Grds	Grounds	Nat	National	Sta	Station
Bdy	Broadway	Cres	Crescent	Grn	Green	PH	Public House	Sts	Streets
Bk	Bank	Ct	Court	Grns	Greens	PO	Post Office	Sub	Subway
Bldgs	Buildings	Cts	Courts	Gro	Grove	Par	Parade	Swim	Swimming
Boul	Boulevard	Ctyd	Courtyard	Gros	Groves	Pas	Passage	TA	Territorial Army
Bowl	Bowling	Dep	Depot	Gt	Great	Pav	Pavilion	TH	Town Hall
Br/Bri	Bridge	Dev	Development	Ho	House	Pk	Park	Tenn	Tennis
Bus	Business	Dr	Drive	Hos	Houses	Pl	Place	Ter	Terrace
C of E	Church of England	Dws	Dwellings	Hosp	Hospital	Pol	Police	Thea	Theatre
Cath	Cathedral	E	East	Hts	Heights	Prec	Precinct	Trd	Trading
Cem	Cemetery	Ed	Education	Ind	Industrial	Prim	Primary	Twr	Tower
Cen	Central, Centre	Elec	Electricity	Int	International	Prom	Promenade	Twrs	Towers
Cft	Croft	Embk	Embankment	Junct	Junction	Pt	Point	Uni	University
Cfts	Crofts	Est	Estate	La	Lane	Quad	Quadrant	Vil	Villa, Villas
Ch	Church	Ex	Exchange	Las	Lanes	Rbt	Roundabout	Vw	View
Chyd	Churchyard	Exhib	Exhibition	Lib	Library	RC	Roman Catholic	W	West
Cin	Cinema	FB	Footbridge	Lo	Lodge	Rd	Road	Wd	Wood
Circ	Circus	FC	Football Club	Lwr	Lower	Rds	Roads	Wds	Woods
Cl/Clo	Close	Fld	Field	Mag	Magistrates	Rec	Recreation	Wf	Wharf
Co	County	Flds	Fields	Mans	Mansions	Res	Reservoir	Wk	Walk
Coll	College	Fm	Farm	Mem	Memorial	Ri	Rise	Wks	Works
Comm	Community	Gall	Gallery	Mkt	Market	S	South	Yd	Yard

Balaclava Rd **SE1** 130 D3
Balcombe St **NW1** 124 F6
Balcorne St **E9** 126 G2
Balderton St **W1** 124 G8
Baldock St **E3** 127 M4
Baldwin Cres **SE5** 130 A7
Baldwin Ter **N1** 126 A4
Baldwin's Gdns **EC1** 125 N7
Bale Rd **E1** 127 J7
Balfe St **N1** 125 L4
Balfern St **SW11** 128 E7
Balfour St **SE17** 130 B3
Balladier Wk **E14** 127 M7
Ballance Rd **E9** 127 H1
Ballantine St **SW18** 128 C10
Ballast Quay **SE10** 131 P4
Ballater Rd **SW2** 129 L10
Balls Pond Rd **N1** 126 B1
Balmer Rd **E3** 127 K4
Balmes Rd **N1** 126 B3
Balmoral Gro **N7** 125 M1
Balmore Cl **E14** 127 N8
Balniel Gate **SW1** 129 K4
Baltic St E **EC1** 126 A6
Baltic St W **EC1** 126 A6
Balvaird Pl **SW1** 129 K4
Banbury Rd **E9** 127 H2
Banbury St **SW11** 128 E8
Bancroft Rd **E1** 126 G5
Banfield Rd **SE15** 130 F9
Bank End **SE1** 126 A10
Bank St **E14** 127 L10
Bankside Av **SE13** 131 M9
Bankton Rd **SW2** 129 N10
Banner St **EC1** 126 A6
Bannerman Ho **SW8** 129 M5
Banstead St **SE15** 130 G9
Bantry St **SE5** 130 B6
Barbers Rd **E15** 127 M4
Barbican, The **EC2** 126 A7
Barchester St **E14** 127 M7
Barclay Cl **SW6** 128 A6
Barclay Rd **SW6** 128 A6
Bardsley La **SE10** 131 N5
Barfleur La **SE8** 131 K3
Barford St **N1** 125 N3
Barforth Rd **SE15** 130 F9
Baring St **N1** 126 B3
Bark Pl **W2** 124 B9
Barker Dr **NW1** 125 J2
Barker Ms **SW4** 129 H10
Barker St **SW10** 128 C5
Barkston Gdns **SW5** 128 B3
Barkworth Rd **SE16** 130 F4
Barlborough St **SE14** 130 G6
Barleycorn Way **E14** 127 K9
Barnaby Pl **SW7** 128 D3
Barnard Ms **SW11** 128 E10
Barnard Rd **SW11** 128 E10
Barnby St **NW1** 125 J4
Barnes St **E14** 127 J8
Barnes Ter **SE8** 131 K4
Barnet Gro **E2** 126 E5
Barnfield Pl **E14** 131 L3
Barnham St **SE1** 130 C1
Barnsbury Gro **N7** 125 M2
Barnsbury Pk **N1** 125 N2
Barnsbury Rd **N1** 125 N4
Barnsbury Sq **N1** 125 N2
Barnsbury St **N1** 125 N2
Barnsbury Ter **N1** 125 M2
Barnsdale Av **E14** 131 L3
Barnsley St **E1** 126 F6
Barnwood Cl **W9** 124 B6
Baron St **N1** 125 N4
Barons Pl **SE1** 129 N1
Barrett St **W1** 124 G8
Barriedale **SE14** 131 J7
Barrington Rd **SW9** 129 P9
Barrow Hill Rd **NW8** 124 E4
Barset Rd **SE15** 130 G9
Barter St **WC1** 125 L7
Bartholomew Cl **EC1** 126 A7
Bartholomew Cl **SW18** 128 C10
Bartholomew Rd **NW5** 125 J1
Bartholomew Sq **EC1** 126 A6
Bartholomew St **SE1** 130 B2
Bartholomew Vil **NW5** 125 J1
Bartlett Cl **E14** 127 L8
Basevi Way **SE8** 131 M5
Basil St **SW3** 128 F2
Basing Ct **SE15** 130 D7
Basingdon Way **SE5** 130 B10
Basinghall Av **EC2** 126 B7
Basinghall St **EC2** 126 A7
Basire St **N1** 126 A3
Basnett Rd **SW11** 128 G9
Bassett St **NW5** 124 G1
Bastwick St **EC1** 125 P6
Basuto Rd **SW6** 128 A7
Batavia Rd **SE14** 131 J6
Batchelor St **N1** 125 N4
Bateman's Row **EC2** 126 C6
Bath St **EC1** 126 B5
Bath Ter **SE1** 130 A2
Bathurst St **W2** 124 D9
Batten St **SW11** 128 E9
Battersea Br **SW3** 128 D6
Battersea Br **SW11** 128 D6
Battersea Br Rd **SW11** 128 E6
Battersea Ch Rd **SW11** 128 D7
Battersea High St **SW11** 128 D7
Battersea Pk **SW11** 128 F6
Battersea Pk Rd **SW8** 129 H7
Battersea Pk Rd **SW11** 128 E8
Battle Br La **SE1** 126 C10
Battle Br Rd **NW1** 125 L4
Batty St **E1** 126 E8
Bavent Rd **SE5** 130 A8
Bawtree Rd **SE14** 131 J6
Baxendale St **E2** 126 E5
Baxter Rd **N1** 126 B1
Bayford St **E8** 126 F2
Bayham Pl **NW1** 125 J3
Bayham St **NW1** 125 J3
Bayley St **WC1** 125 K7
Baylis Rd **SE1** 129 N1
Baynes St **NW1** 125 J2
Bayswater Rd **W2** 124 D9
Baythorne St **E3** 127 K7
Baytree Rd **SW2** 129 M10
Bazely St **E14** 127 N9
Beachy Rd **E3** 127 L2
Beacon Gate **SE14** 131 H9
Beaconsfield Rd **SE17** 130 B4
Beak St **W1** 125 J9
Beale Pl **E3** 127 K4
Beale Rd **E3** 127 K3
Beanacre Cl **E9** 127 K1
Bear Gdns **SE1** 126 A10
Bear La **SE1** 125 P10
Beaton Cl **SE15** 130 D7
Beatrice Pl **W8** 128 B2
Beatrice Rd **SE1** 130 E3
Beatson Wk **SE16** 127 H10
Beatty St **NW1** 125 J4
Beauchamp Pl **SW3** 128 E2
Beauchamp Rd **SW11** 128 E10
Beaufort Gdns **SW3** 128 E2
Beaufort St **SW3** 128 D5
Beaufoy Wk **SE11** 129 M3
Beaulieu Cl **SE5** 130 B9
Beaumont Gro **E1** 127 H6
Beaumont Pl **W1** 125 J6
Beaumont Sq **E1** 127 H6
Beaumont St **W1** 124 G7
Beaumont Wk **NW3** 124 F2
Beccles St **E14** 127 K9
Beck Cl **SE13** 131 M7
Beck Rd **E8** 126 F3
Beckett Ho **SW9** 129 L8
Beckway St **SE17** 130 B3
Bedale St **SE1** 126 B10
Bedford Av **WC1** 125 K7
Bedford Gdns **W8** 124 A10
Bedford Ho **SW4** 129 L10
Bedford Pl **WC1** 125 L7
Bedford Rd **SW4** 129 L9
Bedford Row **WC1** 125 M7
Bedford Sq **WC1** 125 K7
Bedford St **WC2** 125 L9
Bedford Way **WC1** 125 K6
Beech St **EC2** 126 A7
Beechmore Rd **SW11** 128 F7
Beechwood Rd **E8** 126 D1
Beehive Cl **E8** 126 D2
Beehive Pl **SW9** 129 N9
Beeston Pl **SW1** 129 H2
Belfort Rd **SE15** 130 G8
Belgrave Gdns **NW8** 124 B3
Belgrave Ms N **SW1** 128 G2
Belgrave Ms S **SW1** 128 G2
Belgrave Ms W **SW1** 128 G2
Belgrave Pl **SW1** 128 G2
Belgrave Rd **SW1** 129 H3
Belgrave Sq **SW1** 128 G2
Belgrave St **E1** 127 H8
Belgrove St **WC1** 125 L5
Belinda Rd **SW9** 129 P9
Belitha Vil **N1** 125 M2
Bell La **E1** 126 D7
Bell St **NW1** 124 E7
Bell Wf La **EC4** 126 A9
Bell Yd **WC2** 125 N8
Bellefields Rd **SW9** 129 M9
Bellenden Rd **SE15** 130 D8
Bellevue Pl **E1** 126 G6
Bells All **SW6** 128 A8
Bellwood Rd **SE15** 131 H10
Belmont Cl **SW4** 129 J9
Belmont Gro **SE13** 131 P9
Belmont Hill **SE13** 131 P9
Belmont Pk **SE13** 131 P10
Belmont Pk Cl **SE13** 131 P10
Belmont Rd **SW4** 129 J9
Belmont St **NW1** 124 G2
Belmore St **SW8** 129 K7
Belsham St **E9** 126 G1
Belsize Av **NW3** 124 D1
Belsize Gro **NW3** 124 E1
Belsize La **NW3** 124 D1
Belsize Pk **NW3** 124 D1
Belsize Pk Gdns **NW3** 124 E1
Belsize Rd **NW6** 124 B3
Belsize Sq **NW3** 124 D1
Belsize Ter **NW3** 124 D1
Belton Way **E3** 127 L7
Beltran Rd **SW6** 128 B8
Belvedere Ms **SE15** 130 G9
Belvedere Pl **SE1** 129 P1
Belvedere Rd **SE1** 125 M10
Belvedere Twr, The **SW10** 128 C7
Bemerton Est **N1** 125 M2
Bemerton St **N1** 125 M3
Ben Jonson Rd **E1** 127 J7
Benbow St **SE8** 131 L5
Benedict Rd **SW9** 129 M9
Bengeworth Rd **SE5** 130 A9
Benham Cl **SW11** 128 D9
Benhill Rd **SE5** 130 B6
Benjamin Cl **E8** 126 E3
Benjamin St **EC1** 125 P7
Benledi St **E14** 127 P8
Benn St **E9** 127 J1
Bennett Gro **SE13** 131 M7
Bennett Rd **SW9** 129 N8
Bentham Rd **E9** 127 H1
Bentinck St **W1** 124 G8
Benworth St **E3** 127 K5
Berger Rd **E9** 127 H1
Berkeley Ho **E3** 127 L6
Berkeley Sq **W1** 125 H9
Berkeley St **W1** 125 H9
Berkley Rd **NW1** 124 F2
Berkshire Rd **E9** 127 K1
Bermondsey St **SE1** 130 C1
Bermondsey Wall E **SE16** 130 E1
Bermondsey Wall W **SE16** 130 E1
Bernard St **WC1** 125 L6
Bernays Gro **SW9** 129 M10
Berners Ms **W1** 125 J7
Berners Pl **W1** 125 J8
Berners Rd **N1** 125 N4
Berners St **W1** 125 J7
Bernhardt Cres **NW8** 124 E6
Berry St **EC1** 125 P6
Berryfield Rd **SE17** 129 P4
Berthon St **SE8** 131 L6
Bertrand St **SE13** 131 M9
Berwick St **W1** 125 J8
Bessborough Gdns **SW1** 129 K4
Bessborough Pl **SW1** 129 K4
Bessborough St **SW1** 129 K4
Bessemer Rd **SE5** 130 A8
Besson St **SE14** 130 G7
Bestwood St **SE8** 131 H3
Bethnal Grn Est **E2** 126 G5
Bethnal Grn Rd **E1** 126 D6
Bethnal Grn Rd **E2** 126 D6
Bethwin Rd **SE5** 129 P6
Betterton St **WC2** 125 L8
Bevan St **N1** 126 A3
Bevenden St **N1** 126 B5
Beverley Ct **SE4** 131 K9
Bevington St **SE16** 130 E1
Bevis Marks **EC3** 126 C8
Bewdley St **N1** 125 N2
Bewick Ms **SE15** 130 F6
Bewick St **SW8** 129 H8
Bianca Rd **SE15** 130 D5
Bickenhall St **W1** 124 F7
Bicknell Rd **SE5** 130 A9
Bidborough St **WC1** 125 K5
Bidbury Cl **SE15** 130 C5
Biddulph Rd **W9** 124 B5
Bidwell St **SE15** 130 F7
Biggerstaff Rd **E15** 127 N3
Bigland St **E1** 126 F8
Billing Pl **SW10** 128 B6
Billing Rd **SW10** 128 B6
Billing St **SW10** 128 B6
Billingford Cl **SE4** 131 H10
Billington Rd **SE14** 131 H6
Billiter St **EC3** 126 C8
Billson St **E14** 131 N3
Bina Gdns **SW5** 128 C3
Binfield Rd **SW4** 129 L7
Bingfield St **N1** 125 L3
Bingham St **N1** 126 B1
Binney St **W1** 124 G8
Birchfield St **E14** 127 L9
Birchin La **EC3** 126 B8
Birchington Rd **NW6** 124 A3
Bird in Bush Rd **SE15** 130 E6
Birdcage Wk **SW1** 129 J1
Birdhurst Rd **SW18** 128 C10
Birdsfield La **E3** 127 K3
Birkbeck St **E2** 126 F5
Birkenhead St **WC1** 125 L5
Birley St **SW11** 128 G8
Biscoe Way **SE13** 131 P9
Bishop St **N1** 126 A3
Bishops Br **W2** 124 C8
Bishops Br Rd **W2** 124 B8
Bishop's Rd **SW11** 128 E6
Bishops Ter **SE11** 129 N3
Bishops Way **E2** 126 F4
Bishopsgate **EC2** 126 C8
Bisson Rd **E15** 127 N4
Black Friars La **EC4** 125 P9
Black Prince Rd **SE1** 129 M3
Black Prince Rd **SE11** 129 M3
Blackburn Rd **NW6** 124 B1
Blackburne's Ms **W1** 124 G9
Blackfriars Br **EC4** 125 P9
Blackfriars Br **SE1** 125 P9
Blackfriars Rd **SE1** 125 P10
Blackheath Av **SE10** 131 P6
Blackheath Hill **SE10** 131 N7
Blackheath Ri **SE13** 131 N8
Blackheath Rd **SE10** 131 M7
Blackhorse Rd **SE8** 131 J4
Blacklands Ter **SW3** 128 F3
Blackpool Rd **SE15** 130 F8
Blackstone Est **E8** 126 F2
Blackthorn St **E3** 127 L6
Blacktree Ms **SW9** 129 N9
Blackwall Trd Est **E14** 127 P7
Blackwall Tunnel **E14** 127 P10
Blackwall Tunnel Northern App **E3** 127 L4
Blackwall Tunnel Northern App **E14** 127 L4
Blackwall Way **E14** 127 N9
Blackwood St **SE17** 130 B4
Blair Cl **N1** 126 A1
Blair St **E14** 127 N8
Blake Gdns **SW6** 128 B7
Blaker Rd **E15** 127 N3
Blakes Rd **SE15** 130 C6
Blanchard Way **E8** 126 E1
Blanchedowne **SE5** 130 B10
Blandford Sq **NW1** 124 E6
Blandford St **W1** 124 G7
Blantyre St **SW10** 128 D6
Blashford **NW3** 124 F2
Blasker Wk **E14** 131 L4
Blenheim Gro **SE15** 130 E8
Blenheim Rd **NW8** 124 C4
Blenheim Ter **NW8** 124 C4
Blessington Cl **SE13** 131 P9
Blessington Rd **SE13** 131 P9
Bletchley Ct **N1** 126 B4
Bletchley St **N1** 126 A4
Bliss Cres **SE13** 131 M8
Blissett St **SE10** 131 N7
Blithfield St **W8** 128 B2
Blomfield Rd **W9** 124 C7
Blomfield St **EC2** 126 B7
Blomfield Vil **W2** 124 B7
Blondel St **SW11** 128 G8
Blondin St **E3** 127 L4
Bloomfield Pl **W1** 125 H9
Bloomfield Ter **SW1** 128 G4
Bloomsbury Pl **WC1** 125 L7
Bloomsbury Sq **WC1** 125 L7
Bloomsbury St **WC1** 125 K7
Bloomsbury Way **WC1** 125 L8
Blossom St **E1** 126 C7
Blount St **E14** 127 J8
Blucher Rd **SE5** 130 A6
Blue Anchor La **SE16** 130 E3
Blue Anchor Yd **E1** 126 E9
Blundell St **N7** 125 L2
Blythe St **E2** 126 F5
Boardwalk Pl **E14** 127 N10
Boathouse Wk **SE15** 130 D6
Bobbin Cl **SW4** 129 J9
Bocking St **E8** 126 F3
Bohemia Pl **E8** 126 F1
Bohn Rd **E1** 127 J7
Bolden St **SE8** 131 M8
Bolina Rd **SE16** 130 G4
Bolingbroke Gro **SW11** 128 E10
Bolingbroke Wk **SW11** 128 D6
Bolney St **SW8** 129 M6
Bolsover St **W1** 125 H6
Bolton Cres **SE5** 129 P5
Bolton Gdns **SW5** 128 B4
Bolton Gdns Ms **SW10** 128 B4
Bolton Rd **NW8** 124 B3
Bolton St **W1** 125 H10
Boltons, The **SW10** 128 C4
Boltons Pl **SW5** 128 C4
Bombay St **SE16** 130 F3
Bonar Rd **SE15** 130 E6
Bond Ct **EC4** 126 B8
Bondway **SW8** 129 L5
Bonfield Rd **SE13** 131 N10
Bonhill St **EC2** 126 B6
Bonita Ms **SE4** 131 H9
Bonner Rd **E2** 126 G4
Bonner St **E2** 126 G4
Bonnington Sq **SW8** 129 M5
Bonny St **NW1** 125 J2
Bonsor St **SE5** 130 C6
Boot St **N1** 126 C5
Borland Rd **SE15** 130 G10
Borough High St **SE1** 130 A1
Borough Rd **SE1** 129 P2
Borthwick St **SE8** 131 L4
Boscobel Pl **SW1** 128 G3
Boscobel St **NW8** 124 D6
Boston Pl **NW1** 124 F6
Boswell St **WC1** 125 L7
Boulcott St **E1** 127 H8
Boulevard, The **SW6** 128 C7
Boundary La **SE17** 130 A5
Boundary Rd **NW8** 124 B3
Boundary St **E2** 126 D6
Bourdon St **W1** 125 H9
Bourne Est **EC1** 125 N7
Bourne St **SW1** 128 G3
Bourne Ter **W2** 124 B7
Bournemouth Cl **SE15** 130 E8
Bournemouth Rd **SE15** 130 E8
Bousfield Rd **SE14** 131 H8
Boutflower Rd **SW11** 128 E10
Bouverie Pl **W2** 124 D8
Bouverie St **EC4** 125 N8
Bovingdon Rd **SW6** 128 B7
Bow Back Rivers Wk **E15** 127 M2
Bow Br Est **E3** 127 M5
Bow Common La **E3** 127 K6
Bow Ind Pk **E15** 127 L2
Bow La **EC4** 126 A8
Bow Rd **E3** 127 K5
Bow St **WC2** 125 L8
Bowden St **SE11** 129 N4
Bowditch **SE8** 131 K4
Bowen St **E14** 127 M8
Bower St **E1** 127 H8
Bowerdean St **SW6** 128 B7
Bowerman Av **SE14** 131 J5
Bowhill Cl **SW9** 129 N6
Bowl Ct **EC2** 126 C6
Bowland Rd **SW4** 129 K10
Bowling Grn La **EC1** 125 N6
Bowling Grn Pl **SE1** 130 B1
Bowling Grn St **SE11** 129 N5
Bowood Rd **SW11** 128 G10
Bowsprit Pt **E14** 131 L2
Bowyer Pl **SE5** 130 B6
Bowyer St **SE5** 130 A6
Boyd St **E1** 126 E8
Boyfield St **SE1** 129 P1
Boyne Rd **SE13** 131 N9
Boyson Rd **SE17** 130 B5
Brabazon St **E14** 127 M8
Brabourn Gro **SE15** 130 G8
Brackley Av **SE15** 130 F9
Bracklyn St **N1** 126 B4
Bradbourne St **SW6** 128 A8
Bradenham Cl **SE17** 130 B5
Bradmead **SW8** 129 H6
Bradstock Rd **E9** 127 H1
Bradwell St **E1** 127 H5
Brady St **E1** 126 F6
Braes St **N1** 125 P2
Braganza St **SE17** 129 P4
Braham St **E1** 126 D8
Braintree St **E2** 126 G5
Braithwaite Twr **W2** 124 D7
Bramah Grn **SW9** 129 N7
Bramcote Gro **SE16** 130 G4
Bramerton St **SW3** 128 E5
Bramford Rd **SW18** 128 C10
Bramham Gdns **SW5** 128 B4
Bramlands Cl **SW11** 128 E9
Bramshaw Rd **E9** 127 H1
Bramwell Ms **N1** 125 M3
Branch Pl **N1** 126 B3
Branch Rd **E14** 127 J9
Branch St **SE15** 130 C6
Brand St **SE10** 131 N6
Brandon Est **SE17** 129 P5
Brandon Rd **N7** 125 L2
Brandon St **SE17** 130 A3
Brangton Rd **SE11** 129 M4
Branscombe St **SE13** 131 M9
Brassey Sq **SW11** 128 G9
Braxfield Rd **SE4** 131 J10
Bray **NW3** 124 E2
Bray Pl **SW3** 128 F3
Brayards Rd **SE15** 130 F8
Brayburne Av **SW4** 129 J8
Bread St **EC4** 126 A9
Breakspears Rd **SE4** 131 K9
Bream St **E3** 127 L2
Bream's Bldgs **EC4** 125 N8
Breer St **SW6** 128 B9
Bremner Rd **SW7** 128 C1
Brendon St **W1** 124 E8
Brenthouse Rd **E9** 126 F2
Brenton St **E14** 127 J8
Bressenden Pl **SW1** 129 H2
Brewer St **W1** 125 J9
Brewery Rd **N7** 125 L2
Brewhouse La **E1** 126 F10
Brewhouse Wk **SE16** 127 J10
Brewster Ho **E14** 127 K9
Briant St **SE14** 131 H7
Brick La **E1** 126 D7
Brick La **E2** 126 D5
Brick St **W1** 125 H10
Bricklayer's Arms Distribution Cen **SE1** 130 C3
Bride St **N7** 125 M1
Bridewain St **SE1** 130 D2
Bridge App **NW1** 124 G2
Bridge La **SW11** 128 E7
Bridge Meadows **SE14** 131 H5
Bridge Pl **SW1** 129 H3
Bridge Rd **E15** 127 P2
Bridge St **SW1** 129 L1
Bridgefoot **SE1** 129 L4
Bridgeman Rd **N1** 125 M2
Bridgeman St **NW8** 124 E4
Bridgend Rd **SW18** 128 C10
Bridges Ct **SW11** 128 D9
Bridgeway St **NW1** 125 J4
Bridgwater Rd **E15** 127 N3
Bridport Pl **N1** 126 B4
Brief St **SE5** 129 P7
Bright St **E14** 127 M8
Brightlingsea Pl **E14** 127 K9
Brighton Ter **SW9** 129 M10
Brill Pl **NW1** 125 K4
Brindley St **SE14** 131 K7
Brinklow Ho **W2** 124 B7
Brinkworth Way **E9** 127 K1
Brion Pl **E14** 127 N7
Brisbane St **SE5** 130 B6
Bristol Gdns **W9** 124 B6
Britannia Rd **E14** 131 L3
Britannia Rd **SW6** 128 B6
Britannia Row **N1** 125 P3
Britannia St **WC1** 125 M5
Britannia Wk **N1** 126 B5
British St **E3** 127 K5
Britten St **SW3** 128 E4
Britton St **EC1** 125 P6
Brixton Oval **SW2** 129 N10
Brixton Rd **SW9** 129 N8
Brixton Sta Rd **SW9** 129 N10
Broad La **EC2** 126 C7
Broad Sanctuary **SW1** 129 K1
Broad Wk **NW1** 125 H5
Broad Wk **W1** 124 G10
Broad Wk, The **W8** 124 B10
Broadfield La **NW1** 125 L2
Broadhinton Rd **SW4** 129 H9
Broadhurst Gdns **NW6** 124 B1
Broadley St **NW8** 124 E7
Broadley Ter **NW1** 124 E6
Broadwalk Ct **W8** 124 A10
Broadwall **SE1** 125 N10
Broadway **E15** 127 P2
Broadway **SW1** 129 K2
Broadway Mkt **E8** 126 F3
Broadwick St **W1** 125 J8
Brock Pl **E3** 127 M6
Brockham St **SE1** 130 A2
Brockill Cres **SE4** 131 J10
Brocklehurst St **SE14** 131 H6
Brockley Footpath **SE15** 130 G10
Brockley Gdns **SE4** 131 K8
Brockley Rd **SE4** 131 K9
Brodlove La **E1** 127 H9
Broke Wk **E8** 126 E3
Brokesley St **E3** 127 K6
Bromar Rd **SE5** 130 C9
Bromell's Rd **SW4** 129 J10
Bromfelde Rd **SW4** 129 K8
Bromfelde Wk **SW4** 129 K8
Bromfield St **N1** 125 N4
Bromley Hall Rd **E14** 127 N7
Bromley High St **E3** 127 M5
Bromley St **E1** 127 H7
Brompton Pk Cres **SW6** 128 B5
Brompton Pl **SW3** 128 E2
Brompton Rd **SW1** 128 E2
Brompton Rd **SW3** 128 E2
Brompton Rd **SW7** 128 E2
Brompton Sq **SW3** 128 E2
Bromyard Ho **SE15** 130 F6
Bronte Ho **NW6** 124 A5
Bronti Cl **SE17** 130 A4
Bronze St **SE8** 131 L6
Brook Dr **SE11** 129 N3
Brook Gate **W1** 124 F9
Brook St **W1** 125 H8
Brook St **W2** 124 D9
Brookbank Rd **SE13** 131 L9
Brooke St **EC1** 125 N7
Brookfield Rd **E9** 127 J1
Brookmill Rd **SE8** 131 L7
Brook's Ms **W1** 125 H9
Brooksbank St **E9** 126 G1
Brooksby St **N1** 125 N2
Broome Way **SE5** 130 B6
Broomfield St **E14** 127 L7
Broomgrove Rd **SW9** 129 M8
Broomhouse La **SW6** 128 A8
Broomhouse Rd **SW6** 128 A8
Brougham Rd **E8** 126 E3
Brougham St **SW11** 128 F8
Broughton Dr **SW9** 129 N10

Clavell St **SE10** 131 N5
Claverton St **SW1** 129 J4
Claylands Pl **SW8** 129 N6
Claylands Rd **SW8** 129 M5
Claypole Rd **E15** 127 N4
Clayton Cres **N1** 125 L3
Clayton Ms **SE10** 131 P7
Clayton Rd **SE15** 130 E7
Clayton St **SE11** 129 N5
Clearwell Dr **W9** 124 B6
Cleaver Sq **SE11** 129 N4
Cleaver St **SE11** 129 N4
Clemence St **E14** 127 K7
Clement Av **SW4** 129 K10
Clement's Inn **WC2** 125 M8
Clements La **EC4** 126 B9
Clements Rd **SE16** 130 E2
Clephane Rd **N1** 126 A1
Clerkenwell Cl **EC1** 125 N6
Clerkenwell Grn **EC1** 125 P6
Clerkenwell Rd **EC1** 125 N7
Clermont Rd **E9** 126 G3
Cleve Rd **NW6** 124 A2
Cleveland Gdns **W2** 124 C8
Cleveland Rd **N1** 126 B2
Cleveland Row **SW1** 125 J10
Cleveland Sq **W2** 124 C8
Cleveland St **W1** 125 H6
Cleveland Ter **W2** 124 C8
Cleveland Way **E1** 126 G6
Clichy Est **E1** 126 G7
Cliff Rd **NW1** 125 K1
Cliff Ter **SE8** 131 L8
Cliff Vil **NW1** 125 K1
Clifford Dr **SW9** 129 P10
Clifford St **W1** 125 J9
Cliffview Rd **SE13** 131 L9
Clifton Cres **SE15** 130 F6
Clifton Gdns **W9** 124 C6
Clifton Gro **E8** 126 E1
Clifton Hill **NW8** 124 B4
Clifton Pl **W2** 124 D9
Clifton Ri **SE14** 131 J6
Clifton Rd **N1** 126 A1
Clifton Rd **W9** 124 C6
Clifton St **EC2** 126 C7
Clifton Vil **W9** 124 B7
Clifton Way **SE15** 130 F6
Clink St **SE1** 126 A10
Clinton Rd **E3** 127 J5
Clipper Way **SE13** 131 N10
Clipstone Ms **W1** 125 J6
Clipstone St **W1** 125 J7
Clitheroe Rd **SW9** 129 L8
Cliveden Pl **SW1** 128 G3
Cloak La **EC4** 126 A9
Clock Twr Pl **N7** 125 L1
Cloth Fair **EC1** 125 P7
Cloudesley Pl **N1** 125 N3
Cloudesley Rd **N1** 125 N3
Cloudesley Sq **N1** 125 N3
Cloudesley St **N1** 125 N3
Clove Cres **E14** 127 P9
Clove Hitch Quay **SW11** 128 C9
Cloysters Grn **E1** 126 E10
Club Row **E1** 126 D6
Club Row **E2** 126 D6
Cluny Ms **SW5** 128 A3
Clutton St **E14** 127 M7
Clyde St **SE8** 131 K5
Clyston St **SW8** 129 J8
Coate St **E2** 126 E4
Cobb St **E1** 126 D7
Cobbett St **SW8** 129 M6
Coborn Rd **E3** 127 K5
Coborn St **E3** 127 K5
Cobourg Rd **SE5** 130 D5
Cobourg St **NW1** 125 J5
Cochrane St **NW8** 124 D4
Cock La **EC1** 125 P7
Cockayne Way **SE8** 131 J4
Cockspur St **SW1** 125 K10
Code St **E1** 126 D6
Cody Rd **E16** 127 P6
Cody Rd Business Cen **E16** 127 P6
Coin St **SE1** 125 N10
Coity Rd **NW5** 124 G1
Coke St **E1** 126 E8
Colbeck Ms **SW7** 128 B3
Cold Blow La **SE14** 131 H6
Cold Harbour **E14** 131 N1
Coldbath St **SE13** 131 M7
Coldharbour La **SE5** 129 N10
Coldharbour La **SW9** 129 N10
Cole St **SE1** 130 A1
Colebeck Ms **N1** 125 P1
Colebert Av **E1** 126 G6
Colebrooke Row **N1** 125 P4
Colegrove Rd **SE15** 130 D6
Coleherne Ct **SW5** 128 B4
Coleherne Ms **SW10** 128 B4
Coleherne Rd **SW10** 128 B4
Coleman Flds **N1** 126 A3
Coleman Rd **SE5** 130 C6
Coleman St **EC2** 126 B8
Coleridge Cl **SW8** 129 H8
Coleridge Gdns **SW10** 128 B6
Coleridge Sq **SW10** 128 C6
Colestown St **SW11** 128 E8
Coley St **WC1** 125 M6
College App **SE10** 131 N5
College Cres **NW3** 124 D1
College Cross **N1** 125 N2
College Pk Cl **SE13** 131 P10
College Pl **NW1** 125 J3
College Ter **E3** 127 K5
Collent St **E9** 126 G1
Collett Rd **SE16** 130 E2
Collier St **N1** 125 M4
Collingham Gdns **SW5** 128 B3
Collingham Pl **SW5** 128 B3
Collingham Rd **SW5** 128 B3
Collingwood St **E1** 126 F6
Colls Rd **SE15** 130 G7
Colmore Ms **SE15** 130 F7
Colnbrook St **SE1** 129 P2
Cologne Rd **SW11** 128 D10
Colombo St **SE1** 125 P10
Colonnade **WC1** 125 L6
Colonnade Wk **SW1** 129 H3
Colonnades, The **W2** 124 B8
Columbia Rd **E2** 126 D5
Columbine Way **SE13** 131 N8
Colville Est **N1** 126 B3
Colyer Cl **N1** 125 M4
Comber Gro **SE5** 130 A7
Combermere Rd **SW9** 129 M9
Comerford Rd **SE4** 131 J10
Comet Pl **SE8** 131 L6
Comet St **SE8** 131 L6
Comfort St **SE15** 130 C5
Commercial Rd **E1** 126 E8
Commercial Rd **E14** 126 G8
Commercial St **E1** 126 D6
Commercial Way **SE15** 130 D6
Commodore St **E1** 127 J6
Compayne Gdns **NW6** 124 B2
Compton Av **N1** 125 P1
Compton Cl **E3** 127 L7
Compton Rd **N1** 125 P1
Compton St **EC1** 125 P6
Compton Ter **N1** 125 P1
Comus Pl **SE17** 130 C3
Comyn Rd **SW11** 128 E10
Concanon Rd **SW2** 129 M10
Concert Hall App **SE1** 125 M10
Concorde Way **SE16** 131 H3
Condell Rd **SW8** 129 J7
Condray Pl **SW11** 128 E6
Conduit Ms **W2** 124 D8
Conduit Pl **W2** 124 D8
Conduit St **W1** 125 H9
Coney Way **SW8** 129 M5
Congreve St **SE17** 130 C3
Coniger Rd **SW6** 128 A8
Conington Rd **SE13** 131 M8
Coniston Ho **SE5** 130 A6
Conistone Way **N7** 125 L2
Connaught Pl **W2** 124 F9
Connaught Sq **W2** 124 F8
Connaught St **W2** 124 E8
Consort Rd **SE15** 130 F7
Constitution Hill **SW1** 129 H1
Content St **SE17** 130 B3
Conway St **W1** 125 J6
Conyer St **E3** 127 J4
Cook's Rd **E15** 127 M4
Cooks Rd **SE17** 129 P5
Coombs St **N1** 125 P4
Coopers Cl **E1** 126 G6
Coopers La **NW1** 125 K4
Coopers Rd **SE1** 130 D4
Cope Pl **W8** 128 A2
Cope St **SE16** 131 H3
Copeland Dr **E14** 131 L3
Copeland Rd **SE15** 130 E8
Copenhagen Pl **E14** 127 K8
Copenhagen St **N1** 125 L3
Copleston Pas **SE15** 130 D9
Copleston Rd **SE15** 130 D9
Copley St **E1** 127 H7
Copper Row **SE1** 126 D10
Copperas St **SE8** 131 M5
Copperfield Rd **E3** 127 J6
Copperfield St **SE1** 129 P1
Coppock Cl **SW11** 128 E8
Copthall Av **EC2** 126 B8
Copthall Ct **EC2** 126 B8
Coptic St **WC1** 125 L7
Coral St **SE1** 129 N1
Coram St **WC1** 125 L6
Corbden Cl **SE15** 130 D7
Corbiere Ho **N1** 126 C3
Corbridge Cres **E2** 126 F4
Cordelia Cl **SE24** 129 P10
Cordelia St **E14** 127 M8
Corfield St **E2** 126 F5
Coriander Av **E14** 127 P8
Cork St **W1** 125 J9
Corlett St **NW1** 124 E7
Cormont Rd **SE5** 129 P7
Cornelia St **N7** 125 M1
Cornhill **EC3** 126 B8
Cornmill La **SE13** 131 M9
Cornwall Av **E2** 126 G5
Cornwall Gdns **SW7** 128 B2
Cornwall Ms S **SW7** 128 C2
Cornwall Rd **SE1** 125 N10
Cornwall Sq **SE11** 129 P4
Cornwood Dr **E1** 126 G8
Coronet St **N1** 126 C5
Corporation Row **EC1** 125 N6
Corrance Rd **SW2** 129 L10
Corry Dr **SW9** 129 P10
Corsham St **N1** 126 B5
Corsica St **N5** 125 P1
Corunna Rd **SW8** 129 J7
Corunna Ter **SW8** 129 J7
Cossall Wk **SE15** 130 F7
Cosser St **SE1** 129 N2
Costa St **SE15** 130 E8
Cosway St **NW1** 124 E7
Cotall St **E14** 127 L8
Cotleigh Rd **NW6** 124 A2
Cottage Grn **SE5** 130 B6
Cottage Gro **SW9** 129 L9
Cottage Pl **SW3** 128 E2
Cottage St **E14** 127 M9
Cottesmore Gdns **W8** 128 B2
Cottingham Rd **SW8** 129 M6
Cotton Row **SW11** 128 C9
Cotton St **E14** 127 N9
Coulgate St **SE4** 131 J9
Coulson St **SW3** 128 F3
Councillor St **SE5** 130 A6
County Gro **SE5** 130 A7
County St **SE1** 130 A2
Courland Gro **SW8** 129 K7
Courland Gro Hall **SW8** 129 K8
Courland St **SW8** 129 K7
Court Gdns **N7** 125 N1
Courtenay St **SE11** 129 N4
Courtfield Gdns **SW5** 128 B3
Courtfield Rd **SW7** 128 B3
Courthill Rd **SE13** 131 N10
Courtnell St **W2** 124 A8
Courtyard, The **N1** 125 M2
Covent Gdn **WC2** 125 L9
Coventry Rd **E1** 126 F6
Coventry Rd **E2** 126 F6
Coventry St **W1** 125 K9
Coverley Cl **E1** 126 E7
Cowcross St **EC1** 125 P7
Cowdenbeath Path **N1** 125 M3
Cowley Rd **SW9** 129 N7
Cowper St **EC2** 126 B6
Cowthorpe Rd **SW8** 129 K7
Crabtree Cl **E2** 126 D4
Crampton St **SE17** 129 P3
Cranbourn St **WC2** 125 K9
Cranbrook Rd **SE8** 131 L7
Cranbury Rd **SW6** 128 B8
Crane Gro **N7** 125 N1
Crane St **SE10** 131 P4
Crane St **SE15** 130 D7
Cranfield Rd **SE4** 131 K9
Cranford St **E1** 127 H9
Cranleigh Ms **SW11** 128 E8
Cranleigh St **NW1** 125 J4
Cranley Gdns **SW7** 128 C4
Cranley Ms **SW7** 128 C4
Cranley Pl **SW7** 128 D3
Cranmer Ct **SW4** 129 K9
Cranmer Rd **SW9** 129 N6
Cranston Est **N1** 126 B4
Cranswick Rd **SE16** 130 F4
Cranwell Cl **E3** 127 M6
Cranwood St **EC1** 126 B5
Cranworth Gdns **SW9** 129 N7
Craven Hill **W2** 124 C9
Craven Hill Gdns **W2** 124 C9
Craven Hill Ms **W2** 124 C9
Craven Pas **WC2** 125 L10
Craven Rd **W2** 124 C9
Craven St **WC2** 125 L10
Craven Ter **W2** 124 C9
Crawford Est **SE5** 130 A8
Crawford Pl **W1** 124 E8
Crawford Rd **SE5** 130 A7
Crawford St **W1** 124 F7
Crawthew Gro **SE22** 130 D10
Creasy Est **SE1** 130 C2
Credon Rd **SE16** 130 F4
Creechurch La **EC3** 126 C8
Creek Rd **SE8** 131 L5
Creek Rd **SE10** 131 L5
Creekside **SE8** 131 M6
Cremer St **E2** 126 D4
Cremorne Rd **SW10** 128 C6
Crescent Gro **SW4** 129 J10
Crescent Pl **SW3** 128 E3
Crescent St **N1** 125 M2
Crescent Way **SE4** 131 L9
Cresford Rd **SW6** 128 B7
Cresset Rd **E9** 126 G1
Cresset St **SW4** 129 K9
Cressingham Rd **SE13** 131 N9
Cresswell Gdns **SW5** 128 C4
Cresswell Pl **SW10** 128 C4
Cressy Pl **E1** 126 G7
Crestfield St **WC1** 125 L5
Crewdson Rd **SW9** 129 N6
Crews St **E14** 131 L3
Crewys Rd **SE15** 130 F8
Cricketers Ct **SE11** 129 P3
Crimscott St **SE1** 130 C2
Crimsworth Rd **SW8** 129 K7
Crinan St **N1** 125 L4
Cringle St **SW8** 129 J6
Crispin St **E1** 126 D7
Croft St **SE8** 131 J3
Crofters Way **NW1** 125 K3
Crofton Rd **SE5** 130 C7
Crofts St **E1** 126 E9
Crogsland Rd **NW1** 124 G2
Cromer St **WC1** 125 L5
Crompton St **W2** 124 D6
Cromwell Cres **SW5** 128 A3
Cromwell Gdns **SW7** 128 D2
Cromwell Ms **SW7** 128 D3
Cromwell Pl **SW7** 128 D3
Cromwell Rd **SW5** 128 B3
Cromwell Rd **SW7** 128 B3
Cromwell Rd **SW9** 129 P7
Cromwell Twr **EC2** 126 A7
Crondace Rd **SW6** 128 A7
Crondall St **N1** 126 B4
Cronin St **SE15** 130 D6
Crooke Rd **SE8** 131 J4
Crooms Hill **SE10** 131 P6
Crooms Hill Gro **SE10** 131 N6
Cropley St **N1** 126 B4
Cropthorne Ct **W9** 124 C5
Crosby Row **SE1** 130 B1
Cross Av **SE10** 131 P5
Cross Rd **SE5** 130 C8
Cross St **N1** 125 P3
Crossfield Rd **NW3** 124 D2
Crossfield St **SE8** 131 L6
Crossford St **SW9** 129 M8
Crosslet Vale **SE10** 131 M7
Crossley St **N7** 125 N1
Crossmount Ho **SE5** 130 A6
Crossthwaite Av **SE5** 130 B10
Crosswall **EC3** 126 D9
Croston St **E8** 126 E3
Crowder St **E1** 126 F9
Crowhurst Cl **SW9** 129 N8
Crowland Ter **N1** 126 B2
Crown Cl **E3** 127 L3
Crown Cl **NW6** 124 B1
Crown Pas **SW1** 125 J10
Crown Pl **EC2** 126 C7
Crown St **SE5** 130 A6
Crowndale Rd **NW1** 125 J4
Crows Rd **E15** 127 P5
Crucifix La **SE1** 130 C1
Cruden St **N1** 125 P3
Cruikshank St **WC1** 125 N5
Crutched Friars **EC3** 126 C9
Crystal Palace Rd **SE22** 130 E10
Cuba St **E14** 131 L1
Cubitt St **WC1** 125 M5
Cubitt Ter **SW4** 129 J9
Cudworth St **E1** 126 F6
Cuff Pt **E2** 126 D5
Culford Gdns **SW3** 128 F3
Culford Gro **N1** 126 C1
Culford Rd **N1** 126 C2
Culloden Cl **SE16** 130 E4
Culloden St **E14** 127 N8
Culmore Rd **SE15** 130 F6
Culross St **W1** 124 G9
Culvert Pl **SW11** 128 G8
Culvert Rd **SW11** 128 F8
Cumberland Cl **E8** 126 D1
Cumberland Gate **W1** 124 F9
Cumberland Mkt **NW1** 125 H5
Cumberland St **SW1** 129 H4
Cumming St **N1** 125 M4
Cunard Wk **SE16** 131 J3
Cundy St **SW1** 128 G3
Cunningham Pl **NW8** 124 D6
Cupar Rd **SW11** 128 G7
Cureton St **SW1** 129 K3
Curlew St **SE1** 130 D1
Curness St **SE13** 131 N10
Cursitor St **EC4** 125 N8
Curtain Rd **EC2** 126 C6
Curtis St **SE1** 130 D3
Curtis Way **SE1** 130 D3
Curzon Gate **W1** 124 G10
Curzon St **W1** 124 G10
Custom Ho Reach **SE16** 131 K1
Custom Ho Wk **EC3** 126 C9
Cut, The **SE1** 129 N1
Cutcombe Rd **SE5** 130 A8
Cuthbert St **W2** 124 D6
Cuthill Wk **SE5** 130 B7
Cutler St **E1** 126 C8
Cyclops Ms **E14** 131 L3
Cynthia St **N1** 125 M4
Cyntra Pl **E8** 126 F2
Cyprus Pl **E2** 126 G4
Cyprus St **E2** 126 G4
Cyril Mans **SW11** 128 F7
Cyrus St **EC1** 125 P6
Czar St **SE8** 131 L5

D

Dabin Cres **SE10** 131 N7
Dacca St **SE8** 131 K5
Dace Rd **E3** 127 L2
Dacre St **SW1** 129 K2
Dagmar Rd **SE5** 130 C7
Dagmar Ter **N1** 125 P3
Dagnall St **SW11** 128 F8
Dairy Ms **SW9** 129 L9
Daisy La **SW6** 128 A9
Dalberg Rd **SW2** 129 N10
Dalby Rd **SW18** 128 C10
Dalby St **NW5** 125 H1
Dale Rd **SE17** 129 P5
Daleham Ms **NW3** 124 D1
Dalehead **NW1** 125 J4
Daley St **E9** 127 H1
Daley Thompson Way **SW8** 129 H8
Dalgleish St **E14** 127 J8
Daling Way **E3** 127 J3
Dallington St **EC1** 125 P6
Dalrymple Rd **SE4** 131 J10
Dalston La **E8** 126 D1
Dalwood St **SE5** 130 C7
Dalyell Rd **SW9** 129 M9
Dame St **N1** 126 A4
Damien St **E1** 126 F8
Danbury St **N1** 125 P4
Danby St **SE15** 130 D9
Danesdale Rd **E9** 127 J1
Danesfield **SE5** 130 C5
Daneville Rd **SE5** 130 B7
Daniel Gdns **SE15** 130 D6
Daniels Rd **SE15** 130 G9
Dante Rd **SE11** 129 P3
Danvers St **SW3** 128 D5
D'Arblay St **W1** 125 J8
Darien Rd **SW11** 128 D9
Darling Rd **SE4** 131 L9
Darling Row **E1** 126 F6
Darnley Ho **E14** 127 J8
Darnley Rd **E9** 126 F1
Darsley Dr **SW8** 129 K7
Dartford St **SE17** 130 A5
Dartmouth Gro **SE10** 131 N7
Dartmouth Hill **SE10** 131 N7
Dartmouth Row **SE10** 131 N8
Dartmouth St **SW1** 129 K1
Dartmouth Ter **SE10** 131 P7
Darwin St **SE17** 130 B3
Datchelor Pl **SE5** 130 B7
Date St **SE17** 130 A4
Daubeney Twr **SE8** 131 K4
Davenant St **E1** 126 E7
Daventry St **NW1** 124 E7
Davey Cl **N7** 125 M1
Davey Rd **E9** 127 L2
Davey St **SE15** 130 D5
David St **E15** 127 P1
Davidge St **SE1** 129 P1
Davidson Gdns **SW8** 129 L6
Davies St **W1** 125 H9
Dawes St **SE17** 130 B4
Dawson Pl **W2** 124 A9
Dawson St **E2** 126 D4
Dayton Gro **SE15** 130 G7
De Beauvoir Cres **N1** 126 C3
De Beauvoir Est **N1** 126 B3
De Beauvoir Rd **N1** 126 C3
De Beauvoir Sq **N1** 126 C2
De Crespigny Pk **SE5** 130 B8
De Laune St **SE17** 129 P4
De Morgan Rd **SW6** 128 B9
De Vere Gdns **W8** 128 C1
Deacon Ms **N1** 126 B2
Deacon Way **SE17** 130 A3
Deal Porters Way **SE16** 130 G2
Deal St **E1** 126 E7
Deals Gateway **SE13** 131 L7
Dean Bradley St **SW1** 129 L2
Dean Farrar St **SW1** 129 K2
Dean Ryle St **SW1** 129 L3
Dean Stanley St **SW1** 129 L2
Dean St **W1** 125 K8
Dean Trench St **SW1** 129 L2
Deancross St **E1** 126 G8
Deanery St **W1** 124 G10
Deans Bldgs **SE17** 130 B3
Decima St **SE1** 130 C2
Dee St **E14** 127 N8
Deeley Rd **SW8** 129 K7
Deepdene Rd **SE5** 130 B10
Deerdale Rd **SE24** 130 A10
Delaford Rd **SE16** 130 F4
Delamere Ter **W2** 124 B7
Delancey St **NW1** 125 H3
Delaware Rd **W9** 124 B6
Delhi St **N1** 125 L3
Delius Gro **E15** 127 P4
Dell Cl **E15** 127 P3
Dellow St **E1** 126 F9
Deloraine St **SE8** 131 L7
Delverton Rd **SE17** 129 P4
Delvino Rd **SW6** 128 A7
Denbigh Pl **SW1** 129 J4
Denbigh St **SW1** 129 J3
Dene Cl **SE4** 131 J9
Denman Rd **SE15** 130 D7
Denmark Gro **N1** 125 N4
Denmark Hill **SE5** 130 B7
Denmark Hill Est **SE5** 130 B10
Denmark Rd **SE5** 130 A7
Denmark St **WC2** 125 K8
Denne Ter **E8** 126 D3
Dennetts Rd **SE14** 130 G7
Denning Cl **NW8** 124 C5
Dennington Pk Rd **NW6** 124 A1
Dennison Pt **E15** 127 N2
Denny St **SE11** 129 N4
Denyer St **SW3** 128 E3
Deptford Br **SE8** 131 L7
Deptford Bdy **SE8** 131 L7
Deptford Ch St **SE8** 131 L5
Deptford Ferry Rd **E14** 131 L3
Deptford Grn **SE8** 131 L5
Deptford High St **SE8** 131 L5
Deptford Strand **SE8** 131 K3
Deptford Wf **SE8** 131 K3
Derby Rd **E9** 127 H3
Derbyshire St **E2** 126 E5
Dericote St **E8** 126 E3
Dering St **W1** 125 H8
Derry St **W8** 128 B1
Derwent Gro **SE22** 130 D10
Desborough Cl **W2** 124 B7
Desmond St **SE14** 131 J5
Devas St **E3** 127 M6
Deverell St **SE1** 130 B2
Devon St **SE15** 130 F5
Devonia Rd **N1** 125 P4
Devonport St **E1** 126 G8
Devons Est **E3** 127 M5
Devons Rd **E3** 127 L7
Devonshire Cl **W1** 125 H7
Devonshire Dr **SE10** 131 M6
Devonshire Gro **SE15** 130 F5
Devonshire Ms S **W1** 125 H7
Devonshire Ms W **W1** 125 H7
Devonshire Pl **W1** 124 G6
Devonshire St **W1** 125 H7
Devonshire Ter **W2** 124 C8
Dewar St **SE15** 130 E9
Dewberry St **E14** 127 N7
Dewey Rd **N1** 125 N4
D'Eynsford Rd **SE5** 130 B7
Dial Wk, The **W8** 128 B1
Diamond St **SE15** 130 C6
Diamond Ter **SE10** 131 N7
Dibden St **N1** 125 P3
Dickens Est **SE1** 130 D1
Dickens Est **SE16** 130 D1
Dickens Ho **NW6** 124 A5
Dickens Sq **SE1** 130 A2
Dickens St **SW8** 129 H8
Digby Rd **E9** 127 H1
Digby St **E2** 126 G5
Dighton Ct **SE5** 130 A5
Dilke St **SW3** 128 F5
Dimson Cres **E3** 127 L6
Dingle Gdns **E14** 127 L9
Dingley Pl **EC1** 126 A5
Dingley Rd **EC1** 126 A5
Discovery Wk **E1** 126 F10
Diss St **E2** 126 D5
Distaff La **EC4** 126 A9
Distin St **SE11** 129 N3
Ditch All **SE10** 131 M7
Ditchburn St **E14** 127 N9
Dixon Rd **SE14** 131 J7
Dixon's All **SE16** 130 F1
Dobson Cl **NW6** 124 D2
Dock Hill Av **SE16** 131 H1
Dock St **E1** 126 E9
Dockers Tanner Rd **E14** 131 L2
Dockhead **SE1** 130 D1
Dockley Rd **SE16** 130 E2
Docwra's Bldgs **N1** 126 C1
Dod St **E14** 127 K8
Doddington Gro **SE17** 129 P5
Doddington Pl **SE17** 129 P5
Dodson St **SE1** 129 N1
Dog Kennel Hill **SE22** 130 C9
Dog Kennel Hill Est **SE22** 130 C9
Dolben St **SE1** 125 P10
Dolland St **SE11** 129 M4
Dolman St **SW4** 129 M10
Dolphin La **E14** 127 M9
Dolphin Sq **SW1** 129 J4

Dombey St **WC1** 125 M7
Domett Cl **SE5** 130 B10
Don Phelan Cl **SE5** 130 B7
Donegal St **N1** 125 M4
Dongola Rd **E1** 127 J7
Donne Pl **SW3** 128 E3
Dora St **E14** 127 K8
Dora Way **SW9** 129 N8
Doran Wk **E15** 127 N2
Doric Way **NW1** 125 K5
Dorking Cl **SE8** 131 K5
Dorman Way **NW8** 124 D3
Dorney **NW3** 124 E2
Dorothy Rd **SW11** 128 F9
Dorrington St **EC1** 125 N7
Dorset Est **E2** 126 D5
Dorset Pl **E15** 127 P1
Dorset Ri **EC4** 125 P8
Dorset Rd **SW8** 129 M6
Dorset Sq **NW1** 124 F6
Dorset St **W1** 124 G7
Doughty Ms **WC1** 125 M6
Doughty St **WC1** 125 M6
Douglas Rd **N1** 126 A2
Douglas St **SW1** 129 K3
Douglas Way **SE8** 131 K6
Douro Pl **W8** 128 B2
Douro St **E3** 127 L4
Dove Ms **SW5** 128 C3
Dove Rd **N1** 126 B1
Dove Row **E2** 126 E3
Dovehouse St **SW3** 128 D4
Dover St **W1** 125 H9
Dovercourt Est **N1** 126 B1
Doves Yd **N1** 125 N3
Dowgate Hill **EC4** 126 B9
Dowlas St **SE5** 130 C6
Down St **W1** 125 H10
Downfield Cl **W9** 124 B6
Downham Rd **N1** 126 B2
Downing St **SW1** 129 L1
Downtown Rd **SE16** 131 J1
Dowson Cl **SE5** 130 B10
D'Oyley St **SW1** 128 G3
Draco St **SE17** 130 A5
Dragon Rd **SE15** 130 C5
Dragoon Rd **SE8** 131 K4
Drake Rd **SE4** 131 L9
Drakefell Rd **SE4** 131 H8
Drakefell Rd **SE14** 131 H8
Draper Ho **SE1** 129 P3
Drawdock Rd **SE10** 127 P10
Draycott Av **SW3** 128 E3
Draycott Pl **SW3** 128 F3
Draycott Ter **SW3** 128 F3
Drayson Ms **W8** 128 A1
Drayton Gdns **SW10** 128 C4
Dresden Cl **NW6** 124 B1
Driffield Rd **E3** 127 J4
Drovers Pl **SE15** 130 F6
Druid St **SE1** 130 C1
Drummond Cres **NW1** 125 K5
Drummond Gate **SW1** 129 K4
Drummond Rd **SE16** 130 F2
Drummond St **NW1** 125 J6
Drury La **WC2** 125 L8
Dryden Ct **SE11** 129 N3
Drysdale St **N1** 126 C5
Dublin Av **E8** 126 E3
Duchess of Bedford's Wk **W8** 128 A1
Duchess St **W1** 125 H7
Duchy St **SE1** 125 N10
Ducie St **SW4** 129 M10
Duckett St **E1** 127 H6
Dudley St **W2** 124 D7
Duff St **E14** 127 M8
Dufferin St **EC1** 126 A6
Dugard Way **SE11** 129 P3
Duke of Wellington Pl **SW1** 128 G1
Duke of York Sq **SW3** 128 F3
Duke of York St **SW1** 125 J10
Duke St **SW1** 125 J10
Duke St **W1** 124 G8
Dukes La **W8** 128 A1
Dukes Pl **EC3** 126 C8
Duke's Rd **WC1** 125 K5
Dunbridge St **E2** 126 E6
Duncan Rd **E8** 126 F3
Duncan St **N1** 125 P4
Duncan Ter **N1** 125 P4
Duncannon St **WC2** 125 L9
Dundalk Rd **SE4** 131 J9
Dundas Rd **SE15** 130 G8
Dundee St **E1** 126 F10
Dunelm St **E1** 127 H8
Dunloe St **E2** 126 D4
Dunston Rd **E8** 126 D3
Dunston Rd **SW11** 128 G8
Dunston St **E8** 126 D3
Dunton Rd **SE1** 130 D4
Durand Gdns **SW9** 129 M7
Durands Wk **SE16** 131 K1
Durant St **E2** 126 E4
Durham Row **E1** 127 J7
Durham St **SE11** 129 M4
Durham Ter **W2** 124 B8
Durward St **E1** 126 F7
Durweston St **W1** 124 F7
Dutton St **SE10** 131 N7
Dye Ho La **E3** 127 L3
Dylan Rd **SE24** 129 P10
Dylways **SE5** 130 B10
Dymock St **SW6** 128 B9
Dynham Rd **NW6** 124 A2
Dyott St **WC1** 125 K8

E

Eagle Ct **EC1** 125 P7
Eagle St **WC1** 125 M7
Eagle Wf Rd **N1** 126 A4
Eamont St **NW8** 124 E4
Eardley Cres **SW5** 128 A4
Earl St **EC2** 126 B7
Earlham St **WC2** 125 K8
Earls Ct Gdns **SW5** 128 B3
Earls Ct Rd **SW5** 128 A3
Earls Ct Rd **W8** 128 A3
Earls Ct Sq **SW5** 128 B4
Earls Wk **W8** 128 A2
Earlsferry Way **N1** 125 M2
Earlston Gro **E9** 126 F3
Earnshaw St **WC2** 125 K8
East Arbour St **E1** 127 H8
East Cross Cen **E15** 127 L1
East Cross Route **E3** 127 K2
East Cross Route **E9** 127 K2
East Dulwich Rd **SE15** 130 D10
East Dulwich Rd **SE22** 130 D10
East Ferry Rd **E14** 131 M2
East India Dock Rd **E14** 127 L8
East La **SE16** 130 E1
East Mt St **E1** 126 F7
East Rd **N1** 126 B5
East Smithfield **E1** 126 D9
East St **SE17** 130 A4
East Surrey Gro **SE15** 130 D6
East Tenter St **E1** 126 D8
Eastbourne Ms **W2** 124 C8
Eastbourne Ter **W2** 124 C8
Eastbury Ter **E1** 127 H6
Eastcastle St **W1** 125 J8
Eastcheap **EC3** 126 B9
Eastcote St **SW9** 129 M8
Eastdown Pk **SE13** 131 P10
Eastern Rd **SE4** 131 L10
Eastfield St **E14** 127 J7
Eastfields Av **SW18** 128 A10
Eastlake Rd **SE5** 129 P8
Eastney St **SE10** 131 P4
Eastway **E9** 127 K1
Eaton Cl **SW1** 128 G3
Eaton Dr **SW9** 129 P10
Eaton Gate **SW1** 128 G3
Eaton La **SW1** 129 H2
Eaton Ms N **SW1** 128 G2
Eaton Ms S **SW1** 129 H2
Eaton Ms W **SW1** 128 G3
Eaton Pl **SW1** 128 G2
Eaton Row **SW1** 129 H2
Eaton Sq **SW1** 128 G3
Eaton Ter **SW1** 128 G3
Ebbisham Dr **SW8** 129 M5
Ebenezer St **N1** 126 B5
Ebley Cl **SE15** 130 D5
Ebor St **E1** 126 D6
Ebury Br **SW1** 129 H4
Ebury Br Est **SW1** 129 H4
Ebury Br Rd **SW1** 128 G4
Ebury Ms **SW1** 129 H3
Ebury Sq **SW1** 128 G3
Ebury St **SW1** 128 G3
Eccles Rd **SW11** 128 F10
Ecclesbourne Rd **N1** 126 A2
Eccleston Br **SW1** 129 H3
Eccleston Ms **SW1** 128 G2
Eccleston Pl **SW1** 129 H3
Eccleston Sq **SW1** 129 H3
Eccleston Sq Ms **SW1** 129 H3
Eccleston St **SW1** 128 G2
Eckford St **N1** 125 N4
Eckstein Rd **SW11** 128 E10
Edbrooke Rd **W9** 124 A6
Eddystone Twr **SE8** 131 J3
Edenbridge Rd **E9** 127 H2
Edenvale St **SW6** 128 B8
Edgar Kail Way **SE22** 130 C10
Edgar Rd **E3** 127 M5
Edgeley Rd **SW4** 129 K9
Edgware Rd **W2** 124 E8
Edinburgh Gate **SW1** 128 F1
Edinburgh Ho **W9** 124 C5
Edis St **NW1** 124 G3
Edith Gro **SW10** 128 C5
Edith Row **SW6** 128 B7
Edith St **E2** 126 E4
Edith Ter **SW10** 128 C6
Edithna St **SW9** 129 L9
Edmeston Cl **E9** 127 J1
Edmund St **SE5** 130 B6
Edna St **SW11** 128 E7
Edric Rd **SE14** 131 H6
Edrich Ho **SW4** 129 L7
Edward Pl **SE8** 131 K5
Edward St **SE8** 131 K5
Edward St **SE14** 131 J6
Edwardes Sq **W8** 128 A2
Edwards Ms **N1** 125 N2
Edwards Ms **W1** 124 G8
Edwin St **E1** 126 G6
Effie Pl **SW6** 128 A6
Effie Rd **SW6** 128 A6
Effra Rd **SW2** 129 N10
Egbert St **NW1** 124 G3
Egeremont Rd **SE13** 131 M8
Egerton Cres **SW3** 128 E3
Egerton Dr **SE10** 131 M7
Egerton Gdns **SW3** 128 E2
Egerton Gdns Ms **SW3** 128 E2
Egerton Pl **SW3** 128 E2
Egerton Ter **SW3** 128 E2
Egmont St **SE14** 131 H6
Elam Cl **SE5** 129 P8
Elam St **SE5** 129 P8
Eland Rd **SW11** 128 F9
Elbe St **SW6** 128 C8
Elcho St **SW11** 128 E6
Elcot Av **SE15** 130 F6
Elder St **E1** 126 D7
Eldon Rd **W8** 128 B2
Eldon St **EC2** 126 B7
Eleanor Cl **SE16** 131 H1
Eleanor Rd **E8** 126 F2
Eleanor St **E3** 127 L5
Electra Business Pk **E16** 127 P7
Electric Av **SW9** 129 N10
Electric La **SW9** 129 N10
Elephant & Castle **SE1** 129 P3
Elephant La **SE16** 130 G1
Elephant Rd **SE17** 130 A3
Elf Row **E1** 126 G9
Elgar St **SE16** 131 J2
Elgin Av **W9** 124 B5
Elia Ms **N1** 125 P4
Elia St **N1** 125 P4
Elias Pl **SW8** 129 N5
Elim Est **SE1** 130 B2
Eliot Hill **SE13** 131 N8
Eliot Ms **NW8** 124 C4
Eliot Pk **SE13** 131 N9
Eliot Vale **SE3** 131 P8
Elizabeth Av **N1** 126 A2
Elizabeth Br **SW1** 129 H3
Elizabeth Est **SE17** 130 B5
Elizabeth Ms **NW3** 124 E1
Elizabeth St **SW1** 128 G3
Elland Rd **SE15** 130 G10
Ellen St **E1** 126 E8
Ellerdale St **SE13** 131 M10
Ellery St **SE15** 130 F8
Ellesmere Rd **E3** 127 J4
Ellesmere St **E14** 127 M8
Ellingfort Rd **E8** 126 F2
Ellington St **N7** 125 N1
Elliott Rd **SW9** 129 P6
Elliott Sq **NW3** 124 E2
Elliotts Row **SE11** 129 P3
Ellis St **SW1** 128 F3
Ellsworth St **E2** 126 F5
Elm Friars Wk **NW1** 125 K2
Elm Gro **SE15** 130 D8
Elm Pk Gdns **SW10** 128 D4
Elm Pk La **SW3** 128 D4
Elm Pk Rd **SW3** 128 D5
Elm Pl **SW7** 128 D4
Elm Quay Ct **SW8** 129 K5
Elm St **WC1** 125 M6
Elm Tree Cl **NW8** 124 D5
Elm Tree Rd **NW8** 124 D5
Elmfield Way **W9** 124 A7
Elmhurst St **SW4** 129 K9
Elmington Est **SE5** 130 B6
Elmington Rd **SE5** 130 B7
Elmira St **SE13** 131 M9
Elmore St **N1** 126 A2
Elms Ms **W2** 124 D9
Elmslie Pt **E3** 127 K7
Elmstone Rd **SW6** 128 A7
Elmwood Ct **SW11** 129 H7
Elrington Rd **E8** 126 E1
Elsa St **E1** 127 J7
Elsdale St **E9** 126 G1
Elsie Rd **SE22** 130 D10
Elsley Rd **SW11** 128 F9
Elspeth Rd **SW11** 128 F10
Elsted St **SE17** 130 B3
Elswick Rd **SE13** 131 M8
Elswick St **SW6** 128 C8
Elsworthy Ri **NW3** 124 E2
Elsworthy Rd **NW3** 124 E3
Elsworthy Ter **NW3** 124 E2
Elthiron Rd **SW6** 128 A7
Elton Ho **E3** 127 K3
Eltringham St **SW18** 128 C10
Elvaston Ms **SW7** 128 C2
Elvaston Pl **SW7** 128 C2
Elverson Ms **SE8** 131 M8
Elverson Rd **SE8** 131 M8
Elverton St **SW1** 129 K3
Elwin St **E2** 126 E5
Elystan Pl **SW3** 128 E4
Elystan St **SW3** 128 E3
Emba St **SE16** 130 E1
Embankment Gdns **SW3** 128 F5
Embankment Pl **WC2** 125 L10
Emberton **SE5** 130 C5
Embleton Rd **SE13** 131 M9
Emden St **SW6** 128 B7
Emerald St **WC1** 125 M7
Emerson St **SE1** 126 A10
Emery Hill St **SW1** 129 J2
Emma St **E2** 126 F4
Emmott Cl **E1** 127 J6
Emperor's Gate **SW7** 128 B2
Empire Wf Rd **E14** 131 P3
Empress Ms **SE5** 130 A8
Empress Pl **SW6** 128 A4
Empress St **SE17** 130 A5
Empson St **E3** 127 M6
Emu Rd **SW8** 129 H8
Endell St **WC2** 125 L8
Endsleigh Gdns **WC1** 125 K6
Endsleigh Pl **WC1** 125 K6
Endsleigh St **WC1** 125 K6
Endwell Rd **SE4** 131 J8
Enfield Rd **N1** 126 C2
Enford St **W1** 124 F7
Engate St **SE13** 131 N10
Englands La **NW3** 124 F1
Englefield Rd **N1** 126 B1
English St **E3** 127 K6
Enid St **SE16** 130 D2
Ennerdale Ho **E3** 127 K6
Ennismore Gdns **SW7** 128 E1
Ennismore Gdns Ms **SW7** 128 E2
Ennismore Ms **SW7** 128 E1
Ennismore St **SW7** 128 E2
Ensign St **E1** 126 E9
Enterprise Way **SW18** 128 A10
Enterprize Way **SE8** 131 K3
Epirus Ms **SW6** 128 A6
Epping Cl **E14** 131 L3
Epworth St **EC2** 126 B6
Erasmus St **SW1** 129 K3
Eresby Pl **NW6** 124 A2
Eric St **E3** 127 K6
Erlanger Rd **SE14** 131 H7
Ermine Rd **SE13** 131 M9
Ernest St **E1** 127 H6
Errol St **EC1** 126 A6
Erskine Rd **NW3** 124 F2
Esmeralda Rd **SE1** 130 E3
Essendine Rd **W9** 124 A6
Essex Rd **N1** 125 P3
Essex Vil **W8** 128 A1
Essian St **E1** 127 J7
Este Rd **SW11** 128 E9
Esterbrooke St **SW1** 129 K3
Ethelburga St **SW11** 128 E7
Ethnard Rd **SE15** 130 F5
Eton Av **NW3** 124 D2
Eton Coll Rd **NW3** 124 F1
Eton Rd **NW3** 124 F2
Eton Vil **NW3** 124 F1
Etta St **SE8** 131 J5
Ettrick St **E14** 127 N8
Eugenia Rd **SE16** 130 G3
Eustace Rd **SW6** 128 A6
Euston Gro **NW1** 125 K5
Euston Rd **N1** 125 K5
Euston Rd **NW1** 125 H6
Euston Sq **NW1** 125 K5
Euston Sta **NW1** 125 J5
Euston St **NW1** 125 J5
Euston Twr **NW1** 125 J6
Evandale Rd **SW9** 129 N8
Evelina Rd **SE15** 130 G9
Eveline Lowe Est **SE16** 130 E2
Evelyn Gdns **SW7** 128 D4
Evelyn St **SE8** 131 J4
Evelyn Wk **N1** 126 B4
Everest Pl **E14** 127 N7
Evergreen Sq **E8** 126 D2
Everilda St **N1** 125 M3
Eversholt St **NW1** 125 J4
Eversleigh Rd **SW11** 128 F9
Everthorpe Rd **SE15** 130 D9
Evesham Wk **SW9** 129 N8
Evesham Way **SW11** 128 G9
Ewe Cl **N7** 125 L1
Ewer St **SE1** 126 A10
Ewhurst Cl **E1** 126 G7
Excelsior Gdns **SE13** 131 N8
Exchange Sq **EC2** 126 C7
Exeter St **WC2** 125 L9
Exeter Way **SE14** 131 K6
Exhibition Rd **SW7** 128 D2
Exmouth Mkt **EC1** 125 N6
Exmouth Pl **E8** 126 F2
Exon St **SE17** 130 C4
Exton St **SE1** 125 N10
Eythorne Rd **SW9** 129 N7
Ezra St **E2** 126 D5

F

Fairbairn Grn **SW9** 129 N7
Faircharm Trd Est **SE8** 131 M6
Fairclough St **E1** 126 E8
Fairfax Pl **NW6** 124 C2
Fairfax Rd **NW6** 124 C2
Fairfield Rd **E3** 127 L4
Fairfoot Rd **E3** 127 L6
Fairhazel Gdns **NW6** 124 B1
Fairmont Av **E14** 127 P10
Fakruddin St **E1** 126 E6
Falcon Ct **EC4** 125 N8
Falcon Gro **SW11** 128 E9
Falcon La **SW11** 128 E9
Falcon Rd **SW11** 128 E8
Falcon Ter **SW11** 128 E9
Falcon Way **E14** 131 M3
Falkirk Ho **W9** 124 B5
Falkirk St **N1** 126 C4
Falmouth Rd **SE1** 130 A2
Fann St **EC1** 126 A6
Fann St **EC2** 126 A6
Fanshaw St **N1** 126 C5
Farm La **SW6** 128 A5
Farm St **W1** 125 H9
Farmers Rd **SE5** 129 P6
Farncombe St **SE16** 130 E1
Farrance St **E14** 127 K8
Farrell Ho **E1** 126 G8
Farrier St **NW1** 125 H2
Farrier Wk **SW10** 128 C5
Farringdon La **EC1** 125 N6
Farringdon Rd **EC1** 125 N6
Farringdon St **EC4** 125 P7
Farrins Rents **SE16** 127 J10
Farrow La **SE14** 130 G6
Farthingale Wk **E15** 127 P2
Fashion St **E1** 126 D7
Fassett Rd **E8** 126 E1
Fassett Sq **E8** 126 E1
Faulkner St **SE14** 130 G7
Favart Rd **SW6** 128 A7
Fawcett Cl **SW11** 128 D8
Fawcett St **SW10** 128 C5
Fawe St **E14** 127 M7
Feathers Pl **SE10** 131 P5
Featherstone St **EC1** 126 B6
Featley Rd **SW9** 129 P9
Fellows Ct **E2** 126 D4
Fellows Rd **NW3** 124 D2
Felstead St **E9** 127 K1
Felton St **N1** 126 B3
Fenchurch Av **EC3** 126 C8
Fenchurch St **EC3** 126 C9
Fendall St **SE1** 130 C2
Fenham Rd **SE15** 130 E6
Fentiman Rd **SW8** 129 L5
Fenton Cl **SW9** 129 M8
Fenwick Gro **SE15** 130 E9
Fenwick Pl **SW9** 129 L9
Fenwick Rd **SE15** 130 E9
Ferdinand St **NW1** 124 G1
Ferguson Cl **E14** 131 L3
Fern St **E3** 127 L6
Ferndale Rd **SW4** 129 L10
Ferndale Rd **SW9** 129 M9
Ferndene Rd **SE24** 130 A10
Fernshaw Rd **SW10** 128 C5
Ferrey Ms **SW9** 129 N8
Ferrier St **SW18** 128 B10
Ferris Rd **SE22** 130 E10
Ferry St **E14** 131 N4
Ferryman's Quay **SW6** 128 C8
Fetter La **EC4** 125 N8
Ffinch St **SE8** 131 L6
Field St **WC1** 125 M5
Fieldgate St **E1** 126 E7
Fielding Ho **NW6** 124 A5
Fielding St **SE17** 130 A5
Fields Est **E8** 126 E2
Fife Ter **N1** 125 M4
Finborough Rd **SW10** 128 B4
Finch Ms **SE15** 130 D6
Finchley Pl **NW8** 124 D4
Finchley Rd **NW3** 124 C1
Finchley Rd **NW8** 124 D3
Findhorn St **E14** 127 N8
Finland Rd **SE4** 131 J9
Finland St **SE16** 131 J2
Finnis St **E2** 126 F5
Finsbury Circ **EC2** 126 B7
Finsbury Est **EC1** 125 N5
Finsbury Mkt **EC2** 126 C6
Finsbury Pavement **EC2** 126 B7
Finsbury Sq **EC2** 126 B7
Finsbury St **EC2** 126 B7
Finsen Rd **SE5** 130 A9
Fir Trees Cl **SE16** 127 J10
Firbank Rd **SE15** 130 F8
First St **SW3** 128 E3
Fish St Hill **EC3** 126 B9
Fisher St **WC1** 125 M7
Fishermans Dr **SE16** 131 H1
Fisherman's Wk **E14** 127 L10
Fisherton St **NW8** 124 D6
Fitzalan St **SE11** 129 M3
Fitzgerald Ho **E14** 127 M8
Fitzhardinge St **W1** 124 G8
Fitzmaurice Pl **W1** 125 H9
Fitzroy Rd **NW1** 124 G3
Fitzroy Sq **W1** 125 J6
Fitzroy St **W1** 125 J6
Fitzwilliam Rd **SW4** 129 J9
Fiveways Rd **SW9** 129 N8
Flamborough St **E14** 127 J8
Flanders Way **E9** 127 H1
Flaxman Rd **SE5** 129 P8
Flaxman Ter **WC1** 125 K5
Fleet St **EC4** 125 N8
Fleming Rd **SE17** 129 P5
Fleur de Lis St **E1** 126 C6
Flint St **SE17** 130 B3
Flinton St **SE17** 130 C4
Flodden Rd **SE5** 130 A7
Flood St **SW3** 128 E4
Flood Wk **SW3** 128 E5
Flora Cl **E14** 127 M8
Floral St **WC2** 125 L9
Florence Rd **SE14** 131 K7
Florence St **N1** 125 P2
Florence Ter **SE14** 131 K7
Florida St **E2** 126 E5
Flower Wk, The **SW7** 128 C1
Foley St **W1** 125 J7
Folgate St **E1** 126 C7
Follett St **E14** 127 N8
Folly Wall **E14** 131 N1
Fontarabia Rd **SW11** 128 G10
Ford Rd **E3** 127 J3
Ford Sq **E1** 126 F7
Ford St **E3** 127 J3
Fordham St **E1** 126 E8
Fore St **EC2** 126 A7
Foreign St **SE5** 129 P8
Foreshore **SE8** 131 K3
Forest Gro **E8** 126 D1
Forest Rd **E8** 126 D1
Forester Rd **SE15** 130 F10
Forfar Rd **SW11** 128 G7
Formosa St **W9** 124 B7
Forset St **W1** 124 E8
Forsyth Gdns **SE17** 129 P5
Fort Rd **SE1** 130 D3
Forthbridge Rd **SW11** 128 G10
Fortune St **EC1** 126 A6
Fossil Rd **SE13** 131 L9
Foster La **EC2** 126 A8
Foubert's Pl **W1** 125 J8
Foulis Ter **SW7** 128 D4
Foundry Cl **SE16** 127 J10
Fount St **SW8** 129 K6
Fountain Ms **NW3** 124 F1
Fountain Pl **SW9** 129 N7
Fountain Sq **SW1** 129 H3
Four Seasons Cl **E3** 127 L4
Fournier St **E1** 126 D7
Fowler Cl **SW11** 128 D9
Fownes St **SW11** 128 E9
Fox Cl **E1** 126 G6
Foxberry Rd **SE4** 131 J9
Foxcote **SE5** 130 C4
Foxley Rd **SW9** 129 N6
Foxmore St **SW11** 128 F7
Foxwell St **SE4** 131 J9
Frampton Pk Rd **E9** 126 G1
Frampton St **NW8** 124 D6
Francis Chichester Way **SW11** 128 G7
Francis St **SW1** 129 J3
Frankham St **SE8** 131 L6
Frankland Cl **SE16** 130 F2
Franklin Cl **SE13** 131 M7
Franklin Pl **SE13** 131 M7
Franklin St **E3** 127 M5
Franklin's Row **SW3** 128 F4
Frazier St **SE1** 129 N1
Frean St **SE16** 130 E2
Frederick Cl **W2** 124 E9
Frederick Cres **SW9** 129 P6
Frederick St **WC1** 125 M5
Freedom St **SW11** 128 F8
Freemantle St **SE17** 130 C4
Freke Rd **SW11** 128 G9
Fremont St **E9** 126 G3
Frendsbury Rd **SE4** 131 J10
Frensham St **SE15** 130 E5
Frere St **SW11** 128 E8
Freshfield Av **E8** 126 D2
Friars Mead **E14** 131 N2
Friary Est **SE15** 130 E5
Friary Rd **SE15** 130 E6
Friday St **EC4** 126 A8

Friend St EC1 125 P5
Friendly St SE8 131 L7
Friendly St Ms SE8 131 L8
Frimley Way E1 127 H6
Friston St SW6 128 B8
Frith St W1 125 K8
Frogley Rd SE22 130 D10
Frognal Ct NW3 124 C1
Frome St N1 126 A4
Frostic Wk E1 126 D7
Froude St SW8 129 H8
Fulford St SE16 130 F1
Fulham Bdy SW6 128 A6
Fulham Rd SW3 128 C5
Fulham Rd SW10 128 B6
Fulmead St SW6 128 B7
Fulwood Pl WC1 125 M7
Furley Rd SE15 130 E6
Furlong Rd N7 125 N1
Furness Rd SW6 128 B8
Furnival St EC4 125 N8
Furze St E3 127 L7
Fyfield Rd SW9 129 N9
Fynes St SW1 129 K3

G

Gables Cl SE5 130 C7
Gabrielle Ct NW3 124 D1
Gainsford St SE1 130 D1
Gairloch Rd SE5 130 C8
Gaisford St NW5 125 J1
Gaitskell Ct SW11 128 E8
Galbraith St E14 131 N2
Gale St E3 127 L7
Gales Gdns E2 126 F5
Galleywall Rd SE16 130 F3
Galsworthy Av E14 127 J7
Galway St EC1 126 A5
Gambetta St SW8 129 H8
Garden Rd NW8 124 C5
Garden Row SE1 129 P2
Garden St E1 127 H7
Gardens, The SE22 130 E10
Garfield Rd SW11 128 G9
Garford St E14 127 L9
Garlick Hill EC4 126 A9
Garnet St E1 126 G9
Garnies Cl SE15 130 D6
Garrick Cl SW18 128 C10
Garrick St WC2 125 L9
Garsington Ms SE4 131 K9
Gartons Way SW11 128 C9
Garway Rd W2 124 B8
Gascoigne Pl E2 126 D5
Gascony Av NW6 124 A2
Gascoyne Rd E9 127 H2
Gaselee St E14 127 N9
Gaskell St SW4 129 L8
Gaskin St N1 125 P3
Gataker St SE16 130 F2
Gate Ms SW7 128 E1
Gateforth St NW8 124 E6
Gateley Rd SW9 129 M9
Gateway SE17 130 A5
Gateways, The SW3 128 F3
Gatliff Rd SW1 128 G4
Gatonby St SE15 130 D7
Gauden Cl SW4 129 K9
Gauden Rd SW4 129 K8
Gautrey Rd SE15 130 G8
Gawber St E2 126 G5
Gay Rd E15 127 P4
Gaydon Ho W2 124 B7
Gayfere St SW1 129 L2
Gayhurst Rd E8 126 E2
Gayton Ho E3 127 L6
Gaywood Est SE1 129 P2
Gedling Pl SE1 130 D1
Gee St EC1 126 A6
Geffrye St E2 126 D4
Geldart Rd SE15 130 F6
Gellatly Rd SE14 130 G8
General Wolfe Rd SE10 131 P7
Geneva Dr SW9 129 N10
Geoffrey Cl SE5 130 A8
Geoffrey Rd SE4 131 K9
George Beard Rd SE8 131 K3
George Mathers Rd SE11 129 P3
George Row SE16 130 E1
George St W1 124 G8
George Yd W1 124 G9
Georgiana St NW1 125 J3
Gerald Rd SW1 128 G3
Geraldine St SE11 129 P2
Gerards Cl SE16 130 G4
Gernon Rd E3 127 J4
Gerrard Rd N1 125 P4
Gerrard St W1 125 K9
Gerridge St SE1 129 N2
Gertrude St SW10 128 C5
Gervase St SE15 130 F6
Gibbins Rd E15 127 N2
Gibbon Rd SE15 130 G8
Gibraltar Wk E2 126 D5
Gibson Rd SE11 129 M3
Gibson Sq N1 125 N3
Gideon Rd SW11 128 G9
Giffin St SE8 131 L6
Gifford St N1 125 L2
Gilbert Rd SE11 129 N3
Gilbert St W1 124 G8
Gilbeys Yd NW1 124 G2
Gill St E14 127 K8
Gillender St E3 127 N6
Gillender St E14 127 N6
Gillfoot NW1 125 J4
Gilling Ct NW3 124 E1
Gillingham St SW1 129 H3
Gilmore Rd SE13 131 P10
Gilstead Rd SW6 128 B8
Gilston Rd SW10 128 C4
Giltspur St EC1 125 P8
Giraud St E14 127 M8
Gladstone St SE1 129 P2
Gladys Rd NW6 124 A2
Glaisher St SE8 131 L5
Glamis Pl E1 126 G9
Glamis Rd E1 126 G9
Glasgow Ho W9 124 B4
Glasgow Ter SW1 129 J4
Glasshill St SE1 129 P1
Glasshouse Flds E1 127 H9
Glasshouse St W1 125 J9
Glasshouse Wk SE11 129 L4
Glaucus St E3 127 M7
Glebe Pl SW3 128 E5
Gledhow Gdns SW5 128 C3
Glenaffric Av E14 131 P3
Glendall St SW9 129 M10
Glendower Pl SW7 128 D3
Glenfinlas Way SE5 129 P6
Glengall Causeway E14 131 L2
Glengall Gro E14 131 M2
Glengall Rd SE15 130 D5
Glengall Ter SE15 130 D5
Glengarnock Av E14 131 N3
Glenilla Rd NW3 124 E1
Glenloch Rd NW3 124 E1
Glenmore Rd NW3 124 E1
Glenrosa St SW6 128 C8
Glensdale Rd SE4 131 K9
Glentworth St NW1 124 F6
Glenville Gro SE8 131 K6
Glenworth Av E14 131 P3
Globe Pond Rd SE16 127 J10
Globe Rd E1 126 G5
Globe Rd E2 126 G5
Globe Rope Wk E14 131 N3
Globe St SE1 130 A2
Gloucester Av NW1 124 G2
Gloucester Circ SE10 131 N6
Gloucester Cres NW1 125 H3
Gloucester Gate NW1 125 H4
Gloucester Ho NW6 124 A4
Gloucester Ms W2 124 C8
Gloucester Pl NW1 124 F6
Gloucester Pl W1 124 F7
Gloucester Rd SW7 128 C2
Gloucester Sq W2 124 D8
Gloucester St SW1 129 J4
Gloucester Ter W2 124 D9
Gloucester Wk W8 128 A1
Gloucester Way EC1 125 N5
Glycena Rd SW11 128 F9
Godalming Rd E14 127 M7
Godfrey St E15 127 N4
Godfrey St SW3 128 E4
Goding St SE11 129 L4
Godliman St EC4 126 A8
Godman Rd SE15 130 F8
Godson St N1 125 N4
Goffers Rd SE3 131 P7
Golden Jubilee Br SE1 125 L10
Golden Jubilee Br WC2 125 L10
Golden La EC1 126 A6
Golden Sq W1 125 J9
Goldhurst Ter NW6 124 B2
Golding St E1 126 E8
Goldington Cres NW1 125 K4
Goldington St NW1 125 K4
Goldman Cl E2 126 E6
Goldney Rd W9 124 A6
Goldsboro Rd SW8 129 K7
Goldsmith Rd SE15 130 E7
Goldsmith's Row E2 126 E4
Goldsmith's Sq E2 126 E4
Goldsworthy Gdns SE16 130 G3
Goldwin Cl SE14 130 G7
Gomm Rd SE16 130 G2
Gonson St SE8 131 M5
Goodge St W1 125 J7
Goodhart Pl E14 127 J9
Goodinge Cl N7 125 L1
Goodman's Stile E1 126 E8
Goodmans Yd E1 126 D9
Goods Way NW1 125 L4
Goodway Gdns E14 127 P8
Goodwin Cl SE16 130 E2
Goodwood Rd SE14 131 J6
Gopsall St N1 126 B3
Gordon Gro SE5 129 P8
Gordon Pl W8 128 A1
Gordon Rd SE15 130 F8
Gordon Sq WC1 125 K6
Gordon St WC1 125 K6
Gore Rd E9 126 G3
Gore St SW7 128 C2
Gorefield Pl NW6 124 A4
Goring St EC3 126 C8
Gorsuch St E2 126 D5
Gosfield St W1 125 J7
Gosling Way SW9 129 N7
Gosset St E2 126 D5
Gosterwood St SE8 131 J5
Goswell Rd EC1 125 P5
Gough Sq EC4 125 N8
Gough St WC1 125 M6
Goulden Ho App SW11 128 E8
Goulston St E1 126 D8
Gower Ms WC1 125 K7
Gower Pl WC1 125 J6
Gower St WC1 125 J6
Gower's Wk E1 126 E8
Gowlett Rd SE15 130 E9
Gowrie Rd SW11 128 G9
Grace St E3 127 M5
Gracechurch St EC3 126 B9
Grace's All E1 126 E9
Graces Ms SE5 130 C8
Graces Rd SE5 130 C8
Grafton Cres NW1 125 H1
Grafton Ho E3 127 L5
Grafton Pl NW1 125 K5
Grafton Sq SW4 129 J9
Grafton St W1 125 H9
Grafton Way W1 125 J6
Grafton Way WC1 125 J6
Graham Rd E8 126 D1
Graham St N1 125 P4
Graham Ter SW1 128 G3
Granary Rd E1 126 F6
Granary St NW1 125 K3
Granby St E2 126 D6
Granby Ter NW1 125 J4
Grand Junct Wf N1 126 A4
Grand Union Cres E8 126 E2
Grand Union Wk NW1 125 H2
Granfield St SW11 128 D7
Grange, The SE1 130 D2
Grange Gro N1 125 P1
Grange Pl NW6 124 A2
Grange Rd SE1 130 C2
Grange St N1 126 B3
Grange Wk SE1 130 C2
Grange Yd SE1 130 D2
Gransden Av E8 126 F2
Grant Rd SW11 128 D10
Grantbridge St N1 125 P4
Grantham Rd SW9 129 L8
Grantley St E1 127 H5
Grantully Rd W9 124 B5
Granville Ct N1 126 B3
Granville Gro SE13 131 N9
Granville Pk SE13 131 N9
Granville Pl W1 124 G8
Granville Rd NW6 124 A4
Granville Sq SE15 130 C6
Granville Sq WC1 125 M5
Grayling Sq E2 126 E5
Gray's Inn WC1 125 M7
Gray's Inn Rd WC1 125 M5
Grayshott Rd SW11 128 G8
Great Castle St W1 125 J8
Great Cen St NW1 124 F7
Great Chapel St W1 125 K8
Great Chart St SW11 128 D10
Great Coll St SW1 129 L2
Great Cumberland Pl W1 124 F8
Great Dover St SE1 130 A1
Great Eastern Enterprise Cen E14 131 M1
Great Eastern Rd E15 127 P2
Great Eastern St EC2 126 C5
Great George St SW1 129 K1
Great Guildford St SE1 126 A10
Great James St WC1 125 M7
Great Marlborough St W1 125 J8
Great Maze Pond SE1 130 B1
Great Ormond St WC1 125 L7
Great Percy St WC1 125 M5
Great Peter St SW1 129 K2
Great Portland St W1 125 H6
Great Pulteney St W1 125 J9
Great Queen St WC2 125 L8
Great Russell St WC1 125 L7
Great St. Helens EC3 126 C8
Great Scotland Yd SW1 125 L10
Great Smith St SW1 129 K2
Great Suffolk St SE1 125 P10
Great Sutton St EC1 125 P6
Great Titchfield St W1 125 J8
Great Twr St EC3 126 C9
Great Winchester St EC2 126 B8
Great Windmill St W1 125 K9
Greatfield Cl SE4 131 L10
Greatorex St E1 126 E7
Greek St W1 125 K8
Green Bk E1 126 F10
Green Dale SE5 130 B10
Green Hundred Rd SE15 130 E5
Green St W1 124 G9
Greenberry St NW8 124 E4
Greencoat Pl SW1 129 J3
Greencroft Gdns NW6 124 B2
Greenfield Rd E1 126 E7
Greenham Cl SE1 129 N1
Greenland Quay SE16 131 H3
Greenland Rd NW1 125 J3
Greenman St N1 126 A2
Greenwell St W1 125 H6
Greenwich Ch St SE10 131 N5
Greenwich Foot Tunnel E14 131 N4
Greenwich Foot Tunnel SE10 131 N4
Greenwich High Rd SE10 131 M7
Greenwich Pk St SE10 131 P4
Greenwich Quay SE8 131 M5
Greenwich S St SE10 131 M7
Greenwich Vw Pl E14 131 M2
Greenwood Ct SW1 129 J4
Greenwood Rd E8 126 E1
Greet St SE1 125 N10
Gregory Pl W8 128 B1
Grenade St E14 127 K9
Grenard Cl SE15 130 E6
Grendon St NW8 124 E6
Grenville Ms SW7 128 C3
Grenville Pl SW7 128 C2
Grenville St WC1 125 L6
Gresham Rd SW9 129 N9
Gresham St EC2 126 A8
Gresse St W1 125 K7
Greville Pl NW6 124 B4
Greville Rd NW6 124 B3
Greville St EC1 125 N7
Grey Eagle St E1 126 D7
Greycoat Pl SW1 129 K2
Greycoat St SW1 129 K2
Grimwade Cl SE15 130 G9
Grinling Pl SE8 131 L5
Grinstead Rd SE8 131 J4
Grittleton Rd W9 124 A6
Groom Pl SW1 128 G2
Groombridge Rd E9 127 H2
Grosvenor Cres SW1 128 G1
Grosvenor Cres Ms SW1 128 G1
Grosvenor Est SW1 129 K3
Grosvenor Gdns SW1 129 H2
Grosvenor Gate W1 124 F9
Grosvenor Hill W1 125 H9
Grosvenor Pk SE5 130 A5
Grosvenor Pl SW1 128 G1
Grosvenor Rd SW1 129 H5
Grosvenor Sq W1 124 G9
Grosvenor St W1 125 H9
Grosvenor Ter SE5 129 P6
Grosvenor Wf Rd E14 131 P3
Grove Cotts SW3 128 E5
Grove Cres Rd E15 127 P1
Grove End Rd NW8 124 D5
Grove Hill Rd SE5 130 C9
Grove La SE5 130 B7
Grove Pk SE5 130 C8
Grove Pas E2 126 F4
Grove Rd E3 127 H3
Grove St SE8 131 K3
Grove Vale SE22 130 C10
Grove Vil E14 127 M9
Grovelands Cl SE5 130 C8
Groveway SW9 129 M7
Grummant Rd SE15 130 D7
Grundy St E14 127 M8
Guerin Sq E3 127 K5
Guildford Gro SE10 131 M7
Guildford Rd SW8 129 L7
Guildhouse St SW1 129 J3
Guilford Pl WC1 125 M6
Guilford St WC1 125 L6
Guinness Cl E9 127 J2
Guinness Trust Bldgs SE11 129 P4
Guinness Trust Bldgs SW9 129 P10
Gulliver St SE16 131 K2
Gun St E1 126 D7
Gunmakers La E3 127 J3
Gunter Gro SW10 128 C5
Gunthorpe St E1 126 D7
Gunwhale Cl SE16 127 H10
Gurney Rd SW6 128 C9
Gutter La EC2 126 A8
Guy St SE1 130 B1
Gwyn Cl SW6 128 C6
Gwynne Rd SW11 128 D8
Gylcote Cl SE5 130 B10

H

Haberdasher St N1 126 B5
Hackford Rd SW9 129 M7
Hackford Wk SW9 129 M7
Hackney Rd E2 126 D5
Haddo St SE10 131 M5
Haddonfield SE8 131 H3
Hadleigh St E2 126 G6
Hadley St NW1 125 H1
Hadrian Est E2 126 E4
Hafer Rd SW11 128 F10
Haggerston Rd E8 126 D2
Hainford Cl SE4 131 H10
Hainton Cl E1 126 F8
Halcomb St N1 126 C3
Hale St E14 127 M9
Halesworth Rd SE13 131 M9
Half Moon Cres N1 125 M4
Half Moon St W1 125 H10
Halford Rd SW6 128 A5
Halkin Arc SW1 128 F2
Halkin Pl SW1 128 G2
Halkin St SW1 128 G1
Hall Pl W2 124 D6
Hall Rd NW8 124 C5
Hall St EC1 125 P5
Hall Twr W2 124 D7
Hallam St W1 125 H7
Halley Gdns SE13 131 P10
Halley St E14 127 J7
Hallfield Est W2 124 C8
Halliford St N1 126 A2
Halsey St SW3 128 F3
Halsmere Rd SE5 129 P7
Halton Cross St N1 125 P3
Halton Rd N1 125 P2
Hamble St SW6 128 B9
Hamilton Cl NW8 124 D5
Hamilton Gdns NW8 124 C5
Hamilton Pl W1 124 G10
Hamilton Ter NW8 124 B4
Hamlet, The SE5 130 B9
Hamlets Way E3 127 K6
Hammond St NW5 125 J1
Hampson Way SW8 129 M7
Hampstead Rd NW1 125 J4
Hampton Cl NW6 124 A5
Hampton St SE1 129 P3
Hampton St SE17 129 P3
Hanbury St E1 126 D7
Hancock Rd E3 127 N5
Hand Ct WC1 125 M7
Handel St WC1 125 L6
Handforth Rd SW9 129 N6
Handley Rd E9 126 G2
Hankey Pl SE1 130 B1
Hannibal Rd E1 126 G7
Hannington Rd SW4 129 H9
Hanover Gdns SE11 129 N5
Hanover Gate NW1 124 E5
Hanover Pk SE15 130 E7
Hanover Sq W1 125 H8
Hanover St W1 125 H8
Hanover Ter NW1 124 E5
Hans Cres SW1 128 F2
Hans Pl SW1 128 F2
Hans Rd SW3 128 F2
Hanson St W1 125 J7
Hanway St W1 125 K8
Harben Rd NW6 124 C2
Harbet Rd W2 124 D7
Harbinger Rd E14 131 M3
Harbledown Rd SW6 128 A7
Harbour Av SW10 128 C7
Harbour Ex Sq E14 131 M1
Harbour Rd SE5 130 A9
Harbut Rd SW11 128 D10
Harcourt Rd SE4 131 J10
Harcourt St W1 124 E7
Harcourt Ter SW10 128 B4
Harders Rd SE15 130 F8
Hardinge St E1 126 G8
Hardwick St EC1 125 N5
Hare & Billet Rd SE3 131 P7
Hare Row E2 126 F4
Hare Wk N1 126 C4
Harecourt Rd N1 126 A1
Haredale Rd SE24 130 A10
Harefield Ms SE4 131 K9
Harefield Rd SE4 131 K9
Harewood Av NW1 124 E6
Harfield Gdns SE5 130 C9
Harford St E1 127 J6
Hargwyne St SW9 129 M9
Harlescott Rd SE15 131 H10
Harley Gdns SW10 128 C4
Harley Gro E3 127 K5
Harley Pl W1 125 H7
Harley Rd NW3 124 D2
Harley St W1 125 H6
Harleyford Rd SE11 129 M5
Harleyford St SE11 129 N5
Harmood St NW1 125 H2
Harmsworth St SE17 129 P4
Harold Est SE1 130 C2
Harold Pl SE11 129 N4
Harper Rd SE1 130 A2
Harpley Sq E1 126 G5
Harpsden St SW11 128 G7
Harpur St WC1 125 M7
Harrap St E14 127 N9
Harriet Cl E8 126 E3
Harriet Wk SW1 128 F1
Harrington Gdns SW7 128 B3
Harrington Rd SW7 128 D3
Harrington Sq NW1 125 J4
Harrington St NW1 125 J5
Harris St SE5 130 B6
Harrison St WC1 125 L5
Harrow La E14 127 N9
Harrow Pl E1 126 C8
Harroway Rd SW11 128 D8
Harrowby St W1 124 E8
Harrowgate Rd E9 127 J1
Hartfield Ter E3 127 L4
Hartington Rd SW8 129 L7
Hartlake Rd E9 127 H1
Hartland Rd NW1 125 H2
Hartley St E2 126 G5
Harton St SE8 131 L7
Harts La SE14 131 J6
Harvey Rd SE5 130 B7
Harvey St N1 126 B3
Harwood Rd SW6 128 A6
Harwood Ter SW6 128 B7
Haselrigge Rd SW4 129 K10
Hasker St SW3 128 E3
Haslam Cl N1 125 N2
Haslam St SE15 130 D6
Hassett Rd E9 127 H1
Hastings Cl SE15 130 E6
Hastings St WC1 125 L5
Hatcham Pk Rd SE14 131 H7
Hatcham Rd SE15 130 G5
Hatfields SE1 125 P10
Hatherley Gro W2 124 B8
Hathorne Cl SE15 130 F8
Hatton Gdn EC1 125 N7
Hatton Pl EC1 125 N6
Hatton Wall EC1 125 N7
Haul Rd NW1 125 L4
Havannah St E14 131 L1
Havelock St N1 125 L3
Havelock Ter SW8 129 H6
Haverfield Rd E3 127 J5
Haverstock St N1 125 P4
Havil St SE5 130 C6
Hawes St N1 125 P2
Hawgood St E3 127 L7
Hawkstone Est SE16 130 G3
Hawkstone Rd SE16 130 G3
Hawley Cres NW1 125 H2
Hawley Rd NW1 125 H2
Hawley St NW1 125 H2
Hawthorn Av E3 127 K3
Hawthorne Cl N1 126 C1
Hawtrey Rd NW3 124 E2
Hay Currie St E14 127 M8
Hay Hill W1 125 H9
Hay St E2 126 E3
Haydon Way SW11 128 D10
Hayes Gro SE22 130 D10
Hayles St SE11 129 P3
Haymarket SW1 125 K9
Haymerle Rd SE15 130 E5
Hay's Galleria SE1 126 C10
Hay's Ms W1 125 H9
Hazel Cl SE15 130 E8
Hazelmere Rd NW6 124 A3
Hazlebury Rd SW6 128 B8
Head St E1 127 H8
Headfort Pl SW1 128 G1
Headlam St E1 126 F6
Heald St SE14 131 K7
Healey St NW1 125 H1
Hearn St EC2 126 C6
Heath La SE3 131 P8
Heath Rd SW8 129 H8
Heathcote St WC1 125 M6
Heather Cl SW8 129 H9
Heathwall St SW11 128 F9
Heaton Rd SE15 130 E9
Heddon St W1 125 J9
Hedgers Gro E9 127 J1
Heiron St SE17 129 P5
Helmet Row EC1 126 A6
Helmsley Pl E8 126 F2
Helsinki Sq SE16 131 J2
Hemans St SW8 129 K6
Hemberton Rd SW9 129 L9
Hemingford Rd N1 125 M3
Hemming St E1 126 E6
Hemp Wk SE17 130 B3
Hemstal Rd NW6 124 A2
Hemsworth St N1 126 C4
Heneage St E1 126 D7
Henley Dr SE1 130 D3
Henley St SW11 128 G8
Henning St SW11 128 E7

Lauderdale Twr **EC2** 126 A7
Launceston Pl **W8** 128 C2
Launch St **E14** 131 N2
Laurel St **E8** 126 D1
Laurie Gro **SE14** 131 J7
Lauriston Rd **E9** 127 H3
Lausanne Rd **SE15** 130 G7
Lavender Gdns **SW11** 128 F10
Lavender Gro **E8** 126 D2
Lavender Hill **SW11** 128 E10
Lavender Rd **SE16** 127 J10
Lavender Rd **SW11** 128 D9
Lavender Sweep **SW11** 128 F10
Lavender Wk **SW11** 128 F10
Laverton Pl **SW5** 128 B3
Lavington St **SE1** 125 P10
Law St **SE1** 130 B2
Lawford Rd **N1** 126 C2
Lawford Rd **NW5** 125 J1
Lawless St **E14** 127 M9
Lawn Ho Cl **E14** 131 N1
Lawn La **SW8** 129 L5
Lawrence Cl **E3** 127 L4
Lawrence St **SW3** 128 E5
Lawson Est **SE1** 130 B2
Lawton Rd **E3** 127 J5
Laxley Cl **SE5** 129 P6
Layard Rd **SE16** 130 F3
Layard Sq **SE16** 130 F3
Laycock St **N1** 125 N1
Laystall St **EC1** 125 N6
Lea Valley Wk **E3** 127 N6
Lea Valley Wk **E14** 127 M7
Lea Valley Wk **E15** 127 N5
Leabank Sq **E9** 127 L1
Leadenhall St **EC3** 126 C8
Leake St **SE1** 129 M1
Leamouth Rd **E14** 127 P8
Leander Ct **SE8** 131 L7
Leather La **EC1** 125 N7
Leather Rd **SE16** 131 H3
Leathermarket Ct **SE1** 130 C1
Leathermarket St **SE1** 130 C1
Leathwaite Rd **SW11** 128 F10
Leathwell Rd **SE8** 131 M8
Lecky St **SW7** 128 D4
Ledbury Est **SE15** 130 F6
Ledbury St **SE15** 130 E6
Lee Br **SE13** 131 N9
Lee High Rd **SE12** 131 P9
Lee High Rd **SE13** 131 P9
Lee St **E8** 126 D3
Leeke St **WC1** 125 M5
Leerdam Dr **E14** 131 N2
Lees Pl **W1** 124 G9
Leeson Rd **SE24** 129 N10
Leeway **SE8** 131 K4
Lefevre Wk **E3** 127 K3
Leggatt Rd **E15** 127 N4
Legion Cl **N1** 125 N1
Leicester Sq **WC2** 125 K9
Leigh St **WC1** 125 L6
Leinster Gdns **W2** 124 C8
Leinster Ms **W2** 124 C9
Leinster Pl **W2** 124 C8
Leinster Sq **W2** 124 A8
Leinster Ter **W2** 124 C9
Leman St **E1** 126 D8
Lendal Ter **SW4** 129 K9
Lennox Gdns **SW1** 128 F2
Lennox Gdns Ms **SW1** 128 F2
Lenthall Rd **E8** 126 E2
Leo St **SE15** 130 F6
Leonard St **EC2** 126 B6
Leontine Cl **SE15** 130 E6
Leopold St **E3** 127 K7
Leroy St **SE1** 130 C3
Lethbridge Cl **SE13** 131 N7
Lett Rd **E15** 127 P2
Lettsom St **SE5** 130 C8
Levehurst Way **SW4** 129 L8
Leven Rd **E14** 127 N7
Lever St **EC1** 125 P5
Lewey Ho **E3** 127 K6
Lewis Gro **SE13** 131 N9
Lewis St **NW1** 125 H1
Lewisham Cen **SE13** 131 N9
Lewisham High St **SE13** 131 N9
Lewisham Hill **SE13** 131 N8
Lewisham Rd **SE13** 131 M7
Lewisham Way **SE4** 131 K7
Lewisham Way **SE14** 131 K7
Lexham Gdns **W8** 128 B2
Lexham Gdns Ms **W8** 128 B2
Lexham Ms **W8** 128 A3
Lexington St **W1** 125 J8
Leybourne Rd **NW1** 125 H2
Leyland Rd **SE14** 131 H6
Liardet St **SE14** 131 J5
Liberia Rd **N5** 125 P1
Liberty St **SW9** 129 M7
Libra Rd **E3** 127 K3
Library St **SE1** 129 P1
Lichfield Rd **E3** 127 J5
Lidcote Gdns **SW9** 129 N8
Liddell Rd **NW6** 124 A1
Lidlington Pl **NW1** 125 J4
Lighter Cl **SE16** 131 J3
Lighterman Ms **E1** 127 H8
Lightermans Rd **E14** 131 L1
Lilac Pl **SE11** 129 M3
Lilestone St **NW8** 124 E6
Lilford Rd **SE5** 129 P8
Lillie Yd **SW6** 128 A5
Lillieshall Rd **SW4** 129 H9
Lily Pl **EC1** 125 N7
Limburg Rd **SW11** 128 F10
Lime Cl **E1** 126 E10
Lime St **EC3** 126 C9
Limeburner La **EC4** 125 P8
Limeharbour **E14** 131 M2
Limehouse Causeway **E14** 127 K9
Limehouse Flds Est **E14** 127 J7
Limehouse Link **E14** 127 J9
Limerston St **SW10** 128 C5
Limes Gro **SE13** 131 N10
Limes Wk **SE15** 130 F10
Limesford Rd **SE15** 131 H10
Linacre Cl **SE15** 130 F9
Linberry Wk **SE8** 131 K3
Lincoln St **SW3** 128 F3
Lincoln's Inn **WC2** 125 N8
Lincoln's Inn Flds **WC2** 125 M8
Lind St **SE8** 131 M8
Linden Gdns **W2** 124 A9
Linden Gro **SE15** 130 F9
Lindfield St **E14** 127 L8
Lindley St **E1** 126 G7
Lindore Rd **SW11** 128 F10
Lindrop St **SW6** 128 C8
Lindsay Sq **SW1** 129 K4
Lindsell St **SE10** 131 N7
Lindsey Ms **N1** 126 A2
Lindsey St **EC1** 125 P7
Linford St **SW8** 129 J7
Lingards Rd **SE13** 131 N10
Lingham St **SW9** 129 L8
Linhope St **NW1** 124 F6
Link St **E9** 126 G1
Linnell Rd **SE5** 130 C8
Linom Rd **SW4** 129 L10
Linsey St **SE16** 130 E3
Linstead St **NW6** 124 A2
Linton St **N1** 126 A3
Linver Rd **SW6** 128 A8
Linwood Cl **SE5** 130 D8
Lisford St **SE15** 130 D7
Lisle St **WC2** 125 K9
Lisson Grn Est **NW8** 124 E6
Lisson Gro **NW1** 124 E6
Lisson Gro **NW8** 124 D5
Lisson St **NW1** 124 E7
Liston Rd **SW4** 129 J9
Litchfield St **WC2** 125 K9
Lithos Rd **NW3** 124 B1
Little Boltons, The **SW5** 128 B4
Little Boltons, The **SW10** 128 B4
Little Britain **EC1** 125 P7
Little Chester St **SW1** 129 H2
Little Dorrit Ct **SE1** 130 A1
Little Newport St **WC2** 125 K9
Little Portland St **W1** 125 H8
Little Russell St **WC1** 125 L7
Little St. James's St **SW1** 129 J10
Littlebury Rd **SW4** 129 K9
Livermere Rd **E8** 126 D3
Liverpool Gro **SE17** 130 B4
Liverpool Rd **N1** 125 N4
Liverpool St **EC2** 126 C7
Livingstone Rd **E15** 127 N3
Livingstone Wk **SW11** 128 D9
Lizard St **EC1** 126 A5
Lloyd Baker St **WC1** 125 M5
Lloyd Sq **WC1** 125 N5
Lloyd St **WC1** 125 N5
Lloyd's Av **EC3** 126 C8
Loampit Hill **SE13** 131 L8
Loampit Vale **SE13** 131 M9
Lochnagar St **E14** 127 N7
Lockesfield Pl **E14** 131 M4
Lockhart Cl **N7** 125 M1
Lockhart St **E3** 127 K6
Lockington Rd **SW8** 129 H7
Lockmead Rd **SE13** 131 N9
Locksley Est **E14** 127 K8
Locksley St **E14** 127 K7
Lockwood Sq **SE16** 130 F2
Loddiges Rd **E9** 126 G2
Loder St **SE15** 130 G7
Lodge Rd **NW8** 124 D5
Lodore St **E14** 127 N8
Loftie St **SE16** 130 E1
Lofting Rd **N1** 125 M2
Logan Ms **W8** 128 A3
Logan Pl **W8** 128 A3
Lollard St **SE11** 129 M3
Loman St **SE1** 129 P1
Lomas Dr **E8** 126 D2
Lomas St **E1** 126 E7
Lombard Rd **SW11** 128 D8
Lombard St **EC3** 126 B8
Lomond Gro **SE5** 130 B6
Loncroft Rd **SE5** 130 C5
London Br **EC4** 126 B10
London Br **SE1** 126 B10
London Br St **SE1** 126 B10
London Br Wk **SE1** 126 B10
London Flds **E8** 126 F2
London Flds E Side **E8** 126 F2
London Flds W Side **E8** 126 E2
London La **E8** 126 F2
London Rd **SE1** 129 P2
London Silver Vaults **WC2** 125 N7
London St **W2** 124 D8
London Trocadero, The **W1** 125 K9
London Wall **EC2** 126 A7
Long Acre **WC2** 125 L9
Long La **EC1** 125 P7
Long La **SE1** 130 B1
Long Rd **SW4** 129 H10
Long St **E2** 126 D5
Long Yd **WC1** 125 M6
Longbeach Rd **SW11** 128 F9
Longfield Est **SE1** 130 D3
Longford St **NW1** 125 H6
Longhedge St **SW11** 128 G8
Longhope Cl **SE15** 130 C5
Longley St **SE1** 130 E3
Longmoore St **SW1** 129 J3
Longnor Rd **E1** 127 H5
Longridge Rd **SW5** 128 A3
Long's Ct **WC2** 125 K9
Longshore **SE8** 131 K3
Lonsdale Sq **N1** 125 N2
Lord Amory Way **E14** 131 N1
Lord Hills Rd **W2** 124 B7
Lord N St **SW1** 129 L2
Lorden Wk **E2** 126 E5
Lorenzo St **WC1** 125 M5
Loring Rd **SE14** 131 J7
Lorn Ct **SW9** 129 N8
Lorn Rd **SW9** 129 M8
Lorrimore Rd **SE17** 129 P5
Lorrimore Sq **SE17** 129 P5
Lothbury **EC2** 126 B8
Lothian Rd **SW9** 129 P7
Lots Rd **SW10** 128 C6
Loudoun Rd **NW8** 124 C3
Lough Rd **N7** 125 M1
Loughborough Pk **SW9** 129 P10
Loughborough Rd **SW9** 129 N8
Loughborough St **SE11** 129 M4
Louisa St **E1** 127 H6
Louvaine Rd **SW11** 128 D10
Love La **EC2** 126 A8
Love Wk **SE5** 130 B8
Lovegrove St **SE1** 130 E4
Lovegrove Wk **E14** 127 N10
Lovelinch Cl **SE15** 130 G5
Lovell Ho **E8** 126 E3
Lover's Wk **W1** 124 G10
Lowden Rd **SE24** 129 P10
Lowell St **E14** 127 J8
Lower Belgrave St **SW1** 129 H2
Lower Grosvenor Pl **SW1** 129 H2
Lower Marsh **SE1** 129 N1
Lower Merton Ri **NW3** 124 E2
Lower Rd **SE8** 130 G2
Lower Rd **SE16** 130 G2
Lower Sloane St **SW1** 128 G3
Lower Thames St **EC3** 126 B9
Lowfield Rd **NW6** 124 A2
Lowndes Cl **SW1** 128 G2
Lowndes Pl **SW1** 128 G2
Lowndes Sq **SW1** 128 F1
Lowndes St **SW1** 128 F2
Lowth Rd **SE5** 130 A8
Lowther Gdns **SW7** 128 D1
Lubbock St **SE14** 130 G6
Lucan Pl **SW3** 128 E3
Lucas St **SE8** 131 L7
Lucey Rd **SE16** 130 E2
Lucey Way **SE16** 130 E2
Ludgate Hill **EC4** 125 P8
Ludgate Sq **EC4** 125 P8
Ludwick Ms **SE14** 131 J6
Lugard Rd **SE15** 130 F8
Luke Ho **E1** 126 F8
Luke St **EC2** 126 C6
Lukin St **E1** 126 G8
Lulworth Rd **SE15** 130 F8
Lupus St **SW1** 129 H5
Lurline Gdns **SW11** 128 G7
Luscombe Way **SW8** 129 L6
Luton Pl **SE10** 131 N6
Luton St **NW8** 124 D6
Luxborough St **W1** 124 G6
Luxford St **SE16** 131 H3
Luxmore St **SE4** 131 K7
Luxor St **SE5** 129 P8
Lyal Rd **E3** 127 J4
Lyall Ms **SW1** 128 G2
Lyall St **SW1** 128 G2
Lydon Rd **SW4** 129 J9
Lyme St **NW1** 125 J2
Lymington Rd **NW6** 124 B1
Lympstone Gdns **SE15** 130 E6
Lynbrook Gro **SE15** 130 C6
Lyncott Cres **SW4** 129 H10
Lyndhurst Gro **SE15** 130 C8
Lyndhurst Sq **SE15** 130 D7
Lyndhurst Way **SE15** 130 D7
Lynton Rd **SE1** 130 D3
Lyons Pl **NW8** 124 D6
Lytham St **SE17** 130 B4
Lyttelton Cl **NW3** 124 E2

M

Mabledon Pl **WC1** 125 K5
Mabley St **E9** 127 J1
Macaulay Ct **SW4** 129 H9
Macaulay Rd **SW4** 129 H9
Macaulay Sq **SW4** 129 H10
Macauley Ms **SE13** 131 N8
Macclesfield Br **NW1** 124 E4
Macclesfield Rd **EC1** 126 A5
Macclesfield St **W1** 125 K9
Macduff Rd **SW11** 128 G7
Mace St **E2** 127 H4
Macfarland Gro **SE15** 130 C6
Machell Rd **SE15** 130 G9
Mackay Rd **SW4** 129 H9
Mackennal St **NW8** 124 E4
Mackenzie Rd **N7** 125 M1
Mackenzie Wk **E14** 127 L10
Macklin St **WC2** 125 L8
Macks Rd **SE16** 130 E3
Mackworth St **NW1** 125 J5
Macleod St **SE17** 130 A4
Maconochies Rd **E14** 131 M4
Macquarie Way **E14** 131 M3
Maddams St **E3** 127 M6
Maddock Way **SE17** 129 P5
Maddox St **W1** 125 H9
Madinah Rd **E8** 126 E1
Madras Pl **N7** 125 N1
Madrigal La **SE5** 129 P6
Madron St **SE17** 130 C4
Magdalen St **SE1** 126 C10
Magee St **SE11** 129 N5
Maguire St **SE1** 130 D1
Mahogany Cl **SE16** 127 J10
Maida Av **W2** 124 C7
Maida Vale **W9** 124 B4
Maiden La **NW1** 125 K2
Maiden La **WC2** 125 L9
Maidenstone Hill **SE10** 131 N7
Maitland Pk Est **NW3** 124 F1
Maitland Pk Rd **NW3** 124 F1
Maitland Pk Vil **NW3** 124 F1
Major Cl **SW9** 129 P9
Makins St **SW3** 128 E3
Malabar St **E14** 131 L1
Malcolm Pl **E2** 126 G6
Malcolm Rd **E1** 126 G6
Malden Cres **NW1** 124 G1
Maldon Cl **SE5** 130 C9
Malet Pl **WC1** 125 K6
Malet St **WC1** 125 K6
Malfort Rd **SE5** 130 C9
Mall, The **SW1** 129 J1
Mallard Cl **NW6** 124 A4
Mallord St **SW3** 128 D5
Mallory Cl **SE4** 131 J10
Mallory St **NW8** 124 E6
Malmesbury Rd **E3** 127 K5
Malpas Rd **E8** 126 F1
Malpas Rd **SE4** 131 K8
Malt St **SE1** 130 E5
Maltby St **SE1** 130 D1
Malting Ho **E14** 127 K9
Maltings Pl **SW6** 128 B7
Malvern Ct **SW7** 128 D3
Malvern Rd **E8** 126 E2
Malvern Rd **NW6** 124 A5
Malvern Ter **N1** 125 N3
Manaton Cl **SE15** 130 F9
Manchester Gro **E14** 131 N4
Manchester Rd **E14** 131 N4
Manchester Sq **W1** 124 G8
Manchester St **W1** 124 G7
Manciple St **SE1** 130 B2
Mandela St **NW1** 125 J3
Mandela St **SW9** 129 N6
Mandela Way **SE1** 130 C3
Mandeville Pl **W1** 124 G8
Manette St **W1** 125 K8
Manger Rd **N7** 125 L1
Manilla St **E14** 131 L1
Manley St **NW1** 124 G3
Manor Av **SE4** 131 K8
Manor Est **SE16** 130 F3
Manor Gro **SE15** 130 G5
Manor Ms **SE4** 131 K8
Manor Pk **SE13** 131 P10
Manor Pl **SE17** 129 P4
Manresa Rd **SW3** 128 E4
Mansell St **E1** 126 D8
Mansfield St **W1** 125 H7
Mansford St **E2** 126 E4
Mansion Ho **EC4** 126 B8
Manson Ms **SW7** 128 C3
Manson Pl **SW7** 128 D3
Mantle Rd **SE4** 131 J9
Mantua St **SW11** 128 D9
Mantus Rd **E1** 126 G6
Mape St **E2** 126 F6
Maple St **E2** 126 E4
Maple St **W1** 125 J7
Mapledene Rd **E8** 126 D2
Maplin St **E3** 127 K5
Marble Arch **W1** 124 F9
Marble Quay **E1** 126 E10
Marcella Rd **SW9** 129 N8
Marchant St **SE14** 131 J5
Marchmont St **WC1** 125 L6
Marchwood Cl **SE5** 130 C6
Marcia Rd **SE1** 130 C3
Marcon Pl **E8** 126 F1
Marcus Garvey Way **SE24** 129 N10
Marden Sq **SE16** 130 F2
Mare St **E8** 126 F3
Margaret St **W1** 125 H8
Margaretta Ter **SW3** 128 E5
Margery St **WC1** 125 N5
Maria Ter **E1** 127 H7
Marian Pl **E2** 126 F4
Marigold St **SE16** 130 F1
Marinefield Rd **SW6** 128 B8
Mariners Ms **E14** 131 P3
Marischal Rd **SE13** 131 P9
Maritime Quay **E14** 131 L4
Maritime St **E3** 127 K6
Marjorie Gro **SW11** 128 F10
Mark La **EC3** 126 C9
Market Est **N7** 125 L1
Market Ms **W1** 125 H10
Market Pl **W1** 125 J8
Market Rd **N7** 125 L1
Markham Sq **SW3** 128 F4
Markham St **SW3** 128 E4
Marl Rd **SW18** 128 B10
Marlborough Av **E8** 126 E3
Marlborough Ct **W8** 128 A3
Marlborough Gro **SE1** 130 E4
Marlborough Hill **NW8** 124 C3
Marlborough Pl **NW8** 124 C4
Marlborough Rd **SW1** 125 J10
Marlborough St **SW3** 128 E3
Marloes Rd **W8** 128 B2
Marlow Way **SE16** 131 H1
Marlowes, The **NW8** 124 D3
Marmion Rd **SW11** 128 G10
Marmont Rd **SE15** 130 E7
Marney Rd **SW11** 128 G10
Maroon St **E14** 127 J7
Marquess Rd **N1** 126 B1
Marquis Rd **NW1** 125 K1
Marsala Rd **SE13** 131 M10
Marsden Rd **SE15** 130 D9
Marsden St **NW5** 124 G1
Marsh Wall **E14** 127 L10
Marshall St **W1** 125 J8
Marshalsea Rd **SE1** 130 A1
Marsham St **SW1** 129 K2
Marshfield St **E14** 131 N2
Marshgate La **E15** 127 M3
Marshgate Sidings **E15** 127 M3
Marsland Cl **SE17** 129 P4
Marston Cl **NW6** 124 C2
Martello St **E8** 126 F2
Martello Ter **E8** 126 F2
Martha Ct **E2** 126 F4
Martha St **E1** 126 F8
Martineau St **E1** 126 G9
Mary Ann Gdns **SE8** 131 L5
Mary Datchelor Cl **SE5** 130 B7
Mary Grn **NW8** 124 B3
Mary St **N1** 126 A3
Mary Ter **NW1** 125 H3
Marylands Rd **W9** 124 A6
Marylebone High St **W1** 124 G7
Marylebone La **W1** 124 G8
Marylebone Ms **W1** 125 H7
Marylebone Rd **NW1** 124 E7
Marylebone St **W1** 124 G7
Marylee Way **SE11** 129 M3
Maskelyne Cl **SW11** 128 E7
Mason St **SE17** 130 B3
Mason's Pl **EC1** 125 P5
Massingham St **E1** 127 H6
Mast Leisure Pk **SE16** 131 H2
Masterman Ho **SE5** 130 A6
Masters Dr **SE16** 130 F4
Masters St **E1** 127 H7
Masthouse Ter **E14** 131 L3
Mastmaker Rd **E14** 131 L1
Matham Gro **SE22** 130 D10
Matilda St **N1** 125 M3
Matlock Cl **SE24** 130 A10
Matlock St **E14** 127 J8
Matrimony Pl **SW8** 129 J8
Matthew Parker St **SW1** 129 K1
Matthews St **SW11** 128 F8
Maude Rd **SE5** 130 C7
Maunsel St **SW1** 129 K3
Maverton Rd **E3** 127 L3
Mawbey Est **SE1** 130 D4
Mawbey Pl **SE1** 130 D4
Mawbey St **SW8** 129 L6
Maxted Rd **SE15** 130 D9
Maxwell Rd **SW6** 128 B6
Maya Cl **SE15** 130 F8
Maydew Ho **SE16** 130 G3
Mayfair Pl **W1** 125 H10
Mayfield Rd **E8** 126 D2
Mayflower Rd **SW9** 129 L9
Mayflower St **SE16** 130 G1
Maygood St **N1** 125 M4
Maysoule Rd **SW11** 128 D10
Mazenod Av **NW6** 124 A2
McAuley Cl **SE1** 129 N2
McCullum Rd **E3** 127 K3
McDermott Cl **SW11** 128 E9
McDermott Rd **SE15** 130 E9
McDowall Rd **SE5** 130 A7
McEwen Way **E15** 127 P3
McKerrell Rd **SE15** 130 E7
McMillan St **SE8** 131 L5
McNeil Rd **SE5** 130 C8
Mead Pl **E9** 126 G1
Meadcroft Rd **SE11** 129 P5
Meadow Ms **SW8** 129 M5
Meadow Pl **SW8** 129 L6
Meadow Rd **SW8** 129 M5
Meadow Row **SE1** 130 A2
Meadowbank **NW3** 124 F2
Meakin Est **SE1** 130 C2
Meard St **W1** 125 K8
Meath St **SW11** 129 H7
Mecklenburgh Pl **WC1** 125 M6
Mecklenburgh Sq **WC1** 125 M6
Medburn St **NW1** 125 K4
Medlar St **SE5** 130 A7
Medley Rd **NW6** 124 A1
Medway Rd **E3** 127 J4
Medway St **SW1** 129 K2
Medwin St **SW4** 129 M10
Meeting Ho La **SE15** 130 F7
Mehetabel Rd **E9** 126 G1
Melba Way **SE13** 131 M7
Melbourne Gro **SE22** 130 C10
Melbourne Ms **SW9** 129 N7
Melbourne Pl **WC2** 125 M9
Melcombe Pl **NW1** 124 F7
Melcombe St **NW1** 124 F6
Melina Pl **NW8** 124 D5
Melior St **SE1** 130 B1
Mellish St **E14** 131 L2
Melon Rd **SE15** 130 E7
Melton St **NW1** 125 K5
Mendip Rd **SW11** 128 C9
Mentmore Ter **E8** 126 F2
Mepham St **SE1** 125 M10
Mercator Rd **SE13** 131 P10
Mercer St **WC2** 125 L8
Merceron St **E1** 126 F6
Merchant St **E3** 127 K5
Mercia Gro **SE13** 131 N10
Mercury Way **SE14** 131 H5
Mercy Ter **SE13** 131 M10
Meredith Ms **SE4** 131 K10
Meretone Cl **SE4** 131 J10
Meridian Gate **E14** 131 N1
Meridian Pl **E14** 131 M1
Meridian Sq **E15** 127 P2
Mermaid Ct **SE1** 130 B1
Mermaid Ct **SE16** 127 K10
Merriam Av **E9** 127 K1
Merrick Sq **SE1** 130 A2
Merrington Rd **SW6** 128 A5
Merrow St **SE17** 130 A5
Merton Ri **NW3** 124 E2
Mervan Rd **SW2** 129 N10
Messina Av **NW6** 124 A2
Meteor St **SW11** 128 G10
Methley St **SE11** 129 N4
Mews St **E1** 126 E10
Meymott St **SE1** 125 P10
Meynell Cres **E9** 127 H2
Meynell Gdns **E9** 127 H2
Meynell Rd **E9** 127 H2
Meyrick Rd **SW11** 128 D9
Micawber St **N1** 126 A5
Michael Rd **SW6** 128 B7
Micklethwaite Rd **SW6** 128 A5
Middle Fld **NW8** 124 D3
Middle Temple La **EC4** 125 N8
Middlesex St **E1** 126 C7
Middleton Dr **SE16** 131 H1
Middleton Rd **E8** 126 D2
Middleton St **E2** 126 F5
Middleton Way **SE13** 131 P10
Midland Rd **NW1** 125 K4
Midship Pt **E14** 131 L1

Milborne Gro **SW10** 128 C4
Milborne St **E9** 126 G1
Milcote St **SE1** 129 P1
Mildmay Av **N1** 126 B1
Mildmay St **N1** 126 B1
Mile End Pl **E1** 127 H6
Mile End Rd **E1** 126 G7
Mile End Rd **E3** 126 G7
Miles St **SW8** 129 L5
Milford La **WC2** 125 M9
Milk Yd **E1** 126 G9
Milkwell Yd **SE5** 130 A7
Mill Row **N1** 126 C3
Mill St **SE1** 130 D1
Mill St **W1** 125 J9
Millbank **SW1** 129 L2
Millbank Twr **SW1** 129 L3
Millbrook Rd **SW9** 129 P9
Millender Wk **SE16** 130 G3
Millennium Br **EC4** 126 A9
Millennium Br **SE1** 126 A9
Millennium Dr **E14** 131 P3
Millennium Harbour **E14** 131 K1
Millennium Pl **E2** 126 F4
Miller St **NW1** 125 J4
Miller Wk **SE1** 125 N10
Millgrove St **SW11** 128 G8
Millharbour **E14** 131 M2
Milligan St **E14** 127 K9
Millman Ms **WC1** 125 M6
Millman St **WC1** 125 M6
Millmark Gro **SE14** 131 J8
Millstream Rd **SE1** 130 D1
Millwall Dock Rd **E14** 131 L2
Milman's St **SW10** 128 D5
Milner Pl **N1** 125 N3
Milner Sq **N1** 125 P2
Milner St **SW3** 128 F3
Milton Cl **SE1** 130 D3
Milton Ct Rd **SE14** 131 J5
Milton St **EC2** 126 B7
Milverton St **SE11** 129 N4
Mina Rd **SE17** 130 C4
Mincing La **EC3** 126 C9
Minera Ms **SW1** 128 G3
Minerva Cl **SW9** 129 N6
Minerva St **E2** 126 F4
Minet Rd **SW9** 129 P8
Ming St **E14** 127 L9
Minories **EC3** 126 D8
Minson Rd **E9** 127 H3
Mintern St **N1** 126 B4
Mission Pl **SE15** 130 E7
Mitchell St **EC1** 126 A6
Mitchison Rd **N1** 126 B1
Mitre Rd **SE1** 129 N1
Mitre St **EC3** 126 C8
Moat Pl **SW9** 129 M9
Modling Ho **E2** 126 G4
Molesford Rd **SW6** 128 A7
Molesworth St **SE13** 131 N9
Molyneux St **W1** 124 E7
Mona Rd **SE15** 130 G8
Monck St **SW1** 129 K2
Monclar Rd **SE5** 130 B10
Moncrieff St **SE15** 130 E8
Monier Rd **E3** 127 L2
Monkton St **SE11** 129 N3
Monmouth Rd **W2** 124 B8
Monmouth St **WC2** 125 L9
Monnow Rd **SE1** 130 E3
Monson Rd **SE14** 131 H6
Montagu Ms N **W1** 124 F7
Montagu Pl **W1** 124 F7
Montagu Sq **W1** 124 F7
Montagu St **W1** 124 F8
Montague Av **SE4** 131 K10
Montague Cl **SE1** 126 B10
Montague Pl **WC1** 125 K7
Montague St **EC1** 126 A8
Montague St **WC1** 125 L7
Monteagle Way **SE15** 130 F9
Montefiore St **SW8** 129 H8
Montevetro **SW11** 128 D7
Montford Pl **SE11** 129 N4
Montgomery St **E14** 127 M10
Montpelier Pl **E1** 126 G8
Montpelier Pl **SW7** 128 E2
Montpelier Rd **SE15** 130 F7
Montpelier Sq **SW7** 128 E1
Montpelier St **SW7** 128 E1
Montpelier Wk **SW7** 128 E2
Montrose Ct **SW7** 128 D1
Montrose Pl **SW1** 128 G1
Monument St **EC3** 126 B9
Monza St **E1** 126 G9
Moodkee St **SE16** 130 G2
Moody Rd **SE15** 130 D6
Moody St **E1** 127 H5
Moon St **N1** 125 P3
Moor La **EC2** 126 B7
Moore Pk Rd **SW6** 128 B6
Moore St **SW3** 128 F3
Moorfields **EC2** 126 B7
Moorgate **EC2** 126 B8
Moorhouse Rd **W2** 124 A8
Moorland Rd **SW9** 129 P10
Moorlands Est **SW9** 129 N10
Mora St **EC1** 126 A5
Morant St **E14** 127 L9
Morat St **SW9** 129 M7
Moravian St **E2** 126 G5
Mordaunt St **SW9** 129 M9
Morden Hill **SE13** 131 N8
Morden La **SE13** 131 N7
Morden St **SE13** 131 M7
More London Pl **SE1** 126 C10
Morecambe Cl **E1** 127 H7
Morecambe St **SE17** 130 A3
Moreland St **EC1** 125 P5
Moresby Wk **SW8** 129 H8
Moreton Pl **SW1** 129 J4
Moreton St **SW1** 129 K4
Moreton Ter **SW1** 129 J4
Morgan St **E3** 127 J5
Morgans La **SE1** 126 C10
Morley Rd **SE13** 131 N10
Morley St **SE1** 129 N1
Morna Rd **SE5** 130 A8
Morning La **E9** 126 G1
Mornington Cres **NW1** 125 J4
Mornington Gro **E3** 127 L5
Mornington Ms **SE5** 130 A7
Mornington Rd **SE8** 131 K6
Mornington St **NW1** 125 H4
Mornington Ter **NW1** 125 H3
Morocco St **SE1** 130 C1
Morpeth Gro **E9** 127 H3
Morpeth Rd **E9** 126 G3
Morpeth St **E2** 127 H5
Morpeth Ter **SW1** 129 J2
Morris Rd **E14** 127 M7
Morris St **E1** 126 F8
Morrison St **SW11** 128 G9
Morshead Rd **W9** 124 A5
Mortham St **E15** 127 P3
Mortimer Cres **NW6** 124 B3
Mortimer Est **NW6** 124 B3
Mortimer Pl **NW6** 124 B3
Mortimer Rd **N1** 126 C2
Mortimer St **W1** 125 H8
Morton Rd **N1** 126 A2
Morville St **E3** 127 L4
Moscow Rd **W2** 124 A9
Mossbury Rd **SW11** 128 E9
Mossford St **E3** 127 K6
Mossop St **SW3** 128 E3
Mostyn Gro **E3** 127 K4
Mostyn Rd **SW9** 129 N7
Motcomb St **SW1** 128 G2
Moulins Rd **E9** 126 G3
Mount Pleasant **WC1** 125 N6
Mount Row **W1** 125 H9
Mount St **W1** 124 G9
Mountague Pl **E14** 127 N9
Mounts Pond Rd **SE3** 131 P8
Mowlem St **E2** 126 F4
Mowll St **SW9** 129 N6
Moxon St **W1** 124 G7
Mozart Ter **SW1** 128 G3
Mulberry Rd **E8** 126 D2
Mulberry Wk **SW3** 128 D5
Mulvaney Way **SE1** 130 B1
Mundy St **N1** 126 C5
Munro Ter **SW10** 128 D6
Munster Sq **NW1** 125 H5
Munton Rd **SE17** 130 A3
Murdock St **SE15** 130 F5
Muriel St **N1** 125 M4
Murillo Rd **SE13** 131 P10
Murphy St **SE1** 129 N1
Murray Gro **N1** 126 A4
Murray Ms **NW1** 125 K2
Murray St **NW1** 125 K2
Mursell Est **SW8** 129 M7
Musbury St **E1** 126 G8
Muschamp Rd **SE15** 130 D9
Museum St **WC1** 125 L8
Musgrave Cres **SW6** 128 A7
Musgrove Rd **SE14** 131 H7
Mutrix Rd **NW6** 124 A3
Myatt Rd **SW9** 129 P7
Myddelton Sq **EC1** 125 N5
Myddelton St **EC1** 125 N5
Myers La **SE14** 131 H5
Mylne St **EC1** 125 N5
Myrdle St **E1** 126 E7
Myron Pl **SE13** 131 N9
Myrtle Wk **N1** 126 C4
Mysore Rd **SW11** 128 F9

N

N1 Shop Cen **N1** 125 N4
Nairn St **E14** 127 N7
Nankin St **E14** 127 L8
Nansen Rd **SW11** 128 G10
Nantes Cl **SW18** 128 C10
Napier Av **E14** 131 L4
Napier Gro **N1** 126 A4
Napier Ter **N1** 125 P2
Narborough St **SW6** 128 B8
Narrow St **E14** 127 J9
Naseby Cl **NW6** 124 C2
Nash Rd **SE4** 131 H10
Nassau St **W1** 125 J7
Naval Row **E14** 127 N9
Navarino Gro **E8** 126 E1
Navarino Rd **E8** 126 E1
Navarre St **E2** 126 D6
Navy St **SW4** 129 K9
Naylor Rd **SE15** 130 F6
Nazareth Gdns **SE15** 130 F8
Nazrul St **E2** 126 D5
Neal St **WC2** 125 L8
Nealden St **SW9** 129 M9
Neate St **SE5** 130 D5
Nebraska St **SE1** 130 B1
Neckinger **SE16** 130 D2
Neckinger Est **SE16** 130 D2
Neckinger St **SE1** 130 D1
Nectarine Way **SE13** 131 M8
Needleman St **SE16** 131 H1
Nelldale Rd **SE16** 130 G3
Nelson Cl **NW6** 124 A5
Nelson Gdns **E2** 126 E5
Nelson Pl **N1** 125 P4
Nelson Rd **SE10** 131 N5
Nelson Sq **SE1** 129 P1
Nelson St **E1** 126 F8
Nelson Ter **N1** 125 P4
Nelson's Row **SW4** 129 K10
Nepaul Rd **SW11** 128 E8
Neptune St **SE16** 130 G2
Nesham St **E1** 126 E10
Netherford Rd **SW4** 129 J8
Netherhall Gdns **NW3** 124 C1
Netherton Gro **SW10** 128 C5
Nettleton Rd **SE14** 131 H7
Nevada St **SE10** 131 N5
Nevern Pl **SW5** 128 A3
Nevern Rd **SW5** 128 A3
Nevern Sq **SW5** 128 A3
Neville Cl **SE15** 130 E6
Neville St **SW7** 128 D4
Neville Ter **SW7** 128 D4
New Bond St **W1** 125 H9
New Br St **EC4** 125 P8
New Broad St **EC2** 126 C7
New Burlington St **W1** 125 J9
New Butt La **SE8** 131 L6
New Caledonian Wf **SE16** 131 K2
New Cavendish St **W1** 124 G7
New Change **EC4** 126 A8
New Ch Rd **SE5** 130 A6
New Compton St **WC2** 125 K8
New Covent Gdn Mkt **SW8** 129 K6
New Cross Rd **SE14** 130 G6
New Fetter La **EC4** 125 N8
New Globe Wk **SE1** 126 A10
New Inn Yd **EC2** 126 C6
New Kent Rd **SE1** 130 A2
New King St **SE8** 131 L5
New Mt St **E15** 127 P2
New N Rd **N1** 126 B4
New N St **WC1** 125 M7
New Oxford St **WC1** 125 K8
New Pl Sq **SE16** 130 F2
New Quebec St **W1** 124 F8
New Ride **SW7** 128 E1
New River Wk **N1** 126 A1
New Rd **E1** 126 F7
New Row **WC2** 125 L9
New Sq **WC2** 125 M8
New St **EC2** 126 C7
New Union Cl **E14** 131 N2
New Union St **EC2** 126 B7
New Wf Rd **N1** 125 L4
Newark St **E1** 126 F7
Newburgh St **W1** 125 J8
Newburn St **SE11** 129 M4
Newby Pl **E14** 127 N9
Newby St **SW8** 129 H9
Newcastle Pl **W2** 124 D7
Newcomen Rd **SW11** 128 D9
Newcomen St **SE1** 130 B1
Newcourt St **NW8** 124 E4
Newell St **E14** 127 K8
Newent Cl **SE15** 130 C6
Newgate St **EC1** 125 P8
Newington Butts **SE1** 129 P3
Newington Butts **SE11** 129 P3
Newington Causeway **SE1** 129 P2
Newington Grn Rd **N1** 126 B1
Newlands Quay **E1** 126 G9
Newman St **W1** 125 J7
Newport Av **E14** 127 P9
Newport Pl **WC2** 125 K9
Newport St **SE11** 129 M3
Newton Pl **E14** 131 L3
Newton Rd **W2** 124 A8
Newton St **WC2** 125 L8
Nicholas Rd **E1** 126 G6
Nicholl St **E2** 126 E3
Nicholson St **SE1** 125 P10
Nigel Rd **SE15** 130 E9
Nightingale Rd **N1** 126 A1
Nile St **N1** 126 B5
Nile Ter **SE15** 130 D4
Nine Elms La **SW8** 129 J6
Noble St **EC2** 126 A8
Noel Rd **N1** 125 P4
Noel St **W1** 125 J8
Norbiton Rd **E14** 127 K8
Norfolk Cres **W2** 124 E8
Norfolk Pl **W2** 124 D8
Norfolk Rd **NW8** 124 D3
Norfolk Sq **W2** 124 D8
Norman Gro **E3** 127 J4
Norman Rd **SE10** 131 M6
Normandy Rd **SW9** 129 N7
North Audley St **W1** 124 G8
North Bk **NW8** 124 E5
North Carriage Dr **W2** 124 E9
North Colonnade **E14** 127 L10
North Cres **E16** 127 P6
North Cres **WC1** 125 K7
North Gower St **NW1** 125 J5
North Ms **WC1** 125 M6
North Pas **SW18** 128 A10
North Ride **W2** 124 E9
North Rd **N7** 125 L1
North Row **W1** 124 F9
North St **SW4** 129 J9
North Tenter St **E1** 126 D8
North Ter **SW3** 128 E2
North Vil **NW1** 125 K1
North Wf Rd **W2** 124 D7
Northampton Pk **N1** 126 A1
Northampton Rd **EC1** 125 N6
Northampton Sq **EC1** 125 P5
Northampton St **N1** 126 A2
Northbourne Rd **SW4** 129 K10
Northburgh St **EC1** 125 P6
Northchurch Rd **N1** 126 B2
Northchurch Ter **N1** 126 C2
Northcote Rd **SW11** 128 E10
Northdown St **N1** 125 M4
Northey St **E14** 127 J9
Northfields **SW18** 128 A10
Northiam St **E9** 126 F3
Northington St **WC1** 125 M6
Northlands St **SE5** 130 A8
Northpoint Sq **NW1** 125 K1
Northport St **N1** 126 B3
Northumberland All **EC3** 126 C8
Northumberland Av **WC2** 125 L10
Northumberland Pl **W2** 124 A8
Northumberland St **WC2** 125 L10
Northumbria St **E14** 127 L8
Northway Rd **SE5** 130 A9
Northwick Ter **NW8** 124 D6
Norton Folgate **E1** 126 C7
Norway Gate **SE16** 131 J2
Norway St **SE10** 131 M5
Norwich St **EC4** 125 N8
Notley St **SE5** 130 B6
Notre Dame Est **SW4** 129 J10
Notting Hill Gate **W11** 124 A10
Nottingham Pl **W1** 124 G6
Nottingham St **W1** 124 G7
Novello St **SW6** 128 A7
Nuding Cl **SE13** 131 L9
Nugent Ter **NW8** 124 C4
Nunhead Cres **SE15** 130 F9
Nunhead Est **SE15** 130 F10
Nunhead Grn **SE15** 130 F9
Nunhead Gro **SE15** 130 F9
Nunhead La **SE15** 130 F9
Nursery Cl **SE4** 131 K8
Nursery La **E2** 126 D3
Nursery Rd **SW9** 129 M10
Nutbrook St **SE15** 130 E9
Nutcroft Rd **SE15** 130 F6
Nutford Pl **W1** 124 F8
Nutley Ter **NW3** 124 C1
Nutmeg La **E14** 127 P8
Nutt St **SE15** 130 D6
Nuttall St **N1** 126 C4
Nynehead St **SE14** 131 J6

O

Oak La **E14** 127 K9
Oak Tree Rd **NW8** 124 E5
Oakbank Gro **SE24** 130 A10
Oakbury Rd **SW6** 128 B8
Oakcroft Rd **SE13** 131 P8
Oakdale Rd **SE15** 130 G9
Oakden St **SE11** 129 N3
Oakey La **SE1** 129 N2
Oakfield St **SW10** 128 C5
Oakhurst Gro **SE22** 130 E10
Oakington Rd **W9** 124 A6
Oakley Gdns **SW3** 128 E5
Oakley Pl **SE1** 130 D4
Oakley Rd **N1** 126 B2
Oakley Sq **NW1** 125 J4
Oakley St **SW3** 128 E5
Oat La **EC2** 126 A8
Oban St **E14** 127 P8
Oberstein Rd **SW11** 128 D10
Observatory Gdns **W8** 128 A1
Occupation Rd **SE17** 130 A4
Ocean Est **E1** 127 H6
Ocean St **E1** 127 H7
Ocean Wf **E14** 131 K1
Ockendon Rd **N1** 126 B1
Octavia St **SW11** 128 E7
Octavius St **SE8** 131 L6
Odessa St **SE16** 131 K1
Odger St **SW11** 128 F8
Offenbach Ho **E2** 127 H4
Offerton Rd **SW4** 129 J9
Offley Rd **SW9** 129 N6
Offord Rd **N1** 125 M2
Offord St **N1** 125 M2
Oglander Rd **SE15** 130 D10
Ogle St **W1** 125 J7
Old Bailey **EC4** 125 P8
Old Bellgate Pl **E14** 131 L2
Old Bethnal Grn Rd **E2** 126 E5
Old Bond St **W1** 125 J9
Old Broad St **EC2** 126 B8
Old Brompton Rd **SW5** 128 A4
Old Brompton Rd **SW7** 128 A4
Old Burlington St **W1** 125 J9
Old Castle St **E1** 126 D7
Old Cavendish St **W1** 125 H8
Old Ch Rd **E1** 127 H8
Old Ch St **SW3** 128 D4
Old Compton St **W1** 125 K9
Old Ct Pl **W8** 128 B1
Old Ford Rd **E2** 126 G4
Old Ford Rd **E3** 127 J4
Old Gloucester St **WC1** 125 L7
Old Jamaica Rd **SE16** 130 E2
Old James St **SE15** 130 F9
Old Jewry **EC2** 126 B8
Old Kent Rd **SE1** 130 C3
Old Kent Rd **SE15** 130 C3
Old Marylebone Rd **NW1** 124 E7
Old Montague St **E1** 126 E7
Old Nichol St **E2** 126 D6
Old Palace Yd **SW1** 129 L2
Old Paradise St **SE11** 129 M3
Old Pk La **W1** 124 G10
Old Pye St **SW1** 129 K2
Old Quebec St **W1** 124 F8
Old Queen St **SW1** 129 K1
Old Royal Free Sq **N1** 125 N3
Old S Lambeth Rd **SW8** 129 L6
Old Spitalfields Mkt **E1** 126 D7
Old Sq **WC2** 125 N8
Old St **EC1** 126 A6
Old Town **SW4** 129 J9
Old Woolwich Rd **SE10** 131 P5
Oldbury Pl **W1** 124 G6
Oldfield Gro **SE16** 131 H3
O'Leary Sq **E1** 126 G7
Olga St **E3** 127 J4
Oliver Ms **SE15** 130 E8
Oliver-Goldsmith Est **SE15** 130 E7
Ollerton Grn **E3** 127 K3
Olliffe St **E14** 131 N2
Olmar St **SE1** 130 E5
Olney Rd **SE17** 129 P5
O'Meara St **SE1** 126 A10
Omega St **SE14** 131 L7
Ommaney Rd **SE14** 131 H7
Ondine Rd **SE15** 130 D10
Onega Gate **SE16** 131 J2
Ongar Rd **SW6** 128 A5
Onslow Cres **SW7** 128 D3
Onslow Gdns **SW7** 128 D4
Onslow Sq **SW7** 128 D3
Ontario St **SE1** 129 P2
Ontario Way **E14** 127 L9
Opal St **SE11** 129 P3
Ophir Ter **SE15** 130 E7
Oppenheim Rd **SE13** 131 N8
Oppidans Rd **NW3** 124 F2
Orange St **WC2** 125 K9
Oransay Rd **N1** 126 A1
Orb St **SE17** 130 B3
Orbel St **SW11** 128 E7
Orchard, The **SE3** 131 P8
Orchard Cl **N1** 126 A2
Orchard St **W1** 124 G8
Orchardson St **NW8** 124 D6
Orde Hall St **WC1** 125 M6
Ordell Rd **E3** 127 K4
Ordnance Cres **SE10** 131 P1
Ordnance Hill **NW8** 124 D3
Oregano Dr **E14** 127 P8
Oriel Rd **E9** 127 H1
Orkney St **SW11** 128 G8
Orlando Rd **SW4** 129 J9
Orleston Ms **N7** 125 N1
Orleston Rd **N7** 125 N1
Orme Ct **W2** 124 B9
Orme La **W2** 124 B9
Ormonde Gate **SW3** 128 F4
Ormonde Ter **NW8** 124 F3
Ormsby St **E2** 126 D4
Ormside St **SE15** 130 G5
Orpheus St **SE5** 130 B7
Orsett St **SE11** 129 M4
Orsett Ter **W2** 124 C8
Orsman Rd **N1** 126 C3
Orville Rd **SW11** 128 D8
Osborn Cl **E8** 126 E3
Osborn St **E1** 126 D7
Osborne Rd **E9** 127 K1
Oscar St **SE8** 131 L7
Oseney Cres **NW5** 125 J1
Osier St **E1** 126 G6
Osiers Rd **SW18** 128 A10
Oslo Sq **SE16** 131 J2
Osnaburgh St **NW1** 125 H6
Osnaburgh St (north section) **NW1** 125 H5
Osric Path **N1** 126 C4
Ossington St **W2** 124 A9
Ossory Rd **SE1** 130 E4
Ossulston St **NW1** 125 K5
Oswell Ho **E1** 126 F10
Oswin St **SE11** 129 P3
Oswyth Rd **SE5** 130 C8
Otis St **E3** 127 N5
Otter Cl **E15** 127 N3
Otterburn Ho **SE5** 130 A6
Otto St **SE17** 129 P5
Outer Circle **NW1** 125 H4
Outram Pl **N1** 125 L3
Oval, The **E2** 126 F4
Oval Pl **SW8** 129 M6
Oval Rd **NW1** 125 H3
Oval Way **SE11** 129 M4
Overcliff Rd **SE13** 131 L9
Oversley Ho **W2** 124 A7
Overton Rd **SW9** 129 N8
Ovex Cl **E14** 131 N1
Ovington Gdns **SW3** 128 E2
Ovington Ms **SW3** 128 E2
Ovington Sq **SW3** 128 E2
Ovington St **SW3** 128 E2
Oxendon St **SW1** 125 K9
Oxenford St **SE15** 130 D9
Oxenholme **NW1** 125 J4
Oxestalls Rd **SE8** 131 J4
Oxford Rd **E15** 127 P1
Oxford Rd **NW6** 124 A4
Oxford Sq **W2** 124 E8
Oxford St **W1** 125 H8
Oxley Cl **SE1** 130 D4
Oxo Twr Wf **SE1** 125 N9
Oxonian St **SE22** 130 D10
Oyster Wf **SW11** 128 D8

P

Packington Sq **N1** 126 A3
Packington St **N1** 125 P3
Padbury **SE17** 130 C4
Padbury Ct **E2** 126 D5
Paddington Grn **W2** 124 D7
Paddington Sta **W2** 124 C8
Paddington St **W1** 124 G7
Paddington Underground Sta **W2** 124 C8
Padfield Rd **SE5** 130 A9
Padfield Rd **SW9** 130 A9
Pagden St **SW8** 129 H7
Page St **SW1** 129 K3
Pages Wk **SE1** 130 C3
Pagnell St **SE14** 131 K6
Pagoda Gdns **SE3** 131 P8
Pakenham St **WC1** 125 M5
Palace Av **W8** 124 B10
Palace Ct **W2** 124 B9
Palace Gdns Ms **W8** 124 A10
Palace Gdns Ter **W8** 124 A10
Palace Gate **W8** 128 C1
Palace Grn **W8** 128 B1
Palace St **SW1** 129 J2
Palfrey Pl **SW8** 129 M6
Palgrave Gdns **NW1** 124 E6
Pall Mall **SW1** 125 J10
Pall Mall E **SW1** 125 K10
Palmer St **SW1** 129 K2
Palmers Rd **E2** 127 H4
Palmerston Rd **NW6** 124 A2
Pancras Rd **NW1** 125 K4
Pandora Rd **NW6** 124 A1
Parade, The **SW11** 128 F6
Paradise Rd **SW4** 129 L8
Paradise St **SE16** 130 F1
Paradise Wk **SW3** 128 F5
Paragon Rd **E9** 126 G1
Pardoner St **SE1** 130 B2
Parfett St **E1** 126 E7
Paris Gdn **SE1** 125 P10
Park Cl **E9** 126 G3
Park Cl **SW1** 128 F1
Park Cres **W1** 125 H6

Park La W1 124 G9
Park Pl E14 127 L10
Park Pl N1 126 B3
Park Pl SW1 125 J10
Park Pl Vil W2 124 C7
Park Rd NW1 124 E5
Park Rd NW8 124 E5
Park Row SE10 131 P5
Park Sq E NW1 125 H6
Park Sq Ms NW1 125 H6
Park Sq W NW1 125 H6
Park St SE1 126 A10
Park St W1 124 G9
Park Vw Est E2 127 H4
Park Vw Ms SW9 129 M8
Park Village E NW1 125 H4
Park Village W NW1 125 H4
Park Vista SE10 131 P5
Park Wk SW10 128 C5
Parker St WC2 125 L8
Parkfield Rd SE14 131 K7
Parkgate Rd SW11 128 E6
Parkham St SW11 128 E7
Parkholme Rd E8 126 D1
Parkhouse St SE5 130 B6
Parkside Rd SW11 128 G7
Parkway NW1 125 H3
Parliament Sq SW1 129 L1
Parliament St SW1 129 L1
Parliament Vw Apts SE1 129 M3
Parma Cres SW11 128 F10
Parmiter St E2 126 F4
Parnell Rd E3 127 K3
Parr St N1 126 B4
Parry St SW8 129 L5
Parsonage St E14 131 N3
Parsons Grn SW6 128 A7
Parsons Grn La SW6 128 A7
Parson's Ho W2 124 D6
Parthenia Rd SW6 128 A7
Parvin St SW8 129 K7
Pascal St SW8 129 K6
Passmore St SW1 128 G3
Pastor St SE11 129 P3
Patcham Ter SW8 129 H7
Pater St W8 128 A2
Patience Rd SW11 128 E8
Patmore Est SW8 129 J7
Patmore St SW8 129 J7
Patmos Rd SW9 129 P6
Paton Cl E3 127 L5
Patriot Sq E2 126 F4
Patshull Rd NW5 125 J1
Patterdale Rd SE15 130 G6
Pattina Wk SE16 127 K10
Paul Julius Cl E14 127 P9
Paul St E15 127 P3
Paul St EC2 126 B6
Paulet Rd SE5 129 P8
Paul's Wk EC4 126 A9
Paultons Sq SW3 128 D5
Paultons St SW3 128 D5
Paveley Dr SW11 128 E6
Paveley St NW8 124 E6
Pavement, The SW4 129 J10
Pavilion Rd SW1 128 F1
Paxton Ter SW1 129 H5
Payne Rd E3 127 M4
Payne St SE8 131 K5
Peabody Est SW1 129 J3
Peabody Sq SE1 129 P1
Peabody Trust SE1 126 A10
Pear Tree Cl E2 126 D3
Pear Tree Ct EC1 125 N6
Pear Tree St EC1 125 P6
Peardon St SW8 129 H8
Pearman St SE1 129 N1
Pearscroft Ct SW6 128 B7
Pearscroft Rd SW6 128 B7
Pearson St E2 126 C4
Peckford Pl SW9 129 N8
Peckham Gro SE15 130 C6
Peckham High St SE15 130 E7
Peckham Hill St SE15 130 E6
Peckham Pk Rd SE15 130 E6
Peckham Rd SE5 130 C7
Peckham Rd SE15 130 C7
Peckham Rye SE15 130 E9
Peckham Rye SE22 130 E10
Pedlars Wk N7 125 L1
Pedley St E1 126 D6
Peel Gro E2 126 G4
Peel Prec NW6 124 A4
Peel St W8 124 A10
Peerless St EC1 126 B5
Pekin St E14 127 L8
Pelham Cl SE5 130 C8
Pelham Cres SW7 128 E3
Pelham Pl SW7 128 E3
Pelham St SW7 128 E3
Pelican Est SE15 130 D7
Pelling St E14 127 L8
Pelter St E2 126 D5
Pembridge Cres W11 124 A9
Pembridge Gdns W2 124 A9
Pembridge Ms W11 124 A9
Pembridge Pl W2 124 A9
Pembridge Rd W11 124 A9
Pembridge Sq W2 124 A9
Pembridge Vil W2 124 A9
Pembridge Vil W11 124 A9
Pembroke Av N1 125 L3
Pembroke Cl SW1 128 G1
Pembroke Gdns Cl W8 128 A2
Pembroke Pl W8 128 A2
Pembroke Rd W8 128 A3
Pembroke Sq W8 128 A2
Pembroke St N1 125 L2
Pembroke Vil W8 128 A3
Pembroke Wk W8 128 A3
Pembry Cl SW9 129 N7
Penang St E1 126 F10
Penarth St SE15 130 G5
Pencraig Way SE15 130 F5
Pendrell Rd SE4 131 J8
Penfold Pl NW1 124 E7
Penfold St NW1 124 D6
Penfold St NW8 124 D6
Penford St SE5 129 P8
Penn St N1 126 B3
Pennack Rd SE15 130 D5
Pennant Ms W8 128 B3
Pennethorne Rd SE15 130 F6
Pennington St E1 126 E9
Pennyfields E14 127 L9
Penpoll Rd E8 126 F1
Penrose Gro SE17 130 A4
Penrose Ho SE17 130 A4
Penrose St SE17 130 A4
Penryn St NW1 125 K4
Pensbury Pl SW8 129 J8
Pensbury St SW8 129 J8
Penshurst Rd E9 127 H2
Pentland Rd NW6 124 A5
Penton Pl SE17 129 P4
Penton Ri WC1 125 M5
Penton St N1 125 N4
Pentonville Rd N1 125 M4
Pentridge St SE15 130 D6
Penywern Rd SW5 128 A4
Pepper St E14 131 M2
Pepys Rd SE14 131 H7
Pepys St EC3 126 C9
Percival St EC1 125 P6
Percy Circ WC1 125 M5
Percy St W1 125 K7
Peregrine Ho EC1 125 P5
Perkin's Rents SW1 129 K2
Perrymead St SW6 128 A7
Perseverance Pl SW9 129 N6
Peter St W1 125 K9
Peterborough Ms SW6 128 A8
Peterborough Rd SW6 128 A8
Peterborough Vil SW6 128 B7
Petergate SW11 128 C10
Petersham La SW7 128 C2
Petersham Ms SW7 128 C2
Petersham Pl SW7 128 C2
Peto Pl NW1 125 H6
Petticoat La E1 126 C7
Petticoat Sq E1 126 D8
Petty France SW1 129 J2
Petty Wales EC3 126 C9
Petworth St SW11 128 E7
Petyward SW3 128 E3
Peyton Pl SE10 131 N6
Phelp St SE17 130 B5
Phene St SW3 128 E5
Philbeach Gdns SW5 128 A4
Philip Wk SE15 130 E9
Phillimore Gdns W8 128 A1
Phillimore Pl W8 128 A1
Phillimore Wk W8 128 A2
Phillipp St N1 126 C3
Philpot St E1 126 F8
Phipp St EC2 126 C6
Phoenix Pl WC1 125 M6
Phoenix Rd NW1 125 K5
Piccadilly W1 125 H10
Piccadilly Circ W1 125 K9
Pickfords Wf N1 126 A4
Picton St SE5 130 B6
Pier St E14 131 N3
Pigott St E14 127 L8
Pilgrimage St SE1 130 B1
Pilkington Rd SE15 130 F8
Pilot Cl SE8 131 K5
Pilton Pl SE17 130 A4
Pimlico Rd SW1 128 G4
Pinchin St E1 126 E9
Pincott Pl SE4 131 H10
Pindar St EC2 126 C7
Pine St EC1 125 N6
Pinefield Cl E14 127 L9
Pioneer St SE15 130 E7
Piper Cl N7 125 M1
Pitchford St E15 127 P2
Pitfield Est N1 126 B5
Pitfield St N1 126 C5
Pitman St SE5 130 A6
Pitsea St E1 127 H8
Pitt St W8 128 A1
Pitt's Head Ms W1 124 G10
Pixley St E14 127 K8
Plantation Wf SW11 128 C9
Plato Rd SW2 129 L10
Platt St NW1 125 K4
Plaza Shop Cen, The W1 125 J8
Pleasant Pl N1 125 P2
Pleasant Row NW1 125 H3
Plender St NW1 125 J3
Plevna St E14 131 N2
Plough Rd SW11 128 D9
Plough Ter SW11 128 D10
Plough Way SE16 131 H3
Plough Yd EC2 126 C6
Plover Way SE16 131 J2
Plumbers Row E1 126 E7
Plymouth Wf E14 131 P3
Plympton St NW8 124 E6
Pocock St SE1 129 P1
Podmore Rd SW18 128 C10
Point Hill SE10 131 N6
Point Pleasant SW18 128 A10
Pointers Cl E14 131 M4
Poland Ho E15 127 P3
Poland St W1 125 J8
Polesworth Ho W2 124 A7
Pollard Row E2 126 E5
Pollard St E2 126 E5
Polygon Rd NW1 125 K4
Pomeroy St SE14 130 G7
Pond Pl SW3 128 E3
Ponler St E1 126 F8
Ponsford St E9 126 G1
Ponsonby Pl SW1 129 K4
Ponsonby Ter SW1 129 K4
Pont St SW1 128 F2
Pont St Ms SW1 128 F2
Ponton Rd SW8 129 K5
Poole Rd E9 127 H1
Poole St N1 126 B3
Poolmans St SE16 131 H1
Pope St SE1 130 C1
Popes Rd SW9 129 N9
Popham Rd N1 126 A3
Popham St N1 125 P3
Poplar Business Pk E14 127 N9
Poplar High St E14 127 L9
Poplar Pl W2 124 B9
Poplar Rd SE24 130 A10
Poplar Wk SE24 130 A10
Porchester Cl SE5 130 A10
Porchester Gdns W2 124 B9
Porchester Ms W2 124 B8
Porchester Pl W2 124 E8
Porchester Rd W2 124 B7
Porchester Sq W2 124 B8
Porchester Ter W2 124 C9
Porchester Ter N W2 124 B8
Porden Rd SW2 129 M10
Porlock St SE1 130 B1
Portelet Rd E1 127 H5
Porteus Rd W2 124 C7
Portia Way E3 127 K6
Portland Gro SW8 129 M7
Portland Pl W1 125 H7
Portland St SE17 130 B4
Portman Cl W1 124 F8
Portman Ms S W1 124 G8
Portman Pl E2 126 G5
Portman Sq W1 124 F8
Portman St W1 124 G8
Portpool La EC1 125 N7
Portree St E14 127 P8
Portslade Rd SW8 129 J8
Portsoken St E1 126 D9
Portugal St WC2 125 M8
Post Office Way SW8 129 K6
Potier St SE1 130 B2
Pott St E2 126 F5
Potters Rd SW6 128 C8
Pottery St SE16 130 F1
Poultry EC2 126 B8
Pountney Rd SW11 128 G9
Powis Pl WC1 125 L6
Powis Rd E3 127 M5
Pownall Rd E8 126 D3
Poyntz Rd SW11 128 F8
Poyser St E2 126 F4
Praed St W2 124 D8
Prairie St SW8 128 G8
Pratt St NW1 125 J3
Pratt Wk SE11 129 M3
Prebend St N1 126 A3
Prescot St E1 126 D9
Prescott Pl SW4 129 K9
Prestage Way E14 127 N9
Prestons Rd E14 131 N1
Price's Ct SW11 128 D9
Prices Ms N1 125 M3
Price's St SE1 125 P10
Prideaux Pl WC1 125 M5
Prideaux Rd SW9 129 L9
Prima Rd SW9 129 N6
Primrose Cl E3 127 L4
Primrose Gdns NW3 124 E1
Primrose Hill Ct NW3 124 F2
Primrose Hill Rd NW3 124 E2
Primrose Sq E9 126 G2
Primrose St EC2 126 C7
Prince Albert Rd NW1 124 E4
Prince Albert Rd NW8 124 E4
Prince Consort Rd SW7 128 C2
Prince Edwards Rd E9 127 K1
Prince of Wales Dr SW8 129 H6
Prince of Wales Dr SW11 128 F7
Prince of Wales Gate SW7 128 E1
Prince of Wales Rd NW5 124 G1
Prince St SE8 131 K5
Princelet St E1 126 D7
Princes Ct SE16 131 K2
Princes Ct Business Cen E1 126 F9
Princes Gdns SW7 128 D2
Princes Gate SW7 128 E1
Princes Gate Ms SW7 128 D2
Princes Ri SE13 131 N8
Princes Riverside Rd SE16 127 H10
Princes Sq W2 124 B9
Princes St EC2 126 B8
Princes St W1 125 H8
Princess Rd NW1 124 G3
Princess Rd NW6 124 A4
Princess St SE1 129 P2
Princethorpe Ho W2 124 A7
Princeton St WC1 125 M7
Printers Ms E3 127 J3
Prior Bolton St N1 125 P1
Prior St SE10 131 N6
Prioress St SE1 130 B2
Priory Ct SW8 129 K7
Priory Grn Est N1 125 M4
Priory Gro SW8 129 L7
Priory Ms SW8 129 K7
Priory Rd NW6 124 B3
Priory St E3 127 M5
Priory Ter NW6 124 B3
Priory Wk SW10 128 C4
Pritchard's Rd E2 126 E3
Priter Rd SE16 130 E2
Procter St WC1 125 M7
Prospect Pl E1 126 G10
Prospect Quay SW18 128 A10
Providence Ct W1 124 G9
Provost Est N1 126 B4
Provost Rd NW3 124 F2
Provost St N1 126 B5
Prusom St E1 126 F10
Pudding La EC3 126 B9
Pudding Mill La E15 127 M3
Pulross Rd SW9 129 M9
Pulteney Cl E3 127 K3
Pulteney Ter N1 125 M3
Pulton Pl SW6 128 A6
Pump La SE14 130 G6
Pundersons Gdns E2 126 F5
Purbrook St SE1 130 C2
Purcell St N1 126 C4
Purchese St NW1 125 K4
Purdy St E3 127 M6
Purelake Ms SE13 131 P9
Puteaux Ho E2 127 H4
Pytchley Rd SE22 130 C9

Q

Quaker St E1 126 D6
Quality Ct WC2 125 N8
Quarrendon St SW6 128 A8
Quarterdeck, The E14 131 L1
Quebec Way SE16 131 H1
Queen Anne Rd E9 127 H1
Queen Anne St W1 125 H8
Queen Anne's Gate SW1 129 K1
Queen Elizabeth St SE1 130 D1
Queen of Denmark Ct SE16 131 K2
Queen Sq WC1 125 L6
Queen St EC4 126 A9
Queen St W1 125 H10
Queen Victoria St EC4 125 P9
Queenhithe EC4 126 A9
Queen's Cres NW5 124 G1
Queens Gdns W2 124 C9
Queen's Gate SW7 128 D3
Queen's Gate Gdns SW7 128 C2
Queen's Gate Ms SW7 128 C1
Queen's Gate Pl SW7 128 C2
Queen's Gate Pl Ms SW7 128 C2
Queen's Gate Ter SW7 128 C2
Queen's Gro NW8 124 D3
Queen's Gro Ms NW8 124 D3
Queen's Head St N1 125 P3
Queens Ms W2 124 B9
Queens Rd SE14 130 F7
Queens Rd SE15 130 F7
Queen's Row SE17 130 B5
Queen's Ter NW8 124 D4
Queen's Wk SE1 126 C10
Queen's Wk SW1 125 J10
Queensberry Pl SW7 128 D3
Queensborough Ter W2 124 B9
Queensbridge Rd E2 126 D3
Queensbridge Rd E8 126 D2
Queensbury St N1 126 A2
Queensgate Pl NW6 124 A2
Queensmead NW8 124 D3
Queenstown Rd SW8 129 H5
Queensway W2 124 B8
Querrin St SW6 128 C8
Quex Rd NW6 124 A3
Quick St N1 125 P4
Quilter St E2 126 E5
Quince Rd SE13 131 M8
Quixley St E14 127 P9
Quorn Rd SE22 130 C10

R

Racton Rd SW6 128 A5
Radcot St SE11 129 N4
Radlett Pl NW8 124 E3
Radley Ms W8 128 A2
Radnor Pl W2 124 E8
Radnor Rd SE15 130 E6
Radnor St EC1 126 A5
Radnor Wk SW3 128 E4
Radstock St SW11 128 E6
Raeburn St SW2 129 L10
Raglan St NW5 125 H1
Railton Rd SE24 129 N10
Railway App SE1 126 B10
Railway Av SE16 130 G1
Railway St N1 125 L4
Rainbow Av E14 131 M4
Rainbow Quay SE16 131 J2
Rainbow St SE5 130 C6
Raine St E1 126 F10
Rainhill Way E3 127 L5
Rainsborough Av SE8 131 J3
Raleana Rd E14 127 N10
Raleigh St N1 125 P3
Ramillies Pl W1 125 J8
Rampayne St SW1 129 K4
Ramsey St E2 126 E6
Ramsey Wk N1 126 B1
Randall Cl SW11 128 E7
Randall Pl SE10 131 N6
Randall Rd SE11 129 M3
Randell's Rd N1 125 L3
Randolph Av W9 124 C6
Randolph Cres W9 124 C6
Randolph Gdns NW6 124 B4
Randolph Ms W9 124 C6
Randolph Rd W9 124 C6
Randolph St NW1 125 J2
Ranelagh Gdns SW3 128 G4
Ranelagh Gro SW1 128 G4
Rangers Sq SE10 131 P7
Ranwell St E3 127 K3
Raphael St SW7 128 F1
Ratcliffe Cross St E1 127 H8
Ratcliffe La E14 127 J8
Ratcliffe Orchard E1 127 H9
Rathbone Pl W1 125 K8
Rathbone St W1 125 J7
Rattray Rd SW2 129 N10
Raul Rd SE15 130 E7
Raven Row E1 126 F7
Ravensbourne Pl SE13 131 M8
Ravenscroft St E2 126 D4
Ravensdon St SE11 129 N4
Ravenstone SE17 130 C4
Rawlings St SW3 128 F3
Rawstorne St EC1 125 P5
Ray St EC1 125 N6
Raymouth Rd SE16 130 F3
Reading La E8 126 F1
Reardon Path E1 126 F10
Reardon St E1 126 F10
Reaston St SE14 130 G6
Record St SE15 130 G5
Rector St N1 126 A3
Rectory Gro SW4 129 J9
Rectory Sq E1 127 H7
Reculver Rd SE16 131 H4
Red Lion Row SE17 130 A5
Red Lion Sq WC1 125 M7
Red Lion St WC1 125 M7
Red Path E9 127 K1
Red Post Hill SE24 130 B10
Redan Pl W2 124 B8
Redbridge Gdns SE5 130 C6
Redburn St SW3 128 F5
Redcar St SE5 130 A6
Redcastle Cl E1 126 G9
Redchurch St E2 126 D6
Redcliffe Gdns SW5 128 B4
Redcliffe Gdns SW10 128 B4
Redcliffe Ms SW10 128 B4
Redcliffe Pl SW10 128 C5
Redcliffe Rd SW10 128 C4
Redcliffe Sq SW10 128 B4
Redcliffe St SW10 128 B5
Redcross Way SE1 130 A1
Reddins Rd SE15 130 E5
Redesdale St SW3 128 F5
Redfield La SW5 128 A3
Redhill St NW1 125 H4
Redman's Rd E1 126 G7
Redriff Est SE16 131 K2
Redriff Rd SE16 131 H3
Redruth Rd E9 127 H3
Redwood Cl E3 127 L4
Redwood Cl SE16 127 J10
Reece Ms SW7 128 D3
Reed Pl SW4 129 K10
Reedham St SE15 130 E8
Reedworth St SE11 129 N3
Rees St N1 126 A3
Reeves Ms W1 124 G9
Reeves Rd E3 127 M6
Reform St SW11 128 F8
Regan Way N1 126 C4
Regency St SW1 129 K3
Regeneration Rd SE16 131 H3
Regent Sq E3 127 M5
Regent Sq WC1 125 L5
Regent St SW1 125 K9
Regent St W1 125 H8
Regents Br Gdns SW8 129 L6
Regent's Pk, The NW1 124 G4
Regents Pk Rd NW1 124 F3
Regents Row E8 126 E3
Reginald Rd SE8 131 L6
Reginald Sq SE8 131 L6
Regis Pl SW2 129 M10
Relf Rd SE15 130 E9
Rembrandt Cl E14 131 P2
Remington St N1 125 P4
Renforth St SE16 130 G1
Renfrew Rd SE11 129 P3
Rennell St SE13 131 N9
Rennie Est SE16 130 F3
Rennie St SE1 125 P10
Repton St E14 127 J8
Reservoir Rd SE4 131 J8
Retreat Pl E9 126 G1
Revelon Rd SE4 131 J10
Reverdy Rd SE1 130 E3
Rheidol Ter N1 125 P4
Rhodesia Rd SW9 129 L8
Rhodeswell Rd E14 127 J7
Rhondda Gro E3 127 J5
Rhyl St NW5 124 G1
Ricardo St E14 127 M8
Rich St E14 127 K9
Richborne Ter SW8 129 M6
Richmond Av N1 125 M3
Richmond Cres N1 125 M3
Richmond Gro N1 125 P2
Richmond Rd E8 126 D2
Richmond Ter SW1 129 L1
Rick Roberts Way E15 127 N3
Rickett St SW6 128 A5
Ridgdale St E3 127 M4
Ridgeway Rd SW9 129 P9
Riding Ho St W1 125 H7
Rifle Ct SE11 129 N5
Rifle St E14 127 M7
Rigden St E14 127 M8
Rigge Pl SW4 129 K10
Riley Rd SE1 130 D2
Riley St SW10 128 D5
Ring, The W2 124 D9
Ripplevale Gro N1 125 M2
Risdon St SE16 130 G1
Risinghill St N1 125 M4
Rita Rd SW8 129 M6
Ritchie St N1 125 N4
Ritson Rd E8 126 E1
Rivaz Pl E9 126 G1
River Pl N1 126 A2
River St EC1 125 N5
Riverside Ct SW8 129 K5
Riverside Rd E15 127 N4
Riverside Twr SW6 128 C8
Rivington St EC2 126 C5
Roach Rd E3 127 L2
Roan St SE10 131 N5
Robert Adam St W1 124 G8
Robert Dashwood Way SE17 130 A3
Robert Lowe Cl SE14 131 H6
Robert St NW1 125 H5
Roberta St E2 126 E5
Roberts Cl SE16 131 H1
Robertson Rd E15 127 N3
Robertson St SW8 129 H9
Robin Ct SE16 130 E3
Robin Hood La E14 127 N9
Robinson Rd E2 126 G4
Robsart St SW9 129 M8
Rochelle Cl SW11 128 D10
Rochester Ms NW1 125 J2
Rochester Pl NW1 125 J1
Rochester Rd NW1 125 J1

Rochester Row **SW1** 129 J3
Rochester Sq **NW1** 125 J2
Rochester St **SW1** 129 K2
Rochester Ter **NW1** 125 J1
Rockingham Est **SE1** 130 A2
Rockingham St **SE1** 130 A2
Rodmarton St **W1** 124 F7
Rodney Pl **SE17** 130 A3
Rodney Rd **SE17** 130 A3
Rodney St **N1** 125 M4
Roffey St **E14** 131 N1
Roger Dowley Ct **E2** 126 G4
Roger St **WC1** 125 M6
Rokeby Rd **SE4** 131 K8
Roland Gdns **SW7** 128 C4
Roland Way **SE17** 130 B4
Rollins St **SE15** 130 G5
Rolls Rd **SE1** 130 D4
Rolt St **SE8** 131 J5
Roman Rd **E2** 126 G5
Roman Rd **E3** 127 J4
Roman Way **N7** 125 M1
Romford St **E1** 126 E7
Romilly St **W1** 125 K9
Romney Rd **SE10** 131 N5
Romney St **SW1** 129 K2
Rood La **EC3** 126 C9
Rookery Rd **SW4** 129 J10
Rope St **SE16** 131 J3
Ropemaker Rd **SE16** 131 J2
Ropemaker St **EC2** 126 B7
Ropery St **E3** 127 K6
Ropley St **E2** 126 E4
Rosary Gdns **SW7** 128 C3
Rose All **SE1** 126 A10
Rose Sq **SW3** 128 D4
Rosebank Gdns **E3** 127 K4
Roseberry Pl **E8** 126 D1
Roseberry St **SE16** 130 F3
Rosebery Av **EC1** 125 N6
Rosebury Rd **SW6** 128 B8
Rosefield Gdns **E14** 127 L9
Rosemary Dr **E14** 127 P8
Rosemary Rd **SE15** 130 D6
Rosemont Rd **NW3** 124 C1
Rosemoor St **SW3** 128 F3
Rosenau Cres **SW11** 128 E7
Rosenau Rd **SW11** 128 E7
Roserton St **E14** 131 N1
Rosetta Cl **SW8** 129 L6
Rosher Cl **E15** 127 P2
Rosoman St **EC1** 125 N5
Rossendale Way **NW1** 125 J2
Rossetti Rd **SE16** 130 F4
Rossmore Rd **NW1** 124 E6
Rothbury Rd **E9** 127 K2
Rotherfield St **N1** 126 A2
Rotherhithe New Rd **SE16** 130 E4
Rotherhithe Old Rd **SE16** 131 H3
Rotherhithe St **SE16** 130 G1
Rotherhithe Tunnel **E1** 126 G10
Rotherhithe Tunnel App **E14** 127 J9
Rotherhithe Tunnel App **SE16** 130 G1
Rothery Ter **SW9** 129 P6
Rothsay St **SE1** 130 C2
Rothwell St **NW1** 124 F3
Rotten Row **SW1** 128 F1
Rotten Row **SW7** 128 E1
Rotterdam Dr **E14** 131 N2
Rouel Rd **SE16** 130 E2
Rounton Rd **E3** 127 L6
Roupell St **SE1** 125 N10
Rousden St **NW1** 125 J2
Rowcross St **SE1** 130 D4
Rowditch La **SW11** 128 G8
Rowena Cres **SW11** 128 E8
Rowington Cl **W2** 124 B7
Rowley Way **NW8** 124 B3
Rowse Cl **E15** 127 N3
Roxby Pl **SW6** 128 A5
Royal Av **SW3** 128 F4
Royal Cl **SE8** 131 K5
Royal Coll St **NW1** 125 J2
Royal Ct **SE16** 131 K2
Royal Ex **EC3** 126 B8
Royal Hill **SE10** 131 N6
Royal Hosp Rd **SW3** 128 F5
Royal Ms, The **SW1** 129 H2
Royal Mint Ct **EC3** 126 D9
Royal Mint St **E1** 126 D9
Royal Naval Pl **SE14** 131 K6
Royal Oak Rd **E8** 126 F1
Royal Oak Yd **SE1** 130 C1
Royal Opera Arc **SW1** 125 K10
Royal Pl **SE10** 131 N6
Royal Rd **SE17** 129 P5
Royal St **SE1** 129 M2
Royal Victor Pl **E3** 127 H4
Royston St **E2** 126 G4
Rozel Ct **N1** 126 C3
Rozel Rd **SW4** 129 J8
Ruby St **SE15** 130 F5
Rudolph Rd **NW6** 124 A4
Rufford St **N1** 125 L3
Rugby St **WC1** 125 M6
Rugg St **E14** 127 L9
Rum Cl **E1** 126 G9
Rumbold Rd **SW6** 128 B6
Rumsey Rd **SW9** 129 M9
Rupert Gdns **SW9** 129 P8
Rupert St **W1** 125 K9
Rush Hill Rd **SW11** 128 G9
Rushcroft Rd **SW2** 129 N10
Rushton St **N1** 126 B4
Rushworth St **SE1** 129 P1
Ruskin Pk Ho **SE5** 130 B9
Russell Gro **SW9** 129 N6
Russell Sq **WC1** 125 L7
Russell St **WC2** 125 M8
Russia Dock Rd **SE16** 127 J10
Russia La **E2** 126 G4
Russia Wk **SE16** 131 J1
Rust Sq **SE5** 130 B6
Ruston St **E3** 127 K3
Rutherford St **SW1** 129 K3
Rutland Gdns **SW7** 128 E1
Rutland Gate **SW7** 128 E1
Rutland Rd **E9** 126 G3
Rutland St **SW7** 128 E2
Rutts Ter **SE14** 131 H7
Ryder Dr **SE16** 130 F4
Ryder St **SW1** 125 J10
Rye Hill Pk **SE15** 130 G10
Rye La **SE15** 130 E7
Rye Pas **SE15** 130 E9
Rye Rd **SE15** 131 H10
Rycroft St **SW6** 128 B7
Ryland Rd **NW5** 125 H1
Rysbrack St **SW3** 128 F2

S

Sabella Ct **E3** 127 K4
Sabine Rd **SW11** 128 F9
Sable St **N1** 125 P2
Sackville St **W1** 125 J9
Saffron Av **E14** 127 P9
Saffron Hill **EC1** 125 N6
Sail St **SE11** 129 M3
St. Agnes Pl **SE11** 129 N5
St. Albans Gro **W8** 128 B2
St. Alban's Pl **N1** 125 P3
St. Alfege Pas **SE10** 131 N5
St. Alphonsus Rd **SW4** 129 J10
St. Andrew St **EC4** 125 N7
St. Andrew's Hill **EC4** 125 P9
St. Andrews Pl **NW1** 125 H6
St. Andrews Way **E3** 127 M6
St. Ann's St **SW1** 129 K2
St. Ann's Ter **NW8** 124 D4
St. Anthonys Cl **E1** 126 E10
St. Asaph Rd **SE4** 131 H9
St. Augustines Rd **NW1** 125 K2
St. Austell Rd **SE13** 131 N8
St. Barnabas St **SW1** 128 G4
St. Barnabas Vil **SW8** 129 L7
St. Botolph St **EC3** 126 D8
St. Bride St **EC4** 125 P8
St. Chad's Pl **WC1** 125 L5
St. Chad's St **WC1** 125 L5
St. Clements St **N7** 125 N1
St. Cross St **EC1** 125 N7
St. Davids Sq **E14** 131 M4
St. Donatts Rd **SE14** 131 K7
St. Dunstan's Hill **EC3** 126 C9
St. Edmunds Ter **NW8** 124 E3
St. Elmos Rd **SE16** 131 H1
St. Francis Rd **SE22** 130 C10
St. George St **W1** 125 H8
St. George Wf **SW8** 129 L4
St. Georges Circ **SE1** 129 P2
St. George's Dr **SW1** 129 H3
St. Georges Flds **W2** 124 E8
St. Georges Rd **SE1** 129 N2
St. Georges Sq **SE8** 131 K3
St. George's Sq **SW1** 129 K4
St. George's Sq Ms **SW1** 129 K4
St. Georges Way **SE15** 130 C5
St. Giles High St **WC2** 125 K8
St. Giles Rd **SE5** 130 C6
St. Gilles Ho **E2** 127 H4
St. Helena Rd **SE16** 131 H3
St. James Ms **E14** 131 N2
St. James's **SE14** 131 J7
St. James's Av **E2** 126 G4
St. James's Ct **SW1** 129 J2
St. James's Cres **SW9** 129 N9
St. James's Palace **SW1** 125 J10
St. James's Pk **SW1** 129 K1
St. James's Pl **SW1** 125 J10
St. James's Rd **SE1** 130 E4
St. James's Rd **SE16** 130 E2
St. James's Sq **SW1** 125 J10
St. James's St **SW1** 125 J10
St. James's Ter Ms **NW8** 124 F3
St. James's Wk **EC1** 125 P6
St. John St **EC1** 125 P6
St. John's Cres **SW9** 129 N9
St. John's Est **N1** 126 B4
St. John's Hill **SW11** 128 D10
St. John's Hill Gro **SW11** 128 D10
St. John's La **EC1** 125 P6
St. John's Rd **SW11** 128 E10
St. Johns Vale **SE8** 131 L8
St. John's Wd High St **NW8** 124 D4
St. John's Wd Pk **NW8** 124 D3
St. John's Wd Rd **NW8** 124 D6
St. John's Wd Ter **NW8** 124 D4
St. Joseph's Vale **SE3** 131 P8
St. Jude's Rd **E2** 126 F4
St. Katharine's Way **E1** 126 D10
St. Lawrence St **E14** 127 N10
St. Lawrence Way **SW9** 129 N7
St. Leonards Ct **N1** 126 B5
St. Leonards Rd **E14** 127 M7
St. Leonards Sq **NW5** 124 G1
St. Leonards St **E3** 127 M5
St. Leonard's Ter **SW3** 128 F4
St. Loo Av **SW3** 128 E5
St. Luke's Av **SW4** 129 K10
St. Luke's Cl **EC1** 126 A6
St. Luke's Est **EC1** 126 B5
St. Luke's St **SW3** 128 E4
St. Margarets La **W8** 128 B2
St. Margarets Rd **SE4** 131 K10
St. Margaret's St **SW1** 129 L1
St. Mark St **E1** 126 D8
St. Marks Cres **NW1** 124 G3
St. Mark's Gro **SW10** 128 B5
St. Marks Sq **NW1** 124 G3
St. Martins Cl **NW1** 125 J3
St. Martin's La **WC2** 125 L9
St. Martin's Pl **WC2** 125 L9
St. Martin's Rd **SW9** 129 M8
St. Martin's-le-Grand **EC1** 126 A8
St. Mary at Hill **EC3** 126 C9
St. Mary Axe **EC3** 126 C8
St. Marychurch St **SE16** 130 G1
St. Mary's Gdns **SE11** 129 N3
St. Mary's Gate **W8** 128 B2
St. Mary's Gro **N1** 125 P1
St. Marys Mans **W2** 124 C7
St. Marys Path **N1** 125 P3
St. Mary's Pl **W8** 128 B2
St. Mary's Rd **SE15** 130 G7
St. Marys Sq **W2** 124 D7
St. Marys Ter **W2** 124 D7
St. Mary's Wk **SE11** 129 N3
St. Matthew's Rd **SW2** 129 M10
St. Matthew's Row **E2** 126 E5
St. Michael's Rd **SW9** 129 M8
St. Michaels St **W2** 124 D8
St. Norbert Grn **SE4** 131 J10
St. Norbert Rd **SE4** 131 J10
St. Olav's Sq **SE16** 130 G2
St. Oswald's Pl **SE11** 129 M4
St. Pancras Way **NW1** 125 J2
St. Paul St **N1** 126 A3
St. Paul's Av **SE16** 127 H10
St. Paul's Chyd **EC4** 125 P8
St. Paul's Cres **NW1** 125 K2
St. Paul's Ms **NW1** 125 K2
St. Paul's Pl **N1** 126 B1
St. Paul's Rd **N1** 125 P1
St. Paul's Shrubbery **N1** 126 B1
St. Pauls Way **E3** 127 K7
St. Pauls Way **E14** 127 K7
St. Peter's Cl **E2** 126 E4
St. Peters St **N1** 125 P3
St. Peter's Way **N1** 126 C2
St. Petersburgh Ms **W2** 124 B9
St. Petersburgh Pl **W2** 124 B9
St. Philip Sq **SW8** 129 H8
St. Philip St **SW8** 129 H8
St. Philip's Rd **E8** 126 E1
St. Rule St **SW8** 129 J8
St. Saviour's Est **SE1** 130 D2
St. Silas Pl **NW5** 124 G1
St. Silas St Est **NW5** 124 G1
St. Stephens Cres **W2** 124 A8
St. Stephens Gdns **W2** 124 A8
St. Stephens Gro **SE13** 131 N9
St. Stephen's Rd **E3** 127 K4
St. Stephens Ter **SW8** 129 M6
St. Stephen's Wk **SW7** 128 C3
St. Swithin's La **EC4** 126 B9
St. Thomas St **SE1** 126 B10
St. Thomas's Pl **E9** 126 G2
St. Thomas's Sq **E9** 126 F2
Salamanca St **SE1** 129 L3
Sale Pl **W2** 124 E7
Salem Rd **W2** 124 B9
Salisbury Ct **EC4** 125 P8
Salisbury Pl **SW9** 129 P6
Salisbury Pl **W1** 124 F7
Salisbury St **NW8** 124 E6
Salisbury Ter **SE15** 130 G9
Salmon La **E14** 127 J8
Salter Rd **SE16** 127 H10
Salter St **E14** 127 L9
Saltoun Rd **SW2** 129 N10
Saltwell St **E14** 127 L9
Samford St **NW8** 124 E6
Sampson St **E1** 126 E10
Samuel Cl **SE14** 131 H5
Samuel Lewis Trust Dws **SW6** 128 A6
Samuel St **SE15** 130 D6
Sancroft St **SE11** 129 M4
Sandall Rd **NW5** 125 J1
Sandbourne Rd **SE4** 131 J8
Sandgate St **SE15** 130 F5
Sandilands Rd **SW6** 128 B7
Sandison St **SE15** 130 D9
Sandland St **WC1** 125 M7
Sandmere Rd **SW4** 129 L10
Sandpiper Cl **SE16** 131 K1
Sandrock Rd **SE13** 131 L9
Sand's End La **SW6** 128 B7
Sandwell Cres **NW6** 124 A1
Sandwich St **WC1** 125 L5
Sandy's Row **E1** 126 C7
Sanford St **SE14** 131 J5
Sangora Rd **SW11** 128 D10
Sans Wk **EC1** 125 N6
Sansom St **SE5** 130 B6
Santley St **SW4** 129 M10
Saperton Wk **SE11** 129 M3
Sapphire Rd **SE8** 131 J3
Saracen St **E14** 127 L8
Sartor Rd **SE15** 131 H10
Satchwell Rd **E2** 126 E5
Saunders Ness Rd **E14** 131 N4
Saunders St **SE11** 129 N3
Savile Row **W1** 125 J9
Savona Est **SW8** 129 J6
Savona St **SW8** 129 J6
Savoy Ms **SW9** 129 L9
Savoy Pl **WC2** 125 L9
Savoy St **WC2** 125 M9
Sawmill Yd **E3** 127 J3
Sawyer St **SE1** 130 A1
Saxon Rd **E3** 127 K4
Saxton Cl **SE13** 131 P9
Sayes Ct St **SE8** 131 K5
Scala St **W1** 125 J7
Scandrett St **E1** 126 F10
Scarsdale Vil **W8** 128 A2
Scawen Rd **SE8** 131 J4
Scawfell St **E2** 126 D4
Sceaux Est **SE5** 130 C7
Sceptre Rd **E2** 126 G5
Schoolhouse La **E1** 127 H9
Schooner Cl **E14** 131 P2
Sclater St **E1** 126 D6
Scoresby St **SE1** 125 P10
Scott Ellis Gdns **NW8** 124 D5
Scott Lidgett Cres **SE16** 130 E1
Scott St **E1** 126 F6
Scriven St **E8** 126 D3
Scrutton St **EC2** 126 C6
Scylla Rd **SE15** 130 F9
Seacon Twr **E14** 131 K1
Seaford St **WC1** 125 M5
Seagrave Rd **SW6** 128 A5
Searles Cl **SW11** 128 E6
Searles Rd **SE1** 130 B3
Sears St **SE5** 130 B6
Sebastian St **EC1** 125 P5
Sebbon St **N1** 125 P2
Sedding St **SW1** 128 G3
Sedgmoor Pl **SE5** 130 C6
Seething La **EC3** 126 C9
Sekforde St **EC1** 125 P6
Selby St **E1** 126 E6
Selden Rd **SE15** 130 G8
Selsdon Way **E14** 131 M2
Selsey St **E14** 127 L7
Selwood Pl **SW7** 128 D4
Selworthy Ho **SW11** 128 D7
Selwyn Rd **E3** 127 K4
Semley Pl **SW1** 128 G3
Senate St **SE15** 130 G8
Sendall Ct **SW11** 128 D9
Senior St **W2** 124 B7
Senrab St **E1** 127 H8
Serenaders Rd **SW9** 129 N8
Serle St **WC2** 125 M8
Serpentine Rd **W2** 124 F10
Settles St **E1** 126 E7
Settrington Rd **SW6** 128 B8
Severnake Cl **E14** 131 L3
Severus Rd **SW11** 128 E10
Seville Ms **N1** 126 C2
Seville St **SW1** 128 F1
Sevington St **W9** 124 B6
Seward St **EC1** 126 A5
Sewardstone Rd **E2** 126 G4
Sextant Av **E14** 131 P3
Seymour Gdns **SE4** 131 J9
Seymour Ms **W1** 124 G8
Seymour Pl **W1** 124 E7
Seymour St **W1** 124 F8
Seymour St **W2** 124 F8
Seymour Wk **SW10** 128 C5
Seyssel St **E14** 131 N3
Shacklewell St **E2** 126 D6
Shad Thames **SE1** 126 D10
Shaftesbury Av **W1** 125 K9
Shaftesbury Av **WC2** 125 K9
Shaftesbury St **N1** 126 A4
Shafton Rd **E9** 127 H3
Shalbourne Sq **E9** 127 K1
Shalcomb St **SW10** 128 C5
Shamrock St **SW4** 129 K9
Shand St **SE1** 130 C1
Shandy St **E1** 127 H7
Shannon Gro **SW9** 129 M10
Shardeloes Rd **SE4** 131 K9
Shardeloes Rd **SE14** 131 K9
Sharon Gdns **E9** 126 G3
Sharpleshall St **NW1** 124 F2
Sharratt St **SE15** 130 G5
Sharsted St **SE17** 129 P4
Shaw Ct **SW11** 128 D9
Shaw Rd **SE22** 130 C10
Shawfield St **SW3** 128 E4
Shearling Way **N7** 125 L1
Sheep La **E8** 126 F3
Sheepcote La **SW11** 128 F8
Sheffield Ter **W8** 124 A10
Sheldon Pl **E2** 126 E4
Sheldon Sq **W2** 124 C7
Shell Rd **SE13** 131 M9
Shelley Cl **SE15** 130 F8
Shellwood Rd **SW11** 128 F8
Shelmerdine Cl **E3** 127 L7
Shelton St **WC2** 125 L8
Shenfield St **N1** 126 C4
Shenley Rd **SE5** 130 C7
Shepherdess Wk **N1** 126 A4
Sheppard Dr **SE16** 130 F4
Shepperton Rd **N1** 126 A3
Sherborne St **N1** 126 B3
Sheringham Rd **N7** 125 M1
Sherriff Rd **NW6** 124 A1
Sherwin Rd **SE14** 131 H7
Sherwood Gdns **E14** 131 L3
Sherwood Gdns **SE16** 130 E4
Shetland Rd **E3** 127 K4
Ship St **SE8** 131 L7
Shipton St **E2** 126 D5
Shipwright Rd **SE16** 131 J1
Shirbutt St **E14** 127 M9
Shirland Rd **W9** 124 A5
Shirley Gro **SW11** 128 G9
Shoe La **EC4** 125 N8
Shooters Hill Rd **SE10** 131 P7
Shore Pl **E9** 126 G2
Shore Rd **E9** 126 G2
Shoreditch High St **E1** 126 C6
Shorncliffe Rd **SE1** 130 D4
Short Wall **E15** 127 N5
Shorter St **E1** 126 D9
Shorts Gdns **WC2** 125 L8
Shottendane Rd **SW6** 128 A7
Shouldham St **W1** 124 E7
Shrewsbury Rd **W2** 124 A8
Shroton St **NW1** 124 E7
Shrubland Rd **E8** 126 E3
Shuttleworth Rd **SW11** 128 E8
Sibella Rd **SW4** 129 K8
Sidmouth St **WC1** 125 L5
Sidney Rd **SW9** 129 M8
Sidney Sq **E1** 126 G8
Sidney St **E1** 126 F7
Sidworth St **E8** 126 F2
Silex St **SE1** 129 P1
Silk Mills Sq **E9** 127 K1
Silk St **EC2** 126 A7
Silver Rd **SE13** 131 M9
Silver Wk **SE16** 127 K10
Silverthorne Rd **SW8** 129 H8
Silvocea Way **E14** 127 P8
Silwood St **SE16** 130 G3
Simms Rd **SE1** 130 E3
Simpson St **SW11** 128 E8
Simpsons Rd **E14** 127 M9
Sirinham Pt **SW8** 129 M5
Sisters Av **SW11** 128 F10
Sisulu Pl **SW9** 129 N9
Sivill Ho **E2** 126 D5
Six Bridges Trd Est **SE1** 130 E4
Sketchley Gdns **SE16** 131 H4
Skinner St **EC1** 125 N5
Skipworth Rd **E9** 126 G3
Skylines Village **E14** 131 N1
Slaidburn St **SW10** 128 C5
Slaithwaite Rd **SE13** 131 N10
Sleaford Ho **E3** 127 L6
Sleaford St **SW8** 129 J6
Slippers Pl **SE16** 130 F2
Sloane Av **SW3** 128 E3
Sloane Ct W **SW3** 128 G4
Sloane Gdns **SW1** 128 G3
Sloane Sq **SW1** 128 F3
Sloane St **SW1** 128 F1
Sloane Ter **SW1** 128 F3
Smart St **E2** 127 H5
Smeaton St **E1** 126 F10
Smedley St **SW4** 129 K8
Smedley St **SW8** 129 K8
Smeed Rd **E3** 127 L2
Smiles Pl **SE13** 131 N8
Smith Cl **SE16** 127 H10
Smith Sq **SW1** 129 L2
Smith St **SW3** 128 F4
Smith Ter **SW3** 128 F4
Smithy St **E1** 126 G7
Smokehouse Yd **EC1** 125 P7
Smugglers Way **SW18** 128 B10
Smyrks Rd **SE17** 130 C4
Smyrna Rd **NW6** 124 A2
Smythe St **E14** 127 M9
Snow Hill **EC1** 125 P7
Snowbury Rd **SW6** 128 B8
Snowden St **EC2** 126 C6
Snowman Ho **NW6** 124 B3
Snowsfields **SE1** 130 B1
Soames St **SE15** 130 D9
Soho Sq **W1** 125 K8
Solebay St **E1** 127 J6
Solomon's Pas **SE15** 130 F10
Solon New Rd **SW4** 129 L10
Solon Rd **SW2** 129 L10
Solway Rd **SE22** 130 E10
Somerfield St **SE16** 131 H4
Somerford St **E1** 126 F6
Somerford Way **SE16** 131 J1
Somerleyton Pas **SW9** 129 P10
Somerleyton Rd **SW9** 129 N10
Somers Cres **W2** 124 E8
Somerset Est **SW11** 128 D7
Somerset Gdns **SE13** 131 M8
Somerton Rd **SE15** 130 F10
Sondes St **SE17** 130 B5
Sopwith Way **SW8** 129 H6
Sorrel La **E14** 127 P8
Sotheran Cl **E8** 126 E3
Sotheron Rd **SW6** 128 B6
Soudan Rd **SW11** 128 F7
South Audley St **W1** 124 G9
South Bolton Gdns **SW5** 128 B4
South Carriage Dr **SW1** 128 E1
South Carriage Dr **SW7** 128 E1
South Colonnade **E14** 127 L10
South Cres **E16** 127 P6
South Cres **WC1** 125 K7
South Eaton Pl **SW1** 128 G3
South End Row **W8** 128 B2
South Island Pl **SW9** 129 M6
South Kensington Underground Sta **SW7** 128 D3
South Lambeth Pl **SW8** 129 L5
South Lambeth Rd **SW8** 129 L5
South Molton La **W1** 125 H8
South Molton St **W1** 125 H8
South Par **SW3** 128 D4
South Pk **SW6** 128 A8
South Pk Ms **SW6** 128 B9
South Pl **EC2** 126 B7
South Quay Plaza **E14** 131 M1
South Sea St **SE16** 131 K2
South St **W1** 124 G10
South Tenter St **E1** 126 D9
South Ter **SW7** 128 E3
South Vil **NW1** 125 K1
South Wf Rd **W2** 124 D8
Southall Pl **SE1** 130 B1
Southampton Pl **WC1** 125 L7
Southampton Row **WC1** 125 L7
Southampton St **WC2** 125 L9
Southampton Way **SE5** 130 B6
Southbank Business Cen **SW8** 129 K5
Southborough Rd **E9** 126 G3
Southern Gro **E3** 127 K5
Southern St **N1** 125 M4
Southerngate Way **SE14** 131 J6
Southey Rd **SW9** 129 N7
Southgate Gro **N1** 126 B2
Southgate Rd **N1** 126 B3
Southmoor Way **E9** 127 K1
Southolm St **SW11** 129 H7
Southville **SW8** 129 K7
Southwark Br **EC4** 126 A10
Southwark Br **SE1** 126 A10
Southwark Br Rd **SE1** 129 P2
Southwark Pk **SE16** 130 G3
Southwark Pk Est **SE16** 130 F3
Southwark Pk Rd **SE16** 130 D3
Southwark St **SE1** 125 P10
Southwater Cl **E14** 127 K8
Southwell Gdns **SW7** 128 C3
Southwell Rd **SE5** 130 A9
Southwick Pl **W2** 124 E8
Southwick St **W2** 124 E8
Sovereign Cl **E1** 126 F9
Spa Grn Est **EC1** 125 N5
Spa Rd **SE16** 130 D2
Spanby Rd **E3** 127 L6
Spanish Pl **W1** 124 G8
Sparkford Ho **SW11** 128 D7
Sparta St **SE10** 131 M7
Spear Ms **SW5** 128 A3

Speke Ho **SE5** 130 A6
Speldhurst Rd **E9** 127 H2
Spelman St **E1** 126 E7
Spencer Rd **SW18** 128 D10
Spencer St **EC1** 125 P5
Spenser St **SW1** 129 J2
Spert St **E14** 127 J9
Spey St **E14** 127 N7
Spicer Cl **SW9** 129 P8
Spindrift Av **E14** 131 M3
Spital Sq **E1** 126 C7
Spital St **E1** 126 E6
Sporle Ct **SW11** 128 D9
Sprimont Pl **SW3** 128 F4
Spring St **W2** 124 D8
Springall St **SE15** 130 F6
Springfield La **NW6** 124 B3
Springfield Rd **NW8** 124 C3
Springfield Wk **NW6** 124 B3
Springhill Cl **SE5** 130 B9
Springwood Cl **E3** 127 L4
Sprules Rd **SE4** 131 J8
Spur Rd **SE1** 129 N1
Spur Rd **SW1** 129 J1
Spurgeon St **SE1** 130 B2
Spurling Rd **SE22** 130 D10
Squirries St **E2** 126 E5
Stable Yd Rd **SW1** 125 J10
Stables Way **SE11** 129 N4
Stacey St **WC2** 125 K8
Stadium St **SW10** 128 C6
Stafford Cl **NW6** 124 A5
Stafford Ct **W8** 128 A2
Stafford Pl **SW1** 129 J2
Stafford Rd **E3** 127 K4
Stafford Rd **NW6** 124 A5
Stafford St **W1** 125 J10
Stafford Ter **W8** 128 A2
Staffordshire St **SE15** 130 E7
Stag Pl **SW1** 129 J2
Stainer St **SE1** 126 B10
Staining La **EC2** 126 A8
Stainsby Rd **E14** 127 L8
Stalham St **SE16** 130 F2
Stamford Rd **N1** 126 C2
Stamford St **SE1** 125 N10
Stamp Pl **E2** 126 D5
Stanbury Rd **SE15** 130 F7
Stanfield Rd **E3** 127 J4
Stanford Rd **W8** 128 B2
Stanhope Gdns **SW7** 128 C3
Stanhope Gate **W1** 124 G10
Stanhope Ms E **SW7** 128 C3
Stanhope Ms W **SW7** 128 C3
Stanhope Pl **W2** 124 F8
Stanhope St **NW1** 125 J5
Stanhope Ter **W2** 124 D9
Stanley Cl **SW8** 129 M5
Stanley Gro **SW8** 128 G8
Stanley Rd **E15** 127 P3
Stanley St **SE8** 131 K6
Stanmer St **SW11** 128 E7
Stannard Ms **E8** 126 E1
Stannard Rd **E8** 126 E1
Stannary Pl **SE11** 129 N4
Stannary St **SE11** 129 N5
Stansfield Rd **SW9** 129 M9
Stanswood Gdns **SE5** 130 C6
Stanway St **N1** 126 C4
Stanworth St **SE1** 130 D1
Staple Inn Bldgs **WC1** 125 N7
Staple St **SE1** 130 B1
Staples Cl **SE16** 127 J10
Star St **W2** 124 E7
Starboard Way **E14** 131 L2
Starcross St **NW1** 125 J5
Station App **SE1** 129 N1
Station Ct **SW6** 128 C7
Station Pas **SE15** 130 G7
Station Rd **SE13** 131 N9
Station St **E15** 127 P2
Station Ter **SE5** 130 A7
Staunton St **SE8** 131 K5
Stave Yd Rd **SE16** 127 J10
Stayner's Rd **E1** 127 H6
Stead St **SE17** 130 B3
Stean St **E8** 126 D3
Stebondale St **E14** 131 N4
Steeles Rd **NW3** 124 F1
Steers Way **SE16** 131 J1
Stephan Cl **E8** 126 E3
Stephen St **W1** 125 K7
Stephendale Rd **SW6** 128 B8
Stephenson Way **NW1** 125 J6
Stepney Causeway **E1** 127 H8
Stepney Grn **E1** 126 G7
Stepney High St **E1** 127 H7
Stepney Way **E1** 126 F7
Sterling Gdns **SE14** 131 J5
Sternhall La **SE15** 130 E9
Sterry St **SE1** 130 B1
Stevens Av **E9** 126 G1
Stevenson Cres **SE16** 130 E4
Steward St **E1** 126 C7
Stewart St **E14** 131 N1
Stewart's Gro **SW3** 128 D3
Stewart's Rd **SW8** 129 J6
Stillington St **SW1** 129 J3
Stirling Rd **SW9** 129 L8
Stockholm Ho **E1** 126 E9
Stockholm Rd **SE16** 130 G4
Stockholm Way **E1** 126 E10
Stockwell Av **SW9** 129 M9
Stockwell Gdns **SW9** 129 M8
Stockwell Gdns Est **SW9** 129 L8
Stockwell Grn **SW9** 129 M8
Stockwell La **SW9** 129 M8
Stockwell Pk Cres **SW9** 129 M8
Stockwell Pk Est **SW9** 129 M8
Stockwell Pk Rd **SW9** 129 M7
Stockwell Pk Wk **SW9** 129 M9
Stockwell Rd **SW9** 129 M8
Stockwell St **SE10** 131 N5
Stockwell Ter **SW9** 129 M7
Stokenchurch St **SW6** 128 B7
Stone Bldgs **WC2** 125 M7
Stonecutter St **EC4** 125 P8
Stonefield St **N1** 125 N3
Stones End St **SE1** 130 A1
Stoney St **SE1** 126 B10
Stonhouse St **SW4** 129 K9
Stopes St **SE15** 130 D6
Stopford Rd **SE17** 129 P4
Store St **WC1** 125 K7
Storers Quay **E14** 131 P3
Storey's Gate **SW1** 129 K1
Stories Ms **SE5** 130 C8
Stories Rd **SE5** 130 C9
Storks Rd **SE16** 130 E2
Stormont Rd **SW11** 128 G9
Stour Rd **E3** 127 L2
Stourcliffe St **W1** 124 F8
Stowage **SE8** 131 L5
Strafford St **E14** 131 L1
Strahan Rd **E3** 127 J5
Straightsmouth **SE10** 131 N6
Straker's Rd **SE15** 130 F10
Strand **WC2** 125 L9
Stranraer Way **N1** 125 L2
Strasburg Rd **SW11** 129 H7
Stratford Cen, The **E15** 127 P2
Stratford Pl **W1** 125 H8
Stratford Rd **W8** 128 A2
Stratford Vil **NW1** 125 J2
Strath Ter **SW11** 128 E10
Strathblaine Rd **SW11** 128 D10
Strathearn Pl **W2** 124 E9
Strathnairn St **SE1** 130 E3
Strathray Gdns **NW3** 124 E1
Stratton St **W1** 125 H10
Strattondale St **E14** 131 N2
Streatham St **WC1** 125 K8
Streimer Rd **E15** 127 N4
Strickland St **SE8** 131 L8
Stroudley Wk **E3** 127 M5
Strutton Grd **SW1** 129 K2
Stuart Rd **NW6** 124 A5
Stuart Rd **SE15** 130 G10
Stuart Twr **W9** 124 C6
Stubbs Dr **SE16** 130 F4
Studd St **N1** 125 P3
Studdridge St **SW6** 128 A8
Studholme St **SE15** 130 F6
Studley Est **SW4** 129 L7
Studley Rd **SW4** 129 L7
Stukeley St **WC1** 125 L8
Stukeley St **WC2** 125 L8
Sturdy Rd **SE15** 130 F8
Sturgeon Rd **SE17** 130 A4
Sturry St **E14** 127 M8
Sturt St **N1** 126 A4
Stutfield St **E1** 126 E8
Styles Gdns **SW9** 129 P9
Sudeley St **N1** 125 P4
Sudlow Rd **SW18** 128 A10
Sugar Ho La **E15** 127 N4
Sugar Quay Wk **EC3** 126 C9
Sugden Rd **SW11** 128 G9
Sulivan Ct **SW6** 128 A9
Sulivan Rd **SW6** 128 A9
Sullivan Cl **SW11** 128 E9
Sullivan Rd **SE11** 129 N3
Sultan St **SE5** 130 A6
Summercourt Rd **E1** 126 G8
Sumner Pl **SW7** 128 D3
Sumner Rd **SE15** 130 D6
Sumner St **SE1** 126 A10
Sumpter Cl **NW3** 124 C1
Sun St **EC2** 126 B7
Sunbury La **SW11** 128 D7
Sunderland Ter **W2** 124 B8
Sunlight Sq **E2** 126 F5
Sunninghill Rd **SE13** 131 M8
Sunray Av **SE24** 130 B10
Sunset Rd **SE5** 130 A10
Surma Cl **E1** 126 F6
Surrendale Pl **W9** 124 A6
Surrey Canal Rd **SE14** 130 G5
Surrey Canal Rd **SE15** 130 G5
Surrey La **SW11** 128 E7
Surrey La Est **SW11** 128 E7
Surrey Quays Retail Cen **SE16** 131 H2
Surrey Quays Rd **SE16** 130 G2
Surrey Row **SE1** 129 P1
Surrey Sq **SE17** 130 C4
Surrey St **WC2** 125 M9
Surrey Ter **SE17** 130 C4
Surrey Water Rd **SE16** 127 H10
Susannah St **E14** 127 M8
Sussex Gdns **W2** 124 D8
Sussex Pl **NW1** 124 F5
Sussex Pl **W2** 124 D8
Sussex Sq **W2** 124 D9
Sussex St **SW1** 129 H4
Sutherland Av **W9** 124 C5
Sutherland Pl **W2** 124 A8
Sutherland Row **SW1** 129 H4
Sutherland Sq **SE17** 130 A4
Sutherland St **SW1** 129 H4
Sutherland Wk **SE17** 130 A4
Sutterton St **N7** 125 M1
Sutton Est **SW3** 128 E4
Sutton Est, The **N1** 125 P2
Sutton Row **W1** 125 K8
Sutton St **E1** 126 G8
Swain St **NW8** 124 E6
Swallow Cl **SE14** 130 G7
Swan Mead **SE1** 130 C2
Swan Rd **SE16** 130 G1
Swan St **SE1** 130 A2
Swan Wk **SW3** 128 F5
Swandon Way **SW18** 128 B10
Swanfield St **E2** 126 D5
Swaton Rd **E3** 127 L6
Sweden Gate **SE16** 131 J2
Swedenborg Gdns **E1** 126 E9
Sweeney Cres **SE1** 130 D1
Swinford Gdns **SW9** 129 P9
Swinton Pl **WC1** 125 M5
Swinton St **WC1** 125 M5
Swiss Ter **NW6** 124 D2
Sybil Phoenix Cl **SE8** 131 H4
Sycamore Av **E3** 127 K3
Sycamore Ms **SW4** 129 J9
Sydney Cl **SW3** 128 D3
Sydney Ms **SW3** 128 D3
Sydney Pl **SW7** 128 D3
Sydney St **SW3** 128 E3
Sylvan Gro **SE15** 130 F6
Sylvester Rd **E8** 126 F1
Symons St **SW3** 128 F3

T

Tabard Gdn Est **SE1** 130 B1
Tabard St **SE1** 130 B1
Tabernacle St **EC2** 126 B6
Tachbrook Est **SW1** 129 K4
Tachbrook St **SW1** 129 J3
Tack Ms **SE4** 131 L9
Tadema Rd **SW10** 128 C6
Taeping St **E14** 131 M3
Talacre Rd **NW5** 124 G1
Talbot Rd **SE22** 130 C10
Talbot Rd **W2** 124 A8
Talbot Sq **W2** 124 D8
Talfourd Pl **SE15** 130 D7
Talfourd Rd **SE15** 130 D7
Tallis St **EC4** 125 N9
Talma Rd **SW2** 129 N10
Talwin St **E3** 127 M5
Tamworth St **SW6** 128 A5
Tanner St **SE1** 130 C1
Tanners Hill **SE8** 131 K7
Taplow **NW3** 124 D2
Taplow St **N1** 126 A4
Tapp St **E1** 126 F6
Tappesfield Rd **SE15** 130 G9
Tariff Cres **SE8** 131 K3
Tarling St **E1** 126 F8
Tarling St Est **E1** 126 G8
Tarragon Cl **SE14** 131 J6
Tarrant Pl **W1** 124 F7
Tarver Rd **SE17** 129 P4
Tarves Way **SE10** 131 M6
Tasman Rd **SW9** 129 L9
Tatham Pl **NW8** 124 D4
Tatum St **SE17** 130 B3
Taunton Pl **NW1** 124 F6
Tavern La **SW9** 129 N8
Tavistock Pl **WC1** 125 L6
Tavistock Sq **WC1** 125 K6
Tavistock St **WC2** 125 L9
Taviton St **WC1** 125 K6
Tavy Cl **SE11** 129 N4
Tawny Way **SE16** 131 H3
Taybridge Rd **SW11** 128 G9
Tayburn Cl **E14** 127 N8
Taylor Cl **SE8** 131 K5
Tayport Cl **N1** 125 L2
Teak Cl **SE16** 127 J10
Teale St **E2** 126 E4
Tedworth Sq **SW3** 128 F4
Teesdale Cl **E2** 126 F4
Teesdale St **E2** 126 F4
Teignmouth Cl **SW4** 129 K10
Telegraph Pl **E14** 131 M3
Telford Ter **SW1** 129 J5
Tell Gro **SE22** 130 D10
Templar St **SE5** 129 P8
Temple, The **EC4** 125 N9
Temple Av **EC4** 125 N9
Temple Pl **WC2** 125 M9
Temple St **E2** 126 F4
Temple W Ms **SE11** 129 P2
Templecombe Rd **E9** 126 G3
Templeton Pl **SW5** 128 A3
Tench St **E1** 126 F10
Tenison Way **SE1** 125 M10
Tennis St **SE1** 130 B1
Tennyson St **SW8** 129 H8
Tent St **E1** 126 F6
Tenterden St **W1** 125 H8
Teredo St **SE16** 131 H2
Terminus Pl **SW1** 129 H2
Terrace, The **NW6** 124 A3
Terrace Rd **E9** 126 G2
Tessa Sanderson Pl **SW8** 129 H9
Tetcott Rd **SW10** 128 C6
Teversham La **SW8** 129 L7
Teviot St **E14** 127 N7
Thackeray Rd **SW8** 129 H8
Thackeray St **W8** 128 B1
Thalia Cl **SE10** 131 P5
Thame Rd **SE16** 131 H1
Thames Av **SW10** 128 C7
Thames St **SE10** 131 M5
Thanet St **WC1** 125 L5
Thayer St **W1** 124 G7
Theatre St **SW11** 128 F9
Theberton St **N1** 125 N3
Theed St **SE1** 125 N10
Theobald's Rd **WC1** 125 M7
Thermopylae Gate **E14** 131 M3
Thessaly Rd **SW8** 129 J6
Thirleby Rd **SW1** 129 J2
Thirsk Rd **SW11** 128 G9
Thistle Gro **SW10** 128 C4
Thomas Baines Rd **SW11** 128 D9
Thomas Doyle St **SE1** 129 P2
Thomas More St **E1** 126 E9
Thomas Rd **E14** 127 K8
Thompson's Av **SE5** 130 A6
Thorburn Sq **SE1** 130 E3
Thoresby St **N1** 126 A5
Thorncroft St **SW8** 129 L6
Thorndike Cl **SW10** 128 C6
Thorndike Rd **N1** 126 A1
Thorndike St **SW1** 129 J3
Thorne Rd **SW8** 129 L6
Thorney Cres **SW11** 128 D6
Thorney St **SW1** 129 L3
Thorngate Rd **W9** 124 A6
Thornham St **SE10** 131 M5
Thornhaugh St **WC1** 125 K6
Thornhill Cres **N1** 125 M2
Thornhill Rd **N1** 125 N2
Thornhill Sq **N1** 125 M2
Thornton Pl **W1** 124 F7
Thornton St **SW9** 129 N8
Thornville St **SE8** 131 L7
Thorparch Rd **SW8** 129 K7
Thoydon Rd **E3** 127 J4
Thrale St **SE1** 126 A10
Thrawl St **E1** 126 D7
Threadneedle St **EC2** 126 B8
Three Colt St **E14** 127 K9
Three Colts La **E2** 126 F6
Three Kings Yd **W1** 125 H9
Three Mill La **E3** 127 N5
Three Quays Wk **EC3** 126 C9
Throgmorton Av **EC2** 126 B8
Throgmorton St **EC2** 126 B8
Thurland Rd **SE16** 130 E2
Thurloe Cl **SW7** 128 E2
Thurloe Pl **SW7** 128 D3
Thurloe Sq **SW7** 128 E3
Thurloe St **SW7** 128 D3
Thurlow St **SE17** 130 B4
Thurston Rd **SE13** 131 M8
Thurtle Rd **E2** 126 D3
Tibbatts Rd **E3** 127 M6
Tideway Ind Est **SW8** 129 J5
Tidey St **E3** 127 L7
Tidworth Rd **E3** 127 L6
Tileyard Rd **N7** 125 L2
Tiller Rd **E14** 131 L2
Tilney Gdns **N1** 126 B1
Tilney St **W1** 124 G10
Timber Mill Way **SW4** 129 K9
Timber Pond Rd **SE16** 131 H1
Timberland Rd **E1** 126 F8
Timothy Rd **E3** 127 K7
Tindal St **SW9** 129 P7
Tinsley Rd **E1** 126 G7
Tintagel Cres **SE22** 130 D10
Tintern St **SW4** 129 L10
Tinworth St **SE11** 129 M4
Tipthorpe Rd **SW11** 128 G9
Tisdall Pl **SE17** 130 B3
Titchfield Rd **NW8** 124 F3
Tite St **SW3** 128 F4
Tiverton St **SE1** 130 A2
Tivoli Ct **SE16** 131 K1
Tobacco Dock **E1** 126 F9
Tobin Cl **NW3** 124 E2
Toby La **E1** 127 J6
Tollet St **E1** 127 H6
Tollgate Gdns **NW6** 124 B4
Tolpuddle St **N1** 125 N4
Tomlins Gro **E3** 127 L5
Tomlinson Cl **E2** 126 D5
Tonbridge St **WC1** 125 L5
Tooley St **SE1** 126 B10
Topmast Pt **E14** 131 L1
Tor Gdns **W8** 128 A1
Torrens St **EC1** 125 N4
Torridge Gdns **SE15** 130 G10
Torrington Pl **E1** 126 E10
Torrington Pl **WC1** 125 K7
Torrington Sq **WC1** 125 K6
Tothill St **SW1** 129 K1
Tottan Ter **E1** 127 H8
Tottenham Ct Rd **W1** 125 J6
Tottenham Rd **N1** 126 C1
Tottenham St **W1** 125 J7
Totteridge Ho **SW11** 128 D8
Toulmin St **SE1** 130 A1
Toulon St **SE5** 130 A6
Tours Pas **SW11** 128 D10
Towcester Rd **E3** 127 M6
Tower 42 **EC2** 126 C8
Tower Br **E1** 126 D10
Tower Br **SE1** 126 D10
Tower Br App **E1** 126 D10
Tower Br Rd **SE1** 130 C2
Tower Br Wf **E1** 126 E10
Tower Mill Rd **SE15** 130 C6
Tower Millennium Pier **EC3** 126 C10
Tower St **WC2** 125 K8
Town Hall Rd **SW11** 128 F9
Townmead Rd **SW6** 128 C8
Townsend St **SE17** 130 B3
Townshend Est **NW8** 124 E4
Townshend Rd **NW8** 124 E3
Toynbee St **E1** 126 D7
Tradescant Rd **SW8** 129 L6
Trafalgar Av **SE15** 130 D4
Trafalgar Gdns **E1** 127 H7
Trafalgar Gro **SE10** 131 P5
Trafalgar Ms **E9** 127 K1
Trafalgar Rd **SE10** 131 P5
Trafalgar Sq **SW1** 125 K10
Trafalgar Sq **WC2** 125 K10
Trafalgar St **SE17** 130 B4
Trafalgar Way **E14** 127 N10
Trahorn Cl **E1** 126 E6
Transept St **NW1** 124 E7
Transom Sq **E14** 131 M3
Tranton Rd **SE16** 130 E2
Treadway St **E2** 126 F4
Treaty St **N1** 125 M3
Trebovir Rd **SW5** 128 A4
Treby St **E3** 127 K6
Tredegar Rd **E3** 127 K4
Tredegar Sq **E3** 127 K5
Tredegar Ter **E3** 127 K5
Trederwen Rd **E8** 126 E3
Tregarvon Rd **SW11** 128 G10
Trego Rd **E9** 127 L2
Tregothnan Rd **SW9** 129 L9
Tregunter Rd **SW10** 128 C5
Trelawney Est **E9** 126 G1
Tremadoc Rd **SW4** 129 K10
Tremaine Cl **SE4** 131 L8
Trenchard St **SE10** 131 P4
Trenchold St **SW8** 129 L5
Tresco Rd **SE15** 130 F10
Tresham Cres **NW8** 124 E6
Tressillian Cres **SE4** 131 L9
Tressillian Rd **SE4** 131 K10
Trevithick St **SE8** 131 L4
Trevor Pl **SW7** 128 E1
Trevor Sq **SW7** 128 F1
Trevor St **SW7** 128 E1
Triangle Pl **SW4** 129 K10
Triangle Rd **E8** 126 F3
Trident St **SE16** 131 H3
Trigon Rd **SW8** 129 M6
Trim St **SE14** 131 K5
Trinidad St **E14** 127 K9
Trinity Ch Sq **SE1** 130 A2
Trinity Cl **E8** 126 D1
Trinity Cl **SE13** 131 P10
Trinity Gdns **SW9** 129 M10
Trinity Gro **SE10** 131 N7
Trinity Sq **EC3** 126 C9
Trinity St **SE1** 130 A1
Trinity Wk **NW3** 124 C1
Triton Sq **NW1** 125 J6
Trott St **SW11** 128 E7
Troutbeck Rd **SE14** 131 J7
Trowbridge Rd **E9** 127 K1
Troy Town **SE15** 130 E9
Trundleys Rd **SE8** 131 H4
Trundleys Ter **SE8** 131 H3
Truro St **NW5** 124 G1
Tryon Cres **E9** 126 G3
Tryon St **SW3** 128 F4
Tudor Gro **E9** 126 G2
Tudor Rd **E9** 126 F3
Tudor St **EC4** 125 N9
Tufton St **SW1** 129 K2
Tuilerie St **E2** 126 E4
Tunnel Av **SE10** 131 P1
Tunstall Rd **SW9** 129 M10
Turenne Cl **SW18** 128 C10
Turin St **E2** 126 E5
Turks Row **SW3** 128 F4
Turner Cl **SW9** 129 P7
Turner St **E1** 126 F7
Turners Rd **E3** 127 K7
Turnmill St **EC1** 125 N6
Turnpike Ho **EC1** 125 P5
Turnpin La **SE10** 131 N5
Turret Gro **SW4** 129 J9
Tustin Est **SE15** 130 G5
Twelvetrees Cres **E3** 127 N6
Twine Ct **E1** 126 G9
Twyford St **N1** 125 M3
Tyburn Way **W1** 124 F9
Tyers Est **SE1** 130 C1
Tyers St **SE11** 129 M4
Tyers Ter **SE11** 129 M4
Tyler Cl **E2** 126 D4
Tyndale Ct **E14** 131 M4
Tyneham Rd **SW11** 128 G8
Tynemouth St **SW6** 128 C8
Type St **E2** 127 H4
Tyrawley Rd **SW6** 128 B7
Tyrrell Rd **SE22** 130 E10
Tyrwhitt Rd **SE4** 131 L9
Tyssen Pas **E8** 126 D1
Tyssen St **E8** 126 D1

U

Uamvar St **E14** 127 M7
Ufford St **SE1** 129 N1
Ufton Gro **N1** 126 B2
Ufton Rd **N1** 126 B2
Undercliff Rd **SE13** 131 L9
Undershaft **EC3** 126 C8
Underwood Rd **E1** 126 E6
Underwood Row **N1** 126 A5
Underwood St **N1** 126 A5
Undine Rd **E14** 131 M3
Union Gro **SW8** 129 K8
Union Rd **SW4** 129 K8
Union Rd **SW8** 129 K8
Union Sq **N1** 126 A3
Union St **E15** 127 N3
Union St **SE1** 125 P10
University St **WC1** 125 J6
Unwin Cl **SE15** 130 E5
Upcerne Rd **SW10** 128 C6
Upper Bk St **E14** 127 M10
Upper Belgrave St **SW1** 128 G2
Upper Berkeley St **W1** 124 F8
Upper Brockley Rd **SE4** 131 K8
Upper Brook St **W1** 124 G9
Upper Cheyne Row **SW3** 128 E5
Upper Grosvenor St **W1** 124 G9
Upper Grd **SE1** 125 N10
Upper Marsh **SE1** 129 M2
Upper Montagu St **W1** 124 F7
Upper N St **E14** 127 L7
Upper Phillimore Gdns **W8** 128 A1
Upper St **N1** 125 N4
Upper Tachbrook St **SW1** 129 J3
Upper Thames St **EC4** 126 A9
Upper Wimpole St **W1** 124 G7
Upper Woburn Pl **WC1** 125 K5
Upstall St **SE5** 129 P7
Urlwin St **SE5** 130 A5
Urlwin Wk **SW9** 129 N8
Ursula St **SW11** 128 E7
Usborne Ms **SW8** 129 M6
Usher Rd **E3** 127 K4
Usk Rd **SW11** 128 C10
Usk St **E2** 127 H5
Uverdale Rd **SW10** 128 C6
Uxbridge St **W8** 124 A10

V

Vale, The **SW3** 128 D5
Vale Ct **W9** 124 C5
Vale Royal **N7** 125 L2
Valentine Pl **SE1** 129 P1
Valentine Rd **E9** 127 H1
Valentine Row **SE1** 129 P1
Valette St **E9** 126 F1
Vallance Rd **E1** 126 E6
Vallance Rd **E2** 126 E5
Valmar Rd **SE5** 130 A7
Vandon St **SW1** 129 J2

Vanguard St **SE8** 131 L7
Vansittart St **SE14** 131 J6
Vanston Pl **SW6** 128 A6
Varcoe Rd **SE16** 130 F4
Varden St **E1** 126 F8
Vardens Rd **SW11** 128 D10
Varndell St **NW1** 125 J5
Vassall Rd **SW9** 129 N6
Vauban Est **SE16** 130 D2
Vauban St **SE16** 130 D2
Vaughan Rd **SE5** 130 A8
Vaughan St **SE16** 131 K1
Vaughan Way **E1** 126 E9
Vauxhall Br **SE1** 129 L4
Vauxhall Br **SW1** 129 L4
Vauxhall Br Rd **SW1** 129 J3
Vauxhall Gdns Est **SE11** 129 M4
Vauxhall Gro **SW8** 129 L5
Vauxhall St **SE11** 129 M4
Vauxhall Wk **SE11** 129 M4
Vawdrey Cl **E1** 126 G6
Veda Rd **SE13** 131 L10
Velletri Ho **E2** 127 H4
Venables St **NW8** 124 D6
Venetian Rd **SE5** 130 A8
Venn St **SW4** 129 J10
Ventnor Rd **SE14** 131 H6
Venue St **E14** 127 N7
Vere St **W1** 125 H8
Verney Rd **SE16** 130 E5
Verney Way **SE16** 130 F4
Vernon Pl **WC1** 125 L7
Vernon Ri **WC1** 125 M5
Vernon Rd **E3** 127 K4
Vesta Rd **SE4** 131 J8
Vestry Ms **SE5** 130 C7
Vestry Rd **SE5** 130 C7
Vestry St **N1** 126 B5
Viaduct St **E2** 126 F5
Vian St **SE13** 131 M9
Vicarage Cres **SW11** 128 D7
Vicarage Gdns **W8** 124 A10
Vicarage Gate **W8** 128 B1
Vicarage Gro **SE5** 130 B7
Vicars Hill **SE13** 131 M10
Viceroy Rd **SW8** 129 L7
Victoria Embk **EC4** 125 M9
Victoria Embk **SW1** 129 L1
Victoria Embk **WC2** 129 L1
Victoria Gdns **W11** 124 A10
Victoria Gro **W8** 128 C2
Victoria Ms **NW6** 124 A3
Victoria Pk **E9** 127 J2
Victoria Pk Rd **E9** 126 G3
Victoria Pk Sq **E2** 126 G5
Victoria Pl **SW1** 129 H3
Victoria Ri **SW4** 129 H9
Victoria Rd **W8** 128 C2
Victoria Sta **SW1** 129 H3
Victoria St **SW1** 129 J2
Victoria Wf **E14** 127 J9
Victory Pl **SE17** 130 A3
Victory Way **SE16** 131 J1
Vigo St **W1** 125 J9
Viking Ct **SW6** 128 A5
Villa Rd **SW9** 129 N9
Villa St **SE17** 130 B4
Villiers St **WC2** 125 L9
Vince St **EC1** 126 B5
Vincent Cl **SE16** 131 J1
Vincent Sq **SW1** 129 J3
Vincent St **SW1** 129 K3
Vincent Ter **N1** 125 P4
Vine St Br **EC1** 125 N6
Viney Rd **SE13** 131 M9
Vineyard Wk **EC1** 125 N6
Vining St **SW9** 129 N10
Violet Hill **NW8** 124 C4
Violet Rd **E3** 127 M6
Virgil St **SE1** 129 M2
Virginia Rd **E2** 126 D5
Virginia St **E1** 126 E9
Vivian Rd **E3** 127 J4
Voltaire Rd **SW4** 129 K9
Voss St **E2** 126 E5
Vulcan Rd **SE4** 131 K8
Vulcan Ter **SE4** 131 K8
Vulcan Way **N7** 125 M1
Vyner St **E2** 126 F3

W

Wadding St **SE17** 130 B3
Waddington St **E15** 127 P1
Wades Pl **E14** 127 M9
Wadeson St **E2** 126 F4
Wadham Gdns **NW3** 124 E3
Wadhurst Rd **SW8** 129 J7
Wager St **E3** 127 K6
Waghorn St **SE15** 130 E9
Wagner St **SE15** 130 G6
Waite St **SE15** 130 D5
Wakefield St **WC1** 125 L5
Wakeham St **N1** 126 B1
Wakeling St **E14** 127 J8
Wakley St **EC1** 125 P5
Walberswick St **SW8** 129 L6
Walbrook **EC4** 126 B9
Walcot Sq **SE11** 129 N3
Walden St **E1** 126 F8
Walerand Rd **SE13** 131 N8
Wales Cl **SE15** 130 F6
Waley St **E1** 127 H7
Walham Gro **SW6** 128 A6
Wall St **N1** 126 B1
Wallace Rd **N1** 126 A1
Wallbutton Rd **SE4** 131 J8
Waller Rd **SE14** 131 H7
Wallgrave Rd **SW5** 128 B3
Wallis Cl **SW11** 128 D9
Wallis Rd **E9** 127 K1
Wallwood St **E14** 127 K7
Walnut Tree Wk **SE11** 129 N3
Walpole St **SW3** 128 F4
Walsham Rd **SE14** 131 H8
Walter St **E2** 127 H5
Walter Ter **E1** 127 H8
Walton Cl **SW8** 129 L6
Walton Pl **SW3** 128 F2
Walton St **SW3** 128 E3
Walworth Pl **SE17** 130 A4
Walworth Rd **SE1** 130 A3
Walworth Rd **SE17** 130 A3
Wandon Rd **SW6** 128 B6
Wandsworth Br **SW6** 128 B9
Wandsworth Br **SW18** 128 B9
Wandsworth Br Rd **SW6** 128 B7
Wandsworth Rd **SW8** 129 K6
Wanless Rd **SE24** 130 A9
Wanley Rd **SE5** 130 B10
Wansbeck Rd **E3** 127 K2
Wansbeck Rd **E9** 127 K2
Wansey St **SE17** 130 A3
Wapping High St **E1** 126 E10
Wapping La **E1** 126 F9
Wapping Wall **E1** 126 G10
Warburton Rd **E8** 126 F2
Ward Rd **E15** 127 P3
Wardalls Gro **SE14** 130 G6
Warden Rd **NW5** 124 G1
Wardour St **W1** 125 K9
Warham St **SE5** 129 P6
Warley St **E2** 127 H5
Warlock Rd **W9** 124 A6
Warndon St **SE16** 131 H3
Warneford St **E9** 126 F3
Warner Pl **E2** 126 E4
Warner Rd **SE5** 130 A7
Warner St **EC1** 125 N6
Warren St **W1** 125 J6
Warriner Gdns **SW11** 128 F7
Warrington Cres **W9** 124 C6
Warton Rd **E15** 127 N2
Warwick Av **W2** 124 C6
Warwick Av **W9** 124 C6
Warwick Bldg **SW8** 129 H5
Warwick Ct **SE15** 130 E8
Warwick Cres **W2** 124 C7
Warwick Est **W2** 124 B7
Warwick Ho St **SW1** 125 K10
Warwick La **EC4** 125 P8
Warwick Pl **W9** 124 C7
Warwick Pl N **SW1** 129 J3
Warwick Row **SW1** 129 H2
Warwick Sq **SW1** 129 J4
Warwick Sq Ms **SW1** 129 J3
Warwick St **W1** 125 J9
Warwick Way **SW1** 129 J3
Warwickshire Path **SE8** 131 K6
Washington Cl **E3** 127 M5
Wat Tyler Rd **SE3** 131 N8
Wat Tyler Rd **SE10** 131 N8
Water Gdns, The **W2** 124 E8
Water La **SE14** 130 G6
Water Ms **SE15** 130 G10
Waterford Rd **SW6** 128 B7
Watergate St **SE8** 131 L5
Waterloo Br **SE1** 125 M9
Waterloo Br **WC2** 125 M9
Waterloo Est **E2** 126 G4
Waterloo Gdns **E2** 126 G4
Waterloo Pl **SW1** 125 K10
Waterloo Rd **SE1** 129 N1
Waterloo Sta **SE1** 129 N1
Waterloo Ter **N1** 125 P2
Waterman Way **E1** 126 F10
Watermans Wk **SE16** 131 J2
Watermeadow La **SW6** 128 C8
Waterside Cl **E3** 127 K3
Waterside Pt **SW11** 128 E6
Waterside Twr **SW6** 128 C7
Waterson St **E2** 126 C5
Waterview Ho **E14** 127 J7
Watkinson Rd **N7** 125 M1
Watling St **EC4** 126 A8
Watney St **E1** 126 F8
Watson's St **SE8** 131 L6
Watts Gro **E3** 127 M7
Watts St **E1** 126 F10
Watts St **SE15** 130 D7
Waveney Av **SE15** 130 F10
Waverley Pl **NW8** 124 D4
Waverley Wk **W2** 124 A7
Waverton Ho **E3** 127 K3
Waverton St **W1** 124 G10
Wayford St **SW11** 128 E8
Wayman Ct **E8** 126 F1
Wear Pl **E2** 126 F5
Weardale Rd **SE13** 131 P10
Wearside Rd **SE13** 131 M10
Weatherley Cl **E3** 127 K7
Weaver St **E1** 126 E6
Weavers Ter **SW6** 128 A5
Weavers Way **NW1** 125 K3
Webb St **SE1** 130 C2
Webber Row **SE1** 129 P1
Webber St **SE1** 129 N1
Webster Rd **SE16** 130 E2
Weighhouse St **W1** 124 G8
Weir's Pas **NW1** 125 K5
Welbeck St **W1** 124 G7
Welbeck Way **W1** 125 H8
Welby St **SE5** 129 P7
Well St **E9** 126 F2
Welland St **SE10** 131 N5
Wellclose Sq **E1** 126 E9
Wellesley Ct **W9** 124 C5
Wellesley St **E1** 127 H7
Wellesley Ter **N1** 126 A5
Wellington Pl **NW8** 124 E4
Wellington Rd **NW8** 124 D4
Wellington Row **E2** 126 D5
Wellington Sq **SW3** 128 F4
Wellington St **WC2** 125 L9
Wellington Ter **E1** 126 F10
Wellington Way **E3** 127 L5
Wells Ri **NW8** 124 F3
Wells St **W1** 125 J8
Wells Way **SE5** 130 B5
Wells Way **SW7** 128 D2
Welmar Ms **SW4** 129 K10
Welsford St **SE1** 130 E4
Wendle Ct **SW8** 129 L5
Wendon St **E3** 127 K3
Wendover **SE17** 130 C4
Wenlock Rd **N1** 126 A4
Wenlock St **N1** 126 A4
Wennington Rd **E3** 127 H4
Wentworth Cres **SE15** 130 E6
Wentworth St **E1** 126 D8
Werrington St **NW1** 125 J4
Wesley Cl **SE17** 129 P3
Wessex St **E2** 126 G5
West Arbour St **E1** 127 H8
West Carriage Dr **W2** 124 D9
West Eaton Pl **SW1** 128 G3
West End La **NW6** 124 A2
West Gdns **E1** 126 F9
West Gro **SE10** 131 N7
West Halkin St **SW1** 128 G2
West Hampstead Ms **NW6** 124 B1
West India Av **E14** 127 L10
West India Dock Rd **E14** 127 K8
West La **SE16** 130 F1
West One Shop Cen **W1** 125 H8
West Rd **SW3** 128 F5
West Smithfield **EC1** 125 P7
West Sq **SE11** 129 P2
West St **E2** 126 F4
West Tenter St **E1** 126 D8
Westbourne Br **W2** 124 C7
Westbourne Cres **W2** 124 D9
Westbourne Gdns **W2** 124 B8
Westbourne Gro **W2** 124 A8
Westbourne Gro **W11** 124 A8
Westbourne Gro Ter **W2** 124 B8
Westbourne Pk Rd **W2** 124 A7
Westbourne Pk Vil **W2** 124 A7
Westbourne Rd **N7** 125 N1
Westbourne St **W2** 124 D9
Westbourne Ter **W2** 124 D8
Westbourne Ter Ms **W2** 124 C8
Westbourne Ter Rd **W2** 124 C7
Westbridge Rd **SW11** 128 D7
Westbury St **SW8** 129 J8
Westcott Rd **SE17** 129 P5
Western Rd **SW9** 129 N9
Westferry Circ **E14** 127 K10
Westferry Rd **E14** 127 L10
Westfield Cl **SW10** 128 C6
Westfield Way **E1** 127 J5
Westgate St **E8** 126 F3
Westgate Ter **SW10** 128 B4
Westgrove La **SE10** 131 N7
Westminster Br **SE1** 129 L1
Westminster Br **SW1** 129 L1
Westminster Br Rd **SE1** 129 N2
Westminster Gdns **SW1** 129 K3
Westmoreland Pl **SW1** 129 H4
Westmoreland Rd **SE17** 130 A5
Westmoreland St **W1** 124 G7
Westmoreland Ter **SW1** 129 H4
Westmoreland Wk **SE17** 130 B5
Weston Ri **WC1** 125 M4
Weston St **SE1** 130 B2
Westport St **E1** 127 H8
Westway **W2** 124 A7
Westway **W9** 124 A7
Wetherby Gdns **SW5** 128 C3
Wetherby Pl **SW7** 128 C3
Wetherell Rd **E9** 127 H3
Weybridge Pt **SW11** 128 G8
Weymouth Ms **W1** 125 H7
Weymouth St **W1** 125 H7
Weymouth Ter **E2** 126 D4
Wharf Pl **E2** 126 E3
Wharf Rd **N1** 126 A4
Wharf Rd (King's Cross) **N1** 125 L4
Wharfdale Rd **N1** 125 L4
Wharfedale St **SW10** 128 B4
Wharton St **WC1** 125 M5
Wheat Sheaf Cl **E14** 131 M3
Wheatsheaf La **SW8** 129 L6
Wheelwright St **N7** 125 M2
Wheler St **E1** 126 D6
Whidborne St **WC1** 125 L5
Whiskin St **EC1** 125 P5
Whistlers Av **SW11** 128 D6
Whiston Rd **E2** 126 D4
Whitbread Rd **SE4** 131 J10
Whitburn Rd **SE13** 131 M10
Whitcher Cl **SE14** 131 J5
Whitcomb St **WC2** 125 K9
White Ch La **E1** 126 E8
White Hart St **SE11** 129 N4
White Horse La **E1** 127 H6
White Horse Rd **E1** 127 J8
White Horse St **W1** 125 H10
White Lion Hill **EC4** 125 P9
White Lion St **N1** 125 N4
White Post La **E9** 127 K2
White Post La **SE13** 131 L9
White Post St **SE15** 130 G6
Whiteadder Way **E14** 131 M3
Whitear Wk **E15** 127 P1
Whitechapel High St **E1** 126 D8
Whitechapel Rd **E1** 126 E8
Whitecross St **EC1** 126 A6
Whitefriars St **EC4** 125 N8
Whitehall **SW1** 125 L10
Whitehall Ct **SW1** 125 L10
Whitehall Pl **SW1** 125 L10
Whitehead's Gro **SW3** 128 E4
Whiteleys Shop Cen **W2** 124 B8
Whites Grds **SE1** 130 C1
White's Row **E1** 126 D7
Whitethorn St **E3** 127 L6
Whitfield Rd **SE3** 131 P7
Whitfield St **W1** 125 K7
Whitgift St **SE11** 129 M3
Whitmore Est **N1** 126 C3
Whitmore Rd **N1** 126 C3
Whittaker St **SW1** 128 G3
Whitton Wk **E3** 127 L4
Whorlton Rd **SE15** 130 F9
Wick La **E3** 127 L4
Wick Rd **E9** 127 H1
Wickersley Rd **SW11** 128 G8
Wickford St **E1** 126 G6
Wickham Cl **E1** 126 G7
Wickham Gdns **SE4** 131 K9
Wickham Ms **SE4** 131 K8
Wickham Rd **SE4** 131 K10
Wickham St **SE11** 129 M4
Wicklow St **WC1** 125 M5
Wickwood St **SE5** 129 P8
Widdin St **E15** 127 P2
Widley Rd **W9** 124 A5
Wigmore Pl **W1** 125 H8
Wigmore St **W1** 124 G8
Wilbraham Pl **SW1** 128 F3
Wilcox Cl **SW8** 129 L6
Wilcox Rd **SW8** 129 L6
Wild Ct **WC2** 125 M8
Wild Goose Dr **SE14** 130 G7
Wild St **WC2** 125 L8
Wilde Cl **E8** 126 E3
Wild's Rents **SE1** 130 C2
Wilfred St **SW1** 129 J2
Wilkes St **E1** 126 D7
Wilkin St **NW5** 125 H1
Wilkinson St **SW8** 129 M6
Willard St **SW8** 129 H9
Willes Rd **NW5** 125 H1
William Bonney Est **SW4** 129 K10
William Cl **SE13** 131 N8
William IV St **WC2** 125 L9
William Morris Way **SW6** 128 C9
William Rd **NW1** 125 H5
William St **SW1** 128 F1
Williams Bldgs **E2** 126 G6
Willington Rd **SW9** 129 L9
Willis St **E14** 127 M8
Willoughby Pas **E14** 127 L10
Willow Br Rd **N1** 126 A1
Willow Pl **SW1** 129 J3
Willow St **EC2** 126 C6
Willow Wk **SE1** 130 C3
Willowbrook Rd **SE15** 130 D5
Wilman Gro **E8** 126 E2
Wilmcote Ho **W2** 124 A7
Wilmer Gdns **N1** 126 C3
Wilmer Lea Cl **E15** 127 N2
Wilmington Sq **WC1** 125 N5
Wilmington St **WC1** 125 N5
Wilmot Cl **SE15** 130 E6
Wilmot Pl **NW1** 125 J2
Wilmot St **E2** 126 F6
Wilshaw St **SE14** 131 L7
Wilson Gro **SE16** 130 F1
Wilson Rd **SE5** 130 C7
Wilson St **EC2** 126 B7
Wilton Cres **SW1** 128 G1
Wilton Ms **SW1** 128 G2
Wilton Pl **SW1** 128 G1
Wilton Rd **SW1** 129 H2
Wilton Row **SW1** 128 G1
Wilton Sq **N1** 126 B3
Wilton St **SW1** 129 H2
Wilton Ter **SW1** 128 G2
Wilton Vil **N1** 126 B3
Wilton Way **E8** 126 E1
Wiltshire Rd **SW9** 129 N9
Wiltshire Row **N1** 126 B3
Wimbolt St **E2** 126 E5
Wimbourne St **N1** 126 B4
Wimpole Ms **W1** 125 H7
Wimpole St **W1** 125 H8
Winans Wk **SW9** 129 N8
Winchester Cl **SE17** 129 P3
Winchester Rd **NW3** 124 D2
Winchester Sq **SE1** 126 B10
Winchester St **SW1** 129 H4
Winchester Wk **SE1** 126 B10
Wincott St **SE11** 129 N3
Winders Rd **SW11** 128 E8
Windlass Pl **SE8** 131 J3
Windmill Cl **SE13** 131 N8
Windmill La **E15** 127 P1
Windmill Row **SE11** 129 N4
Windmill St **W1** 125 K7
Windmill Wk **SE1** 125 N10
Windrose Cl **SE16** 131 H1
Windsock Cl **SE16** 131 K3
Windsor Gdns **W9** 124 A7
Windsor St **N1** 125 P3
Windsor Ter **N1** 126 A5
Windsor Wk **SE5** 130 B8
Wine Cl **E1** 126 G9
Winford Ho **E3** 127 K2
Winforton St **SE10** 131 N7
Wingfield St **SE15** 130 E9
Wingmore Rd **SE24** 130 A9
Winifred Gro **SW11** 128 F10
Winkley St **E2** 126 F4
Winsland St **W2** 124 D8
Winsley St **W1** 125 J8
Winslow **SE17** 130 C4
Winstanley Est **SW11** 128 D9
Winstanley Rd **SW11** 128 D9
Winterton Ho **E1** 126 F8
Winthrop St **E1** 126 F7
Wise Rd **E15** 127 P3
Wisteria Rd **SE13** 131 P10
Witan St **E2** 126 F5
Wivenhoe Cl **SE15** 130 F9
Wixs La **SW4** 129 H10
Woburn Pl **WC1** 125 K6
Woburn Sq **WC1** 125 K6
Woburn Wk **WC1** 125 K5
Wodeham Gdns **E1** 126 E7
Wodehouse Av **SE5** 130 D7
Wolfe Cres **SE16** 131 H1
Wolftencroft Cl **SW11** 128 D9
Wolseley St **SE1** 130 D1
Wolsey Ms **NW5** 125 J1
Wood Cl **E2** 126 E6
Wood St **EC2** 126 A8
Wood Wf **SE10** 131 M5
Woodbridge St **EC1** 125 P6
Woodchester Sq **W2** 124 B7
Woodchurch Rd **NW6** 124 A2
Woodfall St **SW3** 128 F4
Woodfarrs **SE5** 130 B10
Woodhouse Cl **SE22** 130 E10
Woodland Cres **SE16** 131 H1
Woodpecker Rd **SE14** 131 J5
Woods Ms **W1** 124 F9
Woods Rd **SE15** 130 F7
Woodseer St **E1** 126 D7
Woodstock Ter **E14** 127 M9
Wooler St **SE17** 130 B4
Woolmore St **E14** 127 N9
Woolneigh St **SW6** 128 B9
Woolstaplers Way **SE16** 130 E3
Wooster Gdns **E14** 127 P8
Wootton St **SE1** 125 N10
Worfield St **SW11** 128 E6
Worgan St **SE11** 129 M4
Worgan St **SE16** 131 H2
World's End Est **SW10** 128 C6
Worlingham Rd **SE22** 130 D10
Wormwood St **EC2** 126 C8
Woronzow Rd **NW8** 124 D3
Worship St **EC2** 126 B6
Wotton Rd **SE8** 131 K5
Wren Rd **SE5** 130 B7
Wren St **WC1** 125 M6
Wrexham Rd **E3** 127 L4
Wrigglesworth St **SE14** 131 H6
Wrights Cl **SE13** 131 P10
Wrights La **W8** 128 B1
Wrights Rd **E3** 127 K4
Wroxton Rd **SE15** 130 F8
Wyatt Cl **SE16** 131 K1
Wycliffe Rd **SW11** 128 G8
Wye St **SW11** 128 D8
Wyke Rd **E3** 127 L2
Wyllen Cl **E1** 126 G6
Wymering Rd **W9** 124 A5
Wynan Rd **E14** 131 M4
Wyndham Est **SE5** 130 A6
Wyndham Pl **W1** 124 F7
Wyndham Rd **SE5** 129 P6
Wyndham St **W1** 124 F7
Wynford Rd **N1** 125 M4
Wynne Rd **SW9** 129 N8
Wynnstay Gdns **W8** 128 A2
Wynter St **SW11** 128 C10
Wynyard Ter **SE11** 129 M4
Wyvil Rd **SW8** 129 L5
Wyvis St **E14** 127 M7

Y

Yabsley St **E14** 127 N10
Yalding Rd **SE16** 130 E2
Yardley St **WC1** 125 N5
Yeate St **N1** 126 B2
Yelverton Rd **SW11** 128 D8
Yeo St **E3** 127 M7
Yeoman St **SE8** 131 J3
Yeoman's Row **SW3** 128 E2
York Br **NW1** 124 G6
York Gate **NW1** 124 G6
York Gro **SE15** 130 G7
York Ho Pl **W8** 128 B1
York Pl **SW11** 128 D9
York Rd **SE1** 129 M1
York Rd **SW11** 128 C10
York Rd **SW18** 128 C10
York Sq **E14** 127 J8
York St **W1** 124 F7
York Ter E **NW1** 124 G6
York Ter W **NW1** 124 G6
York Way **N1** 125 L3
York Way **N7** 125 K1
York Way Ct **N1** 125 L3
Yorkshire Rd **E14** 127 J8
Yorkton St **E2** 126 E4
Young St **W8** 128 B1

Z

Zampa Rd **SE16** 130 G4
Zealand Rd **E3** 127 J4
Zenoria St **SE22** 130 D10
Zetland St **E14** 127 M7

INDEX TO GREAT BRITAIN

Administrative area abbreviations

Aber.	Aberdeenshire
Arg. & B.	Argyll & Bute
B'burn.	Blackburn with Darwen
B'pool	Blackpool
B. & H.	Brighton & Hove
B. & N.E.Som.	Bath & North East Somerset
B.Gwent	Blaenau Gwent
Bed.	Bedford
Bourne.	Bournemouth
Brack.F.	Bracknell Forest
Bucks.	Buckinghamshire
Caerp.	Caerphilly
Cambs.	Cambridgeshire
Carmar.	Carmarthenshire
Cen.Beds.	Central Bedfordshire
Cere.	Ceredigion
Chan.I.	Channel Islands
Ches.E.	Cheshire East
Ches.W. & C.	Cheshire West & Chester
Cornw.	Cornwall
Cumb.	Cumbria
D. & G.	Dumfries & Galloway
Darl.	Darlington
Denb.	Denbighshire
Derbys.	Derbyshire
Dur.	Durham
E.Ayr.	East Ayrshire
E.Dun.	East Dunbartonshire
E.Loth.	East Lothian
E.Renf.	East Renfrewshire
E.Riding	East Riding of Yorkshire
E.Suss.	East Sussex
Edin.	Edinburgh
Falk.	Falkirk
Flints.	Flintshire
Glas.	Glasgow
Glos.	Gloucestershire
Gt.Lon.	Greater London
Gt.Man.	Greater Manchester
Gwyn.	Gwynedd
Hants.	Hampshire
Hart.	Hartlepool
Here.	Herefordshire
Herts.	Hertfordshire
High.	Highland
Hull	Kingston upon Hull
I.o.A.	Isle of Anglesey
I.o.M.	Isle of Man
I.o.S.	Isles of Scilly
I.o.W.	Isle of Wight
Inclyde	Inverclyde
Lancs.	Lancashire
Leic.	Leicester
Leics.	Leicestershire
Lincs.	Lincolnshire
M.K.	Milton Keynes
M.Tyd.	Merthyr Tydfil
Med.	Medway
Mersey.	Merseyside
Middbro.	Middlesbrough
Midloth.	Midlothian
Mon.	Monmouthshire
N.Ayr.	North Ayrshire
N.E.Lincs.	North East Lincolnshire
N.Lan.	North Lanarkshire
N.Lincs.	North Lincolnshire
N.P.T.	Neath Port Talbot
N.Som.	North Somerset
N.Yorks.	North Yorkshire
Norf.	Norfolk
Northants.	Northamptonshire
Northumb.	Northumberland
Nott.	Nottingham
Notts.	Nottinghamshire
Ork.	Orkney
Oxon.	Oxfordshire
P. & K.	Perth & Kinross
Pembs.	Pembrokeshire
Peter.	Peterborough
Plym.	Plymouth
Ports.	Portsmouth
R. & C.	Redcar & Cleveland
R.C.T.	Rhondda Cynon Taff
Read.	Reading
Renf.	Renfrewshire
Rut.	Rutland
S'end	Southend
S'ham.	Southampton
S.Ayr.	South Ayrshire
S.Glos.	South Gloucestershire
S.Lan.	South Lanarkshire
S.Yorks.	South Yorkshire
Sc.Bord.	Scottish Borders
Shet.	Shetland
Shrop.	Shropshire
Slo.	Slough
Som.	Somerset
Staffs.	Staffordshire
Stir.	Stirling
Stock.	Stockton-on-Tees
Stoke	Stoke-on-Trent
Suff.	Suffolk
Surr.	Surrey
Swan.	Swansea
Swin.	Swindon
T. & W.	Tyne & Wear
Tel. & W.	Telford & Wrekin
Thur.	Thurrock
V. of Glam.	Vale of Glamorgan
W'ham	Wokingham
W. & M.	Windsor & Maidenhead
W.Berks.	West Berkshire
W.Dun.	West Dunbartonshire
W.Isles	Western Isles (Na h-Eileanan Siar)
W.Loth.	West Lothian
W.Mid.	West Midlands
W.Suss.	West Sussex
W.Yorks.	West Yorkshire
Warks.	Warwickshire
Warr.	Warrington
Wilts.	Wiltshire
Worcs.	Worcestershire
Wrex.	Wrexham

Notes

This index reads in the sequence: Place Name / Postal District / Map Page Number / Grid Reference.

Example: Bishop's Cleeve **GL52** 29 J6

Where there is more than one place with the same name, the index reads in the sequence: Place Name / Administrative Area / Postal District / Map Page Number / Grid Reference.

Example: Prestbury, *Ches.* **SK10** 49 H5
Prestbury, *Glos.* **GL52** 29 J6

Entries in the index shown in **BOLD CAPITALS** indicate the principal post town within a postcode area.
Entries in the index shown in **bold** indicate other post towns.

Example: **GLOUCESTER GL 29 H7**
Example: **Cheltenham GL50 29 J6**

A

Ab Kettleby **LE14** 42 A3
Ab Lench **WR10** 30 B3
Abbas Combe **BA8** 9 G2
Abberley **WR6** 29 G2
Abberley Common **WR6** 29 G2
Abberton *Essex* **CO5** 34 E7
Abberton *Worcs.* **WR10** 29 J3
Abberwick **NE66** 71 G2
Abbess Roding **CM5** 33 J7
Abbey Dore **HR2** 28 C5
Abbey Hulton **ST2** 40 B1
Abbey St. Bathans **TD11** 77 F4
Abbey Town **CA7** 60 C1
Abbey Village **PR6** 56 B7
Abbey Wood **SE2** 23 H4
Abbeycwmhir **LD1** 27 K1
Abbeydale **S7** 51 F4
Abbeystead **LA2** 55 J4
Abbotrule **TD9** 70 B2
Abbots Bickington **EX22** 6 B4
Abbots Bromley **WS15** 40 C3
Abbots Langley WD5 22 D1
Abbots Leigh **BS8** 19 J4
Abbots Morton **WR7** 30 B3
Abbots Ripton **PE28** 33 F1
Abbot's Salford **WR11** 30 B3
Abbots Worthy **SO21** 11 F1
Abbotsbury **DT3** 8 E6
Abbotsfield Farm **WA9** 48 E3
Abbotsham **EX39** 6 C3
Abbotskerswell **TQ12** 5 J4
Abbotsley **PE19** 33 F3
Abbotstone **SO24** 11 G1
Abbotts Ann **SP11** 21 G7
Abbott's Barton **SO23** 11 F1
Abbottswood **SO51** 10 E2
Abdon **SY7** 38 E7
Abdy **S62** 51 G3
Abenhall **GL17** 29 F7
Aber **SA40** 17 H1
Aber Village **LD3** 28 A6
Aberaeron SA46 26 D2
Aberaman **CF44** 18 D1
Aberangell **SY20** 37 H5
Aber-Arad **SA38** 17 G1
Aberarder **PH20** 88 B6
Aberarder House **IV2** 88 D2
Aberargie **PH2** 82 C6
Aberarth **SA46** 26 D2
Aberavon **SA12** 18 A3
Aber-banc **SA44** 17 G1
Aberbargoed **CF81** 18 E1
Aberbeeg **NP13** 19 F1
Aberbowlan **SA19** 17 K2
Aberbran **LD3** 27 J6
Abercanaid **CF48** 18 D1
Abercarn **NP11** 19 F2
Abercastle **SA62** 16 B2
Abercegir **SY20** 37 H5
Aberchalder **PH35** 87 K4
Aberchirder **AB54** 98 E5
Abercorn **EH30** 75 J3
Abercraf **SA9** 27 H7
Abercregan **SA13** 18 B2
Abercrombie **KY10** 83 G7
Abercrychan **SA20** 27 G5
Abercwmboi **CF44** 18 D1
Abercych **SA37** 17 F1
Abercynafon **LD3** 27 K7
Abercynon **CF45** 18 D2
Abercywarch **SY20** 37 H4
Aberdalgie **PH2** 82 B5
Aberdare CF44 18 C1
Aberdaron **LL53** 36 A3
Aberdaugleddau (Milford Haven) SA73 16 B5
ABERDEEN AB 91 H4
Aberdeen Airport **AB21** 91 G3
Aberdesach **LL54** 46 C7
Aberdour **KY3** 75 K2
Aberdovey (Aberdyfi) LL35 37 F6
Aberduhonw **LD2** 27 K3
Aberdulais **SA10** 18 A2
Aberdyfi (Aberdovey) LL35 37 F6
Aberedw **LD2** 27 K4
Abereiddy **SA62** 16 A2
Abererch **LL53** 36 C2
Aberfan **CF48** 18 D1
Aberfeldy PH15 81 K3
Aberffraw **LL63** 46 B6
Aberffrwd **SY23** 27 F1
Aberford **LS25** 57 K6
Aberfoyle **FK8** 81 G7
Abergavenny (Y Fenni) NP7 28 B7
Abergele LL22 47 H5
Aber-Giâr **SA40** 17 J1
Abergorlech **SA32** 17 J2
Abergwaun (Fishguard) SA65 16 C2
Abergwesyn **LD5** 27 H3
Abergwili **SA31** 17 H3
Abergwydol **SY20** 37 G5
Abergwynant **LL40** 37 F4
Abergwynfi **SA13** 18 B2
Abergwyngregyn **LL33** 46 E5
Abergynolwyn **LL36** 37 F5
Aberhafesp **SY16** 37 K6
Aberhonddu (Brecon) LD3 27 K6
Aberhosan **SY20** 37 H6
Aberkenfig **CF32** 18 B3
Aberlady **EH32** 76 C2
Aberlemno **DD8** 83 G2
Aberllefenni **SY20** 37 G5
Aber-llia **CF44** 27 J7
Aberllynfi (Three Cocks) **LD3** 28 A5
Aberlour (Charlestown of Aberlour) AB38 97 K7
Abermad **SY23** 26 E1
Abermaw (Barmouth) LL42 37 F4
Abermeurig **SA48** 26 E3
Aber-miwl (Abermule) **SY15** 38 A6
Abermule (Aber-miwl) **SY15** 38 A6
Abernaint **SY22** 38 A3
Abernant *Carmar.* **SA33** 17 G3
Aber-nant *R.C.T.* **CF44** 18 D1
Abernethy **PH2** 82 C6
Abernyte **PH14** 82 D4
Aberpennar (Mountain Ash) CF45 18 D2
Aberporth **SA43** 26 B3
Aberriw (Berriew) **SY21** 38 A5
Aberscross **KW10** 96 E2
Abersky **IV2** 88 C2
Abersoch **LL53** 36 C3
Abersychan **NP4** 19 F1
ABERTAWE (SWANSEA) SA 17 K6
Aberteifi (Cardigan) SA43 16 E1
Aberthin **CF71** 18 D4
Abertillery NP13 19 F1
Abertridwr *Caerp.* **CF83** 18 E3
Abertridwr *Powys* **SY10** 37 K4
Abertysswg **NP22** 18 E1
Aberuthven **PH3** 82 A6
Aberyscir **LD3** 27 J6
Aberystwyth SY23 36 E7
Abhainnsuidhe **HS3** 100 C7
Abingdon OX14 21 H2
Abinger Common **RH5** 22 E7
Abinger Hammer **RH5** 22 D7
Abington **ML12** 68 E1
Abington Pigotts **SG8** 33 G4
Abingworth **RH20** 12 E5
Ablington *Glos.* **GL7** 20 E1
Ablington *Wilts.* **SP4** 20 E7
Abney **S32** 50 D5
Above Church **ST10** 50 C7
Aboyne AB34 90 D5
Abram **WN2** 49 F2
Abriachan **IV3** 88 C1
Abridge **RM4** 23 H2
Abronhill **G67** 75 F3
Abson **BS30** 20 A4
Abthorpe **NN12** 31 H4
Abune-the-Hill **KW17** 106 B5
Aby **LN13** 53 H5
Acaster Malbis **YO23** 58 B5
Acaster Selby **YO23** 58 B5
Accrington BB5 56 C7
Accurrach **PA33** 80 C5
Acha **PA78** 78 C2
Achacha **PA37** 80 A3
Achadacaie **PA29** 73 G4
Achadh Mòr **HS2** 101 F5
Achadh-chaorrunn **PA29** 73 F5
Achadunan **PA26** 80 D6
Achagavel **PH33** 79 J2
Achaglass **PA29** 73 F6
Achahoish **PA31** 73 F3
Achalader **PH10** 82 C3
Achallader **PA36** 80 E3
Achamore **PA60** 72 D3
Achandunie **IV17** 96 D4
Achany **IV27** 96 C1
Achaphubuil **PH33** 87 G7
Acharacle PH36 79 H1
Achargary **KW11** 104 C3
Acharn *Arg. & B.* **PA35** 80 C4
Acharn *P. & K.* **PH15** 81 J3
Acharonich **PA73** 79 F4
Acharosson **PA21** 73 H3
Achateny **PH36** 86 B7
Achath **AB32** 91 F3
Achavanich **KW5** 105 G4
Achddu **SA16** 17 H5
Achduart **IV26** 95 G1
Achentoul **KW11** 104 D5
Achfary **IV27** 102 E5
Achgarve **IV22** 94 E2
Achiemore *High.* **IV27** 103 F2
Achiemore *High.* **KW13** 104 D3
Achies **KW12** 105 G3
A'Chill **PH44** 85 H4
Achiltibuie **IV26** 95 G1
Achina **KW14** 104 C2
Achindown **IV12** 97 F7
Achinduich **IV27** 96 C2
Achingills **KW12** 105 G2
Achintee **IV54** 95 F7
Achintee House **PH33** 87 H7
Achintraid **IV54** 86 E1
Achlean **PH21** 89 F5
Achleanan **PA34** 79 G2
Achleek **PH33** 79 J2
Achlian **PA33** 80 C5
Achlyness **IV27** 102 E3
Achmelvich **IV27** 102 C6
Achmony **IV63** 88 C1
Achmore *High.* **IV53** 86 E1
Achmore *High.* **IV23** 95 G2
Achmore *Stir.* **FK21** 81 G4
Achnaba **PA31** 73 H2
Achnabat **IV2** 88 C1
Achnabourin **KW14** 104 C3
Achnacairn **PA37** 80 A4
Achnacarnin **IV27** 102 C5
Achnacarry **PH34** 87 H6
Achnaclerach **IV23** 96 B5
Achnacloich *Arg. & B.* **PA37** 80 A4
Achnacloich *High.* **IV46** 86 B4
Achnaclyth **KW6** 105 F5
Achnacraig **PA73** 79 F3
Achnacroish **PA34** 79 K3
Achnadrish **PA75** 79 F2
Achnafalnich **PA33** 80 D5
Achnafauld **PH8** 81 K4
Achnagairn **IV5** 96 C7
Achnagarron **IV18** 96 D4
Achnaha *High.* **PA34** 79 H3
Achnaha *High.* **PH36** 79 F1
Achnahanat **IV24** 96 C2
Achnahannet **PH26** 89 G2
Achnairn **IV27** 103 H7
Achnalea **PH33** 79 K1
Achnamara **PA31** 73 F2
Achnanellan **PH37** 79 J1
Achnasaul **PH34** 87 H6
Achnasheen IV22 95 H6
Achnashelloch **PA31** 73 G1
Achnastank **AB55** 89 K1
Achorn **KW6** 105 G5
Achosnich *High.* **IV25** 96 E2
Achosnich *High.* **PH36** 79 F1
Achreamie **KW14** 105 F2
Achriabhach **PH33** 80 C1
Achriesgill **IV27** 102 E3
Achtoty **KW14** 103 J2
Achurch **PE8** 42 D7
Achuvoldrach **IV27** 103 H3
Achvaich **IV25** 96 E2
Achvarasdal **KW14** 104 E2
Achvlair **PA38** 80 A2
Achvraie **IV26** 95 G1
Ackenthwaite **LA7** 55 J1
Ackergill **KW1** 105 J3
Acklam *Middbro.* **TS5** 63 F5
Acklam *N.Yorks.* **YO17** 58 D3
Ackleton **WV6** 39 G6
Acklington **NE65** 71 H3
Ackton **WF7** 57 K7
Ackworth Moor Top **WF7** 51 G1
Acle **NR13** 45 J4
Acock's Green **B27** 40 D7
Acol **CT7** 25 K5
Acomb *Northumb.* **NE46** 70 E7
Acomb *York* **YO24** 58 B4
Aconbury **HR2** 28 E5
Acre **BB5** 56 C7
Acrefair **LL14** 38 B1
Acrise Place **CT18** 15 G3
Acton *Ches.E.* **CW5** 49 F7
Acton *Dorset* **BH19** 9 J7
Acton *Gt.Lon.* **W3** 22 E3
Acton *Shrop.* **SY9** 38 C7
Acton *Staffs.* **ST5** 40 A1
Acton *Suff.* **CO10** 34 C4
Acton *Worcs.* **DY13** 29 H2
Acton *Wrex.* **LL12** 48 C7
Acton Beauchamp **WR6** 29 F3
Acton Bridge **CW8** 48 E5
Acton Burnell **SY5** 38 E5
Acton Green **WR6** 29 F3
Acton Pigott **SY5** 38 E5
Acton Round **WV16** 39 F6
Acton Scott **SY6** 38 D7
Acton Trussell **ST17** 40 B4
Acton Turville **GL9** 20 B3
Adamhill **KA1** 74 C7
Adbaston **ST20** 39 G3
Adber **DT9** 8 E2
Adderbury **OX17** 31 F5
Adderley **TF9** 39 F2
Adderstone **NE70** 77 K7
Addiewell **EH55** 75 H4
Addingham **LS29** 57 F5
Addington *Bucks.* **MK18** 31 J6
Addington *Gt.Lon.* **CR0** 23 G5
Addington *Kent* **ME19** 23 K6
Addiscombe **CR0** 23 G5
Addlestone KT15 22 D5
Addlethorpe **PE24** 53 J6
Adel **LS16** 57 H6
Adeney **TF10** 39 G4
Adeyfield **HP2** 22 D1
Adfa **SY16** 37 K5
Adforton **SY7** 28 D1
Adisham **CT3** 15 H2
Adlestrop **GL56** 30 D6
Adlingfleet **DN14** 58 E7
Adlington *Ches.E.* **SK10** 49 J4
Adlington *Lancs.* **PR7** 48 E1
Admaston *Staffs.* **WS15** 40 C3
Admaston *Tel. & W.* **TF5** 39 F4
Admington **CV36** 30 D4
Adsborough **TA2** 8 B2
Adscombe **TA5** 7 K2
Adstock **MK18** 31 J5
Adstone **NN12** 31 G3
Adversane **RH14** 12 D4
Advie **PH26** 89 J1
Adwalton **BD11** 57 H7
Adwell **OX9** 21 K2

Adwick le Street **DN6** 51 H2
Adwick upon Dearne **S64** 51 G2
Adziel **AB43** 99 H5
Ae Village **DG1** 68 E5
Affetside **BL8** 49 G1
Affleck **AB21** 91 G2
Affpuddle **DT2** 9 H5
Afon Wen **LL53** 36 D2
Afon-wen **CH7** 47 K5
Afton **PO40** 10 E6
Afton Bridgend **KA18** 68 B2
Agglethorpe **DL8** 57 F1
Aigburth **L17** 48 C4
Aiginis **HS2** 101 G4
Aike **YO25** 59 G5
Aikerness **KW17** 106 D2
Aikers **KW17** 106 D8
Aiketgate **CA4** 61 F2
Aikshaw **CA7** 60 C2
Aikton **CA7** 60 D1
Aikwood Tower **TD7** 69 K1
Ailby **LN13** 53 H5
Ailey **HR3** 28 C4
Ailsworth **PE5** 42 E6
Aimes Green **EN9** 23 H1
Aimster **KW14** 105 G2
Ainderby Quernhow **YO7** 57 J1
Ainderby Steeple **DL7** 62 E7
Aingers Green **CO7** 35 F6
Ainsdale **PR8** 48 C1
Ainsdale-on-Sea **PR8** 48 C1
Ainstable **CA4** 61 G2
Ainsworth **BL2** 49 G1
Ainthorpe **YO21** 63 J6
Aintree **L10** 48 C3
Aird *W.Isles* **HS7** 92 C6
Aird *W.Isles* **HS2** 101 H4
Aird a' Mhachair **HS8** 92 C7
Aird a' Mhulaidh **HS3** 100 D6
Aird Asaig **HS3** 100 D7
Aird Dhail **HS2** 101 G1
Aird Leimhe **HS3** 93 G3
Aird Mhige **HS3** 93 G2
Aird Mhighe **HS3** 93 F3
Aird of Sleat **IV45** 86 B4
Aird Thunga **HS2** 101 G4
Aird Uig **HS2** 100 C4
Airdrie *Fife* **KY10** 83 G7
Airdrie *N.Lan.* ML6 75 **F4**
Aire View **BD20** 56 E5
Airidh a' Bhruaich **HS2** 100 E6
Airieland **DG7** 65 H5
Airies **DG9** 66 D7
Airigh-drishaig **IV54** 86 D1
Airmyn **DN14** 58 D7
Airntully **PH1** 82 B4
Airor **PH41** 86 D4
Airth **FK2** 75 G2
Airton **BD23** 56 E4
Airyhassen **DG8** 64 D6
Aisby *Lincs.* **DN21** 52 B3
Aisby *Lincs.* **NG32** 42 D2
Aisgernis (Askernish) **HS8** 84 C2
Aisgill **CA17** 61 J7
Aish *Devon* **TQ10** 5 G4
Aish *Devon* **TQ9** 5 J5
Aisholt **TA5** 7 K2
Aiskew **DL8** 57 H1
Aislaby *N.Yorks.* **YO21** 63 K6
Aislaby *N.Yorks.* **YO18** 58 D1
Aislaby *Stock.* **TS16** 63 F5
Aisthorpe **LN1** 52 C4
Aith *Ork.* **KW16** 106 B6
Aith *Ork.* **KW17** 106 F5
Aith *Shet.* **ZE2** 107 M7
Aith *Shet.* **ZE2** 107 Q3
Aithsetter **ZE2** 107 N9
Aitnoch **PH26** 89 G1
Akeld **NE71** 70 E1
Akeley **MK18** 31 J5
Akenham **IP1** 35 F4
Albaston **PL18** 4 E3
Albecq **GY5** 3 H5
Alberbury **SY5** 38 C4
Albert Town **SA61** 16 C4
Albourne **BN6** 13 F5
Albourne Green **BN6** 13 F5
Albrighton *Shrop.* **WV7** 40 A5
Albrighton *Shrop.* **SY4** 38 D4
Alburgh **IP20** 45 G7
Albury *Herts.* **SG11** 33 H6
Albury *Oxon.* **OX9** 21 K1
Albury *Surr.* **GU5** 22 D7
Albury End **SG11** 33 H6
Albury Heath **GU5** 22 D7
Albyfield **CA8** 61 G1
Alcaig **IV7** 96 C6
Alcaston **SY6** 38 D7
Alcester B49 30 **B3**
Alciston **BN26** 13 J6
Alcombe **TA24** 7 H1
Alconbury **PE28** 32 E1
Alconbury Hill **PE28** 32 E1
Alconbury Weston **PE28** 32 E1
Aldborough *N.Yorks.* **YO51** 57 K3
Aldborough *Norf.* **NR11** 45 F2
Aldbourne **SN8** 21 F4
Aldbrough **HU11** 59 J6
Aldbrough St. John **DL11** 62 D5
Aldbury **HP23** 32 C7
Aldclune **PH16** 82 A1
Aldeburgh IP15 35 **J3**
Aldeby **NR34** 45 J6
Aldenham **WD25** 22 E2
Alderbury **SP5** 10 C2
Alderford **NR9** 45 F4
Alderholt **SP6** 10 C3
Alderley **GL12** 20 A2
Alderley Edge SK9 49 **H5**
Aldermaston **RG7** 21 J5
Aldermaston Wharf **RG7** 21 K5
Alderminster **CV37** 30 D4
Alderney **GY9** 3 K4
Alderney Airport **GY9** 3 J4
Alder's End **HR1** 29 F5
Aldersey Green **CH3** 48 D7
Aldershot GU11 22 **B6**
Alderton *Glos.* **GL20** 29 J5
Alderton *Northants.* **NN12** 31 J4
Alderton *Suff.* **IP12** 35 H4
Alderton *Wilts.* **SN14** 20 B3
Alderwasley **DE56** 51 F7
Aldfield **HG4** 57 H3
Aldford **CH3** 48 D7
Aldham *Essex* **CO6** 34 D6
Aldham *Suff.* **IP7** 34 E4
Aldie *Aber.* **AB42** 99 J6
Aldie *High.* **IV19** 96 E3
Aldingbourne **PO20** 12 C6
Aldingham **LA12** 55 F2
Aldington *Kent* **TN25** 15 F4
Aldington *Worcs.* **WR11** 30 B4
Aldivalloch **AB54** 90 B2
Aldochlay **G83** 74 B1
Aldons **KA26** 67 F5
Aldous's Corner **IP19** 45 H7
Aldreth **CB6** 33 H1
Aldridge **WS9** 40 C5
Aldringham **IP16** 35 J2
Aldsworth *Glos.* **GL54** 20 E1
Aldsworth *W.Suss.* **PO10** 11 J4
Aldunie **AB54** 90 B2
Aldville **PH8** 82 A4
Aldwark *Derbys.* **DE4** 50 E7
Aldwark *N.Yorks.* **YO61** 57 K3
Aldwick **PO21** 12 C7
Aldwincle **NN14** 42 D7
Aldworth **RG8** 21 J4
Alexandria G83 74 **B3**
Aley **TA5** 7 K2
Aley Green **LU1** 32 D7
Alfardisworthy **EX22** 6 A4
Alfington **EX11** 7 K6
Alfold **GU6** 12 D3
Alfold Crossways **GU6** 12 D3
Alford *Aber.* AB33 90 **D3**
Alford *Lincs.* LN13 53 **H5**
Alford *Som.* **BA7** 9 F1
Alfreton DE55 51 **G7**
Alfrick **WR6** 29 G3
Alfrick Pound **WR6** 29 G3
Alfriston **BN26** 13 J6
Algarkirk **PE20** 43 F2
Alhampton **BA4** 9 F1
Alkborough **DN15** 58 E7
Alkerton **OX15** 30 E4
Alkham **CT15** 15 H3
Alkington **SY13** 38 E2
Alkmonton **DE6** 40 D2
All Cannings **SN10** 20 D5
All Saints South Elmham **IP19** 45 H7
All Stretton **SY6** 38 D6
Allaleigh **TQ9** 5 J5
Allanaquoich **AB35** 89 J5
Allancreich **AB34** 90 D5
Allanfearn **IV2** 96 E7
Allangillfoot **DG13** 69 H4
Allanton *D. & G.* **DG2** 68 E5
Allanton *E.Ayr.* **KA17** 74 E7
Allanton *N.Lan.* **ML7** 75 G5
Allanton *S.Lan.* **ML3** 75 F5
Allanton *Sc.Bord.* **TD11** 77 G5
Allardice **DD10** 91 G7
Allathasdal **HS9** 84 B4
Allbrook **SO50** 11 F2
Allendale Town **NE47** 61 K1
Allenheads **NE47** 61 K2
Allen's Green **CM21** 33 H7
Allensford **DH8** 62 B1
Allensmore **HR2** 28 D5
Allenton **DE24** 41 F2
Aller **TA10** 8 D2
Allerby **CA7** 60 B3
Allercombe **EX5** 7 J6
Allerford *Devon* **EX20** 6 C7
Allerford *Som.* **TA24** 7 H1
Allerston **YO18** 58 E1
Allerthorpe **YO42** 58 D5
Allerton *Mersey.* **L18** 48 D4
Allerton *W.Yorks.* **BD15** 57 G6
Allerton Bywater **WF10** 57 K7
Allerton Mauleverer **HG5** 57 K4
Allesley **CV5** 40 E7
Allestree **DE22** 41 F2
Allet Common **TR4** 2 E4
Allexton **LE15** 42 B5
Allgreave **SK11** 49 J6
Allhallows **ME3** 24 E4
Allhallows-on-Sea **ME3** 24 E4
Alligin Shuas **IV22** 94 E6
Allimore Green **ST18** 40 A4
Allington *Dorset* **DT6** 8 D5
Allington *Lincs.* **NG32** 42 B1
Allington *Wilts.* **SP4** 10 D1
Allington *Wilts.* **SN10** 20 D5
Allington *Wilts.* **SN14** 20 B4
Allithwaite **LA11** 55 G2
Allnabad **IV27** 103 G4
Alloa FK10 75 **G1**
Allonby **CA15** 60 B2
Allostock **WA16** 49 G5
Alloway **KA7** 67 H2
Allowenshay **TA17** 8 C3
Allscot **WV15** 39 G6
Allscott **TF6** 39 F4
Allt na h-Airbhe **IV26** 95 H2
Alltachonaich **PA34** 79 J2
Alltbeithe **IV4** 87 G2
Alltforgan **SY10** 37 J3
Alltmawr **LD2** 27 K4
Alltnacaillich **IV27** 103 G4
Allt-na-subh **IV40** 87 F1
Alltsigh **IV63** 88 B3
Alltwalis **SA32** 17 H2
Alltwen **SA8** 18 A1
Alltyblaca **SA40** 17 J1
Allwood Green **IP22** 34 E1
Almeley **HR3** 28 C3
Almeley Wootton **HR3** 28 C3
Almer **DT11** 9 J5
Almington **TF9** 39 G2
Almiston Cross **EX39** 6 B3
Almondbank **PH1** 82 B5
Almondbury **HD4** 50 D1
Almondsbury **BS32** 19 K3
Alne **YO61** 57 K3
Alness IV17 96 **D5**
Alnham **NE66** 70 E2
Alnmouth **NE66** 71 H2
Alnwick NE66 71 **G2**
Alperton **HA0** 22 E3
Alphamstone **CO8** 34 C5
Alpheton **CO10** 34 C3
Alphington **EX2** 7 H6
Alport **DE45** 50 E6
Alpraham **CW6** 48 E7
Alresford **CO7** 34 E6
Alrewas **DE13** 40 D4
Alrick **PH11** 82 C1
Alsager **ST7** 49 G7
Alsagers Bank **ST7** 40 A1
Alsop en le Dale **DE6** 50 D7
Alston *Cumb.* CA9 61 **J2**
Alston *Devon* **EX13** 8 C4
Alston Sutton **BS26** 19 H6
Alstone *Glos.* **GL20** 29 J5
Alstone *Som.* **TA9** 19 G7
Alstone *Staffs.* **ST18** 40 A4
Alstonefield **DE6** 50 D7
Alswear **EX36** 7 F3
Alt **OL8** 49 J2
Altandhu **IV26** 102 B7
Altanduin **KW11** 104 D6
Altarnun **PL15** 4 C2
Altass **IV27** 96 C1
Altens **AB12** 91 H4
Alterwall **KW1** 105 H2
Altham **BB5** 56 C6
Althorne **CM3** 25 F2
Althorpe **DN17** 52 B2
Alticry **DG8** 64 C5
Altnafeadh **PH49** 80 D2
Altnaharra **IV27** 103 H5
Altofts **WF6** 57 J7
Alton *Derbys.* **S42** 51 F6
Alton *Hants.* GU34 11 **J1**
Alton *Staffs.* **ST10** 40 C1
Alton Barnes **SN8** 20 E5
Alton Pancras **DT2** 9 G4
Alton Priors **SN8** 20 E5
Altonside **IV30** 97 K6
Altrincham WA14 49 **G4**
Altura **PH34** 87 J5
Alva FK12 75 **G1**
Alvanley **WA6** 48 D5
Alvaston **DE24** 41 F2
Alvechurch **B48** 30 B1
Alvecote **B79** 40 E5
Alvediston **SP5** 9 J2
Alveley **WV15** 39 G7
Alverdiscott **EX31** 6 D3
Alverstoke **PO12** 11 H5
Alverstone **PO36** 11 G6
Alverthorpe **WF2** 57 J7
Alverton **NG13** 42 A1
Alves **IV30** 97 J5
Alvescot **OX18** 21 F1
Alveston *S.Glos.* **BS35** 19 K3
Alveston *Warks.* **CV37** 30 D3
Alvie **PH21** 89 F4
Alvingham **LN11** 53 G3
Alvington **GL15** 19 K1
Alwalton **PE2** 42 E6
Alweston **DT9** 9 F3
Alwington **EX39** 6 C3
Alwinton **NE65** 70 E3
Alwoodley **LS17** 57 J5
Alwoodley Gates **LS17** 57 J5
Alyth **PH11** 82 D3
Amalebra **TR20** 2 B5
Ambaston **DE72** 41 G2
Amber Hill **PE20** 43 F1
Ambergate **DE56** 51 F7
Amberley *Glos.* **GL5** 20 B1
Amberley *W.Suss.* **BN18** 12 D5
Amble **NE65** 71 H3
Amblecote **DY8** 40 A7
Ambleside LA22 60 **E6**
Ambleston **SA62** 16 D3
Ambrismore **PA20** 73 J5
Ambrosden **OX25** 31 H7
Amcotts **DN17** 52 B1
Amersham HP6 22 **C2**
Amerton **ST18** 40 B3
Amesbury **SP4** 20 E7
Ameysford **BH22** 10 B4
Amington **B77** 40 E5
Amisfield Town **DG1** 69 F5
Amlwch LL68 46 **C3**
Amlwch Port **LL68** 46 C3
Ammanford (Rhydaman) SA18 17 **K4**
Amotherby **YO17** 58 D2
Ampfield **SO51** 10 E2
Ampleforth **YO62** 58 B2
Ampleforth College **YO62** 58 B2
Ampney Crucis **GL7** 20 D1
Ampney St. Mary **GL7** 20 D1
Ampney St. Peter **GL7** 20 D1
Amport **SP11** 21 G7
Ampthill **MK45** 32 D5
Ampton **IP31** 34 C1
Amroth **SA67** 16 E5
Amulree **PH8** 81 K4
An T-Òb (Leverburgh) **HS5** 93 F3
Anaboard **PH26** 89 H1
Anaheilt **PH36** 79 K1
Ancaster **NG32** 42 C1
Anchor **SY7** 38 A7
Anchor Corner **NR17** 44 E6
Ancroft **TD15** 77 H6
Ancrum **TD8** 70 B1
Ancton **PO22** 12 C6
Anderby **PE24** 53 J5
Anderby Creek **PE24** 53 J5
Andersea **TA7** 8 C1
Andersfield **TA5** 8 B1
Anderson **DT11** 9 H5
Anderton **CW9** 49 F5
Andover SP10 21 **G7**
Andover Down **SP11** 21 G7
Andoversford **GL54** 30 B7
Andreas **IM7** 54 D4
Anelog **LL53** 36 A3
Anfield **L4** 48 C3
Angarrack **TR27** 2 C5
Angarrick **TR3** 2 E5
Angelbank **SY8** 28 E1
Angerton **CA7** 60 D1
Angle **SA71** 16 B5
Angler's Retreat **SY20** 37 G6
Anglesey (Ynys Môn) **LL** 46 B4
Angmering **BN16** 12 D6
Angmering-on-Sea **BN16** 12 D6
Angram *N.Yorks.* **YO23** 58 B5
Angram *N.Yorks.* **DL11** 61 K7
Anick **NE46** 70 E7
Anie **FK17** 81 G6
Ankerville **IV19** 97 F4
Anlaby **HU10** 59 G7
Anmer **PE31** 44 B3
Anmore **PO7** 11 H3
Anna Valley **SP11** 21 G7
Annan DG12 69 **G7**
Annaside **LA19** 54 D1
Annat *Arg. & B.* **PA35** 80 B5
Annat *High.* **IV22** 94 E6
Annbank **KA6** 67 J1
Annesley **NG15** 51 H7
Annesley Woodhouse **NG17** 51 G7
Annfield Plain **DH9** 62 C1
Anniesland **G13** 74 D4
Annscroft **SY5** 38 D5
Ansdell **FY8** 55 G7
Ansford **BA7** 9 F1
Ansley **CV10** 40 E6
Anslow **DE13** 40 E3
Anslow Gate **DE13** 40 D3
Ansteadbrook **GU27** 12 C3
Anstey *Herts.* **SG9** 33 H5
Anstey *Leics.* **LE7** 41 H5
Anstruther KY10 83 **G7**
Ansty *W.Suss.* **RH17** 13 F4
Ansty *Warks.* **CV7** 41 F7
Ansty *Wilts.* **SP3** 9 J2
Ansty Coombe **SP3** 9 J2
Ansty Cross **DT2** 9 G4
Anthill Common **PO7** 11 H3
Anthorn **CA7** 60 C1
Antingham **NR28** 45 G2
Anton's Gowt **PE22** 43 F1
Antony **PL11** 4 D5
Antrobus **CW9** 49 F5
Anvil Corner **EX22** 6 B5
Anvil Green **CT4** 15 G3
Anwick **NG34** 52 E7
Anwoth **DG7** 65 F5
Aoradh **PA44** 72 A4
Apethorpe **PE8** 42 D6
Apeton **ST20** 40 A4
Apley **LN8** 52 E5
Apperknowle **S18** 51 F5
Apperley **GL19** 29 H6
Apperley Bridge **BD10** 57 G6
Appersett **DL8** 61 K7
Appin PA38 80 **A3**
Appin House **PA38** 80 A3
Appleby **DN15** 52 C1
Appleby Magna **DE12** 41 F4
Appleby Parva **DE12** 41 F5
Appleby-in-Westmorland CA16 61 **H4**
Applecross **IV54** 94 D7
Appledore *Devon* **EX39** 6 C2
Appledore *Devon* **EX16** 7 J4
Appledore *Kent* **TN26** 14 E5
Appledore Heath **TN26** 14 E4
Appleford **OX14** 21 J2
Appleshaw **SP11** 21 G7
Applethwaite **CA12** 60 D4
Appleton *Halton* **WA8** 48 E4
Appleton *Oxon.* **OX13** 21 H1
Appleton Roebuck **YO23** 58 B5
Appleton Thorn **WA4** 49 F4
Appleton Wiske **DL6** 62 E6
Appleton-le-Moors **YO62** 58 D1
Appleton-le-Street **YO17** 58 D2
Appletreehall **TD9** 70 A2
Appletreewick **BD23** 57 F3
Appley **TA21** 7 J3
Appley Bridge **WN6** 48 E2
Apse Heath **PO36** 11 G6
Apsey Green **IP13** 35 G2
Apsley **HP3** 22 D1
Apsley End **SG5** 32 E5
Apuldram **PO20** 12 B6
Arberth (Narberth) SA67 16 **E4**
Arbirlot **DD11** 83 G3
Arborfield **RG2** 22 A5
Arborfield Cross **RG2** 22 A5
Arborfield Garrison **RG2** 22 A5
Arbourthorne **S2** 51 F4
Arbroath DD11 83 **H3**
Arbuthnott **AB30** 91 F7
Archdeacon Newton **DL2** 62 D5
Archiestown **AB38** 97 K7
Arclid **CW11** 49 G6
Ard a' Chapuill **PA22** 73 J2
Ardachearanbeg **PA22** 73 J2
Ardacheranmor **PA22** 73 J2
Ardachoil **PA65** 79 J4
Ardachu **IV28** 96 D1
Ardailly **PA41** 72 E5
Ardalanish **PA67** 78 E6
Ardallie **AB42** 91 J1
Ardanaiseig **PA35** 80 B5
Ardaneaskan **IV54** 86 E1
Ardanstur **PA34** 79 K6
Ardantiobairt **PA34** 79 H2
Ardantrive **PA34** 79 K5
Ardarroch **IV54** 94 E7
Ardbeg *Arg. & B.* **PA20** 73 J4
Ardbeg *Arg. & B.* **PA42** 72 C6
Ardbeg *Arg. & B.* **PA23** 73 K2
Ardblair **IV4** 88 C1
Ardbrecknish **PA33** 80 B5
Ardcharnich **IV23** 95 H3
Ardchiavaig **PA67** 78 E6
Ardchonnel **PA37** 80 A4
Ardchonnell **PA33** 80 A6
Ardchrishnish **PA70** 79 F5
Ardchronie **IV24** 96 D3
Ardchuilk **IV4** 87 J1
Ardchullarie More **FK18** 81 G6
Ardchyle **FK21** 81 G5
Arddlin **SY22** 38 B4
Ardechvie **PH34** 87 H5
Ardeley **SG2** 33 G6
Ardelve **IV40** 86 E2
Arden **G83** 74 B2
Ardencaple House **PA34** 79 J6
Ardens Grafton **B49** 30 C3
Ardentallan **PA34** 79 K5
Ardentinny **PA23** 73 K2
Ardeonaig **FK21** 81 H4
Ardersier **IV2** 96 E6
Ardery **PH36** 79 J1
Ardessie **IV23** 95 G3
Ardfad **PA34** 79 J6
Ardfern **PA31** 79 K7
Ardfin **PA60** 72 C4
Ardgartan **G83** 80 D7
Ardgay IV24 96 **D2**
Ardgenavan **PA26** 80 C6
Ardgour (Corran) **PH33** 80 B1
Ardgowan **PA16** 74 A3
Ardgowse **AB33** 90 E3
Ardgye **IV30** 97 J5
Ardhallow **PA23** 73 K3
Ardheslaig **IV54** 94 D6
Ardiecow **AB45** 98 D4
Ardinamar **PA34** 79 J6
Ardindrean **IV23** 95 H3
Ardingly **RH17** 13 G4
Ardington **OX12** 21 H3
Ardington Wick **OX12** 21 H3
Ardintoul **IV40** 86 E2
Ardkinglas House **PA26** 80 C6
Ardlair **AB52** 90 D2
Ardlamont **PA21** 73 H4
Ardleigh **CO7** 34 E6
Ardleigh Green **RM2** 23 J3
Ardleigh Heath **CO7** 34 E5
Ardleish **G83** 80 E6
Ardler **PH12** 82 D3
Ardley **OX27** 31 G6
Ardley End **CM22** 33 J7
Ardlui **G83** 80 E6
Ardlussa **PA60** 72 E2
Ardmaddy **PA35** 80 B4
Ardmair **IV26** 95 H2
Ardmaleish **PA20** 73 J4
Ardmay **G83** 80 D7
Ardmenish **PA60** 72 D3
Ardmhòr **HS9** 84 C4
Ardminish **PA41** 72 E6
Ardmolich **PH36** 86 D7
Ardmore *Arg. & B.* **PA42** 72 C5
Ardmore *Arg. & B.* **PA34** 79 J5
Ardmore *Arg. & B.* **G82** 74 B3
Ardmore *High.* **IV19** 96 E3
Ardnackaig **PA31** 73 F1
Ardnacross **PA72** 79 G3
Ardnadam **PA23** 73 K2
Ardnadrochit **PA64** 79 J4
Ardnagoine **IV26** 95 F1
Ardnagowan **PA25** 80 C7
Ardnahein **PA24** 73 K1
Ardnahoe **PA46** 72 C3
Ardnarff **IV53** 86 E1
Ardnastang **PH36** 79 K1
Ardnave **PA44** 72 A3
Ardno **PA26** 80 C7
Ardo **AB41** 91 G1
Ardoch *D. & G.* **DG3** 68 D3
Ardoch *Moray* **IV36** 97 J6
Ardoch *P. & K.* **PH1** 82 B4
Ardochrig **G75** 74 E6
Ardoyne **AB52** 90 E2
Ardpatrick **PA29** 73 F4
Ardpeaton **G84** 74 A2
Ardradnaig **PH15** 81 J3
Ardrishaig **PA30** 73 G2
Ardroe **IV27** 102 C6
Ardross **IV17** 96 D4
Ardrossan KA22 74 **A6**
Ardscalpsie **PA20** 73 J5

Ardshave IV25 96 E2
Ardshealach PH36 79 H1
Ardshellach PA34 79 J6
Ardsley S71 51 F2
Ardslignish PH36 79 G1
Ardtalla PA42 72 C5
Ardtalnaig PH15 81 J4
Ardtaraig PA23 73 J2
Ardteatle PA33 80 C5
Ardtoe PH36 86 C7
Ardtornish PA34 79 J3
Ardtrostan PH6 81 H5
Ardtur PA38 80 A3
Arduaine PA34 79 K6
Ardullie IV15 96 C5
Ardura PA65 79 H4
Ardvar IV27 102 D5
Ardvasar IV45 86 C4
Ardveenish HS9 84 C4
Ardveich FK19 81 H5
Ardverikie PH20 88 C6
Ardvorlich Arg. & B. G83 80 E6
Ardvorlich P. & K. FK19 81 H5
Ardwall DG7 65 F5
Ardwell D. & G. DG9 64 B6
Ardwell Moray AB54 90 B1
Ardwell S.Ayr. KA26 67 F4
Ardwick M12 49 H3
Areley Kings DY13 29 H1
Arford GU35 12 B3
Argaty FK16 81 J7
Argoed NP12 18 E2
Argoed Mill LD1 27 J2
Argos Hill TN20 13 J4
Argrennan House DG7 65 H5
Arichamish PA31 80 A7
Arichastlich PA33 80 D4
Arichonan PA31 73 F1
Aridhglas PA66 78 E5
Arienskill PH38 86 D6
Arileod PA78 78 C2
Arinacrinachd IV54 94 D6
Arinafad Beg PA31 73 F2
Arinagour PA78 78 D2
Arinambane HS8 84 C2
Arisaig PH39 86 C6
Arivegaig PH36 79 H1
Arkendale HG5 57 J3
Arkesden CB11 33 H5
Arkholme LA6 55 J2
Arkle Town DL11 62 B6
Arkleby CA7 60 C3
Arkleside DL8 57 F1
Arkleton DG13 69 J4
Arkley EN5 23 F2
Arksey DN5 51 H2
Arkwright Town S44 51 G5
Arlary KY13 82 C7
Arle GL51 29 J6
Arlecdon CA26 60 B5
Arlesey SG15 32 E5
Arleston TF1 39 F4
Arley CW9 49 F4
Arlingham GL2 29 G7
Arlington Devon EX31 6 E1
Arlington E.Suss. BN26 13 J6
Arlington Glos. GL7 20 E1
Arlington Beccott EX31 6 E1
Armadale High. KW14 104 C2
Armadale High. IV45 86 C4
Armadale W.Loth. EH48 75 H4
Armathwaite CA4 61 G2
Arminghall NR14 45 G5
Armitage WS15 40 C4
Armitage Bridge HD4 50 D1
Armley LS12 57 H6
Armscote CV37 30 D4
Armshead ST9 40 B1
Armston PE8 42 D7
Armthorpe DN3 51 J2
Arnabost PA78 78 D1
Arnaby LA18 54 E1
Arncliffe BD23 56 E2
Arncliffe Cote BD23 56 E2
Arncroach KY10 83 G7
Arne BH20 9 J6
Arnesby LE8 41 J6
Arngask PH2 82 C6
Arngibbon FK8 74 E1
Arngomery FK8 74 E1
Arnhall DD9 83 H1
Arnicle PA29 73 F7
Arnipol PH38 86 D6
Arnisdale IV40 86 E3
Arnish IV40 94 B7
Arniston Engine EH23 76 B4
Arnol HS2 101 F3
Arnold E.Riding HU11 59 H5
Arnold Notts. NG5 41 H1
Arnprior FK8 74 E1
Arnside LA5 55 H2
Arowry SY13 38 D2
Arrad Foot LA12 55 G1
Arradoul AB56 98 C4
Arram HU17 59 G5
Arran KA27 73 H7
Arras YO43 59 F5
Arrat DD9 83 H2
Arrathorne DL8 62 D7
Arreton PO30 11 G6
Arrington SG8 33 G3
Arrivain FK20 80 D4
Arrochar G83 80 E7
Arrow B49 30 B3
Arscaig IV27 103 H7
Arscott SY5 38 D5
Arthington LS21 57 H5
Arthingworth LE16 42 A7
Arthog LL39 37 F4
Arthrath AB41 91 H1
Arthurstone PH12 82 D3
Artrochie AB41 91 J1
Aruadh PA49 72 A4
Arundel BN18 12 D6
Aryhoulan PH33 80 B1
Asby CA14 60 B4
Ascog PA20 73 K4
Ascot SL5 22 C5
Ascott CV36 30 E5
Ascott d'Oyley OX7 30 E7
Ascott Earl OX7 30 D7
Ascott-under-Wychwood OX7 30 E7
Ascreavie DD8 82 E2
Asenby YO7 57 K2
Asfordby LE14 42 A4
Asfordby Hill LE14 42 A4
Asgarby Lincs. PE23 53 G6
Asgarby Lincs. NG34 42 E1
Ash Dorset DT11 9 H3
Ash Kent CT3 15 H2
Ash Kent TN15 24 C5
Ash Som. TA12 8 D2
Ash Surr. GU12 22 B6
Ash Barton EX20 6 D5
Ash Bullayne EX17 7 F5
Ash Green Surr. GU12 22 C7
Ash Green Warks. CV7 41 F7
Ash Magna SY13 38 E2
Ash Mill EX36 7 F3
Ash Parva SY13 38 E2
Ash Priors TA4 7 K3
Ash Street IP7 34 E4
Ash Thomas EX16 7 J4
Ash Vale GU12 22 B6
Ashampstead RG8 21 J4
Ashbocking IP6 35 F3
Ashbourne DE6 40 D1
Ashbrittle TA21 7 J3
Ashburnham Place TN33 13 K5
Ashburton TQ13 5 H4
Ashbury Devon EX20 6 D6
Ashbury Oxon. SN6 21 F3
Ashby DN16 52 B2
Ashby by Partney PE23 53 H6
Ashby cum Fenby DN37 53 F2
Ashby de la Launde LN4 52 D7
Ashby de la Zouch LE65 41 F4
Ashby Dell NR32 45 J6
Ashby Folville LE14 42 A4
Ashby Hill DN37 53 F2
Ashby Magna LE17 41 H6
Ashby Parva LE17 41 H7
Ashby Puerorum LN9 53 G5
Ashby St. Ledgers CV23 31 G2
Ashby St. Mary NR14 45 H5
Ashchurch GL20 29 J5
Ashcombe Devon EX7 5 K3
Ashcombe N.Som. BS22 19 G5
Ashcott TA7 8 D1
Ashdon CB10 33 J4
Ashe RG25 21 J7
Asheldham CM0 25 F1
Ashen CO10 34 B4
Ashenden TN30 14 D4
Ashendon HP18 31 J7
Ashens PA29 73 G3
Ashfield Arg. & B. PA31 73 F2
Ashfield Here. HR9 28 E6
Ashfield Stir. FK15 81 J7
Ashfield Suff. IP14 35 G2
Ashfield Green Suff. IP21 35 G1
Ashfield Green Suff. CB8 34 B3
Ashfold Crossways RH13 13 F4
Ashford Devon TQ7 5 G6
Ashford Devon EX31 6 D2
Ashford Hants. SP6 10 C3
Ashford Kent TN23 15 F3
Ashford Surr. TW15 22 D4
Ashford Bowdler SY8 28 E1
Ashford Carbonel SY8 28 E1
Ashford Hill RG19 21 J5
Ashford in the Water DE45 50 D5
Ashgill ML9 75 F5
Ashiestiel TD1 76 C7
Ashill Devon EX15 7 J4
Ashill Norf. IP25 44 C5
Ashill Som. TA19 8 C3
Ashingdon SS4 24 E2
Ashington Northumb. NE63 71 H5
Ashington Som. BA22 8 E2
Ashington W.Suss. RH20 12 E5
Ashkirk TD7 69 K1
Ashlett SO45 11 F4
Ashleworth GL19 29 H6
Ashleworth Quay GL19 29 H6
Ashley Cambs. CB8 33 K2
Ashley Ches.E. WA15 49 G4
Ashley Devon EX18 6 E4
Ashley Glos. GL8 20 C2
Ashley Hants. SO20 10 E1
Ashley Hants. BH25 10 D5
Ashley Kent CT15 15 J3
Ashley Northants. LE16 42 A6
Ashley Staffs. TF9 39 G2
Ashley Wilts. SN13 20 B5
Ashley Down BS7 19 J4
Ashley Green HP5 22 C1
Ashley Heath Dorset BH24 10 C4
Ashley Heath Staffs. TF9 39 G2
Ashmanhaugh NR12 45 H3
Ashmansworth RG20 21 H6
Ashmansworthy EX39 6 B4
Ashmore Dorset SP5 9 J3
Ashmore P. & K. PH10 82 C2
Ashmore Green RG18 21 J5
Ashorne CV35 30 E3
Ashover S45 51 F6
Ashover Hay S45 51 F6
Ashow CV8 30 E1
Ashperton HR8 29 F4
Ashprington TQ9 5 J5
Ashreigney EX18 6 E4
Ashtead KT21 22 E6
Ashton Ches.W. & C. CH3 48 E6
Ashton Cornw. TR13 2 D6
Ashton Cornw. PL17 4 D4
Ashton Hants. SO32 11 G3
Ashton Here. HR6 28 E2
Ashton Inclyde PA19 74 A3
Ashton Northants. PE8 42 D7
Ashton Northants. NN7 31 J4
Ashton Peter. PE9 42 E5
Ashton Common BA14 20 B6
Ashton Keynes SN6 20 D2
Ashton under Hill WR11 29 J5
Ashton upon Mersey M33 49 G3
Ashton-in-Makerfield WN4 48 E3
Ashton-under-Lyne OL7 49 J3
Ashurst Hants. SO40 10 E3
Ashurst Kent TN3 13 J3
Ashurst W.Suss. BN44 12 E5
Ashurst Bridge SO40 10 E3
Ashurstwood RH18 13 H3
Ashwater EX21 6 B6
Ashwell Herts. SG7 33 F5
Ashwell Rut. LE15 42 B4
Ashwell End SG7 33 F4
Ashwellthorpe NR16 45 F6
Ashwick BA3 19 K7
Ashwicken PE32 44 B4
Ashybank TD9 70 A2
Askam in Furness LA16 55 F2
Askern DN6 51 H1
Askernish (Aisgernis) HS8 84 C2
Askerswell DT2 8 E5
Askett HP27 22 B1
Askham Cumb. CA10 61 G4
Askham Notts. NG22 51 K5
Askham Bryan YO23 58 B5
Askham Richard YO23 58 B5
Asknish PA31 73 H1
Askrigg DL8 62 A7
Askwith LS21 57 G5
Aslackby NG34 42 D2
Aslacton NR15 45 F6
Aslockton NG13 42 A1
Asloun AB33 90 D3
Aspall IP14 35 F2
Aspatria CA7 60 C2
Aspenden SG9 33 G6
Asperton PE20 43 F2
Aspley Guise MK17 32 C5
Aspley Heath MK17 32 C5
Aspull WN2 49 F2
Asselby DN14 58 D7
Asserby LN13 53 H5
Assington CO10 34 D5
Assington Green CO10 34 B3
Astbury CW12 49 H6
Astcote NN12 31 H3
Asterby LN11 53 F5
Asterley SY5 38 C5
Asterton SY7 38 D6
Asthall OX18 30 D7
Asthall Leigh OX29 30 E7
Astle SK10 49 H5
Astley Gt.Man. M29 49 G2
Astley Shrop. SY4 38 E4
Astley Warks. CV10 41 F7
Astley Worcs. DY13 29 G2
Astley Abbotts WV16 39 G6
Astley Bridge BL1 49 G1
Astley Cross DY13 29 H2
Astley Green M29 49 G3
Astley Lodge SY4 38 E4
Aston Ches.E. CW5 39 F1
Aston Ches.W. & C. WA7 48 E5
Aston Derbys. S33 50 D4
Aston Derbys. DE6 40 D2
Aston Flints. CH5 48 C6
Aston Here. SY8 28 D1
Aston Here. HR6 28 D2
Aston Herts. SG2 33 F6
Aston Oxon. OX18 21 G1
Aston S.Yorks. S26 51 G4
Aston Shrop. SY4 38 E3
Aston Shrop. WV5 40 A6
Aston Staffs. TF9 39 G1
Aston Tel. & W. TF6 39 F5
Aston W'ham RG9 22 A3
Aston W.Mid. B6 40 C7
Aston Abbotts HP22 32 B6
Aston Botterell WV16 39 F7
Aston Cantlow B95 30 C3
Aston Clinton HP22 32 B7
Aston Crews HR9 29 F6
Aston Cross GL20 29 J5
Aston End SG2 33 F6
Aston Eyre WV16 39 F6
Aston Fields B60 29 J2
Aston Flamville LE10 41 G6
Aston Heath WA7 48 E5
Aston Ingham HR9 29 F6
Aston juxta Mondrum CW5 49 F7
Aston le Walls NN11 31 F3
Aston Magna GL56 30 C5
Aston Munslow SY7 38 E7
Aston on Carrant GL20 29 J5
Aston on Clun SY7 38 C7
Aston Pigott SY5 38 C5
Aston Rogers SY5 38 C5
Aston Rowant OX49 22 A2
Aston Sandford HP17 22 A1
Aston Somerville WR12 30 B5
Aston Subedge GL55 30 C4
Aston Tirrold OX11 21 J3
Aston Upthorpe OX11 21 J3
Aston-by-Stone ST15 40 B2
Aston-on-Trent DE72 41 G3
Astwick SG5 33 F5
Astwood MK16 32 C4
Astwood Bank B96 30 B2
Aswarby NG34 42 D1
Aswardby PE23 53 G5
Aswick Grange PE12 43 G4
Atch Lench WR11 30 B3
Atcham SY5 38 E5
Ath Linne HS2 100 D6
Athelhampton DT2 9 G5
Athelington IP21 35 G1
Athelney TA7 8 C2
Athelstaneford EH39 76 D3
Atherington Devon EX37 6 D3
Atherington W.Suss. BN17 12 D6
Athersley North S71 51 F2
Atherstone CV9 41 F6
Atherstone on Stour CV37 30 D3
Atherton M46 49 F2
Atlow DE6 40 E1
Attadale IV54 87 F1
Attenborough NG9 41 H2
Atterby LN8 52 C3
Attercliffe S9 51 F4
Atterley TF13 39 F6
Atterton CV13 41 F6
Attleborough Norf. NR17 44 E6
Attleborough Warks. CV11 41 F6
Attlebridge NR9 45 F4
Attleton Green CB8 34 B3
Atwick YO25 59 H4
Atworth SN12 20 B5
Auberrow HR4 28 D4
Aubourn LN5 52 C6
Auch PA36 80 E4
Auchairne KA26 67 F5
Auchallater AB35 89 J6
Auchameanach PA29 73 G5
Auchamore KA27 73 G6
Aucharnie AB54 98 E6
Aucharrigill IV27 96 B1
Auchattie AB31 90 E5
Auchavan PH11 82 C1
Auchbraad PA30 73 G2
Auchbreck AB37 89 K2
Auchenback G78 74 D5
Auchenblae AB30 91 F7
Auchenbothie PA13 74 B3
Auchenbrack DG3 68 C4
Auchenbreck PA22 73 J2
Auchencairn DG7 65 H5
Auchencrow TD14 77 G4
Auchendinny EH26 76 A4
Auchendolly DG7 65 H4
Auchenfoyle PA13 74 B3
Auchengillan G63 74 D2
Auchengray ML11 75 H5
Auchenhalrig IV32 98 B4
Auchenheath ML11 75 G6
Auchenhessnane DG3 68 D4
Auchenlochan PA21 73 H3
Auchenmalg DG8 64 C5
Auchenrivock DG14 69 J5
Auchentiber KA13 74 B6
Auchenvennel G84 74 A2
Auchessan FK20 81 F5
Auchgourish PH24 89 G3
Auchinafaud PA29 73 F5
Auchincruive KA6 67 H1
Auchindarrach PA31 73 G2
Auchindarroch PA38 80 B2
Auchindrain PA32 80 B7
Auchindrean IV23 95 H3
Auchininna AB53 98 E6
Auchinleck KA18 67 K1
Auchinloch G66 74 E3
Auchinner PH6 81 H6
Auchinroath AB38 97 K6
Auchintoul Aber. AB33 90 D3
Auchintoul Aber. AB54 98 E5
Auchintoul High. IV27 96 C2
Auchiries AB42 91 J1
Auchleven AB52 90 E2
Auchlochan ML11 75 G7
Auchlunachan IV23 95 H3
Auchlunies AB12 91 G5
Auchlunkart AB55 98 B6
Auchlyne FK21 81 G5
Auchmacoy AB41 91 H1
Auchmair AB54 90 B2
Auchmantle DG8 64 B4
Auchmithie DD11 83 H3
Auchmuirbridge KY6 82 D7
Auchmull DD9 90 D7
Auchnabony DG6 65 H6
Auchnabreac PA32 80 B7
Auchnacloich PH8 81 K4
Auchnacraig PA64 79 J4
Auchnacree DD8 83 F1
Auchnafree PH8 81 K4
Auchnagallin PH26 89 H1
Auchnagatt AB41 99 H6
Auchnaha PA21 73 H2
Auchnangoul PA32 80 B7
Aucholzie AB35 90 B5
Auchorrie AB51 90 E4
Auchrannie PH11 82 D2
Auchraw FK19 81 G5
Auchreoch FK20 80 E5
Auchronie DD9 90 C6
Auchterarder PH3 82 A6
Auchtercairn IV21 94 E4
Auchterderran KY5 76 A1
Auchterhouse DD3 82 E4
Auchtermuchty KY14 82 D6
Auchterneed IV14 96 B6
Auchtertool KY2 76 A1
Auchtertyre Angus PH12 82 D3
Auchtertyre High. IV40 86 E2
Auchtertyre Moray IV30 97 J6
Auchtertyre Stir. FK20 80 E5
Auchtubh FK19 81 G5
Auckengill KW1 105 J2
Auckley DN9 51 J2
Audenshaw M34 49 J3
Audlem CW3 39 F1
Audley ST7 49 G7
Audley End Essex CB11 33 J5
Audley End Essex CO9 34 C5
Audley End Suff. IP29 34 C3
Audmore ST20 40 A3
Auds AB45 98 E4
Aughton E.Riding YO42 58 D6
Aughton Lancs. L39 48 C2
Aughton Lancs. LA2 55 J3
Aughton S.Yorks. S26 51 G4
Aughton Wilts. SN8 21 F6
Aughton Park L39 48 D2
Auldearn IV12 97 G6
Aulden HR6 28 D3
Auldgirth DG2 68 E5
Auldhame EH39 76 D2
Auldhouse G75 74 E5
Aulich PH17 81 H2
Ault a'chruinn IV40 87 F2
Ault Hucknall S44 51 G6
Aultanrynie IV27 103 F5
Aultbea IV22 94 E3
Aultgrishan IV21 94 D3
Aultguish Inn IV23 95 K4
Aultibea KW7 105 F6
Aultiphurst KW14 104 D2
Aultmore AB55 98 C5
Ault-na-goire IV2 88 C2
Aultnamain Inn IV19 96 D3
Aultnapaddock AB55 98 B6
Aulton AB52 90 E2
Aultvaich IV4 96 C7
Aultvoulin PH41 86 D4
Aunby PE9 42 D4
Aundorach PH25 89 G3
Aunk EX15 7 J5
Aunsby NG34 42 D2
Auquhorthies AB51 91 G2
Aust BS35 19 J3
Austerfield DN10 51 J3
Austrey CV9 40 E5
Austwick LA2 56 C3
Authorpe LN11 53 H4
Authorpe Row PE24 53 J5
Avebury SN8 20 E4
Avebury Trusloe SN8 20 D5
Aveley RM15 23 J3
Avening GL8 20 B2
Averham NG23 51 K7
Avery Hill SE9 23 H4
Aveton Gifford TQ7 5 G6
Avielochan PH22 89 G3
Aviemore PH22 89 F3
Avington Hants. SO21 11 G1
Avington W.Berks. RG17 21 G5
Avoch IV9 96 D6
Avon BH23 10 C5
Avon Dassett CV47 31 F3
Avonbridge FK1 75 H3
Avoncliff BA15 20 B6
Avonmouth BS11 19 J4
Avonwick TQ10 5 H5
Awbridge SO51 10 E2
Awhirk DG9 64 A5
Awkley BS35 19 J3
Awliscombe EX14 7 K5
Awre GL14 20 A1
Awsworth NG16 41 G1
Axbridge BS26 19 H6
Axford Hants. RG25 21 K7
Axford Wilts. SN8 21 F4
Axminster EX13 8 B5
Axmouth EX12 8 B5
Axton CH8 47 K4
Axtown PL20 5 F4
Aycliffe DL5 62 D4
Aydon NE45 71 F7
Aylburton GL15 19 K1
Ayle CA9 61 J2
Aylesbeare EX5 7 J6
Aylesbury HP20 32 B7
Aylesby DN37 53 F2
Aylesford ME20 14 C2
Aylesham CT3 15 H2
Aylestone LE2 41 H5
Aylmerton NR11 45 F2
Aylsham NR11 45 F3
Aylton HR8 29 F5
Aymestrey HR6 28 D2
Aynho OX17 31 G5
Ayot Green AL6 33 F7
Ayot St. Lawrence AL6 32 E7
Ayot St. Peter AL6 33 F7
Ayr KA7 67 H1
Aysgarth DL8 57 F1
Ayshford EX16 7 J4
Ayside LA11 55 G1
Ayston LE15 42 B5
Aythorpe Roding CM6 33 J7
Ayton P. & K. PH2 82 C6
Ayton Sc.Bord. TD14 77 H4
Aywick ZE2 107 P4
Azerley HG4 57 H2

B

Babbacombe TQ1 5 K4
Babbinswood SY11 38 C2
Babb's Green SG12 33 G7
Babcary TA11 8 E2

Babel SA20 27 H5
Babell CH8 47 K5
Babeny TQ13 5 G3
Bablock Hythe OX29 21 H1
Babraham CB22 33 J3
Babworth DN22 51 J4
Baby's Hill AB37 89 K1
Bac HS2 101 G3
Bachau LL71 46 C4
Back of Keppoch PH39 86 C6
Back Street CB8 34 B3
Backaland KW17 106 E4
Backaskaill KW17 106 D2
Backbarrow LA12 55 G1
Backburn AB54 90 D1
Backe SA33 17 F4
Backfolds AB42 99 J5
Backford CH2 48 D5
Backhill AB53 91 F1
Backhill of Clackriach AB42 99 H6
Backhill of Trustach AB31 90 E5
Backies *High.* KW10 97 F1
Backies *Moray* AB56 98 D5
Backlass KW1 105 H3
Backside AB54 90 C1
Backwell BS48 19 H5
Backworth NE23 71 H6
Bacon End CM6 33 J7
Baconend Green CM6 33 J7
Baconsthorpe NR25 45 F2
Bacton *Here.* HR2 28 C5
Bacton *Norf.* NR12 45 H2
Bacton *Suff.* IP14 34 E2
Bacton Green IP14 34 E2
Bacup OL13 56 D7
Badachro IV21 94 D4
Badanloch Lodge KW11 104 C5
Badavanich IV22 95 H6
Badbea KW7 105 F7
Badbury SN4 20 E3
Badbury Wick SN4 20 E3
Badby NN11 31 G3
Badcall *High.* IV27 102 D4
Badcall *High.* IV27 102 E3
Badcaul IV23 95 G2
Baddeley Green ST2 49 J7
Badden PA31 73 G2
Baddesley Clinton B93 30 C1
Baddesley Ensor CV9 40 E6
Baddidarach IV27 102 C6
Badenscoth AB51 91 F1
Badenyon AB36 90 B3
Badgall PL15 4 C2
Badger WV6 39 G6
Badgerbank SK11 49 H5
Badgers Mount TN14 23 H5
Badgeworth GL51 29 J7
Badgworth BS26 19 G6
Badicaul IV40 86 D2
Badingham IP13 35 H2
Badintagairt IV27 103 G7
Badlesmere ME13 15 F2
Badley IP6 34 E3
Badlipster KW1 105 H4
Badluarach IV23 95 F2
Badminton GL9 20 B3
Badnaban IV27 102 C6
Badnabay IV27 102 E4
Badnafrave AB37 89 K3
Badnagie KW6 105 G5
Badnambiast PH18 88 E7
Badninish IV25 96 E2
Badrallach IV23 95 G2
Badsey WR11 30 B4
Badshot Lea GU9 22 B7
Badsworth WF9 51 G1
Badwell Ash IP31 34 D2
Badworthy TQ10 5 G4
Badyo PH16 82 A1
Bae Cinmel (Kinmel Bay) LL18 47 H4
Bae Colwyn (Colwyn Bay) LL29 47 G5
Bae Penrhyn (Penrhyn Bay) LL30 47 G4
Bag Enderby PE23 53 G5
Bagber DT10 9 G3
Bagby YO7 57 K1
Bagendon GL7 20 D1
Bagginswood DY14 39 F7
Baggrave Hall LE7 41 J5
Baggrow CA7 60 C2
Bàgh a'Chaisteil (Castlebay) HS9 84 B5
Bàgh Mòr HS6 92 D6
Baghasdal HS8 84 C3
Bagillt CH6 48 B5
Baginton CV8 30 E1
Baglan SA12 18 A2
Bagley *Shrop.* SY12 38 D3
Bagley *Som.* BS28 19 H7
Bagmore RG25 21 K7
Bagnall ST9 49 J7
Bagnor RG20 21 H5
Bagpath GL8 20 B2
Bagshot *Surr.* GU19 22 C5
Bagshot *Wilts.* RG17 21 G5
Bagstone GL12 19 K3
Bagthorpe *Norf.* PE31 44 B2
Bagthorpe *Notts.* NG16 51 G7
Baguley M23 49 H4
Bagworth LE67 41 G5
Bagwyllydiart HR2 28 D6
Baildon BD17 57 G6
Baile Ailein (Balallan) HS2 100 E5
Baile a'Mhanaich (Balivanich) HS7 92 C6
Baile an Truiseil HS2 101 F2
Baile Boidheach PA31 73 F3
Baile Gharbhaidh HS8 92 C7
Baile Glas HS6 92 D6
Baile Lion (Balelone) HS6 92 C4
Baile Mhartainn HS6 92 C4
Baile Mhic Phail HS6 92 D4
Baile Mòr *Arg. & B.* PA76 78 D5
Baile Mòr (Balemore) *W.Isles* HS6 92 C5
Baile nan Cailleach HS7 92 C6
Baile Raghaill HS6 92 C5
Bailebeag IV2 88 C3
Baileguish PH21 89 F5
Baile-na-Cille HS6 92 D3
Bailetonach PH36 86 C7
Bailiesward AB54 90 C1
Bailiff Bridge HD6 57 G7
Baillieston G69 74 E4
Bainbridge DL8 62 A7
Bainsford FK2 75 G2
Bainshole AB54 90 E1
Bainton *E.Riding* YO25 59 F4
Bainton *Oxon.* OX27 31 G6
Bainton *Peter.* PE9 42 D5
Bairnkine TD8 70 B2
Bakebare AB55 90 B1
Baker Street RM16 24 C3
Baker's End SG12 33 G7
Bakewell DE45 50 E6
Bala (Y Bala) LL23 37 J2
Balachuirn IV40 94 B7
Balado KY13 82 B7
Balafark G63 74 E1
Balaldie IV20 97 F4
Balallan (Baile Ailein) HS2 100 E5
Balavil PH21 88 E4
Balbeg *High.* IV63 88 B1
Balbeg *High.* IV63 88 B2
Balbeggie PH2 82 C5
Balbirnie KY7 82 D7
Balbithan AB51 91 F3
Balblair *High.* IV7 96 E5
Balblair *High.* IV24 96 C2
Balblair *High.* IV19 96 E3
Balby DN4 51 H2
Balcharn IV27 96 C1
Balcherry IV19 97 F3
Balchers AB45 99 F5
Balchladich IV27 102 C5
Balchraggan *High.* IV5 96 C7
Balchraggan *High.* IV3 88 C1
Balchrick IV27 102 D3
Balcombe RH17 13 G3
Balcurvie KY8 82 E7
Baldernock G62 74 D3
Baldersby YO7 57 J2
Baldersby St. James YO7 57 J2
Balderstone *Gt.Man.* OL16 49 J1
Balderstone *Lancs.* BB2 56 B6
Balderton *Ches.W. & C.* CH4 48 C6
Balderton *Notts.* NG24 52 B7
Baldhu TR3 2 E4
Baldinnie KY15 83 F6
Baldock SG7 33 F5
Baldon Row OX44 21 J1
Baldovan DD3 82 E4
Baldovie *Angus* DD8 82 E2
Baldovie *Dundee* DD5 83 F4
Baldrine IM4 54 D5
Baldslow TN37 14 C6
Baldwin IM4 54 C5
Baldwinholme CA5 60 E1
Baldwin's Gate ST5 39 G1
Baldwins Hill RH19 13 G3
Bale NR21 44 E2
Balelone (Baile Lion) HS6 92 C4
Balemartine PA77 78 A3
Balemore (Baile Mòr) HS6 92 C5
Balendoch PH12 82 D3
Balephuil PA77 78 A3
Balerno EH14 75 K4
Balernock G84 74 A2
Baleromindubh PA61 72 B1
Balerominmore PA61 72 B1
Baleshare (Bhaleshear) HS6 92 C5
Balevulin PA69 79 F5
Balfield DD9 83 G1
Balfour *Aber.* AB34 90 D5
Balfour *Ork.* KW17 106 D6
Balfron G63 74 D2
Balfron Station G63 74 D2
Balgonar KY12 75 J1
Balgove AB51 91 G1
Balgowan *D. & G.* DG9 64 B6
Balgowan *High.* PH20 88 D5
Balgown IV51 93 J5
Balgreen AB45 99 F5
Balgreggan DG9 64 A5
Balgy IV54 94 E6
Balhaldie FK15 81 K7
Balhalgardy AB51 91 F2
Balham SW12 23 F4
Balhary PH11 82 D3
Balhelvie KY14 82 E5
Balhousie KY8 83 F7
Baliasta ZE2 107 Q2
Baligill KW14 104 D2
Baligrundle PA34 79 K3
Balindore PA35 80 A4
Balintore *Angus* DD8 82 D2
Balintore *High.* IV20 97 F4
Balintraid IV18 96 E4
Balintyre PH15 81 H3
Balivanich (Baile a'Mhanaich) HS7 92 C6
Balkeerie DD8 82 E3
Balkholme DN14 58 D7
Balkissock KA26 67 F5
Ball SY10 38 C3
Ball Haye Green ST13 49 J7
Ball Hill RG20 21 H5
Balla HS8 84 C3
Ballabeg IM9 54 B6
Ballacannell IM4 54 D5
Ballacarnane Beg IM6 54 B5
Ballachulish PH49 80 B2
Balladoole IM9 54 B7
Ballafesson IM9 54 B6
Ballagyr IM5 54 B5
Ballajora IM7 54 D4
Ballakilpheric IM9 54 B6
Ballamodha IM9 54 B6
Ballantrae KA26 66 E5
Ballards Gore SS4 25 F2
Ballasalla *I.o.M.* IM9 54 B6
Ballasalla *I.o.M.* IM7 54 C4
Ballater AB35 90 B5
Ballaterach AB34 90 C5
Ballaugh IM7 54 C4
Ballaveare IM4 54 C6
Ballchraggan IV18 96 E4
Ballechin PH9 82 A2
Balleich FK8 81 G7
Ballencrieff EH32 76 C3
Ballidon DE6 50 E7
Balliekine KA27 73 G6
Balliemeanoch PA27 80 C7
Balliemore *Arg. & B.* PA27 73 K1
Balliemore *Arg. & B.* PA34 79 K5
Ballig IM4 54 B5
Ballimeanoch PA33 80 B6
Ballimore *Arg. & B.* PA21 73 H2
Ballimore *Stir.* FK19 81 G6
Ballinaby PA44 72 A4
Ballindean PH14 82 D5
Ballingdon CO10 34 C4
Ballinger Common HP16 22 C1
Ballingham HR2 28 E5
Ballingry KY5 75 K1
Ballinlick PH8 82 A3
Ballinluig *P. & K.* PH9 82 A2
Ballinluig *P. & K.* PH10 82 B2
Ballintuim PH10 82 C2
Balloch *Angus* DD8 82 E2
Balloch *High.* IV2 96 E7
Balloch *N.Lan.* G68 75 F3
Balloch *W.Dun.* G83 74 B2
Ballochan AB31 90 D5
Ballochandrain PA22 73 H2
Ballochford AB54 90 B1
Ballochgair PA28 66 B1
Ballochmartin KA28 73 K5
Ballochmorrie KA26 67 G5
Ballochmyle KA5 67 K1
Ballochroy PA29 73 F5
Ballogie AB34 90 D5
Balls Cross GU28 12 C4
Balls Green *Essex* CO7 34 E6
Ball's Green *Glos.* GL6 20 B2
Balls Hill B71 40 B6
Ballyaurgan PA31 73 F3
Ballygown PA73 79 F3
Ballygrant PA45 72 B4
Ballyhaugh PA78 78 C2
Ballymeanoch PA31 73 G1
Ballymichael KA27 73 H7
Balmacara IV40 86 E2
Balmaclellan DG7 65 G3
Balmacneil PH8 82 A2
Balmadies DD8 83 G3
Balmae DG6 65 G6
Balmaha G63 74 C1
Balmalcolm KY15 82 E7
Balmaqueen IV51 93 K4
Balmeanach *Arg. & B.* PA65 79 H3
Balmeanach *Arg. & B.* PA68 79 F4
Balmedie AB23 91 H3
Balmer Heath SY12 38 D2
Balmerino DD6 82 E5
Balmerlawn SO42 10 E4
Balminnoch DG8 64 C4
Balmore *E.Dun.* G64 74 E3
Balmore *High.* IV12 97 F7
Balmore *High.* IV4 87 K1
Balmore *High.* IV55 93 H7
Balmore *P. & K.* PH16 81 J2
Balmullo KY16 83 F5
Balmungie IV10 96 E6
Balmyle PH10 82 B2
Balnaboth DD8 82 E1
Balnabruaich IV19 96 E4
Balnacra IV54 95 F7
Balnafoich IV2 88 D1
Balnagall IV20 97 F3
Balnagown Castle IV18 96 E4
Balnaguard PH9 82 A2
Balnaguisich IV18 96 D4
Balnahard *Arg. & B.* PA61 72 C1
Balnahard *Arg. & B.* PA68 79 F4
Balnain IV63 88 B1
Balnakeil IV27 103 F2
Balnaknock IV51 93 K5
Balnamoon DD9 83 G1
Balnapaling IV19 96 E5
Balnespick PH21 89 F4
Balquhidder FK19 81 G5
Balsall CV7 30 D1
Balsall Common CV7 30 D1
Balsall Heath B12 40 C7
Balscote OX15 30 E4
Balsham CB21 33 J3
Baltasound ZE2 107 Q2
Balterley CW2 49 G7
Balterley Heath CW2 49 G7
Baltersan DG8 64 E4
Balthangie AB53 99 G5
Balthayock PH2 82 C5
Baltonsborough BA6 8 E1
Baluachraig PA31 73 G1
Balulive PA45 72 C4
Balure *Arg. & B.* PA35 80 B4
Balure *Arg. & B.* PA37 79 K4
Balvaird IV6 96 C6
Balvarran PH10 82 B1
Balvicar PA34 79 J6
Balvraid *High.* IV40 86 E3
Balvraid *High.* IV13 89 F1
Bamber Bridge PR5 55 J7
Bamber's Green CM22 33 J6
Bamburgh NE69 77 K7
Bamff PH11 82 D2
Bamford *Derbys.* S33 50 E4
Bamford *Gt.Man.* OL11 49 H1
Bampton *Cumb.* CA10 61 G5
Bampton *Devon* EX16 7 H3
Bampton *Oxon.* OX18 21 G1
Bampton Grange CA10 61 G5
Banavie PH33 87 H7
Banbury OX16 31 F4
Bancffosfelen SA15 17 H4
Banchor IV12 97 G7
Banchory AB31 91 F5
Banchory-Devenick AB12 91 H4
Bancycapel SA32 17 H4
Bancyfelin SA33 17 G4
Bancyffordd SA44 17 H2
Bandon KY7 82 D7
Bandrake Head LA12 55 G1
Banff AB45 98 E4
Bangor LL57 46 D5
Bangor-is-y-coed LL13 38 C1
Bangor's Green L39 48 C2
Banham NR16 44 E7
Bank SO43 10 D4
Bank End LA20 54 E1
Bank Newton BD23 56 E4
Bank Street WR15 29 F2
Bank Top *Lancs.* WN8 48 E2
Bank Top *W.Yorks.* HX3 57 G7
Bankend DG1 69 F7
Bankfoot PH1 82 B4
Bankglen KA18 67 K2
Bankhead *Aber.* AB33 90 E3
Bankhead *Aber.* AB51 90 E4
Bankhead *Aberdeen* AB21 91 G3
Bankhead *D. & G.* DG6 65 H6
Bankland TA7 8 C2
Banknock FK4 75 F3
Banks *Cumb.* CA8 70 A7
Banks *Lancs.* PR9 55 G7
Bankshill DG11 69 G5
Banningham NR11 45 G3
Bannister Green CM6 33 K6
Bannockburn FK7 75 G1
Banstead SM7 23 F6
Bantam Grove LS27 57 H7
Bantham TQ7 5 G6
Banton G65 75 F3
Banwell BS29 19 G6
Banwen Pyrddin SA10 18 B1
Banyard's Green IP13 35 H1
Bapchild ME9 25 F5
Baptiston G63 74 D2
Bapton BA12 9 J1
Bar End SO23 11 F2
Bar Hill CB23 33 G2
Barabhas (Barvas) HS2 101 F3
Barachander PA35 80 B5
Barassie KA10 74 B7
Barbaraville IV18 96 E4
Barber Booth S33 50 D4
Barber Green LA11 55 G1
Barber's Moor PR26 48 D1
Barbon LA6 56 B1
Barbridge CW5 49 F7
Barbrook EX35 7 F1
Barby CV23 31 G1
Barcaldine PA37 80 A3
Barcaple DG7 65 G5
Barcheston CV36 30 D5
Barclose CA6 69 K7
Barcombe BN8 13 H5
Barcombe Cross BN8 13 H5
Barden DL8 62 C7
Barden Park TN9 23 J7
Bardennoch DG7 67 K4
Bardfield End Green CM6 33 K5
Bardfield Saling CM7 33 K6
Bardister ZE2 107 M5
Bardney LN3 52 E6
Bardon *Leics.* LE67 41 G4
Bardon *Moray* IV30 97 K6
Bardon Mill NE47 70 C7
Bardowie G62 74 D3
Bardsea LA12 55 F2
Bardsey LS17 57 J5
Bardsey Island (Ynys Enlli) LL53 36 A3
Bardwell IP31 34 D1
Bare LA4 55 H3
Barewood HR6 28 C3
Barfad PA29 73 G4
Barford *Norf.* NR9 45 F5
Barford *Warks.* CV35 30 D2
Barford St. John OX15 31 F5
Barford St. Martin SP3 10 B1
Barford St. Michael OX15 31 F5
Barfrestone CT15 15 H2
Bargaly DG8 64 E4
Bargany Mains KA26 67 G3
Bargeddie G69 74 E4
Bargoed CF81 18 E2
Bargrennan DG8 64 D3
Barham *Cambs.* PE28 32 E1
Barham *Kent* CT4 15 H2
Barham *Suff.* IP6 35 F3
Barharrow DG7 65 G5
Barholm PE9 42 D4
Barholm Mains DG8 64 E5
Barkby LE7 41 J5
Barkby Thorpe LE7 41 J5
Barkers Green SY4 38 E3
Barkestone-le-Vale NG13 42 A2
Barkham RG41 22 A5
Barking *Gt.Lon.* IG11 23 H3
Barking *Suff.* IP6 34 E3
Barking Tye IP6 34 E3
Barkisland HX4 57 F7
Barkston NG32 42 C1
Barkston Ash LS24 57 K6
Barkway SG8 33 G5
Barlae DG8 64 C4
Barland LD8 28 B2
Barlaston ST12 40 A2
Barlavington GU28 12 C5
Barlborough S43 51 G5
Barlby YO8 58 C6
Barlestone CV13 41 G5
Barley *Herts.* SG8 33 G5
Barley *Lancs.* BB12 56 D5
Barley Green IP21 35 G1
Barleycroft End SG9 33 H6
Barleyhill NE44 62 B1
Barleythorpe LE15 42 B5
Barling SS3 25 F3
Barlings LN3 52 D5
Barlow *Derbys.* S18 51 F5
Barlow *N.Yorks.* YO8 58 C7
Barlow *T. & W.* NE21 71 G7
Barmby Moor YO42 58 D5
Barmby on the Marsh DN14 58 C7
Barmer PE31 44 C2
Barmolloch PA31 73 G1
Barmoor Lane End TD15 77 J7
Barmouth (Abermaw) LL42 37 F4
Barmpton DL1 62 E5
Barmston YO25 59 H4
Barnaby Green NR34 35 J1
Barnacabber PA23 73 K2
Barnacarry PA27 73 H1
Barnack PE9 42 D5
Barnacle CV7 41 F7
Barnamuc PA38 80 B3
Barnard Castle DL12 62 B5
Barnard Gate OX29 31 F7
Barnardiston CB9 34 B4
Barnard's Green WR14 29 G4
Barnbarroch *D. & G.* DG8 64 D5
Barnbarroch *D. & G.* DG5 65 J5
Barnburgh DN5 51 G2
Barnby NR34 45 J7
Barnby Dun DN3 51 J2
Barnby in the Willows NG24 52 B7
Barnby Moor DN22 51 J4
Barndennoch DG2 68 D5
Barne Barton PL5 4 E5
Barnehurst DA7 23 J4
Barnes SW13 23 F4
Barnes Street TN11 23 K7
Barnet EN5 23 F2
Barnet Gate EN5 23 F2
Barnetby le Wold DN38 52 D2
Barney NR21 44 D2
Barnham *Suff.* IP24 34 C1
Barnham *W.Suss.* PO22 12 C6
Barnham Broom NR9 44 E5
Barnhead DD10 83 H2
Barnhill *Ches.W. & C.* CH3 48 D7
Barnhill *Dundee* DD5 83 F4
Barnhill *Moray* IV30 97 J6
Barnhills DG9 66 D6
Barningham *Dur.* DL11 62 B5
Barningham *Suff.* IP31 34 D1
Barningham Green NR11 45 F2
Barnoldby le Beck DN37 53 F2
Barnoldswick BB18 56 D5
Barns Green RH13 12 E4
Barnsdale Bar WF8 51 H1
Barnsley *Glos.* GL7 20 D1
Barnsley *S.Yorks.* S70 51 F2
Barnsole CT3 15 H2
Barnstaple EX31 6 D2
Barnston *Essex* CM6 33 K7
Barnston *Mersey.* CH61 48 B4
Barnstone NG13 42 A2
Barnt Green B45 30 B1
Barnton *Ches.W. & C.* CW8 49 F5
Barnton *Edin.* EH4 75 K3
Barnwell All Saints PE8 42 D7
Barnwell St. Andrew PE8 42 D7
Barnwood GL4 29 H7
Barons' Cross HR6 28 D3
Barr *Arg. & B.* PA44 72 B4
Barr *High.* PA34 79 H2
Barr *S.Ayr.* KA26 67 G4
Barr *Som.* TA4 7 K3
Barr Hall CO9 34 B5
Barra (Barraigh) HS9 84 B4
Barra (Tràigh Mhòr) Airport HS9 84 B4
Barrachan DG8 64 D6
Barrackan PA31 79 J7
Barraer DG8 64 D4
Barraglom HS2 100 D4
Barrahormid PA31 73 F2
Barraigh (Barra) HS9 84 B4
Barran PA33 80 C5
Barrapoll PA77 78 A3
Barrasford NE48 70 E6
Barravullin PA31 79 K7
Barregarrow IM6 54 C5

Barrets Green CW6 48 E7
Barrhead G78 74 C5
Barrhill KA26 67 G5
Barrington Cambs. CB22 33 G4
Barrington Som. TA19 8 C3
Barripper TR14 2 D5
Barrisdale PH35 86 E4
Barrmill KA15 74 B5
Barrnacarry PA34 79 K5
Barrock KW14 105 H1
Barrow Glos. GL51 29 H6
Barrow Lancs. BB7 56 C6
Barrow Rut. LE15 42 B4
Barrow Shrop. TF12 39 F5
Barrow Som. BA9 9 G1
Barrow Som. BA4 19 J7
Barrow Suff. IP29 34 B2
Barrow Gurney BS48 19 J5
Barrow Hann DN19 59 G7
Barrow Haven DN19 59 G7
Barrow Hill S43 51 G5
Barrow Nook L39 48 D2
Barrow Street BA12 9 H1
Barrow upon Humber DN19 59 G7
Barrow upon Soar LE12 41 H4
Barrow upon Trent DE73 41 F3
Barroway Drove PE38 43 J5
Barrowby NG32 42 B2
Barrowcliff YO12 59 G1
Barrowden LE15 42 C5
Barrowford BB9 56 D6
Barrow-in-Furness LA14 55 F3
Barrows Green LA8 55 J1
Barry Angus DD7 83 G4
Barry V. of Glam. CF62 18 E5
Barsby LE7 41 J4
Barsham NR34 45 H7
Barskimming KA5 67 J1
Barsloisnoch PA31 73 G1
Barston B92 30 D1
Bartestree HR1 28 E4
Barthol Chapel AB51 91 G1
Bartholomew Green CM77 34 B6
Barthomley CW2 49 G7
Bartley SO40 10 E3
Bartley Green B32 40 C7
Bartlow CB21 33 J4
Barton Cambs. CB23 33 H3
Barton Ches.W. & C. SY14 48 D7
Barton Cumb. CA10 61 F4
Barton Glos. GL54 30 B6
Barton Lancs. PR3 55 J6
Barton Lancs. L39 48 C2
Barton N.Yorks. DL10 62 D6
Barton Oxon. OX3 21 J1
Barton Torbay TQ2 5 K4
Barton Warks. B50 30 C3
Barton Bendish PE33 44 B5
Barton End GL6 20 B2
Barton Green DE13 40 D4
Barton Hartshorn MK18 31 H5
Barton Hill YO60 58 D3
Barton in Fabis NG11 41 H2
Barton in the Beans CV13 41 F5
Barton Mills IP28 34 B1
Barton on Sea BH25 10 D5
Barton St. David TA11 8 E1
Barton Seagrave NN15 32 B1
Barton Stacey SO21 21 H7
Barton Town EX31 6 E1
Barton Turf NR12 45 H3
Bartongate OX7 31 F6
Barton-le-Clay MK45 32 D5
Barton-le-Street YO17 58 D2
Barton-le-Willows YO60 58 D3
Barton-on-the-Heath GL56 30 D5
Barton-under-Needwood DE13 40 D4
Barton-upon-Humber DN18 59 G7
Barvas (Barabhas) HS2 101 F3
Barway CB7 33 J1
Barwell LE9 41 G6
Barwhinnock DG6 65 G5
Barwick Herts. SG11 33 G7
Barwick Som. BA22 8 E3
Barwick in Elmet LS15 57 J6
Barwinnock DG8 64 D6
Baschurch SY4 38 D3
Bascote CV47 31 F2
Base Green IP14 34 E2
Basford Green ST13 49 J7
Bashall Eaves BB7 56 B5
Bashall Town BB7 56 C5
Bashley BH25 10 D5
Basildon Essex SS14 24 D3
Basildon W.Berks. RG8 21 K4
Basingstoke RG21 21 K6
Baslow DE45 50 E5
Bason Bridge TA9 19 G7
Bassaleg NP10 19 F3
Bassenthwaite CA12 60 D3
Basset's Cross EX20 6 D5
Bassett SO16 11 F3
Bassingbourn SG8 33 G4
Bassingfield NG12 41 J2
Bassingham LN5 52 C7
Bassingthorpe NG33 42 C3
Basta ZE2 107 P3
Baston PE6 42 E4
Bastonford WR2 29 H3
Bastwick NR29 45 J4
Batavaime FK21 81 F4
Batch BS24 19 G6
Batchley B97 30 B2
Batchworth WD3 22 D2
Batchworth Heath WD3 22 D2
Batcombe Dorset DT2 9 F4
Batcombe Som. BA4 9 F1
Bate Heath CW9 49 F5
BATH BA 20 A5
Bathampton BA2 20 A5
Bathealton TA4 7 J3
Batheaston BA1 20 A5
Bathford BA1 20 A5
Bathgate EH48 75 H4
Bathley NG23 51 K7
Bathpool Cornw. PL15 4 C3
Bathpool Som. TA2 8 B2
Bathway BA3 19 J6
Batley WF17 57 H7
Batsford GL56 30 C5
Batson TQ8 5 H7
Battersby TS9 63 G6
Battersea SW11 23 F4
Battisborough Cross PL8 5 G6
Battisford IP14 34 E3
Battisford Tye IP14 34 E3
Battle E.Suss. TN33 14 C6
Battle Powys LD3 27 K5
Battledown GL52 29 J6
Battlefield SY1 38 E4
Battlesbridge SS11 24 D2
Battlesden MK17 32 C6
Battlesea Green IP21 35 G1
Battleton TA22 7 H3
Battlies Green IP30 34 D2
Battramsley SO41 10 E5
Batt's Corner GU10 22 B7
Bauds of Cullen AB56 98 C4
Baugh PA77 78 B3
Baughton WR8 29 H4
Baughurst RG26 21 J5
Baulds AB31 90 E5
Baulking SN7 21 G2
Baumber LN9 53 F5
Baunton GL7 20 D1
Baveney Wood DY14 29 F1
Baverstock SP3 10 B1
Bawburgh NR9 45 F5
Bawdeswell NR20 44 E3
Bawdrip TA7 8 C1
Bawdsey IP12 35 H4
Bawdsey Manor IP12 35 H5
Bawsey PE32 44 A4
Bawtry DN10 51 J3
Baxenden BB5 56 C7
Baxterley CV9 40 E6
Baxter's Green CB8 34 B3
Bay SP8 9 H2
Baybridge DH8 62 A2
Baycliff LA12 55 F2
Baydon SN8 21 F4
Bayford Herts. SG13 23 G1
Bayford Som. BA9 9 G2
Bayfordbury SG13 33 G7
Bayham Abbey TN3 13 K3
Bayles CA9 61 J2
Baylham IP6 35 F3
Baynards Green OX27 31 G6
Baysham HR9 28 E6
Bayston Hill SY3 38 D5
Bayswater W2 23 F3
Baythorn End CO9 34 B4
Bayton DY14 29 F1
Bayworth OX13 21 J1
Beach High. PA34 79 J2
Beach S.Glos. BS30 20 A4
Beachampton MK19 31 J5
Beachamwell PE37 44 B5
Beacharr PA29 72 E6
Beachley NP16 19 J2
Beacon Devon EX14 7 K5
Beacon Devon EX14 8 B4
Beacon Hill Dorset BH16 9 J5
Beacon Hill Essex CM8 34 C7
Beacon Hill Surr. GU26 12 B3
Beacon's Bottom HP14 22 A2
Beaconsfield HP9 22 C2
Beacravik HS3 93 G2
Beadlam YO62 58 C1
Beadlow SG17 32 E5
Beadnell NE67 71 H1
Beaford EX19 6 D4
Beal N.Yorks. DN14 58 B7
Beal Northumb. TD15 77 J6
Bealach PA38 80 A2
Bealsmill PL17 4 D3
Beambridge CW5 49 F7
Beamhurst ST14 40 C2
Beaminster DT8 8 D4
Beamish DH9 62 D1
Beamsley BD23 57 F4
Bean DA2 23 J4
Beanacre SN12 20 C5
Beanley NE66 71 F2
Beaquoy KW17 106 C5
Beardon EX20 6 D7
Beardwood BB2 56 B7
Beare EX5 7 H5
Beare Green RH5 22 E7
Bearley CV37 30 C2
Bearnie AB41 91 H1
Bearnock IV63 88 B1
Bearnus PA73 78 E3
Bearpark DH7 62 D2
Bearsbridge NE47 61 J1
Bearsden G61 74 D3
Bearsted ME14 14 C2
Bearstone TF9 39 G2
Bearwood Poole BH11 10 B5
Bearwood W.Mid. B66 40 C7
Beattock DG10 69 F3
Beauchamp Roding CM5 33 J7
Beauchief S8 51 F4
Beaudesert B95 30 C2
Beaufort NP23 28 A7
Beaulieu SO42 10 E4
Beauly IV4 96 C7
Beaumaris (Biwmares) LL58 46 E5
Beaumont Chan.I. JE3 3 J7
Beaumont Cumb. CA5 60 E1
Beaumont Essex CO16 35 F6
Beaumont Hill DL1 62 D5
Beaumont Leys LE4 41 H5
Beausale CV35 30 D1
Beauvale NG16 41 G1
Beauworth SO24 11 G2
Beaver Green TN23 14 E3
Beaworthy EX21 6 C6
Beazley End CM7 34 B6
Bebington CH63 48 C4
Bebside NE24 71 H5
Beccles NR34 45 J6
Beccles Heliport NR34 45 J7
Becconsall PR4 55 H7
Beck Foot LA8 61 H7
Beck Hole YO22 63 K6
Beck Row IP28 33 K1
Beck Side Cumb. LA17 55 F1
Beck Side Cumb. LA11 55 G1
Beckbury TF11 39 G5
Beckenham BR3 23 G5
Beckering LN8 52 E4
Beckermet CA21 60 B6
Beckermonds BD23 56 D1
Beckett End IP26 44 B6
Beckfoot Cumb. CA19 60 C6
Beckfoot Cumb. CA7 60 B2
Beckford GL20 29 J5
Beckhampton SN8 20 D5
Beckingham Lincs. LN5 52 B7
Beckingham Notts. DN10 51 K4
Beckington BA11 20 B6
Beckley E.Suss. TN31 14 D5
Beckley Oxon. OX3 31 G7
Beck's Green NR34 45 H7
Beckside LA6 56 B1
Beckton E6 23 H3
Beckwithshaw HG3 57 H4
Becontree RM8 23 H3
Bedale DL8 57 H1
Bedburn DL13 62 B3
Bedchester SP7 9 H3
Beddau CF38 18 D3
Beddgelert LL55 36 E1
Beddingham BN8 13 H6
Beddington SM6 23 F5
Beddington Corner CR4 23 F5
Bedfield IP13 35 G2
Bedfield Little Green IP13 35 G2
Bedford MK40 32 D4
Bedgebury Cross TN17 14 C4
Bedgrove HP21 32 B7
Bedham RH20 12 D4
Bedhampton PO9 11 J4
Bedingfield IP23 35 F2
Bedingfield Green IP23 35 F2
Bedingfield Street IP23 35 F2
Bedingham Green NR35 45 G6
Bedlam Lancs. BB5 56 C7
Bedlam N.Yorks. HG3 57 H3
Bedlar's Green CM22 33 J6
Bedlington NE22 71 H5
Bedlinog CF46 18 D1
Bedminster BS3 19 J4
Bedmond WD5 22 D1
Bednall ST17 40 B4
Bedol CH6 48 B5
Bedrule TD9 70 B2
Bedstone SY7 28 C1
Bedwas CF83 18 E3
Bedwell SG1 33 F6
Bedwellty NP12 18 E1
Bedworth CV12 41 F7
Bedworth Woodlands CV12 41 F7
Beeby LE7 41 J5
Beech Hants. GU34 11 H1
Beech Staffs. ST4 40 A2
Beech Hill RG7 21 K5
Beechingstoke SN9 20 D6
Beechwood WA7 48 E4
Beedon RG20 21 H4
Beeford YO25 59 H4
Beeley DE4 50 E6
Beelsby DN37 53 F2
Beenham RG7 21 J5
Beeny PL35 4 B1
Beer EX12 8 B6
Beer Hackett DT9 9 F3
Beercrocombe TA3 8 C2
Beesands TQ7 5 J6
Beesby Lincs. LN13 53 H4
Beesby N.E.Lincs. DN36 53 F3
Beeson TQ7 5 J6
Beeston Cen.Beds. SG19 32 E4
Beeston Ches.W. & C. CW6 48 E7
Beeston Norf. PE32 44 D4
Beeston Notts. NG9 41 H2
Beeston W.Yorks. LS11 57 H6
Beeston Regis NR26 45 F1
Beeston St. Lawrence NR12 45 H3
Beeswing DG2 65 J4
Beetham Cumb. LA7 55 H2
Beetham Som. TA20 8 B3
Beetley NR20 44 D4
Beffcote ST20 40 A4
Began CF3 19 F3
Begbroke OX5 31 F7
Begdale PE14 43 H5
Begelly SA68 16 E5
Beggar's Bush LD8 28 B2
Beggearn Huish TA23 7 J2
Beggshill AB54 90 D1
Beguildy (Bugeildy) LD7 28 A1
Beighton Norf. NR13 45 H5
Beighton S.Yorks. S20 51 G4
Beili-glas NP7 19 G1
Beinn na Faoghla (Benbecula) HS7 92 D6
Beith KA15 74 B5
Bekesbourne CT4 15 G2
Belaugh NR12 45 G4
Belbroughton DY9 29 J1
Belchalwell DT11 9 G4
Belchalwell Street DT11 9 G4
Belchamp Otten CO10 34 C4
Belchamp St. Paul CO10 34 B4
Belchamp Walter CO10 34 C4
Belchford LN9 53 F5
Belfield OL16 49 J1
Belford NE70 77 K7
Belgrave LE4 41 H5
Belhaven EH42 76 E3
Belhelvie AB23 91 H3
Belhinnie AB54 90 C2
Bell Bar AL9 23 F1
Bell Busk BD23 56 E4
Bell End DY9 29 J1
Bell Heath DY9 29 J1
Bell Hill GU32 11 J2
Bell o' th' Hill SY13 38 E1
Bellabeg AB36 90 B3
Belladrum IV4 96 C7
Bellanoch PA31 73 G1
Bellaty PH11 82 D2
Belle Isle LS10 57 J7
Belle Vue CA2 60 E1
Belleau LN13 53 H5
Belleheiglash AB37 89 J1
Bellerby DL8 62 C7
Bellever PL20 5 G3
Bellfields GU1 22 C6
Belliehill DD9 83 G1
Bellingdon HP5 22 C1
Bellingham Gt.Lon. SE6 23 G4
Bellingham Northumb. NE48 70 D5
Belloch PA29 72 E7
Bellochantuy PA28 72 E7
Bell's Cross IP6 35 F3
Bells Yew Green TN3 13 K3
Bellsbank KA6 67 J3
Bellshill N.Lan. ML4 75 F4
Bellshill Northumb. NE70 77 K7
Bellside ML1 75 G5
Bellsmyre G82 74 C3
Bellsquarry EH54 75 J4
Belluton BS39 19 K5
Belmaduthy IV8 96 D6
Belmesthorpe PE9 42 D4
Belmont B'burn. BL7 49 F1
Belmont Gt.Lon. SM2 23 F5
Belmont Gt.Lon. HA7 22 E2
Belmont Shet. ZE2 107 P2
Belnie PE11 43 F2
Belowda PL26 3 G2
Belper DE56 41 F1
Belper Lane End DE56 41 F1
Belsay NE20 71 G6
Belsford TQ9 5 H5
Belsize WD3 22 D1
Belstead IP8 35 F4
Belston KA6 67 H1
Belstone EX20 6 E6
Belstone Corner EX20 6 E6
Belsyde EH49 75 H3
Belthorn BB1 56 C7
Beltinge CT6 25 H5
Beltingham NE47 70 C7
Beltoft DN9 52 B2
Belton Leics. LE12 41 G3
Belton Lincs. NG32 42 C2
Belton N.Lincs. DN9 51 K2
Belton Norf. NR31 45 J5
Belton Rut. LE15 42 B5
Beltring TN12 23 K7
Belvedere DA17 23 H4
Belvoir NG32 42 B2
Bembridge PO35 11 H6
Bemersyde TD6 76 D7
Bemerton SP2 10 C1
Bempton YO15 59 H2
Ben Alder Cottage PH17 81 F1
Ben Alder Lodge PH19 88 C7
Ben Rhydding LS29 57 G5
Benacre NR34 45 K7
Benbecula (Beinn na Faoghla) HS7 92 D6
Benbecula (Balivanich) Airport HS7 92 C6
Benbuie DG3 68 C4
Benderloch PA37 80 A4
Bendish SG4 32 E6
Benenden TN17 14 D4
Benfield DG8 64 D4
Benfieldside DH8 62 B1
Bengate NR28 45 H3
Bengeo SG14 33 G7
Bengeworth WR11 30 B4
Benhall GL51 29 J6
Benhall Green IP17 35 H2
Benhall Street IP17 35 H2
Benholm DD10 83 K1
Beningbrough YO30 58 B4
Benington Herts. SG2 33 F6
Benington Lincs. PE22 43 G1
Benington Sea End PE22 43 H1
Benllech LL74 46 D4
Benmore Arg. & B. PA23 73 K2
Benmore Stir. FK20 81 F5
Bennacott PL15 4 C1
Bennan Cottage DG7 65 G3
Bennett End HP14 22 A2
Bennetts End HP3 22 D1
Benniworth LN8 53 F4
Benover ME18 14 C3
Benson OX10 21 K2
Benston ZE2 107 N7
Benthall Northumb. NE67 71 H1
Benthall Shrop. TF12 39 F5
Bentham GL51 29 J7
Benthoul AB14 91 G4
Bentlawnt SY5 38 C5
Bentley E.Riding HU17 59 G6
Bentley Essex CM15 23 J2
Bentley Hants. GU10 22 A7
Bentley S.Yorks. DN5 51 H2
Bentley Suff. IP9 35 F5
Bentley W.Mid. WS2 40 B6
Bentley W.Yorks. LS6 57 H6
Bentley Warks. CV9 40 E6
Bentley Heath Herts. EN5 23 F2
Bentley Heath W.Mid. B93 30 C1
Bentley Rise DN5 51 H2
Benton EX32 6 E2
Benton Square NE12 71 J6
Bentpath DG13 69 J4
Bentworth GU34 21 K7
Benvie DD2 82 E4
Benville Lane DT2 8 E4
Benwell NE15 71 H7
Benwick PE15 43 G6
Beoley B98 30 B2
Beoraidbeg PH40 86 C5
Bepton GU29 12 B5
Berden CM23 33 H6
Bere Alston PL20 4 E4
Bere Ferrers PL20 4 E4
Bere Regis BH20 9 H5
Berea SA62 16 A2
Berepper TR12 2 D6
Bergh Apton NR15 45 H5
Berinsfield OX10 21 J2
Berkeley GL13 19 K2
Berkhamsted HP4 22 C1
Berkley BA11 20 B7
Berkswell CV7 30 D1
Bermondsey SE16 23 G4
Bernera IV40 86 E2
Berneray (Eilean Bhearnaraigh) HS6 92 E3
Berners Roding CM5 24 C1
Bernice PA23 73 K1
Bernisdale IV51 93 K6
Berrick Prior OX10 21 K2
Berrick Salome OX10 21 K2
Berriedale KW7 105 G6
Berriew (Aberriw) SY21 38 A5
Berrington Northumb. TD15 77 J6
Berrington Shrop. SY5 38 E5
Berrington Worcs. WR15 28 E2
Berrington Green WR15 28 E2
Berriowbridge PL15 4 C3
Berrow Som. TA8 19 F6
Berrow Worcs. WR13 29 G5
Berrow Green WR6 29 G3
Berry Cross EX38 6 C4
Berry Down Cross EX34 6 D1
Berry Hill Glos. GL16 28 E7
Berry Hill Pembs. SA42 16 D1
Berry Pomeroy TQ9 5 J4
Berryhillock AB56 98 D4
Berrynarbor EX34 6 D1
Berry's Green TN16 23 H6
Bersham LL14 38 C1
Berstane KW15 106 D6
Berthlŵyd SA4 17 J6
Berwick BN26 13 J6
Berwick Bassett SN4 20 E4
Berwick Hill NE20 71 G6
Berwick St. James SP3 10 B1
Berwick St. John SP7 9 J2
Berwick St. Leonard SP3 9 J1
Berwick-upon-Tweed TD15 77 H5
Bescar L40 48 C1
Bescot WS2 40 C6
Besford Shrop. SY4 38 E3
Besford Worcs. WR8 29 J4
Bessacarr DN4 51 J2
Bessels Leigh OX13 21 H1
Besses o' th' Barn M45 49 H2
Bessingby YO16 59 H3
Bessingham NR11 45 F2
Best Beech Hill TN5 13 K3
Besthorpe Norf. NR17 44 E6
Besthorpe Notts. NG23 52 B6
Bestwood Village NG5 41 H1
Beswick E.Riding YO25 59 G5
Beswick Gt.Man. M11 49 H3
Betchworth RH3 23 F6
Bethania Cere. SY23 26 E2
Bethania Gwyn. LL41 37 G1
Bethel Gwyn. LL55 46 D6
Bethel Gwyn. LL23 37 J2
Bethel I.o.A. LL62 46 B5
Bethersden TN26 14 E4
Bethesda Gwyn. LL57 46 E6
Bethesda Pembs. SA67 16 D4
Bethlehem SA19 17 K3
Bethnal Green E2 23 G3
Betley CW3 39 G1
Betley Common CW3 39 G1
Betsham DA13 24 C4
Betteshanger CT14 15 J2
Bettiscombe DT6 8 C5
Bettisfield SY13 38 D2
Betton Shrop. SY5 38 C5
Betton Shrop. TF9 39 F2
Betton Strange SY5 38 E5
Bettws Bridgend CF32 18 C3
Bettws Newport NP20 19 F2
Bettws Bledrws SA48 26 E3
Bettws Cedewain SY16 38 A6

Bettws Gwerfil Goch LL21 37 K1
Bettws Newydd NP15 19 G1
Bettws-y-crwyn SY7 38 B7
Bettyhill KW14 104 C2
Betws SA18 17 K4
Betws Disserth LD1 28 A3
Betws Garmon LL54 46 D7
Betws Ifan SA38 17 G1
Betws-y-coed LL24 47 F7
Betws-yn-Rhos LL22 47 H5
Beulah Cere. SA38 17 F1
Beulah Powys LD5 27 J3
Bevendean BN2 13 G6
Bevercotes NG22 51 J5
Beverley HU17 59 G6
Beverstone GL8 20 B2
Bevington GL13 19 K2
Bewaldeth CA13 60 D3
Bewcastle CA6 70 A6
Bewdley DY12 29 G1
Bewerley HG3 57 G3
Bewholme YO25 59 H4
Bewley Common SN15 20 C5
Bexhill TN40 14 C7
Bexley DA5 23 H4
Bexleyheath DA6 23 H4
Bexwell PE38 44 A5
Beyton IP30 34 D2
Beyton Green IP30 34 D2
Bhalamus HS2 100 E7
Bhaleshear (Baleshare) HS6 92 C5
Bhaltos HS2 100 C4
Bhatarsaigh (Vatersay) HS9 84 B5
Biallaid PH20 88 E5
Bibury GL7 20 E1
Bicester OX26 31 G6
Bickenhall TA3 8 B3
Bickenhill B92 40 D7
Bicker PE20 43 F2
Bickershaw WN2 49 F2
Bickerstaffe L39 48 D2
Bickerton Ches.W. & C. SY14 48 E7
Bickerton Devon TQ7 5 J7
Bickerton N.Yorks. LS22 57 K4
Bickerton Northumb. NE65 70 E3
Bickford ST19 40 A4
Bickham TA24 7 H1
Bickham Bridge TQ9 5 H5
Bickham House EX6 7 H7
Bickington Devon EX31 6 D2
Bickington Devon TQ12 5 H3
Bickleigh Devon PL6 5 F4
Bickleigh Devon EX16 7 H5
Bickleton EX31 6 D2
Bickley BR1 23 H5
Bickley Moss SY13 38 E1
Bickley Town SY14 38 E1
Bicknacre CM3 24 D1
Bicknoller TA4 7 K2
Bicknor ME9 14 D2
Bickton SP6 10 C3
Bicton Here. HR6 28 D2
Bicton Shrop. SY3 38 D4
Bicton Shrop. SY7 38 B7
Bicton Heath SY3 38 D4
Bidborough TN4 23 J7
Biddenden TN27 14 D4
Biddenden Green TN27 14 D3
Biddenham MK40 32 D4
Biddestone SN14 20 B4
Biddick NE38 62 E1
Biddisham BS26 19 G6
Biddlesden NN13 31 H4
Biddlestone NE65 70 E3
Biddulph ST8 49 H7
Biddulph Moor ST8 49 J7
Bideford EX39 6 C3
Bidford-on-Avon B50 30 C3
Bidham Dock ME9 25 F5
Bidlake EX20 6 C7
Bidston CH43 48 B3
Bidwell LU5 32 D6
Bielby YO42 58 D5
Bieldside AB15 91 G4
Bierley I.o.W. PO38 11 G7
Bierley W.Yorks. BD4 57 G6
Bierton HP22 32 B7
Big Sand IV21 94 D4
Bigbury TQ7 5 G6
Bigbury-on-Sea TQ7 5 G6
Bigby DN38 52 D2
Bigert Mire LA20 60 C7
Biggar Cumb. LA14 54 E3
Biggar S.Lan. ML12 75 J7
Biggin Derbys. DE6 40 E1
Biggin Derbys. SK17 50 D7
Biggin N.Yorks. LS25 58 B6
Biggin Hill TN16 23 H6
Biggings ZE2 107 K6
Biggleswade SG18 32 E4
Bigholms DG13 69 J5
Bighouse KW14 104 D2
Bighton SO24 11 H1
Biglands CA7 60 D1
Bignor RH20 12 C5
Bigrigg CA24 60 B5
Bigton ZE2 107 M10
Bilberry PL26 4 A5
Bilborough NG8 41 H1
Bilbrook Som. TA24 7 J1
Bilbrook Staffs. WV8 40 A5
Bilbrough YO23 58 B5
Bilbster KW1 105 H3
Bilby DN22 51 J4
Bildershaw DL14 62 C4
Bildeston IP7 34 D4
Billericay CM12 24 C2
Billesdon LE7 42 A5
Billesley B49 30 C3
Billholm DG13 69 H4
Billingborough NG34 42 E2
Billinge WN5 48 E3
Billingford Norf. IP21 35 F1
Billingford Norf. NR20 44 E3
Billingham TS23 63 F4
Billinghay LN4 52 E7
Billingley S72 51 G2
Billingshurst RH14 12 D4
Billingsley WV16 39 G7
Billington Cen.Beds. LU7 32 C6
Billington Lancs. BB7 56 C6
Billington Staffs. ST18 40 A3
Billister ZE2 107 N6
Billockby NR29 45 J4
Billy Row DL15 62 C3
Bilsborrow PR3 55 J6
Bilsby LN13 53 H5
Bilsby Field LN13 53 H5
Bilsdean TD13 77 F3
Bilsham BN18 12 C6
Bilsington TN25 15 F4
Bilson Green GL14 29 F7
Bilsthorpe NG22 51 J6
Bilsthorpe Moor NG22 51 J7
Bilston Midloth. EH25 76 A4
Bilston W.Mid. WV14 40 B6
Bilstone CV13 41 F5
Bilting TN25 15 F3
Bilton E.Riding HU11 59 H6
Bilton N.Yorks. HG1 57 J4
Bilton Northumb. NE66 71 H2
Bilton Warks. CV22 31 F1
Bilton-in-Ainsty YO26 57 K5
Bimbister KW17 106 C6
Binbrook LN8 53 F3
Bincombe DT3 9 F6
Bindal IV20 97 G3
Bindon TA21 7 K3
Binegar BA3 19 K7
Bines Green RH13 12 E5
Binfield RG42 22 B4
Binfield Heath RG9 22 A4
Bingfield NE19 70 E6
Bingham NG13 42 A2
Bingham's Melcombe DT2 9 G4
Bingley BD16 57 G6
Bings Heath SY4 38 E4
Binham NR21 44 D2
Binley Hants. SP11 21 H6
Binley W.Mid. CV3 30 E1
Binniehill FK1 75 G3
Binsoe HG4 57 H2
Binstead PO33 11 G5
Binsted Hants. GU34 22 A7
Binsted W.Suss. BN18 12 C6
Binton CV37 30 C3
Bintree NR20 44 E3
Binweston SY5 38 C5
Birch Essex CO2 34 D6
Birch Gt.Man. M24 49 H2
Birch Cross ST14 40 D2
Birch Green Essex CO2 34 D7
Birch Green Herts. SG14 33 F7
Birch Grove RH17 13 H4
Birch Heath CW6 48 E6
Birch Vale SK22 50 C4
Birch Wood TA20 8 B3
Bircham Newton PE31 44 B2
Bircham Tofts PE31 44 B2
Birchanger CM23 33 J6
Bircher HR6 28 D2
Bircher Common HR6 28 D2
Birchfield IV24 96 B2
Birchgrove Cardiff CF14 18 E3
Birchgrove Swan. SA7 18 A2
Birchington CT7 25 K5
Birchmoor B78 40 E5
Birchover DE4 50 E6
Birchwood Lincs. LN6 52 C6
Birchwood Warr. WA3 49 F3
Bircotes DN11 51 J3
Bird Street IP7 34 E3
Birdbrook CO9 34 B4
Birdbush SP7 9 J2
Birdfield PA32 73 H1
Birdforth YO7 57 K2
Birdham PO20 12 B6
Birdingbury CV23 31 F2
Birdlip GL4 29 J7
Birdoswald CA8 70 B7
Birds Green CM5 23 J1
Birdsall YO17 58 E3
Birdsgreen WV15 39 G7
Birdsmoor Gate DT6 8 C4
Birdston G66 74 E3
Birdwell S70 51 F2
Birdwood GL19 29 G7
Birgham TD12 77 F7
Birichen IV25 96 E2
Birkby Cumb. CA15 60 B3
Birkby N.Yorks. DL7 62 E6
Birkdale Mersey. PR8 48 C1
Birkdale N.Yorks. DL11 61 K6
Birkenhead CH41 48 C4
Birkenhills AB53 99 F6
Birkenshaw BD11 57 H7
Birkhall AB35 90 B5
Birkhill Angus DD2 82 E4
Birkhill Sc.Bord. TD4 76 D6
Birkhill Sc.Bord. TD7 69 H2
Birkholme NG33 42 C3
Birkin WF11 58 B7
Birks LS27 57 H7
Birkwood ML11 75 G7
Birley HR4 28 D3
Birley Carr S6 51 F3
Birling Kent ME19 24 C5
Birling Northumb. NE65 71 H3
Birling Gap BN20 13 J7
Birlingham WR10 29 J4
BIRMINGHAM B 40 C7
Birmingham International Airport B26 40 D7
Birnam PH8 82 B3
Birsay KW17 106 B5
Birse AB34 90 D5
Birsemore AB34 90 D5
Birstall LE4 41 H5
Birstall Smithies WF17 57 H7
Birstwith HG3 57 H4
Birthorpe NG34 42 E2
Birtle OL11 49 H1
Birtley Here. SY7 28 C2
Birtley Northumb. NE48 70 D6
Birtley T. & W. DH3 62 D1
Birts Street WR13 29 G5
Birtsmorton WR13 29 H5
Bisbrooke LE15 42 B6
Biscathorpe LN11 53 F4
Bish Mill EX36 7 F3
Bisham SL7 22 B3
Bishampton WR10 29 J3
Bishop Auckland DL14 62 D4
Bishop Burton HU17 59 F5
Bishop Middleham DL17 62 E3
Bishop Monkton HG3 57 J3
Bishop Norton LN8 52 C3
Bishop Sutton BS39 19 J6
Bishop Thornton HG3 57 H3
Bishop Wilton YO42 58 D4
Bishopbridge LN8 52 D3
Bishopbriggs G64 74 E3
Bishopmill IV30 97 K5
Bishops Cannings SN10 20 D5
Bishop's Castle SY9 38 C7
Bishop's Caundle DT9 9 F3
Bishop's Cleeve GL52 29 J6
Bishop's Frome WR6 29 F4
Bishops Gate TW20 22 C4
Bishop's Green Essex CM6 33 K7
Bishop's Green Hants. RG19 21 J5
Bishop's Hull TA1 8 B2
Bishop's Itchington CV47 30 E3
Bishop's Lydeard TA4 7 K3
Bishop's Norton GL2 29 H6
Bishops Nympton EX36 7 F3
Bishop's Offley ST21 39 G3
Bishop's Stortford CM23 33 H6
Bishop's Sutton SO24 11 H1
Bishop's Tachbrook CV33 30 E2
Bishop's Tawton EX32 6 D2
Bishop's Waltham SO32 11 G3
Bishop's Wood ST19 40 A5
Bishopsbourne CT4 15 G2
Bishopsteignton TQ14 5 K3
Bishopstoke SO50 11 F3
Bishopston Bristol BS6 19 J4
Bishopston Swan. SA3 17 J7
Bishopstone Bucks. HP17 32 B7
Bishopstone E.Suss. BN25 13 H6
Bishopstone Here. HR4 28 D4
Bishopstone Swin. SN6 21 F3
Bishopstone Wilts. SP5 10 B2
Bishopstrow BA12 20 B7
Bishopswood TA20 8 B3
Bishopsworth BS13 19 J5
Bishopthorpe YO23 58 B5
Bishopton Darl. TS21 62 E4
Bishopton N.Yorks. HG4 57 H2
Bishopton Renf. PA7 74 C3
Bishopton Warks. CV37 30 C3
Bishton NP18 19 G3
Bisley Glos. GL6 20 C1
Bisley Surr. GU24 22 C6
Bispham FY2 55 G6
Bispham Green L40 48 D1
Bissoe TR4 2 E4
Bisterne BH24 10 C4
Bisterne Close BH24 10 D4
Bitchet Green TN15 23 J6
Bitchfield NG33 42 C3
Bittadon EX31 6 D1
Bittaford PL21 5 G5
Bittering NR19 44 D4
Bitterley SY8 28 E1
Bitterne SO18 11 F3
Bitteswell LE17 41 H7
Bitton BS30 19 K5
Biwmares (Beaumaris) LL58 46 E5
Bix RG9 22 A3
Bixter ZE2 107 M7
Blaby LE8 41 H6
Black Bourton OX18 21 F1
Black Bridge SA73 16 C5
Black Callerton NE5 71 G7
Black Carr NR17 44 E6
Black Clauchrie KA26 67 G5
Black Corries Lodge PH49 80 D2
Black Crofts PA37 80 A4
Black Cross TR8 3 G2
Black Dog EX17 7 G5
Black Heddon NE20 71 F6
Black Hill CV37 30 D3
Black Marsh SY5 38 C6
Black Moor LS17 57 H5
Black Mount PA36 80 D3
Black Notley CM77 34 B6
Black Pill SA3 17 K6
Black Street NR33 45 K7
Black Torrington EX21 6 C5
Blackaburn NE48 70 C6
Blackacre DG11 69 F4
Blackadder TD11 77 G5
Blackawton TQ9 5 J5
Blackborough Devon EX15 7 J5
Blackborough Norf. PE32 44 A4
Blackborough End PE32 44 A4
Blackboys TN22 13 J4
Blackbraes Aber. AB21 91 G3
Blackbraes Falk. FK1 75 H3
Blackbrook Derbys. DE56 41 F1
Blackbrook Leics. LE12 41 G4
Blackbrook Mersey. WA11 48 E3
Blackbrook Staffs. ST5 39 G2
Blackburn Aber. AB21 91 G3
BLACKBURN B'burn. BB 56 B7
Blackburn W.Loth. EH47 75 H4
Blackbushe GU17 22 A6
Blackcastle IV2 97 F6
Blackchambers AB32 91 F3
Blackcraig D. & G. DG8 64 E4
Blackcraig D. & G. DG7 68 C5
Blackden Heath CW4 49 G5
Blackdog AB23 91 H3
Blackdown Devon PL19 5 F3
Blackdown Dorset DT8 8 C4
Blackdown Warks. CV32 30 E2
Blacker Hill S74 51 F2
Blackfen DA15 23 H4
Blackfield SO45 11 F4
Blackford Aber. AB51 91 F1
Blackford Cumb. CA6 69 J7
Blackford P. & K. PH4 81 K7
Blackford Som. BA22 9 F2
Blackford Som. BS28 19 H7
Blackford Bridge BL9 49 H2
Blackfordby DE11 41 F4
Blackgang PO38 11 F7
Blackhall Edin. EH4 76 A3
Blackhall Renf. PA1 74 C4
Blackhall Colliery TS27 63 F3
Blackhall Mill NE17 62 C1
Blackhall Rocks TS27 63 F3
Blackham TN3 13 J3
Blackhaugh TD1 76 C7
Blackheath Essex CO2 34 E6
Blackheath Gt.Lon. SE3 23 G4
Blackheath Suff. IP19 35 J1
Blackheath Surr. GU4 22 D7
Blackheath W.Mid. B65 40 B7
Blackhill Aber. AB42 99 J5
Blackhill Aber. AB42 99 J6
Blackhillock AB55 98 C6
Blackhills IV30 97 K6
Blackland SN11 20 D5
Blacklands TA24 7 G2
Blackleach PR4 55 H6
Blackley M9 49 H2
Blacklunans PH10 82 C1
Blackmill CF35 18 C3
Blackmoor Hants. GU33 11 J1
Blackmoor Som. TA21 7 K4
Blackmoor Gate EX31 6 E1
Blackmoorfoot HD7 50 C1
Blackmore CM4 24 C1
Blackmore End Essex CM7 34 B5
Blackmore End Herts. AL4 32 E7
Blackness Aber. AB31 90 E5
Blackness Falk. EH49 75 J3
Blackness High. KW3 105 H5
Blacknest GU34 22 A7
Blackney DT6 8 D5
Blacko BB9 56 D5
Blackpole WR3 29 H3
BLACKPOOL B'pool FY 55 G6
Blackpool Devon TQ6 5 J6
Blackpool Bridge SA67 16 D4
Blackpool Gate CA6 70 A6
Blackpool International Airport FY4 55 G6
Blackridge EH48 75 G4
Blackrock Arg. & B. PA44 72 B4
Blackrock Mon. NP7 28 B7
Blackrod BL6 49 F1
Blackshaw DG1 69 F7
Blackshaw Head HX7 56 E7
Blacksmith's Green IP14 35 F2
Blacksnape BB3 56 C7
Blackstone BN5 13 F5
Blackthorn OX25 31 H7
Blackthorpe IP30 34 D2
Blacktoft DN14 58 E7
Blacktop AB15 91 G4
Blacktown CF3 19 F3
Blackwater Cornw. TR4 2 E4
Blackwater Hants. GU17 22 B6
Blackwater I.o.W. PO30 11 G6
Blackwater Norf. NR9 44 E3
Blackwater Som. TA20 8 B3
Blackwaterfoot KA27 66 D1
Blackwell Darl. DL3 62 D5
Blackwell Derbys. SK17 50 D5
Blackwell Derbys. DE55 51 G7
Blackwell W.Suss. RH19 13 G3
Blackwell Warks. CV36 30 D4
Blackwell Worcs. B60 29 J1
Blackwells End GL19 29 G6
Blackwood (Coed-duon) Caerp. NP12 18 E2
Blackwood D. & G. DG2 68 E5
Blackwood S.Lan. ML11 75 F6
Blackwood Hill ST9 49 J7
Blacon CH1 48 C6
Bladbean CT4 15 G3
Bladnoch DG8 64 E5
Bladon OX20 31 F7
Blaen Clydach CF40 18 C2
Blaenannerch SA43 17 F1
Blaenau Dolwyddelan LL25 46 E7
Blaenau Ffestiniog LL41 37 F1
Blaenavon NP4 19 F1
Blaenawey NP7 28 B7
Blaencelyn SA44 26 C3
Blaencwm CF42 18 C1
Blaendyryn LD3 27 J5
Blaenffos SA37 16 E2
Blaengarw CF32 18 C2
Blaengeuffordd SY23 37 F7
Blaengweche SA18 17 K4
Blaengwrach SA11 18 B1
Blaengwynfi SA13 18 B2
Blaenllechau CF43 18 D2
Blaenos SA20 27 G5
Blaenpennal SY23 27 F2
Blaenplwyf SY23 26 E1
Blaenporth SA43 17 F1
Blaenrhondda CF42 18 C1
Blaenwaun SA34 17 F3
Blaen-y-coed SA33 17 G3
Blagdon N.Som. BS40 19 H6
Blagdon Torbay TQ3 5 J4
Blagdon Hill TA3 8 B3
Blaguegate WN8 48 D2
Blaich PH33 87 G7
Blaina NP13 18 E1
Blair KA24 74 B6
Blair Atholl PH18 81 K1
Blair Drummond FK9 75 F1
Blairannaich G83 80 E7
Blairbuie PA23 73 K3
Blairgowrie PH10 82 C3
Blairhall KY12 75 J2
Blairhoyle FK8 81 H7
Blairhullichan FK8 81 F7
Blairingone FK14 75 H1
Blairkip KA5 74 D7
Blairlogie FK9 75 G1
Blairmore Arg. & B. PA23 73 K2
Blairmore High. IV28 96 E1
Blairmore High. IV27 102 D3
Blairnairn G84 74 A2
Blairnamarrow AB37 89 K3
Blairpark KA24 74 A5
Blairquhan KA19 67 H3
Blairquhosh G63 74 D2
Blair's Ferry PA21 73 H4
Blairshinnoch AB45 98 E4
Blairuskinmore FK8 81 F7
Blairvadach G84 74 A2
Blairydryne AB31 91 F5
Blairythan Cottage AB41 91 H2
Blaisdon GL17 29 G7
Blake End CM77 34 B6
Blakebrook DY11 29 H1
Blakedown DY10 29 H1
Blakelaw Sc.Bord. TD5 77 F7
Blakelaw T. & W. NE5 71 H7
Blakeley WV5 40 A6
Blakelow CW5 49 F7
Blakemere HR2 28 C4
Blakeney Glos. GL15 19 K1
Blakeney Norf. NR25 44 E1
Blakenhall Ches.E. CW5 39 G1
Blakenhall W.Mid. WV2 40 B6
Blakeshall DY11 40 A7
Blakesley NN12 31 H3
Blanchland DH8 62 A1
Bland Hill HG3 57 H4
Blandford Camp DT11 9 J4
Blandford Forum DT11 9 H4
Blandford St. Mary DT11 9 H4
Blanefield G63 74 D3
Blanerne TD11 77 G5
Blankney LN4 52 D6
Blantyre G72 74 E5
Blar a' Chaorainn PH33 80 C1
Blargie PH20 88 D5
Blarglas G83 74 B2
Blarmachfoldach PH33 80 B1
Blarnalearoch IV23 95 H2
Blashford BH24 10 C4
Blaston LE16 42 B6
Blathaisbhal HS6 92 D4
Blatherwycke PE8 42 C6
Blawith LA12 55 F1
Blaxhall IP12 35 H3
Blaxton DN9 51 J2
Blaydon NE21 71 G7
Bleadney BA5 19 H7
Bleadon BS24 19 G6
Bleak Hey Nook OL3 50 C2
Blean CT2 25 H5
Bleasby Lincs. LN8 52 E4
Bleasby Notts. NG14 42 A1
Bleasby Moor LN8 52 E4
Bleatarn CA16 61 J5
Bleathwood Common SY8 28 E2
Blebocraigs KY15 83 F6
Bleddfa LD7 28 B2
Bledington OX7 30 D6
Bledlow HP27 22 A1
Bledlow Ridge HP14 22 A2
Blencarn CA10 61 H3
Blencogo CA7 60 C2
Blencow CA11 61 F3
Blendworth PO8 11 J3
Blennerhasset CA7 60 C2
Blervie Castle IV36 97 H6
Bletchingdon OX5 31 G7
Bletchingley RH1 23 G6
Bletchley M.K. MK3 32 B5
Bletchley Shrop. TF9 39 F2
Bletherston SA63 16 D3
Bletsoe MK44 32 D3
Blewbury OX11 21 J3
Blickling NR11 45 F3
Blidworth NG21 51 H7
Blidworth Bottoms NG21 51 H7
Blindburn Aber. AB41 91 H1
Blindburn Northumb. NE65 70 D2
Blindcrake CA13 60 C3

Blindley Heath RH7 23 G7
Blisland PL30 4 A3
Bliss Gate DY14 29 G1
Blissford SP6 10 C3
Blisworth NN7 31 J3
Blithbury WS15 40 C3
Blitterlees CA7 60 C1
Blo' Norton IP22 34 E1
Blockley GL56 30 C5
Blofield NR13 45 H5
Blofield Heath NR13 45 H4
Blore DE6 40 D1
Blossomfield B91 30 C1
Blount's Green ST14 40 C2
Blowick PR9 48 C1
Bloxham OX15 31 F5
Bloxholm LN4 52 D7
Bloxwich WS3 40 B5
Bloxworth BH20 9 H5
Blubberhouses LS21 57 G4
Blue Anchor *Cornw.* TR9 3 G3
Blue Anchor *Som.* TA24 7 J1
Blue Bell Hill ME5 24 D5
Bluewater DA9 23 J4
Blundellsands L23 48 C3
Blundeston NR32 45 K6
Blunham MK44 32 E3
Blunsdon St. Andrew SN26 20 E3
Bluntington DY10 29 H1
Bluntisham PE28 33 G1
Blunts PL12 4 D4
Blurton ST3 40 A1
Blyborough DN21 52 C3
Blyford IP19 35 J1
Blymhill TF11 40 A4
Blymhill Common TF11 39 G4
Blymhill Lawn TF11 40 A4
Blyth *Northumb.* NE24 71 J5
Blyth *Notts.* S81 51 J4
Blyth Bridge EH46 75 K6
Blyth End B46 40 E6
Blythburgh IP19 35 J1
Blythe Bridge ST11 40 B1
Blythe Marsh ST11 40 B1
Blyton DN21 52 B3
Boarhills KY16 83 G6
Boarhunt PO17 11 H4
Boars Hill OX1 21 H1
Boarsgreave BB4 56 D7
Boarshead TN6 13 J3
Boarstall HP18 31 H7
Boarzell TN19 14 C5
Boasley Cross EX20 6 D6
Boat o' Brig IV32 98 B5
Boat of Garten PH24 89 G3
Boath IV17 96 C4
Bobbing ME9 24 E5
Bobbington DY7 40 A6
Bobbingworth CM5 23 J1
Bocaddon PL13 4 B5
Bochastle FK17 81 H7
Bockhampton RG17 21 G4
Bocking CM7 34 B6
Bocking Churchstreet CM7 34 B6
Bockleton WR15 28 E2
Boconnoc PL22 4 B4
Boddam *Aber.* AB42 99 K6
Boddam *Shet.* ZE2 107 M11
Bodden BA4 19 K7
Boddington GL51 29 H6
Bodedern LL65 46 B4
Bodelwyddan LL18 47 J5
Bodenham *Here.* HR1 28 E3
Bodenham *Wilts.* SP5 10 C2
Bodenham Moor HR1 28 E3
Bodesbeck DG10 69 G3
Bodewryd LL66 46 B3
Bodfari LL16 47 J5
Bodffordd LL77 46 C5
Bodfuan LL53 36 C2
Bodham NR25 45 F1
Bodiam TN32 14 C5
Bodicote OX15 31 F5
Bodieve PL27 3 G1
Bodinnick PL23 4 B5
Bodior LL65 46 A5
Bodle Street Green BN27 13 K5
Bodmin PL31 4 A4
Bodney IP26 44 C6
Bodorgan LL62 46 B6
Bodrane PL14 4 C4
Bodsham Green TN25 15 G3
Bodwen PL26 4 A4
Bodymoor Heath B76 40 D6
Bogallan IV1 96 D6
Bogbain IV2 96 E7
Bogbrae AB42 91 J1
Bogbuie IV7 96 C6
Bogend KA1 74 B7
Bogfern AB33 90 D4
Bogfields AB33 90 D4
Bogfold AB43 99 G5
Boghead *Aber.* AB45 98 E5
Boghead *E.Ayr.* KA18 68 B1
Boghead *S.Lan.* ML11 75 F6
Boghole Farm IV12 97 G6
Bogmoor IV32 98 B4
Bogniebrae AB54 98 D6
Bognor Regis PO21 12 C7
Bograxie AB51 91 F3
Bogroy PH23 89 G2
Bogside FK10 75 H1
Bogston AB36 90 B4
Bogton AB53 98 E5
Bogue DG7 68 B5
Bohemia SP5 10 D3
Bohenie PH31 87 J6
Bohetherick PL12 4 E4
Bohortha TR2 3 F5
Bohuntine PH31 87 J6
Boirseam HS3 93 F3
Bojewyan TR19 2 A5
Bokiddick PL30 4 A4
Bolam *Dur.* DL2 62 C4
Bolam *Northumb.* NE61 71 F5
Bolberry TQ7 5 G7
Bold Heath WA8 48 E4
Bolderwood SO43 10 D4
Boldon NE36 71 J7
Boldon Colliery NE35 71 J7
Boldre SO41 10 E5
Boldron DL12 62 B5
Bole DN22 51 K4
Bolehill DE4 50 E7
Boleigh TR19 2 B6
Bolenowe TR14 2 D5
Boleside TD1 76 C7
Bolfracks PH15 81 K3
Bolgoed SA4 17 K5
Bolham *Devon* EX16 7 H4
Bolham *Notts.* DN22 51 K4
Bolham Water EX15 7 K4
Bolingey TR6 2 E3
Bollington SK10 49 J5
Bolney RH17 13 F4
Bolnhurst MK44 32 D3
Bolshan DD11 83 H2
Bolsover S44 51 G5
Bolsterstone S36 50 E3
Bolstone HR2 28 E5
Boltby YO7 57 K1
Bolter End HP14 22 A2
Bolton *Cumb.* CA16 61 H4
Bolton *E.Loth.* EH41 76 D3
Bolton *E.Riding* YO42 58 D4
BOLTON *Gt.Man.* BL 49 G2
Bolton *Northumb.* NE66 71 G2
Bolton Abbey BD23 57 F4
Bolton Bridge BD23 57 F4
Bolton by Bowland BB7 56 C5
Bolton Houses PR4 55 H6
Bolton Low Houses CA7 60 D2
Bolton Percy YO23 58 B5
Bolton upon Dearne S63 51 G2
Bolton Wood Lane CA7 60 D2
Boltonfellend CA6 69 K7
Boltongate CA7 60 D2
Bolton-le-Sands LA5 55 H3
Bolton-on-Swale DL10 62 D7
Bolventor PL15 4 B3
Bombie DG6 65 H6
Bomere Heath SY4 38 D4
Bonar Bridge IV24 96 D2
Bonawe PA37 80 B4
Bonby DN20 52 D1
Boncath SA37 17 F2
Bonchester Bridge TD9 70 A2
Bonchurch PO38 11 G7
Bondleigh EX20 6 E5
Bonds PR3 55 H5
Bonehill B78 40 D5
Bo'ness EH51 75 H2
Bonhill G83 74 B3
Boningale WV7 40 A5
Bonjedward TD8 70 B1
Bonkle ML2 75 G5
Bonning Gate LA8 61 F7
Bonnington *Edin.* EH27 75 K4
Bonnington *Kent* TN25 15 F4
Bonnybank KY8 82 E7
Bonnybridge FK4 75 G2
Bonnykelly AB53 99 G5
Bonnyrigg EH19 76 B4
Bonnyton *Aber.* AB52 90 E1
Bonnyton *Angus* DD11 83 G4
Bonnyton *Angus* DD10 83 H2
Bonnyton *Angus* DD3 82 E4
Bonsall DE4 50 E7
Bont NP7 28 C7
Bont Dolgadfan SY19 37 H5
Bont Newydd LL40 37 G3
Bontddu LL40 37 F4
Bont-goch (Elerch) SY24 37 F7
Bonthorpe LN13 53 H5
Bont-newydd *Conwy* LL17 47 J5
Bontnewydd *Gwyn.* LL55 46 C6
Bontuchel LL15 47 J7
Bonvilston CF5 18 D4
Bon-y-maen SA1 17 K6
Boode EX33 6 D2
Booham TQ6 5 K5
Booker HP12 22 B2
Booley SY4 38 E3
Boor IV22 94 E3
Boorley Green SO32 11 G3
Boosbeck TS12 63 H5
Boose's Green CO6 34 C5
Boot CA19 60 C6
Boot Street IP6 35 G4
Booth HX2 57 F7
Booth Bank HD7 50 C1
Booth Green SK10 49 J4
Booth Wood HX6 50 C1
Boothby Graffoe LN5 52 C7
Boothby Pagnell NG33 42 C2
Boothstown M28 49 G2
Boothville NN3 31 J2
Bootle *Cumb.* LA19 54 E1
Bootle *Mersey.* L20 48 C3
Booton NR10 45 F3
Boots Green WA16 49 G5
Booze DL11 62 B6
Boquhan G63 74 D2
Boraston WR15 29 F1
Bordeaux GY3 3 J5
Borden *Kent* ME9 24 E5
Borden *W.Suss.* GU30 12 B4
Bordley BD23 56 E3
Bordon GU35 11 J1
Boreham *Essex* CM3 24 D1
Boreham *Wilts.* BA12 20 B7
Boreham Street BN27 13 K5
Borehamwood WD6 22 E2
Boreland *D. & G.* DG11 69 G4
Boreland *D. & G.* DG8 64 D4
Boreland *Stir.* FK21 81 G4
Boreley WR9 29 H2
Boreraig IV55 93 G6
Borgh *W.Isles* HS6 92 E3
Borgh *W.Isles* HS9 84 B4
Borgh (Borve) *W.Isles* HS2 101 G2
Borghastan HS2 100 D3
Borgie KW14 103 J3
Borgue *D. & G.* DG6 65 G6
Borgue *High.* KW7 105 G6
Borley CO10 34 C4
Borley Green *Essex* CO10 34 C4
Borley Green *Suff.* IP30 34 D2
Bornais HS8 84 C2
Borness DG6 65 G6
Bornisketaig IV51 93 J4
Borough Green TN15 23 K6
Boroughbridge YO51 57 J3
Borras Head LL13 48 C7
Borrowash DE72 41 G2
Borrowby *N.Yorks.* TS13 63 J5
Borrowby *N.Yorks.* YO7 57 K1
Borrowdale CA12 60 D5
Borrowfield AB39 91 G5
Borstal ME1 24 D5
Borth SY24 37 F7
Borthwick EH23 76 B5
Borthwickbrae TD9 69 K2
Borthwickshiels TD9 69 K2
Borve *High.* IV51 93 K7
Borve (Borgh) *W.Isles* HS2 101 G2
Borwick LA6 55 J2
Borwick Rails LA18 54 E2
Bosavern TR19 2 A5
Bosbury HR8 29 F4
Boscarne PL30 4 A4
Boscastle PL35 4 A1
Boscombe *Bourne.* BH5 10 C5
Boscombe *Wilts.* SP4 10 D1
Bosham PO18 12 B6
Bosham Hoe PO18 12 B6
Bosherston SA71 16 C6
Bosley SK11 49 J6
Bossall YO60 58 D3
Bossiney PL34 4 A2
Bossingham CT4 15 G3
Bossington *Hants.* SO20 10 E1
Bossington *Som.* TA24 7 G1
Bostadh HS2 100 D4
Bostock Green CW10 49 F6
Boston PE21 43 G1
Boston Spa LS23 57 K5
Boswarthan TR20 2 B5
Boswinger PL26 3 G4
Botallack TR19 2 A5
Botany Bay EN2 23 G2
Botcheston LE9 41 G5
Botesdale IP22 34 E1
Bothal NE61 71 H5
Bothamsall DN22 51 J5
Bothel CA7 60 C3
Bothenhampton DT6 8 D5
Bothwell G71 75 F5
Botley *Bucks.* HP5 22 C1
Botley *Hants.* SO30 11 G3
Botley *Oxon.* OX2 21 H1
Botloe's Green GL18 29 G6
Botolph Claydon MK18 31 J6
Botolphs BN44 12 E6
Botolph's Bridge CT21 15 G4
Bottacks IV14 96 B5
Bottesford *Leics.* NG13 42 B2
Bottesford *N.Lincs.* DN16 52 B2
Bottisham CB25 33 J2
Bottlesford SN9 20 E6
Bottom Boat WF3 57 J7
Bottom of Hutton PR4 55 H7
Bottom o'th'Moor BL6 49 F1
Bottomcraig DD6 82 E5
Bottoms OL14 56 E7
Botton Head LA2 56 B3
Botusfleming PL12 4 E4
Botwnnog LL53 36 B2
Bough Beech TN8 23 H7
Boughrood LD3 28 A5
Boughspring NP16 19 J2
Boughton *Norf.* PE33 44 B5
Boughton *Northants.* NN2 31 J2
Boughton *Notts.* NG22 51 J6
Boughton Aluph TN25 15 F3
Boughton Green ME17 14 C2
Boughton Lees TN25 15 F3
Boughton Malherbe ME17 14 D3
Boughton Street ME13 15 F2
Boulby TS13 63 J5
Bouldnor PO41 10 E6
Bouldon SY7 38 E7
Boulge IP13 35 G3
Boulmer NE66 71 H2
Boulston SA62 16 C4
Boultenstone Hotel AB36 90 C3
Boultham LN6 52 C6
Boundary *Derbys.* DE11 41 F4
Boundary *Staffs.* ST10 40 B1
Bourn CB23 33 G3
Bourne PE10 42 D3
Bourne End *Bucks.* SL8 22 B3
Bourne End *Cen.Beds.* MK43 32 C4
Bourne End *Herts.* HP1 22 D1
Bournebridge RM4 23 J2
BOURNEMOUTH BH 10 B5
Bournemouth Airport BH23 10 C5
Bournheath B61 29 J1
Bournmoor DH4 62 E1
Bournville B30 40 C7
Bourton *Bucks.* MK18 31 J5
Bourton *Dorset* SP8 9 G1
Bourton *N.Som.* BS22 19 G5
Bourton *Oxon.* SN6 21 F3
Bourton *Shrop.* TF13 38 E6
Bourton *Wilts.* SN10 20 D5
Bourton on Dunsmore CV23 31 F1
Bourton-on-the-Hill GL56 30 C5
Bourton-on-the-Water GL54 30 C6
Bousd PA78 78 D1
Boustead Hill CA5 60 D1
Bouth LA12 55 G1
Bouthwaite HG3 57 G2
Bovain FK21 81 G4
Boveney SL4 22 C4
Boveridge BH21 10 B3
Boverton CF61 18 C5
Bovey Tracey TQ13 5 J3
Bovingdon HP3 22 D1
Bovinger CM5 23 J1
Bovington Camp BH20 9 H6
Bow *Cumb.* CA5 60 E1
Bow *Devon* EX17 7 F5
Bow *Devon* TQ9 5 J5
Bow *Ork.* KW16 106 C8
Bow Brickhill MK17 32 C5
Bow of Fife KY15 82 E6
Bow Street *Cere.* SY24 37 F7
Bow Street *Norf.* NR17 44 E6
Bowbank DL12 62 A4
Bowburn DH6 62 E3
Bowcombe PO30 11 F6
Bowd EX10 7 K6
Bowden *Devon* TQ6 5 J6
Bowden *Sc.Bord.* TD6 76 D7
Bowden Hill SN15 20 C5
Bowdon WA14 49 G4
Bower NE48 70 C5
Bower Hinton TA12 8 D3
Bower House Tye CO6 34 D4
Bowerchalke SP5 10 B2
Bowerhill SN12 20 C5
Bowermadden KW1 105 H2
Bowers ST21 40 A2
Bowers Gifford SS13 24 D3
Bowershall KY12 75 J1
Bowertower KW1 105 H2
Bowes DL12 62 A5
Bowgreave PR3 55 H5
Bowhousebog ML7 75 G5
Bowithick PL15 4 B2
Bowker's Green L39 48 D2
Bowland Bridge LA11 55 H1
Bowley HR1 28 E3
Bowley Town HR1 28 E3
Bowlhead Green GU8 12 C3
Bowling *W.Dun.* G60 74 C3
Bowling *W.Yorks.* BD4 57 G6
Bowling Bank LL13 38 C1
Bowlish BA4 19 K7
Bowmanstead LA21 60 E7
Bowmore PA43 72 B4
Bowness-on-Solway CA7 69 H7
Bowness-on-Windermere LA23 60 F7
Bowscale CA11 60 E3
Bowsden TD15 77 H6
Bowside Lodge KW14 104 D2
Bowston LA8 61 F7
Bowthorpe NR5 45 F5
Bowtrees FK2 75 H2
Box *Glos.* GL6 20 B1
Box *Wilts.* SN13 20 B5
Box End MK43 32 D4
Boxbush *Glos.* GL14 29 G7
Boxbush *Glos.* GL17 29 F6
Boxford *Suff.* CO10 34 D4
Boxford *W.Berks.* RG20 21 H4
Boxgrove PO18 12 C6
Boxley ME14 14 C2
Boxmoor HP1 22 D1
Box's Shop EX23 6 A5
Boxted *Essex* CO4 34 D5
Boxted *Suff.* IP29 34 C3
Boxted Cross CO4 34 D5
Boxwell GL8 20 B2
Boxworth CB23 33 G2
Boxworth End CB24 33 G2
Boyden Gate CT3 25 J5
Boydston KA1 74 C7
Boylestone DE6 40 D2
Boyndie AB45 98 E4
Boynton YO16 59 H3
Boys Hill DT9 9 F4
Boysack DD11 83 H3
Boyton *Cornw.* PL15 6 B6
Boyton *Suff.* IP12 35 H4
Boyton *Wilts.* BA12 9 J1
Boyton Cross CM1 24 C1
Boyton End CO10 34 B4
Bozeat NN29 32 C3
Braaid IM4 54 C6
Braal Castle KW12 105 G2
Brabling Green IP13 35 G2
Brabourne TN25 15 F3
Brabourne Lees TN25 15 F3
Brabster KW1 105 J2
Bracadale IV56 85 J1
Braceborough PE9 42 D4
Bracebridge Heath LN4 52 C6
Braceby NG34 42 D2
Bracewell BD23 56 D5
Brachla IV3 88 C1
Bracken Hill WF14 57 G7
Brackenber CA16 61 J5
Brackenbottom BD24 56 D2
Brackenfield DE55 51 F7
Brackens AB53 99 F5
Bracklach AB54 90 B2
Bracklamore AB43 99 G5
Bracklesham PO20 12 B7
Brackletter PH34 87 H6
Brackley *Arg. & B.* PA31 73 G2
Brackley *High.* IV2 97 F6
Brackley *Northants.* NN13 31 G5
Brackley Gate DE7 41 F1
Brackley Hatch NN13 31 H4
Bracknell RG12 22 B5
Braco FK15 81 K7
Bracobrae AB55 98 D5
Bracon Ash NR14 45 F6
Bracora PH40 86 D5
Bracorina PH40 86 D5
Bradbourne DE6 50 E7
Bradbury TS21 62 E4
Bradda IM9 54 A6
Bradden NN12 31 H4
Braddock PL22 4 B4
Bradenham *Bucks.* HP14 22 B2
Bradenham *Norf.* IP25 44 D5
Bradenstoke SN15 20 D4
Bradfield *Devon* EX15 7 J5
Bradfield *Essex* CO11 35 F5
Bradfield *Norf.* NR28 45 G2
Bradfield *W.Berks.* RG7 21 K4
Bradfield Combust IP30 34 C3
Bradfield Green CW1 49 F7
Bradfield Heath CO11 35 F6
Bradfield St. Clare IP30 34 D3
Bradfield St. George IP30 34 D2
Bradford *Cornw.* PL30 4 B3
Bradford *Derbys.* DE45 50 E6
Bradford *Devon* EX22 6 C5
Bradford *Northumb.* NE70 77 K7
Bradford *Northumb.* NE20 71 F6
BRADFORD *W.Yorks.* BD 57 G6
Bradford Abbas DT9 8 E3
Bradford Leigh BA15 20 B5
Bradford Peverell DT2 9 F5
Bradford-on-Avon BA15 20 B5
Bradford-on-Tone TA4 7 K3
Bradiford EX31 6 D2
Brading PO36 11 H6
Bradley *Ches.W. & C.* WA6 48 E5
Bradley *Derbys.* DE6 40 E1
Bradley *Hants.* SO24 21 K7
Bradley *N.E.Lincs.* DN37 53 F2
Bradley (Low Bradley) *N.Yorks.* BD20 57 F5
Bradley *Staffs.* ST18 40 A4
Bradley *W.Mid.* WV14 40 B6
Bradley Fold BL2 49 G2
Bradley Green *Warks.* CV9 40 E5
Bradley Green *Worcs.* B96 29 J2
Bradley in the Moors ST10 40 C1
Bradley Mills HD5 50 D1
Bradley Stoke BS32 19 K3
Bradmore *Notts.* NG11 41 H2
Bradmore *W.Mid.* WV3 40 A6
Bradney TA7 8 C1
Bradninch EX5 7 J5
Bradnop ST13 50 C7
Bradnor Green HR5 28 B3
Bradpole DT6 8 D5
Bradshaw *Gt.Man.* BL2 49 G1
Bradshaw *W.Yorks.* HX2 57 F6
Bradstone PL19 6 B7
Bradwall Green CW11 49 G6
Bradwell *Derbys.* S33 50 D4
Bradwell *Devon* EX34 6 C1
Bradwell *Essex* CM77 34 C6
Bradwell *M.K.* MK13 32 B5
Bradwell *Norf.* NR31 45 K5
Bradwell Grove OX18 21 F1
Bradwell Waterside CM0 25 F1
Bradwell-on-Sea CM0 25 G1
Bradworthy EX22 6 B4
Brae *D. & G.* DG2 65 J3
Brae *High.* IV24 96 B1
Brae *Shet.* ZE2 107 M6
Brae of Achnahaird IV26 102 C7
Braeantra IV17 96 C4
Braedownie DD8 89 K7
Braefoot AB53 99 F6
Braegrum PH1 82 B5
Braehead *D. & G.* DG8 64 E5
Braehead *Glas.* G51 74 D4
Braehead *Moray* AB55 98 B6
Braehead *Ork.* KW17 106 E7
Braehead *Ork.* KW17 106 D3
Braehead *S.Lan.* ML11 75 G7
Braehead *S.Lan.* ML11 75 H5
Braehead of Lunan DD10 83 H2
Braehoulland ZE2 107 L5
Braeleny FK17 81 H6
Braemar AB35 89 J5
Braemore *High.* IV27 96 C1
Braemore *High.* KW6 105 F5
Braemore *High.* IV23 95 H4
Braenaloin AB35 89 K5
Braes of Enzie AB56 98 B5
Braes of Foss PH16 81 J2
Braes of Ullapool IV26 95 H2
Braeswick KW17 106 F4
Braeval FK8 81 G7
Braewick ZE2 107 M7
Brafferton *Darl.* DL1 62 D4
Brafferton *N.Yorks.* YO61 57 K2
Brafield-on-the-Green NN7 32 B3
Bragar HS2 100 E3
Bragbury End SG2 33 F6
Bragenham LU7 32 C6

Bragleenbeg PA34 80 A5
Braichmelyn LL57 46 E6
Braides LA2 55 H4
Braidley DL8 57 F1
Braidwood ML8 75 G6
Braigo PA44 72 A4
Brailsford DE6 40 E1
Brain's Green GL15 19 K1
Braintree CM7 34 B6
Braiseworth IP23 35 F1
Braishfield SO51 10 E2
Braithwaite Cumb. CA12 60 D4
Braithwaite S.Yorks. DN7 51 J1
Braithwaite W.Yorks. BD22 57 F5
Braithwell S66 51 H3
Bramber BN44 12 E5
Brambletye RH18 13 H3
Brambridge SO50 11 F2
Bramcote Notts. NG9 41 H2
Bramcote Warks. CV11 41 G7
Bramdean SO24 11 H2
Bramerton NR14 45 G5
Bramfield Herts. SG14 33 F7
Bramfield Suff. IP19 35 H1
Bramford IP8 35 F4
Bramhall SK7 49 H4
Bramham LS23 57 K5
Bramhope LS16 57 H5
Bramley Hants. RG26 21 K6
Bramley S.Yorks. S66 51 G3
Bramley Surr. GU5 22 D7
Bramley Corner RG26 21 K6
Bramley Head HG3 57 G4
Bramley Vale S44 51 G6
Bramling CT3 15 H2
Brampford Speke EX5 7 H6
Brampton Cambs. PE28 33 F1
Brampton Cumb. CA8 70 A7
Brampton Cumb. CA16 61 H4
Brampton Derbys. S40 51 F5
Brampton Lincs. LN1 52 B5
Brampton Norf. NR10 45 G3
Brampton S.Yorks. S73 51 G2
Brampton Suff. NR34 45 J7
Brampton Abbotts HR9 29 F6
Brampton Ash LE16 42 A7
Brampton Bryan SY7 28 C1
Brampton en le Morthen S66 51 G4
Brampton Street NR34 45 J7
Bramshall ST14 40 C2
Bramshaw SO43 10 D3
Bramshill RG27 22 A5
Bramshott GU30 12 B3
Bramwell TA10 8 D2
Bran End CM6 33 K6
Branault PH36 79 G1
Brancaster PE31 44 B1
Brancaster Staithe PE31 44 B1
Brancepeth DH7 62 D3
Branchill IV36 97 H6
Brand Green GL19 29 G6
Brandelhow CA12 60 D4
Branderburgh IV31 97 K4
Brandesburton YO25 59 H5
Brandeston IP13 35 G2
Brandis Corner EX22 6 C5
Brandiston NR10 45 F3
Brandon Dur. DH7 62 D3
Brandon Lincs. NG32 42 C1
Brandon Northumb. NE66 71 F2
Brandon Suff. IP27 44 B7
Brandon Warks. CV8 31 F1
Brandon Bank PE38 44 A7
Brandon Creek PE38 44 A6
Brandon Parva NR9 44 E5
Brandsby YO61 58 B2
Brandy Wharf DN21 52 D3
Brane TR20 2 B6
Branksome BH12 10 B5
Branksome Park BH13 10 B5
Bransbury SO21 21 H7
Bransby LN1 52 B5
Branscombe EX12 7 K7
Bransford WR6 29 G3
Bransford Bridge WR6 29 H3
Bransgore BH23 10 C5
Bransholme HU7 59 H6
Branson's Cross B98 30 B1
Branston Leics. NG32 42 B3
Branston Lincs. LN4 52 D6
Branston Staffs. DE14 40 E3
Branston Booths LN4 52 D6
Brant Broughton LN5 52 C7
Brantham CO11 35 F5
Branthwaite Cumb. CA7 60 D3
Branthwaite Cumb. CA14 60 B4
Brantingham HU15 59 F7
Branton Northumb. NE66 71 F2
Branton S.Yorks. DN3 51 J2
Brantwood LA21 60 E7
Branxholm Bridgend TD9 69 K2
Branxholme TD9 69 K2
Branxton TD12 77 G7
Brassey Green CW6 48 E6
Brassington DE4 50 E7
Brasted TN16 23 H6
Brasted Chart TN16 23 H6
Brathens AB31 90 E5
Bratoft PE24 53 H6
Brattleby LN1 52 C4
Bratton Som. TA24 7 H1
Bratton Tel. & W. TF5 39 F4
Bratton Wilts. BA13 20 C6
Bratton Clovelly EX20 6 C6
Bratton Fleming EX31 6 E2
Bratton Seymour BA9 9 F2
Braughing SG11 33 G6
Brauncewell NG34 52 D7
Braunston Northants. NN11 31 G2
Braunston Rut. LE15 42 B5
Braunstone LE3 41 H5
Braunton EX33 6 C2
Brawby YO17 58 D2
Brawdy SA62 16 B3
Brawith TS9 63 G6
Brawl KW14 104 D2
Brawlbin KW12 105 F3
Bray SL6 22 C4
Bray Shop PL17 4 D3
Bray Wick SL6 22 B4
Braybrooke LE16 42 A7
Braydon Side SN15 20 D3
Brayford EX32 6 E2
Brayshaw BD23 56 C4
Braythorn LS21 57 H5
Brayton YO8 58 C6
Braywoodside SL6 22 B4
Brazacott PL15 4 C1
Brea TR15 2 D4
Breach Kent CT4 15 G3
Breach Kent ME9 24 E5
Breachwood Green SG4 32 E6
Breacleit HS2 100 D4
Breaden Heath SY13 38 D2
Breadsall DE21 41 F2
Breadstone GL13 20 A1
Breage TR13 2 D6
Breakon ZE2 107 P2
Bream GL15 19 K1
Breamore SP6 10 C3
Brean TA8 19 F6
Breanais HS2 100 B5
Brearton HG3 57 J3
Breascleit HS2 100 E4
Breaston DE72 41 G2
Brechfa SA32 17 J2
Brechin DD9 83 H1
Brecklate PA28 66 A2
Breckles NR17 44 D6
Brecon (Aberhonddu) LD3 27 K6
Breconside DG3 68 D3
Bredbury SK6 49 J3
Brede TN31 14 D6
Bredenbury HR7 29 F3
Bredfield IP13 35 G3
Bredgar ME9 24 E5
Bredhurst ME7 24 D5
Bredon GL20 29 J5
Bredon's Hardwick GL20 29 J5
Bredon's Norton GL20 29 J5
Bredwardine HR3 28 C4
Breedon on the Hill DE73 41 G3
Breibhig HS2 101 G4
Breich EH55 75 H4
Breightmet BL2 49 G2
Breighton YO8 58 D6
Breinton HR4 28 D5
Breinton Common HR4 28 D5
Bremhill SN11 20 C4
Bremhill Wick SN11 20 C4
Brenachoille PA32 80 B7
Brenchley TN12 23 K7
Brendon Devon EX35 7 F1
Brendon Devon EX22 6 B4
Brendon Devon EX22 6 B5
Brenkley NE13 71 H6
Brent Eleigh CO10 34 D4
Brent Knoll TA9 19 G6
Brent Pelham SG9 33 H5
Brentford TW8 22 E4
Brentingby LE14 42 A4
Brentwood CM14 23 J2
Brenzett TN29 15 F5
Brenzett Green TN29 15 F5
Breoch DG7 65 H5
Brereton WS15 40 C4
Brereton Green CW11 49 G6
Brereton Heath CW12 49 H6
Breretonhill WS15 40 C4
Bressay ZE2 107 P8
Bressingham IP22 44 E7
Bressingham Common IP22 44 E7
Bretby DE15 40 E3
Bretford CV23 31 F1
Bretforton WR11 30 B4
Bretherdale Head CA10 61 G6
Bretherton PR26 55 H7
Brettabister ZE2 107 N7
Brettenham Norf. IP24 44 D7
Brettenham Suff. IP7 34 D3
Bretton Derbys. S32 50 D5
Bretton Flints. CH4 48 C6
Brevig HS9 84 B5
Brewood ST19 40 A5
Briach IV36 97 H6
Briantspuddle DT2 9 H5
Brick End CM6 33 J6
Brickendon SG13 23 G1
Bricket Wood AL2 22 E1
Brickkiln Green CM7 34 B5
Bricklehampton WR10 29 J4
Bride IM7 54 D3
Bridekirk CA13 60 C3
Bridell SA43 16 E1
Bridestones CW12 49 J6
Bridestowe EX20 6 D7
Brideswell AB54 90 D1
Bridford EX6 7 G7
Bridge Cornw. TR16 2 D4
Bridge Kent CT4 15 G2
Bridge End Cumb. LA20 55 F1
Bridge End Devon TQ7 5 G6
Bridge End Essex CM7 33 K5
Bridge End Lincs. NG34 42 E2
Bridge End Shet. ZE2 107 M9
Bridge Hewick HG4 57 J2
Bridge o'Ess AB34 90 D5
Bridge of Alford AB33 90 D3
Bridge of Allan FK9 75 F1
Bridge of Avon AB37 89 J1
Bridge of Balgie PH15 81 G3
Bridge of Bogendreip AB31 90 E5
Bridge of Brewlands PH11 82 C1
Bridge of Brown AB37 89 J2
Bridge of Cally PH10 82 C2
Bridge of Canny AB31 90 E5
Bridge of Craigisla PH11 82 D2
Bridge of Dee Aber. AB35 89 J5
Bridge of Dee Aber. AB31 90 E5
Bridge of Dee D. & G. DG7 65 H4
Bridge of Don AB23 91 H4
Bridge of Dun DD10 83 H2
Bridge of Dye AB31 90 E6
Bridge of Earn PH2 82 C6
Bridge of Ericht PH17 81 G2
Bridge of Feugh AB31 90 E5
Bridge of Forss KW14 105 F2
Bridge of Gairn AB35 90 B5
Bridge of Gaur PH17 81 G2
Bridge of Muchalls AB39 91 G5
Bridge of Muick AB35 90 B5
Bridge of Orchy PA36 80 D4
Bridge of Tynet AB56 98 B4
Bridge of Walls ZE2 107 L7
Bridge of Weir PA11 74 B4
Bridge Reeve EX18 6 E4
Bridge Sollers HR4 28 D4
Bridge Street CO10 34 C4
Bridge Trafford CH2 48 D5
Bridgefoot Angus DD3 82 E4
Bridgefoot Cambs. SG8 33 H4
Bridgefoot Cumb. CA14 60 B4
Bridgehampton BA22 8 E2
Bridgehaugh AB55 90 B1
Bridgehill DH8 62 B1
Bridgemary PO13 11 G4
Bridgemere CW5 39 G1
Bridgend Aber. AB54 90 D1
Bridgend Aber. AB53 99 F6
Bridgend Angus DD9 83 G1
Bridgend Arg. & B. PA44 72 B4
Bridgend Arg. & B. PA31 73 G1
Bridgend (Pen-y-bont ar Ogwr) Bridgend CF31 18 C4
Bridgend Cornw. PL22 4 B5
Bridgend Cumb. CA11 60 F5
Bridgend Fife KY15 82 E6
Bridgend Moray AB54 90 B1
Bridgend P. & K. PH2 82 C5
Bridgend W.Loth. EH49 75 J3
Bridgend of Lintrathen DD8 82 D2
Bridgerule EX22 6 A5
Bridges SY5 38 C6
Bridgeton Aber. AB33 90 D3
Bridgeton Glas. G40 74 E4
Bridgetown Cornw. PL15 6 B7
Bridgetown Som. TA22 7 H2
Bridgeyate BS30 19 K4
Bridgham NR16 44 D7
Bridgnorth WV16 39 G6
Bridgtown WS11 40 B5
Bridgwater TA6 8 B1
Bridlington YO16 59 H3
Bridport DT6 8 D5
Bridstow HR9 28 E6
Brierfield BB9 56 D6
Brierley Glos. GL17 29 F7
Brierley Here. HR6 28 D3
Brierley S.Yorks. S72 51 G1
Brierley Hill DY5 40 B7
Brierton TS22 63 F4
Briestfield WF12 50 E1
Brig o'Turk FK17 81 G7
Brigg DN20 52 D2
Briggate NR28 45 H3
Briggswath YO21 63 K6
Brigham Cumb. CA13 60 B3
Brigham E.Riding YO25 59 G4
Brighouse HD6 57 G7
Brighstone PO30 11 F6
Brightgate DE4 50 E7
Brighthampton OX29 21 G1
Brightholmlee S35 50 E3
Brightling TN32 13 K4
Brightlingsea CO7 34 E7
BRIGHTON B. & H. BN 13 G6
Brighton Cornw. TR2 3 G3
Brightons FK2 75 H3
Brightwalton RG20 21 H4
Brightwalton Green RG20 21 H4
Brightwell IP10 35 G4
Brightwell Baldwin OX49 21 K2
Brightwell Upperton OX49 21 K2
Brightwell-cum-Sotwell OX10 21 J2
Brignall DL12 62 B5
Brigsley DN37 53 F2
Brigsteer LA8 55 H1
Brigstock NN14 42 C7
Brill Bucks. HP18 31 H7
Brill Cornw. TR11 2 E6
Brilley HR3 28 B4
Brilley Mountain HR3 28 B3
Brimaston SA62 16 C3
Brimfield SY8 28 E2
Brimington S43 51 G5
Brimington Common S43 51 G5
Brimley TQ13 5 J3
Brimpsfield GL4 29 J7
Brimpton RG7 21 J5
Brims KW16 106 B9
Brimscombe GL5 20 B1
Brimstage CH63 48 C4
Brinacory PH41 86 D5
Brindham BA6 19 J7
Brindister Shet. ZE2 107 N9
Brindister Shet. ZE2 107 L7
Brindle PR6 55 J7
Brindley Ford ST8 49 H7
Brineton TF11 40 A4
Bringhurst LE16 42 B6
Brington PE28 32 D1
Brinian KW17 106 D5
Briningham NR24 44 E2
Brinkhill LN11 53 G5
Brinkley Cambs. CB8 33 K3
Brinkley Notts. NG25 51 K7
Brinklow CV23 31 F1
Brinkworth SN15 20 D3
Brinmore IV2 88 D2
Brinscall PR6 56 B7
Brinsea BS49 19 H5
Brinsley NG16 41 G1
Brinsop HR4 28 D4
Brinsworth S60 51 G3
Brinton NR24 44 E2
Brisco CA4 60 F1
Brisley NR20 44 D3
Brislington BS4 19 K4
Brissenden Green TN26 14 E4
BRISTOL BS 19 J4
Bristol Filton Airport BS10 19 J3
Bristol International Airport BS48 19 J5
Briston NR24 44 E2
Britannia OL13 56 D7
Britford SP5 10 C2
Brithdir Caerp. NP24 18 E1
Brithdir Gwyn. LL40 37 G4
Brithem Bottom EX15 7 J4
Briton Ferry (Llansawel) SA11 18 A2
Britwell SL2 22 C3
Britwell Salome OX49 21 K2
Brixham TQ5 5 K5
Brixton Devon PL8 5 F5
Brixton Gt.Lon. SW2 23 G4
Brixton Deverill BA12 9 H1
Brixworth NN6 31 J1
Brize Norton OX18 21 F1
Broad Alley WR9 29 H2
Broad Blunsdon SN26 20 E2
Broad Campden GL55 30 C5
Broad Carr HX4 50 C1
Broad Chalke SP5 10 B2
Broad Ford TN12 14 C4
Broad Green Cambs. CB8 33 K3
Broad Green Cen.Beds. MK43 32 C4
Broad Green Essex CO6 34 C6
Broad Green Essex SG8 33 H5
Broad Green Mersey. L14 48 D3
Broad Green Suff. IP6 34 E3
Broad Green Worcs. WR6 29 G3
Broad Haven SA62 16 B4
Broad Hill CB7 33 J1
Broad Hinton SN4 20 E4
Broad Laying RG20 21 H5
Broad Marston CV37 30 C4
Broad Oak Carmar. SA32 17 J3
Broad Oak Cumb. CA18 60 C7
Broad Oak E.Suss. TN31 14 D6
Broad Oak E.Suss. TN21 13 K4
Broad Oak Here. HR2 28 D6
Broad Road IP21 35 G1
Broad Street E.Suss. TN36 14 D6
Broad Street Kent ME17 14 D2
Broad Street Kent TN25 15 G4
Broad Street Wilts. SN9 20 E6
Broad Street Green CM9 24 E1
Broad Town SN4 20 D4
Broadbottom SK14 49 J3
Broadbridge PO18 12 B6
Broadbridge Heath RH12 12 E3
Broadclyst EX5 7 H6
Broadfield Lancs. BB5 56 C7
Broadfield Lancs. PR25 55 J7
Broadford IV49 86 C2
Broadford Bridge RH14 12 D4
Broadgate LA18 54 E1
Broadhaugh TD9 69 K3
Broadhaven KW1 105 J3
Broadheath Gt.Man. WA14 49 G4
Broadheath Worcs. WR15 29 F2
Broadhembury EX14 7 K5
Broadhempston TQ9 5 J4
Broadholme LN1 52 B5
Broadland Row TN31 14 D6
Broadlay SA17 17 G5
Broadley Lancs. OL12 49 H1
Broadley Moray AB56 98 B4
Broadley Common EN9 23 H1
Broadmayne DT2 9 G6
Broadmeadows TD7 76 C7
Broadmere RG25 21 K7
Broadmoor SA68 16 D5
Broadnymett EX17 7 F5
Broadoak Dorset DT6 8 D5
Broadoak Glos. GL14 29 F7
Broadoak Kent CT2 25 H5
Broadoak End SG14 33 G7
Broadrashes AB55 98 C5
Broad's Green CM3 33 K7
Broadsea AB43 99 H4
Broadstairs CT10 25 K5
Broadstone Poole BH18 10 B5
Broadstone Shrop. SY7 38 E7
Broadstreet Common NP18 19 G3
Broadwas WR6 29 G3
Broadwater Herts. SG2 33 F6
Broadwater W.Suss. BN14 12 E6
Broadwater Down TN2 13 J3
Broadwaters DY10 29 H1
Broadway Carmar. SA17 17 G5
Broadway Carmar. SA33 17 F4
Broadway Pembs. SA62 16 B4
Broadway Som. TA19 8 C3
Broadway Suff. IP19 35 H1
Broadway Worcs. WR12 30 C5
Broadwell Glos. GL56 30 D6
Broadwell Oxon. GL7 21 F1
Broadwell Warks. CV23 31 F2
Broadwell House NE47 62 A1
Broadwey DT3 9 F6
Broadwindsor DT8 8 D4
Broadwood Kelly EX19 6 E5
Broadwoodwidger PL16 6 C7
Brobury HR3 28 C4
Brocastle CF35 18 C4
Brochel IV40 94 B7
Brochloch DG7 67 K4
Brock PA77 78 B3
Brockamin WR6 29 G3
Brockbridge SO32 11 H3
Brockdish IP21 35 G1
Brockenhurst SO42 10 D4
Brockford Green IP14 35 F2
Brockford Street IP14 35 F2
Brockhall NN7 31 H2
Brockham RH3 22 E7
Brockhampton Glos. GL54 30 B6
Brockhampton Glos. GL51 29 J6
Brockhampton Here. HR1 28 E5
Brockhampton Here. WR6 29 F3
Brockhampton Green DT2 9 G4
Brockholes HD9 50 D1
Brockhurst Hants. PO12 11 G4
Brockhurst W.Suss. RH19 13 H3
Brocklebank CA7 60 E2
Brocklesby DN41 52 E1
Brockley N.Som. BS48 19 H5
Brockley Suff. IP29 34 C3
Brockley Green CO10 34 B4
Brock's Green RG20 21 H5
Brockton Shrop. TF13 38 E6
Brockton Shrop. TF11 39 G5
Brockton Shrop. SY5 38 C5
Brockton Shrop. SY7 38 C7
Brockton Tel. & W. TF10 39 G4
Brockweir NP16 19 J1
Brockwood Park SO24 11 H2
Brockworth GL3 29 H7
Brocton ST17 40 B4
Brodick KA27 73 J7
Brodsworth DN5 51 H2
Brogborough MK43 32 C5
Brogden BB18 56 D5
Brogyntyn SY10 38 B2
Broken Cross Ches.E. SK11 49 H5
Broken Cross Ches.W. & C. CW9 49 F5
Brokenborough SN16 20 C3
Brokes DL11 62 C7
Bromborough CH62 48 C4
Brome IP23 35 F1
Brome Street IP23 35 F1
Bromeswell IP12 35 H3
Bromfield Cumb. CA7 60 C2
Bromfield Shrop. SY8 28 D1
Bromham Bed. MK43 32 D3
Bromham Wilts. SN15 20 C5
BROMLEY Gt.Lon. BR 23 H5
Bromley S.Yorks. S35 51 F3
Bromley Cross BL7 49 G1
Bromley Green TN26 14 E4
Brompton Med. ME7 24 D5
Brompton N.Yorks. DL6 62 E7
Brompton N.Yorks. YO13 59 F1
Brompton Shrop. SY5 38 E5
Brompton on Swale DL10 62 D7
Brompton Ralph TA4 7 J2
Brompton Regis TA22 7 H2
Bromsash HR9 29 F6
Bromsberrow HR8 29 G5
Bromsberrow Heath HR8 29 G5
Bromsgrove B61 29 J1
Bromstead Heath TF10 40 A4
Bromyard HR7 29 F3
Bromyard Downs HR7 29 F3
Bronaber LL41 37 G2
Brondesbury NW6 23 F3
Brongest SA38 17 G1
Bronington SY13 38 D2
Bronllys LD3 28 A5
Bronnant SY23 27 F2
Bronwydd Arms SA33 17 H3
Bronydd HR3 28 B4
Bron-y-gaer SA33 17 G4
Bronygarth SY10 38 B2
Brook Carmar. SA33 17 F5
Brook Hants. SO43 10 D3
Brook Hants. SO20 10 E2
Brook I.o.W. PO30 10 E6
Brook Kent TN25 15 F3
Brook Surr. GU8 12 C3
Brook Surr. GU5 22 D7
Brook Bottom OL5 49 J2
Brook End Bed. MK44 32 D2
Brook End Herts. SG9 33 G6
Brook End M.K. MK16 32 C4
Brook End Worcs. WR5 29 H4
Brook Hill SO43 10 D3
Brook Street Essex CM14 23 J2
Brook Street Kent TN26 14 E4
Brook Street Suff. CO10 34 C4
Brook Street W.Suss. RH17 13 G4
Brooke Norf. NR15 45 G6
Brooke Rut. LE15 42 B5
Brookend Glos. GL15 19 J2

Brookend Glos. GL13 19 K1
Brookfield SK14 50 C3
Brookhampton OX44 21 K2
Brookhouse Ches.E. SK10 49 J5
Brookhouse Denb. LL16 47 J6
Brookhouse Lancs. LA2 55 J3
Brookhouse S.Yorks. S25 51 H4
Brookhouse Green CW11 49 H6
Brookhouses ST10 40 B1
Brookland TN29 14 E5
Brooklands D. & G. DG2 65 J3
Brooklands Shrop. SY13 38 E1
Brookmans Park AL9 23 F1
Brooks SY21 38 A6
Brooks Green RH13 12 E4
Brooksby LE14 41 J4
Brookthorpe GL4 29 H7
Brookwood GU24 22 C6
Broom Cen.Beds. SG18 32 E4
Broom Fife KY8 82 E7
Broom Warks. B50 30 B3
Broom Green NR20 44 D3
Broom Hill Dorset BH21 10 B4
Broom Hill Worcs. DY9 29 J1
Broom of Dalreach PH3 82 B6
Broomcroft SY5 38 E5
Broome Norf. NR35 45 H6
Broome Shrop. SY7 38 D7
Broome Worcs. DY9 29 J1
Broome Wood NE66 71 G2
Broomedge WA13 49 G4
Broomer's Corner RH13 12 E4
Broomfield Aber. AB41 91 H1
Broomfield Essex CM1 34 B7
Broomfield Kent CT6 25 H5
Broomfield Kent ME17 14 D2
Broomfield Som. TA5 8 B1
Broomfleet HU15 58 E7
Broomhall Green CW5 39 F1
Broomhaugh NE44 71 F7
Broomhead AB43 99 H4
Broomhill Bristol BS16 19 K4
Broomhill Northumb. NE65 71 H3
Broomielaw DL12 62 B5
Broomley NE43 71 F7
Broompark DH7 62 D2
Broom's Green GL18 29 G5
Brora KW9 97 G1
Broseley TF12 39 F5
Brotherlee DL13 62 A3
Brothertoft PE20 43 F1
Brotherton WF11 57 K7
Brotton TS12 63 H5
Broubster KW14 105 F2
Brough Cumb. CA17 61 J5
Brough Derbys. S33 50 D4
Brough E.Riding HU15 59 F7
Brough High. KW14 105 H1
Brough Notts. NG23 52 B7
Brough Ork. KW17 106 C6
Brough Shet. ZE2 107 P8
Brough Shet. ZE2 107 N5
Brough Shet. ZE2 107 P6
Brough Shet. ZE2 107 P5
Brough Lodge ZE2 107 P3
Brough Sowerby CA17 61 J5
Broughall SY13 38 E1
Brougham CA10 61 G4
Broughton Bucks. HP20 32 B7
Broughton Cambs. PE28 33 F1
Broughton Flints. CH4 48 C6
Broughton Hants. SO20 10 E1
Broughton Lancs. PR3 55 J6
Broughton M.K. MK16 32 B4
Broughton N.Lincs. DN20 52 C2
Broughton N.Yorks. YO17 58 D2
Broughton N.Yorks. BD23 56 E4
Broughton Northants. NN14 32 B1
Broughton Ork. KW17 106 D3
Broughton Oxon. OX15 31 F5
Broughton Sc.Bord. ML12 75 K7
Broughton V. of Glam. CF71 18 C4
Broughton Astley LE9 41 H6
Broughton Beck LA12 55 F1
Broughton Gifford SN12 20 B5
Broughton Green WR9 29 J2
Broughton Hackett WR7 29 J3
Broughton in Furness LA20 55 F1
Broughton Mills LA20 60 D7
Broughton Moor CA15 60 B3
Broughton Poggs GL7 21 F1
Broughtown KW17 106 F3
Broughty Ferry DD5 83 F4
Browland ZE2 107 L7
Brown Candover SO24 11 G1
Brown Edge Lancs. PR8 48 C1
Brown Edge Staffs. ST6 49 J7
Brown Heath CH3 48 D6
Brown Lees ST8 49 H7
Brown Street IP14 34 E2
Brownber CA17 61 J6
Browndown PO13 11 G5
Brownheath SY12 38 D3
Brownhill AB41 99 G6
Brownhills Fife KY16 83 G6
Brownhills W.Mid. WS8 40 C5
Brownieside NE67 71 G1
Brownlow CW12 49 H6
Brownlow Heath CW12 49 H6
Brown's Bank CW3 39 F1
Brownsea Island BH15 10 B6
Brownshill GL6 20 B1
Brownshill Green CV5 41 F7
Brownsover CV21 31 G1
Brownston PL21 5 G5
Browston Green NR31 45 J5
Broxa YO13 63 J3
Broxbourne EN10 23 G1
Broxburn E.Loth. EH42 76 E3
Broxburn W.Loth. EH52 75 J3
Broxholme LN1 52 C5
Broxted CM6 33 J6
Broxton CH3 48 D7
Broxwood HR6 28 C3
Broyle Side BN8 13 H5
Bru (Brue) HS2 101 F3
Bruachmary IV12 97 F7
Bruan KW2 105 J5
Brue (Bru) HS2 101 F3
Bruera CH3 48 D6
Bruern OX7 30 D6
Bruernish HS9 84 C4
Bruichladdich PA49 72 A4
Bruisyard IP17 35 H2
Bruisyard Street IP17 35 H2
Brumby DN16 52 C1
Brund SK17 50 D6
Brundall NR13 45 H5
Brundish Norf. NR14 45 H6
Brundish Suff. IP13 35 G2
Brundish Street IP13 35 G1
Brunstock CA6 60 F1
Brunswick Village NE13 71 H6
Bruntingthorpe LE17 41 J6
Bruntland AB54 90 C2
Brunton Fife KY15 82 E5
Brunton Northumb. NE66 71 H1
Brunton Wilts. SN8 21 F6
Brushfield SK17 50 D5
Brushford Devon EX18 6 E5
Brushford Som. TA22 7 H3
Bruton BA10 9 F1
Bryanston DT11 9 H4
Bryant's Bottom HP16 22 B2
Brydekirk DG12 69 G6
Brymbo LL11 48 B7
Brympton BA22 8 E3
Bryn Caerp. NP12 18 E2
Bryn Carmar. SA14 17 J5
Bryn Ches.W. & C. CW8 49 F5
Bryn Gt.Man. WN4 48 E2
Bryn N.P.T. SA13 18 B2
Bryn Shrop. SY9 38 B7
Bryn Bwbach LL47 37 F2
Bryn Gates WN2 48 E2
Bryn Pen-y-lan LL14 38 C1
Brynamman SA18 27 G7
Brynberian SA41 16 E2
Brynbuga (Usk) NP15 19 G1
Bryncae CF72 18 C3
Bryncethin CF32 18 C3
Bryncir LL51 36 D1
Bryncoch Bridgend CF32 18 C3
Bryn-côch N.P.T. SA10 18 A2
Bryncroes LL53 36 B2
Bryncrug LL36 37 F5
Bryneglwys LL21 38 A1
Brynford CH8 47 K5
Bryngwran LL65 46 B5
Bryngwyn Mon. NP15 19 G1
Bryngwyn Powys HR5 28 A4
Bryn-henllan SA42 16 D2
Brynhoffnant SA44 26 C3
Bryning PR4 55 H6
Brynithel NP13 19 F1
Brynmawr B.Gwent NP23 28 A7
Bryn-mawr Gwyn. LL53 36 B2
Brynmelyn LD1 28 A1
Brynmenyn CF32 18 C3
Brynna CF72 18 C3
Brynnau Gwynion CF72 18 C3
Brynog SA48 26 E3
Bryn-penarth SY21 38 A5
Brynrefail Gwyn. LL55 46 D6
Brynrefail I.o.A. LL70 46 C4
Brynsadler CF72 18 D3
Brynsaithmarchog LL21 47 J7
Brynsiencyn LL61 46 C6
Bryn-teg I.o.A. LL78 46 C4
Brynteg Wrex. LL11 48 C7
Bryn-y-cochin SY12 38 C2
Brynygwenin NP7 28 C7
Bryn-y-maen LL28 47 G5
Buaile nam Bodach HS9 84 C4
Bualadubh HS8 92 C7
Bualintur IV47 85 K2
Bualnaluib IV22 94 E2
Bubbenhall CV8 30 E1
Bubnell DE45 50 E5
Bubwith YO8 58 D6
Buccleuch TD9 69 J2
Buchan DG7 65 H4
Buchanan Castle G63 74 C2
Buchanhaven AB42 99 K6
Buchanty PH1 82 A5
Buchlyvie FK8 74 D1
Buckabank CA5 60 E2
Buckby Wharf NN11 31 H2
Buckden Cambs. PE19 32 E2
Buckden N.Yorks. BD23 56 E2
Buckenham NR13 45 H5
Buckerell EX14 7 K5
Buckfast TQ11 5 H4
Buckfastleigh TQ11 5 H4
Buckhaven KY8 76 B1
Buckholm TD1 76 C7
Buckholt NP25 28 E7
Buckhorn Weston SP8 9 G2
Buckhurst Hill IG9 23 H2
Buckie AB56 98 C4
Buckies KW14 105 G2
Buckingham MK18 31 H5
Buckland Bucks. HP22 32 B7
Buckland Devon TQ7 5 G6
Buckland Glos. WR12 30 B5
Buckland Hants. SO41 10 E5
Buckland Here. HR6 28 E3
Buckland Herts. SG9 33 G5
Buckland Kent CT16 15 J3
Buckland Oxon. SN7 21 G2
Buckland Surr. RH3 23 F6
Buckland Brewer EX39 6 C3
Buckland Common HP23 22 C1
Buckland Dinham BA11 20 A6
Buckland Filleigh EX21 6 C5
Buckland in the Moor TQ13 5 H3
Buckland Monachorum PL20 4 E4
Buckland Newton DT2 9 F4
Buckland Ripers DT3 9 F6
Buckland St. Mary TA20 8 B3
Buckland-tout-Saints TQ7 5 H6
Bucklebury RG7 21 J4
Bucklerheads DD5 83 F4
Bucklers Hard SO42 11 F5
Bucklesham IP10 35 G4
Buckley (Bwcle) CH7 48 B6
Buckley Green B95 30 C2
Bucklow Hill WA16 49 G4
Buckman Corner RH14 12 E4
Buckminster NG33 42 B3
Bucknall Lincs. LN10 52 E6
Bucknall Stoke ST2 40 B1
Bucknell Oxon. OX27 31 G6
Bucknell Shrop. SY7 28 C1
Buckridge DY14 29 G1
Buck's Cross EX39 6 B3
Bucks Green RH12 12 D3
Bucks Hill WD4 22 D1
Bucks Horn Oak GU10 22 B7
Buck's Mills EX39 6 B3
Bucksburn AB21 91 G4
Buckspool SA71 16 C6
Buckton E.Riding YO15 59 H2
Buckton Here. SY7 28 C1
Buckton Northumb. NE70 77 J7
Buckton Vale SK15 49 J2
Buckworth PE28 32 E1
Budbrooke CV35 30 D2
Budby NG22 51 J5
Buddon DD7 83 G4
Bude EX23 6 A5
Budge's Shop PL12 4 D5
Budlake EX5 7 H5
Budle NE69 77 K7
Budleigh Salterton EX9 7 J7
Budock Water TR11 2 E5
Budworth Heath CW9 49 F5
Buerton CW3 39 F1
Bugbrooke NN7 31 H3
Bugeildy (Beguildy) LD7 28 A1
Buglawton CW12 49 H6
Bugle PL26 4 A5
Bugthorpe YO41 58 D4
Building End SG8 33 H5
Buildwas TF8 39 F5
Builth Road LD2 27 K3
Builth Wells (Llanfair-ym-Muallt) LD2 27 K3
Bulby PE10 42 D3
Bulcote NG14 41 J1
Buldoo KW14 104 E2
Bulford SP4 20 E7
Bulford Camp SP4 20 E7
Bulkeley SY14 48 E7
Bulkington Warks. CV12 41 F7
Bulkington Wilts. SN10 20 C6
Bulkworthy EX22 6 B4
Bull Bay (Porth Llechog) LL68 46 C3
Bull Green TN26 14 E4
Bullbridge DE56 51 F7
Bullbrook RG12 22 B5
Bullen's Green AL4 23 F1
Bulley GL2 29 G7
Bullington LN3 52 D5
Bullpot Farm LA6 56 B1
Bulls Cross EN2 23 G2
Bull's Green Herts. SG3 33 F7
Bull's Green Norf. NR34 45 J6
Bullwood PA23 73 K3
Bulmer Essex CO10 34 C4
Bulmer N.Yorks. YO60 58 C3
Bulmer Tye CO10 34 C5
Bulphan RM14 24 C3
Bulstone EX12 7 K7
Bulverhythe TN38 14 C7
Bulwark AB42 99 H6
Bulwell NG6 41 H1
Bulwick NN17 42 C6
Bumble's Green EN9 23 H1
Bun Abhainn Eadarra HS3 100 D7
Bun Loyne IV63 87 J4
Bunarkaig PH34 87 H6
Bunbury CW6 48 E7
Bunbury Heath CW6 48 E7
Bunchrew IV3 96 D7
Bundalloch IV40 86 E2
Buness ZE2 107 Q2
Bunessan PA67 78 E5
Bungay NR35 45 H7
Bunker's Hill LN4 53 F7
Bunlarie PA28 73 F7
Bunloit IV63 88 C2
Bunmhullin HS8 84 C3
Bunnahabhain PA46 72 C3
Bunny NG11 41 H3
Buntait IV63 87 K1
Buntingford SG9 33 G6
Bunwell NR16 45 F6
Bunwell Street NR16 45 F6
Burbage Derbys. SK17 50 C5
Burbage Leics. LE10 41 G6
Burbage Wilts. SN8 21 F5
Burchett's Green SL6 22 B3
Burcombe SP2 10 B1
Burcot Oxon. OX14 21 J2
Burcot Worcs. B60 29 J1
Burcott LU7 32 B6
Burdale YO17 58 E3
Burdocks RH14 12 D4
Burdon SR3 62 E1
Burdrop OX15 30 E5
Bures CO8 34 D5
Bures Green CO8 34 D5
Burfa LD8 28 B2
Burford Oxon. OX18 30 D7
Burford Shrop. WR15 28 E2
Burg PA74 78 E3
Burgate IP22 34 E1
Burgates GU33 11 J2
Burge End SG5 32 E5
Burgess Hill RH15 13 G5
Burgh IP13 35 G3
Burgh by Sands CA5 60 E1
Burgh Castle NR31 45 J5
Burgh Heath KT20 23 F6
Burgh le Marsh PE24 53 H6
Burgh next Aylsham NR11 45 G3
Burgh on Bain LN8 53 F4
Burgh St. Margaret (Fleggburgh) NR29 45 J4
Burgh St. Peter NR34 45 J6
Burghclere RG20 21 H5
Burghead IV30 97 J5
Burghfield RG30 21 K5
Burghfield Common RG7 21 K5
Burghfield Hill RG7 21 K5
Burghill HR4 28 D4
Burghwallis DN6 51 H1
Burham ME1 24 D5
Buriton GU31 11 J2
Burland CW5 49 F7
Burlawn PL27 3 G2
Burleigh SL5 22 C5
Burlescombe EX16 7 J4
Burleston DT2 9 G5
Burley Hants. BH24 10 D4
Burley Rut. LE15 42 B4
Burley W.Yorks. LS6 57 H6
Burley Gate HR1 28 E4
Burley in Wharfedale LS29 57 G5
Burley Street BH24 10 D4
Burley Woodhead LS29 57 G5
Burleydam SY13 39 F1
Burlingjobb LD8 28 B3
Burlow TN21 13 J5
Burlton SY4 38 D3
Burmarsh TN29 15 G4
Burmington CV36 30 D5
Burn YO8 58 B7
Burn Farm DD9 90 E7
Burn Naze FY5 55 G5
Burn of Cambus FK16 81 J7
Burnage M19 49 H3
Burnaston DE65 40 E2
Burnby YO42 58 E5
Burncross S35 51 F3
Burndell BN18 12 C6
Burnden BL3 49 G2
Burnedge OL2 49 J1
Burnend AB41 99 G6
Burneside LA9 61 G7
Burness KW17 106 F3
Burneston DL8 57 J1
Burnett BS31 19 K5
Burnfoot High. KW11 104 D6
Burnfoot P. & K. FK14 82 A7
Burnfoot Sc.Bord. TD9 70 A2
Burnfoot Sc.Bord. TD9 69 K2
Burnham Bucks. SL1 22 C3
Burnham N.Lincs. DN18 52 D1
Burnham Deepdale PE31 44 C1
Burnham Green AL6 33 F7
Burnham Market PE31 44 C1
Burnham Norton PE31 44 C1
Burnham Overy Staithe PE31 44 C1
Burnham Overy Town PE31 44 C1
Burnham Thorpe PE31 44 C1
Burnham-on-Crouch CM0 25 F2
Burnham-on-Sea TA8 19 G7
Burnhaven AB42 99 K6
Burnhead D. & G. DG7 67 K5
Burnhead D. & G. DG3 68 D4
Burnhervie AB51 91 F3
Burnhill Green WV6 39 G5
Burnhope DH7 62 C2
Burnhouse KA15 74 B5
Burniston YO13 63 K3
Burnley BB11 56 D6
Burnmouth TD14 77 H4
Burnopfield NE16 62 C1
Burn's Green SG2 33 G6
Burnsall BD23 57 F3
Burnside Aber. AB32 91 F3
Burnside Angus DD8 83 G2
Burnside E.Ayr. KA18 67 K2
Burnside Fife KY13 82 C7
Burnside Shet. ZE2 107 L5
Burnside W.Loth. EH52 75 J3
Burnside of Duntrune DD4 83 F4
Burnstones CA8 61 H1
Burnswark DG11 69 G6
Burnt Hill RG18 21 J4
Burnt Houses DL13 62 C4
Burnt Oak HA8 23 F2
Burnt Yates HG3 57 H3
Burntcliff Top SK11 49 J6
Burntisland KY3 76 A2
Burnton E.Ayr. KA18 67 J2
Burnton E.Ayr. KA6 67 J3
Burntwood WS7 40 C5
Burntwood Green WS7 40 C5
Burnworthy TA3 7 K4
Burpham Surr. GU1 22 D6
Burpham W.Suss. BN18 12 D6
Burra ZE2 107 M9
Burradon Northumb. NE65 70 E3
Burradon T. & W. NE23 71 H6
Burrafirth ZE2 107 Q1
Burraland ZE2 107 M5
Burras TR13 2 D5
Burraton Cornw. PL12 4 E4
Burraton Cornw. PL12 4 E5
Burravoe Shet. ZE2 107 P5
Burravoe Shet. ZE2 107 M6
Burray KW17 106 D8
Burrells CA16 61 H5
Burrelton PH13 82 D4
Burridge Devon EX13 8 C4
Burridge Hants. SO31 11 G3
Burrill DL8 57 H1
Burringham DN17 52 B2
Burrington Devon EX37 6 E4
Burrington Here. SY8 28 D1
Burrington N.Som. BS40 19 H6
Burrough Green CB8 33 K3
Burrough on the Hill LE14 42 A4
Burrow Som. TA24 7 H1
Burrow Som. TA12 8 D3
Burrow Bridge TA7 8 C1
Burrowhill GU24 22 C5
Burrows Cross GU5 22 D7
Burry SA3 17 H6
Burry Green SA3 17 H6
Burry Port SA16 17 H5
Burscough L40 48 D1
Burscough Bridge L40 48 D1
Bursea YO43 58 E6
Burshill YO25 59 G5
Bursledon SO31 11 F4
Burslem ST6 40 A1
Burstall IP8 35 F4
Burstock DT8 8 D4
Burston Norf. IP22 45 F7
Burston Staffs. ST18 40 B2
Burstow RH6 23 G7
Burstwick HU12 59 J7
Burtersett DL8 56 D1
Burthorpe IP29 34 B2
Burthwaite CA4 60 F2
Burtle TA7 19 H7
Burtle Hill TA7 19 G7
Burton Ches.W. & C. CH64 48 C5
Burton Ches.W. & C. CW6 48 E6
Burton Dorset BH23 10 C5
Burton Lincs. LN1 52 C5
Burton Northumb. NE69 77 K7
Burton Pembs. SA73 16 C5
Burton Som. TA5 7 K1
Burton Wilts. SN14 20 B4
Burton Wilts. BA12 9 H1
Burton Agnes YO25 59 H3
Burton Bradstock DT6 8 D6
Burton Coggles NG33 42 C3
Burton End CM24 33 J6
Burton Ferry SA73 16 C5
Burton Fleming YO25 59 G2
Burton Green Warks. CV8 30 D1
Burton Green Wrex. LL12 48 C7
Burton Hastings CV11 41 G7
Burton in Lonsdale LA6 56 B2
Burton Joyce NG14 41 J1
Burton Latimer NN15 32 C1
Burton Lazars LE14 42 A4
Burton Leonard HG3 57 J3
Burton on the Wolds LE12 41 H3
Burton Overy LE8 41 J6
Burton Pedwardine NG34 42 E1
Burton Pidsea HU12 59 J6
Burton Salmon LS25 57 K7
Burton Stather DN15 52 B1
Burton upon Stather DN15 52 B1
Burton upon Trent DE14 40 E3
Burton-in-Kendal LA6 55 J2
Burton's Green CM77 34 C6
Burtonwood WA5 48 E3
Burwardsley CH3 48 E7
Burwarton WV16 39 F7
Burwash TN19 13 K4
Burwash Common TN19 13 K4
Burwash Weald TN19 13 K4
Burwell Cambs. CB25 33 J2
Burwell Lincs. LN11 53 G5
Burwen LL68 46 C3
Burwick Ork. KW17 106 D9
Burwick Shet. ZE1 107 M8
Bury Cambs. PE26 43 F7
Bury Gt.Man. BL9 49 H1
Bury Som. TA22 7 H3
Bury W.Suss. RH20 12 D5
Bury End WR12 30 B5
Bury Green SG11 33 H6
Bury St. Edmunds IP33 34 C2
Buryas Bridge TR19 2 B6
Burythorpe YO17 58 D3
Busbridge GU7 22 C7
Busby E.Renf. G76 74 D5
Busby P. & K. PH1 82 B5
Buscot SN7 21 F2
Bush EX23 6 A5
Bush Bank HR4 28 D3
Bush Crathie AB35 89 K5
Bush Green IP21 45 G7
Bushbury WV10 40 B5
Bushby LE7 41 J5
Bushey WD23 22 E2
Bushey Heath WD23 22 E2
Bushley GL20 29 H5
Bushley Green GL20 29 H5
Bushton SN4 20 D4
Bushy Common NR19 44 D4
Busk CA10 61 H2
Buslingthorpe LN8 52 D4

Bussage GL6 20 B1
Busta ZE2 107 M6
Butcher's Common NR12 45 H3
Butcher's Cross TN20 13 J4
Butcher's Pasture CM6 33 K6
Butcombe BS40 19 J5
Bute PA20 73 J4
Bute Town NP22 18 E1
Buthill IV30 97 J5
Butleigh BA6 8 E1
Butleigh Wootton BA6 8 E1
Butler's Cross HP17 22 B1
Butler's Hill NG15 41 H1
Butlers Marston CV35 30 E4
Butlersbank SY4 38 E3
Butley IP12 35 H3
Butley Abbey IP12 35 H4
Butley Low Corner IP12 35 H4
Butley Mills IP12 35 H3
Butley Town SK10 49 J5
Butt Green CW5 49 F7
Butt Lane ST7 49 H7
Butterburn CA8 70 B6
Buttercrambe YO41 58 D4
Butterknowle DL13 62 C4
Butterleigh EX15 7 H5
Butterley DE5 51 G7
Buttermere *Cumb.* CA13 60 C5
Buttermere *Wilts.* SN8 21 G5
Butters Green ST7 49 H7
Buttershaw BD6 57 G6
Butterstone PH8 82 B3
Butterton *Staffs.* ST13 50 C7
Butterton *Staffs.* ST5 40 A1
Butterwick *Dur.* TS21 62 E4
Butterwick *Lincs.* PE22 43 G1
Butterwick *N.Yorks.* YO17 59 F2
Butterwick *N.Yorks.* YO17 58 D2
Buttington SY21 38 B5
Buttonbridge DY12 29 G1
Buttonoak DY12 29 G1
Buttons' Green IP30 34 D3
Butts EX6 7 G7
Butt's Green *Essex* CM2 24 D1
Butt's Green *Hants.* SO51 10 D2
Buttsash SO45 11 F4
Buxhall IP14 34 E3
Buxted TN22 13 H4
Buxton *Derbys.* SK17 50 C5
Buxton *Norf.* NR10 45 G3
Buxton Heath NR10 45 F3
Buxworth SK23 50 C4
Bwcle (Buckley) CH7 48 B6
Bwlch LD3 28 A6
Bwlch-clawdd SA44 17 G2
Bwlch-derwin LL51 36 D1
Bwlchgwyn LL11 48 B7
Bwlch-llan SA48 26 E3
Bwlchnewydd SA33 17 G3
Bwlchtocyn LL53 36 C3
Bwlch-y-cibau SY22 38 A4
Bwlch-y-ddar SY10 38 A3
Bwlchyfadfa SA44 17 H1
Bwlch-y-ffridd SY16 37 K6
Bwlch-y-groes SA35 17 F2
Bwlchyllyn LL54 46 D7
Bwlchymynydd SA4 17 J6
Bwlch-y-sarnau LD6 27 K1
Byers Green DL16 62 D3
Byfield NN11 31 G3
Byfleet KT14 22 D5
Byford HR4 28 C4
Bygrave SG7 33 F5
Byker NE6 71 H7
Byland Abbey YO61 58 B2
Bylane End PL14 4 C5
Bylchau LL16 47 H6
Byley CW10 49 G6
Bynea SA14 17 J6
Byrness NE19 70 C3
Bystock EX8 7 J7
Bythorn PE28 32 D1
Byton LD8 28 C2
Bywell NE43 71 F7
Byworth GU28 12 C4

C

Cabharstadh HS2 101 F5
Cabourne LN7 52 E2
Cabourne Parva LN7 52 E2
Cabrach *Arg. & B.* PA60 72 C4
Cabrach *Moray* AB54 90 B2
Cabus PR3 55 H5
Cackle Street *E.Suss.* TN31 14 D6
Cackle Street *E.Suss.* TN22 13 H4
Cacrabank TD7 69 J2
Cadboll IV20 97 F4
Cadbury EX5 7 H5
Cadbury Barton EX18 6 E4
Cadbury Heath BS30 19 K4
Cadder G64 74 E3
Cadderlie PA35 80 B4
Caddington LU1 32 D7
Caddleton PA34 79 J6
Caddonfoot TD1 76 C7
Cade Street TN21 13 K4
Cadeby *Leics.* CV13 41 G5
Cadeby *S.Yorks.* DN5 51 H2
Cadeleigh EX16 7 H5
Cader LL16 47 J6
Cadgwith TR12 2 E7
Cadham KY7 82 D7
Cadishead M44 49 G3
Cadle SA5 17 K6
Cadley *Lancs.* PR2 55 J6
Cadley *Wilts.* SN8 21 F5
Cadmore End HP14 22 A2
Cadnam SO40 10 D3
Cadney DN20 52 D2
Cadole CH7 48 B6
Cadover Bridge PL7 5 F4
Cadoxton CF63 18 E5
Cadoxton-Juxta-Neath SA10 18 A2
Cadwell SG5 32 E5
Cadwst LL21 37 K2
Cadzow ML3 75 F5
Cae Ddafydd LL48 37 F1
Caeathro LL55 46 D6
Caehopkin SA9 27 H7
Caen KW8 105 F7
Caenby LN8 52 D4
Caenby Corner LN8 52 C4
Caer Llan NP25 19 H1
Caerau *Bridgend* CF34 18 B2
Caerau *Cardiff* CF5 18 E4
Caerdeon LL42 37 F4
CAERDYDD (CARDIFF) CF 18 E4
Caerfarchell SA62 16 A3
Caerfyrddin (Carmarthen) SA31 17 H3
Caergeiliog LL65 46 B5
Caergwrle LL12 48 C7
Caergybi (Holyhead) LL65 46 A4
Caerhun LL32 47 F5
Caer-Lan SA9 27 H7
Caerleon NP18 19 G2
Caernarfon LL55 46 C6
Caerphilly CF83 18 E3
Caersws SY17 37 K6
Caerwedros SA44 26 C3
Caerwent NP26 19 H2
Caerwys CH7 47 K5
Caethle Farm LL36 37 F6
Caggan PH22 89 F3
Caggle Street NP7 28 C7
Caim *High.* PH36 79 G1
Caim *I.o.A.* LL58 46 E4
Caio SA19 17 K2
Cairinis (Carinish) HS6 92 D5
Cairisiadar HS2 100 C4
Cairminis HS5 93 F3
Cairnargat AB54 90 C1
Cairnbaan PA31 73 G1
Cairnbeathie AB31 90 D4
Cairnbrogie AB51 91 G2
Cairnbulg AB43 99 J4
Cairncross *Angus* DD9 90 D7
Cairncross *Sc.Bord.* TD14 77 G4
Cairncurran PA13 74 B4
Cairndoon DG8 64 D7
Cairndow PA26 80 C6
Cairness AB43 99 J4
Cairney Lodge KY15 82 E6
Cairneyhill KY12 75 J2
Cairnhill *Aber.* AB41 91 H2
Cairnhill *Aber.* AB52 90 E1
Cairnie *Aber.* AB32 91 G4
Cairnie *Aber.* AB54 98 C6
Cairnorrie AB41 99 G6
Cairnryan DG9 64 A4
Cairnsmore DG8 64 E4
Caister-on-Sea NR30 45 K4
Caistor LN7 52 E2
Caistor St. Edmund NR14 45 G5
Caistron NE65 70 E3
Cake Street NR17 44 E6
Cakebole DY10 29 H1
Calanais (Callanish) HS2 100 E4
Calbost HS2 101 G6
Calbourne PO30 11 F6
Calceby LN13 53 G5
Calcoed CH8 47 K5
Calcot RG31 21 K4
Calcott *Kent* CT3 25 H5
Calcott *Shrop.* SY3 38 D4
Calcotts Green GL2 29 G7
Calcutt SN6 20 E2
Caldarvan G83 74 C2
Caldback ZE2 107 Q2
Caldbeck CA7 60 E3
Caldbergh DL8 57 F1
Caldecote *Cambs.* CB23 33 G3
Caldecote *Cambs.* PE7 42 E7
Caldecote *Herts.* SG7 33 F5
Caldecote *Northants.* NN12 31 H3
Caldecote *Warks.* CV10 41 F6
Caldecott *Northants.* NN9 32 C2
Caldecott *Oxon.* OX14 21 H2
Caldecott *Rut.* LE16 42 B6
Calder Bridge CA20 60 B6
Calder Grove WF4 51 F1
Calder Mains KW12 105 F3
Calder Vale PR3 55 J5
Calderbank ML6 75 F4
Calderbrook OL15 49 J1
Caldercruix ML6 75 G4
Calderglen G72 74 E5
Caldermill ML10 74 E6
Caldey Island SA70 16 E6
Caldhame DD8 83 F3
Caldicot NP26 19 H3
Caldwell *Derbys.* DE12 40 E4
Caldwell *E.Renf.* G78 74 C5
Caldwell *N.Yorks.* DL11 62 C5
Caldy CH48 48 B4
Calebreck CA7 60 E3
Caledrhydiau SA48 26 D3
Calford Green CB9 33 K4
Calfsound KW17 106 E4
Calgary PA75 78 E2
Califer IV36 97 H6
California *Falk.* FK1 75 H3
California *Norf.* NR29 45 K4
California *Suff.* IP4 35 G4
Calke DE73 41 F3
Callakille IV54 94 C6
Callaly NE66 71 F3
Callander FK17 81 H7
Callanish (Calanais) HS2 100 E4
Callaughton TF13 39 F6
Callerton Lane End NE5 71 G7
Calliburn PA28 66 B1
Calligarry IV45 86 C4
Callington PL17 4 D4
Callingwood DE13 40 D3
Callisterhall DG11 69 H5
Callow HR2 28 D5
Callow End WR2 29 H4
Callow Hill *Wilts.* SN15 20 D3
Callow Hill *Worcs.* DY14 29 G1
Callow Hill *Worcs.* B97 30 B2
Callows Grave WR15 28 E2
Calmore SO40 10 E3
Calmsden GL7 20 D1
Calne SN11 20 C4
Calow S44 51 G5
Calrossie IV19 96 E4
Calshot SO45 11 F4
Calstock PL18 4 E4
Calstone Wellington SN11 20 D5
Calthorpe NR11 45 F2
Calthwaite CA11 61 F2
Calton *N.Yorks.* BD23 56 E4
Calton *Staffs.* ST10 50 D7
Calveley CW6 48 E7
Calver S32 50 E5
Calver Hill HR4 28 C4
Calverhall SY13 39 F2
Calverleigh EX16 7 H4
Calverley LS28 57 H6
Calvert MK18 31 H6
Calverton *M.K.* MK19 31 J5
Calverton *Notts.* NG14 41 J1
Calvine PH18 81 J1
Calvo CA7 60 C1
Cam GL11 20 A2
Camasnacroise PH33 79 K2
Camastianavaig IV51 86 B1
Camasunary IV49 86 B3
Camault Muir IV4 96 C7
Camb ZE2 107 P3
Camber TN31 14 E6
Camberley GU15 22 B5
Camberwell SE15 23 G4
Camblesforth YO8 58 C7
Cambo NE61 71 F5
Cambois NE24 71 J5
Camborne TR14 2 D5
CAMBRIDGE *Cambs.* CB 33 H3
Cambridge *Glos.* GL2 20 A1
Cambridge City Airport CB5 33 H3
Cambus FK10 75 G1
Cambus o'May AB35 90 C5
Cambusbarron FK7 75 F1
Cambuskenneth FK9 75 G1
Cambuslang G72 74 E4
Cambusnethan ML2 75 G5
Camden Town NW1 23 F3
Camel Hill BA22 8 E2
Cameley BS39 19 K6
Camelford PL32 4 B2
Camelon FK1 75 G2
Camelsdale GU27 12 B3
Camer DA13 24 C5
Cameron House G83 74 B2
Camerory PH26 89 H1
Camer's Green WR13 29 G5
Camerton *B. & N.E.Som.* BA2 19 K6
Camerton *Cumb.* CA14 60 B3
Camerton *E.Riding* HU12 59 J7
Camghouran PH17 81 G2
Camis Eskan G84 74 B2
Cammachmore AB39 91 H5
Cammeringham LN1 52 C4
Camore IV25 96 E2
Camp Hill *Pembs.* SA67 16 E4
Camp Hill *Warks.* CV10 41 F6
Campbeltown PA28 66 B1
Campbeltown Airport PA28 66 A1
Camperdown NE12 71 H6
Campmuir PH13 82 D4
Camps EH27 75 K4
Camps End CB21 33 K4
Camps Heath NR32 45 K6
Campsall DN6 51 H1
Campsea Ashe IP13 35 H3
Campton SG17 32 E5
Camptown TD8 70 B2
Camquhart PA22 73 H2
Camrose SA62 16 C3
Camserney PH15 81 K3
Camstraddan House G83 74 B1
Camus Croise IV43 86 C3
Camus-luinie IV40 87 F2
Camusnagaul *High.* PH33 87 G7
Camusnagaul *High.* IV23 95 G3
Camusrory PH41 86 E5
Camusteel IV54 94 D7
Camusterrach IV54 94 D7
Camusurich FK21 81 H4
Camusvrachan PH15 81 H3
Canada SO51 10 D3
Canaston Bridge SA67 16 D4
Candacraig AB35 90 B5
Candlesby PE23 53 H6
Candy Mill ML12 75 J6
Cane End RG4 21 K4
Canewdon SS4 24 E2
Canfield End CM6 33 J6
Canford Bottom BH21 10 B4
Canford Cliffs BH13 10 B6
Canford Magna BH21 10 B5
Canham's Green IP14 34 E2
Canisbay KW1 105 J1
Canley CV4 30 E1
Cann SP7 9 H2
Cann Common SP7 9 H2
Canna PH44 85 H4
Cannard's Grave BA4 19 K7
Cannich IV4 87 K1
Canning Town E16 23 H3
Cannington TA5 8 B1
Cannock WS11 40 B5
Cannock Wood WS15 40 C4
Cannop GL16 29 F7
Canon Bridge HR2 28 D4
Canon Frome HR8 29 F4
Canon Pyon HR4 28 D4
Canonbie DG14 69 J6
Canons Ashby NN11 31 G3
Canon's Town TR27 2 C5
Canterbury *Aber.* AB45 98 D5
CANTERBURY *Kent* CT 15 G2
Cantley *Norf.* NR13 45 H5
Cantley *S.Yorks.* DN3 51 J2
Cantlop SY5 38 E5
Canton CF11 18 E4
Cantray IV2 96 E7
Cantraydoune IV12 96 E7
Cantraywood IV2 96 E7
Cantsfield LA6 56 B2
Canvey Island SS8 24 D3
Canwell Hall B75 40 D5
Canwick LN4 52 C6
Canworthy Water PL15 4 C1
Caol PH33 87 H7
Caolas *Arg. & B.* PA77 78 B3
Caolas *W.Isles* HS9 84 B5
Caolas Scalpaigh (Kyles Scalpay) HS3 93 H2
Caolasnacon PH50 80 C1
Capel *Kent* TN12 23 K7
Capel *Surr.* RH5 22 E7
Capel Bangor SY23 37 F7
Capel Betws Lleucu SY25 27 F3
Capel Carmel LL53 36 A3
Capel Celyn LL23 37 H1
Capel Coch LL77 46 C4
Capel Curig LL24 47 F7
Capel Cynon SA44 17 G1
Capel Dewi *Carmar.* SA32 17 H3
Capel Dewi *Cere.* SY23 37 F7
Capel Dewi *Cere.* SA44 17 H1
Capel Garmon LL26 47 G7
Capel Gwyn *Carmar.* SA32 17 H3
Capel Gwyn *I.o.A.* LL65 46 B5
Capel Gwynfe SA19 27 G6
Capel Hendre SA18 17 J4
Capel Isaac SA19 17 J3
Capel Iwan SA38 17 F2
Capel le Ferne CT18 15 H4
Capel Llanilltern CF5 18 D3
Capel Mawr LL62 46 C5
Capel Parc LL71 46 C4
Capel St. Andrew IP12 35 H4
Capel St. Mary IP9 34 E5
Capel St. Silin SA48 26 E3
Capel Seion SY23 27 F1
Capel Tygwydd SA38 17 F1
Capeluchaf LL54 36 D1
Capelulo LL34 47 F5
Capel-y-ffin NP7 28 B5
Capel-y-graig LL57 46 D6
Capenhurst CH1 48 C5
Capernwray LA6 55 J2
Capheaton NE19 71 F5
Caplaw G78 74 C5
Capon's Green IP13 35 G2
Cappercleuch TD7 69 H1
Capplegill DG10 69 G3
Capstone ME7 24 D5
Capton *Devon* TQ6 5 J5
Capton *Som.* TA4 7 J2
Caputh PH1 82 B3
Car Colston NG13 42 A1
Caradon Town PL14 4 C3
Carbellow KA18 68 B1
Carbeth G63 74 D3
Carbis Bay TR26 2 C5
Carbost *High.* IV51 93 K7
Carbost *High.* IV47 85 J1
Carbrain G67 75 F3
Carbrooke IP25 44 D5
Carburton S80 51 J5
Carcary DD9 83 H2
Carco DG4 68 C2
Carcroft DN6 51 H1
Cardenden KY5 76 A1
Cardeston SY5 38 C4
Cardew CA5 60 E2
CARDIFF (CAERDYDD) CF 18 E4
Cardiff International Airport CF62 18 D5
Cardigan (Aberteifi) SA43 16 E1
Cardinal's Green CB21 33 K4
Cardington *Bed.* MK44 32 D4
Cardington *Shrop.* SY6 38 E6
Cardinham PL30 4 B4
Cardno AB43 99 H4
Cardonald G52 74 D4
Cardoness DG7 65 F5
Cardow AB38 97 J7
Cardrona EH45 76 A7
Cardross G82 74 B3
Cardurnock CA7 60 C1
Careby PE9 42 D4
Careston DD9 83 G2
Carew SA70 16 D5
Carew Cheriton SA70 16 D5
Carew Newton SA68 16 D5
Carey HR2 28 E5
Carfin ML1 75 F5
Carfrae EH41 76 D4
Carfraemill TD2 76 D5
Cargate Green NR13 45 H4
Cargen DG2 65 K3
Cargenbridge DG2 65 K3
Cargill PH2 82 C4
Cargo CA6 60 E1
Cargreen PL12 4 E4
Carham TD12 77 F7
Carhampton TA24 7 J1
Carharrack TR16 2 E4
Carie *P. & K.* PH17 81 H2
Carie *P. & K.* PH15 81 H4
Carines TR8 2 E3
Carinish (Cairinis) HS6 92 D5
Carisbrooke PO30 11 F6
Cark LA11 55 G2
Carkeel PL12 4 E4
Carlabhagh (Carloway) HS2 100 E3
Carland Cross TR8 3 F3
Carlatton CA8 61 G1
Carlby PE9 42 D4
Carlecotes S36 50 D2
Carleen TR13 2 D6
Carleton *Cumb.* CA1 60 F1
Carleton *Cumb.* CA11 61 G4
Carleton *Lancs.* FY6 55 G5
Carleton *N.Yorks.* BD23 56 E5
Carleton *W.Yorks.* WF8 57 K7
Carleton Fishery KA26 67 F5
Carleton Forehoe NR9 44 E5
Carleton Rode NR16 45 F6
Carleton St. Peter NR14 45 H5
Carlin How TS13 63 J5
CARLISLE CA 60 F1
Carloggas TR8 3 F2
Carlops EH26 75 K5
Carloway (Carlabhagh) HS2 100 E3
Carlton *Bed.* MK43 32 C3
Carlton *Cambs.* CB8 33 K3
Carlton *Leics.* CV13 41 F5
Carlton *N.Yorks.* DN14 58 C7
Carlton *N.Yorks.* DL8 57 F1
Carlton *N.Yorks.* YO62 58 C1
Carlton *Notts.* NG4 41 J1
Carlton *S.Yorks.* S71 51 F1
Carlton *Stock.* TS21 62 E4
Carlton *Suff.* IP17 35 H2
Carlton *W.Yorks.* WF3 57 J7
Carlton Colville NR33 45 K6
Carlton Curlieu LE8 41 J6
Carlton Green CB8 33 K3
Carlton Husthwaite YO7 57 K2
Carlton in Lindrick S81 51 H4
Carlton Miniott YO7 57 J1
Carlton Scroop NG32 42 C1
Carlton-in-Cleveland TS9 63 G6
Carlton-le-Moorland LN5 52 C7
Carlton-on-Trent NG23 52 B6
Carluke ML8 75 G5
Carlyon Bay PL25 4 A5
Carmacoup ML11 68 C1
Carmarthen (Caerfyrddin) SA31 17 H3
Carmel *Carmar.* SA14 17 J4
Carmel *Flints.* CH8 47 K5
Carmel *Gwyn.* LL54 46 C7
Carmel *I.o.A.* LL71 46 B4
Carmichael ML12 75 H7
Carmont AB39 91 G6
Carmunnock G76 74 D5
Carmyle G32 74 E4
Carmyllie DD11 83 G3
Carn PA48 72 A5
Carn Brea Village TR15 2 D4
Carn Dearg IV21 94 D4
Carnaby YO16 59 H3
Carnach *High.* IV40 87 G2
Carnach *High.* IV23 95 G2
Carnach *W.Isles* HS6 92 D5
Carnan HS8 92 C7
Carnassarie PA31 79 K7
Carnbee KY10 83 G7
Carnbo KY13 82 B7
Carndu IV40 86 E2
Carnduncan PA44 72 A4
Carnforth LA5 55 H2
Carnhedryn SA62 16 B3
Carnhell Green TR14 2 D5
Carnichal AB42 99 H5
Carnkie *Cornw.* TR16 2 D5
Carnkie *Cornw.* TR13 2 E5
Carnmore PA42 72 B6
Carno SY17 37 J6
Carnoch *High.* IV4 87 K1
Carnoch *High.* IV6 95 J6
Carnoch *High.* IV12 97 F7
Carnock KY12 75 J2
Carnon Downs TR3 3 F4
Carnousie AB53 98 E5
Carnoustie DD7 83 G4
Carntyne G32 74 E4
Carnwath ML11 75 H6
Carnyorth TR19 2 A5
Carol Green CV7 30 D1
Carperby DL8 57 F1
Carr S66 51 H3
Carr Hill DN10 51 J3
Carr Houses L38 48 C2
Carr Shield NE47 61 K2
Carr Vale S44 51 G5
Carradale PA28 73 F7
Carradale East PA28 73 G7
Carragrich HS3 93 G2
Carrbridge PH23 89 G2
Carrefour Selous JE3 3 J7
Carreg-lefn LL68 46 B4
Carreg-wen SA37 17 F1
Carrhouse DN9 51 K2
Carrick PA31 73 H2
Carrick Castle PA24 73 K1

Carriden EH51 75 J2
Carrine PA28 66 A3
Carrington Gt.Man. M31 49 G3
Carrington Lincs. PE22 53 G7
Carrington Midloth. EH23 76 B4
Carroch DG7 68 B4
Carrog Conwy LL24 37 G1
Carrog Denb. LL21 38 A1
Carroglen PH6 81 J5
Carrol KW9 97 F1
Carron Arg. & B. PA31 73 H1
Carron Falk. FK2 75 G2
Carron Moray AB38 97 K7
Carron Bridge FK6 75 F2
Carronbridge DG3 68 D4
Carronshore FK2 75 G2
Carrot DD8 83 F3
Carrow Hill NP26 19 H2
Carrutherstown DG1 69 G6
Carruthmuir PA10 74 B4
Carrville DH1 62 E2
Carry PA21 73 H4
Carsaig PA70 79 G5
Carscreugh DG8 64 C4
Carse PA29 73 F4
Carse of Ardersier IV2 97 F6
Carsegowan DG8 64 E5
Carseriggan DG8 64 D4
Carsethorn DG2 65 K5
Carsgoe KW12 105 G2
Carshalton SM5 23 F5
Carshalton Beeches SM5 23 F5
Carsie PH10 82 C3
Carsington DE4 50 E7
Carsluith DG8 64 E5
Carsphairn DG7 67 K4
Carstairs ML11 75 H6
Carstairs Junction ML11 75 H6
Carswell Marsh SN7 21 G2
Carter's Clay SO51 10 E2
Carterton OX18 21 F1
Carterway Heads DH8 62 B1
Carthew PL26 4 A5
Carthorpe DL8 57 J1
Cartington NE65 71 F3
Cartland ML11 75 G6
Cartmel LA11 55 G2
Cartmel Fell LA11 55 H1
Cartworth HD9 50 D2
Carway SA17 17 H5
Cascob LD8 28 B2
Cas-gwent (Chepstow) NP16 19 J2
Cashel Farm G63 74 C1
Cashes Green GL5 20 B1
Cashlie PH15 81 F3
Cashmoor DT11 9 J3
Caskieberran KY6 82 D7
CASNEWYDD (NEWPORT) NP 19 G3
Cassencarie DG8 64 E5
Cassington OX29 31 F7
Cassop DH6 62 E3
Castell LL32 47 F6
Castell Gorfod SA33 17 F3
Castell Howell SA44 17 H1
Castell Newydd Emlyn (Newcastle Emlyn) SA38 17 G1
Castellau CF38 18 D3
Castell-nedd (Neath) SA11 18 A2
Castell-y-bwch NP44 19 F2
Casterton LA6 56 B2
Castle Acre PE32 44 C4
Castle Ashby NN7 32 B3
Castle Bolton DL8 62 B7
Castle Bromwich B36 40 D7
Castle Bytham NG33 42 C4
Castle Caereinion SY21 38 A5
Castle Camps CB21 33 K4
Castle Carrock CA8 61 G1
Castle Cary BA7 9 F1
Castle Combe SN14 20 B4
Castle Donington DE74 41 G3
Castle Douglas DG7 65 H4
Castle Eaton SN6 20 E2
Castle Eden TS27 63 F3
Castle End CV8 30 D1
Castle Frome HR8 29 F4
Castle Gate TR20 2 B5
Castle Goring BN13 12 E6
Castle Green GU24 22 C5
Castle Gresley DE11 40 E4
Castle Heaton TD12 77 H6
Castle Hedingham CO9 34 B5
Castle Hill Kent TN12 23 K7
Castle Hill Suff. IP1 35 F4
Castle Kennedy DG9 64 B5
Castle Leod IV14 96 B6
Castle Levan PA19 74 A3
Castle Madoc LD3 27 K5
Castle Morris SA62 16 C2
Castle O'er DG13 69 H4
Castle Rising PE31 44 A3
Castle Stuart IV2 96 E7
Castlebay (Bàgh a'Chaisteil) HS9 84 B5
Castlebythe SA62 16 D3
Castlecary G68 75 F3
Castlecraig High. IV19 97 F5
Castlecraig Sc.Bord. EH46 75 K6
Castlefairn DG3 68 C5
Castleford WF10 57 K7
Castlemartin SA71 16 C6
Castlemilk D. & G. DG11 69 G6
Castlemilk Glas. G45 74 E5
Castlemorton WR13 29 G5
Castlerigg CA12 60 D4
Castleside DH8 62 B2
Castlesteads CA8 70 A7
Castlethorpe MK19 31 J4
Castleton Aber. AB45 99 F5
Castleton Angus DD8 82 E3
Castleton Arg. & B. PA31 73 G2
Castleton Derbys. S33 50 D4
Castleton Gt.Man. OL11 49 H1
Castleton N.Yorks. YO21 63 H6
Castleton Newport CF3 19 F3
Castleton Sc.Bord. TD9 70 A4
Castletown Dorset DT5 9 F7
Castletown High. KW14 105 G2
Castletown High. IV2 96 E7
Castletown I.o.M. IM9 54 B7
Castletown T. & W. SR5 62 E1
Castleweary TD9 69 K3
Castlewigg DG8 64 E6
Castley LS21 57 H5
Caston NR17 44 D6
Castor PE5 42 E6
Castramont DG7 65 F4
Caswell SA3 17 J7
Cat & Fiddle Inn SK11 50 C5
Catacol KA27 73 H6
Catbrain BS10 19 J3
Catbrook NP16 19 J1
Catchall TR19 2 B6
Catcleugh NE19 70 C3
Catcliffe S60 51 G4
Catcott TA7 8 C1
Caterham CR3 23 G6
Catfield NR29 45 H3
Catfirth ZE2 107 N7
Catford SE6 23 G4
Catforth PR4 55 H6
Cathays CF24 18 E4
Cathcart G44 74 D4
Cathedine LD3 28 A6
Catherine-de-Barnes B91 40 D7
Catherington PO8 11 H3
Catherston Leweston DT6 8 C5
Catherton DY14 29 F1
Catkin G73 74 E5
Catisfield PO15 11 G4
Catlodge PH20 88 D5
Catlowdy CA6 69 K6
Catmere End CB11 33 H5
Catmore RG20 21 H3
Caton Devon TQ13 5 H3
Caton Lancs. LA2 55 J3
Caton Green LA2 55 J3
Cator Court TQ13 5 G3
Catrine KA5 67 K1
Catsfield TN33 14 C6
Catsfield Stream TN33 14 C6
Catshaw S36 50 E2
Catshill B61 29 J1
Cattadale PA44 72 B4
Cattal YO26 57 K4
Cattawade CO11 34 E5
Catterall PR3 55 J5
Catterick DL10 62 D7
Catterick Bridge DL10 62 D7
Catterick Garrison DL9 62 C7
Catterlen CA11 61 F3
Catterline AB39 91 G7
Catterton LS24 58 B5
Catteshall GU7 22 C7
Catthorpe LE17 31 G1
Cattishall IP31 34 C2
Cattistock DT2 8 E4
Catton N.Yorks. YO7 57 J2
Catton Norf. NR6 45 G4
Catton Northumb. NE47 61 K1
Catton Hall DE12 40 E4
Catwick HU17 59 H5
Catworth PE28 32 D1
Caudle Green GL53 29 J7
Caulcott Cen.Beds. MK43 32 D4
Caulcott Oxon. OX25 31 G6
Cauldcots DD11 83 H3
Cauldhame Stir. FK8 74 E1
Cauldhame Stir. FK15 81 K7
Cauldon ST10 40 C1
Caulkerbush DG2 65 K5
Caulside DG14 69 K5
Caundle Marsh DT9 9 F3
Caunsall DY11 40 A7
Caunton NG23 51 K6
Causeway End D. & G. DG8 64 E4
Causeway End Essex CM6 33 K7
Causeway End Lancs. L40 48 D1
Causewayhead Cumb. CA7 60 C1
Causewayhead Stir. FK9 75 G1
Causey DH9 62 D1
Causey Park NE61 71 G4
Causeyend AB23 91 H3
Cautley LA10 61 H7
Cavendish CO10 34 C4
Cavendish Bridge DE72 41 G3
Cavenham IP28 34 B2
Cavens DG2 65 K5
Cavers TD9 70 A2
Caversfield OX27 31 G6
Caversham RG4 22 A4
Caverswall ST11 40 B1
Cawdor IV12 97 F6
Cawkeld YO25 59 F4
Cawkwell LN11 53 F4
Cawood YO8 58 B6
Cawsand PL10 4 E6
Cawston Norf. NR10 45 F3
Cawston Warks. CV22 31 F1
Cawthorn YO18 58 D1
Cawthorne S75 50 E2
Cawthorpe PE10 42 D3
Cawton YO62 58 C2
Caxton CB23 33 G3
Caxton Gibbet CB23 33 F2
Caynham SY8 28 E1
Caythorpe Lincs. NG32 42 C1
Caythorpe Notts. NG14 41 J1
Cayton YO11 59 G1
Ceallan HS6 92 D6
Ceann a' Bhàigh W.Isles HS6 92 C5
Ceann a' Bhàigh W.Isles HS3 93 F3
Ceann Loch Shiphoirt HS2 100 E6
Ceann Lochroag (Kinlochroag) HS2 100 D5
Ceannaridh HS6 92 D6
Cearsiadar HS2 101 F6
Ceathramh Meadhanach (Middlequarter) HS6 92 D4
Cedig SY10 37 J3
Cefn Berain LL16 47 H6
Cefn Bychan (Newbridge) NP11 19 F2
Cefn Canol SY10 38 B2
Cefn Cantref LD3 27 K6
Cefn Coch LL15 47 K7
Cefn Cribwr CF32 18 B3
Cefn Cross CF32 18 B3
Cefn Einion SY9 38 B7
Cefn Hengoed CF82 18 E2
Cefn Llwyd SY23 37 F7
Cefn Rhigos CF44 18 C1
Cefn-brith LL21 47 H7
Cefn-caer-Ferch LL53 36 D1
Cefn-coch SY10 38 A3
Cefn-coed-y-cymmer CF48 18 D1
Cefn-ddwysarn LL23 37 J2
Cefndeuddwr LL40 37 G3
Cefneithin SA14 17 J4
Cefn-gorwydd LD4 27 J4
Cefn-gwyn SY16 38 A7
Cefn-mawr LL14 38 B1
Cefnpennar CF45 18 D1
Cefn-y-bedd LL12 48 C7
Cefn-y-pant SA34 16 E3
Cegidfa (Guilsfield) SY21 38 B4
Ceidio LL71 46 C4
Ceidio Fawr LL53 36 B2
Ceinewydd (New Quay) SA45 26 C2
Ceint LL77 46 C5
Cellan SA48 17 K1
Cellardyke KY10 83 G7
Cellarhead ST9 40 B1
Cemaes LL67 46 B3
Cemmaes SY20 37 H5
Cemmaes Road (Glantwymyn) SY20 37 H5
Cenarth SA38 17 F1
Cennin LL51 36 D1
Ceos (Keose) HS2 101 F5
Ceres KY15 83 F6
Ceri (Kerry) SY16 38 A6
Cerist SY17 37 J7
Cerne Abbas DT2 9 F4
Cerney Wick GL7 20 D2
Cerrigceinwen LL62 46 C5
Cerrigydrudion LL21 37 J1
Cessford TD5 70 C1
Ceunant LL55 46 D6
Chaceley GL19 29 H5
Chacewater TR4 2 E4
Chackmore MK18 31 H5
Chacombe OX17 31 F4
Chad Valley B15 40 C7
Chadderton OL9 49 J2
Chadderton Fold OL9 49 H2
Chaddesden DE21 41 F2
Chaddesley Corbett DY10 29 H1
Chaddleworth RG20 21 H4
Chadlington OX7 30 E6
Chadshunt CV35 30 E3
Chadstone NN7 32 B3
Chadwell Leics. LE14 42 A3
Chadwell Shrop. TF10 39 G4
Chadwell St. Mary RM16 24 C4
Chadwick End B93 30 D1
Chaffcombe TA20 8 C3
Chafford Hundred RM16 24 C4
Chagford TQ13 7 F7
Chailey BN8 13 G5
Chainhurst TN12 14 C3
Chalbury BH21 10 B4
Chalbury Common BH21 10 B4
Chaldon CR3 23 G6
Chaldon Herring (East Chaldon) DT2 9 G6
Chale PO38 11 F7
Chale Green PO38 11 F6
Chalfont Common SL9 22 D2
Chalfont St. Giles HP8 22 C2
Chalfont St. Peter SL9 22 D2
Chalford Glos. GL6 20 B1
Chalford Wilts. BA13 20 B7
Chalgrove OX44 21 K2
Chalk DA12 24 C4
Chalk End CM1 33 K7
Challacombe EX31 6 E1
Challister ZE2 107 P6
Challoch DG8 64 D4
Challock TN25 15 F2
Chalmington DT2 8 E4
Chalton Cen.Beds. LU4 32 D6
Chalton Hants. PO8 11 J3
Chalvey SL1 22 C4
Chalvington BN27 13 J6
Champany EH49 75 J3
Chancery SY23 26 E1
Chandler's Cross WD3 22 D2
Chandler's Ford SO53 11 F2
Channel Islands GYJE 3 G7
Channel's End MK44 32 E3
Channerwick ZE2 107 N10
Chantry Som. BA11 20 A7
Chantry Suff. IP2 35 F4
Chapel KY2 76 A1
Chapel Allerton Som. BS26 19 H6
Chapel Allerton W.Yorks. LS7 57 J6
Chapel Amble PL27 3 G1
Chapel Brampton NN6 31 J2
Chapel Chorlton ST5 40 A2
Chapel Cleeve TA24 7 J1
Chapel Cross TN21 13 K4
Chapel End MK45 32 D4
Chapel Green Warks. CV7 40 E7
Chapel Green Warks. CV47 31 F2
Chapel Haddlesey YO8 58 B7
Chapel Hill Aber. AB42 91 J1
Chapel Hill Lincs. LN4 53 F7
Chapel Hill Mon. NP16 19 J1
Chapel Hill N.Yorks. LS22 57 J5
Chapel Knapp SN13 20 B5
Chapel Lawn SY7 28 C1
Chapel Leigh TA4 7 K3
Chapel Milton SK23 50 C4
Chapel of Garioch AB51 91 F2
Chapel Rossan DG9 64 B6
Chapel Row Essex CM3 24 D1
Chapel Row W.Berks. RG7 21 J5
Chapel St. Leonards PE24 53 J5
Chapel Stile LA22 60 E6
Chapel Town TR8 3 F3
Chapelbank PH3 82 B6
Chapeldonan KA26 67 F3
Chapelend Way CO9 34 B5
Chapel-en-le-Frith SK23 50 C4
Chapelgate PE12 43 H3
Chapelhall ML6 75 F4
Chapelhill High. IV20 97 F4
Chapelhill P. & K. PH2 82 D5
Chapelhill P. & K. PH1 82 B4
Chapelknowe DG14 69 J6
Chapel-le-Dale LA6 56 C2
Chapelthorpe WF2 51 F1
Chapelton Aber. AB39 91 G6
Chapelton Angus DD11 83 H3
Chapelton Devon EX37 6 D3
Chapelton S.Lan. ML10 74 E6
Chapeltown B'burn. BL7 49 G1
Chapeltown Cumb. CA6 69 K6
Chapeltown Moray AB37 89 K2
Chapeltown S.Yorks. S35 51 F3
Chapmans Well PL15 6 B6
Chapmanslade BA13 20 B7
Chapmore End SG12 33 G7
Chappel CO6 34 C6
Charaton PL14 4 D4
Chard TA20 8 C4
Chard Junction TA20 8 C4
Chardleigh Green TA20 8 C3
Chardstock EX13 8 C4
Charfield GL12 20 A2
Charing TN27 14 E3
Charing Cross SP6 10 C3
Charing Heath TN27 14 E3
Charingworth GL55 30 C5
Charlbury OX7 30 E7
Charlcombe BA1 20 A5
Charlecote CV35 30 D3
Charles EX32 6 E2
Charles Tye IP14 34 E3
Charlesfield TD6 70 A1
Charleshill GU10 22 B7
Charleston DD8 82 E3
Charlestown Aber. AB43 99 J4
Charlestown Aberdeen AB12 91 H4
Charlestown Cornw. PL25 4 A5
Charlestown Derbys. SK13 50 C3
Charlestown Dorset DT3 9 F7
Charlestown Fife KY11 75 J2
Charlestown Gt.Man. M7 49 H2
Charlestown High. IV21 94 E4
Charlestown High. IV1 96 D7
Charlestown W.Yorks. BD17 57 G6
Charlestown W.Yorks. HX7 56 E7
Charlestown of Aberlour (Aberlour) AB38 97 K7
Charlesworth SK13 50 C3
Charleton KY9 83 F7
Charlinch TA5 8 B1
Charlotteville GU1 22 D7
Charlton Gt.Lon. SE7 23 H4
Charlton Hants. SP10 21 G7
Charlton Herts. SG5 32 E6
Charlton Northants. OX17 31 G5
Charlton Northumb. NE48 70 D5
Charlton Oxon. OX12 21 H3
Charlton Som. BA3 19 K6
Charlton Som. BA4 19 K7
Charlton Som. TA3 8 B2
Charlton Tel. & W. TF6 38 E4
Charlton W.Suss. PO18 12 B5
Charlton Wilts. SP7 9 J2
Charlton Wilts. SN16 20 C3
Charlton Wilts. SN9 20 E6
Charlton Worcs. WR10 30 B4
Charlton Abbots GL54 30 B6
Charlton Adam TA11 8 E2
Charlton Down DT2 9 F5
Charlton Horethorne DT9 9 F2
Charlton Kings GL52 29 J6
Charlton Mackrell TA11 8 E2
Charlton Marshall DT11 9 H4
Charlton Musgrove BA9 9 G2
Charlton on the Hill DT11 9 H4
Charlton-All-Saints SP5 10 C2
Charlton-on-Otmoor OX5 31 G7
Charltons TS12 63 H5
Charlwood RH6 23 F7
Charminster DT2 9 F5
Charmouth DT6 8 C5
Charndon OX27 31 H6
Charney Bassett OX12 21 G2
Charnock Richard PR7 48 E1
Charsfield IP13 35 G3
Chart Corner ME17 14 C3
Chart Sutton ME17 14 D3
Charter Alley RG26 21 J6
Charterhouse BS40 19 H6
Charterville Allotments OX29 21 G1
Chartham CT4 15 G2
Chartham Hatch CT4 15 G2
Chartridge HP5 22 C1
Charvil RG10 22 A4
Charwelton NN11 31 G3
Chase End Street HR8 29 G5
Chase Terrace WS7 40 C5
Chasetown WS7 40 C5
Chastleton GL56 30 D6
Chasty EX22 6 B5
Chatburn BB7 56 C5
Chatcull ST21 39 G2
Chatham ME4 24 D5
Chatham Green CM3 34 B7
Chathill NE67 71 G1
Chattenden ME3 24 D4
Chatteris PE16 43 G7
Chattisham IP8 34 E4
Chatto TD5 70 C2
Chatton NE66 71 F1
Chaul End LU1 32 D6
Chavey Down SL5 22 B5
Chawleigh EX18 7 F4
Chawley OX2 21 H1
Chawston MK44 32 E3
Chawton GU34 11 J1
Chazey Heath RG4 21 K4
Cheadle Gt.Man. SK8 49 H4
Cheadle Staffs. ST10 40 C1
Cheadle Heath SK3 49 H4
Cheadle Hulme SK8 49 H4
Cheam SM3 23 F5
Cheapside SL5 22 C5
Chearsley HP18 31 J7
Chebsey ST21 40 A3
Checkendon RG8 21 K3
Checkley Ches.E. CW5 39 G1
Checkley Here. HR1 28 E5
Checkley Staffs. ST10 40 C2
Checkley Green CW5 39 G1
Chedburgh IP29 34 B3
Cheddar BS27 19 H6
Cheddington LU7 32 C7
Cheddleton ST13 49 J7
Cheddon Fitzpaine TA2 8 B2
Chedglow SN16 20 C2
Chedgrave NR14 45 H6
Chedington DT8 8 D4
Chediston IP19 35 H1
Chediston Green IP19 35 H1
Chedworth GL54 30 B7
Chedzoy TA7 8 C1
Cheesden OL12 49 H1
Cheeseman's Green TN24 15 F4
Cheetham Hill M8 49 H2
Cheglinch EX34 6 D1
Cheldon EX18 7 F4
Chelford SK11 49 H5
Chellaston DE73 41 F2
Chells SG2 33 F6
Chelmarsh WV16 39 G7
Chelmondiston IP9 35 G5
Chelmorton SK17 50 D6
CHELMSFORD CM 24 D1
Chelmsley Wood B37 40 D7
Chelsea SW3 23 F4
Chelsfield BR6 23 H5
Chelsham CR6 23 G6
Chelston Heath TA21 7 K3
Chelsworth IP7 34 D4
Cheltenham GL50 29 J6
Chelveston NN9 32 C2
Chelvey BS48 19 H5
Chelwood BS39 19 K5
Chelwood Common RH17 13 H4
Chelwood Gate RH17 13 H4
Chelworth SN16 20 C2
Cheney Longville SY7 38 D7
Chenies WD3 22 D2
Chepstow (Cas-gwent) NP16 19 J2
Cherhill SN11 20 D4
Cherington Glos. GL8 20 C2
Cherington Warks. CV36 30 D5
Cheriton Devon EX35 7 F1
Cheriton Hants. SO24 11 G2
Cheriton Kent CT19 15 G4
Cheriton Pembs. SA71 16 C6
Cheriton Swan. SA3 17 H6
Cheriton Bishop EX6 7 F6
Cheriton Cross EX6 7 F6
Cheriton Fitzpaine EX17 7 G5
Cherrington TF6 39 F3
Cherry Burton HU17 59 F5
Cherry Green CM6 33 J6
Cherry Hinton CB1 33 H3
Cherry Willingham LN3 52 D5
Chertsey KT16 22 D5
Cheselbourne DT2 9 G5
Chesham HP5 22 C1
Chesham Bois HP6 22 C1
Cheshunt EN8 23 G1
Cheslyn Hay WS6 40 B5
Chessington KT9 22 E5
Chestall WS15 40 C4

CHESTER CH 48 D6
Chester Moor DH2 62 D2
Chesterblade BA4 19 K7
Chesterfield Derbys. S40 51 F5
Chesterfield Staffs. WS14 40 D5
Chester-le-Street DH3 62 D1
Chesters Sc.Bord. TD9 70 B2
Chesters Sc.Bord. TD8 70 B1
Chesterton Cambs. CB4 33 H2
Chesterton Cambs. PE7 42 E6
Chesterton Oxon. OX26 31 G6
Chesterton Shrop. WV15 39 G6
Chesterton Staffs. ST5 40 A1
Chesterton Warks. CV33 30 E3
Chesterton Green CV33 30 E3
Chestfield CT5 25 H5
Cheston TQ10 5 G5
Cheswardine TF9 39 G3
Cheswick TD15 77 J6
Cheswick Buildings TD15 77 J6
Cheswick Green B90 30 C1
Chetnole DT9 9 F4
Chettiscombe EX16 7 H4
Chettisham CB6 43 J7
Chettle DT11 9 J3
Chetton WV16 39 F6
Chetwode MK18 31 H6
Chetwynd Aston TF10 39 G4
Chetwynd Park TF10 39 G3
Cheveley CB8 33 K2
Chevening TN14 23 H6
Cheverell's Green AL3 32 D7
Chevington IP29 34 B3
Chevington Drift NE61 71 H4
Chevithorne EX16 7 H4
Chew Magna BS40 19 J5
Chew Moor BL6 49 F2
Chew Stoke BS40 19 J5
Chewton Keynsham BS31 19 K5
Chewton Mendip BA3 19 J6
Chichacott EX20 6 E6
Chicheley MK16 32 C4
Chichester PO19 12 B6
Chickerell DT3 9 F6
Chickering IP21 35 G1
Chicklade SP3 9 J1
Chickney CM6 33 J6
Chicksands SG17 32 E5
Chidden PO7 11 H3
Chidden Holt PO7 11 H3
Chiddingfold GU8 12 C3
Chiddingly BN8 13 J5
Chiddingstone TN8 23 H7
Chiddingstone Causeway TN11 23 J7
Chiddingstone Hoath TN8 23 H7
Chideock DT6 8 D5
Chidham PO18 11 J4
Chidswell WF12 57 H7
Chieveley RG20 21 H4
Chignall St. James CM1 24 C1
Chignall Smealy CM1 33 K7
Chigwell IG7 23 H2
Chigwell Row IG7 23 H2
Chilbolton SO20 21 G7
Chilcomb SO21 11 G2
Chilcombe DT6 8 E5
Chilcompton BA3 19 K6
Chilcote DE12 40 E4
Child Okeford DT11 9 H3
Childer Thornton CH66 48 C5
Childerditch CM13 24 C3
Childrey OX12 21 G3
Child's Ercall TF9 39 F3
Childs Hill NW3 23 F3
Childswickham WR12 30 B5
Childwall L16 48 D4
Childwick Green AL3 32 E7
Chilfrome DT2 8 E5
Chilgrove PO18 12 B5
Chilham CT4 15 F2
Chilhampton SP2 10 B1
Chilla EX21 6 C5
Chillaton PL16 6 C7
Chillenden CT3 15 H2
Chillerton PO30 11 F6
Chillesford IP12 35 H3
Chilley TQ9 5 H5
Chillingham NE66 71 F1
Chillington Devon TQ7 5 H6
Chillington Som. TA19 8 C3
Chilmark SP3 9 J1
Chilson Oxon. OX7 30 E7
Chilson Som. TA20 8 C4
Chilsworthy Cornw. PL18 4 E3
Chilsworthy Devon EX22 6 B5
Chilthorne Domer BA22 8 E3
Chilton Bucks. HP18 31 H7
Chilton Devon EX17 7 G5
Chilton Dur. DL17 62 D4
Chilton Oxon. OX11 21 H3
Chilton Suff. CO10 34 C4
Chilton Candover SO24 11 G1
Chilton Cantelo BA22 8 E2
Chilton Foliat RG17 21 G4
Chilton Polden TA7 8 C1
Chilton Street CO10 34 B4
Chilton Trinity TA5 8 B1
Chilvers Coton CV10 41 F6
Chilwell NG9 41 H2
Chilworth Hants. SO16 11 F3
Chilworth Surr. GU4 22 D7
Chimney OX18 21 G1
Chimney Street CO10 34 B4
Chineham RG24 21 K6
Chingford E4 23 G2
Chinley SK23 50 C4
Chinley Head SK23 50 C4
Chinnor OX39 22 A1
Chipchase Castle NE48 70 D6
Chipley TA21 7 K3
Chipnall TF9 39 G2
Chippenham Cambs. CB7 33 K2
Chippenham Wilts. SN15 20 C4
Chipperfield WD4 22 D1
Chipping Herts. SG9 33 G5
Chipping Lancs. PR3 56 B5
Chipping Campden GL55 30 C5
Chipping Hill CM8 34 C7
Chipping Norton OX7 30 E6
Chipping Ongar CM5 23 J1
Chipping Sodbury BS37 20 A3
Chipping Warden OX17 31 F4
Chipstable TA4 7 J3
Chipstead Kent TN13 23 H6
Chipstead Surr. CR5 23 F6
Chirbury SY15 38 B6
Chirk (Y Waun) LL14 38 B2
Chirk Green LL14 38 B2
Chirmorrie KA26 64 C3
Chirnside TD11 77 G5
Chirnsidebridge TD11 77 G5
Chirton T. & W. NE29 71 J7
Chirton Wilts. SN10 20 D6
Chisbury SN8 21 F5
Chiscan PA28 66 A2
Chiselborough TA14 8 D3
Chiseldon SN4 20 E4
Chiserley HX7 57 F7
Chislehampton OX44 21 J2
Chislehurst BR7 23 H4
Chislet CT3 25 J5
Chiswell Green AL2 22 E1
Chiswick W4 23 F4
Chiswick End SG8 33 G4
Chisworth SK13 49 J3
Chithurst GU31 12 B4
Chittering CB25 33 H1
Chitterne BA12 20 C7
Chittlehamholt EX37 6 E3
Chittlehampton EX37 6 E3
Chittoe SN15 20 C5
Chivelstone TQ7 5 H7
Chivenor EX31 6 D2
Chobham GU24 22 C5
Choicelee TD11 77 F5
Cholderton SP4 21 F7
Cholesbury HP23 22 C1
Chollerford NE46 70 E6
Chollerton NE46 70 E6
Cholsey OX10 21 J3
Cholstrey HR6 28 D3
Cholwell B. & N.E.Som. BS39 19 K6
Cholwell Devon PL19 4 E3
Chop Gate TS9 63 G7
Choppington NE62 71 H5
Chopwell NE17 62 C1
Chorley Ches.E. CW5 48 E7
Chorley Lancs. PR7 48 E1
Chorley Shrop. WV16 39 F7
Chorley Staffs. WS13 40 C4
Chorleywood WD3 22 D2
Chorlton CW2 49 G7
Chorlton Lane SY14 38 D1
Chorlton-cum-Hardy M21 49 H3
Chowley CH3 48 D7
Chrishall SG8 33 H5
Chrishall Grange SG8 33 H4
Chrisswell PA16 74 A3
Christchurch Cambs. PE14 43 H6
Christchurch Dorset BH23 10 C5
Christchurch Glos. GL16 28 E7
Christchurch Newport NP18 19 G3
Christian Malford SN15 20 C4
Christleton CH3 48 D6
Christmas Common OX49 22 A2
Christon BS26 19 G6
Christon Bank NE66 71 H1
Christow EX6 7 G7
Christskirk AB52 90 E2
Chryston G69 74 E3
Chudleigh TQ13 5 J3
Chudleigh Knighton TQ13 5 J3
Chulmleigh EX18 6 E4
Chunal SK13 50 C3
Church BB5 56 C7
Church Aston TF10 39 G4
Church Brampton NN6 31 J2
Church Brough CA17 61 J5
Church Broughton DE65 40 E2
Church Charwelton NN11 31 G3
Church Common IP17 35 H3
Church Crookham GU52 22 B6
Church Eaton ST20 40 A4
Church End Cambs. PE13 43 G5
Church End Cambs. CB24 33 G1
Church End Cambs. PE28 43 F7
Church End Cen.Beds. SG15 32 E5
Church End Cen.Beds. MK17 32 C5
Church End Cen.Beds. LU6 32 C6
Church End Cen.Beds. SG19 32 E3
Church End Cen.Beds. MK43 32 C5
Church End E.Riding YO25 59 G4
Church End Essex CB10 33 J4
Church End Essex CM7 34 B6
Church End Glos. GL20 29 H5
Church End Hants. RG27 21 K6
Church End Herts. AL3 32 E7
Church End Herts. SG11 33 H6
Church End Lincs. PE11 43 F2
Church End Lincs. LN11 53 H3
Church End Warks. CV10 40 E6
Church End Wilts. SN15 20 D4
Church Enstone OX7 30 E6
Church Fenton LS24 58 B6
Church Green EX24 7 K6
Church Gresley DE11 40 E4
Church Hanborough OX29 31 F7
Church Hill Ches.W. & C. CW7 49 F6
Church Hill Derbys. S42 51 G6
Church Houses YO62 63 H7
Church Knowle BH20 9 J6
Church Laneham DN22 52 B5
Church Langley CM17 23 H1
Church Langton LE16 42 A6
Church Lawford CV23 31 F1
Church Lawton ST7 49 H7
Church Leigh ST10 40 C2
Church Lench WR11 30 B3
Church Mayfield DE6 40 D1
Church Minshull CW5 49 F6
Church Norton PO20 12 B7
Church Preen SY6 38 E6
Church Pulverbatch SY5 38 D5
Church Stoke SY15 38 B6
Church Stowe NN7 31 H3
Church Street Essex CO10 34 B4
Church Street Kent ME3 24 D4
Church Stretton SY6 38 D6
Church Town Leics. LE67 41 F4
Church Town Surr. RH9 23 G6
Church Village CF38 18 D3
Church Warsop NG20 51 H6
Church Westcote OX7 30 D6
Church Wilne DE72 41 G2
Churcham GL2 29 G7
Churchdown GL3 29 H7
Churchend Essex SS3 25 G2
Churchend Essex CM6 33 K6
Churchend S.Glos. GL12 20 A2
Churchfield B71 40 C6
Churchgate EN7 23 G1
Churchgate Street CM17 33 H7
Churchill Devon EX31 6 D1
Churchill Devon EX13 8 B4
Churchill N.Som. BS25 19 H6
Churchill Oxon. OX7 30 D6
Churchill Worcs. WR7 29 J3
Churchill Worcs. DY10 29 H1
Churchingford TA3 8 B3
Churchover CV23 41 H7
Churchstanton TA3 7 K4
Churchstow TQ7 5 H6
Churchtown Devon EX31 6 E1
Churchtown I.o.M. IM7 54 D4
Churchtown Lancs. PR3 55 H5
Churchtown Mersey. PR9 48 C1
Churnsike Lodge NE48 70 B6
Churston Ferrers TQ5 5 K5
Churt GU10 12 B3
Churton CH3 48 D7
Churwell LS27 57 H7
Chute Cadley SP11 21 G6
Chute Standen SP11 21 G6
Chwilog LL53 36 D2
Chwitffordd (Whitford) CH8 47 K5
Chyandour TR18 2 B5
Chysauster TR20 2 B5
Cilan Uchaf LL53 36 B3
Cilcain CH7 47 K6
Cilcennin SA48 26 E2
Cilcewydd SY21 38 B5
Cilfrew SA10 18 A1
Cilfynydd CF37 18 D2
Cilgerran SA43 16 E1
Cilgwyn Carmar. SA20 27 G5
Cilgwyn Pembs. SA42 16 D2
Ciliau Aeron SA48 26 E3
Cilldonnain (Kildonan) HS8 84 C2
Cille Bhrighde HS8 84 C3
Cille Pheadair HS8 84 C3
Cilmaengwyn SA8 18 A1
Cilmery LD2 27 K3
Cilrhedyn SA35 17 F2
Cilrhedyn Bridge SA65 16 D2
Cilsan SA19 17 J3
Ciltalgarth LL23 37 H1
Cilwendeg SA37 17 F2
Cilybebyll SA8 18 A1
Cilycwm SA20 27 G4
Cimla SA11 18 A2
Cinderford GL14 29 F7
Cippenham SL1 22 C3
Cippyn SA43 16 E1
Cirbhig HS2 100 D3
Circebost (Kirkibost) HS2 100 D4
Cirencester GL7 20 D1
City Gt.Lon. EC3M 23 G3
City V. of Glam. CF71 18 C4
City Airport E16 23 H3
City Dulas LL70 46 C4
Clabhach PA78 78 C2
Clachaig PA23 73 K2
Clachan Arg. & B. PA26 80 C6
Clachan Arg. & B. PA34 79 K3
Clachan Arg. & B. PA29 73 F5
Clachan High. IV40 86 B1
Clachan W.Isles HS8 92 C7
Clachan Mòr PA77 78 A3
Clachan of Campsie G66 74 E3
Clachan of Glendaruel PA22 73 H2
Clachan Strachur (Strachur) PA27 80 B7
Clachan-a-Luib HS6 92 D5
Clachandhu PA68 79 F4
Clachaneasy DG8 64 D3
Clachanmore DG9 64 A6
Clachan-Seil PA34 79 J6
Clachanturn AB35 89 K5
Clachbreck PA31 73 F3
Clachnabrain DD8 82 E1
Clachnaharry IV3 96 D7
Clachtoll IV27 102 C6
Clackmannan FK10 75 H1
Clackmarras IV30 97 K6
Clacton-on-Sea CO15 35 F7
Cladach a Bhale Shear HS6 92 D5
Cladach a' Chaolais HS6 92 C5
Cladach Chircebost HS6 92 C5
Cladach Chnoc a Lin HS6 92 C5
Cladich PA33 80 B5
Cladswell B49 30 B3
Claggan High. PH33 87 H7
Claggan High. PA34 79 J3
Claigan IV55 93 H6
Claines WR3 29 H3
Clandown BA3 19 K6
Clanfield Hants. PO8 11 J3
Clanfield Oxon. OX18 21 F1
Clannaborough Barton EX17 7 F5
Clanville SP11 21 G7
Claonaig PA29 73 G5
Claonairigh PA32 80 B7
Claonel IV27 96 C1
Clapgate SG11 33 H6
Clapham Bed. MK41 32 D3
Clapham Devon EX2 7 G7
Clapham Gt.Lon. SW4 23 F4
Clapham N.Yorks. LA2 56 C3
Clapham W.Suss. BN13 12 D6
Clapham Green MK41 32 D3
Clapham Hill CT5 25 H5
Clappers TD15 77 H5
Clappersgate LA22 60 E6
Clapton Som. TA18 8 D4
Clapton Som. BA3 19 K6
Clapton-in-Gordano BS20 19 H4
Clapton-on-the-Hill GL54 30 C7
Clapworthy EX36 6 E3
Clara Vale NE40 71 G7
Clarach SY23 37 F7
Clarbeston SA63 16 D3
Clarbeston Road SA63 16 D3
Clarborough DN22 51 K4
Clardon KW14 105 G2
Clare CO10 34 B4
Clarebrand DG7 65 H4
Clarencefield DG1 69 F7
Clarilaw TD9 70 A2
Clark's Green RH5 12 E3
Clarkston G76 74 D5
Clashban IV24 96 D2
Clashcoig IV24 96 D2
Clashdorran IV4 96 C7
Clashgour PA36 80 D3
Clashindarroch AB54 90 C1
Clashmore High. IV25 96 E3
Clashmore High. IV27 102 C5
Clashnessie IV27 102 C5
Clashnoir AB37 89 K2
Clatford SN8 20 E5
Clathy PH7 82 A5
Clatt AB54 90 D2
Clatter SY17 37 J6
Clattercote OX17 31 F4
Clatterford PO30 11 F6
Clatterford End CM5 23 J1
Clatterin Brig AB30 90 E7
Clatteringshaws DG7 65 F3
Clatworthy TA4 7 J2
Claughton Lancs. LA2 55 J3
Claughton Lancs. PR3 55 J5
Clavelshay TA6 8 B1
Claverdon CV35 30 C2
Claverham BS49 19 H5
Clavering CB11 33 H5
Claverley WV5 39 G6
Claverton BA2 20 A5
Claverton Down BA2 20 A5
Clawdd-côch CF71 18 D4
Clawdd-newydd LL15 47 J7
Clawfin KA6 67 K3
Clawthorpe LA6 55 J2
Clawton EX22 6 B6
Claxby LN8 52 E3
Claxby Pluckacre LN9 53 G6
Claxby St. Andrew LN13 53 H5
Claxton N.Yorks. YO60 58 C3
Claxton Norf. NR14 45 H5
Claxton Grange TS22 63 F4
Clay Common NR34 45 J7
Clay Coton NN6 31 G1
Clay Cross S45 51 F6
Clay End SG2 33 G6
Clay Hill BS16 19 K4
Clay of Allan IV20 97 F4
Claybrooke Magna LE17 41 G7
Claybrooke Parva LE17 41 G7
Claydene TN8 23 H7
Claydon Oxon. OX17 31 F3
Claydon Suff. IP6 35 F4
Claygate Kent TN12 14 C3
Claygate Surr. KT10 22 E5
Claygate Cross TN15 23 K6
Clayhanger Devon EX16 7 J3
Clayhanger W.Mid. WS8 40 C5
Clayhidon EX15 7 K4
Clayhill E.Suss. TN31 14 D5
Clayhill Hants. SO43 10 E4
Clayhithe CB25 33 J2
Clayock KW12 105 G3
Claypit Hill CB23 33 G3
Claypits GL10 20 A1
Claypole NG23 42 B1
Claythorpe LN13 53 H5
Clayton S.Yorks. DN5 51 G2
Clayton Staffs. ST5 40 A1
Clayton W.Suss. BN6 13 F5
Clayton W.Yorks. BD14 57 G6
Clayton Green PR6 55 J7
Clayton West HD8 50 E1
Clayton-le-Moors BB5 56 C6
Clayton-le-Woods PR25 55 J7
Clayworth DN22 51 K4
Cleadale PH42 85 K6
Cleadon SR6 71 J7
Clearbrook PL20 5 F4
Clearwell GL16 19 J1
Cleasby DL2 62 D5
Cleat Ork. KW17 106 D9
Cleat W.Isles HS9 84 B4
Cleatlam DL2 62 C5
Cleatop BD24 56 D3
Cleator CA23 60 B5
Cleator Moor CA25 60 B5
Cleckheaton BD19 57 G7
Clee St. Margaret SY7 38 E7
Cleedownton SY8 38 E7
Cleehill SY8 28 E1
Cleestanton SY8 28 E1
Cleethorpes DN35 53 G2
Cleeton St. Mary DY14 29 F1
Cleeve N.Som. BS49 19 H5
Cleeve Oxon. RG8 21 K3
Cleeve Hill GL52 29 J6
Cleeve Prior WR11 30 B4
Cleghorn ML11 75 G6
Clehonger HR2 28 D5
Cleigh PA34 79 K5
Cleish KY13 75 J1
Cleland ML1 75 F5
Clement's End LU6 32 D7
Clench Common SN8 20 E5
Clenchwarton PE34 43 J3
Clennell NE65 70 E3
Clent DY9 29 J1
Cleobury Mortimer DY14 29 F1
Cleobury North WV16 39 F7
Clephanton IV2 97 F6
Clerklands TD6 70 A1
Clermiston EH4 75 K3
Clestrain KW17 106 C7
Cleuch Head TD9 70 A2
Cleughbrae DG1 69 F6
Clevancy SN11 20 D4
Clevedon BS21 19 H4
Cleveland Tontine Inn DL6 63 F7
Cleveley OX7 30 E6
Cleveleys FY5 55 G5
Clevelode WR13 29 H4
Cleverton SN15 20 C3
Clewer BS28 19 H6
Clewer Green SL4 22 C4
Clewer Village SL4 22 C4
Cley next the Sea NR25 44 E1
Cliburn CA10 61 G4
Cliddesden RG25 21 K7
Cliff Carmar. SA17 17 G5
Cliff High. PH36 79 H1
Cliff End TN35 14 D6
Cliff Grange TF9 39 F2
Cliffe Lancs. BB6 56 C6
Cliffe Med. ME3 24 D4
Cliffe N.Yorks. YO8 58 C6
Cliffe Woods ME3 24 D4
Clifford Here. HR3 28 B4
Clifford W.Yorks. LS23 57 K5
Clifford Chambers CV37 30 C3
Clifford's Mesne GL18 29 F6
Cliffs End CT12 25 K5
Clifton Bristol BS8 19 J4
Clifton Cen.Beds. SG17 32 E5
Clifton Cumb. CA10 61 G4
Clifton Derbys. DE6 40 D1
Clifton Devon EX31 6 D1
Clifton Lancs. PR4 55 H6
Clifton N.Yorks. LS21 57 G5
Clifton Northumb. NE61 71 H5
Clifton Nott. NG11 41 H2
Clifton Oxon. OX15 31 F5
Clifton S.Yorks. S66 51 H3
Clifton Stir. FK20 80 E4
Clifton W.Yorks. HD6 57 G7
Clifton Worcs. WR8 29 H4
Clifton York YO30 58 B4
Clifton Campville B79 40 E4
Clifton Hampden OX14 21 J2
Clifton Maybank BA22 8 E3
Clifton Reynes MK46 32 C3
Clifton upon Dunsmore CV23 31 G1
Clifton upon Teme WR6 29 G2
Cliftonville CT9 25 K4
Climping BN17 12 D6
Climpy ML11 75 H5
Clink BA11 20 A7
Clint HG3 57 H4
Clint Green NR19 44 E4
Clinterty AB21 91 G3
Clintmains TD6 76 E7
Clippesby NR29 45 J4
Clippings Green NR20 44 E4
Clipsham LE15 42 C4
Clipston Northants. LE16 42 A7
Clipston Notts. NG12 41 J2
Clipstone NG21 51 H6
Clitheroe BB7 56 C5
Cliuthar (Cluer) HS3 93 G2
Clive SY4 38 E3
Clivocast ZE2 107 Q2
Clixby DN38 52 E2
Clocaenog LL15 47 J7
Clochan AB56 98 C4
Clochtow AB41 91 J1
Clock Face WA9 48 E3
Clockhill AB42 99 G6

Cloddach **IV30** 97 J6
Cloddiau **SY21** 38 A5
Clodock **HR2** 28 C6
Cloford **BA11** 20 A7
Cloichran **FK21** 81 H4
Clola **AB42** 99 J6
Clonrae **DG3** 68 D4
Clophill **MK45** 32 D5
Clopton **NN14** 42 D7
Clopton Corner **IP13** 35 G3
Clopton Green *Suff.* **CB8** 34 B3
Clopton Green *Suff.* **IP13** 35 G3
Close Clark **IM9** 54 B6
Closeburn **DG3** 68 D4
Closworth **BA22** 8 E3
Clothall **SG7** 33 F5
Clothan **ZE2** 107 N4
Clotton **CW6** 48 E6
Clough *Cumb.* **LA10** 61 J7
Clough *Gt.Man.* **OL15** 49 J1
Clough *Gt.Man.* **OL2** 49 J2
Clough *W.Yorks.* **HD7** 50 C1
Clough Foot **OL14** 56 E7
Clough Head **HX6** 57 F7
Cloughfold **BB4** 56 D7
Cloughton **YO13** 63 K3
Cloughton Newlands **YO13** 63 K3
Clounlaid **PA34** 79 J2
Clousta **ZE2** 107 M7
Clouston **KW16** 106 C6
Clova *Aber.* **AB54** 90 C2
Clova *Angus* **DD8** 90 B7
Clove Lodge **DL12** 62 A5
Clovelly **EX39** 6 B3
Clovelly Cross **EX39** 6 B3
Clovenfords **TD1** 76 C7
Clovenstone **AB51** 91 F3
Cloverhill **AB23** 91 H3
Cloves **IV36** 97 J5
Clovullin **PH33** 80 B1
Clow Bridge **BB11** 56 D7
Clowne **S43** 51 G5
Clows Top **DY14** 29 G1
Cloyntie **KA19** 67 H3
Cluanach **PA43** 72 B5
Clubworthy **PL15** 4 C1
Cluddley **TF6** 39 F4
Cluer (Cliuthar) **HS3** 93 G2
Clun **SY7** 38 B7
Clunas **IV12** 97 F7
Clunbury **SY7** 38 C7
Clune *High.* **IV13** 88 E2
Clune *Moray* **AB56** 98 D4
Clunes **PH34** 87 J6
Clungunford **SY7** 28 C1
Clunie *Aber.* **AB53** 98 E5
Clunie *P. & K.* **PH10** 82 C3
Clunton **SY7** 38 C7
Cluny **KY2** 76 A1
Clutton *B. & N.E.Som.* **BS39** 19 K6
Clutton *Ches.W. & C.* **CH3** 48 D7
Clwt-y-bont **LL55** 46 D6
Clwydyfagwyr **CF48** 18 D1
Clydach *Mon.* **NP7** 28 B7
Clydach *Swan.* **SA6** 17 K5
Clydach Terrace **NP23** 28 A7
Clydach Vale **CF40** 18 C2
Clydebank G81 74 **C3**
Clydey **SA35** 17 F2
Clyffe Pypard **SN4** 20 D4
Clynder **G84** 74 A2
Clynderwen SA66 16 **E4**
Clyne **SA11** 18 B1
Clynelish **KW9** 97 F1
Clynfyw **SA37** 17 F2
Clynnog-fawr **LL54** 36 D1
Clyro **HR3** 28 B4
Clyst Honiton **EX5** 7 H6
Clyst Hydon **EX15** 7 J5
Clyst St. George **EX3** 7 H7
Clyst St. Lawrence **EX15** 7 J5
Clyst St. Mary **EX5** 7 H6
Clyst William **EX15** 7 J5
Cnewr **LD3** 27 H6
Cnoc **HS2** 101 G4
Cnoc an Torrain (Knockintorran) **HS6** 92 C5
Cnwch Coch **SY23** 27 F1
Coachford **AB54** 98 C6
Coad's Green **PL15** 4 C3
Coal Aston **S18** 51 F5
Coalbrookdale **TF8** 39 F5
Coalbrookvale **NP13** 18 E1
Coalburn **ML11** 75 G7
Coalburns **NE40** 71 G7
Coalcleugh **NE47** 61 K2
Coaley **GL11** 20 A1
Coalmoor **TF6** 39 F5
Coalpit Heath **BS36** 19 K3
Coalpit Hill **ST7** 49 H7
Coalport **TF8** 39 G5
Coalsnaughton **FK13** 75 H1
Coaltown of Balgonie **KY7** 76 B1
Coaltown of Wemyss **KY1** 76 B1
Coalville LE67 41 **G4**
Coalway **GL16** 28 E7
Coanwood **NE49** 61 H1
Coast **IV22** 95 F2
Coat **TA12** 8 D2
Coatbridge ML5 75 **F4**
Coate *Swin.* **SN3** 20 E3
Coate *Wilts.* **SN10** 20 D5
Coates *Cambs.* **PE7** 43 G6
Coates *Glos.* **GL7** 20 C1
Coates *Lincs.* **LN1** 52 C4
Coates *Notts.* **DN22** 52 B4
Coates *W.Suss.* **RH20** 12 C5
Coatham **TS10** 63 G4
Coatham Mundeville **DL3** 62 D4
Cobairdy **AB54** 98 D6
Cobbaton **EX37** 6 E3
Cobbler's Plain **NP16** 19 H1
Cobby Syke **HG3** 57 G4
Cobden **EX5** 7 J6
Coberley **GL53** 29 J7
Cobhall Common **HR2** 28 D5
Cobham *Kent* **DA12** 24 C5
Cobham *Surr.* KT11 22 **E5**
Cobleland **FK8** 74 D1
Cobley Hill **B60** 30 B1
Cobnash **HR6** 28 D2
Coburty **AB43** 99 H4
Cochno **G81** 74 C3
Cock Alley **S44** 51 G6
Cock Bank **LL13** 38 C1
Cock Bevington **WR11** 30 B3
Cock Bridge **AB36** 89 K4
Cock Clarks **CM3** 24 E1
Cock Green **CM6** 34 B7
Cock Marling **TN31** 14 D6
Cockayne **YO62** 63 H7
Cockayne Hatley **SG19** 33 F4
Cockburnspath TD13 77 **F3**
Cockenzie & Port Seton **EH32** 76 C3
Cocker Bar **PR26** 55 J7
Cockerham **LA2** 55 H4
Cockermouth CA13 60 **C3**
Cockernhoe **LU2** 32 E6
Cockerton **DL3** 62 D5
Cockett **SA2** 17 K6
Cockfield *Dur.* **DL13** 62 C4
Cockfield *Suff.* **IP30** 34 D3
Cockfosters **EN4** 23 F2
Cocking **GU29** 12 B5
Cockington **TQ2** 5 J4
Cocklake **BS28** 19 H7
Cocklaw **NE46** 70 E6
Cockle Park **NE61** 71 H4
Cockleford **GL53** 29 J7
Cockley Beck **LA20** 60 D6
Cockley Cley **PE37** 44 B5
Cockpen **EH19** 76 B4
Cockpole Green **RG10** 22 A3
Cockshutt **SY12** 38 D3
Cockthorpe **NR23** 44 D1
Cockwood *Devon* **EX6** 7 H7
Cockwood *Som.* **TA5** 19 F7
Cockyard **SK23** 50 C4
Codda **PL15** 4 B3
Coddenham **IP6** 35 F3
Coddington *Ches.W. & C.* **CH3** 48 D7
Coddington *Here.* **HR8** 29 G4
Coddington *Notts.* **NG24** 52 B7
Codford St. Mary **BA12** 9 J1
Codford St. Peter **BA12** 9 J1
Codicote **SG4** 33 F7
Codmore Hill **RH20** 12 D5
Codnor **DE5** 41 G1
Codnor Park **NG16** 51 G7
Codrington **BS37** 20 A4
Codsall **WV8** 40 A5
Codsall Wood **WV8** 40 A5
Coed Morgan **NP7** 28 C7
Coed Ystumgwern **LL44** 36 E3
Coedcae **NP4** 19 F1
Coed-duon (Blackwood) NP12 18 **E2**
Coedely **CF39** 18 D3
Coedkernew **NP10** 19 F3
Coedpoeth **LL11** 48 B7
Coedway **SY5** 38 C4
Coed-y-bryn **SA44** 17 G1
Coed-y-caerau **NP18** 19 G2
Coed-y-paen **NP4** 19 G2
Coed-y-parc **LL57** 46 E6
Coed-yr-ynys **NP8** 28 A6
Coelbren **SA10** 27 H7
Coffinswell **TQ12** 5 J4
Cofton **EX6** 7 H7
Cofton Hackett **B45** 30 B1
Cogan **CF64** 18 E4
Cogenhoe **NN7** 32 B2
Cogges **OX28** 21 G1
Coggeshall **CO6** 34 C6
Coggeshall Hamlet **CO6** 34 C6
Coggins Mill **TN20** 13 J4
Cóig Peighinnean **HS2** 101 H1
Coilantogle **FK17** 81 G7
Coileitir **PH49** 80 C3
Coilessan **G83** 80 D7
Coillaig **PA35** 80 B5
Coille Mhorgil **PH35** 87 G4
Coille-righ **IV40** 87 F2
Coillore **IV56** 85 J1
Coity **CF35** 18 C3
Col **HS2** 101 G4
Col Uarach **HS2** 101 G4
Colaboll **IV27** 103 H7
Colan **TR8** 3 F2
Colaton Raleigh **EX10** 7 J7
Colbost **IV55** 93 H7
Colburn **DL9** 62 D7
Colbury **SO40** 10 E3
Colby *Cumb.* **CA16** 61 H4
Colby *I.o.M.* **IM9** 54 B6
Colby *Norf.* **NR11** 45 G2
COLCHESTER CO 34 **D6**
Colchester Green **IP30** 34 D3
Colcot **CF62** 18 E5
Cold Ash **RG18** 21 J5
Cold Ashby **NN6** 31 H1
Cold Ashton **SN14** 20 A4
Cold Aston **GL54** 30 C7
Cold Blow **SA67** 16 E4
Cold Brayfield **MK46** 32 C3
Cold Chapel **ML12** 68 E1
Cold Cotes **LA2** 56 C2
Cold Hanworth **LN8** 52 D4
Cold Harbour **RG8** 21 K3
Cold Hatton **TF6** 39 F3
Cold Hatton Heath **TF6** 39 F3
Cold Hesledon **SR7** 63 F2
Cold Higham **NN12** 31 H3
Cold Inn **SA68** 16 E5
Cold Kirby **YO7** 58 B1
Cold Newton **LE7** 42 A5
Cold Northcott **PL15** 4 C2
Cold Norton **CM3** 24 E1
Cold Overton **LE15** 42 B5
Cold Row **FY6** 55 G5
Coldbackie **IV27** 103 J2
Coldblow **DA5** 23 J4
Coldean **BN1** 13 G6
Coldeast **TQ12** 5 J3
Coldeaton **DE6** 50 D7
Colden Common **SO21** 11 F2
Coldfair Green **IP17** 35 J2
Coldham **PE14** 43 H5
Coldharbour *Glos.* **GL15** 19 J1
Coldharbour *Surr.* **RH5** 22 E7
Coldingham **TD14** 77 H4
Coldrain **KY13** 82 B7
Coldred **CT15** 15 H3
Coldrey **GU34** 22 A7
Coldridge **EX17** 6 E5
Coldrife **NE61** 71 F4
Coldstream TD12 77 **G7**
Coldvreath **PL26** 3 G3
Coldwaltham **RH20** 12 D5
Coldwells **AB42** 99 K6
Cole **BA10** 9 F1
Cole End **B46** 40 D7
Cole Green **SG14** 33 F7
Cole Henley **RG28** 21 H6
Colebatch **SY9** 38 C7
Colebrook **EX15** 7 J5
Colebrooke **EX17** 7 F5
Coleburn **IV30** 97 K6
Coleby *Lincs.* **LN5** 52 C6
Coleby *N.Lincs.* **DN15** 52 B1
Coleford *Devon* **EX17** 7 F5
Coleford *Glos.* GL16 28 **E7**
Coleford *Som.* **BA3** 19 K7
Colegate End **IP21** 45 F7
Colehill **BH21** 10 B4
Coleman Green **AL4** 32 E7
Coleman's Hatch **TN7** 13 H3
Colemere **SY12** 38 D2
Colemore **GU34** 11 J1
Colemore Green **WV16** 39 G6
Colenden **PH2** 82 C5
Coleorton **LE67** 41 G4
Colerne **SN14** 20 B4
Cole's Common **IP21** 45 G7
Cole's Cross **TQ9** 5 H6
Cole's Green **IP13** 35 G2
Colesbourne **GL53** 30 B7
Colesden **MK44** 32 E3
Coleshill *Bucks.* **HP7** 22 C2
Coleshill *Oxon.* **SN6** 21 F2
Coleshill *Warks.* **B46** 40 E7
Colestocks **EX14** 7 J5
Coley *B. & N.E.Som.* **BS40** 19 J6
Coley *Staffs.* **ST18** 40 C3
Colfin **DG9** 64 A5
Colgate **RH12** 13 F3
Colgrain **G82** 74 B3
Colindale **NW9** 23 F3
Colinsburgh **KY9** 83 F7
Colinton **EH13** 76 A4
Colintraive PA22 73 **J3**
Colkirk **NR21** 44 D3
Coll PA78 78 **C2**
Collace **PH2** 82 D4
Collafirth **ZE2** 107 N6
Collamoor Head **PL32** 4 B1
Collaton St. Mary **TQ3** 5 J4
Collessie **KY15** 82 D6
Colleton Mills **EX37** 6 E4
Collett's Green **WR2** 29 H3
Collier Row **RM5** 23 J2
Collier Street **TN12** 14 C3
Collier's End **SG11** 33 G6
Collier's Wood **SW19** 23 F4
Colliery Row **DH4** 62 E2
Collieston **AB41** 91 J2
Collin **DG1** 69 F6
Collingbourne Ducis **SN8** 21 F6
Collingbourne Kingston **SN8** 21 F6
Collingham *Notts.* **NG23** 52 B6
Collingham *W.Yorks.* **LS22** 57 J5
Collington **HR7** 29 F2
Collingtree **NN4** 31 J3
Collins End **RG8** 21 K4
Collins Green *Warr.* **WA5** 48 E3
Collins Green *Worcs.* **WR6** 29 G3
Colliston **DD11** 83 H3
Colliton **EX14** 7 J5
Collmuir **AB31** 90 D4
Collycroft **CV12** 41 F7
Collyhurst **M8** 49 H2
Collynie **AB41** 91 G1
Collyweston **PE9** 42 C5
Colmonell **KA26** 67 F5
Colmworth **MK44** 32 E3
Coln Rogers **GL54** 20 D1
Coln St. Aldwyns **GL7** 20 E1
Coln St. Dennis **GL54** 30 B7
Colnabaichin **AB36** 89 K4
Colnbrook **SL3** 22 D4
Colne *Cambs.* **PE28** 33 G1
Colne *Lancs.* BB8 56 **D6**
Colne Engaine **CO6** 34 C5
Colney **NR4** 45 F5
Colney Heath **AL4** 23 F1
Colney Street **AL2** 22 E1
Colonsay PA61 72 **B1**
Colonsay House **PA61** 72 B1
Colpy **AB52** 90 E1
Colquhar **EH44** 76 B6
Colsterdale **HG4** 57 G1
Colsterworth **NG33** 42 C3
Colston Bassett **NG12** 42 A2
Coltfield **IV36** 97 J5
Colthouse **LA22** 60 E7
Coltishall **NR12** 45 G4
Coltness **ML2** 75 G5
Colton *Cumb.* **LA12** 55 G1
Colton *N.Yorks.* **LS24** 58 B5
Colton *Norf.* **NR9** 45 F5
Colton *Staffs.* **WS15** 40 C3
Colton *W.Yorks.* **LS15** 57 J6
Colva **HR5** 28 B3
Colvend **DG5** 65 J5
Colvister **ZE2** 107 P3
Colwall **WR13** 29 G4
Colwall Green **WR13** 29 G4
Colwall Stone **WR13** 29 G4
Colwell **NE46** 70 E6
Colwich **ST18** 40 C3
Colwick **NG4** 41 J2
Colwinston **CF71** 18 C4
Colworth **PO20** 12 C6
Colwyn Bay (Bae Colwyn) LL29 47 **G5**
Colyford **EX24** 8 B5
Colyton EX24 8 **B5**
Combe *Here.* **LD8** 28 C2
Combe *Oxon.* **OX29** 31 F7
Combe *Som.* **TA10** 8 D2
Combe *W.Berks.* **RG17** 21 G5
Combe Common **GU8** 12 C3
Combe Cross **TQ13** 5 H3
Combe Down **BA2** 20 A5
Combe Florey **TA4** 7 K2
Combe Hay **BA2** 20 A6
Combe Martin **EX34** 6 D1
Combe Pafford **TQ1** 5 K4
Combe Raleigh **EX14** 7 K5
Combe St. Nicholas **TA20** 8 C3
Combeinteignhead **TQ12** 5 J3
Comberbach **CW9** 49 F5
Comberford **B79** 40 D5
Comberton *Cambs.* **CB23** 33 G3
Comberton *Here.* **SY8** 28 D2
Combpyne **EX13** 8 B5
Combridge **ST14** 40 C2
Combrook **CV35** 30 E3
Combs *Derbys.* **SK23** 50 C5
Combs *Suff.* **IP14** 34 E3
Combs Ford **IP14** 34 E3
Combwich **TA5** 19 F7
Comer **FK8** 80 E7
Comers **AB51** 90 E4
Comhampton **DY13** 29 H2
Comins Coch **SY23** 37 F7
Commercial End **CB25** 33 J2
Commins Coch **SY20** 37 H5
Common Edge **FY4** 55 G6
Common Moor **PL14** 4 C3
Common Platt **SN5** 20 E3
Common Side **S18** 51 F5
Common Square **LN4** 52 D5
Commondale **YO21** 63 H5
Commonside **DE6** 40 E1
Compstall **SK6** 49 J3
Compton *Devon* **TQ3** 5 J4
Compton *Hants.* **SO21** 11 F2
Compton *Plym.* **PL3** 4 E5
Compton *Staffs.* **DY7** 40 A7
Compton *Surr.* **GU3** 22 C7
Compton *W.Berks.* **RG20** 21 J4
Compton *W.Suss.* **PO18** 11 J3
Compton *W.Yorks.* **LS22** 57 K5
Compton *Wilts.* **SN9** 20 E6
Compton Abbas **SP7** 9 H3
Compton Abdale **GL54** 30 B7
Compton Bassett **SN11** 20 D4
Compton Beauchamp **SN6** 21 F3
Compton Bishop **BS26** 19 G6
Compton Chamberlayne **SP3** 10 B2
Compton Dando **BS39** 19 K5
Compton Dundon **TA11** 8 D1
Compton Martin **BS40** 19 J6
Compton Pauncefoot **BA22** 9 F2
Compton Valence **DT2** 8 E5
Compton Verney **CV35** 30 E3
Compton Wynyates **CV35** 30 E4
Comra **PH20** 88 C5
Comrie *Fife* **KY12** 75 J2
Comrie *P. & K.* **PH6** 81 J5
Conchra *Arg. & B.* **PA22** 73 J2
Conchra *High.* **IV40** 86 E2
Concraigie **PH10** 82 C3
Conder Green **LA2** 55 H4
Conderton **GL20** 29 J5
Condicote **GL54** 30 C6
Condorrat **G67** 75 F3
Condover **SY5** 38 D5
Coney Weston **IP31** 34 D1
Coneyhurst **RH14** 12 E4
Coneysthorpe **YO60** 58 D2
Coneythorpe **HG5** 57 J4
Conford **GU30** 12 B3
Congash **PH26** 89 H2
Congdon's Shop **PL15** 4 C3
Congerstone **CV13** 41 F5
Congham **PE32** 44 B3
Congleton CW12 49 **H6**
Congresbury **BS49** 19 H5
Congreve **ST19** 40 B4
Conicavel **IV36** 97 G6
Coningsby **LN4** 53 F7
Conington *Cambs.* **PE7** 42 E7
Conington *Cambs.* **CB23** 33 G2
Conisbrough **DN12** 51 H3
Conisby **PA49** 72 A4
Conisholme **LN11** 53 H3
Coniston *Cumb.* LA21 60 **E7**
Coniston *E.Riding* **HU11** 59 H6
Coniston Cold **BD23** 56 E4
Conistone **BD23** 56 E3
Conland **AB54** 98 E6
Connah's Quay **CH5** 48 B6
Connel **PA37** 80 A4
Connel Park **KA18** 68 B2
Connor Downs **TR27** 2 C5
Conock **SN10** 20 D6
Conon Bridge **IV7** 96 C6
Cononish **FK20** 80 E5
Cononley **BD20** 56 E5
Cononsyth **DD11** 83 G3
Consall **ST9** 40 B1
Consett DH8 62 **C1**
Constable Burton **DL8** 62 C7
Constantine **TR11** 2 E6
Constantine Bay **PL28** 3 F1
Contin **IV14** 96 B6
Contlaw **AB13** 91 G4
Contullich **IV17** 96 D4
Conwy LL32 47 **F5**
Conyer **ME9** 25 F5
Conyer's Green **IP31** 34 C2
Cooden **TN39** 14 C7
Coodham **KA1** 74 C7
Cooil **IM4** 54 C6
Cookbury **EX22** 6 C5
Cookbury Wick **EX22** 6 B5
Cookham **SL6** 22 B3
Cookham Dean **SL6** 22 B3
Cookham Rise **SL6** 22 B3
Cookhill **B49** 30 B3
Cookley *Suff.* **IP19** 35 H1
Cookley *Worcs.* **DY10** 40 A7
Cookley Green *Oxon.* **RG9** 21 K2
Cookley Green *Suff.* **IP19** 35 H1
Cookney **AB39** 91 G5
Cook's Green **IP7** 34 D3
Cooksbridge **BN7** 13 G5
Cooksey Green **B61** 29 J2
Cookshill **ST11** 40 B1
Cooksmill Green **CM1** 24 C1
Cookston **AB41** 91 H1
Coolham **RH13** 12 E4
Cooling **ME3** 24 D4
Cooling Street **ME3** 24 D4
Coombe *Cornw.* **PL26** 3 G3
Coombe *Cornw.* **EX23** 6 A4
Coombe *Cornw.* **TR14** 2 D4
Coombe *Cornw.* **TR3** 3 F4
Coombe *Devon* **TQ9** 5 H6
Coombe *Devon* **EX6** 7 G7
Coombe *Devon* **EX10** 7 K6
Coombe *Som.* **TA2** 8 B2
Coombe *Som.* **TA18** 8 D4
Coombe *Wilts.* **SN9** 20 E6
Coombe Bissett **SP5** 10 C2
Coombe End **TA4** 7 J3
Coombe Hill **GL19** 29 H6
Coombe Keynes **BH20** 9 H6
Coombes **BN15** 12 E6
Coombes Moor **LD8** 28 C2
Cooper's Corner *E.Suss.* **TN19** 14 C5
Cooper's Corner *Kent* **TN14** 23 H7
Cooper's Green **AL4** 22 E1
Coopersale **CM16** 23 H1
Coopersale Street **CM16** 23 H1
Cootham **RH20** 12 D5
Cop Street **CT3** 15 H2
Copdock **IP8** 35 F4
Copford Green **CO6** 34 D6
Copgrove **HG3** 57 J3
Copister **ZE2** 107 N5
Cople **MK44** 32 E4
Copley *Dur.* **DL13** 62 B4
Copley *W.Yorks.* **HX4** 57 F7
Coplow Dale **SK17** 50 D5
Copmanthorpe **YO23** 58 B5
Copmere End **ST21** 40 A3
Copp **PR3** 55 H6
Coppathorne **EX23** 6 A5
Coppenhall **ST18** 40 B4
Coppenhall Moss **CW1** 49 G7
Copperhouse **TR27** 2 C5
Coppicegate **DY12** 39 G7
Coppingford **PE28** 42 E7
Coppleridge **SP7** 9 H2
Copplestone **EX17** 7 F5
Coppull **PR7** 48 E1
Coppull Moor **PR7** 48 E1
Copsale **RH13** 12 E4
Copse Hill **SW20** 23 F5
Copster Green **BB1** 56 B6
Copston Magna **LE10** 41 G7
Copt Heath **B93** 30 C1
Copt Hewick **HG4** 57 J2
Copt Oak **LE67** 41 G4
Copthall Green **EN9** 23 H1
Copthorne **RH10** 13 G3
Copy Lake **EX18** 6 E4
Copythorne **SO40** 10 E3
Coralhill **AB43** 99 J4
Corbets Tey **RM14** 23 J3
Corbiegoe **KW1** 105 J4
Corbridge NE45 70 **E7**
Corby NN17 42 **B7**
Corby Glen **NG33** 42 D3
Cordach **AB34** 90 E5
Cordorcan **DG8** 64 D3
Coreley **SY8** 29 F1
Corfcott Green **EX22** 6 B6
Corfe **TA3** 8 B3
Corfe Castle **BH20** 9 J6

Croglin CA4 61 G2
Croick High. IV24 96 B2
Croick High. KW13 104 D3
Croig PA75 79 F2
Crois Dughaill HS8 84 C3
Croit e Caley IM9 54 B7
Cromarty IV11 96 E5
Crombie KY12 75 J2
Crombie Mill DD7 83 G4
Cromblet AB51 91 F1
Cromdale PH26 89 H2
Cromer Herts. SG2 33 F6
Cromer Norf. NR27 45 G1
Cromford DE4 50 E7
Cromhall GL12 19 K2
Cromhall Common GL12 19 K3
Cromore HS2 101 G5
Crompton Fold OL2 49 J1
Cromwell NG23 51 K6
Cronberry KA18 68 B1
Crondall GU10 22 A7
Cronk-y-Voddy IM6 54 C5
Cronton WA8 48 D4
Crook Cumb. LA8 61 F7
Crook Dur. DL15 62 C3
Crook of Devon KY13 82 B7
Crooked Soley RG17 21 G4
Crookedholm KA3 74 C7
Crookham Northumb. TD12 77 H7
Crookham W.Berks. RG19 21 J5
Crookham Eastfield TD12 77 H7
Crookham Village GU51 22 A6
Crooklands LA7 55 J1
Cropredy OX17 31 F4
Cropston LE7 41 H4
Cropthorne WR10 29 J4
Cropton YO18 58 D1
Cropwell Bishop NG12 41 J2
Cropwell Butler NG12 41 J2
Cros (Cross) HS2 101 H1
Crosbie KA23 74 A6
Crosbost HS2 101 F5
Crosby Cumb. CA15 60 B3
Crosby I.o.M. IM4 54 C6
Crosby Mersey. L23 48 C3
Crosby N.Lincs. DN15 52 B1
Crosby Court DL6 62 E7
Crosby Garrett CA17 61 J6
Crosby Ravensworth CA10 61 H5
Crosby Villa CA15 60 B3
Crosby-on-Eden CA6 60 F1
Croscombe BA5 19 J7
Crosemere SY12 38 D3
Crosland Hill HD4 50 D1
Cross Som. BS26 19 H6
Cross (Cros) W.Isles HS2 101 H1
Cross Ash NP7 28 D7
Cross Bank DY12 29 G1
Cross End Bed. MK44 32 D3
Cross End Essex CO9 34 C5
Cross Foxes Inn LL40 37 G4
Cross Gates LS15 57 J6
Cross Green Devon PL15 6 B7
Cross Green Staffs. WV10 40 B5
Cross Green Suff. IP7 34 D3
Cross Green Suff. IP30 34 C3
Cross Green Suff. IP29 34 C3
Cross Hands Carmar. SA14 17 J4
Cross Hands Pembs. SA67 16 D4
Cross Hill DE5 41 G1
Cross Hills BD20 57 F5
Cross Houses SY5 38 E5
Cross in Hand TN21 13 J4
Cross Inn Cere. SA44 26 C3
Cross Inn Cere. SY23 26 E2
Cross Inn R.C.T. CF72 18 D3
Cross Keys SN13 20 B4
Cross Lane PO30 11 G6
Cross Lane Head WV16 39 G6
Cross Lanes Cornw. TR4 2 E4
Cross Lanes Cornw. TR12 2 D6
Cross Lanes N.Yorks. YO61 58 B3
Cross Lanes Wrex. LL13 38 C1
Cross of Jackston AB51 91 F1
Cross o'th'hands DE56 40 E1
Cross Street IP21 35 F1
Crossaig PA29 73 G5
Crossapol PA78 78 C2
Crossapoll PA77 78 A3
Cross-at-Hand TN12 14 C3
Crossbush BN18 12 D6
Crosscanonby CA15 60 B3
Crossdale Street NR27 45 G2
Crossens PR9 48 C1
Crossflatts BD16 57 G5
Crossford D. & G. DG3 68 D5
Crossford Fife KY12 75 J2
Crossford S.Lan. ML8 75 G6
Crossgate Lincs. PE11 43 F3
Crossgate Staffs. ST11 40 B2
Crossgatehall EH22 76 B4
Crossgates Fife KY4 75 K2
Crossgates N.Yorks. YO12 59 G1
Crossgates P. & K. PH2 82 B5
Crossgates Powys LD1 27 K2
Crossgill LA2 55 J3
Crosshands KA5 74 C7
Crosshill Fife KY5 75 K1
Crosshill S.Ayr. KA19 67 H3
Crosshouse KA2 74 B7
Crosskeys NP11 19 F2
Crosskirk KW14 105 F1
Crosslanes SY10 38 C4
Crosslee Renf. PA6 74 C4
Crosslee Sc.Bord. TD7 69 J2
Crossmichael DG7 65 H4
Crossmoor PR4 55 H6
Crossroads Aber. AB31 91 F5
Crossroads E.Ayr. KA1 74 C7
Crossway Mon. NP25 28 D7
Crossway Powys LD1 27 K3
Crossway Green Mon. NP16 19 J2
Crossway Green Worcs. DY13 29 H2
Crossways Dorset DT2 9 G6
Crossways Glos. GL16 28 E7
Crosswell SA41 16 E2
Crosswood SY23 27 F1
Crosthwaite LA8 60 F7
Croston PR26 48 D1
Crostwick NR12 45 G4
Crostwight NR28 45 H3
Crothair HS2 100 D4
Crouch TN15 23 K6
Crouch End N8 23 F3
Crouch Hill DT9 9 G3
Croucheston SP5 10 B2
Croughton NN13 31 G5
Crovie AB45 99 G4
Crow BH24 10 C4
Crow Edge S36 50 D2
Crow Green CM15 23 J2
Crow Hill HR9 29 F6
Crowan TR14 2 D5
Crowborough TN6 13 J3
Crowborough Warren TN6 13 J3
Crowcombe TA4 7 K2
Crowdecote SK17 50 D6
Crowden SK13 50 C3
Crowdhill SO50 11 F2
Crowell OX39 22 A2
Crowfield Northants. NN13 31 H4
Crowfield Suff. IP6 35 F3
Crowhurst E.Suss. TN33 14 C6
Crowhurst Surr. RH7 23 G7
Crowhurst Lane End RH7 23 G7
Crowland Lincs. PE6 43 F4
Crowland Suff. IP31 34 E1
Crowlas TR20 2 C5
Crowle N.Lincs. DN17 51 K1
Crowle Worcs. WR7 29 J3
Crowle Green WR7 29 J3
Crowmarsh Gifford OX10 21 K3
Crown Corner IP13 35 G1
Crownhill PL6 4 E5
Crownthorpe NR18 44 E5
Crowntown TR13 2 D5
Crow's Nest PL14 4 C4
Crows-an-wra TR19 2 A6
Crowsnest SY5 38 C5
Crowthorne RG45 22 B5
Crowton CW8 48 E5
Croxall WS13 40 E4
Croxby LN7 52 E3
Croxdale DH6 62 D3
Croxden ST14 40 C2
Croxley Green WD3 22 D2
Croxton Cambs. PE19 33 F3
Croxton N.Lincs. DN39 52 D1
Croxton Norf. IP24 44 C7
Croxton Staffs. ST21 39 G2
Croxton Green SY14 48 E7
Croxton Kerrial NG32 42 B3
Croxtonbank ST21 39 G2
Croy High. IV2 96 E7
Croy N.Lan. G65 75 F3
Croyde EX33 6 C2
Croyde Bay EX33 6 C2
Croydon Cambs. SG8 33 G4
CROYDON Gt.Lon. CR 23 G5
Cruach PA43 72 B5
Cruchie AB54 98 D6
Cruckmeole SY5 38 D5
Cruckton SY5 38 D4
Cruden Bay AB42 91 J1
Crudgington TF6 39 F4
Crudwell SN16 20 C2
Crug LD1 28 A1
Crugmeer PL28 3 G1
Crugybar SA19 17 K2
Crùlabhig HS2 100 D4
Crumlin NP11 19 F2
Crumpsall M8 49 H2
Crumpsbrook DY14 29 F1
Crundale Kent CT4 15 F3
Crundale Pembs. SA62 16 C4
Crunwere Farm SA67 16 E4
Crutherland Farm G75 74 E5
Cruwys Morchard EX16 7 G4
Crux Easton RG20 21 H6
Crwbin SA17 17 H4
Cryers Hill HP15 22 B2
Crymlyn LL33 46 E5
Crymych SA41 16 E2
Crynant SA10 18 A1
Crystal Palace SE26 23 G4
Cuaig IV54 94 D6
Cubbington CV32 30 E2
Cubert TR8 2 E3
Cubley S36 50 E2
Cublington Bucks. LU7 32 B6
Cublington Here. HR2 28 D5
Cuckfield RH17 13 G4
Cucklington BA9 9 G2
Cuckney NG20 51 H5
Cuckold's Green NR34 45 J7
Cuckoo Bridge PE11 43 F3
Cuckoo's Corner GU34 22 A7
Cuckoo's Nest CH4 48 C6
Cuddesdon OX44 21 J1
Cuddington Bucks. HP18 31 J7
Cuddington Ches.W. & C. CW8 48 E5
Cuddington Heath SY14 38 D1
Cuddy Hill PR4 55 H6
Cudham TN14 23 H6
Cudlipptown PL19 5 F3
Cudworth S.Yorks. S72 51 F2
Cudworth Som. TA19 8 C3
Cuerdley Cross WA5 48 E4
Cuffley EN6 23 G1
Cuidhaseadair HS2 101 H2
Cuidhir HS9 84 B4
Cuidhtinis (Quidinish) HS3 93 F3
Cuidrach IV51 93 J6
Cuilmuich PA24 73 K1
Cuil-uaine PA37 80 A4
Culag G83 74 B1
Culbo IV7 96 D5
Culbokie IV7 96 D6
Culbone TA24 7 G1
Culburnie IV4 96 B7
Culcabock IV2 96 D7
Culcharan PA37 80 A4
Culcharry IV12 97 F6
Culcheth WA3 49 F3
Culdrain AB54 90 D1
Culduie IV54 94 D7
Culford IP28 34 C2
Culfordheath IP31 34 C1
Culgaith CA10 61 H4
Culgower KW8 104 E7
Culham OX14 21 J2
Culindrach PA29 73 H5
Culkein IV27 102 C5
Culkerton GL8 20 C2
Cullachie PH24 89 G2
Cullen AB56 98 D4
Cullercoats NE30 71 J6
Cullicudden IV7 96 D5
Culligran IV4 95 K7
Cullingworth BD13 57 F6
Cullipool PA34 79 J6
Cullivoe ZE2 107 P2
Culloch PH6 81 J6
Culloden IV2 96 E7
Cullompton EX15 7 J5
Culmaily KW10 97 F2
Culmalzie DG8 64 D5
Culmington SY8 38 D7
Culmstock EX15 7 K4
Culnacraig IV26 95 G1
Culnadalloch PA37 80 A4
Culnaknock IV51 94 B5
Culnamean IV47 85 K2
Culpho IP6 35 G4
Culquhirk DG8 64 E5
Culrain IV24 96 C2
Culross KY12 75 H2
Culroy KA19 67 H2
Culsh AB35 90 B5
Culshabbin DG8 64 D5
Culswick ZE2 107 L8
Culter Allers Farm ML12 75 J7
Cultercullen AB41 91 H2
Cults Aber. AB54 90 D1
Cults Aberdeen AB15 91 G4
Cults D. & G. DG8 64 E6
Cultybraggan Camp PH6 81 J6
Culverhouse Cross CF5 18 E4
Culverstone Green DA13 24 C5
Culverthorpe NG32 42 D1
Culvie AB54 98 D5
Culworth OX17 31 G4
Cumberhead ML11 75 F7
Cumberlow Green SG9 33 G5
Cumbernauld G67 75 F3
Cumberworth LN13 53 J5
Cuminestown AB53 99 G6
Cumloden DG8 64 E4
Cummersdale CA2 60 E1
Cummertrees DG12 69 G7
Cummingstown IV30 97 J5
Cumnock KA18 67 K1
Cumnor OX2 21 H1
Cumrew CA8 61 G1
Cumrue DG11 69 F5
Cumstoun DG6 65 G5
Cumwhinton CA4 61 F1
Cumwhitton CA8 61 G1
Cundall YO61 57 K2
Cunninghamhead KA3 74 B6
Cunningsburgh ZE2 107 N10
Cunnister ZE2 107 P3
Cunnoquhie KY15 82 E6
Cupar KY15 82 E6
Cupar Muir KY15 82 E6
Curbar S32 50 E5
Curborough WS13 40 D4
Curbridge Hants. SO30 11 G3
Curbridge Oxon. OX29 21 G1
Curdridge SO32 11 G3
Curdworth B76 40 D6
Curland TA3 8 B3
Curlew Green IP17 35 H2
Curling Tye Green CM9 24 E1
Curload TA3 8 C2
Curridge RG18 21 H4
Currie EH14 75 K4
Curry Mallet TA3 8 C2
Curry Rivel TA10 8 C2
Curteis' Corner TN27 14 D4
Curtisden Green TN17 14 C3
Curtisknowle TQ9 5 H5
Cury TR12 2 D6
Cusgarne TR4 2 E4
Cushnie AB45 99 F4
Cushuish TA2 7 K2
Cusop HR3 28 B4
Cusworth DN5 51 H2
Cutcloy DG8 64 E7
Cutcombe TA24 7 H2
Cutgate OL11 49 H1
Cuthill IV25 96 E3
Cutiau LL42 37 F4
Cutlers Green CM6 33 J5
Cutnall Green WR9 29 H2
Cutsdean GL54 30 B5
Cutsyke WF10 57 K7
Cutthorpe S42 51 F5
Cutts ZE1 107 N9
Cuttyhill AB42 99 J5
Cuxham OX49 21 K2
Cuxton ME2 24 D5
Cuxwold LN7 52 E2
Cwm B.Gwent NP23 18 E1
Cwm Denb. LL18 47 J5
Cwm Ffrwd-oer NP4 19 F1
Cwm Gwaun SA65 16 D2
Cwm Head SY6 38 D7
Cwm Irfon LD5 27 H4
Cwm Penmachno LL24 37 G1
Cwm Plysgog SA43 16 E1
Cwmafan SA12 18 A2
Cwmaman CF44 18 D2
Cwmann SA48 17 J1
Cwmbach Carmar. SA34 17 F3
Cwmbach Carmar. SA15 17 H5
Cwmbach Powys HR3 28 A5
Cwmbach Powys LD2 27 K3
Cwmbach R.C.T. CF44 18 D1
Cwmbelan SY18 37 J7
Cwmbrân NP44 19 F2
Cwmbrwyno SY23 37 G7
Cwmcarn NP11 19 F2
Cwmcarvan NP25 19 H1
Cwm-Cewydd SY20 37 H4
Cwm-cou SA38 17 F1
Cwmcrawnon LD3 28 A7
Cwmdare CF44 18 C1
Cwmdu Carmar. SA19 17 K2
Cwmdu Powys NP8 28 A6
Cwmduad SA33 17 G2
Cwmerfyn SY23 37 G7
Cwmfelin CF46 18 D1
Cwmfelin Boeth SA34 16 E4
Cwmfelin Mynach SA34 17 F3
Cwmfelinfach NP11 18 E2
Cwmffrwd SA31 17 H4
Cwmgiedd SA9 27 G7
Cwmgors SA18 27 G7
Cwmgwili SA14 17 J4
Cwmgwrach SA11 18 B1
Cwmgwyn SA2 17 K6
Cwmhiraeth SA44 17 G2
Cwmifor SA19 17 K3
Cwmisfael SA32 17 H4
Cwm-Llinau SY20 37 H5
Cwmllyfri SA33 17 G4
Cwmllynfell SA9 27 G7
Cwm-mawr SA14 17 J4
Cwm-miles SA34 16 E3
Cwm-Morgan SA38 17 F2
Cwm-parc CF42 18 C2
Cwmpengraig SA44 17 G2
Cwmpennar CF45 18 D1
Cwmsychbant SA40 17 H1
Cwmsymlog SY23 37 F7
Cwmtillery NP13 19 F1
Cwm-twrch Isaf SA9 27 G7
Cwm-twrch Uchaf SA9 27 G7
Cwm-y-glo LL55 46 D6
Cwmyoy NP7 28 C6
Cwm-yr-Eglwys SA42 16 D1
Cwmyrhaiadr SY20 37 G6
Cwmystwyth SY23 27 G1
Cwrt SY20 37 F5
Cwrt-newydd SA40 17 H1
Cwrt-y-cadno SA19 17 K1
Cwrt-y-gollen NP8 28 B7
Cydweli (Kidwelly) SA17 17 H5
Cyffylliog LL15 47 J7
Cyfronydd SY21 38 A5
Cymau LL11 48 B7
Cymmer N.P.T. SA13 18 B2
Cymmer R.C.T. CF39 18 D2
Cyncoed CF23 18 E3
Cynghordy SA20 27 H5
Cynheidre SA15 17 H5
Cynwyd LL21 37 K1
Cynwyl Elfed SA33 17 G3

D

Dabton DG3 68 D4
Daccombe TQ12 5 K4
Dacre Cumb. CA11 61 F4
Dacre N.Yorks. HG3 57 G3
Dacre Banks HG3 57 G3
Daddry Shield DL13 61 K3
Dadford MK18 31 H5
Dadlington CV13 41 G6
Dafen SA14 17 J5
Daffy Green IP25 44 D5
Dagdale ST14 40 C2
Dagenham RM10 23 H3
Daggons SP6 10 C3
Daglingworth GL7 20 C1
Dagnall HP4 32 C7
Dail PA35 80 B4
Dail Beag HS2 100 E3
Dail Bho Dheas (South Dell) HS2 101 G1
Dail Bho Thuath (North Dell) HS2 101 G1
Dail Mòr HS2 100 E3
Dailly KA26 67 G3
Dailnamac PA35 80 A4
Dainton TQ12 5 J4
Dairsie (Osnaburgh) KY15 83 F6
Dairy House HU12 59 J7
Daisy Bank WS5 40 C6
Daisy Green IP31 34 E2
Dalabrog HS8 84 C2
Dalavich PA35 80 A6
Dalballoch PH20 88 D5
Dalbeattie DG5 65 J4
Dalblair KA18 68 B2
Dalbog DD9 90 D7
Dalbreck IV28 104 C7
Dalbury DE6 40 E2
Dalby I.o.M. IM5 54 B6
Dalby Lincs. PE23 53 H6
Dalby N.Yorks. YO60 58 C2
Dalcairnie KA6 67 J3
Dalchalloch PH18 81 J1
Dalchalm KW9 97 G1
Dalchenna PA32 80 B7
Dalchirach AB37 89 J1
Dalchork IV27 103 H7
Dalchreichart IV63 87 J3
Dalchruin PH6 81 J6
Dalcross IV2 96 E7
Dalderby LN9 53 F6
Dalditch EX9 7 J7
Daldownie AB35 89 K4
Dale Cumb. CA4 61 G2
Dale Gt.Man. OL3 49 J2
Dale Pembs. SA62 16 B5
Dale Abbey DE7 41 G2
Dale End Derbys. DE45 50 E6
Dale End N.Yorks. BD20 56 E5
Dale Head CA10 60 F5
Dale of Walls ZE2 107 K7
Dale Park BN18 12 C5
Dalehouse TS13 63 J5
Dalelia PH36 79 J1
Daless IV12 89 F1
Dalestie AB37 89 J3
Dalfad AB35 90 B4
Dalganachan KW12 105 F4
Dalgarven KA13 74 A6
Dalgety Bay KY11 75 K2
Dalgig KA18 67 K2
Dalginross PH6 81 J5
Dalgonar DG3 68 C3
Dalguise PH8 82 A3
Dalhalvaig KW13 104 D3
Dalham CB8 34 B2
Daligan G84 74 B2
Dalinlongart PA23 73 K2
Dalivaddy PA28 66 A1
Daljarrock KA26 67 F5
Dalkeith EH22 76 B4
Dallachulish PA37 80 A3
Dallas IV36 97 J6
Dallaschyle IV12 97 F7
Dallash DG8 64 E4
Dalleagles KA18 67 K2
Dallinghoo IP13 35 G3
Dallington E.Suss. TN21 13 K5
Dallington Northants. NN5 31 J2
Dallow HG4 57 G2
Dalmadilly AB51 91 F3
Dalmally PA33 80 C5
Dalmarnock PH8 82 B3
Dalmary FK8 74 D1
Dalmellington KA6 67 J3
Dalmeny EH30 75 K3
Dalmichy IV27 103 H7
Dalmigavie IV13 88 E3
Dalmore IV17 96 D5
Dalmuir G81 74 C3
Dalmunzie House Hotel PH10 89 H7
Dalnabreck PH36 79 J1
Dalnacarn PH10 82 B1
Dalnaglar Castle PH10 82 C1
Dalnaha PA63 79 H5
Dalnahaitnach PH23 89 F3
Dalnamain IV25 96 E2
Dalnatrat PA38 80 A2
Dalnavert PH21 89 F4
Dalnavie IV17 96 D4
Dalness PH49 80 C2
Dalnessie IV27 103 J7
Dalnigap DG8 64 B3
Dalqueich KY13 82 B7
Dalreoch KA26 67 F5
Dalriech PH8 81 J4
Dalroy IV2 96 E7
Dalrulzian PH10 82 C2
Dalry KA24 74 A6
Dalrymple KA6 67 H2
Dalscote NN12 31 H3
Dalserf ML9 75 F5
Dalsetter ZE2 107 P3
Dalshangan DG7 67 K5
Dalskairth DG2 65 K3
Dalston CA5 60 E1
Dalswinton DG2 68 E5
Daltomach IV13 88 E2
Dalton Cumb. LA6 55 J2
Dalton D. & G. DG11 69 G6
Dalton Lancs. WN8 48 D2
Dalton N.Yorks. YO7 57 K2
Dalton N.Yorks. DL11 62 C6
Dalton Northumb. NE18 71 G6
Dalton Northumb. NE46 62 A1
Dalton S.Yorks. S65 51 G3
Dalton Magna S65 51 G3
Dalton Piercy TS27 63 F3
Dalton-in-Furness LA15 55 F2
Dalton-le-Dale SR7 63 F2
Dalton-on-Tees DL2 62 D6
Daltote PA31 73 F2
Daltra IV12 97 G7
Dalveich FK19 81 H5
Dalvennan KA19 67 H2
Dalvourn IV2 88 D1
Dalwhinnie PH19 88 D6
Dalwood EX13 8 B4

Dam Green NR16 44 E7
Damask Green SG4 33 F6
Damerham SP6 10 C3
Damgate NR13 45 J5
Damnaglaur DG9 64 B7
Damside PH3 82 A6
Danaway ME9 24 E5
Danbury CM3 24 D1
Danby YO21 63 J6
Danby Wiske DL7 62 E7
Dancers Hill EN5 23 F2
Dandaleith AB38 97 K7
Danderhall EH22 76 B4
Dane Bank M34 49 J3
Dane End SG12 33 G6
Dane Hills LE3 41 H5
Danebridge SK11 49 J6
Danehill RH17 13 H4
Danesmoor S45 51 G6
Danestone AB22 91 H3
Daniel's Water TN26 14 E3
Danskine EH41 76 D4
Danthorpe HU12 59 J6
Danzey Green B94 30 C2
Darby End B64 40 B7
Darby Green GU46 22 B5
Darenth DA2 23 J4
Daresbury WA4 48 E4
Darfield S73 51 G2
Dargate ME13 25 G5
Dargues NE19 70 D4
Darite PL14 4 C4
Darland ME7 24 D5
Darlaston WS10 40 B6
Darley HG3 57 H4
Darley Bridge DE4 50 E6
Darley Dale DE4 50 E6
Darley Head HG3 57 G4
Darley Hillside DE4 50 E6
Darlingscott CV36 30 D4
DARLINGTON DL 62 D5
Darliston SY13 38 E2
Darlton NG22 51 K5
Darnabo AB53 99 F6
Darnall S9 51 F4
Darnconner KA18 67 K1
Darnford AB31 91 F5
Darngarroch DG7 65 G4
Darnick TD6 76 D7
Darowen SY20 37 H5
Darra AB53 99 F6
Darracott EX39 6 A4
Darras Hall NE20 71 G6
Darrington WF8 51 G1
Darrow Green IP20 45 G7
Darsham IP17 35 J2
Dartfield AB43 99 J5
DARTFORD DA 23 J4
Dartington TQ9 5 H4
Dartmeet TQ13 5 G3
Dartmouth TQ6 5 J5
Darton S75 51 F1
Darvel KA17 74 D7
Darvell TN32 14 C5
Darwell Hole TN33 13 K5
Darwen BB3 56 B7
Datchet SL3 22 C4
Datchworth SG3 33 F7
Datchworth Green SG3 33 F7
Daubhill BL3 49 F2
Daugh of Kinermony AB38 97 K7
Dauntsey SN15 20 C3
Dauntsey Green SN15 20 C3
Dauntsey Lock SN15 20 C3
Dava PH26 89 H1
Davaar PA28 66 B2
Davan AB34 90 C4
Davenham CW9 49 F5
Davenport Green WA15 49 H4
Daventry NN11 31 G2
Davidstow PL32 4 B2
Davington DG13 69 H3
Daviot Aber. AB51 91 F2
Daviot High. IV2 88 E1
Davoch of Grange AB55 98 C5
Davyhulme M41 49 G3
Dawley TF4 39 F5
Dawlish EX7 5 K3
Dawn LL22 47 G5
Daws Heath SS7 24 E3
Daw's House PL15 6 B7
Dawsmere PE12 43 H2
Day Green CW11 49 G7
Dayhills ST15 40 B2
Dayhouse Bank B62 29 J1
Daylesford GL56 30 D6
Ddôl CH7 47 K5
Deadman's Cross MK45 32 E4
Deadwaters ML11 75 F6
Deal CT14 15 J2
Deal Hall CM0 25 G2
Dean Cumb. CA14 60 B4
Dean Devon TQ11 5 H4
Dean Dorset SP5 9 J3
Dean Hants. SO32 11 G3
Dean Oxon. OX7 30 E6
Dean Som. BA4 19 K7
Dean Bank DL17 62 D3
Dean Cross EX34 6 D1
Dean Head S35 50 E2
Dean Prior TQ11 5 H4
Dean Row SK9 49 H4
Dean Street ME15 14 C2
Deanburnhaugh TD9 69 J2
Deane Gt.Man. BL3 49 F2
Deane Hants. RG25 21 J6
Deanland SP5 9 J3
Deanlane End PO9 11 J3
Deans Bottom ME9 24 E5
Deanscales CA13 60 B4
Deansgreen WA13 49 F4
Deanshanger MK19 31 J5
Deanston FK16 81 J7
Dearham CA15 60 B3
Debach IP13 35 G3
Debate DG11 69 H5
Debden CB11 33 J5
Debden Cross CB11 33 J5
Debden Green Essex CB11 33 J5
Debden Green Essex IG10 23 H2
Debenham IP14 35 F2
Deblin's Green WR2 29 H4
Dechmont EH52 75 J3
Decker Hill TF11 39 G4
Deddington OX15 31 F5
Dedham CO7 34 E5
Dedham Heath CO7 34 E5
Dedworth SL4 22 C4
Deecastle AB34 90 C5
Deene NN17 42 C6
Deenethorpe NN17 42 C6
Deepcar S36 50 E3
Deepcut GU16 22 C6
Deepdale Cumb. LA10 56 C1
Deepdale N.Yorks. BD23 56 D2
Deeping Gate PE6 42 E5
Deeping St. James PE6 42 E5
Deeping St. Nicholas PE11 43 F4
Deepweir NP26 19 H3
Deerhill AB55 98 C5
Deerhurst GL19 29 H6
Deerhurst Walton GL19 29 H6
Deerton Street ME9 25 F5
Defford WR8 29 J4
Defynnog LD3 27 J6
Deganwy LL31 47 F5
Degnish PA34 79 J6
Deighton N.Yorks. DL6 62 E6
Deighton W.Yorks. HD2 50 D1
Deighton York YO19 58 C5
Deiniolen LL55 46 D6
Delabole PL33 4 A2
Delamere CW8 48 E6
Delavorar AB37 89 J3
Delfrigs AB23 91 H2
Dell Lodge PH25 89 H3
Dell Quay PO20 12 B6
Delliefure PH26 89 H1
Delly End OX29 30 E7
Delnabo AB37 89 J3
Delny IV18 96 E4
Delph OL3 49 J2
Delphorrie AB33 90 C3
Delves DH8 62 C2
Delvine PH1 82 C3
Dembleby NG34 42 D2
Denaby DN12 51 G3
Denaby Main DN12 51 G3
Denbigh (Dinbych) LL16 47 J6
Denbury TQ12 5 J4
Denby DE5 41 F1
Denby Dale HD8 50 E2
Denchworth OX12 21 G2
Dendron LA12 55 F2
Denend AB54 90 E1
Denford NN14 32 C1
Dengie CM0 25 F1
Denham Bucks. UB9 22 D3
Denham Suff. IP21 35 F1
Denham Suff. IP29 34 B2
Denham Green UB9 22 D3
Denham Street IP23 35 F1
Denhead Aber. AB51 91 F3
Denhead Aber. AB42 99 J5
Denhead Fife KY16 83 F6
Denhead of Arbirlot DD11 83 G3
Denhead of Gray DD2 82 E4
Denholm TD9 70 A2
Denholme BD13 57 F6
Denholme Clough BD13 57 F6
Denio LL53 36 C2
Denmead PO7 11 H3
Denmill AB51 91 G3
Denmoss AB54 98 E6
Dennington IP13 35 G2
Denny FK6 75 G2
Dennyloanhead FK4 75 G2
Denshaw OL3 49 J1
Denside AB31 91 G5
Densole CT18 15 H3
Denston CB8 34 B3
Denstone ST14 40 C1
Dent LA10 56 C1
Denton Cambs. PE7 42 E7
Denton Darl. DL2 62 D5
Denton E.Suss. BN9 13 H6
Denton Gt.Man. M34 49 J3
Denton Kent CT4 15 H3
Denton Kent DA12 24 C4
Denton Lincs. NG32 42 B2
Denton N.Yorks. LS29 57 G5
Denton Norf. IP20 45 G7
Denton Northants. NN7 32 B3
Denton Oxon. OX44 21 J1
Denton's Green WA10 48 D3
Denver PE38 44 A5
Denvilles PO9 11 J4
Denwick NE66 71 H2
Deopham NR18 44 E5
Deopham Green NR18 44 E6
Depden IP29 34 B3
Depden Green IP29 34 B3
Deptford Gt.Lon. SE8 23 G4
Deptford Wilts. BA12 10 B1
DERBY DE 41 F2
Derbyhaven IM9 54 B7
Dereham (East Dereham) NR19 44 D4
Dererach PA70 79 G5
Deri CF81 18 E1
Derril EX22 6 B5
Derringstone CT4 15 H3
Derrington ST18 40 A3
Derriton EX22 6 B5
Derry FK19 81 H5
Derry Hill SN11 20 C4
Derrythorpe DN17 52 B2
Dersingham PE31 44 A2
Dervaig PA75 79 F2
Derwen LL21 47 J7
Derwenlas SY20 37 G6
Derwydd SA18 17 K4
Derybruich PA21 73 H3
Desborough NN14 42 B7
Desford LE9 41 G5
Detchant NE70 77 J7
Dethick DE4 51 F7
Detling ME14 14 C2
Deuddwr SY22 38 B4
Deunant LL16 47 H6
Deuxhill WV16 39 F7
Devauden NP16 19 H2
Devil's Bridge (Pontarfynach) SY23 27 G1
Devitts Green CV7 40 E6
Devizes SN10 20 D5
Devonport PL1 4 E5
Devonside FK13 75 H1
Devoran TR3 2 E5
Dewar EH38 76 B6
Dewlish DT2 9 G5
Dewsall Court HR2 28 D5
Dewsbury WF12 57 H7
Dewsbury Moor WF15 57 H7
Dhiseig PA68 79 F4
Dhoon IM7 54 D5
Dhoor IM7 54 D4
Dhowin IM7 54 D3
Dhuhallow IV2 88 C2
Dial Green GU28 12 C4
Dial Post RH13 12 E5
Dibden SO45 11 F4
Dibden Hill HP8 22 C2
Dibden Purlieu SO45 11 F4
Dickleburgh IP21 45 F7
Dickleburgh Moor IP21 45 F7
Didbrook GL54 30 B5
Didcot OX11 21 J2
Diddington PE19 32 E2
Diddlebury SY7 38 E7
Didley HR2 28 D5
Didling GU29 12 B5
Didmarton GL9 20 B3
Didsbury M20 49 H3
Didworthy TQ10 5 G4
Digby LN4 52 D7
Digg IV51 93 K5
Diggle OL3 50 C2
Digmoor WN8 48 D2
Digswell AL6 33 F7
Dihewyd SA48 26 D3
Dildawn DG7 65 H5
Dilham NR28 45 H3
Dilhorne ST10 40 B1
Dillington PE19 32 E2
Dilston NE45 70 E7
Dilton Marsh BA13 20 B7
Dilwyn HR4 28 D3
Dilwyn Common HR4 28 D3
Dimple BL7 49 G1
Dinas Carmar. SA33 17 F2
Dinas Gwyn. LL54 46 C7
Dinas Gwyn. LL53 36 B2
Dinas Cross SA42 16 D2
Dinas Dinlle LL54 46 C7
Dinas Powys CF64 18 E4
Dinas-Mawddwy SY20 37 H4
Dinbych (Denbigh) LL16 47 J6
Dinbych-y-pysgod (Tenby) SA70 16 E5
Dinckley BB6 56 B6
Dinder BA5 19 J7
Dinedor HR2 28 E5
Dingestow NP25 28 D7
Dingley LE16 42 A7
Dingwall IV15 96 C6
Dinlabyre TD9 70 A4
Dinnet AB34 90 C5
Dinnington S.Yorks. S25 51 H4
Dinnington Som. TA17 8 D3
Dinnington T. & W. NE13 71 H6
Dinorwig LL55 46 D6
Dinton Bucks. HP17 31 J7
Dinton Wilts. SP3 10 B1
Dinvin DG9 64 A5
Dinwoodie Mains DG11 69 G4
Dinworthy EX22 6 B4
Dipford TA3 8 B2
Dippen Arg. & B. PA28 73 F7
Dippen N.Ayr. KA27 66 E1
Dippenhall GU10 22 B7
Dipple Moray IV32 98 B5
Dipple S.Ayr. KA26 67 G3
Diptford TQ9 5 H5
Dipton DH9 62 C1
Dirdhu PH26 89 H2
Dirleton EH39 76 D2
Discoed LD8 28 B2
Diseworth DE74 41 G3
Dishes KW17 106 F5
Dishforth YO7 57 J2
Dishley LE11 41 H3
Disley SK12 49 J4
Diss IP22 45 F7
Disserth LD1 27 K3
Distington CA14 60 B4
Ditcheat BA4 9 F1
Ditchingham NR35 45 H6
Ditchley OX29 30 E6
Ditchling BN6 13 G5
Ditteridge SN13 20 B5
Dittisham TQ6 5 J5
Ditton Halton WA8 48 D4
Ditton Kent ME20 14 C2
Ditton Green CB8 33 K3
Ditton Priors WV16 39 F7
Dixton Glos. GL20 29 J5
Dixton Mon. NP25 28 E7
Dobcross OL3 49 J2
Dobwalls PL14 4 C4
Doc Penfro (Pembroke Dock) SA72 16 C5
Doccombe TQ13 7 F7
Dochgarroch IV3 88 D1
Dockenfield GU10 22 B7
Docker Cumb. LA8 61 G7
Docker Lancs. LA6 55 J2
Docking PE31 44 B2
Docklow HR6 28 E3
Dockray Cumb. CA11 60 E4
Dockray Cumb. CA7 60 D1
Dodbrooke TQ7 5 H6
Doddenham WR6 29 G3
Doddinghurst CM15 23 J2
Doddington Cambs. PE15 43 H6
Doddington Kent ME9 14 E2
Doddington Lincs. LN6 52 C5
Doddington Northumb. NE71 77 H7
Doddington Shrop. DY14 29 F1
Doddiscombsleigh EX6 7 G7
Doddycross PL14 4 D4
Dodford Northants. NN7 31 H2
Dodford Worcs. B61 29 J1
Dodington S.Glos. BS37 20 A3
Dodington Som. TA5 7 K1
Dodington Ash BS37 20 A4
Dodleston CH4 48 C6
Dods Leigh ST10 40 C2
Dodscott EX38 6 D4
Dodworth S75 51 F2
Doehole DE55 51 F7
Doffcocker BL1 49 F1
Dog Village EX5 7 H6
Dogdyke LN4 53 F7
Dogmersfield RG27 22 A6
Dogsthorpe PE1 43 F5
Dol Fawr SY19 37 H5
Dolanog SY21 37 K4
Dolau Powys LD1 28 A2
Dolau R.C.T. CF72 18 D3
Dolbenmaen LL51 36 E1
Doley ST20 39 G3
Dolfach SY18 27 J1
Dolfor SY16 38 A7
Dolgarreg SA20 27 G5
Dolgarrog LL32 47 F6
Dolgellau LL40 37 G4
Dolgoch LL36 37 F5
Dolgran SA39 17 H2
Doll KW9 97 F1
Dollar FK14 75 H1
Dollarbeg FK14 75 H1
Dolphin CH8 47 K5
Dolphinholme LA2 55 J4
Dolphinton EH46 75 K6
Dolton EX19 6 D4
Dolwen Conwy LL22 47 G5
Dolwen Powys SY21 37 J5
Dolwyddelan LL25 47 F7
Dôl-y-bont SY24 37 F7
Dol-y-cannau HR5 28 A4
Dolyhir LD8 28 B3
Dolywern LL20 38 B2
Domgay SY22 38 B4
DONCASTER DN 51 H2
Donhead St. Andrew SP7 9 J2
Donhead St. Mary SP7 9 J2
Donibristle KY4 75 K2
Doniford TA23 7 J1
Donington Lincs. PE11 43 F2
Donington Shrop. WV7 40 A5
Donington le Heath LE67 41 G4
Donington on Bain LN11 53 F4
Donisthorpe DE12 41 F4
Donna Nook LN11 53 H3
Donnington Glos. GL56 30 C6
Donnington Here. HR8 29 G5
Donnington Shrop. SY5 38 E5
Donnington Tel. & W. TF2 39 G4
Donnington W.Berks. RG14 21 H5
Donnington W.Suss. PO20 12 B6
Donyatt TA19 8 C3
DORCHESTER Dorset DT 9 F5
Dorchester Oxon. OX10 21 J2
Dordon B78 40 E5
Dore S17 51 F4
Dores IV2 88 C1
Dorket Head NG5 41 H1
Dorking RH4 22 E7
Dorley's Corner IP17 35 H2
Dormans Park RH19 23 G7
Dormansland RH7 23 H7
Dormanstown TS10 63 G4
Dormer's Wells UB1 22 E3
Dormington HR1 28 E4
Dormston WR7 29 J3
Dorn GL56 30 D5
Dorney SL4 22 C4
Dorney Reach SL6 22 C4
Dornie IV40 86 E2
Dornoch IV25 96 E3
Dornock DG12 69 H7
Dorrery KW12 105 F3
Dorridge B93 30 C1
Dorrington Lincs. LN4 52 D7
Dorrington Shrop. SY5 38 D5
Dorsell AB33 90 D3
Dorsington CV37 30 C4
Dorstone HR3 28 C4
Dorton HP18 31 H7
Dorusduain IV40 87 F2
Dosthill B77 40 E6
Dotland NE46 62 A1
Dottery DT6 8 D5
Doublebois PL14 4 B4
Dougalston G62 74 D3
Dougarie KA27 73 G7
Doughton GL8 20 B2
Douglas I.o.M. IM1 54 C6
Douglas S.Lan. ML11 75 G7
Douglas & Angus DD5 83 F4
Douglas Water ML11 75 G7
Douglastown DD8 83 F3
Doulting BA4 19 K7
Dounby KW17 106 B5
Doune Arg. & B. G83 74 B1
Doune Arg. & B. FK17 80 E6
Doune High. PH22 89 F3
Doune High. IV24 96 B1
Doune Stir. FK16 81 J7
Dounepark AB45 99 F4
Douneside AB34 90 C4
Dounie High. IV19 96 D3
Dounie High. IV24 96 C2
Dounreay KW14 104 E2
Dousland PL20 5 F4
Dovaston SY10 38 C3
Dove Holes SK17 50 C5
Dovenby CA13 60 B3
Dovendale LN11 53 G4
Dover CT16 15 J3
Dovercourt CO12 35 G5
Doverdale WR9 29 H2
Doveridge DE6 40 D2
Doversgreen RH2 23 F7
Dowally PH9 82 B3
Dowdeswell GL54 30 B6
Dowhill KA26 67 G3
Dowlais CF48 18 D1
Dowland EX19 6 D4
Dowlands DT7 8 B5
Dowlish Ford TA19 8 C3
Dowlish Wake TA19 8 C3
Down Ampney GL7 20 E2
Down End TA6 19 G7
Down Hatherley GL2 29 H6
Down St. Mary EX17 7 F5
Down Thomas PL9 5 F6
Downderry PL11 4 D5
Downe BR6 23 H5
Downend I.o.W. PO30 11 G6
Downend S.Glos. BS16 19 K4
Downend W.Berks. RG20 21 H4
Downfield DD3 82 E4
Downfields CB7 33 K1
Downgate PL17 4 D3
Downham Essex CM11 24 D2
Downham Lancs. BB7 56 C5
Downham Northumb. TD12 77 G7
Downham Market PE38 44 A5
Downhead Cornw. PL15 4 C2
Downhead Som. BA4 19 K7
Downhead Som. BA22 8 E2
Downholland Cross L39 48 C2
Downholme DL11 62 C7
Downies AB12 91 H5
Downley HP13 22 B2
Downs CF5 18 E4
Downside N.Som. BS48 19 H5
Downside Som. BA4 19 K7
Downside Som. BA3 19 K6
Downside Surr. KT11 22 E6
Downton Devon EX20 6 D7
Downton Devon TQ6 5 J5
Downton Hants. SO41 10 D5
Downton Wilts. SP5 10 C2
Downton on the Rock SY8 28 D1
Dowsby PE10 42 E3
Dowthwaitehead CA11 60 E4
Doxey ST16 40 B3
Doynton BS30 20 A4
Drabblegate NR11 45 G3
Draethen NP10 19 F3
Draffan ML11 75 F6
Dragley Beck LA12 55 F2
Drakeland Corner PL7 5 F5
Drakelow DY11 40 A7
Drakemyre KA24 74 A5
Drakes Broughton WR10 29 J4
Drakes Cross B47 30 B1
Draughton N.Yorks. BD23 57 F4
Draughton Northants. NN6 31 J1
Drax YO8 58 C7
Draycot Foliat SN4 20 E4
Draycote CV23 31 F2
Draycott Derbys. DE72 41 G2
Draycott Glos. GL56 30 C5
Draycott Shrop. WV5 40 A6
Draycott Som. BS27 19 H6
Draycott Worcs. WR5 29 H4
Draycott in the Clay DE6 40 D3
Draycott in the Moors ST10 40 B2
Drayford EX17 7 F4
Draynes PL14 4 C4
Drayton Leics. LE16 42 B6
Drayton Lincs. PE20 43 F2
Drayton Norf. NR8 45 F4
Drayton Oxon. OX15 31 F4
Drayton Oxon. OX14 21 H2
Drayton Ports. PO6 11 H4
Drayton Som. TA10 8 D2
Drayton Warks. CV37 30 C3
Drayton Worcs. DY9 29 J1
Drayton Bassett B78 40 D5

Drayton Beauchamp **HP22** 32 C7
Drayton Parslow **MK17** 32 B6
Drayton St. Leonard **OX10** 21 J2
Drebley **BD23** 57 F4
Dreemskerry **IM7** 54 D4
Dreenhill **SA62** 16 C4
Drefach *Carmar.* **SA44** 17 G2
Drefach *Carmar.* **SA14** 17 J4
Dre-fach *Cere.* **SA40** 17 J1
Drefelin **SA44** 17 G2
Dreghorn **KA11** 74 B7
Drem **EH39** 76 D3
Dreumasdal (Drimsdale) **HS8** 84 C1
Drewsteignton **EX6** 7 F6
Driby **LN13** 53 G5
Driffield *E.Riding* YO25 59 G4
Driffield *Glos.* **GL7** 20 D2
Drigg **CA19** 60 B7
Drighlington **BD11** 57 H7
Drimfern **PA32** 80 B6
Drimlee **PA32** 80 C6
Drimnin **PA34** 79 G2
Drimore **HS8** 92 C7
Drimpton **DT8** 8 D4
Drimsdale (Dreumasdal) **HS8** 84 C1
Drimsynie **PA24** 80 C7
Drimvore **PA31** 73 G1
Drinan **IV49** 86 B3
Dringhouses **YO24** 58 B4
Drinisiader **HS3** 93 G2
Drinkstone **IP30** 34 D2
Drinkstone Green **IP30** 34 D2
Drishaig **PA32** 80 C6
Drissaig **PA35** 80 A6
Drointon **ST18** 40 C3
Droitwich Spa WR9 29 H2
Dron **PH2** 82 C6
Dronfield S18 51 F5
Dronfield Woodhouse **S18** 51 F5
Drongan **KA6** 67 J2
Dronley **DD3** 82 E4
Droop **DT10** 9 G4
Dropmore **SL1** 22 C3
Droxford **SO32** 11 H3
Droylsden **M43** 49 J3
Druid **LL21** 37 K1
Druidston **SA62** 16 B4
Druimarbin **PH33** 87 G7
Druimavuic **PA38** 80 B3
Druimdrishaig **PA31** 73 F3
Druimindarroch **PH39** 86 C6
Druimkinnerras **IV4** 88 B1
Drum *Arg. & B.* **PA21** 73 H3
Drum *P. & K.* **KY13** 82 B7
Drumachloy **PA20** 73 J4
Drumbeg **IV27** 102 D5
Drumblade **AB54** 98 D6
Drumblair **AB54** 98 E6
Drumbuie *D. & G.* **DG4** 68 C2
Drumbuie *High.* **IV40** 86 D1
Drumburgh **CA7** 60 D1
Drumchapel **G15** 74 D3
Drumchardine **IV5** 96 C7
Drumchork **IV22** 94 E3
Drumclog **ML10** 74 E7
Drumdelgie **AB54** 98 C6
Drumderfit **IV1** 96 D6
Drumeldrie **KY8** 83 F7
Drumelzier **ML12** 75 K7
Drumfearn **IV43** 86 C3
Drumfern **PH33** 87 F7
Drumgarve **PA28** 66 B1
Drumgley **DD8** 83 F2
Drumguish **PH21** 88 E5
Drumhead **AB31** 90 E5
Drumin **AB37** 89 J1
Drumine **IV2** 96 E6
Drumjohn **DG7** 67 K4
Drumlamford House **KA26** 64 C3
Drumlasie **AB31** 90 E4
Drumlemble **PA28** 66 A2
Drumlithie **AB39** 91 F6
Drummond *High.* **IV16** 96 D5
Drummond *Stir.* **FK17** 81 H7
Drummore **DG9** 64 B7
Drummuir Castle **AB55** 98 B6
Drumnadrochit **IV63** 88 C2
Drumnagorrach **AB54** 98 D5
Drumnatorran **PH36** 79 K1
Drumoak **AB31** 91 F5
Drumore **PA28** 66 B1
Drumour **PH8** 82 A4
Drumrash **DG7** 65 G3
Drumrunie **IV26** 95 H1
Drums **AB41** 91 H2
Drumsturdy **DD5** 83 F4
Drumuie **IV51** 93 K7
Drumuillie **PH24** 89 G2
Drumvaich **FK17** 81 H7
Drumwhindle **AB41** 91 H1
Drumwhirn **DG7** 68 C5
Drunkendub **DD11** 83 H3
Druridge **NE61** 71 H4
Drury **CH7** 48 B6
Drws-y-nant **LL40** 37 H3
Dry Doddington **NG23** 42 B1
Dry Drayton **CB23** 33 G2
Dry Harbour **IV40** 94 C6
Dry Sandford **OX13** 21 H1
Dry Street **SS16** 24 C3
Drybeck **CA16** 61 H5
Drybridge *Moray* **AB56** 98 C4
Drybridge *N.Ayr.* **KA11** 74 B7
Drybrook GL17 29 F7
Dryburgh **TD6** 76 D7
Drygrange **TD6** 76 D7
Dryhope **TD7** 69 H1
Drymen **G63** 74 C2
Drymuir **AB42** 99 H6
Drynoch **IV47** 85 K1
Dryslwyn **SA32** 17 J3
Dryton **SY5** 38 E5
Duachy **PA34** 79 K5
Dubford **AB45** 99 F4
Dubhchladach **PA29** 73 G4
Dubheads **PH7** 82 A5
Dublin **IP23** 35 F2
Dubton **DD8** 83 G2
Duchal **PA13** 74 B4
Duchally **IV27** 103 F7
Duchray **FK8** 81 F7
Duck Bay **G83** 74 B2
Duck End *Bed.* **MK45** 32 D4
Duck End *Cambs.* **PE19** 33 F2
Duck End *Essex* **CM6** 33 K6
Duck Street **HG3** 57 G3
Duckington **SY14** 48 D7
Ducklington **OX29** 21 G1
Duckmanton **S44** 51 G5
Duck's Cross **MK44** 32 E3
Ducks Island **EN5** 23 F2
Duddenhoe End **CB11** 33 H5
Duddingston **EH15** 76 A3
Duddington **PE9** 42 C5
Duddlestone **TA3** 8 B2
Duddleswell **TN22** 13 H4
Duddo **TD15** 77 H6
Duddon **CW6** 48 E6
Duddon Bridge **LA18** 54 E1
Dudleston **SY12** 38 C2
Dudleston Heath (Criftins) **SY12** 38 C2
Dudley *T. & W.* **NE23** 71 H6
DUDLEY *W.Mid.* DY 40 B6
Dudley Port **DY4** 40 B6
Dudlow's Green **WA4** 49 F4
Dudsbury **BH22** 10 B5
Duffield **DE56** 41 F1
Duffryn **SA13** 18 B2
Dufftown **AB55** 90 B1
Duffus **IV30** 97 J5
Dufton **CA16** 61 H4
Duggleby **YO17** 58 E3
Duiar **PH26** 89 J1
Duible **KW8** 104 E6
Duiletter **PA33** 80 C5
Duinish **PH17** 81 H1
Duirinish **IV40** 86 D1
Duisdealmor **IV43** 86 D3
Duisky **PH33** 87 G7
Duke End **B46** 40 E7
Dukestown **NP22** 28 A7
Dukinfield SK16 49 J3
Dulas LL70 46 C4
Dulax **AB36** 90 B3
Dulcote **BA5** 19 J7
Dulford **EX15** 7 J5
Dull **PH15** 81 K3
Dullatur **G68** 75 F3
Dullingham **CB8** 33 K3
Dullingham Ley **CB8** 33 K3
Dulnain Bridge **PH26** 89 G2
Duloe *Bed.* **PE19** 32 E2
Duloe *Cornw.* **PL14** 4 C5
Dulsie **IV12** 97 G7
Dulverton TA22 7 H3
Dulwich **SE21** 23 G4
Dumbarton G82 74 B3
Dumbleton **WR11** 30 B5
Dumcrieff **DG10** 69 G3
Dumeath **AB54** 90 C1
Dumfin **G84** 74 B2
DUMFRIES DG 65 K3
Dumgoyne **G63** 74 D2
Dummer **RG25** 21 J7
Dun **DD10** 83 H2
Dunach **PA34** 79 K5
Dunalastair **PH16** 81 J2
Dunan *Arg. & B.* **PA23** 73 K3
Dunan *High.* **IV49** 86 B2
Dunans **PA22** 73 J1
Dunball **TA6** 19 G7
Dunbar EH42 76 E3
Dunbeath KW6 105 G5
Dunbeg **PA37** 79 K4
Dunblane FK15 81 J7
Dunbog **KY14** 82 D6
Dunbridge **SO51** 10 E2
Duncanston *Aber.* **AB52** 90 D2
Duncanston *High.* **IV7** 96 C6
Dunchideock **EX2** 7 G7
Dunchurch **CV22** 31 F1
Duncote **NN12** 31 H3
Duncow **DG1** 68 E5
Duncraggan **FK17** 81 G7
Duncrievie **PH2** 82 C7
Duncroist **FK21** 81 G4
Duncrub **PH2** 82 B6
Duncryne **G83** 74 C2
Duncton **GU28** 12 C5
DUNDEE DD 83 F4
Dundee Airport **DD2** 82 E5
Dundon **TA11** 8 D1
Dundon Hayes **TA11** 8 D1
Dundonald **KA2** 74 B7
Dundonnell **IV23** 95 G3
Dundraw **CA7** 60 D2
Dundreggan **IV63** 87 K3
Dundrennan **DG6** 65 H6
Dundridge **SO32** 11 G3
Dundry **BS41** 19 J5
Dunearn **KY3** 76 A2
Dunecht **AB32** 91 F4
Dunfermline KY12 75 J2
Dunfield **GL7** 20 E2
Dunford Bridge **S36** 50 D2
Dungate **ME9** 14 E2
Dungavel **ML10** 74 E7
Dungworth **S6** 50 E3
Dunham **NG22** 52 B5
Dunham Town **WA14** 49 G4
Dunham Woodhouses **WA14** 49 G4
Dunham-on-the-Hill **WA6** 48 D5
Dunhampton **DY13** 29 H2
Dunholme **LN2** 52 D5
Dunino **KY16** 83 G6
Dunipace **FK6** 75 G2
Dunira **PH6** 81 J5
Dunkeld PH8 82 B3
Dunkerton **BA2** 20 A6
Dunkeswell **EX14** 7 K5
Dunkeswick **LS17** 57 J5
Dunkirk *Ches.W. & C.* **CH1** 48 C5
Dunkirk *Kent* **ME13** 15 F2
Dunk's Green **TN11** 23 K6
Dunlappie **DD9** 83 G1
Dunley *Hants.* **RG28** 21 H6
Dunley *Worcs.* **DY13** 29 G2
Dunlop **KA3** 74 C6
Dunloskin **PA23** 73 K3
Dunmere **PL31** 4 A4
Dunmore *Arg. & B.* **PA29** 73 F4
Dunmore *Falk.* **FK2** 75 G2
Dunn **KW1** 105 G3
Dunn Street **ME7** 24 D5
Dunnabie **DG11** 69 H5
Dunnet **KW14** 105 H1
Dunnichen **DD8** 83 G3
Dunning **PH2** 82 B6
Dunnington *E.Riding* **YO25** 59 H4
Dunnington *Warks.* **B49** 30 B3
Dunnington *York* **YO19** 58 C4
Dunnockshaw **BB11** 56 D7
Dunoon PA23 73 K3
Dunragit **DG9** 64 B5
Dunrostan **PA31** 73 F2
Duns TD11 77 F5
Duns Tew **OX25** 31 F6
Dunsa **DE45** 50 E5
Dunsby **PE10** 42 E3
Dunscore **DG2** 68 D5
Dunscroft **DN7** 51 J2
Dunsdale **TS14** 63 H5
Dunsden Green **RG4** 22 A4
Dunsfold **GU8** 12 D3
Dunsford **EX6** 7 G7
Dunshalt **KY14** 82 D6
Dunshill **GL19** 29 H5
Dunsinnan **PH2** 82 C4
Dunsland Cross **EX22** 6 C5
Dunsley *N.Yorks.* **YO21** 63 K5
Dunsley *Staffs.* **DY7** 40 A7
Dunsmore **HP22** 22 B1
Dunsop Bridge **BB7** 56 B4
Dunstable LU6 32 D6
Dunstall **DE13** 40 D3
Dunstall Green **CB8** 34 B2
Dunstan **NE66** 71 H2
Dunstan Steads **NE66** 71 H1
Dunster **TA24** 7 H1
Dunston *Lincs.* **LN4** 52 D6
Dunston *Norf.* **NR14** 45 G5
Dunston *Staffs.* **ST18** 40 B4
Dunston Heath **ST18** 40 B4
Dunston Hill **NE11** 71 H7
Dunstone *Devon* **TQ13** 5 H3
Dunstone *Devon* **PL8** 5 F5
Dunsville **DN7** 51 J2
Dunswell **HU6** 59 G6
Dunsyre **ML11** 75 J6
Dunterton **PL19** 4 D3
Duntisbourne Abbots **GL7** 20 C1
Duntisbourne Leer **GL7** 20 C1
Duntisbourne Rouse **GL7** 20 C1
Duntish **DT2** 9 F4
Duntocher **G81** 74 C3
Dunton *Bucks.* **MK18** 32 B6
Dunton *Cen.Beds.* **SG18** 33 F4
Dunton *Norf.* **NR21** 44 C2
Dunton Bassett **LE17** 41 H6
Dunton Green **TN13** 23 J6
Dunton Wayletts **CM13** 24 C2
Duntulm **IV51** 93 K4
Dunure **KA7** 67 G2
Dunure Mains **KA7** 67 G2
Dunvant **SA2** 17 J6
Dunvegan **IV55** 93 H7
Dunwich **IP17** 35 J1
Dura **KY15** 83 F6
Durdar **CA2** 60 F1
Durgan **TR11** 2 E6
Durgates **TN5** 13 K3
DURHAM DH 62 D2
Durham Tees Valley Airport **DL2** 62 E5
Durinemast **PA34** 79 H2
Durisdeer **DG3** 68 D3
Durleigh **TA5** 8 B1
Durley *Hants.* **SO32** 11 G3
Durley *Wilts.* **SN8** 21 F5
Durley Street **SO32** 11 G3
Durlow Common **HR8** 29 F5
Durnamuck **IV23** 95 G2
Durness **IV27** 103 G2
Durno **AB51** 91 F2
Duror **PA38** 80 A2
Durran *Arg. & B.* **PA33** 80 A7
Durran *High.* **KW14** 105 G2
Durrants **PO9** 11 J4
Durrington *W.Suss.* **BN13** 12 E6
Durrington *Wilts.* **SP4** 20 E7
Dursley GL11 20 A2
Dursley Cross **GL17** 29 F7
Durston **TA3** 8 B2
Durweston **DT11** 9 H4
Dury **ZE2** 107 N6
Duston **NN5** 31 J2
Duthil **PH23** 89 G2
Dutlas **LD7** 28 B1
Duton Hill **CM6** 33 K6
Dutson **PL15** 6 B7
Dutton **WA4** 48 E5
Duxford **CB22** 33 H4
Dwygyfylchi **LL34** 47 F5
Dwyran **LL61** 46 C6
Dyce **AB21** 91 G3
Dyfatty **SA16** 17 H5
Dyffryn *Bridgend* **CF34** 18 B2
Dyffryn *Pembs.* **SA64** 16 C2
Dyffryn *V. of Glam.* **CF5** 18 D4
Dyffryn Ardudwy LL44 36 E3
Dyffryn Castell **SY23** 37 G7
Dyffryn Ceidrych **SA19** 27 G6
Dyffryn Cellwen **SA10** 27 H7
Dyke *Devon* **EX39** 6 B3
Dyke *Lincs.* **PE10** 42 E3
Dyke *Moray* **IV36** 97 G6
Dykehead *Angus* **DD8** 82 E1
Dykehead *N.Lan.* **ML7** 75 G5
Dykehead *Stir.* **FK8** 74 D1
Dykelands **AB30** 83 J1
Dykends **PH11** 82 D2
Dykeside **AB53** 99 F6
Dylife **SY19** 37 H6
Dymchurch **TN29** 15 G5
Dymock GL18 29 G5
Dyrham **SN14** 20 A4
Dysart **KY1** 76 B1
Dyserth **LL18** 47 J5

E

Eachwick **NE18** 71 G6
Eadar dha Fhadhail **HS2** 100 C4
Eagland Hill **PR3** 55 H5
Eagle **LN6** 52 B6
Eagle Barnsdale **LN6** 52 B6
Eagle Moor **LN6** 52 B6
Eaglescliffe **TS16** 63 F5
Eaglesfield *Cumb.* **CA13** 60 B4
Eaglesfield *D. & G.* **DG11** 69 H6
Eaglesham **G76** 74 D5
Eaglethorpe **PE8** 42 D6
Eagley **BL1** 49 G1
Eairy **IM4** 54 B6
Eakley **MK16** 32 B3
Eakring **NG22** 51 J6
Ealand **DN17** 51 K1
Ealing **W5** 22 E3
Eamont Bridge **CA10** 61 G4
Earby **BB18** 56 E5
Earcroft **BB2** 56 B7
Eardington **WV16** 39 G6
Eardisland **HR6** 28 D3
Eardisley **HR3** 28 C4
Eardiston *Shrop.* **SY11** 38 C3
Eardiston *Worcs.* **WR15** 29 F2
Earith **PE28** 33 G1
Earl Shilton **LE9** 41 G6
Earl Soham **IP13** 35 G2
Earl Sterndale **SK17** 50 C6
Earl Stonham **IP14** 35 F3
Earle **NE71** 70 E1
Earlestown **WA12** 48 E3
Earley **RG6** 22 A4
Earlham **NR4** 45 F5
Earlish **IV51** 93 J5
Earls Barton **NN6** 32 B2
Earls Colne **CO6** 34 C6
Earl's Common **WR9** 29 J3
Earl's Court **SW5** 23 F4
Earl's Croome **WR8** 29 H4
Earl's Green **IP14** 34 E2
Earlsdon **CV5** 30 E1
Earlsferry **KY9** 83 F7
Earlsford **AB51** 91 G1
Earlsheaton **WF12** 57 H7
Earlston TD4 76 D7
Earlswood *Mon.* **NP16** 19 H2
Earlswood *Surr.* **RH1** 23 F7
Earlswood *Warks.* **B94** 30 C1
Earnley **PO20** 12 B7
Earnshaw Bridge **PR26** 55 J7
Earsairidh **HS9** 84 C5
Earsdon **NE25** 71 J6
Earsdon Moor **NE61** 71 G4
Earsham **NR35** 45 H7
Earsham Street **IP21** 35 G1
Earswick **YO32** 58 C4
Eartham **PO18** 12 C6
Earthcott Green **BS35** 19 K3
Easby **TS9** 63 G6
Easdale **PA34** 79 J6
Easebourne **GU29** 12 B4
Easenhall **CV23** 31 F1
Eashing **GU7** 22 C7
Easington *Bucks.* **HP18** 31 H7
Easington *Dur.* **SR8** 63 F2
Easington *E.Riding* **HU12** 53 G1
Easington *Northumb.* **NE70** 77 K7
Easington *Oxon.* **OX49** 21 K2
Easington *R. & C.* **TS13** 63 J5
Easington Colliery **SR8** 63 F2
Easington Lane **DH5** 62 E2
Easingwold **YO61** 58 B3
Easole Street **CT15** 15 H2
Eassie **DD8** 82 E3
East Aberthaw **CF62** 18 D5
East Acton **W3** 23 F3
East Allington **TQ9** 5 H6
East Anstey **EX16** 7 G3
East Anton **SP11** 21 G7
East Appleton **DL10** 62 D7
East Ardsley **WF3** 57 J7
East Ashey **PO33** 11 G6
East Ashling **PO18** 12 B6
East Auchronie **AB32** 91 G4
East Ayton **YO12** 59 F1
East Barkwith **LN8** 52 E4
East Barming **ME16** 14 C2
East Barnby **YO21** 63 K5
East Barnet **EN4** 23 F2
East Barsham **NR22** 44 D2
East Beckham **NR11** 45 F2
East Bedfont **TW14** 22 D4
East Bergholt **CO7** 34 E5
East Bierley **BD4** 57 G7
East Bilney **NR20** 44 D4
East Blatchington **BN25** 13 H7
East Boldon NE36 71 J7
East Boldre **SO42** 10 E4
East Bolton **NE66** 71 G2
East Bower **TA6** 8 C1
East Brent **TA9** 19 G6
East Bridge **IP16** 35 J2
East Bridgford **NG13** 41 J1
East Brora **KW9** 97 G1
East Buckland **EX32** 6 E2
East Budleigh **EX9** 7 J7
East Burnham **SL2** 22 C3
East Burra **ZE2** 107 M9
East Burrafirth **ZE2** 107 M7
East Burton **BH20** 9 H6
East Butsfield **DL13** 62 C2
East Butterleigh **EX15** 7 H5
East Butterwick **DN17** 52 B2
East Cairnbeg **AB30** 91 F7
East Calder **EH53** 75 J4
East Carleton **NR14** 45 F5
East Carlton *Northants.* **LE16** 42 B7
East Carlton *W.Yorks.* **LS19** 57 H5
East Chaldon (Chaldon Herring) **DT2** 9 G6
East Challow **OX12** 21 G3
East Charleton **TQ7** 5 H6
East Chelborough **DT2** 8 E4
East Chiltington **BN7** 13 G5
East Chinnock **BA22** 8 D3
East Chisenbury **SN9** 20 E6
East Clandon **GU4** 22 D6
East Claydon **MK18** 31 J6
East Clyne **KW9** 97 G1
East Clyth **KW3** 105 H5
East Coker **BA22** 8 E3
East Compton *Dorset* **SP7** 9 H3
East Compton *Som.* **BA4** 19 K7
East Coombe **EX17** 7 G5
East Cornworthy **TQ9** 5 J5
East Cottingwith **YO42** 58 D5
East Cowes PO32 11 G5
East Cowick **DN14** 58 C7
East Cowton **DL7** 62 E6
East Cramlington **NE23** 71 H6
East Cranmore **BA4** 19 K7
East Creech **BH20** 9 J6
East Croachy **IV2** 88 D2
East Darlochan **PA28** 66 A1
East Davoch **AB34** 90 C4
East Dean *E.Suss.* **BN20** 13 J7
East Dean *Hants.* **SP5** 10 D2
East Dean *W.Suss.* **PO18** 12 C5
East Dereham (Dereham) NR19 44 D4
East Down **EX31** 6 D1
East Drayton **DN22** 51 K5
East Dundry **BS41** 19 J5
East Ella **HU5** 59 G7
East End *E.Riding* **HU12** 59 H6
East End *E.Riding* **HU12** 59 J7
East End *Essex* **CM0** 25 G1
East End *Hants.* **RG20** 21 H5
East End *Hants.* **SO41** 10 E5
East End *Herts.* **SG9** 33 H6
East End *Kent* **TN17** 14 D4
East End *Kent* **ME12** 25 F4
East End *M.K.* **MK16** 32 C4
East End *N.Som.* **BS48** 19 H4
East End *Oxon.* **OX29** 30 E7
East End *Poole* **BH21** 9 J5
East End *Som.* **BA3** 19 J6
East End *Suff.* **CO7** 35 F5
East End *Suff.* **IP14** 35 F3
East Farleigh **ME15** 14 C2
East Farndon **LE16** 42 A7
East Ferry **DN21** 52 B3
East Firsby **LN8** 52 D4
East Fleetham **NE68** 71 H1
East Fortune **EH39** 76 D3
East Garston **RG17** 21 G4
East Ginge **OX12** 21 H3
East Goscote **LE7** 41 J4
East Grafton **SN8** 21 F5
East Green *Suff.* **IP17** 35 J2
East Green *Suff.* **CB8** 33 K3
East Grimstead **SP5** 10 D2
East Grinstead RH19 13 G3
East Guldeford **TN31** 14 E5
East Haddon **NN6** 31 H2
East Hagbourne **OX11** 21 J3
East Halton **DN40** 52 E1
East Ham **E6** 23 H3
East Hanney **OX12** 21 H2
East Hanningfield **CM3** 24 D1
East Hardwick **WF8** 51 G1
East Harling **NR16** 44 D7
East Harlsey **DL6** 63 F7
East Harnham **SP2** 10 C2
East Harptree **BS40** 19 J6
East Hartford **NE23** 71 H6
East Harting **GU31** 11 J3
East Hatch **SP3** 9 J2
East Hatley **SG19** 33 F3
East Hauxwell **DL8** 62 C7
East Haven **DD7** 83 G4

Elton *Notts.* **NG13** 42 A2
Elton *Stock.* **TS21** 63 F5
Elton Green **CH2** 48 D5
Elvanfoot **ML12** 68 E2
Elvaston **DE72** 41 G2
Elveden **IP24** 34 C1
Elvingston **EH33** 76 C3
Elvington *Kent* **CT15** 15 H2
Elvington *York* **YO41** 58 D5
Elwick *Hart.* **TS27** 63 F3
Elwick *Northumb.* **NE70** 77 K7
Elworth **CW11** 49 G6
Elworthy **TA4** 7 J2
Ely *Cambs.* CB7 33 **J1**
Ely *Cardiff* **CF5** 18 E4
Emberton **MK46** 32 B4
Embleton *Cumb.* **CA13** 60 C3
Embleton *Hart.* **TS22** 63 F4
Embleton *Northumb.* **NE66** 71 H1
Embo **IV25** 97 F2
Embo Street **IV25** 97 F2
Emborough **BA3** 19 K6
Embsay **BD23** 57 F4
Emerson Park **RM11** 23 J3
Emery Down **SO43** 10 D4
Emley **HD8** 50 E1
Emmington **OX39** 22 A1
Emneth **PE14** 43 H5
Emneth Hungate **PE14** 43 J5
Empingham **LE15** 42 C5
Empshott **GU33** 11 J1
Empshott Green **GU33** 11 J1
Emsworth PO10 11 **J4**
Enborne **RG20** 21 H5
Enborne Row **RG20** 21 H5
Enchmarsh **SY6** 38 E6
Enderby **LE19** 41 H6
Endmoor **LA8** 55 J1
Endon **ST9** 49 J7
Endon Bank **ST9** 49 J7
ENFIELD EN 23 **G2**
Enfield Wash **EN3** 23 G2
Enford **SN9** 20 E6
Engine Common **BS37** 19 K3
Englefield **RG7** 21 K4
Englefield Green **TW20** 22 C4
Englesea-brook **CW2** 49 G7
English Bicknor **GL16** 28 E7
English Frankton **SY12** 38 D3
Englishcombe **BA2** 20 A5
Enham Alamein **SP11** 21 G7
Enmore **TA5** 8 B1
Ennerdale Bridge **CA23** 60 B5
Enniscaven **PL26** 3 G3
Ennochdhu **PH10** 82 B1
Ensay **PA75** 78 E3
Ensdon **SY4** 38 D4
Ensis **EX31** 6 D3
Enson **ST18** 40 B3
Enstone **OX7** 30 E6
Enterkinfoot **DG3** 68 D3
Enterpen **TS15** 63 F6
Enton Green **GU8** 22 C7
Enville **DY7** 40 A7
Eolaigearraidh **HS9** 84 C4
Eorabus **PA67** 78 E5
Eorodal **HS2** 101 H1
Eoropaidh **HS2** 101 H1
Epney **GL2** 29 G7
Epperstone **NG14** 41 J1
Epping CM16 23 **H1**
Epping Green *Essex* **CM16** 23 H1
Epping Green *Herts.* **SG13** 23 F1
Epping Upland **CM16** 23 H1
Eppleby **DL11** 62 C5
Eppleworth **HU16** 59 G6
Epsom KT17 23 **F5**
Epwell **OX15** 30 E4
Epworth **DN9** 51 K2
Epworth Turbary **DN9** 51 K2
Erbistock **LL13** 38 C1
Erbusaig **IV40** 86 D2
Erchless Castle **IV4** 96 B7
Erdington **B24** 40 D6
Eredine **PA33** 80 A7
Eriboll **IV27** 103 G3
Ericstane **DG10** 69 F2
Eridge Green **TN3** 13 J3
Eriff **DG7** 67 K3
Erines **PA29** 73 G3
Erisey Barton **TR12** 2 E7
Eriskay (Eiriosgaigh) **HS8** 84 C3
Eriswell **IP28** 34 B1
Erith DA8 23 **J4**
Erlestoke **SN10** 20 C6
Ermington **PL21** 5 G5
Ernesettle **PL5** 4 E4
Erpingham **NR11** 45 F2
Erringden Grange **HX7** 56 E7
Errogie **IV2** 88 C2
Errol **PH2** 82 D5
Errollston **AB42** 91 J1
Erskine PA8 74 **C3**
Ervie **DG9** 66 D7
Erwarton **IP9** 35 G5
Erwood **LD2** 27 K4
Eryholme **DL2** 62 E6
Eryrys **CH7** 48 B7
Escart **PA29** 73 G4
Escart Farm **PA29** 73 G5
Escomb **DL14** 62 C4
Escrick **YO19** 58 C5
Esgair **SA33** 17 G3
Esgairgeiliog **SY20** 37 G5
Esgyryn **LL31** 47 G5
Esh **DH7** 62 C2
Esh Winning **DH7** 62 C2
Esher KT10 22 **E5**
Eshott **NE65** 71 H4
Eshton **BD23** 56 E4
Eskadale **IV4** 88 B1
Eskbank **EH22** 76 B4
Eskdale Green **CA19** 60 C6
Eskdalemuir **DG13** 69 H4
Eskham **DN36** 53 G3
Eskinish **PA44** 72 B4
Esperley Lane Ends **DL13** 62 C4
Espley Hall **NE61** 71 G4
Esprick **PR4** 55 H6
Essendine **PE9** 42 D4
Essendon **AL9** 23 F1
Essich **IV2** 88 D1
Essington **WV11** 40 B5
Esslemont **AB41** 91 H2
Eston **TS6** 63 G5
Eswick **ZE2** 107 N7
Etal **TD12** 77 H7
Etchilhampton **SN10** 20 D5
Etchingham TN19 14 **C5**
Etchinghill *Kent* **CT18** 15 G4
Etchinghill *Staffs.* **WS15** 40 C4
Etherdwick Grange **HU11** 59 J6
Etherley Dene **DL14** 62 C4
Ethie Mains **DD11** 83 H3
Eton **SL4** 22 C4
Eton Wick **SL4** 22 C4
Etteridge **PH20** 88 D5
Ettiley Heath **CW11** 49 G6
Ettington **CV37** 30 D4
Etton *E.Riding* **HU17** 59 F5
Etton *Peter.* **PE6** 42 E5
Ettrick **TD7** 69 H2
Ettrickbridge **TD7** 69 J1
Ettrickhill **TD7** 69 H2
Etwall **DE65** 40 E2
Eudon George **WV16** 39 F7
Eurach **PA31** 79 K7
Euston **IP24** 34 C1
Euxton **PR7** 48 E1
Evanstown **CF39** 18 C3
Evanton **IV16** 96 D5
Evedon **NG34** 42 D1
Evelix **IV25** 96 E2
Evenjobb **LD8** 28 B2
Evenley **NN13** 31 G5
Evenlode **GL56** 30 D6
Evenwood **DL14** 62 C4
Evenwood Gate **DL14** 62 C4
Everbay **KW17** 106 F5
Evercreech **BA4** 9 F1
Everdon **NN11** 31 G3
Everingham **YO42** 58 E5
Everleigh **SN8** 21 F6
Everley *High.* **KW1** 105 J2
Everley *N.Yorks.* **YO13** 59 F1
Eversholt **MK17** 32 C5
Evershot **DT2** 8 E4
Eversley **RG27** 22 A5
Eversley Cross **RG27** 22 A5
Everthorpe **HU15** 59 F6
Everton *Cen.Beds.* **SG19** 33 F3
Everton *Hants.* **SO41** 10 D5
Everton *Mersey.* **L5** 48 C3
Everton *Notts.* **DN10** 51 J3
Evertown **DG14** 69 J6
Eves Corner **CM0** 25 F2
Evesbatch **WR6** 29 F4
Evesham WR11 30 **B4**
Evie **KW17** 106 C5
Evington **LE5** 41 J5
Ewart Newtown **NE71** 77 H7
Ewden Village **S36** 50 E3
Ewell **KT17** 23 F5
Ewell Minnis **CT15** 15 H3
Ewelme **OX10** 21 K2
Ewen **GL7** 20 D2
Ewenny **CF35** 18 C4
Ewerby **NG34** 42 E1
Ewerby Thorpe **NG34** 42 E1
Ewhurst **GU6** 22 D7
Ewhurst Green *E.Suss.* **TN32** 14 C5
Ewhurst Green *Surr.* **GU6** 12 D3
Ewloe **CH5** 48 C6
Ewloe Green **CH5** 48 B6
Ewood **BB2** 56 B7
Ewood Bridge **BB4** 56 C7
Eworthy **EX21** 6 C6
Ewshot **GU10** 22 B7
Ewyas Harold **HR2** 28 C6
Exbourne **EX20** 6 E5
Exbury **SO45** 11 F4
Exceat **BN25** 13 J7
Exebridge **TA22** 7 H3
Exelby **DL8** 57 H1
EXETER EX 7 **H6**
Exeter International Airport **EX5** 7 H6
Exford **TA24** 7 G2
Exfords Green **SY5** 38 D5
Exhall *Warks.* **B49** 30 C3
Exhall *Warks.* **CV7** 41 F7
Exlade Street **RG8** 21 K3
Exminster **EX6** 7 H7
Exmouth EX8 7 **J7**
Exnaboe **ZE3** 107 M11
Exning **CB8** 33 K2
Exton *Devon* **EX3** 7 H7
Exton *Hants.* **SO32** 11 H2
Exton *Rut.* **LE15** 42 C4
Exton *Som.* **TA22** 7 H2
Exwick **EX4** 7 H6
Eyam **S32** 50 E5
Eydon **NN11** 31 G4
Eye *Here.* **HR6** 28 D2
Eye *Peter.* **PE6** 43 F5
Eye *Suff.* IP23 35 **F1**
Eye Green **PE6** 43 F5
Eyemouth TD14 77 **H4**
Eyeworth **SG19** 33 F4
Eyhorne Street **ME17** 14 D2
Eyke **IP12** 35 H3
Eynesbury **PE19** 32 E3
Eynort **IV47** 85 J2
Eynsford **DA4** 23 J5
Eynsham **OX29** 21 H1
Eype **DT6** 8 D5
Eyre **IV51** 93 K6
Eythorne **CT15** 15 H3
Eyton *Here.* **HR6** 28 D2
Eyton *Shrop.* **SY7** 38 C7
Eyton on Severn **SY5** 38 E5
Eyton upon the Weald Moors **TF6** 39 F4
Eywood **HR5** 28 C3

F

Faccombe **SP11** 21 G6
Faceby **TS9** 63 F6
Fachwen **LL55** 46 D6
Facit **OL12** 49 H1
Faddiley **CW5** 48 E7
Fadmoor **YO62** 58 C1
Faebait **IV6** 96 B6
Faifley **G81** 74 D3
Fail **KA5** 67 J1
Failand **BS8** 19 J4
Failford **KA5** 67 J1
Failsworth **M35** 49 H2
Fain **IV23** 95 H4
Fair Isle **ZE2** 107 K2
Fair Isle Airstrip **ZE2** 107 K2
Fair Oak *Devon* **EX16** 7 J4
Fair Oak *Hants.* **SO50** 11 F3
Fair Oak *Hants.* **RG19** 21 J5
Fair Oak Green **RG7** 21 K5
Fairbourne LL38 37 **F4**
Fairburn **WF11** 57 K7
Fairfield *Derbys.* **SK17** 50 C5
Fairfield *Gt.Man.* **M43** 49 J3
Fairfield *Kent* **TN29** 14 E5
Fairfield *Mersey.* **CH63** 48 B4
Fairfield *Stock.* **TS19** 63 F5
Fairfield *Worcs.* **B61** 29 J1
Fairford GL7 20 **E1**
Fairgirth **DG5** 65 J5
Fairhaven **FY8** 55 G7
Fairhill **ML3** 75 F5
Fairholm **ML9** 75 F5
Fairley **AB15** 91 G4
Fairlie **KA29** 74 A5
Fairlight **TN35** 14 D6
Fairlight Cove **TN35** 14 D6
Fairmile *Devon* **EX11** 7 J6
Fairmile *Surr.* **KT11** 22 E5
Fairmilehead **EH10** 76 A4
Fairnington **TD5** 70 B1
Fairoak **ST21** 39 G2
Fairseat **TN15** 24 C5
Fairstead **CM3** 34 B7
Fairwarp **TN22** 13 H4
Fairwater **CF5** 18 E4
Fairy Cross **EX39** 6 C3
Fairyhill **SA3** 17 H6
Fakenham NR21 44 **D3**
Fala **EH37** 76 C4
Fala Dam **EH37** 76 C4
Falahill **EH38** 76 B5
Faldingworth **LN8** 52 D4
Falfield *Fife* **KY15** 83 F7
Falfield *S.Glos.* **GL12** 19 K2
Falin-Wnda **SA44** 17 G1
Falkenham **IP10** 35 G5
FALKIRK FK 75 **G3**
Falkland **KY15** 82 D7
Falla **TD8** 70 C2
Fallgate **S45** 51 F6
Fallin **FK7** 75 G1
Falmer **BN1** 13 G6
Falmouth TR11 3 **F5**
Falsgrave **YO12** 59 G1
Falstone **NE48** 70 C5
Fanagmore **IV27** 102 D4
Fanans **PA35** 80 B5
Fancott **LU5** 32 D6
Fangdale Beck **TS9** 63 G7
Fangfoss **YO41** 58 D4
Fankerton **FK6** 75 F2
Fanmore **PA73** 79 F3
Fanner's Green **CM3** 33 K7
Fans **TD4** 76 E6
Far Cotton **NN4** 31 J3
Far Forest **DY14** 29 G1
Far Gearstones **LA6** 56 C1
Far Green **GL11** 20 A1
Far Moor **WN5** 48 E2
Far Oakridge **GL6** 20 C1
Far Royds **LS12** 57 H6
Far Sawrey **LA22** 60 E7
Farcet **PE7** 43 F6
Farden **SY8** 28 E1
Fareham PO16 11 **G4**
Farewell **WS13** 40 C4
Farforth **LN11** 53 G5
Faringdon SN7 21 **F2**
Farington **PR25** 55 J7
Farlam **CA8** 61 G1
Farlary **IV28** 96 E1
Farleigh *N.Som.* **BS48** 19 J5
Farleigh *Surr.* **CR6** 23 G5
Farleigh Hungerford **BA2** 20 B6
Farleigh Wallop **RG25** 21 K7
Farlesthorpe **LN13** 53 H5
Farleton *Cumb.* **LA6** 55 J1
Farleton *Lancs.* **LA2** 55 J3
Farley *Derbys.* **DE4** 50 E6
Farley *Shrop.* **SY5** 38 C5
Farley *Staffs.* **ST10** 40 C1
Farley *Wilts.* **SP5** 10 D2
Farley Green *Suff.* **CB8** 34 B3
Farley Green *Surr.* **GU5** 22 D7
Farley Hill **RG7** 22 A5
Farleys End **GL2** 29 G7
Farlington **YO61** 58 C3
Farlow **DY14** 39 F7
Farm Town **LE67** 41 F4
Farmborough **BA2** 19 K5
Farmcote **GL54** 30 B6
Farmington **GL54** 30 C7
Farmoor **OX2** 21 H1
Farmtown **AB55** 98 D5
Farnborough *Gt.Lon.* **BR6** 23 H5
Farnborough *Hants.* GU14 22 **B6**
Farnborough *W.Berks.* **OX12** 21 H3
Farnborough *Warks.* **OX17** 31 F4
Farnborough Street **GU14** 22 B6
Farncombe **GU7** 22 C7
Farndish **NN29** 32 C2
Farndon *Ches.W. & C.* **CH3** 48 D7
Farndon *Notts.* **NG24** 51 K7
Farnell **DD9** 83 H2
Farnham *Dorset* **DT11** 9 J3
Farnham *Essex* **CM23** 33 H6
Farnham *N.Yorks.* **HG5** 57 J3
Farnham *Suff.* **IP17** 35 H2
Farnham *Surr.* GU9 22 **B7**
Farnham Common **SL2** 22 C3
Farnham Green **CM23** 33 H6
Farnham Royal **SL2** 22 C3
Farningham **DA4** 23 J5
Farnley *N.Yorks.* **LS21** 57 H5
Farnley *W.Yorks.* **LS12** 57 H6
Farnley Tyas **HD4** 50 D1
Farnsfield **NG22** 51 J7
Farnworth *Gt.Man.* **BL4** 49 G2
Farnworth *Halton* **WA8** 48 E4
Farr *High.* **KW14** 104 C2
Farr *High.* **IV2** 88 D1
Farr *High.* **PH21** 89 F4
Farr House **IV2** 88 D1
Farraline **IV2** 88 C2
Farringdon **EX5** 7 J6
Farrington Gurney **BS39** 19 K6
Farsley **LS28** 57 H6
Farthing Corner **ME8** 24 E5
Farthing Green **TN12** 14 D3
Farthinghoe **NN13** 31 G5
Farthingstone **NN12** 31 H3
Farthorpe **LN9** 53 F5
Fartown **HD2** 50 D1
Farway **EX24** 7 K6
Fasag **IV22** 94 E6
Fasagrianach **IV23** 95 H3
Fascadale **PH36** 86 B7
Faslane **G84** 74 A2
Fasnacloich **PA38** 80 B3
Fasnakyle **IV4** 87 K2
Fassfern **PH33** 87 G7
Fatfield **NE38** 62 E1
Fattahead **AB45** 98 E5
Faugh **CA8** 61 G1
Fauldhouse **EH47** 75 H4
Faulkbourne **CM8** 34 B7
Faulkland **BA3** 20 A6
Fauls **SY13** 38 E2
Faulston **SP5** 10 B2
Faversham ME13 25 **G5**
Favillar **AB55** 89 K1
Fawdington **YO61** 57 K2
Fawdon **NE3** 71 H7
Fawfieldhead **SK17** 50 C6
Fawkham Green **DA3** 23 J5
Fawler **OX7** 30 E7
Fawley *Bucks.* **RG9** 22 A3
Fawley *Hants.* **SO45** 11 F4
Fawley *W.Berks.* **OX12** 21 G3
Fawley Chapel **HR1** 28 E6
Fawsyde **DD10** 91 G7
Faxfleet **DN14** 58 E7
Faxton **NN6** 31 J1
Faygate **RH12** 13 F3
Fazakerley **L9** 48 C3
Fazeley **B78** 40 E5
Fearby **HG4** 57 G1
Fearn **IV20** 97 F4
Fearnan **PH15** 81 J3
Fearnbeg **IV54** 94 D6
Fearnhead **WA2** 49 F3
Fearnmore **IV54** 94 D5
Fearnoch *Arg. & B.* **PA22** 73 J3
Fearnoch *Arg. & B.* **PA21** 73 H2
Featherstone *Staffs.* **WV10** 40 B5
Featherstone *W.Yorks.* **WF7** 57 K7
Featherstone Castle **NE49** 70 B7
Feckenham **B96** 30 B2
Feering **CO5** 34 C6
Feetham **DL11** 62 A7
Feith-hill **AB53** 98 E6
Feizor **LA2** 56 C3
Felbridge **RH19** 13 G3
Felbrigg **NR11** 45 G2
Felcourt **RH19** 23 G7
Felden **HP3** 22 D1
Felhampton **SY6** 38 D7
Felindre *Carmar.* **SA19** 27 G6
Felindre *Carmar.* **SA32** 17 J3
Felindre *Carmar.* **SA44** 17 G2
Felindre *Carmar.* **SA19** 17 K2
Felindre *Cere.* **SA48** 26 E3
Felindre *Powys* **LD7** 38 A7
Felindre *Powys* **NP8** 28 A6
Felindre *Swan.* **SA5** 17 K5
Felinfach *Cere.* **SA48** 26 E3
Felinfach *Powys* **LD3** 27 K5
Felinfoel **SA14** 17 J5
Felingwmisaf **SA32** 17 J3
Felingwmuchaf **SA32** 17 J3
Felixkirk **YO7** 57 K1
Felixstowe IP11 35 **H5**
Felixstowe Ferry **IP11** 35 H5
Felkington **TD15** 77 H6
Felldownhead **PL19** 6 B7
Felling **NE10** 71 H7
Fellonmore **PA65** 79 H5
Felmersham **MK43** 32 C3
Felmingham **NR28** 45 G3
Felpham **PO22** 12 C7
Felsham **IP30** 34 D3
Felsted **CM6** 33 K6
Feltham TW13 22 **E4**
Felthamhill **TW16** 22 E4
Felthorpe **NR10** 45 F4
Felton *Here.* **HR1** 28 E4
Felton *N.Som.* **BS40** 19 J5
Felton *Northumb.* **NE65** 71 G3
Felton Butler **SY4** 38 C4
Feltwell **IP26** 44 B6
Fen Ditton **CB5** 33 H2
Fen Drayton **CB24** 33 G2
Fen End **CV8** 30 D1
Fen Street *Norf.* **NR17** 44 D6
Fen Street *Norf.* **IP22** 34 E1
Fen Street *Suff.* **IP22** 34 D1
Fen Street *Suff.* **IP14** 35 F2
Fenay Bridge **HD8** 50 D1
Fence **BB12** 56 D6
Fence Houses **DH4** 62 E1
Fencott **OX5** 31 G7
Fendike Corner **PE24** 53 H6
Fenham **TD15** 77 J6
Fenhouses **PE20** 43 F1
Feniscowles **BB2** 56 B7
Feniton **EX14** 7 K6
Fenn Street **ME3** 24 D4
Fenni-fach **LD3** 27 K6
Fenny Bentley **DE6** 50 D7
Fenny Bridges **EX14** 7 K6
Fenny Compton **CV47** 31 F3
Fenny Drayton **CV13** 41 F6
Fenny Stratford **MK2** 32 B5
Fenrother **NE61** 71 G4
Fenstanton **PE28** 33 G2
Fenton *Cambs.* **PE28** 33 G1
Fenton *Lincs.* **LN1** 52 B5
Fenton *Lincs.* **NG23** 52 B7
Fenton *Northumb.* **NE71** 77 H7
Fenton *Notts.* **DN22** 51 K4
Fenton *Stoke* **ST4** 40 A1
Fenton Barns **EH39** 76 D2
Fenwick *E.Ayr.* **KA3** 74 C6
Fenwick *Northumb.* **NE18** 71 F6
Fenwick *Northumb.* **TD15** 77 J6
Fenwick *S.Yorks.* **DN6** 51 H1
Feochaig **PA28** 66 B2
Feock **TR3** 3 F5
Feolin **PA60** 72 D4
Feolin Ferry **PA60** 72 C4
Feorlan **PA28** 66 A3
Feorlin **PA32** 73 H1
Ferguslie Park **PA3** 74 C4
Ferindonald **IV55** 93 G6
Fern **DD8** 83 F1
Ferndale CF43 18 **C2**
Ferndown BH22 10 **B4**
Ferness **IV12** 97 G7
Fernham **SN7** 21 F2
Fernhill Heath **WR3** 29 H3
Fernhurst **GU27** 12 B4
Fernie **KY15** 82 E6
Fernilea **IV47** 85 J1
Fernilee **SK23** 50 C5
Fernybank **DD9** 90 D7
Ferrensby **HG5** 57 J3
Ferrindonald **IV44** 86 C4
Ferring **BN12** 12 D6
Ferry Hill **PE16** 43 G7
Ferrybridge **WF11** 57 K7
Ferryden **DD10** 83 J2
Ferryhill DL17 62 **D3**
Ferryside (Glanyferi) SA17 17 **G4**
Fersfield **IP22** 44 E7
Fersit **PH31** 87 K7
Ferwig **SA43** 16 E1
Feshiebridge **PH21** 89 F4
Fetcham **KT22** 22 E6
Fetlar **ZE2** 107 Q3
Fetterangus **AB42** 99 H5
Fettercairn **AB30** 90 E7
Fetternear House **AB51** 91 F3
Feus of Caldhame **AB30** 83 H1
Fewcott **OX27** 31 G6
Fewston **HG3** 57 G4
Ffairfach **SA19** 17 K3
Ffair-Rhos **SY25** 27 G2
Ffaldybrenin **SA19** 17 K1
Ffarmers **SA19** 17 K1
Ffawyddog **NP8** 28 B7
Ffestiniog (Llan Ffestiniog) **LL41** 37 G1
Ffordd-las *Denb.* **LL16** 47 K6
Fforddlas *Powys* **HR3** 28 B5
Fforest **SA4** 17 J5
Fforest-fach **SA5** 17 K6
Ffostrasol **SA44** 17 G1
Ffos-y-ffin **SA46** 26 D2
Ffridd Uchaf **LL54** 46 D7
Ffrith *Denb.* **LL19** 47 J4
Ffrith *Flints.* **LL11** 48 B7
Ffrwdgrech **LD3** 27 K6
Ffynnon **SA33** 17 G4
Ffynnon Taf (Taff's Well) **CF15** 18 E3
Ffynnongroyw **CH8** 47 K4

Glencoe PH49 80 C2
Glenconglass AB37 89 J2
Glencraig KY5 75 K1
Glencripesdale PH36 79 H2
Glencrosh DG3 68 C5
Glencruitten PA34 79 K5
Glencuie AB33 90 C3
Glendearg D. & G. DG13 69 H3
Glendearg Sc.Bord. TD1 76 D7
Glendessary PH34 87 F5
Glendevon FK14 82 A7
Glendoebeg PH32 88 B4
Glendoick PH2 82 D5
Glendoll Lodge DD8 89 K7
Glendoune KA26 67 F4
Glendrissaig KA26 67 F4
Glenduckie KY14 82 D6
Glenduisk KA26 67 G5
Glendye Lodge AB31 90 E6
Gleneagles Hotel PH3 82 A6
Gleneagles House PH3 82 A7
Glenearn PH2 82 C6
Glenegedale PA42 72 B5
Glenelg IV40 86 E3
Glenfarg PH2 82 C6
Glenfeochan PA34 79 K5
Glenfield LE3 41 H5
Glenfinnan PH37 87 F6
Glenfoot PH2 82 C6
Glengalmadale PH33 79 K2
Glengap DG6 65 G5
Glengarnock KA14 74 B5
Glengarrisdale PA60 72 E1
Glengennet KA26 67 G4
Glengolly KW14 105 G2
Glengrasco IV51 93 K7
Glengyle FK8 80 E6
Glenhead DG2 68 D5
Glenhead Farm PH11 82 D1
Glenhurich PH37 79 K1
Glenkerry TD7 69 H2
Glenkiln KA27 73 J7
Glenkin PA23 73 K2
Glenkindie AB33 90 C3
Glenlair DG7 65 H3
Glenlatterach IV30 97 K6
Glenlean PA23 73 J2
Glenlee Angus DD9 90 C7
Glenlee D. & G. DG7 68 B5
Glenlichorn FK15 81 J6
Glenlivet AB37 89 J2
Glenlochar DG7 65 H4
Glenluce DG8 64 B5
Glenmallan G84 74 A1
Glenmanna DG3 68 C3
Glenmavis ML6 75 F4
Glenmaye IM5 54 B6
Glenmeanie IV6 95 J4
Glenmore Arg. & B. PA20 73 J4
Glenmore High. IV51 93 K7
Glenmore High. PH22 89 G4
Glenmore Lodge PH22 89 G4
Glenmoy DD8 83 F1
Glenmuick IV27 103 F7
Glennoe PA35 80 B4
Glenochar ML12 68 E2
Glenogil DD8 83 F1
Glenprosen Village DD8 82 E1
Glenquiech DD8 83 F1
Glenramskill PA28 66 B2
Glenrazie DG8 64 D4
Glenridding CA11 60 E5
Glenrisdell PA29 73 G5
Glenrossal IV27 96 B1
Glenrothes KY7 82 D7
Glensanda PA34 79 K3
Glensaugh AB30 90 E7
Glensgaich IV14 96 B5
Glenshalg AB31 90 D4
Glenshellish PA27 73 K1
Glensluain PA27 73 J1
Glentaggart ML11 68 D1
Glentham LN8 52 D3
Glenton AB51 90 E2
Glentress EH45 76 A7
Glentrool DG8 64 D3
Glentruan IM7 54 D3
Glentworth DN21 52 C4
Glenuachdarach IV51 93 K6
Glenuig PH38 86 C7
Glenure PA38 80 B3
Glenurquhart IV11 96 E5
Glenwhilly DG8 64 B3
Glespin ML11 68 D1
Gletness ZE2 107 N7
Glewstone HR9 28 E6
Glinton PE6 42 E5
Glooston LE16 42 A6
Glororum NE69 77 K7
Glossop SK13 50 C3
Gloster Hill NE65 71 H3
GLOUCESTER GL 29 H7
Gloup ZE2 107 P2
Gloweth TR1 2 E4
Glusburn BD20 57 F5
Gluss ZE2 107 M5
Glympton OX20 31 F6
Glyn LL24 47 F7
Glyn Ceiriog LL20 38 B2
Glynarthen SA44 17 G1
Glyncoch CF37 18 D2
Glyncorrwg SA13 18 B2
Glyn-Cywarch LL47 37 F2
Glynde BN8 13 H6
Glyndebourne BN8 13 H5
Glyndyfrdwy LL21 38 A1
Glynebwy (Ebbw Vale) NP23 18 E1
Glynneath (Glyn-Nedd) SA11 18 B1
Glyn-Nedd (Glynneath) SA11 18 B1
Glynogwr CF35 18 C3
Glyntaff CF37 18 D3
Gnosall ST20 40 A3
Gnosall Heath ST20 40 A3
Goadby LE7 42 A6
Goadby Marwood LE14 42 A3
Goatacre SN11 20 D4
Goatfield PA32 80 B7
Goathill DT9 9 F3
Goathland YO22 63 K6
Goathurst TA5 8 B1
Gobernuisgeach KW12 104 E5
Gobhaig HS3 100 C7
Gobowen SY11 38 C2
Godalming GU7 22 C7
Goddard's Corner IP13 35 G2
Goddards Green BN6 13 F4
Godden Green TN15 23 J6
Goddington BR6 23 H5
Godford Cross EX14 7 K5
Godington OX27 31 H6
Godleybrook ST10 40 B1
Godmanchester PE29 33 F1
Godmanstone DT2 9 F5
Godmersham CT4 15 F2
Godney BA5 19 H7
Godolphin Cross TR13 2 D5
Godor SY22 38 B4
Godre'r-graig SA9 18 A1
Godshill Hants. SP6 10 C3
Godshill I.o.W. PO38 11 G6
Godstone RH9 23 G6
Godwick PE32 44 D3
Goetre NP4 19 G1
Goff's Oak EN7 23 G1
Gogar EH12 75 K3
Gogarth LL30 47 F4
Goginan SY23 37 F7
Goirtean a' Chladaich PH33 87 G7
Goirtein PA27 73 H2
Golan LL51 36 E1
Golant PL23 4 B5
Golberdon PL17 4 D3
Golborne WA3 49 F3
Golcar HD7 50 D1
Gold Hill Cambs. PE14 43 J6
Gold Hill Dorset DT11 9 H3
Goldcliff NP18 19 G3
Golden Cross BN27 13 J5
Golden Green TN11 23 K7
Golden Grove SA32 17 J4
Golden Pot GU34 22 A7
Golden Valley Derbys. DE55 51 G7
Golden Valley Glos. GL51 29 J6
Goldenhill ST6 49 H7
Golders Green NW11 23 F3
Goldhanger CM9 25 F1
Goldielea DG2 65 K3
Golding SY5 38 E5
Goldington MK41 32 D3
Goldsborough N.Yorks. YO21 63 K5
Goldsborough N.Yorks. HG5 57 J4
Goldsithney TR20 2 C5
Goldstone TF9 39 G3
Goldthorn Park WV2 40 B6
Goldthorpe S63 51 G2
Goldworthy EX39 6 B3
Golford TN17 14 C4
Gollanfield IV2 97 F6
Gollinglith Foot HG4 57 G1
Golspie KW10 97 F2
Golval KW13 104 D2
Gomeldon SP4 10 C1
Gomersal BD19 57 H7
Gometra PA73 78 E3
Gometra House PA73 78 E3
Gomshall GU5 22 D7
Gonachan Cottage G63 74 E2
Gonalston NG14 41 J1
Gonerby Hill Foot NG31 42 C2
Gonfirth ZE2 107 M6
Good Easter CM1 33 K7
Gooderstone PE33 44 B5
Goodleigh EX32 6 E2
Goodmanham YO43 58 E5
Goodmayes IG3 23 H3
Goodnestone Kent CT3 15 H2
Goodnestone Kent ME13 25 G5
Goodrich HR9 28 E7
Goodrington TQ4 5 J5
Goodshaw BB4 56 D7
Goodshaw Fold BB4 56 D7
Goodwick (Wdig) SA64 16 C2
Goodworth Clatford SP11 21 G7
Goodyers End CV12 41 F7
Goole DN14 58 D7
Goom's Hill WR7 30 B3
Goonbell TR5 2 E4
Goonhavern TR4 2 E3
Goonvrea TR5 2 E4
Goose Green Essex CO11 35 F6
Goose Green Essex CO16 35 F6
Goose Green Gt.Man. WN3 48 E2
Goose Green Kent TN11 23 K6
Goose Green S.Glos. BS30 19 K4
Goose Pool HR2 28 D5
Gooseham EX23 6 A4
Goosehill Green WR9 29 J2
Goosewell PL9 5 F5
Goosey SN7 21 G2
Goosnargh PR3 55 J6
Goostrey CW4 49 G5
Gorcott Hill B98 30 B2
Gorddinog LL33 46 E5
Gordon TD3 76 E6
Gordonbush KW9 97 F1
Gordonstoun IV30 97 J5
Gordonstown Aber. AB45 98 D5
Gordonstown Aber. AB51 91 F1
Gore Cross SN10 20 D6
Gore End RG20 21 H5
Gore Pit CO5 34 C7
Gore Street CT12 25 J5
Gorebridge EH23 76 B4
Gorefield PE13 43 H4
Gorey JE3 3 K7
Gorgie EH11 76 A3
Goring RG8 21 K3
Goring Heath RG8 21 K4
Goring-by-Sea BN12 12 E6
Gorleston-on-Sea NR31 45 K5
Gorllwyn SA33 17 G2
Gornalwood DY3 40 B6
Gorrachie AB45 99 F5
Gorran Churchtown PL26 3 G4
Gorran Haven PL26 4 A6
Gors SY23 27 F1
Gorsedd CH8 47 K5
Gorseinon SA4 17 J6
Gorseness KW17 106 D6
Gorseybank DE4 50 E7
Gorsgoch SA40 26 D3
Gorslas SA14 17 J4
Gorsley HR9 29 F6
Gorsley Common HR9 29 F6
Gorstage CW8 49 F5
Gorstan IV23 95 K5
Gorstanvorran PH37 86 E7
Gorsty Hill ST14 40 D3
Gorten PA64 79 J4
Gortenbuie PA70 79 G4
Gorteneorn PH36 79 H1
Gorton Arg. & B. PA78 78 C2
Gorton Gt.Man. M18 49 H3
Gosbeck IP6 35 F3
Gosberton PE11 43 F2
Gosberton Clough PE11 42 E3
Goseley Dale DE11 41 F3
Gosfield CO9 34 B6
Gosford Here. SY8 28 E2
Gosford Oxon. OX5 31 G7
Gosforth Cumb. CA20 60 B6
Gosforth T. & W. NE3 71 H7
Gosland Green CW6 48 E7
Gosmore SG4 32 E6
Gospel End DY3 40 B6
Gosport PO12 11 H5
Gossabrough ZE2 107 P4
Gossington GL2 20 A1
Gossops Green RH11 13 F3
Goswick TD15 77 J6
Gotham NG11 41 H2
Gotherington GL52 29 J6
Gothers PL26 3 G3
Gott ZE2 107 N8
Gotton TA2 8 B2
Goudhurst TN17 14 C4
Goulceby LN11 53 F5
Gourdas AB53 99 F6
Gourdon DD10 91 G7
Gourock PA19 74 A3
Govan G51 74 D4
Goverton NG14 51 K7
Goveton TQ7 5 H6
Govilon NP7 28 B7
Gowanhill AB43 99 J4
Gowdall DN14 58 C7
Gowerton SA4 17 J6
Gowkhall KY12 75 J2
Gowkthrapple ML2 75 F5
Gowthorpe YO41 58 D4
Goxhill E.Riding HU11 59 H5
Goxhill N.Lincs. DN19 59 H7
Goytre SA13 18 A3
Gozzard's Ford OX13 21 H2
Grabhair HS2 101 F6
Graby NG34 42 D3
Gradbach SK17 49 J6
Grade TR12 2 E7
Gradeley Green CW5 48 E7
Graffham GU28 12 C5
Grafham Cambs. PE28 32 E2
Grafham Surr. GU5 22 D7
Grafton Here. HR2 28 D5
Grafton N.Yorks. YO51 57 K3
Grafton Oxon. OX18 21 F1
Grafton Shrop. SY4 38 D4
Grafton Worcs. HR6 28 E2
Grafton Worcs. GL20 29 J5
Grafton Flyford WR7 29 J3
Grafton Regis NN12 31 J4
Grafton Underwood NN14 42 C7
Grafty Green ME17 14 D3
Graianrhyd CH7 48 B7
Graig Carmar. SA16 17 H5
Graig Conwy LL28 47 G5
Graig Denb. LL17 47 J5
Graig-fechan LL15 47 K7
Grain ME3 24 E4
Grainel PA44 72 A4
Grainhow AB53 99 G6
Grains Bar OL4 49 J2
Grainsby DN36 53 F3
Grainthorpe LN11 53 G3
Graiselound DN9 51 K3
Gramisdale (Gramsdal) HS7 92 D6
Grampound TR2 3 G4
Grampound Road TR2 3 G3
Gramsdal (Gramisdale) HS7 92 D6
Granborough MK18 31 J6
Granby NG13 42 A2
Grandborough CV23 31 F2
Grandes Rocques GY5 3 J5
Grandtully PH9 82 A2
Grange Cumb. CA12 60 D5
Grange E.Ayr. KA1 74 C7
Grange High. IV63 87 K1
Grange Med. ME7 24 D5
Grange Mersey. CH48 48 B4
Grange P. & K. PH2 82 D5
Grange Crossroads AB55 98 C5
Grange de Lings LN2 52 C5
Grange Hall IV36 97 H5
Grange Hill IG7 23 H2
Grange Moor WF4 50 E1
Grange of Lindores KY14 82 D6
Grange Villa DH2 62 D1
Grangemill DE4 50 E7
Grangemouth FK3 75 H2
Grangemuir KY10 83 G7
Grange-over-Sands LA11 55 H2
Grangeston KA26 67 G4
Grangetown Cardiff CF11 18 E4
Grangetown R. & C. TS6 63 G4
Granish PH22 89 G3
Gransmoor YO25 59 H4
Granston SA62 16 B2
Grantchester CB3 33 H3
Grantham NG31 42 C2
Grantley HG4 57 H2
Grantlodge AB51 91 F3
Granton EH5 76 A3
Granton House DG10 69 F3
Grantown-on-Spey PH26 89 H2
Grantsfield HR6 28 E2
Grantshouse TD11 77 G4
Grappenhall WA4 49 F4
Grasby DN38 52 D2
Grasmere LA22 60 E6
Grass Green CO9 34 B5
Grasscroft OL4 49 J2
Grassendale L19 48 C4
Grassgarth LA8 60 F7
Grassholme DL12 62 A4
Grassington BD23 57 F3
Grassmoor S42 51 G6
Grassthorpe NG23 51 K6
Grateley SP11 21 F7
Gratwich ST14 40 C2
Gravel Hill SL9 22 D2
Graveley Cambs. PE19 33 F2
Graveley Herts. SG4 33 F6
Gravelly Hill B23 40 D6
Gravels SY5 38 C5
Graven ZE2 107 N5
Graveney ME13 25 G5
Gravesend DA11 24 C4
Grayingham DN21 52 C3
Grayrigg LA8 61 G7
Grays RM17 24 C4
Grayshott GU26 12 B3
Grayswood GU27 12 C3
Grazeley RG7 21 K5
Greasbrough S61 51 G3
Greasby CH49 48 B4
Great Abington CB21 33 J4
Great Addington NN14 32 C1
Great Alne B49 30 C3
Great Altcar L37 48 C2
Great Amwell SG12 33 G7
Great Asby CA16 61 H5
Great Ashfield IP31 34 D2
Great Ayton TS9 63 G5
Great Baddow CM2 24 D1
Great Bardfield CM7 33 K5
Great Barford MK44 32 E3
Great Barr B43 40 C6
Great Barrington OX18 30 D7
Great Barrow CH3 48 D6
Great Barton IP31 34 C2
Great Barugh YO17 58 D2
Great Bavington NE19 70 E5
Great Bealings IP13 35 G4
Great Bedwyn SN8 21 F5
Great Bentley CO7 35 F6
Great Bernera HS2 100 D4
Great Billing NN3 32 B2
Great Bircham PE31 44 B2
Great Blakenham IP6 35 F3
Great Bolas TF6 39 F3
Great Bookham KT23 22 E6
Great Bourton OX17 31 F4
Great Bowden LE16 42 A7
Great Bradley CB8 33 K3
Great Braxted CM8 34 C7
Great Bricett IP7 34 E3
Great Brickhill MK17 32 C5
Great Bridgeford ST18 40 A3
Great Brington NN7 31 H2
Great Bromley CO7 34 E6
Great Broughton Cumb. CA13 60 B3
Great Broughton N.Yorks. TS9 63 G6
Great Buckland DA13 24 C5
Great Budworth CW9 49 F5
Great Burdon DL1 62 E5
Great Burstead CM12 24 C2
Great Busby TS9 63 G6
Great Cambourne CB23 33 G3
Great Canfield CM6 33 J7
Great Canney CM3 24 E1
Great Carlton LN11 53 H4
Great Casterton PE9 42 D5
Great Chalfield SN12 20 B5
Great Chart TN23 14 E3
Great Chatwell TF10 39 G4
Great Chell ST6 49 H7
Great Chesterford CB10 33 J4
Great Cheverell SN10 20 C6
Great Chishill SG8 33 H5
Great Clacton CO15 35 F7
Great Clifton CA14 60 B4
Great Coates DN37 53 F2
Great Comberton WR10 29 J4
Great Corby CA4 61 F1
Great Cornard CO10 34 C4
Great Cowden HU11 59 J5
Great Coxwell SN7 21 F2
Great Crakehall DL8 57 H1
Great Cransley NN14 32 B1
Great Cressingham IP25 44 C5
Great Crosby L23 48 C2
Great Crosthwaite CA12 60 D4
Great Cubley DE6 40 D2
Great Cumbrae KA28 73 K5
Great Dalby LE14 42 A4
Great Doddington NN29 32 B2
Great Doward HR9 28 E7
Great Dunham PE32 44 C4
Great Dunmow CM6 33 K6
Great Durnford SP4 10 C1
Great Easton Essex CM6 33 K6
Great Easton Leics. LE16 42 B6
Great Eccleston PR3 55 H5
Great Edstone YO62 58 D1
Great Ellingham NR17 44 E6
Great Elm BA11 20 A7
Great Eversden CB23 33 G3
Great Fencote DL7 62 D7
Great Finborough IP14 34 E3
Great Fransham NR19 44 C4
Great Gaddesden HP1 32 D7
Great Gidding PE28 42 E7
Great Givendale YO42 58 E4
Great Glemham IP17 35 H2
Great Glen LE8 41 J6
Great Gonerby NG31 42 B2
Great Gransden SG19 33 F3
Great Green Cambs. SG8 33 F4
Great Green Norf. IP20 45 G7
Great Green Suff. IP30 34 D3
Great Green Suff. IP21 35 F1
Great Green Suff. IP22 34 E1
Great Habton YO17 58 D2
Great Hale NG34 42 E1
Great Hallingbury CM22 33 J7
Great Hampden HP16 22 B1
Great Harrowden NN9 32 B1
Great Harwood BB6 56 C6
Great Haseley OX44 21 K1
Great Hatfield HU11 59 H5
Great Haywood ST18 40 C3
Great Heath CV6 41 F7
Great Heck DN14 58 B7
Great Henny CO10 34 C5
Great Hinton BA14 20 C6
Great Hockham IP24 44 D6
Great Holland CO13 35 G7
Great Horkesley CO6 34 D5
Great Hormead SG9 33 H5
Great Horton BD7 57 G6
Great Horwood MK17 31 J5
Great Houghton Northants. NN4 31 J3
Great Houghton S.Yorks. S72 51 G2
Great Hucklow SK17 50 D5
Great Kelk YO25 59 H4
Great Kimble HP17 22 B1
Great Kingshill HP15 22 B2
Great Langton DL7 62 D7
Great Leighs CM3 34 B7
Great Limber DN37 52 E2
Great Linford MK14 32 B4
Great Livermere IP31 34 C1
Great Longstone DE45 50 E5
Great Lumley DH3 62 D2
Great Lyth SY3 38 D5
Great Malvern WR14 29 G4
Great Maplestead CO9 34 C5
Great Marton FY4 55 G6
Great Massingham PE32 44 B3
Great Melton NR9 45 F5
Great Milton OX44 21 K1
Great Missenden HP16 22 B1
Great Mitton BB7 56 C6
Great Mongeham CT14 15 J2
Great Moulton NR15 45 F6
Great Munden SG11 33 G6
Great Musgrave CA17 61 J5
Great Ness SY4 38 D4
Great Notley CM77 34 B6
Great Nurcot TA24 7 H2
Great Oak NP15 19 G1
Great Oakley Essex CO12 35 F6
Great Oakley Northants. NN18 42 B7
Great Offley SG5 32 E6
Great Ormside CA16 61 J5
Great Orton CA5 60 E1
Great Ouseburn YO26 57 K3
Great Oxendon LE16 42 A7
Great Oxney Green CM1 24 C1
Great Palgrave PE32 44 C4
Great Parndon CM19 23 H1
Great Paxton PE19 33 F2
Great Plumpton PR4 55 G6
Great Plumstead NR13 45 H5
Great Ponton NG33 42 C2
Great Potheridge EX20 6 D4
Great Preston LS26 57 J7
Great Purston NN13 31 G5
Great Raveley PE28 43 F7
Great Rissington GL54 30 C7
Great Rollright OX7 30 E5
Great Ryburgh NR21 44 D3
Great Ryle NE66 71 F2
Great Ryton SY5 38 D5
Great Saling CM7 34 B6

Great Salkeld **CA11** 61 G3
Great Sampford **CB10** 33 K5
Great Sankey **WA5** 48 E4
Great Saredon **WV10** 40 B5
Great Saxham **IP29** 34 B2
Great Shefford **RG17** 21 G4
Great Shelford **CB22** 33 H3
Great Smeaton **DL6** 62 E6
Great Snoring **NR21** 44 D2
Great Somerford **SN15** 20 C3
Great Stainton **TS21** 62 E4
Great Stambridge **SS4** 25 F2
Great Staughton **PE19** 32 E2
Great Steeping **PE23** 53 H6
Great Stonar **CT13** 15 J2
Great Strickland **CA10** 61 G4
Great Stukeley **PE28** 33 F1
Great Sturton **LN9** 53 F5
Great Sutton *Ches.W. & C.* **CH66** 48 C5
Great Sutton *Shrop.* **SY8** 38 E7
Great Swinburne **NE48** 70 E6
Great Tew **OX7** 30 E6
Great Tey **CO6** 34 C6
Great Thorness **PO30** 11 F5
Great Thurlow **CB9** 33 K4
Great Torr **TQ7** 5 G6
Great Torrington EX38 6 **C4**
Great Tosson **NE65** 71 F3
Great Totham *Essex* **CM9** 34 C7
Great Totham *Essex* **CM9** 34 C7
Great Tows **LN8** 53 F3
Great Urswick **LA12** 55 F2
Great Wakering **SS3** 25 F3
Great Waldingfield **CO10** 34 D4
Great Walsingham NR22 44 **D2**
Great Waltham **CM3** 33 K7
Great Warley **CM13** 23 J2
Great Washbourne **GL20** 29 J5
Great Weeke **TQ13** 7 F7
Great Welnetham **IP30** 34 C3
Great Wenham **CO7** 34 E5
Great Whittington **NE19** 71 F6
Great Wigborough **CO5** 34 D7
Great Wigsell **TN32** 14 C5
Great Wilbraham **CB21** 33 J3
Great Wilne **DE72** 41 G2
Great Wishford **SP2** 10 B1
Great Witcombe **GL3** 29 J7
Great Witley **WR6** 29 G2
Great Wolford **CV36** 30 D5
Great Wratting **CB9** 33 K4
Great Wymondley **SG4** 33 F6
Great Wyrley **WS6** 40 B5
Great Wytheford **SY4** 38 E4
Great Yarmouth NR30 45 **K5**
Great Yeldham **CO9** 34 B5
Greatford **PE9** 42 D4
Greatgate **ST10** 40 C1
Greatham *Hants.* **GU33** 11 J1
Greatham *Hart.* **TS25** 63 F4
Greatham *W.Suss.* **RH20** 12 D5
Greatness **TN14** 23 J6
Greatstone-on-Sea **TN28** 15 F5
Greatworth **OX17** 31 G4
Green **LL16** 47 J6
Green Cross **GU10** 12 B3
Green End *Bed.* **MK44** 32 E3
Green End *Bucks.* **MK17** 32 C5
Green End *Cambs.* **PE29** 33 F1
Green End *Cambs.* **PE27** 33 G1
Green End *Herts.* **SG12** 33 G6
Green End *Herts.* **SG9** 33 G5
Green End *Warks.* **CV7** 40 E7
Green Hammerton **YO26** 57 K4
Green Hill **SN4** 20 D3
Green Lane **B80** 30 B2
Green Moor **S35** 50 E3
Green Ore **BA5** 19 J6
Green Quarter **LA8** 61 F6
Green Street *E.Suss.* **TN38** 14 C6
Green Street *Herts.* **WD6** 22 E2
Green Street *Herts.* **SG11** 33 H6
Green Street *W.Suss.* **RH13** 12 E4
Green Street *Worcs.* **WR5** 29 H4
Green Street Green *Gt.Lon.* **BR6** 23 H5
Green Street Green *Kent* **DA2** 23 J4
Green Tye **SG10** 33 H7
Greenburn **DD5** 83 F3
Greencroft **DH7** 62 C2
Greendams **AB31** 90 E6
Greendykes **NE66** 71 F1
Greenend **OX7** 30 E6
Greenfaulds **G67** 75 F3
Greenfield *Cen.Beds.* **MK45** 32 D5
Greenfield (Maes-Glas) *Flints.* **CH8** 47 K5
Greenfield *Gt.Man.* **OL3** 50 C2
Greenfield *High.* **PH35** 87 J4
Greenfield *Lincs.* **LN13** 53 H5
Greenfield *Oxon.* **OX49** 22 A2
Greenford UB6 22 **E3**
Greengairs **ML6** 75 F3
Greengates **BD10** 57 G6
Greengill **CA7** 60 C3
Greenhalgh **PR4** 55 H6
Greenhall **AB52** 90 E2
Greenham **RG14** 21 H5
Greenhaugh **NE48** 70 C5
Greenhead **CA8** 70 B7
Greenheads **AB42** 91 J1
Greenheys **BL5** 49 G2
Greenhill *Gt.Lon.* **HA1** 22 E3
Greenhill *High.* **KW9** 97 G1
Greenhill *S.Yorks.* **S8** 51 F4
Greenhithe DA9 23 **J4**
Greenholm **KA16** 74 D7
Greenholme **CA10** 61 G6
Greenhow Hill **HG3** 57 G3
Greenigo **KW15** 106 D7
Greenland **KW14** 105 H2
Greenlands **RG9** 22 A3
Greenlaw *Aber.* **AB45** 98 E5
Greenlaw *Sc.Bord.* **TD10** 77 F6
Greenloaning **FK15** 81 K7
Greenmeadow **NP44** 19 F2
Greenmoor Hill **RG8** 21 K3
Greenmount **BL8** 49 G1
Greenmyre **AB53** 91 G1
Greenock PA16 74 **A3**
Greenodd **LA12** 55 G1
Greens Norton **NN12** 31 H4
Greenscares **FK15** 81 J6
Greenside *T. & W.* **NE40** 71 G7
Greenside *W.Yorks.* **HD5** 50 D1
Greenstead **CO4** 34 E6
Greenstead Green **CO9** 34 C6
Greensted **CM5** 23 J1
Greensted Green **CM5** 23 J1
Greenway *Pembs.* **SA66** 16 D2
Greenway *Som.* **TA3** 8 C2
Greenwell **CA8** 61 G1
Greenwich **SE10** 23 G4
Greet **GL54** 30 B5
Greete **SY8** 28 E1
Greetham *Lincs.* **LN9** 53 G5
Greetham *Rut.* **LE15** 42 C4
Greetland **HX4** 57 F7
Gregson Lane **PR5** 55 J7
Greinetobht (Grenitote) **HS6** 92 D4
Greinton **TA7** 8 D1
Grenaby **IM9** 54 B6
Grendon *Northants.* **NN7** 32 B2
Grendon *Warks.* **CV9** 40 E6
Grendon Common **CV9** 40 E6
Grendon Green **HR6** 28 E3
Grendon Underwood **HP18** 31 H6
Grenitote (Greinetobht) **HS6** 92 D4
Grenofen **PL19** 4 E3
Grenoside **S35** 51 F3
Greosabhagh **HS3** 93 G2
Gresford **LL12** 48 C7
Gresham **NR11** 45 F2
Greshornish **IV51** 93 J6
Gress (Griais) **HS2** 101 G3
Gressenhall **NR20** 44 D4
Gressingham **LA2** 55 J3
Greta Bridge **DL12** 62 B5
Gretna DG16 69 **J7**
Gretna Green **DG16** 69 J7
Gretton *Glos.* **GL54** 30 B5
Gretton *Northants.* **NN17** 42 C6
Gretton *Shrop.* **SY6** 38 E6
Grewelthorpe **HG4** 57 H2
Greygarth **HG4** 57 G2
Greylake **TA7** 8 C1
Greys Green **RG9** 22 A3
Greysouthen **CA13** 60 B4
Greystead **NE48** 70 C5
Greystoke **CA11** 60 F3
Greystone *Aber.* **AB35** 89 K5
Greystone *Angus* **DD11** 83 G3
Greystone *Lancs.* **BB9** 56 D5
Greystones **S11** 51 F4
Greywell **RG29** 22 A6
Griais (Gress) **HS2** 101 G3
Gribthorpe **DN14** 58 D6
Gribton **DG2** 68 E5
Griff **CV10** 41 F7
Griffithstown **NP4** 19 F2
Grigadale **PH36** 79 F1
Grigghall **LA8** 61 F7
Grimeford Village **PR6** 49 F1
Grimesthorpe **S4** 51 F3
Grimethorpe **S72** 51 G2
Griminis (Griminish) **HS7** 92 C6
Griminish (Griminis) **HS7** 92 C6
Grimister **ZE2** 107 N3
Grimley **WR2** 29 H2
Grimmet **KA19** 67 H2
Grimness **KW17** 106 D8
Grimoldby **LN11** 53 G4
Grimpo **SY11** 38 C3
Grimsargh **PR2** 55 J6
Grimsay (Griomsaigh) **HS6** 92 D6
Grimsbury **OX16** 31 F4
Grimsby DN32 53 **F2**
Grimscote **NN12** 31 H3
Grimscott **EX23** 6 A5
Grimshader (Griomsiadar) **HS2** 101 G5
Grimsthorpe **PE10** 42 D3
Grimston *E.Riding* **HU11** 59 J6
Grimston *Leics.* **LE14** 41 J3
Grimston *Norf.* **PE32** 44 B3
Grimstone **DT2** 9 F5
Grimstone End **IP31** 34 D2
Grindale **YO16** 59 H2
Grindiscol **ZE2** 107 N9
Grindle **TF11** 39 G5
Grindleford **S32** 50 E5
Grindleton **BB7** 56 C5
Grindley **ST14** 40 C3
Grindley Brook **SY13** 38 E1
Grindlow **SK17** 50 D5
Grindon *Northumb.* **TD15** 77 H6
Grindon *Staffs.* **ST13** 50 C7
Grindon *Stock.* **TS21** 62 E4
Grindon *T. & W.* **SR4** 62 E1
Gringley on the Hill **DN10** 51 K3
Grinsdale **CA5** 60 E1
Grinshill **SY4** 38 E3
Grinton **DL11** 62 B7
Griomarstaidh **HS2** 100 E4
Griomsaigh (Grimsay) **HS6** 92 D6
Griomsiadar (Grimshader) **HS2** 101 G5
Grisdale **LA10** 61 J7
Grishipoll **PA78** 78 C2
Gristhorpe **YO14** 59 G1
Griston **IP25** 44 D6
Gritley **KW17** 106 E7
Grittenham **SN15** 20 D3
Grittleton **SN14** 20 B4
Grizebeck **LA17** 55 F1
Grizedale **LA22** 60 E7
Grobister **KW17** 106 F5
Groby **LE6** 41 H5
Groes **LL16** 47 J6
Groes-faen **CF72** 18 D3
Groesffordd **LL53** 36 B2
Groesffordd Marli **LL22** 47 J5
Groeslon *Gwyn.* **LL54** 46 C7
Groeslon *Gwyn.* **LL55** 46 D6
Groes-lwyd **SY21** 38 B4
Groes-wen **CF15** 18 E3
Grogport **PA28** 73 G6
Groigearraidh **HS8** 84 C1
Gromford **IP17** 35 H3
Gronant **LL19** 47 J4
Groombridge **TN3** 13 J3
Grosmont *Mon.* **NP7** 28 D6
Grosmont *N.Yorks.* **YO22** 63 K6
Grotaig **IV63** 88 B2
Groton **CO10** 34 D4
Groundistone Heights **TD9** 69 K2
Grouville **JE3** 3 K7
Grove *Bucks.* **LU7** 32 C6
Grove *Dorset* **DT5** 9 F7
Grove *Kent* **CT3** 25 J5
Grove *Notts.* **DN22** 51 K5
Grove *Oxon.* **OX12** 21 H2
Grove End **ME9** 24 E5
Grove Green **ME14** 14 C2
Grove Park **SE12** 23 H4
Grove Town **WF8** 57 K7
Grovehill **HP2** 22 D1
Grovesend *S.Glos.* **BS35** 19 K3
Grovesend *Swan.* **SA4** 17 J5
Gruids **IV27** 96 C1
Grula **IV47** 85 J2
Gruline **PA71** 79 G3
Grumbla **TR20** 2 B6
Grundcruie **PH1** 82 B5
Grundisburgh **IP13** 35 G3
Gruting **ZE2** 107 L8
Grutness **ZE3** 107 N11
Gualachulain **PH49** 80 C3
Guardbridge **KY16** 83 F6
Guarlford **WR13** 29 H4
Guay **PH9** 82 B3
Gubbergill **CA19** 60 B7
Gubblecote **HP23** 32 C7
GUERNSEY GY 3 **J5**
Guernsey Airport **GY8** 3 H5
Guestling Green **TN35** 14 D6
Guestling Thorn **TN35** 14 D6
Guestwick **NR20** 44 E3
Guestwick Green **NR20** 44 E3
Guide **BB1** 56 C7
Guide Post **NE62** 71 H5
Guilden Down **SY7** 38 C7
Guilden Morden **SG8** 33 F4
Guilden Sutton **CH3** 48 D6
GUILDFORD GU 22 **C7**
Guildtown **PH2** 82 C4
Guilsborough **NN6** 31 H1
Guilsfield (Cegidfa) **SY21** 38 B4
Guilthwaite **S60** 51 G4
Guisborough TS14 63 **H5**
Guiseley **LS20** 57 G5
Guist **NR20** 44 E3
Guith **KW17** 106 E4
Guiting Power **GL54** 30 B6
Gulberwick **ZE2** 107 N9
Gullane EH31 76 **C2**
Gulval **TR18** 2 B5
Gulworthy **PL19** 4 E3
Gumfreston **SA70** 16 E5
Gumley **LE16** 41 J6
Gunby *Lincs.* **NG33** 42 C3
Gunby *Lincs.* **PE23** 53 H6
Gundleton **SO24** 11 H1
Gunn **EX32** 6 E2
Gunnersbury **W4** 22 E4
Gunnerside **DL11** 62 A7
Gunnerton **NE48** 70 E6
Gunness **DN15** 52 B1
Gunnislake PL18 4 **E3**
Gunnista **ZE2** 107 P8
Gunnister **ZE2** 107 M5
Gunstone **WV8** 40 A5
Gunter's Bridge **GU28** 12 C4
Gunthorpe *Norf.* **NR24** 44 E2
Gunthorpe *Notts.* **NG14** 41 J1
Gunthorpe *Rut.* **LE15** 42 B5
Gunville **PO30** 11 F6
Gunwalloe **TR12** 2 D6
Gupworthy **TA24** 7 H2
Gurnard **PO31** 11 F5
Gurnett **SK11** 49 J5
Gurney Slade **BA3** 19 K7
Gurnos *M.Tyd.* **CF47** 18 D1
Gurnos *Powys* **SA9** 18 A1
Gushmere **ME13** 15 F2
Gussage All Saints **BH21** 10 B3
Gussage St. Andrew **DT11** 9 J3
Gussage St. Michael **BH21** 9 J3
Guston **CT15** 15 J3
Gutcher **ZE2** 107 P3
Guthram Gowt **PE11** 42 E3
Guthrie **DD8** 83 G2
Guyhirn **PE13** 43 G5
Guynd **DD11** 83 G3
Guy's Head **PE12** 43 H3
Guy's Marsh **SP7** 9 H2
Guyzance **NE65** 71 H3
Gwaelod-y-garth **CF15** 18 E3
Gwaenysgor **LL18** 47 J4
Gwaithla **HR5** 28 B3
Gwalchmai **LL65** 46 B5
Gwastad **SA63** 16 D3
Gwastadnant **LL55** 46 E7
Gwaun-Cae-Gurwen **SA18** 27 G7
Gwaynynog **LL16** 47 J6
Gwbert **SA43** 16 E1
Gweek **TR12** 2 E6
Gwehelog **NP15** 19 G1
Gwenddwr **LD2** 27 K4
Gwendreath **TR12** 2 E7
Gwennap **TR16** 2 E4
Gwenter **TR12** 2 E7
Gwernaffield **CH7** 48 B6
Gwernesney **NP15** 19 H1
Gwernogle **SA32** 17 J2
Gwernymynydd **CH7** 48 B6
Gwern-y-Steeple **CF5** 18 D4
Gwersyllt **LL11** 48 C7
Gwespyr **CH8** 47 K4
Gwinear **TR27** 2 C5
Gwithian **TR27** 2 C4
Gwredog **LL71** 46 C4
Gwrhay **NP12** 18 E2
Gwyddelwern **LL21** 37 K1
Gwyddgrug **SA39** 17 H2
Gwynfryn **LL11** 48 B7
Gwystre **LD1** 27 K2
Gwytherin **LL22** 47 G6
Gyfelia **LL13** 38 C1
Gyre **KW17** 106 C7
Gyrn Goch **LL54** 36 C1

H

Habberley **SY5** 38 C5
Habin **GU31** 12 B4
Habrough **DN40** 52 E1
Haccombe **TQ12** 5 J3
Hacconby **PE10** 42 E3
Haceby **NG34** 42 D2
Hacheston **IP13** 35 H3
Hackbridge **SM6** 23 F5
Hackenthorpe **S12** 51 G4
Hackford **NR18** 44 E5
Hackforth **DL8** 62 D7
Hackland **KW17** 106 C5
Hacklet (Haclait) **HS7** 92 D7
Hacklete (Tacleit) **HS2** 100 D4
Hackleton **NN7** 32 B3
Hacklinge **CT14** 15 J2
Hackness *N.Yorks.* **YO13** 63 J3
Hackness *Ork.* **KW16** 106 C8
Hackney **E9** 23 G3
Hackthorn **LN2** 52 C4
Hackthorpe **CA10** 61 G4
Haclait (Hacklet) **HS7** 92 D7
Hacton **RM14** 23 J3
Hadden **TD5** 77 F7
Haddenham *Bucks.* **HP17** 22 A1
Haddenham *Cambs.* **CB6** 33 H1
Haddington *E.Loth.* EH41 76 **D3**
Haddington *Lincs.* **LN5** 52 C6
Haddiscoe **NR14** 45 J6
Haddon **PE7** 42 E6
Hade Edge **HD9** 50 D2
Hademore **WS14** 40 D5
Hadfield **SK13** 50 C3
Hadham Cross **SG10** 33 H7
Hadham Ford **SG11** 33 H6
Hadleigh *Essex* **SS7** 24 E3
Hadleigh *Suff.* **IP7** 34 E4
Hadleigh Heath **IP7** 34 D4
Hadley *Tel. & W.* **TF1** 39 F4
Hadley *Worcs.* **WR9** 29 H2
Hadley End **DE13** 40 D3
Hadley Wood **EN4** 23 F2
Hadlow **TN11** 23 K7
Hadlow Down **TN22** 13 J4
Hadnall **SY4** 38 E3
Hadspen **BA7** 9 F1
Hadstock **CB21** 33 J4
Hadston **NE65** 71 H4
Hadzor **WR9** 29 J2
Haffenden Quarter **TN27** 14 D3
Hafod Bridge **SA19** 17 K2
Hafod-Dinbych **LL24** 47 G7
Hafodunos **LL22** 47 G6
Hafodyrynys **NP11** 19 F2
Haggate **BB10** 56 D6
Haggbeck **CA6** 69 K6
Haggersta **ZE2** 107 M8
Haggerston *Gt.Lon.* **E2** 23 G3
Haggerston *Northumb.* **TD15** 77 J6
Haggrister **ZE2** 107 M5
Haggs **FK4** 75 F3
Hagley *Here.* **HR1** 28 E4
Hagley *Worcs.* **DY9** 40 B7
Hagnaby *Lincs.* **PE23** 53 G6
Hagnaby *Lincs.* **LN13** 53 H5
Hague Bar **SK22** 49 J4
Hagworthingham **PE23** 53 G6
Haigh **WN2** 49 F2
Haighton Green **PR2** 55 J6
Hail Weston **PE19** 32 E2
Haile **CA22** 60 B6
Hailes **GL54** 30 B5
Hailey *Herts.* **SG13** 33 G7
Hailey *Oxon.* **OX10** 21 K3
Hailey *Oxon.* **OX29** 30 E7
Hailsham BN27 13 **J6**
Haimer **KW14** 105 G2
Hainault **IG6** 23 H2
Haine **CT12** 25 K5
Hainford **NR10** 45 G4
Hainton **LN8** 52 E4
Haisthorpe **YO25** 59 H3
Hakin **SA73** 16 B5
Halam **NG22** 51 J7
Halbeath **KY11** 75 K2
Halberton **EX16** 7 J4
Halcro **KW1** 105 H2
Hale *Cumb.* **LA7** 55 J2
Hale *Gt.Man.* **WA15** 49 G4
Hale *Halton* **L24** 48 D4
Hale *Hants.* **SP6** 10 C3
Hale *Surr.* **GU9** 22 B7
Hale Bank **WA8** 48 D4
Hale Barns **WA15** 49 G4
Hale Nook **PR3** 55 G5
Hale Street **TN12** 23 K7
Hales *Norf.* **NR14** 45 H6
Hales *Staffs.* **TF9** 39 G2
Hales Green **DE6** 40 D1
Hales Place **CT2** 15 G2
Halesgate **PE12** 43 G3
Halesowen B63 40 **B7**
Halesworth IP19 35 **H1**
Halewood **L26** 48 D4
Half Way Inn **EX5** 7 J6
Halford *Devon* **TQ12** 5 J3
Halford *Shrop.* **SY7** 38 D7
Halford *Warks.* **CV36** 30 D4
Halfpenny **LA8** 55 J1
Halfpenny Green **DY7** 40 A6
Halfway *Carmar.* **SA19** 17 K2
Halfway *Carmar.* **SA15** 17 J5
Halfway *Powys* **SA20** 27 H5
Halfway *S.Yorks.* **S20** 51 G4
Halfway *W.Berks.* **RG20** 21 H5
Halfway Bridge **GU28** 12 C4
Halfway House **SY5** 38 C4
Halfway Houses *Kent* **ME12** 25 F4
Halfway Houses *Lincs.* **LN6** 52 B6
Halghton Mill **LL13** 38 D1
HALIFAX HX 57 **F7**
Halistra **IV55** 93 H6
Halket **KA3** 74 C5
Halkirk KW12 105 **G3**
Halkyn **CH8** 48 B5
Hall **G78** 74 C5
Hall Cross **PR4** 55 H7
Hall Dunnerdale **LA20** 60 D7
Hall Green *Ches.E.* **ST7** 49 H7
Hall Green *Lancs.* **PR4** 55 H7
Hall Green *W.Mid.* **B28** 40 D7
Hall Grove **AL7** 33 F7
Hall of the Forest **SY7** 38 B7
Halland **BN8** 13 J5
Hallaton **LE16** 42 A6
Hallatrow **BS39** 19 K6
Hallbankgate **CA8** 61 G1
Hallen **BS10** 19 J3
Hallfield Gate **DE55** 51 F7
Hallglen **FK1** 75 G3
Hallin **IV55** 93 H6
Halling **ME2** 24 D5
Hallington *Lincs.* **LN11** 53 G4
Hallington *Northumb.* **NE19** 70 E6
Halliwell **BL1** 49 F1
Halloughton **NG25** 51 J7
Hallow **WR2** 29 H3
Hallow Heath **WR2** 29 H3
Hallrule **TD9** 70 A2
Halls **EH42** 76 E3
Halls Green *Essex* **CM19** 23 H1
Hall's Green *Herts.* **SG4** 33 F6
Hallsands **TQ7** 5 J7
Hallthwaites **LA18** 54 E1
Hallwood Green **GL18** 29 F5
Hallworthy **PL32** 4 B2
Hallyne **EH45** 75 K6
Halmer End **ST7** 39 G1
Halmond's Frome **WR6** 29 F4
Halmore **GL13** 19 K1
Halmyre Mains **EH46** 75 K6
Halnaker **PO18** 12 C6
Halsall **L39** 48 C1
Halse *Northants.* **NN13** 31 G4
Halse *Som.* **TA4** 7 K3
Halsetown **TR26** 2 C5
Halsham **HU12** 59 J7
Halsinger **EX33** 6 D2
Halstead *Essex* CO9 34 **C5**
Halstead *Kent* **TN14** 23 H5
Halstead *Leics.* **LE7** 42 A5
Halstock **BA22** 8 E4
Halsway **TA4** 7 K2
Haltemprice Farm **HU10** 59 G6
Haltham **LN9** 53 F6
Haltoft End **PE22** 43 G1
Halton *Bucks.* **HP22** 32 B7
Halton *Halton* **WA7** 48 E4
Halton *Lancs.* **LA2** 55 J3
Halton *Northumb.* **NE45** 70 E7
Halton *Wrex.* **LL14** 38 C2
Halton East **BD23** 57 F4
Halton Gill **BD23** 56 D2
Halton Green **LA2** 55 J3
Halton Holegate **PE23** 53 H6
Halton Lea Gate **CA8** 61 H1
Halton Park **LA2** 55 J3
Halton West **BD23** 56 D4
Haltwhistle NE49 70 **C7**
Halvergate **NR13** 45 J5
Halwell **TQ9** 5 H5
Halwill **EX21** 6 C6
Halwill Junction **EX21** 6 C6

Hill Row CB6 33 H1
Hill Side HD5 50 D1
Hill Street SO40 10 E3
Hill Top *Hants.* SO42 11 F4
Hill Top *S.Yorks.* DN12 51 G3
Hill Top *S.Yorks.* S6 50 E4
Hill View BH21 9 J5
Hill Wootton CV35 30 E2
Hillam LS25 58 B7
Hillbeck CA17 61 J5
Hillberry IM4 54 C6
Hillborough CT6 25 J5
Hillbrae *Aber.* AB54 98 E6
Hillbrae *Aber.* AB51 91 F2
Hillbrae *Aber.* AB51 91 G1
Hillbutts BH21 9 J4
Hillcliffiane DE56 40 E1
Hillend *Aber.* AB55 98 C6
Hillend *Fife* KY11 75 K2
Hillend *Midloth.* EH10 76 A4
Hillend *N.Lan.* ML6 75 G4
Hillend *Swan.* SA3 17 H6
Hillend Green GL18 29 G6
Hillersland GL16 28 E7
Hillesden MK18 31 H6
Hillesley GL12 20 A3
Hillfarrance TA4 7 K3
Hillfoot End SG5 32 E5
Hillhead *Devon* TQ5 5 K5
Hillhead *S.Ayr.* KA6 67 J1
Hillhead of Auchentumb
AB43 99 H5
Hillhead of Cocklaw AB42 99 J6
Hilliard's Cross WS13 40 D4
Hilliclay KW14 105 G2
Hillingdon UB10 22 D3
Hillington *Glas.* G52 74 D4
Hillington *Norf.* PE31 44 B3
Hillmorton CV21 31 G1
Hillockhead *Aber.* AB36 90 B4
Hillockhead *Aber.* AB33 90 C3
Hillowton DG7 65 H4
Hillpound SO32 11 G3
Hill's End MK17 32 C5
Hills Town S44 51 G6
Hillsborough S6 51 F3
Hillsford Bridge EX35 7 F1
Hillside *Aber.* AB12 91 H5
Hillside *Angus* DD10 83 J1
Hillside *Moray* IV30 97 J5
Hillside *Shet.* ZE2 107 N6
Hillside *Worcs.* WR6 29 G2
Hillswick ZE2 107 L5
Hillway PO35 11 H6
Hillwell ZE2 107 M11
Hillyfields SO16 10 E3
Hilmarton SN11 20 D4
Hilperton BA14 20 B6
Hilsea PO3 11 H4
Hilston HU11 59 J6
Hilton *Cambs.* PE28 33 F2
Hilton *Cumb.* CA16 61 J4
Hilton *Derbys.* DE65 40 E2
Hilton *Dorset* DT11 9 G4
Hilton *Dur.* DL2 62 C4
Hilton *High.* IV20 97 G3
Hilton *Shrop.* WV15 39 G6
Hilton *Staffs.* WS14 40 C5
Hilton *Stock.* TS15 63 F5
Hilton Croft AB41 91 H1
Hilton of Cadboll IV20 97 F4
Hilton of Delnies IV12 97 F6
Himbleton WR9 29 J3
Himley DY3 40 A6
Hincaster LA7 55 J1
Hinchley Wood KT10 22 E5
Hinckley LE10 41 G6
Hinderclay IP22 34 E1
Hinderton CH64 48 C5
Hinderwell TS13 63 J5
Hindford SY11 38 C2
Hindhead GU26 12 B3
Hindley *Gt.Man.* WN2 49 F2
Hindley *Northumb.* NE43 62 B1
Hindley Green WN2 49 F2
Hindlip WR3 29 H3
Hindolveston NR20 44 E3
Hindon *Som.* TA24 7 H1
Hindon *Wilts.* SP3 9 J1
Hindringham NR21 44 D2
Hingham NR9 44 E5
Hinksford DY3 40 A7
Hinstock TF9 39 F3
Hintlesham IP8 34 E4
Hinton *Glos.* GL13 19 K1
Hinton *Hants.* BH23 10 D5
Hinton *Here.* HR2 28 C5
Hinton *Northants.* NN11 31 G3
Hinton *S.Glos.* SN14 20 A4
Hinton *Shrop.* SY5 38 D5
Hinton Admiral BH23 10 D5
Hinton Ampner SO24 11 G2
Hinton Blewett BS39 19 J6
Hinton Charterhouse BA2 20 A6
Hinton Martell BH21 10 B4
Hinton on the Green WR11 30 B4
Hinton Parva *Dorset* BH21 9 J4
Hinton Parva *Swin.* SN4 21 F3
Hinton St. George TA17 8 D3
Hinton St. Mary DT10 9 G3
Hinton Waldrist SN7 21 G2
Hinton-in-the-Hedges
NN13 31 G5
Hints *Shrop.* SY8 29 F1
Hints *Staffs.* B78 40 D5
Hinwick NN29 32 C2
Hinxhill TN25 15 F3
Hinxton CB10 33 H4
Hinxworth SG7 33 F4
Hipperholme HX3 57 G7
Hipsburn NE66 71 H2
Hipswell DL9 62 C7
Hirn AB31 91 F4
Hirnant SY10 37 K3
Hirst NE63 71 H5
Hirst Courtney YO8 58 C7
Hirwaen LL15 47 K6
Hirwaun CF44 18 C1
Hiscott EX31 6 D3
Histon CB24 33 H2
Hitcham *Bucks.* SL1 22 C3
Hitcham *Suff.* IP7 34 D3
Hitchin SG5 32 E6
Hither Green SE13 23 G4
Hittisleigh EX6 7 F6
Hittisleigh Barton EX6 7 F6
Hive HU15 58 E6
Hixon ST18 40 C3
Hoaden CT3 15 H2
Hoaldalbert NP7 28 C6
Hoar Cross DE13 40 D3
Hoarwithy HR2 28 E6
Hoath CT3 25 J5
Hobarris SY7 28 C1
Hobbister KW17 106 C7
Hobbles Green CB8 34 B3
Hobbs Cross CM16 23 H2
Hobbs Lots Bridge PE15 43 G5
Hobkirk TD9 70 A2
Hobland Hall NR31 45 K5
Hobson NE16 62 C1
Hoby LE14 41 J4
Hockerill CM23 33 H6
Hockering NR20 44 E4
Hockerton NG25 51 K7
Hockley SS5 24 E2
Hockley Heath B94 30 C1
Hockliffe LU7 32 C6
Hockwold cum Wilton IP26 44 B7
Hockworthy TA21 7 J4
Hoddesdon EN11 23 G1
Hoddlesden BB3 56 C7
Hodgehill SK11 49 H6
Hodgeston SA71 16 D6
Hodnet TF9 39 F3
Hodnetheath TF9 39 F3
Hodsoll Street TN15 24 C5
Hodson SN4 20 E3
Hodthorpe S80 51 H5
Hoe NR20 44 D4
Hoe Gate PO7 11 H3
Hoff CA16 61 H5
Hoffleet Stow PE20 43 F2
Hoggard's Green IP29 34 C3
Hoggeston MK18 32 B6
Hoggie AB56 98 D5
Hoggrill's End B46 40 E6
Hogha Gearraidh HS6 92 C4
Hoghton PR5 56 B7
Hognaston DE6 50 E7
Hogsthorpe PE24 53 J5
Holbeach PE12 43 G3
Holbeach Bank PE12 43 G3
Holbeach Clough PE12 43 G3
Holbeach Drove PE12 43 G4
Holbeach Hurn PE12 43 G3
Holbeach St. Johns PE12 43 G4
Holbeach St. Marks PE12 43 G2
Holbeach St. Matthew
PE12 43 H2
Holbeck S80 51 H5
Holbeck Woodhouse S80 51 H5
Holberrow Green B96 30 B3
Holbeton PL8 5 G5
Holborough ME2 24 D5
Holbrook *Derbys.* DE56 41 F1
Holbrook *Suff.* IP9 35 F5
Holbrooks CV6 41 F7
Holburn TD15 77 J7
Holbury SO45 11 F4
Holcombe *Devon* EX7 5 K3
Holcombe *Gt.Man.* BL8 49 G1
Holcombe *Som.* BA3 19 K7
Holcombe Burnell Barton
EX6 7 G6
Holcombe Rogus TA21 7 J4
Holcot NN6 31 J2
Holden BB7 56 C5
Holden Gate OL14 56 D7
Holdenby NN6 31 H2
Holdenhurst BH8 10 C5
Holder's Green CM6 33 K6
Holders Hill NW4 23 F3
Holdgate TF13 38 E7
Holdingham NG34 42 D1
Holditch TA20 8 C4
Hole EX15 7 K4
Hole Park TN17 14 D4
Hole Street BN44 12 E5
Holehouse SK13 50 C3
Hole-in-the-Wall HR9 29 F6
Holford TA5 7 K1
Holgate YO26 58 B4
Holker LA11 55 G2
Holkham NR23 44 C1
Hollacombe *Devon* EX22 6 B5
Hollacombe *Devon* EX17 7 G5
Hollacombe Town EX18 6 E4
Holland *Ork.* KW17 106 D2
Holland *Ork.* KW17 106 F5
Holland *Surr.* RH8 23 H6
Holland Fen LN4 43 F1
Holland-on-Sea CO15 35 F7
Hollandstoun KW17 106 G2
Hollee DG11 69 H7
Hollesley IP12 35 H4
Hollicombe TQ2 5 K4
Hollingbourne ME17 14 D2
Hollingbury BN1 13 G6
Hollingrove TN32 13 K4
Hollington *Derbys.* DE6 40 E2
Hollington *E.Suss.* TN38 14 C6
Hollington *Staffs.* ST10 40 C2
Hollingworth SK14 50 C3
Hollins S42 51 F5
Hollins Green WA3 49 F3
Hollins Lane PR3 55 H4
Hollinsclough SK17 50 C6
Hollinwood *Gt.Man.* OL9 49 J2
Hollinwood *Shrop.* SY13 38 E2
Hollocombe EX18 6 E4
Hollow Meadows S6 50 E4
Holloway DE4 51 F7
Hollowell NN6 31 H1
Holly Bush LL13 38 D1
Holly End PE14 43 H5
Holly Green HP27 22 A1
Hollybush *Caerp.* NP12 18 E1
Hollybush *E.Ayr.* KA6 67 H2
Hollybush *Worcs.* HR8 29 G5
Hollyhurst SY13 38 E1
Hollym HU19 59 K7
Hollywater GU35 12 B3
Hollywood B47 30 B1
Holm *D. & G.* DG13 69 H4
Holm (Tolm) *W.Isles* HS2 101 G4
Holm of Drumlanrig DG3 68 D4
Holmbridge HD9 50 D2
Holmbury St. Mary RH5 22 E7
Holmbush RH12 13 F3
Holme *Cambs.* PE7 42 E7
Holme *Cumb.* LA6 55 J2
Holme *N.Lincs.* DN16 52 C2
Holme *N.Yorks.* YO7 57 J1
Holme *Notts.* NG23 52 B7
Holme *W.Yorks.* HD9 50 D2
Holme Chapel BB10 56 D7
Holme Hale IP25 44 C5
Holme Lacy HR2 28 E5
Holme Marsh HR5 28 C3
Holme next the Sea PE36 44 B1
Holme on the Wolds HU17 59 F5
Holme Pierrepont NG12 41 J2
Holme St. Cuthbert CA15 60 C2
Holme-on-Spalding-Moor
YO43 58 E6
Holmer HR1 28 E4
Holmer Green HP15 22 C2
Holmes PR4 48 D1
Holmes Chapel CW4 49 G6
Holme's Hill BN8 13 J5
Holmesfield S18 51 F5
Holmeswood L40 48 D1
Holmewood S42 51 G6
Holmfield HX2 57 F7
Holmfirth HD9 50 D2
Holmhead *D. & G.* DG7 68 C5
Holmhead *E.Ayr.* KA18 67 K1
Holmpton HU19 59 K7
Holmrook CA19 60 B6
Holmsgarth ZE1 107 N8
Holmside DH7 62 D2
Holmsleigh Green EX14 8 B4
Holmston KA7 67 H1
Holmwrangle CA4 61 G2
Holne TQ13 5 H4
Holnest DT9 9 F4
Holnicote TA24 7 H1
Holsworthy EX22 6 B5
Holsworthy Beacon EX22 6 B5
Holt *Dorset* BH21 10 B4
Holt *Norf.* NR25 44 E2
Holt *Wilts.* BA14 20 B5
Holt *Worcs.* WR6 29 H2
Holt *Wrex.* LL13 48 D7
Holt End *Hants.* GU34 11 H1
Holt End *Worcs.* B98 30 B2
Holt Fleet WR6 29 H2
Holt Heath *Dorset* BH21 10 B4
Holt Heath *Worcs.* WR6 29 H2
Holt Wood BH21 10 B4
Holtby YO19 58 C4
Holton *Oxon.* OX33 21 K1
Holton *Som.* BA9 9 F2
Holton *Suff.* IP19 35 J1
Holton cum Beckering LN8 52 E4
Holton Heath BH16 9 J5
Holton le Clay DN36 53 F2
Holton le Moor LN7 52 D3
Holton St. Mary CO7 34 E5
Holtspur HP9 22 C3
Holtye TN8 13 H3
Holtye Common TN8 13 H3
Holway TA1 8 B2
Holwell *Dorset* DT9 9 F3
Holwell *Herts.* SG5 32 E5
Holwell *Leics.* LE14 42 A3
Holwell *Oxon.* OX18 21 F1
Holwell *Som.* BA11 20 A7
Holwick DL12 62 A4
Holworth DT2 9 G6
Holy Cross DY9 29 J1
Holy Island *I.o.A.* LL65 46 A5
Holy Island *Northumb.*
TD15 77 K6
Holybourne GU34 22 A7
Holyfield EN9 23 G1
Holyhead (Caergybi) LL65 46 A4
Holymoorside S42 51 F6
Holyport SL6 22 B4
Holystone NE65 70 E3
Holytown ML1 75 F4
Holywell *Cambs.* PE27 33 G1
Holywell *Cornw.* TR8 2 E3
Holywell *Dorset* DT2 8 E4
Holywell *E.Suss.* BN20 13 K7
Holywell (Treffynnon)
***Flints.* CH8 47 K5**
Holywell *Northumb.* NE25 71 J6
Holywell Green HX4 50 C1
Holywell Lake TA21 7 K3
Holywell Row IP28 34 B1
Holywood DG2 68 E5
Hom Green HR9 28 E6
Homer TF13 39 F5
Homersfield IP20 45 G7
Homington SP5 10 C2
Homore (Tobha Mòr) HS8 84 C1
Honey Hill CT2 25 H5
Honey Street SN9 20 E5
Honey Tye CO6 34 D5
Honeyborough SA73 16 C5
Honeybourne WR11 30 C4
Honeychurch EX20 6 E5
Honicknowle PL5 4 E5
Honiley CV8 30 D1
Honing NR28 45 H3
Honingham NR9 45 F4
Honington *Lincs.* NG32 42 C1
Honington *Suff.* IP31 34 D1
Honington *Warks.* CV36 30 D4
Honiton EX14 7 K5
Honkley LL12 48 C7
Honley HD9 50 D1
Hoo *Med.* ME3 24 D4
Hoo *Suff.* IP13 35 G3
Hoo Green WA16 49 G4
Hoo Meavy PL20 5 F4
Hood Green S75 51 F2
Hood Hill S35 51 F3
Hooe *E.Suss.* TN33 13 K6
Hooe *Plym.* PL9 5 F5
Hooe Common TN33 13 K5
Hook *Cambs.* PE15 43 H6
Hook *E.Riding* DN14 58 D7
Hook *Gt.Lon.* KT9 22 E5
Hook *Hants.* RG27 22 A6
Hook *Hants.* SO31 11 G4
Hook *Pembs.* SA62 16 C4
Hook *Wilts.* SN4 20 D3
Hook Green *Kent* TN3 13 K3
Hook Green *Kent* DA13 24 C5
Hook Green *Kent* DA13 24 C4
Hook Green *Kent* DA2 23 J4
Hook Norton OX15 30 E5
Hook-a-Gate SY5 38 D5
Hooke DT8 8 E4
Hookgate TF9 39 G2
Hookway EX17 7 G6
Hookwood RH6 23 F7
Hoole CH3 48 D6
Hooley CR5 23 F6
Hoop NP25 19 J1
Hooton CH66 48 C5
Hooton Levitt S66 51 H3
Hooton Pagnell DN5 51 G2
Hooton Roberts S65 51 G3
Hop Pole PE11 42 E4
Hopcrofts Holt OX25 31 F6
Hope *Derbys.* S33 50 D4
Hope *Devon* TQ7 5 G7
Hope *Flints.* LL12 48 C7
Hope *Powys* SY21 38 B5
Hope *Shrop.* SY5 38 C5
Hope *Staffs.* DE6 50 D7
Hope Bagot SY8 28 E1
Hope Bowdler SY6 38 D6
Hope End Green CM22 33 J6
Hope Mansell HR9 29 F7
Hope under Dinmore HR6 28 E3
Hopehouse TD7 69 H2
Hopeman IV30 97 J5
Hope's Green SS7 24 D3
Hopesay SY7 38 C7
Hopkinstown CF37 18 D2
Hopley's Green HR3 28 C3
Hopperton HG5 57 K4
Hopsford CV7 41 G7
Hopstone WV5 39 G6
Hopton *Derbys.* DE4 50 E7
Hopton *Norf.* NR31 45 K6
Hopton *Shrop.* TF9 38 E3
Hopton *Shrop.* SY4 38 C3
Hopton *Staffs.* ST18 40 B3
Hopton *Suff.* IP22 34 D1
Hopton Cangeford SY8 38 E7
Hopton Castle SY7 28 C1
Hopton Wafers DY14 29 F1
Hoptonheath SY7 28 C1
Hopwas B78 40 D5
Hopwood B48 30 B1
Horam TN21 13 J5
Horbling NG34 42 E2
Horbury WF4 50 E1
Horden SR8 63 F2
Horderley SY7 38 D7
Hordle SO41 10 D5
Hordley SY12 38 C2
Horeb *Carmar.* SA15 17 H5
Horeb *Cere.* SA44 17 G1
Horeb *Flints.* LL12 48 B7
Horfield BS7 19 J4
Horham IP21 35 G1
Horkesley Heath CO6 34 D6
Horkstow DN18 52 C1
Horley *Oxon.* OX15 31 F4
Horley *Surr.* RH6 23 F7
Horn Hill SL9 22 D2
Hornblotton BA4 8 E1
Hornblotton Green BA4 8 E1
Hornby *Lancs.* LA2 55 J3
Hornby *N.Yorks.* DL8 62 D7
Hornby *N.Yorks.* DL6 62 E6
Horncastle LN9 53 F6
Hornchurch RM11 23 J3
Horncliffe TD15 77 H6
Horndean *Hants.* PO8 11 J3
Horndean *Sc.Bord.* TD15 77 H6
Horndon PL19 6 D7
Horndon on the Hill SS17 24 C3
Horne RH6 23 G7
Horne Row CM3 24 D1
Horner TA24 7 G1
Horniehaugh DD8 83 F1
Horning NR12 45 H4
Horninghold LE16 42 B6
Horninglow DE13 40 E3
Horningsea CB25 33 H2
Horningsham BA12 20 B7
Horningtoft NR20 44 D3
Horningtops PL14 4 C4
Horns Cross *Devon* EX39 6 B3
Horns Cross *E.Suss.* TN31 14 D5
Horns Green TN14 23 H6
Hornsbury TA20 8 C3
Hornsby CA8 61 G2
Hornsby Gate CA8 61 G1
Hornsea HU18 59 J5
Hornsey N8 23 G3
Hornton OX15 30 E4
Horrabridge PL20 5 F4
Horridge TQ13 5 H3
Horringer IP29 34 C2
Horrocks Fold BL1 49 G1
Horse Bridge ST9 49 J7
Horsebridge *Devon* PL19 4 E3
Horsebridge *Hants.* SO20 10 E1
Horsebrook ST19 40 A4
Horsecastle BS49 19 H5
Horsehay TF4 39 F5
Horseheath CB21 33 K4
Horsehouse DL8 57 F1
Horsell GU21 22 C6
Horseman's Green SY13 38 D1
Horsenden HP27 22 A1
Horseshoe Green TN8 23 H7
Horseway PE16 43 H7
Horsey NR29 45 J3
Horsey Corner NR29 45 J3
Horsford NR10 45 F4
Horsforth LS18 57 H6
Horsham *W.Suss.* RH12 12 E3
Horsham *Worcs.* WR6 29 G3
Horsham St. Faith NR10 45 G4
Horsington *Lincs.* LN10 52 E6
Horsington *Som.* BA8 9 G2
Horsington Marsh BA8 9 G2
Horsley *Derbys.* DE21 41 F1
Horsley *Glos.* GL6 20 B2
Horsley *Northumb.* NE15 71 F7
Horsley *Northumb.* NE19 70 D4
Horsley Cross CO11 35 F6
Horsley Woodhouse DE7 41 F1
Horsleycross Street CO11 35 F6
Horsleygate S18 51 F5
Horsleyhill TD9 70 A2
Horsmonden TN12 23 K7
Horspath OX33 21 J1
Horstead NR12 45 G4
Horsted Keynes RH17 13 G4
Horton *Bucks.* LU7 32 C7
Horton *Dorset* BH21 10 B4
Horton *Lancs.* BD23 56 D4
Horton *Northants.* NN7 32 B3
Horton *S.Glos.* BS37 20 A3
Horton *Shrop.* SY4 38 D3
Horton *Som.* TA19 8 C3
Horton *Staffs.* ST13 49 J7
Horton *Swan.* SA3 17 H7
Horton *Tel. & W.* TF6 39 F4
Horton *W. & M.* SL3 22 D4
Horton *Wilts.* SN10 20 D5
Horton Cross TA19 8 C3
Horton Grange NE13 71 H6
Horton Green SY14 38 D1
Horton Heath SO50 11 F3
Horton in Ribblesdale
BD24 56 D2
Horton Inn BH21 10 B4
Horton Kirby DA4 23 J5
Horton-cum-Studley OX33 31 H7
Horwich BL6 49 F1
Horwich End SK23 50 C4
Horwood EX39 6 D3
Hoscar L40 48 D1
Hose LE14 42 A3
Hoses LA20 60 D7
Hosh PH7 81 K5
Hosta HS6 92 C4
Hoswick ZE2 107 N10
Hotham YO43 58 E6
Hothfield TN26 14 E3
Hoton LE12 41 H3
Houbie ZE2 107 Q3
Houdston KA26 67 F4
Hough CW2 49 G7
Hough Green WA8 48 D4
Hougham NG32 42 B1
Hough-on-the-Hill NG32 42 C1
Houghton *Cambs.* PE28 33 F1
Houghton *Cumb.* CA3 60 F1
Houghton *Devon* TQ7 5 G6
Houghton *Hants.* SO20 10 E1
Houghton *Pembs.* SA73 16 C5
Houghton *W.Suss.* BN18 12 D5
Houghton Bank DL2 62 D4
Houghton Conquest MK45 32 D4
Houghton le Spring DH4 62 E2
Houghton on the Hill LE7 41 J5
Houghton Regis LU5 32 D6
Houghton St. Giles NR22 44 D2
Houghton-le-Side DL2 62 D4
Houlsyke YO21 63 J6
Hound SO31 11 F4
Hound Green RG27 22 A6
Houndslow TD3 76 E6
Houndsmoor TA4 7 K3
Houndwood TD14 77 G4
Hounsdown SO40 10 E3
Hounslow TW3 22 E4

Housebay KW17 106 F5
Househill IV12 97 F6
Houses Hill HD5 50 D1
Housetter ZE2 107 M4
Housham Tye CM17 33 J7
Houss ZE2 107 M9
Houston PA6 74 C4
Houstry KW6 105 G5
Houstry of Dunn KW1 105 H3
Houton KW17 106 C7
Hove BN3 13 F6
Hove Edge HD6 57 G7
Hoveringham NG14 41 J1
Hoveton NR12 45 H4
Hovingham YO62 58 C2
How CA8 61 G1
How Caple HR1 29 F5
How End MK45 32 D4
How Green TN8 23 H7
How Man CA22 60 A5
Howbrook S35 51 F3
Howden DN14 58 D7
Howden Clough WF17 57 H7
Howden-le-Wear DL15 62 C3
Howe *Cumb.* LA8 55 H1
Howe *High.* KW1 105 J2
Howe *N.Yorks.* YO7 57 J1
Howe *Norf.* NR15 45 G6
Howe Green CM2 24 D1
Howe of Teuchar AB53 99 F6
Howe Street *Essex* CM3 33 K7
Howe Street *Essex* CM7 33 K5
Howegreen CM3 24 E1
Howell NG34 42 E1
Howey LD1 27 K3
Howgate *Cumb.* CA28 60 A4
Howgate *Midloth.* EH26 76 A5
Howgill *Lancs.* BB7 56 D5
Howgill *N.Yorks.* BD23 57 F4
Howick NE66 71 H2
Howle TF10 39 F3
Howle Hill HR9 29 F6
Howlett End CB10 33 J5
Howley TA20 8 B4
Hownam TD5 70 C2
Hownam Mains TD5 70 C1
Howpasley TD9 69 J3
Howsham *N.Lincs.* LN7 52 D2
Howsham *N.Yorks.* YO60 58 D3
Howt Green ME9 24 E5
Howtel TD12 77 G7
Howton HR2 28 D6
Howwood PA9 74 C4
Hoxa KW17 106 D8
Hoxne IP21 35 F1
Hoy *High.* KW14 105 H2
Hoy *Ork.* KW16 106 B8
Hoylake CH47 48 B4
Hoyland S74 51 F2
Hoylandswaine S36 50 E2
Hoyle GU29 12 C5
Hubberholme BD23 56 E2
Hubberston SA73 16 B5
Hubbert's Bridge PE20 43 F1
Huby *N.Yorks.* YO61 58 B3
Huby *N.Yorks.* LS17 57 H5
Hucclecote GL3 29 H7
Hucking ME17 14 D2
Hucknall NG15 41 H1
HUDDERSFIELD HD 50 D1
Huddington WR9 29 J3
Huddlesford WS13 40 D5
Hudnall HP4 32 D7
Hudscott EX37 6 E3
Hudswell DL11 62 C7
Huggate YO42 58 E4
Hugglescote LE67 41 G4
Hugh Town TR21 2 C1
Hughenden Valley HP14 22 B2
Hughley SY5 38 E6
Hugmore LL13 48 C7
Hugus TR3 2 E4
Huish *Devon* EX20 6 D4
Huish *Wilts.* SN8 20 E5
Huish Champflower TA4 7 J3
Huish Episcopi TA10 8 D2
Huisinis HS3 100 B6
Hulcote MK17 32 C5
Hulcott HP22 32 B7
HULL HU 59 H7
Hulland DE6 40 E1
Hulland Ward DE6 40 E1
Hullavington SN14 20 B3
Hullbridge SS5 24 E2
Hulme ST3 40 B1
Hulme End SK17 50 D7
Hulme Walfield CW12 49 H6
Hulver Street NR34 45 J7
Hulverstone PO30 10 E6
Humber *Devon* TQ14 5 J3
Humber *Here.* HR6 28 E3
Humberside Airport DN39 52 D1
Humberston DN36 53 G2
Humberstone LE5 41 J5
Humberton YO61 57 K3
Humbie EH36 76 C4
Humbleton *Dur.* DL2 62 B5
Humbleton *E.Riding* HU11 59 J6
Humbleton *Northumb.* NE71 70 E1
Humby NG33 42 D2
Hume TD5 77 F6
Humehall TD5 77 F6
Hummer DT9 8 E3
Humshaugh NE46 70 E6
Huna KW1 105 J1
Huncoat BB5 56 C6
Huncote LE9 41 H6
Hundalee TD8 70 B2
Hundall S18 51 F5
Hunderthwaite DL12 62 A4
Hundleby PE23 53 G6
Hundleton SA71 16 C5
Hundon CO10 34 B4
Hundred Acres PO17 11 G3
Hundred End PR4 55 H7
Hundred House LD1 28 A3
Hungarton LE7 41 J5
Hungate End MK19 31 J4
Hungerford *Hants.* SP6 10 C3
Hungerford *Shrop.* SY7 38 E7
Hungerford *W.Berks.* RG17 21 G5
Hungerford Newtown RG17 21 G4
Hungerton NG32 42 B3
Hunglader IV51 93 J4
Hunmanby YO14 59 G2
Hunningham CV33 30 E2
Hunningham Hill CV33 30 E2
Hunny Hill PO30 11 F6
Hunsdon SG12 33 H7
Hunsingore LS22 57 K4
Hunslet LS10 57 J6
Hunsonby CA10 61 G3
Hunspow KW14 105 H1
Hunstanton PE36 44 A1
Hunstanworth DH8 62 A2
Hunston *Suff.* IP31 34 D2
Hunston *W.Suss.* PO20 12 B6
Hunsworth BD19 57 G7
Hunt End B97 30 B2
Hunt House YO22 63 K7
Huntercombe End RG9 21 K3
Hunters Forstal CT6 25 H5
Hunter's Inn EX31 6 E1
Hunter's Quay PA23 73 K3
Hunterston KA23 73 K5
Huntford TD8 70 B3
Huntham TA3 8 C2
Huntingdon PE29 33 F1
Huntingfield IP19 35 H1
Huntingford SP8 9 H1
Huntington *Here.* HR5 28 B3
Huntington *Here.* HR4 28 D4
Huntington *Staffs.* WS12 40 B4
Huntington *Tel. & W.* TF6 39 F5
Huntington *York* YO32 58 C4
Huntingtower PH1 82 B5
Huntley GL19 29 G7
Huntly AB54 90 D1
Huntlywood TD4 76 E6
Hunton *Hants.* SO21 21 H7
Hunton *Kent* ME15 14 C3
Hunton *N.Yorks.* DL8 62 C7
Hunton Bridge WD4 22 D1
Hunt's Cross L25 48 D4
Huntscott TA24 7 H1
Huntsham EX16 7 J3
Huntshaw EX38 6 D3
Huntshaw Cross EX31 6 D3
Huntshaw Water EX38 6 D3
Huntspill TA9 19 G7
Huntworth TA7 8 C1
Hunwick DL15 62 C3
Hunworth NR24 44 E2
Hurcott *Som.* TA11 8 E2
Hurcott *Som.* TA19 8 C3
Hurdley SY15 38 B6
Hurdsfield SK10 49 J5
Hurley *W. & M.* SL6 22 B3
Hurley *Warks.* CV9 40 E6
Hurley Bottom SL6 22 B3
Hurlford KA1 74 C7
Hurliness KW16 106 B9
Hurlston Green L40 48 C1
Hurn BH23 10 C5
Hursley SO21 11 F2
Hurst *N.Yorks.* DL11 62 B6
Hurst *W'ham* RG10 22 A4
Hurst Green *E.Suss.* TN19 14 C5
Hurst Green *Essex* CO7 34 E7
Hurst Green *Lancs.* BB7 56 B6
Hurst Green *Surr.* RH8 23 G6
Hurst Wickham BN6 13 F5
Hurstbourne Priors RG28 21 H7
Hurstbourne Tarrant SP11 21 G6
Hurstpierpoint BN6 13 F5
Hurstwood BB10 56 D6
Hurtmore GU7 22 C7
Hurworth-on-Tees DL2 62 E5
Hury DL12 62 A4
Husabost IV55 93 G6
Husbands Bosworth LE17 41 J7
Husborne Crawley MK43 32 C5
Husthwaite YO61 58 B2
Hutcherleigh TQ9 5 H5
Huthwaite NG17 51 G7
Huttoft LN13 53 J5
Hutton *Cumb.* CA11 60 F4
Hutton *Essex* CM13 24 C2
Hutton *Lancs.* PR4 55 H7
Hutton *N.Som.* BS24 19 G6
Hutton *Sc.Bord.* TD15 77 H5
Hutton Bonville DL7 62 E6
Hutton Buscel YO13 59 F1
Hutton Conyers HG4 57 J2
Hutton Cranswick YO25 59 G4
Hutton End CA11 60 F3
Hutton Hang DL8 57 G1
Hutton Henry TS27 63 F3
Hutton Magna DL11 62 C5
Hutton Mount CM13 24 C2
Hutton Mulgrave YO21 63 K6
Hutton Roof *Cumb.* LA6 55 J2
Hutton Roof *Cumb.* CA11 60 E3
Hutton Rudby TS15 63 F6
Hutton Sessay YO7 57 K2
Hutton Wandesley YO26 58 B4
Hutton-le-Hole YO62 63 J7
Huxham EX5 7 H6
Huxham Green BA4 8 E1
Huxley CH3 48 E6
Huxter *Shet.* ZE2 107 M7
Huxter *Shet.* ZE2 107 P6
Huyton L36 48 D3
Hwlffordd (Haverfordwest) SA61 16 C4
Hycemoor LA19 54 D1
Hyde *Glos.* GL6 20 B1
Hyde *Gt.Man.* SK14 49 J3
Hyde End *W'ham* RG7 22 A5
Hyde End *W.Berks.* RG7 21 J5
Hyde Heath HP6 22 C1
Hyde Lea ST18 40 B4
Hydestile GU8 22 C7
Hyndford Bridge ML11 75 H6
Hyndlee TD9 70 A3
Hynish PA77 78 A4
Hyssington SY15 38 C6
Hythe *Hants.* SO45 11 F4
Hythe *Kent* CT21 15 G4
Hythe End TW19 22 D4
Hythie AB42 99 J5
Hyton LA19 54 D1

I

Ianstown AB56 98 C4
Iarsiadar HS2 100 D4
Ibberton DT11 9 G4
Ible DE4 50 E7
Ibsley BH24 10 C4
Ibstock LE67 41 G4
Ibstone HP14 22 A2
Ibthorpe SP11 21 G6
Ibworth RG26 21 J6
Icelton BS22 19 G5
Ickburgh IP26 44 C6
Ickenham UB10 22 D3
Ickford HP18 21 K1
Ickham CT3 15 H2
Ickleford SG5 32 E5
Icklesham TN36 14 D6
Ickleton CB10 33 H4
Icklingham IP28 34 B1
Ickwell Green SG18 32 E4
Icomb GL54 30 D6
Idbury OX7 30 D6
Iddesleigh EX19 6 D5
Ide EX2 7 H6
Ide Hill TN14 23 H6
Ideford TQ13 5 J3
Iden TN31 14 E5
Iden Green *Kent* TN17 14 C4
Iden Green *Kent* TN17 14 D4
Idle BD10 57 G6
Idless TR4 3 F4
Idlicote CV36 30 D4
Idmiston SP4 10 C1
Idridgehay DE56 40 E1
Idridgehay Green DE56 40 E1
Idrigil IV51 93 J5
Idstone SN6 21 F3
Idvies DD8 83 G3
Iffley OX4 21 J1
Ifield RH11 13 F3
Ifieldwood RH11 13 F3
Ifold RH14 12 D3
Iford *Bourne.* BH7 10 C5
Iford *E.Suss.* BN7 13 H6
Ifton NP26 19 H3
Ifton Heath SY11 38 C2
Ightfield SY13 38 E2
Ightham TN15 23 J6
Iken IP12 35 J3
Ilam DE6 50 D7
Ilchester BA22 8 E2
Ilderton NE66 71 F1
ILFORD IG 23 H3
Ilfracombe EX34 6 D1
Ilkeston DE7 41 G1
Ilketshall St. Andrew NR34 45 H7
Ilketshall St. Lawrence NR34 45 H7
Ilketshall St. Margaret NR35 45 H7
Ilkley LS29 57 G5
Illey B62 40 B7
Illidge Green CW11 49 G6
Illington IP24 44 D7
Illingworth HX2 57 F7
Illogan TR16 2 D4
Illston on the Hill LE7 42 A6
Ilmer HP27 22 A1
Ilmington CV36 30 D4
Ilminster TA19 8 C3
Ilsington *Devon* TQ13 5 H3
Ilsington *Dorset* DT2 9 G5
Ilston SA2 17 J6
Ilton *N.Yorks.* HG4 57 G2
Ilton *Som.* TA19 8 C3
Imachar KA27 73 G6
Imber BA12 20 C7
Immeroin FK19 81 G6
Immingham DN40 52 E1
Immingham Dock DN40 53 F1
Impington CB24 33 H2
Ince CH2 48 D5
Ince Blundell L38 48 C2
Ince-in-Makerfield WN3 48 E2
Inch Kenneth PA68 79 F4
Inch of Arnhall DD9 90 E7
Inchbae Lodge IV23 96 B5
Inchbare DD9 83 H1
Inchberry IV32 98 B5
Inchbraoch DD10 83 J2
Inchgrundle DD9 90 C7
Inchindown IV18 96 D4
Inchinnan PA4 74 C4
Inchkinloch IV27 103 J4
Inchlaggan PH35 87 H4
Inchlumpie IV17 96 C4
Inchmarlo AB31 90 E5
Inchmarnock PA20 73 J5
Inchnabobart AB35 90 B6
Inchnacardoch Hotel PH32 87 K3
Inchnadamph IV27 102 E6
Inchock DD11 83 H3
Inchrory AB37 89 J4
Inchture PH14 82 D5
Inchvuilt IV4 87 J1
Inchyra PH2 82 C5
Indian Queens TR9 3 G3
Inerval PA42 72 B6
Ingatestone CM4 24 C2
Ingbirchworth S36 50 E2
Ingerthorpe HG3 57 H3
Ingestre ST18 40 B3
Ingham *Lincs.* LN1 52 C4
Ingham *Norf.* NR12 45 H3
Ingham *Suff.* IP31 34 C1
Ingham Corner NR12 45 H3
Ingleborough PE14 43 H4
Ingleby *Derbys.* DE73 41 F3
Ingleby *Lincs.* LN1 52 B5
Ingleby Arncliffe DL6 63 F6
Ingleby Barwick TS17 63 F5
Ingleby Cross DL6 63 F6
Ingleby Greenhow TS9 63 G6
Ingleigh Green EX19 6 E5
Inglesbatch BA2 20 A5
Inglesham SN6 21 F2
Ingleton *Dur.* DL2 62 C4
Ingleton *N.Yorks.* LA6 56 B2
Inglewhite PR3 55 J6
Ingliston EH28 75 K3
Ingmire Hall LA10 61 H7
Ingoe NE20 71 F6
Ingoldisthorpe PE31 44 A2
Ingoldmells PE25 53 J6
Ingoldsby NG33 42 D2
Ingon CV37 30 D3
Ingram NE66 71 F2
Ingrave CM13 24 C2
Ingrow BD21 57 F6
Ings LA8 60 F7
Ingst BS35 19 J3
Ingworth NR11 45 F3
Inhurst RG26 21 J5
Inistrynich PA33 80 C5
Injebreck IM4 54 C5
Inkberrow WR7 30 B3
Inkersall S43 51 G5
Inkersall Green S43 51 G5
Inkhorn AB41 91 H1
Inkpen RG17 21 G5
Inkstack KW14 105 H1
Inmarsh SN12 20 C5
Innellan PA23 73 K4
Innergellie KY10 83 G7
Innerhadden PH16 81 H2
Innerleithen EH44 76 B7
Innerleven KY8 82 E7
Innermessan DG9 64 A4
Innerwick *E.Loth.* EH42 77 F3
Innerwick *P. & K.* PH15 81 G3
Inninbeg PA34 79 H3
Innsworth GL3 29 H6
Insch AB52 90 E2
Insh PH21 89 F4
Inshore IV27 103 F2
Inskip PR4 55 H6
Instow EX39 6 C2
Intake DN2 51 H2
Intwood NR4 45 F5
Inver *Aber.* AB35 89 K5
Inver *Arg. & B.* PA38 80 A3
Inver *High.* IV20 97 F3
Inver *High.* KW6 105 G5
Inver *P. & K.* PH8 82 B3
Inver Mallie PH34 87 H6
Inverailort PH38 86 D6
Inveralligin IV22 94 E6
Inverallochy AB43 99 J4
Inveran IV27 96 C2
Inveraray PA32 80 B7
Inverardoch Mains FK15 81 J7
Inverardran FK20 80 E5
Inverarish IV40 86 B1
Inverarity DD8 83 F3
Inverarnan G83 80 E6
Inverasdale IV22 94 E3
Inverbain IV54 94 D6
Inverbeg G83 74 B1
Inverbervie DD10 91 G7
Inverbroom IV23 95 H3
Inverbrough IV13 89 F2
Invercassley IV27 96 B1
Inverchaolain PA23 73 J3
Invercharnan PH49 80 C3
Inverchorachan PA26 80 D6
Inverchoran IV6 95 J6
Invercreran PA38 80 B3
Inverdruie PH22 89 G3
Inverebrie AB41 91 H1
Invereen IV13 88 E1
Invererne IV36 97 H5
Inveresk EH21 76 B3
Inverey AB35 89 H6
Inverfarigaig IV2 88 C2
Invergarry PH35 87 K4
Invergelder AB35 89 K5
Invergeldie PH6 81 J5
Invergloy PH34 87 J6
Invergordon IV18 96 E5
Invergowrie DD2 82 E4
Inverguseran PH41 86 D4
Inverharroch Farm AB54 90 B1
Inverherive FK20 80 E5
Inverhope IV27 103 G2
Inverie PH41 86 D4
Inverinan PA35 80 A6
Inverinate IV40 87 F2
Inverkeilor DD11 83 H3
Inverkeithing KY11 75 K2
Inverkeithny AB54 98 E6
Inverkip PA16 74 A3
Inverkirkaig IV27 102 C7
Inverlael IV23 95 H3
Inverlauren G84 74 B2
Inverliever PA31 79 K7
Inverliver PA35 80 B4
Inverlochlarig FK19 81 F6
Inverlochy PA33 80 C5
Inverlussa PA60 72 E2
Invermay PH2 82 B6
Invermoriston IV63 88 B3
Invernaver KW14 104 C2
Inverneil PA30 73 G2
INVERNESS IV 96 D7
Inverness Airport IV2 96 E6
Invernettie AB42 99 K6
Invernoaden PA27 73 K1
Inveroran Hotel PA36 80 D3
Inverquharity DD8 83 F2
Inverquhomery AB42 99 J6
Inverroy PH31 87 J6
Inversanda PH33 80 A2
Invershiel IV40 87 F3
Invershore KW3 105 H5
Inversnaid Hotel FK8 80 E7
Invertrossachs FK17 81 G7
Inverugie AB42 99 K6
Inveruglas G83 80 E7
Inveruglass PH21 89 F4
Inverurie AB51 91 F2
Invervar PH15 81 H3
Invervegain PA23 73 J3
Invery House AB31 90 E5
Inverythan AB53 99 F6
Inwardleigh EX20 6 D6
Inworth CO5 34 C7
Iochdar HS8 92 C7
Iona PA76 78 D5
Iping GU29 12 B4
Ipplepen TQ12 5 J4
Ipsden OX10 21 K3
Ipstones ST10 40 C1
IPSWICH IP 35 F4
Irby CH61 48 B4
Irby Hill CH61 48 B4
Irby in the Marsh PE24 53 H6
Irby upon Humber DN37 52 E2
Irchester NN29 32 C2
Ireby *Cumb.* CA7 60 D3
Ireby *Lancs.* LA6 56 B2
Ireland *Ork.* KW16 106 C7
Ireland *Shet.* ZE2 107 M10
Ireland's Cross CW3 39 G1
Ireleth LA16 55 F2
Ireshopeburn DL13 61 K3
Irlam M44 49 G3
Irnham NG33 42 D3
Iron Acton BS37 19 K3
Iron Cross WR11 30 B3
Ironbridge TF8 39 F5
Irons Bottom RH2 23 F7
Ironside AB53 99 G5
Ironville NG16 51 G7
Irstead NR12 45 H3
Irthington CA6 69 K7
Irthlingborough NN9 32 C1
Irton YO12 59 G1
Irvine KA12 74 B7
Isauld KW14 104 E2
Isbister *Ork.* KW17 106 C6
Isbister *Ork.* KW17 106 B5
Isbister *Shet.* ZE2 107 P6
Isbister *Shet.* ZE2 107 M3
Isfield TN22 13 H5
Isham NN14 32 B1
Ishriff PA65 79 H4
Isington GU34 22 A7
Island of Stroma KW1 105 J1
Islawr-dref LL40 37 F4
Islay PA 72 A4
Islay Airport PA42 72 B5
Islay House PA44 72 B4
Isle Abbotts TA3 8 C2
Isle Brewers TA3 8 C2
Isle of Lewis (Eilean Leodhais) HS 101 F3
ISLE OF MAN IM 54 C5
Isle of Man Airport IM9 54 B7
Isle of May KY10 76 E1
Isle of Noss ZE2 107 P8
Isle of Sheppey ME12 25 F4
Isle of Walney LA14 54 E3
Isle of Whithorn DG8 64 E7
Isle of Wight PO 11 F6
Isleham CB7 33 K1
Isleornsay (Eilean Iarmain) IV43 86 C3
Isles of Scilly (Scilly Isles) TR 2 C1
Islesburgh ZE2 107 M6
Isleworth TW7 22 E4
Isley Walton DE74 41 G3
Islibhig HS2 100 B5
Islip *Northants.* NN14 32 C1
Islip *Oxon.* OX5 31 G7
Isombridge TF6 39 F4
Istead Rise DA13 24 C5
Itchen SO19 11 F3
Itchen Abbas SO21 11 G1
Itchen Stoke SO24 11 G1
Itchingfield RH13 12 E4
Itchington BS35 19 K3
Itteringham NR11 45 F2

Itton *Devon* EX20 6 E6
Itton *Mon.* NP16 19 H2
Itton Common NP16 19 H2
Ivegill CA4 60 F2
Ivelet DL11 62 A7
Iver SL0 22 D3
Iver Heath SL0 22 D3
Iveston DH8 62 C1
Ivetsey Bank ST19 40 A4
Ivinghoe LU7 32 C7
Ivinghoe Aston LU7 32 C7
Ivington HR6 28 D3
Ivington Green HR6 28 D3
Ivy Hatch TN15 23 J6
Ivy Todd PE37 44 C5
Ivybridge PL21 5 G5
Ivychurch TN29 15 F5
Iwade ME9 25 F5
Iwerne Courtney (Shroton) DT11 9 H3
Iwerne Minster DT11 9 H3
Ixworth IP31 34 D1
Ixworth Thorpe IP31 34 D1

J

Jack Hill LS21 57 G4
Jackfield TF8 39 F5
Jacksdale NG16 51 G7
Jackstown AB51 91 F1
Jackton G75 74 D5
Jacobstow EX23 4 B1
Jacobstowe EX20 6 D5
Jacobswell GU4 22 C6
Jameston SA70 16 D6
Jamestown *D. & G.* DG13 69 J4
Jamestown *High.* IV14 96 B6
Jamestown *W.Dun.* G83 74 B2
Janefield IV10 96 E6
Janetstown *High.* KW14 105 F2
Janetstown *High.* KW1 105 J3
Jarrow NE32 71 J7
Jarvis Brook TN6 13 J3
Jasper's Green CM7 34 B6
Jawcraig FK1 75 G3
Jayes Park RH5 22 E7
Jaywick CO15 35 F7
Jealott's Hill RG42 22 B4
Jeater Houses DL6 63 F7
Jedburgh TD8 70 B1
Jeffreyston SA68 16 D5
Jemimaville IV7 96 E5
Jericho BL9 49 H1
Jersey ML7 75 G4
JERSEY JE 3 J7
Jersey Airport JE3 3 J7
Jersey Marine SA1 18 A2
Jerviswood ML11 75 G6
Jesmond NE2 71 H7
Jevington BN26 13 J6
Jockey End HP2 32 D7
Jodrell Bank SK11 49 G5
John o' Groats KW1 105 J1
Johnby CA11 60 F3
John's Cross TN32 14 C5
Johnshaven DD10 83 J1
Johnson Street NR29 45 H4
Johnston SA62 16 C4
Johnston Mains AB30 91 F7
Johnstone PA5 74 C4
Johnstone Castle PA5 74 C4
Johnstonebridge DG11 69 F4
Johnstown *Carmar.* SA31 17 G4
Johnstown *Wrex.* LL14 38 C1
Joppa KA6 67 J2
Jordans HP9 22 C2
Jordanston SA62 16 C2
Jordanstone PH11 82 D3
Joy's Green GL17 29 F7
Jumpers Common BH23 10 C5
Juniper Hill NN13 31 G5
Jura PA60 72 D2
Jura House PA60 72 C4
Jurby East IM7 54 C4
Jurby West IM7 54 C4

K

Kaber CA17 61 J5
Kaimes EH17 76 A4
Kames *Arg. & B.* PA21 73 H3
Kames *Arg. & B.* PA34 79 K6
Kames *E.Ayr.* KA18 68 B1
Kea TR3 3 F4
Keadby DN17 52 B1
Keal Cotes PE23 53 G6
Kearsley BL4 49 G2
Kearstwick LA6 56 B2
Kearton DL11 62 B7
Kearvaig IV27 102 E1
Keasden LA2 56 C3
Kebholes AB45 98 E5
Keckwick WA4 48 E4
Keddington LN11 53 G4
Keddington Corner LN11 53 G4
Kedington CB9 34 B4
Kedleston DE22 40 E1
Keelby DN41 52 E1
Keele ST5 40 A1
Keeley Green MK43 32 D4
Keelham BD13 57 F6
Keeres Green CM6 33 J7
Keeston SA62 16 B4
Keevil BA14 20 C6
Kegworth DE74 41 G3
Kehelland TR14 2 D4
Keig AB33 90 E3
Keighley BD21 57 F5
Keil *Arg. & B.* PA28 66 A3
Keil *High.* PA38 80 A2
Keilhill AB45 99 F5
Keillmore PA31 72 E2
Keillor PH13 82 D3
Keillour PH1 82 A5
Keills PA46 72 C4
Keils PA60 72 D4
Keinton Mandeville TA11 8 E1
Keir House FK15 75 F1
Keir Mill DG3 68 D4
Keisby PE10 42 D3
Keisley CA16 61 J4
Keiss KW1 105 J2
Keith AB55 98 C5
Keithick PH13 82 D4
Keithmore AB55 90 B1
Keithock DD9 83 H1
Kelbrook BB18 56 E5
Kelby NG32 42 D1
Keld *Cumb.* CA10 61 G5
Keld *N.Yorks.* DL11 61 K6
Keldholme YO62 58 D1
Keldy Castle YO18 63 J7
Kelfield *N.Lincs.* DN9 52 B2
Kelfield *N.Yorks.* YO19 58 B6
Kelham NG23 51 K7
Kella IM7 54 C4
Kellacott PL15 6 C7
Kellan PA72 79 G3
Kellas *Angus* DD5 83 F4
Kellas *Moray* IV30 97 J6
Kellaton TQ7 5 H7
Kellaways SN15 20 C4
Kelleth CA10 61 H6
Kelleythorpe YO25 59 G4
Kelling NR25 44 E1
Kellington DN14 58 B7
Kelloe DH6 62 E3
Kelloholm DG4 68 C2
Kelly *Cornw.* PL27 4 A3
Kelly *Devon* PL16 6 B7
Kelly Bray PL17 4 D3
Kelmarsh NN6 31 J1
Kelmscott GL7 21 F2
Kelsale IP17 35 H2
Kelsall CW6 48 E6
Kelsay PA47 72 A5
Kelshall SG8 33 G5
Kelsick CA7 60 D1
Kelso TD5 77 F7
Kelstedge S45 51 F6
Kelstern LN11 53 F3
Kelston BA1 20 A5
Keltneyburn PH15 81 J3
Kelton DG1 65 K3
Kelton Hill (Rhonehouse) DG7 65 H5
Kelty KY4 75 K1
Kelvedon CO5 34 C7
Kelvedon Hatch CM15 23 J2
Kelvinside G12 74 D4
Kelynack TR19 2 A6
Kemacott EX31 6 E1
Kemback KY15 83 F6
Kemberton TF11 39 G5
Kemble GL7 20 C2
Kemerton GL20 29 J5
Kemeys Commander NP15 19 G1
Kemeys Inferior NP18 19 G2
Kemnay AB51 91 F3
Kemp Town BN2 13 G6
Kempe's Corner TN25 15 F3
Kempley GL18 29 F6
Kempley Green GL18 29 F6
Kemps Green B94 30 C1
Kempsey WR5 29 H4
Kempsford GL7 20 E2
Kempshott RG22 21 J7
Kempston MK42 32 D4
Kempston Hardwick MK45 32 D4
Kempston West End MK43 32 C4
Kempton SY7 38 C7
Kemsing TN15 23 J6
Kemsley ME10 25 F5
Kenardington TN26 14 E4
Kenchester HR4 28 D4
Kencot GL7 21 F1
Kendal LA9 61 G7
Kenderchurch HR2 28 D6
Kendleshire BS36 19 K4
Kenfig CF33 18 A3
Kenfig Hill CF33 18 B3
Kenidjack TR19 2 A5
Kenilworth CV8 30 D1
Kenknock *P. & K.* PH15 81 G3
Kenknock *Stir.* FK21 81 F4
Kenley *Gt.Lon.* CR8 23 G5
Kenley *Shrop.* SY5 38 E5
Kenmore *Arg. & B.* PA32 80 B7
Kenmore *High.* IV54 94 D6
Kenmore *P. & K.* PH15 81 J3
Kenmore *W.Isles* HS2 100 E7
Kenn *Devon* EX6 7 H7
Kenn *N.Som.* BS21 19 H5
Kennacley HS3 93 G2
Kennacraig PA29 73 G4
Kennards House PL15 4 C2
Kennavay HS4 93 H2
Kenneggy Downs TR20 2 C6
Kennerleigh EX17 7 G5
Kennerty AB31 90 E5
Kennet FK10 75 H1
Kennethmont AB54 90 D2
Kennett CB8 33 K2
Kennford EX6 7 H7
Kenninghall NR16 44 E7
Kennington *Kent* TN24 15 F3
Kennington *Oxon.* OX1 21 J1
Kennoway KY8 82 E7
Kenny TA19 8 C3
Kennyhill IP28 33 K1
Kennythorpe YO17 58 D3
Kenovay PA77 78 A3
Kensaleyre IV51 93 K6
Kensington W8 23 F3
Kenstone TF9 38 E3
Kensworth LU6 32 D7
Kent International Airport CT12 25 K5
Kent Street *E.Suss.* TN33 14 C6
Kent Street *Kent* ME18 23 K6
Kentallen PA38 80 B2
Kentchurch HR2 28 D6
Kentford CB8 34 B2
Kentisbeare EX15 7 J5
Kentisbury EX31 6 E1
Kentisbury Ford EX31 6 E1
Kentish Town NW5 23 F3
Kentmere LA8 61 F6
Kenton *Devon* EX6 7 H7
Kenton *Suff.* IP14 35 F2
Kenton *T. & W.* NE3 71 H7
Kenton Corner IP14 35 G2
Kentra PH36 79 H1
Kents Bank LA11 55 G2
Kent's Green GL18 29 G6
Kent's Oak SO51 10 E2
Kenwick SY12 38 D2
Kenwyn TR1 3 F4
Kenyon WA3 49 F3
Keoldale IV27 103 F2
Keose (Ceos) HS2 101 F5
Keppanach PH33 80 B1
Keppoch *Arg. & B.* G82 74 B3
Keppoch *High.* IV40 86 E2
Keprigan PA28 66 A2
Kepwick YO7 63 F7
Keresley CV6 41 F7
Kernborough TQ7 5 H6
Kerrera PA34 79 K5
Kerridge SK10 49 J5
Kerris TR19 2 B6
Kerry (Ceri) SY16 38 A6
Kerrycroy PA20 73 K4
Kerry's Gate HR2 28 C5
Kerrysdale IV21 94 E4
Kersall NG22 51 K6
Kersey IP7 34 E4
Kersey Vale IP7 34 E4
Kershopefoot TD9 69 K5
Kerswell EX15 7 J5
Kerswell Green WR5 29 H4
Kerthen Wood TR27 2 C5
Kesgrave IP5 35 G4
Kessingland NR33 45 K7
Kessingland Beach NR33 45 K7
Kestle PL26 3 G4
Kestle Mill TR8 3 F3
Keston BR2 23 H5
Keswick *Cumb.* CA12 60 D4
Keswick *Norf.* NR4 45 G5
Keswick *Norf.* NR12 45 H2
Ketley Bank TF2 39 F4
Ketsby LN11 53 G5
Kettering NN16 32 B1
Ketteringham NR18 45 F5
Kettins PH13 82 D4
Kettle Corner ME15 14 C2
Kettlebaston IP7 34 D3
Kettlebridge KY15 82 E7
Kettlebrook B77 40 E5
Kettleburgh IP13 35 G2
Kettlehill KY15 82 E7
Kettleholm DG11 69 G6
Kettleness YO21 63 K5
Kettleshulme SK23 49 J5
Kettlesing HG3 57 H4
Kettlesing Bottom HG3 57 H4
Kettlesing Head HG3 57 H4
Kettlestone NR21 44 D2
Kettlethorpe LN1 52 B5
Kettletoft KW17 106 F4
Kettlewell BD23 56 E2
Ketton PE9 42 C5
Kevingtown BR5 23 H5
Kew TW9 22 E4
Kewstoke BS22 19 G5
Kexbrough S75 51 F2
Kexby *Lincs.* DN21 52 B4
Kexby *York* YO41 58 D4
Key Green CW12 49 H6
Keyham LE7 41 J5
Keyhaven SO41 10 E5
Keyingham HU12 59 J7
Keymer BN6 13 G5
Keynsham BS31 19 K5
Key's Toft PE24 53 H7
Keysoe MK44 32 D2
Keysoe Row MK44 32 D2
Keyston PE28 32 D1
Keyworth NG12 41 J2
Kibblesworth NE11 62 D1
Kibworth Beauchamp LE8 41 J6
Kibworth Harcourt LE8 41 J6
Kidbrooke SE3 23 H4
Kiddemore Green ST19 40 A5
Kidderminster DY10 29 H1
Kiddington OX20 31 F6
Kidlington OX5 31 F7
Kidmore End RG4 21 K4
Kidnal SY14 38 D1
Kidsdale DG8 64 E7
Kidsgrove ST7 49 H7
Kidstones DL8 56 E1
Kidwelly (Cydweli) SA17 17 H5
Kiel Crofts PA37 79 K4
Kielder NE48 70 B4
Kilbarchan PA10 74 C4
Kilbeg IV44 86 C4
Kilberry PA29 73 F4
Kilbirnie KA25 74 B5
Kilblaan PA32 80 C6
Kilbraur KW9 104 D7
Kilbrennan PA73 79 F3
Kilbride *Arg. & B.* PA34 79 K5
Kilbride *Arg. & B.* PA20 73 J4
Kilbride *High.* IV49 86 B2
Kilbride Farm PA21 73 H4
Kilbridemore PA22 73 J1
Kilburn *Derbys.* DE56 41 F1
Kilburn *Gt.Lon.* NW6 23 F3
Kilburn *N.Yorks.* YO61 58 B2
Kilby LE18 41 J6
Kilchattan Bay PA20 73 K5
Kilchenzie PA28 66 A1
Kilcheran PA34 79 K4
Kilchiaran PA48 72 A4
Kilchoan *Arg. & B.* PA34 79 J6
Kilchoan *High.* PH36 79 F1
Kilchoman PA49 72 A4
Kilchrenan PA35 80 B5
Kilchrist PA28 66 A2
Kilconquhar KY9 83 F7
Kilcot GL18 29 F6
Kilcoy IV6 96 C6
Kilcreggan G84 74 A2
Kildale YO21 63 H6
Kildary IV18 96 E4
Kildavie PA28 66 B2
Kildermorie Lodge IV17 96 C4
Kildonan *N.Ayr.* KA27 66 E1
Kildonan (Cilldonnain) *W.Isles* HS8 84 C2
Kildonan Lodge KW8 104 E6
Kildonnan PH42 85 K6
Kildrochet House DG9 64 A5
Kildrummy AB33 90 C3
Kildwick BD20 57 F5
Kilfinan PA21 73 H3
Kilfinnan PH34 87 J5
Kilgetty SA68 16 E5
Kilgwrrwg Common NP16 19 H2
Kilham *E.Riding* YO25 59 G3
Kilham *Northumb.* TD12 77 G7
Kilkenneth PA77 78 A3
Kilkenny GL54 30 B7
Kilkerran *Arg. & B.* PA28 66 B2
Kilkerran *S.Ayr.* KA19 67 H3
Kilkhampton EX23 6 A4
Killamarsh S21 51 G4
Killay SA2 17 K6
Killbeg PA72 79 H3
Killean *Arg. & B.* PA29 72 E6
Killean *Arg. & B.* PA32 80 B7
Killearn G63 74 D2
Killellan PA28 66 A2
Killen IV9 96 D6
Killerby DL2 62 C4
Killerton EX5 7 H5
Killichonan PH17 81 G2
Killiechonate PH34 87 J6
Killiechronan PA72 79 G3
Killiecrankie PH16 82 A1
Killiehuntly PH21 88 E5
Killiemor PA72 79 F4
Killilan IV40 87 F1
Killimster KW1 105 J3
Killin *High.* KW9 97 F1
Killin *Stir.* FK21 81 G4
Killinallan PA44 72 B3
Killinghall HG3 57 H4
Killington *Cumb.* LA6 56 B1
Killington *Devon* EX31 6 E1
Killingworth NE12 71 H6
Killochyett TD1 76 C6
Killocraw PA28 72 E7
Killunaig PA70 79 F5
Killundine PA34 79 G3
Kilmacolm PA13 74 B4
Kilmaha PA35 80 A7
Kilmahog FK17 81 H7
Kilmalieu PH33 79 K2
Kilmaluag IV51 93 K4
Kilmany KY15 82 E5
Kilmarie IV49 86 B3
KILMARNOCK KA 74 C7
Kilmartin PA31 73 G1
Kilmaurs KA3 74 C6
Kilmelford PA34 79 K6
Kilmeny PA45 72 B4
Kilmersdon BA3 19 K6
Kilmeston SO24 11 G2
Kilmichael PA28 66 A1
Kilmichael Glassary PA31 73 G1
Kilmichael of Inverlussa PA31 73 F2
Kilmington *Devon* EX13 8 B5
Kilmington *Wilts.* BA12 9 G1
Kilmington Common BA12 9 G1
Kilmorack IV4 96 B7
Kilmore *Arg. & B.* PA34 79 K5
Kilmore *High.* IV44 86 C4
Kilmory *Arg. & B.* PA31 73 F2
Kilmory *Arg. & B.* PA31 73 F3
Kilmory *High.* PH43 85 J4
Kilmory *High.* PH36 86 B7
Kilmory *N.Ayr.* KA27 66 D1
Kilmote KW8 104 E7
Kilmuir *High.* IV55 93 H7
Kilmuir *High.* IV1 96 D7
Kilmuir *High.* IV18 96 E4
Kilmuir *High.* IV51 93 J4
Kilmun PA23 73 K2
Kilmux KY8 82 E7
Kiln Green *Here.* HR9 29 F7
Kiln Green *W'ham* RG10 22 B4
Kiln Pit Hill DH8 62 B1
Kilnave PA44 72 A3
Kilncadzow ML8 75 G6
Kilndown TN17 14 C4
Kilnhurst S64 51 G3
Kilninian PA74 79 F3
Kilninver PA34 79 K5
Kilnsea HU12 53 H1
Kilnsey BD23 56 E3
Kilnwick YO25 59 F5
Kilnwick Percy YO42 58 E4
Kiloran PA61 72 B1
Kilpatrick KA27 66 D1
Kilpeck HR2 28 D5
Kilphedir KW8 104 E7
Kilpin DN14 58 D7
Kilpin Pike DN14 58 D7
Kilrenny KY10 83 G7
Kilsby CV23 31 G1
Kilspindie PH2 82 D5
Kilstay DG9 64 B7
Kilsyth G65 75 F3
Kiltarlity IV4 96 C7
Kilton *Notts.* S81 51 H5
Kilton *R. & C.* TS13 63 H5
Kilton *Som.* TA5 7 K1
Kilton Thorpe TS12 63 H5
Kiltyrie FK21 81 H4
Kilvaxter IV51 93 J5
Kilve TA5 7 K1
Kilverstone IP24 44 C7
Kilvington NG13 42 B1
Kilwinning KA13 74 B6
Kimberley *Norf.* NR18 44 E5
Kimberley *Notts.* NG16 41 H1
Kimberworth S61 51 G3
Kimble Wick HP17 22 B1
Kimblesworth DH2 62 D2
Kimbolton *Cambs.* PE28 32 D2
Kimbolton *Here.* HR6 28 E2
Kimbridge SO51 10 E2
Kimcote LE17 41 H7
Kimmeridge BH20 9 J7
Kimmerston NE71 77 H7
Kimpton *Hants.* SP11 21 F7
Kimpton *Herts.* SG4 32 E7
Kinaldy KY16 83 G6
Kinblethmont DD11 83 H3
Kinbrace KW11 104 D5
Kinbreack PH34 87 G5
Kinbuck FK15 81 J7
Kincaldrum DD8 83 F3
Kincaple KY16 83 F6
Kincardine *Fife* FK10 75 H2
Kincardine *High.* IV24 96 D3
Kincardine O'Neil AB34 90 D5
Kinclaven PH1 82 C4
Kincorth AB12 91 H4
Kincraig *Aber.* AB41 91 H2
Kincraig *High.* PH21 89 F4
Kincraigie PH8 82 A3
Kindallachan PH9 82 A2
Kindrogan Field Centre PH10 82 B1
Kinellar AB21 91 G3
Kineton *Glos.* GL54 30 B6
Kineton *Warks.* CV35 30 E3
Kineton Green B92 40 D7
Kinfauns PH2 82 C5
King Sterndale SK17 50 C5
Kingarth PA20 73 J5
Kingcoed NP15 19 H1
Kingerby LN8 52 D3
Kingham OX7 30 D6
Kingholm Quay DG1 65 K3
Kinghorn KY3 76 A2
Kinglassie KY5 76 A1
Kingoodie DD2 82 E5
King's Acre HR4 28 D4
King's Bank TN31 14 D5
King's Bromley DE13 40 D4
Kings Caple HR1 28 E6
King's Cliffe PE8 42 D6
King's Coughton B49 30 B3
King's Green WR13 29 G5
King's Heath B14 40 C7
Kings Hill *Kent* ME19 23 K6
King's Hill *W.Mid.* WS10 40 B6
King's Hill *Warks.* CV3 30 E1
Kings Langley WD4 22 D1
King's Lynn PE30 44 A3
King's Meaburn CA10 61 H4
Kings Mills GY5 3 H5
King's Moss WA11 48 E2
Kings Muir EH45 76 A7
King's Newnham CV23 31 F1
King's Newton DE73 41 F3
King's Norton *Leics.* LE7 41 J5
King's Norton *W.Mid.* B30 30 B1
Kings Nympton EX37 6 E4
King's Pyon HR4 28 D3
Kings Ripton PE28 33 F1
King's Somborne SO20 10 E1
King's Stag DT10 9 G3
King's Stanley GL10 20 B1
King's Sutton OX17 31 F5
King's Tamerton PL5 4 E5
King's Walden SG4 32 E6
Kings Worthy SO23 11 F1
Kingsand PL10 4 E5
Kingsbarns KY16 83 G6
Kingsbridge *Devon* TQ7 5 H6
Kingsbridge *Som.* TA23 7 H2
Kingsburgh IV51 93 J6
Kingsbury *Gt.Lon.* HA3 22 E3
Kingsbury *Warks.* B78 40 E6
Kingsbury Episcopi TA12 8 D2
Kingscavil EH49 75 J3
Kingsclere RG20 21 J6
Kingscote GL8 20 B2
Kingscott EX38 6 D4
Kingscross KA27 66 E1
Kingsdale KY8 82 E7
Kingsdon TA11 8 E2
Kingsdown *Kent* CT14 15 J3

Kin - Lai

Kingsdown Swin. SN2 20 E3
Kingsdown Wilts. SN13 20 B5
Kingseat KY12 75 K1
Kingsey HP17 22 A1
Kingsfold Pembs. SA71 16 C6
Kingsfold W.Suss. RH12 12 E3
Kingsford Aber. AB53 99 F6
Kingsford Aber. AB33 90 D3
Kingsford Aberdeen AB15 91 G4
Kingsford E.Ayr. KA3 74 C6
Kingsford Worcs. DY11 40 A7
Kingsgate CT10 25 K4
Kingshall Street IP30 34 D2
Kingsheanton EX31 6 D2
Kingshouse FK19 81 G5
Kingshouse Hotel PH49 80 D2
Kingshurst B37 40 D7
Kingskerswell TQ12 5 J4
Kingskettle KY15 82 E7
Kingsland Here. HR6 28 D2
Kingsland I.o.A. LL65 46 A4
Kingsley Ches.W. & C. WA6 48 E5
Kingsley Hants. GU35 11 J1
Kingsley Staffs. ST10 40 C1
Kingsley Green GU27 12 B3
Kingsley Holt ST10 40 C1
Kingslow WV6 39 G6
Kingsmoor CM19 23 H1
Kingsmuir Angus DD8 83 F3
Kingsmuir Fife KY16 83 G7
Kingsnorth TN23 15 F4
Kingsnorth Power Station ME3 24 E4
Kingstanding B44 40 C6
Kingsteignton TQ12 5 J3
Kingsteps IV12 97 G6
Kingsthorne HR2 28 D5
Kingsthorpe NN2 31 J2
Kingston Cambs. CB23 33 G3
Kingston Cornw. PL17 4 D3
Kingston Devon TQ7 5 G6
Kingston Devon EX10 7 J7
Kingston Dorset DT10 9 G4
Kingston Dorset BH20 9 J7
Kingston E.Loth. EH39 76 D2
Kingston Gt.Man. SK14 49 J3
Kingston Hants. BH24 10 C4
Kingston I.o.W. PO38 11 F6
Kingston Kent CT4 15 G2
Kingston M.K. MK10 32 C5
Kingston Moray IV32 98 B4
Kingston W.Suss. BN16 12 D6
Kingston Bagpuize OX13 21 G2
Kingston Blount OX39 22 A2
Kingston by Sea BN43 13 F6
Kingston Deverill BA12 9 H1
Kingston Gorse BN16 12 D6
Kingston Lisle OX12 21 G3
Kingston Maurward DT2 9 G5
Kingston near Lewes BN7 13 G6
Kingston on Soar NG11 41 H3
Kingston Russell DT2 8 E5
Kingston St. Mary TA2 8 B2
Kingston Seymour BS21 19 H5
Kingston Stert OX39 22 A1
KINGSTON UPON HULL HU 59 H7
KINGSTON UPON THAMES KT 22 E5
Kingston Warren OX12 21 G3
Kingstone Here. HR2 28 D5
Kingstone Here. HR9 29 F6
Kingstone Som. TA19 8 C3
Kingstone Staffs. ST14 40 C3
Kingstone Winslow SN6 21 F3
Kingstown CA3 60 E1
Kingswear TQ6 5 J5
Kingswell KA3 74 D6
Kingswells AB15 91 G4
Kingswinford DY6 40 A7
Kingswood Bucks. HP18 31 H7
Kingswood Glos. GL12 20 A2
Kingswood Here. HR5 28 B3
Kingswood Kent ME17 14 D2
Kingswood Powys SY21 38 B5
Kingswood S.Glos. BS15 19 K4
Kingswood Som. TA4 7 K2
Kingswood Surr. KT20 23 F6
Kingswood Warks. B94 30 C1
Kingthorpe LN8 52 E5
Kington Here. HR5 28 B3
Kington Worcs. WR7 29 J3
Kington Langley SN15 20 C4
Kington Magna SP8 9 G2
Kington St. Michael SN14 20 C4
Kingussie PH21 88 E4
Kingweston TA11 8 E1
Kinharrachie AB41 91 H1
Kinharvie DG2 65 K4
Kinkell G66 74 E3
Kinkell Bridge PH3 82 A6
Kinknockie AB42 99 J6
Kinlet DY12 39 G7
Kinloch Fife KY15 82 D6
Kinloch High. IV27 103 F5
Kinloch High. PA34 79 H2
Kinloch High. PH43 85 K5
Kinloch High. IV16 96 C4
Kinloch P. & K. PH12 82 D3
Kinloch P. & K. PH10 82 C3
Kinloch Hourn PH35 87 F4
Kinloch Laggan PH20 88 C6
Kinloch Rannoch PH16 81 H2
Kinlochan PH37 79 K1
Kinlochard FK8 81 F7
Kinlocharkaig PH34 87 F5
Kinlochbeoraid PH38 86 E6
Kinlochbervie IV27 102 E3
Kinlocheil PH33 87 F7
Kinlochetive PH49 80 C3
Kinlochewe IV22 95 G5
Kinlochlaich PA38 80 A3
Kinlochleven PH50 80 C1
Kinlochmoidart PH38 86 D7
Kinlochmorar PH41 86 E5
Kinlochmore PH50 80 C1
Kinlochroag (Ceann Lochroag) HS2 100 D5
Kinlochspelve PA63 79 H5
Kinloss IV36 97 H5
Kinmel Bay (Bae Cinmel) LL18 47 H4
Kinmuck AB51 91 G3
Kinnaber DD10 83 J1
Kinnadie AB41 99 H6
Kinnaird PH14 82 D5
Kinneff DD10 91 G7
Kinnelhead DG10 69 F3
Kinnell Angus DD11 83 H2
Kinnell Stir. FK21 81 G4
Kinnerley SY10 38 C3
Kinnersley Here. HR3 28 C4
Kinnersley Worcs. WR8 29 H4
Kinnerton LD8 28 B2
Kinnerton Green CH4 48 C6
Kinnesswood KY13 82 C7
Kinnettles DD8 83 F3
Kinninvie DL12 62 B4
Kinnordy DD8 82 E2
Kinoulton NG12 41 J2
Kinrara PH22 89 F4
Kinross KY13 82 C7
Kinrossie PH2 82 C4
Kinsbourne Green AL5 32 E7
Kinsham Here. LD8 28 C2
Kinsham Worcs. GL20 29 J5
Kinsley WF9 51 G1
Kinson BH10 10 B5
Kintarvie HS2 100 E6
Kintbury RG17 21 G5
Kintessack IV36 97 G5
Kintillo PH2 82 C6
Kintocher AB33 90 D4
Kinton Here. SY7 28 D1
Kinton Shrop. SY4 38 C4
Kintore AB51 91 F3
Kintour PA42 72 C5
Kintra Arg. & B. PA42 72 B6
Kintra Arg. & B. PA66 78 E5
Kintradwell KW9 97 G1
Kintraw PA31 79 K7
Kinuachdrachd PA60 73 F1
Kinveachy PH24 89 G3
Kinver DY7 40 A7
Kinwarton B49 30 C3
Kiplaw Croft AB42 91 J1
Kipp FK18 81 G6
Kippax LS25 57 K6
Kippen P. & K. PH2 82 B6
Kippen Stir. FK8 74 E1
Kippenross House FK15 81 J7
Kippford (Scaur) DG5 65 J5
Kipping's Cross TN12 23 K7
Kippington TN13 23 J6
Kirbister Ork. KW17 106 C7
Kirbister Ork. KW17 106 F5
Kirbuster KW17 106 B5
Kirby Bedon NR14 45 G5
Kirby Bellars LE14 42 A4
Kirby Cane NR35 45 H6
Kirby Corner CV4 30 D1
Kirby Cross CO13 35 G6
Kirby Fields LE9 41 H5
Kirby Green NR35 45 H6
Kirby Grindalythe YO17 59 F3
Kirby Hill N.Yorks. DL11 62 C6
Kirby Hill N.Yorks. YO51 57 J3
Kirby Knowle YO7 57 K1
Kirby le Soken CO13 35 G6
Kirby Misperton YO17 58 D2
Kirby Muxloe LE9 41 H5
Kirby Row NR35 45 H6
Kirby Sigston DL6 63 F7
Kirby Underdale YO41 58 E4
Kirby Wiske YO7 57 J1
Kirdford RH14 12 D4
Kirk KW1 105 H3
Kirk Bramwith DN7 51 J1
Kirk Deighton LS22 57 J4
Kirk Ella HU10 59 G7
Kirk Hallam DE7 41 G1
Kirk Hammerton YO26 57 K4
Kirk Ireton DE6 50 E7
Kirk Langley DE6 40 E2
Kirk Merrington DL16 62 D3
Kirk Michael IM6 54 C4
Kirk of Shotts ML7 75 G4
Kirk Sandall DN3 51 J2
Kirk Smeaton WF8 51 H1
Kirk Yetholm TD5 70 D1
Kirkabister ZE2 107 N9
Kirkandrews DG6 65 G6
Kirkandrews-upon-Eden CA5 60 E1
Kirkbampton CA5 60 E1
Kirkbean DG2 65 K5
Kirkbride CA7 60 D1
Kirkbuddo DD8 83 G3
Kirkburn E.Riding YO25 59 F4
Kirkburn Sc.Bord. EH45 76 A7
Kirkburton HD8 50 D1
Kirkby Lincs. LN8 52 D3
Kirkby Mersey. L32 48 D3
Kirkby N.Yorks. TS9 63 G6
Kirkby Fleetham DL7 62 D7
Kirkby Green LN4 52 D7
Kirkby in Ashfield NG17 51 G7
Kirkby la Thorpe NG34 42 D1
Kirkby Lonsdale LA6 56 B2
Kirkby Malham BD23 56 D3
Kirkby Mallory LE9 41 G5
Kirkby Malzeard HG4 57 H2
Kirkby on Bain LN10 53 F6
Kirkby Overblow HG3 57 J5
Kirkby Stephen CA17 61 J6
Kirkby Thore CA10 61 H4
Kirkby Underwood PE10 42 D3
Kirkby Wharfe LS24 58 B5
Kirkby Woodhouse NG17 51 G7
Kirkby-in-Furness LA17 55 F1
Kirkbymoorside YO62 58 C1
KIRKCALDY KY 76 A1
Kirkcambeck CA8 70 A7
Kirkcolm DG9 64 A4
Kirkconnel DG4 68 C2
Kirkconnell DG2 65 K4
Kirkcowan DG8 64 D4
Kirkcudbright DG6 65 G5
Kirkdale House DG8 65 F5
Kirkdean EH46 75 K6
Kirkfieldbank ML11 75 G6
Kirkgunzeon DG2 65 J4
Kirkham Lancs. PR4 55 H6
Kirkham N.Yorks. YO60 58 D3
Kirkhamgate WF2 57 J7
Kirkharle NE19 71 F5
Kirkhaugh CA9 61 H2
Kirkheaton Northumb. NE19 71 F6
Kirkheaton W.Yorks. HD5 50 D1
Kirkhill Angus DD10 83 H1
Kirkhill High. IV5 96 C7
Kirkhill Moray AB38 98 B5
Kirkhope TD7 69 J1
Kirkibost High. IV49 86 B3
Kirkibost (Circebost) W.Isles HS2 100 D4
Kirkinch PH12 82 E3
Kirkinner DG8 64 E5
Kirkintilloch G66 74 E3
Kirkland Cumb. CA10 61 H3
Kirkland Cumb. CA26 60 B5
Kirkland D. & G. DG3 68 D4
Kirkland D. & G. DG4 68 C2
Kirkland D. & G. DG11 69 F5
Kirkland of Longcastle DG8 64 D6
Kirkleatham TS10 63 G4
Kirklevington TS15 63 F5
Kirkley NR33 45 K6
Kirklington N.Yorks. DL8 57 J1
Kirklington Notts. NG22 51 J7
Kirklinton CA6 69 K7
Kirkliston EH29 75 K3
Kirkmaiden DG9 64 B7
Kirkmichael P. & K. PH10 82 B1
Kirkmichael S.Ayr. KA19 67 H3
Kirkmuirhill ML11 75 F6
Kirknewton Northumb. NE71 77 H7
Kirknewton W.Loth. EH27 75 K4
Kirkney AB54 90 D1
Kirkoswald Cumb. CA10 61 G2
Kirkoswald S.Ayr. KA19 67 G3
Kirkpatrick Durham DG7 65 H3
Kirkpatrick-Fleming DG11 69 H6
Kirksanton LA18 54 E1
Kirkstall LS5 57 H6
Kirkstead LN10 52 E6
Kirkstile Aber. AB54 90 D1
Kirkstile D. & G. DG13 69 J4
Kirkstyle KW1 105 J1
Kirkthorpe WF1 57 J7
Kirkton Aber. AB52 90 E2
Kirkton Aber. AB53 98 E5
Kirkton Aber. AB33 90 E3
Kirkton Angus DD8 83 F3
Kirkton Arg. & B. PA31 79 J7
Kirkton D. & G. DG1 68 E5
Kirkton Fife DD6 82 E5
Kirkton High. IV3 88 D1
Kirkton High. KW10 96 E2
Kirkton High. IV2 96 E6
Kirkton High. KW13 104 D2
Kirkton High. IV40 86 E2
Kirkton P. & K. PH3 82 A6
Kirkton Sc.Bord. TD9 70 A2
Kirkton Manor EH45 76 A7
Kirkton of Airlie DD8 82 E2
Kirkton of Auchterhouse DD3 82 E4
Kirkton of Barevan IV12 97 F7
Kirkton of Bourtie AB51 91 G2
Kirkton of Collace PH2 82 C4
Kirkton of Craig DD10 83 J2
Kirkton of Culsalmond AB52 90 E1
Kirkton of Durris AB31 91 F5
Kirkton of Glenbuchat AB36 90 B3
Kirkton of Glenisla PH11 82 D1
Kirkton of Kingoldrum DD8 82 E2
Kirkton of Lethendy PH2 82 C3
Kirkton of Logie Buchan AB41 91 H2
Kirkton of Maryculter AB12 91 G5
Kirkton of Menmuir DD9 83 G1
Kirkton of Monikie DD5 83 G4
Kirkton of Rayne AB51 90 E1
Kirkton of Skene AB32 91 G4
Kirkton of Tealing DD4 83 F4
Kirktonhill Aber. AB30 83 H1
Kirktonhill W.Dun. G82 74 B3
Kirktown AB42 99 J5
Kirktown of Alvah AB45 98 E4
Kirktown of Auchterless AB53 99 F6
Kirktown of Deskford AB56 98 D4
Kirktown of Fetteresso AB39 91 G6
Kirktown of Slains AB41 91 J2
KIRKWALL KW 106 D6
Kirkwall Airport KW15 106 D7
Kirkwhelpington NE19 70 E5
Kirmington DN39 52 E1
Kirmond le Mire LN8 52 E3
Kirn PA23 73 K3
Kirriemuir DD8 82 E2
Kirstead Green NR15 45 G6
Kirtlebridge DG11 69 H6
Kirtleton DG11 69 H5
Kirtling CB8 33 K3
Kirtling Green CB8 33 K3
Kirtlington OX5 31 G7
Kirtomy KW14 104 C2
Kirton Lincs. PE20 43 G2
Kirton Notts. NG22 51 J6
Kirton Suff. IP10 35 G5
Kirton End PE20 43 F1
Kirton Holme PE20 43 F1
Kirton in Lindsey DN21 52 C3
Kiscadale KA27 66 E1
Kislingbury NN7 31 H3
Kismeldon Bridge EX22 6 B4
Kites Hardwick CV23 31 F2
Kitley PL8 5 F5
Kittisford TA21 7 J3
Kittisford Barton TA21 7 J3
Kittle SA3 17 J7
Kitt's End EN5 23 F2
Kitt's Green B33 40 D7
Kitwood SO24 11 H1
Kivernoll HR2 28 D5
Kiveton Park S26 51 G4
Klibreck IV27 103 H5
Knabbygates AB54 98 D5
Knaith DN21 52 B4
Knaith Park DN21 52 B4
Knap Corner SP8 9 H2
Knaphill GU21 22 C6
Knaplock TA22 7 G2
Knapp P. & K. PH14 82 D4
Knapp Som. TA3 8 C2
Knapthorpe NG23 51 K7
Knaptoft LE17 41 J7
Knapton Norf. NR28 45 H2
Knapton York YO26 58 B4
Knapton Green HR4 28 D3
Knapwell CB23 33 G2
Knaresborough HG5 57 J4
Knarsdale CA8 61 H1
Knarston KW17 106 C5
Knaven AB42 99 G6
Knayton YO7 57 K1
Knebworth SG3 33 F6
Knedlington DN14 58 D7
Kneesall NG22 51 K6
Kneesworth SG8 33 G4
Kneeton NG13 42 A1
Knelston SA3 17 H7
Knenhall ST15 40 B2
Knettishall IP22 44 D7
Knightacott EX31 6 E2
Knightcote CV47 31 F3
Knightley ST20 40 A3
Knightley Dale ST20 40 A3
Knighton Devon PL9 5 F6
Knighton Dorset DT9 9 F3
Knighton Leic. LE2 41 J5
Knighton Poole BH21 10 B5
Knighton (Tref-y-clawdd) Powys LD7 28 B1
Knighton Som. TA5 7 K1
Knighton Staffs. ST20 39 G3
Knighton Staffs. TF9 39 G1
Knighton Wilts. SN8 21 F4
Knighton on Teme WR15 29 F1
Knightswood G15 74 D4
Knightwick WR6 29 G3
Knill LD8 28 B2
Knipoch PA34 79 K5
Knipton NG32 42 B2
Knitsley DH8 62 C2
Kniveton DE6 50 E7
Knock Arg. & B. PA71 79 G4
Knock Cumb. CA16 61 H4
Knock High. IV44 86 C4
Knock Moray AB54 98 D5
Knock of Auchnahannet PH26 89 H1
Knockalava PA31 73 H1
Knockally KW6 105 G6
Knockaloe Moar IM5 54 B5
Knockan IV27 102 E7
Knockandhu AB37 89 K2
Knockando AB38 97 J7
Knockarthur IV28 96 E1
Knockbain IV8 96 D6
Knockban IV23 95 J5
Knockbreck IV19 96 E3
Knockbrex DG6 65 F6
Knockdamph IV26 95 J2
Knockdee KW12 105 G2
Knockdow PA23 73 K3
Knockdown GL8 20 B3
Knockenkelly KA27 66 E1
Knockentiber KA2 74 B7
Knockfin IV4 87 K2
Knockgray DG7 67 K4
Knockholt TN14 23 H6
Knockholt Pound TN14 23 H6
Knockin SY10 38 C3
Knockinlaw KA3 74 C7
Knockintorran (Cnoc an Torrain) HS6 92 C5
Knocklearn DG7 65 H3
Knockmill TN15 23 J5
Knocknaha PA28 66 A2
Knocknain DG9 66 D7
Knocknalling DG7 67 K5
Knockrome PA60 72 D3
Knocksharry IM5 54 B5
Knockville DG8 64 D3
Knockvologan PA66 78 E6
Knodishall IP17 35 J2
Knodishall Common IP17 35 J2
Knodishall Green IP17 35 J2
Knole TA10 8 D2
Knolls Green WA16 49 H5
Knolton LL13 38 C2
Knook BA12 20 C7
Knossington LE15 42 B5
Knott End-on-Sea FY6 55 G5
Knotting MK44 32 D2
Knotting Green MK44 32 D2
Knottingley WF11 58 B7
Knotts BD23 56 C4
Knotty Green HP9 22 C2
Knowbury SY8 28 E1
Knowe DG8 64 D3
Knowes of Elrick AB54 98 E5
Knowesgate NE19 70 E5
Knoweside KA19 67 G2
Knowetownhead TD9 70 A2
Knowhead AB43 99 H5
Knowl Green CO10 34 B4
Knowl Hill RG10 22 B4
Knowl Wall ST4 40 A2
Knowle Bristol BS4 19 K4
Knowle Devon EX17 7 F5
Knowle Devon EX33 6 C2
Knowle Devon EX9 7 J7
Knowle Shrop. SY8 28 E1
Knowle Som. TA24 7 H1
Knowle W.Mid. B93 30 C1
Knowle Cross EX5 7 J6
Knowle Green PR3 56 B6
Knowle Hall TA7 19 G7
Knowle St. Giles TA20 8 C3
Knowlton Dorset BH21 10 B3
Knowlton Kent CT3 15 H2
Knowsley L34 48 D3
Knowstone EX36 7 G3
Knox Bridge TN17 14 C3
Knucklas LD7 28 B1
Knutsford WA16 49 G5
Knypersley ST8 49 H7
Krumlin HX4 50 C1
Kuggar TR12 2 E7
Kyle of Lochalsh IV40 86 D2
Kyleakin IV41 86 D2
Kylerhea IV40 86 D2
Kyles Scalpay (Caolas Scalpaigh) HS3 93 H2
Kylesbeg PH38 86 C7
Kylesknoydart PH41 86 E5
Kylesku IV27 102 E5
Kylesmorar PH41 86 E5
Kylestrome IV27 102 E5
Kyloag IV24 96 D2
Kynaston SY10 38 C3
Kynnersley TF6 39 F4
Kyre Park WR15 29 F2

L

Labost HS2 100 E3
Lacasaigh HS2 101 F5
Lacasdal (Laxdale) HS2 101 G4
Laceby DN37 53 F2
Lacey Green HP27 22 B1
Lach Dennis CW9 49 G5
Lacharn (Laugharne) SA33 17 G4
Lackford IP28 34 B1
Lacklee (Leac a' Li) HS3 93 G2
Lacock SN15 20 C5
Ladbroke CV47 31 F3
Laddingford ME18 23 K7
Lade Bank PE22 53 G7
Ladies Hill PR3 55 H5
Ladock TR2 3 F3
Lady Hall LA18 54 E1
Ladybank KY15 82 E6
Ladycross PL15 6 B7
Ladyfield PA32 80 B6
Ladykirk TD15 77 G6
Ladysford AB43 99 H4
Ladywood WR9 29 H2
Laga PH36 79 H1
Lagalochan PA35 79 K6
Lagavulin PA42 72 C6
Lagg Arg. & B. PA60 72 D3
Lagg N.Ayr. KA27 66 D1
Lagg S.Ayr. KA7 67 G2
Laggan Arg. & B. PA43 72 A5
Laggan High. PH34 87 J5
Laggan High. PH20 88 D5
Laggan Moray AB55 90 B1
Laggan Stir. FK18 81 G6
Lagganulva PA73 79 F3
Lagganvoulin AB37 89 J3
Laglingarten PA25 80 C7
Lagnalean IV3 96 D7
Lagrae DG4 68 C2
Laguna PH1 82 C4
Laid IV27 103 G3
Laide IV22 95 F2
Laig PH42 85 K6
Laight KA18 68 B2
Lainchoil PH25 89 H3
Laindon SS15 24 C3
Lair PH10 82 C1
Lairg IV27 96 C1
Lairg Lodge IV27 96 C1
Lairigmor PH33 80 C1
Laisterdyke BD4 57 G6

Llanbadarn Fawr SY23 36 E7
Llanbadarn Fynydd LD1 27 K1
Llanbadarn-y-garreg LD2 28 A4
Llanbadoc NP15 19 G1
Llanbadrig LL67 46 B3
Llanbeder NP18 19 G2
Llanbedr *Gwyn.* **LL45 36 E3**
Llanbedr *Powys* NP8 28 B6
Llanbedr *Powys* LD2 28 A4
Llanbedr Pont Steffan (Lampeter) SA48 17 J1
Llanbedr-Dyffryn-Clwyd LL15 47 K7
Llanbedrgoch LL76 46 D4
Llanbedrog LL53 36 C2
Llanbedr-y-cennin LL32 47 F6
Llanberis LL55 46 D7
Llanbethery CF62 18 D5
Llanbister LD1 28 A1
Llanblethian CF71 18 C4
Llanboidy SA34 17 F3
Llanbradach CF83 18 E2
Llanbryn-mair SY19 37 H5
Llancadle CF62 18 D5
Llancarfan CF62 18 D4
Llancayo NP15 19 G1
Llancynfelyn SY20 37 F6
Llandafal NP13 18 E1
Llandaff CF5 18 E4
Llandaff North CF14 18 E4
Llandanwg LL46 36 E3
Llandawke SA33 17 F4
Llanddaniel Fab LL60 46 C5
Llanddarog SA32 17 H4
Llanddeiniol SY23 26 E1
Llanddeiniolen LL55 46 D6
Llandderfel LL23 37 J2
Llanddeusant *Carmar.* SA19 27 G6
Llanddeusant *I.o.A.* LL65 46 B4
Llanddew LD3 27 K5
Llanddewi SA3 17 H7
Llanddewi Rhydderch NP7 28 C7
Llanddewi Skirrid NP7 28 C7
Llanddewi Velfrey SA67 16 E4
Llanddewi Ystradenni LD1 28 A2
Llanddewi-Brefi SY25 27 F3
Llanddewi'r Cwm LD2 27 K4
Llanddoged LL26 47 G6
Llanddona LL58 46 D5
Llanddowror SA33 17 F4
Llanddulas LL22 47 H5
Llanddwywe LL44 36 E3
Llanddyfnan LL78 46 D5
Llandefaelog Fach LD3 27 K5
Llandefaelog-tre'r-graig LD3 28 A6
Llandefalle LD3 28 A5
Llandegfan LL59 46 D5
Llandegla LL11 47 K7
Llandegley LD1 28 A2
Llandegveth NP18 19 G2
Llandegwning LL53 36 B2
Llandeilo SA19 17 K3
Llandeilo Abercywyn SA33 17 G4
Llandeilo Graban LD2 27 K4
Llandeilo'r-Fan LD3 27 H5
Llandeloy SA62 16 B3
Llandenny NP15 19 H1
Llandevaud NP18 19 H2
Llandevenny NP26 19 H3
Llandinabo HR2 28 E6
Llandinam SY17 37 K7
Llandissilio SA66 16 E3
Llandogo NP25 19 J1
Llandough *V. of Glam.* CF11 18 E4
Llandough *V. of Glam.* CF71 18 C4
Llandovery (Llanymddyfri) SA20 27 G5
Llandow CF71 18 C4
Llandre *Carmar.* SA19 17 K1
Llandre *Carmar.* SA34 16 E3
Llandre *Cere.* SY24 37 F7
Llandrillo LL21 37 K2
LLANDRINDOD WELLS LD 27 K2
Llandrinio SY22 38 B4
LLANDUDNO LL 47 F4
Llandudno Junction LL31 47 F5
Llandudoch (St. Dogmaels) SA43 16 E1
Llandwrog LL54 46 C7
Llandybie SA18 17 K4
Llandyfaelog SA17 17 H4
Llandyfan SA18 17 K4
Llandyfriog SA38 17 G1
Llandyfrydog LL71 46 C4
Llandygai LL57 46 D5
Llandygwydd SA43 17 F1
Llandyrnog LL16 47 K6
Llandyry SA17 17 H5
Llandysilio SY22 38 B4
Llandyssil SY15 38 A6
Llandysul SA44 17 H1
Llanedeyrn CF23 19 F3
Llanedy SA4 17 J5
Llaneglwys LD2 27 K5
Llanegryn LL36 37 F5
Llanegwad SA32 17 J3
Llaneilian LL68 46 C3
Llanelian-yn-Rhos LL29 47 G5
Llanelidan LL15 47 K7
Llanelieu LD3 28 A5
Llanellen NP7 28 C7
Llanelli SA15 17 J5
Llanelltyd LL40 37 G4
Llanelly NP7 28 B7
Llanelly Hill NP7 28 B7
Llanelwedd LD2 27 K3
Llanelwy (St. Asaph) LL17 47 J5
Llanenddwyn LL44 36 E3
Llanengan LL53 36 B3
Llanerfyl SY21 37 K5
Llaneuddog LL70 46 C4
Llaneurgain (Northop) CH7 48 B6
Llanfachraeth LL65 46 B4
Llanfachreth LL40 37 G3
Llanfaelog LL63 46 B5
Llanfaelrhys LL53 36 B3
Llanfaenor NP25 28 D7
Llan-faes *I.o.A.* LL58 46 E5
Llanfaes *Powys* LD3 27 K6
Llanfaethlu LL65 46 B4
Llanfaglan LL54 46 C6
Llanfair LL46 36 E3
Llanfair Caereinion SY21 38 A5
Llanfair Clydogau SA48 27 F3
Llanfair Dyffryn Clwyd LL15 47 K7
Llanfair Talhaiarn LL22 47 H5
Llanfair Waterdine LD7 28 B1
Llanfairfechan LL33 46 E5
Llanfair-Nant-Gwyn SA37 16 E2
Llanfair-Orllwyn SA44 17 G1
Llanfairpwllgwyngyll LL61 46 D5
Llanfair-ym-Muallt (Builth Wells) LD2 27 K3
Llanfairynghornwy LL65 46 B3
Llanfair-yn-neubwll LL65 46 B5
Llanfallteg SA34 16 E4
Llanfaredd LD2 27 K3
Llanfarian SY23 26 E1
Llanfechain SY22 38 A3
Llanfechell LL68 46 B3
Llanfendigaid LL36 36 E5
Llanferres CH7 47 K6
Llanfflewyn LL68 46 B4
Llanfigael LL65 46 B4
Llanfihangel Crucornau (Llanvihangel Crucorney) NP7 28 C6
Llanfihangel Glyn Myfyr LL21 37 J1
Llanfihangel Nant Bran LD3 27 J5
Llanfihangel Rhydithon LD1 28 A2
Llanfihangel Rogiet NP26 19 H3
Llanfihangel Tal-y-llyn LD3 28 A6
Llanfihangel-ar-arth SA39 17 H1
Llanfihangel-nant-Melan LD8 28 A3
Llanfihangel-uwch-Gwili SA32 17 H3
Llanfihangel-y-Creuddyn SY23 27 F1
Llanfihangel-yng-Ngwynfa SY22 37 K4
Llanfihangel-yn-Nhywyn LL65 46 B5
Llanfihangel-y-pennant *Gwyn.* LL51 36 E1
Llanfihangel-y-pennant *Gwyn.* LL36 37 F5
Llanfilo LD3 28 A5
Llanfoist NP7 28 B7
Llanfor LL23 37 J2
Llanfrechfa NP44 19 G2
Llanfrothen LL48 37 F1
Llanfrynach LD3 27 K6
Llanfwrog *Denb.* LL15 47 K7
Llanfwrog *I.o.A.* LL65 46 A4
Llanfyllin SY22 38 A4
Llanfynydd *Carmar.* SA32 17 J3
Llanfynydd *Flints.* LL11 48 B7
Llanfyrnach SA35 17 F2
Llangadfan SY21 37 K4
Llangadog SA19 27 G6
Llangadwaladr *I.o.A.* LL62 46 B6
Llangadwaladr *Powys* SY10 38 A2
Llangaffo LL60 46 C6
Llangain SA33 17 G4
Llangammarch Wells LD4 27 J4
Llangan CF35 18 C4
Llangarron HR9 28 E6
Llangasty-Talyllyn LD3 28 A6
Llangathen SA32 17 J3
Llangattock NP8 28 B7
Llangattock Lingoed NP7 28 C7
Llangattock-Vibon-Avel NP25 28 D7
Llangedwyn SY10 38 A3
Llangefni LL77 46 C5
Llangeinor CF32 18 C3
Llangeitho SY25 27 F3
Llangeler SA44 17 G2
Llangelynin LL36 36 E5
Llangendeirne SA17 17 H4
Llangennech SA14 17 J5
Llangennith SA3 17 H6
Llangenny NP8 28 B7
Llangernyw LL22 47 G6
Llangian LL53 36 B3
Llangiwg SA8 18 A1
Llangloffan SA62 16 C2
Llanglydwen SA34 16 E3
Llangoed LL58 46 E5
Llangoedmor SA43 16 E1
Llangollen LL20 38 B1
Llangolman SA66 16 E3
Llangorse LD3 28 A6
Llangorwen SY23 37 F7
Llangovan NP25 19 H1
Llangower LL23 37 J2
Llangrannog SA44 26 C3
Llangristiolus LL62 46 C5
Llangrove HR9 28 E7
Llangua NP7 28 C6
Llangunllo LD7 28 B1
Llangunnor SA31 17 H3
Llangurig SY18 27 J1
Llangwm *Conwy* LL21 37 J1
Llangwm *Mon.* NP15 19 H1
Llangwm *Pembs.* SA62 16 C5
Llangwnnadl LL53 36 B2
Llangwyfan LL16 47 K6
Llangwyllog LL77 46 C5
Llangwyryfon SY23 27 F1
Llangybi *Cere.* SA48 27 F3
Llangybi *Gwyn.* LL53 36 D1
Llangybi *Mon.* NP15 19 G2
Llangyfelach SA5 17 K6
Llangynhafal LL16 47 K6
Llangynidr NP8 28 A7
Llangyniew SY21 38 A5
Llangynin SA33 17 F4
Llangynog *Carmar.* SA33 17 G4
Llangynog *Powys* SY10 37 K3
Llangynwyd CF34 18 B3
Llanhamlach LD3 27 K6
Llanharan CF72 18 D3
Llanharry CF72 18 D3
Llanhennock NP18 19 G2
Llanhilleth NP13 19 F1
Llanidloes SY18 37 J7
Llaniestyn LL53 36 B2
Llanigon HR3 28 B5
Llanilar SY23 27 F1
Llanilid CF35 18 C3
Llanishen *Cardiff* CF14 18 E3
Llanishen *Mon.* NP16 19 H1
Llanllawddog SA32 17 H3
Llanllechid LL57 46 E6
Llanlleonfel LD4 27 J3
Llanllugan SY21 37 K5
Llanllwch SA31 17 G4
Llanllwchaiarn SY16 38 A6
Llanllwni SA39 17 H1
Llanllyfni LL54 46 C7
Llanllywel NP15 19 G2
Llanmadoc SA3 17 H6
Llanmaes CF61 18 C5
Llanmartin NP18 19 G3
Llanmerewig SY15 38 A6
Llanmihangel CF71 18 C4
Llan-mill SA67 16 E4
Llanmiloe SA33 17 F5
Llanmorlais SA4 17 J6
Llannefydd LL16 47 H5
Llannerch Hall LL17 47 J5
Llannerch-y-medd LL71 46 C4
Llannerch-y-Môr CH8 47 K5
Llannon *Carmar.* SA14 17 J5
Llan-non ***Cere.*** **SY23 26 E2**
Llannor LL53 36 C2
Llanover NP7 19 G1
Llanpumsaint SA33 17 H3
Llanreithan SA62 16 B3
Llanrhaeadr LL16 47 J6
Llanrhaeadr-ym-Mochnant SY10 38 A3
Llanrhian SA62 16 B2
Llanrhidian SA3 17 H6
Llanrhyddlad LL65 46 B4
Llanrhystud SY23 26 E2
Llanrothal NP25 28 D7
Llanrug LL55 46 D6
Llanrumney CF3 19 F3
Llanrwst LL26 47 F6
Llansadurnen SA33 17 F4
Llansadwrn *Carmar.* SA19 17 K2
Llansadwrn *I.o.A.* LL59 46 D5
Llansaint SA17 17 G5
Llansamlet SA7 17 K6
Llansanffraid SY23 26 E2
Llansanffraid Glan Conwy LL28 47 G5
Llansannan LL16 47 H6
Llansannor CF71 18 C4
Llansantffraed LD3 28 A6
Llansantffraed-Cwmdeuddwr LD6 27 J2
Llansantffraed-in-Elwel LD1 27 K3
Llansantffraid-ym-Mechain SY22 38 B3
Llansawel *Carmar.* SA19 17 K2
Llansawel (Briton Ferry) *N.P.T.* SA11 18 A2
Llansilin SY10 38 B3
Llansoy NP15 19 H1
Llanspyddid LD3 27 K6
Llanstadwell SA73 16 C5
Llansteffan SA33 17 G4
Llanstephan LD3 28 A4
Llantarnam NP44 19 G2
Llanteg SA67 16 E4
Llanthony NP7 28 B6
Llantilio Crossenny NP7 28 C7
Llantilio Pertholey NP7 28 C7
Llantood SA43 16 E1
Llantrisant *I.o.A.* LL65 46 B4
Llantrisant *Mon.* NP15 19 G2
Llantrisant *R.C.T.* CF72 18 D3
Llantrithyd CF71 18 D4
Llantwit Fardre CF38 18 D3
Llantwit Major CF61 18 C5
Llantysilio LL20 38 A1
Llanuwchllyn LL23 37 H3
Llanvaches NP26 19 H2
Llanvair-Discoed NP16 19 H2
Llanvapley NP7 28 C7
Llanvetherine NP7 28 C7
Llanveynoe HR2 28 C5
Llanvihangel Crucorney (Llanfihangel Crucornau) NP7 28 C6
Llanvihangel Gobion NP7 19 G1
Llanvihangel-Ystern-Llewern NP25 28 D7
Llanvithyn CF62 18 D4
Llanwarne HR2 28 E6
Llanwddyn SY10 37 K4
Llanwenog SA40 17 H1
Llanwern NP18 19 G3
Llanwinio SA34 17 F3
Llanwnda *Gwyn.* LL54 46 C7
Llanwnda *Pembs.* SA64 16 C2
Llanwnnen SA48 17 J1
Llanwnog SY17 37 K6
Llanwonno CF37 18 D2
Llanwrda SA19 27 G5
Llanwrin SY20 37 G5
Llanwrthwl LD1 27 J2
Llanwrtyd LD5 27 H4
Llanwrtyd Wells LD5 27 H4
Llanwyddelan SY16 37 K5
Llanyblodwel SY10 38 B3
Llanybri SA33 17 G4
Llanybydder SA40 17 J1
Llanycefn SA66 16 E3
Llanychaer Bridge SA65 16 C2
Llanycil LL23 37 J2
Llanycrwys SA19 17 K1
Llanymawddwy SY20 37 H4
Llanymddyfri (Llandovery) SA20 27 G5
Llanymynech SY22 38 B3
Llanynghenedl LL65 46 B4
Llanynys LL16 47 K6
Llan-y-pwll LL13 48 C7
Llanyre LD1 27 K2
Llanystumdwy LL52 36 D2
Llanywern LD3 28 A6
Llawhaden SA67 16 D4
Llawndy CH8 47 K4
Llawnt SY10 38 B2
Llawr-y-dref LL53 36 B3
Llawryglyn SY17 37 J6
Llay LL12 48 C7
Llechcynfarwy LL71 46 B4
Llecheiddior LL51 36 D1
Llechfaen LD3 27 K6
Llechryd *Caerp.* NP22 18 E1
Llechryd *Cere.* SA43 17 F1
Llechrydau SY10 38 B2
Lledrod *Cere.* SY23 27 F1
Lledrod *Powys* SY10 38 B3
Llethrid SA2 17 J6
Llidiad-Nenog SA32 17 J2
Llidiardau LL23 37 H2
Llithfaen LL53 36 C1
Lloc CH8 47 K5
Llong CH7 48 B6
Llowes HR3 28 A4
Lloyney LD7 28 B1
Llundain-fach SA48 26 E3
Llwydcoed CF44 18 C1
Llwydiarth SY21 37 K4
Llwyn *M.Tyd.* CF48 27 K7
Llwyn *Shrop.* SY7 38 B7
Llwyncelyn SA46 26 D3
Llwyn-croes SA33 17 H3
Llwyndafydd SA44 26 C3
Llwynderw SY21 38 B5
Llwyndyrys LL53 36 C1
Llwyneinion LL14 38 B1
Llwyngwril LL37 36 E5
Llwynhendy SA14 17 J6
Llwyn-Madoc LD5 27 J3
Llwynmawr LL20 38 B2
Llwyn-onn SA45 26 D3
Llwyn-y-brain *Carmar.* SA34 16 E4
Llwyn-y-brain *Carmar.* SA20 27 G5
Llwyn-y-groes SY25 26 E3
Llwynypia CF40 18 C2
Llyn Penmaen (Penmaenpool) LL40 37 F4
Llynclys SY10 38 B3
Llynfaes LL65 46 C5
Llysfaen LL29 47 G5
Llyswen LD3 28 A5
Llysworney CF71 18 C4
Llys-y-frân SA63 16 D3
Llywel LD3 27 H5
Load Brook S6 50 E4
Loandhu IV20 97 F4
Loanhead *Aber.* AB41 91 H1
Loanhead ***Midloth.*** **EH20 76 A4**
Loans KA10 74 B7
Lobb EX33 6 C2
Lobhillcross EX20 6 C7
Loch a Charnain HS8 92 D7
Loch Baghasdail (Lochboisdale) HS8 84 C3
Loch Choire Lodge KW11 103 J5
Loch Eil Outward Bound PH33 87 G7
Loch Head *D. & G.* DG8 64 D6
Loch Head *D. & G.* KA6 67 J4
Loch na Madadh (Lochmaddy) HS6 92 E5
Loch Sgioport HS8 84 D1
Lochailort PH38 86 D6
Lochaline PA34 79 H3
Lochans DG9 64 A5
Locharbriggs DG1 68 E5
Lochawe PA33 80 C5
Lochboisdale (Loch Baghasdail) HS8 84 C3
Lochbuie PA62 79 H5
Lochcarron IV54 94 E7
Lochdhu Hotel KW12 105 F4
Lochdon PA64 79 J4
Lochdrum IV23 95 J4
Lochearnhead FK19 81 G5
Lochee DD2 82 E4
Lochend *High.* KW14 105 H2
Lochend *High.* IV3 88 C1
Locheport (Locheuphort) HS6 92 D5
Locheuphort (Locheport) HS6 92 D5
Lochfoot DG2 65 K3
Lochgair PA31 73 H1
Lochgarthside IV2 88 C3
Lochgelly KY5 75 K1
Lochgilphead PA31 73 G2
Lochgoilhead PA24 80 D7
Lochgoyn KA3 74 D6
Lochhill *E.Ayr.* KA18 67 K2
Lochhill *Moray* IV30 97 K5
Lochinch Castle DG9 64 B4
Lochinver IV27 102 C6
Lochlair DD8 83 G3
Lochlane PH7 81 K5
Lochlea KA1 74 C7
Lochluichart IV23 95 K5
Lochmaben DG11 69 F5
Lochmaddy (Loch na Madadh) HS6 92 E5
Lochore KY5 75 K1
Lochportain HS6 92 E4
Lochranza KA27 73 H5
Lochside *Aber.* DD10 83 J1
Lochside *High.* IV27 103 G3
Lochside *High.* KW11 104 D5
Lochside *High.* KW14 105 H2
Lochslin IV20 97 F3
Lochton KA26 67 G5
Lochty KY10 83 G7
Lochuisge PH33 79 J2
Lochurr DG3 68 C5
Lochussie IV7 96 B6
Lochwinnoch PA12 74 B5
Lockengate PL26 4 A4
Lockerbie DG11 69 G5
Lockeridge SN8 20 E5
Lockerley SO51 10 D2
Lockhills CA4 61 G2
Locking BS24 19 G6
Lockington *E.Riding* YO25 59 F5
Lockington *Leics.* DE74 41 G3
Lockleywood TF9 39 F3
Locks Heath SO31 11 G4
Locksbottom BR6 23 H5
Locksgreen PO30 11 F5
Lockton YO18 58 E1
Loddington *Leics.* LE7 42 A5
Loddington *Northants.* NN14 32 B1
Loddiswell TQ7 5 H6
Loddon NR14 45 H6
Lode CB25 33 J2
Loders DT6 8 D5
Lodsworth GU28 12 C4
Lofthouse *N.Yorks.* HG3 57 G2
Lofthouse *W.Yorks.* WF3 57 J7
Loftus TS13 63 J5
Logan *D. & G.* DG9 64 A6
Logan *E.Ayr.* KA18 67 K1
Loganlea EH55 75 H4
Loggerheads TF9 39 G2
Loggie IV23 95 H2
Logie *Angus* DD10 83 H1
Logie *Angus* DD8 82 E2
Logie *Fife* KY15 83 F5
Logie *Moray* IV36 97 H6
Logie Coldstone AB34 90 C4
Logie Hill IV18 96 E4
Logie Newton AB54 90 E1
Logie Pert DD10 83 H1
Logierait PH9 82 A2
Login SA34 16 E3
Lolworth CB23 33 G2
Lonbain IV54 94 C6
Londesborough YO43 58 E5
LONDON E, EC, N, NW, SE, SW, W, WC 23 G3
London Apprentice PL26 4 A6
London Ashford Airport TN29 15 F5
London Beach TN30 14 D4
London City Airport E16 23 H3
London Colney AL2 22 E1
London Gatwick Airport (Gatwick Airport) RH6 23 F7
London Heathrow Airport TW6 22 D4
London Luton Airport (Luton Airport) LU2 32 E6
London Minstead SO43 10 D3
London Southend Airport SS2 24 E3
London Stansted Airport (Stansted Airport) CM24 33 J6
Londonderry DL7 57 H1
Londonthorpe NG31 42 C2
Londubh IV22 94 E3
Lonemore IV25 96 E3
Long Ashton BS41 19 J4
Long Bank DY12 29 G1
Long Bennington NG23 42 B1
Long Bredy DT2 8 E5
Long Buckby NN6 31 H2
Long Clawson LE14 42 A3
Long Compton *Staffs.* ST18 40 A3
Long Compton *Warks.* CV36 30 D5
Long Crendon HP18 21 K1
Long Crichel BH21 9 J3

Lyminster BN17 12 D6
Lymm WA13 49 F4
Lymore SO41 10 D5
Lympne CT21 15 G4
Lympsham BS24 19 G6
Lympstone EX8 7 H7
Lynaberack PH21 88 E5
Lynch TA24 7 G1
Lynch Green NR9 45 F5
Lynchat PH21 88 E4
Lyndale House IV51 93 J6
Lyndhurst SO43 10 D4
Lyndon LE15 42 C5
Lyne Aber. AB51 91 F4
Lyne Sc.Bord. EH45 76 A6
Lyne Surr. KT16 22 D5
Lyne Down HR8 29 F5
Lyne of Gorthleck IV2 88 C2
Lyne of Skene AB32 91 F3
Lyne Station EH45 76 A6
Lyneal SY12 38 D2
Lynegar KW1 105 H3
Lyneham Oxon. OX7 30 D6
Lyneham Wilts. SN15 20 D4
Lyneholmeford CA6 70 A6
Lynemore High. PH26 89 H2
Lynemore Moray AB37 89 J1
Lynemouth NE61 71 H4
Lyness KW16 106 C8
Lynford IP26 44 C6
Lyng Norf. NR9 44 E4
Lyng Som. TA3 8 C2
Lyngate NR28 45 H3
Lynmouth EX35 7 F1
Lynn TF10 39 G4
Lynsted ME9 25 F5
Lynstone EX23 6 A5
Lynton EX35 7 F1
Lyon's Gate DT2 9 F4
Lyonshall HR5 28 C3
Lyrabus PA44 72 A4
Lytchett Matravers BH16 9 J5
Lytchett Minster BH16 9 J5
Lyth KW1 105 H2
Lytham FY8 55 G7
Lytham St. Anne's FY8 55 G7
Lythe YO21 63 K5
Lythe Hill GU27 12 C3
Lythes KW17 106 D9
Lythmore KW14 105 F2

M

Maaruig (Maraig) HS3 100 E7
Mabe Burnthouse TR10 2 E5
Mabie DG2 65 K3
Mablethorpe LN12 53 J4
Macclesfield SK11 49 J5
Macclesfield Forest SK11 49 J5
Macduff AB44 99 F4
Macedonia KY6 82 D7
Machan ML9 75 F5
Machany PH3 81 K6
Macharioch PA28 66 B3
Machen CF83 19 F3
Machrie Arg. & B. PA49 72 A4
Machrie Arg. & B. PA42 72 B6
Machrie N.Ayr. KA27 73 G7
Machrihanish PA28 66 A1
Machrins PA61 72 B1
Machynlleth SY20 37 G5
McInroy's Point PA19 74 A3
Mackerye End AL4 32 E7
Mackworth DE22 41 F2
Macmerry EH33 76 C3
Macterry AB53 99 F6
Madderty PH7 82 A5
Maddiston FK2 75 H3
Madehurst BN18 12 C5
Madeley Staffs. CW3 39 G1
Madeley Tel. & W. TF7 39 G5
Madeley Heath CW3 39 G1
Maders PL17 4 D3
Madford EX15 7 K4
Madingley CB23 33 G2
Madjeston SP8 9 H2
Madley HR2 28 D5
Madresfield WR13 29 H4
Madron TR20 2 B5
Maenaddwyn LL71 46 C4
Maenclochog SA66 16 D3
Maendy Cardiff CF14 18 E4
Maendy V. of Glam. CF71 18 D4
Maenporth TR11 2 E6
Maentwrog LL41 37 F1
Maen-y-groes SA45 26 C3
Maer Cornw. EX23 6 A5
Maer Staffs. ST5 39 G2
Maerdy Carmar. SA19 17 K3
Maerdy Carmar. SA19 17 K3
Maerdy Conwy LL21 37 K1
Maerdy R.C.T. CF43 18 C2
Maesbrook SY10 38 B3
Maesbury Marsh SY10 38 C3
Maes-Glas (Greenfield) Flints. CH8 47 K5
Maes-glas Newport NP20 19 F3
Maesgwynne SA34 17 F3
Maeshafn CH7 48 B6
Maesllyn SA44 17 G1
Maesmynis LD2 27 K4
Maesteg CF34 18 B2
Maes-Treylow LD8 28 B2
Maesybont SA14 17 J4
Maesycrugiau SA39 17 H1
Maesycwmmer CF82 18 E2
Maesyfed (New Radnor) LD8 28 B2
Magdalen Laver CM5 23 J1
Maggieknockater AB38 98 B6
Maggots End CM23 33 H6
Magham Down BN27 13 K5
Maghull L31 48 C2
Magna Park LE17 41 H7
Magor NP26 19 H3
Magpie Green IP22 34 E1
Maiden Bradley BA12 9 G1
Maiden Head BS41 19 J5
Maiden Law DH7 62 C2
Maiden Newton DT2 8 E5
Maiden Wells SA71 16 C6
Maidencombe TQ1 5 K4
Maidenhayne EX13 8 B5
Maidenhead SL6 22 B3
Maidens KA26 67 G3
Maiden's Green RG42 22 B4
Maidensgrove RG9 22 A3
Maidenwell Cornw. PL30 4 B3
Maidenwell Lincs. LN11 53 G5
Maidford NN12 31 H3
Maids' Moreton MK18 31 J5
Maidstone ME14 14 C2
Maidwell NN6 31 J1
Mail ZE2 107 N10
Maindee NP19 19 G3
Mainland Ork. KW 106 B6
Mainland Shet. ZE 107 M7
Mains of Ardestie DD5 83 G4
Mains of Balgavies DD8 83 G2
Mains of Balhall DD9 83 G1
Mains of Ballindarg DD8 83 F2
Mains of Burgie IV36 97 H6
Mains of Culsh AB53 99 G6
Mains of Dillavaird AB30 91 F6
Mains of Drum AB31 91 G4
Mains of Dudwick AB41 91 H1
Mains of Faillie IV2 88 E1
Mains of Fedderate AB42 99 G6
Mains of Glack AB51 91 F2
Mains of Glassaugh AB45 98 D4
Mains of Glenbuchat AB36 90 B3
Mains of Linton AB51 91 F3
Mains of Melgund DD9 83 G2
Mains of Pitfour AB42 99 H6
Mains of Pittrichie AB21 91 G2
Mains of Sluie IV36 97 H6
Mains of Tannachy AB56 98 B4
Mains of Thornton AB30 90 E7
Mains of Tig KA26 67 F5
Mains of Watten KW1 105 H3
Mainsforth DL17 62 E3
Mainsriddle DG2 65 K5
Mainstone SY9 38 B7
Maisemore GL2 29 H6
Major's Green B90 30 C1
Makendon NE65 70 D3
Makeney DE56 41 F1
Makerstoun TD5 76 E7
Malacleit HS6 92 C4
Malborough TQ7 5 H7
Malden Rushett KT9 22 E5
Maldon CM9 24 E1
Malham BD23 56 E3
Maligar IV51 93 K5
Malinbridge S6 51 F4
Mallaig PH41 86 C5
Mallaigmore PH41 86 C5
Mallaigvaig PH41 86 C5
Malleny Mills EH14 75 K4
Malletsheugh G77 74 D5
Malling FK8 81 G7
Mallows Green CM23 33 H6
Malltraeth LL62 46 C6
Mallwyd SY20 37 H4
Malmesbury SN16 20 C3
Malmsmead EX35 7 F1
Malpas Ches.W. & C. SY14 38 D1
Malpas Cornw. TR1 3 F4
Malpas Newport NP20 19 G2
Maltby Lincs. LN11 53 G4
Maltby S.Yorks. S66 51 H3
Maltby Stock. TS8 63 F5
Maltby le Marsh LN13 53 H4
Malting End CB8 34 B3
Malting Green CO2 34 D7
Maltman's Hill TN27 14 D3
Malton YO17 58 D2
Malvern Link WR14 29 G4
Malvern Wells WR14 29 G4
Mambeg G84 74 A2
Mamble DY14 29 F1
Mamhead EX6 7 H7
Mamhilad NP4 19 G1
Manaccan TR12 2 E6
Manadon PL5 4 E5
Manafon SY21 38 A5
Manais (Manish) HS3 93 G3
Manaton TQ13 7 F7
Manby LN11 53 G4
Mancetter CV9 41 F6
MANCHESTER M 49 H3
Manchester Airport M90 49 H4
Mancot Royal CH5 48 C6
Mandally PH35 87 J4
Manea PE15 43 H7
Maneight KA18 67 K3
Manfield DL2 62 D5
Mangaster ZE2 107 M5
Mangerton DT6 8 D5
Mangotsfield BS16 19 K4
Mangrove Green LU2 32 E6
Mangurstadh HS2 100 C4
Manish (Manais) HS3 93 G3
Mankinholes OL14 56 E7
Manley WA6 48 E5
Manmoel NP12 18 E1
Mannal PA77 78 A3
Manningford Abbots SN9 20 E6
Manningford Bohune SN9 20 E6
Manningford Bruce SN9 20 E6
Manningham BD8 57 G6
Mannings Heath RH13 13 F4
Mannington BH21 10 B4
Manningtree CO11 35 F5
Mannofield AB15 91 H4
Manor Park SL2 22 C3
Manorbier SA70 16 D6
Manorbier Newton SA70 16 D5
Manordeifi SA43 17 F1
Manordeilo SA19 17 K3
Manorowen SA65 16 C2
Mansell Gamage HR4 28 C4
Mansell Lacy HR4 28 D4
Mansergh LA6 56 B1
Mansfield NG18 51 H6
Mansfield Woodhouse NG19 51 H6
Manson Green NR9 44 E5
Mansriggs LA12 55 F1
Manston Dorset DT10 9 H3
Manston Kent CT12 25 K5
Manston W.Yorks. LS15 57 J6
Manswood BH21 9 J4
Manthorpe Lincs. PE10 42 D4
Manthorpe Lincs. NG31 42 C2
Manton N.Lincs. DN21 52 C2
Manton Notts. S80 51 H5
Manton Rut. LE15 42 B5
Manton Wilts. SN8 20 E5
Manuden CM23 33 H6
Manwood Green CM5 33 J7
Maolachy PA35 79 K6
Maperton BA9 9 F2
Maple Cross WD3 22 D2
Maplebeck NG22 51 K6
Mapledurham RG4 21 K4
Mapledurwell RG25 21 K6
Maplehurst RH13 12 E4
Maplescombe DA4 23 J5
Mapleton DE6 40 D1
Mapperley Derbys. DE7 41 G1
Mapperley Notts. NG5 41 H1
Mapperton Dorset DT8 8 E5
Mapperton Dorset DT11 9 J5
Mappleborough Green B80 30 B2
Mappleton HU18 59 J5
Mapplewell S75 51 F2
Mappowder DT10 9 G4
Mar Lodge AB35 89 H5
Maraig (Maaruig) HS3 100 E7
Marazion TR17 2 C5
Marbhig HS2 101 G6
Marbury SY13 38 E1
March PE15 43 H6
Marcham OX13 21 H2
Marchamley SY4 38 E3
Marchamley Wood SY4 38 E2
Marchington ST14 40 D2
Marchington Woodlands ST14 40 D3
Marchwiel LL13 38 C1
Marchwood SO40 10 E3
Marcross CF61 18 C5
Marcus DD8 83 G2
Marden Here. HR1 28 E4
Marden Kent TN12 14 C3
Marden T. & W. NE30 71 J6
Marden Wilts. SN10 20 D6
Marden Ash CM5 23 J1
Marden Beech TN12 14 C3
Marden Thorn TN12 14 C3
Marden's Hill TN6 13 H3
Mardon TD12 77 H7
Mardy NP7 28 C7
Mare Green TA3 8 C2
Marefield LE7 42 A5
Mareham le Fen PE22 53 F6
Mareham on the Hill LN9 53 F6
Maresfield TN22 13 H4
Marfleet HU9 59 H6
Marford LL12 48 C7
Margam SA13 18 A3
Margaret Marsh SP7 9 H3
Margaret Roding CM6 33 J7
Margaretting CM4 24 C1
Margaretting Tye CM4 24 C1
Margate CT9 25 K4
Margnaheglish KA27 73 J7
Margreig DG2 65 J3
Margrove Park TS12 63 H5
Marham PE33 44 B5
Marhamchurch EX23 6 A5
Marholm PE6 42 E5
Marian Cwm LL18 47 J5
Mariandyrys LL58 46 E4
Marian-glas LL73 46 D4
Mariansleigh EX36 7 F3
Marine Town ME12 25 F4
Marishader IV51 93 K5
Maristow House PL6 4 E4
Mark TA9 19 G7
Mark Causeway TA9 19 G7
Mark Cross TN6 13 J3
Markbeech TN8 23 H7
Markby LN13 53 H5
Markdhu DG8 64 B3
Markeaton DE22 41 F2
Market Bosworth CV13 41 G5
Market Deeping PE6 42 E4
Market Drayton TF9 39 F2
Market Harborough LE16 42 A7
Market Lavington SN10 20 D6
Market Overton LE15 42 B4
Market Rasen LN8 52 E4
Market Stainton LN8 53 F5
Market Street NR12 45 G3
Market Warsop NG20 51 H6
Market Weighton YO43 58 E5
Market Weston IP22 34 D1
Markethill PH13 82 D4
Markfield LE67 41 G4
Markham NP12 18 E1
Markham Moor DN22 51 K5
Markinch KY7 82 D7
Markington HG3 57 H3
Marks Gate RM6 23 H2
Marks Tey CO6 34 D6
Marksbury BA2 19 K5
Markwell PL12 4 D5
Markyate AL3 32 D7
Marl Bank WR14 29 G4
Marland OL11 49 H1
Marlborough SN8 20 E5
Marlbrook B60 29 J1
Marlcliff B50 30 B3
Marldon TQ3 5 J4
Marle Green TN21 13 J5
Marlesford IP13 35 H3
Marley Green SY13 38 E1
Marley Hill NE16 62 D1
Marlingford NR9 45 F5
Marloes SA62 16 A5
Marlow Bucks. SL7 22 B3
Marlow Here. SY7 28 D1
Marlpit Hill TN8 23 H7
Marlpool DE75 41 G1
Marnhull DT10 9 G3
Marnoch AB54 98 D5
Marple SK6 49 J4
Marple Bridge SK6 49 J4
Marr DN5 51 H2
Marrel KW8 105 F7
Marrick DL11 62 B7
Marrister ZE2 107 P6
Marros SA33 17 F5
Marsden T. & W. NE34 71 J7
Marsden W.Yorks. HD7 50 C1
Marsett DL8 56 E1
Marsh EX14 8 B3
Marsh Baldon OX44 21 J2
Marsh Benham RG20 21 H5
Marsh Gibbon OX27 31 H6
Marsh Green Devon EX5 7 J6
Marsh Green Gt.Man. WN5 48 E2
Marsh Green Kent TN8 23 H7
Marsh Green Tel. & W. TF6 39 F4
Marsh Lane S21 51 G5
Marsh Street TA24 7 H1
Marshall Meadows TD15 77 H5
Marshalsea DT6 8 C4
Marshalswick AL1 22 E1
Marsham NR10 45 F3
Marshaw LA2 55 J4
Marshborough CT13 15 J2
Marshbrook SY6 38 D7
Marshchapel DN36 53 G3
Marshfield Newport CF3 19 F3
Marshfield S.Glos. SN14 20 A4
Marshgate PL32 4 B1
Marshland St. James PE14 43 J5
Marshside PR9 48 C1
Marshwood DT6 8 C5
Marske DL11 62 C6
Marske-by-the-Sea TS11 63 H4
Marsland Green M29 49 F3
Marston Ches.W. & C. CW9 49 F5
Marston Here. HR6 28 C3
Marston Lincs. NG32 42 B1
Marston Oxon. OX3 21 J1
Marston Staffs. ST18 40 B3
Marston Staffs. ST20 40 A4
Marston Warks. B76 40 E6
Marston Wilts. SN10 20 C6
Marston Doles CV47 31 F3
Marston Green B37 40 D7
Marston Magna BA22 8 E2
Marston Meysey SN6 20 E2
Marston Montgomery DE6 40 D2
Marston Moretaine MK43 32 C4
Marston on Dove DE65 40 E3
Marston St. Lawrence OX17 31 G4
Marston Stannett HR6 28 E3
Marston Trussell LE16 41 J7
Marstow HR9 28 E7
Marsworth HP23 32 C7
Marten SN8 21 F5
Marthall WA16 49 G5
Martham NR29 45 J4
Martin Hants. SP6 10 B3
Martin Lincs. LN4 52 E7
Martin Lincs. LN9 53 F6
Martin Drove End SP6 10 B2
Martin Hussingtree WR3 29 H2
Martinhoe EX31 6 E1
Martinscroft WA1 49 F4
Martinstown DT2 9 F6
Martlesham IP12 35 G4
Martlesham Heath IP5 35 G4
Martletwy SA67 16 D4
Martley WR6 29 G2
Martock TA12 8 D3
Marton Ches.E. SK11 49 H6
Marton Cumb. LA12 55 F2
Marton E.Riding HU11 59 H6
Marton E.Riding YO15 59 J3
Marton Lincs. DN21 52 B4
Marton Middbro. TS7 63 G5
Marton N.Yorks. YO51 57 K3
Marton N.Yorks. YO62 58 D1
Marton Shrop. SY21 38 B5
Marton Shrop. SY4 38 D3
Marton Warks. CV23 31 F2
Marton Abbey YO61 58 B3
Marton-in-the-Forest YO61 58 B3
Marton-le-Moor HG4 57 J2
Martyr Worthy SO21 11 G1
Martyr's Green KT11 22 D6
Marwick KW17 106 B5
Marwood EX31 6 D2
Mary Tavy PL19 5 F3
Marybank High. IV6 96 B6
Marybank W.Isles HS2 101 G4
Maryburgh IV7 96 C6
Maryfield Cornw. PL11 4 E5
Maryfield Shet. ZE2 107 N8
Marygold TD11 77 G5
Maryhill Aber. AB53 99 G6
Maryhill Glas. G20 74 D4
Marykirk AB30 83 H1
Marylebone Gt.Lon. W1G 23 F3
Marylebone Gt.Man. WN1 48 E2
Marypark AB37 89 J1
Maryport Cumb. CA15 60 B3
Maryport D. & G. DG9 64 B7
Marystow PL16 6 C7
Maryton DD10 83 H2
Marywell Aber. AB12 91 H5
Marywell Aber. AB34 90 D5
Marywell Angus DD11 83 H3
Masham HG4 57 H1
Mashbury CM1 33 K7
Masongill LA6 56 B2
Mastin Moor S43 51 G5
Mastrick AB16 91 H4
Matchborough B98 30 B2
Matching CM17 33 J7
Matching Green CM17 33 J7
Matching Tye CM17 33 J7
Matfen NE20 71 F6
Matfield TN12 23 K7
Mathern NP16 19 J2
Mathon WR13 29 G4
Mathry SA62 16 B2
Matlaske NR11 45 F2
Matlock DE4 51 F6
Matlock Bank DE4 51 F6
Matlock Bath DE4 50 E7
Matson GL4 29 H7
Matterdale End CA11 60 E4
Mattersey DN10 51 J4
Mattersey Thorpe DN10 51 J4
Mattingley RG27 22 A6
Mattishall NR20 44 E4
Mattishall Burgh NR20 44 E4
Mauchline KA5 67 J1
Maud AB42 99 H6
Maufant JE2 3 K7
Maugersbury GL54 30 C6
Maughold IM7 54 D4
Mauld IV4 87 K1
Maulden MK45 32 D5
Maulds Meaburn CA10 61 H5
Maunby YO7 57 J1
Maund Bryan HR1 28 E3
Maundown TA4 7 J3
Mautby NR29 45 J4
Mavesyn Ridware WS15 40 C4
Mavis Enderby PE23 53 G6
Maw Green CW1 49 G7
Mawbray CA15 60 B2
Mawdesley L40 48 D1
Mawdlam CF33 18 B3
Mawgan TR12 2 E6
Mawgan Porth TR8 3 F2
Mawla TR16 2 E4
Mawnan TR11 2 E6
Mawnan Smith TR11 2 E6
Mawsley NN14 32 B1
Mawthorpe LN13 53 H5
Maxey PE6 42 E5
Maxstoke B46 40 E7
Maxted Street CT4 15 G3
Maxton Kent CT17 15 J3
Maxton Sc.Bord. TD6 76 E7
Maxwellheugh TD5 77 F7
Maxwelltown DG2 65 K3
Maxworthy PL15 4 C1
May Hill GL17 29 G6
Mayals SA3 17 K6
Maybole KA19 67 H3
Maybury GU22 22 D6
Mayen AB54 98 D6
Mayfair W1J 23 F3
Mayfield E.Suss. TN20 13 J4
Mayfield Midloth. EH22 76 B4
Mayfield Staffs. DE6 40 D1
Mayford GU22 22 C6
Mayland CM3 25 F1
Maylandsea CM3 25 F1
Maynard's Green TN21 13 J5
Maypole I.o.S. TR21 2 C1
Maypole Kent CT3 25 H5
Maypole Mon. NP25 28 D7
Maypole Green Essex CO2 34 D6
Maypole Green Norf. NR14 45 J6
Maypole Green Suff. IP13 35 G2
Maypole Green Suff. IP30 34 D3
May's Green N.Som. BS24 19 G5
Mays Green Oxon. RG9 22 A3
Maywick ZE2 107 M10
Mead EX39 6 A4
Mead End SP5 10 B2
Meadgate BA2 19 K6
Meadle HP17 22 B1
Meadow Green WR6 29 G3
Meadowhall S9 51 F3
Meadowmill EH33 76 C3
Meadowtown SY5 38 C5
Meadwell PL16 6 C7
Meaford ST15 40 A2
Meal Bank LA9 61 G7

Mealabost (Melbost Borve) HS2 101 G2
Mealasta HS2 100 B5
Meals LN11 53 H3
Mealsgate CA7 60 D2
Meanley BB7 56 C5
Meanwood LS6 57 H6
Mearbeck BD23 56 D3
Meare BA6 19 H7
Meare Green TA3 8 B2
Mearns G77 74 D5
Mears Ashby NN6 32 B2
Measham DE12 41 F4
Meathop LA11 55 H1
Meavy PL20 5 F4
Medbourne LE16 42 B6
Meddon EX39 6 A4
Meden Vale NG20 51 H6
Medlar PR4 55 H6
Medmenham SL7 22 B3
Medomsley DH8 62 C1
Medstead GU34 11 H1
Meer Common HR3 28 C3
Meer End CV8 30 D1
Meerbrook ST13 49 J6
Meesden SG9 33 H5
Meeson TF6 39 F3
Meeth EX20 6 D5
Meeting House Hill NR28 45 H3
Meggethead TD7 69 G1
Meidrim SA33 17 F3
Meifod Denb. LL16 47 J7
Meifod Powys SY22 38 A4
Meigle PH12 82 D3
Meikle Earnock ML3 75 F5
Meikle Grenach PA20 73 J4
Meikle Kilmory PA20 73 J4
Meikle Rahane G84 74 A2
Meikle Strath AB30 90 E7
Meikle Tarty AB41 91 H2
Meikle Wartle AB51 91 F1
Meikleour PH2 82 C4
Meikleyard KA4 74 D7
Meinciau SA17 17 H4
Meir ST3 40 B1
Meirheath ST3 40 B2
Melbost HS2 101 G4
Melbost Borve (Mealabost) HS2 101 G2
Melbourn SG8 33 G4
Melbourne Derbys. DE73 41 F3
Melbourne E.Riding YO42 58 D5
Melbury EX39 6 B4
Melbury Abbas SP7 9 H3
Melbury Bubb DT2 8 E4
Melbury Osmond DT2 8 E4
Melbury Sampford DT2 8 E4
Melby ZE2 107 K7
Melchbourne MK44 32 D2
Melcombe Bingham DT2 9 G4
Melcombe Regis DT4 9 F6
Meldon Devon EX20 6 D6
Meldon Northumb. NE61 71 G5
Meldreth SG8 33 G4
Meledor PL26 3 G3
Melfort PA34 79 K6
Melgarve PH20 88 B5
Melgum AB34 90 C4
Meliden (Gallt Melyd) LL19 47 J4
Melincourt SA11 18 B1
Melin-y-coed LL26 47 G6
Melin-y-ddol SY21 37 K5
Melin-y-grug SY21 37 K5
Melin-y-Wig LL21 37 K1
Melkinthorpe CA10 61 G4
Melkridge NE49 70 C7
Melksham SN12 20 C5
Melksham Forest SN12 20 C5
Melldalloch PA21 73 H3
Melling Lancs. LA6 55 J2
Melling Mersey. L31 48 C2
Melling Mount L31 48 D2
Mellis IP23 34 E1
Mellon Charles IV22 94 E2
Mellon Udrigle IV22 94 E2
Mellor Gt.Man. SK6 49 J4
Mellor Lancs. BB2 56 B6
Mellor Brook BB2 56 B6
Mells BA11 20 A7
Melmerby Cumb. CA10 61 H3
Melmerby N.Yorks. DL8 57 F1
Melmerby N.Yorks. HG4 57 J2
Melplash DT6 8 D5
Melrose Aber. AB45 99 F4
Melrose Sc.Bord. TD6 76 D7
Melsetter KW16 106 B9
Melsonby DL10 62 C6
Meltham HD9 50 C1
Melton E.Riding HU14 59 F7
Melton Suff. IP12 35 G3
Melton Constable NR24 44 E2
Melton Mowbray LE13 42 A4
Melton Ross DN38 52 D1
Meltonby YO42 58 D4
Melvaig IV21 94 D3
Melverley SY10 38 C4
Melverley Green SY10 38 C4
Melvich KW14 104 D2
Membury EX13 8 B4
Memsie AB43 99 H4
Memus DD8 83 F2
Menabilly PL24 4 A5
Menai Bridge (Porthaethwy) LL59 46 D5
Mendham IP20 45 G7
Mendlesham IP14 35 F2
Mendlesham Green IP14 34 E2
Menethorpe YO17 58 D3
Menheniot PL14 4 C4
Menie House AB23 91 H2
Menithwood WR6 29 G2
Mennock DG4 68 D3
Menston LS29 57 G5
Menstrie FK11 75 G1
Mentmore LU7 32 C7
Meoble PH40 86 D6
Meole Brace SY3 38 D4
Meon PO14 11 G4
Meonstoke SO32 11 H3
Meopham DA13 24 C5
Meopham Green DA13 24 C5
Mepal CB6 43 H7
Meppershall SG17 32 E5
Merbach HR3 28 C4
Mercaston DE6 40 E1
Mere Ches.E. WA16 49 G4
Mere Wilts. BA12 9 H1
Mere Brow PR9 48 D1
Mere Green B75 40 D6
Mere Heath CW9 49 F5
Mereclough BB10 56 D6
Mereside FY4 55 G6
Meretown TF10 39 G3
Mereworth ME18 23 K6
Mergie AB39 91 F6
Meriden CV7 40 E7
Merkadale IV47 85 J1
Merkinch IV3 96 D7
Merkland DG7 65 H3
Merley BH21 10 B5
Merlin's Bridge SA61 16 C4
Merridge TA5 8 B1
Merrifield TQ7 5 J6
Merrington SY4 38 D3
Merrion SA71 16 C6
Merriott TA16 8 D3
Merrivale PL19 5 F3
Merrow GU1 22 D6
Merry Hill Herts. WD23 22 E2
Merry Hill W.Mid. DY5 40 B7
Merry Hill W.Mid. WV3 40 A6
Merrymeet PL14 4 C4
Mersea Island CO5 34 E7
Mersham TN25 15 F4
Merstham RH1 23 F6
Merston PO20 12 B6
Merstone PO30 11 G6
Merther TR2 3 F4
Merthyr SA33 17 G3
Merthyr Cynog LD3 27 J5
Merthyr Dyfan CF62 18 E5
Merthyr Mawr CF32 18 B4
Merthyr Tydfil CF47 18 D1
Merthyr Vale CF48 18 D2
Merton Devon EX20 6 D4
Merton Norf. IP25 44 D6
Merton Oxon. OX25 31 G7
Mervinslaw TD8 70 B2
Meshaw EX36 7 F4
Messing CO5 34 D7
Messingham DN17 52 B2
Metcombe EX11 7 J6
Metfield IP20 45 G7
Metheringham LN4 52 D6
Metherwell PL17 4 E4
Methil KY8 76 B1
Methlem LL53 36 A2
Methley LS26 57 J7
Methley Junction LS26 57 J7
Methlick AB41 91 G1
Methven PH1 82 B5
Methwold IP26 44 B6
Methwold Hythe IP26 44 B6
MetroCentre NE11 71 H7
Mettingham NR35 45 H7
Metton NR11 45 F2
Mevagissey PL26 4 A6
Mewith Head LA2 56 C3
Mexborough S64 51 G3
Mey KW14 105 H1
Meysey Hampton GL7 20 E1
Miabhag W.Isles HS3 93 G2
Miabhag W.Isles HS3 100 C7
Miabhaig (Miavaig) HS2 100 C4
Mial IV21 94 D4
Miavaig (Miabhaig) HS2 100 C4
Michaelchurch HR2 28 E6
Michaelchurch Escley HR2 28 C5
Michaelchurch-on-Arrow HR5 28 B3
Michaelston-le-Pit CF64 18 E4
Michaelston-super-Ely CF5 18 E4
Michaelston-y-Fedw CF3 19 F3
Michaelstow PL30 4 A3
Michelcombe TQ13 5 G4
Micheldever SO21 11 G1
Michelmersh SO51 10 E2
Mickfield IP14 35 F2
Mickle Trafford CH2 48 D6
Micklebring S66 51 H3
Mickleby TS13 63 K5
Micklefield LS25 57 K6
Micklefield Green WD3 22 D2
Mickleham RH5 22 E6
Micklehurst OL5 49 J2
Mickleover DE3 41 F2
Micklethwaite Cumb. CA7 60 D1
Micklethwaite W.Yorks. BD20 57 F5
Mickleton Dur. DL12 62 A4
Mickleton Glos. GL55 30 C4
Mickletown LS26 57 J7
Mickley Derbys. S18 51 F5
Mickley N.Yorks. HG4 57 H2
Mickley Green IP29 34 C3
Mickley Square NE43 71 F7
Mid Ardlaw AB43 99 H4
Mid Beltie AB31 90 E4
Mid Calder EH53 75 J4
Mid Clyth KW3 105 H5
Mid Lambrook TA13 8 D3
Mid Lavant PO18 12 B6
Mid Letter PA27 80 B7
Mid Lix FK21 81 G4
Mid Mossdale DL8 61 K7
Mid Yell ZE2 107 P3
Midbea KW17 106 D3
Middle Assendon RG9 22 A3
Middle Aston OX25 31 F6
Middle Barton OX7 31 F6
Middle Bickenhill B92 40 E7
Middle Bockhampton BH23 10 C5
Middle Claydon MK18 31 J6
Middle Drift PL14 4 B4
Middle Drums DD9 83 G2
Middle Duntisbourne GL7 20 C1
Middle Handley S21 51 G5
Middle Harling NR16 44 D7
Middle Kames PA31 73 H2
Middle Littleton WR11 30 B4
Middle Maes-coed HR2 28 C5
Middle Marwood EX31 6 D2
Middle Mill SA62 16 B3
Middle Quarter TN26 14 D4
Middle Rasen LN8 52 D4
Middle Rigg PH2 82 B7
Middle Salter LA2 56 B3
Middle Sontley LL13 38 C1
Middle Stoford TA21 7 K3
Middle Taphouse PL14 4 B4
Middle Town TR25 2 C1
Middle Tysoe CV35 30 E4
Middle Wallop SO20 10 D1
Middle Winterslow SP5 10 D1
Middle Woodford SP4 10 C1
Middlebie DG11 69 H6
Middlecliff S72 51 G2
Middlecott EX22 6 C5
Middleham DL8 57 G1
Middlehill Aber. AB53 99 G6
Middlehill Cornw. PL14 4 C4
Middlehope SY7 38 E7
Middlemarsh DT9 9 F4
Middlemoor PL19 4 E3
Middlequarter (Ceathramh Meadhanach) HS6 92 D4
Middlesbrough TS1 63 F4
Middlesceugh CA4 60 F2
Middleshaw LA8 55 J1
Middlesmoor HG3 57 F2
Middlestone DL16 62 D3
Middlestone Moor DL16 62 D3
Middlestown WF4 50 E1
Middleton Aber. AB21 91 G3
Middleton Angus DD11 83 G3
Middleton Cumb. LA6 56 B1
Middleton Derbys. DE4 50 E7
Middleton Derbys. DE45 50 D6
Middleton Essex CO10 34 C4
Middleton Gt.Man. M24 49 H2
Middleton Hants. SP11 21 H7
Middleton Here. SY8 28 E2
Middleton Lancs. LA3 55 H4
Middleton Midloth. EH23 76 B5
Middleton N.Yorks. YO18 58 D1
Middleton Norf. PE32 44 A4
Middleton Northants. LE16 42 B7
Middleton Northumb. NE61 71 F5
Middleton Northumb. NE70 77 J7
Middleton P. & K. KY13 82 C7
Middleton P. & K. PH10 82 C3
Middleton Shrop. SY15 38 B6
Middleton Shrop. SY8 28 E1
Middleton Shrop. SY11 38 C3
Middleton Suff. IP17 35 J2
Middleton Swan. SA3 17 H7
Middleton W.Yorks. LS29 57 G5
Middleton W.Yorks. LS10 57 J7
Middleton Warks. B78 40 D6
Middleton Baggot WV16 39 F6
Middleton Bank Top NE61 71 F5
Middleton Cheney OX17 31 F4
Middleton Green ST10 40 B2
Middleton Hall NE71 70 E1
Middleton Moor IP17 35 J2
Middleton of Potterton AB23 91 H3
Middleton on the Hill SY8 28 E2
Middleton One Row DL2 62 E5
Middleton Park AB22 91 H3
Middleton Priors WV16 39 F7
Middleton Quernhow HG4 57 J2
Middleton St. George DL2 62 E5
Middleton Scriven WV16 39 F7
Middleton Stoney OX25 31 G6
Middleton Tyas DL10 62 D6
Middleton-in-Teesdale DL12 62 A4
Middleton-on-Leven TS15 63 F5
Middleton-on-Sea PO22 12 C6
Middleton-on-the-Wolds YO25 59 F5
Middletown Cumb. CA22 60 A6
Middletown Powys SY21 38 C4
Middlewich CW10 49 G6
Middlewood Ches.E. SK12 49 J4
Middlewood S.Yorks. S6 51 F3
Middlewood Green IP14 34 E2
Middlezoy TA7 8 C1
Middridge DL4 62 D4
Midfield IV27 103 H2
Midford BA2 20 A5
Midge Hall PR26 55 J7
Midgeholme CA8 61 H1
Midgham RG7 21 J5
Midgley W.Yorks. WF4 50 E1
Midgley W.Yorks. HX2 57 F7
Midhopestones S36 50 E3
Midhurst GU29 12 B4
Midlem TD7 70 A1
Midloe Grange PE19 32 E2
Midpark PA20 73 J5
Midsomer Norton BA3 19 K6
Midthorpe LN9 53 F5
Midtown High. IV27 103 H2
Midtown High. IV22 94 E3
Midtown of Barras AB39 91 G6
Midville PE22 53 G7
Midway DE11 41 F3
Migdale IV24 96 D2
Migvie AB34 90 C4
Milarrochy G63 74 C1
Milber TQ12 5 J3
Milbethill AB54 98 E5
Milborne Port DT9 9 F3
Milborne St. Andrew DT11 9 G5
Milborne Wick DT9 9 F2
Milbourne Northumb. NE20 71 G6
Milbourne Wilts. SN16 20 C3
Milburn CA10 61 H4
Milbury Heath GL12 19 K2
Milcombe OX15 31 F5
Milden IP7 34 D4
Mildenhall Suff. IP28 34 B1
Mildenhall Wilts. SN8 21 F5
Mile Elm SN11 20 C5
Mile End Essex CO4 34 D6
Mile End Glos. GL16 28 E7
Mile Oak TN12 23 K7
Mile Town ME12 25 F4
Milebrook LD7 28 C1
Milebush TN12 14 C3
Mileham PE32 44 D4
Miles Green ST7 40 A1
Miles Hope WR15 28 E2
Milesmark KY12 75 J2
Miles's Green RG7 21 J5
Milfield NE71 77 H7
Milford Derbys. DE56 41 F1
Milford Devon EX39 6 A3
Milford Shrop. SY4 38 D3
Milford Staffs. ST17 40 B3
Milford Surr. GU8 22 C7
Milford Haven (Aberdaugleddau) SA73 16 B5
Milford on Sea SO41 10 D5
Milkwall GL16 19 J1
Mill Bank HX6 57 F7
Mill Brow SK6 49 J4
Mill End Bucks. RG9 22 A3
Mill End Cambs. CB8 33 K3
Mill End Herts. SG9 33 G5
Mill End Green CM6 33 K6
Mill Green Cambs. CB21 33 K4
Mill Green Essex CM4 24 C1
Mill Green Herts. AL9 23 F1
Mill Green Norf. IP22 45 F7
Mill Green Shrop. TF9 39 F3
Mill Green Staffs. WS15 40 C3
Mill Green Suff. IP13 35 H2
Mill Green Suff. IP14 35 F3
Mill Green Suff. IP14 34 D3
Mill Green W.Mid. WS9 40 C5
Mill Hill B'burn. BB2 56 B7
Mill Hill Cambs. SG19 33 F3
Mill Hill Gt.Lon. NW7 23 F2
Mill Houses LA2 56 B3
Mill Lane GU10 22 A6
Mill of Camsail G84 74 A2
Mill of Colp AB53 99 F6
Mill of Elrick AB41 99 H6
Mill of Fortune PH6 81 J5
Mill of Kingoodie AB21 91 G2
Mill of Monquich AB39 91 G5
Mill of Uras AB39 91 G6
Mill Side LA11 55 H1
Mill Street Kent ME19 23 K6
Mill Street Norf. NR20 44 E4
Milland GU30 12 B4
Millbank AB42 99 J6
Millbeck CA12 60 D4
Millbounds KW17 106 E4
Millbreck AB42 99 J6
Millbridge GU10 22 B7
Millbrook Cen.Beds. MK45 32 D5
Millbrook Cornw. PL10 4 E5
Millbrook Devon EX13 8 C5
Millbrook S'ham. SO15 10 E3
Millburn Aber. AB33 90 D2
Millburn Aber. AB54 90 E1
Millcombe TQ9 5 J6
Millcorner TN31 14 D5
Milldale DE6 50 D7
Millden AB23 91 H3
Milldens DD8 83 G2
Millearne PH7 82 A6
Millend OX7 30 E6
Millenheath SY13 38 E2
Millerhill EH22 76 B4
Miller's Dale SK17 50 D5
Millers Green Derbys. DE4 50 E7
Miller's Green Essex CM5 23 J1
Millgate OL12 56 D7
Millhalf HR3 28 B4
Millhayes Devon EX15 7 K4
Millhayes Devon EX14 8 B4
Millholme LA8 61 G7
Millhouse Arg. & B. PA21 73 H3
Millhouse Cumb. CA7 60 E3
Millhouse Green S36 50 E2
Millhousebridge DG11 69 G5
Millikenpark PA10 74 C4
Millin Cross SA62 16 C4
Millington YO42 58 E4
Millington Green DE6 40 E1
Millmeece ST21 40 A2
Millness IV63 87 K1
Millom LA18 54 E1
Millow SG18 33 F4
Millpool PL30 4 B3
Millport KA28 73 K5
Millthorpe S18 51 F5
Millthrop LA10 61 H7
Milltimber AB13 91 G4
Milltown Aber. AB36 89 K4
Milltown Cornw. PL22 4 B5
Milltown D. & G. DG14 69 J6
Milltown Derbys. S45 51 F6
Milltown Devon EX31 6 D2
Milltown High. IV12 97 G7
Milltown of Aberdalgie PH2 82 B5
Milltown of Auchindoun AB55 90 B1
Milltown of Craigston AB53 99 F5
Milltown of Edinvillie AB38 97 K7
Milltown of Kildrummy AB33 90 C3
Milltown of Rothiemay AB54 98 D6
Milltown of Towie AB33 90 C3
Milnathort KY13 82 C7
Milners Heath CH3 48 D6
Milngavie G62 74 D3
Milnrow OL16 49 J1
Milnsbridge HD3 50 D1
Milnthorpe LA7 55 H1
Milovaig IV55 93 G6
Milrig KA4 74 D7
Milson DY14 29 F1
Milstead ME9 14 E2
Milston SP4 20 E7
Milton Angus DD8 82 E3
Milton Cambs. CB24 33 H2
Milton Cumb. CA8 70 A7
Milton D. & G. DG2 68 D5
Milton D. & G. DG2 65 J3
Milton D. & G. DG8 64 C5
Milton Derbys. DE65 41 F3
Milton High. IV6 95 K6
Milton High. IV18 96 E4
Milton High. IV12 97 G6
Milton High. IV54 94 D7
Milton High. IV6 96 C7
Milton High. KW1 105 J3
Milton High. IV63 88 B1
Milton Moray AB56 98 D4
Milton N.Som. BS22 19 G5
Milton Newport NP19 19 G3
Milton Notts. NG22 51 K5
Milton Oxon. OX15 31 F5
Milton Oxon. OX14 21 H2
Milton P. & K. PH8 82 A4
Milton Pembs. SA70 16 D5
Milton Ports. PO4 11 H5
Milton Som. TA12 8 D2
Milton Stir. FK8 81 G7
Milton Stoke ST2 49 J7
Milton W.Dun. G82 74 C3
Milton Abbas DT11 9 H4
Milton Abbot PL19 4 E3
Milton Bridge EH26 76 A4
Milton Bryan MK17 32 C5
Milton Clevedon BA4 9 F1
Milton Combe PL20 4 E4
Milton Damerel EX22 6 B4
Milton End GL2 29 G7
Milton Ernest MK44 32 D3
Milton Green CH3 48 D7
Milton Hill OX13 21 H2
MILTON KEYNES MK 32 B5
Milton Keynes Village MK10 32 B5
Milton Lilbourne SN9 20 E5
Milton Malsor NN7 31 J3
Milton Morenish FK21 81 H4
Milton of Auchinhove AB31 90 D4
Milton of Balgonie KY7 82 E7
Milton of Buchanan G63 74 C1
Milton of Cairnborrow AB54 98 C6
Milton of Callander FK17 81 G7
Milton of Campfield AB31 90 E4
Milton of Campsie G66 74 E3
Milton of Coldwells AB41 91 H1
Milton of Cullerlie AB32 91 F4
Milton of Cushnie AB33 90 D3
Milton of Dalcapon PH9 82 A2
Milton of Inveramsay AB51 91 F2
Milton of Noth AB54 90 D2
Milton of Tullich AB35 90 B5
Milton on Stour SP8 9 G2
Milton Regis ME10 24 E5
Milton Street BN26 13 J6
Miltonduff IV30 97 J5
Miltonhill IV36 97 H5
Miltonise DG8 64 B3
Milton-Lockhart ML8 75 G6
Milton-under-Wychwood OX7 30 D7
Milverton Som. TA4 7 K3
Milverton Warks. CV32 30 E2
Milwich ST18 40 B2
Mimbridge GU24 22 C5
Minard PA32 73 H1
Minard Castle PA32 73 H1
Minchington DT11 9 J3
Minchinhampton GL6 20 B1
Mindrum TD12 77 G7
Mindrummill TD12 77 G7
Minehead TA24 7 H1
Minera LL11 48 B7
Minety SN16 20 D2
Minety Lower Moor SN16 20 D2

Newton *Bridgend* **CF36** 18 B4
Newton *Cambs.* **PE13** 43 H4
Newton *Cambs.* **CB22** 33 H4
Newton *Cardiff* **CF3** 19 F4
Newton *Ches.W. & C.* **CH3** 48 E7
Newton *Ches.W. & C.* **WA6** 48 E5
Newton *Cumb.* **LA13** 55 F2
Newton *D. & G.* **DG10** 69 G4
Newton *Derbys.* **DE55** 51 G7
Newton *Gt.Man.* **SK14** 49 J3
Newton *Here.* **SY7** 28 C2
Newton *Here.* **HR6** 28 E3
Newton *Here.* **HR2** 28 C5
Newton *High.* **KW1** 105 J3
Newton *High.* **IV2** 96 E7
Newton *High.* **KW1** 105 H3
Newton *High.* **IV27** 102 E5
Newton *High.* **IV6** 96 C6
Newton *High.* **IV11** 96 E5
Newton *Lancs.* **BB7** 56 B4
Newton *Lancs.* **LA6** 55 J2
Newton *Lancs.* **FY3** 55 G6
Newton *Lincs.* **NG34** 42 D2
Newton *Moray* **IV32** 98 B4
Newton *N.Ayr.* **KA27** 73 H5
Newton *Norf.* **PE32** 44 C4
Newton *Northants.* **NN14** 42 B7
Newton *Northumb.* **NE43** 71 F7
Newton *Northumb.* **NE65** 70 E3
Newton *Notts.* **NG13** 41 J1
Newton *P. & K.* **PH8** 81 K4
Newton *Pembs.* **SA62** 16 B3
Newton *Pembs.* **SA71** 16 C5
Newton *S.Glos.* **BS35** 19 K2
Newton *S.Lan.* **ML12** 75 H7
Newton *Sc.Bord.* **TD8** 70 B1
Newton *Shrop.* **SY12** 38 D2
Newton *Som.* **TA4** 7 K2
Newton *Staffs.* **WS15** 40 C3
Newton *Suff.* **CO10** 34 D4
Newton *Swan.* **SA3** 17 K7
Newton *W.Loth.* **EH52** 75 J3
Newton *W.Yorks.* **WF10** 57 K7
Newton *Warks.* **CV23** 31 G1
Newton *Wilts.* **SP5** 10 D2
Newton Abbot TQ12 5 **J3**
Newton Arlosh **CA7** 60 D1
Newton Aycliffe DL5 62 **D4**
Newton Bewley **TS22** 63 F4
Newton Blossomville **MK43** 32 C3
Newton Bromswold **MK44** 32 C2
Newton Burgoland **LE67** 41 F5
Newton by Toft **LN8** 52 D4
Newton Ferrers **PL8** 5 F6
Newton Flotman **NR15** 45 G6
Newton Green **NP16** 19 J2
Newton Harcourt **LE8** 41 J6
Newton Kyme **LS24** 57 K5
Newton Longville **MK17** 32 B5
Newton Mearns **G77** 74 D5
Newton Morrell *N.Yorks.* **DL10** 62 D6
Newton Morrell *Oxon.* **OX27** 31 H6
Newton Mountain **SA73** 16 C5
Newton Mulgrave **TS13** 63 J5
Newton of Affleck **DD5** 83 F4
Newton of Ardtoe **PH36** 86 C7
Newton of Balcanquhal **PH2** 82 C6
Newton of Dalvey **IV36** 97 H6
Newton of Falkland **KY15** 82 D7
Newton of Leys **IV2** 88 D1
Newton on the Hill **SY4** 38 D3
Newton on Trent **LN1** 52 B5
Newton Poppleford **EX10** 7 J7
Newton Purcell **MK18** 31 H5
Newton Regis **B79** 40 E5
Newton Reigny **CA11** 61 F3
Newton St. Cyres **EX5** 7 G6
Newton St. Faith **NR10** 45 G4
Newton St. Loe **BA2** 20 A5
Newton St. Petrock **EX22** 6 C4
Newton Solney **DE15** 40 E3
Newton Stacey **SO20** 21 H7
Newton Stewart DG8 64 **E4**
Newton Tony **SP4** 21 F7
Newton Tracey **EX31** 6 D3
Newton under Roseberry **TS9** 63 G5
Newton Underwood **NE61** 71 G5
Newton upon Derwent **YO41** 58 D5
Newton Valence **GU34** 11 J1
Newton with Scales **PR4** 55 H6
Newtonairds **DG2** 68 D5
Newtongrange **EH22** 76 B4
Newtonhill **AB39** 91 H5
Newton-le-Willows *Mersey.* WA12 48 **E3**
Newton-le-Willows *N.Yorks.* **DL8** 57 H1
Newtonmill **DD9** 83 H1
Newtonmore PH20 88 **E5**
Newton-on-Ouse **YO30** 58 B4
Newton-on-Rawcliffe **YO18** 63 K7
Newton-on-the-Moor **NE65** 71 G3
Newtown *Bucks.* **HP5** 22 C1
Newtown *Ches.W. & C.* **CH3** 48 E7
Newtown *Cornw.* **PL15** 4 C3
Newtown *Cornw.* **TR20** 2 C6
Newtown *Cumb.* **CA6** 70 A7
Newtown *Derbys.* **SK22** 49 J4
Newtown *Devon* **EX36** 7 F3
Newtown *Devon* **EX5** 7 J6
Newtown *Dorset* **DT8** 8 D4
Newtown *Glos.* **GL13** 19 K1
Newtown *Gt.Man.* **WN5** 48 E2
Newtown *Gt.Man.* **M27** 49 G2
Newtown *Hants.* **PO17** 11 H3
Newtown *Hants.* **RG20** 21 H5
Newtown *Hants.* **SO43** 10 D3
Newtown *Hants.* **SO51** 10 E2
Newtown *Hants.* **SO32** 11 G3
Newtown *Here.* **HR8** 29 F4
Newtown *Here.* **HR6** 28 D3
Newtown *High.* **PH35** 87 K4
Newtown *I.o.M.* **IM4** 54 C6
Newtown *I.o.W.* **PO30** 11 F5
Newtown *Northumb.* **NE65** 71 F3
Newtown *Northumb.* **NE66** 71 F1
Newtown *Oxon.* **RG9** 22 A3
Newtown (Y Drenewydd) *Powys* SY16 38 **A6**
Newtown *R.C.T.* **CF45** 18 D2
Newtown *Shrop.* **SY4** 38 D2
Newtown *Som.* **TA6** 8 B1
Newtown *Som.* **TA20** 8 B3
Newtown *Staffs.* **ST8** 49 J6
Newtown *Staffs.* **SK17** 50 C6
Newtown *Staffs.* **WS6** 40 B5
Newtown *Wilts.* **SP3** 9 J2
Newtown *Wilts.* **SN8** 21 G5
Newtown Linford **LE6** 41 H5
Newtown St. Boswells **TD6** 76 D7
Newtown Unthank **LE9** 41 G5
Newtown-in-St-Martin **TR12** 2 E6
Newtyle **PH12** 82 D3
Newyears Green **UB9** 22 D3
Neyland **SA73** 16 C5
Nibley *Glos.* **GL15** 19 K1
Nibley *S.Glos.* **BS37** 19 K3
Nibley Green **GL11** 20 A2
Nicholashayne **TA21** 7 K4
Nicholaston **SA3** 17 J7
Nidd **HG3** 57 J3
Nigg *Aberdeen* **AB12** 91 H4
Nigg *High.* **IV19** 97 F4
Nightcott **TA22** 7 G3
Nilig **LL15** 47 J7
Nilston Rigg **NE47** 70 D7
Nimlet **SN14** 20 A4
Nine Ashes **CM4** 23 J1
Nine Elms **SN5** 20 E3
Nine Mile Burn **EH26** 75 K5
Ninebanks **NE47** 61 J1
Ninemile Bar (Crocketford) **DG2** 65 J3
Nineveh **WR15** 29 F2
Ninfield **TN33** 14 C6
Ningwood **PO30** 11 F6
Nisbet **TD8** 70 B1
Niton **PO38** 11 G7
Nitshill **G53** 74 D4
Niwbwrch (Newborough) **LL61** 46 C6
Nizels **TN11** 23 J6
No Man's Heath *Ches.W. & C.* **SY14** 38 E1
No Man's Heath *Warks.* **B79** 40 E5
No Man's Land **PL13** 4 C5
Noah's Ark **TN15** 23 J6
Noak Hill **RM4** 23 J2
Noblehill **DG1** 65 K3
Noblethorpe **S75** 50 E2
Nobottle **NN7** 31 H2
Nocton **LN4** 52 D6
Noddsdale **KA30** 74 A4
Nogdam End **NR14** 45 H5
Noke **OX3** 31 G7
Nolton **SA62** 16 B4
Nolton Haven **SA62** 16 B4
Nomansland *Devon* **EX16** 7 G4
Nomansland *Wilts.* **SP5** 10 D3
Noneley **SY4** 38 D3
Nonington **CT15** 15 H2
Nook *Cumb.* **CA6** 69 K6
Nook *Cumb.* **LA6** 55 J1
Noonsbrough **ZE2** 107 L7
Noranside **DD8** 83 F1
Norbreck **FY5** 55 G5
Norbury *Ches.E.* **SY13** 38 E1
Norbury *Derbys.* **DE6** 40 D1
Norbury *Gt.Lon.* **SW16** 23 G4
Norbury *Shrop.* **SY9** 38 C6
Norbury *Staffs.* **ST20** 39 G3
Norbury Common **SY13** 38 E1
Norbury Junction **ST20** 39 G3
Norchard **SA70** 16 D6
Norcott Brook **WA4** 49 F4
Nordelph **PE38** 43 J5
Norden *Dorset* **BH20** 9 J6
Norden *Gt.Man.* **OL11** 49 H1
Nordley **WV16** 39 F6
Norham **TD15** 77 H6
Norland Town **HX6** 57 F7
Norley **WA6** 48 E5
Norleywood **SO41** 10 E5
Norlington **BN8** 13 H5
Norman Cross **PE7** 42 E6
Normanby *N.Lincs.* **DN15** 52 B1
Normanby *N.Yorks.* **YO62** 58 D1
Normanby *R. & C.* **TS6** 63 G5
Normanby by Stow **DN21** 52 B4
Normanby le Wold **LN7** 52 E3
Normanby-by-Spital **LN8** 52 D4
Normandy **GU3** 22 C6
Normann's Ruh **PA74** 79 F3
Norman's Bay **BN24** 13 K6
Norman's Green **EX15** 7 J5
Normanston **NR32** 45 K6
Normanton *Derby* **DE23** 41 F2
Normanton *Leics.* **NG13** 42 B1
Normanton *Lincs.* **NG32** 42 C1
Normanton *Notts.* **NG25** 51 K7
Normanton *Rut.* **LE15** 42 C5
Normanton *W.Yorks.* WF6 57 **J7**
Normanton le Heath **LE67** 41 F4
Normanton on Soar **LE12** 41 H3
Normanton on Trent **NG23** 51 K6
Normanton-on-the-Wolds **NG12** 41 J2
Normoss **FY3** 55 G6
Norrington Common **SN12** 20 B5
Norris Green **PL17** 4 E4
Norris Hill **DE12** 41 F4
Norristhorpe **WF15** 57 H7
North Acton **W3** 23 F3
North Anston **S25** 51 H4
North Ascot **SL5** 22 C5
North Aston **OX25** 31 F6
North Baddesley **SO52** 10 E3
North Ballachulish **PH33** 80 B1
North Balloch **KA26** 67 H4
North Barrow **BA22** 9 F2
North Barsham **NR22** 44 D2
North Benfleet **SS12** 24 D3
North Bersted **PO21** 12 C6
North Berwick EH39 76 **D2**
North Boarhunt **PO17** 11 H3
North Bogbain **AB55** 98 B5
North Bovey **TQ13** 7 F7
North Bradley **BA14** 20 B6
North Brentor **PL19** 6 C7
North Brewham **BA10** 9 G1
North Bridge **GU8** 12 C3
North Buckland **EX33** 6 C1
North Burlingham **NR13** 45 H4
North Cadbury **BA22** 9 F2
North Cairn **DG9** 66 D6
North Camp **GU14** 22 B6
North Carlton *Lincs.* **LN1** 52 C5
North Carlton *Notts.* **S81** 51 H4
North Cave **HU15** 58 E6
North Cerney **GL7** 20 D1
North Chailey **BN8** 13 G4
North Charford **SP6** 10 C3
North Charlton **NE67** 71 G1
North Cheriton **BA8** 9 F2
North Chideock **DT6** 8 D5
North Cliffe **YO43** 58 E6
North Clifton **NG23** 52 B5
North Cockerington **LN11** 53 G3
North Coker **BA22** 8 E3
North Collafirth **ZE2** 107 M4
North Common *S.Glos.* **BS30** 19 K4
North Common *Suff.* **IP22** 34 D1
North Commonty **AB53** 99 G6
North Connel **PA37** 80 A4
North Coombe **EX17** 7 G5
North Cornelly **CF33** 18 B3
North Corner **BS36** 19 K3
North Cotes **DN36** 53 G2
North Cove **NR34** 45 J7
North Cowton **DL7** 62 D6
North Crawley **MK16** 32 C4
North Cray **DA14** 23 H4
North Creake **NR21** 44 C2
North Curry **TA3** 8 C2
North Dallens **PA38** 80 A3
North Dalton **YO25** 59 F4
North Dawn **KW17** 106 D7
North Deighton **LS22** 57 J4
North Dell (Dail Bho Thuath) **HS2** 101 G1
North Duffield **YO8** 58 C6
North Elkington **LN11** 53 F3
North Elmham **NR20** 44 D3
North Elmsall **WF9** 51 G1
North End *Bucks.* **LU7** 32 B6
North End *Dorset* **SP7** 9 H2
North End *E.Riding* **YO25** 59 H4
North End *E.Riding* **HU11** 59 H5
North End *E.Riding* **HU12** 59 J6
North End *Essex* **CM6** 33 K7
North End *Hants.* **SO24** 11 G2
North End *Hants.* **SP6** 10 C3
North End *Leics.* **LE12** 41 H4
North End *N.Som.* **BS49** 19 H5
North End *Norf.* **NR16** 44 E6
North End *Northumb.* **NE65** 71 G3
North End *Ports.* **PO2** 11 H4
North End *W.Suss.* **BN14** 12 E5
North End *W.Suss.* **BN18** 12 C6
North Erradale **IV21** 94 D3
North Essie **AB42** 99 J5
North Fambridge **CM3** 24 E2
North Ferriby HU14 59 **F7**
North Frodingham **YO25** 59 H4
North Gorley **SP6** 10 C3
North Green *Norf.* **IP21** 45 G7
North Green *Suff.* **IP19** 35 H1
North Green *Suff.* **IP17** 35 H2
North Green *Suff.* **IP17** 35 H2
North Grimston **YO17** 58 E3
North Halling **ME2** 24 D5
North Harby **NG23** 52 B5
North Hayling **PO11** 11 J4
North Hazelrigg **NE66** 77 J7
North Heasley **EX36** 7 F2
North Heath *W.Berks.* **RG20** 21 H4
North Heath *W.Suss.* **RH20** 12 D4
North Hill **PL15** 4 C3
North Hillingdon **UB10** 22 D3
North Hinksey **OX2** 21 H1
North Holmwood **RH5** 22 E7
North Houghton **SO20** 10 E1
North Huish **TQ10** 5 H5
North Hykeham **LN6** 52 C6
North Johnston **SA62** 16 C4
North Kelsey **LN7** 52 D2
North Kessock **IV1** 96 D7
North Killingholme **DN40** 52 E1
North Kilvington **YO7** 57 K1
North Kilworth **LE17** 41 J7
North Kingston **BH24** 10 C4
North Kyme **LN4** 52 E7
North Lancing **BN15** 12 E6
North Lee **HP22** 22 B1
North Lees **HG4** 57 J2
North Leigh **OX29** 30 E7
North Leverton with Habblesthorpe **DN22** 51 K4
North Littleton **WR11** 30 B4
North Lopham **IP22** 44 E7
North Luffenham **LE15** 42 C5
North Marden **PO18** 12 B5
North Marston **MK18** 31 J6
North Middleton *Midloth.* **EH23** 76 B5
North Middleton *Northumb.* **NE71** 71 F1
North Millbrex **AB53** 99 G6
North Molton **EX36** 7 F3
North Moreton **OX11** 21 J3
North Mundham **PO20** 12 B6
North Muskham **NG23** 51 K7
North Newbald **YO43** 59 F6
North Newington **OX15** 31 F5
North Newnton **SN9** 20 E6
North Newton **TA7** 8 B1
North Nibley **GL11** 20 A2
North Oakley **RG26** 21 J6
North Ockendon **RM14** 23 J3
North Ormesby **TS3** 63 G5
North Ormsby **LN11** 53 F3
North Otterington **DL7** 57 J1
North Owersby **LN8** 52 D3
North Perrott **TA18** 8 D4
North Petherton **TA6** 8 B1
North Petherwin **PL15** 4 C2
North Pickenham **PE37** 44 C5
North Piddle **WR7** 29 J3
North Plain **CA7** 69 G7
North Pool **TQ7** 5 H6
North Poorton **DT6** 8 E5
North Quarme **TA24** 7 H2
North Queensferry **KY11** 75 K2
North Radworthy **EX36** 7 F2
North Rauceby **NG34** 42 D1
North Reston **LN11** 53 G4
North Rigton **LS17** 57 H5
North Rode **CW12** 49 H6
North Roe **ZE2** 107 M4
North Ronaldsay **KW17** 106 G2
North Ronaldsay Airfield **KW17** 106 G2
North Runcton **PE33** 44 A4
North Sandwick **ZE2** 107 P3
North Scale **LA14** 54 E3
North Scarle **LN6** 52 B6
North Seaton **NE63** 71 H5
North Shian **PA38** 80 A3
North Shields NE30 71 **J7**
North Shoebury **SS3** 25 F3
North Side **PE6** 43 F6
North Skelton **TS12** 63 H5
North Somercotes **LN11** 53 H3
North Stainley **HG4** 57 H2
North Stainmore **CA17** 61 K5
North Stifford **RM16** 24 C3
North Stoke *B. & N.E.Som.* **BA1** 20 A5
North Stoke *Oxon.* **OX10** 21 K3
North Stoke *W.Suss.* **BN18** 12 D5
North Stoneham **SO50** 11 F3
North Street *Hants.* **SO24** 11 H1
North Street *Kent* **ME13** 15 F2
North Street *Med.* **ME3** 24 E4
North Street *W.Berks.* **RG7** 21 K4
North Sunderland **NE68** 77 K4
North Tamerton **EX22** 6 B6
North Tarbothill **AB23** 91 H3
North Tawton EX20 6 **E5**
North Third **FK7** 75 F2
North Thoresby **DN36** 53 F3
North Tidworth **SP9** 21 F7
North Togston **NE65** 71 H3
North Town *Devon* **EX20** 6 D5
North Town *Hants.* **GU12** 22 B6
North Town *W. & M.* **SL6** 22 B3
North Tuddenham **NR20** 44 E4
North Uist (Uibhist a Tuath) HS6 92 **D4**
North Walsham NR28 45 **G2**
North Waltham **RG25** 21 J7
North Warnborough **RG29** 22 A6
North Water Bridge **AB30** 83 H1
North Watten **KW1** 105 H3
North Weald Bassett **CM16** 23 H1
North Wembley **HA0** 22 E3
North Wheatley **DN22** 51 K4
North Whilborough **TQ12** 5 J4
North Wick **BS41** 19 J5
North Widcombe **BS40** 19 J6
North Willingham **LN8** 52 E4
North Wingfield **S42** 51 G6
North Witham **NG33** 42 C3
North Wootton *Dorset* **DT9** 9 F3
North Wootton *Norf.* **PE30** 44 A3
North Wootton *Som.* **BA4** 19 J7
North Wraxall **SN14** 20 B4
North Wroughton **SN4** 20 E3
North Yardhope **NE65** 70 E3
Northacre **NR17** 44 D6
Northall **LU6** 32 C6
Northall Green **NR20** 44 D4
Northallerton DL6 62 **E7**
Northam *Devon* **EX39** 6 C3
Northam *S'ham.* **SO14** 11 F3
NORTHAMPTON NN 31 **J2**
Northaw **EN6** 23 F1
Northay *Devon* **EX13** 8 C4
Northay *Som.* **TA20** 8 B3
Northbay **HS9** 84 C4
Northbeck **NG34** 42 D1
Northborough **PE6** 42 E5
Northbourne *Kent* **CT14** 15 J2
Northbourne *Oxon.* **OX11** 21 J3
Northbridge Street **TN32** 14 C5
Northbrook *Hants.* **SO21** 11 G1
Northbrook *Oxon.* **OX5** 31 F6
Northburnhill **AB53** 99 G6
Northchapel **GU28** 12 C4
Northchurch **HP4** 22 C1
Northcote Manor **EX37** 6 E4
Northcott **PL15** 6 B6
Northcourt **OX14** 21 J2
Northdyke **KW16** 106 B5
Northedge **S42** 51 F6
Northend *B. & N.E.Som.* **BA1** 20 A5
Northend *Bucks.* **RG9** 22 A2
Northend *Warks.* **CV47** 30 E3
Northfield *Aber.* **AB45** 99 G4
Northfield *Aberdeen* **AB16** 91 H4
Northfield *High.* **KW1** 105 J4
Northfield *Hull* **HU4** 59 G7
Northfield *Sc.Bord.* **TD14** 77 H4
Northfield *Som.* **TA6** 8 B1
Northfield *W.Mid.* **B31** 30 B1
Northfields **PE9** 42 D5
Northfleet **DA11** 24 C4
Northhouse **TD9** 69 K3
Northiam **TN31** 14 D5
Northill **SG18** 32 E4
Northington *Glos.* **GL14** 20 A1
Northington *Hants.* **SO24** 11 G1
Northlands **PE22** 53 G7
Northleach **GL54** 30 C7
Northleigh *Devon* **EX24** 7 K6
Northleigh *Devon* **EX32** 6 E2
Northlew **EX20** 6 D6
Northmoor **OX29** 21 H1
Northmoor Green (Moorland) **TA7** 8 C1
Northmuir **DD8** 82 E2
Northney **PO11** 11 J4
Northolt UB5 22 **E3**
Northop (Llaneurgain) **CH7** 48 B6
Northop Hall **CH7** 48 B6
Northorpe *Lincs.* **PE11** 43 F2
Northorpe *Lincs.* **DN21** 52 B3
Northorpe *Lincs.* **PE10** 42 D4
Northover *Som.* **BA22** 8 E2
Northover *Som.* **BA6** 8 D1
Northowram **HX3** 57 G7
Northport **BH20** 9 J6
Northpunds **ZE2** 107 N10
Northrepps **NR27** 45 G2
Northton (Taobh Tuath) **HS3** 92 E3
Northtown **KW17** 106 D8
Northway *Glos.* **GL20** 29 J5
Northway *Som.* **TA4** 7 K3
Northwich CW8 49 **F5**
Northwick *S.Glos.* **BS35** 19 J3
Northwick *Som.* **TA9** 19 G7
Northwick *Worcs.* **WR3** 29 H3
Northwold **IP26** 44 B6
Northwood *Gt.Lon.* HA6 22 **D2**
Northwood *I.o.W.* **PO31** 11 F5
Northwood *Kent* **CT12** 25 K5
Northwood *Mersey.* **L33** 48 D3
Northwood *Shrop.* **SY4** 38 D2
Northwood Green **GL14** 29 G7
Northwood Hills **HA6** 22 E2
Norton *Glos.* **GL2** 29 H6
Norton *Halton* **WA7** 48 E4
Norton *Herts.* **SG6** 33 F5
Norton *I.o.W.* **PO41** 10 E6
Norton *Mon.* **NP7** 28 D6
Norton *N.Som.* **BS22** 19 G5
Norton *N.Yorks.* **YO17** 58 D2
Norton *Northants.* **NN11** 31 H2
Norton *Notts.* **NG20** 51 H5
Norton *Powys* **LD8** 28 C2
Norton *S.Yorks.* **DN6** 51 H1
Norton *S.Yorks.* **S8** 51 F4
Norton *Shrop.* **SY4** 38 E5
Norton *Shrop.* **TF11** 39 G5
Norton *Shrop.* **SY7** 38 D7
Norton *Stock.* **TS20** 63 F4
Norton *Suff.* **IP31** 34 D2
Norton *Swan.* **SA3** 17 K7
Norton *V. of Glam.* **CF32** 18 B4
Norton *W.Mid.* **DY8** 40 A7
Norton *W.Suss.* **PO20** 12 C6
Norton *W.Suss.* **PO20** 12 B7
Norton *Wilts.* **SN16** 20 B3
Norton *Worcs.* **WR5** 29 H3
Norton *Worcs.* **WR11** 30 B4
Norton Bavant **BA12** 20 C7
Norton Bridge **ST15** 40 A2
Norton Canes **WS11** 40 C5
Norton Canon **HR4** 28 C4
Norton Disney **LN6** 52 B7
Norton Ferris **BA12** 9 G1
Norton Fitzwarren **TA2** 7 K3
Norton Green *Herts.* **SG1** 33 F6
Norton Green *I.o.W.* **PO40** 10 E6
Norton Green *Stoke* **ST6** 49 J7
Norton Hawkfield **BS40** 19 J5
Norton Heath **CM4** 24 C1
Norton in Hales **TF9** 39 G2
Norton in the Moors **ST6** 49 H7
Norton Lindsey **CV35** 30 D2
Norton Little Green **IP31** 34 D2
Norton Malreward **BS39** 19 K5
Norton Mandeville **CM5** 23 J1

Norton St. Philip **BA2** 20 A6
Norton Subcourse **NR14** 45 J6
Norton Wood **HR4** 28 C4
Norton Woodseats **S8** 51 F4
Norton-Juxta-Twycross **CV9** 41 F5
Norton-le-Clay **YO61** 57 K2
Norton-sub-Hamdon **TA14** 8 D3
Norwell **NG23** 51 K6
Norwell Woodhouse **NG23** 51 K6
NORWICH NR 45 G5
Norwich International Airport **NR6** 45 G4
Norwick **ZE2** 107 Q1
Norwood End **CM5** 23 J1
Norwood Green *Gt.Lon.* **UB2** 22 E4
Norwood Green *W.Yorks.* **HX3** 57 G7
Norwood Hill **RH6** 23 F7
Norwood Park **BA6** 8 E1
Noseley **LE7** 42 A6
Noss Mayo **PL8** 5 F6
Nosterfield **DL8** 57 H1
Nosterfield End **CB21** 33 K4
Nostie **IV40** 86 E2
Notgrove **GL54** 30 C6
Nottage **CF36** 18 B4
Notting Hill **W11** 23 F3
Nottingham *High.* **KW5** 105 H5
NOTTINGHAM *Nott.* NG 41 H1
Nottingham East Midlands Airport **DE74** 41 G3
Nottington **DT3** 9 F6
Notton *W.Yorks.* **WF4** 51 F1
Notton *Wilts.* **SN15** 20 C5
Nottswood Hill **GL17** 29 G7
Nounsley **CM3** 34 B7
Noutard's Green **WR6** 29 G2
Nowton **IP29** 34 C2
Nox **SY5** 38 D4
Noyadd Trefawr **SA43** 17 F1
Nuffield **RG9** 21 K3
Nun Monkton **YO26** 58 B4
Nunburnholme **YO42** 58 E5
Nuneaton CV11 41 F6
Nuneham Courtenay **OX44** 21 J2
Nunney **BA11** 20 A7
Nunnington *Here.* **HR1** 28 E4
Nunnington *N.Yorks.* **YO62** 58 C2
Nunnington Park **TA4** 7 J3
Nunnykirk **NE61** 71 F4
Nunsthorpe **DN32** 53 F2
Nunthorpe *Middbro.* **TS7** 63 G5
Nunthorpe *York* **YO23** 58 B4
Nunton **SP5** 10 C2
Nunwick *N.Yorks.* **HG4** 57 J2
Nunwick *Northumb.* **NE48** 70 D6
Nup End **SG4** 33 F7
Nupend **GL10** 20 A1
Nursling **SO16** 10 E3
Nursted **GU31** 11 J2
Nurton **WV6** 40 A6
Nutbourne *W.Suss.* **RH20** 12 D5
Nutbourne *W.Suss.* **PO18** 11 J4
Nutfield **RH1** 23 G6
Nuthall **NG16** 41 H1
Nuthampstead **SG8** 33 H5
Nuthurst *W.Suss.* **RH13** 12 E4
Nuthurst *Warks.* **B94** 30 C1
Nutley *E.Suss.* **TN22** 13 H4
Nutley *Hants.* **RG25** 21 K7
Nutwell **DN3** 51 J2
Nyadd **FK9** 75 F1
Nybster **KW1** 105 J2
Nyetimber **PO21** 12 B7
Nyewood **GU31** 11 J2
Nymet Rowland **EX17** 7 F5
Nymet Tracey **EX17** 7 F5
Nympsfield **GL10** 20 B1
Nynehead **TA21** 7 K3
Nythe **TA7** 8 D1
Nyton **PO20** 12 C6

O

Oad Street **ME9** 24 E5
Oadby **LE2** 41 J5
Oak Cross **EX20** 6 D6
Oak Tree **DL2** 62 E5
Oakamoor **ST10** 40 C1
Oakbank *Arg. & B.* **PA64** 79 J4
Oakbank *W.Loth.* **EH53** 75 J4
Oakdale *Caerp.* **NP12** 18 E2
Oakdale *Poole* **BH15** 10 B5
Oake **TA4** 7 K3
Oaken **WV8** 40 A5
Oakenclough **PR3** 55 J5
Oakengates **TF2** 39 G4
Oakenhead **IV31** 97 K5
Oakenholt **CH6** 48 B5
Oakenshaw *Dur.* **DL15** 62 D3
Oakenshaw *W.Yorks.* **BD12** 57 G7
Oakerthorpe **DE55** 51 F7
Oakes **HD3** 50 D1
Oakfield *I.o.W.* **PO33** 11 G5
Oakfield *Torfaen* **NP44** 19 F2
Oakford *Cere.* **SA47** 26 D3
Oakford *Devon* **EX16** 7 H3
Oakfordbridge **EX16** 7 H3
Oakgrove **SK11** 49 J6
Oakham LE15 42 B5
Oakhanger **GU35** 11 J1
Oakhill **BA3** 19 K7
Oakington **CB24** 33 H2
Oaklands *Conwy* **LL26** 47 G7
Oaklands *Herts.* **AL6** 33 F7
Oakle Street **GL2** 29 G7
Oakley *Bed.* **MK43** 32 D3
Oakley *Bucks.* **HP18** 31 H7
Oakley *Fife* **KY12** 75 J2
Oakley *Hants.* **RG23** 21 J6
Oakley *Oxon.* **OX39** 22 A1
Oakley *Poole* **BH21** 10 B5
Oakley *Suff.* **IP21** 35 F1
Oakley Green **SL4** 22 C4
Oakley Park **SY17** 37 J7
Oakridge Lynch **GL6** 20 C1
Oaks **SY5** 38 D5
Oaks Green **DE6** 40 D2
Oaksey **SN16** 20 C2
Oakshaw Ford **CA6** 70 A6
Oakshott **GU33** 11 J2
Oakthorpe **DE12** 41 F4
Oaktree Hill **DL6** 62 E7
Oakwoodhill **RH5** 12 E3
Oakworth **BD22** 57 F6
Oare *Kent* **ME13** 25 G5
Oare *Som.* **EX35** 7 G1
Oare *Wilts.* **SN8** 20 E5
Oasby **NG32** 42 D2
Oath **TA7** 8 C2
Oathlaw **DD8** 83 F2
Oatlands **HG2** 57 J4
Oban PA34 79 K5
Obley **SY7** 28 C1
Oborne **DT9** 9 F3
Obthorpe **PE10** 42 D4
Occlestone Green **CW10** 49 F6
Occold **IP23** 35 F1
Occumster **KW3** 105 H5
Ochiltree **KA18** 67 K1
Ochr-y-foel **LL18** 47 J5
Ochtermuthill **PH5** 81 K6
Ochtertyre *P. & K.* **PH7** 81 K5
Ochtertyre *Stir.* **FK9** 75 F1
Ockbrook **DE72** 41 G2
Ockeridge **WR6** 29 G2
Ockham **GU23** 22 D6
Ockle **PH36** 86 B7
Ockley **RH5** 12 E3
Ocle Pychard **HR1** 28 E4
Octon **YO25** 59 G2
Odcombe **BA22** 8 E3
Odd Down **BA2** 20 A5
Oddendale **CA10** 61 H5
Oddingley **WR9** 29 J3
Oddington **OX5** 31 G7
Oddsta **ZE2** 107 P3
Odell **MK43** 32 C3
Odham **EX21** 6 C5
Odie **KW17** 106 F5
Odiham **RG29** 22 A6
Odsey **SG7** 33 F5
Odstock **SP5** 10 C2
Odstone **CV13** 41 F5
Offchurch **CV33** 30 E2
Offenham **WR11** 30 B4
Offerton **SK2** 49 J4
Offham *E.Suss.* **BN8** 13 G5
Offham *Kent* **ME19** 23 K6
Offham *W.Suss.* **BN18** 12 D6
Offley Hoo **SG5** 32 E6
Offleymarsh **ST21** 39 G3
Offord Cluny **PE19** 33 F2
Offord D'Arcy **PE19** 33 F2
Offton **IP8** 34 E4
Offwell **EX14** 7 K6
Ogbourne Maizey **SN8** 20 E4
Ogbourne St. Andrew **SN8** 20 E4
Ogbourne St. George **SN8** 20 E4
Ogil **DD8** 83 F1
Ogle **NE20** 71 G6
Oglet **L24** 48 D4
Ogmore **CF32** 18 B4
Ogmore Vale **CF32** 18 C2
Ogmore-by-Sea **CF32** 18 B4
Oil Terminal **KW16** 106 C8
Okeford Fitzpaine **DT11** 9 H3
Okehampton EX20 6 D6
Okehampton Camp **EX20** 6 D6
Okraquoy **ZE2** 107 N9
Olchard **TQ13** 5 J3
Olchfa **SA2** 17 K6
Old **NN6** 31 J1
Old Aberdeen **AB24** 91 H4
Old Alresford **SO24** 11 G1
Old Arley **CV7** 40 E6
Old Basford **NG6** 41 H1
Old Basing **RG24** 21 K6
Old Belses **TD6** 70 A1
Old Bewick **NE66** 71 F1
Old Blair **PH18** 81 K1
Old Bolingbroke **PE23** 53 G6
Old Bramhope **LS16** 57 H5
Old Brampton **S42** 51 F5
Old Bridge of Urr **DG7** 65 H4
Old Buckenham **NR17** 44 E6
Old Burdon **SR7** 62 E1
Old Burghclere **RG20** 21 H6
Old Byland **YO62** 58 B1
Old Cassop **DH6** 62 E3
Old Church Stoke **SY15** 38 B6
Old Cleeve **TA24** 7 J1
Old Clipstone **NG21** 51 J6
Old Colwyn **LL29** 47 G5
Old Craig **AB41** 91 H2
Old Craighall **EH21** 76 B3
Old Crombie **AB54** 98 D5
Old Dailly **KA26** 67 G4
Old Dalby **LE14** 41 J3
Old Dam **SK17** 50 D5
Old Deer **AB42** 99 H6
Old Dilton **BA13** 20 B7
Old Down *S.Glos.* **BS32** 19 K3
Old Down *Som.* **BA3** 19 K6
Old Edlington **DN12** 51 H3
Old Eldon **DL4** 62 D4
Old Ellerby **HU11** 59 H6
Old Felixstowe **IP11** 35 H5
Old Fletton **PE2** 42 E6
Old Ford **E3** 23 G3
Old Glossop **SK13** 50 C3
Old Goginan **SY23** 37 F7
Old Goole **DN14** 58 D7
Old Gore **HR9** 29 F6
Old Grimsby **TR24** 2 B1
Old Hall **HU12** 53 F1
Old Hall Green **SG11** 33 G6
Old Hall Street **NR28** 45 H2
Old Harlow **CM20** 33 H7
Old Heath **CO2** 34 E6
Old Heathfield **TN21** 13 J4
Old Hill **B64** 40 B7
Old Hurst **PE28** 33 G1
Old Hutton **LA8** 55 J1
Old Kea **TR3** 3 F4
Old Kilpatrick **G60** 74 C3
Old Kinnernie **AB32** 91 F4
Old Knebworth **SG3** 33 F6
Old Leake **PE22** 53 H7
Old Leslie **AB52** 90 D2
Old Malton **YO17** 58 E2
Old Milton **BH25** 10 D5
Old Milverton **CV32** 30 D2
Old Montsale **CM0** 25 G2
Old Netley **SO31** 11 F3
Old Newton **IP14** 34 E2
Old Philpstoun **EH49** 75 J3
Old Poltalloch **PA31** 79 K7
Old Radnor (Pencraig) **LD8** 28 B3
Old Rattray **AB42** 99 J5
Old Rayne **AB52** 90 E2
Old Romney **TN29** 15 F5
Old Scone **PH2** 82 C5
Old Shields **G67** 75 G3
Old Sodbury **BS37** 20 A3
Old Somerby **NG33** 42 C2
Old Stratford **MK19** 31 J4
Old Sunderlandwick **YO25** 59 G4
Old Swarland **NE65** 71 G3
Old Swinford **DY8** 40 B7
Old Thirsk **YO7** 57 K1
Old Town *Cumb.* **LA6** 55 J1
Old Town *I.o.S.* **TR21** 2 C1
Old Town Farm **NE19** 70 D4
Old Tupton **S42** 51 F6
Old Warden **SG18** 32 E4
Old Weston **PE28** 32 D1
Old Windsor **SL4** 22 C4
Old Wives Lees **CT4** 15 F2
Old Woking **GU22** 22 D6
Old Woodhall **LN9** 53 F6
Old Woods **SY4** 38 D3
Oldberrow **B95** 30 C2
Oldborough **EX17** 7 F5
Oldbury *Kent* **TN15** 23 J6
Oldbury *Shrop.* **WV16** 39 G6
Oldbury *W.Mid.* B69 40 B7
Oldbury *Warks.* **CV10** 41 F6
Oldbury Naite **BS35** 19 K2
Oldbury on the Hill **GL9** 20 B3
Oldbury-on-Severn **BS35** 19 K2
Oldcastle *Bridgend* **CF31** 18 C4
Oldcastle *Mon.* **NP7** 28 C6
Oldcastle Heath **SY14** 38 D1
Oldcotes **S81** 51 H4
Oldcroft **GL15** 19 K1
Oldeamere **PE7** 43 G6
Oldfield **WR9** 29 H2
Oldford **BA11** 20 A6
Oldhall *Aber.* **AB34** 90 C5
Oldhall *High.* **KW1** 105 H3
OLDHAM OL 49 J2
Oldham Edge **OL1** 49 J2
Oldhamstocks **TD13** 77 F3
Oldland **BS30** 19 K4
Oldmeldrum **AB51** 91 G2
Oldmill **AB31** 90 D4
Oldpark **TF3** 39 F5
Oldridge **EX4** 7 G6
Oldshore Beg **IV27** 102 D3
Oldshoremore **IV27** 102 E3
Oldstead **YO61** 58 B2
Oldtown **IV24** 96 C3
Oldtown of Aigas **IV4** 96 B7
Oldtown of Ord **AB45** 98 E5
Oldwalls **SA3** 17 H6
Oldways End **EX16** 7 G3
Oldwhat **AB53** 99 G5
Oldwich Lane **B93** 30 D1
Olgrinmore **KW12** 105 G3
Oliver **ML12** 69 G1
Oliver's Battery **SO22** 11 F2
Ollaberry **ZE2** 107 M4
Ollerton *Ches.E.* **WA16** 49 G5
Ollerton *Notts.* **NG22** 51 J6
Ollerton *Shrop.* **TF9** 39 F3
Olmstead Green **CB21** 33 K4
Olney MK46 32 B3
Olrig House **KW14** 105 G2
Olton **B92** 40 D7
Olveston **BS35** 19 K3
Ombersley **WR9** 29 H2
Ompton **NG22** 51 J6
Onchan **IM3** 54 C6
Onecote **ST13** 50 C7
Onehouse **IP14** 34 E3
Ongar Hill **PE34** 43 J3
Ongar Street **HR6** 28 C2
Onibury **SY7** 28 D1
Onich **PH33** 80 B1
Onllwyn **SA10** 27 H7
Onneley **CW3** 39 G1
Onslow Green **CM6** 33 K7
Onslow Village **GU2** 22 C7
Opinan *High.* **IV22** 94 E2
Opinan *High.* **IV21** 94 D4
Orange Lane **TD12** 77 F6
Orasaigh **HS2** 101 F6
Orbliston **IV32** 98 B5
Orbost **IV55** 93 H7
Orby **PE24** 53 H6
Orcadia **PA20** 73 K4
Orchard **PA23** 73 K2
Orchard Portman **TA3** 8 B2
Orcheston **SP3** 20 D7
Orcop **HR2** 28 D6
Orcop Hill **HR2** 28 D6
Ord **IV46** 86 C3
Ordhead **AB51** 90 E3
Ordie **AB34** 90 C4
Ordiequish **IV32** 98 B5
Ordsall **DN22** 51 J5
Ore **TN35** 14 D6
Oreham Common **BN5** 13 F5
Oreston **PL9** 5 F5
Oreton **DY14** 29 F1
Orford *Suff.* **IP12** 35 J4
Orford *Warr.* **WA2** 49 F3
Organford **BH16** 9 J5
Orgreave **DE13** 40 D4
Orkney Islands KW 106 B6
Orlestone **TN26** 14 E4
Orleton *Here.* **SY8** 28 D2
Orleton *Worcs.* **WR6** 29 F2
Orleton Common **SY8** 28 D2
Orlingbury **NN14** 32 B1
Ormacleit **HS8** 84 C1
Ormesby **TS3** 63 G5
Ormesby St. Margaret **NR29** 45 J4
Ormesby St. Michael **NR29** 45 J4
Ormidale **PA22** 73 J2
Ormiscaig **IV22** 94 E2
Ormiston **EH35** 76 C4
Ormlie **KW14** 105 G2
Ormsaigmore **PH36** 79 F1
Ormsary **PA31** 73 F3
Ormskirk L39 48 D2
Oronsay **PA61** 72 B2
Orphir **KW17** 106 C7
Orpington BR6 23 H5
Orrell *Gt.Man.* **WN5** 48 E2
Orrell *Mersey.* **L20** 48 C3
Orrisdale **IM6** 54 C4
Orrok House **AB23** 91 H3
Orroland **DG6** 65 H6
Orsett **RM16** 24 C3
Orsett Heath **RM16** 24 C3
Orslow **TF10** 40 A4
Orston **NG13** 42 A1
Orton *Cumb.* **CA10** 61 H6
Orton *Northants.* **NN14** 32 B1
Orton Longueville **PE2** 42 E6
Orton Rigg **CA5** 60 E1
Orton Waterville **PE2** 42 E6
Orton-on-the-Hill **CV9** 41 F5
Orwell **SG8** 33 G3
Osbaldeston **BB2** 56 B6
Osbaldwick **YO10** 58 C4
Osbaston *Leics.* **CV13** 41 G5
Osbaston *Shrop.* **SY10** 38 C3
Osbaston *Tel. & W.* **TF6** 38 E4
Osbaston Hollow **CV13** 41 G5
Osborne **PO32** 11 G5
Osbournby **NG34** 42 D2
Oscroft **CH3** 48 E6
Ose **IV56** 93 J7
Osgathorpe **LE12** 41 G4
Osgodby *Lincs.* **LN8** 52 D3
Osgodby *N.Yorks.* **YO8** 58 C6
Osgodby *N.Yorks.* **YO11** 59 G1
Oskaig **IV40** 86 B1
Osleston **DE6** 40 E2
Osmaston *Derby* **DE24** 41 F2
Osmaston *Derbys.* **DE6** 40 D1
Osmington **DT3** 9 G6
Osmington Mills **DT3** 9 G6
Osmondthorpe **LS9** 57 J6
Osmotherley **DL6** 63 F7
Osnaburgh (Dairsie) **KY15** 83 F6
Ospringe **ME13** 25 G5
Ossett WF5 57 H7
Ossett Street Side **WF5** 57 H7
Ossington **NG23** 51 K6
Ostend **CM0** 25 F2
Osterley **TW7** 22 E4
Oswaldkirk **YO62** 58 C2
Oswaldtwistle **BB5** 56 C7
Oswestry SY11 38 B3
Oteley **SY12** 38 D2
Otford **TN14** 23 J6
Otham **ME15** 14 C2
Otherton **ST19** 40 B4
Othery **TA7** 8 C1
Otley *Suff.* **IP6** 35 G3
Otley *W.Yorks.* LS21 57 H5
Otter **PA21** 73 H3
Otter Ferry **PA21** 73 H2
Otterbourne **SO21** 11 F2
Otterburn *N.Yorks.* **BD23** 56 D4
Otterburn *Northumb.* **NE19** 70 D4
Otterburn Camp **NE19** 70 D4
Otterden Place **ME13** 14 E2
Otterham **PL32** 4 B1
Otterham Quay **ME8** 24 E5
Otterhampton **TA5** 19 F7
Otternish **HS6** 92 E4
Ottershaw **KT16** 22 D5
Otterswick **ZE2** 107 P4
Otterton **EX9** 7 J7
Otterwood **SO42** 11 F4
Ottery St. Mary EX11 7 J6
Ottinge **CT4** 15 G3
Ottringham **HU12** 59 J7
Oughterby **CA5** 60 D1
Oughtershaw **BD23** 56 D1
Oughterside **CA7** 60 C2
Oughtibridge **S35** 51 F3
Oulston **YO61** 58 B2
Oulton *Cumb.* **CA7** 60 D1
Oulton *Norf.* **NR11** 45 F3
Oulton *Staffs.* **ST15** 40 B2
Oulton *Staffs.* **ST20** 39 G3
Oulton *Suff.* **NR32** 45 K6
Oulton *W.Yorks.* **LS26** 57 J7
Oulton Broad **NR33** 45 K6
Oulton Grange **ST15** 40 B2
Oulton Street **NR11** 45 F3
Oultoncross **ST15** 40 B2
Oundle **PE8** 42 D7
Ousby **CA10** 61 H3
Ousdale **KW7** 105 F6
Ousden **CB8** 34 B3
Ousefleet **DN14** 58 E7
Ouston *Dur.* **DH2** 62 D1
Ouston *Northumb.* **NE18** 71 F6
Out Newton **HU19** 59 K7
Out Rawcliffe **PR3** 55 H5
Out Skerries Airstrip **ZE2** 107 Q5
Outcast **LA12** 55 G2
Outchester **NE70** 77 K7
Outertown **KW16** 106 B7
Outgate **LA22** 60 E7
Outhgill **CA17** 61 J6
Outlands **ST20** 39 G3
Outlane **HD3** 50 C1
Outwell **PE14** 43 J5
Outwood *Surr.* **RH1** 23 G7
Outwood *W.Yorks.* **WF1** 57 J7
Outwoods **TF10** 39 G4
Ouzlewell Green **WF3** 57 J7
Ovenden **HX3** 57 F7
Over *Cambs.* **CB24** 33 G1
Over *Ches.W. & C.* **CW7** 49 F6
Over *Glos.* **GL2** 29 H7
Over *S.Glos.* **BS32** 19 J3
Over Burrows **DE6** 40 E2
Over Compton **DT9** 8 E3
Over Dinsdale **DL2** 62 E5
Over End **DE45** 50 E5
Over Green **B76** 40 D6
Over Haddon **DE45** 50 E6
Over Hulton **BL5** 49 F2
Over Kellet **LA6** 55 J3
Over Kiddington **OX20** 31 F6
Over Monnow **NP25** 28 D7
Over Norton **OX7** 30 E6
Over Peover **WA16** 49 G5
Over Rankeilour **KY15** 82 E6
Over Silton **YO7** 63 F7
Over Stowey **TA5** 7 K2
Over Stratton **TA13** 8 D3
Over Tabley **WA16** 49 G4
Over Wallop **SO20** 10 D1
Over Whitacre **B46** 40 E6
Over Winchendon (Upper Winchendon) **HP18** 31 J7
Over Worton **OX7** 31 F6
Overbister **KW17** 106 F3
Overbrae **AB53** 99 G5
Overbury **GL20** 29 J5
Overcombe **DT3** 9 F6
Overgreen **S42** 51 F5
Overleigh **BA16** 8 D1
Overpool **CH66** 48 C5
Overscaig Hotel **IV27** 103 G6
Overseal **DE12** 40 E4
Overslade **CV22** 31 F1
Oversland **ME13** 15 F2
Oversley Green **B49** 30 B3
Overstone **NN6** 32 B2
Overstrand **NR27** 45 G1
Overthorpe **OX17** 31 F4
Overton *Aber.* **AB51** 91 F3
Overton *Aberdeen* **AB21** 91 G3
Overton *Ches.W. & C.* **WA6** 48 E5
Overton *Hants.* **RG25** 21 J7
Overton *Lancs.* **LA3** 55 H4
Overton *N.Yorks.* **YO30** 58 B4
Overton *Shrop.* **SY8** 28 E1
Overton *Swan.* **SA3** 17 H7
Overton *W.Yorks.* **WF4** 50 E1
Overton (Owrtyn) *Wrex.* **LL13** 38 C1
Overton Bridge **LL13** 38 C1
Overtown *Lancs.* **LA6** 56 B2
Overtown *N.Lan.* **ML2** 75 G5
Overtown *Swin.* **SN4** 20 E4
Overy **OX10** 21 J2
Oving *Bucks.* **HP22** 31 J6
Oving *W.Suss.* **PO20** 12 C6
Ovingdean **BN2** 13 G6
Ovingham **NE42** 71 F7
Ovington *Dur.* **DL11** 62 C5
Ovington *Essex* **CO10** 34 B4
Ovington *Hants.* **SO24** 11 G1
Ovington *Norf.* **IP25** 44 D5
Ovington *Northumb.* **NE42** 71 F7
Ower *Hants.* **SO51** 10 E3
Ower *Hants.* **SO45** 11 F4
Owermoigne **DT2** 9 G6
Owler Bar **S17** 50 E5
Owlpen **GL11** 20 A2
Owl's Green **IP13** 35 G2
Owlswick **HP27** 22 A1
Owmby **DN38** 52 D2
Owmby-by-Spital **LN8** 52 D4
Owrtyn (Overton) **LL13** 38 C1
Owslebury **SO21** 11 G2
Owston **LE15** 42 A5
Owston Ferry **DN9** 52 B2
Owstwick **HU12** 59 J6
Owthorpe **NG12** 41 J2

Oxborough **PE33** 44 B5
Oxcliffe Hill **LA3** 55 H3
Oxcombe **LN9** 53 G5
Oxen End **CM7** 33 K6
Oxen Park **LA12** 55 G1
Oxencombe **TQ13** 7 G7
Oxenhall **GL18** 29 G6
Oxenholme **LA9** 61 G7
Oxenhope **BD22** 57 F6
Oxenpill **BA6** 19 H7
Oxenton **GL52** 29 J5
Oxenwood **SN8** 21 G6
OXFORD OX 21 J1
Oxhey **WD17** 22 E2
Oxhill **CV35** 30 E4
Oxley **WV10** 40 B5
Oxley Green **CM9** 34 D7
Oxley's Green **TN32** 13 K4
Oxnam **TD8** 70 C2
Oxnead **NR10** 45 G3
Oxnop Ghyll **DL8** 62 A7
Oxshott **KT22** 22 E5
Oxspring **S36** 50 E2
Oxted RH8 23 G6
Oxton *Mersey.* **CH43** 48 C4
Oxton *Notts.* **NG25** 51 J7
Oxton *Sc.Bord.* **TD2** 76 C5
Oxwich **SA3** 17 H7
Oxwich Green **SA3** 17 H7
Oxwick **NR21** 44 D3
Oykel Bridge **IV27** 95 K1
Oyne **AB52** 90 E2
Ozleworth **GL12** 20 A2

P

Pabail Iarach (Lower Bayble) **HS2** 101 H4
Pabail Uarach (Upper Bayble) **HS2** 101 H4
Pabbay **HS6** 92 E3
Packington **LE65** 41 F4
Packwood **B94** 30 C1
Padanaram **DD8** 83 F2
Padbury **MK18** 31 J5
Paddington **W2** 23 F3
Paddlesworth **CT18** 15 G3
Paddock **TN25** 14 E2
Paddock Wood **TN12** 23 K7
Paddockhaugh **IV30** 97 K6
Paddockhole **DG11** 69 H5
Paddolgreen **SY4** 38 E2
Padeswood **CH7** 48 B6
Padfield **SK13** 50 C3
Padiham **BB12** 56 C6
Padside **HG3** 57 G4
Padstow PL28 3 G1
Padworth **RG7** 21 K5
Paganhill **GL5** 20 B1
Pagham **PO21** 12 B7
Paglesham Churchend **SS4** 25 F2
Paglesham Eastend **SS4** 25 F2
Paible **HS3** 93 F2
Paignton TQ3 5 J4
Pailton **CV23** 41 G7
Paine's Corner **TN21** 13 K4
Painscastle **LD2** 28 A4
Painshawfield **NE43** 71 F7
Painswick **GL6** 20 B1
Pairc **HS2** 100 E3
PAISLEY PA 74 C4
Pakefield **NR33** 45 K6
Pakenham **IP31** 34 D2
Pale **LL23** 37 J2
Palehouse Common **TN22** 13 H5
Palestine **SP11** 21 F7
Paley Street **SL6** 22 B4
Palgowan **DG8** 67 H5
Palgrave **IP22** 35 F1
Pallinsburn House **TD12** 77 G7
Palmarsh **CT21** 15 G4
Palmers Cross **GU5** 22 D7
Palmers Green **N13** 23 G2
Palmerscross **IV30** 97 K5
Palmerstown **CF63** 18 E4
Palnackie **DG7** 65 J5
Palnure **DG8** 64 E4
Palterton **S44** 51 G6
Pamber End **RG26** 21 K6
Pamber Green **RG26** 21 K6
Pamber Heath **RG26** 21 K5
Pamington **GL20** 29 J5
Pamphill **BH21** 9 J4
Pampisford **CB22** 33 H4
Pan **KW16** 106 C8
Panborough **BA5** 19 H7
Panbride **DD7** 83 G4
Pancrasweek **EX22** 6 A5
Pancross **CF62** 18 D5
Pandy *Gwyn.* **LL36** 37 F5
Pandy *Mon.* **NP7** 28 C6
Pandy *Powys* **SY19** 37 J5
Pandy *Wrex.* **LL20** 38 A2
Pandy Tudur **LL22** 47 G6
Pandy'r Capel **LL21** 47 J7
Panfield **CM7** 34 B6
Pangbourne **RG8** 21 K4
Pannal **HG3** 57 J4
Pannal Ash **HG3** 57 H4
Panshanger **AL7** 33 F7
Pant **SY10** 38 B3
Pant Glas **LL54** 36 D1
Pant Gwyn **LL40** 37 H3
Pant Mawr **SY18** 37 H7
Pantasaph **CH8** 47 K5
Panteg **NP4** 19 G2
Pantglas **SY20** 37 G6
Pantgwyn *Carmar.* **SA19** 17 J3
Pantgwyn *Cere.* **SA43** 17 F1
Pant-lasau **SA6** 17 K5
Panton **LN8** 52 E5
Pant-pastynog **LL16** 47 J6
Pantperthog **SY20** 37 G5
Pant-y-dwr **LD6** 27 J1
Pantyffordd **CH7** 48 B7
Pant-y-ffridd **SY21** 38 A5
Pantyffynnon **SA18** 17 K4
Pantygasseg **NP4** 19 F2
Pantygelli **NP7** 28 C7
Pantymwyn **CH7** 47 K6
Panxworth **NR13** 45 H4
Papa Stour **ZE2** 107 K6
Papa Stour Airstrip **ZE2** 107 K6
Papa Westray **KW17** 106 D2
Papa Westray Airfield **KW17** 106 D2
Papcastle **CA13** 60 C3
Papil **ZE2** 107 M9
Papple **EH41** 76 D3
Papplewick **NG15** 51 H7
Papworth Everard **CB23** 33 F2
Papworth St. Agnes **CB23** 33 F2
Par PL24 4 A5
Parbold **WN8** 48 D1
Parbrook *Som.* **BA6** 8 E1
Parbrook *W.Suss.* **RH14** 12 D4
Parc **LL23** 37 H2
Parcllyn **SA43** 26 B3
Parcrhydderch **SY25** 27 F3
Parc-Seymour **NP26** 19 H2
Parc-y-rhôs **SA48** 17 J1
Pardshaw **CA13** 60 B4
Parham **IP13** 35 H2
Parish Holm **ML11** 68 C1
Park **AB45** 98 D5
Park Close **BB18** 56 D5
Park Corner *E.Suss.* **TN3** 13 J3
Park Corner *Oxon.* **RG9** 21 K3
Park End *Northumb.* **NE48** 70 D6
Park End *Staffs.* **ST7** 49 G7
Park End *Worcs.* **DY12** 29 G1
Park Gate *Hants.* **SO31** 11 G4
Park Gate *W.Yorks.* **LS20** 57 G5
Park Gate *W.Yorks.* **HD8** 50 E1
Park Gate *Worcs.* **B61** 29 J1
Park Green **IP14** 35 F2
Park Hill **S2** 51 F4
Park Lane **LL13** 38 D2
Park Langley **BR4** 23 G5
Park Street **AL2** 22 E1
Parkend *Cumb.* **CA7** 60 E3
Parkend *Glos.* **GL15** 19 K1
Parker's Green **TN10** 23 K7
Parkeston **CO12** 35 G5
Parkfield *Cornw.* **PL14** 4 D4
Parkfield *S.Glos.* **BS16** 19 K4
Parkfield *W.Mid.* **WV4** 40 B6
Parkford **DD8** 83 F2
Parkgate *Ches.W. & C.* **CH64** 48 B5
Parkgate *D. & G.* **DG1** 69 F5
Parkgate *Kent* **TN30** 14 D4
Parkgate *S.Yorks.* **S62** 51 G3
Parkgate *Surr.* **RH5** 23 F7
Parkham **EX39** 6 B3
Parkham Ash **EX39** 6 B3
Parkhead **G31** 74 E4
Parkhill *Angus* **DD11** 83 H3
Parkhill *P. & K.* **PH10** 82 C3
Parkhouse **NP25** 19 H1
Parkhurst **PO30** 11 F5
Parkmill **SA3** 17 J7
Parkmore **AB55** 98 B6
Parkneuk **AB30** 91 F7
Parkside **LL12** 48 C7
Parkstone **BH14** 10 B5
Parkway **BA22** 8 E2
Parley Cross **BH22** 10 B5
Parley Green **BH23** 10 C5
Parlington **LS25** 57 K6
Parracombe **EX31** 6 E1
Parrog **SA42** 16 D2
Parson Cross **S5** 51 F3
Parson Drove **PE13** 43 G5
Parsonage Green **CM1** 33 K7
Parsonby **CA7** 60 C3
Partick **G11** 74 D4
Partington **M31** 49 G3
Partney **PE23** 53 H6
Parton *Cumb.* **CA28** 60 A4
Parton *D. & G.* **DG7** 65 G3
Partridge Green **RH13** 12 E5
Parwich **DE6** 50 D7
Paslow Wood Common **CM4** 23 J1
Passenham **MK19** 31 J5
Passfield **GU30** 12 B3
Passingford Bridge **RM4** 23 J2
Paston **NR28** 45 H2
Paston Street **NR28** 45 H2
Pasturefields **ST18** 40 B3
Patchacott **EX21** 6 C6
Patcham **BN1** 13 G6
Patchetts Green **WD25** 22 E2
Patching **BN13** 12 D6
Patchole **EX31** 6 E1
Patchway **BS34** 19 K3
Pateley Bridge **HG3** 57 G3
Path of Condie **PH2** 82 B6
Pathe **TA7** 8 C1
Pathfinder Village **EX6** 7 G6
Pathhead *Aber.* **DD10** 83 J1
Pathhead *E.Ayr.* **KA18** 68 B2
Pathhead *Fife* **KY1** 76 A1
Pathhead *Midloth.* EH37 76 B4
Pathlow **CV37** 30 C3
Patmore Heath **SG11** 33 H6
Patna **KA6** 67 J2
Patney **SN10** 20 D6
Patrick **IM5** 54 B5
Patrick Brompton **DL8** 62 D7
Patrington **HU12** 59 K7
Patrington Haven **HU12** 59 K7
Patrishow **NP7** 28 B6
Patrixbourne **CT4** 15 G2
Patterdale **CA11** 60 E5
Pattingham **WV6** 40 A6
Pattishall **NN12** 31 H3
Pattiswick **CM77** 34 C6
Paul **TR19** 2 B6
Paulerspury **NN12** 31 J4
Paull **HU12** 59 H7
Paull Holme **HU12** 59 H7
Paul's Green **TR27** 2 D5
Paulton **BS39** 19 K6
Pauperhaugh **NE65** 71 F4
Pave Lane **TF10** 39 G4
Pavenham **MK43** 32 C3
Pawlett **TA6** 19 G7
Pawston **TD12** 77 G7
Paxford **GL55** 30 C5
Paxhill Park **RH16** 13 G4
Paxton **TD15** 77 H5
Payden Street **ME17** 14 E2
Payhembury **EX14** 7 J5
Paythorne **BB7** 56 D4
Peacehaven BN10 13 H6
Peacemarsh **SP8** 9 H2
Peachley **WR2** 29 H3
Peak Dale **SK17** 50 C5
Peak Forest **SK17** 50 D5
Peakirk **PE6** 42 E5
Pean Hill **CT5** 25 H5
Pear Tree **DE23** 41 F2
Pearsie **DD8** 82 E2
Pearson's Green **TN12** 23 K7
Peartree **AL7** 33 F7
Peartree Green *Essex* **CM15** 23 J2
Peartree Green *Here.* **HR1** 29 F5
Pease Pottage **RH11** 13 F3
Peasedown St. John **BA2** 20 A6
Peasehill **DE5** 41 G1
Peaseland Green **NR20** 44 E4
Peasemore **RG20** 21 H4
Peasenhall **IP17** 35 H2
Peaslake **GU5** 22 D7
Peasley Cross **WA9** 48 E3
Peasmarsh *E.Suss.* **TN31** 14 D5
Peasmarsh *Surr.* **GU3** 22 C7
Peaston **EH35** 76 C4
Peastonbank **EH34** 76 C4
Peat Inn **KY15** 83 F7
Peathill **AB43** 99 H4
Peathrow **DL13** 62 C4
Peatling Magna **LE8** 41 H6
Peatling Parva **LE17** 41 H7
Peaton **SY7** 38 E7
Pebble Coombe **KT20** 23 F6
Pebmarsh **CO9** 34 C5
Pebworth **CV37** 30 C4
Pecket Well **HX7** 56 E7
Peckforton **CW6** 48 E7
Peckham **SE15** 23 G4
Peckleton **LE9** 41 G5
Pedham **NR13** 45 H4
Pedmore **DY9** 40 B7
Pedwell **TA7** 8 D1
Peebles EH45 76 A6
Peel *I.o.M.* **IM5** 54 B5
Peel *Lancs.* **FY4** 55 G6
Peening Quarter **TN30** 14 D5
Peggs Green **LE67** 41 G4
Pegsdon **SG5** 32 E5
Pegswood **NE61** 71 H5
Pegwell **CT11** 25 K5
Peighinn nan Aoireann **HS8** 84 C1
Peinchorran **IV51** 86 B1
Peinlich **IV51** 93 K6
Pelaw **NE10** 71 H7
Pelcomb **SA62** 16 C4
Pelcomb Bridge **SA62** 16 C4
Pelcomb Cross **SA62** 16 C4
Peldon **CO5** 34 D7
Pellon **HX2** 57 F7
Pelsall **WS3** 40 C5
Pelton **DH2** 62 D1
Pelutho **CA7** 60 C2
Pelynt **PL13** 4 C5
Pemberton **WN5** 48 E2
Pembrey (Pen-bre) **SA16** 17 H5
Pembridge **HR6** 28 C3
Pembroke (Penfro) SA71 16 C5
Pembroke Dock (Doc Penfro) SA72 16 C5
Pembury **TN2** 23 K7
Penallt **NP25** 28 E7
Penally **SA70** 16 E6
Penalt **HR1** 28 E6
Penare **PL26** 3 G4
Penarlâg (Hawarden) **CH5** 48 C6
Penarran **SY16** 38 A7
Penarth CF64 18 E4
Pen-bont Rhydybeddau **SY23** 37 F7
Penboyr **SA44** 17 G2
Pen-bre (Pembrey) **SA16** 17 H5
Penbryn **SA44** 26 B3
Pencader SA39 17 H2
Pen-cae **SA47** 26 D3
Pen-cae-cwm **LL16** 47 H6
Pencaenewydd **LL53** 36 D1
Pencaitland **EH34** 76 C4
Pencarnisiog **LL63** 46 B5
Pencarreg **SA40** 17 J1
Pencarrow **PL32** 4 B2
Pencelli **LD3** 27 K6
Pen-clawdd **SA4** 17 J6
Pencoed **CF35** 18 C3
Pencombe **HR7** 28 E3
Pencoyd **HR2** 28 E6
Pencraig *Here.* **HR9** 28 E6
Pencraig *Powys* **SY10** 37 K3
Pencraig (Old Radnor) *Powys* **LD8** 28 B3
Pendeen **TR19** 2 A5
Penderyn **CF44** 18 C1
Pendine (Pentywyn) **SA33** 17 F5
Pendlebury **M27** 49 G2
Pendleton **BB7** 56 C6
Pendock **GL19** 29 G5
Pendoggett **PL29** 4 A3
Pendomer **BA22** 8 E3
Pendoylan **CF71** 18 D4
Penegoes **SY20** 37 G5
Penelewey **TR3** 3 F4
Pen-ffordd **SA66** 16 D3
Penffordd-las (Staylittle) **SY19** 37 H6
Penfro (Pembroke) SA71 16 C5
Pengam **NP12** 18 E2
Penge **SE20** 23 G4
Pengenffordd **LD3** 28 A6
Pengorffwysfa **LL68** 46 C3
Pengover Green **PL14** 4 C4
Pen-groes-oped **NP7** 19 G1
Pengwern **LL18** 47 J5
Penhale **TR12** 2 D7
Penhallow **TR4** 2 E3
Penhalvean **TR16** 2 E5
Penhelig **LL35** 37 F6
Penhill **SN2** 20 E3
Penhow **NP26** 19 H2
Penhurst **TN33** 13 K5
Peniarth **LL36** 37 F5
Penicuik EH26 76 A4
Peniel **SA32** 17 H3
Penifiler **IV51** 93 K7
Peninver **PA28** 66 B1
Penisa'r Waun **LL55** 46 D6
Penisarcwm **SY10** 37 K4
Penishawain **LD3** 27 K5
Penistone **S36** 50 E2
Penjerrick **TR11** 2 E5
Penketh **WA5** 48 E4
Penkill **KA26** 67 G4
Penkridge **ST19** 40 B4
Penlean **EX23** 4 C1
Penley **LL13** 38 D2
Penllech **LL53** 36 B2
Penllergaer **SA4** 17 K6
Pen-llyn *I.o.A.* **LL65** 46 B4
Penllyn *V. of Glam.* **CF71** 18 C4
Pen-lôn **LL61** 46 C6
Penmachno **LL24** 47 F7
Penmaen **SA3** 17 J7
Penmaenan **LL34** 47 F5
Penmaenmawr LL34 47 F5
Penmaenpool (Llyn Penmaen) **LL40** 37 F4
Penmaen-Rhôs **LL29** 47 G5
Penmark **CF62** 18 D5
Penmon **LL58** 46 E4
Penmorfa **LL49** 36 E1
Penmynydd **LL61** 46 D5
Penn *Bucks.* **HP10** 22 C2
Penn *W.Mid.* **WV4** 40 A6
Penn Street **HP7** 22 C2
Pennal **SY20** 37 F5
Pennal-isaf **SY20** 37 G5
Pennan **AB43** 99 G4
Pennance **TR16** 2 E4
Pennant *Cere.* **SY23** 26 E2
Pennant *Powys* **SY19** 37 H6
Pennant Melangell **SY10** 37 K3
Pennar **SA72** 16 C5
Pennard **SA3** 17 J7
Pennerley **SY5** 38 C6
Penninghame **DG8** 64 D4
Pennington *Cumb.* **LA12** 55 F2
Pennington *Hants.* **SO41** 10 E5
Pennington Green **WN2** 49 F2
Pennorth **LD3** 28 A6
Pennsylvania **SN14** 20 A4
Penny Bridge **LA12** 55 G1
Pennycross **PL5** 4 E5
Pennyfuir **PA34** 79 K4
Pennygate **NR12** 45 H3
Pennyghael **PA70** 79 G5
Pennyglen **KA19** 67 G2
Pennygown **PA72** 79 H3
Pennymoor **EX16** 7 G4
Penny's Green **NR16** 45 F6
Pennyvenie **KA6** 67 J3
Penparc *Cere.* **SA43** 17 F1
Penparc *Pembs.* **SA62** 16 B2
Penparcau **SY23** 36 E7
Penpedairheol **NP15** 19 G1
Penpethy **PL34** 4 A2
Penpillick **PL24** 4 A5
Penpol **TR3** 3 F5
Penpoll **PL22** 4 B5
Penponds **TR14** 2 D5
Penpont *D. & G.* **DG3** 68 D4
Penpont *Powys* **LD3** 27 J6
Penprysg **CF35** 18 C3
Penquit **PL21** 5 G5
Penrherber **SA38** 17 F2
Penrhiw **SA37** 17 F1
Penrhiwceiber **CF45** 18 D2
Penrhiwgoch **SA32** 17 J4
Penrhiw-llan **SA44** 17 G1
Penrhiw-pâl **SA44** 17 G1
Penrhiwtyn **SA11** 18 A2
Penrhos *Gwyn.* **LL53** 36 C2
Penrhos *I.o.A.* **LL65** 46 A4
Penrhos *Mon.* **NP15** 28 D7
Penrhos *Powys* **SA9** 27 H7
Penrhos-garnedd **LL57** 46 D5
Penrhyn Bay (Bae Penrhyn) **LL30** 47 G4
Penrhyn-coch **SY23** 37 F7
Penrhyndeudraeth LL48 37 F2
Penrhyn-side **LL30** 47 G4
Penrhys **CF43** 18 D2
Penrice **SA3** 17 H7
Penrith CA11 61 G4
Penrose *Cornw.* **PL27** 3 F1
Penrose *Cornw.* **PL15** 4 C2
Penruddock **CA11** 60 F4
Penryn TR10 2 E5
Pensarn *Carmar.* **SA31** 17 H4
Pensarn *Conwy* **LL22** 47 H5
Pen-sarn *Gwyn.* **LL45** 36 E3
Pen-sarn *Gwyn.* **LL54** 36 D1
Pensax **WR6** 29 G2
Pensby **CH61** 48 B4
Penselwood **BA9** 9 G1
Pensford **BS39** 19 K5
Pensham **WR10** 29 J4
Penshaw **DH4** 62 E1
Penshurst **TN11** 23 J7
Pensilva **PL14** 4 C4
Pensnett **DY5** 40 B7
Penston **EH33** 76 C3
Pentewan **PL26** 4 A6
Pentir **LL57** 46 D6
Pentire **TR7** 2 E2
Pentireglaze **PL27** 3 G1
Pentlepoir **SA69** 16 E5
Pentlow **CO10** 34 C4
Pentlow Street **CO10** 34 C4
Pentney **PE32** 44 B4
Penton Mewsey **SP11** 21 G7
Pentonville **N1** 23 G3
Pentraeth LL75 46 D5
Pentre *Powys* **SY10** 37 K3
Pentre *Powys* **SY16** 37 K7
Pentre *Powys* **LD8** 28 B2
Pentre *Powys* **SY15** 38 B6
Pentre *Powys* **SY16** 38 A7
Pentre *R.C.T.* CF41 18 C2
Pentre *Shrop.* **SY4** 38 C4
Pentre *Shrop.* **SY7** 28 C1
Pentre *Wrex.* **LL14** 38 B1
Pentre *Wrex.* **LL14** 38 C1
Pentre Berw **LL60** 46 C5
Pentre Ffwrndan **CH6** 48 B5
Pentre Galar **SA41** 16 E2
Pentre Gwenlais **SA18** 17 K4
Pentre Gwynfryn **LL45** 36 E3
Pentre Halkyn **CH8** 48 B5
Pentre Isaf **LL22** 47 G6
Pentre Llanrhaeadr **LL16** 47 J6
Pentre Maelor **LL13** 38 C1
Pentre Meyrick **CF71** 18 C4
Pentre Poeth **SA6** 17 K6
Pentre Saron **LL16** 47 J6
Pentre-bach *Cere.* **SA48** 17 J1
Pentrebach *M.Tyd.* **CF48** 18 D1
Pentre-bach *Powys* **LD3** 27 J5
Pentrebach *R.C.T.* **CF37** 18 D3
Pentrebach *Swan.* **SA4** 17 J5
Pentre-bont **LL25** 47 F7
Pentre-bwlch **LL11** 38 A1
Pentrecagal **SA38** 17 G1
Pentre-celyn *Denb.* **LL15** 47 K7
Pentre-celyn *Powys* **SY19** 37 H5
Pentre-chwyth **SA1** 17 K6
Pentreclwydau **SA11** 18 B1
Pentre-cwrt **SA44** 17 G2
Pentre-Dolau-Honddu **LD3** 27 J4
Pentredwr *Denb.* **LL20** 38 A1
Pentre-dwr *Swan.* **SA7** 17 K6
Pentrefelin *Carmar.* **SA19** 17 K3
Pentrefelin *Cere.* **SA48** 17 K1
Pentrefelin *Conwy* **LL28** 47 G5
Pentrefelin *Gwyn.* **LL52** 36 E2
Pentrefelin *Powys* **SY10** 38 A3
Pentrefoelas **LL24** 47 G7
Pentregat **SA44** 26 C3
Pentreheyling **SY15** 38 B6
Pentre-llwyn-llŵyd **LD2** 27 J3
Pentre-llyn **SY23** 27 F1
Pentre-llyn-cymmer **LL21** 47 H7
Pentre-piod **LL23** 37 H2
Pentre-poeth **NP10** 19 F3
Pentre'r beirdd **SY21** 38 A4
Pentre'r Felin **LL28** 47 G6
Pentre'r-felin **LD3** 27 J5
Pentre-tafarn-y-fedw **LL26** 47 G6
Pentre-ty-gwyn **SA20** 27 H5
Pentrich **DE5** 51 F7
Pentridge **SP5** 10 B3
Pentwyn *Caerp.* **CF81** 18 E1
Pen-twyn *Caerp.* **NP13** 19 F1
Pentwyn *Cardiff* **CF23** 19 F3
Pen-twyn *Mon.* **NP25** 19 J1
Pentwyn-mawr **NP11** 18 E2
Pentyrch **CF15** 18 E3
Pentywyn (Pendine) **SA33** 17 F5
Penuwch **SY25** 26 E2
Penwithick **PL26** 4 A5
Penwood **RG20** 21 H5
Penwortham **PR1** 55 J7
Penwortham Lane **PR1** 55 J7
Penwyllt **SA9** 27 H7
Pen-y-banc **SA19** 17 K3
Pen-y-bont *Carmar.* **SA20** 27 G5
Pen-y-bont *Carmar.* **SA33** 17 G3
Pen-y-bont *Powys* **SY21** 37 K4
Pen-y-bont *Powys* **SY10** 38 B3
Penybont *Powys* **LD1** 28 A2
Pen-y-bont ar Ogwr (Bridgend) CF31 18 C4
Penybontfawr **SY10** 37 K3
Penybryn *Caerp.* **CF82** 18 E2
Pen-y-bryn *Gwyn.* **LL40** 37 F4
Pen-y-bryn *Pembs.* **SA43** 16 E1

Pen-y-bryn *Wrex.* LL14 38 B1
Pen-y-cae *Powys* SA9 27 H7
Penycae *Wrex.* LL14 38 B1
Pen-y-cae-mawr NP15 19 H2
Pen-y-cefn CH7 47 K5
Pen-y-clawdd NP25 19 H1
Pen-y-coedcae CF37 18 D3
Penycwm SA62 16 B3
Pen-y-Darren CF47 18 D1
Pen-y-fai CF31 18 B3
Penyffordd *Flints.* CH4 48 C6
Pen-y-ffordd *Flints.* CH8 47 K4
Penyffridd LL54 46 D7
Pen-y-gaer NP8 28 A6
Pen-y-garn *Carmar.* SA32 17 J2
Pen-y-garn *Cere.* SY24 37 F7
Penygarn *Torfaen* NP4 19 F1
Penygarnedd SY10 38 A3
Pen-y-garreg LD2 27 K4
Pen-y-Graig *Gwyn.* LL53 36 B2
Penygraig *R.C.T.* CF40 18 D2
Penygroes *Carmar.* SA14 17 J4
Penygroes *Gwyn.* LL54 46 C7
Pen-y-Gwryd Hotel LL55 46 E7
Pen-y-lan CF23 18 E4
Penymynydd CH4 48 C6
Pen-y-parc CH7 48 B6
Pen-y-Park HR3 28 B4
Pen-yr-englyn CF42 18 C2
Pen-yr-heol *Mon.* NP25 28 D7
Penyrheol *Swan.* SA4 17 J6
Pen-y-sarn LL69 46 C3
Pen-y-stryt LL11 47 K7
Penywaun CF44 18 C1
Penzance TR18 2 B5
Penzance Heliport TR18 2 B5
Peopleton WR10 29 J3
Peover Heath WA16 49 G5
Peper Harow GU8 22 C7
Peplow TF9 39 F3
Pepper Arden DL7 62 D6
Pepper's Green CM1 33 K7
Perceton KA11 74 B6
Percie AB31 90 D5
Percyhorner AB43 99 H4
Perham Down SP11 21 F7
Periton TA24 7 H1
Perivale UB6 22 E3
Perkhill AB31 90 D4
Perkins Beach SY5 38 C5
Perkin's Village EX5 7 J6
Perlethorpe NG22 51 J5
Perran Downs TR20 2 C5
Perranarworthal TR3 2 E5
Perranporth TR6 2 E3
Perranuthnoe TR20 2 C6
Perranzabuloe TR4 2 E3
Perrott's Brook GL7 20 D1
Perry Barr B42 40 C6
Perry Crofts B79 40 E5
Perry Green *Essex* CM77 34 C6
Perry Green *Herts.* SG10 33 H7
Perry Green *Wilts.* SN16 20 C3
Perry Street DA11 24 C4
Perrymead BA2 20 A5
Pershall ST21 40 A3
Pershore WR10 29 J4
Persie House PH10 82 C2
Pert AB30 83 H1
Pertenhall MK44 32 D2
PERTH PH 82 C5
Perthcelyn CF45 18 D2
Perthy SY12 38 C2
Perton WV6 40 A6
Pestalozzi Children's Village TN33 14 C6
Peter Tavy PL19 5 F3
PETERBOROUGH PE 42 E6
Peterburn IV21 94 D3
Peterchurch HR2 28 C5
Peterculter AB14 91 G4
Peterhead AB42 99 K6
Peterlee SR8 63 F2
Peter's Green LU2 32 E7
Peters Marland EX38 6 C4
Peters Port (Port Pheadair) HS7 92 D7
Petersfield GU32 11 J2
Petersfinger SP5 10 C2
Peterstone Wentlooge CF3 19 F3
Peterston-super-Ely CF5 18 D4
Peterstow HR9 28 E6
Petham CT4 15 G2
Petrockstowe EX20 6 D5
Pett TN35 14 D6
Pettaugh IP14 35 F3
Petteril Green CA11 61 F2
Pettinain ML11 75 H6
Pettistree IP13 35 G3
Petton *Devon* EX16 7 J3
Petton *Shrop.* SY4 38 D3
Petts Wood BR5 23 H5
Petty AB53 91 F1
Pettycur KY3 76 A2
Pettymuick AB41 91 H2
Petworth GU28 12 C4
Pevensey BN24 13 K6
Pevensey Bay BN24 13 K6
Peverell PL2 4 E5
Pewsey SN9 20 E5
Pheasant's Hill RG9 22 A3
Phesdo AB30 90 E7
Philham EX39 6 A3
Philiphaugh TD7 69 K1
Phillack TR27 2 C5
Philleigh TR2 3 F5
Philpstoun EH49 75 J3
Phocle Green HR9 29 F6
Phoenix Green RG27 22 A6
Phones PH20 88 E5
Phorp IV36 97 H6
Pibsbury TA10 8 D2
Pica CA14 60 B4
Piccadilly Corner IP20 45 G7
Piccotts End HP1 22 D1
Pickerells CM5 23 J1
Pickering YO18 58 D1
Pickering Nook NE16 62 C1
Picket Piece SP11 21 G7
Picket Post BH24 10 C4
Pickford Green CV5 40 E7
Pickhill YO7 57 J1
Picklescott SY6 38 D6
Pickletillem KY16 83 F5
Pickmere WA16 49 F5
Pickney TA2 7 K3
Pickstock TF10 39 G3
Pickston PH1 82 A5
Pickup Bank BB3 56 C7
Pickwell *Devon* EX33 6 C1
Pickwell *Leics.* LE14 42 A4
Pickworth *Lincs.* NG34 42 D2
Pickworth *Rut.* PE9 42 C4
Picton *Ches.W. & C.* CH2 48 D5
Picton *N.Yorks.* TS15 63 F6
Piddinghoe BN9 13 H6
Piddington *Bucks.* HP14 22 B2
Piddington *Northants.* NN7 32 B3
Piddington *Oxon.* OX25 31 H7
Piddlehinton DT2 9 G5
Piddletrenthide DT2 9 G5
Pidley PE28 33 G1
Piercebridge DL2 62 D5
Pierowall KW17 106 D3
Pigdon NE61 71 G5
Pike Hill BB10 56 D6
Pikehall DE4 50 D7
Pikeshill SO43 10 D4
Pilgrims Hatch CM15 23 J2
Pilham DN21 52 B3
Pill BS20 19 J4
Pillaton *Cornw.* PL12 4 D4
Pillaton *Staffs.* ST19 40 B4
Pillerton Hersey CV35 30 D4
Pillerton Priors CV35 30 D4
Pilleth LD7 28 B2
Pilley *Hants.* SO41 10 E5
Pilley *S.Yorks.* S75 51 F2
Pilling PR3 55 H5
Pilling Lane FY6 55 G5
Pillowell GL15 19 K1
Pilning BS35 19 J3
Pilsbury SK17 50 D6
Pilsdon DT6 8 D5
Pilsgate PE9 42 D5
Pilsley *Derbys.* S45 51 G6
Pilsley *Derbys.* DE45 50 E5
Pilson Green NR13 45 H4
Piltdown TN22 13 H4
Pilton *Devon* EX31 6 D2
Pilton *Northants.* PE8 42 D7
Pilton *Rut.* LE15 42 C5
Pilton *Som.* BA4 19 J7
Pilton *Swan.* SA3 17 H7
Pilton Green SA3 17 H7
Pimhole BL9 49 H1
Pimlico HP3 22 D1
Pimperne DT11 9 J4
Pin Mill IP9 35 G5
Pinchbeck PE11 43 F3
Pinchbeck Bars PE11 43 F3
Pinchbeck West PE11 43 F3
Pincheon Green DN14 51 J1
Pinchinthorpe TS14 63 G5
Pindon End MK19 31 J4
Pinehurst SN25 20 E3
Pinfold L40 48 C1
Pinged SA16 17 H5
Pinhay DT7 8 C5
Pinhoe EX1 7 H6
Pinkneys Green SL6 22 B3
Pinley Green CV35 30 D2
Pinminnoch KA26 67 F4
Pinmore KA26 67 G4
Pinn EX10 7 K7
Pinner HA5 22 E3
Pinner Green HA5 22 E2
Pinvin WR10 29 J4
Pinwherry KA26 67 F5
Pinxton NG16 51 G7
Pipe & Lyde HR1 28 E4
Pipe Gate TF9 39 G1
Pipe Ridware WS15 40 C4
Pipehill WS13 40 C5
Piperhall PA20 73 J5
Piperhill IV12 97 F6
Pipers Pool PL15 4 C2
Pipewell NN14 42 B7
Pippacott EX31 6 D2
Pipton LD3 28 A5
Pirbright GU24 22 C6
Pirnmill KA27 73 G6
Pirton *Herts.* SG5 32 E5
Pirton *Worcs.* WR8 29 H4
Pisgah FK15 81 J7
Pishill RG9 22 A3
Pistyll LL53 36 C1
Pitagowan PH18 81 K1
Pitblae AB43 99 H4
Pitcairngreen PH1 82 B5
Pitcairns PH2 82 B6
Pitcaple AB51 91 F2
Pitch Green HP27 22 A1
Pitch Place *Surr.* GU3 22 C6
Pitch Place *Surr.* GU8 12 B3
Pitchcombe GL6 20 B1
Pitchcott HP22 31 J6
Pitchford SY5 38 E5
Pitcombe BA10 9 F1
Pitcot CF32 18 B4
Pitcox EH42 76 E3
Pitcur PH13 82 D4
Pitfichie AB51 90 E3
Pitgrudy IV25 96 E2
Pitinnan AB51 91 F1
Pitkennedy DD8 83 G2
Pitkevy KY6 82 D7
Pitlessie KY15 82 E7
Pitlochry PH16 82 A2
Pitman's Corner IP14 35 F2
Pitmedden AB41 91 G2
Pitminster TA3 8 B3
Pitmuies DD8 83 G3
Pitmunie AB51 90 E3
Pitnacree PH9 82 A2
Pitney TA10 8 D2
Pitroddie PH2 82 D5
Pitscottie KY15 83 F6
Pitsea SS13 24 D3
Pitsford NN6 31 J2
Pitsford Hill TA4 7 J2
Pitstone LU7 32 C7
Pitt *Devon* EX16 7 J4
Pitt *Hants.* SO22 11 F2
Pittendreich IV30 97 J5
Pittentrail IV28 96 E1
Pittenweem KY10 83 G7
Pitteuchar KY7 76 A1
Pittington DH6 62 E2
Pittodrie House AB51 90 E2
Pitton *Swan.* SA3 17 H7
Pitton *Wilts.* SP5 10 D1
Pittulie AB43 99 H4
Pittville GL52 29 J6
Pity Me DH1 62 D2
Pityme PL27 3 G1
Pixey Green IP21 35 G1
Pixley HR8 29 F5
Place Newton YO17 58 E2
Plaidy AB53 99 F5
Plain Dealings SA67 16 D4
Plainfield NE65 70 E3
Plains ML6 75 F4
Plainsfield TA5 7 K2
Plaish SY6 38 E6
Plaistow *Gt.Lon.* E13 23 G3
Plaistow *W.Suss.* RH14 12 D3
Plaitford SO51 10 D3
Plaitford Green SO51 10 D2
Plas SA32 17 H3
Plas Gwynant LL55 46 E7
Plas Isaf LL21 37 K1
Plas Llwyd LL18 47 H5
Plas Llwyngwern SY20 37 G5
Plas Llysyn SY17 37 J6
Plas Nantyr LL20 38 A2
Plashett SA33 17 F5
Plasisaf LL16 47 H6
Plas-rhiw-Saeson SY19 37 J5
Plastow Green RG19 21 J5
Plas-yn-Cefn LL17 47 J5
Platt TN15 23 K6
Platt Bridge WN2 49 F2
Platt Lane SY13 38 E2
Platt's Heath ME17 14 D2
Plawsworth DH2 62 D2
Plaxtol TN15 23 K6
Play Hatch RG4 22 A4
Playden TN31 14 E5
Playford IP6 35 G4
Playing Place TR3 3 F4
Playley Green GL19 29 G5
Plealey SY5 38 D5
Plean FK7 75 G2
Pleasance KY14 82 D6
Pleasant Valley CB11 33 J5
Pleasington BB2 56 B7
Pleasley NG19 51 H6
Pleasleyhill NG19 51 H6
Pleck *Dorset* DT9 9 G3
Pleck *W.Mid.* WS2 40 B6
Pledgdon Green CM22 33 J6
Pledwick WF2 51 F1
Plemstall CH2 48 D5
Plenmeller NE49 70 C7
Pleshey CM3 33 K7
Plockton IV52 86 E1
Plocropol HS3 93 G2
Plomer's Hill HP13 22 B2
Plot Gate TA11 8 E1
Plough Hill CV10 41 F6
Plowden SY7 38 C7
Ploxgreen SY5 38 C5
Pluckley TN27 14 E3
Pluckley Thorne TN27 14 E3
Plucks Gutter CT3 25 J5
Plumbland CA7 60 C3
Plumbley S20 51 G4
Plumley WA16 49 G5
Plumpton *Cumb.* CA11 61 F3
Plumpton *E.Suss.* BN7 13 G5
Plumpton *Northants.* NN12 31 H4
Plumpton Green BN7 13 G5
Plumpton Head CA11 61 G3
Plumstead *Gt.Lon.* SE18 23 H4
Plumstead *Norf.* NR11 45 F2
Plumtree NG12 41 J2
Plungar NG13 42 A2
Plush DT2 9 G4
Plusha PL15 4 C2
Plushabridge PL14 4 D3
Plwmp SA44 26 C3
Plym Bridge PL7 5 F5
PLYMOUTH PL 4 E5
Plymouth City Airport PL6 5 F4
Plympton PL7 5 F5
Plymstock PL9 5 F5
Plymtree EX15 7 J5
Pockley YO62 58 C1
Pocklington YO42 58 E5
Pockthorpe NR20 44 E3
Pocombe Bridge EX2 7 G6
Pode Hole PE11 43 F3
Podimore BA22 8 E2
Podington NN29 32 C2
Podmore ST21 39 G2
Podsmead GL2 29 H7
Poffley End OX29 30 E7
Point Clear CO16 34 E7
Pointon NG34 42 E2
Polanach PA38 80 A2
Polapit Tamar PL15 6 B7
Polbae DG8 64 C3
Polbain IV26 102 B7
Polbathic PL11 4 D5
Polbeth EH55 75 J4
Poldean DG10 69 G4
Pole Moor HD3 50 C1
Polebrook PE8 42 D7
Polegate BN26 13 J6
Poles IV25 96 E2
Polesworth B78 40 E5
Polglass IV26 95 G1
Polgooth PL26 3 G3
Polgown DG3 68 C3
Poling BN18 12 D6
Poling Corner BN18 12 D6
Polkerris PL24 4 A5
Poll a' Charra HS8 84 C3
Polla IV27 103 F3
Pollardras TR13 2 D5
Polldubh PH33 80 C1
Pollie IV28 104 C7
Pollington DN14 51 J1
Polloch PH37 79 J1
Pollok G53 74 D4
Pollokshaws G43 74 D4
Pollokshields G41 74 D4
Polmassick PL26 3 G4
Polmont FK2 75 H3
Polnoon G76 74 D5
Polperro PL13 4 C5
Polruan PL23 4 B5
Polsham BA5 19 J7
Polstead CO6 34 D5
Polstead Heath CO6 34 D4
Poltalloch PA31 73 G1
Poltimore EX4 7 H6
Polton EH18 76 A4
Polwarth TD10 77 F5
Polyphant PL15 4 C2
Polzeath PL27 3 G1
Pomphlett PL9 5 F5
Pond Street CB11 33 H5
Ponders End EN3 23 G2
Pondersbridge PE26 43 F6
Ponsanooth TR3 2 E5
Ponsonby CA20 60 B6
Ponsongath TR12 2 E7
Ponsworthy TQ13 5 H3
Pont Aber SA19 27 G6
Pont Aberglaslyn LL55 36 E1
Pont ar Hydfer LD3 27 H6
Pont Crugnant SY19 37 H6
Pont Cyfyng LL24 47 F7
Pont Dolgarrog LL32 47 F6
Pont Pen-y-benglog LL57 46 E6
Pont Rhyd-sarn LL23 37 H3
Pont Rhyd-y-cyff CF34 18 B3
Pont Walby SA11 18 B1
Pont yr Alwen LL21 47 H7
Pontamman SA18 17 K4
Pontantwn SA17 17 H4
Pontardawe SA8 18 A1
Pontarddulais SA4 17 J5
Pontarfynach (Devil's Bridge) SY23 27 G1
Pontargothi SA32 17 J3
Pont-ar-llechau SA19 27 G6
Pontarsais SA32 17 H3
Pontblyddyn CH7 48 B6
Pontbren Llwyd CF44 18 C1
Pontefract WF8 57 K7
Ponteland NE20 71 G6
Ponterwyd SY23 37 G7
Pontesbury SY5 38 D5
Pontesbury Hill SY5 38 C5
Pontesford SY5 38 D5
Pontfadog LL20 38 B2
Pontfaen *Pembs.* SA65 16 D2
Pont-faen *Powys* LD3 27 J5
Pontgarreg SA44 26 C3
Pont-Henri SA15 17 H5
Ponthir NP18 19 G2
Ponthirwaun SA43 17 F1
Pont-iets (Pontyates) SA15 17 H5
Pontllanfraith NP12 18 E2
Pontlliw SA4 17 K5
Pontllyfni LL54 46 C7
Pontlottyn CF81 18 E1
Pontneddfechan SA11 18 C1
Pontrhydfendigaid SY25 27 G2
Pontrhydyfen SA12 18 A2
Pont-rhyd-y-groes SY25 27 G1
Pontrhydyrun NP44 19 F2
Pontrilas HR2 28 C6
Pontrobert SY22 38 A4
Pont-rug LL55 46 D6
Ponts Green TN33 13 K5
Pontshill HR9 29 F6
Pont-siân SA44 17 H1
Pontsticill CF48 27 K7
Pontwelly SA44 17 H2
Pontyates (Pont-iets) SA15 17 H5
Pontyberem SA15 17 J4
Pont-y-blew LL14 38 C2
Pontybodkin CH7 48 B7
Pontyclun CF72 18 D3
Pontycymer CF32 18 C2
Pontygwaith CF43 18 D2
Pontymister NP11 19 F2
Pontymoel NP4 19 F1
Pont-y-pant LL25 47 F7
Pontypool NP4 19 F1
Pontypridd CF37 18 D2
Pont-y-rhyl CF32 18 C3
Pontywaun NP11 19 F2
Pooksgreen SO40 10 E3
Pool *Cornw.* TR15 2 D4
Pool *W.Yorks.* LS21 57 H5
Pool Bank LA11 55 H1
Pool Green WS9 40 C5
Pool Head HR1 28 E3
Pool of Muckhart FK14 82 B7
Pool Quay SY21 38 B4
Pool Street CO9 34 B5
Poole BH15 10 B5
Poole Keynes GL7 20 C2
Poolend ST13 49 J7
Poolewe IV22 94 E3
Pooley Bridge CA10 61 F4
Pooley Street IP22 44 E7
Poolfold ST8 49 H7
Poolhill GL18 29 G6
Poolsbrook S43 51 G5
Poolthorne Farm DN20 52 D2
Pope Hill SA62 16 C4
Popeswood RG42 22 B5
Popham SO21 21 J7
Poplar E14 23 G3
Porchfield PO30 11 F5
Porin IV6 95 K6
Poringland NR14 45 G5
Porkellis TR13 2 D5
Porlock TA24 7 G1
Porlock Weir TA24 7 G1
Port Allen PH2 82 D5
Port Appin PA38 80 A3
Port Askaig PA46 72 C4
Port Bannatyne PA20 73 J4
Port Carlisle CA7 69 H7
Port Charlotte PA48 72 A5
Port Clarence TS2 63 G4
Port Driseach PA21 73 H3
Port e Vullen IM7 54 D4
Port Ellen PA42 72 B6
Port Elphinstone AB51 91 F3
Port Erin IM9 54 A7
Port Erroll AB42 91 J1
Port Eynon SA3 17 H7
Port Gaverne PL29 4 A2
Port Glasgow PA14 74 B3
Port Henderson IV21 94 D4
Port Isaac PL29 4 A2
Port Logan DG9 64 A6
Port Mòr PH41 85 K7
Port Mulgrave TS13 63 J5
Port na Craig PH16 82 A2
Port nan Giùran (Portnaguran) HS2 101 H4
Port nan Long HS6 92 D4
Port Nis (Port of Ness) HS2 101 H1
Port of Menteith FK8 81 G7
Port of Ness (Port Nis) HS2 101 H1
Port o'Warren DG5 65 J5
Port Penrhyn LL57 46 D5
Port Pheadair (Peters Port) HS7 92 D7
Port Quin PL29 3 G1
Port Ramsay PA34 79 K3
Port St. Mary IM9 54 B7
Port Solent PO6 11 H4
Port Sunlight CH62 48 C4
Port Talbot SA12 18 A2
Port Tennant SA1 17 K6
Port Wemyss PA47 72 A5
Port William DG8 64 D6
Portachoillan PA29 73 F5
Portavadie PA21 73 H4
Portbury BS20 19 J4
Portchester PO16 11 H4
Portencross KA23 73 K6
Portesham DT3 9 F6
Portessie AB56 98 C4
Portfield *Arg. & B.* PA63 79 J5
Portfield *W.Suss.* PO19 12 B6
Portfield Gate SA62 16 C4
Portgate EX20 6 C7
Portgordon AB56 98 B4
Portgower KW8 105 F7
Porth *Cornw.* TR7 3 F2
Porth *R.C.T.* CF39 18 D2
Porth Colmon LL53 36 A2
Porth Llechog (Bull Bay) LL68 46 C3
Porth Navas TR11 2 E6
Porthaethwy (Menai Bridge) LL59 46 D5
Porthallow *Cornw.* TR12 2 E6
Porthallow *Cornw.* PL13 4 C5
Porthcawl CF36 18 B4
Porthcothan PL28 3 F1
Porthcurno TR19 2 A6
Porthgain SA62 16 B2
Porthill ST5 40 A1
Porthkerry CF62 18 D5
Porthleven TR13 2 D6
Porthmadog LL49 36 E2
Porthmeor TR20 2 B5
Portholland PL26 3 G4
Porthoustock TR12 3 F6
Porthpean PL26 4 A5
Porthtowan TR4 2 D4
Porthyrhyd *Carmar.* SA19 27 G5
Porthyrhyd *Carmar.* SA32 17 J4
Porth-y-waen SY10 38 B3
Portincaple G84 74 A1

Reay KW14 104 E2
Reculver CT6 25 J5
Red Ball EX16 7 J4
Red Bull ST7 49 H7
Red Dial CA7 60 D2
Red Hill *Hants.* PO9 11 J3
Red Hill *Warks.* B49 30 C3
Red Lodge IP28 33 K1
Red Lumb OL11 49 H1
Red Oaks Hill CB10 33 J5
Red Point IV21 94 D5
Red Post *Cornw.* EX23 6 A5
Red Post *Devon* TQ9 5 J4
Red Rail HR2 28 E6
Red Rock WN2 48 E2
Red Roses SA34 17 F4
Red Row NE61 71 H4
Red Street ST5 49 H7
Red Wharf Bay (Traeth Coch) LL75 46 D4
Redberth SA70 16 D5
Redbourn AL3 32 E7
Redbourne DN21 52 C3
Redbrook *Glos.* NP25 28 E7
Redbrook *Wrex.* SY13 38 E1
Redbrook Street TN26 14 E4
Redburn *High.* IV16 96 C5
Redburn *High.* IV12 97 G7
Redburn *Northumb.* NE47 70 C7
Redcar TS10 63 H4
Redcastle *Angus* DD11 83 H2
Redcastle *High.* IV6 96 C7
Redcliff Bay BS20 19 H4
Redcloak AB39 91 G6
Reddingmuirhead FK2 75 H3
Reddish SK5 49 H3
Redditch B97 30 B2
Rede IP29 34 C3
Redenhall IP20 45 G7
Redesmouth NE48 70 D5
Redford *Aber.* AB30 91 F7
Redford *Angus* DD11 83 G3
Redford *Dur.* DL13 62 B3
Redford *W.Suss.* GU29 12 B4
Redgrave IP22 34 E1
Redheugh DD8 83 F1
Redhill *Aber.* AB51 90 E1
Redhill *Aber.* AB32 91 F4
Redhill *Moray* AB54 98 D6
Redhill *N.Som.* BS40 19 H5
Redhill *Notts.* NG5 41 H1
REDHILL *Surr.* RH 23 F6
Redhill Aerodrome & Heliport RH1 23 F7
Redhouse *Aber.* AB33 90 D2
Redhouse *Arg. & B.* PA29 73 G4
Redhouses PA44 72 B4
Redisham NR34 45 J7
Redland *Bristol* BS6 19 J4
Redland *Ork.* KW17 106 C5
Redlingfield IP23 35 F1
Redlynch *Som.* BA10 9 G1
Redlynch *Wilts.* SP5 10 D2
Redmarley D'Abitot GL19 29 G5
Redmarshall TS21 62 E4
Redmile NG13 42 A2
Redmire DL8 62 B7
Redmoor PL30 4 A4
Rednal SY11 38 C3
Redpath TD4 76 D7
Redruth TR15 2 D4
Redscarhead EH45 76 A6
Redshaw ML11 68 D1
Redstone Bank SA67 16 E4
Redwick *Newport* NP26 19 H3
Redwick *S.Glos.* BS35 19 J3
Redworth DL5 62 D4
Reed SG8 33 G5
Reed End SG8 33 G5
Reedham NR13 45 J5
Reedley BB10 56 D6
Reedness DN14 58 D7
Reef (Riof) HS2 100 D4
Reepham *Lincs.* LN3 52 D5
Reepham *Norf.* NR10 44 E3
Reeth DL11 62 B7
Regaby IM7 54 D4
Regil BS40 19 J5
Regoul IV12 97 F6
Reiff IV26 102 B7
Reigate RH2 23 F6
Reighton YO14 59 H2
Reinigeadal (Rhenigidale) HS3 100 E7
Reisgill KW3 105 H5
Reiss KW1 105 J3
Rejerrah TR8 3 F3
Releath TR14 2 D5
Relubbus TR20 2 C5
Relugas IV36 97 G7
Remenham RG9 22 A3
Remenham Hill RG9 22 A3
Remony PH15 81 J3
Rempstone LE12 41 H3
Rendcomb GL7 30 B7
Rendham IP17 35 H2
Rendlesham IP12 35 H3
Renfrew PA4 74 D4
Renhold MK41 32 D3
Renishaw S21 51 G5
Rennington NE66 71 H2
Renton G82 74 B3
Renwick CA10 61 G2
Repps NR29 45 J4
Repton DE65 41 F3
Rescobie DD8 83 G2
Rescorla PL26 4 A5
Resipole PH36 79 J1
Resolis IV7 96 D5
Resolven SA11 18 B1
Resourie PH37 86 E7
Respryn PL30 4 B4
Reston TD14 77 G4
Restormel PL22 4 B4
Reswallie DD8 83 G2
Reterth TR9 3 G2
Retew PL26 3 G3
Retford (East Retford) DN22 51 K4
Rettendon CM3 24 D2
Rettendon Place CM3 24 D2
Retyn TR8 3 F3
Revesby PE22 53 F6
Revesby Bridge PE22 53 G6
Rew TQ13 5 H3
Rew Street PO31 11 F5
Rewe *Devon* EX5 7 H6
Rewe *Devon* EX5 7 G6
Reybridge SN15 20 C5
Reydon IP18 35 J1
Reydon Smear IP18 35 K1
Reymerston NR9 44 E5
Reynalton SA68 16 D5
Reynoldston SA3 17 H7
Rezare PL15 4 D3
Rhadyr NP15 19 G1
Rhaeadr Gwy (Rhayader) LD6 27 J2
Rhandirmwyn SA20 27 G4
Rhaoine IV28 96 D1
Rhayader (Rhaeadr Gwy) LD6 27 J2
Rhedyn LL53 36 B2
Rhegreanoch IV27 102 C7
Rheindown IV4 96 C7
Rhelonie IV24 96 C2
Rhemore PA34 79 G2
Rhenigidale (Reinigeadal) HS3 100 E7
Rheola SA11 18 B1
Rhes-y-cae CH8 47 K6
Rhewl *Denb.* LL20 38 A1
Rhewl *Denb.* LL15 47 K6
Rhewl *Shrop.* SY10 38 C2
Rhian IV27 103 H7
Rhicarn IV27 102 C6
Rhiconich IV27 102 E3
Rhicullen IV18 96 D4
Rhidorroch IV26 95 H2
Rhifail KW11 104 C4
Rhigos CF44 18 C1
Rhilochan IV28 96 E1
Rhinduie IV3 96 C7
Rhireavach IV23 95 G2
Rhiroy IV23 95 H3
Rhiston SY15 38 B6
Rhiw LL53 36 B3
Rhiwabon (Ruabon) LL14 38 C1
Rhiwargor SY10 37 J3
Rhiwbina CF14 18 E3
Rhiwbryfdir LL41 37 F1
Rhiwderin NP10 19 F3
Rhiwinder CF39 18 D3
Rhiwlas *Gwyn.* LL57 46 D6
Rhiwlas *Gwyn.* LL23 37 J2
Rhiwlas *Powys* SY10 38 B2
Rhode TA5 8 B1
Rhodes Minnis CT4 15 G3
Rhodesia S80 51 H5
Rhodiad-y-brenin SA62 16 A3
Rhodmad SY23 26 E1
Rhonadale PA28 73 F7
Rhonehouse (Kelton Hill) DG7 65 H5
Rhoose CF62 18 D5
Rhos *Carmar.* SA44 17 G2
Rhos *N.P.T.* SA8 18 A1
Rhos Common SY22 38 B4
Rhosaman SA18 27 G7
Rhoscolyn LL65 46 A5
Rhoscrowther SA71 16 C5
Rhosesmor CH7 48 B6
Rhos-fawr LL53 36 C2
Rhosgadfan LL54 46 D7
Rhos-goch *I.o.A.* LL66 46 C4
Rhosgoch *Powys* LD2 28 A4
Rhos-hill SA43 16 E1
Rhoshirwaun LL53 36 A3
Rhoslan LL52 36 D1
Rhoslefain LL36 36 E5
Rhosllanerchrugog LL14 38 B1
Rhoslligwy LL70 46 C4
Rhosmaen SA19 17 K3
Rhosmeirch LL77 46 C5
Rhosneigr LL64 46 B5
Rhosnesni LL13 48 C7
Rhôs-on-Sea LL28 47 G4
Rhossili SA3 17 H7
Rhosson SA62 16 A3
Rhostrehwfa LL77 46 C5
Rhostryfan LL54 46 C7
Rhostyllen LL14 38 C1
Rhos-y-bol LL68 46 C4
Rhos-y-brithdir SY22 38 A3
Rhosycaerau SA64 16 C2
Rhos-y-garth SY23 27 F1
Rhos-y-gwaliau LL23 37 J2
Rhos-y-llan LL53 36 B2
Rhos-y-mawn LL22 47 G6
Rhos-y-Meirch LD7 28 B2
Rhu G84 74 A2
Rhuallt LL17 47 J5
Rhubodach PA20 73 J3
Rhuddall Heath CW6 48 E6
Rhuddlan LL18 47 J5
Rhue IV26 95 H2
Rhulen LD2 28 A4
Rhumach PH39 86 C6
Rhunahaorine PA29 73 F6
Rhuthun (Ruthin) LL15 47 K7
Rhyd *Gwyn.* LL48 37 F1
Rhyd *Powys* SY17 37 J5
Rhydaman (Ammanford) SA18 17 K4
Rhydargaeau SA32 17 H3
Rhydcymerau SA19 17 J2
Rhyd-Ddu LL54 46 D7
Rhydding SA10 18 A2
Rhydgaled LL16 47 H6
Rhydlanfair LL24 47 G7
Rhydlewis SA44 17 G1
Rhydlios LL53 36 A2
Rhydlydan *Conwy* LL24 47 G7
Rhydlydan *Powys* SY16 37 K6
Rhydolion LL53 36 B3
Rhydowen SA44 17 H1
Rhyd-Rosser SY23 26 E2
Rhydspence HR3 28 B4
Rhydtalog CH7 48 B7
Rhyd-uchaf LL23 37 H2
Rhyd-wen LL23 37 J3
Rhyd-wyn LL65 46 B4
Rhyd-y-ceirw CH7 48 B7
Rhyd-y-clafdy LL53 36 C2
Rhydycroesau SY10 38 B2
Rhydyfelin *Cere.* SY23 26 E1
Rhydyfelin *R.C.T.* CF37 18 D3
Rhyd-y-foel LL22 47 H5
Rhyd-y-fro SA8 18 A1
Rhyd-y-groes LL57 46 D6
Rhydymain LL40 37 H3
Rhydymwyn CH7 48 B6
Rhyd-yr-onnen LL36 37 F5
Rhyd-y-sarn LL41 37 F1
Rhydywrach SA34 16 E4
Rhyl LL18 47 J4
Rhymney NP22 18 E1
Rhyn SY11 38 C2
Rhynd PH2 82 C5
Rhynie *Aber.* AB54 90 C2
Rhynie *High.* IV20 97 F4
Ribbesford DY12 29 G1
Ribchester PR3 56 B6
Ribigill IV27 103 H3
Riby DN37 52 E2
Riccall YO19 58 C6
Riccarton KA1 74 C7
Richards Castle SY8 28 D2
Richings Park SL0 22 D4
Richmond *Gt.Lon.* TW9 22 E4
Richmond *N.Yorks.* DL10 62 C6
Richmond *S.Yorks.* S13 51 G4
Rich's Holford TA4 7 K2
Rickarton AB39 91 G6
Rickerscote ST17 40 B3
Rickford BS40 19 H6
Rickinghall IP22 34 E1
Rickleton NE38 62 D1
Rickling CB11 33 H5
Rickling Green CB11 33 J6
Rickmansworth WD3 22 D2
Riddell TD6 70 A1
Riddings DE55 51 G7
Riddlecombe EX18 6 E4
Riddlesden BD20 57 F5
Ridge *Dorset* BH20 9 J6
Ridge *Herts.* EN6 23 F1
Ridge *Wilts.* SP3 9 J1
Ridge Green RH1 23 G7
Ridge Lane CV10 40 E6
Ridgebourne LD1 27 K2
Ridgeway S12 51 G4
Ridgeway Cross WR13 29 G4
Ridgeway Moor S12 51 G4
Ridgewell CO9 34 B4
Ridgewood TN22 13 H4
Ridgmont MK43 32 C5
Riding Gate BA9 9 G2
Riding Mill NE44 71 F7
Ridley TN15 24 C5
Ridleywood LL13 48 C7
Ridlington *Norf.* NR28 45 H2
Ridlington *Rut.* LE15 42 B5
Ridsdale NE48 70 E5
Riechip PH8 82 B3
Rievaulx YO62 58 B1
Rift House TS25 63 F3
Rigg *D. & G.* DG16 69 H7
Rigg *High.* IV51 94 B6
Riggend ML6 75 F4
Rigifa KW1 105 J1
Rigmaden Park LA6 56 B1
Rigsby LN13 53 H5
Rigside ML11 75 G7
Riley Green PR5 56 B7
Rileyhill WS13 40 D4
Rilla Mill PL17 4 C3
Rillaton PL17 4 C3
Rillington YO17 58 E2
Rimington BB7 56 D5
Rimpton BA22 9 F2
Rimswell HU19 59 K7
Rinaston SA62 16 C3
Ring o' Bells L40 48 D1
Ringford DG7 65 G5
Ringinglow S11 50 E4
Ringland NR8 45 F4
Ringles Cross TN22 13 H4
Ringmer BN8 13 H5
Ringmore *Devon* TQ7 5 G6
Ringmore *Devon* TQ14 5 K3
Ringorm AB38 97 K7
Ring's End PE13 43 G5
Ringsfield NR34 45 J7
Ringsfield Corner NR34 45 J7
Ringshall *Herts.* HP4 32 C7
Ringshall *Suff.* IP14 34 E3
Ringshall Stocks IP14 34 E3
Ringstead *Norf.* PE36 44 B1
Ringstead *Northants.* NN14 32 C1
Ringwood BH24 10 C4
Ringwould CT14 15 J3
Rinloan AB35 89 K4
Rinmore AB33 90 C3
Rinnigill KW16 106 C8
Rinsey TR13 2 C6
Riof (Reef) HS2 100 D4
Ripe BN8 13 J6
Ripley *Derbys.* DE5 51 F7
Ripley *Hants.* BH23 10 C5
Ripley *N.Yorks.* HG3 57 H3
Ripley *Surr.* GU23 22 D6
Riplingham HU15 59 F6
Ripon HG4 57 J2
Rippingale PE10 42 E3
Ripple *Kent* CT14 15 J3
Ripple *Worcs.* GL20 29 H5
Ripponden HX6 50 C1
Risabus PA42 72 B6
Risbury HR6 28 E3
Risby *E.Riding* HU17 59 G6
Risby *Suff.* IP28 34 B2
Risca NP11 19 F2
Rise HU11 59 H5
Riseden TN17 14 C4
Risegate PE11 43 F3
Riseholme LN2 52 C5
Riseley *Bed.* MK44 32 D2
Riseley *W'ham* RG7 22 A5
Rishangles IP23 35 F2
Rishton BB1 56 C6
Rishworth HX6 50 C1
Risinghurst OX3 21 J1
Risley *Derbys.* DE72 41 G2
Risley *Warr.* WA3 49 F3
Risplith HG4 57 H3
Rispond IV27 103 G2
Rivar SN8 21 G5
Rivenhall CM8 34 C7
Rivenhall End CM8 34 C7
River *Kent* CT17 15 H3
River *W.Suss.* GU28 12 C4
River Bank CB7 33 J2
River Bridge TA7 19 G7
Riverford Bridge TQ9 5 H4
Riverhead TN13 23 J6
Riverside CF11 18 E4
Riverton EX32 6 E2
Riverview Park DA12 24 C4
Rivington BL6 49 F1
Roa Island LA13 55 F3
Roach Bridge PR5 55 J7
Road Green NR15 45 G6
Road Weedon NN7 31 H3
Roade NN7 31 J3
Roadhead CA6 70 A6
Roadside *High.* KW12 105 G2
Roadside *Ork.* KW17 106 F3
Roadside of Kinneff DD10 91 G7
Roadwater TA23 7 J2
Roag IV55 93 H7
Roast Green CB11 33 H5
Roath CF24 18 E4
Roberton *S.Lan.* ML12 68 E1
Roberton *Sc.Bord.* TD9 69 K2
Robertsbridge TN32 14 C5
Robertstown *Moray* AB38 97 K7
Robertstown *R.C.T.* CF44 18 D1
Roberttown WF15 57 G7
Robeston Cross SA73 16 B5
Robeston Wathen SA67 16 D4
Robeston West SA73 16 B5
Robin Hood *Derbys.* DE45 50 E5
Robin Hood *Lancs.* WN6 48 E1
Robin Hood *W.Yorks.* LS26 57 J7
Robin Hood Doncaster Sheffield Airport DN10 51 J3
Robin Hood's Bay YO22 63 J2
Robinhood End CO9 34 B5
Robins GU29 12 B4
Roborough *Devon* EX19 6 D4
Roborough *Plym.* PL6 5 F4
Roby L36 48 D3
Roby Mill WN8 48 E2
Rocester ST14 40 D2
Roch SA62 16 B3
Roch Bridge SA62 16 B3
Roch Gate SA62 16 B3
Rochallie PH10 82 C2
Rochdale OL16 49 H1
Roche PL26 3 G2
Rochester *Med.* ME1 24 D5
Rochester *Northumb.* NE19 70 D4
Rochford *Essex* SS4 24 E2
Rochford *Worcs.* WR15 29 F2
Rock *Cornw.* PL27 3 G1
Rock *Northumb.* NE66 71 H2
Rock *Worcs.* DY14 29 G1
Rock Ferry CH42 48 C4
Rockbeare EX5 7 J6
Rockbourne SP6 10 C3
Rockcliffe *Cumb.* CA6 69 J7
Rockcliffe *D. & G.* DG5 65 J5
Rockcliffe Cross CA6 69 J7
Rockfield *Arg. & B.* PA29 73 G5
Rockfield *High.* IV20 97 G3
Rockfield *Mon.* NP25 28 D7
Rockford BH24 10 C4
Rockhampton GL13 19 K2
Rockhead PL33 4 A2
Rockingham LE16 42 B6
Rockland All Saints NR17 44 D6
Rockland St. Mary NR14 45 H5
Rockland St. Peter NR17 44 D6
Rockley SN8 20 E4
Rockside PA49 72 A4
Rockwell End RG9 22 A3
Rockwell Green TA21 7 K4
Rodborough GL5 20 B1
Rodbourne SN16 20 C3
Rodbridge Corner CO10 34 C4
Rodd LD8 28 C2
Roddam NE66 71 F1
Rodden DT3 9 F6
Rode BA11 20 B6
Rode Heath ST7 49 H7
Rodeheath SK11 49 H6
Rodel (Roghadal) HS5 93 F3
Roden TF6 38 E4
Rodhuish TA24 7 J2
Rodington SY4 38 E4
Rodington Heath SY4 38 E4
Rodley GL14 29 G7
Rodmarton GL7 20 C2
Rodmell BN7 13 H6
Rodmersham ME9 25 F5
Rodmersham Green ME9 25 F5
Rodney Stoke BS27 19 H6
Rodsley DE6 40 E1
Rodway TA5 19 F7
Roe Cross SK14 49 J3
Roe Green SG9 33 G5
Roecliffe YO51 57 J3
Roehampton SW15 23 F4
Roesound ZE2 107 M6
Roffey RH12 12 E3
Rogart IV28 96 E1
Rogate GU31 12 B4
Rogerstone NP10 19 F3
Roghadal (Rodel) HS5 93 F3
Rogiet NP26 19 H3
Rokemarsh OX10 21 K2
Roker SR6 63 F1
Rollesby NR29 45 J4
Rolleston *Leics.* LE7 42 A5
Rolleston *Notts.* NG23 51 K7
Rollestone SP3 20 D7
Rolleston-on-Dove DE13 40 E3
Rolston HU18 59 J5
Rolstone BS24 19 G5
Rolvenden TN17 14 D4
Rolvenden Layne TN17 14 D4
Romaldkirk DL12 62 A4
Romanby DL7 62 E7
Romannobridge EH46 75 K6
Romansleigh EX36 7 F3
Romesdal IV51 93 K6
Romford *Dorset* BH31 10 B4
ROMFORD *Gt.Lon.* RM 23 J3
Romiley SK6 49 J3
Romney Street TN15 23 J5
Romsey SO51 10 E2
Romsley *Shrop.* WV15 39 G7
Romsley *Worcs.* B62 29 J1
Rona IV40 94 C6
Ronachan PA29 73 F5
Ronague IM9 54 B6
Ronnachmore PA43 72 B5
Rood End B67 40 C7
Rookhope DL13 62 A2
Rookley PO38 11 G6
Rookley Green PO38 11 G6
Rooks Bridge BS26 19 G6
Rook's Nest TA4 7 J2
Rookwith HG4 57 H1
Roos HU12 59 J6
Roose LA13 55 F3
Roosebeck LA12 55 F3
Roosecote LA13 55 F3
Rootham's Green MK44 32 D3
Rootpark ML11 75 H5
Ropley SO24 11 H1
Ropley Dean SO24 11 H1
Ropley Soke SO24 11 H1
Ropsley NG33 42 C2
Rora AB42 99 J5
Rorandle AB51 90 E3
Rorrington SY15 38 C5
Rosarie AB55 98 B6
Rose TR4 2 E3
Rose Ash EX36 7 F3
Rose Green *Essex* CO6 34 D6
Rose Green *W.Suss.* PO21 12 C7
Rose Hill TN22 13 H5
Roseacre *Kent* ME14 14 C2
Roseacre *Lancs.* PR4 55 H6
Rosebank ML8 75 G6
Rosebrough NE67 71 G1
Rosebush SA66 16 D3
Rosecare EX23 4 B1
Rosecliston TR8 3 F3
Rosedale Abbey YO18 63 J7
Roseden NE66 71 F1
Rosehall IV27 96 B1
Rosehearty AB43 99 H4
Rosehill *Aber.* AB34 90 D5
Rosehill *Shrop.* SY4 38 D4
Roseisle IV30 97 J5
Roselands BN22 13 K6
Rosemarket SA73 16 C5
Rosemarkie IV10 96 E6
Rosemary Lane EX15 7 K4
Rosemount *P. & K.* PH10 82 C3
Rosemount *S.Ayr.* KA9 67 H1
Rosenannon PL30 3 G2
Rosenithon TR12 3 F6
Rosepool SA62 16 B4
Rosevean PL26 4 A5
Roseville WV14 40 B6
Rosewell EH24 76 A4
Roseworth TS19 63 F4
Rosgill CA10 61 G5
Roshven PH38 86 D7
Roskhill IV55 93 H7
Roskorwell TR12 2 E6
Rosley CA7 60 E2
Roslin EH25 76 A4
Rosliston DE12 40 E4

Rosneath G84 74 A2
Ross D. & G. DG6 65 G6
Ross Northumb. NE70 77 K7
Ross P. & K. PH6 81 J5
Ross Priory G83 74 C2
Rossdhu House G83 74 B2
Rossett LL12 48 C7
Rossett Green HG2 57 J4
Rosside LA12 55 F2
Rossie Farm School DD10 83 H2
Rossie Ochill PH2 82 B6
Rossie Priory PH14 82 D4
Rossington DN11 51 J3
Rosskeen IV18 96 D5
Rossmore BH12 10 B5
Ross-on-Wye HR9 29 F6
Roster KW3 105 H5
Rostherne WA16 49 G4
Rosthwaite Cumb. CA12 60 D5
Rosthwaite Cumb. LA20 55 F1
Roston DE6 40 D1
Rosudgeon TR20 2 C6
Rosyth KY11 75 K2
Rothbury NE65 71 F3
Rotherby LE14 41 J4
Rotherfield TN6 13 J3
Rotherfield Greys RG9 22 A3
Rotherfield Peppard RG9 22 A3
Rotherham S60 51 G3
Rothersthorpe NN7 31 J3
Rotherwick RG27 22 A6
Rothes AB38 97 K7
Rothesay PA20 73 J4
Rothiebrisbane AB53 91 F1
Rothienorman AB51 91 F1
Rothiesholm KW17 106 F5
Rothley Leics. LE7 41 H4
Rothley Northumb. NE61 71 F5
Rothney AB52 90 E2
Rothwell Lincs. LN7 52 E3
Rothwell Northants. NN14 42 B7
Rothwell W.Yorks. LS26 57 J7
Rotsea YO25 59 G4
Rottal DD8 82 E1
Rotten Row Bucks. RG9 22 A3
Rotten Row W.Mid. B93 30 C1
Rottingdean BN2 13 G6
Rottington CA28 60 A5
Roud PO38 11 G6
Roudham NR16 44 D7
Rough Close ST3 40 B2
Rough Common CT2 15 G2
Rougham Norf. PE32 44 C3
Rougham Suff. IP30 34 D2
Rougham Green IP30 34 D2
Roughburn PH31 87 K6
Roughlee BB9 56 D5
Roughley B75 40 D6
Roughton Lincs. LN10 53 F6
Roughton Norf. NR11 45 G2
Roughton Shrop. WV15 39 G6
Round Bush WD25 22 E2
Roundbush Green CM6 33 J7
Roundham TA18 8 D4
Roundhay LS8 57 J6
Roundstreet Common RH14 12 D4
Roundway SN10 20 D5
Rous Lench WR11 30 B3
Rousay KW17 106 C4
Rousdon DT7 8 B5
Rousham OX25 31 F6
Rousham Gap OX25 31 F6
Routenburn KA30 73 K4
Routh HU17 59 G5
Rout's Green HP14 22 A2
Row Cornw. PL30 4 A3
Row Cumb. LA8 55 H1
Row Cumb. CA10 61 H3
Row Heath CO16 35 F7
Row Town KT15 22 D5
Rowanburn DG14 69 K6
Rowardennan Lodge G63 74 B1
Rowarth SK22 50 C4
Rowbarton TA2 8 B2
Rowberrow BS25 19 H6
Rowchoish G63 80 E7
Rowde SN10 20 C5
Rowden EX20 6 E6
Rowen LL32 47 F5
Rowfields DE6 40 D1
Rowfoot NE49 70 B7
Rowhedge CO5 34 E6
Rowhook RH12 12 E3
Rowington CV35 30 D2
Rowland DE45 50 E5
Rowland's Castle PO9 11 J3
Rowlands Gill NE39 62 C1
Rowledge GU10 22 B7
Rowlestone HR2 28 C6
Rowley Devon EX36 7 F4
Rowley Dur. DH8 62 B2
Rowley Shrop. SY5 38 C5
Rowley Park ST17 40 B3
Rowley Regis B65 40 B7
Rowly GU5 22 D7
Rowner PO13 11 G4
Rowney Green B48 30 B1
Rownhams SO16 10 E3
Rowrah CA26 60 B5
Rowsham HP22 32 B7
Rowsley DE4 50 E6
Rowstock OX11 21 H3
Rowston LN4 52 D7
Rowthorne S44 51 G6
Rowton Ches.W. & C. CH3 48 D6
Rowton Shrop. SY5 38 C4
Rowton Tel. & W. TF6 39 F4
Roxburgh TD5 77 F7
Roxby N.Lincs. DN15 52 C1
Roxby N.Yorks. TS13 63 J5
Roxton MK44 32 E3
Roxwell CM1 24 C1
Royal British Legion Village ME20 14 C2
Royal Leamington Spa CV32 30 E2
Royal Oak L39 48 D2
ROYAL TUNBRIDGE WELLS TN 13 J3
Royal Wootton Bassett SN4 20 D3
Roybridge PH31 87 J6
Roydon Essex CM19 33 H7
Roydon Norf. IP22 44 E7
Roydon Norf. PE32 44 B3
Roydon Hamlet CM19 23 H1
Royston Herts. SG8 33 G4
Royston S.Yorks. S71 51 F1
Royton OL2 49 J2
Rozel JE3 3 K6
Ruabon (Rhiwabon) LL14 38 C1
Ruaig PA77 78 B3
Ruan Lanihorne TR2 3 F4
Ruan Major TR12 2 D7
Ruan Minor TR12 2 E7
Ruanaich PA76 78 D5
Ruardean GL17 29 F7
Ruardean Hill GL17 29 F7
Ruardean Woodside GL17 29 F7
Rubery B45 29 J1
Ruckcroft CA4 61 G2
Ruckinge TN26 15 F4
Ruckland LN11 53 G5
Rucklers Lane HP3 22 D1
Ruckley SY5 38 E5
Rudbaxton SA62 16 C3
Rudby TS15 63 F6
Rudchester NE15 71 G7
Ruddington NG11 41 H2
Ruddlemoor PL26 4 A5
Rudford GL2 29 G6
Rudge BA11 20 B6
Rudgeway BS35 19 K3
Rudgwick RH12 12 D3
Rudhall HR9 29 F6
Rudheath CW9 49 F5
Rudley Green CM3 24 E1
Rudloe SN13 20 B5
Rudry CF83 18 E3
Rudston YO25 59 G3
Rudyard ST13 49 J7
Rufford L40 48 D1
Rufforth YO23 58 B4
Ruffside DH8 62 A1
Rugby CV21 31 G1
Rugeley WS15 40 C4
Ruilick IV4 96 C7
Ruishton TA3 8 B2
Ruisigearraidh HS6 92 E3
Ruislip HA4 22 D3
Ruislip Gardens HA4 22 D3
Ruislip Manor HA4 22 E3
Rum PH43 85 J5
Rumbling Bridge KY13 75 J1
Rumburgh IP19 45 H7
Rumford PL27 3 F1
Rumleigh PL20 4 E4
Rumney CF3 19 F4
Rumwell TA4 7 K3
Runacraig FK18 81 G6
Runcorn WA7 48 E4
Runcton PO20 12 B6
Runcton Holme PE33 44 A5
Rundlestone PL20 5 F3
Runfold GU10 22 B7
Runhall NR9 44 E5
Runham Norf. NR29 45 J4
Runham Norf. NR30 45 K5
Runnington TA21 7 K3
Runsell Green CM3 24 D1
Runshaw Moor PR7 48 E1
Runswick Bay TS13 63 K5
Runtaleave DD8 82 D1
Runwell SS11 24 D2
Ruscombe Glos. GL6 20 B1
Ruscombe W'ham RG10 22 A4
Rush Green Gt.Lon. RM7 23 J3
Rush Green Herts. SG4 33 F6
Rushall Here. HR8 29 F5
Rushall Norf. IP21 45 F7
Rushall W.Mid. WS4 40 C5
Rushall Wilts. SN9 20 E6
Rushbrooke IP30 34 C2
Rushbury SY6 38 E6
Rushden Herts. SG9 33 G5
Rushden Northants. NN10 32 C2
Rushford Devon PL19 4 E3
Rushford Norf. IP24 44 D7
Rushgreen WA13 49 F4
Rushlake Green TN21 13 K5
Rushmere NR33 45 J7
Rushmere St. Andrew IP5 35 G4
Rushmoor GU10 22 B7
Rushock WR9 29 H1
Rusholme M13 49 H3
Rushton Ches.W. & C. CW6 48 E6
Rushton Northants. NN14 42 B7
Rushton Shrop. TF6 39 F5
Rushton Spencer SK11 49 J6
Rushwick WR2 29 H3
Rushy Green BN8 13 H5
Rushyford DL17 62 D4
Ruskie FK8 81 H7
Ruskington NG34 52 D7
Rusko DG7 65 F5
Rusland LA12 55 G1
Rusper RH12 13 F3
Ruspidge GL14 29 F7
Russ Hill RH6 23 F7
Russel IV54 94 E7
Russell Green CM3 34 B7
Russell's Green TN33 14 C6
Russell's Water RG9 22 A2
Russel's Green IP21 35 G1
Rusthall TN4 13 J3
Rustington BN16 12 D6
Ruston YO13 59 F1
Ruston Parva YO25 59 G3
Ruswarp YO21 63 K6
Rutherend ML10 74 E5
Rutherford TD5 76 E7
Rutherglen G73 74 E4
Ruthernbridge PL30 4 A4
Ruthers of Howe KW1 105 J2
Ruthin (Rhuthun) Denb. LL15 47 K7
Ruthin V. of Glam. CF35 18 C4
Ruthrieston AB10 91 H4
Ruthven Aber. AB54 98 D6
Ruthven Angus PH12 82 D3
Ruthven High. IV13 89 F1
Ruthven High. PH21 88 E5
Ruthvoes TR9 3 G2
Ruthwaite CA7 60 D3
Ruthwell DG1 69 F7
Ruyton-XI-Towns SY4 38 C3
Ryal NE20 71 F6
Ryal Fold BB3 56 B7
Ryall Dorset DT6 8 D5
Ryall Worcs. WR8 29 H4
Ryarsh ME19 23 K6
Rydal LA22 60 E6
Ryde PO33 11 G5
Rydon EX22 6 B5
Rye TN31 14 E5
Rye Foreign TN31 14 D5
Rye Harbour TN31 14 E6
Rye Park EN11 23 G1
Rye Street WR13 29 G5
Ryebank SY4 38 E2
Ryeford HR9 29 F6
Ryehill Aber. AB52 90 E2
Ryehill E.Riding HU12 59 J7
Ryhall PE9 42 D4
Ryhill WF4 51 F1
Ryhope SR2 63 F1
Rylands NG9 41 H2
Rylstone BD23 56 E4
Ryme Intrinseca DT9 8 E3
Ryther LS24 58 B6
Ryton Glos. GL18 29 G5
Ryton N.Yorks. YO17 58 D2
Ryton Shrop. TF11 39 G5
Ryton T. & W. NE40 71 G7
Ryton-on-Dunsmore CV8 30 E1

S

Saasaig IV44 86 C4
Sabden BB7 56 C6
Sabden Fold BB12 56 D6
Sackers Green CO10 34 D5
Sacombe SG12 33 G7
Sacombe Green SG12 33 G7
Sacriston DH7 62 D2
Sadberge DL2 62 E5
Saddell PA28 73 F7
Saddington LE8 41 J6
Saddle Bow PE34 44 A4
Sadgill LA8 61 F6
Saffron Walden CB10 33 J5
Sageston SA70 16 D5
Saham Hills IP25 44 D5
Saham Toney IP25 44 C5
Saighdinis HS6 92 D5
Saighton CH3 48 D6
St. Abbs TD14 77 H4
St. Agnes TR5 2 E3
ST. ALBANS AL 22 E1
St. Allen TR4 3 F3
St. Andrews KY16 83 G6
St. Andrews Major CF64 18 E4
St. Anne GY9 3 K4
St. Anne's FY8 55 G7
St. Ann's DG11 69 F4
St. Ann's Chapel Cornw. PL18 4 E3
St. Ann's Chapel Devon TQ7 5 G6
St. Anthony TR2 3 F5
St. Anthony-in-Meneage TR12 2 E6
St. Anthony's Hill BN23 13 K6
St. Arvans NP16 19 J2
St. Asaph (Llanelwy) LL17 47 J5
St. Athan CF62 18 D5
St. Aubin JE3 3 J7
St. Audries TA4 7 K1
St. Austell PL25 4 A5
St. Bees CA27 60 A5
St. Blazey PL24 4 A5
St. Blazey Gate PL24 4 A5
St. Boswells TD6 76 D7
St. Brelade JE3 3 J7
St. Breock PL27 3 G1
St. Breward PL30 4 A3
St. Briavels GL15 19 J1
St. Brides SA62 16 B4
St. Brides Major CF32 18 B4
St. Bride's Netherwent NP26 19 H3
St. Brides Wentlooge NP10 19 F3
St. Bride's-super-Ely CF5 18 D4
St. Budeaux PL5 4 E5
St. Buryan TR19 2 B6
St. Catherine BA1 20 A5
St. Catherines PA25 80 C7
St. Clears (Sancler) SA33 17 F4
St. Cleer PL14 4 C4
St. Clement Chan.I. JE2 3 K7
St. Clement Cornw. TR1 3 F4
St. Clether PL15 4 C2
St. Colmac PA20 73 J4
St. Columb Major TR9 3 G2
St. Columb Minor TR7 3 F2
St. Columb Road TR9 3 G3
St. Combs AB43 99 J4
St. Cross South Elmham IP20 45 G7
St. Cyrus DD10 83 J1
St. Davids Fife KY11 75 K2
St. David's P. & K. PH7 82 A5
St. David's (Tyddewi) Pembs. SA62 16 A3
St. Day TR16 2 E4
St. Decumans TA23 7 J1
St. Dennis PL26 3 G3
St. Denys SO17 11 F3
St. Dogmaels (Llandudoch) SA43 16 E1
St. Dogwells SA62 16 C3
St. Dominick PL12 4 E4
St. Donats CF61 18 C5
St. Edith's Marsh SN15 20 C5
St. Endellion PL29 3 G1
St. Enoder TR8 3 F3
St. Erme TR4 3 F4
St. Erney PL12 4 D5
St. Erth TR27 2 C5
St. Erth Praze TR27 2 C5
St. Ervan PL27 3 F1
St. Eval PL27 3 F2
St. Ewe PL26 3 G4
St. Fagans CF5 18 E4
St. Fergus AB42 99 J5
St. Fillans PH6 81 H5
St. Florence SA70 16 D5
St. Gennys EX23 4 B1
St. George Bristol BS5 19 K4
St. George Conwy LL22 47 H5
St. Georges N.Som. BS22 19 G5
St. George's Tel. & W. TF2 39 G4
St. George's V. of Glam. CF5 18 D4
St. Germans PL12 4 D5
St. Giles in the Wood EX38 6 D4
St. Giles on the Heath PL15 6 B6
St. Harmon LD6 27 J1
St. Helen Auckland DL14 62 C4
St. Helena NR10 45 F4
St. Helen's E.Suss. TN34 14 D6
St. Helens I.o.W. PO33 11 H6
St. Helens Mersey. WA10 48 E3
St. Helier Chan.I. JE2 3 J7
St. Helier Gt.Lon. SM5 23 F5
St. Hilary Cornw. TR20 2 C5
St. Hilary V. of Glam. CF71 18 D4
St. Hill RH19 13 G3
St. Ibbs SG4 32 E6
St. Illtyd NP13 19 F1
St. Ippollitts SG4 32 E6
St. Ishmael SA17 17 G5
St. Ishmael's SA62 16 B5
St. Issey PL27 3 G1
St. Ive PL14 4 D4
St. Ives Cambs. PE27 33 G1
St. Ives Cornw. TR26 2 C4
St. Ives Dorset BH24 10 C4
St. James South Elmham IP19 45 H7
St. John Chan.I. JE3 3 J6
St. John Cornw. PL11 4 E5
St. John's Gt.Lon. SE4 23 G4
St. John's I.o.M. IM4 54 B5
St. John's Surr. GU21 22 C6
St. John's Worcs. WR2 29 H3
St. John's Chapel Devon EX31 6 D3
St. John's Chapel Dur. DL13 61 K3
St. John's Fen End PE14 43 J4
St. John's Hall DL13 62 B3
St. John's Highway PE14 43 J4
St. John's Kirk ML12 75 H7
St. John's Town of Dalry DG7 68 B5
St. Judes IM7 54 C4
St. Just TR19 2 A5
St. Just in Roseland TR2 3 F5
St. Katherines AB51 91 F1
St. Keverne TR12 2 E6
St. Kew PL30 4 A3
St. Kew Highway PL30 4 A3
St. Keyne PL14 4 C4
St. Lawrence Cornw. PL30 4 A4
St. Lawrence Essex CM0 25 F1
St. Lawrence I.o.W. PO38 11 G7
St. Leonards Bucks. HP23 22 C1
St. Leonards Dorset BH24 10 C4
St. Leonards E.Suss. TN37 14 D7
St. Leonards Grange SO42 11 F5
St. Leonard's Street ME19 23 K6
St. Levan TR19 2 A6
St. Lythans CF5 18 E4
St. Mabyn PL30 4 A3
St. Madoes PH2 82 C5
St. Margaret South Elmham IP20 45 H7
St. Margarets Here. HR2 28 C5
St. Margarets Herts. SG12 33 G7
St. Margarets Wilts. SN8 21 F5
St. Margaret's at Cliffe CT15 15 J3
St. Margaret's Hope KW17 106 D8
St. Mark's IM9 54 B6
St. Martin Chan.I. GY4 3 J5
St. Martin Chan.I. JE3 3 K7
St. Martin Cornw. PL13 4 C5
St. Martin Cornw. TR12 2 E6
St. Martin's I.o.S. TR25 2 C1
St. Martins P. & K. PH2 82 C4
St. Martin's Shrop. SY11 38 C2
St. Mary JE3 3 J6
St. Mary Bourne SP11 21 H6
St. Mary Church CF71 18 D4
St. Mary Cray BR5 23 H5
St. Mary Hill CF35 18 C4
St. Mary Hoo ME3 24 D4
St. Mary in the Marsh TN29 15 F5
St. Marychurch TQ1 5 K4
St. Mary's I.o.S. TR21 2 C1
St. Mary's Ork. KW17 106 D7
St. Mary's Airport TR21 2 C1
St. Mary's Bay TN29 15 F5
St. Mary's Croft DG9 64 A4
St. Mary's Grove BS48 19 H5
St. Maughans Green NP25 28 D7
St. Mawes TR2 3 F5
St. Mawgan TR8 3 F2
St. Mellion PL12 4 D4
St. Mellons CF3 19 F3
St. Merryn PL28 3 F1
St. Mewan PL26 3 G3
St. Michael Caerhays PL26 3 G4
St. Michael Church TA7 8 C1
St. Michael Penkevil TR2 3 F4
St. Michael South Elmham NR35 45 H7
St. Michaels Fife KY16 83 F5
St. Michaels Kent TN30 14 D4
St. Michaels Worcs. WR15 28 E2
St. Michael's on Wyre PR3 55 H5
St. Minver PL27 3 G1
St. Monans KY10 83 G7
St. Neot PL14 4 B4
St. Neots PE19 32 E2
St. Newlyn East TR8 3 F3
St. Nicholas Pembs. SA64 16 C2
St. Nicholas V. of Glam. CF5 18 D4
St. Nicholas at Wade CT7 25 J5
St. Ninians FK7 75 F1
St. Osyth CO16 35 F7
St. Ouen JE3 3 J6
St. Owen's Cross HR2 28 E6
St. Paul's Cray BR5 23 H5
St. Paul's Walden SG4 32 E6
St. Peter JE3 3 J7
St. Peter Port GY1 3 J5
St. Peter's CT10 25 K5
St. Petrox SA71 16 C6
St. Pinnock PL14 4 C4
St. Quivox KA6 67 H1
St. Ruan TR12 2 E7
St. Sampson GY2 3 J5
St. Saviour Chan.I. GY7 3 H5
St. Saviour Chan.I. JE2 3 K7
St. Stephen PL26 3 G3
St. Stephens Cornw. PL12 4 E5
St. Stephens Cornw. PL15 6 B7
St. Stephens Herts. AL1 22 E1
St. Teath PL30 4 A2
St. Thomas EX2 7 H6
St. Tudy PL30 4 A3
St. Twynnells SA71 16 C6
St. Veep PL22 4 B5
St. Vigeans DD11 83 H3
St. Wenn PL30 3 G2
St. Weonards HR2 28 D6
St. Winnow PL22 4 B5
Saintbury WR12 30 C5
Salachail PA38 80 B2
Salcombe TQ8 5 H7
Salcombe Regis EX10 7 K7
Salcott CM9 34 D7
Sale M33 49 G3
Sale Green WR9 29 J3
Saleby LN13 53 H5
Salehurst TN32 14 C5
Salem Carmar. SA19 17 K3
Salem Cere. SY23 37 F7
Salem Gwyn. LL54 46 D7
Salen Arg. & B. PA72 79 G3
Salen High. PH36 79 H1
Salendine Nook HD3 50 D1
Salesbury BB1 56 B6
Saleway WR9 29 J3
Salford Cen.Beds. MK17 32 C5
Salford Gt.Man. M5 49 H3
Salford Oxon. OX7 30 D6
Salford Priors WR11 30 B3
Salfords RH1 23 F7
Salhouse NR13 45 H4
Saline KY12 75 J1
SALISBURY SP 10 C2
Salkeld Dykes CA11 61 G3
Sallachan PH33 80 A1
Sallachry PA32 80 B6
Sallachy High. IV27 96 C1
Sallachy High. IV40 87 F1
Salle NR10 45 F3
Salmonby LN9 53 G5
Salmond's Muir DD11 83 G4
Salperton GL54 30 B6
Salph End MK41 32 D3
Salsburgh ML7 75 G4
Salt ST18 40 B3
Salt Hill SL1 22 C3
Salt Holme TS2 63 F4
Saltaire BD18 57 G6
Saltash PL12 4 E5
Saltburn IV18 96 E4
Saltburn-by-the-Sea TS12 63 H4
Saltby LE14 42 B3
Saltcoats Cumb. CA19 60 B7
Saltcoats N.Ayr. KA21 74 A6
Saltcotes FY8 55 G7
Saltdean BN2 13 G6
Salterbeck CA14 60 A4

Shawhead DG2 65 J3
Shawtonhill ML10 74 E6
Sheanachie PA28 66 B2
Sheandow AB38 89 K1
Shearington DG1 69 F7
Shearsby LE17 41 J6
Shebbear EX21 6 C5
Shebdon ST20 39 G3
Shebster KW14 105 F2
Shedfield SO32 11 G3
Sheen SK17 50 D6
Sheepridge HD2 50 D1
Sheepscombe GL6 29 H7
Sheepstor PL20 5 F4
Sheepwash Devon EX21 6 C5
Sheepwash Northumb. NE62 71 H5
Sheepway BS20 19 H4
Sheepy Magna CV9 41 F5
Sheepy Parva CV9 41 F5
Sheering CM22 33 J7
Sheerness ME12 25 F4
Sheet GU32 11 J2
SHEFFIELD S 51 F4
Sheffield Bottom RG7 21 K5
Sheffield Green TN22 13 H4
Shefford SG17 32 E5
Shefford Woodlands RG17 21 G4
Sheigra IV27 102 D2
Sheinton SY5 39 F5
Shelderton SY7 28 D1
Sheldon Derbys. DE45 50 D6
Sheldon Devon EX14 7 K5
Sheldon W.Mid. B26 40 D7
Sheldwich ME13 15 F2
Sheldwich Lees ME13 15 F2
Shelf Bridgend CF35 18 C3
Shelf W.Yorks. HX3 57 G7
Shelfanger IP22 45 F7
Shelfield W.Mid. WS4 40 C5
Shelfield Warks. B49 30 C2
Shelfield Green B49 30 C2
Shelford NG12 41 J1
Shellachan Arg. & B. PA34 79 K5
Shellachan Arg. & B. PA35 80 B5
Shellbrook LE65 41 F4
Shellbrook Hill SY12 38 C1
Shelley Essex CM5 23 J1
Shelley Suff. IP7 34 E5
Shelley W.Yorks. HD8 50 E1
Shellingford SN7 21 G2
Shellow Bowells CM5 24 C1
Shelsley Beauchamp WR6 29 G2
Shelsley Walsh WR6 29 G2
Shelswell MK18 31 H5
Shelthorpe LE11 41 H4
Shelton Bed. PE28 32 D2
Shelton Norf. NR15 45 G6
Shelton Notts. NG23 42 A1
Shelton Shrop. SY3 38 D4
Shelve SY5 38 C6
Shelwick HR1 28 E4
Shelwick Green HR1 28 E4
Shenfield CM15 24 C2
Shenington OX15 30 E4
Shenley WD7 22 E1
Shenley Brook End MK5 32 B5
Shenley Church End MK5 32 B5
Shenleybury WD7 22 E1
Shenmore HR2 28 C5
Shennanton DG8 64 D4
Shenstone Staffs. WS14 40 D5
Shenstone Worcs. DY10 29 H1
Shenstone Woodend WS14 40 D5
Shenton CV13 41 F5
Shenval AB37 89 K2
Shepeau Stow PE12 43 G4
Shephall SG2 33 F6
Shepherd's Bush W12 23 F4
Shepherd's Green RG9 22 A3
Shepherd's Patch GL2 20 A1
Shepherdswell (Sibertswold) CT15 15 H3
Shepley HD8 50 D2
Sheppardstown KW3 105 H5
Shepperdine BS35 19 K2
Shepperton TW17 22 D5
Shepreth SG8 33 G4
Shepshed LE12 41 G4
Shepton Beauchamp TA19 8 D3
Shepton Mallet BA4 19 K7
Shepton Montague BA9 9 F1
Shepway ME15 14 C2
Sheraton TS27 63 F3
Sherborne Dorset DT9 9 F3
Sherborne Glos. GL54 30 C7
Sherborne St. John RG24 21 K6
Sherbourne CV35 30 D2
Sherbourne Street CO10 34 D4
Sherburn Dur. DH6 62 E2
Sherburn N.Yorks. YO17 59 F2
Sherburn Hill DH6 62 E2
Sherburn in Elmet LS25 57 K6
Shere GU5 22 D7
Shereford NR21 44 C3
Sherfield English SO51 10 D2
Sherfield on Loddon RG27 21 K6
Sherford Devon TQ7 5 H6
Sherford Som. TA1 8 B2
Sheriff Hutton YO60 58 C3
Sheriffhales TF11 39 G4
Sheringham NR26 45 F1
Sherington MK16 32 B4
Shernal Green WR9 29 J2
Shernborne PE31 44 B2
Sherramore PH20 88 C5
Sherrington BA12 9 J1
Sherston SN16 20 B3
Sherwood NG5 41 H1
Sherwood Green EX31 6 D3
SHETLAND ISLANDS ZE 107 M7
Shettleston G32 74 E4
Shevington WN6 48 E2
Shevington Moor WN6 48 E1
Sheviock PL11 4 D5
Shide PO30 11 G6
Shiel Bridge IV40 87 F3
Shieldaig High. IV54 94 E6
Shieldaig High. IV21 94 E4
Shieldhill FK1 75 G3
Shielfoot PH36 86 C7
Shielhill DD8 83 F2
Shiels AB51 90 E4
Shifford OX29 21 G1
Shifnal TF11 39 G5
Shilbottle NE66 71 G3
Shildon DL4 62 D4
Shillingford Devon EX16 7 H3
Shillingford Oxon. OX10 21 J2
Shillingford Abbot EX2 7 H7
Shillingford St. George EX2 7 H7
Shillingstone DT11 9 H3
Shillington SG5 32 E5
Shillmoor NE65 70 D3
Shilstone EX20 6 D5
Shilton Oxon. OX18 21 F1
Shilton Warks. CV7 41 G7
Shimpling Norf. IP21 45 F7
Shimpling Suff. IP29 34 C3
Shimpling Street IP29 34 C3
Shincliffe DH1 62 D2
Shiney Row DH4 62 E1
Shinfield RG2 22 A5
Shingay SG8 33 G4
Shingham PE37 44 B5
Shingle Street IP12 35 H4
Shinness Lodge IV27 103 H7
Shipbourne TN11 23 J6
Shipbrookhill CW9 49 F5
Shipdham IP25 44 D5
Shipham BS25 19 H6
Shiphay TQ2 5 J4
Shiplake RG9 22 A4
Shiplake Row RG9 22 A4
Shipley Northumb. NE66 71 G2
Shipley Shrop. WV6 40 A6
Shipley W.Suss. RH13 12 E4
Shipley W.Yorks. BD18 57 G6
Shipley Bridge Devon TQ10 5 G4
Shipley Bridge Surr. RH6 23 G7
Shipley Common DE7 41 G1
Shipmeadow NR34 45 H6
Shippea Hill CB7 44 A7
Shippon OX13 21 H2
Shipston on Stour CV36 30 D4
Shipton Glos. GL54 30 B7
Shipton N.Yorks. YO30 58 B4
Shipton Shrop. TF13 38 E6
Shipton Bellinger SP9 21 F7
Shipton Gorge DT6 8 D5
Shipton Green PO20 12 B6
Shipton Moyne GL8 20 B3
Shipton Oliffe GL54 30 B7
Shipton Solers GL54 30 B7
Shipton-on-Cherwell OX5 31 F7
Shiptonthorpe YO43 58 E5
Shipton-under-Wychwood OX7 30 D7
Shira PA32 80 C6
Shirburn OX49 21 K2
Shirdley Hill L39 48 C1
Shire Oak WS8 40 C5
Shirebrook NG20 51 H6
Shirecliffe S5 51 F3
Shiregreen S5 51 F3
Shirehampton BS11 19 J4
Shiremoor NE27 71 J6
Shirenewton NP16 19 H2
Shireoaks S81 51 H4
Shirl Heath HR6 28 D3
Shirland DE55 51 F7
Shirley Derbys. DE6 40 E1
Shirley Gt.Lon. CR0 23 G5
Shirley Hants. BH23 10 C5
Shirley S'ham. SO15 11 F3
Shirley W.Mid. B90 30 C1
Shirley Heath B90 30 C1
Shirley Warren SO16 10 E3
Shirleywich ST18 40 B3
Shirrell Heath SO32 11 G3
Shirwell EX31 6 D2
Shirwell Cross EX31 6 D2
Shiskine KA27 66 D1
Shittlehope DL13 62 B3
Shobdon HR6 28 C2
Shobley BH24 10 C4
Shobrooke EX17 7 G5
Shocklach SY14 38 D1
Shocklach Green SY14 38 D1
Shoeburyness SS3 25 F3
Sholden CT14 15 J2
Sholing SO19 11 F3
Shoot Hill SY5 38 D4
Shooter's Hill DA16 23 H4
Shop Cornw. PL28 3 F1
Shop Cornw. EX23 6 A4
Shop Corner IP9 35 G5
Shopnoller TA4 7 K2
Shore OL15 49 J1
Shoreditch N1 23 G3
Shoreham TN14 23 J5
Shoreham Airport BN15 12 E6
Shoreham-by-Sea BN43 13 F6
Shoremill IV11 96 E5
Shoresdean TD15 77 H6
Shoreswood TD15 77 H6
Shoreton IV7 96 D5
Shorley SO24 11 G2
Shorncote GL7 20 D2
Shorne DA12 24 C4
Shorne Ridgeway DA12 24 C4
Short Cross SY21 38 B5
Short Green IP22 44 E7
Short Heath Derbys. DE12 41 F4
Short Heath W.Mid. B23 40 C6
Shortacombe EX20 6 D7
Shortbridge TN22 13 H4
Shortfield Common GU10 22 B7
Shortgate BN8 13 H5
Shortgrove CB11 33 J5
Shorthampton OX7 30 E6
Shortlands BR2 23 G5
Shortlanesend TR4 3 F4
Shorton TQ3 5 J4
Shorwell PO30 11 F6
Shoscombe BA2 20 A6
Shotatton SY4 38 C3
Shotesham NR15 45 G6
Shotgate SS11 24 D2
Shotley Northants. NN17 42 C6
Shotley Suff. IP9 35 G5
Shotley Bridge DH8 62 B1
Shotley Gate IP9 35 G5
Shotleyfield DH8 62 B1
Shottenden CT4 15 F2
Shottermill GU27 12 B3
Shottery CV37 30 C3
Shotteswell OX17 31 F4
Shottisham IP12 35 H4
Shottle DE56 41 F1
Shottlegate DE56 41 F1
Shotton Dur. SR8 63 F3
Shotton Dur. TS21 62 E4
Shotton Flints. CH5 48 C6
Shotton Northumb. NE13 71 H6
Shotton Colliery DH6 62 E2
Shotts ML7 75 G4
Shotwick CH1 48 C5
Shouldham PE33 44 A5
Shouldham Thorpe PE33 44 A5
Shoulton WR2 29 H3
Shover's Green TN5 13 K3
Shrawardine SY4 38 C4
Shrawley WR6 29 H2
Shreding Green SL0 22 D3
Shrewley CV35 30 D2
SHREWSBURY SY 38 D4
Shrewton SP3 20 D7
Shripney PO22 12 C6
Shrivenham SN6 21 F3
Shropham NR17 44 D6
Shroton (Iwerne Courtney) DT11 9 H3
Shrub End CO2 34 D6
Shucknall HR1 28 E4
Shudy Camps CB21 33 K4
Shurdington GL51 29 J7
Shurlock Row RG10 22 B4
Shurnock B96 30 B2
Shurrery KW14 105 F3
Shurrery Lodge KW14 105 F3
Shurton TA5 19 F7
Shustoke B46 40 E6
Shut Heath ST18 40 A3
Shute Devon EX13 8 B5
Shute Devon EX17 7 G5
Shutford OX15 30 E4
Shuthonger GL20 29 H5
Shutlanger NN12 31 J4
Shutt Green ST19 40 A5
Shuttington B79 40 E5
Shuttlewood S44 51 G5
Shuttleworth BL0 49 G1
Siabost (Shawbost) HS2 100 E3
Siabost Bho Dheas HS2 100 E3
Siabost Bho Thuath HS2 100 E3
Siadar Iarach HS2 101 F2
Siadar Uarach HS2 101 F2
Sibbaldbie DG11 69 G5
Sibbertoft LE16 41 J7
Sibdon Carwood SY7 38 D7
Sibertswold (Shepherdswell) CT15 15 H3
Sibford Ferris OX15 30 E5
Sibford Gower OX15 30 E5
Sible Hedingham CO9 34 B5
Sibley's Green CM6 33 K6
Sibsey PE22 53 G7
Sibson Cambs. PE8 42 D6
Sibson Leics. CV13 41 F5
Sibster KW1 105 J3
Sibthorpe NG23 42 A1
Sibton IP17 35 H2
Sibton Green IP17 35 H1
Sicklesmere IP30 34 C2
Sicklinghall LS22 57 J5
Sidbury Devon EX10 7 K6
Sidbury Shrop. WV16 39 F7
Sidcot BS25 19 H6
Sidcup DA14 23 H4
Siddal HX3 57 G7
Siddington Ches.E. SK11 49 H5
Siddington Glos. GL7 20 D2
Sidemoor B61 29 J1
Sidestrand NR27 45 G2
Sidford EX10 7 K6
Sidlesham PO20 12 B7
Sidley TN39 14 C7
Sidlow RH2 23 F7
Sidmouth EX10 7 K7
Sigford TQ12 5 H3
Sigglesthorne HU11 59 H5
Sigingstone CF71 18 C4
Signet OX18 30 D7
Silchester RG7 21 K5
Sildinis HS2 100 E6
Sileby LE12 41 J4
Silecroft LA18 54 E1
Silfield NR18 45 F6
Silian SA48 26 E3
Silk Willoughby NG34 42 D1
Silkstead SO21 11 F2
Silkstone S75 50 E2
Silkstone Common S75 50 E2
Sill Field LA8 55 J1
Silloth CA7 60 C1
Sills NE19 70 D3
Sillyearn AB55 98 D5
Silpho YO13 63 J3
Silsden BD20 57 F5
Silsoe MK45 32 D5
Silver End Cen.Beds. MK45 32 E4
Silver End Essex CM8 34 C6
Silver Green NR15 45 G6
Silver Street Kent ME9 24 E5
Silver Street Som. TA11 8 E1
Silverburn EH26 76 A4
Silvercraigs PA31 73 G2
Silverdale Lancs. LA5 55 H2
Silverdale Staffs. ST5 40 A1
Silvergate NR11 45 F3
Silverhill TN37 14 C6
Silverlace Green IP13 35 H3
Silverley's Green IP19 35 G1
Silvermoss AB51 91 G1
Silverstone NN12 31 H4
Silverton EX5 7 H5
Silvington DY14 29 F1
Silwick ZE2 107 L8
Simister M25 49 H2
Simmondley SK13 50 C3
Simonburn NE48 70 D6
Simonsbath TA24 7 F2
Simonside NE34 71 J7
Simonstone Bridgend CF35 18 C3
Simonstone Lancs. BB12 56 C6
Simprim TD12 77 G6
Simpson MK6 32 B5
Sinclair's Hill TD11 77 G5
Sinclairston KA18 67 J2
Sinderby YO7 57 J1
Sinderhope NE47 61 K1
Sindlesham RG41 22 A5
Sinfin DE24 41 F2
Singdean TD9 70 A3
Singleton Lancs. FY6 55 G6
Singleton W.Suss. PO18 12 B5
Singlewell DA12 24 C4
Singret LL12 48 C7
Sinkhurst Green TN12 14 D3
Sinnahard AB33 90 C3
Sinnington YO62 58 D1
Sinton Green WR2 29 H2
Sipson UB7 22 D4
Sirhowy NP22 28 A7
Sisland NR14 45 H6
Sissinghurst TN17 14 C4
Siston BS16 19 K4
Sithney TR13 2 D6
Sittingbourne ME10 25 F5
Siulaisiadar HS2 101 H4
Six Ashes WV15 39 G7
Six Hills LE14 41 J3
Six Mile Bottom CB8 33 J3
Six Roads End DE6 40 D3
Sixhills LN8 52 E4
Sixmile CT4 15 G3
Sixpenny Handley SP5 10 B3
Sizewell IP16 35 J2
Skail KW11 104 C4
Skaill Ork. KW16 106 B6
Skaill Ork. KW17 106 E7
Skaill Ork. KW17 106 D4
Skares Aber. AB54 90 E1
Skares E.Ayr. KA18 67 K2
Skarpigarth ZE2 107 K7
Skateraw EH42 77 F3
Skaw ZE2 107 P6
Skeabost IV51 93 K7
Skeabrae KW17 106 B5
Skeeby DL10 62 D6
Skeffington LE7 42 A5
Skeffling HU12 53 G1
Skegby NG17 51 H6
Skegness PE25 53 J6
Skelberry Shet. ZE2 107 M11
Skelberry Shet. ZE2 107 N6
Skelbo IV25 96 E2
Skelbo Street IV25 96 E2
Skelbrooke DN6 51 H1
Skeld (Easter Skeld) ZE2 107 M8
Skeldon KA6 67 H2
Skeldyke PE20 43 G2
Skellingthorpe LN6 52 C5
Skellister ZE2 107 N7
Skellow DN6 51 H1
Skelmanthorpe HD8 50 E1
Skelmersdale WN8 48 D2
Skelmonae AB41 91 G1
Skelmorlie PA17 73 K4
Skelmuir AB42 99 H6
Skelpick KW14 104 C3
Skelton Cumb. CA11 60 F3
Skelton E.Riding DN14 58 D7
Skelton N.Yorks. DL11 62 B6
Skelton (Skelton-in-Cleveland) R. & C. TS12 63 H5
Skelton York YO30 58 B4
Skelton-in-Cleveland (Skelton) TS12 63 H5
Skelton-on-Ure HG4 57 J3
Skelwick KW17 106 D3
Skelwith Bridge LA22 60 E6
Skendleby PE23 53 H6
Skendleby Psalter LN13 53 H5
Skenfrith NP7 28 D6
Skerne YO25 59 G4
Skeroblingarry PA28 66 B1
Skerray KW14 103 J2
Skerton LA1 55 H3
Sketchley LE10 41 G6
Sketty SA2 17 K6
Skewen SA10 18 A2
Skewsby YO61 58 C2
Skeyton NR10 45 G3
Skeyton Corner NR10 45 G3
Skidbrooke LN11 53 H3
Skidbrooke North End LN11 53 H3
Skidby HU16 59 G6
Skilgate TA4 7 H3
Skillington NG33 42 B3
Skinburness CA7 60 C1
Skinflats FK2 75 H2
Skinidin IV55 93 H7
Skinnet KW12 105 G2
Skinningrove TS13 63 J5
Skipness PA29 73 G5
Skippool FY5 55 G5
Skipsea YO25 59 H4
Skipsea Brough YO25 59 H4
Skipton BD23 56 E4
Skipton-on-Swale YO7 57 J2
Skipwith YO8 58 C6
Skirbeck PE21 43 G1
Skirbeck Quarter PE21 43 G1
Skirethorns BD23 56 E3
Skirlaugh HU11 59 H6
Skirling ML12 75 J7
Skirmett RG9 22 A3
Skirpenbeck YO41 58 D4
Skirwith Cumb. CA10 61 H3
Skirwith N.Yorks. LA6 56 C2
Skirza KW1 105 J2
Skittle Green HP27 22 A1
Skomer Island SA62 16 A5
Skulamus IV42 86 C2
Skullomie IV27 103 J2
Skyborry Green LD7 28 B1
Skye IV 85 K1
Skye Green CO5 34 C6
Skye of Curr PH26 89 G2
Skyreholme BD23 57 F3
Slack Aber. AB52 90 D1
Slack Derbys. S45 51 F6
Slack W.Yorks. HX7 56 E7
Slackhall SK23 50 C4
Slackhead AB56 98 C4
Slad GL6 20 B1
Slade Devon EX34 6 D1
Slade Devon EX14 7 K5
Slade Pembs. SA61 16 C4
Slade Swan. SA3 17 H7
Slade Green DA8 23 J4
Slade Hooton S25 51 H4
Sladesbridge PL27 4 A3
Slaggyford CA8 61 H1
Slaidburn BB7 56 C4
Slains Park DD10 91 G7
Slaithwaite HD7 50 C1
Slaley NE47 62 A1
Slamannan FK1 75 G3
Slapton Bucks. LU7 32 C6
Slapton Devon TQ7 5 J6
Slapton Northants. NN12 31 H4
Slate Haugh AB56 98 C4
Slatepit Dale S42 51 F6
Slattadale IV22 94 E4
Slaugham RH17 13 F4
Slaughden IP15 35 J3
Slaughterford SN14 20 B4
Slawston LE16 42 A6
Sleaford Hants. GU35 12 B3
Sleaford Lincs. NG34 42 D1
Sleagill CA10 61 G5
Sleap SY4 38 D3
Sledge Green WR13 29 H5
Sledmere YO25 59 F3
Sleights YO22 63 K6
Slepe BH16 9 J5
Slerra EX39 6 B3
Slickly KW1 105 H2
Sliddery KA27 66 D1
Sliemore PH25 89 H2
Sligachan IV47 85 K2
Slimbridge GL2 20 A1
Slindon Staffs. ST21 40 A2
Slindon W.Suss. BN18 12 C6
Slinfold RH13 12 E3
Sling GL16 19 J1
Slingsby YO62 58 C2
Slioch AB54 90 D1
Slip End Cen.Beds. LU1 32 D7
Slip End Herts. SG7 33 F5
Slipton NN14 32 C1
Slitting Mill WS15 40 C4
Slochd PH23 89 F2
Slockavullin PA31 73 G1
Slogarie DG7 65 G4
Sloley NR12 45 G3
Slongaber DG2 65 J3
Sloothby LN13 53 H5
SLOUGH SL 22 C3
Slough Green Som. TA3 8 B2
Slough Green W.Suss. RH17 13 F4
Sluggan PH23 89 F2
Slyne LA2 55 H3
Smailholm TD5 76 E7
Small Dole BN5 13 F5
Small Hythe TN30 14 D4
Smallbridge OL16 49 J1
Smallbrook EX5 7 G6
Smallburgh NR12 45 H3
Smallburn Aber. AB42 99 J6
Smallburn E.Ayr. KA18 68 B1
Smalldale SK17 50 C5

Smalley DE7 41 G1
Smallfield RH6 23 G7
Smallford AL4 22 E1
Smallridge EX13 8 B4
Smallthorne ST6 49 H7
Smallworth IP22 44 E7
Smannell SP11 21 G7
Smardale CA17 61 J6
Smarden TN27 14 D3
Smaull PA44 72 A4
Smeatharpe EX14 7 K4
Smeeth TN25 15 F4
Smeeton Westerby LE8 41 J6
Smerclet HS8 84 C3
Smerral KW5 105 G5
Smestow DY3 40 A6
Smethwick B66 40 C7
Smethwick Green CW11 49 H6
Smirisary PH38 86 C7
Smisby LE65 41 F4
Smith End Green WR13 29 G3
Smithfield CA6 69 K7
Smithies S71 51 F2
Smithincott EX15 7 J4
Smith's End SG8 33 G5
Smith's Green *Essex* CM22 33 J6
Smith's Green *Essex* CB9 33 K4
Smithstown IV21 94 D4
Smithton IV2 96 E7
Smithy Green WA16 49 G5
Smockington LE10 41 G7
Smyrton KA26 67 F5
Smythe's Green CO5 34 D7
Snailbeach SY5 38 C5
Snailwell CB8 33 K2
Snainton YO13 59 F1
Snaith DN14 58 C7
Snape *N.Yorks.* DL8 57 H1
Snape *Suff.* IP17 35 H3
Snape Green PR8 48 C1
Snape Watering IP17 35 H3
Snarestone DE12 41 F5
Snarford LN8 52 D4
Snargate TN29 14 E5
Snave TN29 15 F5
Sneachill WR7 29 J3
Snead SY15 38 C6
Snead's Green DY13 29 H2
Sneath Common NR15 45 F7
Sneaton YO22 63 K6
Sneatonthorpe YO22 63 J2
Snelland LN3 52 D4
Snellings CA22 60 A6
Snelston DE6 40 D1
Snetterton NR16 44 D6
Snettisham PE31 44 A2
Snipeshill ME10 25 F5
Sniseabhal (Snishival) HS8 84 C1
Snishival (Sniseabhal) HS8 84 C1
Snitter NE65 71 F3
Snitterby DN21 52 C3
Snitterfield CV37 30 D3
Snitterton DE4 50 E6
Snittlegarth CA7 60 D3
Snitton SY8 28 E1
Snodhill HR3 28 C4
Snodland ME6 24 D5
Snow End SG9 33 H5
Snow Street IP22 44 E7
Snowden Hill S35 50 E2
Snowshill WR12 30 B5
Soar *Cardiff* CF15 18 D3
Soar *Carmar.* SA19 17 K3
Soar *Devon* TQ7 5 H7
Soay PH41 85 K3
Soberton SO32 11 H3
Soberton Heath SO32 11 H3
Sockbridge CA10 61 G4
Sockburn DL2 62 E6
Sodom LL16 47 J5
Sodylt Bank SY12 38 C2
Softley DL13 62 B4
Soham CB7 33 J1
Soham Cotes CB7 33 J1
Solas (Sollas) HS6 92 D4
Soldon EX22 6 B4
Soldon Cross EX22 6 B4
Soldridge GU34 11 H1
Sole Street *Kent* CT4 15 F3
Sole Street *Kent* DA12 24 C5
Soleburn DG9 64 A4
Solihull B91 30 C1
Solihull Lodge B90 30 B1
Sollas (Solas) HS6 92 D4
Sollers Dilwyn HR4 28 D3
Sollers Hope HR1 29 F5
Sollom PR4 48 D1
Solomon's Tump GL19 29 G7
Solsgirth FK14 75 H1
Solva SA62 16 A3
Solwaybank DG14 69 J6
Somerby *Leics.* LE14 42 A4
Somerby *Lincs.* DN38 52 D2
Somercotes DE55 51 G7
Somerford ST19 40 B5
Somerford Keynes GL7 20 D2
Somerley PO20 12 B7
Somerleyton NR32 45 J6
Somersal Herbert DE6 40 D2
Somersby PE23 53 G5
Somersham *Cambs.* PE28 33 G1
Somersham *Suff.* IP8 34 E4
Somerton *Newport* NP19 19 G3
Somerton *Oxon.* OX25 31 F6
Somerton *Som.* TA11 8 D2
Somerton *Suff.* IP29 34 C3
Sompting BN15 12 E6
Sompting Abbotts BN15 12 E6
Sonning RG4 22 A4
Sonning Common RG4 22 A3
Sonning Eye RG4 22 A4
Sontley LL13 38 C1
Sookholme NG19 51 H6
Sopley BH23 10 C5
Sopworth SN14 20 B3
Sorbie DG8 64 E6
Sordale KW12 105 G2
Sorisdale PA78 78 D1
Sorn KA5 67 K1
Sornhill KA4 74 D7
Soroba PA34 79 K5
Sortat KW1 105 H2
Sotby LN8 53 F5
Sots Hole LN4 52 E6
Sotterley NR34 45 J7
Soudley TF9 39 G3
Soughton CH7 48 B6
Soulbury LU7 32 B6
Soulby CA17 61 J5
Souldern OX27 31 G5
Souldrop MK44 32 C2
Sound *Ches.E.* CW5 39 F1
Sound *Shet.* ZE1 107 N8
Sound *Shet.* ZE2 107 M7
Sourhope TD5 70 D1
Sourin KW17 106 D4
Sourton EX20 6 D6
Soutergate LA17 55 F1
South Acre PE32 44 C4
South Acton W5 22 E4
South Alkham CT15 15 H3
South Allington TQ7 5 H7
South Alloa FK7 75 G1
South Ambersham GU29 12 C4
South Anston S25 51 H4
South Ascot SL5 22 C5
South Baddesley SO41 10 E5
South Ballachulish PH49 80 B2
South Balloch KA26 67 H4
South Bank TS6 63 G4
South Barrow BA22 9 F2
South Bellsdyke FK2 75 H2
South Benfleet SS7 24 D3
South Bersted PO22 12 C6
South Blackbog AB51 91 F1
South Bockhampton BH23 10 C5
South Bowood DT6 8 D5
South Brent TQ10 5 G4
South Brentor PL19 6 C7
South Brewham BA10 9 G1
South Broomhill NE61 71 H4
South Burlingham NR13 45 H5
South Cadbury BA22 9 F2
South Cairn DG9 66 D7
South Carlton LN1 52 C5
South Cave HU15 59 F6
South Cerney GL7 20 D2
South Chard TA20 8 C4
South Charlton NE66 71 G1
South Cheriton BA8 9 F2
South Church DL14 62 D4
South Cliffe YO43 58 E6
South Clifton NG23 52 B5
South Cockerington LN11 53 G4
South Collafirth ZE2 107 M4
South Common BN8 13 G5
South Cornelly CF33 18 B3
South Corriegills KA27 73 J7
South Cove NR34 45 J7
South Creagan PA37 80 A3
South Creake NR21 44 C2
South Crosland HD4 50 D1
South Croxton LE7 41 J4
South Dalton HU17 59 F5
South Darenth DA4 23 J4
South Dell (Dail Bho Dheas) HS2 101 G1
South Duffield YO8 58 C6
South Elkington LN11 53 F4
South Elmsall WF9 51 G1
South End *Bucks.* LU7 32 B6
South End *Cumb.* LA14 55 F3
South End *Hants.* SP6 10 C3
South End *N.Lincs.* DN19 59 H7
South Erradale IV21 94 D4
South Fambridge SS4 24 E2
South Fawley OX12 21 G3
South Ferriby DN18 59 F7
South Field HU13 59 G7
South Flobbets AB51 91 F1
South Garth ZE2 107 P3
South Godstone RH9 23 G7
South Gorley SP6 10 C3
South Green *Essex* CM11 24 C2
South Green *Essex* CO5 34 E7
South Green *Norf.* NR20 44 E4
South Green *Suff.* IP23 35 F1
South Gyle EH12 75 K3
South Hall PA22 73 J3
South Hanningfield CM3 24 D2
South Harefield UB9 22 D3
South Harting GU31 11 J3
South Hayling PO11 11 J5
South Hazelrigg NE66 77 J7
South Heath HP16 22 C1
South Heighton BN9 13 H6
South Hetton DH6 62 E2
South Hiendley S72 51 F1
South Hill PL17 4 D3
South Hinksey OX1 21 J1
South Hole EX39 6 A4
South Holme YO62 58 C2
South Holmwood RH5 22 E7
South Hornchurch RM13 23 J3
South Hourat KA24 74 A5
South Huish TQ7 5 G6
South Hykeham LN6 52 C6
South Hylton SR4 62 E1
South Kelsey LN7 52 D3
South Kessock IV3 96 D7
South Killingholme DN40 52 E1
South Kilvington YO7 57 K1
South Kilworth LE17 41 J7
South Kirkby WF9 51 G1
South Kirkton AB32 91 F4
South Knighton TQ12 5 J3
South Kyme LN4 42 E1
South Lancing BN15 12 E6
South Ledaig PA37 80 A4
South Leigh OX29 21 G1
South Leverton DN22 51 K4
South Littleton WR11 30 B4
South Lopham IP22 44 E7
South Luffenham LE15 42 C5
South Malling BN7 13 H5
South Marston SN3 20 E3
South Middleton NE71 70 E1
South Milford LS25 57 K6
South Milton TQ7 5 G6
South Mimms EN6 23 F1
South Molton EX36 7 F3
South Moor DH9 62 C1
South Moreton OX11 21 J3
South Mundham PO20 12 B6
South Muskham NG23 51 K7
South Newbald YO43 59 F6
South Newington OX15 31 F5
South Newton SP2 10 B1
South Normanton DE55 51 G7
South Norwood SE25 23 G5
South Nutfield RH1 23 G7
South Ockendon RM15 23 J3
South Ormsby LN11 53 G5
South Ossett WF5 50 E1
South Otterington DL7 57 J1
South Owersby LN8 52 D3
South Oxhey WD19 22 E2
South Park RH2 23 F7
South Parks KY6 82 D7
South Perrott DT8 8 D4
South Petherton TA13 8 D3
South Petherwin PL15 6 B7
South Pickenham PE37 44 C5
South Pool TQ7 5 H6
South Queensferry (Queensferry) EH30 75 K3
South Radworthy EX36 7 F2
South Rauceby NG34 42 D1
South Raynham NR21 44 C3
South Redbriggs AB53 99 F6
South Reston LN11 53 H4
South Ronaldsay KW17 106 D9
South Ruislip HA4 22 E3
South Runcton PE33 44 A5
South Scarle NG23 52 B6
South Shian PA37 80 A3
South Shields NE33 71 J7
South Somercotes LN11 53 H3
South Somercotes Fen Houses LN11 53 H3
South Stainley HG3 57 J3
South Stoke *Oxon.* RG8 21 K3
South Stoke *W.Suss.* BN18 12 D6
South Street *E.Suss.* BN8 13 G5
South Street *Gt.Lon.* TN16 23 H6
South Street *Kent* DA13 24 C5
South Street *Kent* CT5 25 H5
South Street *Kent* ME9 24 E5
South Tawton EX20 6 E6
South Thoresby LN13 53 H5
South Tidworth SP9 21 F7
South Tottenham N15 23 G3
South Town *Devon* EX6 7 H7
South Town *Hants.* GU34 11 H1
South Uist (Uibhist a Deas) HS8 84 C1
South Upper Barrack AB41 99 H6
South View RG21 21 K6
South Walsham NR13 45 H4
South Warnborough RG29 22 A7
South Weald CM14 23 J2
South Weston OX9 22 A2
South Wheatley *Cornw.* PL15 4 C1
South Wheatley *Notts.* DN22 51 K4
South Whiteness ZE2 107 M8
South Wigston LE18 41 H6
South Willingham LN8 52 E4
South Wingfield DE55 51 F7
South Witham NG33 42 C4
South Wonston SO21 11 F1
South Woodham Ferrers CM3 24 E2
South Wootton PE30 44 A3
South Wraxall BA15 20 B5
South Yardley B26 40 D7
South Zeal EX20 6 E6
SOUTHALL UB 22 E3
Southam *Glos.* GL52 29 J6
Southam *Warks.* CV47 31 F2
SOUTHAMPTON SO 11 F3
Southampton Airport SO18 11 F3
Southbar PA4 74 C4
Southborough *Gt.Lon.* BR2 23 H5
Southborough *Kent* TN4 23 J7
Southbourne *Bourne.* BH6 10 C5
Southbourne *W.Suss.* PO10 11 J4
Southbrook EX5 7 J6
Southburgh IP25 44 E5
Southburn YO25 59 F4
Southchurch SS1 25 F3
Southcott *Devon* EX20 6 D6
Southcott *Wilts.* SN9 20 E6
Southcourt HP21 32 B7
Southdean TD9 70 B3
Southdene L32 48 D3
Southease BN7 13 H6
Southend *Aber.* AB53 99 F6
Southend *Arg. & B.* PA28 66 A3
Southend *Bucks.* RG9 22 A3
Southend *W.Berks.* RG7 21 J4
Southend *Wilts.* SN8 20 E4
Southend Airport SS2 24 E3
SOUTHEND-ON-SEA SS 24 E3
Southerfield CA7 60 C2
Southerly EX20 6 D7
Southern Green SG9 33 G5
Southerndown CF32 18 B4
Southerness DG2 65 K5
Southery PE38 44 A6
Southfield KY6 76 A1
Southfields SW18 23 F4
Southfleet DA13 24 C4
Southgate *Cere.* SY23 36 E7
Southgate *Gt.Lon.* N14 23 G2
Southgate *Norf.* NR10 45 F3
Southgate *Norf.* PE31 44 A2
Southgate *Swan.* SA3 17 J7
Southill SG18 32 E4
Southington RG25 21 J7
Southleigh EX24 8 B5
Southmarsh BA9 9 G1
Southminster CM0 25 F2
Southmuir DD8 82 E2
Southoe PE19 32 E2
Southolt IP23 35 F2
Southorpe PE9 42 D5
Southowram HX3 57 G7
Southport PR8 48 C1
Southrepps NR11 45 G2
Southrey LN3 52 E6
Southrop GL7 20 E1
Southrope RG25 21 K7
Southsea *Ports.* PO4 11 H5
Southsea *Wrex.* LL11 48 B7
Southstoke BA2 20 A5
Southtown *Norf.* NR31 45 K5
Southtown *Ork.* KW17 106 D8
Southwaite *Cumb.* CA17 61 J6
Southwaite *Cumb.* CA4 61 F2
Southwater RH13 12 E4
Southwater Street RH13 12 E4
Southway BA5 19 J7
Southwell *Dorset* DT5 9 F7
Southwell *Notts.* NG25 51 J7
Southwick *D. & G.* DG2 65 K5
Southwick *Hants.* PO17 11 H4
Southwick *Northants.* PE8 42 D6
Southwick *Som.* TA9 19 G7
Southwick *T. & W.* SR5 62 E1
Southwick *W.Suss.* BN42 13 F6
Southwick *Wilts.* BA14 20 B6
Southwold IP18 35 K1
Southwood BA6 8 E1
Sowden EX8 7 H7
Sower Carr FY6 55 G5
Sowerby *N.Yorks.* YO7 57 K1
Sowerby *W.Yorks.* HX6 57 F7
Sowerby Bridge HX6 57 F7
Sowerby Row CA4 60 E2
Sowerhill TA22 7 G3
Sowley Green CB9 34 B3
Sowood HX4 50 C1
Sowton EX5 7 H6
Soyal IV24 96 C2
Spa Common NR28 45 G2
Spadeadam CA8 70 A6
Spalding PE11 43 F3
Spaldington DN14 58 D6
Spaldwick PE28 32 E1
Spalefield KY10 83 G7
Spalford NG23 52 B6
Spanby NG34 42 D2
Sparham NR9 44 E4
Spark Bridge LA12 55 G1
Sparkford BA22 9 F2
Sparkhill B11 40 C7
Sparkwell PL7 5 F5
Sparrow Green NR19 44 D4
Sparrowpit SK17 50 C4
Sparrow's Green TN5 13 K3
Sparsholt *Hants.* SO21 11 F1
Sparsholt *Oxon.* OX12 21 G3
Spartylea NE47 61 K2
Spath ST14 40 C2
Spaunton YO62 58 D1
Spaxton TA5 8 B1
Spean Bridge PH34 87 J6
Spear Hill RH20 12 E5
Speddoch DG2 68 D5
Speedwell BS16 19 K4
Speen *Bucks.* HP27 22 B1
Speen *W.Berks.* RG14 21 H5
Speeton YO14 59 H2
Speke L24 48 D4
Speldhurst TN3 23 J7
Spellbrook CM23 33 H7
Spelsbury OX7 30 E6
Spen Green CW11 49 H6
Spencers Wood RG7 22 A5
Spennithorne DL8 57 G1
Spennymoor DL16 62 D3
Spernall B80 30 B2
Spetchley WR5 29 H3
Spetisbury DT11 9 J4
Spexhall IP19 45 H7
Spey Bay IV32 98 B4
Speybridge PH26 89 H2
Speyview AB38 97 K7
Spilsby PE23 53 G6
Spindlestone NE70 77 K7
Spinkhill S21 51 G5
Spinningdale IV24 96 D3
Spirthill SN11 20 C4
Spital *High.* KW1 105 G3
Spital *W. & M.* SL4 22 C4
Spital in the Street LN8 52 C3
Spitalbrook EN11 23 G1
Spithurst BN8 13 H5
Spittal *D. & G.* DG8 64 E4
Spittal *D. & G.* DG8 64 D5
Spittal *E.Loth.* EH32 76 C3
Spittal *Northumb.* TD15 77 J5
Spittal *Pembs.* SA62 16 C3
Spittal of Glenmuick AB35 90 B6
Spittal of Glenshee PH10 82 C1
Spittalfield PH1 82 C3
Spixworth NR10 45 G4
Splayne's Green TN22 13 H4
Splott CF24 19 F4
Spofforth HG3 57 J4
Spondon DE21 41 G2
Spooner Row NR18 44 E6
Spoonley TF9 39 F2
Sporle PE32 44 C4
Sportsman's Arms LL16 47 H7
Spott EH42 76 E3
Spratton NN6 31 J1
Spreakley GU10 22 B7
Spreyton EX17 6 E6
Spriddlestone PL9 5 F5
Spridlington LN8 52 D4
Spring Grove TW7 22 E4
Spring Vale PO34 11 H5
Springburn G21 74 E4
Springfield *Arg. & B.* PA22 73 J3
Springfield *D. & G.* DG16 69 J7
Springfield *Fife* KY15 82 E6
Springfield *Moray* IV36 97 H6
Springfield *P. & K.* PH13 82 C4
Springfield *W.Mid.* B13 40 C7
Springfields Outlet Village PE12 43 F3
Springhill *Staffs.* WS14 40 C5
Springhill *Staffs.* WV11 40 B5
Springholm DG7 65 J4
Springkell DG11 69 H6
Springleys AB51 91 F1
Springside KA11 74 B7
Springthorpe DN21 52 B4
Springwell NE9 62 D1
Sproatley HU11 59 H6
Sproston Green CW4 49 G6
Sprotbrough DN5 51 H2
Sproughton IP8 35 F4
Sprouston TD5 77 F7
Sprowston NR7 45 G4
Sproxton *Leics.* LE14 42 B3
Sproxton *N.Yorks.* YO62 58 C1
Sprytown PL16 6 C7
Spurlands End HP15 22 B2
Spurstow CW6 48 E7
Spyway DT2 8 E5
Square Point DG7 65 H3
Squires Gate FY4 55 G6
Sròndoire PA30 73 G3
Sronphadruig Lodge PH18 88 E7
Stableford *Shrop.* WV15 39 G6
Stableford *Staffs.* ST5 40 A2
Stacey Bank S6 50 E3
Stackhouse BD24 56 D3
Stackpole SA71 16 C6
Stacksteads OL13 56 D7
Staddiscombe PL9 5 F5
Staddlethorpe HU15 58 E7
Staden SK17 50 C5
Stadhampton OX44 21 K2
Stadhlaigearraidh (Stilligarry) HS8 84 C1
Staffield CA10 61 G2
Staffin IV51 93 K5
Stafford ST16 40 B3
Stagden Cross CM1 33 K7
Stagsden MK43 32 C4
Stagshaw Bank NE46 70 E7
Stain KW1 105 J2
Stainburn *Cumb.* CA14 60 B4
Stainburn *N.Yorks.* LS21 57 H5
Stainby NG33 42 C3
Staincross S75 51 F1
Staindrop DL2 62 C4
Staines-upon-Thames TW18 22 D4
Stainfield *Lincs.* PE10 42 D3
Stainfield *Lincs.* LN3 52 E5
Stainforth *N.Yorks.* BD24 56 D3
Stainforth *S.Yorks.* DN7 51 J1
Staining FY3 55 G6
Stainland HX4 50 C1
Stainsacre YO22 63 J2
Stainsby *Derbys.* S44 51 G6
Stainsby *Lincs.* LN9 53 G5
Stainton *Cumb.* LA8 55 J1
Stainton *Cumb.* CA11 61 F4
Stainton *Dur.* DL12 62 B5
Stainton *Middbro.* TS8 63 F5
Stainton *N.Yorks.* DL11 62 C7
Stainton *S.Yorks.* S66 51 H3
Stainton by Langworth LN3 52 D5
Stainton le Vale LN8 52 E3
Stainton with Adgarley LA13 55 F2
Staintondale YO13 63 J3
Stair *Cumb.* CA12 60 D4
Stair *E.Ayr.* KA5 67 J1
Stairfoot S70 51 F2
Staithes TS13 63 J5
Stake Pool PR3 55 H5
Stakeford NE62 71 H5
Stakes PO7 11 H4
Stalbridge DT10 9 G3
Stalbridge Weston DT10 9 G3
Stalham NR12 45 H3
Stalham Green NR12 45 H3
Stalisfield Green ME13 14 E2
Stalling Busk DL8 56 E1

Stratford *Cen.Beds.* **SG19** 32 E4
Stratford *Glos.* **GL20** 29 H5
Stratford *Gt.Lon.* **E15** 23 G3
Stratford St. Andrew **IP17** 35 H3
Stratford St. Mary **CO7** 34 E5
Stratford sub Castle **SP1** 10 C1
Stratford Tony **SP5** 10 B2
Stratford-upon-Avon CV37 30 D3
Strath **KW1** 105 H3
Strathan *High.* **IV27** 102 C6
Strathan *High.* **PH34** 87 F5
Strathaven ML10 75 F6
Strathblane **G63** 74 D3
Strathcanaird **IV26** 95 H1
Strathcarron IV54 95 F7
Strathdon AB36 90 B3
Strathgirnock **AB35** 90 B5
Strathkinness **KY16** 83 F6
Strathmiglo **KY14** 82 D6
Strathpeffer IV14 96 B6
Strathrannoch **IV23** 95 K4
Strathtay **PH9** 82 A2
Strathwhillan **KA27** 73 J7
Strathy **KW14** 104 D2
Strathyre **FK18** 81 G6
Stratton *Cornw.* **EX23** 6 A5
Stratton *Dorset* **DT2** 9 F5
Stratton *Glos.* **GL7** 20 D1
Stratton Audley **OX27** 31 H6
Stratton Hall **IP10** 35 G5
Stratton St. Margaret **SN3** 20 E3
Stratton St. Michael **NR15** 45 G6
Stratton Strawless **NR10** 45 G3
Stratton-on-the-Fosse **BA3** 19 K6
Stravanan **PA20** 73 J5
Stravithie **KY16** 83 G6
Strawberry Hill **TW2** 22 E4
Stream **TA4** 7 J2
Streat **BN6** 13 G5
Streatham **SW16** 23 F4
Streatham Vale **SW16** 23 F4
Streatley *Cen.Beds.* **LU3** 32 D6
Streatley *W.Berks.* **RG8** 21 J3
Street *Devon* **EX12** 7 K7
Street *Lancs.* **PR3** 55 J4
Street *N.Yorks.* **YO21** 63 J6
Street *Som.* BA16 8 D1
Street *Som.* **TA20** 8 C4
Street Ashton **CV23** 41 G7
Street Dinas **SY11** 38 C2
Street End **PO20** 12 B7
Street Gate **NE16** 62 D1
Street Houses **LS24** 58 B5
Street Lane **DE5** 41 F1
Street on the Fosse **BA4** 9 F1
Streethay **WS13** 40 D4
Streethouse **WF7** 57 J7
Streetlam **DL7** 62 E7
Streetly **B74** 40 C6
Streetly End **CB21** 33 K4
Strefford **SY7** 38 D7
Strelley **NG8** 41 H1
Strensall **YO32** 58 C3
Strensham **WR8** 29 J4
Stretcholt **TA6** 19 F7
Strete **TQ6** 5 J6
Stretford *Gt.Man.* **M32** 49 G3
Stretford *Here.* **HR6** 28 D3
Stretford *Here.* **HR6** 28 E3
Strethall **CB11** 33 H5
Stretham **CB6** 33 J1
Strettington **PO18** 12 B6
Stretton *Ches.W. & C.* **SY14** 48 D7
Stretton *Derbys.* **DE55** 51 F6
Stretton *Rut.* **LE15** 42 C4
Stretton *Staffs.* **ST19** 40 A4
Stretton *Staffs.* **DE13** 40 E3
Stretton *Warr.* **WA4** 49 F4
Stretton en le Field **DE12** 41 F4
Stretton Grandison **HR8** 29 F4
Stretton Heath **SY5** 38 C4
Stretton Sugwas **HR4** 28 D4
Stretton under Fosse **CV23** 41 G7
Stretton Westwood **TF13** 38 E6
Stretton-on-Dunsmore **CV23** 31 F1
Stretton-on-Fosse **GL56** 30 D5
Stribers **LA12** 55 G1
Strichen **AB43** 99 H5
Strines **SK6** 49 J4
Stringston **TA5** 7 K1
Strixton **NN29** 32 C2
Stroat **NP16** 19 J2
Stromeferry IV53 86 E1
Stromemore **IV54** 86 E1
Stromness KW16 106 B7
Stronaba **PH34** 87 J6
Stronachlachar **FK8** 81 F6
Strone *Arg. & B.* **PA23** 73 K2
Strone *High.* **IV63** 88 C2
Strone *High.* **PH33** 87 H6
Strone *Stir.* **FK17** 81 F6
Stronechrubie **IV27** 102 E7
Stronlonag **PA23** 73 K2
Stronmilchan **PA33** 80 C5
Stronsay **KW17** 106 F5
Stronsay Airfield **KW17** 106 F5
Strontian **PH36** 79 K1
Strontoiller **PA34** 80 A5
Stronvar **FK19** 81 G5
Strood **ME2** 24 D5
Strood Green *Surr.* **RH3** 23 F7
Strood Green *W.Suss.* **RH14** 12 D4
Strood Green *W.Suss.* **RH12** 12 E3
Stroquhan **DG2** 68 D5
Stroud *Glos.* GL5 20 B1
Stroud *Hants.* **GU32** 11 J2
Stroud Common **GU5** 22 D7
Stroud Green *Essex* **SS4** 24 E2
Stroud Green *Glos.* **GL10** 20 B1
Stroude **GU25** 22 D5
Stroul **G84** 74 A2
Stroxton **NG33** 42 C2
Struan *High.* **IV56** 85 J1
Struan *P. & K.* **PH18** 81 J1
Strubby *Lincs.* **LN13** 53 H4
Strubby *Lincs.* **LN8** 52 E5
Strumpshaw **NR13** 45 H5
Struthers **KY15** 82 E7
Struy **IV4** 88 B1
Stryd y Facsen **LL65** 46 B4
Stryt-cae-rhedyn **CH7** 48 B6
Stryt-issa **LL14** 38 B1
Stuartfield **AB42** 99 H6
Stub Place **LA19** 60 B7
Stubber's Green **WS9** 40 C5
Stubbington **PO14** 11 G4
Stubbins **BL0** 49 G1
Stubbs Green **NR14** 45 H6
Stubhampton **DT11** 9 J3
Stubley **S18** 51 F5
Stubshaw Cross **WN4** 48 E2
Stubton **NG23** 42 B1
Stuck *Arg. & B.* **PA20** 73 J4
Stuck *Arg. & B.* **PA23** 73 K1
Stuckbeg **PA24** 74 A1
Stuckgowan **G83** 80 E7
Stuckindroin **G83** 80 E6
Stuckreoch **PA27** 73 J1
Stuckton **SP6** 10 C3
Stud Green **SL6** 22 B4
Studdon **NE47** 61 K1
Studfold **BD24** 56 D2
Studham **LU6** 32 D7
Studholme **CA7** 60 D1
Studland **BH19** 10 B6
Studley *Warks.* B80 30 B2
Studley *Wilts.* **SN11** 20 C4
Studley Common **B80** 30 B2
Studley Green **HP14** 22 A2
Studley Roger **HG4** 57 H2
Stuggadhoo **IM4** 54 C6
Stump Cross *Essex* **CB10** 33 J4
Stump Cross *Lancs.* **PR3** 55 J6
Stuntney **CB7** 33 J1
Stunts Green **BN27** 13 K5
Sturbridge **ST21** 40 A2
Sturgate **DN21** 52 B4
Sturmer **CB9** 33 K4
Sturminster Common **DT10** 9 G3
Sturminster Marshall **BH21** 9 J4
Sturminster Newton DT10 9 G3
Sturry **CT2** 25 H5
Sturton by Stow **LN1** 52 B4
Sturton le Steeple **DN22** 51 K4
Stuston **IP21** 35 F1
Stutton *N.Yorks.* **LS24** 57 K5
Stutton *Suff.* **IP9** 35 F5
Styal **SK9** 49 H4
Styrrup **DN11** 51 J3
Suainebost (Swainbost) **HS2** 101 H1
Suardail **HS2** 101 G4
Succoth *Aber.* **AB54** 90 C1
Succoth *Arg. & B.* **G83** 80 D7
Succothmore **PA27** 80 C7
Suckley **WR6** 29 G3
Suckley Green **WR6** 29 G3
Suckley Knowl **WR6** 29 G3
Sudborough **NN14** 42 C7
Sudbourne **IP12** 35 J3
Sudbrook *Lincs.* **NG32** 42 C1
Sudbrook *Mon.* **NP26** 19 J3
Sudbrooke **LN2** 52 D5
Sudbury *Derbys.* **DE6** 40 D2
Sudbury *Gt.Lon.* **HA0** 22 E3
Sudbury *Suff.* CO10 34 C4
Sudden **OL11** 49 H1
Sudgrove **GL6** 20 C1
Suffield *N.Yorks.* **YO13** 63 J3
Suffield *Norf.* **NR11** 45 G2
Sugarloaf **TN26** 14 E4
Sugnall **ST21** 39 G2
Sugwas Pool **HR4** 28 D4
Suie Lodge Hotel **FK20** 81 F5
Suisnish **IV49** 86 B3
Sulby *I.o.M.* **IM7** 54 C4
Sulby *I.o.M.* **IM4** 54 C5
Sulgrave **OX17** 31 G4
Sulham **RG8** 21 K4
Sulhamstead **RG7** 21 K5
Sullington **RH20** 12 D5
Sullom **ZE2** 107 M5
Sullom Voe Oil Terminal **ZE2** 107 M5
Sully **CF64** 18 E5
Sumburgh **ZE3** 107 M11
Sumburgh Airport **ZE3** 107 M11
Summer Bridge **HG3** 57 H3
Summer Isles **IV26** 95 F1
Summer Lodge **DL8** 62 A7
Summercourt **TR8** 3 F3
Summerfield *Norf.* **PE31** 44 B2
Summerfield *Worcs.* **DY11** 29 H1
Summerhill **LL11** 48 C7
Summerhouse **DL2** 62 D5
Summerlands **LA8** 55 J1
Summerleaze **NP26** 19 H3
Summertown **OX2** 21 J1
Summit **OL15** 49 J1
Sun Green **SK15** 49 J3
Sunadale **PA28** 73 G6
Sunbiggin **CA10** 61 H6
Sunbury TW16 22 E5
Sundaywell **DG2** 68 D5
Sunderland *Cumb.* **CA13** 60 C3
Sunderland *Lancs.* **LA3** 55 H4
SUNDERLAND *T. & W.* SR 62 E1
Sunderland Bridge **DH6** 62 D3
Sundhope **TD7** 69 J1
Sundon Park **LU3** 32 D6
Sundridge **TN14** 23 H6
Sundrum Mains **KA6** 67 J1
Sunhill **GL7** 20 E1
Sunipol **PA75** 78 E2
Sunk Island **HU12** 53 F1
Sunningdale **SL5** 22 C5
Sunninghill **SL5** 22 C5
Sunningwell **OX13** 21 H1
Sunniside *Dur.* **DL13** 62 C3
Sunniside *T. & W.* **NE16** 62 D1
Sunny Bank **LA21** 60 D7
Sunny Brow **DL15** 62 C3
Sunnylaw **FK9** 75 F1
Sunnyside *Aber.* **AB12** 91 G5
Sunnyside *Northumb.* **NE46** 70 E7
Sunnyside *S.Yorks.* **S65** 51 G3
Sunnyside *W.Suss.* **RH19** 13 G3
Sunton **SN8** 21 F6
Sunwick **TD15** 77 G5
Surbiton KT6 22 E5
Surfleet **PE11** 43 F3
Surfleet Seas End **PE11** 43 F3
Surlingham **NR14** 45 H5
Sustead **NR11** 45 F2
Susworth **DN17** 52 B2
Sutcombe **EX22** 6 B4
Sutcombemill **EX22** 6 B4
Suton **NR18** 44 E6
Sutors of Cromarty **IV11** 97 F5
Sutterby **LN13** 53 G5
Sutterton **PE20** 43 F2
Sutton *Cambs.* **CB6** 33 H1
Sutton *Cen.Beds.* **SG19** 33 F4
Sutton *Devon* **EX17** 7 F5
Sutton *Devon* **TQ7** 5 H6
SUTTON *Gt.Lon.* SM 23 F5
Sutton *Kent* **CT15** 15 J3
Sutton *Lincs.* **LN5** 52 B7
Sutton *Norf.* **NR12** 45 H3
Sutton *Notts.* **NG13** 42 A2
Sutton *Notts.* **DN22** 51 J4
Sutton *Oxon.* **OX29** 21 H1
Sutton *Pembs.* **SA62** 16 C4
Sutton *Peter.* **PE5** 42 D6
Sutton *S.Yorks.* **DN6** 51 H1
Sutton *Shrop.* **WV16** 39 G7
Sutton *Shrop.* **TF9** 39 F2
Sutton *Shrop.* **SY2** 38 E4
Sutton *Shrop.* **SY11** 38 C3
Sutton *Staffs.* **TF10** 39 G3
Sutton *Suff.* **IP12** 35 H4
Sutton *W.Suss.* **RH20** 12 C5
Sutton Abinger **RH5** 22 E7
Sutton at Hone **DA4** 23 J4
Sutton Bassett **LE16** 42 A7
Sutton Benger **SN15** 20 C4
Sutton Bingham **BA22** 8 E3
Sutton Bonington **LE12** 41 H3
Sutton Bridge **PE12** 43 H3
Sutton Cheney **CV13** 41 G5
Sutton Coldfield B74 40 D6
Sutton Courtenay **OX14** 21 J2
Sutton Crosses **PE12** 43 H3
Sutton Grange **HG4** 57 H2
Sutton Green *Oxon.* **OX29** 21 H1
Sutton Green *Surr.* **GU4** 22 D6
Sutton Green *Wrex.* **LL13** 38 D1
Sutton Holms **BH21** 10 B4
Sutton Howgrave **DL8** 57 J2
Sutton in Ashfield NG17 51 G7
Sutton in the Elms **LE9** 41 H6
Sutton Ings **HU8** 59 H6
Sutton Lane Ends **SK11** 49 J5
Sutton le Marsh **LN12** 53 J4
Sutton Leach **WA9** 48 E3
Sutton Maddock **TF11** 39 G5
Sutton Mallet **TA7** 8 C1
Sutton Mandeville **SP3** 9 J2
Sutton Montis **BA22** 9 F2
Sutton on Sea **LN12** 53 J4
Sutton on the Hill **DE6** 40 E2
Sutton on Trent **NG23** 51 K6
Sutton Poyntz **DT3** 9 G6
Sutton St. Edmund **PE12** 43 G4
Sutton St. James **PE12** 43 H4
Sutton St. Nicholas **HR1** 28 E4
Sutton Scarsdale **S44** 51 G6
Sutton Scotney **SO21** 11 F1
Sutton upon Derwent **YO41** 58 D5
Sutton Valence **ME17** 14 D3
Sutton Veny **BA12** 20 B7
Sutton Waldron **DT11** 9 H3
Sutton Weaver **WA7** 48 E5
Sutton Wick *B. & N.E.Som.* **BS40** 19 J6
Sutton Wick *Oxon.* **OX14** 21 H2
Sutton-in-Craven **BD20** 57 F5
Sutton-on-Hull **HU7** 59 H6
Sutton-on-the-Forest **YO61** 58 B3
Sutton-under-Brailes **CV36** 30 E5
Sutton-under-Whitestonecliffe **YO7** 57 K1
Swaby **LN13** 53 G5
Swadlincote DE11 41 F4
Swaffham PE37 44 C5
Swaffham Bulbeck **CB25** 33 J2
Swaffham Prior **CB25** 33 J2
Swafield **NR28** 45 G2
Swainbost (Suainebost) **HS2** 101 H1
Swainby **DL6** 63 F6
Swainsthorpe **NR14** 45 G5
Swainswick **BA1** 20 A5
Swalcliffe **OX15** 30 E5
Swalecliffe **CT5** 25 H5
Swallow **LN7** 52 E2
Swallow Beck **LN6** 52 C6
Swallowcliffe **SP3** 9 J2
Swallowfield **RG7** 22 A5
Swallows Cross **CM15** 24 C2
Swampton **SP11** 21 H6
Swan Green *Ches.W. & C.* **WA16** 49 G5
Swan Green *Suff.* **IP19** 35 G1
Swan Street **CO6** 34 C6
Swanage BH19 10 B7
Swanbach **CW3** 39 F1
Swanbourne **MK17** 32 B6
Swanbridge **CF64** 18 E5
Swancote **WV15** 39 G6
Swanland **HU14** 59 F7
Swanlaws **TD8** 70 C2
Swanley BR8 23 J5
Swanley Village **BR8** 23 J5
Swanmore *Hants.* **SO32** 11 G3
Swanmore *I.o.W.* **PO33** 11 G5
Swannington *Leics.* **LE67** 41 G4
Swannington *Norf.* **NR9** 45 F4
Swanscombe DA10 24 C4
SWANSEA (ABERTAWE) SA 17 K6
Swanston **EH10** 76 A4
Swanton Abbot **NR10** 45 G3
Swanton Morley **NR20** 44 E4
Swanton Novers **NR24** 44 E2
Swanton Street **ME9** 14 D2
Swanwick *Derbys.* **DE55** 51 G7
Swanwick *Hants.* **SO31** 11 G4
Swanwick Green **SY13** 38 E1
Swarby **NG34** 42 D1
Swardeston **NR14** 45 G5
Swarkestone **DE73** 41 F3
Swarland **NE65** 71 G3
Swarraton **SO24** 11 G1
Swarthmoor **LA12** 55 F2
Swaton **NG34** 42 E2
Swavesey **CB24** 33 G2
Sway **SO41** 10 D5
Swayfield **NG33** 42 C3
Swaythling **SO18** 11 F3
Swaythorpe **YO25** 59 G3
Sweetham **EX5** 7 G6
Sweethay **TA3** 8 B2
Sweetshouse **PL30** 4 A4
Sweffling **IP17** 35 H2
Swell **TA3** 8 C2
Swepstone **LE67** 41 F4
Swerford **OX7** 30 E5
Swettenham **CW12** 49 H6
Swffryd **NP11** 19 F2
Swift's Green **TN27** 14 D3
Swiftsden **TN19** 14 C5
Swilland **IP6** 35 F3
Swillington **LS26** 57 J6
Swimbridge **EX32** 6 E3
Swimbridge Newland **EX32** 6 D2
Swinbrook **OX18** 30 D7
Swincliffe **HG3** 57 H4
Swincombe **EX31** 6 E1
Swinden **BD23** 56 D4
Swinderby **LN6** 52 B6
Swindon *Staffs.* **DY3** 40 A6
SWINDON *Swin.* SN 20 E3
Swindon Village **GL51** 29 J6
Swine **HU11** 59 H6
Swinefleet **DN14** 58 D7
Swineford **BS30** 19 K5
Swineshead *Bed.* **MK44** 32 D2
Swineshead *Lincs.* **PE20** 43 F1
Swineshead Bridge **PE20** 43 F1
Swineside **DL8** 57 F1
Swiney **KW3** 105 H5
Swinford *Leics.* **LE17** 31 G1
Swinford *Oxon.* **OX29** 21 H1
Swingate **NG16** 41 H1
Swingfield Minnis **CT15** 15 H3
Swingleton Green **IP7** 34 D4
Swinhoe **NE67** 71 H1
Swinhope **LN8** 53 F3
Swining **ZE2** 107 N6
Swinithwaite **DL8** 57 F1
Swinscoe **DE6** 40 D1
Swinside Hall **TD8** 70 C2
Swinstead **NG33** 42 D3
Swinton *Gt.Man.* **M27** 49 G2
Swinton *N.Yorks.* **YO17** 58 D2
Swinton *N.Yorks.* **HG4** 57 H2
Swinton *S.Yorks.* **S64** 51 G3
Swinton *Sc.Bord.* **TD11** 77 G6
Swinton Quarter **TD11** 77 G6
Swintonmill **TD12** 77 G6
Swithland **LE12** 41 H4
Swordale **IV16** 96 C5
Swordland **PH41** 86 D5
Swordle **PH36** 86 B7
Swordly **KW14** 104 C2
Sworton Heath **WA16** 49 F4
Swyddffynnon **SY25** 27 F2
Swyncombe **RG9** 21 K2
Swynnerton **ST15** 40 A2
Swyre **DT2** 8 E6
Sychnant **LD6** 27 J1
Syde **GL53** 29 J7
Sydenham *Gt.Lon.* **SE26** 23 G4
Sydenham *Oxon.* **OX39** 22 A1
Sydenham Damerel **PL19** 4 E3
Syderstone **PE31** 44 C2
Sydling St. Nicholas **DT2** 9 F5
Sydmonton **RG20** 21 H6
Sydney **CW1** 49 G7
Syerston **NG23** 42 A1
Sykehouse **DN14** 51 J1
Sykes **BB7** 56 B4
Sylen **SA15** 17 J5
Symbister **ZE2** 107 P6
Symington *S.Ayr.* **KA1** 74 B7
Symington *S.Lan.* **ML12** 75 H7
Symonds Yat **HR9** 28 E7
Symondsbury **DT6** 8 D5
Synod Inn (Post-mawr) **SA44** 26 D3
Syre **KW11** 103 J4
Syreford **GL54** 30 B6
Syresham **NN13** 31 H4
Syston *Leics.* **LE7** 41 J4
Syston *Lincs.* **NG32** 42 C1
Sytchampton **DY13** 29 H2
Sywell **NN6** 32 B2

T

Taagan **IV22** 95 G5
Tableyhill **WA16** 49 G5
Tabost *W.Isles* **HS2** 101 F6
Tabost (Harbost) *W.Isles* **HS2** 101 H1
Tachbrook Mallory **CV33** 30 E2
Tacher **KW5** 105 G4
Tackley **OX5** 31 F6
Tacleit (Hacklete) **HS2** 100 D4
Tacolneston **NR16** 45 F6
Tadcaster LS24 57 K5
Tadden **BH21** 9 J4
Taddington *Derbys.* **SK17** 50 D5
Taddington *Glos.* **GL54** 30 B5
Taddiport **EX38** 6 C4
Tadley RG26 21 K5
Tadlow **SG8** 33 F4
Tadmarton **OX15** 30 E5
Tadpole Bridge **SN7** 21 G1
Tadworth KT20 23 F6
Tafarnaubach **NP22** 28 A7
Tafarn-y-bwlch **SA41** 16 D2
Tafarn-y-Gelyn **CH7** 47 K6
Taff Merthyr Garden Village **CF46** 18 E2
Taff's Well (Ffynnon Taf) **CF15** 18 E3
Tafolwern **SY19** 37 H5
Taibach *N.P.T.* **SA13** 18 A3
Tai-bach *Powys* **SY10** 38 A3
Taicynhaeaf **LL40** 37 F4
Tain *High.* **KW14** 105 H2
Tain *High.* IV19 96 E3
Tai'n Lôn **LL54** 46 C7
Tai'r Bull **LD3** 27 J6
Tairbeart (Tarbert) **HS3** 100 D7
Tairgwaith **SA18** 27 G7
Tai'r-heol **CF46** 18 E2
Tairlaw **KA19** 67 J3
Tai'r-ysgol **SA7** 17 K6
Takeley **CM22** 33 J6
Takeley Street **CM22** 33 J6
Talachddu **LD3** 27 K5
Talacre **CH8** 47 K4
Talardd **LL23** 37 H3
Talaton **EX5** 7 J6
Talbenny **SA62** 16 B4
Talbot Green **CF72** 18 D3
Talbot Village **BH10** 10 B5
Talerddig **SY19** 37 J5
Talgarreg **SA44** 26 D3
Talgarth **LD3** 28 A5
Taliesin **SY20** 37 F6
Talisker **IV47** 85 J1
Talke Pits **ST7** 49 H7
Talkin **CA8** 61 G1
Talla Linnfoots **ML12** 69 G1
Talladale **IV22** 95 F4
Talladh-a-Bheithe **PH17** 81 G2
Talland **PL13** 4 C5
Tallarn Green **SY14** 38 D1
Tallentire **CA13** 60 C3
Talley (Talyllychau) **SA19** 17 K2
Tallington **PE9** 42 D5
Talmine **IV27** 103 H2
Talog **SA33** 17 G3
Tal-sarn **SA48** 26 E3
Talsarnau LL47 37 F2
Talskiddy **TR9** 3 G2
Talwrn *I.o.A.* **LL77** 46 C5
Talwrn *Wrex.* **LL14** 38 B1
Talwrn *Wrex.* **LL13** 38 C1
Talybont *Cere.* SY24 37 F7
Tal-y-bont *Conwy* **LL32** 47 F6
Tal-y-bont *Gwyn.* LL43 36 E3
Tal-y-bont *Gwyn.* **LL57** 46 E5
Talybont-on-Usk **LD3** 28 A6
Tal-y-Cae **LL57** 46 E6
Tal-y-cafn **LL28** 47 F5
Tal-y-coed **NP7** 28 D7
Talygarn **CF72** 18 D3
Talyllychau (Talley) **SA19** 17 K2
Tal-y-llyn *Gwyn.* **LL36** 37 G5
Talyllyn *Powys* **LD3** 28 A6
Talysarn **LL54** 46 C7
Tal-y-wern **SY20** 37 H5
Tamavoid **FK8** 74 D1
Tamerton Foliot **PL5** 4 E4
Tamworth B79 40 E5
Tamworth Green **PE22** 43 G1
Tan Office Green **IP29** 34 B3
Tandem **HD5** 50 D1
Tandridge **RH8** 23 G6
Tanerdy **SA31** 17 H3
Tanfield **DH9** 62 C1
Tanfield Lea **DH9** 62 C1
Tang **HG3** 57 H4
Tang Hall **YO10** 58 C4
Tangiers **SA62** 16 C4

Tanglandford AB41 91 G1
Tangley SP11 21 G6
Tangmere PO20 12 C6
Tangwick ZE2 107 L5
Tangy PA28 66 A1
Tankerness KW17 106 E7
Tankersley S75 51 F2
Tankerton CT5 25 H5
Tan-lan LL48 37 F1
Tannach KW1 105 J4
Tannachie AB39 91 F6
Tannachy IV28 96 E1
Tannadice DD8 83 F2
Tannington IP13 35 G2
Tannochside G71 74 E4
Tansley DE4 51 F7
Tansley Knoll DE4 51 F7
Tansor PE8 42 D6
Tantobie DH9 62 C1
Tanton TS9 63 G5
Tanworth in Arden B94 30 C1
Tan-y-fron LL16 47 H6
Tan-y-graig LL53 36 C2
Tanygrisiau LL41 37 F1
Tan-y-groes SA43 17 F1
Tan-y-pistyll SY10 37 K3
Tan-yr-allt LL19 47 J4
Taobh a' Deas Loch Baghasdail HS8 84 C3
Taobh Siar HS3 100 D7
Taobh Tuath (Northton) HS3 92 E3
Tapeley EX39 6 C3
Taplow SL6 22 C3
Tapton Grove S43 51 G5
Taransay (Tarasaigh) HS3 100 C7
Taraphocain PA38 80 B3
Tarasaigh (Taransay) HS3 100 C7
Tarbat House IV18 96 E4
Tarbert *Arg. & B.* **PA29 73 G4**
Tarbert *Arg. & B.* PA41 72 E5
Tarbert *Arg. & B.* PA60 72 E2
Tarbert *High.* PH36 79 H1
Tarbert (Tairbeart) *W.Isles* HS3 100 D7
Tarbet *Arg. & B.* G83 80 E7
Tarbet *High.* PH41 86 D5
Tarbet *High.* IV27 102 D4
Tarbock Green L35 48 D4
Tarbolton KA5 67 J1
Tarbrax EH55 75 J5
Tardebigge B60 29 J2
Tardy Gate PR5 55 J7
Tarfside DD9 90 C7
Tarland AB34 90 C4
Tarleton PR4 55 H7
Tarlscough L40 48 D1
Tarlton GL7 20 C2
Tarnbrook LA2 55 J4
Tarnock BS26 19 G6
Tarporley CW6 48 E6
Tarr TA4 7 K2
Tarrant Crawford DT11 9 J4
Tarrant Gunville DT11 9 J3
Tarrant Hinton DT11 9 J3
Tarrant Keyneston DT11 9 J4
Tarrant Launceston DT11 9 J4
Tarrant Monkton DT11 9 J4
Tarrant Rawston DT11 9 J4
Tarrant Rushton DT11 9 J4
Tarrel IV20 97 F3
Tarring Neville BN9 13 H6
Tarrington HR1 29 F4
Tarrnacraig KA27 73 H7
Tarsappie PH2 82 C5
Tarskavaig IV46 86 B4
Tarves AB41 91 G1
Tarvie *High.* IV14 96 B6
Tarvie *P. & K.* PH10 82 B1
Tarvin CH3 48 D6
Tarvin Sands CH3 48 D6
Tasburgh NR15 45 G6
Tasley WV16 39 F6
Taston OX7 30 E6
Tatenhill DE13 40 E3
Tathall End MK19 32 B4
Tatham LA2 56 B3
Tathwell LN11 53 G4
Tatsfield TN16 23 H6
Tattenhall CH3 48 D7
Tattenhoe MK4 32 B5
Tatterford NR21 44 C3
Tattersett PE31 44 C2
Tattershall LN4 53 F7
Tattershall Bridge LN4 52 E7
Tattershall Thorpe LN4 53 F7
Tattingstone IP9 35 F5
Tatworth TA20 8 C4
Tauchers AB55 98 B6
TAUNTON TA 8 B2
Tavelty AB51 91 F3
Taverham NR8 45 F4
Tavernspite SA34 16 E4
Tavistock PL19 4 E3
Taw Bridge EX18 6 E5
Taw Green EX20 6 E6
Tawstock EX31 6 D3
Taxal SK23 50 C5
Tayburn KA3 74 D6
Taychreggan PA35 80 B5
Tayinloan PA29 72 E6
Taylors Cross EX23 6 A4
Taynafead PA33 80 B6
Taynish PA31 73 F2
Taynton *Glos.* GL19 29 G6
Taynton *Oxon.* OX18 30 D7
Taynuilt PA35 80 B4
Tayock DD10 83 H2
Tayovullin PA44 72 A3
Tayport DD6 83 F5
Tayvallich PA31 73 F2
Tea Green LU2 32 E6
Tealby LN8 52 E3
Tealing DD4 83 F4
Team Valley NE11 71 H7
Teanamachar HS6 92 C5
Teangue IV44 86 C4
Teasses KY8 83 F7
Tebay CA10 61 H6
Tebworth LU7 32 C6
Tedburn St. Mary EX6 7 G6
Teddington *Glos.* GL20 29 J5
Teddington ***Gt.Lon.*** **TW11 22 E4**
Tedstone Delamere HR7 29 F3
Tedstone Wafre HR7 29 F3
Teeton NN6 31 H1
Teffont Evias SP3 9 J1
Teffont Magna SP3 9 J1
Tegryn SA35 17 F2
Teigh LE15 42 B4
Teign Village TQ13 7 G7
Teigngrace TQ12 5 J3
Teignmouth TQ14 5 K3
TELFORD TF 39 F5
Telham TN33 14 C6
Tellisford BA2 20 B6
Telscombe BN7 13 H6
Telscombe Cliffs BN10 13 H6
Tempar PH16 81 H2
Templand DG11 69 F5
Temple *Cornw.* PL30 4 B3
Temple *Midloth.* EH23 76 B5
Temple Balsall B93 30 D1
Temple Bar SA48 26 E3
Temple Cloud BS39 19 K6
Temple End CB9 33 K3
Temple Ewell CT16 15 H3
Temple Grafton B49 30 C3
Temple Guiting GL54 30 B6
Temple Herdewyke CV47 30 E3
Temple Hirst YO8 58 C7
Temple Normanton S42 51 G6
Temple Sowerby CA10 61 H4
Templecombe BA8 9 G2
Templeton *Devon* EX16 7 G4
Templeton *Pembs.* SA67 16 E4
Templeton Bridge EX16 7 G4
Templewood DD9 83 H1
Tempsford SG19 32 E3
Ten Mile Bank PE38 44 A6
Tenbury Wells WR15 28 E2
Tenby (Dinbych-y-pysgod) SA70 16 E5
Tendring CO16 35 F6
Tendring Green CO16 35 F6
Tenga PA72 79 G3
Tenterden TN30 14 D4
Tepersie Castle AB33 90 D2
Terally DG9 64 B6
Terling CM3 34 B7
Tern TF6 39 F4
Ternhill TF9 39 F2
Terregles DG2 65 K3
Terriers HP13 22 B2
Terrington YO60 58 C2
Terrington St. Clement PE34 43 J3
Terrington St. John PE14 43 J4
Terry's Green B94 30 C1
Tervieside AB37 89 K1
Teston ME18 14 C2
Testwood SO40 10 E3
Tetbury GL8 20 B2
Tetbury Upton GL8 20 B2
Tetchill SY12 38 C2
Tetcott EX22 6 B6
Tetford LN9 53 G5
Tetney DN36 53 G2
Tetney Lock DN36 53 G2
Tetsworth OX9 21 K1
Tettenhall WV6 40 A5
Tettenhall Wood WV6 40 A6
Tetworth SG19 33 F3
Teuchan AB42 91 J1
Teversal NG17 51 G6
Teversham CB1 33 H3
Teviothead TD9 69 K3
Tewel AB39 91 G6
Tewin AL6 33 F7
Tewkesbury GL20 29 H5
Teynham ME9 25 F5
Thackley BD10 57 G6
Thainston AB30 90 E7
Thainstone AB51 91 F3
Thakeham RH20 12 E5
Thame OX9 22 A1
Thames Ditton KT7 22 E5
Thames Haven SS17 24 D3
Thamesmead SE28 23 H3
Thanington CT1 15 G2
Thankerton ML12 75 H7
Tharston NR15 45 F6
Thatcham RG18 21 J5
Thatto Heath WA9 48 E3
Thaxted CM6 33 K5
The Apes Hall CB6 43 J6
The Bage HR3 28 B4
The Balloch PH7 81 K6
The Banking AB51 91 F1
The Bar RH13 12 E4
The Birks AB32 91 F4
The Bog SY5 38 C6
The Bourne GU9 22 B7
The Bratch WV5 40 A6
The Broad HR6 28 D2
The Bryn NP7 19 G1
The Burf DY13 29 H2
The Burn DD9 90 D7
The Butts BA11 20 A7
The Camp GL6 20 C1
The Chequer SY13 38 D1
The City *Bucks.* HP14 22 A2
The City *Suff.* NR34 45 H7
The Common *Wilts.* SP5 10 D1
The Common *Wilts.* SN15 20 D3
The Craigs IV24 96 B2
The Cronk IM7 54 C4
The Delves WS5 40 C6
The Den KA24 74 B5
The Dicker BN27 13 J6
The Down WV16 39 F6
The Drums DD8 82 E1
The Eaves GL15 19 K1
The Flatt CA6 70 A6
The Folly AL4 32 E7
The Forge HR5 28 C3
The Forstal *E.Suss.* TN3 13 J3
The Forstal *Kent* TN25 15 F4
The Grange *Lincs.* LN13 53 J5
The Grange *Shrop.* SY12 38 C2
The Grange *Surr.* RH9 23 G7
The Green *Arg. & B.* PA77 78 A3
The Green *Cumb.* LA18 54 E1
The Green *Essex* CM8 34 B7
The Green *Flints.* CH7 48 B6
The Green *Wilts.* SP3 9 H1
The Grove WR8 29 H4
The Haven RH14 12 D3
The Headland TS24 63 G3
The Heath ST14 40 C2
The Herberts CF71 18 C4
The Hermitage KT20 23 F6
The Hill LA18 54 E1
The Holme HG3 57 H4
The Howe IM9 54 A7
The Isle SY3 38 D4
The Laurels NR14 45 H6
The Leacon TN26 14 E4
The Lee HP16 22 B1
The Leigh GL19 29 H6
The Lhen IM7 54 C3
The Lodge PA24 73 K1
The Marsh SY5 38 C6
The Moor *E.Suss.* TN35 14 D6
The Moor *Kent* TN18 14 C5
The Mumbles SA3 17 K7
The Murray G75 74 E5
The Mythe GL20 29 H5
The Narth NP25 19 J1
The Neuk AB31 91 F5
The Node SG4 33 F7
The Oval BA2 20 A5
The Polchar PH22 89 G4
The Quarter TN27 14 D3
The Reddings GL51 29 J6
The Rhos SA62 16 D4
The Rookery ST7 49 H7
The Rowe ST5 40 A2
The Sale DE13 40 D4
The Sands GU10 22 B7
The Shoe SN14 20 B4
The Slade RG7 21 J4
The Smithies WV16 39 F6
The Stocks TN30 14 E5
The Swillett WD3 22 D2
The Thrift SG8 33 G5
The Vauld HR1 28 E4
The Wern LL14 48 B7
The Wyke TF11 39 G5
Theakston DL8 57 J1
Thealby DN15 52 B1
Theale *Som.* BS28 19 H7
Theale *W.Berks.* RG7 21 K4
Thearne HU17 59 G6
Theberton IP16 35 J2
Thedden Grange GU34 11 H1
Theddingworth LE17 41 J7
Theddlethorpe All Saints LN12 53 H4
Theddlethorpe St. Helen LN12 53 H4
Thelbridge Barton EX17 7 F4
Thelbridge Cross EX17 7 F4
Thelnetham IP22 34 E1
Thelveton IP21 45 F7
Thelwall WA4 49 F4
Themelthorpe NR20 44 E3
Thenford OX17 31 G4
Therfield SG8 33 G5
Thetford *Lincs.* PE6 42 E4
Thetford ***Norf.*** **IP24 44 C7**
Thethwaite CA5 60 E2
Theydon Bois CM16 23 H2
Theydon Garnon CM16 23 H2
Theydon Mount CM16 23 H2
Thickwood SN14 20 B4
Thimbleby *Lincs.* LN9 53 F6
Thimbleby *N.Yorks.* DL6 63 F7
Thingley SN13 20 B5
Thirkleby YO7 57 K2
Thirlby YO7 57 K1
Thirlestane TD2 76 D6
Thirn HG4 57 H1
Thirsk YO7 57 K1
Thirston New Houses NE65 71 G4
Thirtleby HU11 59 H6
Thistleton *Lancs.* PR4 55 H6
Thistleton *Rut.* LE15 42 C4
Thistley Green IP28 33 K1
Thixendale YO17 58 E3
Thockrington NE48 70 E6
Tholomas Drove PE13 43 G5
Tholthorpe YO61 57 K3
Thomas Chapel SA68 16 E5
Thomas Close CA11 60 F2
Thomastown AB54 90 D1
Thompson IP24 44 D6
Thomshill IV30 97 K6
Thong DA12 24 C4
Thongsbridge HD9 50 D2
Thoralby DL8 57 F1
Thoresby NG22 51 J5
Thoresthorpe LN13 53 H5
Thoresway LN8 52 E3
Thorganby *Lincs.* DN37 53 F3
Thorganby *N.Yorks.* YO19 58 C5
Thorgill YO18 63 J7
Thorington IP19 35 J1
Thorington Street CO6 34 E5
Thorley CM23 33 H7
Thorley Houses CM23 33 H6
Thorley Street *Herts.* CM23 33 H7
Thorley Street *I.o.W.* PO41 10 E6
Thormanby YO61 57 K2
Thornaby-on-Tees TS17 63 F5
Thornage NR25 44 E2
Thornborough *Bucks.* MK18 31 J5
Thornborough *N.Yorks.* DL8 57 H2
Thornbury *Devon* EX22 6 B5
Thornbury *Here.* HR7 29 F3
Thornbury *S.Glos.* BS35 19 K2
Thornbury *W.Yorks.* BD3 57 G6
Thornby NN6 31 H1
Thorncliff HD8 50 E1
Thorncliffe ST13 50 C7
Thorncombe TA20 8 C4
Thorncombe Street GU5 22 D7
Thorncote Green SG19 32 E4
Thorncross PO30 11 F6
Thorndon IP23 35 F2
Thorndon Cross EX20 6 D6
Thorne DN8 51 J1
Thorne St. Margaret TA21 7 J3
Thorner LS14 57 J6
Thorney *Bucks.* SL0 22 D4
Thorney *Notts.* NG23 52 B5
Thorney *Peter.* PE6 43 F5
Thorney *Som.* TA10 8 D2
Thorney Close SR4 62 E1
Thorney Hill BH23 10 D5
Thornfalcon TA3 8 B2
Thornford DT9 9 F3
Thorngrafton NE47 70 C7
Thorngrove TA7 8 C1
Thorngumbald HU12 59 J7
Thornham PE36 44 B1
Thornham Magna IP23 35 F1
Thornham Parva IP23 35 F1
Thornhaugh PE8 42 D5
Thornhill *Cardiff* CF83 18 E3
Thornhill *Cumb.* CA22 60 B6
Thornhill ***D. & G.*** **DG3 68 D4**
Thornhill *Derbys.* S33 50 D4
Thornhill *S'ham.* SO19 11 F3
Thornhill *Stir.* FK8 81 H7
Thornhill *W.Yorks.* WF12 50 E1
Thornhill Lees WF12 50 E1
Thornholme YO25 59 H3
Thornicombe DT11 9 H4
Thornley *Dur.* DH6 62 E3
Thornley *Dur.* DL13 62 C3
Thornley Gate NE47 61 K1
Thornliebank G46 74 D5
Thornroan AB41 91 G1
Thorns CB8 34 B3
Thorns Green WA15 49 G4
Thornsett SK22 50 C4
Thornthwaite *Cumb.* CA12 60 D4
Thornthwaite *N.Yorks.* HG3 57 G4
Thornton *Angus* DD8 82 E3
Thornton *Bucks.* MK17 31 J5
Thornton *E.Riding* YO42 58 D5
Thornton *Fife* KY1 76 A1
Thornton ***Lancs.*** **FY5 55 G5**
Thornton *Leics.* LE67 41 G5
Thornton *Lincs.* LN9 53 F6
Thornton *Mersey.* L23 48 C2
Thornton *Middbro.* TS8 63 F5
Thornton *Northumb.* TD15 77 H6
Thornton *P. & K.* PH8 82 B3
Thornton *Pembs.* SA73 16 C5
Thornton *W.Yorks.* BD13 57 G6
Thornton Bridge YO61 57 K2
Thornton Curtis DN39 52 D1
Thornton Heath CR7 23 G5
Thornton Hough CH63 48 C4
Thornton in Lonsdale LA6 56 B2
Thornton le Moor LN7 52 D3
Thornton Park TD15 77 H6
Thornton Rust DL8 56 E1
Thornton Steward HG4 57 G1
Thornton Watlass HG4 57 H1
Thorntonhall G74 74 D5
Thornton-in-Craven BD23 56 E5
Thornton-le-Beans DL6 63 F7
Thornton-le-Clay YO60 58 C3
Thornton-le-Dale YO18 58 E1
Thornton-le-Moor DL7 57 J1
Thornton-le-Moors CH2 48 D5
Thornton-le-Street YO7 57 K1
Thorntonloch EH42 77 F3
Thornwood CM16 23 H1
Thornyhill AB30 90 E7
Thornylee TD1 76 C7
Thoroton NG13 42 A1
Thorp Arch LS23 57 K5
Thorpe *Derbys.* DE6 50 D7
Thorpe *E.Riding* YO25 59 F5
Thorpe *Lincs.* LN12 53 H4
Thorpe *N.Yorks.* BD23 57 F3
Thorpe *Norf.* NR14 45 J6
Thorpe *Notts.* NG23 51 K7
Thorpe *Surr.* TW20 22 D5
Thorpe Abbotts IP21 45 F7
Thorpe Acre LE11 41 H4
Thorpe Arnold LE14 42 A3
Thorpe Audlin WF8 51 G1
Thorpe Bassett YO17 58 E2
Thorpe Bay SS1 25 F3
Thorpe by Water LE15 42 B6
Thorpe Constantine B79 40 E5
Thorpe Culvert PE24 53 H6
Thorpe End NR13 45 G4
Thorpe Green *Essex* CO16 35 F6
Thorpe Green *Lancs.* PR6 55 J7
Thorpe Green *Suff.* IP30 34 D3
Thorpe Hall YO62 58 B2
Thorpe Hesley S61 51 F3
Thorpe in Balne DN6 51 H1
Thorpe in the Fallows LN1 52 C4
Thorpe Langton LE16 42 A6
Thorpe Larches TS21 62 E4
Thorpe le Street YO42 58 E5
Thorpe Malsor NN14 32 B1
Thorpe Mandeville OX17 31 G4
Thorpe Market NR11 45 G2
Thorpe Morieux IP30 34 D3
Thorpe on the Hill *Lincs.* LN6 52 C6
Thorpe on the Hill *W.Yorks.* WF3 57 J7
Thorpe Row IP25 44 D5
Thorpe St. Andrew NR7 45 G5
Thorpe St. Peter PE24 53 H6
Thorpe Salvin S80 51 H4
Thorpe Satchville LE14 42 A4
Thorpe Street IP22 34 E1
Thorpe Thewles TS21 63 F4
Thorpe Tilney Dales LN4 52 E7
Thorpe Underwood *N.Yorks.* YO26 57 K4
Thorpe Underwood *Northants.* NN6 42 A7
Thorpe Waterville NN14 42 D7
Thorpe Willoughby YO8 58 B6
Thorpefield YO7 57 K2
Thorpe-le-Soken CO16 35 F6
Thorpeness IP16 35 J2
Thorpland PE33 44 A5
Thorrington CO7 34 E6
Thorverton EX5 7 H5
Thrandeston IP21 35 F1
Thrapston NN14 32 C1
Threapland BD23 56 E3
Threapwood SY14 38 D1
Threapwood Head ST10 40 C1
Three Ashes BA3 19 K7
Three Bridges RH10 13 F3
Three Burrows TR4 2 E4
Three Chimneys TN27 14 D4
Three Cocks (Aberllynfi) LD3 28 A5
Three Crosses SA4 17 J6
Three Cups Corner TN21 13 K4
Three Hammers PL15 4 C2
Three Holes PE14 43 J5
Three Leg Cross TN5 13 K3
Three Legged Cross BH21 10 B4
Three Mile Cross RG7 22 A5
Three Oaks TN35 14 D6
Threehammer Common NR12 45 H4
Threekingham NG34 42 D2
Threemilestone TR3 2 E4
Threlkeld CA12 60 E4
Threshfield BD23 56 E3
Threxton Hill IP25 44 C5
Thriepley DD2 82 E4
Thrigby NR29 45 J4
Thringarth DL12 62 A4
Thringstone LE67 41 G4
Thrintoft DL7 62 E7
Thriplow SG8 33 H4
Throapham S25 51 H4
Throckenholt PE12 43 G5
Throcking SG9 33 G5
Throckley NE15 71 G7
Throckmorton WR10 29 J4
Throop DT2 9 H5
Throphill NE61 71 G5
Thropton NE65 71 F3
Througham GL6 20 C1
Throwleigh EX20 6 E6
Throwley ME13 14 E2
Throws CM6 33 K6
Thrumpton *Notts.* NG11 41 H2
Thrumpton *Notts.* DN22 51 K5
Thrumster KW1 105 J4
Thrunton NE66 71 F2
Thrupp *Glos.* GL5 20 B1
Thrupp *Oxon.* OX5 31 F7
Thrupp *Oxon.* SN7 21 F2
Thruscross HG3 57 G4
Thrushelton EX20 6 C7
Thrussington LE7 41 J4
Thruxton *Hants.* SP11 21 F7
Thruxton *Here.* HR2 28 D5
Thrybergh S65 51 G3
Thulston DE72 41 G2
Thunder Bridge HD8 50 D1
Thundergay KA27 73 G6
Thundersley SS7 24 E3
Thunderton AB42 99 J6
Thundridge SG12 33 G7
Thurcaston LE7 41 H4
Thurcroft S66 51 G4
Thurdistoft KW14 105 H2
Thurdon EX23 6 A4
Thurgarton *Norf.* NR11 45 F2
Thurgarton *Notts.* NG14 41 J1
Thurgoland S35 50 E2
Thurlaston *Leics.* LE9 41 H6
Thurlaston *Warks.* CV23 31 F1
Thurlbear TA3 8 B2
Thurlby *Lincs.* PE10 42 E4
Thurlby *Lincs.* LN5 52 C6

Thurlby *Lincs.* LN13 53 H5
Thurleigh MK44 32 D3
Thurlestone TQ7 5 G6
Thurloxton TA2 8 B1
Thurlstone S36 50 E2
Thurlton NR14 45 J6
Thurlwood ST7 49 H7
Thurmaston LE4 41 J5
Thurnby LE7 41 J5
Thurne NR29 45 J4
Thurnham ME14 14 D2
Thurning *Norf.* NR20 44 E3
Thurning *Northants.* PE8 42 D7
Thurnscoe S63 51 G2
Thursby CA5 60 E1
Thursden BB10 56 E6
Thursford NR21 44 D2
Thursley GU8 12 C3
Thurso KW14 105 G2
Thurstaston CH61 48 B4
Thurston IP31 34 D2
Thurston Clough OL3 49 J2
Thurstonfield CA5 60 E1
Thurstonland HD4 50 D1
Thurton NR14 45 H5
Thurvaston *Derbys.* DE6 40 E2
Thurvaston *Derbys.* DE6 40 D2
Thuster KW1 105 H3
Thuxton NR9 44 E5
Thwaite *N.Yorks.* DL11 61 K7
Thwaite *Suff.* IP23 35 F2
Thwaite Head LA12 60 E7
Thwaite St. Mary NR35 45 H6
Thwaites BD21 57 F5
Thwaites Brow BD21 57 F5
Thwing YO25 59 G2
Tibbermore PH1 82 B5
Tibberton *Glos.* GL19 29 G6
Tibberton *Tel. & W.* TF10 39 F3
Tibberton *Worcs.* WR9 29 J3
Tibbie Shiels Inn TD7 69 H1
Tibenham NR16 45 F6
Tibertich PA31 79 K7
Tibshelf DE55 51 G6
Tibthorpe YO25 59 F4
Ticehurst TN5 13 K3
Tichborne SO24 11 G1
Tickencote PE9 42 C5
Tickenham BS21 19 H4
Tickford End MK16 32 B4
Tickhill DN11 51 H3
Ticklerton SY6 38 D6
Ticknall DE73 41 F3
Tickton HU17 59 G5
Tidbury Green B90 30 C1
Tidcombe SN8 21 F6
Tiddington *Oxon.* OX9 21 K1
Tiddington *Warks.* CV37 30 D3
Tiddleywink SN14 20 B4
Tidebrook TN5 13 K4
Tideford PL12 4 D5
Tideford Cross PL12 4 D4
Tidenham NP16 19 J2
Tidenham Chase NP16 19 J2
Tideswell SK17 50 D5
Tidmarsh RG8 21 K4
Tidmington CV36 30 D5
Tidpit SP6 10 B3
Tidworth SP9 21 F7
Tiers Cross SA62 16 C4
Tiffield NN12 31 H3
Tifty AB53 99 F6
Tigerton DD9 83 G1
Tigh a' Gearraidh HS6 92 C4
Tighachnoic PA34 79 H3
Tighnablair PH6 81 J6
Tighnabruaich PA21 73 H3
Tighnacomaire PH33 80 A1
Tigley TQ9 5 H4
Tilbrook PE28 32 D2
Tilbury RM18 24 C4
Tilbury Green CO9 34 B4
Tile Hill CV4 30 D1
Tilehurst RG31 21 K4
Tilford GU10 22 B7
Tilgate RH10 13 F3
Tilgate Forest Row RH10 13 F3
Tillathrowie AB54 90 C1
Tillers' Green GL18 29 F5
Tillery AB41 91 H2
Tilley SY4 38 E3
Tillicoultry FK13 75 H1
Tillingham CM0 25 F1
Tillington *Here.* HR4 28 D4
Tillington *W.Suss.* GU28 12 C4
Tillington Common HR4 28 D4
Tillyarblet DD9 83 G1
Tillybirloch AB51 90 E4
Tillycairn Castle AB51 90 E3
Tillycorthie AB41 91 H2
Tillydrine AB34 90 E5
Tillyfar AB53 99 G6
Tillyfour AB33 90 D3
Tillyfourie AB51 90 E3
Tillygreig AB41 91 G2
Tillypronie AB34 90 C4
Tilmanstone CT14 15 J2
Tiln DN22 51 K4
Tilney All Saints PE34 43 J4
Tilney Fen End PE14 43 J4
Tilney High End PE34 43 J4
Tilney St. Lawrence PE34 43 J4
Tilshead SP3 20 D7
Tilstock SY13 38 E2
Tilston SY14 48 D7
Tilstone Fearnall CW6 48 E6
Tilsworth LU7 32 C6
Tilton on the Hill LE7 42 A5
Tiltups End GL6 20 B2
Timberland LN4 52 E7
Timberland Dales LN10 52 E6
Timbersbrook CW12 49 H6
Timberscombe TA24 7 H1
Timble LS21 57 G4
Timewell EX16 7 H3
Timperley WA15 49 G4
Timsbury *B. & N.E.Som.* BA2 19 K6
Timsbury *Hants.* SO51 10 E2
Timsgearraidh HS2 100 C4
Timworth IP31 34 C2
Timworth Green IP31 34 C2
Tincleton DT2 9 G5
Tindale CA8 61 H1
Tindon End CB10 33 K5
Tingewick MK18 31 H5
Tingley WF3 57 H7
Tingrith MK17 32 D5
Tingwall KW17 106 D5
Tingwall (Lerwick) Airport ZE2 107 N8
Tinhay PL16 6 B7
Tinney EX22 4 C1
Tinshill LS16 57 H6
Tinsley S9 51 G3
Tinsley Green RH10 13 F3
Tintagel PL34 4 A2
Tintern Parva NP16 19 J1
Tintinhull BA22 8 D3
Tintwistle SK13 50 C3
Tinwald DG1 69 F5
Tinwell PE9 42 D5
Tippacott EX35 7 F1
Tipperty *Aber.* AB30 91 F6
Tipperty *Aber.* AB41 91 H2
Tipps End PE14 43 H6
Tiptoe SO41 10 D5
Tipton DY4 40 B6
Tipton St. John EX10 7 J6
Tiptree CO5 34 C7
Tiptree Heath CO5 34 C7
Tirabad LD4 27 H4
Tiree PA77 78 A3
Tiree Airport PA77 78 B3
Tirindrish PH34 87 J6
Tirley GL19 29 H6
Tirphil NP24 18 E1
Tirril CA10 61 G4
Tir-y-dail SA18 17 K4
Tisbury SP3 9 J2
Tisman's Common RH12 12 D3
Tissington DE6 50 D7
Tister KW12 105 G2
Titchberry EX39 6 A3
Titchfield PO14 11 G4
Titchmarsh NN14 32 D1
Titchwell PE31 44 B1
Tithby NG13 41 J2
Titley HR5 28 C2
Titlington NE66 71 G2
Titmore Green SG4 33 F6
Titsey RH8 23 H6
Titson EX23 6 A5
Tittensor ST12 40 A2
Tittleshall PE32 44 C3
Tiverton *Ches.W. & C.* CW6 48 E6
Tiverton *Devon* EX16 7 H4
Tivetshall St. Margaret NR15 45 F7
Tivetshall St. Mary NR15 45 F7
Tivington TA24 7 H1
Tixall ST18 40 B3
Tixover PE9 42 C5
Toab *Ork.* KW17 106 E7
Toab *Shet.* ZE3 107 M11
Tobermory PA75 79 G2
Toberonochy PA34 79 J7
Tobha Mòr (Homore) HS8 84 C1
Tobson HS2 100 D4
Tocher AB51 90 E1
Tockenham SN4 20 D4
Tockenham Wick SN4 20 D3
Tockholes BB3 56 B7
Tockington BS32 19 K3
Tockwith YO26 57 K4
Todber DT10 9 G2
Toddington *Cen.Beds.* LU5 32 D6
Toddington *Glos.* GL54 30 B5
Todenham GL56 30 D5
Todhills *Angus* DD4 83 F4
Todhills *Cumb.* CA6 69 J7
Todlachie AB51 90 E3
Todmorden OL14 56 E7
Todwick S26 51 G4
Toft *Cambs.* CB23 33 G3
Toft *Lincs.* PE10 42 D4
Toft *Shet.* ZE2 107 N5
Toft Hill DL14 62 C4
Toft Monks NR34 45 J6
Toft next Newton LN8 52 D4
Toftcarl KW1 105 J4
Toftrees NR21 44 C3
Tofts KW1 105 J2
Toftwood NR19 44 D4
Togston NE65 71 H3
Tokavaig IV46 86 C3
Tokers Green RG4 21 K4
Tolastadh HS2 101 H3
Tolastadh a' Chaolais HS2 100 D4
Tolastadh Ùr HS2 101 H3
Toll Bar DN5 51 H2
Toll of Birness AB41 91 J1
Tolland TA4 7 K2
Tollard Farnham DT11 9 J3
Tollard Royal SP5 9 J3
Tollcross G32 74 E4
Toller Down Gate DT2 8 E4
Toller Fratrum DT2 8 E5
Toller Porcorum DT2 8 E5
Toller Whelme DT8 8 E4
Tollerton *N.Yorks.* YO61 58 B3
Tollerton *Notts.* NG12 41 J2
Tollesbury CM9 34 D7
Tollesby TS4 63 G5
Tolleshunt D'Arcy CM9 34 D7
Tolleshunt Knights CM9 34 D7
Tolleshunt Major CM9 34 C7
Tolm (Holm) HS2 101 G4
Tolmachan HS3 100 C7
Tolpuddle DT2 9 G5
Tolvah PH21 89 F5
Tolworth KT6 22 E5
Tom an Fhuadain HS2 101 F6
Tomatin IV13 89 F2
Tombreck IV2 88 D1
Tomchrasky IV63 87 J3
Tomdoun PH35 87 H4
Tomdow IV36 97 H7
Tomich *High.* IV4 87 K2
Tomich *High.* IV18 96 E4
Tomich *High.* IV27 96 D1
Tomintoul AB37 89 J3
Tomnacross IV4 96 C7
Tomnamoon IV36 97 H6
Tomnaven AB54 90 C1
Tomnavoulin AB37 89 K2
Tomvaich PH26 89 H1
Ton Pentre CF41 18 C2
Tonbridge TN9 23 J7
Tondu CF32 18 B3
Tonedale TA21 7 K3
Tonfanau LL36 36 E5
Tong *Kent* TN27 14 D3
Tong *Shrop.* TF11 39 G5
Tong *W.Yorks.* BD4 57 H6
Tong Norton TF11 39 G5
Tong Street BD4 57 G6
Tonge DE73 41 G3
Tongham GU10 22 B7
Tongland DG6 65 G5
Tongue IV27 103 H3
Tongue House IV27 103 H3
Tongwynlais CF15 18 E3
Tonmawr SA12 18 B2
Tonna SA11 18 A2
Tonwell SG12 33 G7
Tonypandy CF40 18 C2
Tonyrefail CF39 18 D3
Toot Baldon OX44 21 J1
Toot Hill CM5 23 J1
Toothill *Hants.* SO51 10 E3
Toothill *Swin.* SN5 20 E3
Tooting Graveney SW17 23 F4
Top End MK44 32 D2
Top of Hebers M24 49 H2
Topcliffe YO7 57 K2
Topcroft NR35 45 G6
Topcroft Street NR35 45 G6
Toppesfield CO9 34 B5
Toppings BL7 49 G1
Toprow NR16 45 F6
Topsham EX3 7 H7
Topsham Bridge TQ7 5 H5
Torastan PA78 78 D1
Torbain AB37 89 J3
Torbeg *Aber.* AB35 90 B5
Torbeg *N.Ayr.* KA27 66 D1
Torbothie ML7 75 G5
Torbryan TQ12 5 J4
Torcastle PH33 87 H7
Torcross TQ7 5 J6
Tordarroch IV2 88 D1
Tore IV6 96 D6
Toreduff IV36 97 J5
Toremore *High.* PH26 89 J1
Toremore *High.* KW6 105 G5
Torfrey PL23 4 B5
Torgyle IV63 87 K3
Torksey LN1 52 B5
Torlum HS7 92 C6
Torlundy PH33 87 H7
Tormarton GL9 20 A4
Tormisdale PA47 72 A5
Tormore KA27 73 G7
Tormsdale KW12 105 G3
Tornagrain IV2 96 E6
Tornahaish AB36 89 K4
Tornaveen AB31 90 E4
Torness IV2 88 C2
Toronto DL14 62 C3
Torpenhow CA7 60 D3
Torphichen EH48 75 H3
Torphins AB31 90 E4
Torpoint PL11 4 E5
TORQUAY TQ 5 K4
Torquhan TD1 76 C6
Torr PL8 5 F5
Torran *Arg. & B.* PA31 79 K7
Torran *High.* IV18 96 E4
Torran *High.* IV40 94 B7
Torrance G64 74 E3
Torrance House G75 74 E5
Torrancroy AB36 90 B3
Torre *Som.* TA23 7 J1
Torre *Torbay* TQ1 5 K4
Torrich IV12 97 F6
Torridon IV22 94 E6
Torrin IV49 86 B2
Torrisdale *Arg. & B.* PA28 73 F7
Torrisdale *High.* KW14 103 J2
Torrish KW8 104 E7
Torrisholme LA4 55 H3
Torroble IV27 96 C1
Torry *Aber.* AB54 98 C6
Torry *Aberdeen* AB11 91 H4
Torryburn KY12 75 J2
Torsonce TD1 76 C6
Torterston AB42 99 J6
Torthorwald DG1 69 F6
Tortington BN18 12 C6
Torton DY10 29 H1
Tortworth GL12 20 A2
Torvaig IV51 93 K7
Torver LA21 60 D7
Torwood FK5 75 G2
Torworth DN22 51 J4
Tosberry EX39 6 A3
Toscaig IV54 86 D1
Toseland PE19 33 F2
Tosside BD23 56 C4
Tostarie PA74 78 E3
Tostock IP30 34 D2
Totaig IV55 93 G6
Totamore PA78 78 C2
Tote IV51 93 K7
Tote Hill GU29 12 B4
Totegan KW14 104 D2
Totford SO24 11 G1
Totham Hill CM9 34 C7
Tothill LN13 53 H4
Totland PO39 10 E6
Totley S17 51 F5
Totnes TQ9 5 J4
Toton NG9 41 H2
Totronald PA78 78 C2
Totscore IV51 93 J5
Tottenham N17 23 G2
Tottenhill PE33 44 A4
Tottenhill Row PE33 44 A4
Totteridge *Bucks.* HP13 22 B2
Totteridge *Gt.Lon.* N20 23 F2
Totternhoe LU6 32 C6
Tottington *Gt.Man.* BL8 49 G1
Tottington *Norf.* IP24 44 C6
Totton SO40 10 E3
Toulton TA4 7 K2
Tournaig IV22 94 E3
Toux AB42 99 H5
Tovil ME15 14 C2
Tow Law DL13 62 C3
Towan Cross TR4 2 E4
Toward PA23 73 K4
Towcester NN12 31 H4
Towednack TR26 2 B5
Tower End PE32 44 A4
Towersey OX9 22 A1
Towie *Aber.* AB43 99 G4
Towie *Aber.* AB54 90 D2
Towie *Aber.* AB33 90 C3
Towiemore AB55 98 B6
Town End *Cambs.* PE15 43 H6
Town End *Cumb.* LA11 55 H1
Town End *Mersey.* WA8 48 D4
Town Green *Lancs.* L39 48 D2
Town Green *Norf.* NR13 45 H4
Town of Lowton WA3 49 F3
Town Row TN6 13 J3
Town Street IP27 44 B7
Town Yetholm TD5 70 D1
Townfield DH8 62 A2
Townhead *D. & G.* DG6 65 G6
Townhead *S.Yorks.* S36 50 D2
Townhead of Greenlaw DG7 65 H4
Townhill *Fife* KY12 75 K2
Townhill *Swan.* SA1 17 K6
Towns End RG26 21 J6
Towns Green CW6 49 F6
Townshend TR27 2 C5
Towthorpe *E.Riding* YO25 59 F3
Towthorpe *York* YO32 58 C4
Towton LS24 57 K6
Towyn LL22 47 H5
Toynton All Saints PE23 53 G6
Toynton Fen Side PE23 53 G6
Toynton St. Peter PE23 53 H6
Toy's Hill TN16 23 H6
Trabboch KA5 67 J1
Traboe TR12 2 E6
Tradespark *High.* IV12 97 F6
Tradespark *Ork.* KW15 106 D7
Traeth Coch (Red Wharf Bay) LL75 46 D4
Trafford Centre M17 49 G3
Trafford Park M17 49 G3
Trallong LD3 27 J6
Trallwn SA7 17 K6
Tram Inn HR2 28 D5
Tranent EH33 76 C3
Tranmere CH42 48 C4
Trantlebeg KW13 104 D3
Trantlemore KW13 104 D3
Tranwell NE61 71 G5
Trap SA19 17 K4
Trap Street SK11 49 H6
Traprain EH41 76 D3
Trap's Green B94 30 C2
Traquair EH44 76 B7
Trawden BB8 56 E6
Trawsfynydd LL41 37 G2
Trealaw CF40 18 D2
Treales PR4 55 H6
Trearddur LL65 46 A5
Treaslane IV51 93 J6
Tre-Aubrey CF71 18 D4
Trebanog CF39 18 D2
Trebanos SA8 18 A1
Trebarrow EX22 4 C1
Trebartha PL15 4 C3
Trebarvah TR11 2 E5
Trebarwith PL33 4 A2
Trebeath PL15 4 C2
Trebetherick PL27 3 G1
Trebister ZE1 107 N9
Tre-boeth SA5 17 K6
Treborough TA23 7 J2
Trebudannon TR8 3 F2
Trebullett PL15 4 D3
Treburley PL15 4 D3
Treburrick PL27 3 F1
Trebyan PL30 4 A4
Trecastle LD3 27 H6
Trecott EX20 6 E5
Trecrogo PL15 6 B7
Trecwn SA62 16 C2
Trecynon CF44 18 C1
Tredaule PL15 4 C2
Tredavoe TR20 2 B6
Treddiog SA62 16 B3
Tredegar NP22 18 E1
Tredington *Glos.* GL20 29 J6
Tredington *Warks.* CV36 30 D4
Tredinnick *Cornw.* PL27 3 G2
Tredinnick *Cornw.* PL14 4 C5
Tredogan CF62 18 D5
Tredomen LD3 28 A5
Tredrissi SA42 16 D1
Tredunnock NP15 19 G2
Tredustan LD3 28 A5
Tredworth GL1 29 H7
Treen *Cornw.* TR19 2 A6
Treen *Cornw.* TR20 2 B5
Treesmill PL24 4 A5
Treeton S60 51 G4
Trefaldwyn (Montgomery) SY15 38 B6
Trefasser SA64 16 B2
Trefdraeth *I.o.A.* LL62 46 C5
Trefdraeth (Newport) *Pembs.* SA42 16 D2
Trefecca LD3 28 A5
Trefechan CF48 18 D1
Trefeglwys SY17 37 J6
Trefenter SY23 27 F2
Treffgarne SA62 16 C3
Treffynnon (Holywell) *Flints.* CH8 47 K5
Treffynnon *Pembs.* SA62 16 B3
Trefgarn Owen SA62 16 B3
Trefil NP22 28 A7
Trefilan SA48 26 E3
Trefin SA62 16 B2
Treflach SY10 38 B3
Trefnanney SY22 38 B4
Trefnant LL16 47 J5
Trefonen SY10 38 B3
Trefor *Gwyn.* LL54 36 C1
Trefor *I.o.A.* LL65 46 B4
Treforest CF37 18 D3
Treforest Industrial Estate CF37 18 E3
Trefriw LL27 47 F6
Tref-y-clawdd (Knighton) LD7 28 B1
Trefynwy (Monmouth) NP25 28 E7
Tregadillett PL15 4 C2
Tregaian LL77 46 C5
Tregare NP15 28 D7
Tregarland PL13 4 C5
Tregarne TR12 2 E6
Tregaron SY25 27 F3
Tregarth LL57 46 E6
Tregaswith TR8 3 F2
Tregavethan TR4 2 E4
Tregear TR2 3 F3
Tregeare PL15 4 C2
Tregeiriog LL20 38 A2
Tregele LL67 46 B3
Tregidden TR12 2 E6
Tregiskey PL26 4 A6
Treglemais SA62 16 B3
Tregolds PL28 3 F1
Tregole EX23 4 B1
Tregonetha TR9 3 G2
Tregony TR2 3 G4
Tregoodwell PL32 4 B2
Tregoss PL26 3 G2
Tregowris TR12 2 E6
Tregoyd LD3 28 A5
Tregrehan Mills PL25 4 A5
Tre-groes SA44 17 H1
Treguff CF71 18 D4
Tregullon PL30 4 A4
Tregunnon PL15 4 C2
Tregurrian TR8 3 F2
Tregynon SY16 37 K6
Trehafod CF37 18 D2
Trehan PL12 4 E5
Treharris CF46 18 D2
Treherbert CF42 18 C2
Tre-hill CF5 18 D4
Trekenner PL15 4 D3
Treknow PL34 4 A2
Trelan TR12 2 E7
Trelash PL15 4 B1
Trelassick TR2 3 F3
Trelawnyd LL18 47 J5
Trelech SA33 17 F2
Treleddyd-fawr SA62 16 A3
Trelewis CF46 18 E2
Treligga PL33 4 A2
Trelights PL29 3 G1
Trelill PL30 4 A3
Trelissick TR3 3 F5
Trelleck NP25 19 J1
Trelleck Grange NP16 19 H1
Trelogan CH8 47 K4
Trelowla PL13 4 C5
Trelystan SY21 38 B5
Tremadog LL49 36 E1
Tremail PL32 4 B2
Tremain SA43 17 F1
Tremaine PL15 4 C2
Tremar PL14 4 C4
Trematon PL12 4 D5
Tremeirchion LL17 47 J5
Tremethick Cross TR20 2 B5
Tremore PL30 4 A4

Upper Hawkhillock AB42 91 J1
Upper Hayesden TN11 23 J7
Upper Hayton SY8 38 E7
Upper Heath SY7 38 E7
Upper Heaton HD5 50 D1
Upper Hellesdon NR3 45 G4
Upper Helmsley YO41 58 C4
Upper Hengoed SY10 38 B2
Upper Hergest HR5 28 B3
Upper Heyford *Northants.* NN7 31 H3
Upper Heyford *Oxon.* OX25 31 F6
Upper Hill *Here.* HR6 28 D3
Upper Hill *S.Glos.* GL13 19 K2
Upper Horsebridge BN27 13 J5
Upper Howsell WR14 29 G4
Upper Hulme ST13 50 C6
Upper Inglesham SN6 21 F2
Upper Kilchattan PA61 72 B1
Upper Killay SA2 17 J6
Upper Knockando AB38 97 J7
Upper Lambourn RG17 21 G3
Upper Langford BS40 19 H6
Upper Langwith NG20 51 H6
Upper Largo KY8 83 F7
Upper Leigh ST10 40 C2
Upper Ley GL14 29 G7
Upper Llandwrog (Y Fron) LL54 46 D7
Upper Loads S42 51 F6
Upper Lochton AB31 90 E5
Upper Longdon WS15 40 C4
Upper Longwood SY5 39 F5
Upper Ludstone WV5 40 A6
Upper Lybster KW3 105 H5
Upper Lydbrook GL17 29 F7
Upper Lyde HR4 28 D4
Upper Lye HR6 28 C2
Upper Maes-coed HR2 28 C5
Upper Midhope S36 50 E3
Upper Milovaig IV55 93 G7
Upper Milton OX7 30 D7
Upper Minety SN16 20 D2
Upper Moor WR10 29 J4
Upper Morton BS35 19 K2
Upper Muirskie AB12 91 G5
Upper Nash SA71 16 D5
Upper Newbold S41 51 F5
Upper North Dean HP14 22 B2
Upper Norwood SE19 23 G4
Upper Obney PH1 82 B4
Upper Oddington GL56 30 D6
Upper Ollach IV51 86 B1
Upper Padley S32 50 E5
Upper Pennington SO41 10 D5
Upper Pollicott HP18 31 J7
Upper Poppleton YO26 58 B4
Upper Quinton CV37 30 C4
Upper Ratley SO51 10 E2
Upper Ridinghill AB43 99 J5
Upper Rissington GL54 30 D6
Upper Rochford WR15 29 F2
Upper Sanday KW17 106 E7
Upper Sapey WR6 29 F2
Upper Scolton SA62 16 C3
Upper Seagry SN15 20 C3
Upper Shelton MK43 32 C4
Upper Sheringham NR26 45 F1
Upper Shuckburgh NN11 31 F2
Upper Siddington GL7 20 D2
Upper Skelmorlie PA17 74 A4
Upper Slaughter GL54 30 C6
Upper Sonachan PA33 80 B5
Upper Soudley GL14 29 F7
Upper Staploe PE19 32 E3
Upper Stoke NR14 45 G5
Upper Stondon SG16 32 E5
Upper Stowe NN7 31 H3
Upper Street *Hants.* SP6 10 C3
Upper Street *Norf.* NR12 45 H4
Upper Street *Norf.* IP21 35 F1
Upper Street *Suff.* IP9 35 F5
Upper Street *Suff.* IP6 35 F3
Upper Strensham WR8 29 J5
Upper Sundon LU5 32 D6
Upper Swanmore SO32 11 G3
Upper Swell GL54 30 C6
Upper Tean ST10 40 C2
Upper Thurnham LA2 55 H4
Upper Tillyrie KY13 82 C7
Upper Tooting SW17 23 F4
Upper Town *Derbys.* DE4 50 E6
Upper Town *Derbys.* DE4 50 E7
Upper Town *Derbys.* DE6 50 E7
Upper Town *Here.* HR1 28 E4
Upper Town *N.Som.* BS40 19 J5
Upper Tysoe CV35 30 E4
Upper Upham SN8 21 F4
Upper Upnor ME2 24 D4
Upper Victoria DD7 83 G4
Upper Vobster BA3 20 A7
Upper Wardington OX17 31 F4
Upper Waterhay SN6 20 D2
Upper Weald MK19 32 B5
Upper Weedon NN7 31 H3
Upper Welson HR3 28 B3
Upper Weston BA1 20 A5
Upper Whiston S60 51 G4
Upper Wick WR2 29 H3
Upper Wield SO24 11 H1
Upper Winchendon (Over Winchendon) HP18 31 J7
Upper Witton B23 40 C6
Upper Woodford SP4 10 C1
Upper Woolhampton RG7 21 J5
Upper Wootton RG26 21 J6
Upper Wraxall SN14 20 B4
Upper Wyche WR13 29 G4
Upperby CA2 60 F1
Uppermill OL3 49 J2
Upperthong HD9 50 D2
Upperton GU28 12 C4
Uppertown *Derbys.* S45 51 F6
Uppertown *Ork.* KW1 105 J1
Uppingham LE15 42 B5
Uppington TF6 38 E5
Upsall YO7 57 K1
Upsettlington TD15 77 G6
Upshire EN9 23 H1
Upstreet CT3 25 J5
Upthorpe IP31 34 D1
Upton *Bucks.* HP17 31 J7
Upton *Cambs.* PE28 32 E1
Upton *Ches.W. & C.* CH2 48 D6
Upton *Cornw.* PL14 4 C3
Upton *Cornw.* EX23 6 A5
Upton *Devon* EX14 7 J5
Upton *Devon* TQ7 5 H6
Upton *Dorset* BH16 9 J5
Upton *Dorset* DT2 9 G6
Upton *E.Riding* YO25 59 H4
Upton *Hants.* SP11 21 G6
Upton *Hants.* SO16 10 E3
Upton *Leics.* CV13 41 F6
Upton *Lincs.* DN21 52 B4
Upton *Mersey.* CH49 48 B4
Upton *Norf.* NR13 45 H4
Upton *Northants.* NN5 31 J2
Upton *Notts.* DN22 51 K5
Upton *Notts.* NG23 51 K7
Upton *Oxon.* OX11 21 J3
Upton *Oxon.* OX18 30 D7
Upton *Pembs.* SA72 16 D5
Upton *Peter.* PE5 42 E5
Upton *Slo.* SL1 22 C4
Upton *Som.* TA4 7 H3
Upton *Som.* TA10 8 D2
Upton *W.Yorks.* WF9 51 G1
Upton *Wilts.* SP3 9 H1
Upton Bishop HR9 29 F6
Upton Cheyney BS30 19 K5
Upton Cressett WV16 39 F6
Upton Crews HR9 29 F6
Upton Cross PL14 4 C3
Upton End SG5 32 E5
Upton Grey RG25 21 K7
Upton Hellions EX17 7 G5
Upton Lovell BA12 20 C7
Upton Magna SY4 38 E4
Upton Noble BA4 9 G1
Upton Park E13 23 H3
Upton Pyne EX5 7 H6
Upton St. Leonards GL4 29 H7
Upton Scudamore BA12 20 B7
Upton Snodsbury WR7 29 J3
Upton upon Severn WR8 29 H4
Upton Warren B61 29 J2
Upwaltham GU28 12 C5
Upware CB7 33 J1
Upwell PE14 43 J5
Upwey DT3 9 F6
Upwick Green SG11 33 H6
Upwood PE26 43 F7
Uradale ZE1 107 N9
Urafirth ZE2 107 M5
Urchany IV12 97 F7
Urchfont SN10 20 D6
Urdimarsh HR1 28 E4
Ure ZE2 107 L5
Urgha HS3 93 G2
Urlay Nook TS16 63 F5
Urmston M41 49 G3
Urpeth DH2 62 D1
Urquhart *High.* IV7 96 C6
Urquhart *Moray* IV30 97 K5
Urra TS9 63 G6
Urray IV6 96 C6
Ushaw Moor DH7 62 D2
Usk (Brynbuga) NP15 19 G1
Usselby LN8 52 D3
Usworth NE37 62 E1
Utley BD20 57 F5
Uton EX17 7 G6
Utterby LN11 53 G3
Uttoxeter ST14 40 C2
Uwchmynydd LL53 36 A3
Uxbridge UB8 22 D3
Uyeasound ZE2 107 P2
Uzmaston SA62 16 C4

V

Valley (Y Fali) LL65 46 A5
Valley Truckle PL32 4 B2
Valleyfield *D. & G.* DG6 65 G5
Valleyfield *Fife* KY12 75 J2
Valsgarth ZE2 107 Q1
Vange SS16 24 D3
Vardre SA6 17 K5
Varteg NP4 19 F1
Vatersay (Bhatarsaigh) HS9 84 B5
Vatsetter ZE2 107 P4
Vatten IV55 93 H7
Vaul PA77 78 B3
Vaynor CF48 27 K7
Vaynor Park SY21 38 A5
Veaullt HR5 28 A3
Veensgarth ZE2 107 N8
Velindre *Pembs.* SA41 16 D2
Velindre *Powys* LD3 28 A5
Vellow TA4 7 J2
Veness KW17 106 E5
Venn TQ7 5 H6
Venn Ottery EX11 7 J6
Venngreen EX22 6 B4
Vennington SY5 38 C5
Venny Tedburn EX17 7 G6
Venterdon PL17 4 D3
Ventnor PO38 11 G7
Venton PL7 5 F5
Vernham Dean SP11 21 G6
Vernham Street SP11 21 G6
Vernolds Common SY7 38 D7
Verwood BH31 10 B4
Veryan TR2 3 G5
Veryan Green TR2 3 G4
Vickerstown LA14 54 E3
Victoria PL26 3 G2
Vidlin ZE2 107 N6
Viewfield KW14 105 F2
Viewpark G71 75 F4
Vigo WS9 40 C5
Vigo Village DA13 24 C5
Villavin EX19 6 D4
Vinehall Street TN32 14 C5
Vine's Cross TN21 13 J5
Viney Hill GL15 19 K1
Virginia Water GU25 22 C5
Virginstow EX21 6 B6
Virley CM9 34 D7
Vobster BA3 20 A7
Voe *Shet.* ZE2 107 N6
Voe *Shet.* ZE2 107 M4
Vowchurch HR2 28 C5
Voy KW16 106 B6
Vron Gate SY5 38 C5

W

Waberthwaite CA18 60 C7
Wackerfield DL2 62 C4
Wacton NR15 45 F6
Wadbister ZE2 107 N8
Wadborough WR8 29 J4
Waddesdon HP18 31 J7
Waddeton TQ5 5 J5
Waddicar L31 48 C3
Waddingham DN21 52 C3
Waddington *Lancs.* BB7 56 C5
Waddington *Lincs.* LN5 52 C6
Waddingworth LN10 52 E5
Waddon *Devon* TQ13 5 J3
Waddon *Gt.Lon.* CR0 23 G5
Wadebridge PL27 3 G1
Wadeford TA20 8 C3
Wadenhoe PE8 42 D7
Wadesmill SG12 33 G7
Wadhurst TN5 13 K3
Wadshelf S42 51 F5
Wadworth DN11 51 H3
Wadworth Hill HU12 59 J7
Waen *Denb.* LL16 47 K6
Waen *Denb.* LL16 47 H6
Waen Aberwheeler LL16 47 J6
Waen-fâch SY22 38 B4
Waen-wen LL57 46 D6
Wag KW7 105 F6
Wainfleet All Saints PE24 53 H7
Wainfleet Bank PE24 53 H7
Wainfleet St. Mary PE24 53 H7
Wainford NR35 45 H6
Waingroves DE5 41 G1
Wainhouse Corner EX23 4 B1
Wainscott ME2 24 D4
Wainstalls HX2 57 F7
Waitby CA17 61 J6
WAKEFIELD WF 57 J7
Wakerley LE15 42 C6
Wakes Colne CO6 34 C6
Walberswick IP18 35 J1
Walberton BN18 12 C6
Walbottle NE15 71 G7
Walcot *Lincs.* NG34 42 D2
Walcot *Lincs.* LN4 52 E7
Walcot *N.Lincs.* DN15 58 E7
Walcot *Shrop.* SY7 38 C7
Walcot *Tel. & W.* TF6 38 E4
Walcot Green IP22 45 F7
Walcote *Leics.* LE17 41 H7
Walcote *Warks.* B49 30 C3
Walcott NR12 45 H2
Walcott Dales LN4 52 E7
Walden DL8 57 F1
Walden Head DL8 56 E1
Walden Stubbs DN6 51 H1
Walderslade ME5 24 D5
Walderton PO18 11 J3
Walditch DT6 8 D5
Waldley DE6 40 D2
Waldridge DH2 62 D2
Waldringfield IP12 35 G4
Waldron TN21 13 J5
Wales S26 51 G4
Walesby *Lincs.* LN8 52 E3
Walesby *Notts.* NG22 51 J5
Waleswood S26 51 G4
Walford *Here.* SY7 28 C1
Walford *Here.* HR9 28 E6
Walford *Shrop.* SY4 38 D3
Walford *Staffs.* ST21 40 A2
Walford Heath SY4 38 D4
Walgherton CW5 39 F1
Walgrave NN6 32 B1
Walhampton SO41 10 E5
Walk Mill BB10 56 D6
Walkden M28 49 G2
Walker NE6 71 H7
Walker Fold BB7 56 B5
Walkerburn EH43 76 B7
Walkeringham DN10 51 K3
Walkerith DN21 51 K3
Walkern SG2 33 F6
Walker's Green HR1 28 E4
Walkford BH23 10 D5
Walkhampton PL20 5 F4
Walkingham Hill HG3 57 J3
Walkington HU17 59 F6
Walkwood B97 30 B2
Wall *Cornw.* TR27 2 D5
Wall *Northumb.* NE46 70 E7
Wall *Staffs.* WS14 40 D5
Wall End LA17 55 F1
Wall Heath DY6 40 A7
Wall Houses NE45 71 F7
Wall under Heywood SY6 38 E6
Wallacehall DG11 69 H6
Wallacetown KA19 67 G3
Wallasey CH45 48 B3
Wallaston Green SA71 16 C5
Wallend ME3 24 E4
Waller's Green HR8 29 F5
Wallingford OX10 21 K3
Wallington *Gt.Lon.* SM6 23 F5
Wallington *Hants.* PO16 11 G4
Wallington *Herts.* SG7 33 F5
Wallington *Wrex.* LL13 38 D1
Wallingwells S81 51 H4
Wallis SA62 16 D3
Wallisdown BH12 10 B5
Walliswood RH5 12 E3
Walls ZE2 107 L8
Wallsend NE28 71 J7
Wallyford EH21 76 B3
Walmer CT14 15 J2
Walmer Bridge PR4 55 H7
Walmersley BL9 49 H1
Walmley B76 40 D6
Walmsgate LN11 53 G5
Walpole IP19 35 H1
Walpole Cross Keys PE34 43 J4
Walpole Highway PE14 43 J4
Walpole Marsh PE14 43 H4
Walpole St. Andrew PE14 43 J4
Walpole St. Peter PE14 43 J4
Walrond's Park TA3 8 C2
Walrow TA9 19 G7
WALSALL WS 40 C6
Walsall Wood WS9 40 C5
Walsden OL14 56 E7
Walsgrave on Sowe CV2 41 F7
Walsham le Willows IP31 34 E1
Walshford LS22 57 K4
Walsoken PE13 43 H4
Walston ML11 75 J6
Walsworth SG4 32 E5
Walter's Ash HP14 22 B2
Walterston CF62 18 D4
Walterstone HR2 28 C6
Waltham *Kent* CT4 15 G3
Waltham *N.E.Lincs.* DN37 53 F2
Waltham Abbey EN9 23 G1
Waltham Chase SO32 11 G3
Waltham Cross EN8 23 G1
Waltham on the Wolds LE14 42 A3
Waltham St. Lawrence RG10 22 B4
Walthamstow E17 23 G3
Walton *Bucks.* HP21 32 B7
Walton *Cumb.* CA8 70 A7
Walton *Derbys.* S42 51 F6
Walton *Leics.* LE17 41 H7
Walton *M.K.* MK7 32 B5
Walton *Mersey.* L9 48 C3
Walton *Peter.* PE4 42 E5
Walton *Powys* LD8 28 B3
Walton *Shrop.* SY7 28 D1
Walton *Som.* BA16 8 D1
Walton *Staffs.* ST15 40 A2
Walton *Suff.* IP11 35 H5
Walton *Tel. & W.* TF6 38 E4
Walton *W.Yorks.* WF2 51 F1
Walton *W.Yorks.* LS23 57 K5
Walton *Warks.* CV35 30 D3
Walton Cardiff GL20 29 J5
Walton East SA63 16 D3
Walton Elm DT10 9 G3
Walton Highway PE14 43 H4
Walton Lower Street IP11 35 G5
Walton on the Hill KT20 23 F6
Walton on the Naze CO14 35 G6
Walton on the Wolds LE12 41 H4
Walton Park *D. & G.* DG7 65 H3
Walton Park *N.Som.* BS21 19 H4
Walton West SA62 16 B4
Walton-in-Gordano BS21 19 H4
Walton-le-Dale PR5 55 J7
Walton-on-Thames KT12 22 E5
Walton-on-the-Hill ST17 40 B3
Walton-on-Trent DE12 40 E4
Walwen *Flints.* CH8 47 K5
Walwen *Flints.* CH6 48 B5
Walwick NE46 70 E6
Walworth DL2 62 D5
Walworth Gate DL2 62 D4
Walwyn's Castle SA62 16 B4
Wambrook TA20 8 B4
Wanborough *Surr.* GU3 22 C7
Wanborough *Swin.* SN4 21 F3
Wandel ML12 68 E1
Wandon NE71 71 F1
Wandon End LU2 32 E6
Wandsworth SW15 23 F4
Wandylaw NE67 71 G1
Wangford *Suff.* NR34 35 J1
Wangford *Suff.* IP27 44 B7
Wanlip LE7 41 J4
Wanlockhead ML12 68 D2
Wannock BN26 13 J6
Wansford *E.Riding* YO25 59 G4
Wansford *Peter.* PE8 42 D6
Wanshurst Green TN12 14 C3
Wanstrow BA4 20 A7
Wanswell GL13 19 K1
Wantage OX12 21 G3
Wapley BS37 20 A4
Wappenbury CV33 30 E2
Wappenham NN12 31 H4
Warblebank CA7 60 D2
Warbleton TN21 13 K5
Warblington PO9 11 J4
Warborough OX10 21 J2
Warboys PE28 43 G7
Warbreck FY2 55 G6
Warbstow PL15 4 C1
Warburton WA13 49 F4
Warcop CA16 61 J5
Ward End B8 40 D7
Ward Green IP14 34 E2
Warden *Kent* ME12 25 G4
Warden *Northumb.* NE46 70 E7
Warden Hill GL51 29 J6
Warden Street SG18 32 E4
Wardhouse AB52 90 D1
Wardington OX17 31 F4
Wardle *Ches.E.* CW5 49 F7
Wardle *Gt.Man.* OL12 49 J1
Wardley *Gt.Man.* M27 49 G2
Wardley *Rut.* LE15 42 B5
Wardley *T. & W.* NE10 71 J7
Wardlow SK17 50 D5
Wardsend SK10 49 J4
Wardy Hill CB6 43 H7
Ware *Herts.* SG12 33 G7
Ware *Kent* CT3 25 J5
Wareham BH20 9 J6
Warehorne TN26 14 E4
Waren Mill NE70 77 K7
Warenford NE70 71 G1
Warenton NE70 77 K7
Wareside SG12 33 G7
Waresley *Cambs.* SG19 33 F3
Waresley *Worcs.* DY11 29 H1
Warfield RG42 22 B4
Wargrave *Mersey.* WA12 48 E3
Wargrave *W'ham* RG10 22 A4
Warham *Here.* HR4 28 D5
Warham *Norf.* NR23 44 D1
Wark *Northumb.* NE48 70 D6
Wark *Northumb.* TD12 77 G7
Warkleigh EX37 6 E3
Warkton NN16 32 B1
Warkworth *Northants.* OX17 31 F4
Warkworth *Northumb.* NE65 71 H3
Warland OL14 56 E7
Warleggan PL30 4 B4
Warley *Essex* CM14 23 J2
Warley *W.Mid.* B68 40 C7
Warley Town HX2 57 F7
Warlingham CR6 23 G6
Warmfield WF1 57 J7
Warmingham CW11 49 G6
Warminghurst RH20 12 E5
Warmington *Northants.* PE8 42 D6
Warmington *Warks.* OX17 31 F4
Warminster BA12 20 B7
Warmlake ME17 14 D3
Warmley BS30 19 K4
Warmley Hill BS15 19 K4
Warmsworth DN4 51 H2
Warmwell DT2 9 G6
Warndon WR4 29 H3
Warners End HP1 22 D1
Warnford SO32 11 H2
Warnham RH12 12 E3
Warningcamp BN18 12 D6
Warninglid RH17 13 F4
Warren *Ches.E.* SK11 49 H5
Warren *Pembs.* SA71 16 C6
Warren House PL20 6 E7
Warren Row RG10 22 B3
Warren Street ME17 14 E2
Warrenby TS10 63 G4
Warren's Green SG4 33 F6
Warrington *M.K.* MK46 32 B3
WARRINGTON *Warr.* WA 49 F4
Warroch KY13 82 B7
Warsash SO31 11 F4
Warslow SK17 50 C7
Warsop Vale NG20 51 H6
Warter YO42 58 E4
Warthill YO19 58 C4
Wartle AB31 90 D4
Wartling BN27 13 K6
Wartnaby LE14 42 A3
Warton *Lancs.* LA5 55 J2
Warton *Lancs.* PR4 55 H7
Warton *Northumb.* NE65 71 F3
Warton *Warks.* B79 40 E5
Warton Bank PR4 55 H7
Warwick CV34 30 D2
Warwick Bridge CA4 61 F1
Warwick Wold RH1 23 G6
Warwick-on-Eden CA4 61 F1
Wasbister KW17 106 C4
Wasdale Head CA20 60 C6
Wash SK23 50 C4
Wash Common RG14 21 H5
Washall Green SG9 33 H5
Washaway PL30 4 A4
Washbourne TQ9 5 H5
Washbrook BS28 19 H7
Washfield EX16 7 H4
Washfold DL11 62 B6
Washford *Som.* TA23 7 J1
Washford *Warks.* B98 30 B2
Washford Pyne EX17 7 G4
Washingborough LN4 52 D5
Washington *T. & W.* NE38 62 E1
Washington *W.Suss.* RH20 12 E5
Washmere Green CO10 34 D4
Wasing RG7 21 J5
Waskerley DH8 62 B2
Wasperton CV35 30 D3
Wasps Nest LN4 52 D6

221

INDEX TO NORTHERN IRELAND

Administrative area abbreviations

B'mena Ballymena	*Cooks.* Cookstown	*Dungan.* Dungannon	*Maghera.* Magherafelt	*Newtown.* Newtownabbey
Banbr. Banbridge	*Craig.* Craigavon	*Ferm.* Fermanagh	*New. & M.* Newry & Mourne	*Strab.* Strabane